THE PHILOSOPHY OF
JAAKKO HINTIKKA

THE LIBRARY OF LIVING PHILOSOPHERS

PAUL ARTHUR SCHILPP, FOUNDER AND EDITOR 1939–1981
LEWIS EDWIN HAHN, EDITOR 1981–2001
RANDALL E. AUXIER, EDITOR 2001–

Paul Arthur Schilpp, Editor
THE PHILOSOPHY OF JOHN DEWEY (1939, 1971, 1989)
THE PHILOSOPHY OF GEORGE SANTAYANA (1940, 1951)
THE PHILOSOPHY OF ALFRED NORTH WHITEHEAD (1941, 1951)
THE PHILOSOPHY OF G. E. MOORE (1942, 1971)
THE PHILOSOPHY OF BERTRAND RUSSELL (1944, 1971)
THE PHILOSOPHY OF ERNST CASSIRER (1949)
ALBERT EINSTEIN: PHILOSOPHER-SCIENTIST (1949, 1970)
THE PHILOSOPHY OF SARVEPALLI RADHAKRISHNAN (1952)
THE PHILOSOPHY OF KARL JASPERS (1957; AUG. ED., 1981)
THE PHILOSOPHY OF C. D. BROAD (1959)
THE PHILOSOPHY OF RUDOLF CARNAP (1963)
THE PHILOSOPHY OF C. I. LEWIS (1968)
THE PHILOSOPHY OF KARL POPPER (1974)
THE PHILOSOPHY OF BRAND BLANSHARD (1980)
THE PHILOSOPHY OF JEAN-PAUL SARTRE (1981)

Paul Arthur Schilpp and Maurice Friedman, Editors
THE PHILOSOPHY OF MARTIN BUBER (1967)

Paul Arthur Schilpp and Lewis Edwin Hahn, Editors
THE PHILOSOPHY OF GABRIEL MARCEL (1984)
THE PHILOSOPHY OF W. V. QUINE (1986, AUG. ED., 1998)
THE PHILOSOPHY OF GEORG HENRIK VON WRIGHT (1989)

Lewis Edwin Hahn, Editor
THE PHILOSOPHY OF CHARLES HARTSHORNE (1991)
THE PHILOSOPHY OF A. J. AYER (1992)
THE PHILOSOPHY OF PAUL RICOEUR (1995)
THE PHILOSOPHY OF PAUL WEISS (1995)
THE PHILOSOPHY OF HANS-GEORG GADAMER (1997)
THE PHILOSOPHY OF RODERICK M. CHISHOLM (1997)
THE PHILOSOPHY OF P. F. STRAWSON (1998)
THE PHILOSOPHY OF DONALD DAVIDSON (1999)

Lewis Edwin Hahn, Randall E. Auxier, and Lucian W. Stone, Jr., Editors
THE PHILOSOPHY OF SEYYED HOSSEIN NASR (2001)

Randall E. Auxier and Lewis Edwin Hahn, Editors
THE PHILOSOPHY OF MARJORIE GRENE (2002)
THE PHILOSOPHY OF JAAKKO HINTIKKA

In Preparation:
THE PHILOSOPHY OF ARTHUR C. DANTO
THE PHILOSOPHY OF MICHAEL DUMMETT
THE PHILOSOPHY OF MARTHA NUSSBAUM
THE PHILOSOPHY OF HILARY PUTNAM
THE PHILOSOPHY OF RICHARD M. RORTY

THE LIBRARY OF LIVING PHILOSOPHERS
VOLUME XXX

THE PHILOSOPHY OF
JAAKKO HINTIKKA

EDITED BY

RANDALL E. AUXIER

AND

LEWIS EDWIN HAHN

SOUTHERN ILLINOIS UNIVERSITY CARBONDALE

CHICAGO AND LA SALLE, ILLINOIS • OPEN COURT • ESTABLISHED 1887

To order books from Open Court, call 1-800-815-2280, or visit our website at www.opencourtbooks.com

THE PHILOSOPHY OF JAAKKO HINTIKKA

Open Court Publishing Company is a division of Carus Publishing Company.

Library of Congress Cataloging-in-Publication Data

The philosophy of Jaakko Hintikka / edited by Randall E. Auxier and Lewis Edwin Hahn.
    p. cm. -- (The library of living philosophers ; v. 30)
    Summary: "Addresses Dr. Jaakko Hintikka's work in game-theoretical semantics, philosophy of language, theoretical linguistics, cognitive science, logic, and related fields. Includes twenty-seven critical and descriptive essays by scholars, Hintikka's reply to each essay, his intellectual autobiography, and a bibliography of Hintikka's publications"--Provided by publisher.
    Includes bibliographical references and index.
    ISBN-13: 978-0-8126-9462-8 (cloth : alk. paper)
    ISBN-10: 0-8126-9462-7 (cloth : alk. paper)
    ISBN-13: 978-0-8126-9463-5 (trade paper : alk. paper)
    ISBN-10: 0-8126-9463-5 (trade paper : alk. paper) 1. Hintikka, Jaakko, 1929-
I. Auxier, Randall E., 1961- II. Hahn, Lewis Edwin, 1908- III. Series.
    B4715.H54P45 2006
    198'.8--dc22
                                                    2006006166

The Library of Living Philosophers is published under the sponsorship of Southern Illinois University Carbondale.

GENERAL INTRODUCTION
TO
THE LIBRARY OF LIVING PHILOSOPHERS

Since its founding in 1938 by Paul Arthur Schilpp, the Library of Living Philosophers has been devoted to critical analysis and discussion of some of the world's greatest living philosophers. The format for the series provides for creating in each volume a dialogue between the critics and the great philosopher. The aim is not refutation or confrontation but rather fruitful joining of issues and improved understanding of the positions and issues involved. That is, the goal is not overcoming those who differ from us philosophically but interacting creatively with them.

The basic idea for the series, according to Professor Schilpp's general introduction to the earlier volumes, came from the late F.C.S. Schiller's essay "Must Philosophers Disagree?" While Schiller may have been overly optimistic about ending "interminable controversies" in this way, it seems clear that directing searching questions to great philosophers about what they really mean or how they might resolve or address difficulties in their philosophies can produce far greater clarity of understanding and more fruitful philosophizing than would otherwise exist.

To Paul Arthur Schilpp's undying credit, he acted on this basic thought in launching the Library of Living Philosophers. The general plan for the volumes has sometimes been altered to fit circumstances, but in ways that have well served the mission of the series. The intellectual autobiographies, or, in a few cases, the biographies, shed a great deal of light on both how the philosophies of the great thinkers developed and the major philosophical movements and issues of their time; and many of our great philosophers seek to orient their outlook not merely to their contemporaries but also to what they find most important in earlier philosophers. The critical perspectives of our distinguished contributors have often stood on their own as landmark studies, widely cited and familiar not only to subsequent specialists, but frequently discussed in their own right as pieces of great philosophy. The bibliography helps to provide ready access to the featured scholar's writings and thought.

There is no reason to alter our historical format or mission for the present century. We are pleased that the success of the Library of Living

Philosophers has led to a wider appreciation of the need for dialogue of the type our format creates. We respect the efforts of other academic publishers to employ versions of our format to facilitate pluralistic, meaningful, sharp, constructive, and respectful exchange in philosophical ideas. We are fortunate to have such support from the Open Court Publishing Company, the Edward C. Hegeler Foundation, and the Board of Trustees, College of Liberal Arts, and the Department of Philosophy of Southern Illinois University Carbondale, as to permit us to carry out our purpose with a degree of deliberate thoroughness and comprehensiveness not available to other academic publishers, and we have rededicated ourselves to maintaining the highest standards in scholarship and accuracy anywhere to be found in academic publishing. In recognition of the permanent value that has been accorded our previous volumes, we are committed to keeping our volumes in print and available, and to maintaining our sense of the long-term importance of providing the most reliable source for scholarly analysis by the most distinguished voices of our day about the most important philosophical contributions of the greatest living thinkers.

The Library of Living Philosophers has never construed "philosophy" in a narrow and strictly academic sense. Past volumes have been dedicated both to the leading academic philosophers and to the most visible and influential public philosophers. We renew with each volume our historical orientation to the practice of philosophy as a quest for truth, beauty, and the best life, and we affirm that this quest is a public activity and its results a public possession, both for the present generation and in the future. We seek, with the sober judgment of our Advisory Board, to bring forth volumes on the thought of figures whose ideas have made a genuine difference to the lives of people everywhere. Ideas truly do have consequences, and many of the ideas that have had the broadest impact were indeed best articulated by the figures to whom we have dedicated past volumes. The selfless work of Paul Arthur Schilpp and Lewis Edwin Hahn in realizing this mission stands among the most important scholarly contributions to twentieth-century philosophy. Their judgment regarding how best to pursue the purposes of the Library of Living Philosophers has found constant and continuous confirmation in the reception and ongoing importance accorded this series. Let us continue in their footsteps as well as we may.

RANDALL E. AUXIER

DEPARTMENT OF PHILOSOPHY
SOUTHERN ILLINOIS UNIVERSITY CARBONDALE

FOUNDER'S GENERAL INTRODUCTION[*]
TO
THE LIBRARY OF LIVING PHILOSOPHERS

According to the late F.C.S. Schiller, the greatest obstacle to fruitful discussion in philosophy is "the curious etiquette which apparently taboos the asking of questions about a philosopher's meaning while he is alive." The "interminable controversies which fill the histories of philosophy," he goes on to say, "could have been ended at once by asking the living philosophers a few searching questions."

The confident optimism of this last remark undoubtedly goes too far. Living thinkers have often been asked "a few searching questions," but their answers have not stopped "interminable controversies" about their real meaning. It is nonetheless true that there would be far greater clarity of understanding than is now often the case if more such searching questions had been directed to great thinkers while they were still alive.

This, at any rate, is the basic thought behind the present undertaking. The volumes of the Library of Living Philosophers can in no sense take the place of the major writings of great and original thinkers. Students who would know the philosophies of such men as John Dewey, George Santayana, Alfred North Whitehead, G. E. Moore, Bertrand Russell, Ernst Cassirer, Karl Jaspers, Rudolf Carnap, Martin Buber, et al., will still need to read the writings of these men. There is no substitute for first-hand contact with the original thought of the philosopher himself. Least of all does this Library pretend to be such a substitute. The Library in fact will spare neither effort nor expense in offering to the student the best possible guide to the published writings of a given thinker. We shall attempt to meet this aim by providing at the end of each volume in our series as nearly complete a bibliography of the published work of the philosopher in question as possible. Nor should one overlook the fact that essays in each volume cannot but finally lead to this same goal. The interpretive and critical discussions of the various phases of a great thinker's work and, most

---

[*]This General Introduction sets forth in the founder's words the underlying conception of the Library. L.E.H.

of all, the reply of the thinker himself, are bound to lead the reader to the works of the philosopher himself.

At the same time, there is no denying that different experts find different ideas in the writings of the same philosopher. This is as true of the appreciative interpreter and grateful disciple as it is of the critical opponent. Nor can it be denied that such differences of reading and of interpretation on the part of other experts often leave the neophyte aghast before the whole maze of widely varying and even opposing interpretations. Who is right and whose interpretation shall he accept? When the doctors disagree among themselves, what is the poor student to do? If, in desperation, he decides that all of the interpreters are probably wrong and that the only thing for him to do is to go back to the original writings of the philosopher himself and then make his own decision—uninfluenced (as if this were possible) by the interpretation of anyone else—the result is not that he has actually come to the meaning of the original philosopher himself, but rather that he has set up one more interpretation, which may differ to a greater or lesser degree from the interpretations already existing. It is clear that in this direction lies chaos, just the kind of chaos which Schiller has so graphically and inimitably described.**

It is curious that until now no way of escaping this difficulty has been seriously considered. It has not occurred to students of philosophy that one effective way of meeting the problem at least partially is to put these varying interpretations and critiques before the philosopher while he is still alive and to ask him to act at one and the same time as both defendant and judge. If the world's greatest living philosophers can be induced to cooperate in an enterprise whereby their own work can, at least to some extent, be saved from becoming merely "desiccated lecture-fodder," which on the one hand "provides innocuous sustenance for ruminant professors," and on the other hand gives an opportunity to such ruminants and their understudies to "speculate safely, endlessly, and fruitlessly, about what a philosopher must have meant" (Schiller), they will have taken a long step toward making their intentions more clearly comprehensible.

With this in mind, the Library of Living Philosophers expects to publish at more or less regular intervals a volume on each of the greater among the world's living philosophers. In each case it will be the purpose of the editor of the Library to bring together in the volume the interpretations and criticisms of a wide range of that particular thinker's scholarly contemporaries, each of whom will be given a free hand to discuss the specific phase of the thinker's work that has been assigned to him. All contributed essays will

---

** In his essay "Must Philosophers Disagree?" in the volume of the same title (London: Macmillan, 1934), from which the above quotations were taken.

finally be submitted to the philosopher with whose work and thought they are concerned, for his careful perusal and reply. And, although it would be expecting too much to imagine that the philosopher's reply will be able to stop all differences of interpretation and of critique, this should at least serve the purpose of stopping certain of the grosser and more general kinds of misinterpretations. If no further gain than this were to come from the present and projected volumes of this Library, it would seem to be fully justified.

In carrying out this principal purpose of the Library, the editor announces that (as far as is humanly possible) each volume will contain the following elements:

First, an intellectual autobiography of the thinker whenever this can be secured; in any case an authoritative and authorized biography;

Second, a series of expository and critical articles written by the leading exponents and opponents of the philosopher's thought;

Third, the reply to the critics and commentators by the philosopher himself; and

Fourth, a bibliography of writings of the philosopher to provide a ready instrument to give access to his writings and thought.

PAUL ARTHUR SCHILPP
FOUNDER AND EDITOR, 1939–1981

DEPARTMENT OF PHILOSOPHY
SOUTHERN ILLINOIS UNIVERSITY CARBONDALE

ADVISORY BOARD

ACKNOWLEDGMENTS

The editor hereby gratefully acknowledges his obligation and sincere gratitude to all the publishers of Jaakko Hintikka's books and publications for their kind and uniform courtesy in permitting us to quote—sometimes at some length—from Professor Hintikka.

RANDALL E. AUXIER
LEWIS EDWIN HAHN

Added to Board after the subject of this volume was chosen.

TABLE OF CONTENTS

PREFACE

Jaakko Hintikka, Professor of Philosophy at Boston University, is the most significant philosopher-logician of his generation, and perhaps the second half of the twentieth century, for which title he vies with the likes of Quine and his own teacher von Wright. Hintikka continues to build upon a revolution in logic he started over forty years ago with a sense of purpose that seems ageless. We are pleased to present to the public this comprehensive estimation of his philosophical achievement in this our thirtieth volume. The pages that follow will depict a breadth of thinking and writing that may surprise readers who previously encountered Hintikka's ideas only in some area of their own specialization. I would seek to summarize, however inadequately, Hintikka's remarkable achievement in three exceptional qualities of mind that I have observed in his writing and in our interactions in preparing this volume.

First, I would note that Hintikka is an uncommonly intuitive and close reader of historical texts, a quality not often found among logicians, but as with Quine, von Wright, Peirce, and Leibniz, for example, it is a quality one will find among great logicians. Yet, unlike more typical historians of philosophy, Hintikka not only pieces together what a great thinker is saying, he sees also the structural aspects of the actual thinking and is able, with almost uncanny insight, to present the original arguments in forms not previously understood by earlier interpreters. Perhaps the key to this interpretive power is that Hintikka is a master of formulating and reformulating questions until he comes upon a way of asking the question to which the text genuinely responds. The result of this process is inspiring. Thus, Hintikka has argued that the art of the question is integral to logic as a process of inquiry. Hintikka's interpretive work in historical figures always becomes the center of lively discussion among the specialists in the figures he writes about. His interpretive essays over the years on Aristotle, Descartes, Kant, Peirce, and Wittgenstein have become touchstones no specialized scholar can afford to neglect. And yet, for all this, Hintikka is not primarily a historian of philosophy. Had he taken this path, he would certainly have produced a body of work to compare with Cassirer's, and of like quality. Instead, Hintikka developed this great historical interpretive power as it applies to the philosophical demands of his own day. Thus, not only were the historians of philosophy engaged by Hintikka's work, the past figures themselves sprang again to life in the service of addressing present challenges in human thought. Because of Hintikka's broad and incisive readings, even such neglected figures as Collingwood came back before the attention of our present cutting-edge thinkers and had a say once more. The quality of mind I notice in this case is the capacity to find and follow a valuable idea through many historical and systematic variations and into its applicability in the present.

Second, I would note that Hintikka's endowments include the capacity not only to grasp and use complex formalisms, but to *create* them. I would call this "the formalizing imagination." Whether it is an achievement or a native gift we can only speculate, but that it is uncommon we cannot doubt. Perhaps one in several thousand trained philosophers has any significant power of formalizing imagination, and those who have the ability in a great enough measure to affect all subsequent thinking are exceedingly rare. In terms of formalizing imagination, Hintikka ranks with Aristotle, Descartes, Leibniz, Kant, Peirce, Husserl, Frege, Russell, Whitehead, Gödel, Quine, and Carnap. Excellence in the formalizing imagination is indeed somewhat more common among mathematicians, but even there it is scarce enough. There is surely a link between the capacity for mathematical thinking and the philosophers who have given us our logic, yet this quality of mind is not precisely mathematical. We might pause over what draws those listed above towards philosophy and away from either pure mathematics or mathematical science. All such philosophers seem to have a concern for the world of concrete human problems that is foreign to the temperament of the formalizers who approach their problems exclusively in the mode of *theoria*. Hintikka, as with the other great philosophical formalizers, is grounded in a recognizably concrete world, in a world of actualities that can be transformed through the consideration of possibilities. If Hintikka spends his days investigating mainly formalizable possibilities, they are nevertheless the possibilities which answer to the requirements of actual concrete inquiries; hence, his contributions to the advent of epistemic logic. One never loses sight, in Hintikka's writings, of the place occupied by philosophers in the world, as human beings contributing to the great effort of our living better lives.

In noticing the grounded character of Hintikka's creative formalizing imagination, I am led to the third overarching quality of mind that raises him into the ranks of the immortals of human thought. I worry that my meaning will be missed if I use the word that comes to mind to describe this admirable quality of mind, for that word is "pugnacity," which is often thought of as a character trait one ought really to tame or outgrow. But I mean this in the sense in which William Ernest Hocking discussed it in his masterful *Human Nature and Its Remaking* (1918). Having identified "pugnacity" as the instinctive agent of readjustment in conscious life, a sort of active impulse that proceeds from our response to the way our surroundings change and confront us with the necessity of adapting to new demands, pugnacity matures in human beings. In its highest stage, "apart from competition, discussion, and various sorts of peaceful rivalry, there is the pervasive activity of *critical judgment*," Hocking says. He continues, "wrath against defective persons and institutions, by being circuited through a process of conceptual thought, is made over into an energy for their repair rather than their destruction." This type of constructive pugnacity may be the dominant quality of mind that carries Hintikka's brilliant powers of textual interpretation and formalizing imagination into the ages, for he never met a defect in his own thinking he would not tenaciously confront until it yielded before his intellectual onslaught. The reader will see Hintikka's frank admission throughout this volume of the places in his philosophy where he has not yet succeeded in answering a problem, but always accompanied by an indication of the ways in which he continues to confront it and what progress has been made. But what is even more impressive and singular is that Hintikka has always employed his own mature pugnacity in collaboration with dozens of other philosophers. A short examination of the bibliography in this volume will reveal a staggering number of collaborative publications, and for each collaboration resulting in a publication, there were many more which were preparatory or subsequent to the same sort of work. Hintikka understands as few philosophers ever have, and exemplifies in his work, the true character of transformed pugnacity, reaching out to utilize the intellectual resources of others to transform his problems into theirs and theirs into his, refusing to settle for merely contrived solutions, delving deeper and deeper into the problem until its very root structure is exposed, and digging and surveying in community with other thinkers until the full problem reveals its original seed. Pugnacious collaboration means giving no quarter to the problem, but it also means refusing to accept ideas from any source which go only part of the way towards a solution. Hintikka is so very generous in his willingness to hold up to the light the ideas of others that have resulted in real progress. This is in keeping with his genuinely modest spirit, for solving the problem at hand is the real aim of philosophical activity, not the aggrandizement of the person who may solve it. Thus, Hintikka seeks collaborators while others seek disciples. Those who labor in service of our greater understanding are all on the same side, while the *problem* is on the other.

Perhaps this is the reason Hintikka is unsparing in his critical judgment regarding the value of ideas placed before a problem he is considering. A good idea must pass the test of mature pugnacity. This quality of mind makes Hintikka's critical judgment as much valued as it is feared. But I can honestly say that a philosopher who has placed an idea before Hintikka need fear only for the destiny of the idea, not for the person who thought it. Mature pugnacity transforms our enmity for the problem into a process for its real solution, and in this Hintikka is exceeded by no philosopher I have known.

These are only some of the qualities of mind that one might note in coming to terms with Jaakko Hintikka's important contribution to philosophy and to the world of human thought.

This volume presented a number of challenges, not least of which was the transition from one general editor to another. Professor Hahn launched the volume and invited many of the contributions, but his health did not permit him to edit the volume. Numerous highly technical contributions with a great deal of symbolization have created the necessity for the closest care in creating the text. We have worked tirelessly to eliminate all the errors, but we realize this is too much to hope. For the errors that may remain we assume responsibility and beg pardon of the readers.

We at the Library of Living Philosophers want to thank Professor Hintikka for his kindness, his great patience, and his cheerful co-operation in the long and arduous process of giving birth to this volume. We thank the distinguished contributors for their labor in creating this volume, and we hope that our efforts in their behalf have adequately repaid their time and creativity.

The LLP staff is happy to acknowledge once more the warm support, encouragement, and cooperation of our publisher, Open Court Publishing Company, especially M. Blouke Carus, André Carus, David R. Steele, and Kerri Mommer. And we also very much appreciate continued support, understanding, and encouragement from the administration of Southern Illinois University Carbondale, especially the College of Liberal Arts and Dean Shirley Clay Scott. As always, we are grateful for the friendly and unfailing help in a variety of ways from the staff of Morris Library at SIUC. It is invaluable for our work and that of our fellow scholars. Without the ongoing and unflagging support of the Department of Philosophy at Southern Illinois University Carbondale, and its Chair George Schedler, these volumes could not be published, and we want to thank them for their support. As Editor, my warm gratitude also goes to Jeletta Brant and the Philosophy Department secretariat for help with numerous projects; to Frances Stanley, the LLP Technical Editor, who does nearly everything related to creating these volumes, such as creating the camera-ready proofs, helping with manuscripts, catching many editing points I have missed, and keeping the correspondence with contributors moving and well-ordered. I would also like to thank James Russell Couch, Jason Hills, Tony Giambusso, Brett Carroll, and Aaron Fortune, graduate students at SIUC, for their excellent research, library work, and tireless efforts in tracking down and verifying quotations and citations.

RANDALL E. AUXIER
EDITOR

DEPARTMENT OF PHILOSOPHY
SOUTHERN ILLINOIS UNIVERSITY CARBONDALE
SEPTEMBER 2005

IN MEMORIAM

Lewis Edwin Hahn
September 26, 1908–November 23, 2004

B elow are some words spoken by the present writer at the Memorial Service for Lewis Edwin Hahn, the second editor of the Library of Living Philosophers, serving in that capacity from 1981 until 2001. His years of philosophical service are preserved in the books he gave to the world, in the students he mentored, and in the good name he left behind.

RANDALL E. AUXIER, EDITOR
LIBRARY OF LIVING PHILOSOPHERS

LEWIS E. HAHN MEMORIAL SERVICE
UNITARIAN FELLOWSHIP, CARBONDALE, IL
FEBRUARY 19, 2005

I knew Lewis Hahn from 1987 and have had the unenviable task of attempting to carry on in his place. As his actual shoes were too large for my feet, I feel his symbolic shoes must remain incompletely filled by the feet that follow. We may stand upon his shoulders but we still labor in the shadow he has cast.

Actually, I have come to think of Lewis as a sort of sundial in the world of philosophy, as the light of wisdom moved round him he stood in place and measured it. When the sun shone from the east he looked to the wisdom of the Eastern lands and became an ambassador of West to East, of East to West. He proved at length that at least in him the twain *shall* meet. While eastward lies the direction of daybreak and the future, Lewis was ever building towards the fulfillment of ideals and expectations –many of which were designed to transcend the generations. He gave to future centuries eleven volumes of the Library of Living Philosophers and secured the future existence of another six. Lewis always took the time for the young philosophers around him, lending an ear and offering helpful observation, encouragement and a kind of respect that the young crave in ways that their elders so often forget. But Lewis believed in the future and recognized when it was before him. I was only one among countless young people who took encouragement from Lewis Hahn's vision of the future. Thus he faced the morning sun.

At noonday when not even Lewis cast a shadow, with bright eyes, toothy smile, and a single finger pointed skyward, he stood among his fellows even as he towered over them. Lewis came to be valued as a discerning judge of the qualities that distinguish what is merely good from what is truly great in the world of human thought. His contemporaries responded to his judgment; they waited upon it. He had perfected the art of being both generous and honest in expressing his judgment. What was genuinely to be praised he freely held up to the light, and what was yet to be praiseworthy he sheltered in his own warmth. His was the mentoring touch. His countless students, those who have felt that great but kindly hand upon their shoulders will know that the only fit repayment is to follow Lewis' example. Stand upright among your peers, speak the truth in such a way as to leave each bathed in its light, and let that noonday sun warm your heart even as it gives energy to your thoughts.

As the sun sinks into the west the shadow of the past grows long. In his later days Lewis represented to literally thousands of philosophers a living link to days of wondrous achievement and vital thinking. When I was with Lewis, I was with someone who had known and worked with John Dewey, Stephen Pepper, Edgar Brightman, and so many others of a bygone day. These personages were beyond my reach, but so long as I knew Lewis they were not beyond my imagination; one degree of separation between his amazing memory and the images in my head; the living past facing west.

For so many of us Lewis was the master of context, showing us that the Archimedean point was not a place to stand from which to move the world, but a place from which to grasp the way the world already moves. If we would honor him we must plant our feet and look towards the light.

R.E.A.

PART ONE

INTELLECTUAL AUTOBIOGRAPHY OF JAAKKO HINTIKKA

CHAPTER 1: NATURE OR NURTURE?

How far into one's background should one's intellectual autobiography reach? Psychologists have a great deal to say of the influence of both nature and nurture on one's life. But actual clues to those influences are not easy to spot. They are perhaps easier to identify in the case of influences due to one's background and education than in the case of heredity. In my case, I grew up in a home which was an eminently suitable springboard for a scientific or scholarly career. Books, writing, teaching, science and scholarship were all part of my environment. My father, Toivo Juho Hintikka (1888–1952), usually referred to as T.J. Hintikka

Jaakko Hintikka

INTELLECTUAL AUTOBIOGRAPHY

1. NATURE OR NURTURE?

How far into one's background should one's intellectual autobiography reach? Psychologists have a great deal to say of the influence of both nature and nurture on one's life. But actual clues to those influences are not easy to spot. They are perhaps easier to identify in the case of influences due to one's background and education than in the case of heredity. In my case, I grew up in a home which was an eminently suitable springboard for a scientific or scholarly career. Books, writing, teaching, science, and scholarship were all part of my environment. My father Toivo Juho Hintikka (1888–1952), usually referred to as T. J. Hintikka, had been trained as a biologist, botanist, and plant pathologist, but was making our living by working for a textbook publisher. In spite of not being in academia, scientific and scholarly pursuits undoubtedly were—in the light of psychological hindsight—a need for him, perhaps an escape. He had a wide range of intellectual curiosity. For instance, already in the thirties he was well aware of the new world of viruses and its potential importance, acquiring expensive German books on the subject. Because of disappointments and self-doubts he nevertheless never published much. Occasionally, his self-doubts reached tragic proportions. At one point, he had an already typeset book that he had written destroyed because of his second thoughts.

My father did not take much part in public life, but he was not a loner, either. Among his friends there were several leading Finnish-speaking scientists and scholars in Finland, among them a historian of Finnish literature, Viljo Tarkiainen (1879–1951), a historian, Arno Cederberg (1885–1948), a geologist Väinö Auer (1895–1981), and two biologist-brothers, Paavo Suomalainen (1907–1976) and Esko Suomalainen (1910–1995). Nor did T. J. Hintikka shirk occasional social responsibilities. I remember how he one day during the war surprised his family by showing up for dinner with two Japanese scientists whose temporary host he had somehow ended up becoming. He nevertheless became disillusioned about the credentials of his Asian guests as biologists when one of them asked, "Was bedeutet *flora*? Was bedeutet *fauna*?" His eventual judgment was "spiooneja" ("spies").

I can recognize in myself many of my father's characteristics, both strengths and weaknesses. I am luckier than he was in that in my field one can reach much further than in an empirical science by means of pure thought and creative imagination. As I have noted in an earlier autobiography, I have also been much more fortunate than my father in having had in my early career generous teachers and intellectual sponsors. Equally luckily for me, in fields like logic and its applications one can actually prove one's results, an excellent antidote to the self-doubts which I share with my father but which he obviously found much more difficult to overcome. Such hesitations have nevertheless hurt my career. For instance, in 1962 I managed to formulate a sketch of a proof of a cut elimination theorem for second-order logic. In discussing it with Burt Dreben and Charles Parsons, I found a gap in the argument. I was so discouraged that I gave up the search for a proof. In hindsight, I have come to believe that the gap would probably have been possible to fill.

My mother, Lempi Josefina Hintikka, née Salmi (1895–1988) was an elementary school teacher and in that way involved in the world of learning. (My paternal grandfather, Elias Aukusti Hintikka [1851–1923], had likewise been a schoolteacher.) I was also very fortunate by way of the school I attended, Keravan Yhteiskoulu in Kerava, some twenty miles north of Helsinki, in spite of the fact that the external circumstances were most of the time rather grim because of the war. I began in fact my secondary education the very same day that World War II started. Among my teachers there were several who in one way or other encouraged my intellectual interests or provided role models for intellectual pursuits. The headmaster of the school was Einari Merikallio (1888–1961), nicknamed "Keefas." He was a true scientist in the guise of a pedagogue, later recognized even internationally as a pioneer of ecological ornithology. The first defense of an academic dissertation I witnessed while still a schoolboy in 1946 was of his thesis which instilled in me a healthy sense of the magnitude of efforts needed for a Ph.D. degree. Einari Merikallio had literally counted—of course, strictly speaking estimated the number of—all the birds in Finland, not in the sense of different species but in the sense of actual specimens.

Keefas was an excellent, unconventional teacher. At a relatively late stage of my philosophical career I became interested in the Socratic method of knowledge-seeking by questioning. (See section 7 below.) I cannot help wondering how much of that interest was due to an *anamnesis* of Merikallio's teaching. He was without any comparison the best practitioner of the Socratic *elenchus* that I have ever witnessed. He could take a lad no older than Meno's slaveboy, merely put question after question to him, and at the end impart to him an interesting insight into (say) biological adaptation. When I was in high school, for some irrelevant reason I read at one point everything I could lay my hands on about the different ways of measuring the distances of fixed stars from the earth. Even though it was not part of the curriculum, the subject somehow came up in one of Merikallio's classes. He proceeded to involve me in a lengthy discussion about the subject. I remember walking out of the classroom deeply impressed by the breadth and depth of his knowledge of such an out-of-the-way subject. Only much later did it occur to me to wonder how many questions he asked in comparison with the number of statements he made himself. Was I on that occasion a victim—or a beneficiary—of Socratic irony?

There were other excellent teachers in the same school. Ilmari Salmi, nicknamed "Iisalmi," provided a model of mathematical reasoning. Martti Varsta (1892–1955) and Holger Pohjolan-Pirhonen (1918–1962) helped me to delve into the world of history and historical thinking. Olli Sampola (1912–2002), who taught German and English, was a remarkable personality, a superb teacher who later became a distinguished school administrator. He was still alive when I began to write this autobiography, with memories sharper than mine from my school days.

My interest in philosophy was kindled already when I was at school, in a way that was typical of an entire generation of intellectuals in Finland. The first impulses came from the writings of Eino Kaila (1890–1958). Kaila was an impressive thinker in several respects, a truly charismatic figure in a full sense of this frequently misused word. In historical surveys, he is usually bracketed with the positivists of the Vienna Circle, in whose discussions he in fact participated for a while. This label is nevertheless misleading. By philosophical temperament Kaila was quite unlike Viennese positivists. He was not interested in the epistemological problems of science, or rather was interested in them as a naturalistic psychologist (which he in fact also was professionally). What attracted Kaila to logical empiricists—a term that Kaila seems in fact to have coined—was their interest in contemporary science. Kaila's obsessive interest was nature herself, the secrets of which contemporary science helps to reveal to us, at least in part. In other words, he was a *Naturphilosoph* in a fully romantic sense, but one who took actual science seriously. I once tried to illustrate Kaila's intellectual character by recalling how Keynes called Newton, not the herald of the age of reason, but the last of the magi. Taking the same kind of liberty, I compared Kaila to an arctic shaman who in the Finnish language would be called a *tietäjä,* that is literally, a knower.

As a consequence, Kaila was a staunch realist in his philosophy of science—or should I say, philosophy of nature? In his younger days, he had criticized the version of Machian phenomenalism that was in Finland represented by Rolf Lagerborg (1874–1959) and even temporarily expressed doubts about the special theory of relativity because of what Kaila perceived as its Machian ancestry.

Kaila's character as a *tietäjä* was enhanced by his histrionic temperament that was far removed from the *neue Sachlichkeit* of the Vienna Circle. He had in fact professional interest in theater, among other things as a sometime advisor of the Finnish National Theater. I cannot imagine a sober Rudolf Carnap or Peter Hempel standing in front of an audience, looking up toward the heavens, shaking his fist and shouting, "Answer me, Universe! Answer me!"

Kaila's philosophical ambition nevertheless overran what he could actually accomplish. He inspired an entire generation of philosophers in Finland, prominently including Oiva Ketonen (1913–2000), G. H. von Wright (1916–2003), and Erik Stenius (1911–1990). But all of them had some starting-point different from Kaila's thought. Nobody was able to continue Kaila's own ambitious ideas.

I met Kaila for the first time personally when I was a freshman at the University of Helsinki. I wanted to take a small introductory examination in philosophy and went to Kaila's office for the purpose. The elegant, aristocratic professor was sitting in a haze of cigarette smoke with a long white silk scarf draped around his neck. For a long time he paid no attention to me. But in the end he surprised, not to say overwhelmed, me by taking out time to chat with me and explaining some of his ideas to me. Later, I came to know him personally to some extent.

In the light of hindsight, it seems that the inspiration I received from Kaila was most fortunate. It directed my attention to truly important questions, without saddling me with any easy answers to them. It also gave me a sense of the depth of philosophical and scientific problems and thereby helped me to set high standards for my work. Last but not least, it showed me what an exciting adventure philosophical thinking can be. Eino Kaila was thus another happy environmental influence on my intellectual development.

It is probably only a coincidence, but recently I have occasionally had an eerie impression of having unwittingly returned to the vicinity of one of Kaila's favorite ideas. Kaila's idea was that in areas like quantum theory we need a new conception of causality, dubbed by Kaila "terminal causality." I am trying to avoid the notions of cause and causality, but I have come to believe that in quantum-theoretical phenomena we are dealing with a special, previously unattended pattern of dependencies and independencies between different variables. Did Kaila also perhaps have some kind of vague idea that there is something peculiar about the interaction of factors that "die Welt im innersten zusammenhält"?

But what about nature instead of nurture? Like Kaila I believe in the biological determination of one's life, including intellectual life. However, such determination is difficult to document, especially as far as one's ways of thinking are concerned. The effects of heredity are perhaps easier to spot in one's overall temperament. I have no doubt that the restlessness and ambition in my family is largely due to the genes of my paternal grandmother Sofia (1858–1939). Her father was Iisakki Liimatainen, a well-to-do farmer who represented peasantry in the old-fashioned parliament in the eighteen-sixties. She raised three sons all of whom not only received an academic education but a Ph.D. or equivalent. Sulo Viljo Hintikka (1884–1925) was the first doctor of technology in Finland and later professor of chemistry at the Technical University. Elias Aukusti Hintikka (1892–1936), his father's namesake, was trained as a mathematician and became the chief actuarial mathematician of a big insurance company. (I knew that he had studied in Göttingen, but only recently did I discover that he had listened to Hilbert's lectures on the foundations of mathematics in 1907 and 1911.) I strongly suspect that Sofia Hintikka in some biological sense deserves the credit of her three sons' achievements.

In a purely intellectual realm, too, I am inclined to think that certain predispositions are innate. What I consider my best accomplishment so far is the new, more general logic that I misnamed independence-friendly logic. (See section 7 below.) Now this logic arises when one begins to ask how relations of dependence and independence between variables are expressed in a logical language. In comparison, the precise way of codifying those dependence relations in game-theoretical terms is a much less fundamental matter. In thinking about independence-friendly logic, it has occurred to me that I have always exhibited a spontaneous interest in interaction and in dependence relations. When as a child I played with a Lego-like Meccano set, I was uninterested in most of the suggested constructions because they were static—nothing moved, with no moving parts that would push each other into motion. As a logic student I was especially excited when I learned about the functions, known as Skolem functions, that govern the dependencies of quantifiers on other quantifiers, even if I could not put them to any specific use then. I have studied the history of the old Greek method of analysis, whose essence lies in the study of interdependences of different geometrical objects in a given configuration, spontaneously feeling as I did that this method is somehow especially congenial to me. Does this amount to evidence of an innate predisposition? I do not know what psychologists would say, but I cannot help suspecting that all this consilience is something more than a coincidence.

Are there other similar predispositions that can make a difference to one's thinking? Coleridge thought that there were innate Platonists as distinguished from innate Aristotelians. I have not noticed anyone evoking Coleridge's classification recently (the last example I remember was Gilbert Ryle), but I have sometimes wondered if I perhaps am something of an innate Kantian. In both epistemology and language theory, quite spontaneously, I have been looking for explanations for different phenomena in these areas, not in terms of the objects of knowledge or the objects referred to in language but in terms of what the human knowers or language users have to do (or at least have to be able to do) in order to reach them. This "doing" is of course intended to include using the concepts we need for the purpose. This is in fact the true import of Kant's "Copernican" turn. I am even on the record as maintaining that some of Kant's main arguments are essentially correct. For instance, I have argued that the kind of knowledge Kant thought of as mathematical but which we now consider as first-order logic is indeed due to the structure of the activities we have to carry out to come to know particular objects. But those activities are not, as Kant mistakenly thought, sense perceptions, but language games of seeking and finding. Since I cannot think of any educational explanation for such a Kantian bent of my mind, I am reduced to suspecting it to be due to nature rather than nurture. Unfortunately, I cannot think of much direct evidence, either, for this innateness. Or is this innate Kantianism but another aspect of my preprogrammed interest in relations of functional dependence?

Perhaps the question itself is older. Plato tried to conceptualize mathematical insights as based on *anamnesis*, that is, recollection. This is generally, and probably correctly, taken to be his way of highlighting the *a priori* character of mathematical insights. But it is also tempting to wonder whether Plato might have had experiences like mine, where certain kinds of ideas come to one as if they had arisen naturally and spontaneously, almost as if they had once been known in an earlier life, but meanwhile forgotten.

2. BECOMING A PHILOSOPHER

Eino Kaila was the first philosophical inspiration for me, but he did not play much of a concrete role in my becoming a professional philosopher. That process ran along different lines. While still in high school, I read G. H. von Wright's book *Looginen empirismi* (Swedish original, *Den logiska empirismen,* 1943). It fascinated me in a way different from Kaila's work. It did not have Kaila's pathos, but it had the clarity that a book has only if its author has actually thought his or her way through its ideas. It left in me a lasting impression—and a lasting respect for its author.

When I enrolled in the University of Helsinki in the fall of 1947, I declared a major in mathematics, a safe choice careerwise. (My father recommended that I follow in the footsteps of my uncle and aim at actuarial mathematics.) However, I had decided to try a second major also, in philosophy. With that aim in mind, I began to listen to von Wright's lectures. Some of them were on the history of philosophy, but the ones that changed my life were on logic. Basically von Wright was using the technique of distributive normal forms that every logic student meets in propositional logic and extending it to other applications, to monadic quantification theory and (perhaps in his somewhat later lectures) to special cases of the logic of relations and to modal logic. If his books bear the stamp of an author who had thought his way through the problems he is discussing, in his lectures von Wright was palpably doing just that there and then. Witnessing him in action was thus already a great experience. But there was more. Since von Wright was lecturing in Swedish, very few students were in the audience. Soon they were drawn into that thinking process as more or less active participants. By the end of my first academic year, I had learned some amount of basic logic, but what was much more important, I had learned to think about logic and about philosophy on my own. This was the crucial step in my becoming a philosopher. Or perhaps I should say, the first step. I came to know von Wright in these courses, and I have stayed in touch with him ever since, especially closely in the crucial years from 1949 to 1956. I have only one master in philosophy, and he is Georg Henrik von Wright.

But to go back to the first stages in my becoming a philosopher, it was in the summer of 1948 that I had my first major logico-philosophical insight. I suddenly saw how the idea of a distributive normal form could be extended to the entire first-order logic. (Perhaps I was lucky in that I did not know that Hilbert and Bernays had mistakenly declared such distributive normal forms impossible in general.)

It took me a long time to carry out this idea, for several reasons. I was at the same time engaged in normal studies in mathematics, physics, and philosophy; I was inexperienced and my systematic training was quite spotty; and the subject was in itself new. I had to find a bridge from my semi-intuitive ideas to familiar logical concepts and results. (Half a century later, I have had a similar experience in trying to connect my ideas about quantum logic as independence-friendly logic with the actual mathematical structure of quantum physics.) Nevertheless, by the time I took my first degree in 1952, I had finished a systematic exposition of the distributive normal forms and their basic properties. It was published in the series *Acta Philosophica Fennica*. Because of the liberal (perhaps one should say lax) requirements then prevailing in Helsinki, I was able to defend it as my Ph.D. dissertation already in the spring of 1953.

Gradually, the study of distributive normal forms led me to other insights. By examining the conditions under which the building-blocks of these normal forms are inconsistent, I arrived at the method of dealing with first-order deduction that has become known as the tree method. The outlines of this method were published in 1955. It is closely related to Evert Beth's method of semantical *tableaux,* being a kind of one-sided version of Beth's method. Needless to say, we were both totally unaware of each other's work. In June 1955, out of the blue, just when my paper had come out, I received a registered package from Holland. It contained the proofs of Beth's classical paper "Semantic Entailment and Formal Provability." Beth had heard about my work from Quine, who had given him my address. I corresponded with Beth for a while, among other things pointing out the well-known slip in the first version of his treatment of intuitionistic logic. Alas, Beth did not understand my remark and published his paper, slip and all. Later, I drew considerable inspiration from his other work, especially his ideas about existential instantiation and its precedent in the ancient Greek idea of *ekthesis.*

In hindsight, I seem to have missed a major opportunity opened up by the discovery of distributive normal forms. They provide a highly systematic and highly intuitive approach to the general theory of first-order logic. Each of their building-blocks (disjuncts), called constituents, is but a systematic account of what kinds of ramified sequences of individuals one might come upon in a world in which it is true. From them, a lot of structural information can therefore be read off, putting various model-theoretical results within one's reach. Unfortunately, I was too ignorant of the work that was being done in this direction to ask the right questions. Distributive normal forms are also in general useless for explicit formal manipulation of formulas because of their length. In order to express the insights obtained by their means one is normally well advised to use some suitable game-theoretical conceptualizations, as for instance in Ehrenfeucht's theorem.

In a technically much more modest way, I was also able to put the normal form technique to use in inductive logic, as will be recounted below. In general, I believe that the uses of the theory of distributive normal forms has not yet been exhausted.

But I am now jumping far ahead of my actual life story. To return to its progress, my first year at the University of Helsinki was rather dreary except for von Wright's lectures and a brief glimpse of Eino Kaila. Most of the other lectures were unexciting, and I did not come to know many faculty members or even fellow students. When I found that there was an opportunity to spend a year in the United States under the auspices of the Institute of International Education, I therefore applied for a scholarship for the purpose and received it. Accordingly, I spent the academic year 1948–49 at Williams College, which was my initiation to American life. I was inexperienced and socially awkward, but academically my Finnish education put me well ahead of my American fellow students. A young instructor Henry W. Johnstone discovered my interest in philosophy and logic, encouraged me, and helped me. He also suggested that I meet his former teachers at Harvard and provided me with an introduction. Thus one day I took the train from Williamstown to Cambridge and found my way to Emerson Hall. I met several members of the Harvard Philosophy Department. I remember shaking hands with C. I. Lewis and Henry Sheffer and I remember trying unsuccessfully to explain to Quine the basic ideas of distributive normal forms. (I doubt that he ever internalized the idea.) I met separately some younger philosophers, among them Henry Hiż and Hao Wang. This was my first personal contact with the leaders of the international philosophical community outside Finland.

It was only after my return from the United States that I began to enjoy my studies at the University of Helsinki. I began to find the non-philosophical courses I took more interesting. Thirty years later the prominent physicist Erkki Laurila spontaneously remembered the course in atomic physics which he had taught and which I took and whose other students included three future professors of physics (Matti Nurmia, Jorma Pöyhönen, and Pentti Kauranen). Other future professors among the fellow students I came to know included Ilppo-Simo Louhivaara and Heikki Haahti, both mathematicians, as well a Pentti Pöyhönen, later professor of economics at Helsinki.

Furthermore, through my mathematical studies I came to know the leading mathematicians of Finland, several of whom were truly impressive thinkers and personalities. Much later, in the fall of 1976, I was listening to a lecture at the Finnish Philosophical Society with my future wife Merrill. After the lecture had already started, an elderly gentleman walked in and sat on Merrill's other side. As soon as the speaker had finished, Merrill turned to me and whispered: "Who is that gentleman? He is a remarkable man!" I was not only surprised but deeply moved. The gentleman was Rolf Nevanlinna (1895–1980), the great mathematician and a former teacher of mine. He was literally one of the three or four persons I have admired most—a great scientist and a great personality. Needless to say, I was also impressed and moved by yet another example of Merrill's incredible insight into, and empathy with, other human beings. Nevanlinna's greatness was of course recognized by others, albeit not always equally spontaneously. In some cases, this recognition prompted events of some historical significance, at least significant in the context of the history of Finland. But that is a story for another occasion.

Rolf Nevanlinna's first scientific sojourn abroad had been in Göttingen, and he was in his own thinking very much in the great Hilbertian tradition. Through him, and through other Finnish mathematicians, I came to internalize much of the way of thinking that characterized the Göttingen tradition. I was deeply impressed by Nevanlinna's search for an overview, not to say synthesis, in large areas of mathematics, by his dedication to teaching and by his belief in geometrical intuition as the true psychological source of mathematical insights.

A less tradition-bound professor of mathematics was Gustav Elfving (1908–1984). He had a wide range of intellectual interests. Elfving had a significant impact on my intellectual development in that I was introduced to game theory by one of his lecture courses, which was the first one on this topic in Finland. Gustav Elfving had one of the most independent and inventive minds I have ever witnessed. Once, much later, he proudly told me that he had invented a cocktail of his own. "You would never believe that it is any good, but it is." "What's in it?" "Vodka and tomato juice." He had re-invented the Bloody Mary.

One thing Elfving brought out especially clearly and which immediately fascinated me is the power of game-theoretical analysis to reveal the rationale of certain modes of human behavior that at first sight might be capable of being explained only psychologically, such as the phenomenon of bluffing. From a game-theoretical vantage point, it is nothing more and nothing less than using mixed strategies. The significance of explanations of this kind still does not seem to me to be sufficiently appreciated by philosophers.

To return to my early career, my dissertation was technically in mathematics. Gradually, it nevertheless dawned on me that my talents and inclinations were much better suited for philosophy than for mathematics. I am fascinated by mathematical and logical structures, but I can handle them best when they are instantiated in some concrete medium, be it geometry, physical reality, human behavior, or human consciousness. I have heard of others who have experienced a similar self-discovery concerning their relation to mathematics, among them the mathematical psychologist David Marr.

I have continued to take active interest in mathematical logic, but more so in a few fundamental ideas rather than in detailed technical developments. Sometimes relatively simple ideas have turned out to be fruitful. For instance, for a long time I was fascinated by Leibniz's idea of infinite analysis and expected to find it formalized in some recondite nook or corner of modern logic. Finally, when I learned more, I came to realize that Leibniz's idea had not been captured by the existing forms of logic. I also saw how this could be done. I sketched the basic ideas of what I called infinitely deep logics in a joint paper with Veikko Rantala in 1977. While I have never returned to the subject, some younger logicians in Helsinki took up the idea, with the result that infinitely deep logics were the main subject of the research of a substantial group of logicians in Finland for a decade or so.

It has occurred to me later that there might be a moral in this story for Leibniz scholars in general. Everybody agrees that Leibniz had many brilliant ideas. But there is no agreement as to how they mesh with our own topical concerns. A hundred years ago Russell and Couturat called attention to certain ideas of Leibniz's that are logical in a generous sense of "logic." Some more recent commentators like Robert Adams have seen the interface in a number of fairly routine philosophical and theological concerns. I am convinced that there are other much subtler conceptual issues and ideas in Leibniz that might be worth investigating both for historical and even for topical purposes. I have studied a couple of them in my papers on Leibniz on plenitude and "the reign of law" as well as on Leibniz's allegedly incontinent deity. However, I believe that there are further untapped riches to be uncovered here.

Turning from mathematics to philosophy meant a reorientation in my "life and letters." By force of circumstance more than by conscious choice, I began to look for research and career opportunities in philosophy rather than mathematics. In 1955–56, I applied for the best fellowship then available in Finland, the three-year Rosenberg fellowship, but I lost the competition to Jaakko Suolahti, a learned and successful historian. But unexpectedly, I had the best break of my life—or at least the best break of my career. What had happened was this: Immediately after completing my military service in January 1954, I had gone to Harvard for a semester on a Fullbright-type (ASLA) fellowship. The trip did not begin fortuitously. My plane was twenty-eight hours late, and the first thing I discovered was that Quine, with whom I had expected to work, was in Oxford as the George Eastman Visiting Professor. But fortunately for me Peter Hempel was taking his place. He advised me on what was going on in the Boston area, ending with a recommendation to look up two promising men "of your own age group," to wit, Noam Chomsky and Burton Dreben. I came to know Chomsky, but I have never been very close to him. However, Dreben and I hit it off and became life-long friends. My friendship with him was strong enough to survive fundamental philosophical differences. It should not come as a surprise that I became aware of the contrast between views of language as calculus and language as universal medium (see section 5 below) partly because of our friendly disagreement. My philosophical relation to Burt embodied that contrast for almost half a century.

After I had returned to Finland, unbeknownst to me, Dreben nominated me for the Harvard Society of Fellows. I was elected in 1956 to the usual three-year term. The appointment letter was the only one I have ever received that is signed "Your Obedient Servant." And, as was intended by the founder and endower of the Society, the good President Abbott Lawrence Lowell, being a Junior Fellow turned out to be an excellent basis for a scholarly career. As an additional bonus, my fellow Junior Fellows included several interesting and remarkable people. I regret that I lost touch with most of them after my return to Finland in 1959. They included among others Kurt Gottfried in physics, Dudley Herschbach in chemistry, the scholar and poet John Hollander, another poet Donald Hall, the classical scholar Seth Benardete, Franklin Fisher in economics, and Everett Mendelsohn in the history of biology. There was also an intense economist and game theorist called Daniel Ellsberg. I was struck by his forceful mind but also by a hefty dose of intellectual *hubris* in his thinking. His applications of game-theoretical ideas to international relations turned out to be more important than I realized. In those days Ellsberg was still a dedicated hawk who had re-enlisted as an officer in the Marine Corps and was a consultant to the Rand Corporation, the Air Force think tank. I remember vividly the long arguments Ellsberg had with Everett Mendelsohn, who was an active pacifist. My impression was that the two disagreed much more about the facts of the case than they differed in their values. Maybe the Pentagon Papers provided the facts that persuaded Ellsberg to change his mind.

Still another Junior Fellow with whom I overlapped was Marvin Minsky, one of the founding fathers of artificial intelligence. One day he showed up and declared that he had striking evidence that computers can think better than humans. He had developed a theorem-proving program and then tested it by examining how it could handle the early theorems in Euclid. In the case of Proposition 5, the program produced a proof that was shorter and more elegant than Euclid's own. Can there be better evidence for genuine artificial intelligence?

Unfortunately I had to point out that Minsky's program's "elegant" proof was known already in later antiquity to Pappus. But myths die very hard. In the year 2001, a leading computer scientist is still extolling Minsky's proof which according to him "had not been known in modern times."

Only much later did I realize myself the deeper reason why the Pappus-Minsky proof is not representative of really creative thinking in logic and

mathematics. Such creative thinking turns crucially on the right "constructions" (as they used to be called), that is, on the introduction of the right
new objects into an argument. The problem of discovering what can be
established by means of already introduced objects can be combinationally
difficult (witness the "party problem" in Ramsey theory) but it is decidable.
What happens in Minsky's "elegant" proof is merely that a symmetry
principle is applied to the geometrical objects already under consideration.

Being a Junior Fellow also brought me in contact with a number of
leading philosophers elsewhere in the English-speaking world, among them
some memorable scholars and personalities, especially as I was able to
spend one term of my tenure as a Junior Fellow in Oxford. There I was in
the very center of philosophical activity in the English-speaking world. I
participated in the famous Grice-Strawson seminar in an ice-cold library
room at University College. I came to know Michael Dummett and Hao
Wang. I attended Gwil Owen's seminar. All these were remarkable
philosophers and remarkable personalities. I remember sitting next to Burt
Dreben at one of the earliest papers Owen gave in the United States. (It was
an early version of his paper "Eleatic Questions.") When Owen finished,
Dreben turned to me and said, "I don't know whether he is right or wrong,
but that is one brilliant paper!" As always, Dreben was right, of course. I
also attended John Austin's "Sense and Sensibilia" lectures. (Wags in
Oxford were predicting that next time he gave them, he would highlight one
of the targets of his criticisms and re-name the lectures "Price and Prejudice.") Austin was one of the most forceful, not to say devastating lecturers
I have ever heard. At one point (not recorded in the published version of the
lectures) he quoted Ayer as saying that physical objects are characterized
by a "sharp outline." Austin went to the chalkboard, drew a simple but
expressive picture of a furry cat, looked at the picture, and said, "Let's see,
where is the sharp outline?"

I was interested in Austin's ideas, and subsequently made some use of
them in my best known paper "Cogito ergo sum: Inference or Performance?" However, I have gradually come to doubt their value as a basis of
satisfactory general language theory. But as an intellect and as a person,
Austin was as formidable as anyone as a I have ever met. A knowledgeable
testimony by a third party perhaps conveys something of my impressions.
I happened to be in Uppsala in the fall of 1959 only a couple of weeks after
Austin had visited there. At one point, I was chatting with Ingemar
Hedenius, himself a strong personality, at the time the most feared
polemicist in Sweden. Suddenly he turned the conversation to Austin. "We
had this Englishman called Austin here recently. He gave a talk on what he
called performatives. I did not like the paper." (In fact, it had impressed
Hedenius strongly, so much so that soon afterwards he wrote a paper of his

own on the same subject.) "I told him so, but I must say that he defended himself quite well. *He is a hard man to convince.*"

Later, in 1964, I was able to renew my acquaintance with several Oxford philosophers when I spent a term there giving my John Locke lectures. I greatly enjoyed the experience, even though I did receive the impression that Oxford is a more hospitable environment for visitors than for local scholars. During my sojourn there I was asked to give—strictly speaking, to record—a brief talk for a philosophy series on the famous BBC Third Programme. Before the recording session, I had lunch with the responsible BBC official, a Mr. Thomas. Being a graduate of Oxford himself, he was curious about my impressions of his alma mater. Whom had I met and associated with there? I told Mr. Thomas of having talked with Gilbert Ryle, William and Martha Kneale as well as others, but that the philosophers I had seen most were the members of the Dummett-Kenny-Geach-Anscombe group. The very proper British gentleman gave me a long look and finally said, "But that is not *Oxford.*"

As to my lectures, published in 1974 by the Clarendon Press under the title *Logic, Language-Games and Information*, in the light of hindsight I was far too much concerned with solving my problems instead of relating my solutions to the concerns of other philosophers. Perhaps they were not sufficiently "*Oxford*" either.

Another splendid opportunity to broaden my view on contemporary philosophy and philosophers was the 1960 Congress of Logic, Methodology and Philosophy of Science at Stanford, to which its main organizer Patrick Suppes had invited me. That congress was the first time I saw many of the leading logicians and philosophers of the time. Among many other things, I remember witnessing a symposium on subjective probability with three truly philosophical speakers: "Good, Right, and Savage"—that is, I. J. Good, G. H. von Wright, and L. J. Savage. I was especially impressed by Alfred Tarski listening to paper after paper and in discussion pronouncing in no uncertain terms on them. One of his interventions prompted much later an amusing *déjà vu* experience. It was one of the most impressive papers at the congress, John Addison's survey of his newly minted comparative theory of quantifier hierarchies in different parts of logic and set theory. Addison motivated his work in part by expressing the hope that it would unify the study of logic and foundations. As it happened, John Addison gave a survey lecture on the same topic forty-one years later at the Tarski centennial symposium in Warsaw in June 2001. The framework was the same, and Addison's express motivation was the same. Of course, meanwhile Addison's work had given rise to a research project with lots of new results. Afterwards, I asked John Addison whether he remembered what Tarski had said after his 1960 talk. Tarski had praised Addison's theory, but concluded that it is unrealistic to hope for any real unification in logic and foundational studies.

I cannot possibly list here all the remarkable people I have come across during my intellectual odyssey at Harvard or elsewhere. Some have become close personal friends, among them Dagfinn Føllesdal, Patrick Suppes, and Gabriel Sandu. Others have been fascinating to witness as persons and/or as philosophers. Even a personal fascination has often been for me more than a matter of human interest, in that there are in my view more connections—and subtler connections—between a thinker's personality and his or her thought than what is generally recognized. Hence even a relatively casual acquaintance with someone like Karl Popper, Norman Malcolm, Hans-Georg Gadamer, or Alfred Tarski has often proved to be useful to me in my own work.

My own encounter with Gödel was brief but nonetheless memorable and perhaps also instructive. In 1954 I had a chance of discussing my work in logic with him. The discussion left me in awe, which others have told me they also experienced. I had an impression that I could not tell him anything about logic that he did not already know. I described one line of research of mine to him, and he instantly offered a better formulation of the same result. I described another one, and after a moment's reflection he responded: "Yes, you can do that." Back in Finland I told Kaila about my discussion with Gödel. Kaila commented by saying, "You should have seen him in Vienna in the thirties!"

I have no doubt that my experience was an authentic one. Yet, I had to overcome it in coming to understand the subtle and strong presuppositions on which Gödel was operating in his thinking. These include in the first place what I have called the one-world assumption, and they affected not only his philosophical opinions but also his logical theorizing.

I cannot resist the temptation of recounting another revealing incident. I visited London School of Economics a few times in the sixties and seventies and came to know some of the philosophers there, including Karl Popper, John Watkins, Joe Agassi, and Bill Bartley. It was also at the LSE that I met Amartya Sen for the first time. The most colorful member of the "closed society" of Popperians was nevertheless Imre Lakatos. For all his radical amorality, I found in him a kind of endearing naiveté, and probably because of that I was always on good terms with him. One feature of his character was revealed to me in 1974 at the memorable meeting on history and philosophy of science in Jyväskylä, Finland. (One reason it was memorable is that it was the first time Russian philosophers and historians of science were able to attend a meeting outside the Soviet Union in substantial numbers.) I gave one of the lead papers, and according to the conference format I had two commentators, one a philosopher of science or, in this case, a philosopher of mathematics, and the other a historian of mathematics. The philosopher was Imre Lakatos. Imre made his comments in the style I expected, which was like a passionate political speech. He shouted, he thumped his fist on the desk, he waved his arms—the full works. I replied, whereupon a learned historian of mathematics presented his comments. He was the senior Hungarian scholar Arpad Szabo. I was utterly astounded by his performance. Not only did he, too, present his learned commentary in the style of soapbox oratory; not only did he shout, thump his fist on the lectern and wave his arms; they were the very same gestures and the very same tone of voice as Lakatos's. I was so surprised that my reply was probably not entirely coherent. Was I so nervous that I was imagining things? To test my sanity, I afterwards commented on the weird coincidence to a senior friend. He looked at me and said, "Didn't you know? Imre was a student of Szabo's as a young man."

I suspect that what this incident illustrates is an acquisitive instinct unexpected in a former communist. I cannot help finding other instances of the same instinct elsewhere in Lakatos's behavior. For instance, the linchpin example in Lakatos's *Proofs and Refutations*, the history of the Euler theorem, he acquired from his excountryman Polya, and during his last years his serious hobbies included collecting antique furniture.

Karl Popper was a more significant philosopher by an order of magnitude than his successor Lakatos. I came to know Popper well enough to be invited to visit him at his home in Penn. I was impressed by his truly remarkable intellect, sharp and quick. At the same time I found his writings disappointing in comparison with their author. Popper's Achilles heel was not his intellect, but his intellectual temperament. I could not help having the impression that whatever subject he took up, he immediately had one clever idea about it—which he then spent the rest of his life propagating and defending, often claiming that he is the first thinker in history to have conceived of that idea. It is for this reason that Popper's views are so easy to attach a label to, such as refutation, information, propensity, and the third world. He posed as a critic of logical positivism, but his own thinking used the same conceptual framework as theirs. What would have been required in his historical situation is a substantial enrichment of the logical and other conceptual arsenal wielded by the Vienna Circle, in the first place perhaps a viable model theory (logical semantics) to transcend the "formale Redeweise" of logical positivists. But unlike Carnap, for all of his professed admiration of Tarski, Popper did not even try to develop one.

In 1965, I happened to witness Popper's possessive attitude toward his disciples, which created a personal crisis each time one of them left the closed society of Popperians. A rather strange meeting took place at the University of Denver devoted ambitiously to "Logic, Physics, and History."

The social program included an excursion to the Rockies. For some reason I literally missed the bus and—as a punishment I suspect—I was put into a limousine with Sir Karl, Lady Popper, and Cazimier Lejewski. For the entire hour-long drive, Popper talked compulsively about one thing only, which was how terribly, terribly, terribly Bill Bartley and Joe Agassi had behaved, how terribly, terribly, . . . For a while Lejewski, who had been at LSE, could muster some sort of response, but not knowing anything about what had happened, I was left speechless. I wonder who was more relieved when we finally arrived, I or the driver who was a chainsmoker but had been warned about Popper's notorious intolerance of cigarette smoke.

Naturally I also came to know lots of less famous people who nevertheless also were memorable characters. One amusing memory I have concerns Joe Ullian, whom I met when I was at Harvard and who already then was a confirmed baseball fan. One day I was driving with him to hear a lecture on Gödel. Joe was listening raptly to a game over the radio. When it was over he shouted: "This game will be remembered when Gödel is forgotten!" He was undoubtedly right—it was Don Larsen's one and only perfect game ever pitched in a World Series.

Later, my teaching positions at Stanford, Florida State University, and Boston University gave me a chance of coming to know many interesting and impressive philosophers and other scholars. Especially impressive was the group of philosophers and logicians that were colleagues at Stanford at some time or other. They included in my early days there Patrick Suppes and Donald Davidson in epistemology and philosophy of science, Dana Scott, Solomon Feferman, Georg Kreisel, and William Tait in logic, and later Julius Moravcsik, John Perry, Jon Barwise, Ian Hacking, Nancy Cartwright, and my old friend from Harvard days, Dagfinn Føllesdal, not to try to give an exhaustive list. Working together with Føllesdal kindled my interest in Husserlian phenomenology, even though I have never had a the chance of immersing myself in Husserl's thought in the way I would have liked. I do not receive when reading him the same shocks of recognition as I frequently do when reading Wittgenstein, Peirce, Leibniz, or even Aristotle. Through Føllesdal I came to know others with similar interests, among them Jitendra Mohanty, Claire Hill, and our joint students David W. Smith and Ronald McIntyre.

3. APOLOGIA PRO LOGICA MEA

Being at Harvard and in the Society of Fellows from 1956 to 1959 meant that I was in the middle of the genesis of contemporary philosophical semantics. Quine, the great critic of the semantics of modal logic and of systematic semantics more generally, was a Senior Fellow. Saul Kripke was only an undergraduate, but had a paper on the semantics of modal logic accepted for the *Journal of Symbolic Logic.* Later, he too was elected to the Society. Charles Parsons was likewise a Junior Fellow. Dagfinn Føllesdal was a graduate student writing a dissertation for Quine—brave man that he is—on the semantics of modality, of all things. Some of us were aware of the partly parallel, partly earlier work by Stig Kanger, Marcel Guillaume, and Richard Montague. However, as I recall it, none of us realized how much of our work was in its technical aspects anticipated by Tarski and McKinsey. It is not possible, it seems to me, to understand my ideas except in the context of these many-splendored developments which later led to the doctrines that have been given the label "The New Theory of Reference." My story may perhaps be lent some extra interest by the controversies in which the genesis of this theory has been shrouded.

It all began as an attempt to create an explicit logical theory for modal concepts in the wide sense in which modal logic comprises various intensional logics, such as epistemic, doxastic, and deontic logic, that is, the logics of knowledge, of belief, and of norms. Or so I thought, having been introduced to modal logic through the teaching and through the monograph by my very own teacher von Wright.

Alas, others restricted their attention to what is sometimes inaccurately referred to as alethic modal logic, that is the logic of logical (or perhaps metaphysical) necessity and possibility. That this restriction has turned out to be detrimental to the adequate understanding of the subject should not come as a surprise, for the notions of knowledge and information are much more familiar and much more important in practice than philosophers' semi-technical notions of necessity and possibility. How tricky these notions are is perhaps illustrated by the fact that (as I have shown) Aristotle failed to distinguish from each other the notions of logical (conceptual) necessity and natural (causal) necessity. (See my 1976 monograph.) Simo Knuuttila has since shown that this assimilation persisted long after Aristotle. It was a problem still in the seventeenth century. In general, a study of the history of modal notions is likely to induce a healthy skepticism in any philosopher approaching the logic and epistemology of modal notions.

Right from the beginning I was interested primarily in the semantics and pragmatics of modal and intensional concepts, as witnessed by my 1957 paper "Modality as Referential Multiplicity." For this reason, it was probably a mistake for me to use as the framework of presentation in my early studies the quasi-syntactical technique of model sets and model systems. It seems to have created in some people the impression that I was not trying to get at the actual model theory of modal notions. In any case, initially others focused much more closely on the construction of explicit logical systems and on their properties. Consequently, the problems confronting a logician cutting his or her teeth on modal notions were the formal systems of ordinary alethic modal logic that C. I. Lewis had constructed under the inspiration of Peirce. There were unfortunately too many of them for philosophical comfort, however. A choice between the different Lewis systems was far from obvious in the absence of any sharp intuitions and in the absence of a state-of-the-art treatment. Admittedly, Rudolf Carnap had outlined an explicit treatment of necessity and possibility, but Quine's criticisms had dissuaded philosophers from taking it as a genuine interpretation of modal logic. Indeed, Carnap typically preferred the use of semi-syntactical concepts like state-descriptions to a genuine model theory. Likewise, von Wright's discussion was not geared to the questions mathematical logicians were likely to ask.

In this direction the situation was changed by the introduction of the idea of alternative scenarios or "possible worlds," as they are usually called. It is natural to assume that (i) the usual laws of logic hold in each "world," that (ii) between them there obtains a certain alternativeness or accessibility relation, and (iii) that necessity means truth in all alternative "worlds" (and by the same token that possibility means truth in at least one of them). The initial insight of contemporary modal logic is that this framework serves to distinguish the most important different Lewis systems from each other simply through different assumptions concerning the properties of the alternativeness relation, such as transitivity and symmetry. This insight was reached independently sometime before 1957 by the Swedish logician-philosopher Stig Kanger (who was the first to express this idea in print) and myself. Whether and when it was reached independently by still others, I do not know.

This treatment has become known as possible-worlds semantics (in the wide sense of the word). It quickly led to intensive exploration of different deductive systems and their semantical counterparts. I made only a couple of minor contributions to detailed research in this direction. However, on a general theoretical level this development prompted a host of conceptual problems which still have not been cleared up. What are the "possible worlds" that are postulated in a possible-worlds approach? What is the alternativeness relation like and between which "worlds" does it hold? Answers to these questions are easily forthcoming in the case of epistemic logic. There the worlds alternative to a given one, say W, with respect to a knower b, are all the worlds compatible with what b knows in W. This analysis of the idea of the logical status of knowledge is so natural and so simple that I hesitate to claim it as my own. I have seen it attributed to others, among them David Lewis, but I have never seen any mention of it that predates my first use of the idea. I put it to systematic use us in my monograph *Knowledge and Belief* in 1962.

For logical (conceptual or "alethic") necessity and possibility a reasonable interpretation of the alternativeness relation is nevertheless impossible, I have argued. For the alternative "worlds" ought to be so numerous as to allow any conceptual possibility to be realized. Such a set of possible worlds cannot exist for purely logical reasons any more than the set of all sets.

In this problem situation, Kripke has resorted to an idea of "metaphysical" necessity. It is not a natural necessity, for it can be according to Kripke ascertained by intuition, not by studying the actual laws of nature. No satisfactory account has even been given of either this mysterious faculty of intuition or of the notion of metaphysical necessity. Both are to my mind examples of half-baked ideas that never should have been used in serious philosophy. Such literally metaphysical notions are apt merely to throw us back to the Aristotelian confusions about the relationship of conceptual and natural necessity.

I suspect I might not have been the only philosopher who harbored such misgivings. I have only slowly come to realize that the shrewd Stig Kanger had suspicions about the notion of possible worlds and preferred to ground his thinking on second-order logic rather than on quantification over worlds.

The only viable interpretation of logicians' "possible worlds" is the one that I initially assumed was intended by everyone. That is to understand "possible worlds" as scenarios, that is, applications of our logic, language, or some other theory to some part of the universe that can be actually or at least conceptually isolated sufficiently from the rest. This is how scientific theories are in fact applied, not to the entire universe but to some "system," as physicists are likely to call them. It has always been obvious to me that this is how the ideas of possibility and necessity are in fact used. (This is incidentally also the way Karl Popper spontaneously understood the "possible worlds" idea when I explained it to him in the early childhood of possible-worlds theorizing.) This is how "possible worlds" obviously must be interpreted in epistemic logic, which once again serves as a useful paradigm case for modal logics. Likewise, it is the way of thinking which underlies, for instance, Jimmy Savage's talk about "small worlds" in the foundations of statistics and (in a different terminology) what Montague called "pragmatics." Alas, it slowly dawned on me that this (to me obvious) way of thinking was not what a host of other philosophers had in mind. Some, in the first place "John and Jon" (Perry and Barwise), accepted the idea that what they called "situations" were the natural units of application of our logical notions. However, in their "situation semantics" these situations did not have any genuinely modal alternatives, thus neatly excising modality out of modal logic. I still regret that I did not preclude such a maneuver by labeling what I initially called possible worlds "situations."

Others, for instance David Lewis, took the term "possible world" literally as an entire possible universe (world history). They had a precedent (acknowledged by Carnap) in Leibniz, but that does not make such a speculative theory relevant to our actual use of modal notions. This is reflected by the fact that such a megalomaniac perspective on modal notions precludes several lines of thought that I find indispensable for the understanding of our actual use of modal and intensional notions, for instance understanding the nature of cross-identification (see below).

In such circumstances, a Herculean effort would be needed to clean the stable of received modal logic before it can be expected to yield genuine philosophical insights. I have not found the time and energy to attempt such an operation myself, and hence I have been wary of attempts to extract philosophical insights from the usual forms of modal logic.

Barring such a cleanup in the foundations of modal logics, the philosophical relevance of alethic modal logic—unlike epistemic logic—is therefore very small. Furthermore, by concentrating on the study of alethic modal logic rather than epistemic logic, philosophical logicians have by and large neglected the most important (and timely) applications of their subject, the study of information and cognition for the purposes of the foundations of cognitive science and computer science.

There nevertheless is another syndrome of conceptual problems about possible-worlds semantics (as I will continue to call it, albeit with a "mental reservation," as Jesuits used to say). It rears its ugly head as soon as someone tries to formulate an explicit quantified modal logic. In contemporary philosophy the first such someone was Ruth Barcan Marcus. Her work began even before the semantical discoveries of Kanger and Montague. This work led to the problem situation that confronted philosophical logicians in the late fifties and early sixties. (In some size, shape, and form these problems go partially back to Frege.) The first and foremost interpretational problem was to do justice to the behavior of singular terms and variables of quantification in modal and intensional contexts. The main symptom in this syndrome of problems was that in the context of modal notions they behaved in two different ways. Some of the most important modes of inference, in the first place substitutivity of identity and existential generalization, fail for ordinary singular terms, as Quine was quick to emphasize. However, it was soon realized that for variables of quantification these familiar logical laws must be assumed to hold. As far as I know, this insight was first spelled out explicitly—and apparently indeed reached for the first time—by Ruth Marcus. Whether or not it makes her the inventor of a "New Theory of Reference," it is an achievement of major significance.

Alas, that insight was soon coupled with an inadequate interpretation of quantifiers. This combination led to a disaster. The error has not been eradicated yet. In this day and age, the *modus operandi* of quantifiers is still commonly thought of as being exhausted by their variables "ranging over" a set of values. If so, there presumably must in any overt or covert use of quantifiers exist a range of objects that can serve as such values. Moreover, it is then a cheap thrill—as Kripke and Dana Scott among others have correctly pointed out—to give each of those values a name and then to adopt a substitutional interpretation of quantifiers. If this way of thinking is pushed to the limit, we might as well think of universally quantified sentences as long conjunctions and existentially quantified sentences as long disjunctions as long as there is only one name for each member of the domain of quantification. Since the usual logical laws hold for quantified variables, they must hold for the names in question. Accordingly we can for the purposes of logic—and for other philosophical purposes—apparently assume that there is in any realistic language a set of singular terms, obviously name-like ones, which obey the received first-order laws also in modal contexts. If b is such a name and N for the operator "it is necessary that," then from the logical truth $N(b = b)$ we can infer

(1) $(\exists x)N(b = x)$

In other words, whatever b refers to, it refers to necessarily, that is, in all possible worlds. This mode of reference is what Kripke calls a rigid designation. Kripke has argued correctly that the meaning of such a name cannot be identified with any descriptive content. Moreover, Kripke has sought to identify his rigid designators with the proper names of natural languages. The special kind of reference exhibited by rigid designators is call *de re* reference.

This in a nutshell is the so-called "New Theory of Reference." It has played a major role in philosophical semantics and in philosophy in general—in my considered judgment, a harmful one. It constitutes a remarkable illustration of Santayana's maxim, for it is for all semantical purposes identical with the semantics proposed in Wittgenstein's *Tractatus*. In the spirit of that maxim, I hasten to emphasize that Kripke, like everybody else, seems to be blissfully ignorant of the Wittgensteinian precedent. (The only partial exception to this unawareness that I know of is Hidé Ishiguro, who long ago pointed out perceptively that the objects postulated in the *Tractatus* are little more than values of quantified variables.) Hence I would not dream of accusing Kripke of plagiarism on this score. A major similarity lies already in the fact that Wittgenstein rules out any descriptive meaning of the names of simple objects. Likewise, Wittgenstein insists that in the language envisaged in the *Tractatus* each simple object has precisely one name. More importantly, the simple names postulated in the *Tractatus* refer to their objects necessarily, that is to say, in all possible states of affairs. For their objects are the substance of all possible states of affairs, the same in all of them. Perhaps we should re-dub the "New Theory of Reference" and henceforth call it the "Tractarian Theory of Reference."

This brief account of the essence of the "New Theory of Reference" is not to be found at any one location in the literature. The reason is that its protagonists have never acknowledged their own deeper reasons for holding such a view. (This explains also their unawareness of the Wittgensteinian anticipation.) I did not realize the dialectic of the new theorists' approach until much later, either. This unawareness is also the main reason why the identification of its origin has given rise to an extremely bitter priority dispute, documented in the volume *The New Theory of Reference*, edited by Paul Humphreys and James Fetzer (Kluwer Academic, 1998).

I could not get excited by this controversy, the main reason being that the entire "New Theory of Reference" is in my view evidently false. The largely unrecognized but unmistakable fact is that the meaning of quantifiers cannot be fully captured by reference to quantified variables "ranging over" a class of values, which is the idea the new theoreticians of reference tacitly rely on. This does not capture the other dimension in the semantics of quantifiers, which consists in their relations of dependence and independence to each other, and of other logical notions, such as intensional operators. The simplest counterexample to the exhaustiveness of the "ranging over" idea is offered by the mutually dependent quantifiers which I have recently begun to study. Their semantics simply cannot be understood in terms of quantifiers "ranging over" a class of values. Another part of the job description of quantifiers is to represent relations of dependence and independence between variables through their own relations of dependence on and independence of each other. A better way of conceptualizing quantifiers is to think of them as deputizing the functions that guide the choice of the "witness individuals" that show the truth of a sentence. This kind of logical behavior shows up also in the semantics of modal and intensional notions. There we still have of course only one class of individuals for our variables to "range over." But that does not imply that the choices of witness individuals mandated by quantifiers cannot mix with the choices of possible worlds prescribed by modal or epistemic operators in different ways. Hence the behavior of the variables of quantification in modal and intensional contexts should not be accounted for in terms of their ranging over a fixed class of values, much less in terms of their potential substitution-values referring "rigidly."

The prevalent confusion about the nature of quantifiers has in fact hampered the reception of my ideas. For instance, my treatment of quantifiers in epistemic and modal contexts has often been referred to as a "restricted range" interpretation of quantifiers. There cannot be a neater example of the confusion I am speaking about, for the real point of my interpretation is precisely that quantified variables do not get their full meaning from ranging over any class of entities, restricted or not.

Even though I became cognizant of this deep reason for the failure of the "New Theory of Reference" rather late, I considered this theory seriously inadequate for other reasons right from the beginning. I was convinced that the structure of quantified modal and intensional logics is determined by their being logics whose purpose is that of helping human beings to cope with several different possibilities. Ironically, far too many *soi-disant* possible-worlds semanticists do not in the last analysis take the idea of possible scenarios (worlds) really seriously. When it comes to the theory of reference and identification they operate as if the function of our language and our logic were to speak of the actual world only. Yet in real life much, perhaps most, of our thinking involves a range of possibilities only one of which (at most) can be realized. This fact of life ought to be recognized also as a fact of logic.

From this viewpoint, modal and intensional notions are operators that invite the interpreter to choose one possible scenario to be considered in explicating the meaning of the sentence in question. In other words, they are choice operators like quantifiers, but they govern choices of scenarios, not objects (of any logical type). The puzzling phenomena that prompted the development of the "New Theory of Reference" arose in typical cases through different orderings of choices. For instance, if K means "it is known that" and if the variable x takes as its values human beings,

(2) $K(\exists x)S[x]$

means that it is known that someone satisfies the condition $S[x]$, whereas

(3) $(\exists x)KS[x]$

means that it is known of some particular person that he or she satisfies $S[x]$, in other words that it is known who satisfies $S[x]$. By the same token,

(4) $N(\exists x)(b = x)$

says that b exists necessarily whereas

(5) $(\exists x)N(b = x)$

says that b refers to whatever it refers to necessarily.

Taking our cue from such observations, one can easily formulate the explicit logical laws of quantified modal logic, quantified epistemic logic, and other intensional logics without any great difficulty. The only novelty is the need of extra conditions in logical laws like existential generalization. These conditions require that the term generalized on refers to the same entity in all the relevant scenarios, that is, that it in fact specifies a determinate entity. For instance, a step of existential generalization from $KS[b]$ or $NS[b]$ to $(\exists x)KS[x]$ or $(\exists x)NS[x]$ respectively, is not valid, but can be restored by the extra premise $(\exists x)K(b = x)$ or $(\exists x)N(b = x)$, respectively. Thus the original task of constructing a quantified modal or intensional logic—the task of solving the problem Ruth Marcus in effect posed—can be accomplished (and made model-theoretical sense of) without even speaking of reference.

The real problems begin only when one tries to understand what is involved in such an enterprise, or as one might as well say, what the model theory and pragmatics of such logics is. Now the model theory of modal logics has never been fully appreciated by the new theoreticians. Perhaps I should not blame them, for it took me several years to reach the crucial idea myself. This happened in the winter 1960–61 (if my memory serves me right). The difficulty is to understand the semantical (model-theoretical) realities behind the deductive rules of logic. The basic insight here is that if we take the many-worlds idea seriously, we have to adopt something like Montague's idea that the meaning of an expression is the function that picks out its reference (extension) in each of the relevant possible worlds. But if so, that meaning and those references can be fully determined without determining the relations of identity and nonidentity between the members of different possible worlds. In other words, a theory of reference does not determine fully the semantics of any many-worlds logic. For the purpose, we need also to specify the relations of cross-world identity. For that purpose, no theory of reference, new or old, is enough. It is in fact easy to show that in our actual conceptual systems the reference system does not determine the identification system. Any theory of reference has to be supplemented by a theory of identification. The basic flaw in the "New Theory of Reference" is therefore that it is a theory of reference. For the crucial conditions like $(\exists x)K(b = x)$ and $(\exists x)N(b = x)$ do not rely only on the way the references of b in different scenarios are determined. They also rely on the criteria of identity of those different references in different scenarios ("possible worlds"). And these identity criteria not only do not reduce to any descriptive requirements; they do not reduce to any other ways in which references might be determined.

For instance, the way in which the epistemic conditions $(\exists x)K(b = x)$ can be made true does not affect in the least the way the references of b in different scenarios are determined. The way of making it true is to obtain so much new information that in all the "possible worlds" compatible with what is now known, b, picks out the same individual. In other words, new information affects the class of epistemic alternatives, not references.

As soon as I became familiar with Kripke's ideas, I realized that in view of a realistic model-theoretical analysis of quantified modal and intensional logic, his theories were hopeless. Once again, epistemic logic serves as an instructive test case. For instance, what $(\exists x)K_a(b = x)$ says (where K_a is to be read "a knows that") is that a knows who or what b is. This is a contingent statement about what a knows. It can fail to be true even when "b" is a proper name. Model-theoretically, this means that there are consistent scenarios ("possible worlds") compatible with everything a knows in which b refers to something or someone it in fact refers to. But this means that b does not refer rigidly. Even those allegedly "rigid designators," proper names, are thus readily "bent" in epistemic contexts. This would be impossible if rigid designation were somehow an intrinsic characteristic of proper names.

By the same (or similar) token,

(5) $(\exists x)N(b = x)$

says that b happens to pick out the same individual in all possible worlds. This is contingent on b's having the meaning it in fact has and also contingent (if N expresses natural necessity) upon what the world is like. Hence (5) is by no stretch of imagination a conceptually necessary proposition.

Likewise the notion of a special *de re* reference is a myth. The illusion of such a reference comes about when an individual is chosen for consideration as a value of a term before a scenario is chosen in which that individual is considered. Hence, that one and the same individual has to be available for consideration in all the relevant scenarios. But that is not made possible by a special way in which any name refers to its object in different "possible worlds," but by the criteria of cross-identification.

All told, the "New Theory of Reference" has been an unmitigated disaster, leading most philosophical logicians to work in a wrong direction for two decades. (In particular, it has discouraged philosophical logicians from developing a general epistemic logic that would be useful for application to AI and the rest of information processing in computer science.) Realizing this disaster, I never tried to make any contribution to

it, and in 1995 I tried to expose its weaknesses in a joint paper with Gabriel
Sandu called "The Fallacies of the 'New Theory of Reference'." Unfortunately, I did not at that time yet fully appreciate the role of an inadequate
understanding of quantifiers as the source of the failure of the "New
Theory."

It also took me a long time to discover and to remove another important
obstacle to formulating a truly general theory of modal and intensional
logics, especially epistemic logic. I said above that so-called *de re* reference
is in reality a matter of operator ordering. However, linear ordering and
even tree ordering does not exhaust all the different patterns of dependence
and independence between different quantifiers and other operators. It is
only when we introduce a way of exempting an operator O_2 from its
dependence on another (say O_1) within whose syntactical scope it occurs,
that we can develop a truly general theory of epistemic logic and other
modal and intensional logics. This can be done, for instance, by writing O_2
as (O_2/O_1) when the choice connected with it is independent of the choice
connected with O_1. As an application of such an epistemic logic, we obtain
the first satisfactory general theory of the logic of questions and answers,
capable of defining in general such notions as presupposition and question-
answer relationship, the latter taking the form of a condition of conclusiveness for different kinds of answers. Unfortunately I have not yet had the
opportunity of putting together a book-length exposition of these interesting
developments.

As a small example of the uses of the slash notation, it may be pointed
out that the sentence

(6) $(\exists x)K_a S[x]$

(where x ranges over persons) which means "a knows who satisfies $S[x]$"
can now be written as

(7) $K_a(\exists/K_a)S[x]$.

This is more satisfactory than (6), in that unlike (7) it specifies the content
of a's knowledge. This observation can be generalized to all different kinds
of knowledge with the exception of how- and why-knowledge. (They have
been treated separately in my more recent papers, beginning with Hintikka
and Halonen [1996].)

The superficiality of Kripke's argumentation can be illustrated by
means of a comparison with Wittgenstein. In the *Tractatus*, Wittgenstein
puts forward a similar one-name, one-object, necessary reference theory of
semantics. From the observations made above, it is seen that such a theory,
in effect, presupposes that all the objects named by proper names are
known. Why should Wittgenstein have thought so? Because his objects

were in effect Russellian objects of acquaintance which by definition are the objects given to me in immediate experience. Hence they are known to me *par excellence*. Whether this view is right or wrong, it is an integral part of a fascinating grand philosophical project. And even though Wittgenstein thinks that the structure he is describing is somehow at the bottom of the semantics of an actual discourse, he does not claim that it is exemplified by any natural language.

In contrast, Kripke claims precisely that. In order to make plausible his tacit assumption that we know the references of actual proper names, he indulges in the phantasy that proper names are introduced by some kind of dubbing ceremony which involves actual witnessing of the object to be named. This is pitifully unrealistic as an account of how proper names are in fact used. But even if this were how proper names are introduced into our language, it would not help Kripke. The reason is that a dubbing ceremony does not necessarily help one to come to know what the object is that is being named. And without such knowledge, as was seen, we have to countenance possible scenarios in which the name refers to different objects, that is, is not rigid.

One more comment is in order here. As I have indicated, I consider the entire "New Theory of Reference" radically fallacious. Why, then, have I, in my editorial capacity, encouraged discussions and even controversies about its authorship, in that such discussions have appeared both in the journal *Synthese* and in the series Synthese Library that I was editing? This might seem all the more strange as I have not for a moment believed that the main target of criticism in the priority dispute, Saul Kripke, has ever on purpose appropriated any ideas of other thinkers, no matter how oblivious he may have been to their past history. In fact, the target of my editorial decision was not Saul Kripke but the philosophical community at large. Not only once or twice but three or four times the philosophical community has given Kripke the main credit for ideas that others had put forward earlier or at the same time but independently. This has happened in connection with the semantics of modal logic whose main ideas were put forward in different forms by Kanger, Hintikka, Montague, and others before Kripke. It happened, some people claim, with the "New Theory of Reference." It definitely happened with Kripke's interpretation of Wittgenstein's rule-following discussion, which was unmistakably formulated and published before Kripke by Robert Fogelin. Even Kripke's treatment of truth was put forward at the same time by Hans Hertzberger.

The damage that such misattributions have caused is not the possible injustice that may or may not have been inflicted on a few individuals. What is invidious is that both in the case of the "New Theory of Reference" and in the case of his interpretation of Wittgenstein the philosophical community has uncritically accepted an erroneous theory merely on the strength of Kripke's romantic reputation as an ex-prodigy. Even in the case of Kripke's convergence theory of truth its importance seems to me to have been exaggerated somewhat because of Kripke's reputation. I hoped that an open discussion about the origins of the "New Theory" would serve to demystify this theory and bring about a more balanced judgment concerning the views Kripke has happened to propagate. Whether or not this hope was justified, I still do not know.

When I speak of the opportunities from which the majority of philosophers have been diverted by the New Theorists of Reference, I am not indulging in wishful thinking. Even though many grand opportunities still remain unexplored and even unidentified, I have at least scratched the surface deeply enough to be able to identify some of them. One can in fact distinguish three layers of problems and insights—or are they merely three stages of the development of my thinking?

The first step is obvious. Since the criteria of cross-world identification are largely independent of the principles of reference, they can in principle be chosen differently while keeping our system of references intact. And this is not only possible in principle. One of the most important insights in this area is that in our actual semantics we are constantly, albeit only locally, relying on two different kinds of identification. The clearest example is offered by visual cognition. There we can—and do—identify persons and objects on the one hand via their location in someone's visual space, and on the other hand via their role in public life. More generally speaking, we can speak of perspectivally and publicly identified objects. Even though in any one actual or possible situation there is only one class of objects present, it is tempting to speak of visual objects and public objects, respectively. (Notice that what I call here visual objects are not private in the sense of being accessible only for the perceiver; they are ordinary objects identified from some perceiver's perspective.) In a typical successful public identification, the perceiver finds (on the basis of one's momentary visual information) a slot for some given visual object ("that woman over there") among his or her public objects. This obviously means *seeing who* she is ("Lady Bird Johnson," to use an actual incident from my own experience as an example). In contrast, in a typical visual identification, the perceiver finds a slot for some known public entity among his or her visual objects. ("Are you looking for Dr. Livingston? Dr. Livingston is that gentleman over there.") This is ordinarily expressed in terms of *seeing* with a direct grammatical object, or in terms of *recognizing* the person or object in question. ("You can see Dr. Livingston over there.") Since quantifiers, when used in intensional or modal contexts, rely on some particular mode of identification, two kinds of identification principles correspond to two pairs of quantifiers, each of which behaves on its own in the way explained above. (See, for example, [2]–[3] and [6]–[7].)

This insight into the duality of our actual identification methods is to my mind probably the most important neglected idea in contemporary analytic philosophy. It holds for instance the key to the logic of demonstrative expressions. (They rely on the perspectival mode of identification.) It puts into a perspective several philosophical ideas, for instance, Russell's distinction between objects of acquaintance and objects of description. Among other ideas, it facilitates a neat diagnosis of one of Kripke's mistakes. We can see in the light of the distinction that the idea of rigid designator is relative to a mode of identification. For perspectival identification, a definite individual is captured ostensively, by pointing and saying "this" or "that," Russell, who at bottom considered perspectival identification as the only philosophically correct one, maintained that there are only three "logically proper names" (alias rigid designators, one could perhaps add), viz., "this," "that," and "I." Kripke's theory of naming is a dramatization of such ostensive identification. His mistake is in thinking that such ostensive identification also captures a definite public object. This is of course a fatal confusion, engendered by Kripke's failure to tell the two kinds of identification apart.

Much more generally, one of the most crucial insights in contemporary philosophy is that some of the most important epistemological problems concern at bottom matters of identification of the kind we meet in the semantics of modal and epistemic notions. Indeed, as I tried to indicate in my 1977 paper "Possible-worlds Semantics as a Framework for Comparative and Critical Philosophy," the semantics of intensional logic offers an instructive framework for discussing several interesting developments in twentieth-century philosophy in general. The first philosopher I know who has been aware, however dimly, of these connections is Elizabeth Anscombe. I was in the audience when she gave her Howison lecture "The Intentionality of Sensation: A Grammatical Feature" in Berkeley in 1963. Her lecture opened my eyes to connections between such epistemological problems as, on the one hand, the nature of the objects of perception, and on the other hand, the intensional objects in modal logic. I dealt with some of them, for instance with the problems of Russell's objects of acquaintance, but in the light of hindsight I realize that I should have done much more. How revealing the semantical perspective can be is shown by Russell's quest of the true objects of acquaintance. In the case of perception, they were, for him, sense data. And Russell's sense data were not mere sense impressions. They belonged squarely to the physical world. But what are they? Because of epistemological arguments like the "argument from illusion," Russell could not identify them with ordinary physical objects.

They must be more directly accessible than physical objects. But where are they, then? I have called this quest for the immediately given Russell's "longest philosophical journey." Apart from history, the answer is an ironic one: they are our ordinary objects but identified perspectivally rather than publicly. Interpreted as a search for a special class of actually existing entities, Russell's quest was a wild goose chase.

But even such purely philosophical insights do not exhaust the full import of the distinction between the two modes of identification. Sometime in the eighties I happened to be in conversation with the brilliant neuroscientist Lucia Vaina, who was explaining to me the important distinction between the two cognitive systems known in neuroscience as the "where" system and the "what" system. After a while I stopped her and said, "You are preaching to the converted. Your distinction is a generalization of my distinction between two modes of identification." "How can that be? Your distinction is merely conceptual—logical and semantical. The neuroscientific distinction is not merely functional. It is anatomical; the two systems are implemented by different cortical centers." "Well, if so, I will be the first philosopher since Descartes who is arguing for his theories by means of anatomical evidence."

Seriously speaking, there is by this time no doubt whatsoever that the two distinctions are identical. Neurological evidence concerning patients whose relevant centers have been damaged provides far better illustrations of the conceptual distinction than I ever would have dared to imagine. For instance, Oliver Sacks's "man who mistook his wife for a hat" is a vivid example of a nearly total loss of public identification by visual means, while mistakes in pointing, loss of depth vision, and difficulties in spontaneously distinguishing left and right are symptoms of impaired perspectival visual identification.

This striking connection might even have been of serious professional interest to neuroscientists. The conceptual analysis just adumbrated shows that the distinction between the two systems does not lie in a difference between two different kinds of visual information but in a difference between two kinds of identification. Even syntactically speaking, there is only one epistemic operator involved in the expressions for the two kinds of identification. Admittedly, there are two kinds of quantifiers involved, but they are only codifications of the two modes of identification. Yet some earlier neuroscientists maintained just such an informational distinction and thought that it manifests itself in a difference between two different pathways conveying different kinds of information from the eye to different parts of the cortex. This view ("the two pathways doctrine") has been criticized and largely discredited. My point is that there would have been little temptation to believe in it if the conceptual situation had been clarified

by pointing out that the distinction does not involve a distinction between
two kinds of information in any literal sense.

I have devoted considerable thought to these matters in the last ten-odd
years, but it is only now that I am ready to dare to try to write (together with
John Symons) something for publication. Here I mention the vistas opened
by the idea of two identification methods to illustrate the highly important
interdisciplinary and intradisciplinary possibilities that have been neglected
by philosophers because of their dogmatic faith in the so-called New
Theory of Reference.

4. RELATIONS TO OTHER PHILOSOPHERS: A CASE STUDY

I have always been puzzled by the relationships of different philosophers
to each other, and even more by what historians and other folk say of those
relationships. By "influences," historians seem to refer almost exclusively
to a thinker's adopting the doctrines of another one. It has always seemed
to me that the actual interplay of different philosophers is much subtler than
that. Long ago, a friend expressed to me her surprise that I had not become
a follower of any big name philosopher. My surprise at the comment must
have been much greater than hers. I have never understood the importance
that many people associate with the different "schools" or "movements."
Such terms make sense only when the philosophers and/or scientists in
question actually interact, as for instance in the Vienna Circle. But as that
very example illustrates, such an interaction does not imply very much by
way of shared doctrines or other shared philosophical views. And even
institutionalized cooperation does not guarantee a real meeting of minds.
Heidegger is often said to have begun his philosophical career as a
phenomenologist and as a follower of Husserl. But, as Martin Kusch has
documented, Heidegger's true relationship to his alleged master turns out
to have been quite different. As early as 1923 he wrote to Karl Löwith that
"Husserl was never a philosopher, not for a second in his life. He becomes
ever more ridiculous." With followers like that, Husserl did not need enemies.

Even acknowledged relations of influence between philosophers can be
perplexing. In 1931 Wittgenstein listed ten thinkers who had "influenced"
him. Yet it is impossible to find any traces of specific philosophical ideas
that Wittgenstein had taken over from the last five (Kraus, Loos, Weininger,
Spengler, and Sraffa), and with the exception of Bertrand Russell the
influence of the first five has been considerably exaggerated in the
literature. The doctrinal influences of G. E. Moore and Ernst Mach (neither
of whom is named by Wittgenstein) on his explicit views are much more

pervasive than those of Boltzmann, Hertz, or Schopenhauer (all of whom are listed by him). What Wittgenstein seems to have in mind are the thinkers who posed him problems or otherwise inspired him, not the ones whose views he shared.

It has occurred to me that I could do my readers a service by giving an account of my relationship to one important thinker, to illustrate the complexities and ambiguities of real-life philosophical "influences." The obvious choice for that role is Ludwig Wittgenstein. I do believe that that relationship can illustrate some of the vagaries and subtleties of philosophical "influences" of different thinkers on each other.

I must have come across Wittgenstein's name and a brief description of his *Tractatus* for the first time in von Wright's book *Looginen empirismi*. (Characteristically, Kaila had little use for Wittgenstein.) Some of Wittgenstein's ideas that von Wright expounded immediately struck a responsive chord. If for G. E. Moore, Russell's theory of definite descriptions was a "paradigm of philosophy," I found such a paradigm in Wittgenstein's idea that the logical truths of truth-functional logic are tautological. The combination of conceptual elegance with interpretational clarity impressed me greatly. In hindsight, I have come to realize what is involved and why this paradigm is indeed a fortunate one. Generally speaking, the main weakness of the entire contemporary logical theory is far too poor a grasp of the concrete model-theoretical and pragmatic import of formal concepts and results. In the case of truth-function theory, this import is for once transparently clear. There one can see how each proposition conveys information by literally ruling out certain possibilities concerning the world and admitting others. When it does not rule out anything, it does not convey any information; and that is precisely when the proposition in question is a logical truth of truth-functional logic. Here the concrete meaning of logical truth and of its relation to the notion of information is as robust as it can be.

Indeed, this way of thinking can be thought of as having inspired my work on distributive normal forms. In such a normal form, one literally sees how a first-order proposition admits certain mutually exclusive and collectively exhaustive alternative possibilities and excludes others. One can even see how these alternatives are specified, viz., by listing all the possible ramified sequences of individuals (down to a given quantificational depth) which one could meet in the kind of world in question. Unsurprisingly, by means of such normal forms, I was able to analyze the notion of information in the sixties. Among other things, I was able to distinguish two different kinds of information, which I called depth information and surface information. Deductive reasoning can increase one's surface information, while it cannot increase depth information. These insights have a great deal of general philosophical interest. For one thing, they show that Quine is superficial, if not confused, in claiming that even logical truths cannot be considered analytic in the accepted sense of the term. More generally speaking, Quine's reasons for rejecting analytic-synthetic distinctions do not stand up to the actual logic of information. Unfortunately, in view of the damage Quine's rejection has wrought on the philosophical community, I was too tentative to press the philosophical point at the time, that is to say, in the sixties and seventies.

Thus much of my earliest work was indirectly inspired by Wittgenstein-ian ideas, the mediator being von Wright. When I was asked much later to contribute to the Library of Living Philosophers volume on von Wright, the natural choice for me was to write precisely on the ideas of tautology and normal forms. As it happened, von Wright was also the tool of chance that led me to meet Wittgenstein in person. I spent my second undergraduate year 1948–49 in the United States. As I indicated above, I was already then working with von Wright on logic. On his suggestion I stopped in Cambridge on my way back to Finland for a week or so to discuss my work with him in person. I was invited to stay with the von Wrights. When I arrived there—I can still remember the address: "Strathaird," Lady Margaret Road, Cambridge—I found out that they had another house guest, Ludwig Wittgenstein. Although he was not well and although he spent most of his time working, I saw Wittgenstein at meals and on other social occasions, including two philosophical discussions he had with his friends. Nevertheless I did not exchange more than a couple of words with him directly. I was more or less aware of Wittgenstein's position in philosophy at the time, but his thought was not one of my immediate interests. Yet meeting Wittgenstein was a memorable experience which gave me a per-spective not only on his personality but also on his way of thinking. The strongest experience I had was the almost frightening intensity of his thinking even when he was discussing philosophy with a couple of friends. Von Wright told me that Wittgenstein's doctor had discouraged him from being involved in philosophical discussion too often, because it was taxing his physical strength. Only much, much later did I begin to understand why it was so difficult for Wittgenstein to organize his ideas and to articulate them.

There is little that I can contribute first-hand to Wittgensteiniana. Two vignettes may nevertheless be interesting as corrections to oversimplified myths about his personality. Wittgenstein may have been reclusive and egocentric, but he certainly was enough of a man of the world to enjoy the company and conversation of the aristocratic, well-educated ladies of the house, Mrs. von Wright and her mother, Countess von Troil. At one lunch, I overheard the great philosopher jokingly promise the elegant Elisabeth von Wright to poison Mrs. Braithwaite the next time she came to visit.

Apparently Margaret Masterman was not a favorite character of either of them.

More significantly, once someone steered the conversation to a memorial volume that the friends of the late John Cornford had edited in his memory. John Cornford had studied in Cambridge in the thirties and had become something of an unofficial leader of the young Marxist intelligentsia in Cambridge. Together with Julian Bell he had gone to Spain to help the loyalist cause. Both had died there. To my naïve surprise, Wittgenstein (who had known Cornford in Cambridge) not only knew the volume but said a few kind words about John Cornford. He had been very unhappy at school and in Cambridge, Wittgenstein mused, but had found something to live for and even to die for in Spain.

But then Wittgenstein changed his tone. "Cornford's friends tell me that one reason why he was so unhappy in Cambridge is that old fools like myself did not understand his marvelous ideas. Let me tell you—if I had come to a university when I was a young man and professors had been such fools as to not understand my ideas—I would not have been unhappy at all. That would have been a marvelous opportunity!" I am not now sure that Wittgenstein's counterfactual was true, but it does illustrate a facet of his personality that has not received its due. He was a recluse and something of a mystic, but he was also a proud Bloomsbury intellectual who could condemn a philosopher who never engages in a philosophical argument as being like a boxer who never enters the ring.

Unbeknownst to me, Wittgenstein apparently was working on the final version of both Part I and Part II of the *Philosophical Investigations* during my visit. All I knew of this work were the copies of a few fragments that von Wright gave me while I was in Cambridge. I remember that they included at least paragraphs 253 and 254 of *Philosophical Investigations* I. I pondered on them, but had no framework in which I could see their *Witz*, as their author might have put it. Likewise von Wright gave me copies of some of Wittgenstein's letters to Russell. I was deeply impressed by the passionate search for a genuine friendship that I saw reflected there. I even wrote (in Finnish) a short piece on them with the title "The Limits of Friendship." Alas, for copyright reasons it could not be published. That essay nevertheless prompted an interesting question. I thought I had heard Wittgenstein say something nostalgic about the intellectual climate of pre–World War I Cambridge. Von Wright contradicted me, citing the bleak view Wittgenstein invariably took of his own past. I am still unsure if the comment I ascribed to Wittgenstein really is incompatible with von Wright's undoubtedly correct generalization.

In the first few years of my career I did not work on Wittgenstein's philosophy in any organized manner. I did read the *Tractatus* and the

Philosophical Investigations and thought about them. I felt I understood some aspects of the *Tractatus*, especially the so-called picture theory whose gist I saw in an isomorphic relationship between a sentence and the (possible) fact it represents. When Erik Stenius's thoughtful book on the *Tractatus* came out von Wright said to me: "That is the interpretation of picture theory you have been advocating." I was mildly puzzled, for I had found that "interpretation" so obvious that no proprietary thought had crossed my mind.

In 1958 I did publish a small note on the *Tractatus* (*Mind*, vol. 67, pp. 88–91) which provoked a curious incident. I pointed out that proposition 5.62 of Wittgenstein's *Tractatus* had been mistranslated—as seemed to me fairly obvious—in the original 1922 bilingual edition and that the mistranslation had in fact misled English-speaking philosophers. Wittgenstein is not there speaking of *the language only I understand,* but of *the only language I understand.* I then went on to speculate on the nature of Wittgenstein's self-confessed solipsism, especially about the conceptual connections between my language, my world, and my personal identity.

This note was not a big deal, but I was nevertheless disappointed when G.E.M. Anscombe published in 1959 her book *An Introduction to Wittgenstein's 'Tractatus'* (London: Hutchinson). There Anscombe not only claimed that my translation is wrong and the Ogden-Ramsey translation correct, but cited on her behalf "the decisive and unanimous opinion of people whose native language is German" whom she had reportedly consulted and who had supported her reading "always . . . with certainty." This was either a bluff or—more likely—an example of Elizabeth Anscombe's remarkable powers of suggestion, for purely linguistically my reading was unmistakably the more natural one. However, what could I do? It was apparently my word (my translation) against hers (and Ogden's). Indeed, an observer who reviewed the exchange wrote that the only way of deciding would be for Wittgenstein to rise from his grave and to render judgment. I was luckier than I perhaps deserved, in that Wittgenstein did so, figuratively speaking. What happened is that Casimir Lewy discovered in Cambridge Frank Ramsey's copy of the bilingual edition of the *Tractatus* in which Wittgenstein had penned marginal comments and corrections. One of the corrections was to the very proposition whose translation I had mooted. Guess whose translation Ludwig gave.

Lewy's discovery was published in *Mind* in 1967 (vol. 76, pp. 416–423). Even Elizabeth Anscombe was convinced. The master had spoken himself. In the second edition of her book, she omitted all criticisms of my note, gave the right translation and rewrote her entire interpretation of Wittgenstein's solipsism. For whatever reason, she nevertheless did not bring herself to point out that I had given the right translation before

Lewy's discovery, but simply omitted all mention of my note. Yet she left evidence of my moral victory in her book. She forgot to take me off the index.

One reason why this by itself insignificant episode is worth telling is that it epitomizes the large number of misinterpretations that have been foisted on Wittgenstein even by the best known interpreters. The episode brought vividly home to me at an early stage of my philosophical development the superficiality of most of the current interpretations of Wittgenstein. I hope that it will have the same influence on others. Another early example is provided by the sometime controversy about whether the objects Wittgenstein postulates in the *Tractatus* are all particulars or whether they also include properties and relations. It was clear to me early on that Wittgenstein's view was the latter one. Yet several well-known Wittgensteinians from Elizabeth Anscombe and Irving Copi down strenuously argued that properly speaking only particulars can be objects in the sense of the *Tractatus*. Some of them tried to appeal to *Tractatus* 2.03 where Wittgenstein says that in an atomic proposition objects hang together "like links in a chain," oblivious to what Wittgenstein's point there is, viz., that objects of different logical type "hang together" because of their own respective forms, not because of some additional "logical glue" that keeps them together.

Interpreters of this persuasion were in for a rude surprise, however. Before I had a chance of joining the discussion, their mistake was corrected by the master himself. When Wittgenstein's *Notebooks 1914–1916* were published, they could read there (p. 61) that according to Wittgenstein, "Relations and properties, etc., are *objects* too." [Emphasis in the original.] Some obstinate defenders of the particularist interpretation tried to suggest that Wittgenstein might have changed his mind between the *Notebooks* and the *Tractatus*. Such wishful thinking was quashed when Desmond Lee published in 1980 the explanations that Wittgenstein had given him about the meaning of the *Tractatus*: "'Objects' also include relations; a proposition is not two things connected by a relation. 'Thing' and 'relation' are of the same level. The objects hang as it were in a chain" (*Wittgenstein's Lectures, Cambridge 1930–1932*, p. 120).

In our day and age another massive misinterpretation is rampant. It is the idea that in Wittgenstein, especially in the early Wittgenstein, the "unsayable" (sometimes hyped up as "nonsense") consists predominantly of metaphysical and perhaps ethical and religious views. This line of thought disregards the overwhelming historical and systematic evidence which I have marshaled and which places Wittgenstein squarely in the tradition maintaining the ineffability of semantics. (Cf. here section 5 below and chapter 1 of *Investigating Wittgenstein*.) This ineffability was in fact for him the first and foremost type of the unsayable. In a letter to Schlick on August 8, 1932, Wittgenstein himself relates in so many words "the fundamental idea" of the *Tractatus* to Carnap's notion of the "formal mode of speech," which of course is but a way to avoid speaking of the semantics of language. Wittgenstein's doctrine of the unsayable admittedly served as a bridge to his ethical and religious views, but it was a primarily semantical doctrine, not a metaphysical one. By Wittgenstein's own standards, Carnap was a more faithful follower of his ideas about the unsayable than the "New Wittgensteinians" of today. I may be unkind, but cannot help thinking of what Oscar Wilde might have said of the New Wittgensteinians in analogy with his quip about the great British tradition of foxhunt: "The unspeakable pursuing the uneatable." Now we have another set of unspeakable ones pursuing the unspeakable.

Much later it has occurred to me that my little controversy with Elizabeth Anscombe might perhaps have had unintended consequences. The scholarly identity of two of the original Wittgenstein trustees, Anscombe and Rhees, consisted largely in their being Wittgenstein's ex-students and interpreters. This role of theirs had been put in new light by the discovery of an enormous *Nachlass* which they had not examined. Gradually, they came to realize, possibly jolted by episodes like Lewy's discovery, that they were sitting on a time bomb which might explode their interpretations. This would perhaps explain their strangely secretive behavior *vis-à-vis* the publication of Wittgenstein's posthumous material. Were they trying to have this *Nachlass* published or at some level of awareness trying *not* to have it published? I have no evidence, but it is hard for me to understand the behavior of Anscombe and Rhees otherwise.

To return to chronology, my reading of Wittgenstein gradually inspired important lines of thought in my mind. Probably because of my Kantian ("Copernican") bent of mind I became fascinated by Wittgenstein's notion of language-game and its role in the semantics of our language. Since I had acquired some knowledge of von Neumann's game theory from Gustav Elfving, a simple and perhaps somewhat simple-minded question suggested itself to me: What happens if we apply the basic concepts of the theory of games to Wittgensteinian language-games, or perhaps similar ones? But what are the relevant language games? My latent interest in Skolem functions was activated and suggested an answer. The values of the Skolem functions of a first-sentence S are the "witness individuals" which serve to vouchsafe the truth of S. Hence S is true according to our normal pretheoretical lights if and only if there exists a full set of its Skolem functions. And now the search for appropriate witness individuals can obviously be thought of as a "game against nature" in the sense of the von

Neumann–Morgenstern theory, with sets of Skolem functions playing the role of winning strategies. Since the players of such games cannot be assumed to be initially acquainted with all requisite witness individuals, the "game" of verifying S amounts essentially to a game of seeking and finding. Thus Wittgenstein's idea of language-game was the direct inspiration of the important approach which has come to be known as game-theoretical semantics.

Much later I realized that Wittgenstein had himself come close to this idea when he maintained that a crucial aspect of our notion of object is that an object can be sought for and found. He never connected this idea with logic, however, but rather with the notion of space. As one might put it, he never realized that to be an object is to be a value of a bound variable, to give a new twist to Quine's dictum.

Be that as it may, what is probably the most important idea of my philosophical thought was thus originally inspired by Wittgenstein. At the same time, I realized that I was applying Wittgenstein's ideas not only in a way he had not done himself, but in a way that he would in all likelihood have rejected out of hand. For instance, Wittgenstein maintained that the concept of game is a notion without hard-and-fast boundaries and without any sharp definition operating only by means of "family resemblance." In spirit, if not in letter, von Neumann's game theory can be thought of as providing a refutation of this claim in that it does yield a sharp, explicit characterization of games in general. (Of course, we have first to unpack the unfortunate ambiguity of Wittgenstein's German word *Spiel* which can mean either "game" or "play.")

I was initially rather timid and hesitated to maintain that for the later Wittgenstein language-games were the crucial semantical links between language and the world. For one important example, can the human behavior connected with internal sensations really serve as a language-game constitutive of the meanings of our sensation-vocabulary? I expressed my hesitations in one of my lectures at Stanford in 1977. In the audience was my future wife, Merrill. She contradicted me most vigorously, not only claiming that I had been too timid in not following up the idea of language-games as the alpha and omega of semantics according to Wittgenstein but producing immediately four single-spaced pages of evidence. I was convinced, and that moment was the starting point not only of my cooperation with Merrill on Wittgenstein but of my career as a serious Wittgenstein interpreter.

Some of the results of my work jointly with Merrill were published in our book, *Investigating Wittgenstein*, in 1986, which was truly a labor of love in more than one sense. Of the line of thought and the line of events that led to it, two episodes deserve to be highlighted. One of the few major insights I have ever received from the secondary literature on Wittgenstein is the relationship between Russell's theory of acquaintance and Wittgenstein's picture theory that David Pears pointed out in his perceptive article in the *Philosophical Review* in 1977. From a suitable point of view, the *Tractatus* is little more than Russell's 1913 theory of acquaintance minus logical forms as self-sustaining objects of acquaintance. Together with Merrill, I was able to push this idea further than Pears, who misinterpreted our book as arguing for a phenomenalistic interpretation of the *Tractatus*. Of course, this would have been diametrically opposite to the intentions of Wittgenstein who simply followed Moore and believed that in any experience something is directly given to me, something that is an objective part of reality and which in some cases will even be, like Russell's sense data, part of the physical world. Pears's misreading is an instance of widespread failure by philosophers to appreciate the notion of phenomenology and distinguish it from phenomenalism.

This led us to what might be called a phenomenological interpretation of the *Tractatus*. But what about its relation to Wittgenstein's later ideas? At one time, very early in Merrill's and my work on Wittgenstein, I happened to discuss our interpretation of the *Tractatus* with von Wright. (I can remember vividly the setting, which was "The English Tearoom" on Unioninkatu in Helsinki.) As usual, von Wright was at first noncommittal but eventually said, "That interpretation would explain Wittgenstein's later change of view." Even though I had not studied Wittgenstein's development, scales fell from my eyes and I saw in a flash the tremendous interpretational possibilities that von Wright had in mind. What I did not know at the time is how strikingly his conversion from phenomenological languages to physicalistic ones is reflected in Wittgenstein's notebooks. In reading the crucial entries, especially the entries on October 10–11, 1929, one has the feeling of looking over his shoulder.

I have continued to work on Wittgenstein after Merrill's death. To some extent, the emphasis has moved subtly. Our joint book was intended "only to connect," as its motto reads, that is, to interpret Wittgenstein rather than to judge him. Slowly, as I have come to understand Wittgenstein better, I have found him wanting more and more in important respects. In particular, one of his latest overarching ideas, viz., the conceptual primacy of language-games over their rules, I find unacceptable in its own right.

At the same time, my attitude toward the community of self-appointed Wittgenstein scholars gradually changed. Together with Merrill, I took part in the Second International Wittgenstein Symposium in Kirchberg in 1977. We were happy to be able merely to make a contribution to Wittgenstein studies and to be accepted as Wittgenstein scholars. Over the years, the disappointments with Wittgenstein studies have taken their toll. By the fiftieth anniversary of Wittgenstein's death, I cannot escape the sad feeling that nobody I know (with the exception of von Wright and perhaps a couple of other philosophers) has anything like a firm overall grasp of Wittgenstein's philosophy, including its development. Whether I have one, is best left to others to judge. What is to me unmistakable by this time is that the current state of Wittgenstein interpretation is nothing less than a serious intellectual scandal.

In any case, I have continued to find it most helpful to study Wittgenstein also for the purposes of my own systematic work. It was largely through a study of Wittgenstein that I came to realize the importance of the contrast between the conceptions of language as calculus and language as a universal medium. (More about this contrast in section 5.) And the good old Ludwig keeps surprising me. In the summer 1997, I was chatting with Anna-Maija Hintikka, a psychologist and speech therapist who is married to a cousin of mine. What she was telling me about her patients prompted an unusually forceful *déjà vu* experience. I realized suddenly that Wittgenstein, too, must have been dyslexic, even though I did not at that time remember (or perhaps had not even noticed) that he was a self-confessed one. Wittgenstein had in fact connected what he called his "difficulty in spelling" with "the rest of my character." This psychological diagnosis has turned out to be not only documentable but oddly compelling. One anecdote perhaps conveys a flavor of this consilience of evidence. Anna-Maija Hintikka had been interviewing as a part of her professional work a well-educated lady in Sweden who was dyslexic. When Anna-Maija told her of having begun to study Wittgenstein as a case of dyslexia, she responded: "Didn't everybody know that Wittgenstein was dyslexic?"

Now I had been, and I continue to be, skeptical about attempts to interpret philosophers in terms of their psychological idiosyncrasies. Even in the rare instances when such interpretations are psychologically sound, they are at best shallow and at worst harmful in that they direct scholars' attention away from the real problems. In Wittgenstein's case, too, his dyslexia can be brought to bear on the evaluation of his philosophy only in subtle ways. However, methodologically an insight into his dyslexia is vitally important for the purpose of understanding his thought. Importantly and usefully, but perhaps not very deeply, it not only explains why Wittgenstein wrote about philosophy the way he did, but offers highly useful clues to the structure of his argumentation and thereby to his meaning.

But I have no doubt that the insight into Wittgenstein's dyslexia throws light on his philosophical thinking as well. Shortly before his death von

Wright wrote to me saying that this subject interests him more and more and that in his words, "I have come to believe (only now) that it offers one key for understanding his philosophy."

The following is perhaps a case in point. There is no doubt that one of Wittgenstein's main preoccupations in his philosophy of mathematics and of logic is the relation of purely formal operations ("calculi") and their rules to the applications of mathematics and logic. He had a keen sense of both, but he could not grasp their interconnection. Wittgenstein's awareness of this kind of problem was made especially keen by his dyslexia, which made it hard for him to master such relationships. Unsurprisingly, he never solved this problem. But when I realized this, I also realized what a tremendous achievement it was on Wittgenstein's part to call attention to this problem, which has been neglected or at least underestimated by practically all philosophers and logicians. I have come to think that this is the most timely problem area in the philosophy of logic and mathematics. One reason, but not the only one, for philosophers' neglect has been the unfortunate trichotomy syntax–semantics– pragmatics, which has misled many people into thinking that the use of language cannot be studied by reference to rules that are equally explicit and equally independent of the idiosyncracies of language users as the rules of syntax. Syntax is not a part of graphology, and by the same token pragmatics does not have to be a part of the psychology and sociology of language users.

Be this as it may, once again the study of Wittgenstein has led me to recognize a major research problem and has thus significantly enriched my own work in philosophy and in logic.

Thus several of the main problems and main ideas of my own philosophical work have been prompted by Wittgenstein. These are among the most important impulses I have received. Does that make me his follower? I have never thought so. Has he "influenced" me? The answer depends on the sense of "influence." It was seen that the thinkers Wittgenstein listed as having influenced him are in reality those who had posed him problems or otherwise made him aware of opportunities for philosophical thinking, not those whose assumptions or views he shared. In the same sense, I do not hesitate to acknowledge Wittgenstein's influence on my thinking, even though I have become sharply critical of several of his main views.

It seems to me that historians of philosophy, ancient as well as recent, are well advised to focus their attention on such indirect "influences" much more than is the current par for the course in the history of ideas and in the history of philosophy. The interaction of philosophers is a much subtler matter than most historians of philosophy understand.

5. HISTORICAL EXCURSIONS

Another "nature or nurture" question is posed by my work in the history of philosophy. My father was trained as a straightforward scientist, but his interests gradually turned more and more to the history of biology and to the history of science and learning more generally. My training was not oriented toward history, and yet spontaneous inclinations have led me to work in the history of philosophy and the history of ideas. Or is the appearance of spontaneity an illusion and was my interest in history perhaps originally inspired by my explorations of my father's library?

In purely historical terms, my earliest work in the history of philosophy had in any case a concrete motivation. I was curious to see what the precedents of my own systematic work were and to see whether my own results could throw any light on the history of the subject. In this way, my work on modal logic prompted me to see how the first modal logician in Western philosophy, Aristotle, handled modal concepts. To my surprise, I was able to establish a couple of significant results. Among them was the conceptual tie between modal and temporal concepts in Aristotle and also the related insight that Aristotle did not have any clear distinction between logical (conceptual) and natural (physical) necessity. Much later, I began to wonder how my interpretation of Aristotle was related to the views of the medievals, many of whom were Aristotelians of some kind or other. I knew that I did not have the competence to research the question, but a survey of the secondary literature quickly showed that no clear-cut answer to it was known. At that point Simo Knuuttila was looking for a dissertation topic. Knowing that he had the appropriate background, I told him about the problem. Simo was shrewd enough to realize that my problem was no mean task. He nevertheless took it on, worked on it, and found an interesting answer. My unconventional interpretation of Aristotle turned out to have been the dominating one till the thirteenth century. And even philosophers who like Duns Scotus rejected Aristotle's views usually ascribed them to Aristotle.

Simo Knuuttila thus got a flying start to his subsequent successful career. He was overly generous, however, in giving me some credit for his results. The result was that his views were for a while known among specialists as the Knuuttila-Hintikka interpretation of modalities in the Middle Ages. I had to call him periodically and ask: What am I now being accused of by the medievalists?

A similar pattern was repeated in much of my other work in the history of philosophy. Most of it has started from some specific conceptual insight or other, often facilitated by logical or other systematic insights. For instance, the central role of instantiation rules in contemporary logic led me to explore the tacit or explicit role of instantiation in the history of logic and of the philosophy of mathematics. This role has manifested itself in the form of the ancient Greek notion of *ekthesis*, in the form of so-called auxiliary constructions in geometry, in the use of what Kant called intuitions in his philosophy of mathematics, and in Peirce's notion of a theorematic reasoning as distinguished from a corollarial one. I will return to it below. Here I only mention a beautiful example of historical irony. What Kant meant by appeals to intuitions in mathematics is little more than the use of instantiations. Now the main tool that was later used allegedly to exorcise Kantian intuitions from the philosophy of mathematics was the use of first-order logic to formalize mathematical reasoning. Yet in reality the backbone of first-order logic is the very same idea of instantiation as Kant intended by his references to the use of intuitions in mathematics.

This reliance on conceptual insights does not mean projecting our ideas back into history. Sometimes it can lead to opposite results. Undoubtedly the most important single historical insight I have put forward is the absence of the Frege-Russell ambiguity thesis from philosophical and logical thinking before the nineteenth century. By this thesis, I mean the claim that verbs for being like the English *is* or the ancient Greek *einai* are ambiguous between existence, identity, predication, and subsumption. The key word here is "ambiguous." Every reasonable present or past analyst has been aware that such verbs are used in different ways. However, Frege and Russell went further and attributed this difference in use to an alleged ambiguity of a single word, and not, for instance, to the different contexts of the different kinds of use. The Frege-Russell ambiguity claim has been generally accepted in the last century or even century and a half. Once, when I expressed doubts of it as a feature of natural-language semantics to Leonard Linsky, he looked at me with an expression of mock dismay and said: "Nothing is sacred in philosophy any longer!" What was really sacred for him is probably nonetheless our received first-order logic rather than the Frege-Russell thesis alone. For if this received first-order logic is used as the framework of semantical representation, the Frege-Russell thesis follows as a corollary, in that *is* in its different uses must be translated into it in different ways. But when I developed a game-theoretical semantics for certain parts of the *Sprachlogik* of the English language, I came to realize that the need for the Frege-Russell assumption vanishes automatically in that semantical framework. What resulted was instead something weirdly similar to Aristotle's theory of categories. For example, Aristotle's theory poses to an interpreter a striking question: What is it that his categories at bottom categorize? Is Aristotle's distinction among different categories a distinction among the largest classes of entities over which our quantifiers can range? Or is it a distinction among different uses of verbs for being? Different kinds of predicates that we can attribute to an entity? Or can we take Aristotle literally and interpret categories as being expressed by those different question words and question expressions that Aristotle uses as labels of his categories? The right answer turns out to be: all of the above, in that, surprisingly, a game-theoretical analysis of the logic of natural language shows that in the last analysis all these distinctions go together— at least part of the way.

Conversely, confronting systematic ideas with historical precedents often helps to sharpen the issues and to direct one's attention to interesting issues. It has turned out (or, I should say, Risto Hilpinen has pointed out) that Charles S. Peirce anticipated my game-theoretical treatment of the semantics of quantifiers to a tee. Yet he never put it to systematic use in his logical theory. Why? A plausible and interesting answer is that he lacked the game-theoretical notion of strategy, thus unwittingly illustrating the crucial role of this notion in game-theoretical semantics and in game theory in general.

Here I can nevertheless offer only examples of the variety of historical problems I have discussed. They are not all interrelated, except method-ologically. In this respect, I must offer an apology. The approach to the history of thought I have described bears a close resemblance to the approach that was recommended by A. O. Lovejoy for historians of philosophy and to historians of ideas in general. Lovejoy called it simply "history of ideas," but in his parlance the phrase is to be taken in a much more literal sense than in the current usage. When someone like Isaiah Berlin is called a "historian of ideas," one is mistaken if one expects to find in his writings anything that requires much awareness of the conceptual issues that are the true *métier* of philosophers. What one finds is general intellectual history.

Of course, both approaches have their place. But as a part of the general enterprise of philosophy, history of ideas in Lovejoy's sense has much more to contribute than general intellectual history. If an example is needed, one can simply open a contemporary philosophical book or paper almost at random. One is likely to find there appeals to what the author calls "intuitions." On a closer examination, alas, those alleged intuitions turn out to be such that an author who appeals to them would blush if he or she were familiar with the history of the notion of intuition. (See here my 1999 paper "The Emperor's New Intuitions.")

Unfortunately, instead of acknowledging my debt to the methodology of Lovejoy and his fellow "historians of ideas" in the narrow sense, I reacted to Lovejoy's best known book *ad hominem*. This book is of course his 1936 classic *The Great Chain of Being*. Even though I have always been interested in the role of specific ideas in history, Lovejoy's book was an abject disappointment to me as a philosopher. I found Lovejoy's conception of the philosophically relevant concepts and conceptions that he calls "ideas" oversimplified. He proposes to look at them as combinations of certain "unit ideas," and as a consequence has little to say about their interplay, let alone about the influence of one of them on the role of others. And there are no new insights into the nature or interrelations of different ideas in Lovejoy's writings, and not enough attention is paid by him to larger conceptual structures such as arguments and theories. Worst of all, even though Lovejoy was primarily a historian of philosophy as I am not, I could even on the basis of my spotty research immediately see that Lovejoy had got large portions of the history of his principal case study concept wrong. This sample idea is the so-called "principle of plenitude." This principle asserts, roughly, that each possibility is realized sooner or later. On the abstract level, it is not even obvious that this assumption should be called a principle of plenitude. What it does is merely to assert an equation between possibilities and their realizations. Hence, if someone's conception of what is possible is narrow, the principle is entirely compatible with the paucity of the actual world.

On the historical level, Lovejoy claimed that Plato accepted the principle of plenitude while Aristotle did not. Yet my own studies had revealed incontrovertible evidence of Aristotle's acceptance of the precise literal form of the principle, whereas Plato's attitude toward it is at best unclear. Worst of all, Lovejoy got Leibniz's relation to the idea of the realization of all possibilities diametrically wrong. For Leibniz, the principle of plenitude was "the first falsehood and the source of atheistic philosophy," as he puts it in criticizing Descartes and Spinoza. Moreover, this rejection is deeply rooted in the central ideas of Leibniz's metaphysics.

I expressed my criticisms of Lovejoy in my presidential address to the American Philosophical Association, Pacific Division, in 1976, entitled "Gaps in the Great Chain of Being." Even though I do not have reasons to retract anything in that address, I must admit that it gives the mistaken impression that I am rejecting Lovejoy's approach lock, stock, and barrel, when in reality my own way of thinking is at bottom fairly close to Lovejoy's, especially when his oversimplifications of his own method and his specific historical misinterpretations are corrected. What I do miss in Lovejoy and even more in his successors is a closer cooperation of historical and systematic insights.

There are other differences between Lovejoy's methodology and mine. Lovejoy's "unit ideas" are supposed to include not just concepts, but explicit or implicit assumptions, "more or less unconscious mental habits," what Lovejoy calls "dialectical habits" (for instance, methodological assumptions), "susceptibilities to diverse kinds of metaphysical pathos," and so on. All this I heartily agree with. However, in much of Lovejoy's own historical work, the ideas he considers—the "great chain of being," the "principle of plenitude," and even the idea of primitivism—have predominantly the character of theses or assumptions. This is the case even when Lovejoy studies the role of ideas outside philosophy, for instance, in literature and art. Without belittling what Lovejoy does, it seems to me that the subtlest and most interesting connections between philosophical ideas and literature or art do not concern particular concepts or assumptions, but ways of thinking, questions asked, and perhaps even large "research projects." I have tried to explore some such large-scale connections in twentieth-century thought in my essays on the Bloomsbury group and on cubism. For instance, Virginia Woolf's works are not philosophical novels in the sense that they would illustrate philosophical ideas or contain discussions of philosophical problems. Yet there is a rich indirect philosophical content in them. I was especially forcefully struck by the similarity of Virginia Woolf's technique of constructing—or prompting her reader to construct—her fictional universe from the experiences of her characters, and Bertrand Russell's construction of our external world from the data of immediate experience. Again, Bloomsbury philosophers' quest for the objects of immediate sensory experience, such as sense data, parallels the search for the objects of aesthetic experience by the Bloomsbury theorists of pictorial art. Such connections are not likely to be mere similarities, and they are not captured naturally by reference to "unit ideas," however widely interpreted.

What I ought to have done, instead of getting upset by Lovejoy's mistakes, is to illustrate the importance of conceptual history (Lovejoy's "history of ideas") by reference to a subtler example. Indeed, I would have had—and I still have—available to me excellent test cases. One of them is the role of what a modern logician would recognize as instantiation rules (in particular existential instantiation) in logical and mathematical reasoning. The significance of this role is perhaps not obvious. Even the full role of instantiation rules in our contemporary logic has been recognized only slowly. This role can perhaps be said to have been made explicit only when the semantical meaning of the rules of the so-called natural deduction methods (Gentzen's sequent calculus) was spelled out by E. W. Beth and me in 1955.

Beth also pointed out the identity of existential instantiation with the traditional notion of *ekthesis* that goes back all the way to ancient Greek geometry and to Aristotle. I also realized quickly that it was the use of instantiation rules that made mathematics synthetic and intuitive for the great Immanuel Kant. Kant sought to relate the idea of using particular representatives of general concepts with appeals to what one can find in sense perception. Even though this connection is an illusion, as I have shown in my work, it is eminently natural, historically, going back as it does all the way to Aristotle. At an early stage of this work my claim of a tie between *ekthesis* and the faculty of sense perception was challenged in conversation by an Oxonian scholar. As a reply I quoted what Alexander the Commentator says about *ekthesis* in logic, viz., that it involves an appeal to sense perception. My learned friend was convinced.

More generally speaking, it is the long-term historical role of notions like instantiation that lends more detailed studies, like my studies of Kant's philosophy of mathematics and of the history of the notion of analysis, not only their interest but their persuasiveness as historically relevant interpretations. It is not surprising that some specialists on Kant (and some nonspecialists who have in their studies restricted their attention to Kant) have not been impressed by my interpretation of Kant's theory of the mathematical method. But they have paid a price in the form of parochialism. Not only have they missed an important connection between Kant and contemporary systematic issues in logical theory. They have missed the place of Kant's theory in a wider historical context.

Another earlier philosopher (and practitioner) of history with whom I have had an ambivalent intellectual relationship is R. G. Collingwood. His conception of what he called "the logic of questions and answers" as a major tool in the study of history—and in inquiry in general—I have always found congenial. An especially intriguing component in Collingwood's theory is the notion of the presupposition of a question, which in his treatment leads him to the idea of ultimate presupposition. This idea is designed by Collingwood as a way of approaching the characteristics of the thought of different thinkers, periods, and traditions. Collingwood's theory can be considered as a precedent to my interrogative approach to epistemology, briefly sketched in section 7 below. It is nevertheless badly in need of an explicit implementation as a logic in a full-fledged sense of the word. When I carried out such an implementation one of the victims was Collingwood's crucial idea of ultimate presupposition. (See my forthcoming paper "Presuppositions of Questions and Other Limitations of Inquiry.") For all its fascination and for its connections with a strict logic of questions, Collingwood's notion is fundamentally and hopelessly oversimplified. Did Plato's Socrates need presuppositions when he put questions to his interlocutors?

Yet I have been fascinated by what are hard not to call the ultimate presuppositions of a period or a philosophical tradition. I tried to capture one such presupposition in my essays on the concept of time in the major ancient Greek thinkers. (See the essays collected in the volume *Knowledge and the Known*, 1974.) The Frege-Russell treatment of "is" can be thought of as another major Collingwoodian presupposition. The most important largely tacit presupposition that I have examined is nevertheless the one of which my work on Wittgenstein made me aware.

By examining Wittgenstein's early distinction between saying and showing I became aware of the fundamental difference between different philosophers' attitudes toward language (in its relation to reality and to us) that I proposed to call the contrast between "language as calculus" and "language as a universal medium." I was strongly inspired by van Heijenoort's 1967 essay "Logic as Language and Logic as Calculus," and I tried to align my terminology as closely with his as possible. Alas, both contrasting terms are subject to misunderstanding. The view of language as calculus does not amount to considering language as a formal calculus, only to thinking of language as freely *re*-interpretable like a calculus. The universality intended by the phrase "language as universal medium" does not mean universality with respect to different actual languages, but only the inescapability of my own language. ("A language that I do not understand is no language," Wittgenstein once wrote.)

Misnamed or not, I have found the contrast most instructive as a framework in which to study and to compare with each other twentieth-century philosophers. Martin Kusch extended it in his 1989 book to Continental philosophy, among other things finding it the key to the contrast between Husserl and Heidegger—and to Gadamer's attempt to reconcile the two. An amusing incident perhaps conveys a sense of the prevalence of the ideas involved in the contrast. When I first discussed the contrast with Kusch as a possible leading idea of his dissertation, I noticed that he winced a little whenever I used the phrase "language as a universal medium." Finally I asked for an explanation. Cautiously Kusch said, "Sir, do you know that Gadamer is using the same phrase in the same sense?" He was already then more knowledgeable of the details of the subject than I was.

One of the staunchest believers in the universality of language and its semi-corollary, the one-world view was W. V. Quine. His philosophical *alter ego* Burton Dreben followed Quine in this respect. (Or was it the other way around?) It is an index of the depth of my friendship with Burt that we remained friends in spite of his acceptance and my rejection of the universality view.

The contrast between these two ways of viewing language in its relation to the world and to us is perhaps the most "ultimate presupposition" of late twentieth-century philosophy, even though its role has remained largely undiagnosed. I am therefore glad to see it being discussed as a feature of recent philosophy by Hans Sluga in his essay in the present volume. I believe it serves to illustrate, and perhaps even to demonstrate, the usefulness of Collingwood's idea of ultimate presupposition, even though his analysis of the general notion of presupposition was not on a par with the standards of contemporary logical theory.

6. SEEKING FOR AN OVERVIEW

In the light of hindsight I did not do a good job in my early career of bringing out and spelling out the philosophical implications of my results. My typical mode of operation was to address some specific logical or conceptual problem. Once I had solved it, I often left it to my readers to draw the general philosophical conclusions from the solution. I now recognize this procedure as unsatisfactory. My motives, insofar as I can reconstruct them, were a mixed bunch. By philosophical temperament and undoubtedly because of my lurking insecurity, I preferred lines of thought that yielded a definite conclusion to deliberative or persuasive argumentation. If I had lived in Descartes's time, I would have shared his distaste of "probable syllogisms." In our day and age, one of the methodological ideas I have singularly little sympathy with is Rawls's notion of deliberative equilibrium.

I also thought that to reach a general philosophical position I would have to compare my ideas with other philosophers' theories. Now it is not easy for me to find my way quickly among other people's ideas. Even though I have been editing philosophical journals and books for thirty-five years, I am not a spontaneously good editor, in the sense of finding my way smoothly through the maze of other writers' arguments. For one thing, in order to evaluate them, I would need to know the arguer's tacit presuppositions, which are not easy to tease out of the text. For one important example, I felt comfortable about criticizing the New Theory of Reference only after I had become aware of one of the main sources of the mistakes of the New Theorists, viz., their failure to recognize the role of quantifiers as dependence indicators and to recognize the distinction between the two main modes of cross-identification.

I am also distinctly uncomfortable with philosophical polemics and loath to criticize fellow thinkers unless I know I can do a better job myself—which is what I would like to do anyway rather than to spend my time setting other people's ideas straight.

These are inadequate reasons, I freely admit. They nevertheless serve to explain, if not excuse, my earlier failures. Because of them, I missed several opportunities of making a bigger impact on philosophical discussion. For instance, my very first discovery, the theory of distributive normal forms, is relevant to the question of the uninformativeness, a.k.a. tautologicity, of logical truths. The reason is that they present us a way of expressing the different alternative possibilities that can be expressed in a language. Logical truths have to admit all of them and hence to be tautological in a striking sense. At the same time, on any actual occasion, we may have to consider a number of merely possible-looking possibilities whose elimination by purely logical means increases our information in a different sense of the term. All this shows that Quine's denial of a viable distinction between conceptual and factual truths is based on an inadequate analysis of the logical situation. I spelled out this situation in the late sixties and early seventies, but did not then call attention to the philosophical consequences of my conclusions.

In some cases, my hesitations led to outright misunderstandings. During my years as a professor in Helsinki, I worked in inductive logic and in the theory of semantical information. I was very lucky to attract gifted and interested students, the first of whom were Risto Hilpinen, Raimo Tuomela, and Juhani Pietarinen. That work moved, technically speaking, in the ambit of Carnap's theories. (The first main result was that Carnap's approach could be generalized so as to allow for an explicit treatment of inductive generalization.) As a consequence I have found myself bracketed with Carnap allegedly as a defender of a purely logical conception of probability. The truth is the opposite. In construing his lambda-continuum Carnap showed that even with extremely strong symmetry assumptions one's inductive probability is determined only up to a positive real-valued constant λ. It is not difficult to interpret λ either subjectivistically, as an index of caution, or objectivistically, as a guess concerning the orderliness of the universe. (Indeed, it was shown that the optimal value of λ is a monotonic function of the entropy of one's universe of discourse.) But the very possibility of such interpretations shows that there is no hope whatsoever to fix the value of λ by purely a priori arguments. In this sense, a logical concept of probability is a demonstrable impossibility.

This line of thought was strengthened further by my studies of inductive generalization. They led to the recognition of different kinds of order that there may be in the universe and these had to be codified by different parameters of the same kind as λ.

The failure of purely logical conceptions of probability and information in fact poses intriguing further questions. If our working notions of probability and information are not logical, what are they? Where do we get the prior probabilities that we need for instance in Bayesian inference? If those probabilities are not logical, how are they affected by experience? On a historical level, it is known that von Neumann rejected Carnap's purely logical conception of information. Some writers have viewed this rejection through the spectacles of Quine's rejection of the analytic versus synthetic distinction. In reality, a sharp distinction between logical and physical probabilities can be denied without deviating in the least from the analytic versus synthetic distinction. Furthermore, one cannot escape the problems by switching to epistemic conceptions of probability and information. The very same difficulty of defining unique measures affects epistemic probability quite as much as it does logical probability. Hence the philosophical problems I became aware of in the sixties and seventies are still badly in need of clarification.

This criticism of Carnap's project is not motivated by any animus against its architect. I came to know and to respect Carnap in the sixties. He was then already retired, but lived still in Los Angeles. When he found out that I was working on inductive logic at Stanford (part of each year), he contacted me and asked me to visit him to discuss matters of common interest with him. I did so several times, finding my discussions with him pleasant and rewarding, even though I did not learn much that I did not already know. Carnap, too, had found ways of dealing with the problem of inductive generalization but had not published anything.

I came to admire Carnap greatly as a person and as a philosopher. He was unselfish, modest, and utterly dedicated to his work. He reminded me of an old-fashioned craftsman, perhaps a carpenter who takes great pride in his work and considers no surface or corner too insignificant to be done just right. Carnap was patient to a fault. When I met with him for the first time in Los Angeles, he spent more than an hour, not on the inductive logic problems that I had come to discuss, but on a talk Dana Scott had given in Los Angeles the week before. Carnap was greatly interested in the talk, but had not taken in everything. Since I was a colleague of Dana Scott's at that time, Carnap tried to pick my brains about Scott's ideas.

In the patience-impatience scale Carnap was quite far from some other philosophers I had met. Once a younger American philosopher called me and hesitantly inquired whether he could ask me "a delicate question." Well, you can always ask. . . . After some further hemming and hawing, he came out with the question: Why was it that Wittgenstein and Carnap never got along with each other? The poor questioner undoubtedly expected to find some deep dark secret, perhaps something to do with Wittgenstein's homosexuality. I had a hard time not laughing. There was nothing to explain for anyone who had seen the two men in action. Wittgenstein was as impatient as they come, hating to have to go through the agony of explaining his ideas again to someone who did not grasp them, while Carnap was one of the most patient of men. I can almost hear Carnap asking, "But Herr Wittgenstein, I did not quite understand what you said.

Perhaps you can explain the point again a little more slowly." That would have driven Wittgenstein up the wall.

For all my respect for Carnap and for all the constructive work he did, I do not think that he was a pathbreaker in philosophy. In particular, he did not have deeper insights into the logical tools he used in his own philosophical work. I have used in my own mind as a test case the little and deservedly forgotten paper that Carnap wrote with Bachmann on Hilbert's completeness axiom. In a note I published in 1991 in *Erkenntnis* I showed that, even though the authors did not commit any outright mistakes, they in effect reinterpret the axiom so as to trivialize it.

These remarks have a wider application. Carnap and the other logical empiricists are routinely criticized for relying too much on formal logic in their philosophical work. The truth is the opposite. In the anachronistic and unfair light of hindsight, Carnap and his friends did not use the full power of contemporary logic in their philosophical work. An instructive albeit still anachronistic example is offered by the logical interpolation theorems (Craig's theorem and its improved versions) which have recently turned out to serve as a basis of an interesting theory of explanation, when suitably sharpened.

Gradually, I gained more confidence, at least in my own thinking, if not always in discussion. The reason is that I was able to reach a better grasp of the ideas of my fellow philosophers, including their largely tacit presuppositions, and to put them in a wider perspective. Unexpectedly, but perhaps inevitably, this also led me to take an increasingly more critical view of the current philosophical scene. This does not mean a pessimism as to what can be done in philosophy. On the contrary, I see extremely promising lines of thought in those areas of philosophy that I have been working in. Rather, the cutting edge of my criticism is directed precisely at my fellow philosophers' failure to make use of these possibilities. I am afraid that this makes many of my criticisms unfair by the ordinary human standards. One source of unfairness is that I am not interested in criticizing those *soi-disant* philosophers whom I think least of, such as Derrida and Rorty. By biblical standards, it is easy to forgive them because they do not know what they are talking about. My disappointment is instead prompted by those thinkers who should have known better, by way of intelligence, direction of interests and knowledge.

This process of disillusionment began with the followers and interpreters of Wittgenstein. In a case of an actual flesh-and-blood person, the feeling of disappointment with what others are saying of him was heightened by an experience of intellectual empathy with the thinker in question. More mundanely, my disappointment was also deepened by the failure of most early interpreters of Wittgenstein to make use of his unpublished writings that have repeatedly disproved commentators' views, sometimes quite dramatically. (Some of these failures were discussed in section 4 above.)

In my considered judgment, the overwhelming majority of books and papers on Wittgenstein are hopelessly superficial. They do not evince any real understanding of Wittgenstein as a person or as a philosopher. I am morally incensed by the way philosophers of the widest variety of persuasions have tried to force Wittgenstein to help their pet projects. I have forgotten my choice of words, but Anat Biletzki is undoubtedly right when she reports that she once witnessed me leaving a discussion about the "New Wittgenstein" before it ended, saying, "I cannot stand what they are doing to Wittgenstein."

Perhaps the most striking case in point is the myth of Wittgenstein as representing a view of language as an intrinsically social phenomenon, sometimes even presenting him as a precursor of social constructionism. By debunking this myth I am of course not denying that Wittgenstein might perhaps have answered affirmatively if someone had put to him out of context the question: Is language a social phenomenon? What I mean is that the social character of language does not play any role in his central arguments in his philosophy of language. For him, language does not conceptually presuppose a language community. He would have admitted that a Robinson Crusoe can have a language; in fact he says precisely that repeatedly in his posthumously published writings.

Likewise my consciousness was slowly raised concerning other fundamental but largely neglected presuppositions of various philosophers. In the twentieth century, one can, for instance, come to acknowledge the half-recognized role of such ideas as what I have called the atomistic postulate, the distinction between standard and nonstandard interpretations of higher-order logic, the self-explanatory "one-world" idea, the assumption of compositionality in language theory, and so forth.

When one begins to look at the best known thinkers of the twentieth century in the light of such more or less ultimate presuppositions, one will see that in much of their thought they were seriously restricted by some of those presuppositions. At least this is what I have come to conclude. To take specific examples from thinkers I have myself examined, Tarski was bound by the assumption of compositionality (and perhaps also by his preference for an algebraic way of thinking), Gödel by the one-world assumption, Frege by his nonstandard interpretation of higher-order logic, and so on.

The most representative case in my opinion is Quine. For all his argumentative and expositional elegance and acumen, he never put forward any specific insights that have opened new perspectives in logic, epistemology, or language theory. I have come to believe that this is the case because his thought is restricted by several presuppositions that make it impossible for him to make constructive contributions to logic or epistemology. I have tried to identify the most important presuppositions of this kind, most fully perhaps in my 1999 paper with the Collingwoodian title "Quine's Ultimate Presuppositions." Among them there are the atomistic postulate and the idea of language as the universal medium with its sundry corollaries, including the one-world idea and the inexpressibility of semantics in a large scale.

For a while it was fashionable in some circles to speak of deconstruction and deconstructivism. The basic idea of deconstruction has a great deal of appeal to me, except that I do not believe that deconstruction cannot be followed by reconstruction. I will not be offended if someone describes my systematic and historical analyses of such ideas as language as a universal medium, picture theory of language, induction, principle of plenitude, and quantifier as exercises in deconstruction. However, I do wish the *soi-disant* deconstructivists had directed their attention to several of the crucial ideas that have been popular among English-speaking philosophers recently, including such concepts as intuition, realism, supervenience, and *de re* reference.

I have also been disappointed deeply by the so-called "New Philosophy of Science" of the likes of Thomas Kuhn (another ex–Junior Fellow), Imre Lakatos, and Paul Feyerabend, perhaps even more than by the New Theory of Reference. This disappointment has little to do, contrary to what one might perhaps expect, with their rejection of logical methods in their approach to the philosophy of science in favor of historical, sociological, or perhaps hermeneutical thinking. For one thing, Kuhn did not reject formal techniques out of hand and indeed played for a while with the idea that his own ideas could be explicated by means of the Sneed-Stegmüller structuralist approach. (In helping to organize the 1975 Congress of Logic, Methodology and Philosophy of Science I went out of my way to stage there a symposium with Kuhn, Stegmüller, and Sneed as speakers, and subsequently to publish the contributions in the journal *Synthese.*) For another thing, the rejection of formal methods has always seemed to me a mistake rather than a crime. The new philosophers of science would be better off in their own enterprise if they used concepts and conceptualizations, logical and epistemological, that are sharper than such vague ideas as "paradigm" or "research tradition" which have very little direct explanatory force. Once again, Thomas Kuhn was an atypical Kuhnian. At a relatively early stage of the career of the term he swore to me—admittedly in a light-hearted mood—that he would never, never use the accursed word "paradigm" again.

In the tradition of the New Philosophy of Science it has been fashionable to criticize logical positivists for their use of logic as a tool in epistemology and philosophy of science. My own work, instantiated for instance by the theory of explanation I have developed (with Ilpo Halonen), has convinced me that the Vienna Circle members can be blamed for using too weak logical tools rather than an overdose of logic. Similarly, I have argued (albeit by means of case studies rather than wholesale arguments) that the crucial concepts of the New Philosophers—such as the incommensurability of theories and the theory-ladenness of observations—can be captured in perfectly normal logical and epistemological terms and hence do not in the least motivate dispensing with these conceptual tools in the philosophy and history of science. Needless to say, such Kuhnian concepts also still need a great deal of further analysis (and synthesis) before they can do the job they are supposed to do.

The deeper sources of my disappointment are connected with the failure of the New Philosophers to do a really satisfactory job in their own *métier*, that is, in understanding the methodological ideas that guide the development of actual science. Even Thomas Kuhn misses in his own concrete historical work interesting opportunities of understanding the developments he is studying. One of Kuhn's best achievements was to show that the idea of quantization of energy, which Planck apparently used as a premise in his derivation of the famous radiation law, played an insignificant role in his (and other physicists') thinking until much later than has generally been thought. I believe that this is an important and novel result. But it creates a new perplexing question: How did Planck view his derivation of the radiation law methodologically, if its premises did not merit more attention? It seems to me that Kuhn misses an opportunity here of putting his own discovery in a deeper perspective. For Planck's derivation exemplifies a mode of scientific reasoning that was neither deductive reasoning from premises nor what we now routinely call inductive reasoning (inference from particular uses to a generalization), but inductive reasoning in the old sense of extrapolation and interpolation from partial generalizations. Such inductive generalization could be considered respectable in its own right, independently of what its prima facie premises would have been if it were construed as a deductive argument. This same old concept of induction, in the sense of extrapolation and interpolation of partial generalizations, had in fact played an extremely important role in the methodology of both Aristotle and Newton. (See my 1992 paper on the concept of induction.) Hence, the quantum hypothesis was not for Planck a premise but merely a heuristic crutch that facilitated an "inductive" reconciliation of two different radiation laws.

Similar telling examples can be multiplied. For instance, Kuhn has contrasted what he calls the mathematical and the experimental traditions in early modern science. Even though this may very well be an apt way of describing the gross features of the history of the period in question, it misses what I consider a most interesting suggestion as to what the methodological "secret" of the early modern science was. I am not the only one, nor the first one, to suggest that that methodological key idea was a confluence and not a contrast of the two traditions, viz., what Oskar Becker called the idea of "analytical experiment," that is to say, the idea of considering configurations of interacting physical factors in the same way—and with the same mathematical tools—as interdependent geometrical objects were dealt with in the famous method of analysis of the Greek geometers and by their early modern followers. In other words, the real subtlety of the developments Kuhn is discussing is a synthesis of the two traditions he contrasts to each other.

These examples can be generalized and strengthened. It is my educated belief that the interrogative approach to inquiry would have been much more helpful to Kuhn and his ilk in their historical work than Kuhnian speculations have been to serious philosophy of science, including attempts to understand what actually happens in the work of scientists. Simply saying this may perhaps strike you as a cheap shot. However, what I mean can be illustrated by further examples. One so far unfulfilled hope—most likely forever unfulfilled hope—that I have entertained is to write a study of Newton's methodology, both of what he practiced in his scientific work and of his general pronouncements on the scientific method. At one point I came so close to realizing my pet project as to put together, jointly with a younger colleague, a long paper which my colleague presented at a conference on Newton and realism. In discussion, Ernan McMullin asked whether the assembled Newton scholars believed that Newton's philosophical methodology was anything more than "window dressing." The majority of scholars present did not see anything more than that in Newton's philosophy of science. I find such a view doubly mistaken. First, it shows a failure to understand what Newton was doing, methodologically speaking, and it involves the anti-Socratic mistake of not recognizing one's failure.

From the vantage point of an interrogative approach (see section 7 below), Newton's theory and practice fall into place. Newton's ideas are in fact almost in uncanny agreement with the interrogative model, which reveals the connections not only between Newton's methodological practice and his theory, but between several of his key ideas. They include Newton's notion of experiment, by which he consistently meant controlled experiment; his notion of induction, by which he did not mean inferences from particulars to general statements but the interpolation and extrapolation of already established partial generalizations; his claim to have derived or even deduced laws from "phenomena"; his explanations of the roles of analysis and synthesis in science and in mathematics; the argumentative structure of the *Principia*; and much more. What comparable insights into Newton's thought can we extract from such ideas as a disciplinary matrix or the theory-ladenness of observations?

No one can consider it a major black mark against Kuhn as a historian that he did not tell us everything there is to be told about the precedents of Planck's mode of argumentation, about the idea of controlled experiment or about Newton's methodology. But when the likes of Kuhn tell us that we should dispense with the notions of inference, deduction, induction, and even logic in trying to understand the actual course of science in favor of mare's nest ideas like "disciplinary matrix," I cannot help asking whether a perceptive use of those offending concepts might have helped Kuhn in the historical work that was his primary vocation—and asking what he would have said if he had realized those subtler possibilities of historical understanding. I suspect that he would have been much less sweeping in his philosophical claims if he had been a more perceptive historian.

The New Philosophy of Science is no longer new. Has it delivered what it promised? Has it really deepened our understanding of the scientific process? I do not see that it has. I have myself analyzed a couple of its central concepts—the incommensurability of theories and the theory-ladenness of observations—and found them too unsharp to bear the theoretical burden that they have been assumed to bear. The New Philosophy of Science does not offer us a satisfactory overview of epistemology, philosophy of science or even history of science.

I have likewise been disappointed by another recent movement in the philosophy of science, even though I happened to be an unwitting instrument in its genesis. Logical positivists ostensibly wanted the philosophy of science to be no more and no less than "the logical syntax of the language of science." However, they understood this desideratum in a much wider sense than some of their own followers, in that the borderline between syntax and semantics was for them quite flexible even in the heyday of the group in the early thirties.

Meanwhile, shrewder theorists of science from other backgrounds realized in effect that they had to consider the model theory of scientific theories and not only their proof theory (syntax). Alas, there did not exist in logic a viable model theory as a tool for philosophers to apply to scientific theories until 1960 or thereabouts. Hence some of the best philosophers of science resorted to set theoretical languages as the standardized discourse in the philosophy of science, perhaps because in the case of set theory it seems clear what the intended models are like structurally. Theories define in effect "set theoretical predicates," as one of the slogans of the time went.

One of the shrewd early analysts was Patrick Suppes. One of his doctoral students at Stanford was Joe Sneed, who later joined the Stanford philosophy department as an assistant professor. When his tenure decision was approaching, he put together an able and interesting book, *The Logical Structure of Mathematical Physics* (D. Reidel, 1971), using the approach he had learned from Suppes. But from whom should the department seek evaluation letters? I was at Stanford at the time, and I suggested among others Wolfgang Stegmüller from Munich so that we could get a truly outside opinion. This led to a strange result. For all his mighty learning, Stegmüller had taken the positivistic slogans about the syntax of the language of science at their face value. Reading Sneed's book, he realized for the first time the need of going beyond the purely syntactic viewpoint. Unfortunately, he was familiar neither with the antecedents of Sneed's set-theoretical approach nor with the situation in logical theory, where a genuine model theory had been developed. (Some results from that model theory were in fact used by Sneed.) Stegmüller went overboard. He declared Sneed the greatest American philosopher of science and began to swear by a set-theoretical or, as he labeled it, "structuralist" view of theories as contrasted to positivists' "statement view." Unfortunately, this contrast is due to a confusion. Of course, any theory in any language specifies the structure of its models, a structure that can be discussed model-theoretically in its relation to the theory. (To add the epithet "set-theoretical" is strictly pleonastic.) The entire "statement view" is a figment of confusion. Not only could non-set-theoretical languages have a viable model theory in which these structures can be discussed, by Sneed's time, such a model theory had existed for some ten years.

Of course, one can carry out metascientific studies within a structuralist framework. But such a framework is bound to be clumsy, for the model theory of set theory is much messier than the model theory of (for instance) first-order languages.

The confusion here may have been compounded by the idea that the usual first-order logical languages cannot serve as their own metalanguage. This is true. However, in the light of my own results it is true only because of a historical accident. This accident is that the usual first-order logic is unnecessarily weak. In a suitable independence-friendly first-order language (see below, section 7), one can formulate some of the crucial parts of its model theory, including the notion of truth, in the same language. And if one tries seriously to use first-order axiomatic set theory as its own metalanguage, it is seen that the result is not only incomplete but wrong in that it yields false results.

But did Stegmüller's letter help? Did Sneed get his tenure after all? No, he was faulted on his teaching.

Somewhat similar things can be said of another major research project that is supposed to have important philosophical consequences, to wit, generative linguistics. I have been aware of Noam Chomsky's work ever since Peter Hempel mentioned his name to me in 1954, and I have tried to keep an eye on it. I have especially admired Chomsky's ability to come up with new theoretical ideas again and again. Generative grammar has brought about an impressive body of work. It has been one of the major developments in contemporary science, at least in the human sciences. In spite of all this, I would find Chomsky's general philosophical and methodological suggestions more persuasive if his linguistic theories did justice to what I consider the core area of linguistics, viz., semantics. Chomsky maintains that syntax is the basic part of language, autonomous with respect to semantics. By and large, he has typically approached semantical phenomena via their syntactical counterparts. For instance, his government and binding (GB) theory is supposed to be an exercise in syntax. However, the syntactical regularities it seeks to capture receive their entire interest from their capturing the conditions of such semantical ideas as coreference—insofar as they in fact capture those conditions.

Such an approach seems to me seriously inadequate. I am prepared to believe that there is an autonomous syntactical ground floor in the edifice of language. But it is unmistakable that some syntactical phenomena, including certain phenomena of syntactical acceptability, can only be explained by reference to semantics. The most striking example is perhaps the fact that in typical natural languages negation is a barrier to coreference. This fact turns out to be connected with certain unexpected general features of the logic of negation.

I even found a distributional law in English, called the *any*-thesis, of which it can be argued that it cannot be captured by any possible generative rule. (See my 1980 paper "On Any-thesis and the Methodology of Linguistics.") Chomsky took the challenge seriously enough to respond in print. Even though the presence of several competitive regularities in actual natural language makes the situation somewhat unclear, I still think that it is unmistakable that the *any*-thesis offers an example of a possible distributional regularity that cannot be captured generatively.

Furthermore, there exist in natural languages important semantical notions that are not expressed by any uniform syntactical construction. They are therefore bound to remain inaccessible to a uniform treatment in syntactical terms. The notion of informational independence is the most important case in point. (See here the title essay of my *Selected Papers*, volume 4, "Paradigms for Language Theory.") It is even possible to identify the pragmatic reason for its elusive Cheshire Cat character in syntax. As soon as we can handle the semantics of any notion in game-theoretical terms, it becomes possible for the moves connected with it to be independent of specified other rule applications. Accordingly independence can be a feature of expressions in several different grammatical categories. Hence, it is difficult to think of a syntactical modifier that could attach itself to so many different syntactical constructions.

Even when generative rules do capture the syntactical conditions on which a certain semantical phenomenon is manifested, they do not always explain why this phenomenon occurs. An instructive case study is offered by the study of anaphora in which I have participated since the eighties. As the first approximation, it can be said that in game-theoretical semantics, an anaphoric pronoun prompts a move in which an individual is chosen as its value, not from the whole domain of individuals, but from the individuals so far selected earlier in the same play of the game by the players as values of quantified variables. By means of this idea, suitably implemented, most of the behavior of anaphoric pronouns in English can be understood. I have myself been especially impressed by how this treatment explains certain nonstandard uses of anaphoric pronouns. In them, the intended meaning (or implication, if you wish) comes about by assuming that the conditions of the meaningful use of anaphora are satisfied even though the syntax of the relevant sentences does not by itself show that they are satisfied. Examples are offered by such utterances as the following:

> Of course there is night life in Tallahassee. Unfortunately, this weekend she is in Tampa.

> A suspicious woman to her male companion: You have doubled your daily dose of vitamin E. Who is she?

An anecdote illustrates what I mean here. After I had developed my own account of anaphora in English, I decided to compare its implications with those of Chomsky's "government and binding" (GB) theory. I looked up Chomsky's rules in Andrew Radford's textbook *Transformational Syntax* (Cambridge University Press, 1981). A comparison with the game-theoretical mechanism of anaphora quickly uncovered cases in which the GB rules give a wrong answer. I proudly pointed this out to a colleague, who responded by informing me that Radford's rules were dated and that Chomsky had meanwhile added another rule that eliminated my proposed counterexample. The point that this anecdote illustrates is that, for all his emphasis on deductive depth as a criterion of good explanation, Chomsky's rules are what philosophers of science used to call empirical generalizations, that is, direct generalizations from particular cases. This means that their consequences have little deductive depth. When a counterexample is found, the rules have to be changed—a new epicycle has to be added, so to speak. If Chomsky had reached a real insight into the mechanism of anaphora, he could have predicted the counterexample without any ad hoc adjustment of his rules.

My game-theoretical treatment of anaphora was an extension of a game-theoretical treatment of quantifiers as they operate in natural language. This approach produced other insights of great importance to linguistics and philosophy. The logical form of quantified sentences in natural languages turns out not to be captured by the formulas of the usual first-order logic, even though Chomsky still seems to think of first-order formalism as being close to his LF, a thinly disguised heir to the traditional idea of logical form. There are several different reasons for this failure. For one thing, the received notion of scope, which is one of the cornerstones of the usual notation, is hopelessly ambiguous, indicating both the relative logical priority of different quantifiers (priority scope) and also the limits with which a variable is bound to a given quantifier (binding scope). There is no good reason to think that the two should always go together in natural language, and plenty of good reasons to think that they do not. This insight shows among other things the limitations of linguists' labeled tree notation.

Most importantly, as was pointed out in the preceding section, in a game-theoretical treatment of natural-language quantifiers we do not need to assume that verbs for being like *is*, *ist*, *estin*, and so on are ambiguous between identity, existence, and predication as Frege and Russell thought. Instead, Aristotle's theory of categories is a good first approximation to the logic of quantifiers in ordinary language. Since Chomsky relies on logicians' received notation, his ideas of logical form of the quantifier sentences of a natural language like English are hopelessly oversimplified.

I am not criticizing Chomsky in order to belittle his achievements or the methodological revolution he started in theoretical linguistics. However, as long as generative linguists do not have their own semantical house in order, their philosophical and other general theoretical suggestions carry little conviction in philosophy or even in language theory at large.

I have likewise been immediately disappointed with other, less sweeping intellectual fashions, even though it has sometimes taken me a lot of time and effort to figure out precisely what is wrong with them. It is nevertheless possible to refute or at least "deconstruct" them, to use "derridaspeak." I have found reasons to think that the fascinating "cognitive fallacies" studied by Tversky and Kahneman need not be fallacious at all, notwithstanding the enormous attention they have received as alleged examples of built-in irrationality of human information processing. What Tversky and Kahneman miss is the fact that the message one receives is itself part of the data on the basis of which one judges its reliability.

As to the fad called fuzzy logic, it may offer practical advantages in handling low-level information-processing tasks. However, when it is compared with the "fuzzy logic" that we had available to us well before Lofti Zadeh in the form of the probability calculus, its main theoretical advantage is its conformity with the principle of compositionality. But this principle can for independent reasons be shown to be too restrictive for our logical reasoning always to conform to. It is also turning out that the independence-friendly logic I have developed (together with Gabriel Sandu and others) offers a far simpler representation of the kind of "fuzzy reasoning" we spontaneously use, for instance, when we reject the sorites paradox. I believe that independence-friendly logic is the actual "fuzzy logic" of everyday thinking.

Even some of the specific guidelines that we are supposed to follow in logical and philosophical analysis have proved illusory in my experience. A great deal of logical, linguistic, and philosophical theorizing has recently been characterized by an attempt to follow what is known as the principle of compositionality. In its most general form, this principle says that the semantical attributes of a complex expression are determined by the semantical attributes of its constituent expressions plus its structure. With my predilection to dependence analysis, I saw immediately that compositionality amounts to semantical context-independence. The main thrust of the principle is that the meaning of a complex expression depends *only* on the meanings of its constituent expressions (plus its structure, of course) thus excluding all dependence on the context. I was therefore surprised, not to say astounded, to see how thinkers as acute as Donald Davidson were averring that the compositionality of a language is a precondition of its learnability. It seemed to me—and it still seems to me—a veritable instance of intellectual *chutzpa* to claim on a priori grounds that human beings cannot learn context-sensitive semantical rules. I kept quiet, however, because I also realized that by hook or crook compositionality could always be implemented in a formal semantics. Context-sensitive semantical rules deal with the semantical interaction of different expressions in a sentence or discourse. If one is sufficiently ruthless, one can build the laws of such interaction into the respective meanings of the interacting expressions. Indeed, in a public discussion about compositionality sometime in the eighties, Michael Arbib tried to dispel my doubts about compositionality by declaring that he can always make his computer languages compositional.

Meanwhile, Richard Montague had used compositional methods in his logical and linguistic work, and partly through his work compositionality was widely accepted as a methodological guideline among theoretical linguists. A particularly forceful defender of compositionality was Barbara Partee. I had to bide my time and try to find logico-linguistic phenomena regarding which an attempt to enforce compositionality would lead to interpretational absurdity. Eventually, I discovered such phenomena in the form of independent quantifier structures. In such structures, the force of a quantifier depends on its context, viz., on which quantifiers outside its scope it depends or does not depend on.

This violation of compositionality is not an obvious one. At the meeting on "Integrating Logic and Linguistics" held at the University of Amsterdam in 1992 an early version of my 1997 joint survey paper (with Gabriel Sandu) on game-theoretical semantics was discussed. Our preassigned commentator was the shrewd and personable British logician Wilfrid Hodges. In our paper draft, we had mentioned rather casually that our independence-friendly logic was not compositional. Before the session, Hodges took us aside to warn us, saying that we were wrong and that there existed a simple compositional semantics for independence-friendly logic. We looked at each other, and in a couple of minutes were able to point out the flaw in Hodges's semantics. He took up the challenge and in the next several years he carried out ingenious studies of the unexpected intricacies of the game-theoretical semantics and of independence-friendly logic. The upshot of his impressive work nevertheless was that there does not after all exist a compositional semantics for independence-friendly logic that does not violate our normal assumptions about quantifiers.

Slowly I have come to understand what a handicap the assumption of compositionality has been in semantical theorizing. Once it is given up, there is, for instance, no difficulty in formulating truth predicates for suitable first-order languages in the same language. This also shows that there are no obstacles in principle to defining truth for ordinary language sentences in the same language, either. So why did Tarski think that this was impossible?

A modicum of historical detective work (together with Gabriel Sandu) revealed the answer: Because he was committed to compositionality, Tarski's own truth definitions were compositional, and he was perceptive enough to realize that ordinary language is not compositional. Small wonder, therefore, that Tarski disapproved of Davidson's attempt to use Tarski-type compositionality methods in the semantics of natural language!

Thus it is because of a misplaced faith in compositionality that logical semantics was stuck with the limitations of Tarski-type truth definitions for sixty years. I am convinced that a liberation from the fetters of compositionality will open dramatic new applications to logic and logical analysis.

7. WORK IN PROGRESS

This rejection of most of the current approaches to the philosophy of logic and mathematics, epistemology and philosophy of language meant that I had to strike out on my own. Or, historically speaking, it was the result of working on my own that led me to become wary of the ideas of others. What are the unmarked paths I have taken? One of the two most important such lines of thought concerns the nature of our basic logic, variously known as first-order logic, quantification theory, elementary logic, or predicate calculus. In section 4, I described how I was inspired by Wittgenstein's idea of language-game. But what are the language-games that are the logical home of quantifiers? Wittgenstein never provides a clear answer, even though he came close to the right one. Instead of quantifiers, he spoke of their values, that is, of objects. Wittgenstein believed that in order for something to be an object, it must be capable of being looked for and found. I applied this idea to the quantifiers whose values are precisely those discoverable objects, and I quickly saw that the truth conditions of quantified sentences can be expressed in terms of certain simple games in the strict sense of the mathematical theory of games. I called them semantical games. They can be considered the logical home of quantifiers.

This basic idea of what came to be known as game-theoretical semantics (GTS) was put forward for the first time in my 1968 paper "Language-games for Quantifiers." Perhaps the most characteristic idea of GTS is to define the truth of a sentence S as the existence of a winning strategy for the verifier in the correlated game $G(S)$. The verifier's winning strategies are then codified by what are known as complete sets of Skolem functions for S. Intuitively speaking, the Skolem functions are ways of finding the "witness individuals" that testify to the truth of S. The truth of a sentence S can thus be defined as the existence of a full set of its Skolem functions. It is vitally important to realize that this analysis is not a logician's artifice, but a faithful explication of our pretheoretical notion of truth.

This game-theoretical treatment of first-order logic is so natural that it did not come to me as a distinct new idea but rather as a way of spelling out what the logic of quantifiers is on any account. I was in any case made familiar early in my career with Skolem functions by the work of the Hilbert school. One might even initially think of the entire game-theoretical approach as little more than a dramatization of the role of Skolem functions in first-order logic. Furthermore, the structure of distributive normal forms, my first love in logic, with its alternating existential and universal quantifiers, strongly suggests the implicit presence of some kind of seeking-

and-finding game. Indeed, as was mentioned, the technique of distributive normal forms is roughly equivalent with the technique of Ehrenfeucht games. Undoubtedly my contemplation of distributive normal forms thus made me receptive to game-theoretical ideas in logic.

The precise mathematical structure of the truth constituting games refutes ipso facto a plausible-looking initial objection to the idea that semantical games of seeking and finding are constitutive of the meaning of quantifiers, viz., the objection that the notions of seeking and finding are too fuzzy to serve the purposes of a stringent logical theory. In a more general perspective, a similar objection can be made—and can be refuted—to the use of the notion of game. This notion, too, can be made explicit and precise. Perhaps the most clear-cut conceptual mistake Wittgenstein ever committed is to claim that the word "game" operates semantically by means of "family resemblance." The mathematical theory of games is a live refutation of any such simplistic view. Of course any concept is rough at the edges, but the operative question is whether one can identify a rule-governed core meaning. I suspect that the price Wittgenstein paid for this mistake is that he never realized what the language-games are that serve as the logical home of quantifiers.

Wittgenstein was not the only one who is mistaken here. Most linguists and philosophers of language seem to think that language-games belong to the pragmatics of language. (A sophisticated recent form of this mistake is to approach game-theoretical semantics as a study of how certain kinds of games can or could be played in an intuitively natural way.) And pragmatics is far too often for them, in Yehoshua Bar-Hillel's phrase, the "wastepaper basket" to which to relegate those problems that cannot be dealt with in terms of explicit syntax and semantics. Yet in Wittgenstein's overall vision of language, language-games take over the hopelessly unrealistic notion of intentionality in that they mediate the meaning relations between language and the world. Therefore semantics can be precise only insofar as the theory of language-games is.

How natural the game-theoretical interpretation of quantifiers is, is shown among many other things by the fact (first noted by Risto Hilpinen) that it was put forward completely explicitly already by Charles S. Peirce. The main difference is that Peirce did not have access to the concepts of von Neumann's game theory. For another item of anecdotal evidence, Erik Stenius once challenged in a discussion my suggested connection between the idea of existence (as expressed by the existential quantifier) and the ideas of seeking and finding. In response I said: "Erik, your first language is Swedish. In Swedish, how do you express existence? You say, *det finns*—literally, *one can find*."

In the light of critical hindsight, however, what I perceived as the naturalness of game-theoretical semantics was a fortunate combination of insights. Perhaps I just happened to be in the right place at the right time. Possibly because of my predilection to look for functional dependencies, I was already aware at an early stage of the game (no pun intended) of the semantical role of the Skolem functions of a sentence. The existence of a full set of such Skolem functions codifies our pretheoretical notion of truth. The lessons in game theory that I had first learned from Gustav Elfving enabled me to interpret Skolem functions as the strategy functions for one of the two players ("the verifier") in certain games which are known as semantical games. Putting the two ideas together resulted in a definition of truth as the existence of a winning strategy for a verifier.

From this it follows that semantical games are not, literally speaking, games of verification and falsification, even though I have myself used these word to describe them. Our actual activities of truth-seeking are not attempts to win a semantical game. They can be conceptualized as games, but they have to be distinguished sharply from semantical games. A speaker also who asserts the truth of S is not playing a semantical game, nor is the recipient of his or her message playing one. In this respect, semantical games differ from what Peirce seems to have envisaged. Semantical games are not games in language. Their moves are not language acts, and the study of game-theoretical semantics is not a study of games people actually play in using language. Semantical games constitute the links between language and the world that give our language its meanings. We rely on (but do not play) them when we speak. This function of semantical games happened to be precisely the role that Wittgenstein's language-games had in his semantics according to the interpretation I had reached earlier. (Here is yet another concrete example of how my work on Wittgenstein has facilitated my systematic thinking.) In order to understand a sentence S, one need not play the game $G(S)$ associated with it, but one has to master conceptually $G(S)$. This showed me that the practical implementation of semantical games is largely irrelevant, as long as such implementation is possible in principle. Nor does the greater or lesser naturalness of the implementation of different potential semantical games matter *per se*. (For instance, it suffices for semantical games to be defined only in their normal form, independently of what the extensive form might look like.) Thus the happy consilience of several different insights helped me to avoid different mistaken or at least distracting perspectives or game-theoretical semantics.

Once I grasped the idea of semantical games with quantified sentences, all sorts of matters fell into place. An example is offered by Gödel's *Dialectica* interpretation. I had read Gödel's paper, but failed to make heads or tails of it. Gödel presents his interpretation in the form of a translation of first-order logic and arithmetic into a higher-order language. The translation rules were not motivated by him in any way, and I could not see any reason why they should have been chosen in preference to dozens of equally plausible-looking ones. But once I appreciated the game-theoretical idea, it was clear to me that Gödel's rules could be understood in terms of certain nonstandard semantical games. The translation of a given sentence S will then assert the existence of a winning strategy in the correlated nonstandard game. After I realized this, I found out that my sometime Stanford colleague Dana Scott had unbeknownst to me pointed out the same game-theoretical interpretation of Gödel's rules in a seminar talk in 1968. His note was published in the *Yearbook* of the Gödel Society in 1991.

But the treatment of quantifiers in terms of semantical games of seeking and finding was only the first step in a longer line of thought. One direction of further work is to develop a game-theoretical treatment of other notions. I did some work in this direction in the eighties with Jack Kulas, a former student of mine from Florida State University. It turns out that one can formulate interesting game-theoretical rules for such English expressions and constructions as negation, "only," anaphoric pronouns, genitives, and even proper names. This success of game-theoretical semantics had for me a more general meaning. Having developed a viable theory of anaphora of my own I had a vantage point from which to judge other theories for their theoretical significance.

One potential advantage of game-theoretical semantics is that it can in a sense eliminate the hard-and-fast boundary that often is thought to separate logical and nonlogical concepts from each other. For assume that the semantics of some nonlogical concept can be formulated by means of certain games which generalize the semantical games of first-order logic. Then we can typically hang on to the all-important definition of truth as the existence of at least one winning strategy for the "verifier." This enables us to extend notions of logical (analytical) truth and of logical consequence to many sentences containing nonlogical constants. The most comprehensive example of such extensions of game-theoretical semantics beyond first-order languages is the second-generation epistemic logic which uses the slash (—/K).

The possibility of such conservative extensions of game-theoretical semantics undercuts neatly the criticisms of Tarski's treatment of logical consequence and logical truth proposed by my former student John Etchemendy. This kind of extension of semantical games is not limited by a boundary between logical and nonlogical words but by the limits of the game-theoretical approach to semantics in general.

Furthermore, once one begins to think of first-order logic in game-theoretical terms, one faces a host of questions of a general game-theoretical nature. One of them is likely to occur to any game theorist worthy of her utility matrix. Are semantical games games with perfect information or not? It soon became obvious to me that one can easily stage semantical games with imperfect information. The crucial first step in this direction was taken in my 1973 paper "Quantifiers vs. Quantification Theory." It did not take much contemplation, either, for me to realize that semantical games with imperfect information play an interesting role in the semantics of natural languages. A part of this interest is due to the fact that the widespread phenomenon of informational independence is not indicated in most natural languages by any uniform syntactical construction. The methodological consequences of this fact, which I discussed briefly in my 1989 paper, "Paradigms for Language Theory," remain largely to be drawn.

The impact of the new logic on the languages of mathematics and science (and of epistemology) are nevertheless even greater. I made a multiple tactical mistake when I proposed to call the new logic independence-friendly (IF) first-order logic. As I have since repeatedly pointed out, it is a mistake to characterize the new logic by any particular epithet. It is *the* unrestricted first-order logic (*the* quantification theory), unencumbered by any unnecessary restrictions. It is the received form of first-order logic that needs to be qualified terminologically, perhaps as dependence-handicapped logic or perhaps, politically correctly, as independence-challenged logic.

By the same token, IF logic is not "nonclassical." It does not involve any changes in the interpretation of our logical concepts, as reflected by the fact that the same semantical game rules for connectives and for quantifiers are used in IF logic as are relied on in the received first-order logic, of course with the exception that informational independence is allowed. Thus IF logic is in a sense fully as classical as the received first-order logic, but wider in its applicability. In a different perspective, it nevertheless also comes close to intuitionistic logic.

But progress in as fundamental an area as the logic of quantifiers is inevitably slow. The mere realization of the possibility of quantifier independence does not automatically yield a full-fledged IF first-order logic. Initially many logicians, including myself, thought that quantifiers must exhibit a partially ordered dependence structure. It seems that many philosophers still think of IF logic as the logic of such "branching quantifier" structures.

In fact it took me a while to realize the deepest reason for IF first-order logic. It finally crystallized in my mind in the last few of years of the last millennium. The relations of dependence and independence between quantifiers are important because they are the only way of expressing relations of dependence and independence between variables on the first-order level. Since we obviously want to express all possible patterns of dependence and independence between variables in our logical language, IF first-order languages are the languages of choice in looking for a fully explicit scientific or mathematical language at least on the first-order level.

Thus IF logic does not only allow one to express patterns of independence between quantifiers that cannot be expressed in the old dependence-handicapped logic, but new patterns of dependence as well, in particular, patterns of mutual dependence. In brief, it is as much or as little dependence-friendly logic as it is independence-friendly logic.

To put the general point negatively, the received Frege-Russell treatment of quantifiers is seen to be seriously limited in what can be expressed by its means, and therefore inadequate as a logic of science or mathematics. Technically speaking, the Frege-Russell treatment of quantifiers is inadequate because dependence relations between quantifiers are in the received logic indicated by inclusion relations between their scopes. The usual scope relations cannot express all possible patterns of dependence and independence between quantifiers. (For instance, such inclusion relations are transitive and antisymmetric, and thus rule out lots of possible structures.) This throws, in fact, sharp critical light on the notion of scope, including its uses in linguistics. In my 1997 paper "No Scope for Scope" I pointed out that realizing and overcoming the restrictions of this notion helps us to deal with specific linguistic problems, especially anaphora, and in particular the hoary "donkey sentences" problem. The cautionary punch line of my paper was, "In linguistics, once a day with scope does not do it."

As indicated earlier, the same point can be expressed in another way. The meaning of quantifiers is usually taken to be exhausted by their "ranging over" a certain class of values. If there are enough names available, we could think of quantified sentences as long disjunctions and conjunctions. But this simply does not work, as is most clearly seen by considering mutually dependent quantifiers. We have to acknowledge the relations of dependence and independence as an integral part of the semantics of quantifiers. In brief, our ideas about the meaning of quantifiers have to be reconsidered in the light of GTS.

This point can be illustrated by an example. What I have said implies that there can be a two-sorted quantification theory where quantifiers of the two sorts range over mutually exclusive classes of values and yet can be dependent and independent of each other quite as freely as quantifiers ranging over the same class of values. Whoever appreciates this fact should not be surprised by the nonlocality problems in quantum theory.

These developments have opened an almost incredible embarrassment of potential riches. I am using the word "embarrassment" here advisedly, for I am keenly aware that I will never have the time, energy, and the background knowledge to utilize these possibilities myself.

Undoubtedly the slow absorption of my ideas into the mainstream of discussion is to be expected, not only because of my limitations as an expositor, but also because the consequences of these new insights are so radical as to make it difficult for thinkers to readjust their ideas all of a sudden. A mere list of some of these arguable consequences is enough to show their revolutionary character.

Among other consequences, IF logic (when suitably enriched) enables us to reconstruct all normal mathematical reasoning on the first-order level. This aids and abets mightily the cause of logicism in the philosophy of mathematics. It nevertheless does not lead to any axiomatic reduction of mathematics to logic, for IF first-order logic is inevitably semantically incomplete: the set of valid formulas is not recursively enumerable. But it does mean that several crucial concepts can now be dealt with on the level of first-order (IF) logic, for instance, the notions of equicardinality and infinity. More generally speaking, my observations show that in the foundations of mathematics we can in principle dispense with all the perplexing questions concerning the existence of higher-order entities.

As an aficionado of game theory is likely to expect, the semantical games of IF logic are not determinate. In plain English, this means that in IF logic the law of excluded middle fails. Since we can extend the basic IF logic by adding to it a sentence-initial contradictory negation, it can be seen that our very concept of negation has an unavoidable Janus face. The negation which we are primarily interested in and which is codified in natural language negation is contradictory negation, but the only negation we can have semantical game rules for is the strong (dual) negation. This puts the entire concept of negation to a new light, including its behavior in natural languages.

In the early nineties I realized that in a suitable applied IF first-order language we can define a truth predicate for that language in the language itself. (This insight first came to me in the middle of a seminar I was conducting at Boston University.) This seems to contradict Tarski's impossibility theorem that has dominated logico-philosophical discussions of truth for more than a half-century. The contradiction is seen to be merely apparent when we realize that Tarski is assuming that the concept of negation he is dealing with is the contradictory negation. Similar comments can be made on Lindström's well-known theorem. This theorem cannot any longer be said to show that the received first-order logic is the strongest possible first-order logic. It shows this maximal strength only on the assumption that the only negation present is the contradictory one. For a brief while I wondered whether a similar maximal strength theorem could be proved for IF logic, discussed the possibility with Lindström and even looked for a proof, until I realized that by restricting the strategy sets available to the verifier in a semantical game one can easily formulate increasingly stronger first-order logics. Furthermore, I have argued (together with Sandu) that Tarski's belief in the impossibility of a coherent use of the concept of truth in our actual working language is due to his commitment to compositionality, which is but another casualty of IF logic.

The most surprising observation in this general direction is independent of most of the technicalities of IF logic. One does not even need IF logic to realize that according to our pretheoretical concept of truth, the truth of a quantified sentence S amounts to the existence of a full set of Skolem functions for S. As one can put it, Skolem functions of S produce as their values the "witness individuals" that vouchsafe the truth of S. What follows when this is applied to any first-order axiomatic set theory? The existence of the Skolem functions for S can be expressed in a self-applied set theory. Hence, we seem to be able to formulate a truth definition for first-order axiomatic set theory in the same theory. But this is impossible by Tarski's famous result. Now the only way in which the proposed truth definition can fail (barring inconsistency) is that some sentence S is true even though not all its Skolem functions exist. But even though this does not result in a formal contradiction in a first-order treatment of set theory, it is contrary to our ordinary concept of truth, and not only to our pretheoretical notion of truth, but also to the combinational idea of truth that is codified in the standard interpretation of quantification over sets (in Henkin's sense of standardness) on which such set-theoretical statements as the continuum hypothesis are based. In this sense, there are false statements in any model of a first-order axiomatic set theory. What is worse, such false statements cannot be blamed on the presence of "too big" sets, as the old paradoxes of set theory are often blamed. They make their appearance already in cardinalities that are used in ordinary mathematics. The general result is therefore that truth according to first-order axiomatic set theory, that is, literal first-order truth in the models of the theory, is not an infallible guide to real (combinatorial) set-theoretical truth. For instance, the independence results of Gödel and Paul Cohen do not by themselves show anything whatsoever about the truth or falsity of the continuum hypothesis.

Another new opening is created by the theory of mutually dependent variables. I am trying to show that this theory is the true logic of quantum theory. Unsurprisingly, this has turned out to be the most difficult problem area I have ever approached.

Although most of the concrete nitty-gritty work probably remains to be done, I can thus look with deep satisfaction to that part of my intellectual life that has led to these new insights. If I am asked where my new ideas have come from, my playful yet serious answer is: from my older ideas. As

I have indicated, in the development of my thinking about our basic logic and its semantics, one thing has almost literally led to another.

I have another major source of professional satisfaction in that a new line of thought I have developed is promising to revolutionize epistemology in somewhat the same way game-theoretical semantics and IF logic are promising to revolutionize philosophical logic and the foundations of mathematics. Or perhaps I should not speak here of a new line of thought, because in a sense its basic idea is truly old, older than logic and epistemology in Western thought. This basic idea is codified already in the Socratic *elenchus*, his method of questioning, which in my youth I witnessed Einari Merikallio practicing. Plato turned the *elenchus* into a general method of inquiry and philosophical training, and his student Aristotle began to develop a systematic theory of Socratic questioning games. He saw in interrogative reasoning a general method of inquiry, including a way of finding the first premises of any science. I have suggested that Aristotle was still in his two *Analytics* thinking of the entire scientific process as a question-answer sequence. I have also tried to show how Aristotle was led from the Platonic questioning games to his logic. The most important strategic consideration in any questioning game is to anticipate the answers. Aristotle realized that there is a class of answers that are fully predictable, viz., those that (as we would now put it) are logically implied by earlier answers. By trying to analyze such answers in relation to earlier ones Aristotle became the first theoretical logician in Western thought.

Aristotle also anticipated the architectonic step that distinguishes the modern interrogative approach to inquiry from the questioning games of Plato's Academy. When an answer to a question is logically implied by earlier answers, the entire step is conceptually different from ordinary question-answer moves. As Aristotle would have said, such steps must be judged *ad argumentum*, not *ad hominem*. The answerer and his or her (or its, if we are dealing with a database) epistemic state are irrelevant. All that matters is the logical relation of the question and its answer to earlier answers. Hence it is reasonable to separate such moves from ordinary question-answer steps and label them "logical inference steps."

Indeed, the interrogative model of knowledge-seeking differs from the Socratic method basically only in that the predictable answers Aristotle studied are separated, in my model, into a class of logical inference moves as distinguished from interrogative (question-answer) moves. It can be argued —I have done so in my abduction paper (1998)—that any rational knowledge-seeking reasoning can be represented as such a questioning-cum-inference form. By rational I here mean "subject to rational evaluation."

The project of modeling inquiry in general as a questioning process can only be successful if we have at our disposal an explicit general logic of questions and answers. And such a logic can only be developed as a branch of an adequate logic of knowledge, also known as epistemic logic.

I developed the basic ideas of an epistemic logic as a part of my work on modal and intensional logic from 1956 to 1962 and published them in *Knowledge and Belief* in 1962. It dawned on me slowly, however, that the treatment given them was not fully general. It worked for simple wh-questions, but not for all complex (multi-quantifier) questions. I became gradually aware that epistemic logic was really needed in the theory of questioning processes, and equally slowly aware that my 1962 epistemic logic was only part of the story. The latter insight was first prompted by the work by Elisabeth Engdahl, reported in her 1986 book *Constituent Questions*. The questions she put to me in preparing her book showed me that my 1962 logic was not able to deal with complex questions with an outside universal quantifier on the first-order level. Fortunately I had meanwhile developed other ideas that turned out to be what I needed to extend my model. The new insight was that the correct formal expression of the question ingredient is the "slash" that indicates that an existential quantifier or a disjunction is independent of a sentence-initial "knows that" operator K. (For a brief explanation of this idea, see section 3 above.) In this way, the most crucial concepts relating to questions and answers can be captured, especially the notion of the presupposition of a question and the conditions that conclusive answers to a given question have to satisfy—in brief, the notion of answer. Unfortunately I have not been able to expound this interrogative logic at monographic length. (But see the 1999 paper by myself, Halonen, and Mutanen.) The other ideas needed here are in any case the same as are required to overcome the mistakes of the New Theory of Reference. They are discussed briefly above in section 3.

This interrogative approach to epistemology throws sharp light on its rivals. Nevertheless, its scope might seem to be seriously limited. Admittedly, even Thomas Kuhn is willing to consider normal science as a series of exercises in problem-solving. But how can the interrogative approach do justice to the discovery of new laws and theories? Presumably good old mother nature can only tell how things are here and now, not what they are always and everywhere, at least if empiricists are right. What that means is that the input to interrogative reasoning consists only of particular propositions. And from them no general conclusions ensue without strong a priori assumptions. Hence there seem to be three main ways of looking at theory formation in science.

The first is to add to the logical (deductive) rules of inference suitable inductive rules. The second is to allow strong a priori premises. The third is to give up the attempt to analyze theory formation altogether and adopt something like the hypothetico-deductive model of science. These three alternatives characterize three main ways of looking at the scientific process in philosophical literature.

The interrogative approach suggests a much more satisfactory answer: None of the above. In actual scientific practice, the input into scientific reasoning is not restricted to particular (quantifier-free) propositions. Indeed, the most important kind of question put to nature in actual science is a controlled experiment. Now the question asked in such an experiment concerns the mode of dependence of the observed variable on the controlled variable. An answer to such a question specifies the function that codifies the mode of dependence. Such an answer can only be formulated by means of a two-quantifier sentence. In brief, the answer to an experimental question is not a particular (singular) proposition, but has nontrivial quantificational complexity. Such propositions can very well entail general laws and even theories.

Hence the proposals to go in effect beyond the interrogative model are not only unnecessary but mistaken in that they overlook the most important feature of the conceptual situation. This feature is the fact that the input into scientific reasoning includes what, logically speaking, are propositions of some generality. One explanation why this fact has not been appreciated is the foundationalist search for indubitable premises for scientific inferences. But there are plenty of collateral reasons, some of them supplied by the game-theoretical semantics, to adopt a fallibilist epistemology in any case. And if so, there is no reason to discriminate against general propositions as a part of the input into scientific reasoning.

This puts a number of the classical issues in epistemology in a new light. For instance, it shows that Hume's problem of induction only arises on strictly limited conditions. Not only did Hume have to rule out innate ideas; he had to rule out general answers to empirical questions. There could not have been Hume's problem before Hume, and there is no problem of induction for anyone accepting an experimentalist methodology. For instance, Newton had no problem of induction in Hume's sense. Indeed, for an experimentalist like Newton, Hume's problem of induction as an inference from particulars to generalizations is replaced by the problem of extending and combining partial generalizations (generalizations restricted to certain intervals of argument values). It even turns out that this "replacement" is not a figure of speech but literally an item of conceptual history in that such extrapolation and interpolation is what Newton (and before him Aristotle) in effect meant by induction (or *epagoge*). As it happened, I had reached (in my 1980 paper) essentially this diagnosis of Aristotle's notion of *epagoge* already before I had developed the interrogative framework.

In this way, the interrogative approach leads to important insights in epistemology, philosophy of science and even history of science. But there are even more general repercussions of the interrogative approach. They require a new viewpoint, however. This viewpoint is also old. It is implicit in the idea of considering inquiry as a game. Hence it is foreshadowed, if not by Socrates, then by Plato's systematization of *elenchus* into the practice of interrogative *games*. The word "game" is not my invention. It is used commonly by classicists discussing the development of the Socratic *elenchus* into a general philosophical method of reasoning in Plato's Academy.

But once again, the full utilization of an old idea is possible only with the help of modern methods, which in this case are the ways of thinking and conceptualization codified in the mathematical theory of games. One of the patron saints of the new epistemology is thus John von Neumann, the father of contemporary game theory. We met game theory already in connection with game-theoretical semantics. However, the interrogative games are, of course, different from the semantical games that are the logical home of quantifiers, and also different from the formal games of theorem-proving. Perhaps I should not say "of course," for confusion about the three kinds of games is one of the most persistent mistakes in recent epistemology. For instance, Dummett's so-called intuitionism is little more than an unfortunate attempt to assimilate semantical and interrogative games to each other, and also to assimilate them to the formal games of theorem-proving that should be distinguished from both.

Many of the repercussions of the interrogative approach are connected with a distinction which is as important as it is neglected by philosophers. In all games of strategy, in most other games and in many goal-directed processes we can distinguish—and have to distinguish—from each other two different kinds of rules or principles. I have called them *definitory rules* and *strategic rules*. For instance, in the game of chess the definitory rules tell you how chessmen are moved on the board, what counts as checking and mating, and so on. These rules define the game of chess. In a sense, you cannot break them. If you try to move a piece in a way contrary to them, you are not playing chess. Your attempted move has to be taken back. It is null and void.

But if you only know the definitory rules of chess, you cannot even claim that you know how to play chess. For the purpose, you have to have some grasp of the strategic rules (or principles, if you prefer the term) of chess. That is, you must have some idea what better and worse moves of chess are, how to try to win a play of the game.

This distinction can obviously be extended to other strategic games. One reason why it is important is shown by the mathematical theory of games. From this theory, it can be seen that in a rock-bottom sense, only entire strategies can be evaluated, not particular moves, except in a derived sense via the strategies of which they are parts. This is contrary to the tactics of most philosophers working in formal philosophy of science, in that they are thinking of the rules of scientific reasoning as if they were definitory rules in some process or other. The supposed rules of inductive logic are cases in point.

This strategic viewpoint throws sharp light on a wide variety of important issues in epistemology and in philosophy of science. Among them there are the following:

(1) The so-called rules of inference of deductive logic are definitory rules of the game of formal proof. They do not tell what inferences one should draw in a situation in which several inferences are possible, nor what inferences people always or generally draw in such circumstances. They are not rules of inference in either a descriptive or a prescriptive sense. They are merely permissive. They are rules for avoiding fallacies.

(2) It follows that human deductive behavior cannot be modeled in any interesting sense by the so-called rules of inference. Such behavior should be studied by reference to the strategic rules of deductive logic.

(3) Similar things can be said of the rules of ampliative reasoning, including interrogative reasoning. Its definitory rules should merely rule out such behavior as is always ill-advised. For the rest, the definitory rules are merely permissive. For instance, in order to deal with answers that can be false, it is enough for these rules to authorize the inquirer to reject tentatively ("bracket") an earlier answer, together with everything that depends on it in reasoning. The choice of an answer to bracket can only be determined by strategic rules. Naturally we must also have a rule for unbracketing.

The (permissive) rule for questioning says simply that any question can be raised whose presuppositions have been established. For this purpose, we need a general notion of presupposition which is provided by the logic of questions and answers. Similarly conclusiveness conditions help to define what it means to have an answer to a given question. The fact that these two notions can now be defined for the first time in my second-generation logic of questions and answers explains why the Socratic questioning method was not systematized much earlier.

(4) Scientific reasoning must be modeled by means of strategic rules, not definitory rules.

(5) The definitory rules governing logical inference and the definitory rules governing question-answer steps are quite different. However, there are interesting connections between the strategic rules governing the two kinds of steps. These are especially clear in the case in which all answers are true and are all known to be true. This case typifies purely truth-seeking reasoning, sometimes characterized as a context of discovery, as distinguished from critical or evaluative reasoning. On this assumption, consider a situation at some given stage of inquiry. The inquirer has reached a number propositions which can be used either as premises of a logical inference step or as

presuppositions of a question. If one is arguing purely deductively, one has to ask which proposition serves best the purposes of deductive argumentation. If one is carrying out interrogative argumentation, one has to ask which proposition serves best as the presupposition of the next question. There is in general no computable answer to either question. However, there is a striking connection between the two questions, at least in a context of pure discovery, subject only to certain further explanations. *The answer is the same in both cases.*

This result is highly interesting philosophically. What it means is that, strategically speaking, deductive logic is the key to all good reasoning, at least in reasoning involved in pure discovery. I have called the idea that logic and deduction are the gist of all good thinking the "Sherlock Holmes conception of logic." What has been found is that Sherlock Holmes was right at least in contexts of discovery.

(6) This result puts into a new light the entire job description of epistemology. An influential tradition restricts the task of epistemology to the study of what have been called contexts of justification, that is to say, to the study of the reliability of already reached theories, hypotheses, and other propositions. On this view, which is closely related to the hypothetico-deductive conception of science, contexts of discovery cannot be dealt with by means of logic or by means of any other kind of rational epistemology. Even though more and more dissenting voices have been heard in recent years, the overwhelming majority of actual work in epistemology still deals with contexts of justification rather than contexts of discovery.

This view has now been refuted for good. Not only is a logic of discovery possible; we already know what it is like. It is a special case of the strategic logic of question-answer sequences, viz., the case in which all answers are known to be true, so that no problem of justification can arise. This case of pure discovery is admittedly a special case, but it is enough for the purpose of a demonstration of the possibility of a logic of discovery. In the strategic sense, the logic of discovery is in this case nearly tantamount to the strategic aspects of ordinary deductive logic.

One thing that all this implies is that epistemologists will have to study seriously information-seeking and not just the justification of already reached truths. Of course, this is in keeping with what theoretical scientists are doing. Naturally, they are interested in knowing to what extent so far available evidence supports their already formulated hypotheses and theories. However, it is of even greater interest to them to ask what further information might be available that would support or perhaps refute the hypothesis or theory in question, which in terms of the interrogative model means deciding what questions to have.

(7) The game-theoretical approach upsets in an even more fundamental

way the traditional distinction between contexts of discovery and contexts of justification. In an actual scientific process, an inquirer is usually looking at one and the same time both for new knowledge and for justification for old and new putative knowledge. This process can be considered as a game. The double character of the process only means that the payoffs depend on the informativeness and on the reliability of the answers obtained and accepted as well as on their truth. As was pointed out above, the evaluation of such a process must pertain in the last analysis to entire strategies. In these strategies, we cannot in general tell apart the truth-seeking and the justificatory components. Hence the true overall situation in realistic epistemology is diametrically opposed to the traditional view. There is a marvelously clear-cut logic of discovery, although it applies directly only to the idealized case in which the problem of justification is assumed not to come up. The shoe is now on the other foot. It is the process of justification that cannot be studied in isolation—because epistemological strategies have to be at one and the same time strategies of justification and strategies of discovery. We cannot study the justification problem apart from the problem of discovery, which is what the overwhelming majority of epistemological studies are still attempting to do. Of course, such attempts may be successful in that they yield results that are valid on certain assumptions, just as Carnapian λ-continuum yields an optimal inductive method in the special case in which his symmetry assumptions hold and, which is the crucial assumption, the total amount of order in the universe of discourse is known. (Otherwise we do not know what value of λ to choose.) But as an ultimate epistemological truth, methods of justification cannot be evaluated, and hence individual justificatory moves cannot be evaluated, independently of the component of discovery in the scientific process. There is in the last analysis no adequate theory of justification separated from a theory of discovery.

(8) In order to theorize about interrogative searches of information, we need to understand the logic of questions and answers, as well as of question-answer sequences such as (tentative) acceptance and (tentative) rejection, and at some stage also probabilistic notions. What we do not need are the notions of knowledge and belief. Hence most of what seems to me the most important questions of epistemology can be dealt with without speaking of knowledge or belief. The notion of knowledge enters into the picture only in connection with the question as to when the interrogative process has been carried far enough. And the answer to this question might perhaps be relative to the particular inquiry one is engaged in. Thus it can even be suggested that in concentrating heavily on the notion of knowledge and its definition philosophers are simply asking the wrong questions. As I may put my rhetorical question: Do we need the concept of knowledge in epistemology?

This list could be continued. What it shows already in its present shape is that we have here the ingredients of a radical revolution in epistemology. This revolution involves both the conceptual tools used in epistemology and the central questions to be raised there.

The two new approaches outlined in this chapter are a source of a deep professional satisfaction for me. At the same time, they are also a source of intense frustration. Even though most of the leading ideas of the two new approaches have already proved their mettle, I cannot expect them to be generally accepted before they have been carried out systematically and before their main consequences have been established. And this task is too great for any single individual to carry out.

What is more, I have at the present time relatively few students or other close collaborators that can contribute to this task. This is not because I shun cooperation in philosophy. On the contrary, I probably have more co-authored publications to my credit than any other active philosopher. In Finland, I helped to train an entire generation of philosophers in a wide sense of the word, mostly as sometime members of the research group I led under the auspices of the Academy of Finland. Later, I have worked very closely with a few individuals, especially with Gabriel Sandu. But in the last decade or so, I have found it hard to engage in a genuinely cooperative work with graduate students or junior faculty, admittedly with some pleasant and rewarding exceptions. Undoubtedly I must accept much of the blame myself. However, it is unmistakable that the intellectual climate in most departments of philosophy in the United States is not hospitable to genuine cooperation in philosophical research. The main reason is the career pressure under which most graduate students and most untenured faculty members are struggling. Graduate students can expect economic support only for a restricted number of years. In order to finish their dissertations in the expected time, they choose a safe subject that does not require new ideas or discoveries for their completion. They have of course a good reason to do so, for genuine discoveries are unpredictable and topics that would require them are risky. The result is a slew of dissertations that are descriptive rather than problem-oriented. They do not deal with the problems of a Kripke, Kuhn, Quine, Wittgenstein, or Husserl, but with what other philosophers have said of these problems. Anachronistic work used to be branded in Oxbridge by saying that the author dealt with historical figures as if they were "fellows of another college." In much of recent philosophical literature the converse mistake is committed: members of other contemporary universities are dealt with as if they were historical figures.

A contributing factor is that there are no major research projects in philosophy going on at this time in which graduate students and their advisors could meaningfully cooperate and whose results could be anticipated. This is connected with what I said in section 6 about the failure of the ostensible leaders of our profession to come up with breakthrough projects.

The same can be said of the pressures on untenured faculty. These pressures are due to the greater requirements for tenure, reported for instance in the *Chronicle of Higher Education* on January 5, 2001. And these requirements are in turn reflections of the intellectual insecurity of most departments and universities. The do not trust their own judgment of quality and promise. Only the most secure institutions dare to look away from formal criteria, such as publication record. In my own experience, I have seen how well such courage can pay off. Such legendary figures as Burton Dreben and Rogers Albritton never published very much. All the publications of Gwil Owen—an academic triple crown winner—fit into one medium-sized volume. Isaac Levi and James Higginbotham were originally promoted on a relatively slim publication record. But the overwhelming issue is not the personal injustice done to the mute inglorious Miltons of philosophy nor my frustration in trying to revolutionize contemporary philosophy, but the damage to the entire philosophical community. It is the philosophical community, not myself, that is missing an opportunity here.

I do have a belief, however, unrealistic though it may be, that the merits of the two new approaches I have sketched in this section are sufficiently obvious to perceptive philosophers to be adopted by them and utilized to the extent they deserve.

Thus in the light of hindsight the main lines of my intellectual efforts appear to show continuity, progress, and success. However, at the time when the work was originally carried out, things looked entirely different. Continuity and progress can be perceived (or imagined) only *post factum*. In the course of actual inquiry, one is keenly aware of obstacles and failures. Repeatedly, from my earliest work on distributive normal forms to my ongoing work on the logical structure of quantum theory, I have found—or at least felt—that I am charting a new territory for which I do not have any maps and for the exploration of which I do not have as good a training as I could have. Even when one reaches some specific new insight, it often leads to new problems. Thus at the time of the actual work I have always felt that my progress, if any, was very slow.

EPILOGUE

By definition, an intellectual autobiography does not cover the other aspects of one's life. Hence much that has been important in my life history is left out here. Thus my relation to religion, literature, and to the arts as well as my *éducation sentimentale* do not belong to this essay, even though there inevitably is some overlap. Perhaps it suffices to make a few concessions to the interconnections of different walks of one's life and letters. My marriage to the late Merrill Bristow Hintikka (1939–1987) was not only personally the most important period of my life, it was also an exciting intellectual adventure. I hope to tell her extraordinary life story one of these days.

Several of the people I have personally known and respected have been religious, but I am not sure what an operative definition of religious belief could be and how it could possibly apply in my own case. Maybe one cannot live without some religious myth, but if I could choose one for myself, it would not be that of any organized religion but perhaps rather something like what the Swedish poet Hjalmar Gullberg envisages in his memorable poem "Åt halvgudarna" ("To Demigods"). I can imagine what it would be like to encounter one of Gullberg's demigods who are characterized by him as "the intolerable saviors in our need" distinguished by "their goodness and their violent death." I can even imagine myself fantasizing about having met such creatures, at least if I replace their goodness by their creativity and the violence of their death by cruelty in a wider sense. Was Gödel such a demigod? Was Merrill one? But I cannot seriously envisage gods who would take personal interest in human lives. As to the "consolation of philosophy" one needs in the midst of trials and tribulations of one's personal and professional life, I am likewise tempted to borrow a phrase or two from professional writers. I am not as heroic as Sten Selander's proverbial *bondestudent* who defended himself against desperation "med stålblanka romarcitat" ("with shining steel lines from the Romans"). As I would reply to Selander, my name just is not Linnaeus or Tegnér. Most of the time I merely try to recall the closing words of Toivo Pekkanen's remarkable *Bildungsroman* entitled *Tehtaan varjossa*:

> His task was to live here in the world, to take part in its joys and sorrows and to grow taller than his father had been and to see farther than his father had seen.

JAAKKO HINTIKKA

BOSTON UNIVERSITY
FEBRUARY 2003

ACKNOWLEDGMENT

In composing this autobiography and in checking the data presented there, I have been helped by Veikko Hintikka and by Soili Hintikka.

PART TWO

DESCRIPTIVE AND CRITICAL ESSAYS WITH REPLIES

1

Simo Knuuttila

HINTIKKA'S VIEW OF
THE HISTORY OF PHILOSOPHY

Jaakko Hintikka is one of the few contemporary philosophers who are well known for their systematic works and studies of the history of Western philosophy. The history of philosophy is not the main item of Hintikka's interest, but his historical contributions are found both philosophically and historically valuable and highly stimulating and original. There is not a very sharp distinction between the historical and systematic approaches in Hintikka's works: "This interplay between topical and historical work is one of the characteristic features of my philosophical work. It is truly a two-way interaction, for purely historical insights frequently enhance our awareness of important systematic issues especially of our own conceptual assumptions."[1] This is not very common in the analytic tradition that is Hintikka's main orientation. In any case, his studies of ancient thought, Descartes, Leibniz, Kant, and twentieth-century philosophy are innovative just because they combine historical knowledge with new systematic approaches to the foundations of rational discourse. Historical texts are put in a new perspective by comparing their conceptual presuppositions with alternative ways of thinking about the same things.[2]

My aim is to make some remarks on Hintikka's conception of the history of philosophy. The phrase is ambiguous because it may refer to philosophy in history or, as here, to historical research. Hintikka has not written much about philosophy as a historical institution or about the nature of the historical work in philosophy, apparently thinking that his views can be seen in his investigations of particular themes. This is what

I shall try to do in what follows. Let us first have a look at Hintikka's studies on Aristotle's modal theory, which illustrate his attitude to the history of philosophy in general.[3]

I. INVESTIGATING ARISTOTLE

Recent studies of the modalities in Aristotle and other ancient authors have received much impetus from Hintikka's studies on Aristotle's modal theories. Some of them have long been among the most quoted references in the discussion of Aristotle's modal conceptions.[4] In "Necessity, Universality, and Time in Aristotle," first published in 1957, Hintikka paid attention to certain systematic relations between time and modality in Aristotle and formulated the main variants of the principle of plenitude in Aristotle's works. The term "the principle of plenitude," coined by A. O. Lovejoy in his famous work *The Great Chain of Being*, takes the basic form:

(P)   no genuine possibility remains eternally unrealized.[5]

In addition to (P), Hintikka mentions the following Aristotelian variants of the principle of plenitude:

(P)*   that which never is, is impossible,

(P)**   what always is, is by necessity

and

(P)***   nothing eternal is contingent.

In this early paper Hintikka restricted (P) and its variants in Aristotle to discussions of everlasting beings, kinds of individuals, and types of events. In later works he calls this group of assumptions, with certain further specifications, a statistical model of modality in Aristotle. That something is possible must be shown by its happening sometimes, and what is always is by necessity. Applications of modal notions understood in this way reduce to comparisons of frequencies of what happens at different moments in time. According to Hintikka, this model codifies some of the more or less conscious conceptual presuppositions on which Aristotle based his modal thought, but it was not the only one of Aristotle's modal paradigms and hence did not yield definitions of the various modal terms to him.[6]

Some authors have argued that even though (P) and its variants played a role in Aristotle, they are metaphysical principles based on special ontological and metaphysical views, not modal principles derived from the meaning of modal terms.[7] Hintikka stresses that Aristotle did not draw any systematic distinction between what we call logical or conceptual necessity or possibility on the one hand and metaphysical or natural necessities or possibilities on the other. He is also inclined to think that in some form the principle of plenitude is embedded in all the modal paradigms of Aristotle and that it was just this feature of his modal conceptions which tended to cause problems in certain philosophical contexts.[8] Many scholars have thought, following Alexander of Aphrodisias and Boethius, that, in addition to modal paradigms which involved (P), Aristotle also operated with a conception of alternative prospective singular possibilities which remain open options until the moment of time to which they refer.[9] Because of their assumption of the necessity of the present, the later Aristotelians did not develop any idea of synchronic alternatives. If there are transient alternative possibilities with respect to a particular future event, they disappear when the future is fixed. It seems that Aristotle suggested something like this in *Metaphysics* VI.3 (1027a29–1027b16) (and in some other places).[10]

The most discussed part of Hintikka's studies on Aristotle's modal theory is his interpretation of *De interpretatione* 9 (18a28–19b4). In his paper "The Once and Future Sea Fight," reprinted as chapter 8 in *Time and Necessity*, Hintikka wanted to show that Aristotle's main problem in *De interpretatione* 9 was created by his tacitly equating possibility with truth at some times and necessity with omnitemporal truth. The problems of this statistical model came to the surface when Aristotle tried to define the modal status of temporally definite sentences referring to individual historical events. He was not well prepared to do this, since he regarded temporally indefinite token reflexive sentences as the paradigm types of informative sentences, and since he was strongly committed to certain habits of thinking which were based on this view.[11] According to Hintikka, Aristotle expresses his basic problem in *De interpretatione* 9 by stating that "it was always true to say of anything that has happened that it is or will be so." Aristotle's heavy reliance on the statistical model is seen in his moving from the infinite past truth of a statement to its necessity: "But if it was always true to say that it is or will be so, it could not be not so, or not be going not to be so" (18b10–13). On this interpretation, Aristotle's real problem is that temporally definite statements, if they are true, are always and unchangingly true and as such necessarily true. The problem is not really solved. All that Aristotle could do, Hintikka argues, was to transpose the question to a level at which it could be discussed in terms of temporally indefinite sentences. This happens in passage 19a23–27. Aristotle says that what is, necessarily is, when it is, and the meaning of this remark is that what is, immutably is what it is, when it is. Aristotle says that when something is necessary in this sense, it does not follow that it would be necessary "without qualification," that is, actual at all times. In the same way a true temporally determinate sentence, which as such seems to be necessarily true, may become contingent when the temporal specification is removed. This is no solution to the deterministic problem which immediately arises when statistically interpreted modal notions are applied to temporally definite sentences or events. If what happens at a given time cannot not happen then, this necessity is not removed by saying what can take place at other times.[12]

The question of the truth and falsity of future contingent sentences was one of the themes occurring in ancient discussions of Diodorus Chronus's famous argument for determinism. This Master Argument, as it was called, is incompletely known to us through Epictetus's description.[13] According to Epictetus, the point of the argument was to demonstrate that the conjunction of (1) everything past and true is necessary and (2) the impossible does not follow from the possible, which is accepted as evidently true, is incompatible with (3) what neither is nor will be is possible. In his paper "Aristotle and the 'Master Argument' of Diodorus," Hintikka noted structural similarities between the background assumptions in Diodorus's argument and in Aristotle's modal theories.[14]

Arthur Prior put forward a fairly complicated tense logical reconstruction of the 'Master Argument' in 1955.[15] Hintikka's interpretation is more straightforward. He asserts that Diodorus Chronus thought that what is now future will be past and hence necessary. Therefore, to say that a future event can be other than what it in fact will be is to say something from which an impossibility follows, that is, that it could be true to say that such a thing has not happened of which it will be necessarily true to say that it has happened.[16] Although their interpretations are based on different views about the nature of some background assumptions of the argument, both Prior and Hintikka see the basic problem in the fact that possibilities are taken to refer to what is actual in our universe considered as a definite whole. The argument is in this sense based on determinism. Hintikka argues that the Master Argument can be regarded as a variant of Aristotle's argument in *De caelo* I.12.[17] The difference between Aristotle and Diodorus was that Diodorus had nothing against determinism, while for Aristotle it was an unintended side-effect of his modal assumptions, which he unsuccessfully tried to turn aside in various ways.[18]

The problematic implications of Aristotle's modal paradigms were not restricted to the statistical model. They were also embedded in Aristotle's second modal paradigm which was that of possibility as potency. In *Metaphysics* V.12 (1019a15–20, 33–b7) and IX.1 (1046a19–26) potency is said to be the principle of motion or change either as an activator (in

Latin *potentia activa*) or as the receptor of a relevant influence (in Latin *potentia passiva*). The types of potency-based possibilities belonging to a species are recognized as possibilities because of their sometime actualization—no natural potency type remains eternally frustrated (*De caelo* I.12). The model of possibility as potency *prima facie* allowed Aristotle to speak about all kinds of unrealized singular possibilities by referring to various levels of potentiality or by treating passive and active potencies separately.

Hintikka argues that this move did not help Aristotle. Active and passive potencies are generic capacities and do not as such guarantee that their actualization can take place. More is required for a real singular potency-based possibility. According to Aristotle, a singular dynamic possibility can be actualized only when the active and passive potency are in contact; in such a case the possibility is necessarily realized if there are no external hindrances (*Metaphysics* IX.5, 1048a5–21). If partial singular possibilities cannot be realized before having first become full possibilities, i.e., before having all the constituents just mentioned, the borderline between real possibility and actuality seems to disappear. Aristotle thought that the real difference between a singular possibility and its actuality is clearly seen in time-taking motions and changes (*kinēsis*). In order to stress this point he defined process as the actuality of the potentiality (of the end) *qua* potentiality (*Physics* III.1, 201a10–11). In this way Aristotle could maintain that there are unrealized singular possibilities in the world, but this maneuver did not help him more than offering a place for the full potential of what will be.[19]

According to Hintikka, the sources of Aristotle's problems with modal notions are clearly seen from how he operates with his definition of possibility as that which can be assumed to be actual without any impossibility resulting from his assumption (*Prior Analytics* I.13, 32a18–20). This "logical" definition occurs in Aristotle's corpus in conjunction with other ideas of which the most important is that the realization must pertain to some moment of time in our actual world. In *De caelo* I.12 (281a28– b25) Aristotle excludes from the realm of genuine possibilities those which remain eternally frustrated, because one cannot assume them to be realized at any time without contradiction. If this view is applied to temporally definite possibilities, its deterministic implications become obvious.[20]

In his diagnoses of Aristotle's modal thought Hintikka has been particularly interested in its extensional presuppositions and the absence of the idea of modality as involving reference to simultaneous alternatives. Because of these features Aristotle's theory represents an approach which is quite different from intensionally oriented modal conceptions which, since medieval times, have offered an alternative to extensional theories.[21]

The intensional interpretation forms the core of contemporary possible worlds semantics according to which the meaning of basic modal notions can be spelled out only by considering several alternative states of affairs and their relation to each other at the same time. Hintikka was one of the first to put forward the basic ideas of possible worlds semantics in "Modality as Referential Multiplicity" which appeared in 1957.[22] His paper "Necessity, Universality and Time in Aristotle" also appeared in the same year. This is not a mere coincidence. It is characteristic of Hintikka's studies of Aristotle's modal paradigms that they are analyzed as philosophical positions with special assumptions and related to other possible assumptions, mainly to those of possible worlds semantics. The comparisons are seldom explicitly formulated, but they do shape the general lines of discussion. It is often stressed that certain ideas are not found in Aristotle and that certain solutions become understandable for just this reason.

Hintikka's work on Aristotle's modal theory shows how the conceptual assumptions of a philosophical theory can be discerned against the background provided by another theory and how this comparison can also shed light on the special features of both theories. The interpretational context of Hintikka's studies in the history of modal theories has been the leading contemporary approach, and it is clear that this philosophical orientation has greatly added to the interest which these works have aroused among philosophers and the historians of philosophy.

The same combination between historical scholarship and consciousness of various topical philosophical possibilities also occurs in Hintikka's other historical works. In 1961 he published an often quoted paper on Descartes in which he argued that Descartes's *cogito ergo sum* is not an inference from *cogito* to *sum*.[23] Its special character is due to the self-defeating character of an attempt to think that I do not exist, analogous to the self-defeating character of the assertion "I do not exist." Hence 'cogito' does not express a premise, but refers to the act through which the self-defeating or self-verifying character of certain thought-acts is manifested. The very act of thinking or saying "I exist" shows that what one says or thinks is true. This is said to throw light on several aspects of the *cogito* of Descartes, for example, the curiously momentary character of its formulation in Meditation II: "*I am, I exist* is necessarily true each time it is uttered by me or conceived mentally." Even here Hintikka's interpretive questions were associated with central systematic themes such as the nature of indexicals and the question of self-reference in epistemic logic. The latter topic Hintikka discusses, with some further historical examples, in his book *Knowledge and Belief*, which was published a year later.[24]

Most of Hintikka's other historical papers from Plato's and Aristotle's epistemology to Leibniz's modal metaphysics and Kant's philosophy of mathematics and transcendental knowledge provide similar examples of explicating and evaluating philosophical theories by analyzing their conceptual properties in relation to possible alternatives.[25] A particularly representative example is Hintikka's analysis of Aristotle's concept of being; I shall return to it in section 4.

II. HISTORICAL VERSUS RATIONAL RECONSTRUCTION

Before having a closer look at some aspects of Hintikka's approach to the history of philosophy, it is proper to make some general remarks on the methodological issues. In her book *The Hellenistic Aesthetic* Barbara Hughes Fowler describes, among other things, Hellenistic poems and paintings that include, as she says, the pathetic fallacy. For example, Theocritus says that wild animals mourned at Daphnis's death, and in some paintings trees and mountains are presented as expressing the emotional gestures of people. Fowler says that these poets and artists attributed human sentiments to animals and other things of nature. This is what she calls the pathetic fallacy.[26] In historical explanations of this kind it is assumed that certain *prima facie* strange modes of thought in ancient texts are fallacies. It is believed that the poets and other artists mistakenly extrapolated from human emotional experiences to similar states in other beings. This attitude has been part of what could be called the Enlightenment conception of intellectual history. Historical documents are seen as expressions of the lower stages of the development of human cognitive capacities. We mainly learn from them how insufficient conceptual tools and mistaken beliefs have influenced habits of thinking and how certain questions have puzzled people before the solutions were ultimately found.

The Enlightenment model is often applied by the historians of science and it is not uncommon among the historians of philosophy. Its adherents are not merely critical. They may be impressed by some historical achievements which in their opinion anticipated the more advanced contemporary views or theories. In the history of logic, they may help past masters by formalizing their "intuitive" results by modern formal tools which unfortunately were not available to earlier generations. In other areas of philosophy, they pick up the "valuable" parts of the classics and rewrite them "in modern language" so that they can be read as contributions to contemporary discussions. It is assumed that we can easily see what is important in historical texts and what is rubbish. Bertrand Russell's *History of Western Philosophy* is an example of this approach.

As far as the adherents of the Enlightenment model think that there is something valuable in philosophical classics, their approach to them can be characterized as purely rational reconstruction without historical sensitivity. A common criticism of this approach is that historical texts are read and evaluated as if they were answers to the systematic questions that the interpreters happen to have in their minds. It is seldom the case that these texts actually aim at providing such answers. The meaning and significance of a text in its historical context may have been very different from the impression the text makes on somebody who reads it from a point of view which was beyond the purview of its original readers. The purely rational reconstruction is said to dismiss the basic interpretive task which is historical reconstruction without anachronism. An often quoted rule pertaining to this topic, formulated by Quentin Skinner in 1969, was that one should not maintain that a historical person said or did something that he or she would not accept as a correct description of what he or she meant or intended. Correspondingly, serious studies of the works of past masters should reconstruct them as answers to questions that were actual or possible in their historical contexts. The historical meaning is understood by studying the texts in relation to the intellectual or social institutions of their time. It is only after this historical reconstruction of the meaning of the text that we are entitled to discuss its possible significance in our contemporary intellectual milieu.[27]

In a slightly modified form this view is defended by Richard Rorty, Alasdair MacIntyre, Quentin Skinner, and some others in a collection of essays published in 1984 under the title *Philosophy in History*.[28] Referring to this two-level model Rorty argues that historical reconstructions tend to converge and systematic constructions tend to diverge. This remark is in line with his view that there is no common philosophical rationality. Rorty does not believe that historical studies can really explicate the original meanings of texts written in different periods or cultures, but regards historiography as an important institution that enables us to have contact with different ways of thought and to become more conscious of the contingent nature of our basic certainties. Rorty refers approvingly of the idea of the hermeneutic circle in interpretation, but he does not discuss Gadamer's criticism of the traditional division between historical interpretation and philosophical interpretation which he and some others in this collection employ.

In criticizing German historicism and its "purely historical approach" Gadamer does not maintain that the distinction between the historical and systematic approach is useless. His point is that these approaches are dialectically related to each other. What is called an objective historical study of the original meaning is always conditioned by the contingent historical situation of the interpreters. As all studies of historical texts are interplays between interpretive presuppositions and texts, it is better to be conscious of this fact and not to pretend that historical meanings are revealed as such in new contexts. According to Gadamer, avoiding anachronism can be characterized as a conscious attempt to refrain from reading our ideas into texts. The historical horizon of ancient philosophical texts is a reconstruction made from the point of view of contemporary scholarship. As far as its purpose is to make room for ideas different from ours, we succeed better in this attempt the more we know about philosophy and the more we are conscious of our own modes of thinking. Instead of two levels of interpretation, it is more proper to speak about different moments of one process of interpreting and understanding.[29]

Regarding something as being either anachronistic or not anachronistic is obviously conditioned by our contemporary beliefs, but this is somewhat trivial and does not qualify the significance of the distinction, which is easily understood without any great sophistication. Gadamer's point is that one should not confuse this distinction with the distinction between the historical and systematic strands of interpretation. As for these strands, if historical research into past philosophy is philosophical and not, say, philological, psychological, or sociological, the question of whether the levels of interpretation are separate looks academic. Suppose that an author on Aristotle's *De Anima* stresses that he or she does not employ the notion of philosophy of mind at the level of historical reconstruction, but makes use of it at the level of rational reconstruction and comparison. This sounds pedantic, and so does the response that in fact it is tacitly employed at the alleged level of historical reconstruction. However, discussions of this kind are not uncommon, since they are associated with the institutional question of whether systematic philosophy and the history of philosophy belong together or should live separate lives. The authors who reject any sharp division between philosophy and its history as disciplines are sympathetic to the dialectical conception of the relationship between the levels of interpretation, while those who argue for this division have no special reason for sharing their sympathies.[30] It is understandable that the former group sees philosophy as essentially historical and temporal activity while the latter separates its historical aspect from its intellectual core. The authors who believe in some sort of incommensurability between different cultures and traditions, such as Peter Winch, are inclined to think that non-anachronistic historical reconstructions of past meanings should be understood as partial descriptions of alien forms of thinking and that this reconstruction takes place, so to speak, through learning a totally new conceptual system from inside.[31] This is a problematic methodological view since avoiding anachronistic interpretive tools or deriving alien meanings presupposes some sort of systematic comparison.

III. HINTIKKA ON HISTORICAL INTERPRETATION

Hintikka, like Gadamer, argues that there is no sharp distinction between historical and systematic levels in investigations of historical philosophical texts. Reading is interpretation, and it is better to be conscious of the interpretive patterns than to ignore them. Furthermore, it is not only the philosophical interest, but also the scholarly accuracy of historical work that can be enhanced by one's awareness of the constructive tools and ideas of systematic philosophy.[32]

In a Finnish study from 1961 Hintikka discusses C. S. Lewis's book *Studies in Words*, commenting on the history of terms such as "intuition," "irony," "sympathy," "sense," and "experiment."[33] It is obvious that in certain historical texts these words are not used in the same way as they are used nowadays. But it is also trivially true that speaking about their historical meanings implies comparison with contemporary usage. This shows why the anachronism rule that simply denies comparisons with later ideas should be revised. As the terms "experience" and "experiment" began to be used in different senses in early modern science, it is informative for us to know whether a seventeenth-century author used them synonymously, even though the possibility that they are not synonymous was not considered by that author. Another example that Hintikka discusses is the term "sympathy" in eighteenth-century authors. A historian of thought soon notices that, as distinct from the contemporary usage, the term did not refer to any particular emotion at that time. This difference with respect to the later meanings of the word was beyond the purview of eighteenth-century authors, of course, but it is an essential part of the historical conception of the eighteenth-century term "sympathy."

These examples show that it is legitimate and even imperative to formulate historical conceptions by attending to what can and what cannot be found in historical texts. If it is simply thought that anachronism is best avoided by not relating historical texts with what is historically later, the results may be absurd. How can we study Plato's concept of justice, for example, without having any idea of what justice might be? Studies of justice in Plato are usually initiated by a more or less conscious preliminary conception of justice with the help of which the authors identify the texts in which Plato treats questions related to what might be called justice. Suppose that our initial model of justice includes the elements A, B, and C which are usually associated with the notion of justice. We may notice that Plato does not discuss C at all, but he connects A and B with D which does not occur in our contemporary concept of justice. This is a rough sketch of how a historical concept of Plato's notion of justice could be formed. It involves a reference to what is not found in Plato, but it does not anachronistically maintain that there is something in Plato's works that they do not involve.

Hintikka does not explicate this model, but, as is clear from what is stated in section (1), he often formulates historical concepts in accordance with it. He also comments on some special questions which are associated with this model. When it is stated that a distinction introduced later or some later ways of thinking are not used in a historical text, no serious anachronism problems are involved in these remarks; on the contrary, they may be very important in avoiding anachronism. When it is noticed, for example, that Aristotle did not operate with the distinction between logical and physical modalities, this helps us to understand some of his arguments better and to avoid anachronistic misconstructions of them.[34] Negative remarks of this kind can, of course, be more or less adequate. As for the positive similarities with later views, one can distinguish among first, the interpretive ideas that are compatible with what is said in the texts without having any close resemblance to what was probably meant by the authors; second, the ideas that are not mentioned in the text but could have been, since they were introduced by other authors at the same time or later on the same basis without many additional premises; and third, those ideas that can be regarded as congenial elaborated conceptualizations of what was originally meant.[35]

One of the widely recognized conclusions of Hintikka's Aristotle studies is the explication of Aristotle's preference for temporally indefinite statements as the paradigmatic cases of information-carrying propositions. In Hintikka's view Aristotle shared this line of thinking with other Greek philosophers. Even though Aristotle was not fully aware of its role in his philosophy, it is not anachronistic to refer to it in analyzing Aristotle's philosophical arguments. Hintikka thinks that the conceptual teleology of Plato's theory of knowledge and Aristotle's inclination to speak about possibilities from the point of view of their actualizations in history are further examples of partially unconscious, culturally conditioned habits of thinking.[36] These are interesting examples from the point of view of the task of philosophy, which Hintikka sees as improving consciousness about the foundations of our cognitive attitudes and tools.

There are lots of beliefs which are automatically accepted in a culture and which are realized as particular contingent assumptions by external observers, but not as easily realized by those who share them. It is possible to find unconscious assumptions in historical texts, but they can also make the present interpreters aware of taking for granted something which can be otherwise. According to Hintikka, several generations of scholars have

used the Frege-Russell distinction between allegedly different senses of
"is" as one of their main interpretive tools in studies of the notion of being
in Plato and Aristotle. What makes this situation strange is that the distinction was not assumed in ancient philosophy. Some historians have not
noticed this at all, and some of those who have realized it have criticized
ancient thinkers for not applying the distinction, without thinking that it is
in itself a highly problematic doctrine. When a systematic idea is not found
in historical works, it can also lead one to consider the reasons why it was
later introduced, particularly if it is problematic or obviously wrong.[37]

The terms "conceptual assumption" and "habit of thinking" often
figure in Hintikka's works on the history of philosophy. The habits of
thinking, one might say, are more or less conscious formal or material
regulative principles of discourse. In reading historical texts we may notice
that the arguments include assumptions that are not explicitly formulated
and that the author takes for granted. Detecting them may be of great
importance for historical understanding, but they may also help the interpreters to identify some features of their own conceptual models and to
make them conscious of the alternative conceptual structures. These strands
of interpretation are connected with each other. We do not notice special
conceptual presuppositions of historical texts different from those of our
own without thinking that alternative presuppositions are possible. One of
the best ways of realizing that our habits of thinking are contingent is to
compare them to ideas in the history of philosophy.[38]

I began this section by comparing Hintikka's views to those of
Gadamer. Even the last remark is not very far from Gadamer's idea of the
hermeneutic circle, but it is appropriate to note that Hintikka does not
discuss Gadamer's philosophy at all. There are some similarities, but also
profound differences in their approaches.[39] Hintikka is much more interested in the varieties of ways in which things are referred to, concepts are
used, and arguments are developed than are Gadamer and his followers in
hermeneutic philosophy, but the difference is not merely a matter of
degree—it is associated with differing views of language as a whole and of
the conditions of understanding.

In a series of papers Hintikka has studied the opposition between the
conceptions of "language as the universal medium" and "language as
calculus" which in his view dominated twentieth-century philosophy.
Contrary to the hermeneutic view of language as the universal medium of
understanding, Hintikka thinks that the basic meaning relations are not
simply given. We can study how they are formed in various historical
contexts and also in our cognitive culture. The adherents of the conception
of language as the medium of understanding think that semantics is ultimately ineffable, because one cannot, as it were, look at one's language and

describe it from outside; language is always presupposed in our attempts to understand it. The conception of language as calculus (the model-theoretical view) is that language is a tool that can be reinterpreted, changed, and replaced, at least step by step. Semantics is neither ineffable nor inaccessible, though it may be inexhaustible.[40] These visions are associated with opposite conclusions concerning various philosophical issues, including the question of the goal of interpretation. In hermeneutic philosophy, philosophical texts are read as articulations of the experience of human being-in-the-world and they are taken to speak to philosophical interpreters through a dialogical and nonobjectifying search for joint language. Identifying various prejudices or presuppositions is part of Gadamer's conception of the fusion of the horizons that takes place in understanding, but these are epistemic attitudes rather than structural presuppositions of historical texts or interpreters. Hintikka is attracted by the structural elements of historical attempts to understand things.[41] To analyze these presuppositions is to understand some basic constituents of human understanding itself—contrary to the tenets of the medium conception of meaning.

Michael Frede, Jorge Gracia, and Calvin Normore are three well-known authors in this field who have recently written about their views on what the history of philosophy should be. They think that the history of philosophy can be useful for systematic philosophy, provided that it concentrates on historical construction of philosophical ideas and the reasons given for them in their original historical context and that the approach is internal. Sociological or cultural connections are irrelevant to the philosophical theories and arguments. This view is hostile to the attempts to apply nonphilosophical analysis to philosophy, such as the sociology of philosophical knowledge.[42]

Hintikka's view of the history of philosophy is not as puritanical as that of Frede, Gracia, and Normore. Hintikka's works do not contain discussions of the psychology or sociology of philosophy, to be sure, but the conceptual connections between the modes of thinking in philosophy and in other areas are often attended. The philosophers of the past have shared some common conceptual presuppositions of their culture without always noticing it. The same is probably true now, although it is not as easily realized as in historical studies. When philosophers write about art, science, politics, or business, it is useful for them to realize the extent to which their own tools of analysis are conditioned by the habits of thinking embedded in the phenomena they are discussing. According to Hintikka, raising consciousness by analytic means belongs among the tasks of philosophy, but philosophy itself is not separated from the cognitive structures which it tries to explicate. Philosophy is not provided with an

Archimedean point, but is itself part of the cognitive reality which it analyzes.[43] This dialectical approach makes the scope of Hintikka's philosophy broader than what is typical of the analytically oriented philosophy in general.

IV. HINTIKKA VERSUS LOVEJOY

Arthur O. Lovejoy's book *The Great Chain of Being* was one of the most read works on the history of ideas in the last century. Hintikka has often discussed its content and method; actually his only paper which explicitly concentrates on the methods of the history of philosophy is a discussion of Lovejoy's conception of the history of ideas.[44] Lovejoy called his book a study of the history of three "unit ideas" from Plato to the nineteenth century. He asserts that there are historical entities called "unit ideas." These are certain basic units of meaning, relatively independent of each other, which survive through the centuries. The task of a historian of ideas is to shed light on past forms of thinking by analyzing its structural elements, that is, by isolating unit ideas and tracing their occurrences in different combinations from one thinker to another. The three unit ideas studied in *The Great Chain of Being* are treated as conjoints of a complex idea which Lovejoy calls the idea of the great chain of being. The first unit idea of this complex is *the principle of plenitude* (P) mentioned above. Lovejoy thinks that one can find its initial form in Plato. The other two ideas pertaining to the chain of being were introduced in the works of Aristotle. *The principle of continuity* states that all theoretically possible intermediate types between two given natural species are realized, and *the principle of unilinear gradation* is the thesis that all beings belong to a single *scala naturae* in which their status is determined by their degree of perfection. The rest of the book consists of the story of the supposed complex idea of the great chain of being in Western thought.

In his studies on the history of modal conceptions Jaakko Hintikka has argued that the principle of plenitude, whatever it may be, is not a unit idea.[45] For one thing, different authors accepting this kind of balance sheet between possibility and actuality have applied it to quite different conceptions of possibilities and the principle has correspondingly different meanings for them. Second, some authors have associated the principle with the meaning of modal notions, but it may also be embedded in various conceptual presuppositions. For example, it is found in Aristotle's works partly because of his habit of treating possibilities from the point of view of their actualization in time without the idea of synchronic alternatives. Third, it is easily seen that the further implications of the alleged unit idea are not independent of its conceptual and theoretical environment.[46]

The collapse of the unit idea approach in the case which should have been its main example shows that this kind of historical Platonism is not warranted. However, the history of the principle of plenitude illustrates an important feature of our intellectual tradition in Hintikkas's view. It seems that there are lots of ideas that have repeatedly appeared in philosophical works. Some historians have been satisfied with making a list of them and of the authors applying them. But when these occurrences are analyzed, it may be realized that these *prima facie* similar views can have quite different meanings depending on how they are influenced by general presuppositions and related to surrounding ideas. "This allegedly unit-like building-block as it were changes its shape under the pressure of the rest of the structure into which it is being built."[47]

Hintikka's criticism of the unit ideas is related to what was said above about the relation between his philosophy and the hermeneutic philosophy. Lovejoy's conception of the history of ideas is certainly different from Gadamer's approach to history, but both of them think that the tradition consists of meanings that are ultimate units of understanding and cannot be analyzed further. In Hintikka's theory of language as calculus, semantic relations are seen as inexhaustible rather than ineffable. Correspondingly he thinks, *pace* Lovejoy, that we are not obliged to take any allegedly unchanging units of meaning as our starting point. We can also investigate how different conceptual assumptions have resulted in similar ideas. And as distinct from Gadamer Hintikka stresses that analyzing the changing forms and strategies of signifying and synthesizing in past philosophical texts may sometimes tell us more about human understanding than discussing the theses put forward in them.

SIMO KNUUTTILA

UNIVERSITY OF HELSINKI
JANUARY 2002

NOTES

1.   Jaakko Hintikka, "Self-Profile," in *Jaakko Hintikka*, ed. R. J. Bogdan, Profiles 8 (Dordrecht: Reidel, 1987), p. 38.

2.   See also Hintikka, "Replies and Comments," in *Jaakko Hintikka*, ed. Bogdan, p. 333.

3.   Hintikka's main work on Aristotle's modal conception is *Time and Necessity: Studies in Aristotle's Theory of Modality* (Oxford: Clarendon Press,

1973). Many of its central chapters are based on studies which appeared earlier. Chapter 4 was published under the title "Time, Truth, and Knowledge in Ancient Greek Philosophy" in the *American Philosophical Quarterly* 4 (1967): 1–14. Chapter 5, "Aristotle and the Realization of Possibilities in Time," is a rewritten and extended version of "Necessity, Universality, and Time in Aristotle," *Ajatus* 20 (1957): 65–90. Chapter 8, "The Once and Future Sea Fight: Aristotle's Discussion of Future Contingents in *De interpretatione* 9," first appeared in the *Philosophical Review* 73 (1964): 461–92, and chapter 9, "Aristotle and the 'Master Argument' of Diodorus," in the *American Philosophical Quarterly* 1 (1964): 101–14. There are some additions to the first versions in chapters 8 and 9. Some parts of chapter 7, "Aristotle's Modal Syllogistic," were first published in "An Aristotelian Dilemma," *Ajatus* 22 (1959): 87–92.

    4.   See, e.g., Richard Sorabji, *Necessity, Cause, and Blame: Perspectives on Aristotle's Theory* (Ithaca: Cornell University Press, 1980); Sarah Waterlow, *Passage and Possibility: A Study of Aristotle's Modal Concepts* (Oxford: Clarendon Press, 1982); Jeroen van Rijen, *Aspects of Aristotle's Logic of Modalities*, Synthese Historical Library 35 (Dordrecht: Kluwer, 1989); Simo Knuuttila, *Modalities in Medieval Philosophy* (London: Routledge, 1993); Richard Gaskin, *The Sea Battle and the Master Argument* (Berlin: de Gruyter, 1995). There are many references to other relevant studies in these works.

    5.   A. O. Lovejoy, *The Great Chain of Being: A Study of the History of an Idea* (Cambridge, Mass.: Harvard University Press, 1936). Hintikka has often discussed Lovejoy's book; see also section 4 below.

    6.   Hintikka, *Time and Necessity*, chapter 5. There is a survey of Aristotle's various modal paradigms in Jaakko Hintikka (in collaboration with U. Remes and S. Knuuttila), *Aristotle on Modality and Determinism*, Acta Philosophica Fennica 29, no. 1 (Amsterdam: North-Holland, 1977).

    7.   Waterlow, *Passage and Possibility*; van Rijen, *Aspects of Aristotle's Logic of Modalities*.

    8.   *Aristotle on Modality and Determinism* (note 6 above).

    9.   See the works mentioned in note 4 above.

    10. *Metaphysics*, a revised text with introduction and commentary by W. D. Ross (Oxford: Clarendon Press, 1924). See also Knuuttila, *Modalities in Medieval Philosophy*, pp. 31–34, 38, 57. Other works by Aristotle used in the text are as follows: *De Interpretatione*, ed. L. Minio-Paluello (Oxford: Clarendon Press, 1949), *De caelo*, ed. D. J. Allan (Oxford: Clarendon Press, 1936), *Physics*, a revised text with introduction and commentary by W. D. Ross (Oxford: Clarendon Press, 1936), and *Prior and Posterior Analytics*, a revised text with introduction and commentary by W. D. Ross (Oxford: Clarendon Press, 1949). All passages from Aristotle can also be found in *The Complete Works of Aristotle*, ed. Jonathan Barnes (Princeton: Princeton University Press, 1984).

    11. For a discussion of this assumption in Aristotle and other ancient thinkers,

see Hintikka, *Time and Necessity*, ch. 4.

12. Another possible interpretation makes use of the idea of diachronic modality—Aristotle wanted to show that the necessity of an event at a certain moment of time does not imply that it would have been antecedently necessary. See e.g., G. H. von Wright, *Truth, Knowledge, and Modality* (Oxford: Blackwell, 1984), pp. 72–78.

13. Epictetus, *Dissertationes*, ed. H. Schenk (Leipzig: Teubner, 1916), II.19, 1–5.

14. Hintikka, *Time and Necessity*, ch. 9.

15. Arthur Prior, "Diodorian Modalities," *Philosophical Quarterly* 5 (1955): 205–13.

16. Hintikka, *Time and Necessity*, pp. 191–93.

17. Ibid., pp. 205–13.

18. In chapter 2 of *Aristotle on Modality and Determinism* Hintikka deals with Aristotle's attempts to escape from the deterministic consequences of his conceptual framework.

19. Ibid., pp. 35–39, 50–77.

20. Ibid., pp. 32–35.

21. See Knuuttila, *Modalities in Medieval Philosophy*.

22. Jaakko Hintikka, "Modality as Referential Multiplicity," *Ajatus* 20 (1957): 46–64.

23. Jaakko Hintikka, "*Cogito, ergo sum*: Inference or Performance," *The Philosophical Review* 72 (1961): 3–32. According to Gareth Matthews, there are three main interpretations of Descartes's cogito: the simple intuition interpretation, the inference interpretation, and Hintikka's performative interpretation. See Gareth Matthews, *Thought's Ego in Augustine and Descartes* (Ithaca and London: Cornell University Press, 1992), pp. 16–22.

24. Jaakko Hintikka, *Knowledge and Belief: An Introduction to the Logic of Two Notions* (Ithaca: Cornell University Press, 1962).

25. For some examples see the discussions of Plato's concept of knowledge and Kant's views of analyticity, mathematics, and intuition in Jaakko Hintikka, *Knowledge and the Known: Historical Perspectives in Epistemology*, Synthese Historical Library 11 (Dordrecht: Reidel, 1974); Aristotle's views of science and induction in "On the Ingredients of an Aristotelian Science," *Nous* 6 (1972): 55–69 and in "Aristotelian Induction," *Revue Internationale de Philosophie* 34 (1980): 422–39; Leibniz's modal theory in "Leibniz, Plenitude and the 'Reign of Law'," *Ajatus* 31 (1970): 117–44 (reprinted with changes and additions in *Leibniz: A Collection of Critical Essays*, ed. H. G. Frankfurt [Garden City, N.Y.: Doubleday, 1972], pp. 155–90 and in *Reforging the Great Chain of Being*, ed. S. Knuuttila, Synthese Historical Library 20 [Dordrecht: Reidel, 1980], pp. 1–17), and in "Was Leibniz's Deity an *Akrates*" in *Modern Modalities: Studies of the History of Modal Theories from Medieval Nominalism to Logical Positivism*, ed. S. Knuuttila, Synthese Historical Library 33 (Dordrecht-Boston: Kluwer, 1988), pp. 85–108; and

transcendental knowledge in "Kant's Transcendental Method and His Theory of
Mathematics," *Topoi* 3 (1984): 99–108, and in "The Paradox of Transcendental
Knowledge" in *An Intimate Relation*, ed. J. R. Brown and J. Mittelstrass
(Dordrecht-Boston: Kluwer, 1989), pp. 243–57. The Greek geometrical method of
analysis and synthesis and its significance to the experimental method of early
modern scientists is analysed in Jaakko Hintikka and Unto Remes, *The Method of
Analysis: Its Geometrical Origin and Its General Significance*, Boston Studies in
the Philosophy of Science 25 (Dordrecht-Boston: Reidel, 1974); see also Jaakko
Hintikka and Unto Remes, "Ancient Geometrical Analysis and Modern Logic" in
Essays in Memory of Imre Lakatos, ed. R. S. Cohen et al. (Dordrecht: Reidel,
1975), pp. 253–76.

26. Barbara Hughes Fowler, *The Hellenistic Aesthetic* (Bristol: The Bristol
Press, 1989), pp. 104–9. According to J. L. Mackie, the pathetic fallacy is treating
as belonging to some external states of affairs the feeling that the state of affairs
arouses in us; see "Fallacies," *The Encyclopedia of Philosophy*, vol. 3, ed. P.
Edwards (London-New York: Macmillan, 1967), p. 176.

27. Quentin Skinner, "Meaning and Understanding in the History of Ideas,"
History and Theory 8 (1969): 3–53.

28. Richard Rorty, Jerome B. Schneewind, Quentin Skinner, eds., *Philosophy
in History* (Cambridge: Cambridge University Press, 1984).

29. Hans-Georg Gadamer, *Wahrheit und Methode*, 2nd impression (Tübingen:
J. C. B. Mohr, 1965).

30. For a concise discussion of contemporary German argument for the
division, see Volker Peckhaus, "The Contextualism of Philosophy" in *The
Sociology of Philosophical Knowledge*, ed. M. Kusch, The New Synthese
Historical Library 48 (Dordrecht-Boston: Kluwer, 2000), pp. 171–91.

31. Peter Winch, *The Idea of a Social Science and Its Relation to Philosophy*
(London: Routledge and Kegan Paul, 1958).

32. Hintikka, "Self-Profile," pp. 37–38.

33. Jaakko Hintikka, "Käsitteilläkin on kohtalonsa," *Suomalainen Suomi* 29
(1961): 459–64, also in *Tieto on valtaa ja muita aatehistoriallisia esseitä* (Helsinki:
WSOY, 1969), pp. 35–46.

34. This is one of the themes in *Aristotle on Modality and Determinism* (note
6 above).

35. Hintikka, *Time and Necessity*, pp. 72, 84, 139.

36. Hintikka, *Knowledge and the Known*, chs. 1–3.

37. "The Varieties of Being in Aristotle" in *The Logic of Being*, ed. Simo
Knuuttila and Jaakko Hintikka, Synthese Historical Library 28 (Dordrecht-Boston:
Reidel, 1986), pp. 81–114; Jaakko Hintikka, "On Aristotle's Notion of Existence,"
Review of Metaphysics 52 (1999): 779–805.

38. Hintikka, *Time and Necessity*, pp. 62–68, 149–53; "The Varieties of Being
in Aristotle," pp. 81–85.

39. Both authors take up R. G. Collingwood's remarks on the logic of question, answer and presupposition and Collingwood's view that to understand an opinion is to understand it as an answer to a question. See Gadamer, *Wahrheit und Methode*, pp. 352–60, 485–87; Hintikka often refers to Collingwood, but has not discussed his views in detail prior to the present volume.

40. Jaakko Hintikka, *Lingua Universalis vs. Calculus Ratiocinator: An Ultimate Presupposition of Twentieth-Century Philosophy* (J. Hintikka: *Selected Papers*, vol. 2), Dordrecht-Boston: Kluwer 1996. See also Merrill B. Hintikka and Jaakko Hintikka, *Investigating Wittgenstein* (Oxford: Blackwell, 1986), and Martin Kusch, *Language as Calculus vs. Language as Universal Medium: A Study in Husserl, Heidegger and Gadamer* (Dordrecht-Boston: Kluwer, 1989).

41. Hintikka, *Knowledge and the Known*, p. 1, "Replies and Comments," p. 333.

42. Michael Frede, "The History of Philosophy as a Discipline," *Journal of Philosophy* 85 (1988): 666–72; Calvin Normore, "Doxology and the History of Philosophy," *Canadian Journal of Philosophy*, supp. vol. 16 (1990): 203–26; Jorge Gracia, *Philosophy and Its History: Issues in Philosophical Historiography*, (Albany, N.Y.: State University of New York Press, 1992); Jorge Gracia, "Sociological Accounts and the History of Philosophy" in *The Sociology of Philosophical Knowledge*, ed. M. Kusch, The New Synthese Historical Library 48 (Dordrecht: Kluwer Academic Publishers, 2000), pp. 193–211. The approaches of Frede, Normore, and Gracia are discussed in Martin Kusch, *Psychologism: A Case Study in the Sociology of Philosophical Knowledge* (London: Routledge, 1995), pp. 17–23.

43. See Hintikka's opening essay in *Tieto on valtaa*, chapters 1–3 of *Knowledge and the Known*, and the discussion about the analogies between the problem of representation in modern art and meaning theory in chapter 11 of *The Intentions of Intentionality and Other New Models for Modalities* (Dordrecht-Boston: Reidel, 1975).

44. Jaakko Hintikka, "Gaps in the Great Chain of Being: An Exercise in the Methodology of the History of Ideas," *Proceedings and Addresses of the American Philosophical Association* 49 (1976): 22–38, reprinted in *Reforging the Great Chain of Being*, ed. S. Knuuttila, Synthese Historical Library 20 (Dordrecht: Reidel, 1981), pp. 1–17.

45. In addition to the works mentioned above (notes 3 and 44), see also Jaakko Hintikka and Heikki Kannisto, "Kant on 'The Great Chain of Being' or the Eventual Realization of All Possibilities: A Comparative Study," in *Reforging the Great Chain of Being*, ed. S. Knuuttila, Synthese Historical Library 20 (Dordrecht: Reidel, 1981), pp. 287–308.

46. Hintikka, "Gaps in the Great Chain of Being" (note 44 above).

47. Ibid., p. 6.

REPLY TO SIMO KNUUTTILA

The contributions of both Simo Knuuttila and Gabriel Motzkin (see chapter 2) deal with my views on the methodology of history and philosophy and of history of ideas, and hence my response to one of them is inevitably also an answer to the other. I am afraid that in one respect I have unwittingly made the task of both of them more difficult than that of most of the other contributors. I have dealt with the methodology of the history of ideas only in one essay, which is my APA Presidential Address of 1976. Most of my views on this subject therefore have to be teased out from my historical practice. Moreover, as I confess in my intellectual autobiography, I now consider that particular essay to be formulated far too much *ad hominem* to give a balanced account of my views at the time, let alone of my reconsidered views of the 2003 vintage.

This change of emphasis (and perhaps to some extent change of views) takes us straight into the problematic discussed by Knuuttila and Motzkin. This problematic concerns in the first place the interplay of systematic conceptual insights with historical interpretation. Knuuttila connects it in an illuminating way with discussions of the prospects of historical interpretation by such thinkers as Quentin Skinner, Richard Rorty, and Hans-Georg Gadamer.

In my 1976 essay I criticized, on the face of it, A. O. Lovejoy's approach to the history of ideas.[1] His approach relies on what he called unit ideas, and he sees much of the history of thought as a drama in which these unit ideas are the actors. The main thrust of my essay was to argue that the actual import of such unit ideas is very much context-dependent. Their primary significance is often in their interaction with other ideas, not in their intrinsic immutable nature. And I illustrated the importance of this context-dependence by arguing that Lovejoy had himself neglected it in his case study devoted to the idea that he called the Principle of Plenitude.

I am totally unrepentant concerning the specific historical criticisms of Lovejoy that I have put forward. But on a methodological level, I was in 1976 grossly deficient in self-awareness. The fact is that the methodology that I have used in my own work is very close to what Lovejoy preaches (though perhaps does not practice entirely successfully). Whatever success I may have had in my historical work has depended on being able to identify more or less specific concepts or conceptual assumptions in historical material and to follow them through longer periods of the history of thought. These concepts or conceptual assumptions are not as atomistic as Lovejoy's "unit ideas" but like him I have considered them as the focal points of the history of ideas. And Knuuttila is quite right in tracing such ideas typically back to my systematic work.

In order for this kind of "idea-centered" approach to work, the concepts and conceptual assumptions in question—in other words, Lovejoy's "ideas"—must enjoy independent life at least to the extent of being identifiable independent of the context and hence being possible to follow through longer sequences of the history of philosophy. In order for this approach to be truly interesting these "ideas" must have played a significant role in the history of thought. I believe that the identification both of the relevant ideas of their career is possible. As was pointed out, my own work instantiates the strategy of following "ideas" throughout longer periods of thought. The operative significance of such "ideas" might at first seem debatable. Yet I have no doubt of the significant role of ideas even in the narrower sense of concepts and conceptual assumptions. If an example is needed, one is provided by what the real "Crime of Galileo" (to borrow De Santillana's phrase) was.[2] For why did the infamous trial and condemnation come about? Neither party wanted confrontation. The Catholic church was willing to let the Copernican system be taught, if only as a way of "saving the phenomena." Awkward passages in the Bible could always be explained away. The good Cardinal Bellarmine even tried to offer advice to Galileo as to how to stay in his good theological graces. And what Galileo wanted was certainly not to create any conflict with the church. All he was trying to do was to discover mathematical laws of nature holding *de facto*. But therein was the rub. If a natural law can be formulated mathematically, it cannot be metaphysically necessary, for another mathematical formula will automatically codify another metaphysically possible way in which things might happen. And most unfortunately, Cardinal Bellarmine happened to be basing his "natural theology" on the idea which Lovejoy dubbed "The Principle of Plenitude," according to which every metaphysical possibility is sometimes realized, as apparently required by God's generosity and his nature as *actus purus*. *Ergo* there cannot be exceptionless mathematical laws of nature; *ergo* Galileo trying to restrict God's freedom by proposing such laws; *ergo* inquisition. . . . The conflict here is between ideas in Lovejoy's narrow sense, not between the religious social or political attitudes of the two men. One of my daydreams has for a long time been to spell out and document this supreme example of the irony of the history of ideas. Doing so would be a timely task in view of a flood of new books and articles explaining Galileo's conflict with the Church in political, social, or psychological terms. In dealing with Galileo, too many intellectual historians have failed to see the philosophical wood for diplomatic, theological, or temperamental trees.

These remarks can be elaborated further. How can we identify the concepts other thinkers use or have wielded so that we can understand them and use them to discuss their views? The autonomy of concepts that I am defending implies that the first and foremost instrument of so doing is systematic conceptual analysis, combined with the identification of those concepts in other thinkers. This is the reason for the fruitfulness of systematic insights in historical applications. Admittedly there are other considerations, of course. For instance, Gadamer emphasizes the importance in our hermeneutical task of identifying the cultural horizons of different thinkers and their roots in different traditions. Charting such genealogies of concepts is an interesting and worthwhile enterprise, but in the actual history of philosophy doing so does not accomplish much.

An example might illustrate the point I am making. In any normal sense, Isaac Newton and David Hume shared the same cultural horizon, and any attempt to explain their philosophical differences by reference to their respective overall intellectual horizons would be jejeune. Hume even thought that he was extending Newton's ideas to "moral sciences." The subtle differences between their views are due to different conceptual assumptions, and these differences show up in their understanding of the words they shared and used. Experiment meant in Newton's methodological pronouncements controlled experiment; for Hume it meant any observation resulting from an interference in the course of events. Induction meant for Hume inference from particulars to general laws. For Newton, it meant extrapolating and interpolating partial generalizations. Such differences are not matters of cultural background, but of conceptual foreground. An unintended *reductio ad absurdum* of the emphasis on the background was provided *anno dazumal* by Gerard Radnitzky in his two-volume study of and comparison between what he called "continental schools of metascience" and "Anglo-Saxon schools of metascience."[3] At one point he raises the question as to what differences in the cultural background of the two schools of thinkers might help to account for the differences—a puzzling question in view of the index of Radnitzky's book where it turns out that his most frequently quoted "Anglo-Saxon" metascientists are Rudolf Carnap, Karl Popper, C. G. Hempel, and Gustav Bergmann.

The possibility of an idea-centered approach is even easier to defend, for there I can point to many actual case studies. The reader will find examples in this volume discussed in this volume by Webb, Knuuttila, and Motzkin. Others are mentioned in my autobiography, and still further ones exist only in my wishful plans for future work. Whatever a critical reader may think of the details of these studies, it is incontrovertible that the issues I have taken up are as central in the history of philosophy as any. The most striking result reached in them is perhaps the total absence from pre-nineteenth-century philosophy of the Frege-Russell thesis that verbs for being are ambiguous between existence, identity, predication, and subsumption.

Some of the most interesting conceptual assumptions we can ascribe to different philosophical figures are so fundamental that the thinkers themselves did not acknowledge them in so many words. This might seem to lead to methodological problems, but I do not see them as being unsurmountable.

By identifying other philosophers' presuppositions, we can in fact sometimes ascribe to them views that they themselves did not express and sometimes would have denied if they had been proposed to them. Knuuttila quotes Quentin Skinner's rule (anticipated by Richard Robinson in his book on Plato's early dialectic) that "one should not maintain that a historical person said or did something that he or she would not accept as a correct description of what he or she meant or intended." This rule is of little use because of its counterfactual character, especially when it is applied to the most basic conceptual presuppositions. These ultimate presuppositions are seldom formulated explicitly just because they are so fundamental. But even so there are counter examples to Skinner's rule. A clear-cut case in point is found in the history of mathematics where some of the early critics of the axiom of choice turned out to have used it in their own mathematical reasoning. In my own work I have come across another example. In *Metaphysics* IX, 3 Aristotle criticizes Megarian philosophers for holding that "a thing can act only when it is acting." Yet an examination of Aristotle's theory of modality reveals that he in effect agrees with the targets of his criticism. He differs from them only in that he wants to reinterpret what is meant by possibility. Aristotle wants to deal only with statistically interpreted modalities. As is shown by *Met.* IX, 3, 1047a10 ff., Aristotle says that what is capable in his sense is what will happen or will be true. But there is no reason to believe that this is what the Megarians meant by possibility, and Aristotle says himself in *De Interpretatione* 9 that "what is, necessarily is when it is."

I may have stumbled on this approach to the history of philosophy and history of ideas, but on reflection I believe that it is one of the most promising methods in the history of thought. I have been personally surprised how we can gain sharp insights into the thought of different thinkers and different eras by recognizing the manifestations of one and the same idea in different thinkers in different periods and relating these manifestations to each other.

The feasibility of such strategy presupposes, and provides evidence for, an assumption that is a generalized form of the assumption on which Lovejoy's approach rests. This assumption is the reality and context-independence of ideas or concepts. For instance, if we do not recognize that Greek geometers' notion of *ecthesis*, Kant's notion of construction and modern logicians' instantiation are literally the same notion—or at least have an identifiable common conceptual element—we cannot compare the views of different thinkers from different periods of history on them, which in my view would mean not being able to understand some of the most fascinating subjects in the history of philosophy. My criticism of Lovejoy is enough to show that I am aware of the problems one encounters in such an identification. However, I do not have any doubts about the reality and identifiability of the concepts and conceptual assumptions that Lovejoy called "ideas." Indeed I can think of sharp questions concerning them that might very well be among the ones whose answers will mark some of the next substantial advances in serious history of philosophical ideas.

As specific examples, perhaps I can mention two. It can be shown that in Aristotle the allegedly different Frege-Russell meanings of *estin* were only so many components in the meaning of the verb, but how do these different components interact in Aristotle's metaphysics? Another problem that is close to Knuuttila's interest is the following: Since we have for systematic reasons to distinguish the interrogative games that serve the pursuit of factual truths from the formal games in which we are looking for proofs of logical truth and which can also be formulated as questioning processes, how should we in the light of this distinction look upon the medieval questioning games, the famous *obligationes* games?[4] As long as this question remains unanswered our understanding of this important segment of medieval thought is incomplete.

For another example, I do not think that we have grasped the deeper meaning of the controversies about geometrical constructions in antiquity (and later) until we have understood the issues involved in these discussions of the problem of the status of functions. Are they only a way of speaking of certain relations between objects or do they codify genuine dependence relations between the objects in question?

If this faith in the reality and identifiability of concepts or "ideas" makes me a Platonist, I will gladly wear the badge, at least whenever I have put on my historian's cap. This faith also seems to align my approach with what Knuuttila and others have called systematic rather than historical interpretations. However, I think that this entire contrast is mistaken. What the defenders of purely historical interpretation are trying to avoid is projection of our conceptions to historical figures. But what can be meant here by "conceptions"? Concepts or assumptions? Of course we must not assume that earlier thinkers share our assumptions, but the fact is that we need not assume this in order to share their concepts. This has been denied by many recent philosophers, often following Quine's fallacious rejection of the analytic-synthetic distinction, which goes hand in hand with his thesis that there is no determinate way of expressing another person's meaning in my language. I have criticized Quine's views elsewhere from a systematic point of view.[5] What we have here is in fact a vivid illustration of the mess that has been caused by Quine's and other philosophers' failure to separate conceptual presuppositions from substantial assumptions.

Quine's theses and arguments have to be dealt with in topical terms. However, it is, in a general philosophical perspective, instructive to see how the consequences of Quine's views that I have argued are fallacious show up in another branch of philosophy as a source of confusion and methodological uncertainty.

The distinction between concepts (as well as conceptual assumptions) and theses disarms among other objections "a common criticism of this approach" noted by Knuuttila, viz., that in it "historical texts are read and evaluated as if they were answers to the systematic questions that the interpreters happen to have in their minds." Concepts and conceptual presuppositions are simply not answers to questions, be these questions historically correct or anachronistic. This is especially clear when the presupposition is the meaningfulness and importance of a certain contrast, which typically means the meaningfulness of a certain question.

This point is made very well by Knuuttila when he notes that conceptual history presupposes comparisons with current meanings. Rather, unawareness of such constructive comparisons is a much more dangerously anachronistic procedure. Such comparisons have inevitably something of the character of a contrast in them. *Pace* Motzkin, I nevertheless agree with Knuuttila that claiming such contrasts does not make one's work ahistorical.

Quine is not the only philosopher whose views have to be taken with more than a pinch of salt or whatever antidote might work here. Philosophers who appeal to Wittgenstein in defense of cultural relativism misunderstand the thrust of his remarks. It may very well be the case that our thinking and our language, like everybody else's, are limited by our own preconceptions. But this is not anything we can express in our actual language according to Wittgenstein. "A language that I do not understand is no language." It is true that he tried to convey indirectly ("tried to show") to us certain insights that cannot literally be said, but they typically concern the limits of what can be said in our language, rather than what can be said in some other tongue. Hence the critics of the supposedly "systematic" interpretations cannot very well appeal to Wittgenstein in defending their position.

Rather than try to utter the unsayable, the hermeneutically oriented philosophers should encourage each other—and themselves—to deepen these systematic conceptual insights, as it were to extend their own language. By doing so, they can open new possibilities of understanding and even evaluating earlier thinkers—and other thinkers more generally. It seems to me that an interesting example is forthcoming from cutting-edge work in logic. Leibniz's monadological metaphysics seems to rely on a rather elementary logico-mathematical idea. If each monad is characterized by the function that specifies its state as a function of time, then the entire world's history is determined by the totality of such functions taken one by one, without any need to speak of the interaction among different monads. In Leibniz's terms, we can always consider monads as if they were "windowless." And this seems to be possible anyway, without any special assumption of pre-established harmony. However, from the nascent logic by which we can study mutual dependence relations (known as IF logic), it turns out that such "windowlessness" is possible only if the mutual dependence relations are "synchronized" in the sense that a's dependence on b is always the inverse of b's dependence on a. This is a very strong assumption on which Leibniz's monadology is entirely dependent. Thus Leibniz's assumption of "pre-established harmony" is not an innocent dramatization of a trivially possible representation of reality, but is seen to be for logical reasons an extremely consequential metaphysical axiom.

One might be tempted to conclude from what I just said that IF logic has shown Leibniz to be "mistaken." Perhaps he was *sub specie aeternitatis*. I prefer to emphasize that Leibniz's idea (tacit assumption, if you prefer) was so incredibly deep that only in the twenty-first century do we have the logical tools to diagnose it.

J. H.

NOTES

1. The most important formulation and application of Lovejoy's ideas is in A. O. Lovejoy, *The Great Chain of Being* (Cambridge: Harvard University Press, 1936).

2. Cf. here Giorgio de Santillana, *The Crime of Galileo* (Chicago: University of Chicago Press, 1955).

3. Gerard Radnitzky, *Contemporary Schools of Metascience*, 1-2 (Gothenburg: Akademiförlaget, 1968).

4. Cf. here Mikko Yrjönsuuri, *Obligationes: 14ᵗʰ Century Logic of Disputational Duties*, Acta Philosophica Fennica 55 (Helsinki: Societas Philosophica, 1994).

5. See especially my 2003 paper, "A Distinction Too Few or Too Many?"

2

Gabriel Motzkin

HINTIKKA'S IDEAS ABOUT THE HISTORY OF IDEAS

Jaakko Hintikka, throughout his career, has evinced a strong interest in historical questions that used to be rare among analytic philosophers and philosophers of mathematics. This interest is not an accident of personality; it is intimately bound up with Hintikka's philosophical interests. While some of his work reveals an almost metaphysical general fascination with the ontological implications of logic, his interest in historical research stems from a quite specific set of motives. These are rooted in Hintikka's conception of language as calculus or as model, and his consequent commitment to the expressibility or "effability" of the language-reality connection. In turn, the idea that the semantic determinations of a language should be expressible in that language itself leads Hintikka to favor the contextual determination of the meaning of ideas. The context in question, however, is the logical and systematic context: a different system is constructed when given ideas have not yet been discovered, but that system can nonetheless be a rigorous system, one which can be compared to contemporary systems precisely because of the different solutions that develop from the lack of availability of a given option, different solutions that can then illumine and be illumined by a comparison with contemporary solutions. The enterprise of a systematic investigation of the embedded contextual meaning of ideas mandates not just a passing interest in the history of ideas, but a major epistemological commitment to it. In turn, if the conception of language as calculus can be shown to work for the history of ideas, i.e., for our relations to the past, then the ineffability arguments are well and truly dismissible.

Hintikka then does not conceive of the history of philosophy as a tale of inferior past attempts or a narrative of anticipations of present positions.

On the contrary, the history of ideas should serve as a source for alternative blueprints to contemporary models of the links between ideas. Such a view of the past as possibly providing alternative solutions to contemporary problems means that Hintikka's method is not quite historical (as can be seen in his essays on Wittgenstein).[1] He is not interested in the past for its own sake. His method is reconstructive. Its aim is to show differences in meaning between arguments that are apparently formulated with identical ideas and terms.

Hintikka's insight into Kant's non-Copernican revolution, his essay comparing Husserl and Picasso, and his analysis of Lovejoy's principle of plenitude all reveal what one could call a dialectical interest in pre-suppositional architecture. It is as if a philosopher's set of arguments form a building that must be analyzed by a specific comparison to the opposite building. This comparison is not just the operation of opposing one argument to another. It is rather opposing one set to another set of arguments, when both claim to occupy the same field, focusing on the joints between different arguments. This is a profoundly unhistorical method, for no philosopher has ever simply built one counter-building to another. The counter-building is Hintikka's hypothetical historical counter-building, the reverse picture of the philosophy under analysis.

Thus in "Gaps in the Great Chain of Being"[2] it is not the internal coherence of the principle of plenitude that is questioned; rather the idea of plenitude is analyzed by embedding it in the matrix of a set of contrasting assumptions to plenitude. Since Lovejoy's principle of plenitude is both a metaphysical and a historical principle, Hintikka subjects it to both a metaphysical and a historical analysis. But while the consequences of Hintikka's analysis are important for our understanding of the history of philosophy, his analysis is unhistorical because the principle of interpretation is not continuity or development: rather like Burckhardt static buildings are compared with each other. Nonetheless, it is a philosophy of the history of philosophy. If this method can be used to analyze philosophical texts, it lets us view the history of philosophy as a slide show, one in which, however, the slides shown are negatives or holograms. Hintikka's continuing interest in the problem of representation is not coincidental.

Contrasting *gaps* in the great chain of being to the principle of *plenitude* has several consequences, not just the failure of the principle of plenitude as a dynamic principle according to which all possibilities will be realized. The metaphor of the gap shows that Lovejoy not only assumed a principle of plenitude but also a principle of continuity, i.e., that there would be an incremental growth in plenitude. Now one could believe in the principle of plenitude and also believe that it would obtain one moment before the end of creation, like a balloon payment on a mortgage, but that say only 0.0001 percent of all possibilities will have been realized until that moment. Generalizing that point, there is no reason to assume that the principle of plenitude also assumes a principle of historical continuity, but Lovejoy does make that assumption, and Hintikka's metaphor shows what is wrong with it. What Hintikka has observed is not just a logical fault in Lovejoy's argument, but rather an architectural fault. As a historian of ideas, Hintikka is an architect, much as Kant was a philosophical architect.

In Hintikka's terms, I have already sinned, for I have referenced the principle of plenitude to possible sequences of events, whereas Hintikka is careful to point out that it can also be referenced to possible states of affairs, i.e., that one must pay attention to the scope and field of application of a given principle.[3] The question then ensues whether the principle is the same in different fields of application. The essence of Hintikka's argument is that it is not: by implication principles derive their meaning from their fields of application. "The Principle fails to be an atom-like unit also because its implications are not independent of its conceptual and theoretical environment."[4] Thus Hintikka pleads for contextuality without historicism, just as he rejects the continuity beloved of historicists. The architect continues: "This allegedly unit-like building-block as it were changes its shape under the pressure of the rest of the structure into which it is being built."[5]

Hintikka immediately applies his other principle of interpretation, imposing a holographic negative, by which a perspective painting can be viewed in reverse perspective, as if it were a Russian icon. For the historian, this methodological procedure has significant implications: it replaces the controversial and rejected idea of a counterfactual history by the idea of reverse modeling; it is not facts that are being denied; rather the structures that connect them are isomorphically constructed (in Hintikka's history of ideas the links are structural, but there many different kinds of structures). "It [the principle of plenitude] does not assert the plenitude of actual realizations, but only an equation between possibilities and their realizations. It is as much or as little a Principle of the Paucity of Possibilities as a Principle of Plenitude of their Realizations."[6] Here Hintikka views the principle from the point of view of possibility rather than realization, and provides the historian with an interpretative question: under which conditions is the field of possibility restricted? As Hintikka puts it, the reason for someone espousing this principle may lie somewhere between a "belief in the richness of the real world" and a "narrow view of the hidden possibilities that lurk behind the ontological backdrop of our actual world."[7]

Thus the historical point that Hintikka extracts from the history of the decline in belief in this alleged principle is not that of the expansion of the real world, but rather the expansion of the field of possibilities. And he points out that this expansion meant a widening of the gap between reality and the field of possibilities, now recast as the gap between logical and physical possibility.

However, Hintikka does accept one tenet of the historical canon: actors do not have to be aware of the process in which they are engaged. On the contrary, he views most thinkers as conservatives who struggle to fit in what is new about their thought into the principles that they have inherited. Thus their statements about the implications of their thought must be treated with suspicion, because they are misleading. That is because a principle such as the principle of plenitude not only has different fields of application, but can also serve as an answer to different questions.

While Hintikka rejects the notion of unit-ideas and its implicit Platonism, it does not lead him to disdain the pursuit of the history of ideas. The history of ideas is philosophically relevant and not just historically interesting in the same way that the history of architecture is relevant for architects. Since thinkers like architects do not formulate explicitly many of their assumptions and conceptions, these must be "inferred" from "their indirect effects, from their joint implications together with other ideas."[8] Since ideas in that case cannot be depicted in isolation, but only in context, Hintikka rejects the unit-ideas. The context in question, however, is one of other ideas; the effects can be read at the joints. Thus instead of a universe composed of individuals we obtain a universe of idea-forces, which, however, only exist in impure conditions, and in those impure conditions actually have different meanings. In the texts, the joints or connections must be explicit, not the presuppositions. In turn, however, the presuppositions serve as a "mirror" for the connections.[9] The point about this interplay of substructure (presuppositions) and superstructure (connections) is that the one provides a mirror-image for the other; moreover, each does not have just one mirror-image, but many, in the way that we can obtain different mirror-images from different angles. The interest in philosophical history lies in exposing these connections between ideas, i.e., why a connection may occur even when it does not seem plausible, in this way widening the scope of philosophical appreciation. The need is not to isolate ideas, but rather to find ideas which "reflect" differences between philosophical positions.

This distinction can be seen clearly at one point in Hintikka's *Knowledge and the Known* (1974).[10] Hintikka queries what Kant had in mind in comparing his philosophy to Copernicus's new astronomy.[11] It could not have been a strict comparison, since Copernicus removed man from the center of the universe, while Kant's aim was to place man at its center. This is a deceptively simple observation; it stems from what I have termed an architectural sensitivity, which can perhaps be specified here as a sensitivity to philosophical geometry. Hintikka shows that despite this radical architectural difference, Kant was right in thinking that he shared something in common with Copernicus, namely locating the observed movement in the spectator. It is the consequence of locating observation in the spectator that is the opposite. The identity and the difference between the two points of view can be specified: the focus of attention is the same, but the direction beyond that focus is quite different.

I would now like to turn to an earlier essay by Hintikka: "Concept as Vision: On the Problem of Representation in Modern Art and in Modern Philosophy," in order to show how the principle of architectural mirror-imaging can be applied across different fields.[12] In this essay Hintikka queries whether a philosophical understanding can clarify the alleged turn to abstract, nonrepresentational art at the turn of the last century. Hintikka disagrees with the interpretation of this art as nonrepresentational, claiming that the Cubists had a well-thought-out idea of representation, and asserting that "the aim of Cubists was to restore to painting the sense of concrete, solid reality which had been lost by the impressionists and by the symbolists."[13] Of course, the philosophical question here is what is meant by reality.

Hintikka's aim is to show that Edmund Husserl and the Cubists approached this question in a similar spirit. Laying the groundwork, he analyzes Husserl's distinction between noema and object as an application of Frege's distinction between sense and reference, between the sense, which is like the noema in that it enables us to pick out the object, and the reference, which is like Husserl's object. The noemata are "meaning entities."[14] As meaning entities, the noemata are not subjective; however abstract, the noemata are objective entities.

The Cubists were "representing noemata, not objects."[15] "Cubism is the art of the noemata."[16] The point here is that according to Hintikka this art is neither about objects nor about subjects but rather about the objective, or intended, or projected element of meaning, as if the eye were an agent rather than a recipient. Cubism is the opposite of Impressionism. The eye projects a meaning onto an object. Then however, the function of art also changes, for art does not depict what the eye sees or even projects. Art itself projects a noema or a meaning onto a canvas: "Cubist paintings are a sort of concretizations of noemata."[17]

The question we have for Hintikka, however, is not whether art can be illumined by philosophy. That is an old enterprise, common among philosophers since Hegel, although Hintikka has something new to say here. The question is rather the reverse one: can philosophy be illumined by art? In the comparison-game, philosophy has an advantage over art in that it professionally generates concepts, which can then be applied to anything. Thus philosophy can always say something about art. The question implicit in this universal applicability of philosophy is whether the comparison stems from the philosophy's internal architecture or from the transformative power of the act of application. The question here, however, is the inverse question of whether art can *show* something about philosophy (since it cannot say it). In this case, we must ask whether we can better understand noemata through seeing their depiction or indeed their production in Cubist art?

Hintikka has little difficulty in showing that Cubists were not only realists, but also conceptualists, i.e., that they viewed the senses as "sources of error."[18] In their account, we should disregard perspective and visual perception because they cannot show how we conceive of an object, only how we presume that we see it. The task is to *show* the conception. In this sense the Cubists were realists even while being anti-naturalistic and anti-illusionistic.[19] The Cubists were reacting against the Impressionists, just as Husserl was reacting against Ernst Mach's focus on sense-impressions.

Hintikka's point is that both Husserl and the Cubists were rejecting concrete perception, "the way it happens to be perceived."[20] The illuminating distinction that Hintikka makes, following Husserl, is one between the perspective variations, and the perspected variables, i.e., between the conditions of our viewing an object, and the object's possibilities of being viewed. His point is that both Husserl and the Cubists were interested in the perspected variables, how an object could be seen, and not how it is seen from a particular point. Thus in the strict sense the Cubists did not give up on perspective. On the contrary, they sought to expand its meaning by distinguishing between perspectives and the subjective point of view. Hintikka terms the Cubists realists because of this distinction: they believe they can investigate perspective without a reference to the subjective point of view. In the same way. Husserl's noemata are not subjective pictures.[21]

Hintikka thus infers that both Husserl and the Cubists were concerned about the relation between representation and reality. Here he engages in a two-step procedure. First, he creates criteria that make a comparison possible: Husserl would have denied that the noema is a representation, but that does not mean that seen in comparison, or indeed from Hintikka's point of view, it does not function like a representation, thus permitting a functional comparison. Second, this comparison allows Hintikka to inject his own philosophical preoccupations into the comparison, a procedure that is fully in accord with his idea about how the history of ideas ought to be done. The test of this procedure is whether the adoption of his own point of view can prove illuminating for the elucidation of the two positions, and for their comparison.

There are two models here; one according to which the relations between representation and reality can be freely varied, and one according to which they cannot. Hintikka links these two to the distinction he draws between two logical models, one of logic as language, and one of logic as calculus. The logic as language model is the one in which we cannot get out of our language rules for articulating the relations between representation and reality, and the logic as calculus model is the one in which we can. Unsurprisingly, it is in the logic as calculus model, the one in which we can get out of language rules, that we can freely vary the rules. It is not that Hintikka believes that we can get out of language, but his endorsement of the possibility of semantic self-referentiality provides a model that can also be usefully applied on the basis of realist assumptions, unlike the model of logic as language, which must assume semantic ineffability. Applying Hintikka's model on the basis of realist assumptions, we reach the paradoxical conclusion that the rules can be varied on realist assumptions, but not on linguistically-bound ones. Normally, the limitation to language has been taken as the sign of greater freedom, freeing us from Platonic essentialism and determinism. In the essay on the Great Chain of Being, Hintikka indicated what is wrong with this conception of realism as also implying determinism. That same argument is anticipated here, showing that the position of a metalanguage, or rather of a meta-non-language, is necessary for safeguarding this variability. This is the opposite of Derrida's position, but it is also a quest for freedom. Hintikka's conclusion: individuals can be constituted "in more than one way."[22]

The model that then is determinist is the one which accords with naturalistic and illusionistic pictorial representation. Other systems of representation are possible, which is not the same as saying that a system of links to reality without representation is possible. Hintikka's point: the free creation of other conventional systems for linking representation to reality is a kind of realism. For such a realism, the best expression is a "language with invented signs."[23] Moreover, Hintikka implies that cultures have often employed such nonnaturalistic systems of representation. The innovation of Cubism was to assert that the artist has a free choice of inventing his own nonnaturalistic system of representation. Underlying this point, however, is Hintikka's assumption that what one must have is a *system* of representation, i.e., an architecture, something with coherent internal relations. Thus what one has here is not just a language, but rather a language that assumes that it is not enclosed, and is therefore inherently relative. However, that openness does not make such a language dependent on external reality. On the contrary, because of its relativity it can be treated independently of that reality so long as it is not taken as being absolute.

I would now like to turn to Hintikka's "Contemporary Philosophy and the Problem of Truth."[24] In this article Hintikka states that there are "hidden problems and assumptions that cut across the artificial boundaries between different philosophical traditions."[25] The "hidden" problems and assumptions are then not embedded in the specific hermeneutic method or the explicit arguments adopted by a given tradition, but function in terms of that specific tradition as if they were prelinguistic or metalinguistic. Hintikka's point is that these hidden problems and assumptions, despite this special position with regard to the system in which they are applied, cannot be ineffable for a given tradition of philosophical argument, for otherwise that tradition could never question its own axioms: generalizing, human beings could not question the axioms of thought, or of language.

Moreover, if the axioms for a given tradition were inexpressible, there could be no crossover between traditions, for what are axioms in one tradition are not necessarily axioms in another tradition, unless one assumes that there are axioms which are universal for all traditions, thus denying to some degree the philosophical legitimacy of given traditions. Cross-fertilization between traditions assumes the specificity of traditions and their capacity for transformation. "It is actually possible for a philosopher to reach specific results which put to an essentially new light issues that affect all the different philosophical traditions."[26] A key point of Hintikka's conception of philosophical history is his conscious belief, in contrast to the view of historians, in the methodological importance of anachronism. That does not mean that the results of the past should be misrepresented; rather, since we are dealing with philosophical architecture, knowing new construction techniques can make us reevaluate older construction techniques. In this restricted sense he agrees with Derrida that the point of view to be adopted is not the suppositious point of view of the past, but a point of view which was never adopted in the past. However, there are two differences between them. First, they respond differently to the question of what it is about past constructions that this conscious adoption of an anachronistic position will reveal. Unlike Derrida, Hintikka's aim is not subversive. On the contrary, his position is more "aesthetic" and less "ethical" than Derrida's: past constructions of the past should not be gauged primarily in terms of how they can be dismantled, but rather how they can be constructed. This is in accord with his basic reconstructive aim: Hintikka disagrees with Tarski, but seeks to trump him by adopting a point of view which restricts Tarski's results. In comparison to Derrida, Hintikka emerges as the more synthetic philosopher. Thus, second, the past is not rendered obsolete by the present. In a funny way, both Heidegger and Derrida constantly turn to past texts with the aim of showing their obsolescence, and that very aim of showing that they are obsolete binds them to the past, since their own claim of being more than obsolete can only be shown in comparison to those texts. In contrast, Hintikka is more expansive: he almost never disavows past results, but seeks rather to trump them through wider generalization, in this way locating the exception to which the result does not apply. This is done by isolating elements of results, and then questioning the possible generalizations of each element, and not only of the final result.

It is logical for Hintikka to assert that "such Lovejoyful unit ideas are not independent of their context and that their study therefore ought to pay attention to their interaction and not only to their different possibilities of being combined with each other."[27] Here again the option is taken twice for history. First, Hintikka does not restrict himself to the results of generalization, but then *on that basis* looks for the actual interactions. Second, ideas can only be studied in relation to other ideas, not on their own. He had already shown that ideas have different meanings when associated with different ideas. One could even argue that the self-sameness of an idea can be shown by studying it in its variability. Conversely, the assumption is made, in contrast to Derrida, that this variability is not infinite.

Thus Hintikka does not oppose the aim of deconstruction, but rather the strategy. It is of the essence of Derrida's project that he eschews historical method, since his deconstruction is based on the rejection of the history of ideas, precisely because he understands the history of ideas as maintaining the importance of the origin in relation to the supplement. Since Hintikka does not at all have that view of the history of ideas, but rather advocates a history that does not look for origins, he sees no reason to reject the historical method. He can endorse traditional historical means because he does not have traditional historical aims.

Second, Hintikka endorses reconstruction after deconstruction: this is a cardinal distinction between Hintikka and both Derrida and Rorty. Hintikka does not believe that philosophy is dead. This is a central point: the question to be posed to Heidegger is "what next?" Heidegger's philosophy may be true, but it is also a *cul-de-sac*. Derrida showed that Heidegger had been insufficiently radical by making his own philosophy into the same kind of *cul-de-sac*. Thus the inner dynamic of this kind of philosophy is to assimilate its predecessors to the so-called tradition, and thence to adopt a point of view by which that tradition is negated. As Gadamer intuited, this move does not so much negate the (original) tradition as create a negative bonding to the tradition, since overcoming the tradition can only be shown in relation to the tradition. Moreover, this philosophy in a *cul-de-sac* creates an anti-tradition of successive closures, a privative tradition, which subsists by negating its forebears, not in some dialectical setting of oppositions, but rather through the impetus to constant radicalization. Insofar, however, as new impetuses come in from other disciplines, however, whether science or culture, such a tradition is ultimately incapable of assimilating them, for it cannot base its negation except on the (original) tradition. Such attempts to assimilate extra-philosophical ideas have been made, e.g., to conscript deconstruction for politically correct positions of various stripes. But this stance is then arbitrary unless it can be shown to emerge, if only negatively, from the tradition itself, as Foucault was always careful to maintain.

The use of historical methods in philosophy is not only a question of the relation to the past. It is also a question of the degree to which philosophy is capable of confronting new results stemming from other fields, whether mathematics, physics, neurobiology, or cultural studies. Confronting such results has always been a problem for philosophy, but the point is that a model can be constructed which allows for such assimilations. Such a model must be capable of proving itself in relation to already-obtained results. This all sounds perilously like neo-Kantianism, but neo-Kantianism was both imprecise in its historical analyses and also wedded to definite ideas about what the past contains. It is of the essence of Hintikka's model of historical studies that it is not wedded to any definite ideas about what the past contains, since this past must be reinterpreted in relation to new results.

The point is this: the past can only be studied contextually. However, the context is itself not determinate, since it is determined in relation to the (always shifting) point of view. However, the noemata of past ideas, which serve as the objects for Hintikka's history of ideas, are not infinitely variable. He objects to Derrida's choice of objects such as postcards for deconstruction because he believes that deconstructive procedures should focus on the noemata that have already been given, major historical themes and ideas, such as intuition or induction. However, maybe the value of a method may first be proved in relation to an arbitrary object. In contrast, Hintikka's focus on these past noemata emancipates him from the texts of the past even while it binds him historically to their ideas.

The essence of the paper under discussion is the link Hintikka makes between his qualified criticism of Derrida and his already-noted distinction between language as the universal medium and language as calculus or language as a model. Hintikka somewhat confusingly calls these the universalist assumption and the model-conception. It should be noted that the universalist assumption here does not mean an attachment to universals, it means only the idea that language is universal. The idea that language is the universal medium means that reality is encased within language, whereas the model-conception of language raises the possibility that there may be a coherent concept of a reality external to language (it is unclear whether or not a model-conception is ontologically neutral). The essence of Hintikka's point is that it is the first model which is ultimately mystical despite its seeming clarity, and it is the second model which is actually the more transparent one.

If conceptual truths are taken to be beyond language, then any conception of language as totality must believe that such concepts are inexpressible. The connections to reality in this conception must exist in a funny way before language (unless one denies that such exist), and then these connections to reality cannot be the object of knowledge, if knowledge is set as being within language. There are two chimeras in this conception, which Hintikka bundles into one, by stating that "a realistic metalanguage in which we could discuss our own working language is a chimera according to the universalists."[28] One chimera is that of a metalanguage: could one have according to the universalists' conception a universalist metalanguage or not? Such a universal metalanguage seems possible on universalist assumptions, but Hintikka indicates that he thinks that the universalist assumption about the ineffability of some reality eventually vitiates any idea of a metalanguage. The other chimera is about the sense of "realistic": i.e., if the assumption is made that such a metalanguage should be realistic, then that clearly is not allowed according to this conception, since the realistic basis is denied, or even the idea that a language can be realistic. But left unanswered is the question of whether what encases that language, which is a universal medium, is a world which itself is linguistic or a world which is not linguistic. Concepts may be formulated in a metalanguage, but are they intrinsically part of that metalanguage? This will be a question for the second conception, that of language as a model. That conception does not provide an axiomatic answer to the question of whether or not concepts preexist the model. One does not have to be a semi-Platonist to agree to the conception of language as a model.

There is a further point. Linguistic universalism is not the same as ontological universalism. In a sense Hintikka fastens on that distinction in order to show that the consequence of the idea of the inexpressibility of what is beyond language is that our prejudices would not be understandable to us, if they too are defined as being beyond language. Therefore the consequence of this kind of universalism must be self-opacity. That same sense of the self-opacity of the traditional subject (which was not a linguistic subject) is at the heart of Derrida's critique. The disagreement lies in the notion of whether and how self-transparency can be achieved. Derrida takes the position that it can never be completely achieved; rather this opacity must always be highlighted, like negative theology in relation to statements about God, and should never be simply ignored. Hintikka takes the position that self-transparency is a worthwhile project using traditional means so long as we understand that our language is a model. From Hintikka's perspective, there is no point to doing philosophy on the assumption of opacity. Unlike Rorty, his attitude to the history of philosophy is not elegiac.

Having read his Collingwood, Hintikka, in contrast to Hegel, accepts the notion that the past has vanished. The past is not some Platonic meta-reality because it *is not*. The question is whether the nonexistence of the past also implies its ineffability. On universalist claims, one could argue the case either way. On the one hand, what is beyond language is ineffable. On the other hand, precisely the nonexistence of the past may be more similar to the kind of existence that obtains within language, i.e., a past that is encased within language. Such a past, however, is then not characterized by temporal pastness, it is simply a virtual reality. Moreover, the kind of history that would then be preferable would be one of linguistic usage rather than one of geometrical models. And indeed recent history of ideas and of philosophy has tended in that direction, as if the foundation of historical issues lies in linguistic ones.

Hintikka would oppose this approach. The effability of the past, which is the presupposition of our ability to say something about it, depends neither on its continued existence (Plato and Hegel) nor on its being a linguistic construct. A further prepoint: showing our ability to say something about the past that is not a linguistic construct is tantamount to being able to talk about our language as the product of human activity without falling prey to the idea that we cannot do that because we are bound by language. By doing *history* we assume a world that was. Now we can do history without believing in the existence of the past, and that would be the conclusion of someone who would do history while believing in being encased by language. He would reply that he does believe in the existence of the past, but that this belief is an act of faith, something that cannot be examined because the grounds for this belief are inexpressible. But these grounds are not at all the point. It is not that we must believe in the existence of the past to do history; it is that we must believe that history is effable in the strong sense; otherwise we are just not doing history. Now that does not mean that history is a valid pursuit. History may not be valid, but on this argument it has to be done in a certain way to qualify as history. Can one do theology without believing in God? On my argument one can, but using theological methods makes one behave as if one believes in God. One cannot do theology without behaving as if one believes in God, without behaving as if the question of God is a serious question. Even if one is in the business of constantly deconstructing theology, in which case one simply applies the same deconstructive method to text after text after text, one believes that God is a serious question, even though one cannot create a negative counter-theology in this fashion. In the same way, one cannot create a negative counter-history that is based on a method that treats the past as if it is ineffable (even though one can continue to believe just that). Put another way, Hintikka's notion of language as a model fails if it is inapplicable to the past.

My subject here is not Hintikka's analysis of the problem of truth, but rather the way that analysis reflects his view of the possibility and desirability of doing history, and what doing history could mean on his assumptions. First, it drives Hintikka to look for reconceptualizations of the history of philosophy. He is fully aware that such reconceptualizations are self-justificatory, but his point about the method of doing the history of philosophy is that it must be undertaken from partisan positions that reveal new connections. In that respect, he is in accord with one of the foremost contemporary theoreticians of history, Reinhart Koselleck, who has pointed out that modern history could only develop in the eighteenth century once the idea of a nonperspectival impartial master narrative was abandoned.[29]

Second, Hintikka's position on language as a model makes him reject a synthetic view of the history of philosophy despite his synthetic views on other topics. In other words, just as he does not believe that principles can be isolated, but only viewed in interdependence, he does not believe in only one possible world, or only one metalanguage. If he did, he would also believe that the history of philosophy is totalizable, that different ways of viewing the history of philosophy can eventually be reduced to one way of viewing the history of philosophy that is appropriate for one world. That is what he does not and cannot believe, since he does not believe in the philosophical validity of the principle of plenitude.

However, we come now to the following interesting result: Hintikka believes, unlike Gadamer, in the cogency of what have traditionally been metalinguistic issues, but unlike Habermas, he does not believe that one standard metalanguage could be formulated that would be distinct from our ordinary everyday language. The possibility of a metalanguage can be conceived with three different resolutions: no metalanguage, one metalanguage, or many metalanguages (if there are different possible worlds, and if there are metalanguages, then each possible world can have its own metalanguage). Having no metalanguage has the effect of assigning metalinguistic considerations to the impenetrable realm beyond language, and thus making them ineffable. Having only one metalanguage divorces our ordinary working language from the metalanguage and drives us to seek to compare our many working languages with the metalanguage (unless we believe that there is only one ordinary working language). If however, there are many possible metalanguages, then we can use our ordinary working language as the metalanguage (there is no reason to think that meta-linguistical considerations cannot then be expressed in ordinary language). Using our ordinary working language makes it possible to deal with allegedly metalinguistic concerns within language instead of excluding them. That is the meaning of the idea that the assumptions of a given language can be made transparent within that language itself. Consequently, Hintikka does not believe in just one metalanguage, which is the usual belief of those who believe in metalanguages. The limited similarity between Hintikka and Derrida stems from their shared belief in a plurality of languages, but because Hintikka denies ineffability, his conception of this plurality is even more radical than Derrida's. The ideal of the transparency of metalinguistic considerations, then, does not necessarily entail a belief in only one metalanguage. However, then one must ask: is not the assumption of only one metalanguage essential to the belief in metalanguage? Hintikka's answer is negative because he has the theory of language as model: one metalanguage on that assumption would imply only one model. Still, the metalanguage must be emancipated from Platonism, so that there can coexist several different idea-worlds. Assuming there are several different possible idea-worlds, for each of those worlds there is a different constructible history. The transworld heir lines for the different histories are not identical with the identification of the transworld lines between the different possible worlds themselves, and it is this difference which is essential for Hintikka's idea of how the history of philosophy can be done fruitfully.

Thus, in Hintikka's rehistory Peirce, Hilbert, and Gödel belong together,[30] and from this point of view (which language is adopted) there was no real break in Wittgenstein's career. It should be emphasized that this sort of denial of such a break means rather that Wittgenstein$_1$ and Wittgenstein$_2$ had certain beliefs in common, from which, however, it would be an error to claim that their philosophies were identical. However, neither does that mean that such distinctions are immutable; rather, they will be rearranged from another point of view. The point is that none of these distinctions is ineffable, nor does something ineffable exist on the other side of these distinctions. But the rejection of ineffability does not return Hintikka to Platonism. Platonism and the belief in the metalinguistic transparency of ordinary working language are poles apart. Hintikka's quasi-phenomenological conception of language helps explain his lifelong attraction to Husserl.

In the same way, Cassirer and Carnap are bedfellows in that they did not believe in what Hintikka calls the universality of language.[31] It is clear that Cassirer believed in the key role of language, devoting much specula-tive energy to explaining how it may have come about, without believing in the universal medium assumption. It is because he did not believe in ineffability that he felt he had to give an account of the origin of language, for if history and language are effable, the origin of language must also be effable. The "we don't know" with which we confront this issue is not the same as "we could not know in any possible world." Can we think the question of the origin of language in a different sense than we can think the existence of God? We believe the origin of language is an empirical fact about which we lack information, we believe that we can never obtain empirical information about God's existence. Cassirer believes that we can reconstruct the origin of language.[32] Historical studies are all about reconstructing past worlds on the basis of lack of information. That is even true of well-documented events, but books are even written about prehistoric times and ancient cultures which have a thin empirical basis. How could such books be written and still be "scientific?" Only if we accept the validity of modeling procedures may we consider them so.

And yet: Hintikka criticizes Derrida for the "ineffability of the results of deconstruction."[33] Certainly Derrida goes too far in applying ineffability everywhere (both sources and results: there is no point of view from which intelligibility criteria can be applied that can be understood outside that point of view. There are no transworld lines). But does that mean that there is ineffability nowhere? Or that whereof one cannot speak, one should remain silent? Is Hintikka so far from Wittgenstein's fear of irrationality? The opposite point of view to Hintikka's is exemplified in Paul Frankl's *System der Kunstwissenschaft*, in which he states that "Sinn ist immer irrational."[34] Frankl wanted to distinguish between *Sinn* and *Wissenschaft*, content and form, the latter being rational. His point was that we must create sciences for what is itself irrational, never however thinking that the rationality of our science (in this case the history of art) is identical with the rationality of its object. Clearly one *must* speak of that of which one "cannot" speak. In that case, however, one could both believe in the ineffability of something and still believe in the necessity of effability. But is that not theology? It is only theology if we do not adopt the model-conceptualization of language.

Let us see where this leads us. A truth definition for a formal language can only be given in a stronger metalanguage. There is no stronger metalanguage than our actual working language. Hence truth definitions are impossible. One cannot discuss the semantics of a language in that language itself. That language would have to be context-independent, and both Tarski and Hintikka agree that it is not. But that is only true if we are in agreement about the concept of truth, if we are in agreement about the relation of logic to language. Hintikka believes he has shown that there is a logic which makes it possible to "give a complete truth-definition for that language in the language itself."[35]

I cannot argue the validity of the issue, but it is interesting that belief in the ineffability thesis leads to a lack of interest in both historical and philosophical questions. The period in which mathematicians were seriously interested in the philosophy of mathematics as part of their mathematics can be said to have ended with Gödel. If Hintikka is right, the relevance of metamathematical issues for mathematicians once again becomes paramount. But that shows the force of the effability thesis. The point of this discussion has been to show the force of this thesis whatever our assumption about the object being discussed.

In his later work, Hintikka has changed his interpretation of Husserl in two different ways that can be summed up as "uneasiness with the noema." This uneasiness stems from his insight that exclusive concentration on noemata can render opaque their relation to whatever is outside of them. Pursuing this direction, in contrast to Husserl's intentions, we merely replicate the pervasive modern sense of the opacity of external reality, including the opacity of the past. While Hintikka had earlier focused on the noema ("Concept as Vision") because of his interest in the contribution of the act to the constitution of the object, he has lately emphasized in "The Longest Philosophical Journey: Quest of Reality as a Common Theme in Bloomsbury" the *hyle*, the sense data basis that *precedes* the constitution of noemata.[36] As he puts it: "For a phenomenologist, the forms involved in an aesthetic experience cannot be spontaneously given to me, because in the sensory domain the given has no form. The form has to be imposed on us by the *hyle*."[37] In "The Phenomenological Dimension," he emphasizes the implementive relations that *follow* the constitution of the noemata, i.e., the relations of noemata to objects ("it does not follow that one can understand the noema-object relationship merely by examining noemata.")[38] Perhaps Hintikka no longer wants to think that effability is more a property of the noema than it is of the sense datum or the object.

But can this line of thought be applied to the contemplation of the past? Only if we believe that the past is immediately given does this model work. If appearances are no less objects than any other objects, the appearances of the past are effable in precisely this way. In that case, however, we return from an interest in the noemata through which the past is constructed to the *hyle* (if there be such) which is provided by the past, and to past objects. If we look at the past from this point of view, however, there is no *hyle* except in an uninteresting sense (the feel of the parchment that I am holding right now). Nor can we say that the objects of the past are given in the same immediate sense except in a way that is indistinguishable from present objects. The fundamental question is whether an absent object is immediately given in the same sense as a present object.[39] If the absent object is not given in the same sense, then the noemata occupy a privileged role with result to absent objects, a non-Husserlian result. The absent objects are rescued only because the noemata can be taken to assume intended objects. If we adopt Hintikka's position on Husserl, we must either conclude that doing history is not primarily aesthetic in the modern sense, since the *hyle* and the object are given, or that aesthetic experience is not Kantian in nature. If we wish to apply the phenomenological model to historical research, the earlier model that emphasized the noemata is simpler (which is not to say that it is more correct), although its validity presumes the validation of the link between noema and intended object.

The underlying question is whether or not the adoption of language as model versus language as universal medium is more like or unlike an aesthetic view of the world and of history. One could argue that it is language as universal medium that leads to a more aesthetic view, since ineffability is of the essence of the aesthetic experience. Already in "Concept as Vision," Hintikka had argued against that position, claiming rather that art is all about the capacity to express the schema or noema of the intended object. In that sense historiography must also be able to reproduce the schema of the intended object; it must assume the expressibility of noemata of past objects. Then, however, there must be a primacy of the noema over the *hyle*, for the schema of the object over the schema of the sense data. On the other hand, one could argue that the idea of language as model is profoundly anti-aesthetic in that the element of choice that is hereby introduced into our capacity to construct is at bottom an ethical question.

Beyond the old idea of linking aesthetics to ethics (as Kant did at the end of the *Critique of Judgment*) there is one net gain here: historians often feel frustration that they cannot construct possible worlds. The reason is that any counterfactual has unforeseen effects on all other facts and that at two removes the number of possibilities is already too large to be described coherently, even if it could be grasped. The appeal of contextual explanation for historians is that it gives them one world for the reference of everything within it. Being historians, they usually define that one enclosing world in terms of time, for example, the Renaissance, the Stuart Monarchy, and so forth. This kind of conception is especially invidious for the history of ideas. A context-free history of ideas, on the other hand, cannot specify how and why ideas combine and divorce, for there is nothing inherent in those ideas that makes them do this. Even the elective affinities of ideas are just that, *pace* Goethe: elective.

Why does this dissatisfaction of historians exist? Because the meaning of events (and of ideas) cannot be understood without contrasting them to something else. The impracticality of counterfactuals and the incomparability consequent upon periodization makes historians dubious about the validity of comparison. Hintikka offers a way out of this dilemma. The key insight is that ideas are not constant individuals; hence he opposes unit-ideas. Neither are ideas accidents. Rather, their past cross-individuation between different worlds is not the same as their present cross-individuation. Adopting ineffability would mean that past cross-individuation would be indecipherable because we are embedded in present cross-individuation as a semantic presupposition. Hintikka himself has shown that we can distinguish between past and present cross-individuation. These are not merely aesthetic constructions, they are different possibilities of logical connections between ideas. This capacity to make the past effable is not the same as a possibility of our stepping out of context; it rather assumes that we can decipher our own context, which is the opposite of historicism, but may be necessary for rendering the history of ideas intelligible.

GABRIEL MOTZKIN

THE HEBREW UNIVERSITY OF JERUSALEM
JULY 2000

NOTES

1. Jaakko Hintikka, *Ludwig Wittgenstein: Half-Truths and One-and-a-Half-Truths* (Dordrecht: Kluwer Academic Publishers, 1996).

2. Jaakko Hintikka, "Gaps in the Great Chain of Being: An Exercise in the Methodology of the History of Ideas," in *Reforging the Great Chain of Being: Studies of the History of Modal Theories*, ed. Simo Knuuttila (Dordrecht: D. Reidel, 1981).

3. Ibid., p. 4.

4. Ibid., p. 6.

5. Ibid.

6. Ibid.

7. Ibid.

8. Ibid., p. 13.

9. Ibid., p. 14.

10. Jaakko Hintikka, *Knowledge and the Known: Historical Perspectives in Epistemology* (Dordrecht: D. Reidel, 1974).

11. Ibid., p. 127.

12. Jaakko Hintikka, "Concept as Vision: On the Problem of Representation in Modern Art and Modern Philosophy," in Jaakko Hintikka, *The Intentions of*

Intentionality and Other New Models for Modalities (Dordrecht: D. Reidel, 1975).
13. Ibid., p. 223.
14. Ibid., p. 228.
15. Ibid., p. 229.
16. Ibid.
17. Ibid.
18. Ibid.
19. Ibid., p. 230.
20. Ibid., p. 232.
21. Ibid., p. 235.
22. Ibid., p. 239.
23. Ibid., p. 244. Hintikka quoting Daniel-Henry Kahnweiler (in discussion with Picasso) on 22 June 1946, as reported in "Voice of the Artist III," *The Observer*, 8 December 1957.
24. Jaakko Hintikka, "Contemporary Philosophy and the Problem of Truth," in Jaakko Hintikka, *Lingua Universalis vs. Calculus Ratiocinator: An Ultimate Presupposition of Twentieth-Century Philosophy* (Dordrecht: Kluwer Academic Publishers, 1997).
25. Ibid., p. 1.
26. Ibid.
27. Ibid., p. 2.
28. Ibid., p. 4.
29. Reinhart Koselleck, *Vergangene Zukunft: zur Semantik geschichtlicher Zeiten* (Frankfurt am Main: Suhrkamp, 1979).
30. Hintikka, op. cit., pp. 7–8.
31. Ibid., p. 11.
32. Ernst Cassirer, *Philosophie der symbolischen Formen. 1. Teil: Die Sprache* (Berlin: B. Cassirer, 1923).
33. Hintikka, op. cit., p. 12.
34. Paul Frankl, *Das System der Kunstwissenschaft* (Brünn, Leipzig: Rudolf M. Rohrer, 1938, repr. Berlin: Gebr. Mann Verlag, 1998), p. 64.
35. Hintikka, op. cit., p. 15.
36. Jaakko Hintikka, "The Longest Philosophical Journey: Quest of Reality as a Common Theme in Bloomsbury," in *The British Tradition in 20th Century Philosophy. Proceedings of the 17th International Wittgenstein-Symposium*, ed. Jaakko Hintikka and Klaus Puhl (Vienna: Verlag Hölder-Pichler-Tempsky, 1995).
37. Ibid., p. 20.
38. Jaakko Hintikka, "The Phenomenological Dimension," in *The Cambridge Companion to Husserl*, ed. Barry Smith and David Woodruff Smith (Cambridge: Cambridge University Press, 1995), p. 80.
39. On absent and nonexistent objects see Pierre Keller, *Husserl and Heidegger on Human Experience* (Cambridge: Cambridge University Press, 1999), pp. 25–30.

REPLY TO GABRIEL MOTZKIN

As was noted in my reply to Simo Knuuttila, he and Gabriel Motzkin deal with essentially the same problematic, wherefore my response to one of them cannot help being partly also a response to the other one. Both commentators note the crucial importance of a self-enforcing interplay of topical ("systematic") and historical viewpoints in my work. Both of them also note the relative rarity of such a combination of approaches among analytic philosophers. As intellectual historians, they might nevertheless have added that the combination of interests in question has not been a rarity in Finland. Among the philosophers of the preceding generation or two in Finland, Eino Kaila, Erik Stenius, Oiva Ketonen, and G. H. von Wright were all deeply interested in the history of thought and wrote about it, even though they were not centrally involved in scholarship in the history of philosophy.

Both my commentators approve of this cooperation of systematic and historical ideas. However, I cannot help finding that even in their admittedly most congenial and perceptive comments they still underestimate the relevance of topical viewpoints, and in particular of conceptual analysis, to the kind of work they themselves do as practicing historians. Admittedly, Knuuttila defends in a persuasive manner the legitimacy of using systematic ideas in historical interpretation. Yet he leaves me somewhat dissatisfied in a deeper sense with his paper. I want to go much further than he does in arguing not only for the legitimacy but also for the need of systematic ideas and viewpoints in a purely historical work.

In the same spirit, it seems to me, Motzkin finds my method not quite historical, involving (as he sees it) a search for "alternative solutions to contemporary problems." In my view, much more than this is involved. I would go so far as to claim that the continued vitality of several different types of historical research depends on their cooperation with systematic studies, including comparisons with contemporary developments.

There might even be more to be said for occasionally resorting to what might look like an application of what Knuuttila calls the enlightenment model, in the sense of discussing the views of earlier thinkers by reference to what has since turned out to be correct and incorrect. An important example can illustrate what I have in mind. At the present time, there exists a veritable scholarly industry on Frege. What is its *raison d'être* as a part of the cultivation of philosophy and of the history of philosophy? Frege is admittedly a central figure eminently worth studying in detail. However, one does not have to be overly critical to think that this industry is by this time producing rapidly diminishing marginal returns insofar as the task of simply understanding what Frege said and did not is concerned. Indeed, many ostensibly historical studies of Frege are beginning to resemble projections of the author's own concepts and problems to his texts. In contrast, extremely interesting, largely unsolved problems concern Frege's failures. The alleged ambiguity he found between the different meanings of verbs for being has turned out not to be indispensable and even to be probably wrong as a piece of ordinary language semantics, notwithstanding the fact that Frege incorporated it in his logic. Frege's treatment of existence as a higher-order predicate is dubious. Frege assumed in his semantics the principle of compositionality which cannot always be upheld. The expressive force of Frege's logic of quantifiers is subject to important limitations that have to be removed. Frege does not seem to leave any room for the all important standard interpretations of higher-order logic. And most subtly, his treatment of identity is seriously handicapped because he does not admit into his logic the most important mathematical use of identity, viz., as expressing functional dependencies. The truly important task in Frege studies is to recognize these shortcomings in their historical context so as to see how they can be overcome. Otherwise the entire Frege industry will soon lapse into pedantry. Yet in the deluge of papers and books on Frege, these truly vital issues—vital also for the deeper historical understanding of Frege—are conspicuously absent.

Similar things can also be said of some of the other figures of early analytic philosophy. For instance, surely it will make a difference to historical studies of Hilbert when it is shown that his original foundational project can be carried out to his own presumed satisfaction. (See here my forthcoming paper, "How to Carry Out Hilbert's Project.")

Of course, this does not mean contradicting the rightly understood criticisms of the enlightenment model. We are here not dealing with self-congratulating classification of past views into more or less "valuable" ones, but with questions as to what the work of thinkers like Frege really amounts to. It does not mean asking systematic questions that we have in mind but Frege did not. Frege was concerned with the very same problems as we are, in the first place with the problem of constructing a general logic of quantifiers.

By and large, there is very little that I can disagree with in Motzkin's essay. Yet, somewhat in the same way as with Knuuttila's contribution, there is a massive unspoken feature of the story that they never get around to telling or at least emphasizing. This underlying fact is that conceptual and other topical assumptions are needed by a historian for the very first purpose of understanding what earlier thinkers said in the sense of what their views actually amounted to. This point is easier to convey by means of examples than by means of verbal explanations. Here I could call as my first witness Judson Webb. Webb's testimony is his essay in the present volume. He traces, as I had earlier done more superficially, the connections, sometimes veritable identities, between such ideas as the *ecthesis* of Aristotelian logic, its namesake in Euclid, Kant's notion of intuition as it is used in mathematical proofs, Peirce's conception of the iconicity of reasoning, and the notion of instantiation used in contemporary logic. One simply does not understand any of these ideas if one does not grasp their kinship (sometimes amounting to virtual identity) with each other.

I myself underestimated earlier this dependence of the hermeneutical task on a historian's own topical awareness. Perhaps I ought to have formulated my criticism of Lovejoy differently. Perhaps I ought to have blamed him, not so much for not realizing the context-dependence of his "unit ideas" as for not identifying them correctly in the different historical contexts in which they have occurred. Perhaps the reason why Lovejoy ended up misinterpreting some of the crucial characters in the (hi)story of the principle of plenitude is that he was not focused keenly enough on the precise content of this unit idea. It may not be entirely accidental that the thinkers Lovejoy misinterpreted worst are Aristotle and Leibniz, both of whom were exceptionally sophisticated in their handling of concepts and conceptual assumptions. And perhaps there is a moral here for other historians of ideas, too.

In any case, my misdirected criticism of Lovejoy has led Motzkin to overemphasize the contextualism of my approach to the history of ideas. In so far as there is misunderstanding here, I am to be blamed for it, not Motzkin. I want to go on record in any case as *not* believing in "the contextual determination of the meaning of ideas." I would not say, either, that the principle of plenitude is "both a metaphysical and a historical principle." It is a metaphysical assumption, and it is a good historical maxim to pay special attention to the role of this metaphysical principle in the history of thought.

The (admittedly heavily qualified) independence of Lovejoyful "ideas" of context should make it possible to use them also counterfactually. I think that such speculative ventures can sometimes be instructive and prompt interesting questions. For instance, I cannot help wondering what would have happened if Gödel had applied to set theory the same kinds of arguments as he applied to arithmetic in 1931. I doubt that he would have spent nearly as much time and energy on axiomatic set theory if he had done so, nor otherwise paid to set theory the attention he did. And if so, what would the subsequent history of the foundations of mathematics have been like? Or is the only serious question here why Gödel did not apply his own ideas to set theory?

Motzkin believes that historians reject all such counterfactual speculations. I am sure that he is right about intellectual history, but as the example of Niall Ferguson shows,[1] counterfactual or "virtual" history, as it is now called, is by no means a lost art among serious practicing historians.

J. H.

NOTE

1. Cf. Niall Ferguson, ed., *Virtual History: Alternatives and Counterfactuals* (New York: Basic Books, 1999).

3

Juliet Floyd

ON THE USE AND ABUSE OF LOGIC IN PHILOSOPHY: KANT, FREGE, AND HINTIKKA ON THE VERB "TO BE"

Clown: . . . as the old hermit of Prague, that never saw pen and ink, very wittily said to a niece of King Gorboduc, 'That that is is;' so I, being Master Parson, am Master Parson; for, what is 'that' but 'that,' and 'is' but 'is'?

Twelfth Night, act 4, scene 2

Jaakko Hintikka is a radical and wildly ambitious philosopher. Over the course of more than forty years he has attempted to refashion the whole of logic and philosophy in his own image, urging the overthrow of most everything analytic philosophy inherited from Frege and Russell. He argues that the correct philosophical Logic (with a capital "L" to designate "the real Logic") is his "independence-friendly" logic, wedded to his construals of modal and epistemic logic in the context of game-theoretic semantics, and he calls for a reappraisal of every philosophical problem in light of this conception. Hintikka thereby rejects what became for philosophers (after Hilbert, Gödel, and Quine) the standard answer to the question, What is Logic?, viz., first-order logic, unmoved by its commonly supposed advantages: topic-neutrality, wide curricular, mathematical, and philosophical acceptance, general (if not universal) applicability, recursively axiomatizable completeness with respect to deductive validity, and classical syntax and semantics for negation. He is not swayed either by the expressive power of second-order logic. He wants a system that is, expressively speaking, somewhere in between. To understand him as a philosopher is to be able to fathom why.

It is not the aim of this essay to come fully to grips with Hintikka's persistent campaign to overthrow the present order of things. Instead, I shall try to characterize his self-conception in broad brushstrokes. Section 1 of the essay aims to situate Hintikka's thought within the context of recent analytic philosophy. Section 2 canvasses his criticisms of Frege's and Russell's fundamental logical notions. Section 3 assesses his treatment of the classical Ontological Argument for God's existence in light of these criticisms. First, I contrast his treatment of the argument with that of Michael Dummett. Next, I consider what Hintikka has left out of philosophical account in his particular reconstruction of the argument, suggesting that it is precisely this which is most telling with respect to his own philosophy. In section 4 I delve into a more detailed analysis of Hintikka's treatment of Kant's philosophy of logic, with the aim of showing how his own philosophical preconceptions shape his historical readings.

1. INTRODUCTORY OVERVIEW OF HINTIKKA'S PHILOSOPHY

Hintikka's philosophy is difficult to survey in brief, because his arguments are legion and divide into unexpected groups along multiple fronts. In general, however, it may be said that his overarching strategy is to stress the potentially fruitful applications of his (continually evolving conception of) Logic to a wide array of as yet unresolved philosophical problems, both historical and contemporary. His philosophical creativity and ingenuity within this framework are remarkable, his willingness to speculate within its terms unfettered, his boldness in overthrowing nearly all that is taken for granted in contemporary philosophy unhesitating. He is an opportunistic revolutionary: recasting and solving as many contemporary problems as he can in the light of his Logic, he aims to capitalize on those outstanding (and seemingly intractable) conceptual problems contemporary philosophers have inherited from the commonly accepted logical frameworks of first- and second-order logic as they try to apply those frameworks to an analysis of the semantics and syntax of natural languages. In exploiting unclarities at work in much contemporary philosophy, Hintikka paints in bold, outline strokes; he is not a detail man, and he speaks unguardedly and programmatically, as if determined not to be slowed down by technical precision. Indeed, the most basic philosophical fact about him is his impatience for new vistas, inquiries, and ideas. This attitude is reflected not only in the sheer quantity and style of his output, but also in his manner of styling himself a revolutionary. At the center of his vision is an overarching theory of inquiry, a codification constructed around the notion that it is better, Logically speaking, to commit errors in the pursuit of many different ideas than to guard oneself too closely from error. As he puts the point, he would rather indulge in sins of commission than sins of omission.[1] Clarity for its own sake, even truth, is less important to him than epistemological ambition, creativity, and sagacity. This fundamental instinct is wedded to a conviction in, and fascination with, Logic—by which I mean, not simply formal or modern mathematical logic, but Logic conceived of as an inherited science, proper to philosophy, with a lineage stretching back to the Presocratics.[2]

Hintikka often makes it sound as if the virtues of his IF logic might primarily be seen via its logico-mathematical properties. But this, I believe, is misleading. His primary arguments on behalf of his logic—on behalf of the notion that IF logic constitutes *the* correct Logic—are philosophical and historical, ultimately not purely logico-mathematical at all, even if mathematical questions may be and have been raised about this logic (and about his earlier versions of modal and epistemic logics, now subsumed within the IF program), and even if, in order to sway the prevailing philosophical community to his side, he realizes that he must give technical reasons as to why philosophers ought to prefer its logical properties. In purely technical terms, expressive equivalencies may be seen between IF logic and Henkin's earlier treatment of branching quantifiers, or even first-order quantification over functions.[3] This Hintikka dismisses as logically irrelevant, even while he remains interested in articulating the formal logico-mathematical properties of his system. Why? Because ultimately his arguments answering the question "What is Logic?" turn on his insistence on affiliating himself with a longstanding philosophical tradition about Logic stretching back to Aristotle, Kant, and Peirce—all thinkers on whom, not accidentally, he has written, sometimes critically, but always in such a way as to take them to have prepared the way (sometimes through their errors) for the adoption of his own point of view. His readings of history are essential to his self-conception as a philosopher, even if he will occasionally say that the historical pedigree and coherence of a philosophical idea is no guarantee of its truth.

His heady dream, his vision of Logic itself, is a general theory of inquiry, formally codified, that will frame and contribute to our understanding of all of contemporary science, from mathematics to physics to psychology to linguistics, history, and philosophy itself.[4] The success of this program, for Hintikka, depends upon its fruitfulness for future scientific research. But it also depends centrally on its ability to recover those philosophical insights from the tradition that are worth preserving. Hintikka's philosophy is thus a grand, interconnected system of thought, not a collection of independent theses, despite the fact that he himself often argues as if one could take or leave his arguments piecemeal. Given his game-theoretic semantics, his formalization cannot express classical negation, and the law of the excluded middle fails within it. This is enough to make many readers skeptical about his approach.[5] Rather than arguing the merits of that (kind of) question here, I shall be trying to spell out the metaphors and overarching pictures that make Hintikka prepared to swim against the tide, showing that localized disagreements are difficult even to formulate in relation to his framework.

My point, then, is that Hintikka's assault on recent conceptions of how first-order or second-order quantification theory should form the true Logic is best compared, not with the discovery of new logical theorems or techniques concerning existing frameworks (such as model theory, game theory, or the theorems of Gödel or Hilbert or Cohen), nor with the invention of new formalizations of portions of modal and psychological discourse (even though Hintikka has himself contributed to these), but instead, with philosophical revolutions on the order of, say, Hegel's attack on Kant. Hegel built upon and radicalized his immediate predecessors' philosophy of logic, praising Kant's aim to transform Logic from an empty, formal syllogistic to a fruitful, synthetic science, while simultaneously accusing Kant of not having gone far enough. In a similar vein, Hintikka builds upon yet radicalizes his immediate predecessors' philosophies of logic. He takes a leaf out of Frege's and Russell's books, adopting (the first-order part of) their quantificational logic as part of the story, while simultaneously accusing them of having mistaken a mere fragment of Logic for the whole. Despite his respect and praise for their formal achievements, then, he takes Frege and Russell to have had a negative influence on philosophy of logic. His view is that by setting in place a host of conceptual dogmas—most centrally the dogma that Logic consists primarily of a formulation of the laws of valid deductive inference—they held back the development of an engaged, productive Logic of rational inquiry. After Frege and Russell, Hintikka claims, Logic came too often to be conceived, at least in philosophy, as primarily a limitative framework, a negative touchstone, a means of organizing the purely deductive justificatory order of truth, rather than an instrument for producing new truths and questioning received ones in all branches of science. To the extent that it was construed as a general theory of inquiry, it failed. The Frege-Russell framework, whether first- or second-order, is in Hintikka's mind ill-suited to the task of showing us in general how Logic aids, structures, and represents our efforts to produce new truths and question received ones, in all branches of knowledge. He does not deny that Frege and Russell inaugurated a fruitful new area of logical research. He does deny that their particular ways of conceiving Logic were on anything like the right path.

It must be said that there is not a skeptical bone in Jaakko Hintikka's body; he has never been *moved* by skepticism, religious, epistemic, ethical, or otherwise, and he is therefore not aiming to diagnose or respond to it.

Logic, as Hintikka conceives it, frames all of inquiry, and it requires no defense. But Hintikka has never been concerned to chart, explore, and emphasize the limits of logic or the limits of meaningful expression *überhaupt*. This is not because he believes that we have infallible insight into the logical structure of language—far from it. Hintikka takes (the logical structure of) meaning to be, while not ineffable, inexhaustible and open-ended.[6] At the same time, while it is not immediately transparent, it is transparent enough to admit of formal representation. His readings of Wittgenstein (several with Merrill Hintikka)[7] reflect this picture: they celebrate (the later) Wittgenstein's idea of a multiplicity of language-games and the (early and later) Wittgenstein's commitment to an immediacy of contact between mind and world, and downplay the idiosyncrasy of Wittgenstein's concern with exploring the limits of sense and the complexities and vagaries of human expressiveness. Similarly with Hintikka's interpretations of Kant: he has written extensively about Kant's views on logic, knowledge, and mathematical intuition, but never emphasizes Kant's dialectical fascination with probing the sources of metaphysical illusion. It is not that Hintikka is an uncritical metaphysician or ontologist; he has incorporated into his philosophy much of the post-critical tendencies of both Wittgenstein and Kant. What is distinctive in Hintikka's view is that he never was and never shall be bothered enough by the ineffable, the illusory, and the nonsensical to focus thematically or dialectically on their sources and nature.

Thus, oddly enough, Hintikka must be classified—and indeed classifies himself—as a thinker affiliated with, and inspired by, a certain scientific and constructive way of taking the teachings of J. L. Austin.[8] It was Austin who called for a detailed investigation and classification of the complexities of our uses of the verbs "to know" and "to believe," Austin who insisted on the importance of performance and action to our very notion of *knowledge*, and Austin who—whether out of his own sense of profundity, under a mask, or not—evinced something akin to impatience with skepticism. Hintikka's interrogative model of inquiry, though a more general, formalized structure than any Austin contemplated, is Austinian in an Aristotelian way: it *assumes* that humans achieve a certain degree of success in querying nature and other interlocutors. It urges us to adopt a perspective on knowledge *sub specie humanitatis*, and then see what insight we can gain from looking at our applications of the epistemic verbs.

For Hintikka, then, Logic is assumed to be an applied branch of knowledge, but the application of Logic is understood according to his analogies with games. He conceives of inquiry as an activity of organizing what is deemed (locally, for present intents and purposes) relevant and credible information in an interlocking series of steps according to certain deductive and strategic (types of questioning) rules.[9] In inquiry, we pose questions and we reach answers. In scientific inquiry, we pose questions to nature, and nature responds as an oracle. We have a choice, in any given instance, about whether it seems plausible to treat the oracle's deliverances as reliable. But we have no general choice about whether to use nature as an oracle ever, at all. Differently put, the very fact that the oracle has been reliable in the past is enough, strategically, for us to go on: we play, most all of us, the game. Hintikka takes attempts to formulate skepticism in ordinary language to be self-defeating. And he rejects as wrong-headed all epistemological theories that presume to analyze the locution "a knows that p" in terms of a two-place relation between a and the content *what a knows* (e.g., a proposition or Fregean *Gedanke*).[10] Knowledge for Hintikka is a kind of performative achievement, a laudable or especially sagacious step in human inquiry. It is neither a transcendent nor a merely psychological state.

This way of framing the Logical has bothered many. Michael Dummett finds that Hintikka's philosophy of logic offers far too limited an account of the commitments involved in a speaker's making an assertion. In Dummett's words, Hintikka treats assertion as too easily discardable, "a kind of gamble that the speaker will not be proved wrong."[11] Dummett's (Fregean) concern is that the notions of *truth* and *justification* are not deeply and directly enough embedded in Hintikka's philosophy of logic. And it is true that neither notion plays a constitutive, fundamentally privileged role in the interrogative model's game-theoretic analysis of reasoning. But what is instructive here is that Hintikka is self-consciously rejecting the very criteria of the Logical that shape Dummett's characterization of his point of view. He rejects altogether Dummett's particular conception of the way in which Logic is applied. For Hintikka, there is no point in trying to hold on to the guiding (Fregean) idea that the logical structure of assertion (judgment) is based upon nothing more, and nothing less, than acknowledgment of the True. For him, unlike for Frege or Dummett, there is no ultimate, universal context of justification in which the application of logic is taken to turn on the structure of deductive inference, or even a general theory of meaning. Hintikka's ideal of assertion (and of semantics) is framed by the context, not merely of justification, but also of discovery and persuasion. Hintikka's ideal is uniformly applicable to fictional and non-fictional contexts of language use, for it is designed so as to engage epistemic situations in which the flow of information may be imperfect. This ideal localizes the uses of *all* sentences (fictional or not) to their place in dialogues of questioning. This way of handling knowledge hearkens back to a Socratic image of philosophy. Logic, as Hintikka conceives it, is applicable in situations in which sharing of (purported) information is humanly and practically structured as an ongoing, cooperative game of inquiry, situations in which different participants may have access to different epistemic possibilities and in which it is not necessary always to assume the presence of an omniscient player. One of Hintikka's favorite examples is the situation of information-gathering in a court of law, where rules of evidence, procedure, and questioning structure the flow of information in a context in which plausible reasoning is the best that may be hoped for as a gateway to truth.

A clarification is in order here. Hintikka's contextualism about statements is not forwarded primarily to defend a general thesis of the kind that Putnam has called the "thesis of contextualism" about knowledge, viz., the notion that the truth-evaluable content of sentences depends both on what they mean, and on the particular context of their use.[12] Instead Hintikka seeks, in a sense, to "logicize" this thesis itself. On his conception the whole of logic and knowledge are humanized, in a certain sense psychologized and contextualized, but not in any viciously mentalist, subjectivist or intensionalist way, and not at the expense, but for the profit, of formalization. On his view assertions are made, Logically speaking, from within particular interrogative contexts in answer to specific questions. Once this view is applied to the modalities, Hintikka has no use for a notion of *essence* or *absolute necessity*: Hintikka's contextualism about doubt and knowledge neither supports nor undercuts nor invites realism, idealism, or skepticism; in Wittgenstein's famed words, it "passes them by." Hintikka holds that human activities of seeking and finding should be fully acceptable to any (reasonable?) philosopher of inquiry, even to a behaviorist, so long as it is granted that these activities take place in specific contexts of questioning, contexts which may be classified in the theory of question and answer, which according to the interrogative model constitutes the most general methodological framework of science. Hintikka's contextualism does not exclude, but rather entails, that the notions of *knowledge* and *belief*, connected with human action, have a relative logic of their own, a logic that Hintikka has worked at formalizing.[13]

That games of inquiry lead more often than not to the truth is thus a presupposition of Hintikka's view of inquiry, but not one reduced in the model to a series of explicit assertions, nor one applied across the board to all the relevant uses of declarative sentences of the language at once. Error, even radical error, is perfectly compatible with the interrogative model. This is not, of course, to say that Hintikka is uninterested in truth. One of the presumed advantages of IF logic over first-order quantification theory is, according to him, that IF logic can define its own truth predicate. This Hintikka takes to be a formal advantage, for it allows him to fix once and for all the language in which the logical theory is framed relative to truth.

At the same time, it allows for a rich open-endedness of semantics: so rich, in fact, that IF logic is neither axiomatizeable nor complete. Why, he asks, should we want it to be? Some would say that there is an odd clash here between what Hintikka allows himself to take for granted at the metalevel and what his logic cannot capture deductively (e.g., classical negation). This is symptomatic, however, of his conception of Logic. Hintikka does not privilege formal *deduction*.

Hintikka is asking us to question that which we tend to take for granted in treating first-order Logic as a canonical framework for Logic. He is asking why we *ought* to restrict ourselves to a set of logical laws that are axiomatizeable and uniformly applicable, whose general laws' application is fixed in advance, once and for all. For Hintikka, rules of deduction such as Frege's are *definatory* rules in any game of inquiry: flaunt them and you are not playing such a game. On the other hand Hintikka fails to see the project of analyzing our intuitive notion of deductive validity as a free-standing one. For him, these deductive rules must always be treated in light of their applications, in light of *strategic* rules of inquiry. The price of insisting on axiomatizing Logic is, on his view, that we then have no workable (sufficiently context-relative yet formally powerful) notion of *information* to apply in modeling actual human inquiry.[14] Hintikka does not question Gödel's completeness theorem for first-order quantification theory. But he does question whether we should aspire to a Logic that is deductively complete.

A fortiori Hintikka has not much use for what are often viewed as the most important insights of recent philosophy of science. He rejects the hypothetico-deductive model's focus on the deductive articulation of scientific theories and empiricism. He takes Humean inductive worries to be the product of a misguided conception of inquiry: as he sees it, the Humean has an arbitrarily narrow conception of the Logic of inquiry in which only Yes-No questions are permitted to be posed at the atomic level. On the other hand, a Humean construes generalizations acontextually, as fully universal generalizations.[15] From Hintikka's perspective, Kuhn's and Hanson's twin emphases on the theory-ladenness of observations and the importance of models in the discovery of scientific theories seem like jejune, rather localized criticisms in comparison to his own bold alternative. From his point of view neither traditional methodologists of science nor their critics sufficiently emphasize how much general structure there is to the strategic element in reasoning, the savoir-faire of a good question in context. Hintikka freely admits that on his own view, the notion of *information* is an empirical, evolving one, localized to the particular game context at hand. He does not aspire to a general doctrine of content, internalist or externalist. A fortiori he sees no point in appealing to a general notion of "common sense" or the biological theory of evolution to explain human epistemic success. He is especially critical of a priori appeals to general semantical "intuitions."[16] He does not need to defend or criticize metaphysical realism, for he does not worry that our theories might turn out to be nothing but put-up jobs. He has never sought to do justice to the quest for legitimate evidential anchor-points for our theories in the perceptual world that avoid imposing our local preferences on reality. As I have said, he is not inclined to dwell—as did Kant, Wittgenstein, Frege, Carnap, and even Quine—on the points at which language or our claims to knowledge lead us astray.

This does not mean that he has not written extensively about the distinction between (what he calls) perspectivally identified objects and publicly identified objects: he has worked to show how identity and individuation might be understood in terms of this distinction,[17] and tried to fit these notions coherently into the semantics of modal logic. Nevertheless, on the whole, Hintikka's concerns in philosophy have always been primarily a matter of system-building within formal logic so as to square it in a transparent way with as much of "ordinary" language and inquiry (including scientific language and inquiry) as he can. He has never been concerned to give a wholesale philosophical defense of claims made from an overarching standpoint with minimal or austere presuppositions. In this respect, he is more like Hegel and Peirce than like Frege or Wittgenstein or Quine. For Hintikka, Logic is a study of inquiry in general, and it must therefore be, at its most basic level, reflective of the psychological and linguistic structures of the inquirers who investigate. There is no harm or danger he sees in building into Logic itself what general epistemological structure seems to be given in common applications of our concept of *knowledge*. The only harm that can be done is to leave this structure *out*. If we seek to do this—as, say, Frege and Quine do—we sell Logic conceptually short, we treat it as a merely limitative canon for thought, an empty, wholly negative science.

Hintikka's construal of the logic of statements mirrors his overarching theory of inquiry: it is saturated with images and metaphors of inquiry as a human activity, immanent within language, of seeking and finding, a game of asking and answering questions that are meaningfully posed and resolved in specific interrogative contexts where certain assumptions (empirical and conceptual) are locally fixed. There is nothing God-like, crystalline, impersonal or axiomatic about this conception of how to conceive and present Logic. Classical negation is not central to it because calling falsehoods falsehoods is, on its own, a largely one-sided focus for Hintikka, with much less interesting systematicity to it than formal logicians have traditionally thought.

In his way then, like Austin, Hintikka makes no pretense of drawing ahuman limits to thought or Reality or Being. This pits him against most of his contemporaries vis-à-vis the modalities.[18] He rejects at the outset all views that take the notions of *necessity, essence,* and *possibility* to be clear apart from their human range of possible application. At the same time, he rejects a universalist view of logic which would disallow any fundamental role for the notion of *necessity* by embracing the ideal of a unique, topic-neutral, and amental interpretation of the range of the quantifiers (a view such as Frege's or Quine's). In contrast to both these approaches, Hintikka's philosophy of logic is self-consciously deeply Kantian, deeply indebted to the notion that the application of formal logic, and hence Logic itself, must be conceived of as working only subject to certain human conditions and limits. Logical possibilities are, in an important sense, restricted and not absolute, according to him.[19] At the same time, he decries Kant's insistence that the notions of *possibility* and *necessity* form no systematic logical part of the content of judgments (for more on this point, see section 4 below).

Thus—to choose but one illustration—Hintikka is simply not attracted to Quine's project of building "an enduring and impersonal formulation of a system of the world." This is witnessed by Quine himself, responding to Hintikka's criticisms of his views:

> Jaakko Hintikka has concerned himself with my remarks regarding the intensional idioms of modal logic and the propositional attitudes. In my view these idioms are semantically dependent upon the circumstances of utterance, much in the manner of the indexicals. Thus relativized, they make sense and are useful. Necessity, for instance, may typically be said of a sentence that follows logically from acceptances shared by the parties to the particular dialogue or inquiry. . . . In the case of the propositional attitudes the indexical character is instructively pinpointed, under Hintikka's approach, in the key idiom of believing or knowing who or what someone or something is; for the question who or what someone or something is depends for its force on the purposes and background information of the moment. . . .
>
> Indexicals present no major logical or semantic problems, and furthermore they are indispensable to daily discourse. Still, for obvious reasons, they would be out of place in an enduring and impersonal formulation of a system of the world. Now in my view this last is true equally of the intensional idioms of modality and propositional attitude. They differ from the indexicals, or from other indexicals, only in not enjoying so transparent a logic and semantics.
>
> Where I consequently disagree with many philosophers, though perhaps not Hintikka, is in scouting any notion of objective or metaphysical necessity. The logic and semantics of necessity and the propositional attitudes is of interest only as a study in linguistics and psychology, and not as a reflection of broad structures of reality.[20]

But of course Hintikka rejects the notion that linguistics and psychology do not reflect "broad"—that is, logical—features of reality. What are true or false, and what have presuppositions, are for Hintikka statements—that is, actions or events of utterance made by individuals on particular occasions in particular epistemic situations, addressing their remarks to a particular audience in a particular context of inquiry—not (as for Quine) sentences, abstract sets of sets of phonemes.[21] Hintikka is quite happy to see logic and ontology as studies continuous with and indebted to linguistics and psychology, as well as methodology. And he relishes the picture of the contextually sensitive application of semantical notions. In fact, he imposes a grammatical relativity across the board upon *all* the traditional apparatus of quantification theory, making relative and fluctuating all the usual logico-grammatical distinctions and terms worked with in contemporary philosophy of logic (see especially section 3.3 below for details). Hintikka construes the very structure of a statement itself in game-theoretic psychological terms borrowed from observable linguistic behavior. He firmly believes that this semantics should be accepted even by behaviorists. For he believes, as Quine never did, that there is such a thing as the Logic of scientific inquiry. And this is so even if, as is also true, his conception of science, of knowledge, is, like Quine's, very broad and open-ended—so that he can agree with Quine that a philosopher does best not to focus on developing any kind of a priori, principled criterion of science, of knowledge, or of philosophy.

    Within formal logic proper, the fundamental notion for Hintikka is that of a *dependent* (embedded, alternated) quantifier, conceived as replaceable by a term for a Skolem function.[22] In, for example, "$(x)(\exists y)Fxy$" we may think of replacing the "$(\exists y)$" with a functional term "$f_1(x)$," whose value is a "function of," i.e., *dependent as a value upon* our "choice" of a value for "x," as in "$(x)Fxf_1(x)$" (note well here Hintikka's comfort with eliding the categorial boundaries between the contribution of a quantifier, a singular term, and a variable—a point that I shall emphasize in sections 2 and 3 below). The moral Hintikka draws from this is not the need of our quantifying, in a first-order way, over functions. Instead, he takes Skolem's technique to license our reading a formal representation of a natural language sentence with a string of quantifiers out front as a representation of a game of inquiry conducted by an (idealized) individual player working through the sentence from left to right, weeding out "model sets" (possible models) for the sentence as she goes. Hintikka's understanding of the content and application of a quantifier is thus contextual, both without and within the sentence, relativized to its mutual behavior in relation to other quantifiers within the structure of the particular sentence in which it appears.

Hintikka has often stressed the ways in which at least some of his philosophical views can only be seen as natural outgrowths of Frege's. In particular, he has always praised Frege's quantificational conception of generality. Like Frege, Hintikka resists understanding existential commitment in terms of any kind of primary or brute fact (psychological or epistemic or semantic or intuitive) holding between a mind and an object independently of the apparatus of quantification; indeed, his readings of the (Kantian) notions of *intuition* and *syntheticity* are refracted through his understanding of the existential quantifier. Nevertheless, his image of instantiation—unlike Quine's or Frege's—is game-theoretic, controlled by the strategic possibilities available to an idealized player facing and choosing from an array of possible worlds or models for the sentence. The modalities are intrinsic to Logic, on this view. Hence Hintikka's hostility to what he calls "actualism," or "one-world" views of the interpretation of the range of the quantifiers, such as Frege's, Russell's, Quine's, or even (as he reads him) Gödel's.[23]

At the same time Hintikka seeks by means of his Logic to replace the application of purely modal notions with epistemic notions, thereby treating the notions of *possibility* and *necessity* as also context-dependent, a matter of their specific sequential place in the structure of the sentence. Compositionality, along with a univocal interpretation of the quantifiers and modalities, goes by the board: for Hintikka "all" and "exists" do not always have the same semantical force across the sentences of a theory—a point on which he explicitly differs with, for example, Quine. Thus, however—as Quine supportively notes in the passage quoted above—any enduring, absolute (or "objective") sense of necessity and possibility goes by the board. For Hintikka replaces the unrestricted notions of *necessity* and *possibility* with epistemic counterparts, to wit, with the notions of *knowing that* and *knowing who (or what) something is*. On this view, "it is possible that" is replaced by "for all that is known (by A), it is possible that." Quine can wholeheartedly applaud Hintikka's admission that the modalities and propositional attitudes have no acontextual, "objective" metaphysical force. But he cannot do so on grounds that Hintikka could possibly accept. For Quine's whole philosophy of logic is designed to preserve the ideal of a univocal, acontextual interpretation of language, a "system of the world" to which our theories, ideally, commit themselves. Like Frege, Quine is an "actualist," brooking no serious (scientific) use of the notion of *a possible world*.

Performance, action, successful inquiry—these are, then, the basic metaphors and concepts of Hintikka's vision, the basic notions in terms of which he understands the logic of statements, as well as the history and nature of philosophy as a whole. For Quine, contexts of modality and propositional attitude are too contextually sensitive, too opaque, and should hence be left out of pure logic altogether. Quine could write that "'Know' is like 'big': useful and unobjectionable in the vernacular where we acquiesce in vagueness, but unsuited to technical use because of lacking a precise boundary."[24] For Hintikka, the logic of "it is known that" must be mastered, localized to the state of information available to a particular inquirer at a particular point in a particular process of inquiry and its contextual sensitivity made primary for logic, shedding light across the board on all fundamental logical distinctions. Like Quine, Hintikka considers it folly to attempt to include explicit analyses or definitions of "knowledge" and "belief" in one's general theory of inquiry. Ironically, Hintikka's is a formalized theory of inquiry *without* any (absolute or generally applicable) notions of *knowledge, belief, justification,* or *information.*[25] He rejects, however, Quine's skeptical analogy between these notions and indexicals and demonstratives. Instead, like Austin, Hintikka takes the notion of *knowledge* to be connected with evaluative, action-oriented investigations *in situ,* evincing structure of an interesting, systematic kind. That structure is in no way exhausted by the approach of rational choice theory,[26] but is spelled out in the formal articulation of Hintikka's interrogative model of inquiry.

Armed with this aerial snapshot of Hintikka's place within recent philosophy, let us turn to a case study in Hintikkean history of philosophy. My focus shall be Hintikka's interpretation of the traditional Ontological Argument for God's existence, but before we examine that treatment we must understand why it matters to him. For Hintikka it is a case study demonstrating how the Frege-Russell treatment of Logic can (and has) distorted our understanding of the history of philosophy. A perspective on history that does not anachronistically or dogmatically assume that the Frege-Russell philosophy of logic is correct yields a more subtle understanding of history, on Hintikka's view, because it does not import into our assessment of earlier historical contexts distinctions that would have been alien to earlier philosophers' way of thinking. But Hintikka hopes for more; he hopes that if we consider these figures in the light of his alternative contemporary analysis of logic, this may point us toward a better understanding of the intrinsic limitations of the Frege-Russell conception of logic, and of the philosophical virtues of his alternative proposal. He is using history to further his own point of view, and to condemn Frege's and Russell's as partial and limited. This means that he practices history as rational reconstruction, picking and choosing from his predecessors just those ideas that he thinks are correct, and openly condemning those ideas that do not fit in with his own overarching scheme. He is a strong reader in Harold Bloom's sense. This is precisely why, if one wishes to understand his overall perspective, it is especially crucial to examine his historical work.

2. Hintikka on Frege and Russell (I): The "Ambiguity Thesis" about "Is"

Let us first revisit the modern logical context within which the Ontological Argument has come to be placed. From the standpoint of Frege-Russell logic (treated as one "logic" and restricted to its first-order portion) the Ontological Argument—along with most other traditional questions about Being—turns on a series of conflations among different uses of "is." As Bill Clinton rightly said, "it depends on what 'is' is." However self-serving, Clinton's point was logically impeccable, as present-day notational distinctions display. For in present-day logical notation we sharply distinguish between at least four fundamentally different uses of the word:

(a) Predication	Venus is a planet.	Pv
(b) Identity	Venus is Phospherus.	$v = p$
(c) Existence	Humans are (exist).	$(\exists x)Hx$
	Venus is (exists).	$(\exists x)(x = v)$[27]
(d) Subordination	A whale is a mammal.	$(x)(Wx \supset Mx)$

In this notation, the surface appearance of "is" does not find a constant notational correlate; its paraphrase is dependent upon its particular use. As a consequence there is no uniformity to the grammatical (notational) lens we apply to the traditional copula. Instead, the verb "to be" is subject to a contextual analysis, an analysis wholly dependent upon and designed to isolate and explicate its precise contribution to the deductive role of the sentence in which it appears.

This contrasts with analyses given in traditional syllogistic logic, even if it has been customary at least since Aristotle to note the ways in which the verb "to be" equivocates in different contexts of use. For in logic before Frege, a quantificational conception of generality was absent. The forms of judgment were construed as analogous in terms of their root subject-predicate structure, "S is P," even those handled in the theory of syllogisms. The content of "An A is a B" (subordination) is thereby assimilated to "A is" (existence) and to "This A is a B" (predication). Even the limiting case of content, "A is A" (or any instance of the so-called Law of Identity), was not sharply distinguished.[28] On this view the logical differences among uses of the verb for *Being* are driven by the nature of the specific terms filled in for the subject and the predicate, but singular and general terms are still conceived in a parallel way. Identity is treated as a limiting case of predication and inclusion. This is of course quite different from the post-Frege-Russell analysis of identity statements, in which "A is A" is treated with a distinct symbol, "=," interpreted as a term denoting a purely logical relation of (strictly numerical) identity. Grammatically speaking the "is" of identity can occur *only* between singular terms: "="cannot not be placed on a single continuum, as traditionally it had been, with subordination.[29] And thus, in terms of this large historical perspective, it is intrinsic to Frege's and Russell's quantificational analysis of identity to differentiate sharply in the notation between singular terms and predicates.[30] This is connected with the fact that their logic, unlike traditional syllogistic logic, is capable of presenting instantiation of quantifiers, the move from particular (e.g., "Fb") to general (e.g., "($\exists$x)Fx") and capable as well of expressing multiple generality and inferences concerning relations.

So much Hintikka will fully accept: he has written that "instantiation rules are the secret of the systematic logic of quantification."[31] Yet he ardently rejects the usual post-Fregean understanding of instantiation, the formal interplay between names and variables. Frege and Russell conceived the fundamental logical distinction to be that between function and argument, and so, as we have seen, does Hintikka. Each takes this language to be inspired by the modern mathematical notation "$f(x) = y$." But each reads this notation in a distinctive way. For Hintikka, Frege's and Russell's reading of "=" is far too Procrustean. For him, Frege and Russell did not take seriously enough the mathematician's original intuitive notion of a function as marking the *dependence* of one value on another. In casting all equalities, whether mathematical or not, as assertions of numerical identity, neither Frege nor Russell left room for a primitive notion of *dependence* of the kind Hintikka champions. Of course, to take such a notion as logically fundamental is to reject the usual conception of how identity is to be conceived. And Hintikka has become more and more open about his rejection of this as time has gone on, more and more strident in his insistence that we must not too sharply separate between numerical identity and our working, epistemologically sensitive apparatus of individuation *via* predication—an apparatus, as we have seen, that he regards as fully Logical, and not merely epistemological.

Here is where Hintikka's reading of history enters, at least rhetorically, into the heart of his philosophy. By generalizing his notion of *functional dependence* to all the most basic logical notions—including identity—Hintikka takes himself to have reunified the workings of the verb "to be" under a single banner, thus imitating the uniformity of the logicians' traditional (pre-Fregean) grammatical lens. Indeed, Hintikka regards as a signal achievement his ability to recover, grammatically speaking, the unity of template characteristic of pre-Fregean formal logic. On his view, "is" always means the same, but is subject to different uses: identity, inclusion, existence, and predication are seen to lie on a continuum reflected in the uniform grammar of all statements. A correct analysis, according to Hintikka, should therefore adhere to the traditional idea that *Being* is a simple notion, though subject to different uses.

Thus, on the view of his "game-theoretic semantics," there is a parallel between the grammatical divisibility of all the traditional forms of declarative statement, for they all may be said to instantiate "the same" form, viz.,

$$X \text{ is} - a(n) \ Y - \text{who } Z - W.$$

In "Socrates is mortal" (predication), the parts "X" and "Y" are used. In "Socrates is the teacher of Plato" (identity), "X" and "W" alone are used. In "Socrates is" (or "philosophers are (exist)"), "X" alone is used, and in "All philosophers are wise" (subordination), "X" is universally quantified (with "every") in relation to (every) "Y". The formal semantics of this scheme have been investigated by Hintikka at great length; the details need not occupy us here. The important point is to see how Hintikka aims to argue within the terms of his framework that a correct analysis of "is" should adhere to the traditional idea of the copula as a unifying participle of the sentence—that is to say, how he tries to use an appeal to the historical tradition to picture Frege and Russell as outlanders among the pioneers of Logic at the end of the nineteenth century.

In some essays Hintikka has been inclined to speak of the "relativity" of logical analyses, holding that there is no clear reason for preferring the Frege-Russell philosophy of logic to his.[32] Yet in other works, and increasingly as time has worn on, this pluralistic tone has given way to an uncompromising insistence on the correctness of his own point of view. This is largely because problem after problem in what came to be thought of as standard philosophy of language seems to Hintikka to vanish in the face of his recasting of the grammar of sentences. Furthermore, his alternative IF world came to seem to him more and more fruitful in generating questions and answers. Contemporary problems with the semantics of identity statements, proper names, truth and existence claims came to appear to Hintikka more and more like misbegotten pseudo-problems thrown up by the limitations of Frege's and Russell's analyses. From his present point of view, the Frege-Russell logic is but an expressive fragment of Logic in which one may express only linear series of quantificational dependencies. And for Hintikka, expressive flexibility at the level of the individual sentence is all in philosophy of logic; he is willing to overturn basic understandings of the variable, of identity, of negation, and otherwise unquestioned assumptions about what we mean by a logical deduction in order to enrich it.[33] Hintikka always stresses the expressive (as opposed to formal deductive) power, at the level of the sentence and of the theory as a whole, that comes from his dependence-friendly point of view. He seems proudest of having at least presented an *alternative* to present-day logic, and to have suggested by its means some novel solutions to outstanding philosophical questions. Yet fundamentally the appeal of his alternative lies, as I have said, in its way of reuniting him, at least verbally, with the past.

The rhetoric of his attack on Frege and Russell turns on his attributing to them (what he calls) an erroneous "ambiguity" thesis about the verb "to be," a thesis that, he claims, sets them apart from all logicians who preceded them.[34] The thesis, as I understand it, is a thesis about meaning, namely, that the verb "to be," or "is," is lexically ambiguous, like the English words "bank" and "dive." In general, of course, the different meanings of such words have no systematic logical interconnections among them, and it seems to be part of Hintikka's intent to accuse Frege and Russell of surrendering a properly unified logical conception of how the copula works. Hintikka objects that no logician before Frege and Russell ever insisted on a difference of *meaning* between the "is" of identity and the "is" of predication. Instead, logicians appreciated—rightly, on Hintikka's view—that "is" always "means the same," though it is "subject to different uses" and has differing "force," depending upon the particular context in which it appears.[35]

Russell did broach talk of meaning when he wrote of the "terribly ambiguous" character of "is."[36] This notion of ambiguity can seem misleading: there is, first, the difficulty that no one has ever produced a lexically ambiguous sentence containing the verb "to be," whereas it seems intrinsic to the lexical ambiguity of most ordinary nouns that they be able to produce ambiguous, grammatically correct sentences ("What a dive!!!" or "The bank is up high above the river").[37] But the real difficulty does not concern our notion of *lexical ambiguity*. Our difficulty is that if one rests satisfied with mention of lexical ambiguity alone, one seems vastly to underestimate the most important feature of the quantificational analysis itself, viz., the systematic logical interconnections among the different uses of the verb "to be."

Hintikka's charge is, however, difficult to pin squarely upon either Frege or Russell, who certainly understood the logical interconnections among these different uses. Perhaps Hintikka's remarks on the ambiguity thesis ought best to be read as pointing out a weakness in Russell's broaching talk of meaning in the first place. Hintikka's attribution of this thesis is, in fact, especially tendentious in the case of Frege, who by Hintikka's own lights explicitly eschewed any semantical perspective from which he might pronounce generally on features of words such as lexical ambiguity.[38] Moreover, Frege does not hold any lexical ambiguity thesis explicitly. And he would certainly have agreed with what every logician in the tradition granted, namely, that the force of the linguistic appearance of the verb "to be" equivocates depending upon its contextual occurrence in a statement. Fundamentally it is unclear precisely what Hintikka can mean in drawing such a sharp distinction between the (incorrect) thesis that the verb is ambiguous and the (correct) thesis that "is" always "means the same," but is subject "to different uses."

In reality the alleged "ambiguity thesis" is a shorthand, orienting label for Hintikka's expression of his dissatisfaction with Frege's and Russell's entire conception of what Logic is. Hintikka's rhetoric makes it sound as if his own semantical approach is alone in relating these notions to one another in a systematic way, but it would be better to say that his way of conceiving the formalization of the systematic interplay is just different from Frege's and Russell's. What we have is a difference in overarching perspective, rather than an isolated disagreement about the ambiguous meaning of a word. Hintikka's whole vision of Logic depends for its cogency upon a conception of the internal contextual relativity of the logico-categorial notions so sharply distinguished within Frege's and Russell's (respective) philosophies of logic.

Yet it is internal to Hintikka's self-conception that we should aim to affiliate ourselves, at least rhetorically, with the pre-Fregean tradition in logic, in which identity, predication, existence, and subordination are treated as lying on a single continuum, distinguished from one another by the particular (relative) character of the terms figuring in the statement. All parties to this dispute agree that it is the logical interplay among the notions of *existence, predication, subordination*, and *identity* that any logical system worthy of scrutiny must make explicit. Where they differ is in the precise distribution of the notions across statements couched in the formal notation. Hintikka, as we shall see, insists on a specific interpretation of the relation between identity claims and predication.

3. HINTIKKA ON FREGE AND RUSSELL (II): THE FAILURE OF THE ONTOLOGICAL ARGUMENT

My aim in this section is to situate Hintikka's analysis of the traditional Ontological Argument for God's existence against the wider background of his philosophy. Hintikka is not an advocate of the Ontological Argument

—he thinks it fails. But the most widely-cited ground given for its failure, since Kant, seems to Hintikka to be ill-formed and misbegotten, an index of lack of logical sharpness. So many different reconstructions of Anselm's Ontological Argument have been put forward since Anselm that an overview of them is quite impossible; it is no part of my plan to try to press the historical accuracies and inaccuracies of Hintikka's reading of it here.

The focus of Hintikka's criticisms has been the idea, originated with Kant, that the Ontological Argument fails because existence is not a predicate. This position was apparently accepted by Frege, who took his own codification of logic to display the sense in which Kant's doctrine is true.[39] And since Frege it has been widely agreed that Kant's slogan that "existence is not a (real) predicate" constitutes a clear, purely logical explication of the failure of the Ontological Argument. It has been widely agreed, in fact, that:

1. Kant's slogan is correct, and is shown to be correct by the Frege-Russell analysis, which draws a sharp distinction between the "is" of existence and the "is" of predication.

2. The principal logical flaw in the ontological argument is best analyzed in terms of its committing its proponents to a denial of Kant's slogan; Kant's critique is best seen as directed at this commitment.

3. Kant and Frege agree on the meaning of Kant's slogan; thus Kant was a precursor of the Frege-Russell ambiguity thesis, at least in his sharply separating the "is" of existence from that of predication. Kant's conception of general logic must therefore be said to be quite modern, and closer to Frege's conception than, e.g., to Aristotle's.

Hintikka rejects all three of these claims. But before we turn to his arguments against them, it will be useful to examine a contemporary analysis of the Ontological Argument that more or less aims to vindicate the above three claims. Michael Dummett's analysis of the Ontological Argument, precisely because it is Fregean in spirit, will serve to illustrate how these claims might fit together.

3.1 Dummett's Analysis of the Ontological Argument

On Dummett's view, the Ontological Argument is schematized thus:[40]

1. The object which is God has the property Φ.

2. Anything that has the property Φ also has the property of existing.

3. God exists.

This reconstruction of the Argument:

(a) Assumes we can use a proper name to pick out a possibly nonexisting object (premise 1).

(b) Uses existence as a (first-level) concept true of objects (premise 2, conclusion).

(c) Does not assume the Argument uses irreducibly modal notions.

For Frege premise (b) represents an intrinsic barrier to this argument's success, for it is simply nonsensical. It pretends to attach the notion of *existence* directly to an object, rather than attributing it via a concept, presupposing that this attachment can be in itself informative in a substantial way. Frege's universalist view was that Logic, a maximally general science, presupposes that the singular terms we use are not empty, that they have meaning. For him singular existential judgments such as "Socrates exists" or "Socrates is" are otiose, and in so being, grammatically illegitimate. What content could they express, he asked, except to call attention to the fact that a name, "Socrates," has significance? Thus for Frege the fact that his notation cannot obviously express such singular existence claims leaves no logically interesting content out of account.

But it has seemed to many, both before and after Frege, that singular existence claims make perfect sense: can it not be informative to learn that a name has or does not have reference? Must we not be able meaningfully to deny that a name has reference? Though he is a Fregean, Dummett does not wish to proscribe such singular assertions. So he at least partially endorses an idea framed (though ultimately rejected) by Frege himself, namely, that "Venus exists (is)" may be said to be expressed by "$(\exists x)(x = $ Venus)."[41] Thus may singular existence be asserted or denied.

As for fictional discourse, Dummett endorses Frege's account of it in terms of a notion of *sense*, building on work of Gareth Evans. Like Kant, Frege refused to grant that modal notions such as *possibility* and *necessity* make an unambiguous, systematic logical contribution to the content of judgments. And Frege did not countenance alternative (possible) universes of discourse, much less genuine quantification over unactualized possibilities: he insisted upon a univocal understanding of the application of the quantifier, and a univocal understanding of assertion as acknowledgment of the True. In fictional contexts he regarded language as operating on a different level, in which the references of terms became their ordinary senses. Dummett, following Frege and Evans, urges that fictional claims of existence be relegated to "make-believe" uses of language, a Fregean doctrine of *sense* spelling out a notion of significance for such discourse.

Dummett's analysis of the Ontological Argument proceeds, then, without any appeal to modal notions in spelling out Anselm's reasoning.

3.2 Hintikka's Analysis of the Ontological Argument

In contrast to Frege and Dummett, Hintikka claims to be able to make perfect sense of the notion of *an existentially greatest being*, hence, of existence as a property and a legitimate first-level concept. The Ontological Argument fails, according to his analysis of it, but not because "existence is not a predicate"—for on Hintikka's view, existence *can* be expressed in predication (see section 3.3 below for an explanation).[42] Instead, as Hintikka sees it the Argument turns on a confusion about the necessary existence of such a greatest being. In brief, it equivocates on a modal operator switch of quantifiers—a contextualist fault of "dependence."

Thus, unlike Dummett, Hintikka takes modal notions to be intrinsic to the Ontological Argument. His analysis turns on a contrast he draws—using "N" for the necessity operator—between

(1) $N(\exists x)[(y)(y \text{ exists} \supset x \text{ exists})]$

which is, Hintikka argues, trivially or tautologically true—since necessarily, for anything that exists, we can find something that exists, if only it itself—and

(2) $(\exists x)N[(y)(y \text{ exists} \supset x \text{ exists})]$

a much stronger claim. Hintikka takes (2) rather than (1) to be the aim of advocates of the Ontological Argument, for it asserts that there exists at least one individual that exists in all worlds in which anything at all exists. (1) is not strong enough to prove (2), for from the assumption that in each possible world in which anything at all exists, there is some existentially greatest being, it does not follow that in every possible world the said being is always the same. If an advocate of the Ontological Argument tries to divide the problem in two, by arguing first, that there must be at least one existentially greatest being and second, that there is only one such being, then Hintikka will respond that the first task is trivial, and the second indefensible.

Hintikka's diagnosis of the Argument's failure in terms of an unjustified operator switch sheds some light on the traditional language in which the Ontological Argument was cast, though it glosses over certain distinctions that are, logically speaking, fundamental. Nowadays one would naturally distinguish between a concept of God as a *maximal* and God as a *greatest* being. The two notions coincide only if the relation under discussion is assumed to be a linear ordering; if it is not, then there may be more than one maximal being. Such a notion of maximality seems to me better to fit Anselm's original language of a "being greater than which none can be conceived": Anselm's thought is compatible with God's bearing no relation at all to other elements of the universe. Hintikka explicitly assumes that the being whose existence is to be proved must be unique, in accordance with the traditional idea that Anselm's argument may be taken to be the culmination of a certain conception of monotheism.[43] Of course, his own rendition of the argument's true aim holds that it commits its proponents to the existence of *at least one* being that exists in any possible world in which anything at all exists, and does not rule out that there may be more than one such being. Here he takes himself to be as charitable to the advocates of the Argument as he can be.[44] But his independence-friendly conception of the relation between possible and actual individuals is reflected in the ease with which he moves between the notions of *maximal* and *greatest* in this context.

Hintikka is then suggesting that a sentence such as "there necessarily is some individual which is such that if anything exists, it does" is ambiguous between (1) and (2). We are revealed not to know *who* God is, in a certain sense. For the premise that would be required to prove the stronger claim (2) is, Hintikka points out, the equally strong claim that

(3) $(\exists x) N(g = x)$

i.e., there exists something that is necessarily identical to God, the existentially greatest being. And if we replace the modal operator with the epistemic one (as Hintikka is so often inclined to do), we see that the strong claim requires the premise

(4) $(\exists x) K(g = x)$

i.e., there is something known to be God.[45] Hintikka's own preferred ways of expressing existential commitment and identity figure, not surprisingly, in his analysis of the Argument (see section 3.3 below). But he believes that his analysis alone shows why it is that an "actualist" prejudiced against the reality of possible world talk is so perennially tempted to find something deeply convincing about the Ontological Argument: the "actualist" is, according to Hintikka, unable to recognize the kind of operator switch that Hintikka takes to be essential to the logic of the argument.[46]

On the other hand, we see that absolute construals of the notions of *essence* and of *necessity*, unrestricted by broadly epistemic considerations —construals in which Hintikka has so little faith—are viewed by him as will-o'-the-wisps as far as any charitable reconstruction of Anselm is concerned: he does not depend upon them in his formulation of the argument.[47] There occurs here no purportedly "real" definition of God, as in Dummett's Fregean version of the Argument.

3.3 *Hintikka's Contextual Treatment of Identity and Existence*

For Hintikka our ability to speak meaningfully of nonexistent individuals is fundamental to our ordinary methods of inquiry as they actually apply. And for him Frege's global application of his notion of *Sinn* to fictional discourse, celebrated (with modifications) by Dummett and many others, cannot do justice to the logically fundamental role of such talk. A brief segue into Hintikka's application of his analysis of the modalities to questions of identity and existence will help make his disagreements with a Fregean approach clearer.

In general Hintikka has no need and no room for Frege's doctrine of sense or for any conception according to which fictional names (or sentences employing them) concern a separate, wholly distinct level of meaning. A fortiori he does not need even to consider the epistemic demand that proper names be treated as having genuine reference only when their senses determine their references. Hintikka has ruled out from the start an approach to identity statements and propositional attitude expressions accounting for their cognitive content in terms of the notion of *Sinn*. This is because, even more fundamentally, he has rejected the contemporary logical conception of identity as a relation holding between every object and itself.

Early on Hintikka advocated the development of a "free logic" in which a rule of existential generalization would not be taken to express existential commitment without independent support from an identity claim of the form "$(\exists x)x = a$."[48] Like Dummett and many others, Hintikka was concerned with being able to revise Frege's logic so as to be able to express the non-existence and existence of particular individuals. And Hintikka's free-logic way of handling existential presupposition and commitment gave him not only an expressive solution to this problem, but also a way around difficulties associated with Russell's theory of descriptions as an analysis of nonreferring names. For it bypassed all "descriptive" predicates aside from identity itself. As Hintikka wrote:

> Existence can be a predicate in the sense that it is possible to use a formal expression containing the free individual symbol a as a translation of the phrase 'a exists' [namely, the expression "$(\exists x)(x = a)$"], without running into any logical difficulties. . . . [w]e can now meaningfully deny the existence of individuals; formulas of the form $\neg(\exists x)(x = a)$ are not all disprovable any more. Hence such sentences as 'Homer does not exist' can be translated into

our symbolism without any questionable interpretation of the proper name 'Homer' as a hidden description. If anybody should set up a chain of arguments in order to show the non-existence of Homer, we could hope to translate it into our symbolism without too many clumsy circumlocutions. In this sense, the use of an expression for existence is not only possible but serves a purpose. Existence is, if you want, a predicate definable in terms of the existential quantifier.[49]

Later on Hintikka presented his analysis as a development of Frege:

There is one superficial aspect of Frege's and Russell's formalism which misleadingly encourages the idea that Kant's thesis "existence is not a predicate" is an anticipation of Frege. In the most literal sense, existence is not a predicate for Frege, either, viz. in the sense of being an explicit predicate of individuals. [For Frege] we cannot take a free singular term (Frege's "proper name"), say "b," and go on to assert "b exists." However, this is a merely contingent feature of Frege's notation. What is more, it partially hides one of the most fundamental features of his treatment of existence, viz. that existence is expressed only by the existential quantifier.

In fact, the reason why Frege can get along without a predicate of existence is that he assumes that all proper names (free singular terms) are nonempty. This is reflected by the validity of existential generalization in Frege's system: from any proposition F(b) containing "b" we can infer $(\exists x)Fx$. This obviously presupposes that b exists. If we do not make this assumption, we have to amplify the rule of existential generalization and formulate it as saying that from the two premises

(9)   F(b) and b exists

we may infer

(10) $(\exists x)F(x)$.

From certain eminently natural assumptions one can show . . . that the extra premise "b exists" must be equivalent with

(11) $(\exists x)(b = x)$

We can now see that Frege's distinction [between the 'is' of existence and the other uses of 'is'] does not presuppose that "existence is not a predicate." On the contrary, the full import of Frege's approach cannot be spelled out without a "predicate of existence." Hence Kant's thesis [that existence is not expressed in the real use of a predicate] does not make him into a precursor of Frege and Russell.[50]

So far we see apparent agreement with Dummett on how to express singular existence claims via the use of identity and an associated proper name. Yet this agreement is, in the end, only apparent. Dummett is prepared to countenance that a "free" logic (in which it is not assumed that every term has an actual denotation) might be an improvement over Frege's.[51] Yet, as we have seen, he wishes to retain Frege's idea of sense as (in Dummett's

words) a "semantical feature" of an expression "in virtue of which it contributes to determining the truth or falsity of any sentence in which it
occurs."[52] And a sentence, true or false, expresses a proposition, on his
view. For Dummett, the free logician's assignment of truth values to
sentences containing empty names is "somewhat arbitrary,"[53] for "it must
be in principle possible that the question of existence should be settled,
affirmatively or negatively, to the satisfaction of all."[54] But Hintikka rejects
this demand for semantical determination in the form Dummett understands
it, locating questions of existence within the context of an idealized
inquirer's point of view within a particular game of inquiry or investigative
problem situation. On Hintikka's view, questions of existence are settled
relative to a language whose scope, mode of application, and existential
commitments evolve over time. For Dummett "there *are* no game-
propositions: expressing a proposition in the [hypothetical or make-believe]
game is no more to be described as actually expressing a game-proposition
than eating a mango in a dream is actually eating a dream-mango."[55] But for
Hintikka there *are* no Fregean propositions in Dummett's sense: all there
are are "language-games."

The contrast with much contemporary philosophy of language is stark.
Dummett is inclined to take seriously Evans's suggestion that properly to
understand the content of singular existential claims—including those in
fictional or counterfactual discourse—we should postulate a systematic
global distinction between non-make-believe and make-believe uses of our
terms.[56] Hintikka takes this approach to be, not merely artificial and
unnecessary, but logically misconceived. The notion of a distinct realm of
"make-believe" uses of language is anathema to him, unable to do justice
to the (to Hintikka) very natural idea of a possibly existing object given
through a scenario the inquirer constructs in order to reason.

Yet Hintikka's interpretation of such modal notions is highly contextual, not absolute. For Hintikka, not only does essence never contain
existence, but existence never contains essence. He argues that we ought to
surrender the notion that in order to know *who* someone is we must first
know *that* that someone does or does not exist.[57] More importantly, he
insists that the "who" and the "that" depend upon one another (another
"dependence" metaphor). He takes it to be a deeply embedded feature of
discourse that we are able to consider a merely possible individual and
attribute to it predicates definable only in terms of the actual world, and
then later attribute actual existence to *it* (the very same individual). Such a
view of counterparts seems naturally, and happily from Hintikka's
"dependence-friendly" point of view, to demand an independence-friendly
treatment of modal operators as "backward" looking.[58]

The examples Hintikka adduces to defend the naturalness of his analysis are everyday and ordinary, child-like in their simplicity: an actor may, within the setting of a play or TV show, make a cameo appearance as his actual self; here he speaks the same language to the audience, not a radically different (kind of) language. Hamlet, who is introduced to most of us as a fictional character, is (one and the same as the person) only *later* revealed (to many of us) as (a possible) someone with a real-life (actual) counterpart, that is, as someone such that *he* enjoys the predicate of (actual) existence.

Hintikka fails to see why we should take ourselves to have made a global switch in our (uses of) language when we make the step of identification. He argues that sameness of language is a perfectly coherent and natural assumption here, that there is no need for a sharp logical distinction between the "make-believe" and the "non-make-believe" uses of (the same) language. The point is as if devilishly simple. Not since Derrida has so influential a philosopher deconstructed the notion of "serious" (as opposed to "non-serious" or "make-believe") uses of language.[59]

All this shows how far Hintikka is breaking with currently received logical tradition. His early claims to have analyzed the notion of *existence* in a basically Fregean or even Quinean way, by means of the existential quantifier, tell only part of the story. For Hintikka, the existential presupposition or commitment of using a proper name is multiply context relative, relative to a speaker's use of a sentence at a specific point in a specific argumentative context of inquiry and—even more—within a specific point in the understanding of the sentence itself. This context-dependency undercuts what on Frege's (or Russell's) view was fundamental: the relation between generality and instance, expressed in the (instantial) use of a variable, a relation constrained by the principle of identity (that if a and b coincide, then whatever holds of a also holds of b and vice versa). As Hintikka has been insisting with ever-increasing stridency in recent papers, his position entails a rejection of the post-Fregean conception of identity statements as *logical* identities expressing the co-reference of two otherwise independent, self-sufficient singular terms ("self-sufficient" in the sense that such terms figure in predication as the arguments of functions). He therefore has no need and indeed no room for a notion of Fregean *sense*.

Perhaps, as Wiggins has argued, identity is such a fundamental notion that it can only be elucidated.[60] But Hintikka presses against the limits of such a position, suggesting that what can only be elucidated, in Wiggins' sense, may be no notion worth saving as fundamental to Logic. Hintikka has been glad to point out that there were some after Frege who maintained the traditional division between mathematical equations and logical identities, refusing to accept Frege's logical treatment of the equality sign.[61] These were among an even wider group of philosophers who rejected Frege's distinction between *Sinn* and *Bedeutung* as a misplaced shadow of his talk of concepts and objects, of functions and arguments.[62] Hintikka bemoans the fact that none of these philosophers developed such insights in a suitably systematic fashion, as he has tried to do. But he praises their willingness to break with Frege and Russell.

Unlike any of his analytic predecessors, Hintikka is logicizing notions by breaking down the usual distinctions between logical and nonlogical notions. And thus, despite surface appearances to the contrary, Hintikka cannot enter into the terms in which contemporary philosophers debate Frege's claim that *existence* is a notion that, properly speaking, can only be predicated of a concept, and never of an object. For how we understand such a debate will depend crucially on what we take the basis of the concept/object distinction to be. Hintikka does not have the wherewithal to provide an account of concepts that would engage with Frege's. So much the worse for contemporary philosophy of logic and language, on his view. Hintikka cares little for the rehabilitation of fundamental categorial notions such as *concept*, *object*, and *proposition*, preferring to focus, in developing his theory of inquiry, on more localized categorial notions.[63] He finds Frege's primitive logical notions too few and coarse to be useful at the categorial foundation.[64] This allows him to pose a fascinating and very central question, viz., To what purpose, and on what grounds, should we aim to preserve, update, and make systematic sense of the traditional logical vocabulary Frege felt he had still to maintain ("concept," "object," "extension," and "proposition")? Perhaps, as was already suggested by Wittgenstein and Quine, such notions cannot survive with anything like a systematic usage the advent of modern mathematical logic with its vastly more complex modes of distinction and analysis.

4. HINTIKKA ON KANT

It must be said that the overarching framework that Hintikka brings to bear in his reconstruction of the Ontological Argument bypasses altogether some of Kant's deepest philosophical concerns. We need to appreciate this lack of engagement in order fully to appreciate Hintikka's mind: here as elsewhere, Hintikka picks and chooses what he likes best, and what he leaves behind in Kant is as important as what he chooses to revitalize. In the final sections of this essay, I shall try to characterize the significance of some of his discussions of Kant's philosophy of logic. I shall highlight what

Hintikka has left out of his treatment of Kant's philosophy, hoping to triangulate, by subtraction, some further elements of Hintikka's general philosophical attitude.

4.1 *Hintikka on Being and Existence*

Hintikka can write that it is "time to lay to rest the myth that 'existence is not a predicate',"[65] but nevertheless praise some of Kant's insights. Even if *existence* is, logically speaking, said to be expressed in the use of a genuine predicate, according to Hintikka, that predicate is trivial, legitimizing in general the application of no *other* truly "ampliative" predicates to the thing, beyond its mere existence. Existence cannot, according to Hintikka, be used implicitly or explicitly in the definition of a thing: we do not possess any substantial knowledge of individual essence. This is an unquestionably Kantian aspect of Hintikka's philosophy, closely related to his (and to Kant's) criticisms of the Ontological Argument.[66]

In his precritical *Beweisgrund* (1763) Kant had written the following:

> Take any subject you please, for example, Julius Caesar. Draw up a list of all the predicates which may be thought to belong to him, not excepting even those of space and time. You will quickly see that he can either exist with all these determinations, or not exist at all. The Being who gave existence to the world and to our hero within that world could know every single one of these predicates without exception, and yet still be able to regard him as a merely possible thing which, in the absence of that Being's decision to create him, would not exist.[67]

Kant's most fundamental aim was to deny that the notion of *existence as such* is a notion able to be voiced in a predicate like any other: he is distinguishing God's act of bringing the world into existence, and the order of the world that is brought about. He was careful enough to admit, in the same essay, that on purely grammatical grounds the expression "exists" *can* occur as a predicate in judgments concerning the existence of particular things (as in, e.g., "Immanuel Kant is"). Yet, he insisted, if it does, it is a predicate "not so much of the thing itself as of the thought which one has of the thing . . . it means that the representation is an empirical concept, i.e., it is the representation of an existent thing."[68]

Kant thus was led to distinguish between two uses of the copula "is": the merely "logical" or "relative" ("comparative") use and the "real" or "absolute" ("determining") use. In the former, we "compare" subject and predicate. But no existence claim can follow from merely logical, reflective comparison of the notions (as in, e.g., "God is omnipotent"). In contrast, the absolute use of the copula is one in which existence alone is asserted to hold of a particular individual subject (as in "Immanuel Kant exists"). Kant denies that a merely "logical" ("comparative," "relative") use of the verb "to be" can ever on its own license a logical inference to its "real" ("absolute") use, for there is nothing contradictory in supposing any particular individual not to exist. Differently put, for Kant, as for Hintikka, "real" definitions of individual essence are never able to secure existential commitment, only singular existence claims can. Logically speaking it is this distinction between the "relative" and "absolute" uses of the copula, first voiced in Kant's "New Elucidation,"[69] that forms the heart of his explicit rejection of Descartes's version of the Ontological Argument and provides the basis for his later argument in the *Beweisgrund* and in the first *Critique* (1781/1878) that existence is not a predicate of a thing.[70] In Kant's postcritical philosophy, the merely logical use of the copula is divided into two sorts: if the predicate is already "contained" in the subject term, we regard the judgment as analytic and true. If the predicate goes beyond the subject, the judgment is "ampliative" and hence synthetic. No purely analytic judgment can have existential consequences.

For Hintikka, it is telling that Kant draws his distinction between the "relative" and "absolute" uses of the copula against the background of a unitary notion of the copula's meaning. That meaning, in general, is the simple notion of *Being*. In Hintikka's words, "Kant did not assume the Frege-Russell [ambiguity thesis]."[71] Hence "something subtler was involved [for Kant] than a denial that 'existence is a predicate' in the simplest possible sense of the expression."[72]

Ultimately, as Hintikka sees it, Kant was relying on the quite traditional view, shared by Aristotle, that *Being* is not a predicate that can serve as an ordinary term in a syllogism. Neither Kant nor Aristotle would have accepted an inference of the form

Every B is (i.e., has existence)

Every C is B

Every C is (i.e., exists)

as valid, because they assume that *Being* (hence existence) is not a species of a genus. For Aristotle *Being* cannot be the essence of anything, for it is too general a notion, unrestricted to a particular category or class of *predicabilia*. On this point Kant and Frege explicitly follow Aristotle, holding that *Being* is, as a concept with an unlimited extension, empty and therefore not predicable on its own. As Kant puts it, this "highest" concept is that which is "indeterminate" in all things, and "lacking in content," because content diminishes as the logical *sphaera* of a concept grows, just as when "a leaf of gold stretches it loses in thickness."[73] Frege goes a step further in rejecting the notion of *Being* altogether as a concept. A predicate without content, for Frege, expresses nothing more than a "quasi-concept."[74] This seems to confirm Hintikka's sense that Frege is breaking with the tradition on the interpretation of "is": for Aristotle and Kant, "is" denoted a simple concept, whereas Frege denies that we have any such concept at all.

In fact, Hintikka believes that in criticizing the Ontological Argument Kant made a crucial conceptual contribution to the development of logic. In particular, as we have seen, Hintikka is sympathetic to Kant's rejection of the idea that "real" definitions of objects can give us substantial knowledge of individual essence. Traditional syllogistic logicians, as well as proponents of the Ontological Argument, were quite comfortable taking existential commitment to be voiced in the application of a predicate to an individual, so long as that predicate spelled out the essence of the subject term. Thus for Aristotle

Homer is a poet

Homer is

is not valid, because the premise does not give us a definition of Homer's essence, though in a case where we *do* frame an essential predication of an individual, existential commitment trickles downward to the conclusion through the application of the predicate. Kant made a genuine step forward, according to Hintikka, in questioning whether "real" definitions of individuals could ever support existential commitment in this way. This illustrates an indirect contribution that Anselm made to the history of Logic *via* the Ontological Argument. As Hintikka tells this history, only after Anselm had featured existence as one among the (essential) attributes of a Being greater than which none can be conceived was it natural for logicians to focus on the question whether existence *is* an attribute reflected in a predicative use of the copula like any other.[75] In Descartes's version of the Argument, the question of whether existence could be part of the essential definition of an individual object becomes explicit. This opened the way for Kant to distinguish between predication and existence in his rejection of the Ontological Argument: Kant rejects Descartes's assumption that essential definitions of individuals can contain existential consequences.[76]

Of course, we must note here that Hintikka's own preferred way of expressing existential commitment is tied, not to a definition of an individual by way of properties, but to an identity claim involving only a proper name. And also we should note that the situation is different, according to Hintikka, with "real" definitions of properties or kind words. These, he believes, can have substantial, ampliative consequences vis-à-vis existence. Here he takes himself to be breaking with Kant and siding with Aristotle. For Aristotle, when the major term in a syllogism voices the most general categorial principle of a subject kind or a part of science, existential commitment may form part and parcel of a deductive inference, as in this syllogism:[77]

Every B is (an existing) A

Every C is B

Every C is (an existing) A

For Hintikka this gives a clue as to the right way of conceiving the role of general assumptions in scientific Inquiry.

Thus for Hintikka, once Kant had separated predication and existence, he left early nineteenth-century thinkers with a problem: Where was existential commitment to be explicitly lodged in the representation of deductive inferences?[78] As Hintikka sees it, Kant overreacted in emptying general (deductive) logic of all synthetic and ampliative power, in calling it "analytic." For Hintikka, as we know, formal logic is ampliative in several different senses, once the quantifier's fruitfulness is systematically understood. At the same time, Kant's rejection of the expression of *existence* in a predicate, coupled with his insistence on the analyticity (lack of existential import) of pure (general) logic, had the distinct advantage of leaving utterly to the side, as "an orphan," how it was that the formal logician was to voice existential commitment in the context of a syllogistically developed science.[79] The solution—to lodge existential force in the particular judgment "Some A's are B's"—eluded Kant, according to Hintikka. But at least Kant provided a problem-context within which Peirce and Frege could provide a solution, with their innovation of the existential quantifier.[80]

Moreover, by Hintikka's lights Kant was on legitimate ground in holding that *syllogistic* logic is analytic:

> [In holding that existence is not a predicate] Kant is not only rejecting the view that existence can serve as an independent syllogistic term. . . . He was also denying that the idea of existence can be part of the force of a syllogistic term, in other words, that it adds something to concepts, presumably including the major terms of syllogisms, when conjoined with them. In other words, proper syllogisms cannot carry any existential force of the kind explained [as in Aristotle].[81]

Kant's mistake, as Hintikka sees it, was to overgeneralize from the syllogistic logic of his day: that logic, which is essentially "monadic" (without multiple generality expressed), is indeed "analytic" for Hintikka. But with the modern quantifier, "syntheticity" is produced through the expression of multiple generality, and hence, "dependent" constructions ("choices") of individuals in existential instantiation. Existential import cannot be banished from the content of general logical principles, on this view. Thus, Hintikka argues,

> I think it is the time to lay to rest the myth that "existence is not a predicate." It is embarrassingly clear what Kant's grounds for maintaining this thesis were. They were largely due to the paucity of the logics and languages he was contemplating. He envisaged only two types of judgment relevant here, viz., what I shall call here judgments of "essential" predication and judgments of existence. . . . In the former, exemplified by "God is omnipotent," a necessary connection is asserted to obtain between the subject and the predicate, without prejudicing the existence of either. . . . The other kind of judgment Kant mentions is the existential one, e.g., "God exists." In neither one is existence a predicate, Kant says in effect. A judgment of essential predication has no existential force, whereas in an existential one we take a subject as it were all ready-made with its essential predicates and simply assert that this particular complex of predicates is in fact instantiated in reality. Here existence is not one of the configuration of predicates; it is what is asserted of the configuration.[82]

At the same time, Hintikka complains, "Where contingent predication was supposed to find a niche was not explained by the good Immanuel."[83] This charge is unfair to the good Immanuel, as I shall explain in section 4.2 below. But it is significant that Hintikka makes it. For Hintikka, the price of an insistence on the global analyticity of formal logic is one's having to abandon the idea that we apply formal logic directly in our efforts to obtain knowledge of nature. This leaves Logic with only a negative role of logic as a canon, rather than an organon—just as the postcritical Kant insisted. And this is not a view that Hintikka can, in general, accept: his own theory of inquiry everywhere turns on such applications.[84]

4.2 *Kant on Contingent Predication*

As Hintikka is fully aware, Kant did not rest with an account of general logic, but developed transcendental logic precisely in order to try to capture the synthetically fruitful uses of logic in the sphere of scientific inquiry. In transcendental logic, Kant argued, we do gain substantial, synthetic knowledge through general principles laying out our concept of an object (of human knowledge) in general. Thus, for example, it is one of the first general principles of science, according to Kant, that for every event there is some cause or other. This is a piece of synthetic a priori knowledge in which the predicate goes beyond the subject concept and determines it via a universal categorial principle of science. Here the existence of at least some universally applicable laws governing all objects of possible experience *is* something we can infer from pure transcendental logic alone. For Aristotle, the particular judgment "Some A's are B's" does not always express existential force: whether it does so or not depends upon the place of the claim among the premises of arguments given in a syllogistically developed science.[85] Kant would have fully agreed. For him, as for Aristotle, judgments of the form "Some A's are B's" and "Every A is a B" *do* sometimes express existential force through predication, namely, when they are tied in with the premises of arguments given in a syllogistically developed science, and ideally with the universal categorial principles of a science. *Pace* Hintikka, then, Kant was not objecting to Aristotle's image of fruitful syllogisms *überhaupt*. He viewed *transcendental* logic as a fruitful science in application to the phenomenal world.

In fact, ideally, for Kant, just as for Aristotle, the force of *all* the existential assumptions of a science are vested in general premises about its particular kind of objects, or, at least, in the universality of these premises applications to their objects.[86] This comes out perhaps most vividly in Kant's third *Critique*, the *Critique of Judgment*,[87] a work on which Hintikka has not, so far as I know, ever commented.

In the introductions to the third *Critique* Kant investigates the structure of *Urteilskraft*, the human power of judgment. This is for him our capacity to make sagacious contingent judgments about nature, including those which draw empirical generalizations about kinds of object and the laws governing them. Kant concedes to Hume that we have no a priori guarantee that the generalizations we draw will in the long run fit together into a unity, or even that the empirical concepts we devise will hold up forever. It is perfectly possible, so far as our concept of Nature goes, that nature's most fundamental universal laws will lie forever beyond human reach, and that nature could be for us a "crude, chaotic aggregate."[88] Nevertheless, Hume's correct insistence that induction cannot be converted into (a priori) deduction only brings out the importance of our fundamental assumption that we possess the capacity for judgment, for sagacious exercise of our powers of knowing. What we concoct and apply are rules of epistemological thumb, and we must learn to apply these rules with discernment. For this we use what Kant calls "reflective" ("comparative") judgment constructively, making limited generalizations where we can find them—generalizations that may well depend upon prior empirical generalizations we have made—always aiming where we can at a unity and systematicity in our overall theory of nature. We must in the end relegate to the status of a regulative ideal the image of the total unity of experience derived from a small number of fundamental, universal principles. But on the basis of our ability to use reflective judgment in the unification of individual existence claims within a general conceptual structure, our generalizations can have genuine existential import: in Kant's phrase, our empirical conceptual generalizations are "empirical," just as are our singular existence claims about (concepts of) individuals when we make a "real" use of the copula.

This account of contingent predication and of scientific inquiry is in certain respects closer to Aristotle's than to Hume's. Indeed, Kant is a precursor of Hintikka in thinking that we should jettison the Humean empiricist model and return to something more like Aristotle's picture of inquiry. On that picture, the existential assumptions of a science are vested in its generic (categorial) premises. These are never absolutely universal, for Aristotle, but are always restricted to a particular kind of object.[89] For Kant, the fundamental principles of science are universal for objects in the phenomenal world. It is true that Kant is more of an empiricist than Aristotle when it comes to specific empirical classifications that group objects as to their particular individual structure. As Kant sees it, we are never in possession of the specification of laws derived from the universal principles. So the existential commitments of our available scientific theories are held tentatively, for the moment, in light of what reflective judgment can construct. But this fits in with Hintikka's reading of Aristotle as well. For both Aristotle and Kant, as for Hintikka, the picture is that in inquiry we begin with an hypothesis of limited generality and then test to see how far it holds up. Nature is assumed from the outset to have given us some meaningful empirical generalizations. We are thus in practice never faced with the Humean situation in which we are expected to be able to draw absolutely universal generalizations *ab initio* from a finite stock of particular (atomic) premises that have been obtained independently of any prior commitments to empirical classification. On this picture the force of existence claims is always categorially structured and is framed within the context of a syllogistic development of a specific part of science.[90]

Of course, Kant's Newtonian (Maupertuisian) ideal of nature being governed by a small number of universally applicable laws is hardly Aristotelian. It is hardly Hintikkean either. Hintikka's model of inquiry surrenders this ideal of unity for logic, for mathematics, and for empirical science generally as a *necessary* ideal. He believes that the Euclidean axiomatic tradition has for too long been badly misused as a model, in both logic and in philosophy. Moreover, Hintikka cannot accept Kant's empiricism. Kant's regulative ideal of the systematicity of Nature is for

Hintikka, in the end, just an empty fiction insofar as it remains nothing more than a limiting ideal forever beyond our reach.

4.3 *Kant's Critique of the Notions of Existence and Possibility*

I have so far argued that Hintikka's rejection of Kant's critique of formal (general) logic leads him to downplay Kant's more constructive theory of transcendental logic, a theory which should be in broad outline acceptable to Hintikka insofar as it is, at least to a certain extent, a "logic" of inquiry. But in the end Kant's motives in critiquing the application of formal logic in metaphysics are motives Hintikka cannot share. Perhaps this can best be brought out by revisiting the philosophical and historical context in which Kant's rejection of the Ontological Argument is embedded.

Kant's explicit criticism of the Ontological Argument proceeds as if it turns on purely logical considerations, on relatively straightforward logico-grammatical analysis of existence claims. But this way of advancing his critique is misleading in the context of his postcritical philosophy. In fact Kant's logical distinction between "relative" and "absolute" uses of the copula was originally drawn, as I have said, in his precritical phase, in his 1755 essay. But Kant's attitude toward purely logical distinctions, and also his attitude toward proofs of God's existence, evolved greatly over time. In the postcritical period, Kant's view centered, most fundamentally, on his critique of the transcendent, that is, on his exploration of how and why human beings are driven, *despite* the logical flaws in the philosophical arguments, to know and to claim the existence of God. Kant's famed post-critical answer is that it is human Reason's internal drive toward what he calls "the Unconditioned"—toward totality, completeness, and ultimate systematicity in human knowledge—that generates the impulse to an idea of God in the first place. This drive is reflected in what the later Kant came to see as a pernicious form of metaphysical rationalism. For every ground or principle given, Reason demands another ground to be given for that ground. We are, on Kant's view, humanly unable to complete this regress of grounds. Yet the demand for the regress is internal to our capacity for Reason itself. And thus are naturally produced unrestricted Ideas of totality—of God, the World, and the Soul—as a kind of imaginary focus for our Reason. Collectively these Ideas aim at a unity of what is and what ought to be, of theoretical and practical reason, of happiness and virtue, what Kant sometimes calls the unity of Reason.[91] This ideal, however, carries within it the innate human tendency toward fanaticism and dogmatism, from which only skepticism and misology are bound to result.

Precisely in order that our most ultimate demands achieve a positive orienting use, Kant insists on a "critique": Reason itself must curb its own application of its ideals, showing that they cannot be applied directly within the realm of human experience. Reason's ideals—including the ideal of an ultimately unified syllogistically developed science—have only an indirect regulative use. Their legitimate application within the empirical realm requires an ineliminable use of judgment.

Kant's postcritical "transcendental logic," the synthetic a priori part of our knowledge, was designed precisely in order to curb the excesses of those who claim to found metaphysics on principles of pure logic alone. Transcendental logic is restricted in application to our humanly conditioned forms of possible experience. Unrestricted knowledge of the true essences of things-in-themselves—including *existence* and *possibility* as such—is, for Kant, humanly impossible. Accordingly Kant tries to expose a deep ambiguity at work in our most natural ways of thinking about basic metaphysical notions like *substance, causality, possibility, necessity,* and *existence.* On the one hand, there is the conception of these notions applied to things-in-themselves, apart from their human conditions of application. This conception is inherently dialectical, according to Kant, giving rise to hopeless metaphysical perplexity. On the other hand there is a conception of these notions as given through their applications within the realm of possible human experience, subject to the categorial laws of human understanding. This conception forms the basis for metaphysics as a possible branch of knowledge.

In the first *Critique* Kant's purely logical critique of Anselm's argument pushed this wider, diagnostic part of his vision into the background; as did the purely logical analyses of the Argument we have considered by Frege, Hintikka, and Dummett. To dispense with Anselm by maintaining that "existence" is (or is not) a predicate is to ignore those aspects of Anselm's argument that have been taken by many to break or render problematic our understanding of the limits of logic, the limits of understanding, and/or the limits of being. These aspects are, for another longstanding tradition that partly includes Kant himself, absolutely central. Anselm may best be read as insisting upon the riddle-like quality of our very notion of *understanding who God is.* Hintikka acknowledges this, but does not make it central to his understanding of the Ontological Argument.[92] He does not, for example, take the argument to threaten the rule-governedness of our grasp on its grammar, of our very notions of *object, understanding,* and *Being* as such.[93] Yet the centrality to Kant of the elusiveness and illusoriness of these notions—as well as the notions of *possibility, existence,* and *reality*—cannot be overemphasized. Kant's major philosophical move was to draw a sharp contrast between the notion of *object* conceived absolutely (as *noumenon* or thing-in-itself) and the notion of *object* conceived relative to human powers of cognition (as *phenomenon*). His aim was to read off from the contrast a particular conception of human knowledge and value as given through critical struggle, through continual efforts to reconcile ourselves to pursuing goodness and knowledge in a world in which the hope of gaining total knowledge is vanishing but eternal. For Kant, knowledge and freedom are realized, if at all, only partially, and only contingent upon the successful exercise of human judgment, a capacity that is not a gift of pure Reason (or pure logic) alone.

Thus when Kant hived the notion of *existence* off from predication, it was for more than one reason, and not for the sake of logic alone. This may be seen by considering Kant's own development. Following Leibniz, the early Kant held to the idea that though the existence of the world as such is contingent, its order is intrinsic to it, hence necessary. The notion of *existence* is naturally relegated, on any such view, to a distinctive conceptual status of its own, attached to God's act of will in bringing the world as such into being. That there is any Being at all, hence any *existence* of anything *as* anything, ultimately depends, in this picture, upon God's creative act. It is not for Kant *logically* inconsistent for nothing ever to have been anything at all.

Hintikka claims that the perennial conceptual appeal of the Ontological Argument should be surrendered in the face of his analysis of the argument's assumptions, which include a logical rendering of the modal notions. Any remaining appeal to the argument would then appear to lie in an "actualism" biased against a proper understanding of the modalities. But another aspect of the Argument's perennial seductiveness is, Kant would say, the appeal of an argument that would explain certain forms of skepticism away. First and foremost among questions about *existence* is the wonder that anything or anyone at all *is* (exists, is the case, is *what* it is, is anything at all). This wonder has spawned much philosophy, much theology and much skepticism, both about the world and our ability to make claims about it. It has always been connected with concerns about the limits of sense, of human understanding: it is no accident that Anselm himself first framed his argument as a response to a *fool* who "says in his heart, 'There is no God'" (Psalms 13:1).[94] Wittgenstein described our wonder at existence as such as a prime example of "ethics";[95] for him, it was ultimately connected with the limits of philosophy to argue over questions of absolute value. How things stand or might stand, as a matter of fact, is one thing; that there is any possibility of things standing in any particular way at all is quite another, something beyond the limits of what logic (or perhaps philosophy) alone can argue.[96] The Kantian tradition—to which Wittgenstein belongs at least in this respect—has always retained an interest in charting forms of human illusion, in emphasizing the difficulties human beings have in coming to terms with the limits of knowledge and understanding. This is a project that a purely logical analysis cannot hope to come to terms with.

This point has long (if tacitly) been appreciated. For Hintikka—as for Frege, Quine, Dummett, and many others who followed them in the analytic tradition—the traditional wonder at there being anything at all that is what it is evaporates in the face of logical analysis, and, in particular, in the face of the quantifier. The question becomes a matter of what bound variables range over, existential commitment being revealed in the interplay between quantified variables, the identity sign, and genuinely (for Hintikka, possibly) referring proper names. It is thus granted at the outset that there is no general way that logic can help us to answer the question why something rather than nothing exists, apart from our participation in, and acceptance of, the use of language in which at least some proper names refer—and that is no "justified" "answer" to the Great Riddle of why something rather than nothing exists.

In Kant's Leibnizian era, philosophers were more comfortable stepping in with a bit more to say about this riddle. And it is to Kant's great credit that he persuaded rationalist philosophers in his day to ask themselves whether they could coherently picture the absoluteness of existence and of value in the ways they had pictured them before him. Kant's appreciation of the difficulties was profound partly because he had struggled in his early career to articulate such pictures himself. Though he had rejected the logic of the Ontological Argument already in his 1755 essay, "New Elucidation" (by drawing a sharp distinction between the "absolute" and the "relative" use of the verb "to be"), eight years later in his *Beweisgrund* he argued that God must exist precisely *because* existence is not a mere predicate, precisely *because* we have a notion of *Being* admitting of an *absolute* use, and no merely "logical" or "relative" use. In a move anticipating his post-critical attitude, he sharply distinguished between the notions of *logical possibility* and *real possibility*. But he then tried to erect a proof of God's existence on the basis of this distinction. He argued as follows:

> *It is absolutely impossible that nothing at all should exist.*
> [T]he complete cancellation of all existence whatever involves no internal contradiction. However, the means by which the material element, the data, of all that is possible is cancelled, is also the means by which all possibility itself is negated. Now, this is effected by the cancellation of all existence. Thus, when all existence is denied, then all possibility is cancelled as well. As a consequence, it is absolutely impossible that nothing at all should exist.[97]

Given that it is impossible that nothing should be, Kant concludes that "*There exists an absolutely necessary being.*"[98]

For Kant at this time the question "Why is there anything at all?" is a meaningful question, but a necessarily closed one, in light of the absolute necessity of the existence of something, in order for anything at all to be really possible—something presupposed in the very asking of the question "Why?" It was left to the postcritical Kant to reject such reasoning on the ground that it pretends that we have a coherent notion of *the sum total of all possibilities*. That Idea, for the postcritical Kant, is a "mere fiction," and it becomes philosophy's primary task to explore the question why it is that human Reason is tempted, perhaps inevitably, to mistake this fiction (however useful) for a fact.[99]

I have already said that Hintikka has never felt the force of skepticism, nor has he been especially interested in charting the limits of sense. The closest he has come to engaging with these more obscure, diagnostic aspects of Kant's philosophy is in his historical treatment of (what Lovejoy called) the Principle of Plenitude, viz., the doctrine that all (genuine) possibilities must in the long run eventually realize themselves.[100] In his usual way (following Lovejoy, though critically), Hintikka treats the principle as a freestanding conceptual doctrine, and asks whether or not Kant subscribed to its truth. Hintikka emphasizes that for Kant the principle is bound up with Kant's attitude toward (in Hintikka's words) "the venerable problem of theodicy."[101] But from Hintikka's point of view, that problem is a function of the logic of Kant's conceptual situation, not a problem about the bounds of sense. When the precritical Kant rejected Leibniz's picture of an array of possible worlds from which God chooses to bring into existence the best, he was forced, according to Hintikka, to say why he was not obliged to subscribe to the Principle of Plenitude: intuitively, this principle seems to leave no way out of the problem of evil short of insisting that on the whole, those evils that God brings into existence as real possibilities form part of a larger, more perfect order.[102] Hintikka construes Kant ultimately to have been driven to restrict the *range* of possibilities in order to solve the problem. By distinguishing between purely intellectual notions and sensible notions, Kant can rightly—from Hintikka's point of view—admit a form of the Principle of Plenitude back into his philosophy, but without the disastrous implications for the problem of evil that might otherwise have resulted from its adoption. Precisely by narrowing down the domain of our humanly applicable notion of *possibility* to those phenomena subject to the (sensible) conditions of possible experience, Kant can maintain that possibility is, though undetermined except as given through these conditions, still a viable philosophical notion. Kant's empiricism drives this restriction.

Hintikka is open about his attraction to the overall thrust of Kant's ideas:[103] as we have seen, he does not himself wish to rely on uncritical, absolute construals of the quantifiers or the modalities. Yet his difficulties with Kant are philosophically decisive. He has no use for Kant's empiricism, for his Humean side, the side by means of which the "restriction" (as Hintikka calls it) of genuine possibility is carried through. And most fundamentally Hintikka has no sympathy with Kant's notion of an Idea of Reason or a *noumenon*. He admits that it is *this* part of Kant's philosophy, and not the mere thesis that existence is not a predicate, that underpins and necessitates Kant's rejection of the Ontological Argument.[104] But unlike Kant he feels no need either to critique or to save a role for an Idea of the Unconditioned. Kant's relegation of an Idea of Reason (such as *God*) to regulative status is a way, for Hintikka, to cast it off into "outer darkness"[105] and not a way, as it was for Kant, to preserve its indirect use in orienting us, and thereby to protect us from both skepticism and from fanaticism.

Kant's restrictions on the notions of *existence, possibility*, and *necessity* are thus fundamentally *qualitative*, not quantitative. This qualitative aspect is, however, pushed to the side in Hintikka's reading of Kant, confirming something I have already said is deeply important in understanding the spirit of Hintikka's philosophy. Hintikka is simply not interested in skepticism: he has never seen it as anything like an inevitable threat. Nor, therefore, is he especially concerned to battle the kind of uncritical rationalism Kant feared would result from the threat of skepticism. For Hintikka such concerns stem fundamentally from an illegitimate perspective on human knowledge claims that we should simply live without.

5. CONCLUSION

Hintikka is fond of quoting Lord Acton's sayings that historians ought to study problems, not periods, and that history is a hanging judge. As I hope I have shown, his treatments of thinkers such as Aristotle, Anselm, Kant, Frege, and Quine use as a conceptual touchstone his own theories of logic and language, gauging the distances and affinities between them and the most influential texts of the past. The kind of conceptual history he practices is not terribly fashionable these days: he brings to bear on historical figures his own *Fragestellung*, and he is not shy about telling us just where he takes Aristotle or Kant or Frege or Quine to have gone wrong in light of (his) modern Logic. This approach might seem marred with *hubris*, as if he dares to put his own conception on a par with Kant's or Aristotle's. It undoubtedly runs the risk of miscasting earlier philosophers' aims by emphasizing certain problems at the expense of others. It may be viewed, ultimately, as irrelevant to the truth of his views. But Hintikka's brand of conceptual history, frankly opinionated and systematically partial though it is, has the great benefit of taking historical texts seriously, of reading them without condescension, to contain lessons for present-day concerns. He never engages in simplistic logic-chopping. On the contrary, he often succeeds in unmasking the naïveté of contemporary historians of philosophy who, enthralled by present-day philosophy of logic, unwittingly impose alien distinctions upon traditional texts.

Writing of the human as burdened with consciousness of history, Nietzsche stressed that in reading history—and the history of philosophy in particular—it is our fate to have to navigate among multiple and competing yet unavoidable intellectual impulses and values, each one of which, too uncritically pursued, will lead us astray. He spoke of a triad of temptations: the *heroizing* "Great Man" impulse that treats everything the most well-known philosophers wrote as perfect, superior, and unalterable; the courageous *critical* impulse that rejects as bunk all that the so-called "great" thinkers had to say; and the *antiquarian*, ecumenical impulse that celebrates all curious oddities of past philosophies as each of equal value.[106] Few contemporary analytic theorists of logic, language, and science care or dare to try to negotiate a subtle compromise with each of these impulses; few remain, as Hintikka does, willing and able to see conversations about the history and development of philosophy as internal to philosophy itself. Hintikka's method has the signal virtue of getting us to look at the entire philosophical tradition—both "analytic" and "continental"—in new ways.[107] On this score, the novelty and idiosyncrasies of his own perspective on logic are a help, not a hindrance. He belies the caricature of the analytic philosopher as willfully ignorant of history. Indeed, his work shows that if we are to grasp the full complexity of present-day philosophical debates about the nature of logic, we cannot lose sight of the ways in which traditional usages cling, sometimes unbeknownst, to our most basic logical notions. When we ask, "What is Logic?," we do not pose a question resolvable by mathematical means alone, but a question mired, inevitably, in a long and vexed history. Nor do we pose a question whose answer may comfortably rest on the utterly unselfevident notion of *self-evidence*. We have no neutral place to stand in answering it apart from our own philosophical habits, our own present conceptions of what Logic is and ought to be. Hintikka's work demonstrates this philosophical point beautifully.

JULIET FLOYD

BOSTON UNIVERSITY
MARCH 2003

I should like to express special gratitude for conversations with Henry Allison, Jan Harald Alnes, Burton Dreben, Peter Hylton, Montgomery Link, Hilary Putnam,

Thomas Ricketts, Camilla Serck-Hanssen, Irving Singer, Hans Sluga, David Wiggins, and especially Akihiro Kanamori, each of whom helped me think more clearly about issues treated here, as well as the audiences at the Norwegian Kant Society 2000, in Oslo, Norway; the Department of Philosophy Colloquium, University of Tromsø, Norway, and the Boston Colloquium for the History and Philosophy of Science. Most of all, of course, I must thank Jaakko Hintikka for his many inspiring philosophical contributions and for the stimulation I have received from my conversations with him over the last dozen years.

NOTES

1. Jaakko Hintikka, "Quine as a Member of the Tradition of the Universality of Language," in *Perspectives on Quine*, ed. R. Barrett and R. Gibson (Oxford: Blackwell, 1990), p. 172.
2. Cf. Jaakko Hintikka, "Parmenides' *Cogito* Argument," *Ancient Philosophy* (Fall 1980): 5–16.
3. See W. V. Quine, "Response to Hintikka," *Revue Internationale de Philosophie* 51 (1997): 567–68.
4. See Jaakko Hintikka, Ilpo Halonen, and Arto Mutanen, "Interrogative Logic as a General Theory of Reasoning," in Jaakko Hintikka, *Inquiry as Inquiry: A Logic of Scientific Discovery, Selected Papers V* (Dordrecht: Kluwer Academic Publishers, 1999), pp. 47–90.
5. See Neil Tennant, "Review of Jaakko Hintikka, *The Principles of Mathematics Revisited*," *Philosophia Mathematica* 6, no. 1 (1998): 90–115.
6. Hintikka, "Quine as a Member of the Tradition of the Universality of Language," p. 171.
7. See Jaakko Hintikka and Merrill Hintikka, *Investigating Wittgenstein* (Oxford: Basil Blackwell, 1986); Jaakko Hintikka, *Ludwig Wittgenstein: Half-Truths and One-and-a-Half-Truths*, *Selected Papers*, vol. 1 (Dordrecht: Kluwer Academic Publishers, 1996).
8. See, e.g., Jaakko Hintikka, *Knowledge and Belief* (Ithaca: Cornell University Press, 1962); *Models for Modalities* (Dordrecht: D. Reidel, 1969), p. vi.
9. See Jaakko Hintikka, "Knowledge Representation and the Interrogative Model of Inquiry," in *Knowledge and Skepticism*, ed. Marjorie Clay and Keith Lehrer (Boulder, Colo.: Westview Press, 1989), pp. 155–83; "Epistemology without Knowledge and without Belief?" (forthcoming).
10. See Hintikka, *Knowledge and Belief*; compare, e.g., Jaakko Hintikka, "'Is', Semantical Games, and Semantical Relativity," *Journal of Philosophical Logic* 8 (1979): 433–68. Reprinted in Jaakko Hintikka, *Selected Papers*, vol. 4, pp. 71–106.
11. Michael Dummett, "What is a Theory of Meaning? II," in *The Seas of Language* (Oxford University Press, 1993), p. 84.
12. See Hilary Putnam, "Skepticism, Stroud and the Contextuality of

Knowledge" in *Philosophical Explorations*, vol. 4, no. 1 (2001): 2–16; compare Charles Travis, *The Uses of Sense* (Oxford, 1989) and *Unshadowed Thought: Representation in Thought and Language* (Cambridge, Mass.: Harvard University Press, 2000).

13. See Hintikka, *Knowledge and Belief.*

14. See Jaakko Hintikka, "Who Has Kidnapped the Notion of Information?" (forthcoming).

15. See Jaakko Hintikka, "The Concept of Induction in the Light of the Interrogative Approach to Inquiry," in *Inquiry as Inquiry: Toward a Logic of Scientific Discovery* (Dordrecht: Kluwer Academic Publishers, 1999), pp. 161–81.

16. See Jaakko Hintikka, "The Theory-Ladenness of Intuitions," in *Logique en perspective: Mélanges offerts à Paul Gochet*, ed. François Beets and Éric Gillet (Bruxelles: Ouisia, 2000), pp. 259–87.

17. See Jaakko Hintikka: "The Cartesian *cogito*, Epistemic Logic and Neuroscience: Some Surprising Interrelations," in *The Logic of Epistemology and the Epistemology of Logic*, ed. J. Hintikka and M. Hintikka (Dordrecht: Kluwer Academic, 1989), pp. 113–36; "Knowledge Representation and the Interrogative Model of Inquiry," pp. 155–83; "Cogito, Ergo Quis Est?" *Revue Internationale de Philosophie* 1, no. 195 (1996): 5–21; and "Perspectival Identification, Demonstratives and 'Small Worlds'," in Jaakko Hintikka, *Paradigms for Language Theory and Other Essays, Selected Papers* IV (Dordrecht: Kluwer Academic Publishers, 1998), pp. 219–49 (Appears also in *Synthese* 114, no.2 (1998): 203–232.).

18. Hintikka's attitude toward modal logic and its uses in analyzing the modalities metaphysically, logically, and in the semantics of natural language has met vehement resistance in certain contemporary circles. Readers interested in untangling the issues should consult J. H. Fetzer and P. W. Humphreys, eds., *Varia, With a Symposium on The New Theory of Reference*, special issue of *Synthese*, vol. 104, no. 2 (1995); and also J. P. Burgess, "Which Modal Logic is the Right One?" *Notre Dame Journal of Formal Logic* 40 (1999): 81–93, and "Which Models are the Right Ones (for Logical Necessity)?" (forthcoming). Burgess, in particular, sets out a useful framework for thinking through the issue of modeling what he calls "logical" modalities, which he sharply distinguishes from "metaphysical" modalities. Readers of Hintikka should be struck by how far Hintikka's own (in many ways very loose) conception of the "Logical" is from Burgess's.

19. See Jaakko Hintikka, "Gaps in the Great Chain of Being: An Exercise in the Methodology of the History of Ideas," *Proceedings and Addresses of the American Philosophical Association* 49 (1976): 22–38, 28. (Also appears in *Reforging the Great Chain of Being*, ed. S. Knuuttila [Dordrecht: D. Reidel, 1980], pp. 1–17.)

20. W. V. Quine, "Reply to Hintikka," in *The Philosophy of W. V. Quine*, The Library of Living Philosophers, vol. 18, expanded edition, ed. L. E. Hahn and P. A. Schilpp (Chicago, Ill.: Open Court, 1998; 1st ed. 1986), p. 227.

21. Hintikka, *Knowledge and Belief*; Hintikka, Halonen, and Mutanen, "Interrogative Logic as a General Theory of Reasoning." Compare Burton Dreben, "Quine and Wittgenstein: The Odd Couple," in *Wittgenstein and Quine*, ed. R.

Arrington and H.-J. Glock (London: Routledge, 1996), pp. 39–61 on Quine's conception of a sentence.

22. Cf. Jaakko Hintikka, "On the Different Identities of Identity: A Historical and Critical Essay" (forthcoming), pp. 14–15.

23. Hintikka, "Quine as a Member of the Tradition of the Universality of Language"; Jaakko Hintikka, *On Gödel* (Belmont, Calif.: Wadsworth Philosophers Series, 2000), p. 53.

24. W. V. Quinne, "Relativism and Absolutism," *Monist* 67 (1984): 295.

25. Hintikka, "Epistemology without Knowledge and without Belief" (forthcoming).

26. Compare Hintikka, "Who Has Kidnapped the Notion of Information?" and "A Fallacious Fallacy?" *Synthese* 140 (2004): 25–35.

27. Frege did not accept this as a paraphrase of "Venus is," for he rejected as ill-formed all such purportedly singular existential claims. I abstract from this historical point here, but shall return to it below.

28. The fruitfulness of such identities was, however, often doubted. For more on this history, see Burton Dreben and Juliet Floyd, "Tautology: How Not to Use a Word," *Synthese* 87, no. 1 (1991): 23–50.

29. Of course, in set theory membership in the singleton of a, {a}, is, in general, equivalent to identity—so that identity can be defined in terms of membership and singleton. This was done, for example, by Peano. Akihiro Kanamori, in "The Empty Set, the Singleton, and the Ordered Pair" (forthcoming), points out Peano's attention to the surface grammar of the copula in so defining identity: Peano parses the phrase "is equal to" by means of the "is" of subordination (thereby lending the surface grammar of "is" a certain uniform interpretation) and the "equal to" of membership in the singleton.

30. Russell's theory of descriptions, which analyzes away proper names as primitives, does not contradict this: the only way Russell may be said to have promoted an *analysis* of proper names is that he distinguished them in the first place. Of course, the depth of intellectual difficulty involved in settling on a philosophically stable understanding of the respective roles of singular terms and predicates is shown by present-day debates over identity, especially in modal contexts. Perhaps this is not surprising: even from the purely extensional perspective of set theory, a clear distinction between the notions of *membership*, *subordination*, *existence*, and *unit set* arrived surprisingly late, as Kanamori recounts in "The Empty Set, the Singleton, and the Ordered Pair." Compare Hintikka, "How Did Modern Logic Evolve?" (forthcoming), "Epistemology without Knowledge and without Belief?"

31. Hintikka, "How Did Modern Logic Evolve?" p. 11.

32. Such as "'Is', Semantical Games, and Semantical Relativity"; "Semantical Games, the Alleged Ambiguity of 'Is', and Aristotelian Categories," *Synthese* 54 (1983): 443–68.

33. An early indication of this willingness is J. Hintikka, "Identity, Variables and Impredicative Definitions," *Journal of Symbolic Logic* 21 (1956): 225–45,

where he examines the "exclusive" interpretation of quantified variables, derived from Wittgenstein, *Tractatus Logico-Philosophicus*, trans. C. K. Ogden (London: Routledge & Kegan Paul, 1922), in which identity is eliminated as a primitive notion.

34. See Jaakko Hintikka: "'Is', Semantical Games, and Semantical Relativity"; "Frege's Hidden Semantics," *Revue Internationale de Philosophie* 33 (1979): 716–22; "Semantical Games, the Alleged Ambiguity of 'Is', and Aristotelian Categories"; "The Varieties of Being in Aristotle," in *The Logic of Being: Historical Studies*, ed. S. Knuuttila and J. Hintikka, Synthese Historical Library, vol. 28 (Dordrecht and Boston: D. Reidel, 1986), pp. 81–114; "Kant on Existence, Predication, and the Ontological Argument," in *The Logic of Being*, pp. 249–68; "On Aristotle's Notion of Existence," *Review of Metaphysics* 52 (1999): 779–805; "How Did Modern Logic Evolve?"; "On the Different Identities of Identity: A Historical and Critical Essay."

35. See especially Hintikka: "The Varieties of Being in Aristotle"; "Kant on Existence, Predication, and the Ontological Argument"; "How Did Modern Logic Evolve?"

36. See Bertrand Russell, *The Principles of Mathematics* (Cambridge University Press, 1903), p. 64n, (reprinted 1937, London: George Allen and Unwin). The remark occurs in the context of Russell's discussion of the information conveyed in identity statements, a discussion framed by his general notion of a *term*. He cites DeMorgan as a precedent, but in "'Is', Semantical Games, and Semantical Relativity" Hintikka argues that DeMorgan's understanding of the ambiguity is not the same as Russell's. Compare Hintikka, "Semantical Games, the Alleged Ambiguity of 'Is', and Aristotelian Categories."

37. Hintikka, "Semantical Games, the Alleged Ambiguity of 'Is', and Aristotelian Categories."

38. See Hintikka, "Frege's Hidden Semantics."

39. See Gottlob Frege, *The Foundations of Arithmetic*, trans. J. L. Austin (Oxford: Blackwell, 1953), §53; G. Frege, *Collected Papers on Mathematics, Logic, and Philosophy,* ed. B. McGuinness, trans. M. Black, et al. (Oxford: Blackwell, 1984), p. 153n; G. Frege, *Gottlob Frege: Philosophical and Mathematical Correspondence*, ed. G. Gabriel, et.al., trans. H. Kaal (Chicago: University of Chicago, 1980), p. 108; G. Frege, "Frege's *Begriffsschrift* Lectures, Winter semester 1910/11," ed. G. Gabriel, *History and Philosophy of Logic* 17, no. 1 (1996), p. 18.

40. Dummett, "Existence," p. 278.

41. Ibid., p. 283; cf. G. Frege (pre-1884), "Dialogue with Pünjer on Existence," in Frege, *The Foundations of Arithmetic*, pp. 53–67. Frege expressed doubts about the rendering of existence in terms of this ("predicative") use of the identity sign: he felt it necessary to deny that the content of an existential claim could be lodged in the verb alone (i.e., in "exists" or "is") and then predicated contentually of a subject independently conceived (see Frege pre-1884). His primary aim, I take it, was to jettison altogether the lens of the "S is P" template. Frege had to *argue*, as

we today do not, that his existential quantifier may serve adequately to express the traditional particular judgment form.

42. See Hintikka, *Models for Modalities*, and "Kant on Existence, Predication, and the Ontological Argument."

43. Ibid.

44. Hintikka, *Models for Modalities*, p. 45:

> If what we are trying to do is to establish that there exists a unique being "than which nothing greater can be conceived"—in short, a unique supremely perfect Being—surely the great difficulty is to show that there exists *at least one* such being, whereas we can face the problem of uniqueness with relative calm.

45. See Hintikka, "Kant on Existence, Predication, and the Ontological Argument."

46. For Hintikka's criticisms of Gödel along these lines, see his *On Gödel*.

47. Failure to take into account this aspect of Hintikka's larger perspective mars, it seems to me, the criticisms of his treatment of the Ontological Argument offered in James Tomberlin, "A Definition of 'God' Examined," *Sophia* 13 (1974): 30–32; William Vallicella, "A Note on Hintikka's Refutation of the Ontological Argument," *Faith and Philosophy* 6, no. 2 (1989): 215–17; and Graham Oppy, *Ontological Arguments and Belief in God* (Cambridge: Cambridge University Press, 1995).

48. See Hintikka, *Models for Modalities*.

49. Jaakko Hintikka, "Studies in the Logic of Existence and Necessity. I: Existence," *Monist* 50 (1966): 55–76. An updated version is printed in *Models for Modalities* under the title "Existential Presuppositions and Their Elimination," pp. 23–44. Quote is from p. 34.

50. Hintikka, "Kant on Existence, Predication, and the Ontological Argument," in *The Logic of Being*, pp. 259–61.

51. Dummett, "Existence," in the *Seas of Language*, p. 285.

52. Ibid.

53. Ibid., p. 295.

54. Ibid., p. 297.

55. Ibid., p. 304.

56. Ibid., p. 295; compare for a recent (different) development of the same suggestion, R. M. Sainsbury and David Wiggins, "Names, Fictional Names and 'Really'," *Nottingham Joint Session* (1999), pp. 271–86; D. Wiggins, "The Kant-Frege-Russell View of Existence: Toward the Rehabilitation of the Second-Level View," in *Modality, Morality and Belief: Essays for Ruth Barcan Marcus*, ed. W.S. Armstrong, D. Raffman, N. Asher (Cambridge: Cambridge University Press, 2002), pp. 93–113.

57. Hintikka, *Models for Modalities*, p. 49.

58. Hintikka, "Kant on Existence, Predication, and the Ontological Argument," p. 258ff.

59. Hintikka goes so far as to rely on his analysis of existence to explain the

workings of Gödel's arithmetization of syntax, a technique crucial to the proof of the incompleteness theorem. A so-called Gödel sentence may be interpreted either as a purely number-theoretic statement or as a statement about syntax. This has struck some as paradoxical. But on Hintikka's view there is no paradox here, and no "self-reference" of a mysterious kind. Gödel's proof turns, from a purely logical point of view, on nothing more surprising than watching an actor make a cameo appearance as himself on a TV show and speak his mother tongue, or a player in the play turn to the audience and speak to them out of character (*On Gödel*, p. 31ff). This is Hintikka's particular way of deflating the philosophical significance of Gödel's theorem, and denying that it turns on any kind of logical "paradox." It also offers him a way to criticize Gödel for having been too much of an "actualist."

60. David Wiggins, *Sameness and Substance Renewed* (Cambridge: Cambridge University Press, 2002).

61. See Jaakko Hintikka, "On the Different Identities of Identity" (forthcoming). Among these were the early Wittgenstein and A. N. Whitehead, according to Hintikka.

62. Among this group are to be counted Russell and Frank Ramsey.

63. This does not mean that he shies away from offering an interpretation of Frege's notion of *concept* in which Frege is held to have deliberately rejected the notion of an *arbitrary function* in his understanding of the second-order quantifier (J. Hintikka, and G. Sandu, "The Skeleton in Frege's Cupboard: The Standard versus Nonstandard Distinction," *Journal of Philosophy* 89 [1992]: 290–315). This reading of Frege's concept/object distinction has met with resistance from careful readers of Frege and historians of set theory: historically and philosophically, the situation is far less clear than Hintikka and Sandu make it sound. See J. P. Burgess, "Hintikka *et* Sandu *versus* Frege *in re* Arbitrary Functions," *Philosophia Mathematica* 3, no. 1 (1993): 50–65; William Demopoulos and J. L. Bell, "Frege's Theory of Concepts and Objects and the Interpretation of Second-order Logic," *Philosophia Mathematica* 3, no. 1 (1993): 139–56; R. G. Heck Jr. and J. Stanley, "Reply to Hintikka and Sandu: Frege and Second-Order Logic," *Journal of Philosophy* 90, no. 8 (1993): 416–24. This is an important index, it seems to me, of the polemical/philosophical picture lying behind their historical work.

64. Hintikka, "Frege's Hidden Semantics," p. 722.

65. Hintikka, "Kant on Existence, Predication, and the Ontological Argument," p. 253.

66. Starting as he does with the assumption that knowledge of "real" identity is possible, Wiggins leaves this rather crucial point out of account when he lays at Hintikka's feet the doctrine that (real) identity can be "reduced somehow to other properties and relations" (*Sameness and Substance Renewed*, p. 183). Wiggins is not especially concerned, as I am here, to give a proper exposition of Hintikka's philosophy of logic. But it is quite clear that Hintikka would reject both of the empiricistic ideas Wiggins suggests lie at the root of the (alleged) doctrine: (1) the worry that identity is not observable and (2) that identity is inscrutable *except* as resemblance. Hintikka's rejection of "real" essence turns on his rejection of the

Frege-Russell suggestion about how to read "=". This is a rejection of something fundamental to their conception of logic, as Hintikka is admitting more and more freely of late. It has nothing to do with empiricism, which Hintikka roundly rejects.

67. Immanuel Kant (1763), "The Only Possible Argument in Support of a Demonstration of the Existence of God," in *Kants Gesammelte Schriften*: vol. 1–22, Preussische Akademie der Wissenschaften; vol. 23, Deutsche Akademie der Wissenschaften zu Berlin; vol. 24, Akademie der Wissenschaften zu Göttingen (Berlin: Reimer, 1900– [reprinted Dordrecht: Walter de Gruyter & Co., 1979–]); and Kant, *Theoretical Philosophy*, trans., ed., D. Walford, F. Meerbote (Cambridge: Cambridge University Press, 1992), pp. 107–202. Hereafter references to the *Akademie* edition will be abbreviated AA (*Akademie Ausgabe*), followed by volume and page numbers. The extract mentioned here is AA 2:72.

68. Kant, AA 2:72.

69. Kant (1755), "A New Elucidation of the First Principles of Metaphysical Cognition," in *Theoretical Philosophy*, pp. 1–46. Page references are to vol. 1 of Kant 1900–.

70. I. Kant (1763), "The Only Possible Argument" in Kant 1900–, vol. 1, pp. 71ff; and I. Kant (1781/1787), *Kritik der Reinen Vernunft*, in Kant 1900–, 1st ed., A 598/B 626 [("A" page number) vol. 4, second edition ("B" page number) vol. 3].

71. Hintikka, "Kant on Existence, Predication, and the Ontological Argument," p. 258.

72. Hintikka, "On Aristotle's Notion of Existence," p. 790.

73. I. Kant (early 1770s), "Blomberg Logic," in Kant 1900–, vol. 24, pp. 7–301, translation in Kant, *Lectures on Logic*, trans., ed., J. Michael Young (Cambridge: Cambridge University Press, 1992), pp. 5–250. Page references are to Kant 1900–, pp. 911–12.

74. Frege, "Dialogue with Pünjer on Existence." See Leila Haaparanta, *Frege's Doctrine of Being, Acta Philsophica Fennica*, vol. 39 (Helsinki, 1985) for a lengthy discussion.

75. See Jaakko Hintikka, "How Did Modern Logic Evolve?" (forthcoming).

76. Ibid., p. 12.

77. Frege appears to be following this tradition when he writes:

> But if the content of what is predicated in the judgement 'Men exist' does not lie in the 'exist', where then does it lie? I answer: in the form of the particular judgement. Every particular judgement is an existential judgement that can be converted into the 'there is' form. E.g. 'Some bodies are light' is the same as 'there are light bodies'. . . . It becomes more difficult if we try to put 'There are men' into the form of a particular judgement. If we define man = rational living being, we may say 'Some living beings are rational' and, assuming the definition to be correct, this means the same as 'there are men'.
>
> This recourse is only open to us when the concept can be analysed into two characteristic marks. E.g. if we have to convert 'There are negroes', we may say that negro = negro that is a human, because the

concept 'negro' is subordinate to the concept 'human'. . . . But this works only in the particular case of the concept 'negro'. For 'There are birches' we should have to select a different superordinate concept, such as 'tree'. (Frege, "Dialogue with Pünjer on Existence," p. 63)

78. Assuming that it *was* so to be lodged—which is, of course, an assumption that is, perhaps, anachronistic with respect to syllogistic logic.

79. Hintikka, "How Did Modern Logic Evolve?" p. 12.

80. Cf. Hintikka, "Kant on Existence, Predication, and the Ontological Argument," "How Did Modern Logic Evolve?"

81. Hintikka, "On Aristotle's Notion of Existence," p. 789.

82. Hintikka, "Kant on Existence, Predication, and the Ontological Argument," pp. 253–54.

83. Ibid., p. 254.

84. Cf. Jaakko Hintikka, *Logic, Language-Games, and Information: Kantian Themes in the Philosophy of Logic* (Oxford: Oxford University Press, 1973).

85. See Hintikka, "On Aristotle's Notion of Existence" and "On the Different Identities of Identity."

86. Cf. Hintikka, "On Aristotle's Notion of Existence," p. 797.

87. I. Kant (1790), *Kritik der Urteilskraft*, in AA 5 and (for the First Introduction, unpublished) in AA 20. References are to this pagination.

88. See Kant (1790), AA 20, p. 209; cf. AA 5, p. 183. For a discussion see J. Floyd, "Heautonomy and the Critique of Sound Judgment: Kant on Reflective Judgment and Systematicity," *Kants Ästhetik/Kant's Aesthetics/ L'Esthétique de Kant*, Herman Parret, Hrsg./ed. (Berlin, New York: Walter de Gruyter Verlag, 1998): 192–218; "The Fact of Judgment: The Kantian response to the Humean Condition," in *From Kant to Davidson: Philosophy and the Idea of the Transcendental*, ed. Jeffrey Malpas (London: Routledge, 2003), pp. 22–47.

89. See Hintikka, "On Aristotle's Notion of Existence."

90. In this account of Kant's theory of science I am leaving to the side Kant's notions of *intuition* and *construction*, which are essential to his account of the syntheticity and existential commitments of mathematics. For a very useful discussion of the relation between Kant's philosophy of logic and his notion of *intuition* in mathematics that is indebted to Hintikka's work on this topic, see Michael Friedman, *Kant and the Exact Sciences* (Cambridge, Mass.: Harvard University Press, 1992), ch. 1. I agree with Friedman that Hintikka's account of existential commitment and of syntheticity through Skolemization of functional terms is somewhat at odds with Kant's conception of categorial construction through a priori intuitions, that is, with Kant's conception of the role of transcendental logic.

91. Susan Neiman, *The Unity of Reason: Rereading Kant* (Oxford: Oxford University Press, 1994) emphasizes this as a central feature of Kant's overarching philosophy.

92. See Hintikka, "Kant on Existence, Predication, and the Ontological Argument," p. 253. Hintikka had written earlier that "the purposes of religious

discourse are not normally defeated by the speaker's failure to know what he is saying in the way the purposes of scientific (factual) discourse are thereby defeated" (*Knowledge and Belief*, p. 100).

93. As do, for example, Karl Barth, 1960, *Anselm: Fides Quaerens Intellectum* (*Faith in Search of Understanding*), trans. Ian W. Robertson (Cleveland: World Publishing Co.); and Cora Diamond, "Riddles and Anselm's Riddle" in *The Realistic Spirit: Wittgenstein, Philosophy, and the Mind* (Cambridge, Mass.: MIT Press, 1991). I take Wittgenstein's explicit discussion of the ontological argument in *Culture and Value*, ed. G. H. von Wright, trans. Peter Winch (Chicago: University of Chicago Press, 1980), p. 82, to stand partly within this tradition. See note 100 below.

94. In his history of the fate of the Ontological Argument in modern philosophy, Dieter Henrich suggests three conditions for the possibility of the Argument's articulation (Henrich, *Der Ontologische Gottesbeweis: Sein Problem und seine Geschichte in der Neuzeit* [Tübingen: J.C.B. Mohr (Paul Siebeck), 1960], pp. 263–64). First, the thought of a first principle of all questions, an ultimate ground for what can be thought, must be framed: a self-sufficient ground that takes care of itself, so to speak, that cannot in turn be taken to be based upon any choice or action or will. Second, the thought of such a principle must also presuppose an "ontological difference" between "What is" (*Wassein*) and "That (what is) is" (*Dassein*), a distinction between fact and principle that the Argument purports to overcome. Finally, the Argument must presuppose the concept of a true essence of things, that it is what it is independently of any subject's cognition of it, but which all the same perfectly coincides with what the subject thinks in thinking it, and which does not wholly outstrip the limits of (human) thought. The Argument, in short, must postulate an absolute limit for Reality and Thought, conceived as a totality of some kind, and then show how our thought of God may coincide with it. God must be *absolutely* total, *absolutely fundamental*, and hence unique.

95. Wittgenstein (1929), "A Lecture on Ethics," in Wittgenstein, *Ludwig Wittgenstein: Philosophical Occasions 1912–1951*, ed. J. Klagge and A. Nordmann (Indianapolis: Hackett Publishing, 1993), pp. 36–44.

96. As I see it, part of Wittgenstein's ethical point in writing the *Tractatus* was to show that there is no purely logical approach to dissolving wonder at existence (or value) as such. In the *Tractatus* the point is marked by the distinction between "the What" and "the How" (1922 3.221, 5.552ff, 6.432ff). "The What," connected with the notions of *object* and *substance*, has to do with the wonder that anything at all is as it is, with the "es" and the "sich verhalten" in "Es verhält sich so." "The How" has to do with how things are, with the "so." That there are objects that are any way at all is part of "the "What"; how things stand is part of "the How." This distinction is adapted from Schopenhauer. In *The World as Will and Representation* "the What" (*das Was*) is connected with things-in-themselves, with the *Ding an sich*, with the Ultimate Ground of Being, or substance as such. "The How" (*das Wie*) is connected with what Schopenhauer calls, after Kant, the phenomenal world, the world subjected to human forms of knowing, with objects inhering in certain

relations to one another—see Schopenhauer (1859), *The World as Will and Representation*, trans. E.F.J. Payne (New York: Dover Publications, 1958), vol. 1, p. 121. Compare note 94 above.

97. Kant, AA 2:79, p. 124.

98. Kant, AA 2:82, p. 127.

99. See Kant (1781/1787) A 324/B 381ff, A 572/B 600ff, especially A 580/B 608; compare G. Buchdahl, *Metaphysics and the Philosophy of Science: The Classical Origins, Descartes to Kant* (Lanham, Md.: University Press of America, 1988), chapter VIII, for a very useful analysis of the *Beweisgrund* essay.

100. Hintikka, "Gaps in the Great Chain of Being."

101. Ibid., p. 292.

102. This is what Kant appears to hold in his 1755 essay (AA 1: 404 and compare Hintikka, "Gaps in the Great Chain of Being").

103. Hintikka, ibid., p. 288.

104. Hintikka, "Kant on Existence, Predication, and the Ontological Argument," p. 262.

105. Ibid.

106. F. Nietzsche (1874), *Unzeitgemässe Betrachtungen,* in English as "On the Uses and Disadvantages of History for Life," in *Untimely Meditations*, trans. R. J. Hollingdale (Cambridge: Cambridge University Press, 1983).

107. Compare Jaakko Hintikka, "Ernst Mach at the Crossroads of Twentieth-Century Philosophy," in *Future Pasts: The Analytic Tradition in Twentieth-Century Philosophy*, ed. J. Floyd and S. Shieh (New York: Oxford University Press, 2001), pp. 81–100.

REPLY TO JULIET FLOYD

Juliet Floyd calls me a "wildly ambitious philosopher." It seems to me that I can return the compliment—which I do take as a compliment. In her contribution, she offers nothing less than an overview of my philosophy, plus an examination of my views on Frege and Russell, on the purported ambiguity of being, on existence, possibility, and identity, as well as on the ontological argument and, as if this were not ambitious enough, on my use of history. I feel more than a little overwhelmed by the rich details of her analysis and comparisons, unable to take up all the interesting points she raises. The best I can do is to describe my reaction to the main points she is making from the perspective of my current ideas.

The first topic will thus be Juliet Floyd's examination of my overall approach to logical studies. She captures very well the overall thrust of my work. I consider it a major shortcoming of logical and epistemological studies in the past and in the present that they have not shown the *raison d'être* of logic for the purpose of argumentation and discovery in general. Sherlock Holmes claimed to have reached his brilliant solutions by means of "logic" and "deductions," and ordinary usage seems to concur. But philosophers have never before offered any real justification for this view. Among other observations, the connection between strategies of deduction and strategies of interrogative discovery that I have pointed out goes a long way towards such a justification and towards a vindication of Floyd's overall perspective on my logical and epistemological work.

In a wider historical perspective Floyd is thus right in saying that for me logic is a general theory of inquiry. But this identity is, strictly speaking, more a happy consilience of different developments in logical and epistemological research than a conscious aim or assumption, even though Floyd may be ultimately right in speaking of a single "vision" underlying these different developments.

Thus I differ from the overall picture Floyd offers in that I consider the epistemological and metaphysical significance of logic as a product of fortunate cooperation of different studies each of which has its own intrinsic nature and independent justification, not a product of a single holistic entity called my Philosophical Logic. For instance, independence-friendly logic has its significance as a way of representing previously inexpressible patterns of dependence and independence between variables. The success of the interrogative approach to inquiry is based on advances in epistemic logic, which again are due to the use of the notion of independence. My primary arguments for the importance of IF logic may be philosophical and historical, but I insist that IF logic has an ample rationale in purely logical and mathematical terms. Admittedly, intriguing connections between IF logic and epistemic logic have come to light. For instance, what I call extended IF logic turns out to be extremely closely related to epistemic logic, but I do not consider epistemic logic as having been "subsumed" under IF first-order logic. I consider it as clarifying to keep the main relevant "language games" sharply separated, viz., on the one hand the "game" of applied first-order logic and on the other hand the "questioning games" of interrogative inquiry. There can even be alternatives to the latter. I have explored tentatively the kinds of language-games of exploration that are in certain respects closest in letter and in spirit to the general ideas of game-theoretical semantics. (See my forthcoming paper "An Epistemology for Game-theoretical Semantics.") While I am glad as a philosopher that Floyd has recognized the connecting links unifying the different lines of thought that I have pursued in logic, foundations of mathematics, and epistemology, as a logician I must distinguish from each other at the very least the project of IF logic and its applications and the project of the interrogative approach of inquiry with its applications and with its backing in epistemic logic.

Furthermore, I would like to insist that the sense of logic in "independence-friendly logic" is logic in quite as pure a sense as the received first-order logic, and not "philosophical logic" in the present sense of this phrase as meaning sundry logical systematizations of the logical behavior of philosophically interesting concepts. I consider this prevalent use of the term "philosophical logic" misleading, not the least because I believe that at this time the most philosophically interesting insights are in the offing in the basic "symbolic" logic than in the misnamed "philosophical logic."

Floyd speaks of how I am striving to "humanize" logic and knowledge. Even with all due attention to the pitfalls of self-knowledge, I would like to think of her attribution as showing impressive sensitivity to my motives. She is apparently also aware of the link between this humanization and

Kant's transcendental stance, which amounts to concentrating on what we humans do to reach our knowledge and what (conceptual) means we need in order to do so. Likewise, Floyd is aware, even though she does not emphasize it, that this attempted humanization does not mean a concession to subjectivity. The main idea by means of which this transcendental stance is implemented is the reconstructed idea of language games. Now language games can be thought of as being played by human beings, as was in fact done by the first thinker to conceptualize our basic logical notions, the quantifiers, in game-theoretical terms. These games are in any implementation "games" of seeking and finding, which obviously are basic, recognizable modes of human behavior.

But saying this is not incompatible with saying that the only things about language-games that matter for logical and semantical purposes (at least as far as the basic abstract meanings of our expressions are concerned) are the rules of these language-games. And they are completely objective, independent of the idiosyncrasies of language users. This illustrates the sense in which the humanization Floyd speaks of does not make logic and semantics subjective in the least.

This objectivity carries over to the conceptualizations that can be thought of as further developments of the same game idea. They include IF logic which results simply from the admission of informational independence into semantical games. Thus I reject lock, stock, and barrel all conventionalism in logic, including all deliberation of the "advantages" and "disadvantages" of different logics.

One of the focal issues in the philosophy of logic that I have taken up is the claim that ordinary-language verbs for being are lexically ambiguous. One of the most important implications of game-theoretical semantics is that this ambiguity assumption is not an unavoidable feature of every correct implementation of our basic logic, which is the logic of quantifiers. Indeed, I have argued in some detail that this ambiguity assumption does not characterize the logical behavior of quantifiers in natural language. I have attributed the ambiguity thesis to Frege and Russell. Floyd nevertheless says that "Frege does not hold any lexical ambiguity thesis explicitly" and that it is "difficult to pin squarely upon either Frege or Russell." But what does it mean in practice to consider a word ambiguous in the first place? The best answer I can think of is that on different occasions such a word has to be translated differently into the right semantical framework, the framework of representation that brings out the true logical form of our sentences. Now there is no doubt whatsoever that Frege and Russell considered their respective logical languages, Frege's "Begriffsschrift" and the symbolism of the *Principia Mathematica*, as being such a codification of the true logical forms of our propositions. And in this framework the verb "to be" is to be expressed differently on the different occasions of its use. In this clear-cut sense verbs for being are unmistakably ambiguous for these logicians and for most of their followers. It seems to me that this translation to a canonical notation is a more important question than whether Frege and Russell said in so many words that "to be" is ambiguous.

Floyd says that on my view "'is' always means 'the same'." Whatever I may have written, my current view of the Frege-Russell ambiguity claim is more agnostic. Floyd is undoubtedly right in considering as the crucial thing here the logical relations between the different uses of "is," even though I am not sure that I understand precisely what these logical relations are supposed to be. For instance, whenever a logician rules out empty singular terms from his or her language, an implication from the predicative "is" to the existential "is" is thereby established. However, I maintain that among the most interesting relations between the different uses of *is* are their logical differences. For instance, identity is always transitive and symmetric whereas predication is neither. It is in fact instructive to see how these differences led Aristotle into difficulties when he tried to use a unified notion of being. Such difficulties might very well be used to argue for a logical distinction between the different uses of "is." Likewise even the usual treatment of first-order logic seems to show that the different uses of "is" are relatively independent of each other. For instance, when existential presuppositions have to be spelled out, existence can be expressed only by means of existential quantifier. All these argue for some kind of logical differences between the different uses of "is." Further thought may very well be needed here.

Floyd has chosen to discuss my views of being and existence by reference to the ontological argument and to what I have said about it. This is in one sense an inspired choice. Several important lines of thought cross each other in this famous argument. Furthermore, I have in fact tried to make several different points about the problematic of the ontological argument. However, I am not sure that these points are the best signposts to my overall views of being and existence. The fault is here squarely mine, for I do not think that I have presented a satisfactory overall interpretation of the argument either systematically or historically. For instance, I have not dealt adequately with Anselm's use of the idea of existence in the mind, which has to be seen in the context of an Aristotelian conception of thinking.

Even though I am far from sure about the overall interpretation of the ontological argument, several specific observations can be made about its problematic. First, Kant's thesis that "existence is not a predicate" has to be understood against the background of Aristotle's treatment of existence in a syllogistic context. There Aristotle treated existence by allowing existence to be sometimes a part of the predicate term of a syllogistic premise. Such a premise might thus have the logical form of either

(1)   every B is an A (existent or not)

or

(2)   every B is an existent A

For Aristotle, existence nevertheless could not alone operate as a predicate, for it is not restricted in any one genus.

Hence, literally speaking Aristotle already maintained that "existence is not a predicate." In fact Kant's real thesis was stronger. As his formulations clearly show, existence could not even be a part of the force of a predicate term. This had the effect of forcing the notion of existence out of all syllogistic contexts. Subsequent logicians found a home for it in the existential quantifier.

In systematic terms, existence can operate as a predicate in intensional contexts as soon as objective criteria of cross-identification are available. One way of seeing this is to go along for a moment with Kripke and to think that names are given a meaning by an act of dubbing. Now we can easily imagine a possible world in which a certain object is given a name in such a way. Since cross-identification is objective, it makes sense to ask whether the object so dubbed exists in the actual world.

It seems that neglect of the realities of cross-identification has played a role in the ontological argument. It is perhaps not difficult to buy an argument to the effect that in each possible world there exists a most perfect being. But whether those beings are (or are not) manifestations of the same being is not obvious—or, rather, is easily seen to be a gratuitous assumption.

The subtlest feature of these problematics is that there are certain assumptions built into the usual first-order logic that tend to encourage the ontological argument. These are illustrated by the logical validity of propositions of the form

(3) $(\exists x)(A[x] \supset (\forall y) A[y])$

which have as their special case the conditional

(4) $(\exists x)((\exists z)(z = x) \supset (\forall y)(\exists z)(z = x))$

which I have discussed and which Floyd comments on. What is interesting about (4) is that it seems to show that there in fact is "an existentially greatest" being. And this result seems to result already from our generally accepted first-order logic without considering any modalities. I suspect that a tacit recognition of the logical truth of (4) has been instrumental in encouraging the acceptance of the ontological argument.

It turns out, however, that this logic should not be generally accepted. In a forthcoming paper "Truth, Negation and other Main Concepts of Logic" I have argued that whenever the basic predicates of an applied first-order logic admit of truth-value gaps, then we must use IF logic rather than the traditional first-order logic. This is the case with the predicate of existence involved in (4). But in IF first-order logic (4) is no longer a logical truth, as can easily be seen. Hence, the discovery of IF logic eliminates what I consider the most serious temptation to accept something like the ontological argument.

J. H.

4

Judson C. Webb

HINTIKKA ON ARISTOTELEAN CONSTRUCTIONS, KANTIAN INTUITIONS, AND PEIRCEAN THEOREMS

What makes the work of Jaakko Hintikka so distinctive if not unique among the major living philosophers is that he has so often applied his own research at the cutting edge of logical theory, philosophy of mathematics, philosophy of language, and analytic epistemology to the interpretation and reconstruction of some of the major themes of the great philosophers of the distant as well as the near past. This historical orientation has resulted, among many other fine things, in a series of substantial papers that examine the conception and role of intuition in other major thinkers, central among which are those presenting Hintikka's well-known but controversial interpretation of Kantian intuitions, which he reconstructs as singular representations resulting from existential instantiations, typically comprising the auxiliary constructions introduced in a Euclidean-style proof. This interpretation is directed against the thesis of Russell that Kant's intuitions essentially served only to compensate for gaps in Euclid's axiomatic system which, once filled by Hilbert's complete set of axioms, no longer needed such intuitions to guide its proofs. Since, however, the key to Hintikka's case against Russell is that he wrongly believed that Kantian intuitions must "lie outside the axiomatic and deductive frameworks" of Euclid's system, a just appreciation of the relative merits of these two interpretations will require not only a careful consideration of Kant's relation to Euclid but also a clear understanding of some essential details of Euclid's geometry itself, including its own historical setting as well as its relation to Hilbert.

Crucial to the historical understanding of Euclid is the vexed question

of the relation of his *Elements* to Aristotle's theory of demonstrative science
on which Hintikka has written extensively and we shall find that much of
this work is not only interesting in its own right but provides a nearly
perfect backdrop for the very appreciation of Kant's own historical context
for which Hintikka has pleaded. In fact, the notion of "ecthesis" goes back
to Aristotle's logic and, as Hintikka has put it, "an attempt to explain and
justify the mathematical ecthesis from an Aristotelian point of view also
easily gives rise to striking anticipations of Kantian doctrine."[1] In particular,
Hintikka has suggested that the connection of Kantian intuitions with their
singularity has its roots in the Aristotelean doctrine that particulars can only
be grasped in perception.

    Central to these analyses is Hintikka's assimilation of the use of
auxiliary constructions to the introduction of ever new constants via
existential instantiation by which he tries to explain, for example, why the
ancient writers found the subject of such constructions so difficult: in view
of the undecidability of first-order logic, it was never possible to predict
effectively how many such auxiliaries might be necessary to prove a given
theorem. It is remarkable how much reconstructive mileage he has gotten
from this and kindred purely metalogical ideas, and nowhere has he applied
it more convincingly than in his analysis of what Peirce called his "most
important discovery," namely, his distinction between truly "theorematic"
reasoning and merely "corollarial" reasoning. We may characterize much
of this work by Hintikka as a logical analysis of intuition and, as such, view
it as a generalization of the "logical analysis of our spatial intuition" that
Hilbert gave in his *Festschrift*—which Hintikka has also analyzed
extensively. The aim of this paper is a critical appreciation of the light that
Hintikka's analyses have thrown and can throw on the role of logic and
intuition in the philosophy of geometry of each of these great figures and
as a further test for them, on Kant's philosophy of time.

    In their classic study of analysis in ancient geometry, Hintikka and
Remes conjectured that the intrinsic difficulty revealed by modern proof
theory of deciding how to rearrange the order of construction steps, when
reversing the order of the steps in an analysis for a synthesis, might explain
the relative insignificance of such "resolutions" in the practice of ancient
geometers such as Pappus. As evidence they cited "the general uneasiness
of ancient geometers *vis-à-vis* the role and justification of auxiliary
constructions," the need for which "puzzled them."[2] Their main example of
such "ambivalence" was Proclus who claimed in his commentary on Euclid
that such constructions were only needed in exceptional cases, since "in
most theorems there is no construction, because the exposition is sufficient,
without the addition of anything else, to prove the proposed conclusion

from the given."[3] Hintikka and Remes attribute "a philosophically motivated suspicion of constructions"[4] deriving from his neoplatonist aversion to genesis in geometry, but they overlook what will be seen below to be a crucial observation of Proclus about constructions in geometry. Hintikka has also argued for Aristotle's own ambivalence about auxiliary constructions stemming from his reservations over the use of ecthesis in logic and the problem of incontinence in logic.[5]

Aristotle held logical inferences to be psychologically necessary inasmuch as whenever both premises of a syllogism are present in the soul, "the soul must . . . affirm the conclusion."[6] Hintikka argues that this is only plausible for arguments which are analytic in the sense of being surface tautologies, but that their alleged necessity vanishes when existential instantiations are needed, for "if we have to do something ourselves before we can draw the conclusion, namely, to introduce new auxiliary individuals into the argument, then the drawing of the conclusion cannot be necessary in the sense that one cannot avoid drawing it."[7] Hintikka claims that the "setting out" procedure of ecthesis employed by Aristotle in his logic closely approximates the rule of existential instantiation and that "it is not impossible that Aristotle connected this logical procedure with the *ecthesis* of the geometers which he also knew and commented on."[8] He stresses Aristotle's awareness of the importance of auxiliary constructions evinced in his claim concerning the proof of the angle-sum theorem by means of an auxiliary parallel that "it is by actualization also that geometrical relations are discovered; for it is by dividing the given figures that people discover them. If they had been already divided, the relations would have been obvious; but as it is the divisions are present only potentially" (*Metaphysics* 1051a21–24).[9]

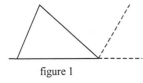

figure 1

Hintikka associates this insight with his own rejection of a subjective explanation of our frequent failure to perceive the conclusions of logical arguments:

> This failure may be due to the perfectly objective fact that the argument can only be carried out in terms of further geometrical objects which simply are not there in the given figure, but which have to be introduced by a preparatory construction. Aristotle may have been unduly optimistic when he claimed that geometrical propositions are obvious as soon as the right constructions have been made. He displayed his usual shrewdness, however, in refraining from making any claim of this sort *before* the appropriate constructions had been discovered and executed.[10]

Nevertheless Hintikka believes that Aristotle was just as "suspicious" of the need of auxiliary constructions as Proclus, citing as evidence Aristotle's claim about ecthesis in *Prior Analytics* that "we use the process of setting out terms like perception by sense, in the interest of the student—not as though it were impossible to demonstrate without them, as it is to demonstrate without the premises of the deduction" (50a1–4).[11] But any ambivalence Aristotle felt about constructions in geometry was inevitable before the kind of proofs found by Hilbert and others that certain constructions are or are not eliminable from the proofs of various theorems. Two examples should make this clear.

The first example concerns the reducibility of *reductio ad absurdum* proofs to "universal deductions in the first figure," by which every syllogism can be perfected. Aristotle's example is the proof that "the diagonal of the square is incommensurate with the side, because odd numbers are equal to evens if it is supposed to be commensurate" (*Prior Analytics* 41a25–27). Such an argument succeeds in "proving something impossible by means of [the] hypothesis conceded at the beginning" (41a31–32), but Aristotle believes it to be reducible to universal proofs in the first figure. Indeed, "in every deduction . . . universality must be present" (41b6–7), since otherwise deduction is either impossible, irrelevant to the proposed subject, or will beg the original question. His example is the proof of Thales's theorem on the equality of the base angles of an isosceles triangle invoking an elaborate auxiliary construction which, Aristotle emphasizes, depends on universal assumptions, e.g., the equality of all "angles of semicircles."[12] This complicated proof of a simple theorem stands in striking contrast to the relatively simple proof Aristotle describes for the far more complicated theorem of the incommensurability of the diagonal and side of a square. How could the proof of such an obvious theorem about a triangle require not only an auxiliary circle but obscurely understood "angles between straight and curved lines" as well? Looking at an isosceles triangle the first thing one sees is the equality of its base

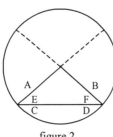

figure 2

angles—without looking at anything *but* the triangle. Aristotle would never have said of *this* theorem that if only the circle had already been drawn it would have been obvious! Why is such a contraption necessary? Looking at a square one could never *see* that however finely we divide the side into units, the diagonal could never be measured by an integral number of them. Only our intellect can prove this impossibility, which elicits initial wonder from everyone, says Aristotle, "for it seems wonderful to all men who have not yet perceived the explanation that there is a thing which cannot be measured even by the smallest unit" (*Metaphysics* 983a16–18).

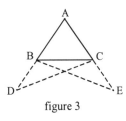

figure 3

The career of Thales's theorem helps explain the attitudes of Pappus and Proclus. In a proof unknown to Aristotle, Euclid eliminates the use of angles in a semicircle by extending the equal sides of an isosceles triangle by an equal amount, joining the endpoints of these extensions to its vertices, and applying his SAS-congruence theorem to the triangles *ABE* and *ACD* (figure 3). One may ask if even this auxiliary construction is necessary, and in analyzing Euclid's proof of his congruence theorem Proclus finds the key to a still simpler proof of Thales's theorem, found by Pappus, using no construction at all. Euclid used his "common notion" that "things which coincide with one another are equal to one another," but to do so he has to "apply" one triangle to another and must invoke, as Proclus points out, the *converse* of this notion: that two equal triangles can be made to coincide. Whereas such "application" will later be seen to presuppose a rigid motion, Proclus says that "visible equality . . . in things of the same form is manifestly the ground of the entire proof."[13] Still, he agrees with Carpus who, anticipating this later understanding, says that Euclid "in a sense takes the same triangle as lying in different places."[14] Proclus notes that "this is the simplest and most fundamental of the theorems (for it is demonstrated without artifice from the primary notions alone)."[15] This explains how Pappus could prove Thales's theorem without *any* construction: given an isosceles triangle *ABC*, says Proclus, "let us think of this triangle as two triangles and reason thus: Since *AB* is equal to *AC* and *AC* is equal to *AB*, the two sides of *AB* and *AC* are equal to the two sides of *AC* and *AB*, and the angle *BAC* is equal to the angle *CAB* (for they are the same); therefore, all the corresponding parts are equal, *BC* to *CB*, the triangle *ABC* to the triangle *ACB*, and angle *ACB* to angle *ABC*."[16] Proclus remarks that "it looks as if he discovered this method of proof when he noted that in the fourth theorem it was by uniting the two triangles so that they coincide with each other, thus making them one instead of two, that the author of the *Elements* perceived their equality in all respects. In the same way, then, it is possible for us, by assumption, to see two triangles in this single one and so prove the equality of the angles at the base."[17] We now describe this "method of proof" as a rigid reflection in space, and indeed one sees that in Euclid's own proof the triangles *ACD* and *ABE* can only be made to coincide by such reflection since they are of opposite orientation.[18] No one with

Proclus's awareness of such *elimination* of auxiliary constructions from the proof of a basic theorem can be blamed for envisaging their dispensability generally: they are out of place in a proof of the basic congruence theorem and possibly eliminable from the proof of any theorem depending solely on congruence.

Aristotle never mentions congruence or the elimination of constructions, so any belief he had that they were avoidable would have stemmed from his hope that all geometrical proofs could be recast in his syllogistic.[19] His apparent exclusion of motion from geometry is taken by some to reflect his acquiescence in Plato's scorn for "the absurd language of geometers" who speak "as if they were doing something and as if all their words were directed toward action. For all their talk is of *squaring* and *applying* and *adding* and the like, whereas in fact the real object of the entire study is pure knowledge."[20] Yet his invocation in *Metaphysics* at 1051a of the geometer's actualization of potential constructions suggests that Aristotle rejected Plato's posit of eternal geometric objects independent of the geometer's activity.[21] But if, as Hintikka argues, Aristotle lies in Euclid's trajectory, why does he never mention congruence, the basic relation of geometry, the theory of *measure*?

According to Aristotle "measure is that by which quantity is known." But "knowledge also, and perception, we call the measure of things, for the same reason, because we know something by them—while as a matter of fact they are measured rather than measure other things. But it is with us as if some one else measured us and we came to know how big we are by seeing that he applied the cubit-measure a certain number of times to us" (*Metaphysics* 1053a31–35). Aristotle would agree with Proclus that our knowledge that an object was one cubit long depends on the "visible equality" of the object and the cubit-measure, that is, the perception that their endpoints coincide when the latter is applied to it. Measuring by the application of a cubit-rule r is a case of Euclid's common notion that "things which coincide with one another are equal." If we want to know if objects s and t are equal: apply s to t and if they coincide, sCt for short, we pronounce them equal. If s and t are far apart we may apply r first to s and then to t, and if we find that rCs and rCt, we commonly infer that s and t are equal. This assumes the transitivity of equality formulated in Euclid's common notion that "things which are equal to the same thing are equal to each other," which together with common notion 4 implies the transitivity of "coincides with." This depends on the rigid mobility of r: even if rCs and rCt, we might not have sCt if r shrank in transport from s to t.

To minimize appeals to superposition, Euclid only uses his coincidence notion to prove the congruence of triangles: to lay off a segment equal to a given segment or cut off smaller ones from it, he gives "constructions" appealing to his circle postulate "to describe a circle with any center and radius." Euclid does not explain how to "describe" a circle, a void Proclus fills by claiming that "if we think of a finite line as having one extremity stationary and the other moving about this stationary point, we shall have produced the third postulate; for the stationary point will be the center and the straight line the distance."[22] While Euclid hid this appeal to motion behind his term "describe," he could not do so in the congruence theorem. This bears on Hintikka's thesis of ancient ambivalence over geometric constructions. The lack of clarity about congruence made it seem that more auxiliary constructions were required than were really necessary, so that anyone who notices their eliminability from any proof was bound to question their necessity. The language of "drawing," "describing," and "producing" in Euclid's construction postulates also obscured the status of his geometry as *mixed* mathematics. His geometry is an *applied* theory: its key common notion, providing an empirical criterion of "coincidence" for the primitive idea of "equal," might be called his "application axiom" since he can only use it by "applying" one figure to another. That it mixes Euclid's geometric language with the physical language of "coincidence" is clear from the conspicuous absence of this term from his definitions, while the term "placed" occurs only in the proof of the congruence theorem to facilitate the use of the coincidence criterion. This common definition of "equal" illustrates Aristotle's tenet that "the principles of demonstrations are definitions" (*Posterior Analytics* 90b25) as well as the "atomic premises" that Hintikka sees as essential to his science: "coincide" and "equal" are too close for the insertion of any middle term between them.

But congruence alone cannot ground the kind of indirect measurement of distance made possible by the theory of parallels, and Hintikka has argued in a classic paper that this side of Euclid's geometry, with its commitment to infinite space, is incompatible with Aristotle's finite cosmos and theory of potential infinity.[23] His main thesis is that Aristotle's rejection of actual in favor of potential infinity was not intended to deny the actualization of a possibility, and hence not meant to deny the principle of plenitude which Hintikka is at pains to show that Aristotle upheld. Our concern is with his argument that Aristotle's account of infinity was irreconcilable with Greek mathematical practice, wherein he motivated Aristotle's ambivalence over auxiliary constructions, and took a unique position in the controversy over his "prophetic idea" of non-Euclidean geometry.

Aristotle canvassed several reasons for belief in the actual existence of the infinite, including the need for infinite divisibility in mathematics. But "most of all, a reason which is peculiarly appropriate and presents the difficulty that is felt by everybody—not only number but also mathematical magnitudes and what is outside the heaven are supposed to be infinite because they never give out in our thought" (*Physics* 203b22–26). Belief that what is "outside the heaven" is infinite also leads to belief in infinite bodies, which Aristotle purports to disprove. Yet he insists that

> our account does not rob the mathematicians of their science, by disproving the actual existence of the infinite in the direction of increase, in the sense of the untraversable. In point of fact they do not need the infinite and do not use it. They postulate only that a finite straight line may be produced as far as they wish. It is possible to have divided into the same ratio as the largest quantity another magnitude of any size you like. Hence, for the purposes of proof, it will make no difference to them whether the infinite is found among existent magnitudes. (*Physics* 207b27–34)

Hintikka took this to mean that one could always avoid arbitrarily large extensions of straight lines by rescaling the relevant geometrical magnitudes.[24] But this, he claims, depends on the existence of sufficiently small figures similar to any given figure still lacking any axiomatic foundation. Euclid's parallel postulate supplied this but requires the unbounded extendability of straight lines, so Aristotle's account does not "guarantee that the resulting geometry is Euclidean."[25] If his doctrine of maximal spatial extensions is taken literally, says Hintikka, "his physical universe is non-Euclidean: the axiom of parallels is not satisfied in it."[26] Nor can Aristotle's physical universe accommodate all the auxiliary constructions required by Euclid's postulate, leaving us to "doubt whether the indispensability of this postulate was realized in Aristotle's time . . . as clearly as it was realized by Euclid."[27]

If *U* is any circle representing Aristotle's finite universe there will be lines *AC* and *BD* making angles α and β with a transversal less than 2R whose intersection as required by Euclid's postulate only occurs on their extensions "outside the heaven." According to Hintikka, the most that one can say "on Aristotle's principles" is that under these conditions "there is a point *A'* on *AB* sufficiently near *A* such that a parallel to *BD* through *A'* meets *AC* on the side Euclid specifies."[28] Since we can find parallels to *BD* meeting *AC* *within U* only through points *A'* that are close to *A*, Euclid's postulate fails for converging

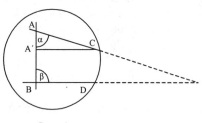

figure 4

lines whose intersections with a transversal are too far apart. This illustrates the "compunctions about geometric constructions" that Hintikka attributes to Aristotle, especially those that "may require the existence of longer lines than any of the ones involved in the given figure."[29] This is how he reads Aristotle's "difficulty that is felt by everybody" that magnitudes "outside the heaven are supposed to be infinite because they never give out in thought." This brings us to Hintikka's analysis of Aristotle's idea of deductive science and its relation to Euclid.

Aristotle identifies magnitudes as the basic genus of mathematics: arithmetic deals with discrete magnitude, geometry with continuous magnitude. They begin with the meaning of their "primitives": for example, "we must assume what a unit or what straight and triangle signify, and that the unit and magnitude *are*; but we must prove that the others are" (*Posterior Analytics* 76a35–36, author's emphasis). Geometry must assume the definition of things "proper" to it, "e.g. that a line is *such and such*, and straight so and so" (76a40–41). But "proper too are the things which are assumed to be, about which the science considers what belongs to them in themselves—as e.g. arithmetic is about units, and geometry is about points and lines. For they assume these to be and to be *this*" (76b3–5). Given Aristotle's maxim that "a science is one if it is of one genus" (87a38), Hintikka proposed that the apex of an Aristotelean science is the assumption of the existence of its genus, thus establishing its "widest term," together with "generic premises" which define narrower terms for species of its genus.[30] So "the existential force is carried downward from wider terms to narrower ones in a sequence of scientific syllogisms. Hence the only ultimate existential assumption needed in a science concerns the existence of the members of the genus which is its subject matter."[31] Dorothea Frede objected that "in cases where you have not one but two or more basic entities which are not subordinate to one another, like the point and line . . . one would wind up with more than one widest, i.e., generic premise."[32] This depends, however, on how Aristotle *would define* points and lines, which he recognized as problematic. Frede thinks an indication of how Aristotle "could have thought to build up a science like geometry" could clarify the matter, but Hintikka replied that his "top down" reconstruction of Aristotle's existence assumptions is dictated by his "syllogistic mold" for a science, stressing that geometrical axioms do not fit into it.[33]

Aristotle identifies an obstacle to treating geometry deductively when he recommends that "you should divide the genus into what is atomic in species—the primitives— . . . then in this way attempt to get definitions of these (e.g. of straight line and circle and right angle)" (*Posterior Analytics*

96b15–19). He knew the difficulty of defining *these* items, having prefaced
his discussion of them at 76b by warning: "It is difficult to be aware of
whether one knows or not. For it is difficult to be aware of whether we
know from the principles of a thing or not—and that is what knowing is"
(76a25–8). Since these "principles" must, Hintikka stresses, be *definitions*,
this difficulty is one of *framing* suitable definitions. Aristotle imposed strict
demands on definitions, as seen from his critique of the definition of a line
as "a length without breadth" (*Topics* 143b11–34). Nor does the Platonic
definition of *straight* line satisfy a modularity condition he imposes:

> Suppose now that a definition has been rendered of some complex, take away
> the account of one of the elements in the complex, and see if the rest of the
> account defines the rest of it: if not, it is clear that neither does the whole
> account define the whole complex. Suppose, e.g., that some one has defined
> a finite straight line as the limit of a finite plane, such that its centre is in a line
> with its extremes; if now the account of a finite line is the limit of a finite
> plane, the rest (viz., "such that its centre is in line with its extremes") ought to
> be an account of *straight*. But an infinite straight line has neither centre nor
> extremes and yet is straight, so that the remainder is not an account of the
> remainder. (*Topics* 148b24–32, my emphasis)

Nor did the current definition of circle satisfy his demand that a definition
of x make possible a proof that x exists.[34] What satisfied Euclid as
definitions of "line" and "straight" did not satisfy Aristotle. But would
Euclid's definition of *parallels* satisfy him?

This is related to the issue of inklings of non-Euclidean geometry in
Aristotle. Hintikka claimed that Aristotle's universe was unwittingly non-
Euclidean: he was unaware that it failed to satisfy the infinitistic Euclidean
assumptions of the geometry he tacitly accepted. He explicitly rejected the
suggestion that Aristotle had a "sort of prophetic idea" of non-Euclidean
geometry which Heath found in his explanation of necessity in
mathematics: "Since a straight line is what it is, it is necessary that the
angles of a triangle should equal two right angles. But not conversely;
though if the angles are *not* equal to two right angles, then the straight line
is not what it is either."[35] Heath took this to mean that, if $\Sigma = 2R$ failed, "the
original assumptions on which the whole of Euclidean geometry is based
must be revised, including the definition, or the generally accepted notion,
of a straight line. It is as if he had a sort of prophetic idea of some geometry
based on other than Euclidean principles such as the modern 'non-
Euclidean' geometries."[36] Far from evincing any such idea, says Hintikka,
"this passage might on the contrary indicate that the role of the axiom of
parallels was not particularly clear to Aristotle." For "Aristotle traces one

of the theorems that turns on the axiom of parallels to the straight line's being 'such as it is' without specifying its nature in any more detail and without mentioning the axiom of parallels."[37] But some find better evidence of Aristotle's inkling of non-Euclidean geometry in passages not mentioned by Hintikka. These are best read in light of the connections discerned by Ross between 1051a22–27 (*Metaphysics*) on auxiliary constructions, 48a31–9 (*Prior Analytics*) on middle terms for geometrical theorems, and 200a16–19 (*Physics*) itself that shed light on Aristotle's view of the nature of straight lines, as well as his "syllogistic mold."

Ross noted that when Aristotle claims at 200a that $\Sigma = 2R$ holds necessarily if the straight line "is what it is," he means the proof in 1051a where he asks, "Why are the angles of a triangle equal to two right angles? Because the angles about a point are equal to two right angles. If then the line parallel to the side had already been drawn, the theorem would have been evident to anyone as soon as he saw the figure." It is the fact that a straight line makes "about a point" of intersection with another line, angles adding up to $2R$ that, in light of the auxiliary parallel, explains why $\Sigma = 2R$, and whose proof, says Ross, "depends on the understanding of the nature of the straight line."[38] The supplementary angles "about a point" sum to $2R$ because the straight line "is what it is." It is such a complex of words as "figure which has its angles equal to the angles about a point," says Ross, that Aristotle intends when he explains why the middle term for a demonstration cannot always be an individual word by reference to this very theorem:

> Let A stand for two right angles, B for triangle, C for isosceles triangle. A then belongs to C because of B; but A belongs to B not in virtue of anything else (for the triangle in virtue of its own nature contains two right angles); consequently there will be no middle term for AB, although it is demonstrable. For it is clear that the middle must not always be assumed to be an individual thing, but sometimes a phrase, as happens in the case mentioned. (*Prior Analytics* 48a31–39)

$\Sigma = 2R$ follows quasi-syllogistically from

(1) The angle sum of every triangle is equal to that of a figure having its angles equal to the angles about a point.

(2) Any figure having angles equal to the angles about a point has angles equal to $2R$.

To prove (1), however, one must construct a parallel to a side and invoke the equality of alternate angles, and according to Aristotle, *geometers who draw such parallels actually beg the question.* We beg the question, says Aristotle, when we prove A by B and B by C in cases where it is natural to prove C by A, since we are then proving A by means of itself: "This is what those persons do who suppose that they are constructing parallel lines; for they fail to see that they are assuming facts impossible to demonstrate unless the parallels exist. So it turns out that those who reason thus merely say a particular thing is, if it is: in this way everything will be known by means of itself. But that is impossible" (*Prior Analytics* 65a4–8). This remarkable passage raises two questions: (i) what *kind* of fallacy is begging the question for Aristotle, a logical one of a mistaken inference, or one of epistemic logic? and (ii) what question *were* geometers begging?

Hintikka answers (i) in terms of his interrogative model of an Aristotelean science, a key idea of which is that its first premises are discovered "by means of a kind of interrogative process."[39] He reconstructs the Aristotelean fallacies within the framework of dialogical games, wherein

> the aim of the entire game can be to answer a "big" initial or principal question; on the other hand, this "big" question is to be answered by means of a number of replies to "small" questions the Inquirer puts to his or her interlocutor. If a distinction between the two is not maintained, one can try to trivialize the entire questioning procedure by posing the "big" question to the Answerer without further ado. If a conclusive answer is forthcoming, the entire game is reduced to a single move.[40]

Hintikka analyzes Aristotle's idea that begging the question results in accepting something "known by means of itself" in terms of an interrogative game in which the inquirer is allowed to pose tautological questions of the form "$S \vee -S$." Aristotle was not pointing to any kind of mistaken inference, claims Hintikka, who suggests that

> a proposition's, say S's, being knowable through itself can be taken to amount to its being knowable as an answer to the question "S or not S?", while its not being knowable through itself means that answers to *other* questions are needed to come to know it. Indeed, this way of reading Aristotle lends his words a much better sense than on the assumption that he is thinking of coming to know S through an inference. For to infer S from S is not even to do anything.[41]

A crucial fact about Hintikka's games, which makes this interpretation so interesting, is that while such tautological statements cannot increase the deductive consequences of given premises, they *do* increase their interrogative consequences, a consequence of Gentzen's *Hauptsatz* establishing the eliminability of "cut rules" from deductive logical proofs which violate the subformula principle. The use of tautologies of the form $S \vee -S$ is typical of such rules. Hintikka admits that "Aristotle never points out in so many words the role of tautological premises (14.4) in questioning. His remarks on *petitio principi* nevertheless show amply his sensitivity to the issues. . . . Even if he did not anticipate Gentzen's problem, he came remarkably close to it."[42] We will study Hintikka's model after we address question (ii) which he does not discuss.

What "fact" T did Aristotle think constructors of parallels presupposed that could only be proved if "parallels exist"? What proposition S were they begging? Clearly we cannot identify T or S without knowing what Aristotle *meant* by "parallel lines," i.e., how he would try to *define* them. Thus a plausible candidate for T would be $\Sigma = 2R$ since Aristotle saw its proof as depending on the existence of parallels, but if they are defined as Euclid did this is not enough: their *uniqueness* is also required. Nor is $\Sigma = 2R$ *needed* for the existence of Euclidean parallels: mere congruence will suffice. But if he took parallels as lines making equal angles with a transversal, then $\Sigma = 2R$ *would* be needed for their "existence" (see below) but could not be proved unless they do exist. But most commentors uncritically assume that Aristotle defined parallels as Euclid did, whereupon it is their uniqueness that is begged and I, 29 of Euclid the fact that proves and is proved by it.[43]

Euclid defined parallels globally as "straight lines which, being in the same plane and, being produced indefinitely in both directions, do not meet one another in either direction," hardly the definition of someone bent on "disproving the actual existence of the infinite in the direction of increase, in the sense of the untransversable." Such parallels are untransversable, and their definition provides *no hint of how to prove their existence*, as Aristotle requires. There is a close fit between Euclid's definition and his postulate: his global criterion of nonintersection despite infinite extension obliges the postulation of the intersection of straight lines making angles with a transversal $< 2R$ which by contraposition makes angles $= 2R$ if they never meet however far extended. Hintikka's argument that Aristotle would reject Euclid's postulate casts doubt on his acceptance of Euclid's definition, as does his Aristotelean motivation for the classical critique of the postulate: "The gist of many of these criticisms is that Euclid's postulate does not give the essence of the straight line . . . otherwise the objection that the converse of the fifth postulate is provable would not make much sense. In slightly different words, the complaint was that the fifth postulate could not be conceived of as a definition."[44] Euclid's definition makes no Aristotelean sense.

Several passages on parallels are puzzling if meant in Euclid's sense.

Aristotle says that "thinking that parallels meet is geometrical in a sense and non-geometrical in another way. For . . . one way of being non-geometrical is by not having geometrical skill . . . and the other [is] by having it badly" (*Posterior Analytics* 77b23–26). But if parallels are *defined* as lines that don't meet, then thinking that they do is not just lacking in geometrical skill but *contradictory*.[45] Aristotle's example of the fallacy of demonstrating by cases suggests that he understood parallels as lines making the *same angle* with a transversal: "If someone were to prove that right angles do not meet, the demonstration would seem to hold of this because of its holding of all right angles. But that is not so, if it comes about not because they are equal in *this* way but in so far as they are equal in any way at all" (*Posterior Analytics* 74a13–17).[46] This seems to mean that the fact that parallels making right angles with another line do not meet is not because they make equal right angles with it but simply the *same* angle. Nor is it easy to square Euclid's definition with Aristotle's striking example of the same false conclusion following from different assumptions, "since it is not perhaps absurd that the same false result should follow from several suppositions, e.g., that parallels meet, both on the assumption that the interior angle is greater than the exterior and on the assumption that a triangle contains more than two right angles" (*Prior Analytics* 66a11–15). For such "non-Euclidean" results there are proofs Aristotle could plausibly have known, if he understood parallels locally as lines making the same angle with another.[47]

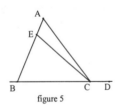

figure 5

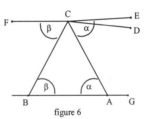

figure 6

If $\angle ACD < \angle ABC$, then at C on CD lay off an angle equal to $\angle ABC$, whose other side will thus be parallel to AB (by definition). But given the assumed angle inequality, it must also lie inside triangle ABC and thus cut AB in a point E (figure 5). So as Aristotle says, if the exterior is less than the interior angle, parallels meet. More problematic is how geometers of his day may have demonstrated his second claim that parallels meet if $\Sigma > 2R$. Given triangle ABC, lay off $\angle\beta$ at C on BC and $\angle\alpha$ at C on CA, with free sides CF and CE respectively (figure 6). If the angle sum of triangle ABC

> $2R$, then the line FCE is "inflected" (cf. *Posterior Analytics* 76b10) at C, and the extension of FC to D lies between CE and CA. Now $FD \parallel AB$ (since they make the same angle β with BC) and $CE \parallel BG$ (since they make the same angle α with AC). Thus the line CD between CE and BG must be "approaching" BG, and geometers of Aristotle's day commonly assumed that such lines will eventually meet. This follows from Euclid's postulate which implies the uniqueness of the parallel to BG through C, but Dehn claims that it would not have satisfied Aristotle's understanding of a postulate, to say nothing of his different idea of parallels.

This reconstruction shows the difficulty of defining parallels as lines equally inclined to a transversal: FC and BA make the same angle with BC but *not* with CA. Dehn thinks Aristotle realized that the consistent existence of such parallels, that is, the equal inclination of two lines to *every* transversal if so inclined to one, is *equivalent* to $\Sigma = 2R$, thus explaining the charge of question begging he brought against geometers. They constructed a parallel to a given line by choosing a transversal making some angle with it and then *laying off that angle* at a given point on this transversal. They could prove the independence of this parallel from the transversal chosen by appeal to $\Sigma = 2R$ which, however, they could only prove by the construction of a parallel whose independent existence they presupposed. Dehn claims that when Posidonius's dissatisfaction with Euclid's postulate led him to redefine parallels as lines everywhere equidistant, he lacked "Aristotle's insight" that the existence of such lines had to be demonstrated.[48] In terms of Hintikka's interrogative model, Aristotle resisted trivializing geometry by posing at the outset the question whether such parallels exist or not. On Dehn's reconstruction, Aristotle may have anticipated the charge of some geometers centuries later, that Euclid had begged the question with his postulate after all. Together with further observations of Hintikka, Dehn's view also illuminates the famous passage on relative necessity in mathematics in the *Eudemian Ethics*.

Aristotle argues that principles of mathematics have only the relative necessity associated with deductive inference, since if they were changed their consequences would change:

> For if, supposing the triangle to have its angles equal to two right angles, the quadrilateral must have them equal to four right angles, it is clear that the property of the triangle is the cause of this last. And if the triangle should change, then so must the quadrilateral, having six right angles if the triangle has three, and eight if it has four: but if the former does not change but remains as it was before, so must the quadrilateral. . . . Supposing there were no further cause for the triangle's having the above property, then the triangle would be a sort of principle or cause of all that comes later. (*Eudemian Ethics* 1222b31–41).

This confirms what Dehn's reconstruction of the results of 66a and the question begged at 65a suggest, that Aristotle seriously considered *taking* $\Sigma = 2R$ *itself as a basic principle of geometry not caused by anything else.* This *had* been demonstrated, he knew, by the construction of parallels, but he evidently believed that this construction depends on $\Sigma = 2R$—thereby begging the question. But how could he reconcile such a choice with his requirement that the basic premises of a demonstrative science be "better known" than its theorems? "Better known" is asymmetrical but the search for axioms by analysis depends on "conversions" of propositions that confront Aristotle with symmetrical "equivalences" between them which he sees as depending on constructions that beg the question. Not only did he appreciate the importance of conversion, says Hintikka, but also "the fact that establishing convertability of the different steps of analysis is the main burden in justifying analysis synthetically," as well as "the role of auxiliary constructions in geometrical heuristics."[49] It is difficult to understand Aristotle's views on these matters without also heeding Hintikka's claim *that he had no clear notion of logical equivalence.*[50]

Aristotle is led to consider $\Sigma = 2R$ as a basic principle of geometry by reflection on

(a) If $\Sigma = 2R$, then the angles of a square must sum to 4R

If $\Sigma = 2R$ holds for the triangles into which a diagonal divides a square, it is immediate that its angles must sum to $4R$. Given the importance of squares for the area concept of geometry—whose figures are said by Aristotle to "constitute a series, each successive term of which potentially contains its predecessor, e.g., the square, the triangle . . ." (*On the Soul* 414b30–31)—it is tempting to convert (a). But from the premise that squares have $4R$, $\Sigma = 2R$ follows immediately on their division only for *isosceles* right triangles and to prove it generally requires a "proof by cases" that Aristotle insists cannot establish the angle sum "universally" for triangles. For

> even if you prove of each triangle either by one or by different demonstrations that each has two right angles—separately of the equilateral and the scalene and the isosceles—you do not yet know of the triangle that it has two right angles, except in the sophistic fashion; nor do you know it of triangle[s] universally, not even if there is no other triangle apart from these. (*Posterior Analytics* 74a25-31)

To Aristotle the $4R$ property of squares would not appear as good a candidate for a basic principle of geometry as the $2R$ property of triangles.

But (a) *does* convert, as is explicitly claimed in the *Magna Moralia*,[51] raising the specter of circularity.

Aristotle observed that "if it were impossible to prove truth from falsehood, it would be easy to make an analysis; for they [the propositions] would convert from necessity. For let *A* be something that is the case; and if this is the case, then *these* are the case (things which I know to be the case—call them *B*). From these, therefore, I shall prove that the former is the case" (*Posterior Analytics* 78a7–11). This makes analysis harder, but "in mathematics things convert more because they assume nothing accidental—and in this too they differ from argumentations—but only definitions" (78a11–14). But he argues that knowledge proceeding from immediate propositions has no place for *circular* reasoning by claiming that such conversions are *very rare*, insisting that *we already indulge in such reasoning* when we purport to show of two propositions A and B both that 'If A, then necessarily B' *and* 'If B, then A,' since "that is what being circular is" (73a1).[52] That Aristotle sees circularity in a proof of convertability is clear from his account in the *Topics* "of the ways in which a questioner may postulate the point at issue" (*Topics* 162b31). One does this "if he postulates the one or the other of a pair of statements that necessarily follow one another, e.g., if he had to prove that the diagonal is incommensurable with the side, and were to postulate that the side is incommensurable with the diagonal" (*Topics* 163a11–14). This brings us to non-Euclidean geometry and back to Hintikka's interrogative model.

Non-Euclidean geometry emerged after centuries of attempts to prove Euclid's postulate were seen to have depended on tacit or unconscious assumptions "equivalent" to it, and hence to have begged the question! Many tried to derive a contradiction from the denial of this postulate (or some equivalent) and we have no reason to deny that such attempts were being made by geometers in Aristotle's time. In fact, the second result he mentions in *Prior Analytics* at 66a was later proved by Saccheri in his attempt to reduce $\Sigma > 2R$ to absurdity. Though he proved theorems of elliptic geometry, he did not believe in the "possibility" of this geometry, having proved to his satisfaction that it was contradictory (using the extension postulate, which is not assumed in this geometry). Only Lambert's discovery of a *model* for this geometry on a sphere gave any reason to believe in its consistency, something unknown in antiquity.[53] But the consistency of a set of geometrical sentences need not convince one that it comprises *geometry* as Aristotle understood it: a study of demonstrations of things that surveyors learn by dividing estates and use to "deal with all other properties of areas and regions."[54] A system containing no theorem for measuring the *area* of any figure would not be taken as geometry, and it was not until Lambert discovered the area theorem that geometers began taking the consequences of $\Sigma \neq 2R$ seriously as geometries.[55] This was unknown to the ancients but Aristotle's observation that the angles of a square must be greater than $4R$ if $\Sigma > 2R$ may have led them to wonder how such "squares" could fit flush enough to serve as units of area of larger squares.[56] But these results are too immediate to witness serious pursuit of the consequences of $\Sigma \neq 2R$. Did they find deeper consequences of it?

Aristotle illustrates the hypothetical use of "possible" and "impossible" by saying "It is impossible, for instance, on a certain hypothesis that the triangle should have its angles equal to two right angles, and on another [hypothesis] the diagonal is commensurable" (*On the Heavens* 281b5–7). We have from 66a a hypothesis implying $\Sigma > 2R$: the exterior angle < the interior angle. What other hypothesis did Aristotle know that would entail the commensurability of the diagonal? A possibility suggested by Heath is that "all lines are made up of *indivisible* elements, for then the indivisible element would be a common measure of both."[57] Now the Aristotelean tract "On Indivisible Lines" records several consequences of the existence of such lines, including the commensurability of all lines: the diagonal of a square would not be incommensurable with its side, "nor will the area which is the square on the diagonal be double the square on the indivisible line" (*On Indivisible Lines* 970a16–17). Aristotle surely intended such results when he warned: "Admit, for instance, the existence of a minimum magnitude, and you will find that the minimum which you have introduced causes the greatest truths of mathematics to totter" (*On the Heavens* 271b9–11). The incommensurability of the diagonal is a great truth for him, "for it seems wonderful to all men who have not yet perceived the explanation that there is a thing which cannot be measured even by the smallest unit" (*Metaphysics* 983a16–18). But did he know a hypothesis that entails the commensurability of the diagonal and side *without denying their infinite divisibility*? According to Toth, what Aristotle *said* in *On the Heavens* at 281b5–7 is that $\Sigma \neq 2R$ *is* such a hypothesis, i.e.,

   (b) If $\Sigma \neq 2R$, then the diagonal of a square *is* commensurable with its side

which states "a very important non-Euclidean theorem."[58] But in view of (a) he also knew

   (c) If $\Sigma = 2R$, then the diagonal of a square is *in*commensurable with its side

which would confront Aristotle with the *aporia* of how two propositions, one only an auxiliary parallel away from being self-evident and another too implausible to believe initially, could still be equivalent.[59] Could both be equivalent to the *existence of a square that a slave boy knew*?[60]

Aristotle objected to the "argument in the *Meno* that learning is recollection" that one never has "foreknowledge of the particular" but only after knowledge of it by induction, "for we know some things directly; e.g. that the angles are equal to two right angles, if we see that the figure is a triangle" (*Prior Analytics* 67a24–6). He distinguishes "universal knowledge" from either "knowledge proper to the matter in hand or actualizing such knowledge" (67b5–6), presumably intending that Socrates had actualized the slave boy's potential knowledge of properties of a square. Hintikka gives a striking interrogative gloss on this analysis in which Socrates is said to

> show how the slave boy knew a certain geometrical truth without knowing that he knew, in the sense of knowing it deductively and hence potentially but not actively. This potential knowledge and its activation through Socrates' skillful questioning (interrogative game) is all the more impressive as it is not virtual knowledge but requires a construction of the fuller diagram by Socrates, i.e., the introduction of several new auxiliary geometrical objects into the argument. From this point of knowledge activation Plato lets Socrates infer that the initially unknown knowledge was remembered knowledge, thus supporting the idea of *anamnesis*. The assumption is that the geometrical knowledge in question was tacit knowledge and hence not known.[61]

But the boy's deductive knowledge of a square is undermined on Aristotle's view by Socrates's failure to give an adequate definition of *what* a square is. Why did Socrates not give such a definition? Plato was unable to give a correct definition of his idea of square. We easily forget the difficulty of formulating good definitions and how slowly they crystallize in the genesis of a science. Consider the definition of square as a quadrilateral all of whose sides are equal, whose opposite sides are parallel, and all of whose angles are right angles. Nowhere does Plato mention, let alone define parallel lines, and we saw how hard it is to extract a definition of them from the few places they are discussed in Aristotle. The parallelism condition can be dropped but not the right angle condition. But Plato never defines right angles, and Aristotle says that to treat geometry deductively one should try to get definitions of straight line, circle, and right angle. We saw his dissatisfaction with Platonic definitions of the straight line and "current definers" of the circle, but what about the right angle? Euclid's definition of it as an angle equal to its supplementary angle still eluded him.[62]

What can be said about Aristotle's relation to Euclid in interrogative terms? Hintikka explains the distinction between tacit and potential knowledge of geometry by saying that:

I am likely to give the right answer to each question concerning the truth or falsity of an axiom of elementary geometry. In other words, I know them tacitly. In contrast, I often cannot answer without further inquiry a question concerning the theoremhood of some complicated geometrical proposition, even if it follows logically from the axioms. Such propositions are known to me potentially but not tacitly.[63]

Active knowledge of axioms is represented by an explicit list of initial premises, which are true *in the model* relative to which the game is being played and can guide the interrogative process in the selection of questions. Tacit knowledge consists of a less well-defined set of propositions available only as answers to questions that may activate them but which in general is difficult to probe.[64] The *choice* of the model can affect which "tacit assumptions" made by a geometer count as "true." Thus in the countable algebraic field constructed by Hilbert to prove the consistency of elementary Euclidean geometry the tacit assumption made by Euclid in his first theorem, that circles intersect, is false, as would be the tacit assumption of someone trying to trisect an angle with ruler and compass that there *is* an angle which is one-third of any given angle.

The most important "gaps" in Euclid concern his tacit knowledge of the order axioms. If asked how many of three collinear points could lie between the other two, Euclid would surely have said one, and so had tacit knowledge of this axiom as well as that of Pasch who activated this tacit topological knowledge of triangles. Euclid actively knew both the line and parallel postulates while Aristotle, in view of (a), knew the line postulate tacitly and the parallel postulate potentially. Aristotle's knowledge of congruence is tacit insofar as he nowhere mentions it but does tacitly appeal to SSS-congruence in a proof he presents.[65] His tacit knowledge of Euclid's common notion that "things which coincide are equal" for segments is implicit in his description of the application of a cubit-rule to measure his size. Though much of Aristotle's knowledge of axioms is only tacit, the difference between his axiomatization of geometry and Euclid's would not have been as great as many assume. In explaining where Aristotle fell short on this score, Ross wrote that "he should have recognized among the principles peculiar to one science certain which are neither definitions nor assumptions of the existence of certain entities—such propositions as Euclid's fourth axiom, that things which coincide are equal, and his fourth and fifth postulates."[66] But he considered $\Sigma = 2R$ as a principle which, together with the Archimedean principle he also actively knew, implies Euclid's fifth postulate, while the fourth is implicit at *Posterior Analytics* 74a13–16. Euclid's "mixed axiom" of coincidence was an important advance over Aristotle's tacit knowledge of the use of rulers.

Hintikka does find a basic difference between them: Euclid's axiomatic system is purely deductive whereas Aristotle "is treating the entire inquiry, including deductive steps, as an interrogative process."[67] Once we recognize "the dialectical character of Aristotelean science," says Hintikka, it is clear that

> there need not be any one stage of scientific inquiry at which all the first principles have been found so as to be ready to serve as premises of scientific syllogisms. The mistake of thinking that there must be such a stage according to Aristotle might be called the "Euclidean fallacy." It has come about by projecting the Euclidean, not to say Hilbertian, idea of an axiomatic science back to Aristotle.[68]

Hintikka grants that Aristotle pursues first principles in the *Posterior Analytics*, "but nowhere does he say or imply that there is a stage in the development of a science when those principles are all known to the scientist in such a way that all the rest could be proved syllogistically from those premises, and those premises only."[69] But what else could "all the rest" have meant to him than the *known* theorems?[70] Aristotle did envisage sufficient first principles to prove *them*: he saw this possibility when he concluded from his analysis of $\Sigma = 2R$ in (a) that "supposing there is no further cause for the triangle's having this property, then the triangle would be a sort of principle or cause of all that comes later." Knowing that this principle, together with the straight angle theorem, is the main cause of these other theorems, he knew that it was "most true" in the sense that "that which causes derivative truths to be true is most true" (*Metaphysics* 993b26–27). Given his active knowledge of the Archimedean principle, we cannot deny that he was within reach of an experimentally complete set of premises for geometry. What eluded him were good definitions: of straight lines, circles, right angles, and parallels. We shall appreciate Aristotle's problem with them more when we see them still haunting Kant centuries after Euclid seemed to have solved them.

Hintikka has challenged the view that the "syntheticity" of a mathematical theorem is ultimately as an inheritance from the *axioms*, claiming that it is rather a matter of the way it is proved. He finds the roots of Kant's thoughts in Euclid, but in the methodology of his geometry rather than its content: his notions of intuition and construction are both rooted in his recognition of the need for "auxiliary constructions" in Euclid's proofs. According to Hintikka, a Kantian intuition is just a "representation of a particular entity in the mind," while a construction is merely "the introduction of such a particular to instantiate a general concept."[71] He proposes that for Kant "a mathematical argument is synthetic if it involves the use of 'auxiliary constructions', i.e., the introduction of new particulars over and above those given in the conditions of the argument,"[72] and stresses the role of the postulates in guaranteeing such constructions. He concludes "the syntheticity of a geometrical *theorem* is on my account recognized from the use of auxiliary constructions in its proof,"[73] relating Kant's difficult notions of intuition and construction to "procedures which are closely related to the instantiation rules of modern logic."[74] Having located the syntheticity of theorems "squarely within the framework of the Euclidean axiomatic and deductive treatment of geometry," says Hintikka, we "need not pursue the rainbow of syntheticity back to the axioms."[75] The objection that such a pursuit is implied by Kant's claim at B14 in the first *Critique*, that a synthetic proposition can be proved analytically only if another synthetic proposition is presupposed, cannot hold for mathematics generally, argues Hintikka, in view of Kant's denial that arithmetic *has* any axioms.[76]

Hintikka's identification of intuitions as singular representations is geared to his denial that for Kant they are pictures seen in the mind's eye or represented in the imagination.[77] Hintikka sometimes says more provocatively that Kantian intuitions are "not very intuitive." Many have objected that Kant characterized intuitions not only by their singularity but by their *immediacy*, which is epistemologically more important. Hintikka recognizes both attributes but argues that the immediacy of an intuition is a corollary of its singularity; and that intuitions yield certain knowledge for Kant not by virtue of their immediate reference to an object but rather by virtue of their *ideality*, that is, by not representing things in themselves.[78] As evidence that Kant actually *excludes* the appeal to vulgar intuition in geometry, Hintikka cites his famous description of how

> a new light broke upon the first person who demonstrated the isoceles triangle . . . he found that what he had to do was not to trace what he saw in this figure, or even trace its mere concept, and read off, as it were, from the properties of the figure; but rather that he had to produce the latter from what he himself thought into the object and presented (through construction) according to *a priori* concepts, and that in order to know something securely *a priori* he had to ascribe to the thing nothing except what followed necessarily from what he himself had put into it in accordance with its concept.[79]

Hintikka reads this as excluding appeal to any intuition except the singular instantiations of postulates.[80] In fact, Kant realized by 1787 that the question of what the geometer *could* think into his figure and "present by construction" that "necessarily followed from his concept" required a *suitable definition* of his concept, something he now appreciated as more problematic than he realized in 1781.[81] Hintikka's reading of Kant is more convincing if Kant's circumspect formulation of the geometer's method in the first *Critique,* at Bxii, reflects an awareness of these Aristotelean difficulties that emerged after 1781. We will explore this later.

Hintikka rejects Russell's thesis that "Kant, having observed that the geometers of his day could not prove their theorems by unaided argument, but required an appeal to the figure, invented a theory of mathematical reasoning according to which the inference is never strictly logical, but always requires the support of what is called 'intuition'."[82] Hintikka admits that this interpretation "is not without relevance as an objection to Kant's full fledged theory of space, time, and mathematics as it appears in the Transcendental Aesthetic,"[83] but claims that *it ignores the precritical origin of this theory that Kant incorporated intact in the Doctrine of Method.* Hintikka sees two levels of Kant's theory: the original theory of mathematical method amenable to logical reconstruction and a superimposed theory of the transcendental ideality of space and time insuring a priori the applicability of mathematics to sensible objects. Let us examine this.

In 1763 Kant wrote his *Prize Essay* on the question of whether metaphysics could ever attain the degree of certainty found in geometry, which both he and Mendelssohn attributed to its use of concrete figures: "For since signs in mathematics are sensible means to cognition," wrote Kant, "it follows that one can know that no concept has been overlooked. . . . And these things can be known with the degree of assurance characteristic of seeing something with one's own eyes."[84] Whereas the philosopher represents universals *in abstracto* by words, the geometer represents them *in concreto* with symbols: "Suppose, for example, that the geometer wishes to demonstrate that space is infinitely divisible. He will take, for example,

figure 7

a straight line standing vertically between two parallel lines; from a point on one of these parallel lines he will draw lines to intersect the other two lines. By means of this symbol he recognises with the greatest certainty that the division can be carried on *ad infinitum.*"[85] Kant's geometer here violates the ban he later imposes on "reading off" properties of the object from those of the figure. He can literally *see* only five lines intersecting in seven points in it. Nor is the certainty of this infinite divisibility a matter of "intuition" in any sense explained in the *Essay.*

Hintikka believes that intuition plays no role here and that "the use of general concepts *in concreto,* i.e., in the form of individual instances, was the starting point of Kant's more elaborate views on mathematics."[86] Kant attributes the certainty insured by concrete symbols to their being "more intuitive" than words, but as in earlier precritical references to intuition, this serves only to gauge the *clarity* of impressions.[87] There *is* intuition in philosophical cognition, but

> the intuition involved in this cognition is, as far as its exactitude is concerned, greater in mathematics than it is in philosophy. And the reason for this is the fact that, in mathematics, the object is considered under sensible signs *in concreto*, whereas in philosophy the object is only ever considered in universal abstracted concepts; and the clarity of the impression made by such abstracted concepts can never be as great as that made by signs which are sensible in character.[88]

It is objected to Hintikka that even *here* intuition is "tied to sensibility," but he says that "this explicit doctrine is formulated without using the *problematic* concept of an intuition, and is therefore free of all the ambiguities of this difficult concept."[89] He means the *immediate* or *pure* intuition derived from the very "form of sensibility," which is hardly meant in the *Essay*. Seeing symbols with one's eyes is *mediated*, though according to Kant, sight is "the sense in which we are least aware of the organ's being affected. . . . So sight comes closest to a *pure intuition* (an immediate representation of the given object, with no admixture of sensation noticeable in it)."[90] In the *Essay* it is only with *subjective* necessity that "the degree of certainty increases with the degree of intuition to be found in the cognition of this necessity."[91] The *objective* certainty of mathematics depends on its *definitions*.

Mathematical definitions are "*arbitrary combinations* of concepts," says Kant, as when I baptize a surface bounded by four lines whose opposite sides are not parallel a "trapezium": "The concept which I am defining is not given prior to the definition itself; on the contrary, it only comes into existence as a result of that definition."[92] Since mathematics defines concepts synthetically, says Kant, "it can say with certainty that what it did not intend to represent in the object by means of the definition is not contained in that object. For the concept of what has been defined only comes into existence by means of the definition; the concept has no other significance at all apart from that which is given to it by the definition."[93] This is the bedrock of the *Doctrine of Method* that "mathematical definitions can never err. For since the concept is first given through the definition, it contains just that which the definition would think through it."[94] So the two-levels thesis must be taken seriously. An interesting test of it is Kant's account of the biangle.

Nothing in the *Prize Essay* theory of arbitrary definitions would disqualify biangles as objects of mathematics, and while the *Doctrine of Method* adds the proviso that its definitions be "constructed in intuition," it provides *no* reason why a biangle is *not* so constructible. Kant appeals to his *Postulate of Empirical Thought*, that "whatever agrees with the formal conditions of experience in accordance with intuition and concepts is possible," to rule out biangles, claiming that "their impossibility rests not on the concept in itself, but on its construction in space, i.e., on the conditions of space and its determinations."[95] But this "space" is the problematic "form of outer intuition," of the Transcendental Aesthetic. Kant's treatment of the biangle fits the two-levels thesis.

It also fits Hintikka's reading of Kant's doctrine of the synthetic character of mathematical reasoning "essentially as saying that much of the non-trivial reasoning codified in mathematical logic is not tautologous in the sense of surface tautology."[96] To prove deeper tautologies below the surface one must unearth hidden inconsistencies by introducing more and more individuals. So, says Hintikka,

> on the one hand, this idea is related to Kant's notion of a construction. On the other hand, it is connected with non-trivial provability as follows: all the non-trivially inconsistent constituents can be discovered by a systematic procedure which consists essentially in raising the degree of our constituents more and more. The element of undecidability is due to the fact that we often do not know how deep we have to go to uncover whatever inconsistencies there may be in a given constituent.[97]

As far as these ideas may seem from Kant's methodology, his contemporaries *were* beginning to appreciate the problem of recognizing inconsistency. Kant argued that for the objective reality of a concept it was not sufficient that it contain no contradictions: "Thus in the concept of a figure that is enclosed between two straight lines there is no contradiction, for the concepts of two straight lines and their intersection contain no negation of a figure."[98] But what he means by saying that the concept of a biangle "contains no negation of a figure" is that its two component concepts, (i) two straight lines and (ii) their intersecting twice, are not contradictory. Kant is simply noting that these two concepts do not explicitly contradict each other: one is not the denial of the other. In Hintikka's terms, (i) and (ii) are not trivially inconsistent. But others were aware that the contradiction in a mathematical concept *could indeed lie deeply hidden from their eyes*. In explaining the inadequacy of the modal postulate that "possible is, what contains no contradiction in itself," Lambert observed that "this principle is negative and tells us only what is not possible, namely, where a contradiction occurs. Since, however, we are not able to find all contradictions immediately, and indeed contradictory things are often believed for centuries, this principle is of little use for the *positive* determination of what is possible."[99] Hintikka's reconstruction of

Kant fits Lambert like a glove, so we must gauge his influence on Kant.

The superiority of Mendelssohn's account of the certainty of geometry over Kant's is seen in his insistence, as formulated in the Academy's official abridgement of his essay, that

> a distinction must be made between pure mathematics and applied or mixed mathematics. The former is restricted to the world of the understanding and the realm of possibilities. Here, the highest degree of certainty is to be found, for all that one needs to do is to compare ideas, and to demonstrate that the derived notions are identical with the primitive notion. But when this science is transposed to the real world, it needs sensory experience; without it, all its operations are suspended.[100]

Without such experience of *coincidence* the operation of measuring with a ruler included in Euclid's mixed axiom of congruence is suspended. But Mendelssohn no sooner received his prize than he became aware of the weakness of his own account of geometrical reasoning upon reading Lambert, confessing in a letter to Thomas Abbt that "had I read Mr. Lambert's *New Organon* some years ago, my prize essay would certainly have remained in my drawer or else it would have felt the wrath of Vulcan."[101] Let us peek at Lambert's account of the certainty of geometry in the manuscript he wrote for the competition but kept in *his* drawer.

Lambert proposes that "the certainty of geometrical proofs is based on 1. deductions and the necessity of their conclusions, and 2. that one cannot *so* easily go astray from the concepts of the figures because they are simple, lay before the eyes, and can even be distinguished by the blind by touch."[102] He stressed the logical validity of geometrical proofs while allowing that, however useful for following such proofs, eyes were not necessary. Nor more importantly, and contrary to what Kant claimed, do figures prevent errors in them. Indeed, says Lambert,

> it is not that one cannot err in geometry. One can: just consider, e.g., all those misbegotten squarings of the circle of which a 100 can be counted, all containing specifiable paralogisms. Gregorius, who was certainly a great and insightful geometer, died in the conviction that he had found it, and how difficult it was to find just where he had gone astray![103]

It was clear to him that concrete figures often hid fallacies from the eyes of geometers rather than revealed the truth to them, though he grants it is easier to recognize paralogisms in geometry since "at least, one is agreed as to the axioms."[104] Lambert attributed the certainty geometry enjoyed to this agreement, but the publication of so many fallacious proofs for squaring the circle showed how illusory such certainty can be.

Lambert soon learned from Klügel's dissertation of 1763 that geometers had also produced scores of fallacious proofs of the axiom of parallels in which the question was begged unconsciously by assumptions equivalent to it or even more obscure. The *uncertainty* whether this axiom *was* provable from Euclid's "other axioms" prompted Lambert's penetrating study of the problem in which he "discovered" non-Euclidean geometry. This new spate of paralogisms exposed by Klügel obliged him to formulate a formal criterion of proof in geometry, independent of the meaning of its concepts and figures, in order to distinguish *two* aspects of the problem:

> *Can this axiom be derived correctly from Euclid's postulates and remaining axioms?* Or, *if these premises are not sufficient, can we produce other postulates, or axioms, no less evident than Euclid's, from which this axiom can be derived?* In dealing with the first part of this question we may wholly ignore what I have called the *representation of the subject matter* (Vorstellung der Sache). Since Euclid's postulates and remaining axioms are stated in words, we can and should demand that no appeal be made anywhere in the proof to the matter itself, but that the proof be carried out—if it is at all possible—in a thoroughly symbolic fashion. In this respect, Euclid's postulates are, so to speak. like so many given algebraic equations, which we must solve for x, y, z, etc. without ever looking back to the matter itself. Since the postulates are not quite such formulas, we can allow the drawing of a figure as a guiding thread to direct the proof. On the other hand, it would be preposterous to forbid consideration of the subject matter in the second part of the question, and to require that the *new* postulates and axioms be found without reflecting on their subject matter, off the cuff, so to speak.[105]

As Torretti noted, Lambert's method "combines a would-be total formalism in the derivation of theorems with a healthy appeal to intuition in the search for postulates and axioms," especially in his discovery of *models* of non-Euclidean propositions.[106]

Both the formalist and the intuitionist prongs of Lambert's method enter his letter of 1766 to Kant that, Hintikka suggests, crystalized Kant's associations of intuition with the introduction of individual examples in geometric proofs.[107] Here Lambert proposes that *the matter as opposed to the form of a science* must be formulated in axioms and postulates containing only "simple concepts" and that the "objectively simple concepts must be found by direct intuition [Anschauen] of them, that is, we must, in good anatomical fashion, assemble all the concepts and let each one pass through inspection, in order to see whether, when we ignore all the relations of a given concept to other concepts, there are several concepts included in it or it is indeed simple."[108] Lambert had already formulated new axioms for geometry, for as he explained to Kant, "Euclid does not derive his elements from either the definition of space or that of geometry but begins instead with lines, angles, and so on, the simple elements in the dimensions of space."[109] Lambert agrees with Kant on the importance of "individual cases" to illustrate the principles of natural philosophy, which are so abstract when "expressed logically," and claims that "examples perform the same job that figures do in geometry, for the latter, too, are actually examples or special cases."[110] Lambert was paraphrasing a passage on Euclid's method from his *Architectonic* linking this idea of figures as individual examples with their ability to represent concepts:

> Euclid had complete freedom, in the figure—which is actually only a special or individual case of a general theorem, thereby serving as an *example*—to disregard everything that did not properly belong to it, or was not present in the concept. The figure then represents the concept completely and clearly. However, since it does not provide for the possibility of the concept, Euclid took care to consider this carefully, and to this end he used his postulates, which introduce general, unconditional, and simple possibilities or constructions that are conceivable in themselves, and which he presents in the form of problems. But along with the combination of the simple possibilities come limitations, and Euclid decides upon these mostly with his ninth and twelfth postulates.[111]

This is essentially Kant's method in the first *Critique*, Bxii.

Kant pondered Lambert's remarks on Euclid's method and failure to relate his elements to space, as well as the question he proposed for their joint study—to what extent knowing the *form* of knowledge leads to knowing its *matter*—for four years before answering his letter with his *Dissertation*, in which he answers this question and makes good on Euclid's failure in one fell swoop.[112] He explains that space is a pure intuition because it is a *singular* concept not "compounded from sensations, although it is the fundamental form of all outer sensation. Indeed, this pure intuition can easily be seen in the axioms of geometry, and in any mental construction of postulates, even of problems."[113] How is such intuition "easily seen" in the axioms of geometry: what have *they* to do with the singularity of this pure intuition? That there is but *one* straight line between two points, that a circle can be described with a given radius around a given point, these things *cannot*, says Kant, "be derived from some universal concept of space; they can only be *apprehended* concretely, so to speak, in space itself."[114] Does the uniqueness of the lines and circles in space derive from the singularity that qualifies *it* as a pure intuition? Hintikka cited the claim, that the singularity of space proves it to be an intuition, as evidence that singularity is the essential mark of a Kantian intuition, but this cannot explain such intuitions as auxiliary individuals in Euclidean proofs, for as Lambert says, none of Euclid's axioms mentions space. The line axiom yields auxiliary lines which Kant later calls "guiding intuitions," but he never relates their uniqueness to that of space. We need the distinction made by Parsons between "intuitions *of*" and "intuitions *that*": it is one thing to have an intuition *of* a straight line through two points and another to intuit *that* it is unique. The former is individual, the latter is propositional.[115]

Geometry studies relations in space comprising "the very form of all sensory intuition," but, as in the *Essay*, geometry still demonstrates universal propositions "by placing [an object] before the eyes by means of a singular intuition, as happens in the case of what is sensitive."[116] What is "pure" about the intuition of a concrete figure "before the eyes"? The geometer abstracts from the sensation he has of this figure, leaving only *its* form, but this form is not yet tied to space as "the form of outer sensation."[117] Still, Kant answers Lambert's question affirmatively: since Kant has identified the "principle" of geometry as the study of relations in the *form* of outer sensory intuition, the axioms comprising its "matter" must hold of this form. So *in geometry* at least, knowing the form of knowledge *does* lead to knowing its matter: its axioms can be "easily seen" from its principle. What about chronometry: would knowing its principle lead to *its* axioms? What *is* its principle?

Kant says little about how the pure intuition of time relates to "the axioms which can be known about time," except that "all motions and all internal changes" necessarily agree with them and thus it would be contradictory "to wish to arm reason against the first postulates of pure time."[118] This refers to Lambert's provisional formulation in the *Neues Organon* of axioms and postulates for *chronometry*, the science he viewed as bearing *the same relation to time as geometry bears to space*. Kant expounds two such axioms: "that time has one dimension" and "different times are earlier and later and not simultaneous." Lambert based the latter on the awareness of the flow of our thoughts, but argued that their succession can never *measure* time as accurately as the lawful motion of bodies, owing to the inherently uneven clarity and distinctness of our consciousness of them.[119] Kant, however, having not yet decided between the monadic time of Leibniz and the absolute time of Newton, keeps both these chronometrical options open: "That we are only able to calculate the *quantity* of time in the concrete, namely, either by *motion* or by a *series of thoughts*, is due to the fact that the concept of time rests exclusively on an internal law of the mind, and is not some kind of innate intuition."[120] Time is not yet the "form of inner intuition."

Kant also uses incongruous counterparts to argue that space is a pure intuition: two similar spherical triangles of equal size but opposite orientation are indiscernible "in respect of everything which may be expressed by means of characteristic marks intelligible to the mind through speech," and yet cannot be proved congruent by superposition. "It is, therefore, clear that in these cases the difference, namely, the incongruity, can only be apprehended by a certain pure intuition."[121] This is Kant's wedge between the sensible and intelligible worlds: such a difference cannot be conceived by the intellect, only grasped by the senses. Yet this argument does not invoke a *singular* intuition of an object but only "a certain pure intuition" *that two* objects are not congruous, something the intellect cannot conceive. One can only intuit *that* these triangles can never coincide. Here Hintikka's case for Kantian intuitions as auxiliary individuals in a Euclidean proof seems weak: since geometers still had no order axioms, Kant's intuition had to remain "outside the axiomatic framework" of Euclid. But Hintikka argues that only his interpretation of this argument can explain "the fact that at different times Kant drew from it conclusions which are apparently contrary to each other."[122] Hintikka says that *here*, coming right after the "axioms of geometry" argument, it is just another proof of the *singularity of space* based on the pure intuition of a difference which the intellect cannot conceive, from which, says Hintikka, "he concludes that their difference is due to their relation to some third *individual* thing."[123] He has a point, for though Kant does not explicitly say this in the *Dissertation*, he did infer from his earlier analysis of incongruity in 1768 that this third thing was absolute space. But from both of his uses of the incongruities in the *Prolegomena* and *Metaphysical Foundations*, he infers the ideality of space. This fits the two-levels thesis and Hintikka concludes that the conflicting consequences Kant drew in 1768 and 1783 from the same premises cannot be understood "unless the peculiar implications of the term 'Anschauung' in the first *Critique* and in the *Prolegomena* are recognized."[124]

Let us compare Kant's proof that time is a pure intuition with his incongruity argument. Time is singular since all times must be thought as parts of the same time, so we must represent any two years in a definite order relation to each other: "But among different times, the time which is *earlier* and the time which is *later* cannot be defined in any way by any characteristic marks which can be conceived by the understanding. . . . The mind only discerns the distinction between them by a singular intuition" (§14). This resembles the incongruity argument for the intuitivity of space: in each case a pair of objects too similar to be distinguished by marks is intuited to be incapable of superposition. But there is a crucial difference: in intuiting the discongruity the mind sees both spherical triangles *at once*, whereas with time *memory* has to count as part of the pure intuition, since two times cannot be intuited simultaneously. Kant's claim that we perceive which of two times is earlier by a singular, hence pure, intuition stretches his definition of the purity of an intuition beyond recognition, since time is not the singular *form* of any " sense"—yet.[125] Nor can the intuition of the difference between two times be *immediate*, leaving only its singularity.[126] The full transcendental theory of mathematics is not in place in the *Dissertation*, since time is only "an internal law of the mind," not yet the form of inner *sense*. The impetus for this step, in order to base the ideality of time on the a priori necessity of the axioms of time, will be Lambert.

Lambert takes Kant's thesis that "all our intuition is bound to a certain principle of form, and it is only under this form that anything can be *apprehended* by the mind immediately or as *singular*" (§10), along with the arguments of §§14, 15, to show that space and time *individuate* objects. But, says Lambert, the judgments from which Kant concludes that time is a *pure* intuition, such as "this year is earlier than that year," are accidental truths of chronology: "The truths of geometry and chronometry, however, involve time and location essentially, not merely accidentally; and insofar as the *concepts* of space and time are eternal, the truths of geometry and chronometry belong to the class of eternal, immutable truths also."[127] Lambert thus doubts that these truths are based on sensibility and he objects to Kant's *inference*, from his proposition that time is a pure intuition, that it is "not something objective and real" (§14). Lambert argued that this conclusion is incompatible with the reality of *change*: "All changes are bound to time and are inconceivable without time. *If changes are real, then time is real*, whatever it may be. *If time is unreal, then no change can be real*. I think, though, that even an idealist must grant at least that changes really exist and occur in his representations, for example, their beginning and ending."[128] The most we can say, Lambert thinks, in view of the indefinability of time, is that time is "a finite determination of duration, and like duration, it is somehow real in whatever this reality may consist."[129] Implicit in Lambert's argument (explicit in Mendelssohn's) is that "even the idealist" must admit he observes a succession of changes in his *self*, and hence knows an object undergoing real changes in time. Kant cannot answer this from the standpoint of the *Dissertation*, for here time is "an internal Law of the mind" which knows things of the intelligible world as they *are*, not just as they appear. He will have to invent an "inner *sense*" for time to be the "form" of, so he can say that even an idealist can apprehend himself only as changes in his representations appear to this "sense," and can only establish those "finite determinations of duration" Lambert said were inseparable from his existence by means of the motions of external

bodies needed to measure it. This "refutation of idealism" is implicit in
Lambert's analysis of the dependence of chronometry on dynamics, but
closed to Kant as long as he allowed, as he did in the *Dissertation*, that we
could measure duration "either by motion *or* by a series of thoughts."[130] The
path to this refutation will confront Kant with the delicate problem of the
mathematical status of Lambert's chronometry, whose axioms and
postulates for a *one* dimensional time cannot yield the plethora of
constructions found in geometry—and will invite Hintikka's analysis.

Lambert's main criticism of the *Dissertation* was directed against
Kant's complete separation of the sensible and intellectual worlds, so that
"knowledge that comes from the senses thus is and remains sensible, just as
knowledge that comes from the understanding remains peculiar to the
understanding."[131] He argued that a science with intellectual concepts could
not be *tested* unless they are "contaminated" by propositions connecting
them with sensible concepts.[132] He also suggested to Kant that "I should
think that the counterpart of space and time in the intelligible world could
also be considered in the theory you have in mind. It is a facsimile of real
space and real time and can readily be distinguished from them."[133] Such
models would relieve the need to proliferate further worlds beyond the
sensible and intellectual ones which our *symbolic* knowledge would otherwise require, since "our symbolic knowledge is a thing half way between
sensing and actual pure thinking,"[134] which actually extends our knowledge.
In Lambert's opinion

> no one has yet formed himself a clear representation of all the members of an
> infinite series, and no one is going to do so in the future. But we are able to do
> arithmetic with such series, to give their sum and so on, by virtue of the laws
> of *symbolic* knowledge. We thus extend ourselves far beyond the borders of
> our actual [*wirklichen*] thinking. The sign $\sqrt{-1}$ represents an unthinkable non-
> thing. And yet it can be used very well in finding theorems. What are usually
> regarded as specimens of pure understanding can be viewed most of the time
> as specimens of symbolic knowledge."[135]

The idea of $\sqrt{-1}$ often entered into proofs of theorems not containing this
symbol as a symbolic auxiliary construction. This brings us to Kant's view
of the relation of geometry to algebra and their "constructions," and
Hintikka's challenge to make sense of Kant's claims about algebra without
his austere reading of intuition.

Kant writes in 1781 that

> mathematics does not merely construct magnitudes (*quanta*), as in geometry,
> but also mere magnitude (*quantitatem*), as in algebra, where it entirely

abstracts from the constitution of the object that is to be thought in accordance with such a concept of magnitude. In this case it chooses a certain notation for all construction of magnitudes in general (numbers), as well as addition, subtraction, extraction of roots, etc. . . . . It then exhibits all the procedures through which magnitude is generated and altered in accordance with certain rules in intuition; where one magnitude is to be divided by another, it places their symbols together in accordance with the form of the notation for division, and thereby achieves by a symbolic construction equally well what geometry does by an ostensive or geometrical construction (of the objects themselves), which discursive cognition could never achieve by means of mere concepts.[136]

Hintikka argues that Kant's claim that algebra exhibits its operations in intuitions is natural on his interpretation of them but unintelligible if the Transcendental Aesthetic is logically prior to the Methodology of mathematics. In the Aesthetic all intuitions derive from the two forms of sensibility, leaving no room in mathematics for nonsensible intuitions, but Hintikka says that the discrepancy between the Aesthetic and the Methodology belies his reading only if this corollary of the Aesthetic *is correct*: "If there now are intuitions, say the individual variables or 'intuitions' of algebra, which have no relation to our sensibility, then the only possible conclusion is not that these alleged intuitions are not intuitions at all in Kant's sense. The other possibility is to say that they are genuine intuitions but that Kant just was wrong in saying that all the intuitions used in mathematics are . . . due to our sensibility."[137] When algebra does confront Kant with such an example as $\sqrt{2}$ he tries to ground it in sensibility via the constructions of geometry.[138]

The association of intuition with auxiliary construction occurs in Kant's famous discussion of $\Sigma = 2R$ in the Methodology in which he tries to distinguish the conceptual analysis of the philosopher from the intuitive construction of the geometer that Hintikka takes as paradigmatic of Kant's view of intuition. The philosopher, says Kant, would analyze his concept of triangle in vain for its angle sum:

But now let the geometer take up this question. He begins at once to construct a triangle. Since he knows that two right angles together are exactly equal to all of the adjacent angles that can be drawn at one point on a straight line, he extends one side of his triangle, and obtains two adjacent angles that together are equal to two right angles. Now he divides the external one of these angles by drawing a line parallel to the opposite side of the triangle, and sees that here there arises an external adjacent angle which is equal to an internal one, etc. In such a way, through a chain of inferences that is always guided by intuition, he arrives at a fully illuminating and at the same time general solution of the question.[139]

Hintikka's identification of the intuitions that guide Kant's geometer here with the individual extension and parallel instantiated from postulates is borne out by Kant's reiteration of the *Essay* theme that philosophy is bound to its abstract universal concepts, "while mathematics can assess the universal *in concreto* (in the individual intuition) and yet through pure *a priori* intuition, where every false step becomes visible."[140] But Kant was unaware of the many false steps taken by geometers in trying to prove the postulate needed to justify the equality of the internal and external angles made by this auxiliary parallel.

Kant's description of the proof of $\Sigma = 2R$ is similar to Aristotle's in that both focus on the same two crucial points: the straight angle theorem and the construction of an auxiliary parallel to exploit it. However, Aristotle

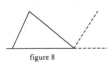

figure 8

charged his contemporary geometers with begging the question when they drew parallels, since they justified their construction only by appeal to $\Sigma = 2R$, which they could only prove by drawing parallels. Euclid cut this Gordian knot with a postulate that Lambert claimed "we can only represent with more effort and less evidence"

than his other axioms,[141] but whose truth "can be shown by way of all the evident and necessary consequences that for all purposes can be drawn from it,"[142] such as similar figures and finite trigonometric tables. The problem begins with Euclid's *definition* of parallels: "a definition of a concept must provide for its possibility" writes Lambert in 1765 to Holland, but "with respect to parallel lines this policy is even more obvious, since their definition gives no indication at all of their possibility. For one must be able to imagine extending them straight into the infinite in both directions."[143] Nor does it help to define parallels as *equidistant* lines, as Wolff did in order to prove Euclid's postulate, for then, says Lambert, "the difficulty is only *removed from the axiom* and *smuggled into the definition*."[144] Given Euclid's failure to derive his elements from the definition of space, Lambert replaces his postulate with an axiom about space,

(A) Space has no determinate unit (bestimmte Einheit)[145]

Although the measure of angles is absolute and thus "intelligible without having to be presented," linear magnitude and size must be "immediately presented and perceived, not conceived," says Lambert, which he motivates by quoting Wolff's metaphysical "theorem"

(Q) "Quantitas dari sed non per se intelligi potest"[146]

But he observes that *angles comprise an exception to (Q)*, and uses his area theorem to construct a 1-1 correspondence between angles and Lambert quadrilaterals to prove

(L) If Σ < 2R, "there is *an absolute measure for every line, area, and volume in space.*"[147]

As the angle G, e.g., goes from 90° to 0, the area of $ADGB$ goes from 0 to infinity, and similarly for the angle $J < G$ and $ACJE$. Thus G is the "absolute measure" of $ADGB$ since, as an angle, it is intrinsically definable in geometry itself and uniquely correlated with this quadrilateral (figure 9).

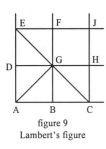

figure 9
Lambert's figure

If a Paris foot happens to correspond to 80°, says Lambert, "one has to increase the quadrilateral $ABGD$ until the angle $G = 80°$: in this way one gets to have the absolute length of the Paris foot on $AB = AD$," a consequence Lambert found so "alluring" that he would just as soon "wish that the third hypothesis [Σ < 2R] were true."[148] Theoretically such a magnitude, taken as a unit, would not have to be exemplified by a physical object whose length varied with temperature but could be specified forever by a pure number.

Among the "inconveniences," as Lambert called them, one would have to tolerate as a price of such an a priori unit of magnitude, he cited the need for infinite series in trigonometry and the absence of similar figures, so that "no figure could be represented in other than its absolute magnitude."[149] Though the existence of such a unit contradicts (A), a proposition, says Lambert, which "up to now no one has doubted,"[150] it cannot be refuted by appeal to (Q) without begging the question why (Q) should hold for linear but not angular magnitudes. Would such a unit inconvenience Kant's transcendental basis for geometry? Does it follow from the ideality of space that the figures we synthesize in it cannot be represented in their absolute magnitude? Does it preclude Lambert's figure being an *absolutely small* Lambert quadrilateral?

In 1781 Kant concluded his proof that space is a pure intuition by claiming that "space is represented as a given infinite magnitude. A general concept of space (which is common to a foot as well as an ell) can determine nothing in respect to magnitude. If there were not boundlessness in the progress of intuition, no concept of relations could bring with it a principle of their infinity."[151] He presumably meant that units of magnitude such as a foot or ell must be given in empirical intuition, not conceptually defined in accordance with (A) and (Q). If so, he was ruling out the possibility of absolute units in infinite space, though not with (L) in mind, which had not yet been published.[152] Kant was soon informed of the problem of parallels, and the uncertainty whether Euclid's postulate was provable engendered by scores of fallacious proofs of it, by Johann Schultz, who set himself to prove it. The need to see why the intuition that, as Kant had just publicized, "secures all inferences against mistakes" and through which "every false step becomes visible," had not prevented these paralogisms, prompted him to try his own hand at such a proof.[153]

Kant's Reflections on proving the parallel postulate support Hintikka's analysis of his intuition, and may even motivate the more conceptual formulation of the geometer's method of Bxii that he takes to rule out a geometer's appeal to vulgar intuitions. Hintikka claims that "there is nowhere in Kant's speculations about geometry (he tried for instance to prove the postulate of parallels) any sign that he considered appeal to geometrical intuition (in the twentieth-century sense) as an admissible procedure in geometrical arguments."[154] Hintikka motivates his idea of constructions as "anticipations of existence" depending on postulates by observing that "the main construction needed in Kant's favorite example, the theorem about the internal angles of a triangle, is based on the postulate of parallels which Kant himself tried to prove."[155] But neither Kant's efforts nor what he meant by "constructing concepts in intuition" are intelligible apart from his theory of *definition*, for he insists that definitions *are* constructions which "*make* the concept itself."[156] To say that Apollonius "constructed a parabola in intuition," Kant explains to Reinhold in 1789, means that the *definition* of a parabola "is itself the exhibition of a concept in intuition, viz., the intersection of a cone under certain conditions. In establishing the objective reality of the concept, here as always in geometry, the definition is at once a construction of the concept."[157] When a mathematician "constructs a concept" he activates a definition of which, *if appropriate*, as in the case of the circle, the construction is a "practical corollary." But as Lambert explained to Holland, Euclid's definition of parallels offered no basis for their possibility.[158] As Kant put it in his notes on parallels, "I think that from a definition which does not at the same time contain the construction of the concept itself, nothing follows that would be a synthetic predicate."[159] He adopts Wolff's definition of parallels as "straight lines which are everywhere equidistant," but finds these harder to construct a priori than Euclid's, whose postulate is equivalent to the *existence* of Wolff-parallels. Kant's notes never mention "Anschauung" and reach only what he calls a "philosophical proof from concepts" of this postulate.[160] They are best understood in relation to Schultz's proof of it.

Schultz's proof is based on the idea that "the magnitude of a plane angle is determined by the amount of the plane that lies between its sides

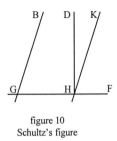

figure 10
Schultz's figure

prolonged without end."[161] Suppose ∠BGH = ∠KHF and $DH \perp GH$. To prove that BG must intersect OH if both are produced indefinitely, Schultz introduces two kinds of infinite objects based on this idea. The area in ∠DHK when its sides are produced without end is called an "infinite area," which Schultz claims to bear a definite ratio to the whole plane, the ratio of ∠DHK to 360°. The infinite area bounded by GH and the parallels BG and HK prolonged without end is called a "strip." Schultz argues that strips all bear vanishing ratios to infinite areas, since unlike such areas, no finite number of strips covers the whole plane. The strip $BGHK$ has such a ratio to the infinite area KHF because the latter is equal to the infinite area BGH. But the infinite area DHK has a finite ratio to that of KHF, hence the strip $BGHK$ has a vanishing ratio to the infinite area DHK. It follows, according to Schultz, that BG must eventually meet DH, otherwise the infinite area would be *part* of the strip.

His proof that the infinite areas BGH and KHF *are* equal presupposes that BG and HK are not just Euclid-parallels, but also Wolff-parallels, which is equivalent to Euclid's postulate, though no one realized this at the time.[162] Kant wrote to Schultz in 1784 that "I have no doubts that your book, as also your ingenious theory of parallel lines, will broaden and extend human knowledge and contribute to your deserved fame."[163]

It is clear from Kant's notes on parallels, however, that he preferred a proof without infinite areas: they are not "entirely given," obscuring how a geometer invoking them was "guided throughout by intuition." But he could find only a "philosophical proof" of Euclid's postulate, not a "mathematical" or a "purely geometric" one.[164] Specifically, the theorem that a line perpendicular to one of two Wolff-parallels is perpendicular to the other, says Kant, "cannot be represented mathematically, but rather follows merely from concepts," namely, that of such parallels which alone among pairs of lines "have a determinate distance between them."[165] Such a proof appeals to neither intuition nor construction: "Since this geometrical proof (without dragging in infinite areas) rests only on these propositions, thus on the concepts of determinate distance and parallels as lines whose distance is determinate, which cannot be constructed, it is no mathematical proof."[166] Kant allows that a proof like Schultz's using infinite areas is *mathematical*, even "better than merely philosophical ones," but neither are *geometrical* proofs, in which "the magnitudes whose relations are to be established can be entirely given."[167] These distinctions mark Kant's awareness that his exposition of space as "an infinite given magnitude" is problematic, heightened by Schultz's claim that his infinite areas are "given in pure intuition" in view of it! But any mention of intuition is conspicuously absent from Kant's notes on these proofs, leaving it doubtful that he accepted this claim. Since he accepted Schultz's proof, he must have meant to accommodate it with his more liberal characterization of the geometer's method of Bxii. Kant's acquiescence in a conceptual proof of parallels "foregoing any construction" may also explain why the Transcendental Exposition that replaces the 1781 third space argument expounding the "apodictic certainty of all geometrical principles and the possibility of their *a priori* construction" drops any reference to construction.[168]

In his controversy with Eberhard, who challenged Kant's doctrine of the synthetic a priori in mathematics, Schultz's theory of parallels and the infinite was a target of criticism, creating a difficult situation for Kant. Kästner objected to his proof of Euclid's postulate that only the potential, not the actual infinite is admissible in geometry.[169] But in replying to Eberhard's critique of Euclid, Kant wrote that:

> Euclid himself is supposed to have among his axioms propositions which are certainly in need of demonstration, but are nevertheless presented without proof. . . . If only this *obliging philosophy* . . . had been obliging enough to produce an example from Euclid, where he presents a proposition which is *mathematically* demonstrable as an axiom; for of what can be demonstrated merely philosophically (from concepts), e.g., the whole is greater than the parts, the proof does not belong to mathematics, if its method is stated in a fully rigorous way.[170]

Kant was perhaps disingenuous here, for he knew by now that geometers tried to prove Euclid's postulate because they believed it to lack the evidence of an axiom but accepted Shultz's proof of it as mathematical and his own proof of it from concepts as philosophical. In the *Opus Postumum* he acknowledges this breach in his system, claiming that mathematics still consists of synthetic a priori propositions but admitting that "if one attempted to progress in this science by proceeding analytically from concepts, one would breach its principles, that is, its formal element as a science within philosophy, although not demonstrating falsely."[171] Indeed, Kant adds, "Euclid's proposition regarding two parallel lines which are intersected by a third *can be proved quite rigorously by a philosophical treatment*."[172] Such were the final reverberations of Kant's "crisis of syntheticity" and his own go at the problem of parallels. To gauge Hintikka's gloss on syntheticity we look at the objections made to the synthetic a priori and its Kantian defense.

The focal point of the dispute over syntheticity was the proof of the triangle inequality that Hintikka chose to exemplify "Euclid as a Paradigm for Kant."[173] Schwab argued that if Euclid's proof is based on a suitable definition of a triangle it can be established analytically from concepts that, given triangle ABC, the sum of the sides AB and AC is greater than BC.

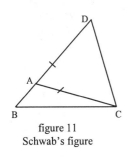

figure 11
Schwab's figure

Euclid extended AB to a point D such that $AC = AD$, so by Thales's theorem, $\angle ADC = \angle ACD$. Also $\angle BCD > \angle ACD$ by Euclid's axiom that the whole is greater than the part, hence $\angle BCD > \angle ADC$. Since the greater angle subtends the greater side, we have $BD > BC$, and Euclid's inequality follows. For Schwab the crux of the matter was threefold: (i) To derive Euclid's postulate "to extend a straight line indefinitely" from the definition of a triangle as a "plane bounded by three straight lines," which implies analytically, he thinks, that it has a finite area and hence finite sides.[174] Since it is also analytic that "any finite magnitude can increase,"[175] Euclid's postulate follows. (ii) To prove Thales's theorem analytically from concepts: in addition to the extension postulate, Euclid's proof of it uses only the axiom that "two straight lines cannot enclose a space" and the congruence theorem for triangles. (iii) The obvious analyticity of the part-whole axiom. Rehberg objected on Kant's behalf to Schwab's *use of the figure*: "a proof from concepts must be conducted entirely with mere words, for everything contained in a concept can be unfolded in words."[176] Rehberg doubted the extension postulate could be proved with mere words without any figure, but admitted that Schwab had revealed more analytic steps in the proof than met the eye. The only proposition needed that could not be proved analytically, said Rehberg, was the axiom that two straight lines cannot enclose a space, for as Kant had remarked, the concept of two such straight lines "contains no negation of a figure."[177] He granted that both the part-whole axiom *and* the congruence theorem were analytic, following Kant with respect to the former but agreeing with Eberhard on the analyticity of the latter. So an analytic demonstration of this theorem could use neither figure, nor extension, nor congruence, and indeed the first two are *the very sources of individual instances and auxiliary constructions in this proof that Hintikka says makes it synthetic for Kant.*[178] But Kant's own view of congruence does pose a problem.

In 1781 Kant said that motion, like all concepts involving *both* space and time, presupposes something empirical, "for this presupposes the perception of something movable. In space, considered in itself, there is nothing movable; hence the movable must be found *in space only through experience*; thus an empirical datum."[179] How then, asked C. G. Schutz, can geometry be the a priori science of space if, as Kant also says, to know anything in space I must *draw* it? "Drawing is, however, a kind of motion; motion is an empirical concept; thus it appears that even lines, consequently figures, and the conic sections need empirical support in order to be represented."[180] Kant replied to this in 1787 by distinguishing the motion of an *object* in space from motion as an *act* of describing space: "Motion of an *object* in space does not belong in a pure science, thus also not in geometry; for that something is movable cannot be cognized *a priori* but only through experience. But motion, as *description* of a space, is a pure act of the successive synthesis of the manifold in outer intuition in general through productive imagination, and belongs not only to geometry but even to transcendental philosophy."[181] But in the *Prolegomena*, Kant claimed that "All proofs of the complete congruence of two given figures . . . finally come down to this: that they coincide with one another which obviously is nothing other than a synthetic proposition based on immediate intuition. This intuition must be given pure and *a priori*, otherwise the proposition could not hold as apodictically certain, but would have only empirical certainty" (§12). *This intuition cannot be of auxiliary constructions, for they do not occur in such proofs.*[182] But in 1783 Kant overlooked that the motion implicit in Euclid's proof violated Kant's own principle in the Transcendental Aesthetic that "motion is found in space only through experience," which was thus incompatible with his claim about congruence. To avoid contradiction Kant revised his claim about intuition that impugned Hintikka's gloss of it in terms of auxiliary construction by invoking "acts of description" that no longer do so.[183] This brings us to Hintikka's crucial argument for severing Kantian intuition from sensibility, the support for it in the second edition, and its bearing on Kant's account of time.

Hintikka's reliance on the definition of an intuition as "a singular representation" allows him to say that it is "not very intuitive."[184] He admits that "later in his system Kant came to make intuitions intuitive again, by arguing that all our human intuitions are bound up with sensibility," but denies that this bond follows from his definition: "On the contrary, Kant insists all through the *Critique of Pure Reason* that it is not incomprehensible that other beings might have intuitions by means other than senses."[185] Kant's admission of the possibility of beings with *intellectual intuition* shows that intuition is not *necessarily* tied to sensibility: he allows that "the concept of a *noumenon*, i.e., of a thing that is not to be thought of as an object of the senses but rather as a thing in itself . . . is not at all contradictory; for one cannot assert of sensibility that it is the only possible kind of intuition."[186] Kant allowed for such beings in the second edition when he inserted the qualification "at least for us humans" in the definition of intuition as something given immediately to sensibility.[187] But how can his admission of such intuition touch his transcendental theory of mathematics, if human intuitions *are* sensible?

A cardinal point requiring a being with intellectual intuition is the crux of Kant's Elucidation of the transcendental ideality of time by which he resolves the conflict between causality and freedom.[188] Kant grants that Lambert's argument from change shows that time is *empirically* real, but he wants to "dispute all claim of time to absolute reality, namely where it would attach to things absolutely as a condition or property even without regard to the form of our sensible intuition."[189] From the exposition of time as a pure intuition he "concluded" that time could not "attach to things as an objective determination, and thus remain if one abstracted from all subjective conditions of the intuitions of things," for then time could not be "cognized and intuited *a priori* through synthetic propositions."[190] Kant *tries to elucidate such an abstraction* by claiming that "if I or another being could intuit myself without this condition of sensibility, then these very determinations, which we now represent to ourselves as alternations, would yield us a cognition in which the representation of time and thus also of alteration would not occur at all."[191] But the counterfactual claim, that *I* could intuit my inner state as changeless if freed from the bondage of sensibility, begs the question. Kant can only deny the "absolute reality" of time by arguing that *there is* "another being" who could intuit my inner state as changeless: namely, a "primordial being" like God with an intellectual intuition of my self as it is in itself.[192] The point is not just that Kant's need to acknowledge a being with intellectual intuition to elucidate the ideality of time justifies Hintikka's denial that Kantian intuition is tied necessarily to sensibility, but to identify a third problem, in addition to motion and parallels, which Kant found in his formulations of 1781, that prompted those of 1787 that are more favorable to Hintikka's austere reading.

Kant admitted in the B-Preface that his account of time left something to be desired.[193] His proof that time is a pure intuition was especially weak, as Christian Garve pointed out in his review of the *Critique*. Kant noticed that the certainty peculiar to mathematics was due to its ability to make its concepts "intuitable in all their purity," says Garve, and in exploring this "believed that he had discovered a special type of intuition he called intuition *a priori*." Consequently, "this peculiarity of Mathematics and particularly of Geometry, he inferred, cannot come from anywhere but the special nature of its object, *space*, and because space and time are

completely analogous concepts, this *a priori* intuition must be special to
both of them and only them."[194] Garve demurred, for "as similar as space
and time supposedly are, and even though both, as the author puts it, are
intuited *a priori*, how is it that the intuitable aspect of time has hardly led
us to any particular proposition, whereas that of space has allowed us to
develop a whole science, Geometry?"[195] Here Garve fingered a weak link
in the *Critique*: having argued that space had to be a pure intuition for
geometry to prove so many synthetic a priori propositions about it, Kant
tries to assign the same status to time on the strength of the axiom that "it
has only one dimension: different times are not simultaneous but
successive."[196] Worse, critics and followers alike were convinced that the
successiveness of different times was *analytic*, despite Kant's claim that the
validity of such axioms is needed for experiences to be possible.[197] Garve's
question bears on the familiar one of what science Kant bases on time:
arithmetic, mechanics, or what? He was clearly unaware that Kant's paltry
"axiom of time" was only a sample of the four axioms and three postulates
Lambert had formulated for chronometry.[198] We must try then to understand
Kant's silence about this even while trying to integrate it into his system in
order to prove ideality and refute idealism. Kant eventually realizes that he
must walk a fine line between marshaling enough a priori knowledge of
time to prove that it is a pure intuition while showing that we have *not*
enough of it for an idealist to "determine his existence in time."[199] What
light can Hintikka shed on this?

Hintikka finds confirmation of his reliance on singularity in the
argument that space is a pure intuition because, Kant says, "one can only
represent a single space, and if one speaks of many spaces, one understands
by that only parts of one and the same unique space."[200] Hintikka thinks his
view better frames the "active force" of Kant's intuitions implicit in his
transcendental arguments about space and time than does vulgar intuition
keyed to passive perception. He argues that Kant's conclusion from the
intuition argument, that "space represents no property at all of any things
in themselves . . . nor determinations of them,"[201] is best seen as making the
point that "intuitions used *a priori* (that is to say, used so as to precede their
objects) can yield knowledge only if they pertain to the subjective
conditions of knowledge, that is, to our knowledge-seeking activities and
their products."[202] Hintikka claims that "essentially the same things" can be
said of Kant's conclusions about *time*, but despite his effort to frame his
time arguments parallel to those of space, they are very different. The
argument that time is a pure intuition also rests on its singularity, but when
we see Kant in his transcendental conclusions still trying to prove that time
is an intuition, we may doubt his confidence in this argument.

Kant concludes that time is nothing but the form of inner sense, of the intuition of our self and our inner state:

> For time cannot be a determination of outer appearances; it belongs neither to a shape or a position, etc., but on the contrary determines the relation of representations in our inner state. And just because this inner intuition yields no shape we also attempt to remedy this lack through analogies, and represent the temporal sequence through a line progressing to infinity, in which the manifold constitutes a series that is of only one dimension, and infer from the properties of this line to all the properties of time, with the sole difference that the parts of the former are simultaneous but those of the latter always exist successively. From this it is also apparent that the representation of time is itself an intuition, since all its relations can be expressed in an outer intuition.[203]

When we isolate from an empirical intuition everything the understanding thinks about it as well as all sensation, Kant said we were left with a shape: a pure intuition occurring "*a priori* . . . as a mere form of sensibility in the mind."[204] To confirm that time is a pure intuition by "isolating" a suitable "shape" from it he appeals to its linear representation, but this obliges him to go beyond Lambert to claim that we can infer *all* the properties of time except successiveness from those of the line representing it.[205] But the *intuitivity* of time itself hardly follows that of its *representation*. Kant can only cling to its singularity, but Thompson questioned whether time really *can* be "a genuinely singular term for Kant" in view of its need for such outer representation.[206] Hintikka's reliance on singularity can be shored up by appeal to the *formal intuitions* Kant explicitly introduced in 1787 when he stressed that the B-deduction requires space and time to *be* intuitions themselves and not merely *forms* of it, for "space, represented as an *object* (as is really required in geometry) contains more than the mere form of intuition, namely, the *comprehension* of the manifold given in accordance with the form of sensibility in an *intuitive* representation, so that the *form of intuition* merely gives the manifold, but the *formal intuition* gives *unity* of representation."[207] Kant does not identify what the formal intuition of time is the object of, but he presumably took its representing line to *be* its singular formal intuition.[208]

Hintikka's reading fits the transcendental exposition of space since it arose from his analysis of Kant's accounts of geometrical reasoning, but it should also clarify the more problematic transcendental exposition of time if it is "especially true of what Kant calls the transcendental expositions of the basic mathematical concepts" that we can analyze them in terms of modern quantification theory.[209] We see that Garve's objection did not catch

Kant by surprise when we read in the first edition that he will show "that there is a large number of *a priori* apodictic and synthetic propositions about both [space and time], but especially about space, which we will therefore here investigate as our primary example."[210] But the newly minted transcendental exposition of time simply refers to the metaphysical exposition with its "one or two propositions" that Garve questioned.[211] Kant adds that, since it underlies the principle of contradiction, "our concept of time therefore explains the possibility of as much synthetic *a priori* cognition as is presented by the general theory of motion, which is no less fruitful."[212] But time is hardly mentioned in the text of *Metaphysical Foundations*: the Preface, however, presents a curious argument why there cannot really *be* a substantial science based on time that is quite natural on Hintikka's analysis.

Kant argues that the "doctrine of the soul" can never be a science, for "in any special doctrine of nature there can be only as much *proper* science as there is mathematics therein."[213] But *mathematics is not applicable to inner sense*, says Kant, so

> the only option one would have would be to take the *law of continuity* in the flux of inner changes into account—which, however, would be an extension of cognition standing to that which mathematics provides for the doctrine of body approximately as the doctrine of the properties of the straight line stands to the whole of geometry. For the pure intuition in which the appearances of the soul are supposed to be constructed is *time*, which has only one dimension.[214]

This is Kant's fallback answer to Garve: with its one dimension time cannot be expected to yield any more synthetic a priori propositions than the geometry of a straight line as opposed to the rich store of theorems of plane geometry.[215] In his final formulation of this *dimensionality argument*, Kant says of the doctrines of body and soul that, "in both there can be science only insofar as mathematics, i.e., the construction of concepts, can be applied therein, and hence the spatiality of objects can do more *a priori* for physics, than the form of time which underlies intuition through inner sense, since the latter has only one dimension."[216] But Garve questioned how one could prove that time *was* an intuition with so few a priori propositions about it. On Hintikka's analysis Kant's position hangs together: time is an intuition because it is *singular*, but its one-dimensionality leaves no more room for proving synthetic chronometrical theorems by *auxiliary constructions* than one would have in the geometry of a straight line. Kant knew when he wrote his makeshift transcendental exposition of time not only that Lambert formulated seven axioms and postulates for chronometry but that Schultz intended to meet Garve's challenge with his *own* axioms and postulates for time in his commentary on the *Critique*.[217] But it is unclear if Kant ever pondered the differences in their formulations, and hence difficult to know if he ever consciously felt confronted with "alternative chronometries" differing enough to make him doubt the existence of a unique axiomatic "science of time" sufficient to answer Garve squarely. If we apply Hintikka's reading to this argument in the context of his own argument that his reading is confirmed by the role of the Axioms of Intuition, we can further focus Kant's response to this problem as well as some puzzling aspects of his doctrine of the Axioms.

Hintikka sees the Axioms as "a reluctant and indirect admission of the conceptual fact that the logic of our knowledge of particulars (intuitions) is the logic of existence and universality," that is, first-order logic which deals with the different quantities of judgment: universality, particularity, and singularity.[218] It may seem surprising, says Hintikka, that the principle for the categories of quantity would be the *axioms of intuition*, but "it is merely Kant's oblique recognition of the fact that the logic of existence and universality is the 'logic' of the axioms of intuition, i.e., of the axioms for particular representations."[219] He takes Kant's Principle that "all intuitions are extensive magnitudes," to mean that "all particulars are subject to geometrical and kinematical conditions," objecting to this otherwise apt marriage of intuition to the logic of particulars that "it is certainly easier to argue in terms of our concepts of existence and universality than in terms of the idea of intuitions as always being given to us in sense perception."[220] This global analysis of the Axioms ignores curious gaps they betray in the otherwise impeccable tripartite architecture of Kant's interlocking system of categories, schemata, and principles which have puzzled commentators. Why only *one* principle for the three categories of quantity? And why only one *schema* for them?[221]

The schema for a category is a "transcendental time determination" which "rests on a rule *a priori*" making it applicable to appearances.[222] The pure schema of the category of quantity "is *number*, which is a representation that summarizes the successive addition of one (homogeneous) unit to another. Thus number is nothing other than the unity of the synthesis of the manifold of a homogeneous intuition in general, because I generate time itself in the apprehension of the intuition."[223] But why not three schemas, as we have for the three categories of relation and modality? If Kant held Euclid's definition of number as "a plurality of units," the use of the categories of unity, plurality, and totality in many acts of counting and measuring would follow from Kant's combination principle, namely, that "*allness* (totality) is nothing other than plurality considered as a unity." He says that the concept of number "belongs to the category of allness," i.e., totality.[224] But this fails for measurements yielding a quantity of *one* unit, say a stick one foot long, perhaps explaining why Kant provided *no schema for the category of unity*. This would be "nothing but [an] *a priori* time-determination in accordance with rules"[225] making the category of unity applicable in its quantitative sense: a unit of measurement such as a minute, or inch. How could there be an a priori rule for determining a unit of *time*? We can only pick a unit *arbitrarily*, and Lambert's scale invariance axiom of chronometry states explicitly that a priori determinate units of time *do not exist*. Nor could such a schema for determining such units.[226] This is implied by Hintikka's motivation for the dimensionality argument.

Kant uses his account of quantity as schematized by number to prove that all intuitions have extensive magnitudes.[227] The idea is that since all intuitions are in space and time, they are determined by the *same kind of successive synthesis of their parts by virtue of which they have quantity*. He gives two examples: "I cannot represent to myself any line, no matter how small it may be, without drawing it in thought, i.e., successively generating all its parts from one point, and thereby first sketching this intuition. It is exactly the same with even the smallest time. I think therein only the successive progress from one moment to another, where through all parts of time and their addition a determinate magnitude of time is finally generated."[228] Kant passes over an essential point: the magnitude of a temporal interval is hardly "determinate" with a definite value unless the "parts" added are either *equal* or contain a definite number of *units* of time. My "successive advance" through seven days adds up to a "determinate week" if they are all equal, just as the successive applications of a ruler only determine that a board is ten feet long if it is divisible into ten equal parts each congruent with the ruler. But temporal advance precludes such application, prompting Locke to claim that we can never *know*, by any *intuitive* evidence, that two parts of duration *are* equal or some process truly *periodic*.[229] Lambert, following Newton, grants there may really *be* no perfectly periodic process in nature but argues that one can determine the inequalities of clocks by means of the dynamical laws of motion *for whose independent variable of time we must presuppose an absolute congruence*.[230] Since Kant's example of the Axioms rehearses the main point of the A-deduction of quantity for temporal intervals without joining the issue of temporal congruence, there is justice in Hintikka's claim that his attempt "to give a deeper foundation of the alleged connection between particulars and sensibility by means of his examination of the threefold synthesis" is unsatisfactory.[231] What about a priori chronometrical construction?

In a passage in the Methodology that seems to count against the two-levels thesis, Kant says that, "of all intuition none is given *a priori* except the mere form of appearances, space and time, and a concept of these, as *quanta*, can be exhibited *a priori* in pure intuition, i.e., constructed, together with either its quality (its shape), or else merely its quantity (the mere synthesis of the homogeneous manifold) through number."[232] This patch of the transcendental idealism in the Methodology may blur the two-levels thesis, but the a priori construction of *shapes* in pure intuition is equivalent to Kant's a priori proof of $\Sigma = 2R$, which is grist for Hintikka's logic mill. But it is also equivalent to Lambert's axioms, excluding a priori units, and this passage suggests we can, a priori, construct *quantities* in violation of such axioms, as does Kant's elaboration of mathematical construction: "But to determine an intuition *a priori* in space (shape), to divide time (duration), or merely to cognize the universal in the synthesis of one and the same thing in time and space and the magnitude of an intuition in general (number) which arises from that: that is the *concern* of *reason* through the construction of concepts, and is called *mathematical*."[233] Lambert proved that $\Sigma < 2R$ allowed the a priori measure of angles to be geometrically transferred to lengths, but the one dimension of time provides no angles or any other a priori constructible pegs for durations. Kant might agree that his "divisions of time" could only comprise the construction of durations *bearing a prescribed ratio to given durations*, but this includes the a priori construction of equal durations. He says that temporal constructions are *mathematical*, but on what axioms are they based, those of Lambert or Schultz? Why are they not mentioned in the Axioms of Intuition? Kant avoided such questions with a dimensionality argument that seems natural on Hintikka's reading.[234]

We can now summarize the main points of our analysis of Hintikka's interpretation of Kantian intuition. He observed that the intuition invoked by Kant in his favorite demonstration of a synthetic a priori proposition was said to emanate from the auxiliary parallel drawn by the geometer. He noted that this assimilation of intuition to singular representations in the Methodology is adumbrated in the *Prize Essay* with its emphasis on the geometer's use of concrete symbols, and he pointed to Lambert's 1766 letter as a plausible catalyst for Kant's early associations of intuition with individual examples in geometrical proofs. Hintikka argues that this notion of intuition, which lends itself to logical analysis, is prior to and independent of the doctrine of the Transcendental Aesthetic that ties intuitions immediately to our forms of sensibility. But like the *Essay*, the *Critique* was geared to explain the certainty that Kant uncritically assumed to invariably attach to geometrical proofs, innocent of all the paralogisms and uncertainty resulting from the actual efforts of geometers. Kant realized this by the time he revised the *Critique* in 1787 and Hintikka's reading relies on many passages in this edition, so we can hardly evaluate it adequately without asking why.

Four problems were not addressed sufficiently, if at all, in 1781, the 1787 formulations of which are more favorable to Hintikka's austere logical reading: the ideality of time, the paucity of axioms of time, the problem of parallels, and the status of motion in geometry. Thus, the second edition is more explicit in acknowledging the possibility of intellectual intuition needed to elucidate the ideality of time against Lambert's objection to it, thereby severing the bond of necessity between intuition and sensibility seen by many as inimical to Hintikka's reading. Garve asked how one could prove that time *is* a pure intuition with so few "axioms of time" compared with those of geometry. Kant replied in 1786 that a science based on time can be no more extensive than the geometry of the straight line, as one would expect on Hintikka's reading: there would be no room within a line of one dimension for proofs by auxiliary constructions. This leaves the intuitivity of time hanging by the slender thread of its representing line. In 1781 Kant became aware of the problem of parallels. On reflection he saw that Euclid's parallels were not constructible in intuition and that the only proof of his postulate based on them was J. Schultz's invoking infinite areas that few accepted. Kant defined parallels as equidistant lines but had to settle for a "philosophical proof" from concepts, foregoing any construction, of Euclid's postulate. This liberalization of geometrical proofs is reflected in the formulation of the true method of geometry in the B-Preface that Hintikka cites as Kant's denial that vulgar intuition is any part of that method. But C. G. Schutz asked how motion could be known only from experience and still play its role in the a priori science of geometry. While unaware of this conflict, Kant claimed in the *Prolegomena* that proofs of congruence rested on immediate a priori intuition despite using no auxiliary constructions, in conflict with Hintikka's analysis. But in 1787 Kant distinguished motion of an object in space from acts of describing space, assigning to the latter a kinematical interpretation in accord with Hintikka's reading of the Axioms of Intuition.

Hintikka takes the basic insight of Kant's theory of mathematics to be his realization that "*certain arguments simply cannot be carried out without the use of auxiliary constructions.*"[235] Kant thereby anticipated, he believes, what Peirce called his "first real discovery about mathematical procedure," namely, the distinction between *corollarial* and *theorematic* reasoning. In the formulation Hintikka took as typical, Peirce says that *corollarial deduction* is where it is only necessary to imagine any case in which the premises are true in order to perceive immediately that the conclusion holds in that case. . . . *Theorematic deduction* is deduction in which it is necessary to experiment in imagination upon the image of the premiss in order for the result of such experiment to make corollarial deductions to the truth of the conclusion.[236]

Peirce relates his distinction to the anatomy of Euclidean proofs, making it clear that by "experiment" he meant an auxiliary construction, but Hintikka stresses that his "brilliant insight is that this geometrical distinction can be generalized to *all deductive reasoning*."[237] Indeed, "What makes a deduction theorematic according to Peirce is that in it we must envisage other individuals than those needed to instantiate the premise of the argument."[238] By formalizing proofs of geometry, says Hintikka,

we obtain a good reconstruction of Peirce's theorematic-corollarial distinction for deductions using the tools of modern quantification theory: a valid deductive step is theorematic if it increases the number of layers of quantifiers in the proposition in question. This is, apart from the possibility of a minor sharpening of the definition, precisely my distinction between non-trivial and trivial logical arguments (surface tautologies and depth tautologies).[239]

Hintikka embraces Peirce's claim of the importance of his distinction for resolving puzzles about human reasoning and identifies their common core as Aristotle's problem of logical incontinence: "How can anyone fail to see all the logical consequences of premises one is aware of?"[240] This in turn is essentially the problem of "logical omniscience" pressed by critics of "possible worlds" approaches to epistemic logic, but:

These problems are all solved by the Peirce-Hintikka distinction. There may indeed be a problem as to how anyone can fail to carry out a corollarial deduction. . . . But there is not even a problem as to how one can fail to draw a theorematic conclusion. Since such a conclusion is characterized by the need of introducing the right auxiliary individuals into the argument, it can fail not only because of a wrong choice of auxiliary individuals but more importantly by a simple failure to consider the more complicated configurations of individuals obtainable by introducing auxiliaries.[241]

Hintikka succeeded in making model-theoretical sense of "the number of individuals considered in an argument" with his game-theoretical semantics, the roots of which he also finds in Peirce.[242] His broader interpretive aim is to *place Peirce within the model-theoretic "language as calculus" tradition in logic.*

Hintikka faults Peirce for thinking that "perhaps when any branch of mathematics is worked up into its most perfect form all its theorems will be converted into corollaries."[243] He shows that with certain "natural" rules of first-order logic we could not convert all theorems of an *undecidable* theory into corollaries in Peirce's sense.[244] As Hookway has observed, "Given Peirce's interest in whether the future work of necessary reasoning could be left to machines, it is tempting to construe Peirce's doctrine as an early dim anticipation of the undecidability of the logic of relations. Thus Hintikka has seized upon the Peircean distinction as an anticipation of his own distinction between depth and surface tautologies."[245] While granting the relevance of this reconstruction Hookway doubts that it can "get to the heart" of Peirce's thought since "he is somewhat ambivalent about the relation between the logic of relations and issues of decidability."[246] Hintikka replied that "not only is it the case that corollarial reasoning is mechanizable and decidable. On my reconstruction, the decidability of a theory becomes simply the problem of telling which 'auxiliary constructions' to carry out—or even how many of them will be needed for a proof. Predicting this number is equivalent to the decision problem of the theory in question."[247] To evaluate Hintikka's reconstruction and critique of Peirce, as well as Hookway's and other objections to it, we need to see how Peirce came to make this distinction and the problems he saw in maintaining it. Analysis of his examples of theorematic reasoning reveal two different notions he never clearly distinguished, one of which was central in Hilbert's work on the foundations of geometry. Peirce's formulation above is from his Carnegie application of 1902 for support for his research on logic and mathematics including theorematic and corollarial deductions; but he framed this distinction and the related theme of mechanical reasoning in various ways over many years that are by no means equivalent, nor are some plausibly explicated in Hintikka's terms. The issue of mechanical reasoning in turn was closely related for Peirce to the logic of relations. Let us track how he braided these three strands of theorematic, nonmechanical, and relational reasoning as he developed.

In his 1883 paper on the logic of relatives Peirce notes that because of multiple quantification "this algebra cannot be subjected to hard and fast rules like those of the Boolean calculus; and all that can be done in this place is to give a general idea of the way of working with it."[248] This admission gives way to the claim in his 1885 paper that "I shall not be able to perfect the algebra sufficiently to give facile methods of reaching logical conclusions. I can only give a method by which any legitimate conclusion may be reached and any fallacious one avoided."[249] If "legitimate" and "fallacious" conclusions are valid and invalid ones respectively, he was claiming a complete method that will soundly "avoid" invalid inferences. Peirce stressed that his extension of Boole's algebra with notations such as "l_{ijk}" for "points i, j, k lie on one line" allowed his logic to "express relations of considerable complexity," and gives this example of his *sixth icon*:[250]

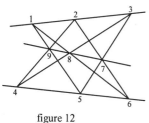

figure 12

$$l_{159} \prec l_{267} \prec l_{348} \prec l_{249} \prec l_{186} \prec l_{375} \prec l_{123} \prec l_{456} \prec l_{789}$$

He also saw his logic as "a first step toward the resolution of one of the main problems of logic, that of producing a method for the discovery of methods in mathematics."[251] Before seeing what sort of "methods" Peirce hoped to discover with his logic, let us see how he thought it resolved an old paradox of mathematics.

It had long been "a puzzle how it could be that, on the one hand, mathematics is purely deductive . . . and draws its conclusions apodictically, while on the other hand, it presents as rich and apparently unending series of surprising discoveries as any observational science." Peirce's solution was that "all deductive reasoning . . . consists in constructing an icon or diagram the relations of whose parts shall present a complete analogy with those of the parts of the object of reasoning, of experimenting upon this image in the imagination, and of observing the result so as to discover unnoticed and hidden relations among the parts."[252] In 1887 he uses this idea to explain to Marie Noble why reasoning always "involves observation": the mathematician "draws a diagram . . . conforming to certain general conditions, and then he observes certain relations among the parts of his diagram, over and above those which were used to determine the construction of it."[253] That she may see such a proof of an "interesting proposition" Peirce explains Desargues's theorem: if two coplanar triangles are in perspective from a point, they must also have an axis of perspective, i.e., the three points of intersection of corresponding sides must be collinear. He sketches von Staudt's long proof that begins by connecting the given configuration with a new point "over and above" the plane in which it lies and constructing a spatial configuration of planes, three of which determine the center of perspective and two its axis. This proof will become Peirce's paradigm for theorematic reasoning and as such an anchor of Hintikka's reading.

He soon invokes this proof in connection with the problem of whether such reasoning could be executed by *logical machines* and concludes that although such machines do reason, since their operations conform to truth-preserving rules, they are "destitute of all originality and initiative." For, says Peirce, "the simplest proposition of projective geometry, about ten straight lines in a plane, is proved by von Staudt from a few premises and by reasoning of extreme simplicity, but so complicated is the mode of compounding these premises and rules of inference, that there are no less than 70 or 80 steps in the demonstration. How can we make a machine

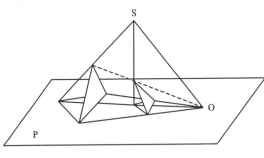

figure 13

that would automatically thread its way through such a labyrinth as that?"[254] Given the central perspectivity of two coplanar triangles, the machine would have to "take the initiative" in introducing spatial objects "over and above" the plane to determine their axis. This proof will ever be Peirce's paradigm for what is "unmechanical" in mathematical reasoning, which he later calls "theoric" for exploiting "the power of looking at facts from a novel point of view."[255] Though this graphical theorem says nothing about lengths, for long the only known proof of it calculated lengths: "Since this introduced an idea to which, indeed, no doubt attached, yet which was in nowise involved in the premises, the demonstration was of the kind called theoric."[256] This "new point of view" was "ill chosen," but finally, "von Staudt had the idea, equally simple, indubitable, and penetrating, that the three rays in the plane passing through the arbitrarily chosen point, might be regarded as a perspective representation of three rays through the same point."[257] This idea that the plane figure is a projection of a three dimensional one is not corollarial, and "the notion of any such idea being furnished by turning the crank of a logical machine is simply ludicrous."[258] Only one's familiarity with perspective "would bring this theoric step to his mind." But was it *logically necessary*?

For Peirce the above proofs for the plane case made it "a truly remarkable theorem."[259] They exemplified what in 1903 he called "theorematic" as opposed to corollarial ones which merely "represent the conditions of the conclusion in a diagram" and finds from the observation of this diagram *as it is*, the truth of the conclusion: going beyond the observation of the diagram "as it is," such a proof "performs an ingenious experiment upon the diagram, and by observation of the diagram, so modified, ascertains the truth of the conclusion."[260] He had long viewed von

Staudt's proof as a most "ingenious experiment" on a planar diagram, but in 1898 he was still unclear about the generality of his distinction. Further inspiration came from Boole's widow who, Peirce enthuses, "has lately written a little book in which she points out that, in solving a mathematical problem, we usually introduce some part or element into the construction which, when it has served our purpose, is removed."[261] She gave striking examples of such constructions, but Peirce prefers the plane Desargues's theorem: "The demonstration of it which is now usual, that of von Staudt, introduces a third dimension, and the utility of that arises from the fact that a ray, or unlimited straight line, being the intersection of two planes, these planes show us exactly where the ray runs, while, as long as we confine ourselves to the consideration of a single plane, we have no easy method of describing precisely what the course of the ray is."[262] But this hardly shows that this case can *only* be proved by such reasoning.

The need for relations to *express* Desargues's theorem plays no role in Peirce's analyses of its nonmechanical proofs. In 1887 he wrote:

> I do not think there would be any great difficulty in constructing a machine which should work the logic of relations with a large number of terms. But owing to the great variety of ways in which the same premises can be combined to produce different conclusions in that branch of logic, the machine, in its first state of development, would be no more mechanical than a hand-loom for weaving in many colors with many shuttles. The study of how to pass from such a machine as that to one corresponding to a Jacquard loom, would be likely to do very much for the improvement of logic.[263]

But he never pursued this and by 1896 is convinced that "the old syllogistic inference can be worked by machinery, but characteristic relative inferences cannot be performed by any mere mechanical rule whatever."[264] Only *one* conclusion follows from syllogistic premises, but in relative logic, "at every step . . . there are different courses which reason may pursue; so that the conduct of the reasoning far transcends the powers of any machine."[265] Peirce invoked this nonmechanical aspect of such reasoning to stem what he saw by 1900 as the alarming invasion of machinery in every aspect of culture:

> Consider Mathematics, as a field where, if anywhere, it might be supposed that machinery would be of little avail. In the early eighteenth century the greatest geometers in Europe were still 'stumping' one another with problems, and the discovery of a theorem might raise a man to greatness. . . . Subsequently, it must be a *method*, no longer a mere *theorem*, to impress the world so power-fully. Nowadays, methods of the greatest power and profundity are turned out at such an astonishing rate that nobody but professional mathematicians ever

hear of them singly, at all. Hermann Schubert's Calculus of Geometry, which enables us, for example, by a brief computation, to determine that the number of cubic curves each of which shall touch any twelve given spheroids, is just 5 billion 819,539 million, 783,680 hardly makes a ripple in the ocean of modern mathematics.[266]

This calculus exemplified the "methods" whose discovery he thought his logic could facilitate—but also the regrettable eclipse of theorems by mechanical methods as discoveries that could "raise a man to greatness." Only a "major theorem" could still do this, and Peirce felt he *had* discovered such a theorem.

Peirce's proof of his "theorem about multitudes" was perhaps the first that he explicitly called "theorematic," in an effort to classify it as "major."[267] It says that "every multitude is less than a multitude. That is, given any multitude, as that of the Xs, there is a collection, which we may call the Ys such that there is a relation, ρ, such that every X is ρ to a Y to which no other X is ρ; but any relation, σ, whatsoever is either such that some Y is not σ to any X or else is such that two different Ys σ to the same X."[268] Peirce denies that this claim could be proved by "a straight forward application of the definition of fewer" since it appears to be false. He called his labored diagonal proof that there is no 1-1 correspondence between the Xs and "the possible collections of Xs," theorematic "inasmuch as it requires the invention of an idea not at all forced upon us by the terms of the thesis."[269] But he does not identify the "idea" so required in his proof, insisting only that it differs essentially from corollarial reasoning which "consists merely in carefully taking account of the definitions of the terms occurring in the thesis to be proved."[270] Since Peirce did *not* define the terms of his thesis, one could object that he had not really given corollarial reasoning a chance, and he admits that "one cannot see how a first premiss of mathematics can have any other origin than as the definition of a term or the definition of what shall be regarded as involved in the idea of the general subject of discussion."[271] He even grants that on a *suitable definition* of "collection" his theorem *might reduce to a corollary*, but "if that proof is to be made corollarial, it can only be by a deeper study of possibility; I have not neglected this study; but I have not as yet reached sufficiently matured conclusions."[272] Hintikka's analysis of Peirce's doubt in terms of undecidability hardly explains what puzzled him here, as another such case will make clear.

Thales's theorem was proved by ever simpler constructions until Pappus proved it without any at all by a reflection. Given Peirce's association of the "unmechanical" element in reasoning with the "theoric" introduction of such constructions, one might expect him to see this proof as corollarial. But he calls it theorematic because it could not be carried out "without imagining something more than what the condition supposes to exist."[273] Specifically, it can be proved "by first proving that a rigid triangle may be exactly superposed on the isosceles triangle, and that it may be turned over and reapplied to the same triangle. But since the enunciation of the Pons says nothing about such a thing and since the Pons cannot be demonstrated without some such hypothesis . . . it is a theorem."[274] But we could *define* congruence by means of displacements of rigid bodies: "Were such a definition admitted, we may admit that the idea of a rigid triangle being turned over and reapplied to the fixed isosceles triangle would be so nearly suggested in the enunciation that the proposition might well be called a corollary."[275] Peirce could not rule out *the possibility that such definitions might always exist in a 'perfected' branch of mathematics.*

It was in his Carnegie application that Peirce wrote that his "first real discovery" about mathematical proofs was his notion of theorematic reasoning that "considers something not implied at all in the conceptions so far gained, which neither the definition of the object of research nor anything yet known about could of themselves suggest, although they give room for it. Euclid, for example, will add lines to his diagram which are not at all required or suggested by any previous proposition, and which the conclusion that he reaches by this means says nothing about."[276] Earlier in the application Peirce says rather that theorematic reasoning "consists in so introducing a foreign idea, using it, and finally deducing a conclusion from which it is eliminated. Every such proof rests, however, upon judgments in which the foreign idea is first introduced, and which are simply self evident."[277] We saw Peirce in 1907 call the old metrical proof of Desargues's theorem "theoric" since it "introduced an idea [of length] . . . which was in nowise involved in the premises." In 1909 he instructs James that metrical ideas "are utterly irrelevant" to the projective theorems of Desargues and Pascal and that the space construction to prove the former is "a very good example" of theorematic reasoning.[278] There are thus two distinct kinds of things we can introduce into a proof that do not appear in such a theorem: auxiliary *lines* and the idea of *length*. The former are only new *objects* of the same kind occurring in the theorem, while the latter is a new *concept* that is "foreign" to it. Had Peirce discussed these theorems in his application, he would have said that the idea of length was foreign to them and that von Staudt's proof of Desargues's was theorematic in that it "adds lines to the diagram . . . which the conclusion that he reaches says nothing about." But in 1902 he had no logical basis for thinking that such a construct was *necessary* to prove this theorem. Peirce was also struggling to write a book on non-Euclidean geometry treated as special cases of projective geometry.[279] In response to his request for advice about the best recent works on non-Euclidean geometry, E. H. Moore recommended and actually sent Peirce a copy of Hilbert's *Grundlagen der Geometrie*, wherein Peirce could find "theorems" answering some of his questions about these theorematic proofs.[280] This brings us to Hintikka's analysis of Peirce's model-theoretic credentials, which he motivates by an interesting comparison of them with those of Hilbert.

Hintikka sees the essential idea of the model-theoretic as opposed to the universalist tradition in logic as the view that language is "like a calculus" that can be freely reinterpreted.[281] He believes that Peirce placed himself in this tradition "with perfect clarity" when he said of his existential graphs that "this system is not intended to serve as a universal language for mathematicians or other reasoners like that of Peano."[282] Peano illustrated his claim that all of mathematics could be expressed in his universal symbolic language with a book in which all the axioms and theorems of descriptive geometry were written.[283] Hilbert, however, *consciously avoided the use of any such logical symbolism* in his *Festschrift*, believing that he could thereby better exercise the "ground rule" of modern mathematics:

> In this investigation the ground rule was to discuss every question that arises in such a way as to find out . . . whether it can be answered in a specified way with some limited means . . . if in the course of mathematical investigations, a problem is encountered, or a theorem is conjectured, the drive for knowledge is then satisfied only if either the complete solution of the problem and the rigorous proof of the theorem are demonstrated successfully, or the basis for the impossibility of success and hence inevitability of failure are clearly seen. The *impossibility* of certain solutions and proofs thus plays a prominent role in modern mathematics, and the drive to answer questions of this kind is often the cause for the discovery of new and fruitful areas of investigation."[284]

In fact, "the logical analysis of spatial intuition" for which Hilbert framed his axiomatic system required knowing exactly from what axioms a theorem can and *cannot* be proved.

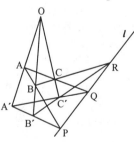

figure 14

Hilbert separated his twenty-three axioms into five groups, "each of which expresses certain basic facts of our intuition which belong together": axioms of incidence (plane and space), order, congruence, parallelism, and continuity. The simplest and most direct expressions of our spatial intuition are the space incidence axioms, for example, that any three noncollinear points lie in a plane, and that it is unique. Desargues theorem (D) in space is an immediate consequence of these two axioms and may thus be said to be evident to space intuition.[285] On Hintikka's reconstruction of Peirce this proof would still be theorematic since it uses three auxiliary planes beyond the two occurring in the theorem.[286] In the case of coplanar triangles von Staudt's space construction also follows from Hilbert's axioms but requires many more auxiliary individuals, so Hintikka's gloss gives it a greater degree of theorematicity than the space theorem—in keeping with Peirce's own opinion. In his lectures Hilbert cited this case and proof to illustrate the bearing of his "ground rule" on the problem of auxiliary constructions:

> *The content of Desargues' theorem belongs entirely to plane geometry; for its proof, however, we have used space.* Here therefore we are for the first time in a position to pursue a critique of the auxiliary devices of a proof. Such a critique is often pursued in modern mathematics, where the endeavor is to safeguard the purity of methods, that is, to use in the proof of a theorem, wherever possible, only such auxiliary means as are closely related to the content of the theorem. This endeavor often succeeds and has been fruitful for the progress of science.[287]

As Peirce recommended: "Demonstration should be *Corollarial* when it can."[288] But he did not believe (D) could be proved in the plane in this manner: as he informed James, "for more than two centuries . . . the greatest mathematicians have tried to prove *that* by the diagram required to exhibit it *alone*, and hence have tried in vain."[289] Hilbert verified this by proving

(I) (D) cannot be proved from the axioms of plane incidence, order, parallels, and continuity.

by constructing a model in which all these axioms hold while (D) along with the congruence axiom for triangles fails. This axiom is necessary to prove (D) in the plane, so that any proof of this case *must* use either a space construction or the idea of congruence foreign to the theorem.[290]

(D) is the basic theorem on the two-dimensional representation of three-dimensional scenes in linear perspective giving a geometrical criterion for one triangle in space to be the perspective image of another. To isolate what (D) implies about space simpliciter, Hilbert considers affine planes in which the axioms of plane incidence, order, and parallels hold and proves

(E) An affine plane can be embedded in space iff (D) holds in it.

Together with (I) this shows, as Hilbert put it in his lectures, that "Desargues' theorem is the only one which the plane gains for itself from space, and we could say that everything is provable with Desargues's in the plane that is provable in space generally."[291] This can be proved synthetically by defining, solely in terms of the points and lines of the given plane, "space points," "space lines," and "planes" and using (D) to prove the space axioms for them. Hilbert gave an algebraic construction of the embedding space based on his co-ordinatization theorem

(C) An affine plane can be represented by a skew field iff (D) holds in it.

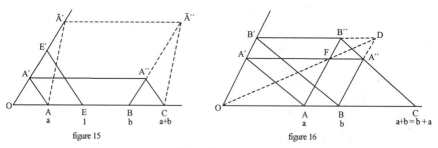

figure 15   figure 16

Hilbert's Figures

For any pair of segments a and b, Hilbert uses the axioms of plane incidence and parallels to define, by a purely geometrical construction, two further segments '$a + b$' and '$a \cdot b$' and uses (D) alone without axioms of congruence or continuity to prove that this 'sum' and 'product' satisfy all the algebraic laws except the commutativity of multiplication, dispelling the illusion that analytic geometry must presuppose a pre-existing algebraic structure.[292] The *Streckenrechnung* exemplifies what Hilbert intended when he opposed the prevailing view, that rigor resides only in arithmetic and algebra, not in geometry, by observing that "the arithmetic symbols are written diagrams and the geometrical figures are graphic formulas; and no mathematician could spare these graphic formulas, any more than in calculation the insertion and removal of parentheses or the use of other analytic signs."[293] As Peirce explained, icons resemble what they represent: "Thus, an algebraic formula is an icon, rendered such by the rules of commutation, association, and distribution of the symbols."[294] Hilbert calls the "graphic formulas" drawn by the geometer "mnemonic symbols of space intuition" (ibid.) and who would forego those he drew showing how (D) implies that his *Streckenrechnung* satisfies these algebraic rules? Certainly not Peirce, who motivated his anticipation of Hintikka's thesis, that Kant's philosophy of mathematics depends on its method rather than its content, by noting that "even in algebra, the great purpose which the symbolism subserves is to bring a skeleton representation of the relations concerned in a problem before the mind's eye in a schematic shape, which can be studied much as a geometrical figure is studied."[295] However, (D) does not imply the commutativity of multiplication by itself unless the assumption of continuity is made in the tradition of von Staudt.

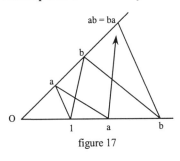

figure 17

Hilbert defines the multiplication of segments in his calculus just as Descartes had introduced his linear notion of multiplication in his analytic geometry, and he shows that they form a field only in the presence of Pascal's theorem (P), which he proves equivalent to the commutativity of this multiplication. Indeed, says Hilbert, "from the accompanying figure it becomes immediately clear that the commutative law of multiplication is none other than Pascal's theorem for the two axes."[296] He then constructs a complicated non-Archimedean geometry to prove that

(I′) (P) cannot be proved from the axioms of incidence, order, and parallels even if (D) is assumed.

showing that Pascal's theorem is not a corollary of Desargues's, as Peirce apparently believed.[297]

Hilbert was *certainly more active* model-theoretically than Peirce, who never constructs a model to show that some geometrical proposition is *not* a logical consequence of others. What better use to make of the freedom to reinterpret a language than to prove the impossibility of deriving important propositions from others from which they were *believed* to follow? Hintikka explains that Peirce "distinguishes his interests from those of the logical algebraists. They were merely looking for rules to facilitate the drawing of actual logical inferences; Peirce was deeply concerned with the model-theoretic basis of such inferences, especially with analyzing them into the shortest and most obvious steps."[298] Peirce did implicitly claim the soundness of his logic of relatives, which would justify Hilbert's results had he been using such a logic. But as Hintikka says, "Not a single symbol of formal logic disfigures Hilbert's pages."[299] Peirce insisted that "in the science of the logic of science it will not do to rely upon our instinctive judgments of logicality merely; it is necessary to prove that, from the nature of things, the given method of reasoning will conduce to the truth in the sense in which it professes to do so."[300] Hilbert had relied on his "instinctive judgments of logicality" in deriving theorems *and* in exercising his "ground rule" that to fully discern the significance of a theorem one must show what it cannot be derived from. *Prima facie nothing would seem further beyond a machine than the construction of models to establish nonderivability.*

Despite his opposition to the notion that necessary reasoning can no more deviate from its course than could a machine, Peirce admits that "even the logic of relations fails to eradicate that notion completely, although it does show that much unexpected truth may often be brought to light by the repeated reintroduction of a premise already employed."[301] However often one finds alternative paths open in reasoning, the tendency of even the logic of relations "is to insinuate the idea that in necessary reasoning one is always limited to a narrow choice between quasi-mechanical processes; so that little room is left for the exercise of invention."[302] Poincaré even claimed that the prospects of machines proving things had been improved by Hilbert, who had "put his axioms into such a form" that one who could not understand them because he had never *seen* points, lines, or planes, could still *use* them for deduction:

> It should be possible, according to [Hilbert], to reduce reasoning to purely mechanical rules, and it should suffice, in order to create geometry, to apply these rules slavishly to the axioms without knowing what the axioms mean. We shall be able to construct all geometry, I will not say precisely without understanding it at all, since we shall grasp the *logical* connections of the propositions, but at any rate without *seeing* it at all. We might put the axioms into a reasoning apparatus like the logical machine of Stanley Jevons, and see all geometry come out of it.[303]

But Peirce denied that Jevons's machine could "take initiative" in adding new points outside the plane of a Desargues configuration or see it in perspective as a spatial configuration. What "form" had Hilbert given his axioms to make this possible? As an example Poincaré quoted the incidence axioms: "On every straight line there are at least two points; on every plane there are at least three points not in a straight line; in space there are at least four points which are not in the same plane."[304] So it was *not* their "form" but their *explicitness* that made Hilbert's axioms machine friendly in Poincaré's eyes, and granted, for a machine to find von Staudt's proof, it would have to be told that "in space there are at least four points which are not in the same plane." Hardly cause to fear an invasion of machinery in geometry, but another *theorem* of Hilbert is.

To prove the commutativity of multiplication from his other axioms for the real ordered field, Hilbert found that one must use the Archimedean axiom and mathematical induction. Since (P) can be used to *construct* a field, it comprises, in the context of elementary geometry, a "finite" replacement for number, induction, and continuity. To pursue this Hilbert formulates the idea of a "pure point of intersection theorem" or *Schnittpunktsatz* dealing with only a finite number of points and lines and their incidence relations, which take the following form:

> Choose an arbitrary set of a finite number of points and lines. Then draw in a prescribed manner any parallels to some of these lines. Choose any points on some of the lines and draw any lines through some of these points. Then, if connecting lines, points of intersection and parallels are constructed through the points existing already in the prescribed manner, a definite set of finitely many lines is eventually reached, about which the theorem asserts that they either pass through the same point or are parallel.[305]

(D) is such a *Schnittpunktsatz* but cannot be proved in the plane without the 'foreign idea' of congruence while (P) is another, but cannot be derived from (D) without continuity. Could one find *Schnittpunktsätze* from which all others could be logically derived without using congruence or continuity? Hilbert finds that (P) alone suffices. Call a geometry Pascalian if the axioms of plane incidence, order, and parallels, as well as (P), hold in it. Then

> **(M)** Any *Schnittpunktsatz* that holds in a Pascalian geometry can be proved "by the construction of suitable auxiliary points and lines from a finite number of Pascalian configurations."

This leads to a decision procedure for *Schnittpunktsätze* and is known in the literature on computer theorem proving as "Hilbert's Mechanization Theorem."[306] Hilbert's original proof of (M) reduced the conditions for a *Schnittpunktsatz* to hold to the vanishing of a certain algebraic expression for all values of the parameters, which could be decided "by means of the *formal rules of calculation* based on Desargues and Pascal."[307] Later Hilbert seeks a similar result for arithmetic: to show by a finitary consistency proof that a finitary theorem always has a finitary proof. (M) shows that for a significant class of geometrical theorems the introduction of auxiliary constructions needed to prove them can be mechanized, revealing an ambiguity in Hintikka's characterization of nontrivial mathematical reasoning by means of a distinction depending for its significance on the undecidability of first-order logic. This motivates his idea of the "unpredictability" of the number of auxiliary individuals needed to prove a theorem logically from axioms, but the set of geometrical sentences holding in a geometry characterized by first-order axioms may be mechanically provable.

Hintikka argues that Hilbert's model theoretic credentials depend on his belief in the completeness of logic that comprised "formalism" in logic, *not* in mathematics:

Hilbert the axiomatist conceived of his axioms as interpretable systems. They served a purpose as soon as they had one realization, one interpretation which made all the axioms true. But how can we be sure that a given axiom system has such an interpretation? If we have available to us, as Hilbert thought, a complete and completely formal system of logic, then it would suffice to study the axiom system purely formally to answer the question. If it can be shown that one can never derive a contradiction from the axioms in a purely formal way, then the axiom system is consistent in the interpretability sense, granted of course the completeness of one's formalized logic.[308]

Hintikka's point is well taken, but his failure to acknowledge the continuity of Hilbert's later "program" with the earlier one centering on geometry skews the account he gives of Hilbert's later focus on first-order logic and its completeness.

Whereas Peirce chose Pascal's theorem to illustrate the expressive powers of relatives, Hilbert and Ackermann chose (I') to illustrate the importance of first-order logic *before* it had been proved complete, to emphasize the significance of the *Entscheidungsproblem*.[309] They construct a first-order formula, $\mathcal{A} \rightarrow \mathcal{P}$, which would be logically valid were (I') not the case, so that a positive solution to this problem would have enabled Hilbert to have discovered a model establishing (I') purely mechanically! In the second edition they attribute no less significance to its negative solution found by Church than to Gödel's completeness proof while continuing to emphasize the importance of the former for difficult questions such as "the independence of Pascal's theorem" from certain axioms. They stressed the *limitations* of first-order logic and the need for second-order logic to express important mathematical notions such as the equicardinality of sets, as well as the notions of validity and satisfiability for first-order sentences, despite being proved incomplete by Gödel. In fact, *the incompleteness of second-order logic is a corollary of the undecidability of first-order logic*, which, in view of its completeness, underscores the basic difficulty of trying to mechanize the discovery of models for establishing nonderivability in first-order theories.[310]

Peirce was convinced that mathematics "is as far as possible from being purely mechanical work" and that consequently there could be "no room to doubt that there is *some* theoric reasoning, something unmechanical, in the business of mathematics. I hope that, before I cease to be useful in this world, I may be able to define better than I now can what the distinctive essence of theoric thought is."[311] Since he connects the unmechanical business with the need for the logic of *relations*, he may have vaguely felt that the introduction of the appropriate number of auxiliary individuals in this logic may be difficult to predict or mechanize. He never realized that *exactly the same difficulty may be encountered in trying to predict the behavior of a deterministic machine.*[312] The notion of undecidability, as a property of an infinite class of questions, never occurred to Peirce. He did formulate a decision procedure for the propositional α-part of his existential graphs of which he wrote that it would be "easy to devise a machine that would perform" it since it was a "comprehensive routine."[313] But, as Roberts points out, Peirce believed he could reduce the full system of first order β graphs to the α graphs, its undecidability being "one thing Peirce seems not to have anticipated."[314] What Peirce regards as beyond a machine, as he conceives it, is the ability of a geometer not just to intuit a diagram but to view it as a *perspective* drawing.[315] But the inability of a machine to discover *such* a "theoric step" in a demonstration has nothing to do with decidability in the modern sense. Desargues's theorem can be proved in certain complete and decidable systems of elementary geometry, but the Turing machine which exists for churning out *all* the proofs of such a system would hardly convince Peirce that a "machine" was capable of such intuition. This brings us to the interesting way Hintikka ties his case for placing Peirce and Hilbert in the model-theoretic tradition to intuition.[316]

Hintikka develops his case for Peirce in connection with his theme of *intuitions as model-theoretic insights*, articulated in terms of the Beth-Hintikka formalization of first-order deductions as "frustrated counter-model constructions." He admits that the letter of this approach is not found in Peirce but does find its spirit in his claims about icons in logic, for example, that "there is one assurance that the Icon does afford in the highest degree. Namely, that which is displayed before the mind's gaze—the Form of the Icon, which is also its object—must be *logically possible*."[317] Hintikka sees this as his realization that "a completed construction will *ipso facto* show that a *counter-example* is indeed logically possible," but what is "displayed before the mind's gaze" that could assure Peirce that a tree *must go on endlessly* without closing? Hintikka cites as evidence of Peirce's anticipation of this way of looking at deduction and intuition his claim that

the whole Weierstrassian mathematics—that is to say the way mathematicians reason since Weierstrass showed how loose most geometrical reasoning is, showing for example that it does not follow that because a real function is continuous that it must have a differential coefficient, which he did by simply giving an obvious instance of its falsity—well, the whole Weierstrassian mathematics is characterized by a *distrust of intuition*. Therein it betrays ignorance of a principle of logic of the utmost practical importance; namely, that every deductive inference is performed, and can only be performed, by imagining an instance in which the premises are true and *observing* by contemplation of the image, that the conclusion is true.[318]

But Weierstrass's example concerns the impossibility of such an inference from continuity (c) to differentiability (d) which no contemplation of the image of (c) can show us. Peirce says he gave "an obvious instance" of its falsity, *not* that it was "intuitive."

Did Peirce believe that Weierstrass *had* constructed a counterexample to this "manifest truth" that everyone once believed? No:

> Weierstrass and the general body of mathematicians denied that, because, they said, a line may be wavy in such a way that on every wave there are smaller waves, and *therefore* on those waves still smaller ones without end. It is undeniable that a line, once formed, can become crinkly; and we can in a general way admit that every crinkle can attain crinkles on it. There is, thus, no contradiction, in thinking that this crinkling goes on endlessly; but whether it means anything to say that this endless crinkling is *completed* is not quite clear to me. A line is a path of a moving point. Now whether it means anything to say that a point starts to move without starting to move in any particular direction, is to me *more* than doubtful. I declare that we have no such idea at all. A *possibility* may be endless; but I cannot admit that an endless series ever actually gets ended.[319]

In Hintikka's terms Peirce admits that a tree beginning with (c) & ~(d) may well go on endlessly without closing (since there is "no contradiction" in supposing such a function) but still denies that it exists, since the collection of the "model" wrongly assumes the existence of a *completed* infinite path through the tree. He would deny the conclusion of the completeness theorem, perhaps even König's lemma. In explaining how this perspective on logical deductions accords with Hilbert's later "formalism" in arithmetic, Hintikka stresses that the rules for generating trees "refer only to the signs (symbols) involved. Not only can the rules which govern the countermodel . . . construction be formulated purely formally. If the countermodel construction does succeed, one can use a device originating from Henkin's completeness proof and use the set of formulas (configurations of symbols) which results from the constructions as its own model."[320] True, "some countermodels take an infinite number of steps to complete," says Hintikka, but "every step and every initial segment of the process is finite, and governed by purely formal rules."[321] But Peirce would apparently reject this basic principle of model theory.

Hilbert agrees with Hintikka concerning the completeness of first-order logic and the assimilation of intuition to model-theoretic insights, though the latter's "vindication" of him by means of his IF-extension of this logic may betray some difference in their views of logic.[322] To compare the views of these three thinkers, we note that in denying Weierstrass's counter-example Peirce had disallowed the Hilbert problem that, more than any other, revealed the utility of set theory for mathematical research and perhaps the need for second-order logic in the axiomatic method, namely, the Fifth problem on eliminating the differentiability assumptions from Lie's theory of continuous groups. Indeed, if continuous nondifferentiable functions did not exist, there would be no such problem! But they do and Hilbert's solution of it for plane geometry in his 1902 memoir was more revolutionary than the *Festschrift* to which it soon became an appendix.[323] Hilbert then explained the difference between his two "foundations": in the *Festschrift*

> the arrangement of the axioms is such that continuity is required *last* among the axioms so that the question as to what extent the well known theorems and arguments of elementary geometry which are independent of continuity arises in the foreground in a natural way. In the present investigation, however, continuity is required *first* among the axioms for the definition of the plane and a motion so that here the most important task has been rather to determine the least number of conditions from which to obtain by the most extensive use of continuity the elementary figures of geometry (circle and line) and their properties necessary for the construction of geometry.[324]

Hilbert soon realized that these two complementary "foundations" for geometry required different faces of logic: an "algorithmic logic" for elementary geometry and a slice of the "general theory of sets" for his topological treatment of the Raumproblem.[325] In his 1905 lectures on "Logical Principles of Mathematical Thought" he proposed a generalization of this twofold axiomatic approach to a science, one beginning with "the simplest things" in its domain connected by laws reproducing "facts of intuition," the other with "fundamental things" in it already introduced by axioms including continuity.[326] The eventual realization, published in 1928, of the need for both first and second-order logic shows that Hintikka's paraphrase of Hilbert's genesis of mathematics in the sign—"In the beginning there was first-order logic"—has to be taken with a grain of salt.[327] This logic was important for putting the finishing touches on results such as (C) and (M) by providing a language in which one can formulate a continuity schema for elementary geometry from which one can no longer derive the Archimedean axiom "logically," resulting in a complete and decidable axiomatization of it.[328]

Hintikka knows that any assessment of the logical significance of the *Festschrift* must face the fact that "not a single symbol of formal logic disfigures Hilbert's pages." He argues that its use of first-order logic is "tacit" but characterizes the point of Hilbert's axiomatic system by observing that "if you have reached in your investigation . . . a complete axiom system, then the rest of your work will consist in merely teasing out the logical consequences of the axioms . . . you no longer need to study the reality they represent."[329] That this overlooks Hilbert's "ground rule" is clear when Hintikka says that "this idea [a purely logical axiom system] may be taken to be the gist of the entire axiomatic method."[330] But this is only *one half* of his method, viz. finding sufficient conditions for theorems: the other more difficult half was to establish their necessary conditions. That this remained the goal of Hilbert's method is clear when he explains in 1922 that "to proceed axiomatically is simply to think with consciousness of what one is doing: in earlier times when the axiomatic method was not used men naively believed in certain interconnections as if they were dogmas; the axiomatic method removes this naivete, but leaves us with the advantages of belief."[331] These "interconnections" are indeed purely logical, and the half of his method devoted to removing "naive dogmatic beliefs" in them is precisely that of *models*, for example, believing that the parallel axiom followed from Euclid's other axioms. Removing other such beliefs required tracking the need for continuity and comprised a critique of "solutions" to Lambert's problem of finding other axioms as evident as Euclid's, from which it can be derived. Geometers found various candidates, such as $\Sigma = 2R$, the existence of similar figures, and the existence of Wolff-parallels, but Dehn showed that *none* of these are really *equivalent* to Euclid's postulate.[332] He constructed non-Archimedean models in which all three of these propositions held but in which through any point not on a given line an infinity of parallels to it passed. Since one could prove these propositions from Euclid's postulate without the Archimedean axiom it was indeed "naive" to believe them "equivalent" to it. Hilbert saw in this a vindication of Euclid's choice of his axiom for parallels, while in the report Moore recommended to Peirce, Halstead extolled it as "a marvellous triumph for Euclid."[333]

What must Pierce have thought of the slender *Festschrift* that Moore recommended and sent to him? It would have confirmed his belief that the mathematician does not need a notation or theory of logic, only his *logica utens*. It confirmed his belief that (D) can *only* be proved theorematially in the plane. And it demonstrated his belief in the underlying iconicity common to both algebra and geometry in a more direct manner than he perhaps ever imagined. Why then did the name 'Hilbert' never fall from Peirce's pen? Earlier in 1902 Moore sent Peirce a copy of his paper "On the Projective Axioms of Geometry" devoted to an analysis and discussion of Hilbert's incidence and order axioms and their relation to those of Pasch and Peano.[334] This paper contains the first discussion in English of proofs of the independence of axioms, explaining that they require "the exhibition of a particular geometry" in which certain axioms "hold" while another "does not hold." Such proofs, says Moore, occur in the work of Peano, and "they play a brilliant part in the work of Hilbert."[335] But in response to Moore's request for comments on his paper Peirce would only say that the postulates for projective geometry could not be "intelligently considered" until those of topical geometry had been "perfectly stated."[336] Peirce simply would not talk about models, making it impossible for him to arrive at any definite idea about the necessary conditions of theorems and hence any such idea about the necessity of theorematic reasoning. Moore also discusses a difference between Hilbert's axiomatization and others that not only illuminates how his later approach to logic differs from that of Frege and Russell but also facilitates its comparison with that of Hintikka.

Russell found inspiration for his logicist project of reducing mathematics to the *smallest possible number* of logical concepts and principles in the work of the Italians who created a logical symbolism for expressing arithmetic and geometry using ever fewer primitives. As he explained in January of 1901, Peano had already "reduced the greater part of mathematics . . . to strict symbolism."[337] This was most important for geometry, since before Peano

> it was held by philosophers and mathematicians alike that proofs in Geometry depended on the figures; nowadays, this is known to be false. In the best books there are no figures at all. The reasoning proceeds by the strict rules of formal logic from a set of axioms laid down to begin with. If a figure is used, all sorts of things seem obviously to follow which no formal reasoning can prove from the explicit axioms. By banishing the figure it became possible to discover *all* the axioms that are needed.[338]

Russell contrasted such rigor with "the countless errors" in Euclid's first eight propositions and famously concluded that "the proof that all pure mathematics, including Geometry, is nothing but formal logic, is a fatal blow to the Kantian philosophy. Kant, rightly perceiving that Euclid's propositions could not be deduced from Euclid's axioms without the help of the figures, invented a theory of knowledge to account for this fact. . . . The doctrine of *a priori* intuitions . . . is wholly inapplicable to mathematics in its present form."[339] What must Russell have thought, one month later, on opening a book on geometry that began by quoting Kant on how "all human knowledge begins with intuitions, proceeds to concepts and ends with ideas," described the aim of axiomatic geometry as "the logical analysis of spatial intuition," and contained more figures per page than even Euclid, but no logical symbols? But, alas, it was the first to contain *all* the axioms that Euclid needed! Indeed, this unlikely book proved to be Russell's only source of answers to three questions about geometry and Euclid he had pondered, and he was forced to add three references to it after the manuscript of the *Principles* had been sent to the printer.[340] Had Hilbert papered over his axioms with logical symbolism, Russell would still have preferred those Italian works, for his project fed off axiomatizations formulated with a *minimum number of primitives*: many pages of the *Principles* are devoted to polishing their definitions of straight lines and planes in terms of points and some relation. Hilbert had preserved these three primitives of Euclid as well as his notion of congruence and formulated five groups of axioms to facilitate the search for the *necessary* conditions of theorems in accord with his Kantian theme: thus, our knowledge of space begins with the simplest *intuitions* of planes, which yield (D) immediately in space; but to prove it in the plane it is necessary to introduce a *concept* of congruence "foreign" to (D), while to prove (P) from it without this concept it is necessary to introduce an *idea* of continuity involving infinity. In the *Principia* Russell described the goal of mathematical logic as "diminishing to the utmost the number of undefined ideas and undemonstrated propositions" in accord with his aim with respect to *theorems* "that the axioms stated by us are *sufficient* to prove them."[341]

When Hilbert turned to the axiomatic study of logic itself in the 1920s, he approached it exactly as he had geometry, formulating several groups of logical axioms, each isolating different properties of a given logical constant in order to clarify its role in deductions. He studied a subsystem of "positive logic" comprising axioms for implication, conjunction, and disjunction and showed that new positive theorems, such as Peirce's law, $((A \to B) \to A) \to A$ became provable when the system is "closed" by axioms for negation. As Bernays put it: "We recognize here very clearly, that the role of negation is that of an *ideal element*, whose introduction has the significance of rounding off the logical system as a whole, just as the system of real numbers is extended to a more surveyable totality by the introduction of imaginaries."[342] Hilbert also compared the quantifiers with ideal elements, and indeed it was precisely the application of negation to the universal quantifier that became the focus of the intuitionistic critique of the resulting "idealized" classical logic. He also analyzed quantifiers, as Hintikka has emphasized, in terms of choice functions, a move in the direction of his game-theoretical understanding of quantifiers. But to assess Hintikka's proposal to "vindicate" Hilbert in terms of IF logic it is more instructive just to compare Hilbert's analysis of the paradoxes and problem of truth using "dependence handicapped" first-order logic with Hintikka's using independence-friendly logic.

Hilbert and Bernays use arithmetization to "mathematically sharpen" the Liar and Richard's paradox by determining precisely the conditions on a formal language under which analogues of them might occur. Using the diagonal fixed-point lemma, they show that in a consistent arithmetical formalism Z based on classical logic with negation, there cannot exist a predicate $T(x)$ for which

(**T**) $\vdash_z T(\bar{n}) \leftrightarrow A_n$,

the formal expression of Tarski's criterion for T to be a truth predicate for Z. If T were such a predicate, the fixed point for $\neg T$ would express the contradictory "I am not true." They explicitly disclaim any philosophical implications for our concept of truth in this result:

> By means of this formal version of the paradox it is made immediately clear that this antinomy has nothing to do with the question of objective truth as an epistemological problem; that on the contrary, for the occurrence of the contradiction all that is needed of the concept of correctness (truth) of a statement is formulated in the assumption (**T**), which can be formulated in everyday language roughly as: A sentence of the form 'the sentence A is true' is itself a sentence, from which the sentence A can be derived, and conversely, from the sentence A that sentence.[343]

Though denying that (**T**) could clarify any epistemological problem about truth, Hilbert and Bernays do use arithmetization to construct, for each n a predicate T_n of Z, defined with $n + 1$ quantifiers, that provably satisfies (**T**) for all sentences A^n with $\leq n$ quantifiers, viz. $\vdash_z T_n(\bar{r}) \leftrightarrow A^n_r$. So Z can define an infinite sequence for ever wider 'local truth predicates' for itself; in particular, T_{10} defines truth for the infinitely many sentences of Z with 10 or fewer quantifiers, so a fixed point for $\neg T_{10}$ would be a sentence with 11 quantifiers saying truly "I am not a truth with 10 quantifiers." The common claim that Tarski showed that such a formal language cannot express the truth of its sentences is thus clearly an exaggeration. Nor do Hilbert and Bernays see any philosophical clarification of truth in their detailed construction of a truth predicate for Z: "The expression 'truth definition' should not mislead us into expecting any philosophical illumination of the concept of truth. It simply makes precise the interpretation of the formulas presupposed in the customary uses of the formalism and the purpose of such a definition consists solely in expressing this interpretation in a general way that *depends on their form*. But such definitions are not in general capable of a finitary interpretation."[344] The moral they draw from Tarski's theorem is that the material content of the law of excluded middle as applied to the integers is not completely formalized. As for Hintikka's question "Who's Afraid of Alfred Tarski?" we must answer: obviously not Hilbert and Bernays.

Hintikka shows that in IF first-order arithmetic there *is* a single formula T defining truth for sentences with any number of quantifiers. Here there is no classical negation but only a "dual negation" $\sim$ with the property that the fixed point for $\sim T$ yields only a sentence which is neither true nor false in the sense of the game-theoretical semantics: any strategy for either its verification or its falsification can be frustrated. Like Hilbert and Bernays, Hintikka sees here a failure of the law of excluded middle, though it is fair to say that in IF logic such a failure is more directly motivated by the semantics itself. Hintikka admits that the contradictory negation ¬ is indeed "natural" but argues that it cannot be applied in extended IF logic to open formulas. One also hears an echo of Hilbert and Bernays in Hintikka's suggestion that "in some sense, the liar paradox has more to do with our concept of negation than with our concept of truth."[345] Certainly they see no more philosophical significance in Tarski's result than does Hintikka despite having analyzed it in first-order logic. This brings us to Hintikka's most interesting argument for the superiority of IF logic over first-order logic, namely, the fact that it is incomplete, his point being that it is the very incompleteness of this logic which enables it to formulate its own truth predicate, which is equivalent to a Σ_1^1 formula.

In looking back over Hintikka's manifold uses of first-order logic to explicate the ideas of ancient geometers, Aristotle, Kant, and Peirce, we see that most of them depend for their significance on the undecidability of this logic. Indeed, he even suggested in connection with the problem of recognizing the inconsistency of surface models that: "Here we are perhaps beginning to get a feeling for what the undecidability of first-order logic means in terms of fairly straightforward, down to earth handling of logical problems."[346] Elsewhere he observes that "virtually all logical problems concerning our language could be solved if we could locate all inconsistent constituents in the tree structure."[347] Here Hintikka echoes the realization of Hilbert and others in the 1920s we have alluded to above: that a positive solution of the *Entscheidungsproblem* would, as von Neumann put it, replace mathematicians with an "absolutely mechanical procedure."[348] Hilbert claimed in 1926 that a method for solving all mathematical problems did not exist and von Neumann claimed a year later that the *Entscheidungsproblem* was unsolvable. A year later Hilbert and Ackerman even pointed to the equivalence of statements of satisfiability of first-order sentences and Σ_1^1 sentences of second-order logic, without, however, trying to prove anything to this effect. If we let $\mathcal{A}$ be any first-order sentence, U be the Σ_1^1 sentence existentially quantifying the relation variable of some first-order sentence satisfiable only in an infinite domain, and $\exists\neg\ \mathcal{A}$ the Σ_1^1 sentence existentially quantifying all the relations and predicate variables of $\neg\ \mathcal{A}$, then the relevant theorem is

(**H**) not $\Vdash_1 \mathcal{A}$ iff $\Vdash_2 U \rightarrow \exists\neg\ \mathcal{A}$

which can be used to deduce the incompleteness of second-order logic almost immediately from the undecidability of first-order logic.[349] Hintikka denies that second-order logic is suitable for "critically reviewing" mathematical inferences because it is not axiomatizable and hence subject to "uncertainties" concerning higher order entities.[350] He believes that the incompleteness of second-order logic is more basic to the failure of Hilbert's program than that of elementary arithmetic. But the incompleteness of all three—arithmetic, IF logic, and second-order logic—follows from the undecidability of first-order logic, which itself was proved directly by Turing without appealing to any incompleteness theorem.[351] Much of the "uncertainty" that attends second-order logic then must stem from the very uncertainty about how many auxiliary individuals may be needed in a first-order proof that motivates and justifies several of Hintikka's ingenious reconstructions.

What about his reconstruction of Peirce's notions of corollarial and theorematic reasoning? We have seen that not all of Peirce's examples of and claims about these notions are in accord with it. In particular, his reconstruction does not analyze Peirce's conflation of the introduction of new objects in a proof with that of foreign concepts. Still, it is easy to underestimate the resources of Hintikka's reconstruction.[352] He has been accused of ignoring Peirce's claim that abstract reference is often essential to theorematic reasoning, but he replies that "in reality it is the introduction of new objects by existential instantiation that creates the most interesting problem of abstract reference, namely, the problem of the status of the 'arbitrary objects' or 'witness individuals' that are apparently referred to by the 'dummy names' introduced in existential instantiations."[353] Indeed, for suitable equivalence relations R, instantiations of $\exists \alpha \forall x (x \in \alpha \leftrightarrow aRx)$ yield such witnesses to some of Peirce's examples of abstraction such as numbers and infinite points that may clearly figure into theorematic reasoning. Perice himself admitted of one of his many attempts to capture his distinction that "this may exclude some propositions called theorems. But I do not think mathematicians will object to that, in view of my making a sharp distinction between a corollary and a theorem, and thus furnishing the logic of mathematics with two exact and convenient technical terms in place of vague unscientific words."[354] Given Peirce's later admission that he had not succeeded in making these terms altogether precise, this surely belies the objection that Hintikka's proposals for making them so are "too technical."[355]

JUDSON C. WEBB

BOSTON UNIVERSITY
MARCH 2003

NOTES

1. Jaakko Hintikka, "Kant on the Mathematical Method," in *Kant's Philosophy of Mathematics: Modern Essays*, ed. C. J. Posy (Dordrecht: Kluwer, 1992), p. 92.

2. Jaakko Hintikka and Unto Remes, *The Method of Analysis* (Dordrecht: D. Reidel, 1974), p. 65.

3. Proclus, *A Commentary on the First Book of Euclid's Elements*, trans. Glenn R. Morrow (Princeton: Princeton University Press, 1970), p. 159. Hereafter we refer to this as *Commentary*.

4. Hintikka and Remes, *The Method of Analysis*, p. 98.

5. This theme is first broached by Hintikka in the paper "Kant Vindicated," published in Jaakko Hintikka, *Logic, Language Games, and Information: Kantian Themes in the Philosophy of Logic* (Oxford: Clarendon Press, 1973), p. 197, and developed at length in "Aristotle's Incontinent Logician," *Ajatus* 37 (1978): 48–65.

6. Aristotle, *Nicomachean Ethics* 1147a27. All our quotations of Aristotle are from *The Complete Works of Aristotle: The Revised Oxford Translation*, ed. Jonathan Barnes (Princeton: Princeton University Press, 1984), hereafter cited in text by the standard pagination.

7. Hintikka, *Logic, Language Games, and Information*, p. 197.

8. Ibid., p. 216.

9. The figure is from W. D. Ross, *Aristotle's Metaphysics: A Revised Text with Introduction and Commentary*, 2 vols. (Oxford: Oxford University Press, 1924, rev. 1958), vol. 2, p. 269. Ross explains that "dividing" a figure means in this case that the space around the given triangle is divided up by the auxiliary parallel (as well as by the extension of its base).

10. Hintikka, *Logic, Language Games, and Information*, p. 217.

11. Not all scholars agree that Aristotle has *geometrical* proofs in mind in this passage. See Robin Smith for a clear presentation of the different readings of it, in Aristotle, *Prior Analytics* (Indianapolis: Hackett, 1989), p. 173.

12. For Aristotle's full formulation, see *Prior Analytics*, 41b15–22. See also Ross's marginal notes on this passage in *The Works of Aristotle*, vol. 1 (London: Oxford University Press, 1928).

13. Proclus, *Commentary*, p. 188.

14. Ibid., p. 189.

15. Ibid., p. 190.

16. Ibid., p. 195.

17. Ibid.

18. David Hilbert's memoir on Thales's theorem (*Foundations of Geometry*, [La Salle, Ill.: Open Court, 1971], Appendix II) was the first serious study of such proofs. Using his axioms of order he defines the notion of orientation and formulates a "weak" form of the SAS-congruence axiom restricted to triangles of the same orientation. His main results are that Thales's theorem is equivalent to reflections in space whereas the Pythagorean theorem can be proved without presupposing such reflection but that incommensurability does not follow from it without the Archimedean axiom.

19. Theokritos Kouremenos argues persuasively that Aristotle did not assume

that all geometrical proofs are syllogistically formalizable; but rather recognized those that proceed by constructions as resisting such formalization. See "Aristotle on Syllogistic and Mathematics," *Philologus* 142 (1998): 220–40.

20. Plato, *Republic* 527a, in *The Collected Dialogues of Plato*, ed. E. Hamilton and H. Cairns (New York: Pantheon Books, 1961). My emphasis.

21. So argued Anders Wedberg, *Plato's Philosophy of Mathematics* (Stockholm: Almquist and Wiksell, 1955), p. 53. He claims that Euclid also rejected Plato's "static" conception of geometry in favor of a "dynamic" one driven by his "construction postulates." That this can hardly be the whole story, however, is clear from Euclid's invocation of infinite straight lines in I, 12, 22.

22. Proclus, *Commentary*, p. 145.

23. Jaakko Hintikka, "Aristotelean Infinity," *Philosophical Review* 75 (1966). The page references below are to its reprinting in Jaakko Hintikka, *Time and Necessity: Studies in Aristotle's Theory of Modality* (Oxford: Clarendon Press, 1973).

24. In *Mathematics in Aristotle* (Oxford: Oxford University Press, 1949), Sir Thomas Heath observed, however, that the bisection principle on which Eudoxos based his method of exhaustion "was framed precisely in accordance with the principle enunciated by Aristotle in this passage" (p. 111), which he shows by analyzing his other discussions of division 'in the same ratio' in connection with infinite series. Heath's reading has been strengthened by further analysis of these passages by Theokritos Kouremenos, *Aristotle on Mathematical Infinity* (1995), pp. 21–24. But even if it is the successively smaller differences arising from the exhaustion method that Aristotle intends to be divided "in the same ratio" rather than the rescaling argument attributed to him by Hintikka, it is clear that no mere refinement of the bisection principle can relieve the conflict between the extension and parallel postulates and Aristotle's finite cosmos that Hintikka stresses. Heath suggested that Aristotle was thinking of *physical* magnitudes in these passages and that he had left open the question "whether the existence of the infinite is possible in mathematical objects and in the objects of thought which have no magnitude" (p. 112).

25. Hintikka, *Time and Necessity*, p. 119.

26. Ibid., p. 120.

27. Ibid.

28. Ibid., p. 119. I have drawn this figure to depict Hintikka's argument and labeled it to match his text.

29. Ibid., p. 120. If triangle *AA'C* is large enough, the auxiliary line needed by Euclid to prove the exterior angle theorem for it will protrude outside *U*.

30. Jaakko Hintikka, "Ingredients of an Aristotelean Science," *Nous* 6 (1972): 63.

31. Ibid.

32. "Comment on Hintikka's Paper 'On the Ingredients of an Aristotelian Science,'" *Synthese* 28 (1974): 87; and Jaakko Hintikka, "Reply to Dorothea Frede," *Synthese* 28 (1974): 91–96. His analysis is reworked in "On the Development of Aristotle's Ideas of Scientific Method and the Structure of Science" in *Aristotle's Philosophical Development*, ed. W. Wians (Lanhem, Md.: Roman and Littlefield, 1996).

33. Aristotle followed the demand to define points and lines by claiming that

"as to what are *attributes* of these in themselves . . . geometry [assumes] what irrational or inflexion or verging signifies and they prove that they are" (*Posterior Analytics* 76b5–11). But these "attributes" are all rather complicated *relations* between straight lines.

34. For, "it is clear that, in the current methods of definition, definers do not prove that anything exists. Even if there is something equidistant from the middle, *why* does what has been defined exist? And why is this a circle?—You could say that it was a definition of mountain-copper. Definitions do not show that what they describe is possible, nor that the definitions are of what they say they are—it is always possible to ask why" (*Posterior Analytics* 92b19–25).

35. Aristotle, *Physics* 200a15–20. Hereafter we write '$\Sigma = 2R$' for Euclid's angle-sum theorem.

36. Heath, *Mathematics in Aristotle*, p. 101.

37. Hintikka, "Aristotelean Infinity," p. 204. Hintikka also argues that Aristotle would not have accepted Euclid's postulate as a definition of straight line, since its converse was provable.

38. Ross, *Commentary on Aristotle's Physics*, p. 532.

39. Hintikka, "The Fallacy of Fallacies," *Argumentation* 1 (1987): 216. Hintikka builds a persuasive case that Aristotle's notion of deductive science emerged from and remained embedded within his interrogative conception of inquiry in "Commentary on Smith," *Proceedings of the Boston Area Colloquium in Ancient Philosophy* 9 (1993): 275–86.

40. Ibid., p. 219.

41. Ibid., p. 237, author's italics.

42. Ibid., p. 224.

43. This is the conclusion of Imre Toth, "Das Parallelenproblem im Corpus Aristotelicum," *Archive for History of Exact Sciences* 3 (1967): 249–422. Despite his very thorough analysis of all the Aristotelean texts bearing on this issue, he assumes without any discussion that Aristotle defined parallels as Euclid did, apparently following Heath. See *Euclid: The Thirteen Books of the Elements*, vol. 1, p. 190.

44. Jaakko Hintikka, "Aristotelean Axiomatics and Geometrical Axiomatics," in *Theory Change, Ancient Axiomatics, and Galileo's Methodology: Proceeding of the 1978 Pisa Conference on the History and Philosophy of Science*, vol. 1, ed. J. Hintikka, D. Gruender, and E. Agazzi (1980), pp. 133–44; pp. 142–43.

45. Aristotle never says that "parallels meet" is impossible, as it should be if they are *defined* as not meeting.

46. See Jonathan Barnes's commentary on this passage in Aristotle, *Posterior Analytics* (Oxford: Clarendon Press, 1993), pp. 123–24. As for what it implies for Aristotle's understanding of parallel lines, I have followed the analysis of Max Dehn "Beziehungen zwischen der Philosophie und der Grundlegung der Mathematik im Alterum," *Quellen und Studien zur Geschichte der Mathematik, Astronomie, und Physik*, Abteilung 8, Band 4 (1937), pp. 1–29.

47. As Dehn has shown on pp. 13–16. Figures 5 and 6 are his. Dehn's reconstructions of these results are more plausible, if less rigorous, than Toth's. Another reconstruction was given by Hans Freudenthal, "Nichteuklidische Geo-

metrie im Alterum?" *Archive for History of Exact Sciences* 43 (1991/2): 188–97.

48. Dehn, pp. 17–18. Dehn argued, however, that Euclid's postulate is superior to assuming either the existence of equidistant lines or the independence of Aristotelean parallels from transversals, since only from it can one develop the theory of proportion and area without recourse to the Archimedean axiom as Hilbert did. This follows from Dehn's results in "Die Legendreschen Sätze über die Winkelsumme im Drieck," *Mathematische Annalen* 53 (1900): 405–39.

49. Hintikka and Remes, *The Method of Analysis*, p. 87.

50. Hintikka, *Time and Necessity*, pp. 45–55. We shall see that this is also true in the case of Kant.

51. There we read that the principle of "like begetting like" by virtue of their first principles "can be seen more clearly in matters of geometry. For there also when certain principles are assumed . . . so are what follows the principles; for instance, if the triangle has its angles equal to two right angles, and the quadrilateral to four, then according as the triangle changes, so does the quadrilateral share in its changes (for it is convertible), and if the quadrilateral has not its angles equal to four right angles, neither will the triangle have its angles equal to two right angles" (*Magna Moralia* 1187a36–64).

52. The considered opinion of Robin Smith, "Immediate Propositions and Aristotle's Proof Theory," *Ancient Philosophy* 6 (1986), is that "convertible terms are simply disastrous for the entire project of refuting the agnostics and the circular demonstrators on proof-theoretic grounds, as Aristotle wants to do" (p. 62).

53. Johann H. Lambert, "Theorie der Parallellinien," in *Theorie der Parallellinien von Euclid bis auf Gauss*, ed. F. Engel and P. Stäckel (Leipzig: B. G. Teubner, 1895). Hereafter, "Theory of Parallel Lines."

54. Protrepticus, in *The Works of Aristotle* (Oxford: Clarendon Press, 1952), vol. 12, p. 31.

55. Lambert proved that the area of a hyperbolic triangle is proportional to its defect, that is, the amount by which its angle sum differs from $2R$. He also showed that defects of triangulated figures are additive.

56. The way Socrates purports to fit his "squares" together to make larger ones for the slave boy.

57. Heath, *Mathematics in Aristotle*, p. 169. Author's italics.

58. Toth, "Das Parallelenproblem im Corpus Aristotelicum," pp. 317–23. Toth bases this claim on an analysis of various Vatican manuscripts that were available to Bekker. It has been challenged by G. J. Kayas, "Aristotle et le géométries non-euclidiennes avant et aprés Euclide," *Revue des questiones scientifiques* 147 (1976): 175–84, 281–301 (see 281–84).

59. The commensurability of the diagonal is repeatedly said by Aristotle to be absolutely impossible. If he knew (b) as well as (c), why does he never say that $\Sigma \neq 2R$ is impossible?

60. But recall that Socrates did *not adequately define* a square for the boy, telling him only that it has all four sides equal. See G. J. Boter, "Plato, Meno 82c2–3," *Phronesis* 33 (1988): 209–15.

61. Jaakko Hintikka, "Knowledge Representation and the Interrogative Model of Inquiry," in *Knowledge and Scepticism*, ed. M. Clay and K. Lehrer (Boulder,

Colo.: Westview Press, 1989), p. 179. This illustrates Hintikka's thesis that the acceptance of reflexive knowledge in epistemic logic reflects the assumption that all knowledge is active knowledge. He analyzes this episode further in "Socratic Questioning, Logic, and Rhetoric," *Revue Internationale de Philosophie* 47 (1993): 5–30.

62. Aristotle asks: "Why is the angle in a semicircle a right angle? It is right if *what* holds? Well, let right be *A*, half of two rights *B*, the angle in the semicircle *C*. Thus *B* is the explanation of why *A*, right, belongs to *C*, the angle in the semicircle. For this is equal to *A*, and *C* to *B*, for it is half of two rights. So if *B*, half of two rights, holds, then *A* belongs to *C* (that is, the angle in the semicircle is right). And what it is to be it is the same as this, since this is what its account means" (*Posterior Analytics* 94a28–34). He apparently entertained "half of two rights" as a definition of right angle, and indeed Ross translates the last sentence as "*B* is identical with (b), the defining form of *A*, since it is what *A*'s definition signifies." In his *Commentary* Ross calls this indefensible but "not unnatural" (p. 639) in view of its analogy with Euclid's definition. J. A. Novak (*Aperion* 12 [1978]: 31) claimed that this definition would be "a paradigm case of a useless circular definition" were it not *exactly equivalent* to Euclid's. But if we try to *use* it in Euclid's proof of I, 13, we can't get past the first case where one line makes equal angles with another: by Euclid's definition they are right angles but Aristotle's would only tell us that they are right *if* each is half of two right angles, which is just what we are trying to prove. That someone with Aristotle's sensitivity to begging the question would eschew this definition is confirmed by his later directive in *Posterior Analytics* at 96b to "try to get a definition of a right angle."

63. Hintikka, "Knowledge Representation and the Interrogative Model of Inquiry," p. 165.

64. Hintikka compares this difficulty with that of the notorious frame problem of AI.

65. Aristotle, *Meteorologica*, 376a ff. He also tacitly appeals to the line, plane, and circle postulates here.

66. Ross, *Commentary on Aristotle's Prior and Posterior Analytics*, p. 59.

67. Hintikka, "On Aristotle's Notion of Existence," *Review of Metaphysics* 52 (1999):780.

68. Ibid., p. 781. See also A. Seidenberg, "Did Euclid's Elements, Book 1, Develop Geometry Axiomatically?" *Archive fir History of Exact Sciences* 14 (1974/5): 263–95, which argues that this was *not* Euclid's aim.

69. Hintikka, "On Aristotle's Notion of Existence," p. 781.

70. Such as Thales's, Pythagoras's, the semicircular angle theorem, 4*R* squares, and the like.

71. Hintikka, "Kant's Theory of Mathematics Revisited," p. 201.

72. Ibid.

73. Ibid., p. 213.

74. Ibid., p. 207. This leads to Hintikka's "vindication" of Kant's claim that nontrivial mathematical reasoning is synthetic, namely that it "is not tautologous in the sense of being a surface tautology" (*Logic, Language Games, and Information*, p. 23). We consider the historical plausibility of this aspect of Hintikka's reconstruction below.

75. Ibid., pp. 207, 213. This is directed against Russell.

76. A deft and convincing analysis of Hintikka's reconciliation of his interpretation with B14 can be found in Sun-Joo Shin, "Kant's Syntheticity Revisited by Peirce," *Synthese* 113 (1997): 1–41.

77. Hintikka, *Kant on the Mathematical Method*, p. 21ff. Hintikka agrees that on this vulgar reading of Russell, modern developments in logic and geometry have indeed refuted Kant's theory. See Hintikka, *Knowledge and the Known: Historical Perspectives in Epistemology* (Dordrecht: Reidel, 1974), p. 130.

78. A classic statement of immediacy as the essential property of Kant's intuitions is by Charles Parsons in the "Postscript" to his paper on "Kant's Philosophy of Arithmetic," in *Kant's Philosophy of Mathematics*, ed. Carl J. Posy (Dordrecht: Kluwer, 1992), pp. 69–75. Hintikka replied to Parsons in "Kantian Intuitions," *Inquiry* 15 (1972): 341–45, basing his claim that it is not immediacy but ideality by virtue of which intuitions yield knowledge on Kant's claim in the *Prolegomena* that "in one way only can my intuition anticipate the actuality of the object, and be a cognition *a priori*, namely: if my intuition contains nothing but the form of sensibility" (§8). A lucid sketch of the rationale of Hintikka's interpretation can be found in Stewart Shapiro, *Thinking About Mathematics* (New York: Oxford University Press, 2000), pp. 81–87.

79. Kant, *Critique of Pure Reason*, trans. Paul Guyer and Allen W. Woods (Cambridge University Press, 1998), Bxii. Further references to Kant are to titles in the Cambridge Edition of his works, unless otherwise specified.

80. See Hintikka, "Russell, Kant, and Coffa," *Synthese* 46 (1981): 266 and "Kant's Transcendental Method and Theory of Mathematics," in *Kant's Philosophy of Mathematics*, p. 345.

81. Kant realized this when he worked on the problem of parallels after publishing the first edition of the first *Critique* in 1781.

82. Bertrand Russell, *Introduction to Mathematical Philosophy* (London: George Allen and Unwin, 1919), p. 145.

83. Hintikka, "Kant on the Mathematical Method," p. 22.

84. Kant, *Theoretical Philosophy, 1755–1770*, trans. and ed. David Walford and Ralf Meerbote (Cambridge University Press, 1992), p. 265. Moses Mendelssohn's essay won first prize. [An abridgement of Mendelssohn's essay is included in *Theoretical Philosophy*, pp. 276–86.]

85. Ibid., p. 251. This "symbol" simplifies the figure Kant drew in the *Physical Monadology* (ibid., p. 54) to prove the infinite divisibility of space, and is found in Kant's Reflexion 5091 (*Kant's gesammelte Schriften, herausgegeben von der Deutschen Akademie der Wissenschaften*, 29 vols. [Berlin: Walter de Gruyter, 1902], vol. 18, p. 379; hereinafter cited as *AA* and volume) where he relates this infinite divisibility to an "absolute magnitude" for space, though not in the precise sense Lambert will give this idea.

86. Hintikka, *Kant on the Mathematical Method*, p. 25. Kant himself says that the geometer "handles individual signs rather than the universal concepts of the things themselves," p. 251.

87. As observed by Kent E. Robson, "Kant's Concept of Intuition," *Akten des 4. Internationalen Kant-Kongresses (Fourth International Kant Congress)*, ed.

Gerhard Funke (Berlin: Walter de Gruyter, 1974), p. 244.

88. Kant, *Theoretical Philosophy, 1755–1770*, p. 265.

89. Hintikka, *Logic, Language Games, and Information*, p. 145. This objection was made by Parsons ("Kant's Philosophy of Mathematics," p. 66) and elaborated along with others by Mirella Cappozi Celluci, "J. Hintikka e il metodo della matematica in Kant," *Il Pensiero* 18 (1973): 232–67. Though it is not convincing for the reason given in the text, she shows that Kant's logic does not match the anatomy of Euclidean proofs as nicely as Hintikka suggests. She points out (p. 253) that Euclid's proof of the congruence theorem should be analytic by Hintikka's lights since it introduces no auxiliary individuals. I analyze this below.

90. Kant, *Anthropology from a Pragmatic Point of View*, trans. Mary J. Gregor (The Hague: Martinus Nijhoff, 1974), p. 35.

91. Kant, *Theoretical Philosophy, 1755–1770*, p. 264.

92. Ibid., p. 248. Kant adds that definitions are always "a result of *synthesis*."

93. Ibid., p. 264. "Der Mathematicus in seiner definition sagt: sic volo, sic iubeo" (*AA* 16, p. 579).

94. Kant, *Critique of Pure Reason* A731/B759. Later we examine the full import of this: that the definition of a concept *is* its construction.

95. Ibid., A221/B268. Kant makes no attempt to explain why biangles are not constructible in space.

96. Hintikka, *Logic, Language Games, and Information*, p. 23.

97. Ibid.

98. Kant, *Critique of Pure Reason* A221/B268. It is often suggested that this claim reveals Kant's awareness of the consistency of non-Euclidean geometry gained from Lambert. See e.g., Gordon Brittan, *Kant's Theory of Science* (Princeton: Princeton University Press, 1978), p. 70. We shall see below, however, that the evidence is against this. See also my paper "Immanuel Kant and the Greater Glory of Geometry," in *Naturalistic Epistemology*, ed. A. Shimony and D. Nails (Dordrecht: D. Reidel, 1987), pp. 17–70.

99. Johann H. Lambert, *Anlage zur Architectonic, oder Theorie des Einfachen und des Ersten in der philosophischen und mathematischen Erkenntnis* (Riga: Hartknoch, 1771), §19 (hereafter, just *Architectonic*). [This is my translation. Hereafter, unless otherwise noted, excerpts from texts cited only in German editions are translated by me.]

100. Mendelssohn's essay, in Kant's *Theoretical Philosophy, 1755–1770*, p. 279. Mendelssohn adds that "it is not that mixed geometry loses its self-evidence. If one were to concede to the idealists that the external world was nothing, and that bodies were only phenomena or appearances, geometry would not be any less fallible" (ibid.). We shall see that Kant's idealism in the Transcendental Aesthetic incurs inconsistency by obscuring the mixed character of Euclid's geometry.

101. Moses Mendelssohn, *Gesammelte Schriften Jubiläumsausgabe* (Stuttgart-Bad Cannstatt: Friedrich Frommann Verlag, 1971), Band 12, 1, p. 49.

102. Johann H. Lambert, "Über die Methode die Metaphysik, Theologie und Moral richtiger zu beweisen," aus dem Manuscript herausgegeben von K. Bopp, *Kantstudien*, Erganzungshefte 42 (1918): 7.

103. Ibid., p. 11.

104. Ibid. One reason for not submitting his essay was that Lambert could not yet formulate axioms he could expect comparable agreement on for *chronometry*, a science he believed belongs as much to mathematical science as does geometry. His aim was to distill axiomatically the purely chronometrical from the chronological aspects of Newton's arguments for absolute time.

105. Lambert, *Theory of Parallel Lines*, p. 153. This translation is by Roberto Torretti, *Philosophy of Geometry from Riemann to Poincaré* (Dordrecht: D. Reidel, 1978), p. 49. For a striking echo of Lambert's formulation in Hilbert see note 330.

106. Ibid., p. 49. Lambert recognized that familiar geometrical truths may still be "fulfilled" or fail, when *reinterpreted in a different structure*. Thus he proved under his second hypothesis $\Sigma > 2R$ that the area of triangles would be proportional to their excess which, in view of the formula $A = r^2(\alpha + \beta + \gamma - \pi)$ for spherical triangles, prompts his famous observation that "here it seems to me remarkable that the second hypothesis is fulfilled when instead of a plane triangle one takes a spherical one, because in this both the sum of the angles is greater than 180° and the area of the triangle is also proportional to its excess. Even more remarkable, it appears that what I say here can be proved without consideration of the difficulty of parallel lines" (ibid., p. 202). So despite having "easily refuted" $\Sigma > 2R$ by a *purely symbolic* proof (using the extension postulate to derive a contradiction from it), Lambert's intuition finds a *model* for it, a structure in which it is fulfilled, though without mentioning that the extension postulate fails in it. Since upon substituting '$\sqrt{-1}r$' for 'r' the formula above becomes $A = r^2(\pi - \alpha - \beta - \gamma)$, a special case of what he proved for plane triangles under the third hypothesis $\Sigma < 2R$, Lambert *explains the difficulty he had trying to refute it* with his famous suggestion that "I should almost conclude from this that the third hypothesis holds in an imaginary sphere. At least there must always exist *something*, to show why it cannot be refuted nearly as easily on the plane as in the case of the second hypothesis" (ibid., p. 203). Here Lambert anticipates the completeness principle for "purely logical" refutations, suggesting that: if you cannot derive a contradiction from an hypothesis using other axioms in a "thoroughly symbolic way," then there must exist a sphere or structure (however imaginary!) in which it is fulfilled—and which explains *why* you cannot. He was not anticipating any *proof* of this principle but simply demanding a *sufficient reason* for nonderivability.

107. See Jaakko Hintikka, "On Kant's Notion of Intuition (Anschauung)," in *The First Critique: Reflections on Kant's Critique of Pure Reason*, ed. Terrence Penelhum and J. J. Macintosh (Belmont, Calif.: Wadsworth, 1969), pp. 43–44. Hintikka also suggests the influence on Kant of Lambert's *Architectonic* of which we have already seen evidence and which we further explore below.

108. Kant, *Correspondence*, trans. and ed. Arnulf Zweig, p. 86. *The Cambridge Edition of the Works of Immanual Kant*, general ed. Paul Guyer and Allen W. Wood (Cambridge: Cambridge University Press, 1999). I have translated "Anschauen" as "intuition" rather than "inspection" as in the Cambridge edition.

109. Ibid., p. 87. We consider his replacement for the parallel postulate below. Kant was especially interested in the deficiencies Lambert found in Euclid. In fact, Kant not only believed that Aristotle had completed logic but that Euclid did something comparable for geometry. As he puts it in his *Lectures on Logic*, "We have no one who has exceeded Aristotle or enlarged his <pure> logic (which is

274 JUDSON C. WEBB

fundamentally impossible) just as no mathematician has exceeded Euclid" (p. 438). In an earlier lecture he admitted that "mathematicians sometimes go wrong with their concepts, especially *modern* ones, but Euclid never did it" (p. 364).

110. Kant, *Correspondence*, p. 87.

111. Lambert, *Architectonic*, §12. This was written in 1764 but was not published until 1771, with Kant's help.

112. Kant writes: "I am taking advantage of the opportunity I have of sending you my Dissertation . . . At the same time, I should like to destroy an unpleasant misunderstanding caused by my protracted delay in answering your valued letter. The reason was none other than the striking importance of what I gleaned from that letter, and this occasioned the long postponement of a suitable answer. Since I had spent much time investigating the science on which you focused your attention there . . . it could not have pleased me more that a man of such discriminating acuteness and universality of insight, with whose method of thinking I had often been in agreement, should offer his services for a joint project of tests and investigations, to map the secure construction of this science" (*Correspondence*, p. 107).

113. Kant, *Theoretical Philosophy, 1755–1770*, p. 396.

114. Ibid.

115. This distinction was first made by Charles Parsons, "Mathematical Intuition," *Proceedings of the Aristotelean Society*, New Series, vol. 80 (1980), pp. 145–69, where he remarks that it seems to be required by Kant's arguments even if it was never an official part of his doctrine. Parsons has considerably refined and deepened this distinction in "Intuition and the Abstract," in *Philosophie in synthetischer Absicht*, ed. M. Stamm (Stuttgart: Klett-Cotta, 1998), pp. 155–87.

116. Kant, *Theoretical Philosophy, 1755–1770*, p. 397. He adds that it is easy to demonstrate the infinite divisibility of space in this way, alluding to the "proof" he described in the *Prize Essay* based on figure 7.

117. Kant prepares for this in the *Critique* at A20-1 by isolating the "Gestalt" of an empirical intuition, but he never explicitly associates it with the "pure" shape or form independent of size characteristic of Euclidean geometry. When Lambert posed the problem of deriving the matter of knowledge from its form to Kant, he explained that "only that part of metaphysics that deals with form has remained indisputable, whereas strife and hypotheses have arisen when material knowledge is at issue. The basis of material knowledge has not, in fact, been adequately shown. Wolff assumed nominal definitions [as it were gratis] and, without noticing it, shoved aside or concealed all the difficulties in them" (*Correspondence*, p. 85). Lambert intended primarily Wolff's definition of parallels as equidistant lines in which, as he explains a few months later, the problem of Euclid's axiom of parallels is only concealed and which "cannot be proved without this axiom" (*Theory of Parallel Lines*, p. 159). Wolff thus unknowingly concealed the material knowledge comprised by Euclid's axiom in his definition, thereby unconsciously taking it and such pure form gratis. (See below and note 160.)

118. Kant, *Theoretical Philosophy, 1755–1770*, p. 395.

119. In the *Architectonic* Lambert had already formulated a fuller set of axioms and postulates for chronometry, which he says *must use the laws of motion and deal with Newton's distinction between "apparent and true time."* Indeed, says Lambert,

"I take this occasion to remark that those who take time for only a phenomenon are prone to confuse apparent time with the true" (§63). His axioms and postulates in §83 are

A1. The moments of time are outside one another, or the moments of time are not simultaneous. (Order Axioms)

A2. Time has no determinate units. (Scale-invariance Axiom)

A3. All times have determinate beginning.

A4. Duration and time have only one dimension. (Dimensionality Axiom)

P1. Any instant can be taken as a beginning of a time.

P2. Any duration can be taken as a unit and extended or added to itself as much as we please, forwards or backwards.

P3. Any time can be represented by a line, and any such line can be extended forwards or backwards as much as we please. (Representation Postulate)

The representation postulate, P3, uses lines for the purpose of representing *temporal congruence*: "Since time is not as evident to the senses as space, it provides us with fewer metaphorical and transcendent expressions and concepts. Even the *ideal* transport of intervals of time, in order to determine their equality, falls into fantasy, and we rather use a line for this in accordance with the third postulate" (§84). As in his geometry, Lambert deals with temporal congruence outside the pure axioms of chronometry as a problem of formulating empirical criteria for the equality of temporal intervals. This is more difficult than in geometry where one needs only the likes of Euclid's "coincidence": "To measure time, however, we must use motion, like that which, by virtue of its uniform velocity, represents intervals of time by the intervals of space traversed; with pendulums, however, units of time are counted out by their oscillations" (§774). Chronometry thus faces the problem of *consistency* (i.e., linear relation between) of essentially different kinds of criteria of temporal congruence. It must also clarify and generalize the astronomical equation of time to which Newton appeals in his argument for distinguishing absolute true time from relative measures of it, as Lambert will do later in his "Anmerkungen über die Zeitgleichung," *Astronomisches Jahrbuch für 1780* (Berlin, 1777), pp. 23–25.

120. Kant, *Theoretical Philosophy, 1755–1770*, p. 394. Allowing a "series of thoughts" to measure time opens the door to the idealist's determination of his existence in time, but Lambert's scale-invariance axiom makes reference to the motion of bodies for the definition of units of duration, such as seconds, days, and years unavoidable, leaving it hard to conceive how he could construct such units from the flow of his thoughts or perceptions. Though the absolute time of English philosophers is "a most absurd fiction," Kant does find Leibniz's treatment of simultaneity inferior to Newton's emphasis on the *ubiquity* of time which "adds a further dimension to the magnitude of actual things, insofar as they hang, so to speak, from the same point of time. For, if you were to represent time by a straight line extended to infinity, and simultaneous things at any point in time by lines drawn perpendicular to it, the surface thus generated would represent the *phenomenal* world in respect both of substance and of accidents" (ibid.). Thus, Kant wholly embraced the very property of Newtonian time that is rejected by relativity theory: absolute simultaneity.

121. Ibid., p. 396.

122. Hintikka, "On Kant's Notion of Intuition," pp. 52–53.

123. Ibid., p. 53.

124. Ibid.

125. For an incisive and sympathetic discussion of how Kant took this fateful step of adding inner sense to the doctrine of the *Dissertation*, see Béatrice Longuenesse: *Kant and the Capacity to Judge*, trans. Charles T. Wolfe (Princeton: Princeton University Press, 1998), pp. 233ff.

126. In the first *Critique* Kant wisely abandons this appeal to pure intuition in determining relations of temporal order in favor of a *causal* criterion in the Second Analogy. The similarity of this appeal to the incongruity argument may help explain why Kant also withheld this favorite argument from the first *Critique*.

127. *Correspondence*, p. 115. Lambert later implores Kant to "find a way of showing more deeply the ground and origin of the truths of geometry and chronometry."

128. Ibid., p. 116. For excellent discussions of the impact on Kant of this argument, see L. Falkenstein, "Kant, Mendelssohn, Lambert, and the Subjectivity of Time," *Journal of the History of Philosophy* 29 (1991): 227–51, and James van Cleve, *Problems From Kant* (New York: Oxford University Press, 1999), pp. 52–61.

129. *Correspondence*, p. 116. In a review of Herz's presentation of Kant's inference, Lambert emphasized more strongly that the reality of change entails that of duration, arguing that "time is necessarily required for *measuring* changes and their duration is in reality determinable in time" (*Allgemeine deutsche Bibliothek* 20 [1773], p. 227). Time is also absolute for Lambert because of its order structure: "Since time and all its parts are in a way absolute, that every instant has an absolute individuality, we can take in it an arbitrary beginning and from it count years, days, hours, minutes, etc., forwards and backwards, and in this way name the noteworthy events of every instant" (*Architectonic*, §218). While the re-identifiability of an instant from "the present" makes time absolute, Lambert grants that spatial positions can also identify individuals but not that they are absolute. We can identify an event as occurring in Berlin but we cannot re-identify next year the position "in space" where it occurred, even assuming that the earth returned to the same position in relation to the solar system—for the whole solar system may have moved, and must have in Lambert's cosmology. While time is absolute in ways that space is not, he argues that both comprise *ideal* relations as opposed to real ones such as causality, for "neither are in things, rather things are in them. This implies, firstly, that space and time are considered without respect to things, and that relations between their parts can be determined in and of themselves" (ibid., §416). Kant uses this independence of space and time from things to prove their a priori nature in the Transcendental Aesthetic, but Lambert pursued a different argument: "Secondly, space and time alter nothing in the things themselves, despite the spatial changes occurring in composite things and the temporal ones occurring in everything. Nor are things necessarily bound to this or that space and time, despite having always to be at some place and time. Hence a thing can remain in itself completely the same despite changes in time and place" (ibid., §416). From this, says Lambert, we derive in mechanics the principle "that the common rectilinear motion of all parts of a system of bodies, in which there is no change brought about in relative motion among them, can be left out of consideration" (ibid., §417).

Galilean relativity is based on the fact that space and time comprise ideal relations. Such a system, says Lambert, is the solar system in Newton's theory, allowing us to regard its center of gravity as at rest. Lambert's claim that the instants of time have an absolute individuality, something he appears to withhold from spatial locations because of Galilean relativity, shows how close he was to the explicit and correct claim that Newton's theory was really only committed to absolute time, *not* to absolute locations.

130. For the bearing of Lambert's argument on Kant's problem of refuting idealism, see Luis Eduardo Hoyos Jaramillo, *Kant und die Idealismusfrage* (Mainz: Gardez! Verlag, 1995), pp. 21–26. Just as he had taken four years to answer Lambert's letter of 1766 with his *Dissertation*, Kant took seven years to prepare his reply to this letter, which consisted of nothing less than the version of the *Critique of Pure Reason* he announced for publication in 1776, for which he wrote the following dedication to Lambert: "You have honored me with your letters. The endeavor, to give at your request an idea of the method of pure philosophy has given rise to a series of reflections on how to develop this idea lying still obscurely within me, and as the possibilities widen with each step forward, my answers have been continually delayed. This work can serve in lieu of an answer, as far as the speculative part is concerned. Since it is due to your instigation and pointers, I would hope that it could always be with you by the endeavor to add to it in your research. . . . It is hardly necessary to add that this work borrows a suggestion from your letter and is not the end" (*AA*, 18, p. 64). But Lambert died suddenly in 1777 and Kant took four more years to add to his first *Critique* himself before he published it in 1781. However, some of Lambert's points did not have any impact on Kant until 1787 and even later.

131. Kant, *Correspondence*, p. 115. Kant sought to protect intellectual knowledge from "contamination" by sensible concepts.

132. Euclid's fourth common notion is a good example, contaminating equality with coincidence. Kant acknowledged this point in the *Critique* by incorporating the apparatus of *Schematism* into his epistemology.

133. Kant, *Correspondence*, p. 118.

134. Ibid.

135. Ibid. This is aimed at Kant's claim that a superhuman understanding "might distinctly apprehend" an infinite series "at a glance" (§1). Later Kant hails Lambert's proof using such series that π is irrational as evidence that mathematics "can demand and expect clear and certain solutions to all its problems" (A480/B508), without trying to explain how it could have been "guided by intuition." Actually, this proof was less than half of Lambert's achievement in his pathbreaking "Mémoire sur quelques propriétés remarquables des quantités transcendentes circulaires et logarithmiques," *Academie de Berlin*, vol. 17 (1768), pp. 265–322, wherein he introduced the hyperbolic functions by allowing the circular functions to take imaginary arguments, enabling him to find a completely analogous proof of the irrationality of e exemplifying the symbolic use of $\sqrt{-1}$ (cf. note 106). Lambert concluded that if, as he conjectured, π was transcendental, it would "not admit of a geometrical construction" (p. 322). This would seem to preclude its "construction in intuition" in any but Hintikka's sense.

136. Kant, *Critique of Pure Reason* A717. For a discussion of these two kinds

of "constructions," see G. Brittan, "Algebra and Intuition," in *Kant's Philosophy of Mathematics*, ed. Carl J. Posy (Dordrecht: Kluwer, 1992), pp. 315–39.

137. Hintikka, "Kant on the Mathematical Method," p. 33. In "The Notion of Intuition in Husserl," *Revue Internationale de Philosophie* 57 (2003): 172, Hintikka infers that "there was for Kant no definitory link between intuition and sense-perception or imagination. Purely symbolic algebraic symbols could be 'intuitive' merely because they represent particular numbers."

138. Geometry constructs a square ostensively while algebra symbolically constructs the ratio √2 of its diagonal to its side, as a solution to $x^2 = 2$. For Kant there was *no such number* though its magnitude could be approximated asymptotically by numbers. But why, Rehberg will ask, cannot the understanding *produce* this number if it can *think* of it? Kant answers that the understanding must content itself with an asymptotic approach to it because of *time*, "the successive progression as form of all counting and of all numerical quantities" (*Correspondence*, p. 357). What perplexes the understanding, says Kant, "is that this concept √2 can be constructed geometrically, so that it is not merely thinkable but also adequately visualizable, and the understanding is unable to see the basis of this" (ibid., p. 358). He never confronts Lambert's claim to our symbolic knowledge via √-1. Kant could still say in 1790 that geometry constructs √2 in intuition because he had not fully absorbed the implications of the problem of parallels he confronted after 1781. He admits that he can only give a "philosophical" proof of Euclid's postulate that foregoes any construction, without realizing that this postulate is equivalent to the construction of a square.

139. Kant, *Critique of Pure Reason* A716/B744. Kant's justification of the *generality* of this proof based on "an individual drawn figure" (A714) on the grounds that it "abstracts" from differences in size and angles shows that he had not read Lambert's memoir on parallels wherein he uses congruence to reprove Saccheri's *theorem* that if one triangle satisfies $\Sigma = 2R$ they all must do so. The generality of $\Sigma = 2R$ is a matter of the homogeneity (i.e., constant curvature) of space imposed by the congruence axioms and cannot be explained by mere logical analysis or abstraction.

140. Kant, *Critique of Pure Reason* A734/B762.

141. Lambert, *Architectonic*, §685.

142. Lambert, *Theory of Parallel Lines*, p. 160.

143. *Johann Heinrich Lamberts deutscher gelehrter Briefwechsel*, ed. Johann Bernoulli, Band 1 (Berlin, 1781), p. 31.

144. Lambert, *Theory of Parallel Lines*, p. 159.

145. Lambert, *Architectonic*, §79. Lambert means a unit definable entirely in geometrical terms, an idea that only became clear to his contemporaries when they saw his proof below that such units must actually exist if $\Sigma < 2R$ holds in space.

146. Lambert, *Architectonic*, §701, and *Theory of Parallel Lines*, p. 200. Kant later used these words to characterize the difference between incongruities.

147. Lambert, *Theory of Parallel Lines*, p. 199.

148. Ibid., p. 200. This was also the main allure of hyperbolic geometry for Gauss and Lobachevsky, though the latter admitted that "we are not in a position to conceive what kind of relation between things could hold in nature that would

bind such different things as lines and angles" (*Zwei geometrischen Abhandlungen*, ed. F. Engel [Leipzig: B. G. Tuebner, 1898], p. 24).

149. Lambert, *Theory of Parallel Lines*, p. 201. Astronomy would also be hampered in its search for parallax, thought Lambert, since the measurement of two angles of an astronomical triangle would no longer permit the calculation of the third angle.

150. Ibid., p. 200.

151. Kant, *AA*, vol. 14, pp. 31–52.

152. To express Lambert's axiom (A) as a synthetic a priori proposition most naturally in the language of intuition, Kant would have to use the of/that distinction to claim that we have a pure intuition *that* any unit of length must be given immediately as an object *of* empirical intuition.

153. Kant, *Critique of Pure Reason* A734/B762.

154. Hintikka, "Russell, Kant, and Coffa," *Synthese* 46 (1981): 266.

155. Hintikka, *Kant on the Mathematical Method*, p. 36. It is often objected to Hintikka's reconstruction that its dependence on existential quantification is belied by Kant's disclaimer that "in mathematical problems the question is not about this nor about existence as such at all, but about the properties of the objects in themselves, solely insofar as these are combined with the concept of them" (*Critique of Pure Reason*, A719). But Kant means that mathematical objects do not enter into *causal* relations, as becomes clear when he later explains that "since in pure mathematics there can never be an issue of the existence of things, but only of their possibility, namely the possibility of an intuition corresponding to their concept, and hence there can never be an issue of cause and effect, all of the purposiveness that has been noted there must therefore be considered merely as formal, never as a natural end" (*Critique of the Power of Judgment*, trans. P. Guyer and E. Matthews [Cambridge: Cambridge University Press, 2000], p. 239). Hintikka's notion of Kantian constructions as "anticipations of existence" does not look for claims of mathematical existence in Kant, but rather for those of possibility.

156. Kant, *Critique of Pure Reason* A730/B758. This is perhaps the most striking confirmation of Hintikka's two-levels thesis. But Hintikka's neat gloss of Kantian construction as merely "the introduction of a particular to instantiate a concept" sanctioned by a postulate is clouded by Kant's insistence that the definition of a geometrical concept *is* its construction, since unlike a postulate it does not explicitly state the possibility of the object it defines.

157. Kant, *Correspondence*, p. 306. Kant asks: "If a circle is defined as a curve all of whose points are equidistant from a mid-point, is not this concept given in intuition? And this even though the practical proposition that follows, viz., to *describe a circle* . . . is not even considered" (ibid.). He writes to Herz that the "possibility is *given* in the definition of the circle, since the circle is actually constructed by means of the definition, that is, it is exhibited in intuition, not actually on paper (empirically) but in the imagination (*a priori*)" (ibid., p. 315). But Kant knew by now that this failed in a crucial case: Euclid's postulate was *not* given by his definition of parallels, which is no construction of them. Worse, for the crucial axiom that a plane passes through any three noncollinear points in space —the *only* example of an axiom given in the Methodology—Kant knows *no definition at all for a plane*, leaving high and dry his claim that mathematics is

capable of *such* axioms because it "constructs concepts in intuition" (*CPR*, A732). He can say that we "draw a line in thought" through two points but what would it mean to draw a *plane* in thought through three points in space, without the conventions of perspective? Without an answer to this, Kant's account of Apollonius's "construction in intuition" of a parabola collapses.

158. Kant reviewed Lambert's correspondence which included this letter. See *AA*, vol. 8, pp. 2–4.

159. Kant, *AA*, vol. 14, p. 31. His adoption of Wolff's definition is further evidence that he had not seen Lambert's work on parallels wherein he had so clearly explained the futility of reverting to it.

160. Kant possibly found a seductive but illusory rationale for Wolff's definition in Leibniz's justification of it as "the *real* definition" of parallels, as opposed to Euclid's merely *nominal* definition, on the grounds that "once we understand that we can draw a straight line in a plane, parallel to a given straight line, by insuring that the point of the stylus drawing the parallel remains at the same distance from the given line, we can see at once that the thing is possible, and why the lines have the property of never meeting, which is their nominal definition" (*New Essays on Human Understanding*, trans. and ed. Peter Remnant and Jonathan Bennett [Cambridge: Cambridge University Press, 1981], p. 295).

161. Kant, *AA*, vol. 13, p. 132.

162. See Gert Schrubring, "Ansatze zur Begrundung theoretischen Terme in der Mathematik—Die Theorie des Unendlichen bei Johann Schultz," *Historia Mathematica* 9 (1982): 441–84, for a full analysis of Schultz's theory of the infinite and his attempts to prove Euclid's postulate by means of it.

163. Kant, *Correspondence*, p. 216. Kant's controversy with Eberhard later severely tested his confidence in Schultz's proof.

164. Kant, *AA*, vol. 14, pp. 44–48.

165. Ibid., pp. 44–45.

166. Ibid., p. 48. In a later note Kant remarks: "How one can demonstrate, with complete rigor, although not in Euclidean fashion, the proposition 'If two parallel lines are intersected by a third line, etc.', by means of a philosophical representation by concepts foregoing any construction" (ibid., p. 52). An intuition *of* a pair of Wolff-parallels would be equivalent to an intuition *that* Euclidean parallels are unique.

167. Ibid., p. 48.

168. Kant, *CPR*, A24/B39. Though Kant found only a philosophical proof from concepts, foregoing any construction, of the parallel postulate, he still makes claims suggesting that he only slowly, if ever, fully appreciated the implications of this revelation, e.g., in his replies to Rehberg's question and Eberhard's critique of Euclid. In addition to replacing Euclid's definition of parallels for the sake of his conceptual proof, he also envisaged other definitions of a circle in order to ground more theorems conceptually in the definition of circle. Thus he considers defining a circle as "a line in the plane to which all lines drawn from one (definite) point are perpendicular" (*AA*, 14, p. 23), which is essentially III 18 of Euclid stating that lines drawn from the center of a circle are perpendicular to the tangent at the point of their intersection with it, a theorem on the way to Euclid's proof of III 35, *the* most

important geometrical theorem for Kant. He formulates another definition: "the circle is a curved line all of whose arcs are bisected by lines which are perpendicular to and bisect their chords," and asks "*how much follows from this definition of circle?*" (ibid., p. 31). This would make III 3 true by definition, a theorem crucial to Euclid's proof of III 35. That Kant wanted to prove III 35 solely from the definition of circle is clear when he asks in the *Prolegomena*:

> Does this law lie in the circle or does it lie in the understanding? i.e., does this figure, independently of the understanding, contain the ground of the law in itself, or does the understanding put into it the law of the chords cutting each other in geometrical proportion when it constructs the figure itself according to its concepts (namely of the equality of the radii)? One soon perceives, if one pursues the proof of this law, that it can be deduced solely from the condition which the understanding placed at the ground of the construction of this figure, namely, the equality of the radii (§38). (*Prolegomena to Any Future Metaphysics that Will Be Able to Present Itself as a Science*, trans. Peter G. Lucas [Manchester University Press, 1959], pp. 82–83.)

Did Kant convince himself that he did not have to build either III 3 or III 18 into the definition of circle to prove the law of chords, that it follows from Euclid's definition alone? In fact, III 35 depends on the Pythagorean theorem which in turn depends on the "description" of squares, which depends on Euclid's postulate. Perhaps Kant decided that his conceptual proof of it justified his claim to prove the law of chords conceptually from just Euclid's definition of circle. Bxii seems framed to accommodate such proofs.

169. These points are set out in three papers: "Was heisst in Euklids geometrie möglich?" *Philosophisches Magazin*, Bd. 2 (1790): 391–402, "Über den mathematischen Begriff des Raums," ibid.: 403–19, "Über die geometrische Axiome," ibid.: 420–31. One would never guess from reading just Kant's reply (*AA*, vol. 20, pp. 411–23) that Kästner questioned the validity of a specific proof of the main axiom of geometry. But Kant's position with Schultz was delicate: the man who had worked tirelessly and unselfishly to expound and defend the critical philosophy was now, in the crisis created by Eberhard, tying its reputation too closely to his proof of the parallel postulate for the peace of mind of Kant, who would prefer to prove it "ohne Herbeiziehung unendlicher Flächen" (*AA*, vol. 14, p. 45). On August 2, 1790 Kant wrote to Schultz, who was working on his reply suggesting that he not deal with those places where Kästner alluded to his own theory of the infinite, but save his self-defense for his commentary on the *Critique*. Kant had sent him a copy of his own response to Kästner, suggesting that it might enable Schultz to "bring [his] theory into agreement with what the *Critique* says in the section on the Antinomy dealing with the infinite in space" (Johann Schultz, *Exposition of Kant's 'Critique of Pure Reason'*, trans. J. C. Morrison [Ottawa: University of Ottawa Press, 1995], p. 160). Upon reading through Schultz's review, however, Kant wrote to Schultz again on August 16 expressing a "doubt": "It concerns the passage about your theory of parallel lines" (ibid., p. 161). Kant was afraid that over-dependence on Schultz's proof would provide additional targets for the mathematicians Eberhard had enlisted as "borrowed plumage" to dignify his attacks on the *Critique*.

170. Kant, *Theoretical Philosophy after 1781*, pp. 290–91.

171. Kant, *Opus Postumum*, trans. Eckart Förster and Michael Rosen

(Cambridge: Cambridge University Press, 1993), p. 188.

172. Ibid., (my emphasis). He says that transcendental philosophy "contains principles of a *synthetic* cognition from concepts and [is], to that extent, analogous to mathematics—to the latter's formal principles, however, not its material (the object). (Of a philosophical proof of Euclid's 12th proposition.)" (ibid., p. 247).

173. This is the title of §8 of "Kant on the Mathematical Method." Kant concluded from the third space argument that "all geometrical principles, e.g., that in a triangle two sides together are always greater than the third, are never derived from general concepts of line and triangle, but rather are derived from intuition and indeed derived *a priori* with apodictic certainty" (*CPR*, A25).

174. J. Schwab, "Über die geometrischen Beweise aus Gelegenheit einer Stelle in der A. L. Z.," *Philosophische Magazin*, Bd. 3 (1791): 399.

175. Ibid., p. 400.

176. August Wilhelm Rehberg, "Über die Natur der Geometrische Evidenz," *Philosophische Magazin*, Bd. 4 (1792): 449. The *reason* the figure is needed here, however, was obscured by the analyticity of the part-whole axiom: without any *order* axioms a figure is needed to *apply* this axiom, specifically to show that ∠ *ACD is* part of ∠ *BCD*. My *concept* of whole implies that ∠ *BCD* > ∠ *ACD if it is* the whole, but only the figure shows me *that* it is. This is what Russell meant when he said that Kant invoked intuition to explain why the geometers of his day could not deduce theorems without the use of figures. But Hintikka argues that figures *can* be considered within the axiomatic framework of geometry as "an alternative symbolism parallel to that of first-order geometry" ("The Emperor's New Intuitions," *Journal of Philosophy* 96 [1999]: 143). Note that this use of the figure to intuit the inclusion of these angles violates Kant's prohibition at *CPR*, Bxii against "tracing what we see in the figure" of the concept.

177. Kant, *CPR* A221/B268. Kant contradicts *himself* on this point when he says that "the object of a concept that contradicts itself is nothing because the concept is nothing, like a rectilinear figure with two sides" (A291/B348). For the roots of this contradiction in Kant's earlier acceptance of the Leibniz-Wolff theory of modality, see Gottfried Martin, "Das geradlinige Zwieck, ein offener Widerspruch in der *Kritik der reinen Vernunft*" in *Tradition und Kritik* (Stuttgart: Friedrich Frommann Verlag, 1967), pp. 229–36.

178. This roughly fits Hintikka's suggestion that "the distinction between intuitive and logical ways of reasoning was for Kant . . . equivalent with the distinction between the use of postulates, i.e., principles of construction, and the use of axioms, i.e., principles of proof" ("Kant on the Mathematical Method," p. 36).

179. Kant, *Critique of Pure Reason*, A41/B58.

180. C. G. Schutz's review of Schultz's *Erlauterungen* and Kant's *Prolegomena* in the *Allgemeine Literatur-Zeitung* 162 (1785), p. 43.

181. Kant, *CPR*, B155.

182. That Kant regarded as synthetic a number of Euclid's theorems that he proved without any auxiliary constructions was pointed out by Howard Duncan in a sympathetic but critical study of Hintikka's interpretation, "The Euclidean Tradition in Kant's Thoughts on Geometry," *Canadian Journal of Philosophy* 17 (1987): 23–48.

183. Kant's disciple George S. A. Mellin uses this idea in his *Wörterbuch der Kritischen Philosophie*, vol. 4 (Lena: Friedrich Frommann, 1801), p. 798ff. to reconstruct Euclid's congruence proof in just the format Hintikka says is important for Kant, where the auxiliary construction is a "transcendental motion." Michael Friedman (*Kant and the Exact Sciences* [Cambridge, Mass.: Cambridge University Press, 1992], p. 42) suggests a kinematical interpretation of descriptions of space, based on Kant's explanation in *Metaphysical Foundations* where he reaffirms that the motion of an object in space can be known only by experience. But, "in Phoronomy, since I am acquainted with matter through no other property than its movability, and may thus consider it only as a point, motion can be considered as the describing of a space, in such a way, however, that I attend not solely, as in geometry, to the space described, but also to the time in which, and thus to the speed with which, a point describes the space" (*Theoretical Philosophy after 1781*, p. 202). Since matter considered only for its movability may be considered as a point, it need not be regarded as an *object* moving in space. One sees how difficult it was for readers of the B-deduction to understand what Kant meant by "describing space" without having read the *Metaphysical Foundations*!

184. Hintikka, "Kant on the Mathematical Method," p. 23.

185. Ibid.

186. Kant, *Critique of Pure Reason*, A254/B310.

187. Ibid., B33. At B72 Kant makes clear that God is the only "original being," with intellectual intuition, from which Hintikka concludes that "God could have 'intellectual intuitions' unmediated by sense-perception. In them, God's creative relation to objects is the immediate link that justifies the use of the term 'intuition'" ("The Notion of Intuition in Husserl," p. 172).

188. Ibid., A540/B568. He does so by distinguishing our "empirical character," or self as it appears to us, from our "intelligible character," or self as it is in itself, claiming that only the former is governed by causality; indeed, "this acting subject, in its intelligible character, would not stand under any condition of time, for time is only the condition of appearances, not of things in themselves. In that subject no *action* would *arise* or *perish*, hence it would not be subject to the law of everything alterable in its time-determination, that everything *that happens* must find its cause in the *appearances* of the previous state" (A540/B568).

189. Ibid., A35–36.

190. Ibid., A33. Kant's example is the axiom that "different times are not simultaneous but successive." In his authorized commentary on the *Critique*, Schultz tells us that Kant took this axiom from Lambert's *Architectonic* (see note 217), although Lambert's axiom simply says that "the moments of time are not simultaneous" (see note 119). But in §158 of the *Architectonic* he infers from it that the non-simultaneity of moments of time implies that they are "necessarily different," and since one moment precedes or succeeds another only if they are different, Kant's formulation does indeed correctly express the intended content of Lambert's axioms.

191. Ibid., A37/B54.

192. In 1781 Kant said only that such a being would have "intellectual intuition" and that such a notion is by no means contradictory, but that if *we* had such a faculty, we would not be human but rather "beings that we cannot even say are

possible, let alone how they are constituted" (A278). Since God is the only being who for Kant can indubitably be said to intuit things intellectually, it is plausible that the thing in itself is just "the thing for God," as argued by Merold Westphal, "In Defense of the Thing in Itself," *Kantstudien* 59 (1968). See also Karl Ameriks, *Kant's Theory of Mind: An Analysis of the Paralogisms of Pure Reason* (Oxford: Clarendon Press, 1982), p. 265ff, for an illuminating discussion of this move. Kant's elucidation of the ideality of time seems to depend as much on God as does Berkeley's ideality of external objects in space.

193. Kant claimed that he could not alter even the smallest parts of his system without introducing contradictions into it as well as human reason: "Yet in the *presentation* there is still much to do, and here is where I have attempted to make improvements in this edition, which should remove first the misunderstanding of the *Aesthetic*, chiefly the one in the concept of time" (Bxxxviii). In particular, the introduction of a "Transcendental Exposition" of time was intended to answer the objection of Garve we are about to consider, as was suggested by Hans Vaihinger, *Commentar zu Kants Kritik der reinen Vernunft*, vol. 2 (Stuttgart: Union Deutsche Verlagsgesellschaft, 1922), p. 387ff.

194. *Kant's Early Critics*, ed. and trans. Brigitte Sassen (Cambridge: Cambridge University Press, 2000), p. 75.

195. Ibid.

196. Kant, *CPR*, A31/B47. Neither Garve nor some modern commentators are sure whether Kant was proposing one or two "axioms of time." See Jonathan Bennett, *Kant's Analytic* (Cambridge: Cambridge University Press, 1966), pp. 52–53.

197. Kant, *CPR*, A31/B47. Lambert's discussion of this axiom reveals it to be anything but analytic, stating the total ordering of moments in time by the 'before and after' relation, though he admitted to Kant that his attempt in §§81, 87 of *Neues Organon* to derive from it the necessity of a unique chronological ordering of events in time was not satisfactory. Kant later tried to establish this in the Second Analogy.

198. See note 119 for Lambert's axioms and postulates for chronometry. He had formulated only seven axioms and five postulates for geometry!

199. See Ameriks, *Kant's Theory of Mind*, p. 265.

200. Kant, *CPR*, A25/B39.

201. Ibid., A26/B42.

202. Hintikka, "Kant's Transcendental Method and Theory of Mathematics," p. 350. The assimilation of the "active force" of Kantian intuitions to game theoretical semantics is seriously questioned by Christopher Russell, "Hintikka on Kant and Logic," *Erkenntnis* 33 (1990): 23–38.

203. Kant, *CPR*, A33/B50.

204. Ibid., A21/B35.

205. Lambert motivated his postulate by the possibility of representing temporal congruence by inertial motion, which Kant may intend with his kinematical notion of describing space (see Friedman, *Kant and the Exact Sciences*, p. 131ff), but he argues in the B-deduction that it allows us to represent other chronometrical axioms in intuition as well.

206. See Manley Thompson, "Singular Terms and Intuitions in Kant's Epistemology," *Review of Metaphysics* 26 (1972): 335ff.

207. Kant, *CPR*, B160n.

208. An elegant reconstruction of his formal intuitions incorporating this idea is given by Friedman who suggests we gloss the time Kant seeks to construct in the Analytic as *space-time*: "space and time as mere forms of intuition comprise a one-dimensional sequence of three-dimensional Euclidean spaces: a four-dimensional space-time structure comprising a one-dimensional ordering of three-dimensional 'planes of simultaneity'" (Friedman, *Kant and the Exact Sciences*, p. 179). He remarks that the description of Newton's "ubiquity of time" in the *Dissertation* (see note 120) shows that this way of presenting space-time structure "was not entirely foreign to Kant himself." For space and time as *formal intuitions* "one considers the *relations* between such instantaneous Euclidean three-spaces" (ibid., p. 199), where we have the choice between the relation of being-at-the-same-spatial-location between pairs of points in different instantaneous spaces or an affine structure yielding only the relation lying-on-the-same-inertial-trajectory between triples of points in different such spaces. Since Friedman denies that the formal intuition of space is concerned with the transition from topological to metrical structure, he cannot take Kant's claim that it it is simply the object of geometry at face value but must gloss it as leading "in the end to the dynamical structure of *physical* space" (ibid., p. 199). But crucial for our understanding of Kant's philosophy of space and time would be *his choice* of the alternative ways of conceiving space that Friedman leaves open to him: either as the rigging in which points persist as reidentifiable over time or the affine structure allowing the identification of inertial paths but no longer the same points at different times. Can this gloss clarify Kant's view of Newton's absolute space *versus* his absolute time? The affine alternative is one in which, unlike the rigging that represents Newton's official view that both space and time are absolute, only time remains absolute. Thus his dynamics does not *require* absolute space, only absolute time. If Kant "was to see farther than anyone the philosophical implications of the Newtonian achievement" (ibid., p. 210), one would expect some indication of this most important fact about Newtonian space-time. But while we have seen such in Lambert (note 129), tied indeed to the Galilean relativity on which the construction of the affine alternative depends, we find none in Kant. A profound analysis of formal intuition can be found in Longuenesse (*Kant and the Capacity to Judge*, pp. 215–25), but she does not analyze the formal intuition of time.

209. Hintikka, *Logic, Language Games, and Information*, p. 220. See also p. 121.

210. Kant, *CPR*, A46/B64.

211. Kant explains that "in order to be brief, I have placed that which is properly transcendental under the heading of the metaphysical exposition" (*CPR*, B48).

212. Ibid., B49.

213. *Theoretical Philosophy after 1781*, p. 185.

214. Ibid., p. 186.

215. He later says, "time does not furnish enough material for an entire science, unlike the pure theory of space, geometry" (*Critique of the Power of Judgement*, p. 38). This is another critical point needed to comprehend the second edition that readers could only find in the *Metaphysical Foundations*. See note 183.

216. *Theoretical Philosophy after 1781*, pp. 375–76.

217. Kant wrote to Johann Schultz about it that "time, as you correctly notice, has no influence on the properties of numbers" so that arithmetic is "a pure intellectual synthesis" not depending on time (*Correspondence*, pp. 284–85). Schultz explained in Part I of his *Prüfung der Kantischen Critik der reinen Vernunft* (Königsberg: Hartung, 1789) that, while his postulates depend on our consciousness of synthesis in time, his *axioms*, such as the commutativity of addition, depend only on a *concept* of quantity formed by the intellect, so time "has no influence" on the commutative property of numbers. Having clarified the relation of arithmetic to time, Schultz can answer Garve, for "I have been fortunate enough to discover the real axioms and postulates of time,

A1. Between two points of time there is *only one time*.
A2. All parts of time are *similar* to each other, and so two equal parts of time are *congruent*.

P1. Between two points of time there is always a time.
P2. Any given part of time can be *extended* forward and backward without end," (p. 235).

Formulated to support Kant's dimensionality argument, "these axioms and postulates of time correspond exactly to the axioms and postulates of the straight line" (ibid.). Garve overlooked that "we have a *whole pure science of time* of considerable scope, namely, *pure mechanics*, whose main purpose is the measure of time. It is all the more remarkable that the science with time as its object has scope, for time has but one dimension and thus corresponds to just an infinite straight line" (ibid.). But Schultz ignores the *order* properties of time. As he informs readers of Part II in 1792, he was gratified, having been led to P2 by its analogy with the extension postulate of geometry, to have found it also among those of Lambert which were not available to him in 1789. A2 betrays Schultz's incomprehension of the problem of temporal congruence. When he read the *Architectonic* Schultz realized he had fallen short, for "Lambert formulated two other propositions that were used in the *Critique of Pure Reason* as axioms, namely, that time is continuous, and that two different times cannot be simultaneous. But this last proposition, in my opinion, is a purely identical one, for it says nothing more than *different* parts of time are not the *same* parts of time. The former is, however, obviously synthetic and hence a real axiom . . . as are the following: there exists only *one* time which is infinite, time is an *extended* magnitude, time has only one dimension, the order in which the parts of time follow one another is determined in one unchangeable way. . . . So I hold it necessary in chronometry or time science to add to the two axioms already formulated by me the five propositions just enunciated: these seven axioms and two postulates of time are now *so many proofs that time is an intuition*, indeed an *a priori* intuition" (*Prüfung II*, pp. 263–64).

218. Hintikka, "The Paradox of Transcendental Knowledge," pp. 244–45.
219. Ibid., p. 245.
220. Ibid. Kant's preference for the latter is seen by Hintikka as his "Aristotelean mistake."
221. For the first question, see Paul Guyer, *Kant and the Claims of Knowledge* (Cambridge: Cambridge University Press, 1987), p. 190ff. For the second question see Longuenesse, *Kant and the Capacity to Judge*, pp. 253–54.

222. Kant, *CPR*, A138/B178.

223. Kant, *CPR*, A142–43/B182. Kant distinguished the 'qualitative' from the 'quantitative' sense of "unity" in 1787.

224. Kant, *CPR*, B111. By "combination principle" we mean Kant's claim that the third category in each of the four triplets of categories arises by a combination of the first two.

225. Kant, *CPR*, A145/B184.

226. Such a schema would have to comprise a rule for constructing a temporal interval a priori, as we have in geometry for angles.

227. These are magnitudes "in which the representation of the parts makes possible the representation of the whole" (Kant, *CPR*, A162/B203), following Lambert who introduced them in §688–§695 of the *Architectonic*.

228. Kant, *CPR*, A162–63/B203.

229. *Essay Concerning Human Understanding*, Bk. II, chapter 14, §21; Bk. IV, chapter 3, §§2,3.

230. Locke's challenge foreshadowed the famous argument for chronometrical conventionalism of Henri Poincaré that "time should be defined so that the equations of mechanics may be as simple as possible. In other words, there is not one way of measuring time more true than another; that which is generally adopted is only more *convenient*. Of two watches, we have no right to say that one goes true, the other wrong. We can only say that it is advantageous to conform to the indications of the first" (Henri Poincaré, *The Value of Science* [New York: Dover, 1958], p. 228). Poincaré rules out a choice based on intuition, claiming even more emphatically than Locke that "*we have no direct intuition of the equality of two intervals of time*. Those who believe they possess this intuition are dupes of an illusion. When I say, from noon to one the same time passes as from two to three, what meaning has this?" (ibid., p. 224).

231. Hintikka, "The Paradox of Transcendental Knowledge," p. 245. See Longuenesse, *Kant and the Capacity to Judge*, ch. 2, for a thorough analysis of the threefold synthesis and A-deduction of quantity. Kant pursues the basis of chronometry in the B-deduction to protect the ideality of time from *the paradox of inner sense* spawned by his Elucidation of it. He distinguished apperception as the source of active synthesis sharply from the passivity of inner sense to argue that "we cannot even represent time without, in *drawing* a straight line (which is to be the external figurative representation of time), attending merely to the action of the synthesis of the manifold through which we successively determine the inner sense, and thereby attending to the succession of this determination in inner sense" (B154–55). To defuse the paradox of inner sense he must explain how I can be an object of myself in inner sense and *this*, says Kant, is explained by "the fact that time, although it is not itself an object of outer intuition at all, cannot be made representable to us except under the image of a line, insofar as we draw it, without which sort of presentation we could not know the unity of its measure at all, or likewise from the fact that we must always derive the determination of the length of time or also of the positions in time for all inner perceptions from that which presents external things to us as alterable" (B156). Here Kant resolves the chronometrical disjunction of the *Dissertation*: measuring the duration between "inner perceptions" requires *external things*, viz. the motion of bodies, as

articulated in the Refutation and General Note.

232. Kant, *CPR*, A720/B748.

233. Ibid., A724/B752.

234. This argument would restrict the "auxiliary constructions" to the selection of arbitrary points in time bearing only ordinal relations to given points—unless inertial motion is somehow constructible a priori. See Friedman, *Kant and the Exact Sciences*, p. 131ff for this possibility.

235. *Kant's Theory of Mathematics Revisited*, p. 205. He grants that Kant was unclear about the logical basis of the phenomenon.

236. Charles Peirce, *The New Elements of Mathematics*, 4 vols., ed. Carolyn Eisele (The Hague: Mouton, 1976), vol. 4, p. 38. We shall come back to the circumstances of this formulation, which was written in 1902.

237. Jaakko Hintikka, "C. S. Peirce's 'First Real Discovery' and its Contemporary Relevance," *The Monist* 63 (1980): 306. This point is lost on Kenneth Laine Ketner who argues in "How Hintikka Misunderstood Peirce's Account of Theorematic Reasoning," *Transactions of the Charles S. Peirce Society* 21 (1985): 413–14, that Hintikka sought to paint Peirce as a geometrical constructionist tied to Euclidean figures.

238. Ibid., p. 307.

239. Ibid. In his later paper on "The Place of C. S. Peirce in the History of Logical Theory" Hintikka recalls, "A long time ago . . . I came independently upon the same distinction in my work on the philosophy of logic, only to discover that the same insight had been reached by Peirce" (in *The Rule of Reason: The Philosophy of Charles Sanders Peirce*, ed. Jacqueline Brunning and Paul Forster [Toronto: University of Toronto Press, 1997], p. 26).

240. Hintikka, "Peirce's 'First Real Discovery,'" p. 311.

241. Ibid.

242. See his "Impossible Worlds Vindicated," *Journal of Philosophical Logic* 4 (1975): 475–84.

243. Peirce, *The New Elements of Mathematics*, vol. 4, p. 289.

244. See *Language, Logic Games, and Information*, pp. 278–82. For a critique of Hintikka's relativization of Peirce's distinction to the choice of logical rules, see Christiane Chauviré, "Schématisme et Analyticité chez C. S. Peirce," *Archives de Philosophie* 50 (1987): 413–37.

245. Christopher Hookway, *Peirce* (London: Routledge, 1985), p. 199. A very careful and informative analysis of Peirce's possible "premonitions" of the undecidability of his logic of relations is given by Randall R. Dipert, "Peirce, Frege, the Logic of Relations, and Church's Theorem," *History and Philosophy of Logic* 5 (1984): 49–66. Dipert gives an especially clear account of Hintikka's use of his distinction between surface and depth information to analyze Peirce's notion of theorematic reasoning, concluding that "Pierce's insight is not, however, altogether as 'sharp' as Hintikka would have it" (p. 62). We shall find a certain justification for this judgment in our analysis of Peirce's notion below.

246. Ibid., p. 200. On this ambivalence see also Dipert, "Peirce, Frege, the Logic of Relations, and Church's Theorem." Another critique of Hintikka's reconstruction of Peirce's distinction can be found in Gerhard Heinzmann, "Mathematical

CONSTRUCTIONS, INTUITIONS, AND THEOREMS   289

Reasoning and Pragmatism in Pierce," in *Logic and Philosophy of Science in Uppsala*, ed. D. Prawitz and D. Westerstähl (Dordrecht: Kluwer, 1994), pp. 297–310. He cites Peirce's claim that his proof of the associativity of addition in arithmetic is corollarial despite introducing formulas whose quantificational depth exceeds that of the theorem itself. But he calls it corollarial, I believe, because he uncritically assumed without justification that the recursion equations for addition give its *meaning*. See also Stephen H. Levy, "Peirce's Theoremic/Corollarial Distinction and the Interconnections between Mathematics and Logic" in *Studies in the Logic of Charles Sanders Peirce*, ed. N. Houser, D. Roberts, and J. van Erva (Bloomington: Indiana University Press, 1997), pp. 85–117.

247. "The Place of C. S. Peirce in the History of Logical Theory," p. 27.

248. *CP* 3.342. *Collected Papers of Charles Sanders Peirce*, vols. 1–6, ed. Charles Hartshorne and Paul Weiss (1931–1935); vols. 7–8, ed. Arthur Burks (Cambridge: Belknap Press, 1958). Our references are by volume and paragraph number.

249. *CP*, 3.364. Peirce intends no decision procedure here; see Jay Zeman, "Peirce on the Algebra of Logic: Some Comments on Houser," *Transactions of the Charles S. Peirce Society* 25 (1989): 53.

250. *CP*, 3.392. This is Pascal's theorem. In words: If the six vertices of a hexagon lie three and three on two straight lines, the three points of intersection of opposite sides lie on a straight line. We have drawn the figure and labeled its points to match Peirce's formula. '—<' is Peirce's symbol for implication which associates to the right.

251. Ibid., 3.364.

252. Ibid., 3.363.

253. *The Writings of Charles S. Peirce: A Chronological Edition*, vol. 6 (Bloomington: Indiana University Press, 1993), p. 37.

254. Peirce, *The New Elements of Mathematics* 3, p. 630. For a comprehensive and informative account of how Peirce's analysis of machines figures into his philosophy of mind, see Claudine Tiercelin, "Peirce on Machines, Self-Control, and Intentionality" in *The Mind and the Machine*, ed. S. B. Torrance (New York: Halsted Press, 1984), pp. 99–113.

255. *M* 318, p. 50. Written in 1907. This refers to the numbering of Peirce's manuscripts in the *Annotated Catalogue of the Papers of Charles S. Peirce* by Richard S. Robin (Amherst: University of Massachusetts Press, 1967).

256. Ibid., p. 52.

257. Ibid., p. 53. Given two triangles in perspective from O on the plane P, connect two corresponding vertices and O with a point S in space. One then constructs a pair of triangles in space, also in perspective from O, of which the given coplanar triangles are a projection on P from S. The planes of the space triangles must intersect in a straight line (not shown), their axis of perspective, whose projection on P from S will be the perspective axis of the coplanar triangles. The key point is that all incidence relations are preserved under central projection. (Figure 13 is from David Hilbert and Stefan Cohn-Vossen, *Geometry and the Imagination [Anschauliche Geometrie]*, trans. P. Nemenyi [New York: Chelsea Publishing Co., 1952], p. 122.)

258. Ibid., p. 53.

259. Peirce, *The New Elements of Mathematics*, vol. 2, p. 214. In a manuscript on geometry in 1895.

260. *CP*, 2.267.

261. *CP*, 3.561. Mary E. Boole, *The Mathematical Psychology of Gratry and Boole*, 1895, in *Collected Works*, vol. 2 (London: Daniel, 1931), pp. 693–765.

262. *CP*, 3.561.

263. Peirce, *The New Elements of Mathematics*, vol. 3, pp. 631–32. Peirce apparently was unaware that Babbage had done precisely this in designing his Analytical Engine: incorporate an adaptation of the punched cards of the Jacquard loom, which he says "is capable of weaving any design which the imagination of man may conceive," into his engine to vastly widen its range of computations (*Charles Babbage and his Calculating Engines*, ed. Philip and Emily Morrison [New York: Dover, 1961], p. 55). When the engine is in its initial state, as his assistant Lady Lovelace explained, "it is ready to receive at any moment, by means of cards constituting a portion of its mechanism (and applied on the principle of those used in the Jacquard loom), the impress of whatever *special* function we may desire to develop or tabulate. These cards contain within themselves . . . the law of development of the particular function that may be under consideration, and they compel the mechanism to act accordingly in a certain corresponding order" (ibid., pp. 254–56). Jacquard's idea, she says, "has rendered it possible to endow mechanism with such extensive faculties as bid fair to make this engine the executive right-hand of abstract algebra" (ibid., p. 251). The principle of *backing* these cards (repetition of sub-routines) suggests further uses which "seem likely to place *algebraical* combinations no less completely within the province of mechanism, than are all those varied intricacies of which *intersecting threads* are susceptible" (ibid., p. 265). Finally, in view of the existence of functions whose computation requires such complicated processes as to be almost practically impossible, says Lady Lovelace, "we may conceive there being some results which it may be *absolutely impossible* in practice to attain with any accuracy, and whose precise determination it may prove highly important for some of the future wants of science, in its manifold, complicated and rapidly developing fields of inquiry, to arrive at" (ibid., p. 283). When Turing gave a precise mathematical description of his universal Turing machine he immediately used a diagonal argument to prove the absolute unsolvability of its halting problem and then used coding to design a Turing machine K that automatically finds all the provable formulas of Hilbert's functional calculus. Indeed, K does "work the logic of relatives" and the unsolvability of its halting problem implies that of the *Entscheidungsproblem*.

264. Review of Schröder, in *Contributions to the Nation*, 3 vols., ed. K. L. Ketner and J. E. Cook (Lubbock: Texas Tech University Press, 1975–79), vol. 1, p. 132.

265. Ibid. Peirce adds: "Nor can our ordinary procedure of thinking possibly be mapped out in advance by turning the crank of a machine."

266. *CP*, 7.263. Peirce praised Schubert's calculus as "the most extensive application of Boolean algebra which has ever been made."

267. Peirce, *The New Elements of Mathematics*, vol. 4, p. 1.

268. Ibid., p. 5. We now call this Cantor's theorem but Peirce did not believe he

had proved it rigorously.

269. Ibid., p. 8.

270. Ibid. Peirce says that "theorematic reasoning, at least the most efficient of it, works by abstraction. . . . I proved that there is no maximum multitude by considering the collection of all possible collections of a given multitude. Now a *collection* is an abstraction. For what is an abstraction but an object whose being consists in facts about other things?" (ibid., p. 11). But what "abstraction" did Peirce see at work in his "very good example" of theorematic reasoning in Staudt's proof of (D)?

271. Ibid., p. 8. This, of course, was just what Aristotle could not see either.

272. Ibid., p. 9. In a later unpublished manuscript Peirce writes that "the more I consider the matter, the more I am convinced that corollarial reasonings are the highest. Among these is my proof about multitude" (M754).

273. Ibid, p. 289.

274. Ibid.

275. Ibid.

276. Ibid., p. 49.

277. Ibid., p. 42.

278. Peirce, *The New Elements of Mathematics*, vol. 3, p. 870. In 1903 Peirce had seized on the theorems of Desargues and Pascal as his two specific examples of the failure of Kempe's graphical representation of mathematical form to adequately represent Thirdness, viz. their relational properties. See *The Essential Peirce: Selected Philosophical Writings*, vol. 1, ed. Nathan Houser and Christian Kloesel (1992); vol. 2, ed. The Peirce Edition Project (1998) (Bloomington: Indiana University Press, 1998), vol. 2, pp. 173–75.

279. He wrote to Story in 1901: "It begins with a long logical introduction which I have written twice and am still not satisfied with it. It then takes up the theory of numbers with particular attention to logic. I then take up algebra, and develop with strict logic and in a somewhat novel way, the fundamental ideas, first of rational fractions and then of continuous real quantity. My definition of continuity is some improvement upon Cantor" (*New Elements of Mathematics*, vol. 2, p. v.).

280. E. H. Moore to Peirce, August 13, 1902, (L299).

281. "The Place of C. S. Peirce in the History of Logical Theory," pp. 15–16.

282. *CP*, 4.424.

283. *Principii della geometria logicamente espositi* (Turin: Bocca, 1889). Peirce had been content to illustrate the power of his new logic of relatives to "express relations of considerable complexity" by translating Pascal's theorem into it.

284. *Foundations of Geometry*, p. 106. This "ground rule" was inspired by an accelerating accumulation of impossibility proofs that also comprised the basis of Hilbert's argument for the solvability of all definite mathematical problems in his famous lecture on "Mathematical Problems," *Bulletin of the American Mathematical Society* 6 (1901): 444. In his *Lectures* Hilbert identifies "the modern principle" as "the principle of the proof of unprovability" (*David Hilbert's Lectures on the Foundations of Geometry, 1891–1902*, ed. M. Hallett and U. Majer [New York: Springer, 2004], p. 284, hereafter *Lectures*).

285. If the triangles *ABC* and *A' B' C'* in perspective from *O* lie in *different*

planes, *AB* and *O* determine a plane that contains *A ′B ′* which meets *AB* at *P*, and similarly for the points *Q* and *R*. Thus each of *P*, *Q*, *R* lie in *both* of the planes of our triangles and so must be collinear, since otherwise these planes would not intersect in a line. Indeed, it is obvious by viewing the figure *perspectively* that the line must be their intersection. Like Peirce, Hilbert saw projective theorems as expressions of the 'optical properties' of space; in this case, that two triangles are optically indistinguishable from a point in space if and only if they optically vanish from any point on a unique line in space.

286. The three individuals introduced by existential instantiation of the space axiom are literally Kantian space intuitions. Since this was the sole example of an axiom given by Kant in the *Methodology*, despite having no definition at all of a plane, and hence no construction of one, one has little leverage for objecting to Hintikka's gloss on the Kantian intuition of this fundamental "space theorem," as Hilbert called it.

287. *Lectures*, pp. 315–16.

288. *The Essential Peirce: Selected Philosophical Writings*, vol. 2, p. 442.

289. Peirce, *The New Elements of Mathematics*, vol. 3, p. 871.

290. This logically confirmed a common belief for which, however, only vague reasons like Peirce's had been given. Thus Russell answers the question why (D) could not be "projectively proved in Flatland" by explaining that "in order to prove three points collinear, we must not define our straight line by points, but by planes. For when defined by two points, it is simply an aspect of their relation, and though any plane containing the two points contains the straight line, yet nothing can be said as to points on this straight line. Thus to get three collinear points, we must define the straight line as the intersection of two planes, and prove the three to lie each in both planes" (Bertrand Russell, *Philosophical Papers: 1896-99*, ed. Nicholas Griffin and Albert C. Lewis, vol. 2 of *The Collected Papers of Bertrand Russell* [Boston: Unwin Hyman, 1990], pp. 344–45). Russell formulated axioms for the projective plane from which (I) shows (D) to be independent, and as such affords a better comparison with the independence of Gödel's sentence than that of the parallel postulate. For it shows that, while the plane case of (D) may be evidently true when considered via projection from space (where it is evident), it is no longer provable in a plane contained in space without new axioms. Similarly, we say of Gödel's formal sentence, that while it is evident when considered via the Gödel-numbering as the projection of an evidently true metalinguistic statement, it is no longer provable in the formal language contained in its metalanguage unless wholly new kinds of axioms are added to it. A Gödel-sentence can be read either as a metalinguistic statement about proofs or as a formal statement about numbers, and while it can be evident when read in the former mode, it cannot be seen directly as a literal truth about numbers. Similarly, a Desargues figure can be viewed perspectively as a picture of lines and planes in space or literally as a flat configuration of lines (see Hilbert, *Lectures*, p. 171). In the former view it can picture an evident truth about the lines of intersection of planes, but when these lines are seen as a flat configuration, we have no clue as to the meaning of their relations—as Peirce and Russell realized.

291. *Lectures*, p. 240. In the *Festschrift* Hilbert describes the "significance of Desargues's theorem" as "so to speak, the result of eliminating the space axioms."

We have already described Hilbert's use of the order and congruence axioms to analyze the sense of 'spatial intuition' presupposed by Thales's theorem (note 18), whose significance we could express, by analogy with this characterization, as 'the result of eliminating reflections in space.'

292. We describe the Streckenrechnung on the horizontal of two axes intersecting at O (figure 15). Choose a 'unit line' EE'. To construct the 'sum' of $a + b$ of two segments $a = OA$ and $b = OB$, draw the parallel to EE' through A, intersecting OE in A'. Then draw the parallel OA through A', letting it intersect the parallel to OA' through B at A''. The parallel to EE' through A'' will meet the axis at the end point C of a segment OC we call '$a + b$.' To see the independence of this construction from our choice of the unit line EE', consider that choosing another such line (not shown) would yield another point $\bar{A}'$ on the vertical axis to start with, through which we would draw the parallel to the axis and then the parallel to $A\bar{A}'$ through $\bar{A}''$. To show that it must meet the axis in the *same* point C as before we must prove $C\bar{A}'' \parallel AA''$. This follows by applying (D) to the triangles $AA'\bar{A}'$ and $CA''\bar{A}s''$. Since the lines joining their corresponding vertices are parallel and we have $AA' \parallel CA''$ and $A'\bar{A}' \parallel A''\bar{A}''$ by construction, $C\bar{A}'' \parallel AA''$ follows by (D). To prove commutativity (figure 16), the construction of $a + b$ ends as before with the parallel to AA' through A'' intersecting the axis at C. The construction of $b + a$ begins with the parallel to a unit line through B intersecting the vertical axis at B'. Then let the parallel to the axis through B' meet the parallel to the vertical axis through A at B'', and draw the parallel to BB' through B'', which meets the axis at the endpoint of $b + a$. To show that this must be C we must prove $A''B'' \parallel AA'$. Let F be the intersection of $A'A''$ and AB'' and D the intersection of $B'B''$ and BA''. Then the three points O, F, D must be collinear since the corresponding sides of the triangles $AA'F$ and $BB'D$ are parallel; so by (D) must be in central perspective from O. It follows that the triangles OAA' and $DA''B''$ are in central perspective from F, and since we have $OA \parallel DB''$ and $OA' \parallel DA''$ by construction, $AA' \parallel A''B''$ follows by (D).

293. "Mathematical Problems," p. 5. As K. Reidemeister observed: "Durch eine geringe Änderung der Grundbegriffe wird die alte Theorie der Konstruktionen mit Zirkel und Lineal in Hilberts Händen nun so gelenkig, das sich die Konstruktionen mit dem Lineal herausheben lassen und einige elementare geometrische Figuren zu den—mit dem Lineal—*gezeichneten Formeln* für das Rechnen mit Strecken werden. Und dieser so anschauliche Sachverhalt ergibt sich gerade durch die als abstrakt verschrieene systematische Untersuchung der Beweiszusammenhänge (*Hilbert Gedenkband* [Berlin: Springer-Verlag, 1971], p. 5).

294. *CP*, 2.279. On this see Sun-Joo Shin, *The Iconic Logic of Peirce's Graphs* (Cambridge, Mass.: M.I.T. Press, 2002), pp. 19–22.

295. *CP*, 3.556. Hilbert's calculus illustrates Hintikka's claim that what occurs in an algebraic construction for Kant is at bottom what occurs in a geometric one, namely, "that we have introduced a representative for a new individual. And such an introduction of new representations for new individuals, i.e., new intuitions, was just according to Kant's definition what happens when we construct something. The new individuals may be said to represent the concepts 'the sum of a and b', 'the product of a and b', etc." ("Kant on the Mathematical Method," p. 27). Any doubt about the dependence of the calculus on the axiom of parallels would have been

dispelled by another of Moore's recommended readings: the "Report on Non-Euclidean Geometry" in *Science*, vol. 14 (1901) of Halsted, to whom Peirce had written in 1892 of his own project of "a modern synthetic-geometry treatment of non-Euclidean geometry" (Peirce, *The New Elements of Mathematics*, vol. 2, p. x). From this report he would have learned that Anne Bosworth had succeeded in her dissertation, *Begründung einer von Parallelenaxiome unabhängigen Strecken-rechnung* (Göttingen, 1900), under Hilbert in showing how to dispense with the use of this axiom: "This is a beautiful piece of non-Euclidean geometry and is, so far as I know, the first feminine contribution to our fascinating subject" (p. 715). She uses only (D) and (P) to construct a Strekenrechnung in a remarkable display of synthetic geometrical reasoning that would be very hard to follow without the forty figures that fill her fifty-seven pages.

296. *Foundations of Geometry*, p. 94. This is the weak affine case of Pascal. In his lecture Hilbert remarked that "just as Desargues is so to speak the elimination of the space axioms, so Pascal emerges as the elimination of the congruence axioms, that is, Pascal is the sufficient condition for a congruence relation to be possible." For with it, "calculation with segments or analytic geometry can be established, where the letters of course signify segments, not numbers" (*Lectures*, p. 261).

297. In notes for his "Second Talk on Deduction" of 1907, Peirce writes: "The ten point problem. The stupidity of early ways of treating it. von Stadt. How the ten-point problem establishes a kind of measurement. The nine point problem then becomes corollarial" (M754).

298. "The Place of C. S. Peirce in the History of Logical Theory," p. 22.

299. *The Principles of Mathematics Revisited*, 1996, p. 2. Hilbert suggested that any 'new statements' beyond his axioms for real arithmetic, including his 'completeness' axiom, would "be valid only if one can deduce them from those axioms by a finite number of logical inferences" ("Über den Zahlbegriff," *Jahresbericht der Deutschen Mathematiker-Vereinigung* 8 [1900]: 192). But on reflection his uncertainty *what logic was* led him to doubt this inference in a lecture in Göttingen on which extensive notes were taken by Husserl, in which he recounted "Hilbert's Objection.—Am I justified in saying that every proposition containing only the positive integers would be either true or false on the basis of the axioms for the positive integers? Here one would add the following: When we claim, that a proposition is decided by the axioms of a domain, what may we use besides these axioms? Everything logical. What is that? All principles that are free of anything specific to a domain of knowledge, that holds independently of all 'specific axioms,' of all material knowledge. Here one confronts an embarrassing dilemma: in the domain of algorithmic logic, in the domain of number, in the domain of combinatorial theory, in the domain of the general theory of ordinal numbers. And finally, is not the most general theory of manifolds or sets itself purely logical?" (Edmund Husserl, *Philosophie der Arithmetik* [The Hague: Martinus Nijhoff, 1970], p. 445.)

300. Peirce, *The New Elements of Mathematics*, vol. 4, p. 38. He never actually tries to prove the soundness of his logic of relatives.

301. *CP* 4.611.

302. Ibid.

303. "Poincaré's Review of Hilbert's 'Foundations of Geometry,'" *Bulletin of the American Mathematical Society* 8 (1902): 4–5. But could such a machine inform us of (I) or (I')? That is the question.

304. Ibid., p. 5. According to Poincaré, "anyone who had left any place for intuition, however small it might be, would not have dreamed of saying that on every straight line there are at least two points, or rather he would have added at once that there are an infinite number of them; for intuition would have revealed to him both facts immediately and simultaneously" (ibid., p. 5). One should compare these remarks with Kant's about his figure 7.

305. *Foundations of Geometry*, p. 97.

306. That (M) is "closely connected with the problem of completeness" was noted by Alfred Tarski, *The Completeness of Elementary Algebra and Geometry*" (Paris: Institut Blaise Pascal, 1967), p. 342. That (M) leads directly to a decision procedure for *Schnittpunktsätze* was shown in detail by Wu Wen-Tsun, "Toward Mechanization of Geometry: Some Comments on Hilbert's 'Grundlagen der Geometrie,'" *Acta Mathematica Scientia* 2 (1982): 124–38. For the role of (M) in modern automated theorem proving see his "Basic Principles of Mechanical Theorem Proving in Elementary Geometries," *Journal of Automated Reasoning* 3 (1986): 221–52. For the relation between mechanical theorem proving based on Wu's methods and those based on Tarski's, see Deepak Kapur, "Geometry Theorem Proving Using Hilbert's Nullstellensatz," *Proceedings of the 1986 Symposium on Symbolic and Algebraic Computation* (New York: ACM Press, 1986), pp. 202–8. On the relation of algebraic to formal synthetic proofs in Hilbert's *Festschrift*, see Shang-Ching Chou and Mahesh Rathi, "Machine Proofs of Geometry Theorems" in *Computing in Euclidean Geometry*, ed. D. Du and F. Hwang (Singapore; River Edge, N.D.: World Scientific, 1995), pp. 144–45. For the relation of (M) to Tarski's model theory of elementary geometry, see Wolfgang Rautenberg, "Hilberts Schnittpunktsätze und einige modelltheoretische Aspekte der formalisierten Geometrie," *Wissenschaftliche Zeitschrift der Homboldt-Universität zu Berlin. Mathematisch-Naturwissenschaftliche Reine*, *XIV* (1965), pp. 409–15.

307. *Lectures*, p. 283. This was before Hessenberg discovered in 1905 how to derive (D) from (P) after which Hilbert could simply say that "in proving the point of intersection theorem with the aid of Pascal's theorem it is then no longer necessary to revert to the congruence and continuity axioms" (*Foundations of Geometry*, p. 98).

308. "The Place of C. S. Peirce in the History of Logical Theory," p. 22. Hintikka stresses that neither Hilbert's interest in syntactical consistency proofs nor Peirce's purely formal study of existential graphs "mark any lapse from model-theoretic virtue" (p. 23). He elaborates his case for the *Festschrift* as "one of the main gateways of model-theoretical thinking into twentieth-century logic and philosophy" in his paper "On the Development of the Model-Theoretic Viewpoint," *Synthese* 77 (1988): 1–36.

309. *Grundzüge der theoretischen Logik* (Berlin: Julius Springer, 1928), pp. 74ff. They emphasize that such a decision procedure may not be feasible even if it existed.

310. As Weyl remarked, Hilbert's construction of models was "a wonderful trick to avoid analyzing the mechanism of deduction itself," but still required "all his amazing wealth of invention." See "David Hilbert and his Mathematical Work,"

Bulletin of the American Mathematical Society 50 (1944): 612–54.

311. Peirce, *The New Elements of Mathematics*, vol. 3, p. 622. Written in 1908.

312. He did not realize that this was true of Babbage's new machine. Though granting that "Babbage's analytical engine would perform considerable feats in mathematics" (*CP*, 2.56), Peirce proceeded to lump his machine together with the logical machines designed by Jevons and Marquand to grind out syllogisms in a way that shows no awareness of how fundamentally it differed from them in principle. (See note 263.) This point is misunderstood by Kenneth Laine Ketner, "Peirce and Turing: Comparisons and Conjectures," *Semiotica* 68 (1988), where he motivates Peirce's anticipation of Turing's result by distinguishing a "deterministic" (Turing) machine from a "theorematic" (Peirce) machine, "a nondeterministic machine that could accomplish the theorematic method" (pp. 50–51), whose "nondeterministic element" implies that "in our present state of knowledge we knew of no way to predict its output, knowing only its input" (p. 51). This is just what Turing proved of the *deterministic* machine that 'works the logic of relatives': one cannot even effectively predict whether it will yield any output at all from a given input—even if you know its whole program!

313. M462. See Don Roberts, "A Decision Method for Existential Graphs," in Houser et al., pp. 387–401 for a thorough discussion of Peirce's method.

314. Roberts, ibid., p. 388.

315. According to Peirce, "the study of geometry ought to begin with the theory of perspective" (*CP*, 8.94).

316. Hintikka admits that membership in this tradition must in some cases be taken with a grain of salt. For the difficulty of excluding even Frege completely from the logic as calculus tradition, see Juliet Floyd, "Frege, Semantics, and the Double Definition Stroke," in *The Story of Analytic Philosophy*, ed. A. Biletzki and A. Matar (London; New York: Routledge, 1998).

317. *CP* 4.531. Hintikka quotes and analyzes this and similar passages in "The Place of C. S. Peirce in the History of Logical Theory," pp. 24–25. He carries the analysis further in "Intuitions as Model-theoretical Insights," in *Intuitive Formation of Meaning: Symposium Held in Stockholm, April 21–21, 1998*, ed. S. Sondström, Konferenser 48 (Stockholm: Almqvist & Wiksell, 2000): 75–90.

318. Peirce, *The New Elements of Mathematics*, vol. 3.2, p. 968.

319. Peirce, *The New Elements of Mathematics*, vol. 2, p. 579. It has been suggested that Peirce's rejection of Weierstrass's nondifferentiable curve was motivated by his belief that calculus and differential topology are best developed by appeal to infinitesimals. See R. V. Dusek, "Peirce as Philosophical Topologist," in *Charles S. Peirce and the Philosophy of Science*, ed. Edward C. Moore (Tuscaloosa: University of Alabama Press, 1993), pp. 49–59.

320. "Hilbert Vindicated?" *Synthese* 110 (1997): 24.

321. Ibid.

322. In the *Anschauliche Geometrie* Hilbert stressed the use of models enabling one to see that certain propositions hold in a theory. Thus, it is obvious that (D) can be proved in elliptic geometry (given that any two lines intersect): "But if we attempt to give a direct proof of Desargues' theorem in the hyperbolic plane, without recourse to our model, we are faced with difficulties similar to those in

Euclidean and projective geometry." Specifically, "in the hyperbolic plane, a unified formulation of the theorems of incidence is possible only if two kinds of ideal points are adjoined—points corresponding in our model to the points on the circumference of the circle and points corresponding to points in the exterior of the circle. For example, if a Desargues configuration in the plane is given, we can always draw the fundamental circle of our model in such a way that nine points of the configuration are interior to the circle and that the tenth point is on the circumference of or exterior to the circle" (p. 247).

323. Also entitled "Foundations of Geometry." See Torretti, *Philosophy of Geometry from Riemann to Poincaré*, p. 185ff for a modern appreciation of Hilbert's breakthrough. Hilbert now *defines* the concept of a plane as a *set* π of points, all of which have neighborhoods comprised of the sets of points inside a Jordan curve, and which can be mapped homeomorphically into an auxiliary number-plane; that is, so that the now familiar neighborhood axioms are satisfied. A motion of π is a continuous mapping of π onto itself preserving the sense of Jordan curves, and a 'true circle' through Q centered on P is the set of all motions taking Q somewhere and leaving P fixed. Hilbert formulates three axioms: (1) the motions form a group, (2) a true circle is an infinite set, and (3) if motions exist that bring corresponding vertices of two triangles (point triples) arbitrarily close together, then there is a motion making them coincide. (This combines topological completeness with Helholz' idea of rigid mobility.) Hilbert uses (2) to prove that the points on a circle comprise a perfect set in Cantor's sense, i.e., one that is dense in itself and closed. His main result is that any plane satisfying (1) – (3) must either be Euclidean or hyperbolic. Though nonelementary, this system represents a considerable simplification of the solutions of Helmholtz and Lie of the Raumproblem for the plane, eliminating any need for the differential calculus and depending almost wholly on Cantor's point-set theory. Indeed, it convinced Hilbert and others of the indispensability of Cantor's theory for mathematical research.

324. *Foundations of Geometry*, p. 189.

325. See note 299.

326. Volker Peckhaus, *Hilbertprogramm und Kritische Philosophie* (Göttingen: Vanenhoeck and Ruprecht, 1990), pp. 60–61.

327. Thus van Heijenoort had it exactly right when he wrote that "Hilbert's position is somewhat between that of Frege-Russell and that of Peirce-Schröder-Lowenheim. Like the former, he works with axioms and rules. With his mathematician's instinct, however, he is inclined to consider quantifiers ranging not over 'everything,' but rather over well defined collections of objects. He also feels that the jump from first-order to second-order logic marks an important change in complexity; and though second-order logic may be indispensable at a certain stage, it is important to see what can be done in first-order logic," *Selected Essays*, 1985, pp. 45–46. That Hilbert explicitly distinguished first- from second-order logic by 1917 is made clear in the highly informative paper by Wilfried Sieg, "Hilbert's Programs: 1917–1922," *Bulletin of Symbolic Logic* 5 (1999): 1–44.

328. On this see P. Bernays, "Die Mannigfaltigkeit der Directiven für die Gestaltung geometrischer Axiomensysteme," in *The Axiomatic Method*, ed. L. Henkin, P. Suppes, and A. Tarski (Amsterdam: North-Holland, 1959), pp. 7–8.

329. *Principles of Mathematics Revisited*, p. 1. Sun-Joo Shin ties her valuable

critical analysis of Hintikka's gloss on Kantian constructions to the questionable claim that any step in a Euclidean proof requiring the construction of a figure corresponds to a proof step in Hilbert's system "using modern logic" ("Kant's Syntheticity Revisited by Peirce," p. 13). But if, as Hintikka says, no symbol of modern logic disfigures his pages, how *could* it be that "with the help of modern logic, Hilbert formalized Euclid's axioms *plus* Euclid's construction processes . . . to axiomatize the system" (ibid., p. 7). There is no more "modern logic" in Hilbert's pages than in Euclid's, though there are *many more axioms* from which to derive his theorems, using what we can only call with Peirce his *logica utens*. It is true that "Hilbert's axiomatization of Euclidean geometry has been considered as evidence that geometry can be free from the construction of figures" (ibid., p. 13). But try to follow his proofs of the algebraic laws for his *Streckenrechnung* without his Desargues figures. It is often said that Hilbert replaced Euclid's "construction postulates" with "existence axioms," but he formulates the congruence axiom for segments that is crucial for grasping the relation of his system to Euclid's by saying that, given any two points on a given line and another point on another line, "it is possible to find a point" on that other line for which the segments determined by the two point pairs are congruent, explaining that "this axiom requires the possibility of *constructing* segments" (*Foundations of Geometry*, p. 10). This removes the "gap" in Euclid's first proposition, wherein he tacitly assumes that circles must intersect in order to "construct" an equilateral triangle, which he immediately uses to *re*construct segments equal to given ones in Proposition 2. Hilbert's axiom postulates the possibility of this construction, thereby avoiding the prior construction of an equilateral triangle depending on the intersection of circles. Indeed, in the first edition of the *Festschrift* Hilbert could no more *prove* their intersection than Euclid, having only the Archimedean axiom. Later he adds the axiom of completeness that does entail their intersection, but the point is moot since the *Festschrift* aims to show that *no continuity assumptions at all are necessary in elementary geometry*.

330. Ibid., p. 2. Hintikka says Hilbert was "merely highlighting the purely logical nature" of geometrical proofs when he said they would hold of chairs and beer mugs as well as of points and planes, but his point is best seen in his reply to Frege's charge that his axioms failed to fix the meaning of "point": "If in speaking of my points I think of some system of things, e.g., the system: love, law, chimneysweeps . . . and then assume all my axioms as relations between these things, then my propositions . . . are also valid for these things. In other words: any theory can always be applied to infinitely many systems of basic elements. One only needs to apply a reversible one-one transformation and lay it down that the axioms shall be correspondingly the same for the transformed things. This circumstance is in fact frequently made use of, e.g., in the principle of duality, etc. and I have made use of it in my independence proofs . . . and it is in any case unavoidable" (Gottlob Frege, *Philosophical and Mathematical Correspondence* [Chicago: University of Chicago Press, 1980], pp. 40–41). Hilbert claims that axioms can at best characterize their subject only up to isomorphism and thus that definitions cannot uniquely fix the meaning of their primitives, though as a logicist Frege may have felt there was a better chance of defining points in purely logical terms than love or chairs. Hilbert's rationale for his proof of (M) suggests that he

conceived the "formal" aspect of his system algebraically and he may well have followed Lambert's idea of formal proofs. Thus in a review of the *Festschrift* his assistant J. Sommer explains: "J. H. Lambert compares the axioms to as many equations that can be combined in innumerable ways. Professor Hilbert, to decide the question of consistency, imagines the domain of an enumerable ensemble of numbers, and represents a point by two numbers of the domain, a straight line by the ratios of three numbers" (*Bulletin of the American Mathematical Society* 6 [1900]: 291). Where Lambert thinks of axioms as "algebraic equations that we must solve for x, y, z . . . without looking back to their subject matter," Hilbert proves their consistency in just this way: emphasizing that they are solved in a *countable* algebraic field. Dreben and Kanamori describe this "as arguably the first instance of the Löwenheim-Skolem phenomenon, a 'Skolem paradox' for the continuum" ("Hilbert and Set Theory," *Synthese* 110 [1997]: 82). In fact, this model plays a crucial role in the proofs of Hilbert's theorems giving criteria for the solvability of geometric construction problems using various means such as ruler and compass. The importance of Hilbert's work in algebraic number fields for his analysis of constructions as well as the "formality" of the *Festschrift* is cogently analyzed by Hourya Sinaceur, "De la géométrie formelle à l'algèbre abstraite," in *1830–1930: A Century of Geometry, Epistemology, History and Mathematics*, ed. L. Boi, D. Flament, J. M. Salanskis (Berlin: Springer-Verlag, 1992), pp. 167–74.

331. "Neubegründung der Mathematik: Erste Mitteilung," *Abhandlungen aus dem mathematischen Seminar der Hamburgischen Universität* 1 (1922): 161.

332. See note 48.

333. Bruce Halsted, "Report on Non-Euclidean Geometry," *Science* 14 (1901): 712. One sees from these results some continuity between Hilbert's early program of establishing necessary conditions of theorems and the partial realizations of his later program in Stephen Simpson, "Partial Realizations of Hilbert's Program," *Journal of Symbolic Logic* 53 (1988). Thus in the "subsystem" of Hilbert's system comprising just the axioms of incidence, order, and congruence one could prove the equivalence of various pairs of theorems that could not be proved from these axioms, but *not* the equivalence of Euclid's postulate and Σ= 2R.

334. *Transactions of the American Mathematical Society* 3 (1902): 142–58.

335. Ibid., p. 142.

336. Peirce, *The New Elements of Mathematics*, vol. 3/2, p. 924. E. V. Huntington also sought comments from Peirce on his paper "Set of Independent Postulates for the Algebra of Logic." Peirce wrote to him early in 1904: "Please understand me. I have no reason to doubt that you are substantially right from your point of view. But I think my telling you at large that I can make neither head nor tail of your postulates will lead to a discussion that must be useful to me and may probably be so to you. I am old, and notwithstanding my never relaxing my studies, don't take up new points of view so readily as many men I have known. I studied mathematics in preweierstrassian days" (L210). In short, before the days of counterexamples and models.

337. "Recent Work on the Principles of Mathematics," *International Monthly* 4 (1901): 87.

338. Ibid., p. 99.

339. Ibid., p. 101.

340. See *Toward the "Principles of Mathematics," 1900–1902*, vol. 3 of *The Collected Papers of Bertrand Russell* (Boston: Unwin Hyman, 1933), p. 466.

341. Bertrand Russell and Alfred North Whitehead, *Principia Mathematica* (Cambridge: University Press, 1910), vol. 1, p. vi. Just how important and lasting this drive for logical economy was for Russell can be seen in his remarkable claim in the Preface to the 1925 edition that "the most definite improvement resulting from work in mathematical logic during the past fourteen years" (p. xiii) was Scheffer's reduction of his two truth-functional primitives to one, making possible Nicod's reduction of his five primitive propositions to one.

342. Paul Bernays, "Probleme der theoretischen Logik," *Unerrichtsblätter für Mathematik und Naturwissenschaften*, vol. 33 (1927), pp. 369–77. This approach to propositional logic is carried out in detail by David Hilbert and Paul Bernays, *Grundlagen der Mathematik* 2 Aufl. (Berlin: Springer, 1968–70), vol. 1, pp. 63–86, where Peirce's law is shown to be underivable in certain axiomatizations of positive logic. In general, they pose "entirely analogously to the deductive development of elementary geometry, the problem of choosing the simplest and most natural system of axioms in which the role played by each of the propositional connectives is thrown into the clearest possible relief" (ibid., p. 64). They formulate a complete set of axioms "corresponding to the axiom groups of Hilbert's *Grundlagen*" in which the negation axioms come last in analogy with those of continuity.

343. Hilbert and Bernays, *Grundlagen der Mathematik*, vol. 2, p. 267.

344. Ibid., p. 278. To formalize Richard's paradox they formulate two further conditions: (t) that all closed terms represent unique numbers (hence that all function terms represent total functions), and (d) that there is a term $e(x)$ of Z for which $\vdash_z e(\overline{n}) = t_n$, which formalizes the "value concept" of a function. They show that (1) under (t) and (d) Z becomes inconsistent, and (2) that any such Z satisfying (d) must have a predicate T satisfying (**T**). They prove (1) by composing $e(x)$ with the diagonalization of the substitution function to construct a fixed point for the successor function, the nonexistence of which is immediate from the Peano axioms of Z. Unless one makes the questionable assumption that an e satisfying (d) would be an objective "denotation" function for Z, how can (T) be thought to be a criterion for objective truth in view of (2)? However, just such an assumption is made by Graham Priest in his interesting paper "On a Paradox of Hilbert and Bernays," *Journal of Philosophical Logic* 28 (1997): 45–56.

345. *Principles of Mathematics Revisited*, p. 144.

346. "Surface Semantics: Definition and its Motivation," in *Truth, Syntax, and Modality: Proceedings of the Temple University Conference on Alternative Semantics*, ed. H. Leblanc (Amsterdam: North-Holland, 1973), p. 138.

347. *Language, Logic Games and Information*, p. 226.

348. "Zur Hilbertschen Beweistheorie," *Mathematische Zeitschrift* 26 (1927): 10.

349. See Hans Hermes, *Enumerability, Decidability, Computability* (New York: Springer-Verlag, 1965), pp. 173ff. He attributes this proof to G. Hasenjaeger.

350. "Independence-Friendly Logic and Axiomatic Set Theory," *Annals of Pure and Applied Logic* 126 (2004): 313–33.

351. If there was something that Hilbert "overlooked," it was presumably the implications of (H) in view of his belief that the *Entscheidungsproblem* was

unsolvable. In any case, it may be said on behalf of first-order logic that its two basic properties of completeness and undecidability faithfully reflect the basic asymmetry in mathematical research invoked by Hilbert between finding sufficient axioms to prove a theorem and demonstrating which axioms are necessary to prove it. The greater expressive power of neither IF logic nor second-order logic are able to overcome the impossibility of effectively constructing models for first-order sentences. The best informed evaluation of Hilbert's program that I know of is by W. Sieg, "Beyond Hilbert's Reach?" in *Reading Natural Philosophy: Essays in the History and Philosophy of Science and Mathematics*, ed. D. Malament (Chicago: Open Court, 2002).

352. Levy has argued that "some of the mathematical theorematic ideas that introduce new axioms do not introduce additional quantification. Some non-Euclidean geometries are cases in point: they deny an axiom such as Euclid's fifth postulate and do not add another axiom that adds more quantifiers. Simply to deny an existential quantifier is to change it into a universal quantifier followed by a negation, not to introduce yet another quantifier" ("Peirce's Theoremic/Corollarial Distinction," p. 103). But Euclid's postulate asserts the existence of a unique parallel through a point not on a line while Hilbert's axiom of hyperbolic parallels asserts the existence of two such parallels, so the formalization of his hyperbolic axioms will clearly increase the number of existential quantifiers found in that of his Euclidean axioms.

353. "The Place of C. S. Peirce in the History of Logical Theory," p. 27.

354. *The Essential Peirce*, vol. 2, p. 303.

355. Editor's note: Due to circumstances beyond the control of the Library of Living Philosophers, it has not been possible to verify all the references, quotations, and translations in Professor Webb's contribution.

REPLY TO JUDSON C. WEBB

I used to wonder what Kant would have thought if he had known what industry the study of his writings was going to become, including what is known in German as *Kant-Philologie*. Reading Judson Webb's monumental examination of one line of my work I am beginning to have a taste of an answer. I appreciate greatly the penetrating scholarship with which Webb examines my ideas about the history of interconnected notions concerning the mathematical method, especially the use of what used to be called constructions, the notion of intuition and the logical technique of instantiation. Webb has dug into their history in certain directions in much greater detail than I have managed to do, often offering corrections and amplifications to what I have written.

Independently of the compliment which such an attention means, I have a specific reason to be pleased by Webb's essay. This reason is methodological. As I have tried to spell out (among other occasions) in my response to Knuuttila and Motzkin in this volume, the main strategy I have pursued in my historical work is to use the heightened awareness that systematic conceptual studies can develop in us for the purpose of identifying different concepts, ideas, assumptions, and problems in historical material and then to follow them from one thinker to another. As I have pointed out, such a strategy can only succeed if we are really dealing with the same concepts and ideas in the various philosophers, mathematicians, and scientists in question. No matter how accurate or inaccurate my discussions of Aristotle, Euclid, Pappus, Descartes, Kant, and Peirce are or may be, Webb's essay leaves no doubt that this methodological presupposition is satisfied in the historical studies that he is examining. In other words, Webb shows directly and indirectly that the concepts and problems of the different thinkers I have studied are indeed the same ones. As far as the methodology of history of philosophy and history of ideas is concerned, I could not have hoped for better judgments than Webb puts forward, for instance, when he writes that "we shall appreciate Aristotle's problem with them more when we see them still haunting Kant centuries after Euclid seemed to have solved them." I am tempted to go even farther and submit that a historian who does not realize what the relation of Aristotle's and Euclid's *ecthesis* bears on Kant's notion of intuition and to our contemporary notion of instantiation is bound to tell us only part of the true (hi)story.

This methodological satisfaction does not by itself mean that the details of my work are correct or that I agree with everything Webb says. The best way I can think of showing my appreciation of what he has done is to suggest a number of ways of pushing our thinking even further in several directions. I will begin with systematic problems. Indeed, even after his heroic efforts there still remains more to be said—and to be asked—about some of the topics in question. For instance, it is to my mind unmistakable that the problematic Webb discusses is largely the same as the one connected with our present-day logical notion of instantiation. But is the latter completely understood philosophically? For instance, the use of instantiation in logic has been discussed by some philosophical logicians under the heading "reasoning with arbitrary individuals." Unfortunately, I have never seen, touched, or kissed an arbitrary individual, nor could I recognize one if I met her (him? it?) in the street. I was first made aware of the connection between *ecthesis* and instantiation by the writings of Evert W. Beth. But Beth thought that he could dismiss the problems that had been raised earlier in history concerning *ecthesis* simply by showing that *ecthetic* reasoning can be reconstructed in modern logic. I do not think that this really solves the philosophical problems concerning *ecthesis*, for many of the same questions as were asked about it can be raised concerning our present-day notion of instantiation. It seems to me that all through the history that Webb so ably analyzes there prevails something of an uncertainty as to what at bottom makes such reasoning as involves *ecthesis* (or instantiation or any other form of reference to John Doe–like individuals) applicable to reality. As Webb spells out, several early thinkers thought that *ecthesis* amounts to an appeal to sense perception, and were therefore suspicious of it as a mode of logical reasoning. As late a thinker as Peirce held that reasoning "always involves observation." Instead of trying to escape this connection with sense perception, Kant made it the basis of his explanation of the applicability of *ecthetic* reasoning to reality. This applicability he tried to explain by connecting mathematical reasoning to the form of sense perception. For that link is established by ourselves (our faculty of sense perception), which gives us a chance of projecting the requisite relations on the objects of perception. Such a link was foreshadowed already in antiquity, as the testimony of Alexander the Commentator shows. But sense perception is not the only link between our language and our thinking and reality.

Peirce already saw this connection in the case of our logical (quantificational) discourse as being constituted by certain games. He did not take the analogy with Kant to its natural conclusion, however. This "logical" conclusion would have been to see the foundation of instantiating reasoning, not in the forms of sense perception, but in the forms of such meaning-constitutive games. It is the latter idea that I have tried to spell out in my "Quantifiers, Language-games and Transcendental Arguments"[356] and subsequent papers on transcendental arguments. This is a good example of what I have in mind when in my intellectual autobiography I speak of the Kantian streak in my thinking. This analogy between on the one hand Kantian forms (the outer and the inner sense) and on the other hand language games of seeking and finding is of course not complete. For one thing, as comes up in my response to Kusch, the structure of such language-games is less rigidly fixed than the forms of sensation according to Kant.

Thus under the surface of the actual uses of *ecthesis*, auxiliary constructions or other forms of instantiation, there is an important deeper and equally protracted story concerning justification of such procedures, a story that extends to the present day. This story has richly ironic overtones. It is still widely believed that the regimentation of mathematical reasoning in terms of symbolic reasoning disproved Kant's theses of the use of intuitions as a mainstay of the mathematical method and of the synthetic character of mathematical truths. Now the gist of present-day symbolic logic is the use of instantiations. But it turns out that this very use of instantiations is what Kant intended by saying that we use intuitions in mathematical reasoning and this is what, according to Kant, makes mathematics synthetic. Thus the same use of instantiations which Kant took to be a mark of the syntheticity and intuition-ladenness of mathematics was in effect taken to disprove Kant's views. This is a telling example of how systematic insights are needed in order to uncover what is really going on in the history of philosophy.

The delicacy of the conceptual matters we are dealing with here is shown by the fact that in some parts of logic instantiation rules become complicated. The reason is that unqualified instantiation may disturb the dependence and independence relations that hold in a given sentence. In the last analysis, in spite of the role of instantiation in contemporary logic, Skolem functions and instantiation by their means takes us deeper into the heart of logic than ordinary instantiation. Thus Webb's essay takes us already on the systematic level to a number of deep problems.

Some of the further historical questions prompted by Webb's essay apply to several different characters in the long-range history he examines. There are certain perennial questions that accompany the ideas of intuition, instantiation, and auxiliary construction throughout their history. They are not unrelated to the question of the ultimate justification of *ecthesis* and of auxiliary constructions. The first and foremost one is the dispensability or indispensability of these proof methods. Aristotle apparently tried to get rid of *ecthesis* in his logical theory.[357] Did he think that we do not need *ecthesis* in mathematical proofs, either? There was a major controversy in antiquity concerning the nature of what are known as constructions in geometry. Some thinkers tried to interpret them (as a modern axiometist would) by appeals to existence assumptions and existence theorems. Does such a view presuppose the dispensability of auxiliary constructions as proof steps? If so, the existence view is a lost cause, for modern logic shows that we cannot avoid the introduction of new individuals into logical arguments.

In the course of history, some thinkers came to believe in the indispensability of auxiliary constructions, while others believed in their dispensability. It would be extremely interesting to know more about the explicit and implicit reasons of both kinds of thinkers.

An interesting case study in this respect is offered by Charles S. Peirce. Webb discusses Peirce's fascinating ideas about these matters with impressively close attention to Peirce's various texts and to his development. He criticizes me in effect for oversimplifying Peirce's ideas in certain respects, especially when it comes to the possibility of replacing theorematic arguments by corollarial ones. His criticisms are well taken. The systematic situation has nevertheless been clarified meanwhile, principally through the new, stronger interpolation theorem for the usual first-order logic that I have recently proved (together with Ilpo Halonen).[358] This interpolation theorem distinguishes three parts in any first-order deduction after it has been converted into a suitable normalized form. Thus in a deduction of G from F we can distinguish first a derivation of an interpolation formula I_1 from F, third a derivation of G from another interpolation formula I_2 and between these two a derivation of I_2 from I_1. The first and the third part are typically theorematic, but the middle one is in a suitable perspective corollarial in the sense that no new individuals are introduced. Now the introduction of new individuals in the proof of $F_1 \vdash I_1$ or of $I_2 \vdash F_2$ could admittedly be avoided so to speak by building them into the premise F_1 or into the conclusion F_2, for the intermediate part $I_1 \vdash I_2$ is corollarial in essentially Peirce's sense. Thus by means of the new interpolation theorem I can do better justice to Peirce's thought than I could do earlier. To use Webb's formulation, the kind of analysis provided by the new interpolation theorem cuts much deeper than any "analysis of Peirce's doubt in terms of undecidability." What we do not get is any reason that all theorems can be made corollarial; and indeed we get a reason to think that this cannot be done in general. For the anticipatory introduction can only be carried out ad hoc, not uniformly. The definitions needed for the purpose would have to be of a complexity unpredictable on the basis of prima facie formulation of the theorem in the first place.

Another group of questions concerns the nature of the instantiating "arbitrary objects." Some thinkers, among them Kant, were completely clear about the fact that the "intuitions" introduced in *ecthesis* and in auxiliary constructions could be merely symbolic like variables in algebra. Is this view a complete novelty in Kant or does it have precedents? Aristotle already defended geometrical *ecthesis* by saying that a geometrician is not uttering a falsehood when he says that the line he has drawn is precisely one foot long. Aristotle's defense turns on the claim that the precise length of the line introduced in *ecthesis* or in an auxiliary construction is not used as a premise in the geometrician's argument. But a geometer's argument might very well turn on the assumption that one *ecthetic* line in a figure is precisely twice as long as another one. Is this incompatible with Aristotle's defense?

One of the most intriguing large-scale developments in mathematics that is connected with the issues figuring in Webb's essay is mentioned in my reply to Garrett. How can a geometer hope to find an ordinary "synthetic" proof of a theorem by analyzing the given figure specified in the statement of a theorem? Does the figure instantiate only the given figure specified by the theorem? If so, a proof cannot always be discovered by analysis, for the proof may depend on auxiliary constructions not mentioned in the statement of a theorem. But how can these constructions be included in the figure, for they are part of what is being looked for? The brilliant answer by people like Fermat and Descartes was to include the looked-for auxiliary constructions in the figure to be analyzed *as unknowns*. (Wallis thought that lawyers' parlance with Jane Does and Richard Roes might be the model for this introduction of unknowns into reasoning.) This idea of instantiating variables with respect to unknowns is closely related to the method of analysis which can be seen as the methodological "secret" of early modern science. It also touches the question of the very nature of "arbitrary individuals." Are there precedents to this idea of instantiating objects in the earlier mathematical or philosophical literature?

Webb's discussion of Kant's ideas in the light of mine is a significant contribution to Kantian scholarship in its own right. I am especially impressed by the way Webb relates Kant's ideas in the context of the views of others, especially those of Lambert and Garve. There is little that I can criticize or improve on in Webb's examination of Kant. However, certain further questions can be raised.

Webb agrees with me that strong evidence for my interpretation of Kant's notion of intuition comes from Kant's comments on nonsensory or "intellectual" intuition. He follows Kant's explicit statements and connects intellectual intuition with the possibility of intuiting my inner states as nonsuccessive, without subjecting them to a temporal framework. I wonder if much more is involved here. Intuitions have a direct relationship to their objects. In the case of intellectual intuition, that direct relationship cannot be sensory. The only obvious alternative open for Kant seems to be to make that relation a creative one. This is in keeping with Kant's attribution of intellectual intuition to God, who has an immediate creative relation to all objects. One reason why this interpretation is of historical interest is that it would link Kant with the tradition of "maker's knowledge" and also with Newton's idea of space as God's sensorium.[4]

In reading Webb's discussion of Kant's ideas of the nature and of the one-dimensional structure of time I could not help having an anachronistic *déjà vu* experience. At one point Webb writes: "This is Kant's fallback answer to Garve: with its one dimension time cannot be expected to yield any more synthetic a priori propositions than the geometry of a straight line as opposed to the rich store of theorems of plane geometry." I remember having once made similar remarks about the poverty of a theory of continuous linear ordering. I was severely criticized by Dana Scott who emphasized what intricate mathematical structure even a one-dimensional continuum has. I suspect that all mathematicians who, like Hilbert, have striven to express axiomatically the continuity properties of a straight line will appreciate Dana Scott's point. But this point is probably anachronistic, for Kant was not aware of the vexing problems of continuity in which the rich structure of even a one-dimensional continuum manifests itself.

I wish that Webb would have commented on the semantic history of the term "intuition" and its cognates. C. S. Lewis has argued that words like *conscientia* for a long time referred only to a sinner's guilty co-knowledge of his or her transgressions and that the idea of conscience as "an internal lawgiver" developed relatively late.[5] Likewise, intuition seems to have referred originally only to one's in-sighting, and only later acquired the meaning of one's internal intellectual advisor, that is, a special mental faculty. I do not know, but would dearly like to know, when and how this semantic development took place.

Webb seems to give me too much credit when it comes to the help we can expect from the interrogative model of inquiry in understanding deductive reasoning. Or perhaps I should say that such help is likely to be either purely historical or else strategic. One thing that is historically crucial is that in the Platonic questioning games as well as in Aristotle's logic and epistemology even purely deductive steps were thought of as being prompted by questions.

In this respect, the deductive reasoning carried out by Meno's slaveboy is an eloquent example. But such prima facie reliance on questioning also when carrying out what we would take to be a purely logical (deductive) argument does not make these arguments any less strict or any less provable from geometrical axioms. Thus what I have said does not imply that Aristotle was not "able to marshal sufficient first principles to prove the main theorems" in Euclid.

These questions are not criticisms of Webb's remarkable essay. They are prompted by a desire to get more mileage out of his essay than he covers in so many words.

Even independently of the main lines of my work in the history of philosophy, Webb's research produces results that dovetail neatly with my ideas. In my autobiography I tell how Marvin Minsky gleefully noted that their theorem-proving programs are so clever that they have produced a proof of Thales's theorem (Proposition 5 in Euclid) that is more "elegant" than Euclid's. In the autobiography, I point out that the supposed improvement by Minsky's program over Euclid is not indicative of any really strategic superiority. Now it is turning out that the apparent awkwardness of Euclid's proof was not due to any inability on his part of formulate an "elegant" proof but resulted from Euclid's pursuit of other Webb desiderata than "elegance." For Webb shows that the "clumsiness" of Euclid's proof was probably deliberate, in that he was trying to avoid—for reasons rooted in questions of logic and philosophy—those very symmetry assumptions that the computer programmers flaunt.

In the last part of his essay Webb extends his discussion of auxiliary constructions and of the theorematic vs. corollarial distinction to more recent questions concerning the mechanization of logic and concerning Hilbert's axiomatization projects. Webb finds an ambiguity in my characterization of nontrivial mathematical and logical reasoning. There are indeed several ambiguities present here, but they are located in the subject matter rather than the concepts I have been using, even though I am undoubtedly guilty of not having disentangled them more clearly. Webb examines how Hilbert tries to avoid auxiliary constructions unless they "are closely related to the content of the theorem." Webb compares such elimination of auxiliary constructions with Hilbert's later project of dispensing with ideal elements in mathematical theories. Furthermore, Webb sees the elimination of auxiliary constructions as being relevant to the program of mechanizing mathematical reasoning.

There are in fact interesting relationships here. In particular, Webb makes a fascinating point in relating Hilbert's early axiomatizing efforts to his later metamathematical projects. It is also of interest to see how early the idea of mechanizing logical and mathematical reasoning came up. However, the conceptual situation is more complex than logicians realized at the time. The very notion of mechanization is ambiguous. In our contemporary terminology, the mechanization of logical reasoning may mean either that the set of logical truths is recursive or that it is recursively enumerable. These two kinds of mechanization were not distinguished until much later. The use of auxiliary individuals is perfectly compatible with the latter sense of mechanizability, and it is incompatible with the former sense only when it is recursively unpredictable how many new individuals (instantiations) are needed. Moreover, Hilbertian ideal entities are often, perhaps typically, higher-order entities, not individuals (first-order entities) introduced by instantiation. Insofar as applications of the law of excluded middle can be said to introduce (or presuppose) ideal elements, they are higher-order entities, viz., sets of values over which quantified variables range.

This entire range of problems has to be discussed from a general systematic point of view. Here a new perspective is offered by my forthcoming paper "Truth, Negation and other Basic Notions of Logic."[6] There I argue that in logic appeals to completed infinite sets are introduced by unrestricted appeals to the law of excluded middle, not by the completeness of first-order logic or by König's lemma. Indeed, this lemma is a logical truth of IF logic, which can be viewed as a realization of intuitionists' idea of logic. Hence someone's attempted rejection of the construction of models by the tree method or equivalent are not very interesting systematically. Likewise, however historically interesting Peirce's rejection of Weierstrass's continuous but undifferentiable function may be, it is not a viable position.

Webb is right in that this entire complex of issues needs a thorough re-examination. I have made a beginning in such unpublished papers as "Truth, Negation and other Basic Notions of Logic" as well as "How to Prove the Consistency of Arithmetic" and "Hilbert was an Axiomatist, not a Formalist."[7] I am convinced that the results of such an examination will bear out what I am suggesting here.

Webb argues that Peirce was not interested in model theory in the same way as Hilbert. However, I have been speaking of model theory in a much wider sense than Webb seems to do, in a sense in which Peirce's game-theoretical interpretation of quantifiers is a fragment of a certain kind of model theory (semantics). Even more obviously, Peirce's logical graphs constitute a kind of model theory of logic. In any case, even if Webb is right, it does not make Peirce any less of a member of the tradition of "logic as calculus" tradition in the sense in which I have used this *terminus technicus*. Virtually all the other symptoms of this syndrome are found in Peirce, and are related to his central ideas about logic and meaning.

J. H.

NOTES

1. Published as chapter 5 of my *Logic, Language-Games and Information* (Oxford: Clarendon Press, 1973).

2. See my 1978 paper "Aristotle's Incontinent Logician," *Ajatus* 37:48–65.

3. See our 1999 paper "Interpolation as Explanation," *Philosophy of Science* 66:414–23.

4. It has repeatedly been suggested that this idea of Newton's, well known to everybody in the eighteenth century, was an especially close anticipation of Kant's theory. All that Kant had to do, so to speak, was to replace God by man.

5. C. S. Lewis, *Studies in Words* (Cambridge: Cambridge University Press, 1958).

6. "Truth, Negation and other Basic Notions of Logic," forthcoming in *The Age of Alternative Logics: Assessing Philosophy of Logic and Mathematics Today*, ed. J. van Benthem et al. (Dordrecht: Springer).

7. "How to Prove the Consistency of Arithmetic," co-authored with Besim Karakadilar; "Hilbert was an Axiomatist, not a Formalist," forthcoming in a *Festschrift* for Ilkka Niiniluoto.

5

R. M. Dancy

HINTIKKA, ARISTOTLE, AND EXISTENCE

1. INTRODUCTION

Jaakko Hintikka has, over the years, made a number of large contributions to our understanding of ancient Greek philosophy: he has discussed Parmenides, Plato, and, most extensively, Aristotle. I shall here focus on his work on Aristotle. So far, though, that is not much of a focus, for Hintikka has written about a large variety of topics in Aristotle, such as: time, modality, induction, dialectic, methodology in general, theory of science, philosophy of mind, categories, and being and existence. I shall focus on the last of these topics, being and existence.

I do this with a twinge of regret, since, long before I met him, a paper of Hintikka's was the inspiration for my own Ph.D. dissertation: his paper was "Necessity, Universality, and Time in Aristotle," which appeared in 1957.[1] In it Hintikka claimed (to put it very baldly) that Aristotle supposed that all possibilities must be realized sooner or later. At first I disagreed. In the end my dissertation (none of it ever published) was devoted to the question why Aristotle might have held this view, to which he was committed. Hintikka has returned to this topic since, and more remains to be said on it.

But perhaps a discussion of being and existence will be more useful at this point in time, for Hintikka has quite recently returned to this.[2] In the early 1980s Hintikka and I, at Florida State University, taught a stimulating joint seminar on Aristotle's *Posterior Analytics*, and this topic figured large in our discussions then. He had already published material on the topic,[3] and

I published a paper of my own on it,[4] derived in part from my contributions to our discussions. Hintikka did the same;[5] subsequently Knuuttila and he reprinted my paper,[6] and Hintikka added another of his own in the same volume.[7] My discussion here will be pretty much confined to these papers, including Hintikka's most recent contribution.

Hintikka and I were not, at least not obviously, in complete agreement in that seminar, but we seemed to coincide over a large stretch of the terrain, and I recall being puzzled as to just what we were disagreeing over. I think I may have a better understanding now, and perhaps at least some of the disagreement is unreal. But I fear not all of it is.

I begin with an area of what is, on the face of it, agreement. First, we both reject a claim Hintikka refers to as "the alleged ambiguity of 'is'"[8] or the "Frege Trichotomy."[9] Let us simply call it "the Trichotomy." Second, we both hold that Aristotle did not accept the Trichotomy either. Our failure to reach complete agreement has to do with what Aristotle does accept.

Consider these points one by one. In taking up the first one, considerations that have a bearing on Aristotle's Greek will come in, but most of those will be shelved until we take up the second.

2. THE ALLEGED AMBIGUITY OF 'IS'

It is a matter of street wisdom (if anything in philosophy can be so characterized) that 'is' is ambiguous, at least among existence, identity, and predication:[10] this is the Trichotomy. Hintikka's rejection of the Trichotomy is carried out using Game-Theoretical Semantics (GTS). At Florida State, I was more than once a reader of dissertations directed by Hintikka on GTS, but I have never become adept in the use of this tool, so I am going to put it in my own terms. It is my hope that Hintikka and I converge, albeit from different directions, but I shall have to leave it to him and to the reader to determine that.

There are substantive questions here, and they must not be swept aside. First, my way of getting at the rejection of the Trichotomy is sufficiently different from Hintikka's to motivate the question whether the point I am making really is the same as the one he is making. Second, even if he and I do manage to converge on the same point, there will, later on, be some divergence, at least potentially. And perhaps some clue to the source of that divergence is to be found in our different ways of getting at the rejection of the Trichotomy.

The Trichotomy can obviously enough be divided into three Dichotomies; I will consider two of them, reject them, and suppose that the third has thereby been dispatched as well.

2.1. *The First Dichotomy: Identity vs. Predication*

Consider the first Dichotomy: the ambiguity alleged to obtain between the 'is' of identity and the 'is' of predication. I take it that this Dichotomy is supposed to appear between the two 'is'es of:[11]

(1) Socrates is {a}[12] man.[13]

or

(2) Socrates is pale.

on the one hand, and

(3) Socrates is the son of Sophroniscus.

Before we get any further, let me say that I take (1) and (2) to be predications, and (3) to be a statement of identity. My disagreement with defenders of the Dichotomy is not over this point.

I think the same is true of Hintikka's disagreement with defenders of the Dichotomy; that is, I think he would agree that (1) and (2) are predications and (3) an identity statement. But I am not completely sure, for the following reason.

Sometimes people have spoken as if, although (2) is a predication, (1) is actually a (quantified) identity statement: it tells us that

(1') Socrates is identical with some man or other.

And they have sometimes supposed, in addition, that the distinction between accidental and essential predication (terms we use in discussing Aristotle: they do not exactly occur in Aristotle, although the distinction certainly does) can be brought out in this way: essential predications are really (slightly) disguised identity statements (and so are essential 'predications' only in a Pickwickian sense).

And some of the things Hintikka has said make it sound as if he has at least been tempted by one or both of these ideas.[14] Hence the uncertainty just mentioned. I think we should not give into temptation on either score.

To take the latter one first, consider that (2) amounts to:

(2') Socrates is {a} pale {thing}.

and that if it is legitimate to rewrite (1) as (1') it is equally legitimate to rewrite (2'), and hence (2), as:

(2") Socrates is identical with some pale {thing} or other.

And then the alleged clarification of the distinction between essential 'predications' and accidental predications evaporates: if essential 'predications' are really identity statements, so are accidental 'predications'.[15]

I shall come back later to the suggestion that Aristotle himself differentiates between accidental and essential predications in something like this way. For the present, let us turn to the former temptation, the one that would lead us to treat (1) as an identity statement. Let us grant that (1′) is equivalent to (1); certainly I do not see any relevant difference, except for a perfectly obvious one: (1′) is a quantified identity statement, of the form:

(1″) $(\exists x)(Mx \ \& \ s=x)$,

whereas (1) is a predication, of the form:

(1‴) Ms.

Differently put, the equivalence of (1) and (1″), and the corresponding equivalence of (2) and (2″), show that predications may be rewritten as quantified identity statements. This does not show that predications are "really" identity statements. It should, in fact, cause us a twinge of doubt over the alleged Dichotomy between the 'is' of identity and the 'is' of predication, but it is hardly decisive by itself.

So I return to my original idea that (1) and (2) are predications and (3) is an identity statement. I shall also assume that Hintikka would agree; if this is an erroneous assumption, he will surely correct it.

But the Dichotomy is not simply one between the types of statement; it goes on from the correct claim that (1) and (2) are predications and (3) an identity statement to the conclusion that the 'is' of (1) and (2) is the 'is' of predication and the 'is' of (3) is the 'is' of identity: that 'is' has different senses in (1) and (2) and in (3). This conclusion seems to me, and, I take it, to Hintikka as well, quite unwarranted. It does not follow from the fact that

(4) My love is a red, red rose.

is a poetic statement and

(5) That flower is a red, red rose.

a (slightly odd) prosaic one that (4) employs the 'is' of poetry and (5) the 'is' of (slightly odd) prose.

No doubt a defender of the Dichotomy would accuse me, in connection with this treatment of (4) and (5), of parody of reasoning. But it raises an obvious question: what would it take to show that the 'is' of (1) and (2) has a different sense from that of (3)? To the extent that this requires a general analysis of ambiguity, of what it is for a word to have more than one sense, it is not going to get an answer here: that is a large question, way too large for present treatment. But something can be said without going that far.

One paradigm way in which the ambiguity of a word shows itself is when it renders a sentence ambiguous, especially when it does so by making the sentence express a truth under one reading in one situation but a falsehood under another reading in that same situation. Think of a philosophically uncontroversial case such as

(6) Socrates owns a cape.

Suppose there is no problem over settling the reference of 'Socrates', and suppose the individual referred to does own a cape of the sort that Superman and others wear on certain occasions, but does not own any real estate at all, much less a cape such as the Cape of Good Hope. In this situation, (6) gives a truth under one reading and a falsehood under the other. (6) is ambiguous.

Furthermore, it owes its ambiguity to the word 'cape', which picks out two quite different ranges of thing under its two meanings. That it does so is not what makes it ambiguous, for 'animal' picks out a number of different ranges of things without being ambiguous: to confine it to two, think of dogs and donkeys, and consider

(7) Socrates owns an animal.

This will give us truth if Socrates owns a dog. Suppose he does not own a donkey: that does not give us a "reading" of (7) in which it comes out *false*; it is just plain true. And if he does in fact own a donkey, then he will own two animals. But if we change the situation for (6) so that Socrates owns both a piece of land jutting out into the water and a piece of clothing of the flowing wraparound sort, that will not make it so that he owns two capes, except as a sort of joke.

And further, the ambiguity of (6) cannot be explained as a syntactic ambiguity, as in

(8) Visiting relatives can be a nuisance.

This could be true under one reading and false under another (many of the native speakers I have consulted find it true under both readings, but are prepared to acknowledge the remote possibility that it might under one or the other reading turn out false). Here there is no single word that is lexically ambiguous; the ambiguity turns (to put it roughly) on whether 'relatives' is construed as the subject or the object of 'visiting'. But in (6) we have a lexical ambiguity, and 'cape' is the obvious culprit.

I have not argued, and cannot argue, that the only way ambiguity can show up is in that way (that would require the general analysis of ambiguity skirted above), but it is a pretty good way, and where we cannot find an ambiguous sentence that owes its ambiguity to a word, we have not got much of a case for the ambiguity of the word.

Now do we have such an ambiguous sentence for the 'is'es of predication and identity? Let us think about

(9) Green is green.[16]

A Dichotomizer might be tempted to say: well now, there it is. Read as an identity, it is true; read as a predication, it is false: the color green is not itself colored green. So 'is' is ambiguous.

But that does not follow. For to read (9) as an identity, you must read its right-hand complement (the second "green") as a noun, indeed as a definite singular noun, and to read it as a predication, you must read its right-hand complement as an adjective. That is where the ambiguity lies, and it is in some ways more like a syntactic ambiguity than a lexical one. In any case, it does not rest on the word 'is'. You can stare at the little word 'is' until the cows come home, but it will not get you anything but a bunch of cows in the yard. For it is a perfectly general truth that for a sentence of the form

(10) S is P.

to count as an identity statement 'P' must be replaced by a definite singular noun. Adjectives and indefinite singular nouns produce predications every time.

To put it differently, the apparatus for settling the ambiguity of (9) is already in place, since it is a feature of all color words and other words as well that they can figure as nouns or as adjectives. That has to be said in any case, whatever one ends up doing with 'is'. But then insisting on the ambiguity of 'is' is a duplication of effort. Where possible, we should keep the lexicon as simple as we can, and not multiply distinctions beyond necessity. The identity-predication Dichotomy appears to me totally unnecessary: there are no philosophical confusions that turn on misunderstanding one of the allegedly distinct 'is'es from the other.

Of course the case I have made against the Dichotomy is not airtight. Perhaps Game-Theoretical Semantics can make a better case. The strategies I rely on make no appeal to GTS, but I take it that Hintikka would not rule them out, for he himself employs such strategies by way of confirming the result he himself reaches *via* GTS.[17] So far, I think, he and I are on the same wavelength.

2.2. *The Second Dichotomy: Existence vs. Predication*

The Trichotomy involves a second Dichotomy: that between the 'is' of predication and the 'is' of existence. So let us look at that. Here what we must deal with is another inference from the function assigned to certain sentences containing 'is' to the 'is'es they contain. The predications are once again (1) and (2), but now we are to contrast those predications with existence claims, and our paradigm here is:

(11) Socrates is.

To English-speaking ears (pardon my synecdoche) this sounds odd: we expect something more like

(12) Socrates exists.

(There is something still not quite right about that; we will get to it shortly.) But (11) is more like the way existence claims appear in Greek,[18] and especially in Aristotle, who does not employ separate verbs for 'is' and 'exists':[19] εἶναι, 'to be', does for both. And it is hardly unintelligible English. So, since, ultimately, our target is going to be Aristotle, we should try as far as possible to talk like him, short of doing everything in Greek.

Aristotle speaks of the occurrence of 'is' (εἶναι) in (11) as "'is' just by itself" (εἶναι ἁπλῶς: the quotation marks of course do not occur in the Greek), by contrast with "is something" (εἶναι τι), that is, "'is' + predicate" as in (1) or (2). So we could say that Aristotle characterizes the existential 'is' as "'is' just by itself," but that might be misleading, for it becomes clear that "the existential 'is'," for Aristotle, is not 'is' with a special sense: it is just 'is' not followed by a predicate. We can get closer to this starting from English.

As just parenthetically noted, (12), our current English approximation to (11), sounds funny, just on its own, and we can see why if we try to imagine a situation in which we would spontaneously utter it. Consider the question whether God exists; this is a question that is quite straightforward, at least for its linguistic propriety. If there were doubters about Socrates, people who wanted to say that there was never any such person, that he was a fabrication of the authors of Socratic dialogues, we can easily imagine entering a dispute with a past-tense version of (12): "no, Socrates *existed*," one might heatedly say.

But then it is clear that 'Socrates' is not merely a linguistic counter. Another large question to be avoided on the present occasion is that of the meaning of proper names. But plainly 'Socrates' carries some freight in our quarrel with the Socratic skeptics, whether as part of its meaning or as dictated by the pragmatics of our conversational situation or whatever. There stands in back of our conversation an implicit agreement as to what Socrates would be (or would have been): a predication. (Among the most frustrating conversations I can recall is one with a librarian friend of mine who was telling me about her "Plato project"—anyway, that is the way I heard it, and I could make no sense of it until I realized that I should have heard it as "PLATO project," where "PLATO" was an acronym for a computer language. Until that point, there was no such implicit agreement standing in back of this conversation.)

In English, the most comfortable locution for framing an existence claim using 'is' employs the existential prefix "there is." But, once again, the oddity of (12), just by itself, is reflected in the even greater oddity of

(13) There is Socrates.

where this is not read as an ostension ("*There* is Socrates; I thought he was back here."). What we need, to fill this out, is an explicit appeal to the predication or predications that render our argument with the Socratic skeptics intelligible: we need something such as

(14) There is such a man as Socrates.

No doubt we need more than that, but this is an absolute minimum: if we do not know whether the question has to do with a human being or a computer language, we do not know much of anything about the question.

But then (14) derives from (1) in a way that is quite common in English: just as we can rewrite

(15) An implicit agreement as to . . . stands in back of our conversation.
as
(16) There stands in back of our conversation an implicit agreement as to . . .

we can start from (1) and get (14).

And, as far as I can see, just as the sense of "stands in back of" in (16) is no different from the sense of "stands in back of" in (15), so also the sense of 'is' involved in (14) is simply that of 'is' in (1). It is not a special "existential sense" of 'is'.

So we have a somewhat incomplete case against the second Dichotomy that figures in the Frege-Russell Trichotomy to which Hintikka and I are opposed. The case is somewhat incomplete, since it has not yet covered the 'is' in (11), "Socrates is." When we turn to that, we turn toward Greek, and in particular toward Aristotle.

We do have a natural use, in English, for the words of (11): for example, in a conversation in which someone says "Socrates is wise" and someone else says, in agreement, "Socrates is." Here "Socrates is" is elliptical for "Socrates is wise." But then it is not giving us (11) construed as an assertion of Socrates's existence. Still, the idea of ellipsis is going to be useful. Unfortunately, it looks as if it is over this idea that Hintikka and I to some extent diverge.

Let us turn to Aristotle.

3. ARISTOTELIAN BEINGS

An "essentialist" is someone who thinks that at least some things have essences. An essence of one of those things is what that thing's being (existence) consists in: what it is for that thing to be. The phrase, "what it is for . . . to be," is an almost[20] exact translation of the Greek phrase, 'τὸ τί ἦν εἶναι . . . ' (with '. . .' in the dative case), standardly translated as "essence" in Aristotle. Above we were saying that discussion of Socrates's existence takes place against a background assumption or set of assumptions as to what Socrates might be: some sort of description, perhaps quite inchoate, of what Socrates is supposed to be. An essentialist is going to say that there are certain privileged descriptions: those that tell you what Socrates's being consists in, that give you his essence.

His essence, what it is for him to be, in Aristotle, is: for him to be a man.[21] Aristotle is an essentialist in that sense.[22] And one way to put that is this: Aristotle would understand (11), when taken as an existence claim, is as something that cashes in on (1), or is elliptical for (1): (11) tells us that Socrates is, and (1) tells us what it is for him to be.

But if we put the point by saying that (11) is elliptical for (1), we put it in one way misleadingly. For when we say "Socrates is" in the course of agreeing with someone else who has said "Socrates is wise," the way to fill in the ellipsis is obvious from the conversational context. But essences are not necessarily that obvious: getting at a thing's essence may require a certain amount of work. Granted, we cannot very well assert the existence of something without having available *some* way of saying what it is whose existence is in question, but if we are working in biology, say, we may have a ways to go before we nail down what is essential to the organism we are studying. This point will come back toward the end of this paper.

Shelving the concern for the time being, we might represent what is happening here by an entailment:

(17) Socrates is a man $\rightarrow$ Socrates is.

And then we could see Aristotle as telling us that it is from (1) that (11) derives, mediated by (17). But a certain amount of care is required. For Aristotle unambiguously tells us, in *Categories* 10.13b12–35, that when Socrates does not exist, positive predications such as "Socrates is healthy" and "Socrates is sick" are false, and their negations are true. So, in general, he is committed to all statements of the form

(18) S is P $\rightarrow$ S is.

Of course, (17) is a statement of that form. But so is

(19) Socrates is wise $\rightarrow$ Socrates is.

And however prominent a part of our picture of Socrates his wisdom may be, we can hardly say that his being consists in his wisdom.

So we want to be able to 'say, on Aristotle's behalf, that although (11) in fact follows from any true predication about Socrates, its actual content derives only from (1): an essential predication about him. (18) is, we might say, an entailment mediated by an argument: where "S is P" is true but not an essential predication, there is an essential predication "(S is P′)ₑ," and that is what warrants the existence claim "S is." By contrast, the entailments licensed by

(20) (S is P)ₑ ⊢ S is.

are immediate.

At any rate, this idea makes an otherwise problematic text a good deal less problematic. This is in *De interpretatione* 11. There Aristotle says, enigmatically (but does he ever say anything any other way?), in 21a25–28:

> ... for example, Homer is something, e.g., a poet; and so is he, therefore, or not? For 'is' is predicated of Homer accidentally; for because he is {a} poet, not by-virtue-of itself, 'is' is predicated of Homer.
> ... ὥσπερ Ὅμηρός ἐστί τι, οἷον ποιητής· ἆρ' οὖν καὶ ἔστιν, ἢ οὔ; κατὰ συμβεβηκὸς γὰρ κατηγορεῖται τὸ ἔστιν τοῦ Ὁμήρου· ὅτι γὰρ ποιητής ἐστιν, ἀλλ' οὐ καθ' αὐτό, κατηγορεῖται κατὰ τοῦ Ὁμήρου τὸ ἔστιν.[23]

Aristotle is not here making some sort of point about the "Homeric question": he is not asking whether Homer existed or not.[24] He is asking what follows from what. The standard way of reading this passage (followed most recently by Hintikka[25]) is a perfectly natural one: Aristotle is telling us that

(21) Homer is a poet.

does not entail

(22) Homer is.

Aristotle's question is not "does Homer exist?" but "does Homer *therefore* exist?" that is, "does it follow from 'Homer is a poet' that Homer is?" According to the standard reading, that is what he is asking, and that is all he is asking.

The trouble is that this reading brings us into conflict with *Categories* 10.[26] We can avoid that conflict by building a little more into Aristotle's question. If this is the same Aristotle that wrote *Categories* 10, his answer to the question whether (22) follows from (21) is "yes." But perhaps what Aristotle is asking about is the particular *type* of inference that might get one from (21) to (22). *De interpretatione* 11 has to do with the logical relations between predications in which a term in predicate position occurs "just by itself" (ἁπλῶς, 21a5 *et passim*) and ones in which such a term appears "in combination" with others (συντιθέμενα, 20b31; cf. συμπλοκάς, 21a5). We may call one of the sorts of inferences Aristotle considers "simplification," and illustrate it by the example Aristotle discusses in 21a18–21, where he has pronounced the following inference acceptable:

(23) Socrates is {a} pale man ⊢ Socrates is pale.

In the preceding he had discussed the converse rule, "addition," that would allow

(24) Socrates is pale, Socrates is {a} man ⊢ Socrates is {a} pale man.

In 20b35–36 he rejected an instance of that rule, namely:

(*25) Socrates is good, Socrates is {a} cobbler ⊢ Socrates is {a} good cobbler.[27]

The occurrence of 'good' in the premise for (*25) is a case of "'good' just by itself" (ἁπλῶς ἀγαθός, 21a15). Plainly Aristotle would also reject the simplification

(*26) Socrates is {a} good cobbler ⊢ Socrates is good.

in which the conclusion contains 'good' just by itself.

　　Aristotle would reject it for the same reason he rejects the addition in (*25). No doubt it is tempting to say that he rejects it because 'good' does not have the same sense in the premise as in the conclusion and would reject (*26) for the same reason. But this really is misleading: there are not two different lexical entries for 'good' one of which defines the sense of 'good' in the premise and the other that in the conclusion. 'Good' is a word the application of which to a man requires attention to features of the man in question different from those that must be attended to when it is applied to a cobbler: what makes someone a good man is pretty clearly not the same as what makes him a good cobbler. But if this made for different lexical entries under 'good' there would have to be a different entry under 'good' for every noun in the language: not only 'man' and 'cobbler', but 'thief', 'car', 'theory', 'sunset', 'piece of music', ...[28] We need not go to such lengths to reject (*26). We need only point out that 'good' requires construal with a noun or noun phrase; the noun 'cobbler', is given in the premise of (*26), but not in the conclusion. When 'good' occurs just by itself as predicate with a human being as subject, and the context does not restrict us to cobblers or thieves, we will supply 'man' as the missing noun. If we do that, we will make (*26) conclude from Socrates's being a good cobbler that he is a good man, and that obviously does not follow.

And that is the build-up to 21a25–28, quoted above. But there is a twist. For if Aristotle means to be rejecting the inference

(?27) Homer is a poet $\vdash$ Homer is.

on grounds exactly parallel to those for rejecting (*26), he is going to have to say that in the conclusion of (?27) we have 'is' just by itself, and where we have that we will supply the completion ' {a} man'. So far, so good: that is indeed, in his view, what we should supply, at least as I construe him. But can he go on to say in the case of (?27) what we made him say in the case of (*26), "that obviously does not follow"? Apparently not. For in fact it does follow from (21), "Homer is a poet," given one or another unavoidable subsidiary premises, that

(28) Homer is a man.

For poets are, like Sappho and Tyrtaeus, men. One might perhaps think of gods or muses, who also seem to have written poetry, and hope to avoid the inference of (28) from (21) on some such grounds. But that would be at best a stopgap measure, for if we are going to count gods and muses among our possible poets, we shall be able to infer from (21) that Homer is either a man or a god or a muse, and from each of those it will again follow that Homer is. In any case, sooner or later we shall have a replacement for (28) from which it will follow by one or more acceptable simplifications that Homer is, (22). So (22) follows from (21) after all, just as the *Categories* led us to expect.

But even so, it does not follow directly from (21); rather (21) has to be routed through (28) or some more elaborate replacement for (28); and even if that inference is acceptable, it is an additional step: (22) does not follow from (21) just by simplification. And that is what I take to be the message of this passage. That is, to recall the way I put it a little earlier, 'is' just by itself, which is used to assert existence in (22), is given its content by the essential predication (28), not by the accidental predication (21).[29]

In this I have gone beyond what Hintikka has said about this passage, which he treats as at least relatively impenetrable.[30] But I take it to be a reading of the passage that is, at least broadly speaking, sympathetic to his views on existence in Aristotle.

4. GRAY AREAS

But perhaps I am wrong, for Hintikka has rather vehemently rejected "ellipsis theories" of 'is' just by itself.[31] Most of what Hintikka has to say against such theories has to do with the interpretation of the *Posterior Analytics*, and I have not left myself enough room to give a reasonable exposition and critique of Hintikka's views about that formidable book; I will confine myself to the briefest of terms. Hintikka thinks that, in *Posterior Analytics* B 1–2 Aristotle unambiguously distinguishes existential from predicative questions, and characterizes the former as employing "a purely existential use of εἰ ἔστι."[32] And Hintikka thinks that, in an Aristotelian science, there are purely existential presuppositions or major premises standing at the top of the syllogistic chains that constitute the science: there are, in some sense, "existential syllogisms" embedded in the science, inferences of the form:[33]

(29) Every B is.

(30) Every C is B.

∴ (31) Every C is.

As for the latter claim, Hintikka has himself more than once admitted Aristotle never formulates such syllogisms.[34] And although he thinks that "[t]he explanation is that he does not need to do so,"[35] I find this less than fully convincing. The strongest evidence that I can see for such syllogisms is that provided by *Posterior Analytics* B 2.89b37–38, which tells us that when we investigate whether something "is just by itself" (i.e., where the 'is' occurs just by itself) we are asking for a middle term. But it seems to me that the kind of structure Aristotle is seeking is best illustrated by his treatment of thunder in B 10:[36] we start with what we might call a "nominal" definition for thunder, such as

thunder $=_{df}$ a noise in the clouds,

and then end up showing that there is such a thing by supplying a 'syllogism' such as:

(32) Fire is extinguished in the clouds.

(33) Noise takes place whenever fire is extinguished.

∴ (34) Noise takes place in the clouds.

It is clear that casting this as a syllogism is going to take some rewriting; this is far from unusual. But, broadly speaking, the extinguishing of fire provides a middle term that shows us why such noises take place, that is, why there is such a thing as thunder. And it does that by telling us what it is for there to be thunder. So the middle term is associated with unpacking the 'is' in "thunder is."

No doubt that is too brief. But it is enough to raise the question whether the treatment of 'is' just by itself in *Posterior Analytics* B is not in the long run quite compatible with the idea that 'is' just by itself unpacks into the 'is' of essential predication.

I wonder at this point once again whether Hintikka and I are really in disagreement. He says, about the view that 'is' just by itself is elliptical:[37]

> There is a sense in which it probably comes close to being a true representation of what things are like according to Aristotle's last and final conclusions. Roughly, for any entity to *exist* is for it to be *what it is*, i.e., what it *essentially* is.

But immediately he goes on:

> However, admitting this does not mean that the force of the term *esti* in Aristotle's actual argumentation is tacitly predicative.

And then I want to ask: what would be wrong with supposing that it *is* tacitly predicative?

I will raise a pair of small final questions. First, Hintikka, as just noted, wants to make 'is' just by itself a "purely existential use." Here I am bothered, as I was in our joint seminar years ago, by the term 'use'. I wanted then to ask: what differentiates between 'use' and 'sense'?[38] I think the best answer to this may just be: different uses involve different syntactic environments. The predicative use of 'is' occurs when the word appears in one syntactic environment; the identifying use when that same word, with the same sense, occurs in another. The only difference is the environments. Is that enough to cover the ground Hintikka wants covered in talking about uses?[39]

Second, Hintikka often supposes that, even though the Frege Trichotomy is not to be found in Aristotle, there is a distinction among senses of 'is' associated with the different categories of being. And it is perfectly true that Aristotle often tells us that being "is said in many ways" (πολλαχῶς λέγεται: e.g., the opening of *Metaphysics* Z). But in a paper published as far back as 1959[40] Hintikka made the extremely valuable point that this strange phrase need not be understood as "has many senses." (Aristotle has *no* expression that translates in the latter way.) So a question along the same lines as the preceding one is worth raising: what individuates senses, as opposed to uses? That, of course, is a question I refused to embark on earlier. But we can get a narrower one by confining the question to Aristotle alone: why should we say that *Aristotle* takes 'is' to show any ambiguity at all?

R. M. Dancy

Department of Philosophy
Florida State University
July 2003

NOTES

1. Jaakko Hintikka, "Necessity, Universality, and Time in Aristotle," *Ajatus* 20 (1957): 65–90; rewritten as chapter 5, "Aristotle on the Realization of Possibilities in Time," in Jaakko Hintikka, *Time and Necessity: Studies in Aristotle's Theory of Modality* (Oxford: Clarendon Press, 1973), pp. 93–113.

2. Jaakko Hintikka, "On Aristotle's Notion of Existence," *Review of Metaphysics* 52 (1998/99): 779–805.

3. See esp. Jaakko Hintikka, "'Is', Semantical Games, and Semantical Relativity," *Journal of Philosophical Logic* 8 (1979): 433–68.

4. R. M. Dancy, "Aristotle and Existence," *Synthese* 54 (1983): 409–42; reprinted in *The Logic of Being: Historical Studies*, ed. Simo Knuuttila and Jaakko Hintikka (Dordrecht: D. Reidel Publishing Company, 1986), pp. 49–80; followed in the same issue of *Synthese* by Hintikka (see note 5).

5. Jaakko Hintikka, "Semantical Games, the Alleged Ambiguity of 'Is', and Aristotelian Categories," *Synthese* 54 (1983): 443–68.

6. Knuuttila and Hintikka, *The Logic of Being*.

7. Jaakko Hintikka, "The Varieties of Being in Aristotle," in Knuuttila and Hintikka, *The Logic of Being*.

8. See, for example, Hintikka, "Semantical Games, the Alleged Ambiguity of 'Is', and Aristotelian Categories," pp. 443, 448.

9. See, for example, Hintikka, "'Is', Semantical Games, and Semantical Relativity," pp. 434, 443.

10. Hintikka frequently adds, as Russell does, class inclusion. That will not be of present concern.

11. The following examples should be thought of as translations from the Greek; they are fairly common Aristotelian fare. Bracketed words are ones that would not appear in Greek, from which the examples ultimately derive; the brackets are curly, '{' and '}', rather than square brackets, '[' and ']', or angle brackets, '<' and '>', because the latter types have special uses in Greek texts.

12. The indefinite article would not appear in Greek, which has none. Articles are about to become important, so it seems best to keep track of this fact.

13. Where "man" is to be thought of as a translation of the Greek ἄνθρωπος: just "human being," not "male human being"; "Xanthippe is a man" would do as well. So why not translate it as "human being"? Because this is a paper about being, and beings are not here to be multiplied beyond necessity. Then why not "human"? Because "human" is an adjective, unlike the original, but like the predicate in (2).

14. I have in mind such passages as Hintikka, "The Varieties of Being in Aristotle," pp. 94–95.

15. Does it help to point out that "man" individuates while "pale," even "pale {thing}," does not? That is certainly a difference between "man" and "pale," but it does not, on the face of it, make for a relevant difference between (1′) and (2″).

16. The example comes from Wittgenstein's *Tractatus* 3.323 ¶ 3, except that

Wittgenstein takes the first "Green" as the name of a person. The same point could be made taking it that way; indeed, perhaps that is the point Wittgenstein means to be making. But in ¶ 2 he subscribes to the Trichotomy.

17. See Hintikka, "'Is', Semantical Games, and Semantical Relativity," pp. 460–64.

18. For documentation, see Charles H. Kahn, *The Verb Be in Ancient Greek* [*Foundations of Language*, Supplementary Series 16] (Dordrecht: D. Reidel Publishing Company, 1973), ch. vi.

19. At least Aristotle does not *officially* use different verbs for 'is' and 'exists': the verb ὑπάρχειν is sometimes used by Aristotle to mean 'exist', but he shows no second-order awareness of this.

20. The qualification has to do with the fact that the occurrence of 'is' replaces the Greek word ἦν, which is a past tense. Why Aristotle uses a past tense is a matter of dispute that does not affect us here: none of the competing explanations would overthrow the idea that "what it is for . . . to be" is an acceptable paraphrase for the Greek.

21. At least, so I think. Hintikka, on p. 86 of "The Varieties of Being in Aristotle," adverts to Balme as having "shown" something different: that "for Socrates to exist is not so much for him to exemplify . . . the species-characteristic form of man, but rather to exemplify . . . the particular nature which consists in his likeness to his parents. And it is not clear at all that Socrates's exemplifying *this* particular form is a predicative relation rather than an identity." This is not the place to take up Balme's views in any detail, but I do not think he has shown what he claims here, and, even if he had, the fact that Socrates would share that particular form with his twin brother Schmocrates would detract a good deal from treating his exemplifying it as a matter of identity. See David M. Balme, "Aristotle's Biology Was Not Essentialist," *Archiv für Geschichte der Philosophie* 62 (1980): 1–12; reprinted, revised and expanded, in *Philosophical Issues in Aristotle's Biology*, ed. Allan Gotthelf and James G. Lennox (Cambridge: Cambridge University Press, 1987), pp. 291–312.

22. Is he an essentialist in some stronger sense, that postmodernists, feminists, and others take to be a pejorative sense of "essentialist"? That depends on one's interpretation of some passages in Aristotle's biological works and in the *Politics*, and I suspect the answer is "yes." Fortunately, that is not part of our present concern. Here I use "essentialist" only in the minimal way described above. In that sense, I suspect that many of us, even those who would reject Aristotle's sexist leanings, such as I do, would be amenable to essentialism.

23. In 1801 Gottfried Hermann ruled that the accentuation of the existential ἔστι was to be different from that of the ordinary predicative ἐστὶ; this has become known as "Hermann's rule," and, so as not to beg any questions, I have followed the text of Lorenzo Minio-Paluello, *Aristotelis Categoriae et Liber de interpretatione* (Oxford: Clarendon Press, 1949) in this passage (he attempts to follow the rule). Hintikka and I follow Charles Kahn in rejecting Hermann's rule (see Hintikka, "On Aristotle's Notion of Existence," p. 784, and Dancy, "Aris-

totle and Existence," p. 50, both referring to Kahn, *The Verb **Be** in Ancient Greek*, pp. 420–34, esp. 422–24). It is, then, worth noting that there is no way consistently to apply the rule to this passage; it amounts to a *prima facie* counterexample to that rule: if the two allegedly distinct types of ἐστι actually *sounded* different to Aristotle, what could his question be in this passage? And if we look at the last two occurrences in this passage, we see that Minio-Paluello has got Aristotle saying that, in "Homer is$_p$ a poet," 'is$_e$' is predicated of Homer. There is, in fact, no consistent way of accenting the last occurrence.

24. Nor is Aristotle addressing the view that Homer *does* not exist, because he is dead (C. W. A. Whitaker, *Aristotle's De Interpretatione: Contradiction and Dialectic* [Oxford: Clarendon Press, 1996], pp. 154–55): in that case he would no longer be a poet either. There are no poets in the Dead Poets' Society.

25. Hintikka, "On Aristotle's Notion of Existence," p. 786.

26. This is a notorious crux; the classic treatment of it is Manley Thompson, "Aristotle's Square of Opposition," *Philosophical Review* 62 (1953): 251–65, still very much worth reading. Reprinted in J.M.E. Moravcsik, *Aristotle: A Collection of Critical Essays* (Garden City, N.Y.: Anchor Books, 1967), pp. 51–72.

27. The asterisks mark the inferences rejected by Socrates. The question mark in (?27) indicates the ambiguity of that inference.

28. See Peter Geach, "Good and Evil," *Analysis* 17 (1956): 33–42; reprinted in *Theories of Ethics*, ed. Philippa Foot (New York: Oxford University Press, 1967), pp. 64–73.

29. See here Hermann Weidemann, *Aristoteles: **Peri Hermeneias**, übersetzt und erläutert. Aristoteles: Werke in deutscher Übersetzung*, ed. E. Grumach and H. Flashar [Band I Teil II.] (Berlin: Akademie Verlag, 1994), pp. 386–87.

30. See Hintikka, "On Aristotle's Notion of Existence," p. 786.

31. See Hintikka, "The Varieties of Being in Aristotle," pp. 85–92. The objection there is directed at Alfonso Gomez-Lobo, "The So-Called Question of Existence in Aristotle's *An. Post.* 2. 1–2," *Review of Metaphysics* 34 (1980/81): 71–89, but I take it that my paper, reprinted in the same collection immediately before Hintikka's, has much in common with Gomez-Lobo's, at least as far as the "ellipsis theory" goes. See also Hintikka, "On Aristotle's Notion of Existence," pp. 793–95.

32. Hintikka, "The Varieties of Being in Aristotle," p. 89, citing *Posterior Analytics* B 1.89b33: "I mean 'if it is' or 'is not' just by itself, not 'if it is or is not white'" (τὸ δ' εἰ ἔστιν ἢ μὴ ἁπλῶς λέγω, ἀλλ' οὐκ εἰ λευκὸς ἢ μή). I hope it is clear that the reading I have proposed for *De interpretatione* 11 applies, *mutatis mutandis*, to this passage as well.

33. Ibid., p. 87; Hintikka, "On Aristotle's Notion of Existence," p. 787.

34. Hintikka, "The Varieties of Being in Aristotle," p. 88; Hintikka, "On Aristotle's Notion of Existence," pp. 787–88. In the latter passage, he actually says that "purely existential syllogisms are impossible for Aristotle." This, I take it, he subsequently qualifies.

35. Hintikka, "The Varieties of Being in Aristotle," p. 88.

36. For this see R. M. Dancy, *Sense and Contradiction: A Study in Aristotle* (Dordrecht: D. Reidel Publishing Company, 1975), pp. 131–34.

37. Hintikka, "The Varieties of Being in Aristotle, p. 86.

38. This comes from no naïve, procrustean Wittgensteinianism about uses and senses. I simply want to get hold of whatever distinction Hintikka intends between 'use' and 'sense'. I am not helped by what I take to be a bit of careless writing on occasion, as in Hintikka, "'Is', Semantical Games, and Semantical Relativity," p. 444 ¶ 1, which begins by insisting that "there are differences between different uses of 'is'," which it illustrates by two different syntactical environments for 'is', and then concludes by saying that this syntactic difference "suffices to explain the surface difference between the two without postulating different uses {*sic!*} of 'is'." Hintikka, "Semantical Games, the Alleged Ambiguity of 'Is', and Aristotelian Categories," p. 459, at (iii)–(v), appears to ascribe the Trichotomy to Aristotle himself.

39. See here Hintikka, "Semantical Games, the Alleged Ambiguity of 'Is', and Aristotelian Categories," pp. 457–59; Hintikka, "The Varieties of Being in Aristotle," pp. 82–83, 85, *et passim.*

40. Reprinted as chapter 1 of Hintikka, *Time and Necessity.*

REPLY TO R. M. DANCY

When I first read Russ Dancy's nostalgic and quietly witty contribution, my first impression was that we agree so much that an interesting response might be difficult to produce. On re-reading it, however, I realize that there is much that remains to be said on the topic of Dancy's paper. It may seem presumptuous to think that one has something new to say about as difficult and as old a topic as Aristotle's view of being and existence. I nevertheless believe that the lines of thought that Dancy and I have been pursuing do lead to fresh perspectives on Aristotle's conception of being. For this purpose, it may be useful to broaden Dancy's perspective somewhat and relate what he and I have said to Aristotle's ideas of metaphysics and of the structure of science.

We—meaning Dancy and I—both reject the unavoidability of the Frege-Russell ambiguity claim that Dancy calls "the Trichotomy." This is the claim that verbs for being, like *is* or *estin*, are ambiguous regarding the notions of existence, identity, and predication. We also agree that there is no such trichotomy of meanings or senses in Aristotle. Of course there are different uses of *is* or *estin*, but they cannot be explained as being due to the ambiguity of a single verb.

Saying this nevertheless leaves a number of interpretational loose ends hanging. One pertinent question is raised by Dancy at the end of his paper. What is a difference in use, and how does it differ from difference in sense? Here I have apparently been sloppy in my explanations. One can—and should—distinguish the different Frege-Russell senses from each other, but they are not, systematically speaking, or in Aristotle, different meanings that a verb for being could have on different occasions. Rather, in Aristotle they are components of the unequivocal meaning of *einai*. In principle, Aristotle seems to think that these different meaning components all go together. In *Metaphysics* IV, 2 he says that *to on* (τό ὄν) and *to hen* (τό ἕν) go together just like *arkke* and *arition*, so that *one man* (εἷς ἄνθρωπος), *existing man* (ὢν ἄνθρωπος), and *man simpliciter* (ἄνθρωπος) are the same.

This suggests that all three Frege-Russell senses should be present whenever we use a word for being.

But this just is not possible, a fact that leads Aristotle into problems. For one thing, the identity sense is transitive whereas the predication sense is not. To use Aristotle's own examples from *De Soph. El.* v, the following inferences are not valid even though they ought to be valid if *is* had there the identity force:

> Coriscus is not a certain man
> Coriscus is a man
> _____
> ergo: Coriscus is not Coriscus

> Coriscus is not Socrates
> Socrates is a man
> _____
> ergo: Coriscus is not a man

According to the diagnosis I am offering, the gist of these fallacies is that the first *is* in both of them expresses identity, while the second one expresses predication. Aristotle expresses the second of these points by saying that the second premise in both cases expresses an accident. This cannot be true in the usual sense of 'accident', for neither Coriscus nor Socrates is a man by accident in the same sense in which they may for instance be pale accidentally. What he means is that the second premise in each case does not identify Socrates or Coriscus respectively, with any particular man. In our contemporary jargon this amounts to admitting that the *is* does not have an identifying force.

In other cases the existential force is missing. This explains Aristotle's fuss about how one can in a syllogistic theory prove a *that* before proving *why*. In any chain of syllogistic inferences, existential force trickles from the top down, establishing the existence of the event to be explained. In order to prove the *why*, the chain of syllogisms must consist of immediate (atomic) inferences. Hence, as Aristotle puts it, one can know the *that* before one knows the *why*.

For this interpretation of Aristotle's "eclipse" discussion in *Posterior Analytics* I do not need to postulate purely existential syllogisms like Dancy's (29)–(31). As Dancy points out, there are no such existential syllogisms in Aristotle, and Aristotle in effect rules them out in 92b12–15. It suffices for my interpretation to assume that in a syllogistic major premise like "every B is A" the *is* may or may not have an existential force, thus lending or not lending an existential content to that particular occurrence of the major term A. On other occasions, the predicative sense can be missing. The beginning of *Posterior Analytics* B seems to offer examples of such existential uses of *estin*.

Thus the different Frege-Russell senses should not be talked about as different *uses* of *is* or *estin*. Rather, in Aristotle, the different uses of *estin* involve different selections of the Frege-Russell component senses. If I have said something different in the past, I am hereby revoking it.

Dancy points out that what in practice enables us to tell the different "senses" or "uses" of verbs for being from each other is the syntactical environment, and asks whether this context could do the whole job here. I think that he is right as to how the distinction is actualized in natural languages. However, it is to my mind more informative to speak of component senses here. (This may even be a reason for saying that Frege and Russell were up to something important in their trichotomy.) For the environment does not always separate the different senses from each other. This can be seen most dramatically in the instantiation rules for natural-language quantifiers. Hence speaking of component senses seems to me a sharper tool for analysis here than referring to context or to uses.

These interpretations do not strike me as being especially daring, even though they can undoubtedly be challenged. But more difficult problems remain. First and foremost, if I am right about the missing senses, how could Aristotle insist that all the three senses go together? We are here dealing with some of the most difficult problems of Aristotle's metaphysics. I cannot hope to solve them here, but perhaps I can make some suggestions.

My main conjecture is that there is in Aristotle a link among the ideas of essence, subsistence, and the identity sense of *estin*. This link is evidenced in Aristotle's solution to the puzzle about Coriscus where the identity sense of *estin* is expressed by Aristotle by speaking of accidental attribution. Again in *Posterior Analytics* B vii, 92b12–15 Aristotle makes it clear that the *estin* of existence does not imply *estin* of identification by saying that existence is not the *ousia* of anything.

Why, then, does Aristotle seem to insist that all the different senses of *estin* go together? My conjecture is that he thinks that any statement must be about something. And this something must be an identifiable substance. However, the statement itself may not identify it. If it is true to say "pale man is sitting," pallor must belong to some particular substance or other. This is what it means for the *is* to have an identificatory component. But the job of identification is not done by the terms for pallor or sitting.

When the predicate term does identify a particular substance the statement is essential. "The pale [object] is man" is a case in point. If this conjecture should turn out to be true, additional conclusions ensue. Aristotle holds that the identity sense of *estin* implies existence: "It is impossible to know what a thing is if we do not know whether it exists" (*Posterior Analytics* B viii, 93a20–21).

This throws light on one of the main problems Dancy discusses. When is it that we can, according to Aristotle, infer "A is" from "A is B"? To us Aristotle's own example, why does "Homer is a poet" not imply "Homer is," i.e. "Homer exists"? Clearly any old predicative *is* does not support the inference. Dancy thinks that the inference is valid whenever B expresses the essence of A. I agree with him verbally, but it seems to me that we are looking at the semantical situation differently. Take a case in which A is a proper name, say 'Socrates'. Then, when we use this name, "there stands in the back of our conversation an implicit agreement as to what Socrates would be (or would have been): a predication," as Dancy puts it. But all that such agreement has to accomplish is to make sure that we are speaking of the same person. In other words, the *is* must be an *is* of identification. According to my hypothesis, this is what it means for the *is* to express essential predication. But if so, the use of the term 'predication' is somewhat out of place here, for the crucial point is that the relevant *is* does not only express predication but also identity.

Maybe Dancy holds that the only way identity can be expressed is by means of some predicative (descriptive) content. This is an arguable position in semantic theory, but it is not connected with the interpretation of Aristotle. I am prepared to argue that to identify A is not to tell what A is like, but rather to locate it within some agreed-on framework, as it were, on a certain map (or "chart," to use Peirce's word). Thus both Dancy and I agree that what sustains the inference is something like essential predication, but we seem to understand differently what such an essential predication amounts to.

A general point that emerges here is the importance of the identificatory component of the meaning of *is* or *estin*. Its role in Aristotle and in the later history of philosophy seems to deserve much more attention than it has received so far. I have made a stab at charting this role in my paper "On the Different Identities of Identity."[1] Among important features of this role there is the presence of the identity sense in the generic premises in Aristotle. This apparently implies that each Aristotelian science deals with a genus of known entities. If so, it will be hard to deal with in an Aristotelian framework with a science that aims at the discovery of previously unknown entities, and indeed hard to deal with the notion of an unknown quantity in general. This suggests an interesting perspective on the genesis of modern mathematics and modern science, where a crucial role was played by the manipulation of unknowns to the extent that we can set up equations relating them to the knowns or to the "data" as Greek geometers would have called them. After setting up suitable equations, we can then find the unknown by solving these equations.

Whether or not my conjectures prove to be viable, they illustrate the tremendous interest and importance of the questions Russ Dancy is asking. I am grateful to him for an opportunity to return to some of them after all these years.

J. H.

NOTE

1. "On the Different Identities of Identity: A Historical and Critical Essay," in *Language, Meaning, Interpretation*, ed. Guttorm Fløistad (Dordrecht: Kluwer Academic Publishers, 2004), pp. 117–39. (Appears also in French translation in the *Proceedings of Societé Française de Philosophie*.)

6

Aaron Garrett

THE METHOD OF THE ANALYST

In 1974 Jaakko Hintikka and Unto Remes published a monograph entitled *The Method of Analysis*.[1] The purpose of the book was to argue for the pervasiveness of the method of analysis, particularly the ancient geometrical conception of analysis, in ancient and modern philosophy. Although the book was co-written by Hintikka and Remes, Hintikka had the larger hand in the speculative first and last chapters on the importance of analysis in modern philosophy and Remes the middle sections on Pappus and ancient geometry. The two were interconnected of course. Descartes, the paradigmatic modern analyst, exhibited the power and extension of his analytical geometry by solving one of the outstanding problems of ancient mathematics known as "Pappus' problem." Hintikka and Remes argued that the connections went much deeper, through the continuity of an analytical method shared by ancient geometers and early modern scientists and philosophers.

Method and analysis are considered and reconsidered throughout Hintikka's diverse corpus. In this essay I would like to treat the question of the interconnection between method and analysis quite locally. In the first section I will very briefly present some themes in *The Method of Analysis* and show how Hintikka proposes to extend them to the Cartesian method as presented in the *Meditations*. In the second section I will turn to Hintikka's wellknown treatment of Descartes's *cogito*, and consider how it fits in with his discussions of analysis. Hintikka has suggested that the connection arises from "Descartes's identification of the essence of any one thing with a kind of efficient cause."[2] In the third section I will argue for the pervasiveness and centrality of analysis among early modern philosophers and attempt to extend Hintikka's discussions beyond Descartes to the paradigmatic early modern geometrical philosopher, Spinoza. I will conclude with two questions for Hintikka.

I. THE METHOD OF ANALYSIS

In the opening chapter of *The Method of Analysis*, Hintikka presents analysis as a means of "looking for proofs of theorems (theoretical analysis) and for constructions to solve problems (problematical analysis)."[3] Pappus, for example, sought to prove geometrical theorems and to provide geometrical constructions resulting in proofs. Ancient analysis and its modern descendants and variants did not seek to "discover" wholly new entities. Geometers sought new theorems, of course, but these were understood as drawing out intrinsic features of geometrical objects via proof and construction, as opposed to discovering them in the sense one discovers new planets and new continents. Analytic "discovery" was rather the discovery of middle terms or causes that explain the thing and, for Aristotle, ultimately gave rise to a definition.

More colloquially, ancient geometers and analysts began with a fact, a thing, or a state of affairs, and sought to explain what the fact, thing, or state of affairs is. Analysis normally took the form of breaking something into constituent parts or elements and then considering "the interrelations and interdependencies of entities in a definite configuration."[4] By means of this analysis the analyst came to understand the structure of and necessity in the fact, thing, or state of affairs that initially prompted the analysis—a virtuous explanatory circle. Beginning with a phenomenon, thunder, for example, we would then analyze the thunder into constituent parts—clouds, lightning, and rain—and discover the causes of the thunder that prompted the analysis. For Aristotle and Aristotelians the cause would be the quenching (rain) of fire (lightning) accessed through the analysis of constituent parts (for example, *Posterior Analytics* II.8; 113b15–114a26). Aristotle pursued this sort of explanation in many of his works, in particular in his biological explanations of the motion and reproduction of animals. Given Aristotle's influence it is unsurprising that analysis would have been central to ancient and medieval mathematics and science. Through the influence of Jacobo Zabarella and other methodologists, these basic features of Aristotle's theory of analysis were disseminated to many Renaissance and early modern logicians and methodologists. Of course, Galileo cannot be understood simply as offering an extension of this methodology since the mathematization of physical laws is something that is not considered in Zabarella's far more biologically centered Renaissance Aristotelianism; rather, such mathematizing constitutes a central feature of Galileo's innovation. However, as has often been pointed out, the framework of analysis and synthesis constitutes a general framework within which Galileo operated and through which he could successfully present his own mathematical philosophy by "mathematizing" the middle term. Galileo's use of mathematics in physical explanation disrupts many of the central features of the Aristotelian picture, but does not necessarily disrupt the method of synthesis and analysis.

I am writing as if there is straightforward continuity between Aristotle and the geometers, but there are important differences. A particularly notable difference is that nontrivial arguments in geometry, unlike Aristotle's analysis of the eclipse, often demand auxiliary constructions. In most interesting geometrical demonstrations one needs to utilize something more than just the object under consideration, for example, a triangle. Consequently, geometers use auxiliary constructions that draw out essential features of the object being considered and further orient the analysis (for example, tangent lines *et alia*). Hintikka places particular emphasis on auxiliary constructions as they are "one of the very few situations in which traditional philosophers of mathematics were confronted by the consequences of the nontriviality of logical reasoning."[5] Auxiliary constructions can be considered as allowing for concrete, complex strategies for solving problems and bringing essential properties of geometrical objects to the fore.

Hintikka and Remes have convincingly argued for the importance of auxiliary construction in ancient geometry and the way in which such construction relies on complex reasoning. Furthermore, auxiliary construction is not central only for ancient geometers. There are modern analogues of geometrical construction that in part explain the great efficaciousness of Renaissance and early modern science, for example, scientific and mental instruments. Bacon, Hobbes, and Descartes all seemed to view scientific instruments and methodological scientific constructions in this way, as instruments augmenting human power that clarify our understanding of the problems and objects to be considered in ways that a mere survey of the objects without said instruments would not. This would fit well with Hintikka's account of analysis.

Although a case can be made for auxiliary construction throughout Descartes's scientific works, in particular in the *Optics*,[6] it is far less evident how auxiliary constructions might apply to Descartes's *Meditations*. Is it not a crucial methodological point throughout the *Meditations* that one can analytically investigate the real structure of the mind independent of any auxiliary constructions, that is, of any constructions auxiliary to the human mind itself? Furthermore, in the "Second Replies" Descartes explicitly contrasted the analysis of *Meditations* with synthetic geometrical presentation in the "Second Replies." Perhaps Hintikka should have argued that the method of the *Meditations* differs from ancient geometrical analysis on this point. But Hintikka seems to hold that all Cartesian analysis (and the *Meditations* is, according to Descartes, the paradigmatic example of

Cartesian analysis) is in line with ancient geometrical analysis (AT VII, 156; *PWD* 2, 110–11).[7] For example, Hintikka emphasized that Descartes's method, including the *Meditations*, "can be profitably considered as a variant of the method of analysis."[8] So does this mean then that the *Meditations* results in a trivial analysis?

II. THE *COGITO* AND ANALYSIS

Finally, emphasizing analysis in early modern science and philosophy would seem to be at odds with Hintikka's best-known discussion of Descartes. In his classic paper "*Cogito, Ergo Sum*: Inference or Performance?" Hintikka argued that Descartes's *cogito* is best understood not as a syllogistic or logical inference but instead as a sort of mental performative utterance. Each reader of the *Meditations* must perform the *cogito*, must think it through and thus engage in (or even be) a mental act which itself provides the verification of the certitude of the *cogito*. Any presentation of the *cogito* as a syllogistic inference is derivative of the prior performative establishment of the certitude of the *cogito*. In other words, it is placing a noninferential insight into syllogistic form. This is clear from the fact that the formula "*cogito ergo sum*" (in which the "*ergo*" marks the formula as an inference) is only one of a number of ways that Descartes expresses his crucial insight.[9] The inferential "*ergo form*" of the *cogito* appears in the *Discourse on Method* (AT VI, 32; *PWD* 1, 127) and the *Principles* (AT VIIIA, 25; *PWD* 1, 210–11) but not in the *Meditations*. In the *Meditations* Descartes first concludes "I think, I am" and only later draws out the fact that "I am a thinking thing." Since Descartes considered the *Principles* to offer a synthetic presentation of his philosophy (*Conversations with Burman*, AT V, 153), and since the introductory essay to the *Discourses* was meant to provide only a synthetic glimpse of the *Meditations*, we can quite sensibly consider the inferential formula as a derivative syllogistical presentation of an insight Descartes had *in more analytico*.[10] Even in the *Principles*, the "*cogito ergo sum*" formula derives from Descartes's prior assertion that "it is a contradiction to suppose that what thinks does not, at the very time when it is thinking, exist" (AT VIIIA, 25; *PWD* 1, 195). But it is then incumbent on Descartes's interpreters to explain how the *cogito* argument functions as a result of analysis in the *Meditations* if it is not an inference.[11]

For Hintikka, the key to understanding the *cogito* as a performative is in appreciating the restricted conditions under which the *cogito* can be asserted. Just as for J. L. Austin there are conditions where "I christen this ship" could not be asserted—"I christen this ship the H.M.S. Stalin"—so there are clearly conditions under which the declaration "X does not exist" is consistently false. "Jack exists" may or may not hold or fail under a wide variety of circumstances, for example, each and every Jack might change his name to "Jill" and then the sentence would fail. This is not failure *qua* performative though; Austin's example of christening a ship "H.M.S. Stalin" and the example of Jack notably differ when considered as performatives. Success or lack of success in ship christening is due to following or violating social rules, whereas whenever Jack utters the sentence "Jack does not exist," independent of external circumstances, it fails. Now the capacity to christen a ship will always fail when one is not the christener, but "Jack does not exist" fails precisely when the proposition is uttered by Jack. Hintikka diagnoses this type of failure as signaling an existentially inconsistent utterance: an utterance which when uttered by the person referred to is inconsistent.[12]

The consistency or inconsistency of this type of sentence does not seem to depend on its being uttered or not uttered by a particular individual, this Jack, but rather being uttered by the individual or an example of the class of individuals asserted not to exist in the proposition or utterance: "Jacks." "Concertina players do not exist" would be inconsistent when uttered by any concertina player. What is important is that whatever the proposition refers to as not existing is the being uttering the proposition and is capable of doing so.[13] "Stardust does not exist" is neither here nor there as an existentially inconsistent utterance since stardust, unlike concertina players, cannot form a mental sentence or mental words. For Hintikka the "I" that can form such a mental sentence engages in a thought act that insures its own existence as a performance, that is, by enacting the conditions assumed in the thought act through the very thought act.

In the case of the *cogito* we have a sentence where the X is a generic subject of a verb, an "I," for instance, "I think, I am," "I am a thinking thing." Why? First it seems important for Descartes's argument that any reader of the *Meditations*, as well as anyone who might independently formulate such a mental sentence, would also be formulating an existentially inconsistent sentence. This is basic for what the *Meditations* sets out to accomplish, not only an investigation of *my* soul/mind but also an investigation of the human soul/mind. Consequently, Descartes seems to assume, whether legitimately or not, that what we are doing when we work through the *Meditations* is analyzing the structure of the human soul and its relation to God in an appropriate order—and in the process of this analysis resolving a number of difficult problems.

This is related to a second point. In one sense the "I" of Descartes's *Meditations* that comes to formulate the *cogito* is a placeholder that can be filled by any actual human being (or even any thinking creature) capable of understanding a simple argument. But is the *cogito* then a general formula which can be satisfied by various "I's"? And if an existential inconsistency is discovered in relation to the "I" will the inconsistency then hold of each and every being capable of filling the place of "I," just as each and every Jack when uttering "Jack does not exist" will utter an existentially inconsistent sentence? Since the class of beings able to fill the place of "I" is the class of all rational, thinking beings, the existential inconsistency will be coextensive with this class, and conversely will be exhaustively certain. So if each and every thinker can not think and not exist, then each and every thinker who thinks must exist. This is why both "concertina players play therefore they exist" and "I walk therefore I exist" are unsatisfactory due to their limited extensions.[14]

But construing the *cogito* as a general formula runs into one of Hintikka's objections. In *"Cogito, Ergo Sum"* Hintikka criticizes attempts to consider the *cogito* as holding for any beings beyond those who undergo the process of thinking it through for themselves. This point is amplified in *"Cogito Ergo Quis Est?"* where Hintikka emphasizes that the *cogito* rests on perspectival as opposed to public modes of identification, modes which "cannot support any inference to the existence of a public object."[15] It seems evident that the *cogito* and the argument of the *Meditations* in general has a strongly particular and perspectival character. It seems evident as well that Descartes thinks we all need to think it through for ourselves once in our lives. Hintikka further amplifies this point by claiming "Descartes clearly was painfully (or blissfully) aware of the restriction of the *cogito* to a single moment of time and to have tried to overcome this limitation."[16]

Yet, that Descartes wished to generalize the insights of the *Meditations* seems indisputable as well. Hintikka draws the conclusion that Descartes was incapable of successfully generalizing the *cogito*, even though he seems to have thought that he had done just this. The proofs of God in the Third and Fifth Meditations are the failed attempt, and here Descartes attempts to move from the perspectival and individual to the public, external world with God as anchor.

While this failure is certainly part of the story, Descartes also had other grounds for thinking himself successful in generalizing the *cogito*, having to do with the method of analysis considered by Hintikka in *The Method of Analysis*. Why this is the case will be discussed at greater length in a moment, but it seems reasonable to make a distinction between, on one side, that which is assumed in a performative utterance (the stuff that enters into it) which can be generalities holding of all souls, and, on the other side, the actual performative act through which each individual must make his or her own perspectival acquaintance with the generalities. This distinction can be made clear if we look at the parallel in the famous wax argument that concludes the Second Meditation. In the wax arguments Descartes claims that the mind can recognize generic features of material objects through a particular analysis of a particular piece of wax and that the knowledge of said generic features is essential to understanding both our minds and the material world. As in the wax argument, so also in the *cogito* we recognize essential features and interdependences found in human minds via the analysis of a particular mind. Insofar as we discover essential features and interdependences they can be said to hold of all possible actual minds (as opposed to all thinkable minds).[17]

Even if this is an accurate way of representing Descartes's assumptions —and I am not claiming that they are warranted, just that this seems to be the sort of thing Descartes had in mind—I have not really explained how the *cogito* argument is to be construed not as an inference but as a performance, if Descartes's method is understood as analytic in Hintikka's sense. In order to make sense of how this performance works (or if it works) in these terms, I would like to look very briefly at one of the most discussed arguments in the history of philosophy.

In the opening of the Second Meditation Descartes (and each potential reader) lists off a sample of things, concepts, and powers the certainty of which has been challenged in the First Meditation (sight, memory, body, shape, extension, movement, and place). He goes on to demonstrate that there is no necessary interconnection between the nonexistence of the external world or my body and my own nonexistence; rather he shows that they are distinct. From this it follows:

> [I]f I convinced myself of something I certainly existed. But there is a deceiver of supreme power and cunning who is deliberately and constantly deceiving me. In that case I too undoubtedly exist, if he is deceiving me; and let him deceive me as much as he can, he will never bring it about that I am nothing so long as I think that I am something. So after considering everything very thoroughly, I must finally conclude that this proposition, *I am, I exist*, is necessarily true whenever it is put forward by me or conceived in my mind. (AT VII, 25; *PWD* 2, 17)

There are many different ways to construe this argument but I take Hintikka's claims to warrant the following interpretation. The First Meditation demonstrated that one could doubt the existence of the body, the external world and more. Doubting the body, the external world, and so on (in other words thinking that they do not exist), is independent of doubting my own nonexistence. Why? Whereas in the former cases I can clearly formulate my doubt without contradiction, in the latter case when I attempt to formulate my doubt I am led to an existential inconsistency. Hintikka emphasizes that this interpretation is supported by the concluding statement of the passage above—"I must finally conclude that this proposition, *I am, I exist*, is necessarily true whenever it is put forward by me or conceived in my mind."

Reaching this conclusion is a crucial function of the *cogito* argument, but something else seems to be going on as well. The passage begins:

> [I]f I convinced myself of something I certainly existed. But there is a deceiver of supreme power and cunning who is deliberately and constantly deceiving me. In that case I too undoubtedly exist, if he is deceiving me. (AT VII, 25; *PWD* 2, 17)

In Descartes's argument, "I too undoubtedly exist" clearly derives from the fact that *either* I am deceiving myself *or* another is deceiving me. This exhaustive disjunction leads to the conclusion that in both cases there is an "I" being deceived. That Descartes saw the *cogito* argument as responding to such an exhaustive disjunction is telling for one aspect of his project in the *Meditations*. Richard Popkin has stressed the importance for Descartes of finding a response to Pyrrhonian skepticism. In the *Outlines of Pyrrhonism*, Sextus Empiricus presents the main principle of skepticism as "opposing to every proposition or reason an equally valid opposed proposition or reason" (*Outlines* I.12), that is, the ability to maintain the either side of a disjunction when one side is dogmatically asserted. So if someone presents the skeptic with a thesis, the skeptic has the means to show that the opposite side of the disjunction is equally tenable. For Sextus the ultimate goal of this sort of argumentative strategy is to undermine dogmatism, suspend judgment, and consequently attain *ataraxia*.

The Cartesian argument is, notably, incapable of being undermined by Pyrrhonian techniques because both sides of the disjunction (deceiver *or* no deceiver) still assume the same underlying thesis. Like the Pyrrhonian Descartes emphasizes suspension, and like the Pyrrhonian he argues for a kind of *ataraxia*, but unlike the Pyrrhonian suspension must give way to the assertion by the will of a central philosophical thesis—I am, I exist—and many theses arising from it. So Descartes's argument points towards his struggle with skepticism and his countering of skepticism with his own scientistic philosophical voluntarism and its form of ataraxia—the scientific transformation of the world.

Descartes seems to give this counter-skeptical claim a prominence of place in the argument, but, of course, the obvious objection to placing any weight on this passage is that there need not be anyone deceiving me, so my existence is dependent on a contingent deceiver. One response is that in the absence of an external deceiver, I am deceiving myself, with the same net result.

What is the efficacy of the external deceiver? It seems that this is the example we were seeking of an auxiliary construction functioning in Descartes's *Meditations*! The evil genius is a construction, quite literally. He is an extension of various properties of my mind, a construction, to an external entity. This construction functions to reveal essential interdependences in the object under investigation from which the construction was derived—my mind. The construction functions analytically, by ruling out a variety of things that I thought might be features of the object under consideration—body, space, and so on—and leaving intact the basic constituents and their interdependences. Deception, like doubt, is a kind of thought, a special case of thinking. So the constant in the "I" which allows it to exist is that whether being deceived by another or by the self, it is thinking.

The auxiliary construction of the evil genius clearly involves nontrivial reasoning. But does such a construction not violate one of the important principles of Descartes's analysis by positing something beyond my mind and independent? No, because it is in the end a *reductio ad absurdum* argument—Descartes ultimately shows the construction to be absurd given what necessarily follows from it. What remains are the essential interdependences in the object in relation to which it was constructed.

Descartes teases these interdependences out when he considers "what 'this' I is." He rules out a range of conventional possibilities until arriving at the conclusion:

> Thinking? At last I have discovered it—thought; this alone is inseparable from me. I am, I exist—that is certain. But for how long? For as long as I am thinking. For it could be that were I totally to cease from thinking, I should totally cease to exist. At present I am not admitting anything except what is necessarily true. I am, then, in the strict sense only a thing that thinks. (AT VII, 27; *PWD*2, 18)

This passage is for the most part consistent with Hintikka's performative interpretation. For example, Descartes seems to be emphasizing that "I am, I exist" holds just insofar as "this" I thinks, and conversely were this I not to think it would not necessarily be the case that I would exist. Furthermore his claim in the *Principles* that "it is a contradiction to suppose that what thinks does not, at the very time when it is thinking, exist" might be construed as synthetic shorthand for the far more complex argument in the *Meditations* with its many dialectical twists and turns. But in addition to these performative aspects, Descartes is maintaining not just that my existence is secure through my thinking, but that thinking is an essential predicate of each and every actual "I." For example, Descartes phrases a crucial passage of the argument—"were I totally to cease from thinking, I should totally cease to exist"—in a way that satisfies the basic criterion for a Cartesian essential predicate, were it to be taken away (no thinking) the thing (I) would be taken away.

This leads me to the following conclusion concerning the *cogito* argument of the *Meditations*: The *cogito* is a performance, but a performance that depends on a prior analysis. More strongly, the *cogito* argument can be understood as an analysis from a different perspective. Through the devices of the evil genius and the deceiver God, Descartes makes apparent just what the essential features are of the objects under investigation: our minds. These auxiliary constructions reveal essential interdependences in the objects under consideration. And they function quite like auxiliary constructions in geometry and are extensions of the principles that underlie and constitute the object (tangent lines versus hyperbolic metaphysical tangents!). Finally, these constructions allow for nontrivial arguments that reveal essential interdependences (between thinking and being, for example) in the object, dictating the ebb and flow the argument, the questions asked and the answers proferred.

Take the section of the *cogito* argument considered above:

> [I]f I convinced myself of something I certainly existed. But there is a deceiver of supreme power and cunning who is deliberately and constantly deceiving me. In that case I too undoubtedly exist, if he is deceiving me. (AT VII, 25; *PWD* 2, 17)

How does the auxiliary construction function in this passage? It will help to locate something common to both "deception" and "deceiving"— thinking—through showing how both underpin my "undoubted" existence. This is just one small example; the extended catalogues of all of the things that "I" am not (body, spirit, and so on) and the justifications of why "I" am not these things would be far less trivial examples.

Finally, the *cogito* can be generalized in a limited way, as an essential property holding of all thinkers insofar as they think. Hintikka ascribes this kind of generalization to Descartes, the conversion of "the intuitive insight concerning a particular case into a general premise."[18] Hintikka presents this conversion as Aristotelian, whereas I think that it depends on the assumption that the essential predicates entering into the *cogito* argument are intrinsically general which I view as being an analytic assumption in line with some aspects of Descartes's Scotism.[19] Regardless, this only holds of thinkers, not of material things, and consequently Descartes needs the proofs of God to anchor publicly identified objects in the external world.

But in my presentation have I not analyzed the performative right out of the *Meditations*? As noted previously, Hintikka has suggested that the connection arises from "Descartes's identification of the essence of any one thing with a kind of efficient cause."[20] In the Fourth Replies, to Arnauld, Descartes remarks:

> in between 'efficient cause' in the strict sense and 'no cause at all', there is a third possibility, namely 'the positive essence of a thing', to which the concept of an efficient cause can be extended. In the same way in geometry the concept of the arc of an indefinitely large circle is customarily extended to the concept of a straight line. (AT VII, 239; *PWD* 2, 167)

Descartes is attempting to circumvent Arnauld's objection that if, for Descartes, God's existence is derived from its essence, and all causes are efficient causes, then God is *causa sui*. This response suggests that Arnauld is incorrect in thinking that Descartes assumes God's essence is the efficient cause of its existence as a cause prior in time. To illustrate how one might think about essence causing existence differently Descartes suggests that the efficient cause of some thing's existence bears a sort of asymptotic relation to the positive essence of a thing.

We need not worry about what precisely Descartes meant by applying efficient causes to God (although clearly Spinoza worried about that). What is important for understanding the *cogito* is that Descartes draws a connection between the positive essence of something and the efficient cause of its existence. Now in the case of the *cogito* Descartes could not entertain that we, *qua* minds that go through the process of formulating the *cogito* argument, are the efficient cause of our existence. Existence can only be said to belong to the divine essence. But Descartes could hold that when an analytic investigation into the human mind reveals an intrinsic relation among essential properties, a relation between thinking and existence, for example, the positive essence as a whole can be construed as an efficient cause.

In other words, grasping the interrelation between aspects of my particular essence leads to an understanding of the ways in which I exist and the connection between my mode of existing and my thinking. Only God can be cause of my existence, but in performing the *cogito* I can grasp the essence of my existence, so to speak. Consequently, the *cogito* involves analysis and synthesis, analysis of my positive essence and the synthetic causal interconnection of aspects of my essence in a particular, performative act. But can the performance and the analysis ultimately be reconciled in the asymptotic sense defined above, or are they always at odds? And does the performance involve something additional, the faculty of will? Despite the suggestion offered above, I think Hintikka is right in seeing that there is a discrepancy between the *cogito* and analysis. I will return to this issue again in the final section, but in order to develop this problem further I would like to turn to a philosopher who took Descartes's treatment of geometry so seriously that he thought it ended up making the *cogito* irrelevant for analysis at best (and destructive at worst): Spinoza.

III. SPINOZA, THE GEOMETRICAL METHOD, AND THE WILL

Although a Cartesian in some important senses, Spinoza diverged from Descartes on method and analysis. Spinoza's most important work, the *Ethics*, is presented as a linear deductive, geometrical, and synthetic argument. This would seem to imply that for Spinoza Euclidean geometrical presentation was to be equated not with analysis but with synthesis. The identification of geometry with synthesis is not surprising since in the Second Replies Descartes himself equated Euclidean geometrical presentation with synthesis.

   In the introduction to his geometrical presentation of Descartes's *Principles of Philosophy*, Spinoza criticized Descartes for having presented his philosophy analytically and not allowing the reader to follow easily his complex arguments. Of course, Descartes thought that his *Principles* were a synthetic presentation of material that had been previously arrived at analytically, so Spinoza's criticism of analysis seems inappropriate. Furthermore since Descartes criticized synthetic geometrical presentation as always derivative of prior analysis—the true method of discovery hidden by the ancients and made widely accessible by Descartes—Spinoza appears to have entirely missed the point.

   Yet Spinoza clearly read the *Objections and Replies* with great care, so it is far more likely that he was criticizing how Descartes conceived of synthesis. Descartes ordered the *Principles of Philosophy* synthetically, moving from causes to effects, but in the unrigorous manner of early modern university textbooks. Furthermore, that the *Principles* opens with Spinoza's synthetic ordering of a work already in a synthetic order can be understood as an attempt to make it more rigorous and accessible. In other words there is synthetic ordering in general, and then there is the rigorous method of synthetic geometrical presentation.

   But how could Spinoza really have thought that his rigorous geometrical presentation could possibly make the *Principles*—already written in a familiar style and hence probably fairly easy for its intended audience to read—any easier going? Spinoza's *Principles of Descartes's Philosophy* is clumsy going at best, and would have been so for seventeenth-century readers as well, however skilled they were in Euclidean geometry. So what was Spinoza's justification for providing a synthetic "representation" of Descartes's *Principles*?

I think that Spinoza saw an additional function of the Euclidean method—rigorously applied—beyond those that Descartes emphasized in the Second Replies. The function of a geometrical presentation is not just to communicate difficult subject matters clearly and easily. Geometry makes problematic inferences apparent in two ways. First geometry makes it apparent that a certain interpretation of a nominal definition cannot hold. For example, let us say my geometrically rendered philosophy begins with a definition of substance, a doxic definition much like the definitions with which Euclid began his geometry. I begin with other definitions as well. As I proceed in my geometrically rendered philosophy I may discover that assumptions I made about the initial definitions were incorrect; let us say I assumed that there were three substances in nature and each was a substance in a sense that I laid out in my original definition. As I examined various consequences of my definitions I might have come to the conclusion that I was mistaken in assuming that my initial definition warranted the conclusion that there were three substances.

This is one central aspect of how I think Spinoza thinks that Euclidean geometry functions.[21] In the *Principles of Descartes's Philosophy* Spinoza uses Descartes's definitions of basic features of mind and his metaphysics to undermine Descartes's claims about the will. Only a rigorous Euclidean geometrical method is able to exhibit whether a philosopher has mistakenly believed that he is warranted on the basis of his premises to come to the conclusion that he does. Consequently there is reason to place a synthetic philosophy in a different synthetic form.

Is this view a function of synthesis or analysis? Hintikka has quite correctly emphasized that the ancient geometer's analytic method is to be understood as both analytic and synthetic, although the analysis must be prior in some sense to the synthesis. Descartes assumes that analysis is prior in the sense that a pure analytic investigation must precede and be independent of any synthetic content. But Descartes primarily emphasized analysis to the almost complete detriment of synthesis, and hence the independence of the analytic method *qua* method. Synthesis for Descartes was more of an ordering procedure than an authentic method.

But in presenting Descartes's *Principles* in a geometrical manner Spinoza points toward something else. Synthesis and analysis cannot be nearly as independent as Descartes holds them to be. For a synthetic procedure can coexist with analytic discovery, in Spinoza's case the discovery of the inadequacy of the will as a philosophical concept and the consequent clarification of other important concepts. Of course, there would be no need for such clarificatory synthesis if Cartesian analysis had been successful.

Furthermore, Spinoza seems to be suggesting that Cartesian synthesis will be in principle unsuccessful, insofar as the Cartesian priority of analysis depends on the will. The skeptical argument that generates and allows for Cartesian analysis assumes that the will has the capacity neither to assent to nor dissent from ideas we experience (*PP* I/146), what Descartes calls the indifference of the will (AT VII, 58; *PWD* 2, 40–41). Spinoza implies that this is just the feature of the will that careful readers of the *Principles of Philosophy* should call into scrutiny through his own geometrical presentation (AT I/132, 173–76). Descartes could in theory pursue analysis independent of doubt, but it would only be successful if the analyst were without prejudices (which is impossible).[22] The procedure would be limited by the prejudices of the analyst and consequently fail to provide an adequate basis for Cartesian science.

Yet if Spinoza's criticisms are well founded, the proposed science will be well served in replacing an analytic method centered on the will with a method that emphasizes the mutual dependence of both analysis and synthesis. That analysis and synthesis were not independent seemed a common assumption among early modern philosophers, particularly Hobbes and Hobbesians. Descartes differs from Hobbes in combining analysis with a neo-Augustinianism that is at odds with some of his most exciting discoveries.

How does this relate to the *cogito*? Descartes arrives at the *cogito* via analysis, but the *cogito* is different from many of the other things one arrives at through analysis; it is—as Hintikka has shown—at least in part performative. From where does its performative character derive?

I think that ultimately the differences of kind between the *cogito* as performance and the other things we analyze and call into doubt arise from the stress Descartes lays on the will throughout the *Meditations*. The will comes to the foreground only in the Fourth Meditation, but it is important for the *cogito* argument. How? In his treatment of the will Descartes emphasizes:

> [T]he will simply consists in our ability to do or not to do something (that is, to affirm or deny, to pursue or avoid); or rather, it consists simply in the fact that when the intellect puts something forward for affirmation or denial or for pursuit or avoidance, our inclinations are such that we do not feel we are determined by any external force. In order to be free, there is no need for me to be inclined both ways; on the contrary, the more I incline in one direction—either because I clearly understand that reasons of truth and goodness

point that way, or because of a divinely produced disposition of my inmost thoughts—the freer is my choice. (AT VII, 57–58; *PWD* 2, 40)

This is the function of the will I just alluded to in considering analysis. It seems also to be a precise explanation of the force of the performative character of the *cogito* as analyzed by Hintikka. The *cogito* is the freest act of the will, insofar as the "reasons of truth" incline us as strongly as we may possibly avow it. But the *cogito* is also based on the capacity of the will to separate the soul or mind from its intentional objects. For example, the precondition of the *cogito* argument that I am able to recognize that "nothing is certain" rests on the capacity to set aside or bracket the contents of mind. Here we meet again the consequence of the indifference of the will. So perhaps the problems of the *cogito* which have been clearly identified by Hintikka are endemic to a theory which places such strategic importance on the distinctness between analysis and synthesis.

My Spinozist criticism does not invalidate the *cogito*, but rather stresses that Descartes's centralizing of the *cogito* and the failures of the arguments built upon this centralizing of the *cogito* result from the manner in which Descartes conceives of the independence of analysis and of the *cogito* as the result of said analysis. When Descartes coyly remarked that the ancient geometers were not ignorant of analysis but rather kept it as a sacred mystery, one might respond that in fact the ancient geometers had no mysteries but rather did not conceive of analysis as radically distinct from synthesis.

IV. QUESTIONS FOR HINTIKKA

I am curious whether or not Hintikka considers my presentation of early modern philosophical analysis to be accurate, both in conveying Descartes's consistency with the ancient geometers and his voluntarist divergences from them? If so, is Descartes, and the *cogito*, more exception than rule in the history of early modern scientific philosophical inquiry?

AARON GARRETT

BOSTON UNIVERSITY
JANUARY 2003

NOTES

1. Jaakko Hintikka and Unto Remes, *The Method of Analysis* (Dordrecht: Reidel, 1974).

2. Jaako Hintikka, "A Discourse on Descartes's Method," in *Descartes: Critical and Interpretative Essays*, ed. Michael Hooker (Baltimore: The Johns Hopkins University Press), p. 78.

3. Hintikka and Remes, *The Method of Analysis*, p. 1.

4. Ibid., p. 4.

5. Ibid., p. 5.

6. Thanks to Bret Doyle for helping me with this point.

7. See Charles Adam and Paul Tannery, eds., *Oeuvres de Descartes*, 12 vols. (Paris: L. Cerf, 1910), hereafter cited as AT; trans. by John Cottingham, et al., *The Philosophical Writings of Descartes*, 3 vols. (Cambridge: Cambridge University Press, 1984, 1985, 1991), hereafter cited as *PWD*.

8. Hintikka, "A Discourse on Descartes's Method," p. 74.

9. Jaakko Hintikka, "*Cogito, Ergo Sum*: Inference or Performance," *Philosophical Review* 72, no. 4 (1962): 15.

10. Harry Frankfurt claims that Descartes's response to Gassendi supports the view that Descartes viewed the *cogito* as an inference. But as far as I can tell Descartes's response only shows as far as I can tell that the *cogito supports* inferences and is superior to other possible supports for inferences insofar as it is certain. In other words Descartes takes over Gassendi's formulation of the *cogito* as an inference, and shows that a successful presentation of the *cogito* as an inference depends on the certainty of "I think." But this does not mean that the *cogito* is an inference. See Harry Frankfurt, "Descartes's Discussion of his Existence in the Second Meditation," *Philosophical Review* 75, no. 3 (1966): 337.

11. By "*cogito* argument" I mean the argument in the *Meditations*. By "*cogito* arguments" I will mean the cluster of arguments in the *Meditations*, *Objections and Replies*, *Discourse on Method*, and the *Principles*.

12. Hintikka, "*Cogito, Ergo Sum*: Inference or Performance," p. 11.

13. Frankfurt points out that an existentially inconsistent sentence ("EI") can have another independent proposition attached to it and will still fail ("EI & X"). This is true but seems not really to damage Hintikka's argument, as Frankfurt admits.

14. They are unsatisfactory for other reasons as well catalogued in the "Objections and Replies."

15. Jaakko Hintikka, "*Cogito, Ergo Quis Est?*" *Revue Internationale de Philosophie* (1996): 14.

16. Ibid., 15.

17. Another response to the problem of the specificity of the *cogito* is offered by Jean Beyssade in *La Philosophie Première de Descartes* (Paris: Flammarion, 1979). Beyssade accepts that the *cogito* is performative but suggests that the *cogito*

is discursive and temporal as opposed to momentary; it is a performance in time.

18. Hintikka, "*Cogito, Ergo Quis Est?*" 19.

19. This is the same as saying that a particular can be understood as a bundle of univocal properties plus *haecceitas* or thisness. For the importance of Scotus for Descartes see Roger Ariew, *Descartes and the Last Scholastics* (Ithaca: Cornell University Press, 1999).

20. Hintikka, "A Discourse on Descartes's Method," p. 78.

21. For an in-depth discussion see Aaron Garrett, *Meaning in Spinoza's Method* (Cambridge: Cambridge University Press, 2003).

22. See AT VII, 157–58; *PWD* 2, 111–12.

REPLY TO AARON GARRETT

By mundane criteria, my two papers on the Cartesian *cogito* have been
the most successful ones. They have even received the ultimate
compliment of being republished in France in a French translation. Frankly,
I nevertheless do not consider them my best philosophical achievements,
and I feel that whatever credit they deserve belongs to Rene Descartes. For
it is the rich lode of insights, proposals, and ideas that is hidden in that
apparently simple argument that has enabled me to mine materials for my
papers. These riches—I almost wrote, this embarrassment of riches—is so
great that it should not be a surprise that Garrett has come up with
interesting perspectives on the *cogito* which complement and correct what
I have said.

Eminently appropriately, Garrett considers in his contribution my ideas
about Descartes and his contemporaries by references to what was known
as the method of analysis. The original home of this method was Greek
mathematics, especially geometry. (One can find anticipation of the method
of analysis in Plato and Aristotle, but the most characteristic features of the
method emerge only from the Greek mathematical practice.) In geometrical
proofs an important and usually indispensable role is played by what were
called auxiliary constructions, which in the eyes of a logician are nothing
but steps of instantiation, that is, introductions of new individuals into an
argument. Using my own ideas to correct me, Garrett perceptively points
out that Descartes's overall argumentative strategy involves a line of
thought which I had not taken into account. After having initially convinced
himself of his existence, Descartes introduces the possibility that these
apparent insights were due to the wiles of some cunning deceiver. "In that
case too I undoubtedly exist, if he is deceiving me."

As far as I can see, Garrett is here absolutely right. I did not cover this
Cartesian line of thought in my earlier writings. Furthermore, it is not only
possible but instructive to consider the entry of the evil demon as being,
logically speaking, a step of instantiation. Such a step of logical instantiation introduces an entity we know or assume to exist without knowing what

or who that entity is. Such an "arbitrary object" will have to be referred to by a "dummy name" like lawyers' "Jane Doe" or "Richard Roe." Now obviously Descartes does not know who that "supreme power" is or might be, as little as a lawyer knows who she is talking about in arguing about Jane Doe or Richard Roe.

But what follows from this correction? Since it leaves the other branch of Descartes's argument intact, nothing very much seems to be affected. But a closer look at Garrett's observations prompts several second thoughts, some of them noted by him, some not. Indeed, the role of the deceitful demon can be seen as a prelude to the most important point Garrett makes. He examines Spinoza's objections to Descartes's skeptical argument.

The central one is directed against Descartes's voluntarism. The Cartesian argument "assumes that the will has the capacity neither to assent to nor dissent from ideas we experience." Spinoza rejects this assumption. Garrett argues with Spinoza here, and sees in the failure of Descartes's assumption the reason why Descartes's analytic argument cannot be converted into a synthetic one. I tend to agree with Garrett here, but I wonder if further analysis (and synthesis) might be needed. After all, Descartes claimed, in so many words, that his metaphysical argumentation can be organized synthetically.

This observation does not make Garrett's point any less illuminating. It seems to me that an unspoken voluntaristic assumption explains the need for Descartes to evoke the devious demon in the first place. Isn't what Descartes is thinking something like this: Suppose I muster my will and try to assert that I don't exist. Then that very act of assertion shows that I exist. But what if my act and its conclusion are affected by some deceiver's will? Then again I must exist, for otherwise I could not be affected by the deceiver.

Garrett's observations about Descartes's voluntarism are interesting also in that they invite comparisons with yet other thinkers, in the first place Aristotle. In my old (1978) paper, "Aristotle's Incontinent Logician," I called attention to an analogy between practical and theoretical syllogisms in Aristotle. Practical syllogisms are necessary for Aristotle, not just in the sense that the holding of the conclusion is necessitated by the premises, but in the sense that whoever realizes the premises in his or her mind must act accordingly. This is a puzzling view, among other things because it implies the impossibility of *akrasia*. But even more puzzling is the parallel view of Aristotle's according to which the full actual contemplation of the premises necessitates the drawing of the conclusion of a theoretical syllogism. Whatever one can say here, the Cartesian *cogito* cannot be a logical inference in this Aristotelian sense, in that it results from a deliberate, voluntary thought-act on Descartes's part. Moreover, its conclusion cannot have Aristotelian timeless necessity, for the initial certainty of the *cogito* is restricted to the moment of that act. How close Spinoza was in this respect to Aristotle I must leave for Garrett to tell me.

Some comparisons between Cartesian and Aristotelian theories of thinking throw light also on the history of the method of analysis. A stumbling-block for Aristotelian necessitarianism in the theory of logical and mathematical reasoning is constituted by the need of auxiliary constructions. These constructions are not determined by the statement of the theory to be proved, not even in conjunction with axioms, postulates, and earlier theorems. Auxiliary constructions do not occur to a geometrician automatically; they have to be deliberately chosen. Their role in geometrical and indeed all logical reasoning is not easy to reconcile with Aristotle's idea of syllogistic necessity.

Even though Garrett does not mention it, the role of auxiliary constructions in the analytic method is at odds with Aristotelian thinking in other ways, too. Such constructions are needed in order to prove a theorem or find the object to be constructed in a problem. Hence they have to be present in the configuration of objects whose mutual dependencies are literally analyzed in a geometrical analysis. But auxiliary constructions are not known, sight unseen. They are not part of the "data" of a theorem or a problem. Hence it is somewhat oversimplified when Garrett says that analysis "began with a fact, a thing, or a state of affairs." The nagging complication forced on geometers by the unavoidable need of auxiliary constructions is that they are not given in the theorem but introduced only in the course of the unknown synthetic proof that is being sought. (Indeed, in mathematical jargon the word "synthetic" still connotes the use of constructions, in contradistinction to "analytic.") You can see here, incidentally, that the Aristotelian necessitarianism tended to hide this problematic.

So where do the constructions come from? This question was especially poignant for a follower of Aristotle, according to whom the widest premises of any one science served to identify the very class of entities studied in that science. Hence the "auxiliary objects" introduced in a construction should be known, for they obviously must lie within the known genus studied by the science in question.

The brilliant novelty of early modern mathematicians was to include the prospective results of auxiliary constructions into an analysis *as unknowns*. Indeed, this approach is very much in the spirit of the idea of instantiation. We can argue about a "Jane Doe" even though we do not know who she is, for the term is really a name for an unknown. (The British mathematician Wallis surmised that the legal "John Doe" parlance was in fact the source of the use of symbols for unknowns by algebraists.)[1] The method of analysis thus became, in effect, the theory of equations and of ways of solving them. Garrett writes that "ancient analysis, and its modern descendants and variants did not seek to 'discover' wholly new entities." This is undoubtedly true of ancient analysis, in the sense in which it is intended. But since auxiliary constructions are typically indispensable, even an ancient analyst had to find them somehow in order to include them in the figure to be analyzed. Garrett's contrast is nevertheless apt. The kind of analysis practiced by the likes of Descartes could succeed only because the new entities—which they were trying to discover and which were intended to serve in the role of auxiliary objects—had been introduced into the analysis right from its beginning in the form of *unknowns*. (In this sense, they were not "*wholly* new.")

Thus Garrett not only corrects and complements what I have said about Descartes and his contemporaries; he calls our attention to questions that are crucial to our understanding of the development of philosophy and mathematics in a grand scale.

J. H.

NOTE

1. According to Jacob Klein, *Greek Mathematical Thought and the Origin of Algebra* (Cambridge: M.I.T. Press, 1968), p. 321.

7

Karl-Otto Apel

SPECULATIVE-HERMENEUTIC REMARKS ON HINTIKKA'S PERFORMATORY INTERPRETATION OF DESCARTES'S *COGITO, ERGO SUM*

I. Announcement of a Speculative-Hermeneutic Approach to Descartes and to Hintikka

From my first reading of Hintikka's essay on Descartes[1] in the early seventies I retained the impression that this was a completely novel approach to Descartes's philosophy made possible by the paradigmatic (often so-called "linguistic") turn of philosophy in the twentieth century, more precisely by speech-act theory. I will not revoke this early opinion, but in rereading the essay I realized with a certain astonishment that Hintikka did not mention any such inspiration of his own approach by a paradigmatic turn of recent philosophy but rather tried carefully to reconstruct Descartes's own tendential intentions, even if they were incoherent or even inconsistent with each other.

Thus one could say that Hintikka's essay is an example of historical hermeneutics, although he did not dispense with investing notions which could allow us to understand Descartes better than he understood himself—to appeal to a traditional *topos* of hermeneutics that was called into question by H.-G. Gadamer.[2]

In principle I agree with Hintikka's methodical approach but, for my own comments on his comments in what follows, I will take the license to keep at a greater distance from Descartes's text in speculating about the paradigmatic presuppositions in the history of occidental philosophy (especially *prima philosophia*). Such presuppositions may, on the one hand, have determined the background of Descartes's way of thinking and, on the other hand, may have been inaugurated by Descartes's new beginning, but among them may even be those features that, in my opinion, had to be overthrown by the paradigmatic turn of philosophy in the twentieth century. Roughly speaking, my speculation will be inspired by the supposition of a historical sequence of three paradigms of *prima philosophia*, namely (1) ontological metaphysics, (2) (transcendental) philosophy of consciousness, and (3) (transcendental) philosophy of language (or semiotics).[3] Thereby it may be possible, I hope, even to increase the scale of significance of Hintikka's novel approach to Descartes's philosophy.

II. How to Interpret Descartes's Transition from "*Cogito, Ergo Sum*" to "*Sum Res Cogitans*"?

Following my speculative heuristics of the three successive paradigms of *prima philosophia*, I will first consider the often discussed question of Descartes's transition from his fundamental insight of *cogito, ergo sum* to his conclusion, grounding a new type of ontological metaphysics, that he is a *res* or *substantia cogitans*, excluding everything that belongs to an outside (extramental) world of *res extensæ*. Hintikka approaches this problem after having already proposed his performatory interpretation of the *cogito, ergo sum*, and he even supports this latter—most innovative—interpretation by his account of Descartes's response to the question "what, then, am I?" by the thesis "I am a *res cogitans*."[4]

This does not mean that Hintikka defends the correctness of this (often criticized) conclusion, but in Hintikka's view it means the following: It was the performatively self-verifying function of the act of *cogito* (expressing itself as well in the self-defeating function of *cogito* that I do not exist) that in the first place suggested to Descartes the transition from *cogito* to *sum* that he expressed by the "*ergo*." For this transition could not be conveyed by any nonintellectual verb (as e.g., by Gassendi's "*ambulo*," and in a sense still to be clarified not even by verbs like "*volo*" or "*sentio*").

This same function of the *cogito* was also the main reason for answering the question "what, then, am I?" for Descartes by the thesis "I am a *res cogitans*." Thus the performatory interpretation of the *cogito, ergo sum*, according to Hintikka, provides the main reason why Descartes had to give a privileged position to *cogitatio* and hence also to *res cogitans*, in his response to the question "what, then, am I?" Up to this point the conception of a "*res cogitans*" for him was a necessary consequence of the performative evidence of his fundamental insight.[5]

This hermeneutic conjecture, within the horizon of its leading question, seems to me, quite plausible. But considering the problematic inauguration of a novel paradigm of ontological metaphysics by the internal connection of "*res*" and "*cogitans*" in the conception of a "*res cogitans*," one could also ask a more radical question with regard to the very question Descartes asked and wanted to answer.

Why did he—obviously quite naturally—ask: "What, then, am I?" and gave his response by introducing a (novel) "*res*" or "*substantia*"? Heidegger[6] and Gadamer[7] suggested that Descartes, not withstanding his intention to keep himself free from prejudices, quite naturally, so to speak, fell victim to the Greek ontology of asking for the substance of being (a paradigm of *prima philosophia* that was passed down to Descartes through his scholastic education in La Flèche.) Now, in order to understand critically and judge the logical dichotomy between res cogitans and res extensa, which became the metaphysical paradigm of modern philosophy and physics, I think, we have to take into consideration the Heideggerian suggestion as well as Hintikka's arguments for understanding Descartes's giving priority to the *cogito* (or at least to intellectual terms like *dubito*) in distinguishing the function of the indubitable.

First it seems clear that on Hintikka's interpretation we can easily understand Descartes was eager to stress that only as often, or only as long, as he was thinking he could be certain of his existence. This point, according to Hintikka, cannot be explained by a syllogism that supposes the general premise "whatever is thinking must exist" (since we can suppose by fiction that Hamlet thinks a lot but nevertheless does not exist[8]), but only by the fact that by somebody's performance of thinking the existential inconsistency of the conclusion "I do not exist" comes about (or rather is brought about). If this performatory interpretation is correct, it is clear that one cannot put the words "*ambulo*" or even "*volo*" or "*sentio*" in the place of "*cogito*."

But there is also the fact that Descartes himself in his conclusive ontological definition of the "*res cogitans*" subsumes also "*volo*" and "*sentio*" under the term "*res cogitans*." This cannot immediately be explained by Hintikka's performative account of *cogito* but, I think, rather by the fact—also taken into account by Hintikka[9]—that Descartes distinguished between the external, corporeal meaning of "*sentio*" and the internal, mental meaning of it that can be identified and claimed as being indubitable by the reflection that even in the case of a sensory illusion it seems to me that I have a certain sensation.

Descartes himself gives a very clear explication of this answer to our problem which is also quoted by Hintikka:

Suppose I say *I see* or *I am walking, therefore I exist*. If I take this to refer to vision or walking as corporeal action, the conclusion is not absolutely certain; for, as often happens during sleep, I may think I am seeing though I do not open my eyes, or think that I am walking although I do not change my place; and it may even be that I have no body. But if I take it to refer to the actual sensation or awareness [*sensu sive conscientia*] of seeing or walking, then it is quite certain; for in that case it has regard to the mind, and it is the mind alone that has sense or thought [*sentit sive cogitat*] of itself seeing or walking.[10]

How should we interpret this whole conception, which through its separation between the "corporeal action" and the "actual sensation or awareness of seeing or walking" provides the foundation for Descartes's prioritization of internal experience and thereby becomes a paradigmatic presupposition for the subsequent philosophy of consciousness?

III. Hintikka's Interpretation of "The Ambiguity of Cartesian *Cogito*" in Light of an Alternative Interpretation

Hintikka explains the "*prima facie* paradox" of Descartes's "ambiguous" use of the term *cogitatio*—differing between the narrow sense of an intellectual verb and the wide sense that includes willing, feeling, imagination, and perception (sensation)—by recourse to two interpretations of the *cogito* argument that are not clearly distinguished but rather confused by Descartes. The one interpretation of the fundamental argument, which makes it really *cogent*, is made clear by the performatory interpretation, but the other one, which is suggested by the logic of deduction, supposes that Descartes by perceiving that he thinks, obtains a premise of the form B (a) for a conclusion of the form B (a) $\supset$ E $(x)(x = a)$. Thus he seems to be able to deduce his existence from his being an individual (a) that receives the attribute (B), i.e., "thinking."

As Hintikka argues, along with Leibniz, this syllogism does not show that thinking entails existence, for to think and to be thinking is the same thing, hence to say "I am thinking" is already to say "I am."[11] On the other hand, an attempt at deducing the existence of an individual solely from its attribute "thinking" without presupposing already its existence, must fail, as is shown by the example, already mentioned, of Shakespeare's *Hamlet*. Thus far only the performatory interpretation can ensure the conclusiveness of the *cogito, ergo sum* argument.

But Hintikka presumes that Descartes, when he tried to interpret the nature of a *res cogitans* and, in accordance with the philosophical tradition, wanted to take into account all senses of the "acts of consciousness," might have been led not so much by the performative meaning of his basic argument but at least also by its deductive interpretation, which indeed presupposed the wide sense of "being *cogitans*" that covered all acts of consciousness.

Nevertheless, Hintikka thinks, Descartes reserved a privileged position for the verbs of intellection like *cogitare*, since only these verbs can convey the performative interpretation of the *cogito, ergo sum* argument.[12] However, if this thesis of the privileged status of the verbs of intellection meets Descartes's position, how could Hintikka say previously that for Descartes—obviously because of his confusion of two interpretations of his basic argument—the reason why sensation belonged to the nature of *res cogitans* was "exactly the same as the reason why he could argue *sentio, ergo sum*"?[13] Could he in fact argue in this way, if he has taken into account the privileged status of the verbs of intellection?

Or, to ask a closely related question: could Descartes argue *sentio, ergo sum* in the sense of a performatory interpretation of this argument, if he, or even because he, according to his own justification of the subsumption of sensation under the definition of *res cogitans*, could claim that only "actual sensation or awareness [*sensu sive conscientia*] of seeing or walking" (i.e., the fact that I seem to see or walk even in case of a deception by dream) is in any case "quite certain," because "it is the mind alone that has sense or thought [*sentit sive cogitat*] of itself seeing or walking"?

It seems to me that the point of this argument is very different from the point of the performatory interpretation of the *cogito ergo sum* argument. This is shown especially by the fact, also stressed by Hintikka,[14] that for the performatory interpretation of Descartes's basic argument the difference between the (alleged) internal, private sense of *cogito* and the external, public sense of a corresponding speech act of affirming and thereby trying to persuade somebody is completely irrelevant.

This, I think, is obviously not the case with regard to the quoted argument by Descartes; for this argument is a consequence of Descartes's preceding separation between vision (or walking) as "corporeal action" and "the actual sensation or awareness of seeing or walking," which is a matter of the mind. Precisely this separation between an external, corporeal sphere and an internal, mental sphere, which is so characteristic of Descartes's novel paradigm of ontological metaphysics, I suggest, must not be presupposed by a performatory interpretation of the act of thinking as equivalent to an act of uttering sentences in addressing somebody else in a dialogue (say, in an argumentative discourse).

This thesis is even strongly supported by Hintikka himself, namely by his important hint that one cannot say either: "You do not exist," since in this case the speech act of addressing somebody that is performatively implied is canceled by the propositional content of the sentence. I am indeed convinced that the performatory interpretation of the *cogito ergo sum* argument belongs together with the performatory interpretation of the verdict against "You do not exist" because they both must be originally based on the public use of language. Therefore, in both cases the performatory interpretation is not applied to a private, internal act of my consciousness (which, according to Husserl's account in the *Cartesian Meditations*, has to be understood and accepted as the basis of a "transcendental" or "methodical solipsism"). For even trying to persuade oneself by a voiceless act of thinking that one does not exist is trying to apply the structure (i.e., the claim to intersubjective validity) of a public act of arguing and therefore is doomed to fail by producing a performative self-contradiction.

Descartes's separation of the "external, corporeal acts" of sensation and the actual, internal acts of sensation as acts of the mind and his prioritization of the latter acts as paradigm of certainty does not fit the equivalence of thinking and public arguing that, as Hintikka shows, even Descartes must sometimes presuppose in his basic argument.[15] Descartes's "recourse to the private certainty" of "my actual thinking" that includes even the certainty of my sensation in the case of a sensory illusion, in my opinion, is rather one of the origins of modern times' paradigmatical prejudice of "methodical solipsism" of thought whose last classic proponent was Edmund Husserl[16] (Another origin of this paradigm—and thus even of Descartes's conception of the *res cogitans* that excluded the external world of the *res extensæ* and of the other minds—may have been Ockhamism by its substitution of internal [intuitive] experience brought about by causal affection of the senses in the place of "intentionality." Husserl therefore had the problem of reconciling a solipsistic conception of "intentionality" with the Kantian postulate of objective, i.e., intersubjective, validity of experience.)

Another argument in favor of the discrepancy between the performatory interpretation of the *cogito ergo sum* argument and Descartes's prioritization of internal experience is provided, it seems to me, by Hintikka's rejection of the interpretation of Descartes's basic argument in terms of introspection.[17] For the recourse to introspection is very closely related to the recourse to private, internal experience in that it completely fails to account for the self-verifying or, respectively, self-defeating function of the performance of saying or thinking "I exist" or "I do not exist," and this again is obviously a consequence of the fact that "introspection" as gazing into my consciousness is conceived as being independent of the medium of public language. Thus introspection may indeed be compared to the reflection on one's internal experience as being separated from any external experience and thus far also from a language and communication with other people.

However, is not Descartes's paradigmatical separation of external, corporeal and internal, purely mental experience the only possible response to his argument that possibly every supposed experience of the external world might be only my dream? Thus far Descartes could at least suggest that the existence of the sphere of *res cogitans* (consciousness and its contents) is certain before the existence of the external world of *res extensæ* could be proved (with the aid of the proof of God's existence). (Even Kant has taken this problematic situation very seriously by his talk about "problematic idealism" and his demand for a proof of the existence of the "external world" and thus far of objectively valid experience.)[18]

I think this whole conception indeed constitutes the case of modern times' paradigm of *prima philosophia* (as philosophy of consciousness) in so far as it is brought about by Descartes. But this paradigm has to be radically surmounted, it seems to me, by the new paradigmatic presupposition that public argumentation—expressed, or at least semantically mediated, by language—is the last resort of critical reflection of valid thought. Such reflection is characterized by the performative-propositional "double structure"[19] of forwarding truth claims in a discourse and thus far is the point of reference for the performative interpretation of the Cartesian basic argument *cogito, ergo sum*. But, how then should it be possible, on this basis, to cope with the Cartesian dream argument and the fact that internal experience in Descartes's sense seems to be immune to all kinds of perceptual deceptions?

I think, we have first to distinguish between the Cartesian (paradigmatic) interpretation of the above argument which connects it with a totalizing doubt about the existence of an external world and an other interpretation which expresses only a virtually universal doubt (in the sense of the principle of fallibilism) with regard to all of our experiences. By this distinction, relying on a sense critique of arguing, we can today dissolve the dramatic point of the Cartesian dream argument by showing that, in contradistinction to the principle of fallibilism, the dream argument abolishes itself by its universalization, since it thereby destroys the semantic presupposition of the phrase "only my dream." At the same time we may also abolish the dramatic point of the priority of internal experience by showing that at least its meaning for us is dependent of the use of public language and—thus far—its possibility is parasitic upon external experience, which is indeed fallible, but "by and large" (to speak along

with Davidson) must be reliable if there should be a functioning public
language for its interpretation.[14]

IV. HINTIKKA'S "PERFORMATORY" INTERPRETATION OF "*COGITO, ERGO
SUM*" AS SAVING THE TRUTH OF DESCARTES'S BASIC INSIGHT IN LIGHT
OF A POSTMETAPHYSICAL PARADIGM OF *PRIMA PHILOSOPHIA*

My arguments in favor of the paradigmatic difference between the
performative interpretation of the *cogito, ergo sum* argument and Descartes's connection of this conception of *res cogitans* with the
epistemological prioritization of internal experience could suggest to the
reader that I would, as a consequence, refuse Hintikka's performatory
interpretation of the *cogito, ergo sum* as an interpretation of Descartes's
own point, conceiving of it rather as a paradigmatic conception of the
linguistic turn of philosophy in the twentieth century. This would of course
not invalidate the systematic philosophical point of Hintikka's approach but
it would at least be incompatible with Hintikka's obvious intention to
reconstruct hermeneutically Descartes's own tendential intentions. But, I
think, the situation is not so simple. For I have not yet considered an
argument that seems strongly to support the narrowly hermeneutic claim of
Hintikka's interpretation of Descartes's basic argument.

Hintikka stresses the fact that the performatory interpretation of *cogito,
ergo sum* fits in very well with the whole spirit of Descartes's method of
doubting, which is completely different from the passive doubts of classical
skepticism which consist in "the giving up of all opinions."[21] By contrast,
Descartes actively and intentionally constructs doubts as questioning all we
usually believe, thereby trying to reach the point where the questioning
becomes a *reductio ad absurdum* of all skepticism. This aim of a methodical doubt in Descartes's sense, in my opinion, can indeed only be reached
by an argument that shows its certainty through the self-defeating of its own
negation.

Especially important, in this context, is the fact that a performatory
interpretation of *cogito, ergo sum* is apt to defend the point of Descartes's
insight against those many arguments, from Lichtenberg through Nietzsche,
that were used to show the illusionary character of Descartes's alleged
introspective insight. These arguments point to the fact that we know so
little of the essential nature of thinking that it might perhaps be more
plausible to say "It is thinking within myself" ("Es denkt in mir") than "I
think." Now, I think, the (performatory-reflective) interpretation of the
cogito as "I hereby argue that . . ." shows that all interpretations that

conceive of Descartes's basic argument as a report, based on introspection, about some occurrence within my consciousness are completely beside the point. Such interpretations are irrelevant because they do not meet the performance of responsible arguing (explicitly expressed e.g., by the phrase "I hereby assert . . .") as being noncircumventible (in German: "nichthin-tergehbar") by a self-reflection of the discourse. These interpretations are instead concerned with a metaphysical-ontological problem which can be ignored by the strictly reflective recourse to the performance of arguing (and its existential and normative presuppositions that cannot be denied without committing a performative self-contradiction.[23])

I would indeed not simply deny that Descartes by his basic insight was in a sense anticipating this (on my account) postmetaphysical point of a performatory interpretation of the *cogito, ergo sum*. But, in the face of Descartes's use of his basic insight in the construction of his whole system of philosophy, I would think that Hintikka's performatory interpretation of the *cogito, ergo sum* is not a historical-hermeneutic interpretation in the usual sense; it is rather an interpretation that presupposes a novel paradigm of *prima philosophia* which transcends that very paradigm of it that was in fact initiated by Descartes (i.e., by the whole of his system), namely (transcendental) metaphysics of consciousness.

Hintikka's interpretation may, nevertheless, still be considered an example of understanding a philosophical author better than he understood himself. I say this because I neither accept the complete discontinuity—"incommensurability" (Kuhn)—of "paradigms" in philosophy nor the continuity of the history of philosophy as being merely one of change (Gadamer). Thus far, as one should understand, I wholeheartedly agree with Hintikka.

KARL-OTTO APEL

JOHANN-WOLFGANG-GOETHE UNIVERSITY
NOVEMBER 2002

NOTES

1. See Jaakko Hintikka, "*Cogito, Ergo Sum*: Inference or Performance?" in *Descartes: A Collection of Critical Essays* (Notre Dame, Ind.: University of Notre Dame Press, 1967), pp. 108–39.

2. See Hans-Georg Gadamer, *Wahrheit und Methode* (Tübingen: J.C.B. Mohr [F. Siebeck], 1960); and Karl-Otto Apel, "Regulative Ideas or Truth-Happening? An Attempt to Answer the Question of the Conditions of the Possibility of Valid

Understanding," in *The Philosophy of Hans-Georg Gadamer*, ed. Lewis E. Hahn, The Library of Living Philosophers, vol. 24 (Chicago, Ill.: Open Court, 1997), pp. 67–94.

3. Cf. Karl-Otto Apel, "Transcendental Semiotics as First Philosophy," in *Selected Essays, vol. I: Towards a Transcendental Semiotics* (New Jersey: Humanities Press, 1994), pp. 112–31; and "Erste Philosophie heute?" in *K.-O. Apel*, ed. V. Hösle, R. Simon-Schäfer), *Globalisierung: Herausforderung für die Philosophie* (Universitätsverlag Bamberg, 1998), pp. 21–74.

4. Cf. Hintikka, *"Cogito, Ergo Sum:* Inference or Performance?" p. 135.

5. Cf. ibid., pp. 129ff, 132ff.

6. Cf. Martin Heidegger, *Sein und Zeit*, 5th ed. (Halle: Niemeyer, 1941), 83ff.

7. Cf. Gadamer, *Wahrheit und Methode*, p. 254.

8. One may perhaps object that only real thinking, not thinking supposed by fiction, must be supposed in the general premise and that this supposition means not the same as supposing "whatever is thinking and exists, exists" (as is suggested by Hintikka). But this objection would not change the problem situation; for one could ask for a justification of the truthclaim of the corrected general premise, and the answer to this question can only be provided, I would suggest, by recourse to Hintikka's performatory interpretation of the *cogito, ergo sum*.

9. Hintikka, *"Cogito, Ergo Sum:* Inference or Performance?" p. 138.

10. Principia I, 9; cf. Descartes's similar reply to Gassendi's objections to the *Cogito*, in *Œuvres de Descartes*, ed. C. Adam and P. Tannery (Paris, 1897–1913, VII), p. 352; and *The Philosophical Works of Descartes*, trans. E. S. Haldane and G. R. T. Ross (London 1931, II, 137). Quotation according to Hintikka, *"Cogito, Ergo Sum:* Inference or Performance?" p. 138.

11. Hintikka, ibid., p. 113.

12. Ibid., p. 138f.

13. Ibid., p. 138.

14. Ibid., pp. 119f. and 123f.

15. See ibid., p. 123.

16. Cf. Karl-Otto Apel, "Erste Philosophie heute?" (see note 3); and "Husserl, Tarski oder Peirce? Für eine transzendentalsemiotische Konsenstheorie der Wahrheit," in *I forste, andre og tredje person* (Festskrift til Audun Øfsti), ed. S. Bøe, B. Molander, B. Strondhagen (Trondheim: NTNU Filosofisk Institutt, 1999), pp. 3–14.

17. Hintikka, *"Cogito, Ergo Sum:* Inference or Performance?" p. 125.

18. Cf. Immanuel Kant, *Kritik der reinen Vernunft*, 2nd ed. (Riga 1787), 275; and Heidegger's critique of Kant's demand in *Sein und Zeit*, p. 204ff.

19. Cf. Jürgen Habermas, "Was heißt Universalpragmatik?" in *Sprachpragmatik und Philosophie*, ed. K.-O. Apel (Frankfurt a.M.: Suhrkamp, 1976), pp. 174–272; and K.-O. Apel, "Die Logosauszeichnung der menschlichen Sprache. Die philosophische Tragweite der Sprechakttheorie," in *Perspektiven auf Sprache*, ed. H.-G. Bosshardt (Berlin and New York: de Gruyter, 1986), pp. 45–87.

20. Cf. Donald Davidson, "The Method of Truth in Metaphysics," in *Studies in the Philosophy of Language*, ed. P. A. French, T. E. Uehling Jr., and J. K. Wettstein (The University of Minnesota Press, 1977).

21. Hintikka, "*Cogito, Ergo Sum*: Inference or Performance?" p. 124. I would add that Hintikka's performatory interpretation is also completely different from a certain pragmatistic conception of our day which only admits as relevant contextual doubts that can be dispelled (disposed of) with regard to the same context of praxis.

22. Ibid.

23. Cf. K.-O. Apel, "Das Problem der philosophischen Letztbegründung im Lichte einer transzendentalen Sprachpragmatik," in *Auseinandersetzungen—in Erprobung des transzendentalpragmatischen Ansatzes* (Frankfurt a.M.: Suhrkamp, 1998), pp. 33–80 (Engl. transl.: "The Problem of Philosophical Fundamental Grounding in Light of a Transcendental Pragmatics of Language," in *Man and World*, vol.8/3, 1975, 239–75, repr. in *After Philosophy: End or Transformation?*, ed. K. Baynes et al. (Cambridge, Mass.: MIT Press, 1987), pp. 250–90.

REPLY TO KARL-OTTO APEL

Deep philosophical ideas are characterized by their conceptual richness. Several different insights are usually intertwined in such an idea, and a knowledgeable interpreter can therefore relate the original formulation of the idea to different systematic developments. Inevitably, but not necessarily unfairly, a reader's knowledge of these collateral developments will influence his or her construal of the original idea. Or perhaps I should say that such anticipations, parallels, and further developments offer to an interpreter objects of comparison which can help one see the initial idea more clearly.

Descartes's *cogito* argument—if it is an argument—offers a well-known example of such a many-faceted idea. Karl-Otto Apel's essay provides an illustration of the multiple bridges from Descartes's idea to other ideas and currents in philosophy.

In my papers on the Cartesian *cogito*, my aim has been to understand Descartes's thought. Apel's focus is somewhat different. What he is interested in are the leading ideas of Western philosophy that are reflected in Descartes's insight. The conceptual richness of the *cogito* does in fact make it an excellent case study for the purpose.

For reasons of space I follow Apel's example and assume my 1962 "performatory" interpretation of the *cogito* to be familiar to the reader. Very briefly, the leading idea was a parallelism between the certainty of the *cogito* and the self-verifying character of someone's uttering "I exist." This contrast is even more striking when we turn the tables. Descartes's attempt to doubt his existence defeats itself just as an utterance "I don't exist" only serves to demonstrate its negation.

What collateral developments does this interpretation suggest? I related my interpretation to Austin's notion of a performatory utterance. Apel recalls his astonishment at my failure to acknowledge as my inspiration "the paradigmatic (often so-called linguistic) turn of philosophy in the twentieth century," more specifically, the so-called speech act theory. The reason for this underemphasis is that I simply do not consider speech-act theories especially powerful theories of language or typical of what might be called the linguistic turn in philosophy, interesting though they might be on a small scale. Here my reasons can be formulated in Wittgensteinian terms. What is crucial in language theory are the language-games that relate language to reality. The fact that moves in these "games" can sometimes be made by uttering something is an interesting but marginal matter. Performatory utterances should be thought of as utterable performances, to borrow a pun of Roderick Chisholm's.

My treatment of the *cogito* can also be related to developments within analytic philosophy other than speech-act theory. It is not always noted that a treatment of the Cartesian *cogito* with the help of modern logical tools presupposes the acceptability of some kind of "free logic," that is to say, of a logic free of existential presuppositions concerning individual constants. One kind of significance that my analysis of the *cogito* seems to have had is to help to show the philosophical relevance of presupposition-free logics.

As is eminently appropriate, Apel focuses his attention on Descartes's intriguing step from *cogito ergo sum* to *sum res cogitans*. How does this step fit into the performatory interpretation? Apel sees the crucial connection in the fact that according to Descartes, we can argue *cogito ergo sum* but cannot thereby replace reference to thinking, introduced by the verb *cogitare* with a reference mediated by a nonintellectual verb. And this is not the whole story. The performatory interpretation offers us—or, rather, offers Descartes—a stronger reason. In an Aristotelian chain of explanatory syllogisms, it is the middle term of the last atomic syllogism demonstrating the explanandum that shows the proximate cause of the explanandum. Insofar as Descartes thought that his insight could be formulated in similar syllogistic terms, thought would have to be taken to be "my" nature in that it is, in a sense, the proximate cause of my existence. Notice how well this Aristotelian perspective fits in with the performative interpretation according to which Descartes literally produces the evidence for his existence by doing something, viz., thinking. I suspect that in Cartesian self-knowledge there is more than a touch of the old idea of makers' knowledge.[1] To what extent this amounts to a concession on Descartes's part to Greek ontology requires a separate examination.

From this point of view, it becomes immediately clear why Descartes cannot use a verb of external action, for instance, and argue *ambulo ergo sum*, even though at first sight it might seem that on the performatory interpretation he ought to do so, since this interpretation relies on an analogy between external and internal acts. We do not have guaranteed power over our external actions in the same way we have over our thoughts. We do not, so to speak, create external objects or even external actions *ex nihilo*. To put the same point in epistemological terms, I can imagine that I am walking without actually doing so, but I cannot actively imagine that I am thinking without doing so. Furthermore, verbs for internal action qualify for a variant of the *cogito* argument insofar, but only insofar, as they involve an actual thought-act. As Descartes puts it, mind must have "sense or thought [*sentit sive cogitat*] of itself seeing or walking." (Notice the little word *sive* here.)

Thus it does not seem to me that Descartes's admittance of verbs like *volo* or *sentio* into a *cogito*-type argument makes any difference to the performatory interpretation, rightly understood. Perhaps it can also be alleged on Descartes's behalf that he does not have to reach the conclusion *sum res cogitans* by means of each and every variant of the *cogito* argument. It suffices to reach it via the regulation formula *cogito ergo sum*.

We do not need to postulate a distinction between two different senses of *volo* or *sentio*, but we do have to recognize that willing or sensing involves a kind of thought-act. This is not an unheard-of idea but is in fact reminiscent of Kant's omnipresent *Ich denke* and of Sartre's prereflective *cogito*.

Apel is convinced that the analogy which forms the backbone of the performatory interpretation is due to the fact that both its terms "must be originally based on the public use of language." I agree, but I do not find that common origin nearly as important as the analogies between thought-acts and public utterances. One such analogy is examined in my more recent (1996) paper on the *cogito*.

In the case of a self-defeating speech-act of uttering: "I do not exist," the effect presupposes that the hearer is in the position of actually witnessing the act. In terms of the important but neglected distinction between the two modes of identification, the public and the perspectival one (explained by Hilpinen in his contribution to this volume), the entity whose existence can be proved performatively must be a perspectivally identified one. Analogously, Descartes can hope to prove by means of the *cogito* only the existence of a perspectivally identified entity, of an *I* rather than of the public entity called Cartesius. Indeed, the attempted argument *cogito, ergo Cartesius est* becomes literally a linguistic joke. (I have seen it being put forward as one.)

This observation shows again the interest of the *cogito* emphasized by Apel as revealing some of the presuppositions (Apel's "paradigms") of Western philosophy. The tacit restriction on Descartes's conclusion exemplifies the subjectivism that is characteristic of the Cartesian tradition. At the same time we can see the conceptual basis of this subjectivism. Descartes is looking at the entire reality as if it were his personally accessible cognitive neighborhood.

Thus it seems to me that, Apel notwithstanding, Descartes's "prioritiz-ation of internal experience" does not create a discrepancy with the performatory interpretation of the *cogito*. Rather, what is referred to as Descartes's subjectivism is made understandable by the performatory interpretation.

This does not mean that we have to consider Descartes's line of thought as unobjectionable. At least two different objections can be raised. First, like virtually all his fellow philosophers, Descartes does not acknowledge the difference between the two modes of identification, but tries to extend what can be said of perspectivally identified entities to public ones. He is not alone in trying to do so. The latest important parallel fallacy is Saul Kripke's unspoken attempt to extend the way perspectival entities are initially identified, viz., by ostension ("dubbing") to public identification.

Second, Descartes moves from the requirement of direct access to the entities that can be proved by a *cogito* type argument to the priority of internal experience. This step is not justified by the performatory interpre-tation, of course, but this interpretation helps to explain the temptation to take this step.

Thus I can agree, in a sense, with Apel's overall judgment of my performatory interpretation. It does rest on a paradigmatic insight of twentieth-century logical semantics. However, I locate the crucial aspect of this insight in a way different from Apel's. The crucial aspect does not lie so much in speech-act theory or even in the active character of the *cogito* performance. It lies in the distinction between the two modes of identification. It is insight into the unavoidability of this distinction that tells us what the *cogito* can and cannot accomplish, and thereby throws light on the entire philosophical tradition started by Descartes.

This distinction creates a certain discrepancy between Descartes's actual thoughts and what they ought to look like, so to speak, on the performatory interpretation. But it is this very same interpretation that leads us to see the relevance of the difference between different modes of identification to Descartes's philosophy.

J. H.

NOTE

1. Cf. here my 1974 paper "Practical vs. Theoretical Reason—an Ambiguous Legacy."

8

Dagfinn Føllesdal

HINTIKKA ON PHENOMENOLOGY

Jaakko Hintikka's first article on Husserl's phenomenology was the title essay of *The Intentions of Intentionality and Other New Models for Modalities* in 1975.[1] Since then he has written half a dozen articles on the interpretation of Husserl and made major independent contributions to several of the themes that engaged Husserl, such as the theory of intentionality, perception, action theory, language and meaning, the philosophy of art, and *Anschauung* and its role in mathematics.

As always in Hintikka's work, the historical work and the systematic work go hand in hand. The systematic concerns motivate many of his historical studies, and the historical discussions kindle, illustrate, and refine the systematic insights.

There are, in particular, two areas where Hintikka's systematic interests and his work on Husserl are intimately connected: the study of intentionality and the analysis of the given in perception.

In the former of these two areas Hintikka and I start out from almost identical, Frege-inspired interpretations of Husserl. However, Hintikka gives this interpretation a special twist by connecting it with his own possible-world semantics. This possible-world interpretation of Husserl's theory of intentionality risks coming into conflict with some of Husserl's basic insights, for example, that the object of an act of perception is a full-fledged physical object. Mohanty, who shares the Frege-inspired interpretation of Husserl, sees the same kind of difficulties in the possible-world interpretation of intentionality as I see, and has carried out a careful, critical discussion of that interpretation. His objections have in turn been responded to by Hintikka. Several other philosophers have followed up the discussion, partly in response to Hintikka, partly in response to David W. Smith and Ronald McIntyre's book *Husserl and Intentionality: A Study of Mind, Meaning and Language*.[2] While I agree with Mohanty's arguments and find that we interpret Husserl in much the same way, some of the other critics' criticism of the possible world interpretation of intentionality is based on an interpretation of Husserl's notion of intentionality which I regard as problematic.[3] I will not go into this discussion here, but instead turn to the second area of Hintikka's work on Husserl's phenomenology.

This second area, Hintikka's interpretation of Husserl's view on the given in perception, has not been discussed earlier. This is also the area where Hintikka has made his most recent contribution to the study of phenomenology, in his chapter "The Phenomenological Dimension" in *The Cambridge Companion to Husserl*. This chapter is a particularly apt setting for a general discussion of Hintikka's work on phenomenology since Hintikka here gives his most comprehensive presentation and discussion of Husserl's phenomenology.

In this essay, Hintikka addresses the most general problem confronting a philosopher reading Husserl: "How is his approach to philosophy to be understood? What was Husserl trying to do?" Many of us will respond that Husserl's phenomenology is primarily a theory of intentionality and that this in turn is intimately connected with a theory of meaning. Hintikka does not disagree with this, but points out that this answer leaves open the question of how the vehicles of meaning are linked up with whatever it is that they in fact mean. "For instance, no analysis of the structure of the *noema*, however detailed and accurate, can tell you what its relation is to its object. This does not fault the analysis in the least, but it does show that such an analysis of *noema* structure is not the whole story of Husserlian phenomenology."[4]

I agree with Hintikka that an analysis of *noema* structure is not the whole story, it is only part of Husserl's phenomenology, although a central part. I will now present a fuller picture, put forward as a running commentary on Hintikka's presentation of Husserl's phenomenology in "The Phenomenological Dimension." The commentary will expand upon and partly modify the points made by Hintikka. My observations have been made in print before, with detailed evidence from Husserl's texts, and have been more fully worked out in courses I have given on Husserl over the past forty years, but they will here be presented in a new context, that of Hintikka's discussion of "how the meaning entities manage to accomplish their intentional or referential function." I will follow the order Hintikka follows in his chapter.

THE TRANSCENDENTAL REDUCTION

Hintikka starts his discussion by examining Husserl's notion of the transcendental reduction. He holds that it is this reduction and not Husserl's other reductions, such as the eidetic reduction, that is crucial for the issue at hand, and I agree. Hintikka quotes Husserl's description of the transcendental reduction in the *Ideas,* where the main point is that in this reduction one directs one's attention "on the sphere of consciousness" and "study what is immanent in it."

Hintikka then continues:

> From the viewpoint of a self-sufficient intentionality, the only reasonable sense one can make of these reductions is to aver that what is "bracketed" in them is the very reality which can be interpreted by means of the vehicles of intentionality. A phenomenologist's entire attention is on this view concentrated on *noemata* or whatever meaning bearers we are considering.[5]

Hintikka distances himself from this view:

> The main difficulty with an account of phenomenological reductions which sees in them a method of concentrating one's attention exclusively on *noemata* is that far too much will end up being bracketed. Such an exclusive concentration inevitably brackets, not merely objects, but the relation of *noemata* to objects. You simply cannot be aware of a relation's holding between two terms if you are not aware of both of the two terms.[6]

I have two remarks on this. One of them may seem rather pedantic, but I think it is important and I will get back to it in a moment: What is left after the transcendental reduction is not just *noemata*, but also *noeses* and *hyle*.[7] While the *noema* is a timeless structure that can in principle be instantiated in several acts, the *noeses* and *hyle* are experiences. They begin at a certain time and end at some later time, and will never be the same in two acts. The *noema* is, roughly, the meaning given in an act, the *noesis* is the meaning-giving ingredient in our experience, and the *hyle* are experiences we typically have when our senses are affected. These *hyletic* experiences are constraints on the *noeses* and *noemata* in acts of perception. We shall get back to this.

My second remark is that one of Husserl's main concerns when he discusses intentionality is to understand how consciousness relates to objects. This is also Hintikka's concern in this essay. However, while Hintikka insists that in order to understand this we need to have access to both terms of the relation, consciousness and object, Husserl warned that assuming from the start that there are two terms and a relation between them may easily engender an illusion of understanding. We have to ask more specifically exactly what that relation consists in and how it comes about. Thus, when Brentano defined intentionality by stating that for every act there is an object towards which it is directed, Husserl raised two objections. First, he observed that there are acts which to the agent seem to have an object, like other acts, but where there is no object. As examples he mentioned acts where we hallucinate, certain acts of grave misperception, and acts of thinking which have no object, such as when early mathematicians tried to calculate the largest prime number. From the point of view of the subject, such acts may seem perfectly like acts which have an object; they are *as if of* some object. It is this *as if of* character of acts Husserl wants to throw light on in his study of the intentionality of consciousness. Husserl's second objection against Brentano is that Brentano had not seen the need for such an analysis. By focusing immediately and exclusively on acts that have an object Brentano had never become aware of the need for accounting for the directedness of consciousness. To do this was for Husserl just the main challenge for an understanding of intentionality.

Hintikka's central question: How are the vehicles of meaning linked up with whatever it is that they in fact mean, and in particular, how does the *noema* relate to its object?—is therefore also a key question for Husserl. Husserl thinks that at least a major part of the answer to that question has to be found by a careful analysis of *noema*, *noeses*, and *hyle*, that is, the three ingredients that we are focusing on when we are performing the transcendental reduction. Some reflection shows that the *as if of* feature of consciousness must be something that we can clarify without bringing in the second term of the relation, that is the objects of acts—the reason for this simply being that acts have this *as if of* character even where there is no object for them to relate to. There may be something more to the relationship between act and object in those cases in which the act has an object. This remains to be seen, and it also remains to be seen whether that extra that comes in when the act has an object requires for its elucidation that we have access to the objects in our analysis.

The *Noematic Sinn*

Let us now see how far we can get in answering Hintikka's and Husserl's basic question by studying the *noema*. The *noema* has two main components, the *noematic* sense (*Sinn*) and the thetic component. In the *noematic Sinn*, in turn, one may distinguish two parts, one corresponding to the various features of the object and one, which Husserl calls "the determinable *X*" and which reflects the fact that an object is not a collection of properties, but something that has properties. We will get back to the determinable *X* and the thetic component later. Let us now first consider the feature part of the *noematic Sinn*.

The *noematic Sinn* can be compared to a set of anticipations of the various features of the object, such as its having a certain shape, color, weight, taste, duration, location, and so on. The anticipations include not only anticipations about these various features of the object, but also concerning how these features will be experienced by us when we move around and change or if the object moves around and changes. Thus if we take the object to be a cube, we anticipate how this cube's appearance will change as we move around it, or if it turns or in other ways moves in space. We also anticipate how the color of an object will change as the light conditions change and how the sound of an orchestra will change while we move around in the concert hall.

"Anticipations" is an inappropriate word for what is going on. The overtones of conscious expectations are too strong. Most of the "anticipations" that are involved in our experience of the world and its objects go unnoticed, and we might even have difficulties bringing them to consciousness. The word "set" as we use it, for example, in "mind set" might be better. However, the anticipations involve also bodily sets or settings. Thus, for example, when we walk on a soft trail every morning and a stretch of it is frozen during the night, we might notice this through our feet and legs and our manner of moving. In general all movements of our body involve "anticipations" in this sense, our adaptations to gravitation, to acceleration, the fine movements involved in our throwing an object, and so forth. There are also numerous examples of how what happens within one sensory realm, for example, touch, guides our "anticipations" for other senses, for example, taste or vision. Gestalt psychology, which was strongly influenced by Husserl, emphasized this, and it is a phenomenon widely studied in current neurophysiology.

We are aware of some few of the "anticipations" and these could be called "anticipations" or "expectations" in the proper sense of these words. Others we can become aware of through reflection, and these were the ones Husserl tended to concentrate on. Our anticipations are, however, so many and so varied that it would be an unmanageable task to try to map them out even in the case of very simple acts. The large multitude of anticipations we therefore become aware of only when something "goes wrong," as in the case of the frozen path. Sometimes our anticipations are so unknown to us that we just notice that there is something strange, something "fishy," without being able to say immediately what it is that we find disturbing. "Queer" and "peculiar" may be English words that capture some of this.

Although the *noemata* are exceedingly rich and we anticipate many more features of the object than the ones that currently meet the eye, the objects we are experiencing are experienced as going far beyond our experience of them. They are "transcendent," Husserl held. This does not mean that we cannot experience them, the objects of our acts are just these full-fledged objects that surround us. But these objects are experienced as having many more features than ever anticipated by us. They are experienced as having the features that we are currently seeing, touching, smelling, and so on for the other senses. Then there are those further features that we consciously are aware of; still further there are all those features that we unconsciously or tacitly "anticipate." And then there are, finally, all those features that we are not anticipating in any way, but that are only part of that great unknown world that we gradually come to anticipate and eventually experience, features that the object has, but that are unknown to us.

The *Sinn* component of the *noema* hence tells us what we consciously or tacitly "anticipate" the object to be like. Our further experience may confirm and refine some of these anticipations, but it may also lead us to modify or revise them. In serious cases we may not only change our view of what the object is like, but even give up our belief that there is such an object there. We may experience a switch to another object or to no object at all. In such cases Husserl would say that our *noema* "explodes." Given that the *noemata* are timeless entities, this is clearly a metaphorical way of speaking; all that is meant is that the original act comes to an end and we get a new act, with a new *noema*.

Kant, who was an important influence on Husserl, held that we have anticipations concerning time and space that are the same for all rational beings, independent of their former experience and background, and that these anticipations are *a priori*, in the sense that they cannot be falsified by empirical observations. Husserl's view is different. He held that the anticipations relate not only to space and time and a few other notions discussed by Kant, but to all aspects of what we experience. He further regarded these anticipations as largely sedimentations from past experience. They might hence differ from person to person, dependent upon their personal history. The dynamics of this sedimentation process is a major theme in Husserl. An important subtheme is the adaptations that yield intersubjectivity. And finally, although Husserl, like Kant, called these anticipations *a priori*, he did not mean by this that they could never turn out to be wrong, but that they were *prior* to our sensory experience and would have to be revised if we encountered recalcitrant experience.

These anticipations are crucial for our experiencing objects and not just a chaos of disconnected features, if there can be such a thing—we will return to this in the discussion of *hyle* below. It therefore seems to me that this facet of the *noematic Sinn* already has brought us a step forward illuminating the issue that Hintikka was missing in Husserl, the relation between *noema*, or consciousness, and object. It even indicates that the issue of the relation between consciousness and object is intimately connected with the question of what it is to be an object.

THE DETERMINABLE X

This however, is not yet the whole story. The *Sinn* contains, in addition to components corresponding to the properties of the object, also the idea, through the so-called "determinable X," that an object is not a collection of properties, but something that has properties. The contents of the *noematic Sinn* is organized around the determinable X in such a way that we do not experience free floating properties, but an object that has various properties. Further, the determinable X reflects the idea that two objects may be very similar and still not identical, while one and the same object may display quite different properties at different times or when seen from different points of view. The determinable X is hence crucial for our ability to distinguish similarity from identity, and difference from distinctness (sometimes called numerical difference as opposed to qualitative difference). It is what makes sense of the question: Is this object that looks just the same as the one I saw yesterday really the same? The determinable X reflects the "indexical" element in the *noema*. The determinable X does not keep track of the object or tell us whether we are experiencing the right object. But it reminds us that questions of identity are something to be right or wrong about even when they go beyond questions of similarities and differences.

THE THETIC ELEMENT

After having considered the two elements in the *noematic Sinn*: the various determinations and the determinable X, let us now turn to the final element in the *noema*, the thetic component. If we compare an act of perception and an act of imagination, we find a striking difference: I experience the object of the act of perception as real, while I do not experience the object of the act of imagination as real. We do not think that in perception we happened to focus on an existing object, while in imagination we failed to do so. Imagination is not just unsuccessful perception; it differs from perception in its very *claim* to deal with reality. This reality claim is what Husserl draws attention to and explores under the label "thetic." One of the aims of phenomenology is to throw light on how our consciousness differs when we regard the object of our act as real, as we do in perception and memory, and when we do not think that there is any real object for our act, as we do in imagination.[8]

It seems to me that this thetic element of consciousness is highly relevant to Hintikka's question: How are the vehicles of meaning linked up with whatever it is that they in fact mean, and in particular, how does the *noema* relate to its object? We are not only interested in the fact that an act relates to some particular object, we also want to understand *in what manner* the act relates to it. Is the object regarded by us as real, or do we consider the object of the act as merely a figment of our imagination?

THE *NOESIS*

All the elements I have mentioned until now are contained in the *noema*: the *noematic Sinn* with its determinations and the determinable *X*, and the thetic component. As I mentioned at the beginning of the essay, Husserl held that there are two more elements connected with our consciousness that remain after the transcendental reduction: the *noesis* and the *hyle*. They are, as we noted, experiences.

The *noesis* is the meaning-giving ingredient in our experience. It gives meaning, or structure, to the act. As one should expect, there is a thoroughgoing parallelism between *noema* and *noesis*. An example Husserl gives in order to clarify the two notions is that of a judgment. Philosophers since Bolzano have learned that what we study in logic are abstract entities called judgments and not the acts through which we make the judgments. The former has to do with the *noema*, the latter with the *noesis*.

THE *HYLE*

The third element of the act, in addition to the timeless *noema* and the temporal *noesis*, is the *hyle*. Like the *noeses* the *hyle* are experiences. Typically, we have *hyle* when our sense organs are affected, but we also can have *hyle* in special other situations, for example, when we are affected by fever, drugs, or nervous disturbances. The *hyle* form a kind of boundary condition for the kind of *noesis* we can have in acts of perception. For perception to take place, the *noesis* and the *hyle* must fit harmoniously together. When this happens, the *hyle* we are experiencing are said to "fill" anticipations in the *noema*. The object perceived must be experienced as being placed in a position that enables it to have an effect on our sensory organs appropriate for the *hyle* we are experiencing. The causal relations involved in this, like all other relations in the world that we experience, are reflected in the structure of the *noema*, as anticipations of what happens in this world. In acts of perception, the *hyle* therefore plays a role in determining, in interplay with the *noesis*, what object we see, hear, smell, or feel. Thereby the *hyle* also has an influence on the meaning-component of the *noema*. This concerns not only the *hyle* we have now. The *noema* is, as mentioned, very rich, and most of the anticipations are not filled, but concern *hyle* that we do not presently have, but will have if we move around, follow the object through time, and so on.

Note that the presence of *hyle* is not enough to make an act an act of perception. We may keep our eyes open and think about something else, for example, a philosophical or a mathematical problem. In the latter case, the object of our act may be an abstract entity, or we may think of a person or an object presently inaccessible to our senses. In such a case we may have *hyle*, but the *hyle* does not play any role in determining the object of our act. The thetic character of the act is not that of perception, but that of thinking. We are not perceiving. One characteristic of the thetic component in perception is hence that in perception the *hyle* play a role, and the *noesis* and *hyle* must harmonize with one another.

Remembering is different. We may remember an object we once perceived, but the *hyle* we now have will normally be irrelevant to the act of remembering. In some cases the *hyle* we have may be relevant; there may be something about the present situation that reminds me of the object. Also the object I remember may be likely to have left traces, which I may now look for and that may help corroborate what I remember or may make it less plausible. In either case there is a connection between memory and present sensation that constrains us, and this gives memory, as it gives perception, a reality-character. What is remembered, and what is perceived, is experienced as real. Remembering and perceiving are here unlike imagining or fantasizing, which is unencumbered by my *hyle*. I can fantasize whatever I want. I may fantasize that there is a horse in this room, but I cannot perceive a horse now, however hard I try. Unlike fantasy, perception is not up to us; neither is memory. The price we have to pay for this freedom of fantasy is that what we fantasize is not real. The recalcitrance that is present in perception and in memory plays an important part in giving these kinds of acts their reality character.

A central point in Husserl's theory of perception, which I shall not discuss here, is that the *noesis* is never uniquely determined by the *hyle*. We can have very different *noeses*, and perceive very different objects, while what reaches our sensory organs may be the same. One should not say that the *hyle* are the same in such a case. The *hyle* are experiences, and not only is the *noesis* dependent on the *hyle*, also the *hyle* will depend on the *noesis*. There are no *hyle* that can be compared from act to act where the *noeses* are different. The important points for Husserl are that perception is underdetermined by what reaches our sensory organs, and that there are no sense data or other intermediaries given in perception. Perception is directly of objects, and there are no intermediary steps. Neither the *hyle* nor the *noesis* nor the *noema* are objects that we perceive. The former two are experiences, not objects experienced (except, of course, when we are turning them into objects of study in the phenomenological reduction). And the *noema* includes a structure that the perceived object has, but it also includes much more, such as the thetic component. And it is definitely not the same as the physical object that we perceive (see note 3).

HINTIKKA'S CRITICISM OF HUSSERL'S PHENOMENOLOGY

All these elements we have examined one by one are crucial parts of Husserl's account of how the act relates to its object: the *noematic* Sinn with the determinations and the determinable X, the thetic component of the *noema*, the *noesis* and the *hyle*. Hence they seem to provide an answer to Hintikka's crucial question. But is the answer satisfactory? Hintikka thinks not. Let us now consider his various objections.

First there is the objection I already mentioned, that according to Hintikka only the *noema* remains after the transcendental reduction. "The main difficulty with . . . concentrating one's attention exclusively on *noemata* is that far too much will then end up being bracketed. Such an exclusive concentration inevitably brackets, not merely objects, but the relation of *noemata* to objects."[9] As we have seen, also the *noesis* and the *hyle* remain after the transcendental reduction, and the *noema* itself is rather rich in its characterization of the *as if of* relation.

Then there is a series of more interesting objections, which have to do with a fundamental tension and lack of clarity in Husserl's notion of *hyle*. The *hyle* is a particularly tricky notion in Husserl. Husserl's view on the constraints in perception developed from his first phenomenological work, the *Logical Investigations* in 1900, to his *Ideas* in 1913, where he introduces the term "*hyle*" for these constraints. In the *Logical Investigations* he calls them "sense data" (*Sinnesdaten*) and although he does not regard them as building blocks of reality, they come dangerously close to belonging to the object side of the act, having colors and extension. Husserl is emphasizing that it is only when we are experiencing something as an object that a sense datum can be experienced as an adumbration (*Abschattung*) of the thing experienced. There are no "raw" sense data; without the structure imposed by consciousness there is neither extension nor color. Hintikka interestingly contrasts Husserl with Russell on this point and writes:

> for the mature Husserl, unlike Russell, the self-given is not structured categorically into particulars, their properties, their interrelations, etc. For instance, what is given in visual perception is not an articulated structure of visual objects but something like (in Quine's phrase) "a two-dimensional

continuum of colors and shades." Only one's articulating and "informing" *noesis* turns it into perceptions of objects (of different logical types), that is to say, into perceptions of the kinds of objects we can have *noemata* of.[10]

However, even the early Husserl of the *Logical Investigations* could hardly be said to hold that something colored and spatially extended is *given* in perception. And the mature Husserl of the *Ideas* definitely rejected that there could be something spatially extended without the "informing" *noesis*. Even the temporality of the *hyle* is of a rather special kind, so that the normal temporal notions that we use when we talk about the physical world are inappropriate when we talk about the *hyle*. Even more inappropriate is it to apply color words to the *hyle*. After all, the *hyle* are experiences, and this should serve as a warning bell when we are tempted to attribute spatial extension and colors to them. In fact, even Quine moved in a Husserlian direction in his later years and would be reluctant to hold that "a two-dimensional continuum of colors and shades" is given in visual perception. According to Quine, a main task of his own philosophy

> is [the] rational reconstruction of the individual's and/or the race's actual acquisition of a responsible theory of the external world. It would address the question how we, physical denizens of the physical world, can have projected our scientific theory of that whole world from our meager contacts with it: from the mere impacts of rays and particles on our surfaces and a few odds and ends such as the strain of walking uphill.[11]

So, for Quine, the reconstruction does not start from sense data or a two-dimensional continuum of colors and shades, but from afflictions of our body, including the strain of walking uphill, which does not seem so unlike the bodily adaptations to gravitation discussed by Husserl that I mentioned above. Also, like Husserl, Quine regards space and time as a result of our structuring and not merely as *given*:

> Our sophisticated concept of recurrent objects, qualitatively indistinguishable but nevertheless distinct, involves our elaborate schematism of intersecting trajectories in three-dimensional space, out of sight, trajectories traversed with the elapse of time. These concepts of space and time, or the associated linguistic devices, are further requisites on the way to substantial cognition.[12]

Also Quine's holism has similarities with that of Husserl. Quine writes: "I picture our concepts of body, space and time as evolving interdependently."[13] Hence there seems to have been a convergence between Quine and Husserl on many points. However, let us now return to Husserl. Hintikka asks:

What is it that fills a *noema*? And even more pertinently, whatever it is, does it belong to the sphere of objects or to the sphere of *noemata*? Either answer lands you in trouble. For if the filling is done by something that belongs to the realm of objects, it must have been bracketed in the phenomenological reductions. This would make the entire phenomenon of filling inaccessible to a phenomenologist. But if the filling is done by something that belongs to the realm of the vehicles of intentionality, that is, to the world of *noemata*, then filling cannot help to link *noemata* and reality to each other as it is obviously intended by Husserl to do.[14]

As we have seen in the sketch of the basics of Husserl's theory of perception that I gave above, Husserl clearly rejected the first horn of the dilemma. He did not regard the *hyle* as belonging to the realm of objects. The *hyle* are experiences that we undergo, not objects of acts (except the reflective acts that we carry out when we perform a transcendental reduction and reflect upon our own consciousness). What, then, about the second option Hintikka leaves us with? The *hyle* do belong to the realm of the vehicles of intentionality (although it is misleading to call this whole realm "the world of *noemata*," since, as we have seen, it also contains *hyle* and *noeses*, which are temporal entities, quite different from the *noemata*). Is not Hintikka then quite right that "filling cannot help to link *noemata* and reality to each other as it is obviously intended by Husserl to do"? This is a most interesting question. Clearly, Husserl's view cannot be written off just by stating that "if the filling is done by something that belongs to the realm of the vehicles of intentionality . . . then filling cannot help to link *noemata* and reality to each other as it is obviously intended by Husserl to do." The *hyle* are experiences, they are intimately connected with our body and our sense organs through the causal structures whose *noematic* counterparts we are studying in phenomenology. The *noemata* and the *hyle* must adapt to one another, and it is this recalcitrance that underlies our notion of reality and makes sense of the idea that our acts of perception are directed towards real objects.[15]

Rather than taking the notions of object and reality for granted and then asking how our consciousness relates to objects in the real world, Husserl regards these two notions as part of a package to which also acts, consciousness, *noema*, *noesis*, *hyle*, and our bodies belong. It is only by seeing them as part of this package that we can make sense of each one of these notions. The relation between consciousness and objects emerges as part of this same package: to understand the notions of reality and object we need to understand how consciousness relates to objects, and conversely. We are lifting ourselves by the bootstraps, but that is what one must expect from holists like Husserl.[16]

In my opinion, Husserl's carefully worked out framework of *noemata*, *hyle*, and so on is exceptionally well suited for analyzing and discussing the various manifestations of consciousness, in perception, action, communication, and so forth, including the relationship between act and object. Husserl arrived at this framework through analyses of a variety of detailed examples. The terminology may be abstruse, but the basic notions and distinctions enabled him to work out a theory of perception that steered clear of a multitude of problems besetting theories of perception that were proposed later in the twentieth century. His theory also seems to be a suitable framework for clarifying many of the problems that have come up in contemporary cognitive science. We may be dissatisfied with the holistic interdependence of his basic notions and the resulting circularity when he tries to explain them, and we may of course disagree with Husserl. However, we must first find out exactly what his view is. Only then can there be disagreement, and only then can it be fruitful.

DAGFINN FØLLESDAL

DEPARTMENT OF PHILOSOPHY
STANFORD UNIVERSITY
AUGUST 2003

NOTES

1. Jaakko Hintikka, "The Intentions of Intentionality," in *The Intentions of Intentionality and Other New Models for Modalities*, Synthese Library, vol. 90 (Dordrecht: D. Reidel Publishing Co., 1975).
2. See J. N. Mohanty, "Intentionality and Possible Worlds: Husserl and Hintikka," in *Husserl, Intentionality and Cognitive Science*, ed. Hubert L. Dreyfus (Cambridge, Mass.: MIT Press, 1982), pp. 233–51, and Hintikka's "Response," ibid., pp. 251–55. David W. Smith and Ronald McIntyre, *Husserl and Intentionality: A Study of Mind, Meaning and Language* (Dordrecht: Reidel, 1982). Lloyd J. Carr, "Review of Smith and McIntyre," *Husserl Studies* 1 (1984): 113–23. Bernard Waldenfels, "Mens sive cerebrum. Intentionalität in mentalistischer Sicht," *Philosophische Rundschau* 31 (1984): 22–52. Charles Harvey, "Husserl's Phenomenology and Possible World Semantics: A Reexamination," *Husserl Studies* 3 (1986): 191–207. Peter Hutcheson, "Transcendental Phenomenology and Possible World Semantics," *Husserl Studies* 4 (1987): 225–42. Thomas M. Seebohm, "Phenomenology of Logic and the Problem of Modalizing," *Journal of the British Society for Phenomenology* 19 (1988): 235–51. Thomas M. Seebohm, "Possible 'Worlds': Remarks about a Controversy," in *Phenomenology – East and West*, ed. F. M. Kirkland and D. P. Chattopadhyaya (Dordrecht: Reidel, 1993), pp. 129–43. A survey of the discussion may be found in Daniel Schmicking, "Intensionale

Semantik und Intentionsanalyse: Die Hintikka-Mohanty-Kontroverse (1975–1993)," *Phänomenologische Forschungen, Neue Folge* 1 (1996), second Halbband: 297–316.

3. What these interpretations have in common, is that they maintain that the noema is the same as the object of the act, but looked upon in a special way. One of the clearest formulations of this view may be found in William McKenna's review of Izchak Miller's book *Husserl, Perception, and Temporal Awareness* in *Husserl Studies* 2 (1985): 294:

> I do not think it can be maintained that the noematic *Sinn* is in no way identical to the object of a perceptual act. When the transcendental phenomenological reduction is carried out our reflective glance is directed, in noematic reflection, towards the *object* of our perception, now called the *Sinn* of our act. . . .

This interpretation is incompatible with a number of clear and precise passages in Husserl's text. These passages are not discussed by the proponents of this and similar interpretations and one wonders how they would interpret them. Also this interpretation raises philosophical difficulties. Thus, for example: what happens if the act has no object? According to Husserl this is the case in hallucination, in many acts of thinking and also in serious cases of misperception. If the noema is the object seen or reflected upon in a certain way, do then such acts not have a noema? This kind of issue is never discussed by the proponents of this kind of interpretation, and they may not have seen it as a difficulty. However, they should not attribute this view to Husserl, who was criticizing Brentano for taking it for granted that every act has an object.

4. Jaakko Hintikka, "The Phenomenological Dimension," in *The Cambridge Companion to Husserl*, ed. Barry Smith and David Woodruff Smith (Cambridge: Cambridge University Press, 1995), p. 79.

5. Ibid.

6. Ibid., p. 80.

7. For evidence of this and a fuller discussion, see, for example, my "Phenomenology." Chapter 19 of Edward C. Carterette and Morton P. Friedman, eds., *Handbook of Perception*, vol. I (New York: Academic Press, 1974), pp. 377–86. An excerpt is included in Dreyfus, *Husserl, Intentionality and Cognitive Science*, pp. 93–96.

8. A fuller presentation and discussion of the thetic component may be found in my article "The Thetic Role of Consciousness," in *Husserl's Logical Investigations Reconsidered*, ed. Denis Fisette, Contributions to Phenomenology, vol. 48 (Dordrecht: Kluwer Academic Publishers, 2003), pp. 11–20.

9. Hintikka, "The Phenomenological Dimension," pp. 79–80.

10. Ibid., p. 98.

11. W. V. Quine, *From Stimulus to Science* (Cambridge, Mass.: Harvard University Press, 1995), p. 16.

12. W. V. Quine, [unpublished] lectures at Lehigh University Oct. 15, 1990, and at Franklin and Marshall College April 17, 1992. A similar observation is made

in W. V. Quine, "Reactions," in *On Quine*, ed. Paolo Leonardi and Marco Santambrogio (Cambridge: Cambridge University Press, 1993), p. 350.

13. Quine, *From Stimulus to Science*, p. 36.

14. Hintikka, "The Phenomenological Dimension," p. 81.

15. See my article "Husserl's Notion of Intentionality," in *The Logical Foundations of Cognition*, ed. John Macnamara and Gonzalo E. Reyes (New York and Oxford: Oxford University Press, 1994), pp. 296–308.

16. Husserl's holism also extends to his theory of evidence and justification. See my "Husserl on Evidence and Justification," in *Edmund Husserl and the Phenomenological Tradition: Essays in Phenomenology* (Proceedings of a lecture series in the Fall of 1985), ed. Robert Sokolowski. *Studies in Philosophy and the History of Philosophy* 18 (Washington, D.C.: The Catholic University of America Press, 1988), pp. 107–29.

REPLY TO DAGFINN FØLLESDAL

I owe my old friend Dagfinn Føllesdal a great intellectual debt in that he first kindled my interest in phenomenology. I must confess, however, that I have never experienced the same meeting of minds in reading Husserl as I have sometimes experienced with other major past philosophers—the feeling that I understand some of their ideas as well as—and occasionally better than—they understood these ideas themselves. Perhaps it is because of this lingering alienation that Føllesdal has to correct several details in my discussions of Husserl. It is only very recently that I have begun to understand (it seems to me) what drives the entire phenomenological movement. And this understanding I have gained not so much by analyzing the texts of Husserl or Brentano as by a deeper look at the historical roots of phenomenologists' way of thinking. I am making an attempt to sketch the perspective I have reached in a paper entitled "Phenomenologists—Raiders of the Lost Forms?" forthcoming (in French translation) in a *Festschrift* for Paul Ricoeur.

From a suitable perspective, what I am doing now is raising again the same questions I raised in earlier papers discussed by Føllesdal. Føllesdal is one of the most prominent representatives of a tradition that sees phenomenology as being primarily a theory of intentionality, as a kind of general theory of meaning. The vehicles of this intentionality are the noemata. I do not have to try to describe noemata, for Føllesdal does it better in his contribution to this volume (and in his other work) than I could ever do.

The critical questions that I have raised earlier and which Føllesdal discusses concern the relation of noemata to their objects. What mediates this relation? How is it related to phenomenological reductions, and how is it related to constitution? Such questions inevitably face anybody who interprets phenomenology as a theory of intentionality. They are not illuminated by Føllesdal's famous analogy between Husserl's notion of noema and Frege's notion of *Sinn*, for the same or similar critical questions can be levelled at Frege's theory of meaning.

Føllesdal's basic response to my critical questions is to suggest that they are not well posed. "Rather than taking the notions of object and reality for granted and then asking how our consciousness relates to objects in the real world, Husserl regards these two notions as part of a package to which also acts, consciousness, *noema*, *noesis*, *hyle*, and our bodies belong." I agree with this statement both as a description of Husserl's views and as a pointer to what is important in phenomenology. Indeed, in my own thinking about phenomenology I have been led to emphasize the interwovenness of consciousness and its objects. But saying that Husserl was a holist does not answer my critical questions, it only moves them to another location. One can still ask how a noema is related to its object. One can still ask questions about the relationship, however holistic, between consciousness and its objects. Føllesdal points out that for Husserl the objects of perception are "full-fledged physical objects." How are they related to consciousness? How can they be parts of the same package as noemata and noesis? The different parts of the Husserlian package cannot be completely inseparable conceptually, for otherwise the phenomenological reductions would not seem to be possible. Even if the epistemic acts of the human mind are bootstrapping operations, we still need a rational account of them.

One phenomenological idea that I find especially intriguing is that we can have immediate access in our consciousness to some objects. (This idea already shows the interwovenness of objects and consciousness according to Husserl.) As Husserl puts it, an intuitively grasped object can be "personally" present to my consciousness in its totality. I am beginning to suspect that it is this idea of the direct givenness, almost the presence of an object in my consciousness, that is the true root idea of phenomenology, rather than the idea of intentionality. Unfortunately, this assumption of immediate givenness is so alien to most philosophers *anno domini* 2004 that its role in thinkers like Husserl (or G. E. Moore, for that matter) easily escapes their attention. In contrast, a kind of immediate givenness is the centerpiece of the most influential theorist of mind in the history of philosophy, Aristotle. (See here my paper, "Aristotle's Theory of Thinking and its Consequences for his Methodology.")[1] For Aristotle, for me to think of *X* is for the form of *X* to be present in my soul, not as somehow being represented there, but being there in full reality quite as much as in the realizations of the same form outside the soul. It has the same necessary concomitants and the same potentialities and powers.[2] Because of this reality, I can read off the properties of this form when it is realized in my own mind. Scientific method does not consist in drawing conclusions from data provided by sense experience, but in using the materials provided by perception to assemble the relevant forms in one's soul.

The historical perspective I am suggesting is that this Aristotelian theory of thinking is phenomenologists' paradise lost. Philosophers were driven from this paradise partly by a rejection of the Aristotelian idea of form and partly by the realization that not all forms—even if there were such entities—can be actually present in consciousness. But from the perspective I am suggesting, phenomenologists can be seen as maintaining the immediate givenness of some entities, and as trying to bring all the others as close to these intuitively given objects as possible by showing how such objects can be constituted from the intuitively given. Brentano-style inexistence of an object in one's mind is nothing but a reconstructed version of the actual presence of the form of X when I am thinking of X according to Aristotle. Phenomenologists are raiders of the lost Aristotelian forms.

This interpretation does not necessarily imply that the real-life twentieth-century phenomenologists were unsuccessful. Nor does the perspective I am suggesting by itself contradict other interpretations. However, the emphases it leads to are distinctly different from some of the usual ones, and should in my judgment motivate a critical scrutiny of some of the main features of the usual interpretations. For one thing, in the perspective I have suggested the very notion of intentionality becomes suspect or at least turns out to have limits. When an object is actually present in my mind, I do not intend it. It is in my consciousness; I do not have to point beyond my consciousness in order to think of it. I do not need any meaning entities to refer to it.

Likewise, the *as if* character of acts aptly described by Føllesdal seems to fall into the category of "virtue out of necessity." The closer we come in our reductions to self-given objects, the thinner the "as if" aspect becomes. If I may exaggerate this point, I am tempted to suggest that the unspoken aim of phenomenologists should not be a theory of intentionality, but an elimination of intentionality in favor of immediate awareness.

In order to round out this response, it may be in order to repeat what Føllesdal points out and to make it clear that he is dealing with only a part of my work on phenomenology. Another part deals with the relation of intentionality to possible-worlds semantics. Føllesdal may be well advised not to discuss this relation. In the best of circumstances this subject matter deserves a much more extensive discussion than I can give it here. However, I strongly disagree with the one reason Føllesdal gives for not discussing a possible-worlds approach to intentionality. He says that this approach "risks coming into conflict with some of Husserl's basic insights, for example that the object of an act of perception is a full-fledged physical object." It is my educated view that neglecting the possible-worlds angle runs the risk of failing to understand adequately the highly complex notion of "a full-fledged physical object." (Cf. here my response to Sandu in this volume.)

At the end of his contribution Føllesdal expresses the view that Husserl's theory of perception helps to clarify problems that have come up in contemporary cognitive science. This may be true, but I cannot extend this optimism to the field that is philosophically even more important potentially than typical so-called cognitive science. By this field I mean neuroscience. What has evolved there is a massive realization that by far most causal structures in cognition do not have noematic counterparts in consciousness and hence are not amenable to phenomenological study.

J. H.

NOTES

1. Jaakko Hintikka, "Aristotle's Theory of Thinking and its Consequences for his Methodology," in *Analogies of Aristotle, Selected Papers* 6 (Dordrecht: Kluwer Academic Publishers, 2004), pp. 45–75.

2. See especially, Aristotle, *De Anima* II, 7–8.

9

David Pears

PRIVATE LANGUAGE

Privacy and publicity are central topics in Wittgenstein's later work and it gives me great pleasure that this essay is published in the volume of the Library of Living Philosophers devoted to Jaakko Hintikka, whose extensive *oeuvre* includes many acute studies of Wittgenstein's philosophy.

The interpretation of Wittgenstein's "Private Language Argument" turns on the question, "What are the essential resources that a private language would lack?" A private language would be a necessarily unteachable language and the reason why it would be necessarily unteachable would be that it was restricted to reporting the speaker's sensations and the contents of his mind. It would be a language in which nothing could be said about the physical causes of his sensations or about his physical reactions to them. His use of this language would be isolated because the usual links with the physical world, *including his own body*, would have been severed. This is a very strong sense of the word "private."[1]

Wittgenstein's critique of private language was an attempt to subvert the Cartesian philosophy that had dominated the field for several centuries, and it was aimed at any isolationist account of the contents of the mind. But its main target was the account of perception and language current in the Vienna Circle and especially the account given by Carnap in *Die Logische Aufbau der Welt*.[2] According to Carnap our sensations are bracketed between stimuli and responses and each of us really speaks two languages about them, one specifying them in physical terms based on the stimuli that produce them and on the responses that they then produce, and the other specifying them in purely sensory terms. It is easy to understand how we communicate with one another in the first of these two languages but the second one would be private in the strong sense investigated by Wittgenstein.

This account of perception and language is criticized by Wittgenstein in *Philosophical Investigations*:

The essential thing about private experience is really not that each person possesses his own exemplar, but that nobody knows whether other people also have *this* or something else. The assumption would thus be possible—though unverifiable—that one section of mankind had one sensation of red and another section another.

What am I to say about the word "red"?—that it means something 'confronting us all' and that everyone should really have another word, besides this one, to mean his *own* sensation of red?[3]

There is an element of self-criticism in this passage, because Wittgenstein himself had once been attracted by the kind of theory that he criticizes here. In *Philosophical Remarks* (1929–31) he had written:

We could adopt the following way of representing matters: If I, L. W., have toothache, then that is expressed by means of the proposition 'There is toothache'. But if that is so, what we now express by the proposition 'A has toothache' is put as follows: 'A is behaving as L. W. does when there is toothache'. [Note the absence of any mention of the stimulus: more about that later]. Similarly, we shall say 'It is thinking' and 'A is behaving as L.W. does when it is thinking'. . . . It's evident that this way of speaking is equivalent to ours when it comes to questions of intelligibility and freedom from ambiguity. But it's equally clear that this language could have anyone at all at its center.[4]

This is followed by a discussion of some of the details of the theory about the two levels of language, one specifying sensations by the stimuli and responses that bracket them while the other specifies them directly in purely sensory terms. The difficulty that threatens the theory is that there is nothing to guarantee the identity of a sensation of A's specified in B's indirect physical way with a sensation of A's specified in A's direct sensory way.

The difficulty was not new: it had been pointed out by Russell in 1917.[5] Russell accepted it as inevitable but, of course, it raises a further question: "What then is the role of sensations when they are specified directly in sensory terms?" Wittgenstein's later answer to this question was that they have no role at all *if they are treated as independent inner objects*, and so, since they obviously do have a role, they must be treated in some other way. (This answer is easily misunderstood as the unconditional assertion that they have no role at all.) In this earlier text he had not yet reached that point, because he had not yet formulated his argument against the possibility of a private language. It makes its first appearance in 1936 in *Notes for Lectures on 'Private Experience' and 'Sense-data'*.[6]

I am going to discuss three questions about the interpretation of Wittgenstein's critique of private language. First, what exactly is the force of his contention that the would-be private linguist would have no criterion of correctness?[7] Second, what resources would have given him a criterion of correctness, if only he had had them? Third, what does he mean when he says that a sensation is not a *something* but not a *nothing* either?[8]

A short answer to the first question is that Wittgenstein is rejecting the assumption that reports of sensations in a private language would have definite meanings in spite of lacking a criterion of correctness. An equally short answer to the second question is that the would-be private linguist's basic lack is access to the things that, in Carnap's theory, bracket his sensations. The third question is more difficult to answer briefly but informatively. What it asks is how sensations can support meanings when they occur between the two brackets, and yet provide no support at all when they occur in isolation.

Before these questions are tackled in detail they need to be connected with some of the discussions of Wittgenstein's critique of private language. My first question is about the identification of the premises from which he deduced the impossibility of such a language. When *Philosophical Investigations* first appeared, it was immediately assumed that he was relying on the verification principle for his rejection of the possibility of a private language. However, though there is a strong verificationist vein in his later philosophy, he never subscribed to the principle. So perhaps it would be more plausible to regard his critique as a deduction from the narrower premise, that speaking a language is something that we do intentionally and, therefore, necessarily with knowledge of what would count as succeeding in doing it. This would be a large part of the point of his insistence that speaking a language is a practice.

My second question is connected with recent discussions of Wittgenstein's verdict on the possibility of a solitary language, invented by its speaker for his own use and so not learned but not, therefore unteachable.[9] The most obvious resource that this would-be solitary linguist would lack is communication with other people, especially with his parents, who would have taught him their public language if they had had a chance to do so. But this child had been solitary from birth and we may assume that he is a lucky survivor. The question is, "Could he really have developed a language for formulating his own thoughts relying on the resources provided by the physical world, without those provided by other people (roughly speaking, relying on the material constituting Carnap's first bracket without the intersubjectivity attainable through the material constituting his second bracket)?"

My third question is connected with the most frequent objection to Wittgenstein's critique of private language. He argued that reports of sensations can acquire meaning only by being made in their appropriate physical contexts and never independently of the two brackets. But if phenomenalism is true, statements about the physical world are reducible without remainder to reports of sensations. So Wittgenstein's contextual requirement can be met without recourse to anything beyond the sensory world. Nor is this surprising. For all our knowledge of the physical world comes through our sensations, and a sensation can avoid being a nothing only by being an independently recognizable something.[10]

I will now try to answer the three questions in detail beginning with the first one: "What is the force of Wittgenstein's contention that the would-be speaker of a private language would have no criterion of correctness?" It is an objection to the claim that in a private language the connection between a sign and a sensation could be established by an isolated ostensive definition:

> But I speak, or write the sign down, and at the same time I concentrate my attention on the sensation—and so, as it were, point to it inwardly.—But what is this ceremony for? for that is all it seems to be! A definition surely serves to establish the meaning of a sign.—Well, that is done precisely by the concentration of my attention; for in this way I impress on myself the connection between the sign and the sensation.—But "I impress it on myself" can only mean: this process brings it about that I remember the connection *right* in the future. But in the present case I have no criterion of correctness. One would like to say: whatever is going to seem right to me is right. And that only means that here we can't talk about 'right'.[11]

This is an apt criticism of Carnap's account of the foundations of language. According to Carnap, the first step, taken in what may be called "the original position," is to react to the remembered similarity of a present sensation to a previous one by naming their common property. The name is defined ostensively, because the pioneer points inwardly to his own sensation and relies on his memory of its similarity to an earlier sensation.

Barry Stroud has argued convincingly that this criticism of private language is based on Wittgenstein's contention that an isolated ostensive definition leaves it largely unclear how the defined word is to be applied in the future.[12] It is also based on his requirement that memories must be independently checkable.[13] So two questions arise at this point. First, is there any reason to suppose that the would-be private linguist is unable to go on and apply the word to further sensations and so is worse off than someone who can follow up an ostensive definition by applying the defined word to further physical objects? Second, is there any reason to suppose that the would-be private linguist is unable to check his memory-claims?

There seems to be nothing to stop him disambiguating his ostensive definition by going on to apply his word to further sensations. So I take this criticism to be a point made *ad hominem* against Carnap, who had naively relied on isolated ostensive definitions. But the uncheckability of the would-be private linguist's memory-claims is a more serious objection. The very concept of memory requires that there must sometimes be an independent identification of the point of input of the original experience and that is something that is never available in Carnap's original position (unless he is entitled to assume that phenomenalism is true).[14]

This raises a more general question of interpretation: why does Wittgenstein assume that the would-be speaker of a private language needs any criterion of correctness? His reason might have been a general acceptance of the verification principle: lack of a criterion would leave his reports of his sensations meaningless. That would be a fault that would make them unusable and so make their retention in his memory and in the memories of others who heard them absolutely useless. But Wittgenstein's criticism has a different emphasis. He focuses on the production of his reports rather than their reception and argues that, if the speaker had no criterion of correctness, he would not be *doing* anything, and he means that his utterances would not be examples of intentional action. This is an argument that identifies a fault in the production of a private report of a sensation and we can appreciate its force without supposing that it is based on a general acceptance of the verification principle. Reporting a sensation is an intentional shot at the truth and if you do not know what would count as hitting the target, you cannot know what you are engaged in doing intentionally and therefore cannot be doing it intentionally.

In 1941, when Wittgenstein reviewed his critique of private language, he wrote:

[I]n order to establish a name relation we have to establish a technique of use. And we are misled if we think that it is a peculiar process of christening an object which makes a word the word for an object. This is a kind of superstition. So it's no use saying that we have a private object before the mind and give it a name. There is a name only where there is a technique of using it and that technique can be private; but this only means that nobody but I know about it, in the sense in which I can have a private sewing machine. But in order to be a private sewing machine, it must be an object that deserves the name "sewing machine," not in virtue of its privacy but in virtue of its similarity to sewing machines, private or otherwise.[15]

To practice a technique is to perform a series of actions intentionally and it is characteristic of Wittgenstein to make that point by using a mechanical analogy. (When he was a boy, he made a sewing machine that worked.) Of course, it is only an analogy and not a reductive thesis. Earlier he had used a similar analogy to illustrate the effect of severing the criterial connection between sensations and the physical world. If the engine of a motor-roller were simply a piston mounted rigidly inside the drum, it would not only fail to produce any effect outside the drum but would also be doing nothing inside the drum. The first of these two faults is like the failure to serve as the basis for any conclusions about the physical world and the second fault is like the failure to record anything within the mind.[16]

My second question is, "What resources would have given the would-be private linguist a criterion of correctness, if only he had had them? On the face of it there seem to be two important resources on which we public linguists rely, the corroboration provided by successful communication with other people and the reinforcement of our self-imposed linguistic regularities that is provided by their success in tracking the identities of objects in the world around us and their regular connections with one another and with our own bodies. (Our regularity is an investment that earns the discovery of their regularities.) The would-be private linguist would lack the first of these two resources, but he would still have the second one, for what it would be worth. But what would it be worth? Would it support a solitary language? Or would his lack of the first resource leave him unable to exploit the second one?

This is a difficult question and Wittgenstein does not give a clear answer to it. He insists on the need for "agreement in judgments" with other people as well as "agreement in definitions," but only conditionally: "If language is to be a means of communication there must be agreement not only in definitions but also, (queer as this may sound) in judgments."[17] In a parallel, but more explanatory passage, he remarks, "We say that, in order to communicate, people must agree with one another about the meanings of words. But the criterion for this agreement is not just agreement with reference to definitions, . . . but *also* an agreement in judgments. It is essential for communication that we agree in a large number of judgments."[18]

But what if there is nobody else with whom to communicate? Would the solitary vocalizations of a private linguist necessarily fail to count as a language? Wittgenstein side-steps this question and asks, instead, the related question, whether it would be possible that there should have been only one occasion on which someone obeyed a rule (e.g., a linguistic rule). He gives this question an unqualified negative answer, and he takes the same line about mathematical calculation: "But what about this consensus—doesn't it mean that *one* human being by himself could not calculate? Well, *one* human being could at any rate, not calculate just *once* in his life."[19]

This is an evasion. Of course, it is difficult to imagine a language invented by a person solitary from birth solely to register his own thoughts, instead of evolving from a system of natural expressions first used for communication between people and only later internalized to register their users' thoughts. However, that still falls short of conceptual impossibility. If we found what seemed to be a case of a solitary language, we would not immediately reject it as a logical impossibility. So why does Wittgenstein not confine himself to saying that the case would be marginal?

What he actually says is, "If language is to be a means of communication . . .," and that certainly suggests that a language might never be used for communication between one person and another. He never says outright that an apparent case of that kind would not count as a language, and in his treatment of the question, whether a single human being by himself would be able to calculate, he shows a similar caution. He feels sure of the central area of the application of these concepts and when he moves out from the center along some radius, he does not always feel it necessary to find the exact point at which it crosses the circumference and moves from sense to nonsense. He says that his "aim is: to teach you to pass from a piece of disguised nonsense to something that is patent nonsense."[20]

That said, it must be admitted that his treatment of sensation-language is tilted towards the necessity of communication between people. On first reading his account in *Philosophical Investigations* one feels that one is standing on level ground with equal emphasis on Carnap's two brackets. But his concentration on pain really does focus attention on the effects of the sensation rather than its causes. For pain is a sensation with a great variety of causes but fairly uniform effects, viz., action taken to terminate it or avoid it and, among social animals, a vocalization established as its natural expression, a cry for help. Obviously a visual impression of a color has no uniform natural effect and the unity of the concept depends on its cause. Pain is a special case and Wittgenstein uses it to illustrate the social function of its natural expression and of the word that has been substituted for it.[21] We are now well on the way to concluding that communication is not only an original function of language but also a necessary one.

This tendency reaches its extreme point in a passage in *Philosophical Investigations*, where Wittgenstein imagines someone saying

"Oh, I know what 'pain' means; what I don't know is whether *this*, that I have now, is pain"—we should merely shake our heads and be forced to regard his words as a queer reaction which we have no idea what to do with. (It would be rather as if we heard someone say seriously: "I distinctly remember that some time before I was born I believed. . . .")
    That expression of doubt has no place in the language-game; but if we cut out human behavior, which is the expression of sensation, it looks as if I might *legitimately* begin to doubt afresh. My temptation to say that one might take a

> sensation for something other than what it is arises from this: if I assume the
> abrogation of the normal language-game with the expression of a sensation, I
> need a criterion of identity for the sensation; and then the possibility of error
> also exists.[22]

His point is that if we separate pain from its natural expression, we will
credit it with an independent criterion of identity, because we will model the
inner world on the outer world. So he asks, "'What would it be like if
human beings showed no outward signs of pain (did not groan, grimace,
etc.)?'"[23] Now many pains are caused by identifiable stimuli which the
sufferer can learn to avoid, but this important fact is not mentioned here.
Instead, the suggested answer to the question is, "Then it would be
impossible to teach a child the use of the word 'tooth-ache'."[24] True, both
question and answer are segregated by inverted commas and this may
indicate that it is not Wittgenstein who is giving the answer, but his
interlocutor. However, the comments that follow are Wittgenstein's and
they do not contain any mention of the possibility of learning the meaning
of the word "pain" through the stimuli that cause the sensation. §257
continues: "—Well, let's assume that the child is a genius and itself invents
a name for the sensation! . . . — So does he understand the name, without
being able to explain its meaning to anyone?"

Obviously Wittgenstein was not unaware of the causes of pain and their
use as criteria. Nevertheless his concentration on pain, with its natural
expressions and their connection with communication, does tilt the balance
of the critique of private language in *Philosophical Investigations* and so
leads to a neglect of the only resource available to the solitary linguist. His
defense would probably have been that his method was to explore separate
lines of inquiry without generalizing their results. Also, the choice of pain
for special attention was originally not his but his Cartesian adversaries'.
They chose it because it is the clearest example of a type of sensation with
a phenomenal property recognizable independently of any specific cause
and philosophers as different as Galileo and Berkeley argued that some, or
perhaps all properties that seemed to belong to physical objects were really
properties like phenomenal painfulness.

Finally, to complete my answer to my second question, something
needs to be said about the only resource available to the solitary linguist,
the primitive science that would shape his rudimentary linguistic efforts
and confirm their success. If we were supposing that he could quickly
develop a language with the complexity of ours we would be envisaging a
miracle. But if we only credit him with a very minimal language for
recording objects in his immediate environment and their effects on each
other and on his own body, he would not even need to be a genius. For his

life in space would already have provided him with a conceptual framework of identifiable points for the attachment of symbols. Then the self-imposed regularity of his linguistic practices would be reinforced by its success in tracking the identities of objects and the regularities of their behavior.

There seem to be two things that made Wittgenstein avoid this kind of neo-Kantian inquiry. First, it is highly theoretical and he believed that it is not the task of philosophy to theorize. Second, it would be an inquiry into the origin of our concepts and he regarded such inquiries as scientific rather than philosophical.[25] But exactly the same objection could be made against his own use of natural expression. Anyway, whatever the explanation, there is a clear change of emphasis between the *Notes for Lectures on 'Private Experience' and 'Sense-data'*[26] and *Philosophical Investigations*: in the earlier work much more is said about what I have been calling "Carnap's first bracket" and in the later work the emphasis shifts to his "second bracket," and this change would naturally be accompanied by a heavier emphasis on communication between people.

My third and last question is, "What does Wittgenstein mean when he says that 'a sensation is not a something but not a nothing either'?" When I first asked this question, I pointed out that it is connected with a common objection to his critique of private language. The objection is that if phenomenalism is true, our account of the physical world is reducible without remainder to a record of our sensations, and so when Wittgenstein argues that a word can be given a meaning by being applied to a sensation only when it is applied to it in a physical context, this contextual requirement can be met without recourse to anything beyond the sensory world.[27]

It is hardly self-explanatory to proclaim that "a sensation is not a *something* but not a *nothing* either." The point is made more perspicuously by a much-discussed analogy—the collectors, each with a beetle in his box but each only able to look into his own box. Wittgenstein's comment is that "if we construe the grammar of expression of sensation on the model of 'object and designation' the object drops out of consideration as irrelevant."[28] We can contrapose this and say that, if the sensation is going to be relevant, it must not be treated as an object, and that means that it must not be treated like a physical object. Berkeley's philosophy of perception, the first stage on the road to phenomenalism, is a perfect example of the wrong treatment. What physical objects have, but sensations lack, is independent identifiability and re-identifiability. We may express Wittgenstein's thesis by saying that sensations are not objects in the strong sense of that word.

The point that Wittgenstein is making is fatally apt to be misunderstood because it is so easy to confuse this strong sense of the word "object" with a weaker sense in which it merely means "thing designated by a noun." This confusion always makes his argument seem more paradoxical than it really is. For example, he imagines that he can tell when his blood pressure is rising because it gives him a particular sensation, and that when a manometer is used, it confirms his judgment.

> And now it seems quite indifferent whether I have recognized the sensation *right* or not. Let us suppose that I regularly identify it wrong; it does not matter in the least. And that alone shows that the hypothesis that I make a mistake is mere show. (We as it were turn a knob which looked as if it could be used to turn on some part of the machine; but it was a mere ornament; not connected with the mechanism at all.)[29]

This is a paradoxical thing to say, given that it is through his sensation that he recognizes that his blood pressure is rising. His point must be that that, then, is the way to put it, and that it is a mistake to say that I recognize the quality of the sensation. For that suggests that my sensation is an object with a property recognizable independently of its original connection with the physical world.

The same point is made in his discussion of seeing aspects: "Always get rid of the idea of a private object in this way: assume that it constantly changes, but that you do not notice the change because your memory constantly deceives you."[30] This too would be a paradoxical thing to say if it meant that my visual sensation (or impression) was irrelevant. His point is that it *would be* irrelevant if it were treated as an independently identifiable object.

Finally, there is the question of the validity of the phenomenalist's objection to Wittgenstein's critique of private language. The objection is that if phenomenalism is true, any statement about physical objects is reducible without remainder to a series of statements about sensation, and so when Wittgenstein insists on the need for a physical context if anyone is going to succeed in setting up a sensation-language, his requirement can be met without recourse to anything beyond the sensory world.

The natural response to this objection is to point out that it is not legitimate to assume that phenomenalism is true in order to rebut an objection to it. But this invites the retort that neither is it legitimate to assume that it is false in order to rebut the rebuttal. But this is only skirmishing and we need to understand what lies behind it.

What lies behind it is a confusion about the rules governing a controversy about a reductive philosophical theory. The critic of the theory will ask its supporter to defend a certain step in his argument—in this case, to defend Carnap's claim that in the original position the pioneer could learn to classify his sensations relying only on their remembered similarities. The onus of proof now lies on the supporter of the reductive theory and, in order to discharge this obligation, he cannot legitimately use the conclusion that he is going to draw in the next step of his argument—in this case, the reductive thesis, that statements about physical objects amount to no more than statements about sensations. For that step has not yet been taken and so its result is not yet available for use in defense of the first step.

To put this in another way, the first step must be taken autonomously, without reliance on what we all know is going to be the second step. Carnap's account of the original position must rely on its own merits as a description of a situation that will strike us immediately and on its own merits as a possible one; it must not rely on something that is going to be established that will convince us that when independent physical objects have been eliminated from the scene, we can still classify our sensations relying only on their remembered similarities. At this stage in his argument, his conclusion, that physical objects *are* sensations, cannot be used to dislodge us from the point of view of common sense.

The phenomenalist's objection to Wittgenstein's critique of private language depends on a trick that is easy to detect when an argument moves on a single level of reality. But when two levels are involved, as they are in this case, the trick is more insidious. After all, what lies in the future in the argument belongs to the present in reality. So why should the critic not be allowed to borrow against the future? So we forget that the original position has to be a possible one when it is described simply as we would describe it in real life. That is a condition of the success of the argument that is intended to liberate us from the restricted point of view of common sense. So I conclude that Wittgenstein was right to reject untestable memories, and right to insist on the need of independently identifiable objects to support the very concept of memory.

DAVID PEARS

OXFORD UNIVERSITY
FEBRUARY 2003

NOTES

1. See Ludwig Wittgenstein, *Philosophical Investigations*, trans. G.E.M. Anscombe (New York: Macmillan, 1970), I, §243.
2. Rudolf Carnap, *Der Logische Aufbau der Welt* (Berlin, 1928).
3. Wittgenstein, *Philosophical Investigations* I, §§272–73.
4. Ludwig Wittgenstein, *Philosophical Remarks*, ed. Rush Rhees, trans. Raymond Hargreaves and Roger White (Oxford: Blackwell, 1975), VI, §58.

5. See Bertrand Russell, "The Philosophy of Logical Atomism" in *Logic and Knowledge: Essays 1901-1950 / Bertrand Russell*, ed. Robert Charles Marsh (London: Unwin Hyman, 1988; originally published: London: Allen & Unwin, 1956), p. 195.

6. See Ludwig Wittgenstein, *Philosophical Occasions: 1912–1951*, ed. James C. Klagge and Alfred Nordmann (Indianapolis: Hackett, 1993), pp. 202–88.

7. See Wittgenstein, *Philosophical Investigations*, I, §304.

8. See ibid.

9. See C. Verheggen, "Wittgenstein on Solitary Language," *Philosophical Investigations* 18 (October 1995).

10. See A. J. Ayer, *Wittgenstein* (London: Weidenfeld and Nicolson, 1985; New York: Random House, 1985), pp. 74–75. Reprinted by University of Chicago Press, 1986.

11. Wittgenstein, *Philosophical Investigations*, I, §258.

12. Barry Stroud, "Private Objects, Physical Objects and Ostension," in *Wittgensteinian Themes: Essays in Honour of David Pears*, ed. David Charles and William Child (Oxford: Clarendon Press, 2001), pp. 143–62.

13. Wittgenstein, *Philosophical Investigations*, I, §265.

14. See below, pp. 17–20.

15. "Notes for the 'Philosophical Lecture,'" in *Philosophical Occasions*, p. 448.

16. Wittgenstein, "Philosophical Grammar" §141, *Remarks on the Philosophy of Psychology*, vol. I, §397.

17. Wittgenstein, *Philosophical Investigations*, I, §242.

18. Wittgenstein, *Remarks on the Foundations of Mathematics*, 3rd ed., ed. von Wright, Rhees, and Anscombe, trans. Anscombe (New York: Macmillan, 1978), VI, §39.

19. Ibid., II, §67.

20. Wittgenstein, *Philosophical Investigations*, I, §464.

21. Ibid., I, §§244–45; and Ludwig Wittgenstein, *Zettel*, ed. Anscombe and von Wright, trans. Anscombe (Oxford: Blackwell, 1967), §§540–43.

22. Wittgenstein, *Philosophical Investigations*, I, §288.

23. Ibid., §257.

24. Ibid.

25. See ibid., II, xii.

26. Ludwig Wittgenstein (1936), "Notes for Lectures on 'Private Experience' and 'Sense-data'," *Philosophical Review* 77 (1968): 275–320; and "Notes for Lectures on 'Private Experience' and 'Sense-data'," computer version in VIEWS text (Pittsboro, N.C.: InteLex Corp., 1992).

27. See e.g., A. J. Ayer, *Wittgenstein*, pp. 74–75.

28. Wittgenstein, *Philosophical Investigations*, I, §293.

29. Ibid., §270.

30. Ibid., II, xi, p. 207.

REPLY TO DAVID PEARS

David Pears is one of the very few Wittgenstein interpreters from whom I have actually acquired genuine insights into Wittgenstein's philosophy. For one important example, it was Pears's 1977 study that first opened my eyes to the connection between Russell's theory of acquaintance,[1] especially in the version presented in the posthumously published book *Theory of Knowledge*,[2] and Wittgenstein's picture theory. Together with Merrill Hintikka, I pushed this interpretation further and argued that the simple objects of the *Tractatus* are nothing but Russellian objects of acquaintance, with the important exception that Wittgenstein rejected Russell's idea of logical forms as a separate class of objects of acquaintance. We tried to express this idea by calling the objects postulated in the *Tractatus* phenomenological. This caused a major misunderstanding among other interpreters of the *Tractatus* who had mistakenly assimilated to each other the notions of "phenomenological" and "phenomenalistic." Among others, in his book *The False Prison* David Pears criticizes our interpretation of the Tractarian objects.[3] This criticism is based on a misunderstanding of our intentions and more specifically of what we meant by calling the objects of the *Tractatus* "phenomenological." Perhaps this is an occasion to try to set the record straight. Admittedly in the early usage there was a good deal of confusion about what the terms "phenomenological" and "phenomenalistic" meant. But a distinction in meaning between these terms is not only possible, but crucial for the proper understanding of thinkers in the period. Such thinkers include Mach, Boltzmann, Planck, and other physicists and philosophers of science. For scientists of that period, the distinction is between what can be directly observed and what can only be inferred from the phenomena. According to this usage, which was well known to Wittgenstein from the writings of philosophers of science like Boltzmann, an object is phenomenological if I can be directly aware of it. A phenomenalist thinks that the only objects we can be so aware of are our own impressions and ideas. But a phenomenologist need not be a phenomenalist if he or she believes that we can be directly aware of objects in the actual mind-independent world. And this is precisely what some important thinkers who figure in Wittgenstein's background did. Moore believed that in any one of my experiences I can distinguish the immediate object of that experience from the merely psychological event in my consciousness. That object belongs according to Moore to the objective (no pun intended) world. Likewise, Russell maintained that his objects of acquaintance belong to the actual world and are not only contents of our consciousness.[4] For instance, Russell staunchly maintained at the time that sense data belong to the physical world.

Hence the point of calling the objects of the *Tractatus* phenomenological is not that they are mere phenomena, but that I can experience them directly. They are thus distinguished, not from things in themselves, but from objects that cannot be directly experienced, for instance, from the theoretical entities postulated by physicists.

I have suggested that behind this contrast there is a deeper conceptual distinction between two kinds of frameworks in which objects can be identified. Wittgenstein, at a later stage of his development, was aware to some extent of this distinction, as is evidenced especially by *The Blue Book*.[5] But unsurprisingly he did not fully master this subtle distinction that even now has not been acknowledged by the majority of philosophers. In any case, it does not play any overt role in the *Tractatus*, and most importantly it only reinforces my point that phenomenological objects can in the matter of contrast between consciousness and reality belong squarely on the objective side.

When this confusion is cleared up, there remain no objections to our vision of the *Tractatus* as a variant of Russell's theory of acquaintance. The objects assumed there are phenomenological in the sense that they are directly known by me.

But why did Wittgenstein not himself in the *Tractatus* call his position phenomenological? I believe that a historical answer can be given. In the *Tractatus*, Wittgenstein's Viennese background plays a role. If he had used the label "phenomenological," whose ideas would his views have been assimilated to, at least in Vienna? The terminology mentioned earlier yields an answer: to the views of Ernst Mach. This assimilation would not have been totally unjustified, as I have shown in my 2002 paper "Ernst Mach at the Crossroads of Twentieth-century Philosophy." But it so happened that Wittgenstein personally detested Mach as a thinker and writer. In a letter to Russell, he goes as far as to say that reading Mach makes him sick. For this reason, Wittgenstein glossed over all his less than elective affinities with Mach. One of them was the use of the label "phenomenological" for the views he shared with Mach.

Revealingly, when Wittgenstein later had in a sense given up these shared views, he begins to refer to Mach and to criticize Mach.[6] When Wittgenstein came back to philosophy in the twenties, the terminological situation had changed in general philosophy, if not in physics and in the philosophy of physics, where the old sense of "phenomenological" still prevails. The main association would now have been to Husserl's phenomenology, which Wittgenstein found objectionable on other grounds, but which was not perceived by the majority of readers to be closely related to Mach's phenomenology and to which he did not evince the same gut-level antipathy as displayed toward Mach. Thus Wittgenstein began to refer to his own views as phenomenological.

It is crucial for understanding Wittgenstein's overall thought to realize that those views were indeed in the relevant respects the same as the views expressed in the *Tractatus*. I am astonished that this fact has not been generally acknowledged. For one indication of the obviousness of the identity, Wittgenstein's Viennese friends like Waismann and Schlick never thought otherwise. They were in a much better position to judge the matter than later interpreters.

Even though Wittgenstein changed his view in this matter beginning in October 1929, it is important to realize the precise nature of his phenomenology. One reason is that it provides a crucial key to his later philosophy. This is the case in two different respects. First, it is vital to understand precisely how he changed his views. Second, many theses expressed in his later philosophical writings are little more than criticisms of his earlier views. In the preface to the *Philosophical Investigations*,[7] Wittgenstein encourages his readers to read it by comparing it with the *Tractatus*. Few interpreters have nevertheless followed up this clue.

In his contribution, David Pears discusses Wittgenstein's so-called "private language argument."[8] It may therefore be in order to use this interesting line of thought as a test case. Wittgenstein introduces the subject by raising the question as to how we can refer to our internal experiences and speak about them. How would he have answered this question in the *Tractatus*? Since the objects referred to in a Tractarian language are the objects of our experiences, Wittgenstein's question pertains to experienced inner sensations, experiences of colors, and the like. They are according to the *Tractatus* actual objects. They are as little subjective as Moore's objects of experiences or Russell's sense data. They are named ostensively, just like the objects designated by Russell's "logically proper names" *this* and *that*. (Wittgenstein does not refer in so many words to ostensive definitions in the *Tractatus*, but the criticism of ostension in the *Philosophical Investigations* is unmistakably aimed at the views expressed in the *Tractatus*.) However, and this is a general point about the Tractarian objects, they are given to me only momentarily, as ingredients of a specious present. As I have shown in my 1996 paper "Wittgenstein on Being and Time," in the *Tractatus* he defended a kind of temporal solipsism. "Propositions are verified in the present." To use his own later terminology, the only kind of time assumed by Wittgenstein in the *Tractatus* is memory-time. This does not make his objects any less real than bona fide physical objects or any less members of the external world. However, it makes a difference to their re-identification in time. It forces Wittgenstein to consider all identification of objects not presently given to me a matter of memory. In all these respects, objects of internal sensations are in the *Tractatus* on a par with objects of other experiences.

Now what happens when Wittgenstein gives up the primacy of phenomenological languages? First of all, it does not mean rejecting the reality of phenomenological objects. Even after the crucial switch of linguistic priorities, for Wittgenstein "the world we live in is the world of sense-data"—i.e., generally speaking, of phenomenological objects.[9] Accordingly, Wittgenstein is not rejecting the reality of internal experiences or of their objects, their knowability or our ability to speak about them and give them names. His problem is how we can do so. And this is a problem for the later Wittgenstein because the entities referred to by our linguistic expressions are typically now everyday physical objects, which need not be direct objects of any experience. What is especially important, the criteria of identity of such objects as can be referred to in language must be public. Hence, memory cannot serve to constitute the ultimate criterion of identification of internal sensations. Hence, Wittgenstein's point in criticizing memory in the course of his "private language argument" is not the trite and old saw that memory can be deceptive, but rather a general theoretical rejection of the Tractarian conception of memory as providing the medium of identification for objects of experience. This explains Wittgenstein's comments on memory in the "private language argument." This point is independent of the status of internal experiences as internal. What sets the objects of such experiences apart is that other people do not have access to them. If there were external objects accessible only to their owners, the conceptual situation would be the same. Indeed, in *Philosophical Investigations I*,[10] Wittgenstein envisages such a situation as a thought experiment. In all these different cases, the normal meaning of our terms presupposes a framework that is interpersonally available. In the case of internal experiences, this framework is constituted by certain modes of public behavior ("language-games") associated with our vocabulary for such experiences.

From this a *prima facie* paradoxical conclusion follows. If an expression functions in the same way in the respective language-games of two different people, its meaning is the same for both of them. This, Wittgenstein argues, is a general fact about language. But it implies that the experienced character of two objects is in a sense irrelevant to the realities of actual language. This is one of the morals of Wittgenstein's story of "experience S."[11] The perceived identity of the objects of internal experiences plays no role in the realities of language. "The assumption would thus be possible—though unverifiable—that one section of mankind had one sensation of red and another section another."[12] Such a paradoxical sounding assumption would have been not only unverifiable but also inexpressible for Wittgenstein.

This paradoxical air is to some extent dispelled by further observations. Of course, Wittgenstein realizes that our language would not function properly unless there were in normal cases an agreement between an expression and its accompanying behavior. His point is merely that such agreement is neither conceptually necessary nor expressible in language. This is what Wittgenstein means when he writes: "If language is to be a means of communication there must be agreement not only in definitions, but also . . . in judgments . . . what we call 'measuring' is partly determined by a certain constancy in the results of measurement."[13]

Wittgenstein is in some unspeakable sense assuming that different people actually associate similar sensations with our words for internal experiences. Otherwise our language-games would go haywire. For instance, a jungle linguist would be in for considerable hermeneutical difficulties in the translation of pain vocabulary if he were to chance upon a sick tribe in which the majority of members are masochists. But it is a contingent, albeit inexpressible, fact that most of the speakers of my language are not masochists.

Given such a contingent consilience of experiences and the associated behavior, we can in a sense talk about our experiences even in their qualitative sense. And this is possible only courtesy of certain regularities which are not guaranteed by language.

The apparent strangeness of Wittgenstein's view can also be partly eliminated by considering what it amounts to when applied to concepts other than internal sensations. Wittgenstein says in *Remarks on Colour* that color words are used in the same way as words for sensations.[14] This may sound strange, for there are no characteristic modes of color behavior as there are obvious modes of pain behavior. But the relevant behavior can be simply a reaction to different color words. "'Red' means the color that occurs to me when I hear the word 'red'. . . ."[15] But this does not guarantee that I know what occurs to you when you hear the word. What Wittgenstein means is that in the language-game with color words we have been trained to react to different colors in a certain way. In all such cases the directly and experientially given objects—the phenomenological object—is inexpressible. But all that this means is that the colors we speak of in our language are physical (public) colors, not experienced ("phenomenological") colors. The analogous conclusion for words for pains and for other internal sensations need not be any more paradoxical.

Furthermore, the direct inexpressibility of the phenomenological objects of experiences according to the later Wittgenstein has a precedent in the *Tractatus* in the form of the inexpressibility of all simple objects. Since such an object must be given to me before I can speak of it, I can neither meaningfully and nontrivially say that it exists, nor can I define it, for then I could say that there exists an object so defined. All this is anticipated already in Russell's *Theory of Knowledge*. Hence it should not be surprising to find a similar view in later Wittgenstein.

The reader is invited to compare what Pears says about the private language argument with this brief sketch of its position in Wittgenstein's development. Whatever such a comparison may bring out, it will illustrate the main difference between my approach to Wittgenstein and that of practically all others. What I am trying to do is to find the leading ideas of Wittgenstein's philosophy and the overall dynamics of his developments, and then use them to understand the details of his work.

J. H.

NOTES

1. David Pears, "The Relation Between Wittgenstein's Picture Theory of Propositions and Russell's Theories of Judgment," *Philosophical Review* 86 (1977): 190–212.

2. Bertrand Russell, *Theory of Knowledge: The 1913 Manuscript*, Collected Papers of Bertrand Russell, vol. 7, ed. Elizabeth R. Eames in collaboration with Kenneth Blackwell (London: Allen and Unwin, 1984).

3. David Pears, *The False Prison: A Study of the Development of Wittgenstein's Philosophy* 1–2 (Oxford: Clarendon Press, 1987).

4. See especially Bertrand Russell, "The Relation of Sense-data to Physics," in *Mysticism and Logic* (London: Longmans, 1917), ch. 8.

5. Ludwig Wittgenstein, *The Blue and Brown Books* (Oxford: Blackwell, 1958), pp. 58–68.

6. See especially Ludwig Wittgenstein, *Philosophical Remarks*, ed. Rush Rhees (Oxford: Blackwell, 1975), sec. 213.

7. Ludwig Wittgenstein, *Philosophical Investigation* (Oxford: Blackwell, 1953).

8. Ibid., secs. 243–315.

9. See Ludwig Wittgenstein, *Wittgenstein's Lectures, Cambridge 1930–1932*, ed. Desmond Lee (Oxford: Blackwell, 1980), p. 82.

10. Wittgenstein, *Philosophical Investigations*, sec. 293.

11. Ibid., secs. 258–261, 270.

12. Ibid., sec. 272.

13. Ibid., sec. 242.

14. Ludwig Wittgenstein, *Remarks on Colour* (Oxford: Blackwell, 1977), Part III, secs. 171–172.

15. Wittgenstein, *Philosophical Investigations*, sec. 239.

10

Mathieu Marion

PHENOMENOLOGICAL LANGUAGE, THOUGHTS, AND OPERATIONS IN THE *TRACTATUS*

I. INTRODUCTION

Analytic philosophy is often construed as being narrowly ahistorical. However, it is not unusual for analytic philosophers to produce substantive, perceptive, albeit controversial, interpretations of past philosophers, for example, Strawson on Kant or Dummett on Frege. Jaakko Hintikka has been unusually productive and wide-ranging in the field of history of philosophy, with significant contributions on Aristotle, Descartes, Kant, Frege, Husserl, and Wittgenstein. In almost all of these cases, his ideas have turned out to be remarkably fruitful, even when limited to a few papers, as in the case of his interpretation of Descartes's *cogito*.[1] It is perhaps Hintikka's interpretation of Wittgenstein that stands out as the most substantive. His writings on Wittgenstein extend for almost half a century, beginning in the 1950s with a pair of papers that contributed significantly to the understanding of identity[2] and solipsism[3] in the *Tractatus Logico-Philosophicus*.[4] This work culminated in a book jointly written with Merrill B. Hintikka, *Investigating Wittgenstein*;[5] some of the themes of the book were further developed in numerous papers.[6]

The most significant feature of Hintikka's interpretation[7] is that it offers an explanation of the reasons for Wittgenstein's ill-understood move from his earlier to his later philosophy.[8] In a nutshell, it has to do with a change of "basic" or "operative" language. This change, which occurred in 1929, occupies a central position within Hintikka's interpretation:

It is our thesis . . . that the decisive turning-point in Wittgenstein's philosophical development in 1929 was *the replacement of this phenomenological
language by an everyday physicalistic language* as his operative language, and,
indeed, as the only viable basic language in philosophy. Moreover, we shall
argue that this was the *only* clear-cut initial change in Wittgenstein's views and
that the other developments of his philosophical ideas during his so-called
middle period can be viewed, at least genetically, as further consequences of
this first new step.[9]

The gist of this remark is that, at the time of writing the *Tractatus*,
Wittgenstein had in mind the idea that the meaning of sentences in ordinary
language could be made explicit through an analysis which would
ultimately transcribe them in a "phenomenological" language (I shall try
and explain later what is meant by that expression) but, in 1929, he realized,
as a result of a "deduction,"[10] that there is in fact no such thing as a
phenomenological language and he gave it up, along with the concomitant
conception of analysis. According to Hintikka, this change of "operative"
language forced Wittgenstein to rethink the basic semantical links between
language and reality and he was ultimately led to the realization that
language games are not derived from but constitutive of these links. The
original argument for the abandonment of phenomenological languages
being unconvincing, Wittgenstein is said to have set about finding a better
one, ultimately coming up with the "private language argument," while the
"rule-following argument" is the result of Wittgenstein's attempt at getting
rid of the phenomenological conception of rules. It is a great pity that,
unlike, say, Saul Kripke's book,[11] Hintikka's interpretation has not attracted
its proper share of critical scrutiny.[12] It is not possible within the compass
of this paper to provide an overall assessment of it and I shall merely
concentrate on one aspect of the main thesis concerning the change of
"operative" language. Unlike Hintikka, I do not see Wittgenstein's
philosophy as evolving through global, spectacular changes but I do not
wish to discuss this point here. I instead shall press on a little bit farther on
the path pioneered here by Hintikka and explore some of the consequences
of the idea that the language of elementary propositions of the *Tractatus*
might, after all, be "phenomenological." I shall therefore focus on
Hintikka's writings on the *Tractatus*, which form his contribution to an
unusually rich Finnish tradition of commentaries on that book.[13] I shall
argue that it is in a sense right to describe the "operative" language of
Tractatus as "phenomenological" but also that this is not the whole story.
I hope to draw some conclusions that are of relevance from a wider
perspective. What will emerge should be reasons to believe that, in the end,
Hintikka's emphasis on underlying semantical issues provides us with an

incomplete account of the *Tractatus* and a more accurate picture shows that there are other ideas at stake, ideas that can be characterized roughly as proof-theoretical, to which Hintikka appears to be somewhat impervious.

II. PHENOMENOLOGICAL AND PHYSICALIST LANGUAGE IN THE *TRACTATUS*

In trying to show that the "operative" language of the *Tractatus* is "phenomenological," I shall avoid Hintikka's controversial detour through the identification of its "simple objects" with Russell's "objects of acquaintance," because I wish to steer clear of the many complications that it brings about. I shall use another detour, through the so-called middle period. I should begin, however, with two very brief remarks concerning the alleged change of "operative" language, in 1929. First, that it is a fact that something happened is not something open to doubt, since we have Wittgenstein's repeated testimony. For example, in December 1929, Wittgenstein announces to Schlick and Waismann:

> I used to believe that there was the everyday language that we all usually spoke and a primary language that expressed what we really knew, namely phenomena. I also spoke of a first system and a second system. . . . I do not adhere to that conception any more. I think that essentially we have only one language, and that is our everyday language. We need not invent a new language or construct a new symbolism, but our everyday language already is *the* language, provided we rid it of the obscurities that lie hidden in it.[14]

This remark is confirmed by the first paragraph of the *Philosophical Remarks*, a typescript collated in 1930:

> I do not now have phenomenological language, or "primary language" as I used to call it, in mind as my goal. I no longer hold it to be necessary. All that is possible and necessary is to separate what is essential from what is inessential in *our* language. . . . A recognition of what is essential and what is inessential in our language if it is to represent, a recognition of which parts of our language are wheels turning idly, amounts to the construction of a phenomenological language.[15]

Secondly, it is clear that in passages such as these, Wittgenstein is referring to views that he held at the time of writing the *Tractatus* and not to some hypothetical theory that he had presumably concocted some time in 1929 before throwing it out within a matter of months. There is simply not a shred of textual evidence to support such a claim. There is at any rate a more direct hint that the matter was dealt with within the *Tractatus*, in a letter to Schlick dated August 8, 1932, concerning a paper by Carnap, "Die physikalische Sprache als Universalssprache der Wissenschaft."[16] Wittgenstein had previously accused Carnap of stealing a number of his ideas, and the latter defended himself by claiming that Wittgenstein had not dealt with the question of "physicalism" in the *Tractatus*. Wittgenstein's reply was simply this: "It is not true that I have not dealt with the questions of 'physicalism' (albeit not under this—horrible—name) and with the same brevity with which the entire *Tractatus* is written."[17]

It seems in order, therefore, to look seriously at the possibility that there is such a thing as a "phenomenological" and/or "physicalist" language in the *Tractatus*. One must first try and ascertain what is meant by this "phenomenological" and "physicalist" in this context. Those expecting definitions in accordance with today's high standards of precision will of course be disappointed, but what is important here is to re-enact Wittgenstein's train of thought.

Since Wittgenstein did not use these terms in the *Tractatus*, it is better to look at material from the middle period, where these expressions occur. In Waismann's *Theses*, one finds the following remark:

> The purpose of our ordinary language is to describe what goes on in the world around us. Its end is not to reproduce the logical structure of phenomena. It does, however, speak of the events in our environment by talking of objects (things, bodies), ascribing properties to them, or relating them to each other, etc.[18]

This is a clear indication that Wittgenstein saw the use of terms referring to "objects" (I shall leave aside properties) as the defining feature of ordinary, everyday language. It is also clear that here "objects" means "moderate-size specimens of dry goods," to use Austin's expression.[19] Wittgenstein's examples, when talking about analysis, from watches[20] to lark eggs[21] and brooms,[22] are indeed nearly always of that kind; in this passage from the *Theses*, it is a table.[23] Now the key point, repeated over and over by Wittgenstein in the early 1930s, is that "the concept of an object involves an hypothesis."[24] The hypothesis connects different aspects (*Aspekte*): "The structuring achieved by our language consists, therefore, in assembling all those innumerable aspects in an hypothetically assumed connection."[25] And ordinary language "uses a system of hypotheses" and does so "by means of using nouns."[26] As Wittgenstein would say in his Cambridge lectures: "'Propositions' about physical objects and most of the things we talk about in ordinary life are always really hypotheses."[27] The distinction is assumed to be a strict one, since propositions about physical objects "are not elementary propositions."[28] In the late 1920s and early 1930s, Wittgenstein was holding a form of verificationism: "To analyze a proposition means to consider how the proposition is to be verified."[29] Verification is done by elementary propositions, which "deal with reality immediately."[30] The elementary propositions that verify hypotheses are also called, at times, "phenomenological."[31]

Wittgenstein's terminology has nothing mysterious in it. His notion of "phenomenology" is clearly derived from that of physicists such as Ernst Mach or Ludwig Boltzmann, whose works were known to him. In physics, the idea of a phenomenology has nothing to do with a contrast between entities such as "ideas," "sense impressions," or "sense data" and some "material objects," as is the case with the various philosophical forms of "phenomenalism"; it has to do with the possibility of a self-sufficient description of experience, e.g., a thermodynamics that does not assume molecules.[32] This is what Wittgenstein had in mind, for example, when he writes that he needs for his investigations a "psychological or rather phenomenological colour theory" which is a "theory in *pure* phenomenology in which mention is only made of what is actually perceptible and in which no hypothetical objects—waves, rods, cones and all that—occur."[33]

Wittgenstein's conceptions are also closely linked with the "physicalism" of Neurath and Carnap. The origin of the latter is a matter of controversy, since Wittgenstein claimed, in the above-mentioned letter, that Carnap, who refers instead to Neurath, has stolen his ideas from him.[34] This is not the place to settle this matter but one should note an ambiguity in the writings of Neurath and Carnap. Indeed, "physicalism" is described at times as the thesis that the universal language of science is the "language of physics," while on other occasions, the language referred to is a "thing-language," that is, roughly, the language of terms referring to "moderate-size specimens of dry goods."[35] This second definition became the preferred one but this was, as we just saw, the essential characteristic of Wittgenstein's "physicalist" language.

I have appealed so far to reasonably well-known, incontrovertible facts about Wittgenstein's views after 1929. But, what about the *Tractatus*? Why not simply see a similar model at work in that book? Now it would be utter nonsense to claim that when Wittgenstein wrote about philosophy being a "critique of language" (4.0031) or about the "analysis" of propositions (e.g., at 3.25), he was talking about something else than or excluded from their scope propositions of ordinary, everyday language. So why not see as the *terminus a quo* of analysis propositions of ordinary language, understood in the above sense as having as their primary feature that they talk of "moderate-size specimens of dry goods," and as its *terminus ad quem* phenomenological propositions? I contend that there are no valid objections to this. There are, of course, elements of the 1929 picture that do not carry over. For example, there is no trace of verificationism. Moreover,

Wittgenstein describes "hypothesis" as "a law for constructing statements" (or "expectations"); hypotheses are therefore not constructed as truth-functions of a finite number of such statements.[36] There is no hint of this in the *Tractatus*. The idea appears to have been adopted by Wittgenstein in 1929; it originates in the writings of Hermann Weyl and Frank Ramsey.[37]

However, when such necessary adjustments are made, the above model could serve to explicate the *Tractatus*. It certainly fits a number of uncontroversial facts about it. For example, it is hard indeed not to recognize that the level of elementary propositions is that of immediate experience or "acquaintance." Wittgenstein does speak of "knowing" an object at 2.0123, and when answering a query by C. K. Ogden about the translation of the German *kennen*, Wittgenstein wrote that he meant: "I know *it* but I needn't know anything *about* it."[38] As Norman Malcolm pointed out, this corresponds exactly to Russell's definition of "knowledge by acquaintance."[39] It makes sense at any rate to think in this way, since to know something *about* an object, as it occurs in a proposition, implies knowing the truth of another proposition and such mediation would indicate that the original proposition is not elementary.[40]

It is of course not possible here to convince skeptics—I assume that Hintikka is not one of them—but at least I have now stated my case: in the *Tractatus*, the unanalyzed proposition is a proposition of the ordinary, physicalist language, while the result of its analysis is a bunch of (jointly negated) propositions in phenomenological language. This much is sufficient for the present purposes.

III. THOUGHTS AND OPERATIONS IN THE *TRACTATUS*

Why should the language at the end of analysis be a *phenomenological* language and not a physicalist language of the sort Neurath and Carnap envisaged? There are many ways to answer this and I shall give only one answer here, which will bring out the role of thought in the *Tractatus*. I have qualms with Hintikka's interpretation at least insofar as it relies, at bottom, on a one-sided picture of the *Tractatus*. For reasons that are obvious given his own logical background, Hintikka is primarily interested in semantical relations. Therefore, the picture of the *Tractatus* that comes out of his writings is that of a theory built solely around language-world relations. To my mind, insufficient attention is paid here to thoughts (*Gedanken*) and the thinking (*das Denken*) as the third element of a semiotic "triad."[41] In order to see what I mean by this, one has to go to paragraphs 3.1–3.2 of the *Tractatus* and do a bit of explaining. A thought

(*Gedanke*) is defined at 3.5 as "A propositional sign, applied and thought out." Keeping this in mind, we read:

> 3.11—We use the perceptible sign of a proposition (spoken or written, etc.) as a projection of a possible situation. The method of projection is the thinking (*das Denken*) of the sense of the proposition.[42]

> 3.12—I call the sign with which we express a thought a propositional sign.—And a proposition is a propositional sign in its projective relation to the world.

> . . .

> 3.14— . . . A propositional sign is a fact.

> . . .

> 3.2—In a proposition a thought can be expressed in such a way that elements of the propositional sign correspond to the objects of the thought.

There are three elements here, the "propositional sign," the "proposition," and the "situation" (*Sachlage*), which are united by the "projective relation." (Actually, although it does not appear clearly in these passages, Wittgenstein is merely talking about one thing, namely the [propositional] sign: it can be seen as either a "fact" [3.14], which is perceptible by the senses [3.1 and 3.11] or a "proposition," when projected as the picture of a situation [3.12], or as a "thought," when applied [3.5].)

Wittgenstein distinguishes at 3.32 between "sign" and "symbol": "A sign is what can be perceived of a symbol." Two symbols can share the same sign and to recognize the symbol, one must "observe how it is used with a sense" (3.326). At 3.11, the "perceptible sign of a proposition" is said to be used as "a projection of a possible situation" and at 3.14 this "propositional sign" is said to be a "fact" (*Tatsache*), because only facts can express sense (3.142). From these explanations, it comes out quite clearly that the "propositional sign" is but the *physical* aspect of the proposition, the sounds or marks on the paper.[43] Wittgenstein defines the proposition as "a propositional sign in its projective relation to the world" (3.12) and the latter is defined as "the thinking of the sense of the proposition" (3.11). Since a proposition has sense when it is a picture of a situation, all this amounts to saying that we use a linguistic fact (the "propositional sign") as the picture of a worldly fact, possible or real (a "situation"). Following again 3.326, it is my use of the linguistic fact which shows what I meant by it. This last idea is couched in a different terminology in the *Philosophical Remarks*:

> How is a picture meant? The intention never resides in the picture itself, since, no matter how the picture is formed, it can always be meant in different ways. ... [T]he intention is already expressed in the way I *now* compare the picture with reality.[44]

The expression "method of projection" may be taken from Hertz, but in the context of the analysis of ordinary language, what it is really about is the intentional aspect. This conception can be understood using the example of rules since it seems natural to think that the symbolic expression of a rule cannot serve, of itself, as a guide for its application and, therefore, that any action according to that rule must contain an interpretation of the rule. That is why Wittgenstein spoke in his Cambridge lectures in 1930 of the rule as "contained in our intention."[45] This comes out quite clearly in another passage where Wittgenstein discusses copying, which is a basic form of rule-following:

> The method of projection must be contained in the process of projecting; the process of representation reaches up to what it represents by means of a rule of projection. ... The total result—i.e. the copy *plus the intention*—is the equivalent of the original. The actual result—the mere visible copy—does not represent the whole process of copying; we must include the intention. The *process* contains the rule, the *result* is not enough to describe the process.[46]

I should like to introduce here a short digression on situations. I think that it is important to see how the above comments on 3.1–3.2 fit perfectly within Wittgenstein's formal ontology, properly understood,[47] so that their central place within the *Tractatus* will be recognized. One could clarify the thought expressed at 2.06 by saying that, if an elementary proposition is true, then there obtains or exists (*besteht*) a state of affairs (*Sachverhalt*), this being in itself a "positive fact," which is an atomic one, since it is not the product of simpler ones. If an elementary proposition is false, then the non-existence (*nichtbestehen*) of a state of affairs is an (atomic) "negative fact." Elementary propositions cannot depict only "positive facts," as they all are true. One needs some entities that can be represented by elementary propositions independently of their truth value. This is the role played by situations (*Sachlage*); they are to be identified by the possibility of existence or non-existence of states of affairs. (One is reminded here of Meinong's "objectives.") Wittgenstein also silently distinguishes between "to depict" (*abbilden*) and "to represent" (*darstellen*):[48] a proposition "depicts" a fact or reality, but it "represents" a situation. This distinction is quite visible at 2.201:

> 2.201—A proposition depicts (*abbildet*) by representing (*darstellt*) a possibility of existence or non-existence of states of affairs.

Thus propositions "represent" their sense (2.221) independently of their truth value (2.22). To use a metaphor from the *Notebooks*, the proposition thus casts its "shadow" on the world.[49] It is important that one sees readily that the casting of the shadow here is nothing else than "the thinking of the sense of the proposition" at 3.11. It is also worth noticing that it is at this very juncture that the notion of "logical space," which makes room for the truth tables, comes in:

> 2.11—A picture presents (*stellt*) a situation in logical space, the existence and non-existence of states of affairs.

(I believe, however, that the truth tables are part of a "combinatorics," and not a semantics.[50] I shall give some justification for this below.)

Now, with the propositional sign, the proposition and the situation, we are dealing here not with simple language-world relations, but with three-termed language-thought-world relations. None of the elements can be seen as independent from the others. I cannot argue this here, but there is no asymmetry in the terms, thus no priority of one over the others.[51] It is thus wrong, for example, to believe in the priority of thought and to liken the *Tractatus* to some enterprise à la Fodor, as Norman Malcolm did.[52] Wittgenstein did not put forward a substantial notion of "thought": it is identical to the proposition with sense (3.03–3.032, and 5.61). It does not have properties of its own.[53] Thus the intentional aspect cannot be identified with a process of thinking that would be independent from propositions with sense. And "thought" cannot be understood as the origin of meaning, since there is no substantial notion of "subject": "There is no such thing as the subject that thinks or entertains ideas" (5.631).

It is also wrong to exclude the intentional aspect and to reduce the scaffoldings of the *Tractatus* to mere language-world relations. If the intentional element were to be superfluous, then a proposition should be able to do the job by itself, so to speak, and represent of its own bat what makes it into a picture of a given situation. This is categorically excluded by Wittgenstein at 3.332, 4.12–4.121, and 4.442. This important fact is at the basis of the saying/showing distinction. After all, it takes someone to see (*ersehen*) what shows itself![54] I do not think that in the *Philosophical Remarks* Wittgenstein was expressing a newly acquired idea when he wrote, "If you exclude the element of intention from language, its whole function then collapses."[55]

In conversation with Schlick and Waismann, Wittgenstein expressed thoughts remarkably similar to those of the *Tractatus* (although he is referring, within that conversation, to a manuscript from 1931):

> I again and again concern myself with the question, What does it mean to

> *understand* a proposition? This is connected with the general question of what
> it is what people call *intention, to mean, meaning*. . . . I now believe [for my
> part] that understanding is not a particular psychological process at all that is
> there in addition, supplementary to the perception of a propositional picture.
> . . . I understand a proposition by *applying* it. Understanding is thus not a
> particular process; it is operating with a proposition. *The point of a proposition
> is that we should operate with it.* (What I do, too, is an operation.) . . .
> Understanding a word or a proposition is calculating. . . . What I am doing with
> the words of a language in *understanding* them is exactly the same thing I do
> with a sign in the calculus: I operate with them.[56]

One should recall that in the *Tractatus* "intuition" or other mental processes
of the sort were already excluded from "calculation" (6.233–6.2331).
Keeping in mind the parallels here with key passages such as 3.5, there is
no reason to believe that in the *Tractatus* Wittgenstein did not hold such a
combinatory view of intentionality *as mere manipulations of or operations
with signs*. Now I would like to insist on this: granted that there is no
substantial "subject" in the *Tractatus*, it remains that the "seeing" at 5.13,
6.1221 or 6.232, the "projecting," at, for instance, 3.11, the "thinking" of
the sense of the proposition at 3.12, the "applying" of the propositional sign
at 3.5, and so forth, are all *activities* or *operations* by a (generic) user of (the
system of) signs.

One should note that, if operating with signs requires an agent, to this
agent the propositions must of necessity be "phenomenological" entities. In
this sense of the expression "phenomenological," the *Tractatus* is indeed
phenomenological through and through.

An "operation" is defined as "what has to be done to the one proposition in order to make the other out of it" (5.23); in non-Wittgensteinian
terms, it is the *act* by which one obtains a proposition from another
proposition.[57] This is not an extensional concept. The concept of "operation" plays a fundamental role in the *Tractatus*, which can immediately be
seen by pointing out that the most important "variables" of the book, the
general form of a truth function at 6 and the general form of an integer at
6.021 are variants on the general term, given at 5.2522, for a series of forms
generated by operations. First, the concept of operation allows Wittgenstein
to introduce the calculus of truth functions in logic. Indeed, the truth
functions of elementary propositions are defined by Wittgenstein as "results
of operations with elementary propositions as bases" (5.234). These
particular operations, "denial," "negation," "logical addition," "logical
multiplication" (5.2341), he calls "truth-operations" (*Warheitsoperationen*)
(5.234). For Frege, logical connectives such as 'and' or 'or' were terms
denoting functions whose domains were pairs of truth values and co-
domains the values True and False. The connectives were thus conceived
of as functions like any other function but for Wittgenstein "Truth-

Functions are not material functions" (5.44), they are the "results of successive applications to elementary propositions of a finite number of truth-operations" (5.32). This is one reason among many for believing that there is no set-theoretical, "functional" semantics such as Frege's in the *Tractatus*. One finds instead a constructivist, Leibnizian *Ars combinatoria*.

Second, Wittgenstein defines the natural numbers (6.02–6.031) and the elementary arithmetical operations (addition and multiplication) on them (6.241) in terms of "operations," actually in terms of successive application of an operation—as he says: "exponent[s] of an operation" (6.021)—which prefigure the definition of Church numerals in the λ-calculus. The implication here is that Wittgenstein rejects the logicist reduction of arithmetic to some class-theoretical system (6.031). Again, the intensional nature of the notion of operation is evident.[58]

One of the least understood dimensions of the *Tractatus* is its implicit distinction between what could be termed the static and the dynamical. The ontology of the *Tractatus* is about "simple objects" and "states of affairs," not even "events." It is static. However, there are *acts* or *operations* such as "denying," "adding," and the like. These are never captured by Wittgenstein's ontology. They are not part of the furniture of the world, so to speak. To use a terminology foreign to Wittgenstein, operations pertain to the domain of "doing," not to that of "being." The key feature of the concept of operation is that an operation does not assert anything; only its result does (see 5.25). If one has a proposition p, stating, say, that it rains, one can use the operation of negation and turn it into $\neg p$, which states that it is not the case that it rains. Both p and $\neg p$ assert something. Both are also propositional signs, hence facts, but *operations are never facts*. The notion of "thought" is complicated by this very distinction, since it is both an act, as in "the thinking of the sense of the proposition" but also, as a *Gedanke*, it is a fact.[59]

IV. Semantics?

Analytic philosophers are often criticized for not clearly separating their historical inquiries from their own philosophical preoccupations. Anachronism is a definite risk. To this, I would merely reply that there are also limits to historicism, limits that ought to be learned by those interested in the history of analytical philosophy. It is hard indeed to carry on making unsophisticated appeals to the author's "intention" or to even more far-fetched incommensurability claims about the impossibility of philosophers to understand each other. These limits leave ample room for fruitful re-appropriation of past philosophies that shed at the same time new light on them. This is what Hintikka has done with Wittgenstein and I have no quarrels with the appropriateness of this maneuver. I believe that his writings on Wittgenstein are full of gems.[60]

It is useful indeed that we look at Hintikka's writings on Wittgenstein from his own angle of approach, that is, from the point of view of a logician who has made landmark contributions to semantics. Not unlike Carnap, with his concept of "state-description,"[61] Hintikka developed some of his most fruitful ideas, such as the concept of "model set," in connection with his thinking about the *Tractatus*.[62] It is a logician with a very acute sense of underlying semantical issues who reads Wittgenstein. Hintikka's interest in Wittgenstein is not incidental: he agrees with some of the key ideas such as the idea of meaning as being mediated by language games,[63] which is fundamental to Hintikka's own game-theoretical semantics. He even described the latter as "the true Wittgensteinian semantics for first-order logic."[64] As he pointed out, Beth's tableau method and his own version of it—which led to his game-theoretical semantics—"capture the spirit of Wittgenstein's guiding ideas."[65] It is not possible fully to discuss this issue here, but it seems to me that, although Hintikka is entitled to such claims, they cannot be the whole story about Wittgenstein.

I shall conclude by supporting these claims with a broad sketch of two lines of argument, in line with the remarks from the previous section. It seems to me that the purpose of Hintikka's interpretation of the *Tractatus* is not truly to try and recover the gist of his logical ideas, but rather to show how he moved away from his earlier views, which he himself finds at any rate mistaken, towards some insights that, in turn, can be seen as fundamental for Hintikka's own conceptions. Again, I see nothing wrong in principle in this maneuver, but I think that, in order to perform it, Hintikka has to rely on an "extensional" interpretation of the *Tractatus* and that some of the logical ideas in the *Tractatus* are thereby passed over in silence.

I have hinted in the previous section at the idea that there is no semantics but rather a "combinatorics" in the *Tractatus*. I cannot pursue this idea here, nor can I discuss its implications vis-à-vis Hintikka's thesis that Wittgenstein is a semanticist without a semantics. I should say a few things, however, about the extensional viewpoint. Work by Wolfgang Stegmüller, André Maury, and the late Georg Henrik von Wright has considerably undermined the validity of interpretations of the *Tractatus* relying on the "principle of extensionality."[66] It is clear, for example, that 5.525 cannot provide support for a reduction of modal notions to extensional notions, in accordance with Carnap's "thesis of extensionality."[67] Hintikka's stand on the intensional aspects of the *Tractatus* is not immediately clear. That he has not sufficiently dealt with this issue is shown for example by his identification of the "simple objects" with Russellian "objects of acquaintance": Russellian sense data are purely extensional, while Wittgenstein's concept of simple object is intensional. To see this, one merely has to consider again 2.0123, which states that "if I know an object I also know all its possible occurrences in states of affairs." Furthermore, Russell defines "objects" in a purely extensional manner as classes of sense data[68] but in 1929 Wittgenstein defines them as "hypotheses," again in a non-extensional manner, and he criticizes Russell's definition.[69] Admittedly, this is not relevant to the discussion of the *Tractatus*, but it is not clear to me to which extent Hintikka's semantical concepts can be viewed as genetically linked with Wittgenstein's ideas. Perhaps the genetic link would be clear if, *inter alia*, quantifiers had been reduced extensionally in the *Tractatus*, to begin with, as (finite or infinite) conjunctions or disjunctions. This is a possible reading, which has strong textual support, but one should not forget that Wittgenstein is also at pains at 5.521 to distinguish generality from truth functions. At any rate, even if it were true that Wittgenstein's position in the *Tractatus* is "extensional," von Wright has pointed out that this would be true only as far as what can be said is concerned, and not about what shows itself.[70] But, as I shall presently claim, some of the most intriguing ideas of the *Tractatus* concern inferential acts, and these can only be seen.

The central role of operations in the *Tractatus* points in another direction, namely a reflection on inference. The parallels here with Gentzen's conceptions, and thus with a proof-theoretical tradition, are striking indeed.[71] First, Wittgenstein rejects the axiomatic conception of logic. At 6.127 he wrote that all propositions of logic are of "equal status": "it is not the case that some of them are essentially primitive propositions and others essentially derived propositions." This is strangely reminiscent of Gentzen's calculi of natural deduction. Secondly, at 6.1223 Wittgenstein indicated correctly that logical truths are to be seen as *by-products* of the derivation of true sentences from true sentences,[72] and at 6.1271 Wittgenstein mocks Frege's appeal to evidence in order to justify them. At 6.1224, he reaffirms the traditional view of logic as dealing with (valid) inference and not with truth (as Frege believed). Again, all this is conceptually nearer to Gentzen's calculi. Finally, at 5.132 Wittgenstein wrote that "Laws of Inference," such as the modus ponens used by Frege and Russell, "have no sense, and would be superfluous." Here, Wittgenstein aims at the transgression of the saying/showing distinction—in other words: at the language/metalanguage distinction—at work in the axiomatic conception of logic. These aspects of the *Tractatus* are somewhat occulted by a reading of the *Tractatus* which focuses merely on the language-world relations.

MATHIEU MARION

CANADA RESEARCH CHAIR
    IN PHILOSOPHY OF LOGIC AND MATHEMATICS
UNIVERSITY OF QUEBEC AT MONTREAL
AUGUST 2003

NOTES

1. See Jaakko Hintikka, "'*Cogito Ergo Sum*': Inference or Performance,"
Philosophical Review 71 (1962): 3–32 and "'*Cogito Ergo Sum*' as an Inference and
a Performance," *Philosophical Review* 72 (1963): 487–96. For an example of the
sustained interest in Hintikka's thoughts on this topic see: S. Bourgeois-Gironde,
Reconstruction analytique du cogito (Paris: Vrin, 2001).

2. Jaakko Hintikka, "Identity, Variables and Impredicative Definitions,"
Journal of Symbolic Logic 21 (1956): 225–45.

3. Jaakko Hintikka, "On Wittgenstein's Solipsism," *Mind* 64 (1958): 88–91.

4. In this paper, I refer to the Pears-McGuinness translation of Ludwig
Wittgenstein, *Tractatus Logico-Philosophicus* (London: Routledge & Kegan Paul,
1961) by paragraph number in the text.

5. Merrill B. Hintikka and Jaakko Hintikka, *Investigating Wittgenstein*
(Oxford: Blackwell, 1986).

6. Some of them are now collected in Jaakko Hintikka, *Selected Papers 1*,
Ludwig Wittgenstein: Half Truths and One-and-a-Half Truth (Dordrecht: Kluwer,
1996).

7. For reasons of convenience, I shall speak hereafter of Jaakko Hintikka's
interpretation of Wittgenstein, when I should, strictly speaking, refer more often
than not to joint work with the late Merrill B. Hintikka.

8. As Hintikka says himself, a lack of proper understanding of this transition
will lead only to half-truths about Wittgenstein's philosophy. See Hintikka, *Selected
Papers 1*, p. 80.

9. Hintikka and Hintikka, *Investigating Wittgenstein*, p. 138.

10. "In briefest possible terms, Wittgenstein's 'deduction' thus ran as follows:
the basic sentences of our language must be compared directly with (virtually,
superimposed on) the facts they represent. But since language itself belongs to the
physical world . . . such comparisons must take place in the physical world. Hence
only what there is in the physical world can be represented directly in the language"
(Hintikka and Hintikka, *Investigating Wittgenstein*, p. 166). That Wittgenstein
reasoned in these terms is, according to textual evidence, incontrovertible. In what
follows, I shall not discuss this point but I should point out that since M. B. and J.
Hintikka wrote those lines, more textual evidence became public, in the form of one
of Wittgenstein's dictations to Waismann, "phänomenale Sprache," where one finds
another statement of that "deduction." See G. Baker, ed., *The Voices of Wittgenstein:
The Vienna Circle* (London and New York: Routledge, 2003), pp. 313–37.

11. Saul Kripke, *Wittgenstein on Rules and Private Language* (Cambridge
Mass.: Harvard University Press, 1982).

12. Among the relatively small literature on the topic, I should point out a pair
of articles by David Pears: "Hintikka's Interpretation of Wittgenstein's Treatment
of Sensation-Language," *Grazer philosophische Studien* 49 (1994/5): 1–18 and "Le
Wittgenstein de Hintikka," in *Jaakko Hintikka: Questions de Logique et de*

phénoménologie, ed. E. Rigal (Paris: Vrin, 1998), pp. 259–74.

13. Erik Stenius, *Wittgenstein's* Tractatus*: A Critical Exposition of the Main Lines of Thought* (Oxford: Blackwell, 1960); André Maury, *The Concepts of* Sinn *and* Gegenstand *in Wittgenstein's* Tractatus, *Acta Philosophica Fennica* 29 (1977); Heikki Kannisto, *Thoughts and their Subject: A Study of Wittgenstein's* Tractatus, *Acta Philosophica Fennica* 40 (1986); Georg Henrik von Wright, *Wittgenstein* (Oxford: Blackwell, 1982).

14. Ludwig Wittgenstein, *Ludwig Wittgenstein and the Vienna Circle*, ed. Brian McGuinness, trans. Joachim Schulte and Brian McGuinness (Oxford: Blackwell, 1979), p. 45.

15. Ludwig Wittgenstein, *Philosophical Remarks* (Oxford: Blackwell, 1975), §1. One should immediately note that Wittgenstein's alternatives are between having or not having a "basic" language that expresses "what we really knew," and not, as was the case within the Vienna Circle, a choice between two "protocol" languages, that of the "physical objects" and that of the "autopsychological objects," to use Carnap's expressions. See Rudolf Carnap, *The Logical Structure of the World* (Berkeley/Los Angeles: University of California Press, 1967; Chicago: Open Court, 2003).

16. Rudolf Carnap, "Die physikalische Sprache als Universalssprache der Wissenschaft," *Erkenntnis* 2 (1931): 432–65; English translation: *The Unity of Science* (Bristol: Thoemmes, 1995).

17. This passage is quoted in Jaakko Hintikka, "Ludwig's Apple Tree: On the Philosophical Relations Between Wittgenstein and the Vienna Circle," reprinted in Jaakko Hintikka, *Selected Papers 1*, p. 137.

18. *Wittgenstein and the Vienna Circle*, p. 254. In order not to burden the reader with too many quotations, I shall stick mainly to that text. But all ideas contained in it are to be found elsewhere in the writings or notes from the transitional period.

19. J. L. Austin, *Sense and Sensibilia* (Oxford: Oxford University Press, 1962), p. 8.

20. Wittgenstein, *Notebooks 1914–1916*, 2nd ed., ed. G. H. von Wright and G.E.M. Anscombe, trans. G.E.M. Anscombe (Oxford: Blackwell, 1979), p. 61.

21. Wittgenstein, *Wittgenstein and the Vienna Circle*, p. 101.

22. Wittgenstein, *Philosophical Investigations* (Oxford: Blackwell, 1953), §60.

23. Wittgenstein, *Wittgenstein and the Vienna Circle*, p. 256.

24. Ibid., p. 256. I have discussed this notion of "hypothesis" in great detail in Mathieu Marion, *Wittgenstein, Finitism, and the Foundations of Mathematics* (Oxford: Clarendon Press, 1998), chs. 4 and 5.

25. Wittgenstein, *Wittgenstein and the Vienna Circle*, p. 256.

26. Ibid.

27. Ludwig Wittgenstein, *Wittgenstein's Lectures: Cambridge 1930–1932*, ed. Desmond Lee (Oxford: Blackwell, 1980), p. 53.

28. Wittgenstein, *Wittgenstein and the Vienna Circle*, p. 249.

29. Ibid.

30. Ibid., p. 248.

31. Ibid., p. 101.

32. For an early occurrence of the term "phenomenology," see Ernst Mach, "On the Principle of Comparison in Physics: An Address delivered before the General Session of the German Association of Naturalists and Physicians, at Vienna, Sept. 24, 1894," later published in *Popular Scientific Lectures* (La Salle, Ill.: Open Court, 1943), p. 250. For Boltzmann's understanding of Mach, see Ludwig Boltzmann, *Theoretical Physics and Philosophical Problems* (Dordrecht: D. Reidel, 1974), pp. 93f. Here again, Hintikka has explored the connections, see "The Idea of Phenomenology in Wittgenstein and Husserl," in *Selected Papers 1*, pp. 55–77; see also pp. 212f.

33. Wittgenstein, *Philosophical Remarks*, §218.

34. For opposite points of view in this dispute, see Friedrich Stadler, *The Vienna Circle: Studies in the Origins, Development, and Influence of Logical Empiricism* (Vienna/New York: Springer, 2001), pp. 429–38; Hintikka, "Ludwig's Apple Tree," pp. 125–44.

35. The contrast can be seen, for example, in Neurath's writings. Indeed, at times he presents the universal language as the language of physics. See Otto Neurath, *Philosophical Papers 1913–1946* (Dordrecht: D. Reidel, 1983), pp. 54–55. On the other hand, Neurath speaks of the universal language as a purified version of everyday language, which he identifies with the language of physics. See Neurath, *Philosophical Papers 1913–1946*, pp. 62, 91. On this terminological matter, see Wolfgang Stegmüller, *Main Currents in German, British and American Philosophy* (Bloomington: Indiana University Press, 1969), pp. 292–95.

36. Wittgenstein, *Wittgenstein and the Vienna Circle*, p. 255.

37. For a detailed discussion, see Marion, *Wittgenstein, Finitism, and the Foundations of Mathematics*, chs. 4, 5.

38. Wittgenstein, *Letters to C. K. Ogden* (Oxford/London: Blackwell/Routledge Kegan Paul, 1973), p. 59.

39. Norman Malcolm, *Nothing is Hidden* (Oxford: Blackwell, 1986), pp. 8–9.

40. I should point out further that Wittgenstein's simple objects are not mere appearances or impressions, as opposed to the "real" objects; there is no trace of phenomenalism in Wittgenstein's philosophy and there need not be any, although reference to Russell might mislead here. As pointed out above in reference to the meaning of "phenomenology" in physics, the contrast here is not between sense-impressions or the like and some "material" objects but between a self-sufficient phenomenology and the appeal to "hypotheses." As Wittgenstein himself wrote, "the point of talking of sense-data and immediate experience is that we're after a description that has nothing hypothetical in it" (*Philosophical Remarks*, §226). Strangely enough, this mistake is often imputed to Hintikka himself, although he repeatedly warned his readers. See, e.g., *Selected Papers 1*, pp. 58, 128, or 194.

41. See François Latraverse, "Signe, proposition, situation : éléments pour une lecture du *Tractatus logico-philosophicus*," *Revue internationale de philosophie*

219 (2002): 125–40. I had expressed similar views in Mathieu Marion, "Operations and Numbers in the Tractatus," *Wittgenstein Studien* 2 (2000): 105–123.

42. I modify slightly the Pears-McGuinness translation. For reasons for doing so, see P.M.S. Hacker, "Naming, Thinking and Meaning in the *Tractatus*," *Philosophical Investigations* 22 (1999): 119–35.

43. I am aware that this meaning of "physical" is not exactly the same as the above (i.e., as in the definition of "physicalist" language). But the two meanings are not unrelated.

44. Wittgenstein, *Philosophical Remarks*, §24.

45. Wittgenstein, *Wittgenstein's Lectures*, p. 40.

46. Ibid., pp. 36–37.

47. To my mind, the best paper on the topic is Peter Simons, "The Old Problem of Complex and Fact," reprinted in *Philosophy and Logic in Central Europe from Bolzano to Tarski: Selected Essays* (Dordrecht: Kluwer, 1992), pp. 319–38.

48. I owe this distinction to conversations with J. Plourde.

49. Wittgenstein, *Notebooks*, pp. 27, 30.

50. Peter Simons is nearer the mark when he speaks of a "combinatorial" semantics. See Peter Simons, "Wittgenstein and the Semantics of Combination," in *Philosophy of Mind/Philosophy of Psychology*, ed. R. Chisholm, J. C. Marek, J. T, Blackmore, A. Hübner (Vienna: Hölder-Pichler-Tempsky, 1985), pp. 446–49.

51. See Latraverse, "Signe, Proposition, Situation," p. 130.

52. N. Malcolm, *Nothing is Hidden*, p. 67.

53. See Latraverse, "Signe, Proposition, Situation," p. 136.

54. On the other hand, the relation between a thought and a fact is "internal" and there is no need for an extra element of recognition (*Philosophical Remarks*, §21).

55. Ibid., §20.

56. Wittgenstein, *Wittgenstein and the Vienna Circle*, pp. 167–70.

57. On "operations" in the *Tractatus*, see Marion, "Operations and Numbers in the *Tractatus*."

58. On these points, see Pasquale Frascolla, *Wittgenstein's Philosophy of Mathematics* (London: Routledge, 1994), ch. 1; Pasquale Frascolla, "The *Tractatus* System of Arithmetic," *Synthese* 112 (1997): 353–78; and my "Operations and Numbers in the *Tractatus*."

59. See Kannisto, *Thoughts and their Subject: A Study of Witgenstein's* Tractatus, p. 99.

60. One such gem, that I did not discuss here, is a set of remarks concerning the origin of Wittgenstein's finitism. See *Selected Papers 1*, pp. 85–88, 158, 166–67. One can see my *Wittgenstein, Finitism, and the Foundations of Mathematics* as an independent vindication of these remarks.

61. Rudolf Carnap, *Meaning and Necessity* (Chicago: University of Chicago Press, 1956), pp. 9–10.

62. See, e.g., the remarks on his concept of "model set" in Jaakko Hintikka, *Logic, Language-Games and Information: Kantian Themes in the Philosophy of*

430   MATHIEU MARION

Logic (Oxford: Clarendon Press, 1973), ch. 2.

63. See, e.g., Hintikka, *Selected Papers 1*, pp. 151, 156, 174.

64. Ibid., p. 166. However, according to Hintikka, Wittgenstein has misunderstood the nature of quantifiers, by not tying them, as he did, to seeking-and-finding games.

65. E. W. Beth, "Semantic Entailment and Formal Derivability," *Medelingen van de Koninklijke Nederlandse Akademie van Wetenschappen, Afdeling Letterkunde, n.r.* 18 (1955): 309–42; Jaakko Hintikka, "Form and Content in Quantification Theory," *Two Papers on Symbolic Logic*, Acta Philosophica Fennica 8 (Helsinki: Philosophical Society of Finland, 1955), pp. 11–55; Hintikka, *Selected Papers 1*, p. 100. I remember, for example, a conversation with Kreisel where it became clear that the idea of Herbrand expansion, which is related to Hintikka's method, was close to Wittgenstein's own preoccupations as late as after the war.

66. Wolfgang Stegmüller, "Ein modelltheoretische Präzisierung der wittgensteinschen Bildtheorie," *Notre Dame Journal of Formal Logic* 7 (1966): 181–95; André Maury, *The Concepts of* Sinn *and* Gegenstand *in Wittgenstein's* Tractatus; G. H. von Wright, *Wittgenstein*. For the "principle of extensionality" in the *Tractatus*, see, e.g., Max Black, *A Companion to Wittgenstein's Tractatus* (Ithaca: Cornell University Press, 1964), pp. 280–81, 298.

67. This thesis was perceived by Carnap as a generalization of Wittgenstein's thesis at 5, that "A proposition is a truth-function of elementary propositions." Rudolf Carnap, *Logical Syntax of Language* (London: Routledge & Kegan Paul, 1937), p. 245 or *Meaning and Necessity*, p. 141.

68. Bertrand Russell, *Our Knowledge of the External World* (London: Routledge, 1993), pp. 107, 115–16.

69. Wittgenstein, *Wittgenstein and the Vienna Circle*, p. 257.

70. Von Wright, *Wittgenstein*, p. 186.

71. These parallels are discussed in Gilles-Gaston Granger, "Wittgenstein et la métalangue," *Revue internationale de philosophie* 23 (1969): 77–87 and Mathieu Marion, "Qu'est-ce que l'inférence? Une relecture du Tractatus logico-philosophicus, *Archives de philosophie* 64 (2001): 545–67.

72. On this point, see Ian Hacking, "What is Logic?" *Journal of Philosophy* 76 (1979): 285–319, especially pp. 288–89.

REPLY TO MATHIEU MARION

I have read Mathieu Marion's lucid and knowledgeable essay with pleasure. There is much in his paper that I can agree with. However, it seems to me that some of his main theses require qualifications and modifications. My task in this response is therefore to put forward those qualifications. This format should not mislead the readers to overlook the large area of agreement between the two of us, agreement which Marion generously spells out. For one important example, we agree that the phenomenological objects Wittgenstein speaks of in the late twenties are nothing but the simple objects of the *Tractatus*.[1]

One of Marion's main theses is that "in the *Tractatus*, the unanalyzed proposition is a proposition of the ordinary physicalist language, while the result of its analysis is a bunch of . . . propositions in phenomenological language." The notion of analysis used here can be seen from Marion's statement that "The meaning of sentences in ordinary language could be made explicit which would ultimately transcribe them in a 'phenomenological' language." I see this notion of analysis (attributed to the *Tractatus*) as revealing the meaning of ordinary language sentences in need of further scrutiny. In the last analysis, the *Tractatus* recognizes one and only one way in which a sentence in any language can have meaning, viz., being a picture of a state of affairs. Of course the word "picture" has to be taken in a special sense. It serves to highlight that according to Wittgenstein the vehicle of linguistic representation is the form of a sentence, the form that it shares with the corresponding fact when it is true. This applies to sentences of ordinary language as well as those of the purified language envisaged in the *Tractatus*. (Let us call languages of the latter kind "Tractarian languages.") What makes the difference is that in a Tractarian language this representative form is captured by the syntactical form of the sentence in question, whereas the representative forms of ordinary language expressions have to be gathered from their use. To use Wittgenstein's jargon when one understands the meaning of an ordinary language sentence, one sees the sentence as a picture.

Hence, whatever it is in the analysis that brings out the meaning of ordinary discursive sentences, its function is to reveal their pictorial forms. Now there is in the *Tractatus* an argument to show that the meaning of all sentences can be thus understood pictorially.

This argument forms in fact the plot of Wittgenstein's work. But what is being analyzed is not natural language meaning, but meaning in a Tractarian language. Wittgenstein thought that he already had an almost fully analyzed universal language at his disposal, viz., the language of *Principia Mathematica*. It was not completely satisfactory, but by and large it served as the target of his analysis.[2] What Wittgenstein argued was that such a language can be seen as being pictorial. First, quantifiers are analyzed in terms of truth-functions. Second, the picture interpretation is extended from elementary sentences to all their truth-functions. But this analysis—if "analysis" is the right word—is not analysis of ordinary language except in so far as it has already been translated in the *Begriffsschrift* presented in the *Principia Mathematica*.

This evidence shows that the main analysis actually offered in the bulk of the *Tractatus* is not an analysis of propositions of ordinary language into a phenomenological language. The main analysis is a proof that the propositions of an already regimented language can—and must—be seen as pictorial. This account does not show that the *Tractatus* does not presuppose an analysis of the propositions of ordinary language in phenomenological terms. Such an analysis will amount to a translation of our everyday language into a regimented notation not unlike Russell's and Whitehead's *Principia Mathematica*.[3]

Much of Russell's work just before World War I dealt with such translation, or rather with its mirror image, logical construction. Wittgenstein may very well have been so impatient as to leave all the details of such "logical construction of the world" to Russell. Perhaps in some sense he did. But even if he did, there are a number of things that remain to be said about the *Tractatus*.

I can in a sense agree with Marion that for Wittgenstein ordinary language is physicalistic and that he envisages a kind of translation of it into a phenomenological language. But if so, we have to clarify the distinction between phenomenological and physical objects. I am dealing with this distinction also in my response to David Pears, and hence I can be brief here. The upshot of the discussion there is that the distinction between the two kinds of objects does not concern their metaphysical status in a dimension like the mental vs. the physical, but their availability to immediate awareness. Now Marion obviously sees some sort of metaphysical distinction here. I do not find any such distinction in Wittgenstein.

This point can be put in a historical perspective. The background of the distinction in Wittgenstein is Moore's and Russell's deep conviction that our consciousness can reach all the way to some objects in the real world, not only to "phenomena." According to Moore's "Refutation of Idealism" one can in any one experience distinguish the experience itself as an event in one's consciousness from its object, which is present in my mind but at the same time part of the real world. Of course, not all objects in the external world can be such objects. For instance, much as Russell and Moore would perhaps have liked to think of ordinary physical objects as potential direct objects of sensory experience, the fallibility of sense experience concerning them dissuaded them from so doing. Hence the objects of sense perception, dubbed "sense data" by Moore and Russell, are something more immediately present to our senses. But sense sdata belong nevertheless firmly to the external physical world.

It seems to me that by and large the same can be said of the objects assumed in the *Tractatus*. For Wittgenstein in the *Tractatus*, objects are objects of experience, but this does not imply any relation to an experiencing person. "All experience is world and does not need the subject."[4] The distinction between phcnomenological and physical objects in Wittgenstein is simply the difference between objects that can be, in Russell's and Moore's sense, objects of our experience and those that cannot serve in such a capacity. It is in this sense that all the simple objects of the *Tractatus* are phenomenological. Wittgenstein's view is expressed clearly in his *Notebooks 1914–1916*: "What seems to be given us a priori is the concept: *This*. —Identical with the concept of the *object*."[5] Phenomenological objects in this sense are not intentional or mental. It is this inaccessibility of physical (nonphenomenological) entities to immediate awareness that Wittgenstein refers to as their "hypothetical" character.

Needless to say, there is in the historical texts, including Wittgenstein's writings, plenty of confusion concerning the distinction. In the last analysis, we should not think of it as a distinction between two kinds of objects, but as a distinction between two modes of identifying objects. Actually, Wittgenstein was in this respect much more insightful than any of his contemporaries, as is shown by *The Blue Book*.[6] In any case, the distinction cannot be identified with a contrast between "phenomena" and "moderate-size specimens of dry goods."

Thus a translation or paraphrase of ordinary language statements into phenomenological ones could not have been a translation of an extensional discourse to an intensional one or have involved any kind of replacement of physical objects in the ordinary sense of the word by mind-dependent entities. The translation is purely and simply a reduction to acquaintance in Russell's sense. At the same time when we realize what the contrast between phenomenological and everyday physical objects meant for Wittgenstein, we can appreciate better the peculiarities of this reduction.

Somewhat surprisingly, it seems that Russell—and presumably Wittgenstein, too—thought of the reduction to acquaintance as being tantamount to expressing the content of ordinary language sentences in the logical language of the *Principia*. Among other things, we are in a position to register an important tacit assumption that the early Wittgenstein and Russell shared. There is a statement at the end of Russell's "On Denoting" that completely boggled my mind when I first read it. Russell says there that his theory of definite descriptions serves to prove the reducibility to acquaintance. What can Russell possibly have in mind here? The theory of definite descriptions is a piece of logico-linguistic analysis quite innocent of the epistemological, ontological, and semantical implications of the reducibility thesis. Yet we can understand what Russell had in mind. The theory of definite description is a sermon on the text "to be is to be a value of a quantifier." It shows that the only entities we have to postulate are the ones we quantify over. But why should these values be objects of acquaintance? We begin to understand Russell when we realize that for him the only possible kind of quantification is over the objects given to us in experience, that is, over phenomenological objects. In other words (of which Russell was blissfully ignorant), the only possible mode of identification was for him the perspectival one. Accordingly, the only logically proper names of English are the ones that identify an object perspectivally, viz., "this," "that," and (according to Russell) "I." A more common name for the simplest forms of such an identification is ostensive identification.

There is no reason to believe that this, as it were, logical preference of phenomenological objects was not shared by Wittgenstein. It is an important part of what Wittgenstein gave up in October 1929.

Wittgenstein's preference in the *Tractatus* of phenomenological objects is relevant here because it shows that Marion has indeed seen something important when he speaks of the Wittgensteinean reduction in the *Tractatus* as a reduction to phenomenological entities. Unfortunately, the targets of the reduction in question are not intensional entities, but objects of acquaintance.

Marion says that I should have paid more attention to the intensional aspect of the *Tractatus*. I must confess that I find it very hard to understand what he means. Marion never spells out fully what he means by "intensional." What seems to be the case is that what is intensional must somehow involve human thinking. But it is not at all clear that all the senses of "intensional" relied on by Marion really involve human consciousness. For one thing, the kind of intensionality emphasized by Stegmüller and von Wright amounts to assuming the existence of many alternative possibilities. Wittgenstein makes such an assumption, and the only reason why he does not express it by speaking of possible worlds is that according to him one cannot speak of any worlds, real or possible, as closed totalities. But one can deal with such multiplicity of possible states of affairs conceptually without any reference to human consciousness.

The most common meaning of intensionality is the failure of the logical law of the substitutivity of identity. But in this sense the logic of the *Tractatus* is extensional, no matter how we understand his technical treatment of identity, because for Wittgenstein a name refers to the same object in all possible states of affairs.

It may be that in one sense Wittgenstein's simple objects involve thinking, for they are defined ostensively. (This is shown by his criticism of ostensive definitions in the beginning of *Philosophical Investigations*, for what he is there criticizing is fairly obviously the philosophy of the *Tractatus*.) But in the same sense Russell's objects of acquaintance are "intensional," named as they are by "this" and "that." All told, I fail to find in Marion's paper any real evidence against my near-identification of Wittgenstein's simple objects and Russell's objects of acquaintance. The only respect in which this identification must be qualified is that for Wittgenstein logical forms were not a subclass of objects of acquaintance, as they were for Russell in 1913.

Wittgenstein's conception of meaning has two components. Propositional meaning is pictorial. The truth of a proposition is ascertained purely objectively by comparing its structure with that of facts, by "putting it on the top of a fact," as Wittgenstein later expressed himself. The only place where thinking comes in is in the meaning of simple names. But this symbol meaning should be thought of as having only the kind of intentionality that is involved in an ostensive definition.

A couple of further remarks may be in order here. Marion compares Gentzen's systems of logical inference to Wittgenstein's idea of operations. I find such a comparison less convincing than another way of relating Gentzen's rules to Wittgenstein's ideas. If you invert Gentzen's rules, you can understand them as rules of attempted model construction by means of E. W. Beth's tableaux. This comes very close to the view Wittgenstein sometimes expressed during his middle-period, the idea of propositions, not as pictures, but as recipes of picture construction.

Marion writes that "If operating with signs requires an agent, to this agent the propositions must of necessity be 'phenomenological' entities." I suspect that this claim touches the rawest of all raw nerves in Wittgenstein's thinking. Wittgenstein had a sense of the possibility of mechanical operating with signs that a machine can carry out. He tried to understand human rule-following by means of an analogous rule-following by a machine. But he never felt that he understood the connection between such blind rule-following and the actual applications of calculation or of other ways of operating with signs. Marion's "of necessity" was for Wittgenstein an impossibility, or at best a dire difficulty, in the light of psychological hindsight undoubtedly caused by his dyslexia. I am afraid that here Marion has not fully grasped what it would be like to think like Wittgenstein.

J. H.

NOTES

1. Ludwig Wittgenstein, *Tractatus Logico-Philosophicus* (London: Kegan Paul, 1922).

2. See Wittgenstein, *Tractatus* 3.325.

3. Bertrand Russell and Alfred North Whitehead, *Principia Mathematica* (Cambridge: Cambridge University Press, 1910–1913).

4. Ludwig Wittgenstein, *Notebooks 1914–1916* (Oxford: Blackwell, 1961), p. 89.

5. Ibid., p. 61.

6. Ludwig Wittgenstein, *The Blue & Brown Books* (Oxford: Blackwell, 1958), pp. 58–68.

11

Raymond M. Smullyan

A LOGICAL MISCELLANY

The pioneering work of Hintikka[1] on tableaux and model sets was a major influence on my own work in first-order logic. I shall now present some themes that I hope will be of interest to Hintikka. Part I consists of some topics in propositional logic. Part II (the "fun" part) and Part III on paradoxes can each be read independently of Part I.

I. SOME PROPOSITIONAL TIDBITS

1. *Some Interrelations between Logical Connectives*

It is, of course, well known that all logical connectives are definable from ~ and any one of the connectives $\wedge$, $\vee$, and $\supset$. Perhaps a trifle less well known is the fact that $\vee$ is definable from $\supset$ alone. [p $\vee$ q is equivalent to (p $\supset$ q) $\supset$ q.] I have observed several other relations of interest that I will pose as a problem that the reader might have fun trying to solve prior to reading the solutions that follow.

Problem: Prove the following facts:
    (1) $\wedge$ is definable from $\supset$ and $\equiv$.
    (2) $\wedge$ is definable from $\vee$ and $\equiv$.
    (3) $\wedge$ is definable from $\not\supset$ alone [p $\not\supset$ q $\underset{\mathrm{df}}{=}$ ~(p $\supset$ q)].

    (4) $\vee$ is definable from $\wedge$ and $\equiv$.
    (5) $\vee$ is definable from $\wedge$ and $\not\equiv$ [p $\not\equiv$ q $\underset{\mathrm{df}}{=}$ ~(p $\equiv$ q)].

Thus $\neq$ is *strong* disjunction, and so weak disjunction is definable from strong disjunction and conjunction.

(6) $\lor$ is definable from $\neq$ and $\not\supset$.
(7) $\not\supset$ is definable from $\lor$ and $\neq$.

Solutions: (1) $p \land q$ is equivalent to $p \equiv (p \supset q)$.
(2) $p \land q$ is equivalent to $(p \lor q) \equiv (p \equiv q)$.
(3) $p \land q$ is equivalent to $p \not\supset (p \not\supset q)$.
(4) $p \lor q$ is equivalent to $(p \land q) \equiv (p \equiv q)$.
(5) $p \lor q$ is equivalent to $(p \land q) \neq (p \neq q)$.
(6) $p \lor q$ is equivalent to $p \neq (q \not\supset p)$.
(7) $p \not\supset q$ is equivalent to $(p \lor q) \neq q$.

Discussion: The discovery of (1)—that conjunction is definable from the conditional and biconditional—came about as follows: Consider an imaginary island in which each inhabitant is of one of two types—type T or type F. Those of type T make only true statements; those of type F make only false ones. A prospector visits the island because of a rumor that gold is buried there. He asks a native whether there is gold on the island. The native only answers: "If I am of type T, then there is gold here." What can be inferred? Well, suppose he is of type T. Then it is really true that if he is of type T then there is gold there, and this, in conjunction with his being of type T, implies there is gold there. Thus, the assumption that he is of type T leads to the conclusion that there is gold there, which proves that *if* he is of type T, then there is gold there. Well, that is just what the native asserted, hence what he asserted is true, so he is really of type T. It then follows that there is gold there. And so his asserting what he did, implies that he is of type T and that there is gold on the island.

The above argument is valid intuitionistically as well. The following simpler argument is valid classically: If he were of type F, then the antecedent of his statement would be false, hence the whole statement would be true, but those of type F don't make true statements, hence he must be of type T.

Now, how is this related to the fact that $\land$ is definable from $\supset$ and $\equiv$? Well, let p be the proposition that the speaker is of type T. Then for any proposition q, if the speaker asserts q, the reality of the situation is that p is equivalent to q. (He is of type T if and only if his assertion q is true). Now, he has asserted $p \supset q$, where q is the proposition that there is gold on the island, and so the reality of the situation is $p \equiv (p \supset q)$, from which we can infer both p and q. Thus $p \equiv (p \supset q)$ implies $p \land q$, and the converse implication is trivial. Thus, I discovered that $p \equiv (p \supset q)$ is equivalent to $p \land q$.

This equivalence is also closely related to the Curry paradox which enables one to prove any proposition whatsoever, and unlike Russell's paradox, does not use negation: Suppose we wanted to prove, say, that Santa Claus exists. Well, consider the following sentence S:

If this sentence is true, then Santa Claus exists.

Let q be the proposition that Santa Claus exists and let p be the proposition that S is true. Thus, S asserts that if S is true, then q, and so S is true if and only if (if S is true then q), and thus p is equivalent to (p ⊃ q) from which we have both p and q.

A more humorous version of this paradox arises in the following conversation between two friends:

A: Santa Claus exists, if I am not mistaken.
B: Well, of course Santa Claus exists *if you are not mistaken*!
A: So what I said was right!
B: Of course!
A: Hence, I was not mistaken.
B: Right.
A: Hence you agree that Santa Claus exists if I am not mistaken, and you agree that I am not mistaken. How then can you consistently deny that Santa Claus exists?

2. Two Immediately Complete Axiom Systems for Propositional Logic

System I: It is best to present this system in uniform notation: We will take ~, ∧, ∨ and ⊃ as independent primitives. We let α be any formula of one of the four forms $X \wedge Y$, $\sim(X \vee Y)$, $\sim(X \supset Y)$, $\sim\sim X$, and by α_1 we mean X, $\sim X$, X, X respectively, and by α_2 we mean Y, $\sim Y$, $\sim Y$, X respectively. Under any interpretation, α is true if and only if α_1 and α_2 are both true. We let β be any formula of one of the three forms $X \vee Y$, $\sim(X \wedge Y)$, $X \supset Y$, and by β_1, we mean X, $\sim X$, $\sim X$ respectively, and by β_2 we mean Y, $\sim Y$, Y respectively. Under any interpretation, β is true if and only if at least one of β_1, β_2 is true. Every formula is either an α, a β, or a propositional variable, or the negation of a propositional variable. Now, here is the system:

Axioms: All formulas of the form $(X_1 \wedge \ldots \wedge X_n) \supset X_i \ (i \leq n)$

Inference Rules: <u>Rule A_1</u> - $\dfrac{X \supset \alpha_1 \qquad X \supset \alpha_2}{X \supset \alpha}$

<u>Rule A_2</u> - (1) $\dfrac{X \supset \beta_1}{X \supset \beta}$ (2) $\dfrac{X \supset \beta_2}{X \supset \beta}$

$$\text{Rule } B_1 - \frac{(X \wedge Y) \supset Z \qquad (X \wedge \sim Y) \supset Z}{X \supset Z}$$

$$\text{Rule } B_2 - \frac{X \supset Z \qquad \sim X \supset Z}{Z}$$

Consider now a formula X in the propositional variables $p_1, \ldots, p_n$. By a *basic* conjunction in the variables $p_1, \ldots, p_n$ is meant a conjunction $q_1 \wedge \ldots \wedge q_n$, where for each $i \leq n$, the formula q_i is either p_i or $\sim p_i$. Now, for any basic conjunction B in the variable of X, if $B \supset X$ is a tautology, then $B \supset X$ is provable using just rules A_1 and A_2, as is easily seen by induction on the degree of X. (The proof mirrors the construction of one row of the truth table for X. Actually, the only instances of the axioms needed in this system are those in which $X_1 \wedge \ldots \wedge X_n$ is a basic conjunction.) If now X is a tautology, then for each of the 2^n basic conjunctions $B_1, \ldots, B_n$ in the variables of X, each formula $B_i \supset X$ $(i \leq 2^n)$ is a tautology, hence provable, and then X is provable using n-1 applications of rule B_1, and one application of rule B_2. Thus, the system is complete.

Remarks: One could alternatively replace the axiom scheme by $X_1 \supset (\ldots \supset (X_n \supset X_i) \ldots$ $(i \leq n)$, in which case Rule B_1 would not be needed. Or one could replace that axiom scheme by the simpler scheme $X \supset X$, and add the rules:
$$\frac{X}{Y \supset X} \qquad \frac{X \supset Z}{X \supset (Y \supset Z)}$$

It is obvious how to further modify the system so that modus ponens is the only inference rule, if desired.

System II: For this system, it is best to use the propositional constants t and f, and (say) $\supset$. [Of course, we could take t as an abbreviation of $f \supset f$, but I would rather not].

Axiom: t

This is the only axiom.

Inference Rule 1: One may replace any occurrence of t by any one of $t \supset t$, $f \supset t$ or $f \supset f$, and any occurrence of f by $t \supset f$.

From just this rule, one obviously can get all tautologies that involve no propositional variables. To get *all* tautologies, we need add only:

Inference Rule 2: $\dfrac{\phi(t), \phi(f)}{\phi(p)}$. [$\phi(p)$ is any formula involving the propositional variable p, and $\phi(t)$ ($\phi(f)$) is the result of substituting t (respectively f) for all occurrences of p in $\phi(p)$.]

For example, suppose ɸ(p, q) is a tautology involving just the two propositional variables p and q. By Rule 1, we can obtain the four tautologies ɸ(t, t), ɸ(t, f), ɸ(f, t), ɸ(f, f). Then from the first two, using Rule 2, we can get ɸ(t, q). From the last two, we can get ɸ(f, q). Then from ɸ(t, q) and ɸ(f, q) we can get ɸ(p, q).

Remark: A well-known philosopher to whom I showed this system said that it seemed to him *evil*!

II. SOME PHILOSOPHICAL TIDBITS

1. *Some Logical Sophistry, or How to Prove Anything*

As Socrates said about the sophists: "So great is their skill, that they can refute any proposition, true or false."

Well, one who can refute anything can also prove anything (by refuting its negation, assuming classical logic, of course!). Now, we have seen Curry's method of proving anything. Here are two others:

Method 1: Consider the following two sentences:
    (1) This sentence and sentence (2) are both false.
    (2) Santa Claus exists.

If sentence (1) were true, we would have a contradiction, hence (1) must be false. Therefore, it is *not* the case that (1) and (2) are both false, hence at least one of them is true, but since (1) is false, it must be (2) that is true. Therefore, Santa Claus exists.

Method 2: I call this the "legerdelogical method." Unfortunately, only a magician can use it. I first say to you: "Do you agree that if a proposition p is true, then for any proposition q, at least *one* of the propositions p, q is true? Of course, you agree. I then take a deck of cards, remove the queen of hearts which I show you, and place it face down on your palm and say: "Since this card is red, then *either* this card is red, or Santa Claus exists. At least one of those two alternatives holds." Of course, you agree. I then turn over the card, and you see that it is really the queen of spades, which is black. I then say triumphantly: Therefore Santa Claus exists."

In my student days, I once used this prank on my teacher, Rudolf Carnap to prove that God exists. Carnap's reaction was delightful: "Ah yes, proof by *legerdemain*. Same as the theologians use!"

Before leaving the subject of sophistry, I would like to tell you the following: In one of the Plato dialogues, Socrates criticized the sophist

Protagoras for taking money for imparting wisdom. Protagoras then explained that at the end of the instruction period, if the student was not completely satisfied, Protagoras would refund the money in full. Well, on reading this, it occurred to me that it would be funny if after the instruction period, a student claimed that he hadn't learned enough, and hence demanded his money back. Protagoras then asks him whether he can give a really good argument why Protagoras should give him his money back. The student then gives an excellent argument upon which Protagoras says: "You see the dialectical skill that I have taught you!"

It would be still funnier if a second student demands his money back, and again Protagoras asks whether he can give a good argument why he should get his money back. After a thoughtful pause, the student says: "No." Upon which Protagoras says: "Okay, here's your money back."

2. Ontology and Anti-Ontology

Descartes tried to prove the existence of God, or a perfect being, by taking certain properties called *perfections*, one of which was the property of *existence*, and defined *God* as a being having *all* perfections, and therefore God exists by definition. Kant rejected this proof on the grounds that existence is not a property. I don't believe that this objection comes to the heart of the matter; even if we assume that existence is a property, Descartes's argument fails, for the following reasons:

To begin with, Descartes's method (if valid) could prove the existence of *anything*: Suppose I wish to prove the existence of a unicorn. To do this, let us put ourselves in the frame of mind of some of the medieval philosophers who believed in nonexistent entities as well as existent ones, and that nonexistent entities can also have various properties. Then, let us define a *kunicorn* as a unicorn that has the additional property of existence. Thus a kunicorn is a unicorn that exists. Now, if I can prove the existence of a kunicorn, then I have a-fortiori proved the existence of a unicorn (since every kunicorn is also a unicorn). Well, either a kunicorn exists or a kunicorn does not exist, but the latter alternative is clearly a contradiction. Therefore, a kunicorn must exist.

What is wrong with this argument? Leaving aside the question of whether or not existence is a property, the fault lies in the ambiguity of the phrase "a kunicorn exists." Does the word "a" here mean *all* or *at least one*? Does the phrase mean *all* kunicorns exist, or that there exists a kunicorn? If the former, then the argument is correct: Of course, all kunicorns exist by definition, but that does not mean that there exists a unicorn. Similarly, Descartes's argument shows that all perfect beings exist, but not that there exists a perfect being.

Now for some (what might be termed) *antiontology*: A dual of Descartes's argument shows that there is no devil, if we define a *devil* as a being that *lacks* all perfections. Thus, any devil lacks the perfection of existence, hence there cannot exist any devil!

Curiously enough, I just received a letter from Joshua M. Epstein who quite independently gave a basically similar proof of the nonexistence of the Devil: His proof, unlike mine, is a dualization of Anselm's argument, instead of that of Descartes. Anselm defined God as a being than whom no greater being can be conceived. Well, an existent being is greater than a nonexistent one, hence a nonexistent God is contradictory; therefore, God exists. Well, Epstein defined the *Devil* as a being than whom no *lesser* being is possible. Now, an *existent* Devil cannot be the *least* of all possible beings, hence the Devil cannot exist.

In short, my claim is that the main error of the arguments of Descartes and Anselm is not that existence is not a property, but simply a confusion of quantifiers. What properly results from their approaches is that *all* perfect beings exist, not that there exists a perfect being; whereas Epstein's and my arguments correctly show that no completely imperfect being can exist.

All this, of course, presupposes that existence is a property (which is certainly questionable). Now, wouldn't it be interesting if some of the medieval philosophers were right in that there were nonexistent entities as well as existent ones. If this is so, then maybe God was originally a nonexistent being, yet powerful enough to will himself into existence! Thus, before saying "Let there be light," He said: "Let Me exist!" and lo and behold, He then came into existence!

III. SOME OLD PARADOXICAL WINES IN NEW BOTTLES

1. *Hintikka's Moral Paradox, and a Variant*

Hintikka has given the following remarkable proof that one is morally obligated not to do anything that is impossible: Suppose an act is such that if one performs it the human race will be destroyed. Isn't one then morally obligated not to do it? Of course one is! Well, any impossible act is such that if one does it, the human race will be destroyed (since a false proposition implies any proposition). Therefore, one is morally obligated not to do any impossible act.

I propose a variant: I will prove that one is morally obligated to perform *all* impossible acts! Now, suppose an act is such that if one performs it, the human race will be saved from destruction. Surely one is morally obligated to perform such an act! Well, any impossible act satisfies that condition!

2. *Newcombe's Paradox without a Predictor*

What now follows is intended for both those who know Newcombe's paradox about a perfect predictor and those who do not. When I present this paradox to those who don't know it, I do so in the following diabolical manner: "Suppose you are in front of a chest of two drawers. Either there is $100 in each drawer, or $1,000 in each drawer. You have the choice of taking either the money in both drawers or the money in just the bottom drawer. Which of the alternatives would you take; which one will gain you the more money?" Naturally, the person says: "Both drawers." I then say: "Is there any further information I could give you that would make you change your mind—any further information that would convince you that if you choose only the bottom drawer, you will find more money than if you choose both drawers?" The usual answer is: "No." I then explain that what I have not yet told you is that there exists a being—either a human, or a computer, or maybe a god—who is a *perfect* predictor, and at all times knows the entire future of the universe. This perfect predictor knew in advance how you would choose and was in complete control of how much money was to be put into the drawers. If the being predicts that you would chose both drawers, then $100 was put into each drawer, but if it was predicted that you would choose just the bottom drawer, then $1,000 was put into each drawer. I then ask: "With this additional information, would you still choose both drawers?" The answers I have gotten have been mixed. One argument is that one should choose just the bottom drawer, since you will then get $1,000, whereas if you choose both drawers, you will get only $200. (This is my position, by the way). The other argument is that the money is already there, and there is twice as much money in both drawers than in just the bottom drawer; hence, one should obviously choose both drawers. This is the so-called "paradox." Some have claimed that this paradox proves that there cannot be such a thing as a perfect predictor. I don't agree with this at all! In fact, the essential idea behind the so-called "paradox" can be reformulated in a manner that leaves out the predictor entirely! So here is my variant:

Again, there is a chest of two drawers, and either there is $1,000 in each drawer or $100 in each drawer, and again you are to choose either both drawers, or just the bottom drawer. We are also given the following:

Proposition: Either you will choose both drawers and there will be $100 in each drawer, or you will choose just the bottom drawer and there will be $1,000 in each drawer.

Please note that nothing has been said about any predictor! Newcombe's version with the predictor *implies* the above proposition, but the above proposition is more general and makes no reference to a predictor.

The question now is this: Is the above proposition consistent? Well, I will first prove that the proposition is inconsistent, and then I will prove that it is consistent. This is my version of the paradox.

Proof that the proposition is inconsistent: Regardless of whether there is $1,000 or $100 in each drawer, the fact remains that there is twice as much money in both drawers as in just the bottom drawer, and so if you take the money in both drawers, you will get more money than if you take the money from just the bottom drawer. On the other hand, the above proposition implies that if you choose both drawers, you will get only $200, whereas if you choose only the bottom drawer, you will get $1,000, and hence more than if you choose both drawers. This is clearly inconsistent, hence the proposition must be inconsistent.

Proof that the proposition is consistent: If there is any possibility that the proposition is true, then the proposition must obviously be consistent. Well, there are two such possibilities: (i) It is possible that you choose both drawers and that there be $100 in each drawer; (ii) it is equally possible that you choose just the bottom drawer and that there is $1,000 in each drawer. Both possibilities validate the proposition, hence the proposition is consistent.

3. The Prisoner's Dilemma Revisited

The prisoner's dilemma is not traditionally stated as a paradox, but I will show how it can be converted into one. I will consider the *positive* version in which the players are rewarded instead of punished: You and I are the players and there is also a rewarder. Each of us has two options—to *cooperate* or *defect*. If we both cooperate, we each get $3. If we both defect, we each get $1. But if one of us cooperates and the other defects, the defector gets $5 and the cooperator gets nothing! What is your best strategy? Well, either I will cooperate or defect. If I cooperate, you will get more by defecting than by cooperating ($5 versus $3). Also if I defect, then again you will get more by defecting than cooperating ($1 versus nothing). So regardless, of what I do, you will be better off defecting than cooperating, and so you are better off defecting. By the same reasoning, I am better off defecting than cooperating, and so you and I both defect, and as a result, we each get $1, whereas if we had both cooperated, we would each have gotten \$3. And so, the curious thing is that we are better off if we both cooperate, yet each of us individually would be better off defecting!

I had an interesting argument with a friend about this: I claimed that I would earn more by defecting than by cooperating. He claimed that I would earn more by cooperating, assuming that you and I are both completely rational. His argument was that if you and I are both rational, then the condition is symmetrical and hence you and I will play alike. Knowing that we will play alike, we should obviously cooperate (thus earning \$3 instead of \$1). Yet by the first argument, each of us should defect! Isn't this an inconsistency? Well, let us assume that we will play alike. Then the following propositions hold:

Proposition 1: (a) If we both cooperate we each get \$3; (b) If we both defect, then we each get \$1; (c) If one of us cooperates and the other defects, the defector gets \$5 and the cooperator gets nothing.

Proposition 2: You and I will play alike—that is, either we will both cooperate or both defect.

Are these two propositions consistent? Well, I will first prove that they are inconsistent and then I will show that they are consistent, thus getting a paradox of the same form as the preceding one. To prove that they are inconsistent, we see that from the first proposition alone, it follows, by the same argument already given, that regardless of what I do, you will get more by defecting than by cooperating. Yet from the two propositions together, it follows that you will get more by cooperating than by defecting (\$3 versus \$1). This is clearly an inconsistency. Yet the propositions are both realizable—if we play alike, regardless of whether we cooperate or defect, both propositions will be validated. Thus, the propositions are jointly consistent. This is the paradox.

RAYMOND M. SMULLYAN

DEPARTMENT OF PHILOSOPHY
INDIANA UNIVERSITY
OCTOBER 1999

NOTE

1. K. J. J. Hintikka, "Form and Content in Quantification Theory," *Acta Philosophica Fennica* 8 (1955): 7–55.

REPLY TO RAYMOND M. SMULLYAN

My professional path as a logician and as a philosopher has crossed Ray Smullyan's repeatedly. In his early work, reported in *First-Order Logic*,[1] he took the tree method of first-order deduction that I had formulated in 1955 and showed its potentialities in a much more impressive way than I have ever done. I included his paper "Languages in Which Self Reference Is Possible" in the little anthology on the philosophy of mathematics I edited for Oxford University Press in 1969. Later I made use of, and admired, his books on the Gödelian problematic.[2] I have also found his famous puzzle books a rich source of examples and ideas both in my research and in my teaching. His essay gives me a welcome occasion to meditate on the relation of his work to mine.

As I see it, there is a multiplicity of different kinds of connections between our respective works. One kind of relationship comes up in connection with the details of the products of Ray Smullyan's ingenuity. In some of his puzzles Smullyan has already proceeded further than the fully formal logical analyses found in the literature. In such cases, sometimes my recent or ongoing work can serve to uncover the logical mechanism that produces his clever puzzles. Take, for instance, Smullyan's beautiful but desperate Scheherazade who is allowed to address one last question to the King and have it honestly answered.[3] One possible question she could ask is: "Will you either answer *no* to this question or spare my life?" As a moment's thought (or a glimpse at Smullyan's book) shows, the King will have to answer yes and spare Scheherazade's life.

A sober analysis of the presuppositions of the question shows where the surprise comes from. The presupposition of a propositional question of the logical form "Is it the case that A or the case that B?" is $(A \lor B)$. (See e.g., my 1992 article "Knowledge-seeking by Questioning.")

In Scheherazade's case, the presupposition is "You will answer *no* to the question 'Will you either answer *no* to this question or spare my life' or spare my life." Assuming the King's avowed veracity, this turns out to imply "You will spare my life." In strict interrogation, a question may be asked only if its presupposition has been established. But this presupposition is precisely what the lady is trying to make true by asking the question. Hence the proper conclusion is that Scheherazade's charms have led the king to overlook the need of presuppositions in asking questions.

This explanation does not make Smullyan's puzzle any less intriguing or any less ingenious. What it shows is that one can give a precise logical analysis of the puzzle. Among other things it shows that what is crucial in the puzzle is not self-reference *per se*, but a violation of the presupposition of the question.

Most of the other puzzles constructed by Smullyan and involving questions can be analyzed in a similar way. In brief, Smullyan's "coercive logic" is but a chapter of my logic of questions and answers based on epistemic logic.

More interesting than such specific logical glosses one can give of Smullyan's puzzles and paradoxes are certain general features of his puzzle constructions (and of his solutions to the puzzles). One of them, illustrated by the presupposition puzzles just diagnosed, is the prevalence of self-referentiality in his thinking. Raymond Smullyan is, it seems to me unmistakable, the great theoretician and practitioner of self-reference in logic and in the theory of logic. It also seems to me that the most useful thing I can do in my comments on him is to show how my ideas can reinforce his ideas and put them into a perspective.

One point that can be made in the service of this project is to clarify the conceptual nature of the specific kind of self-referentiality that is involved in Gödel's first incompleteness theorem. If this conceptual nature is not appreciated, there will be no end of problems left open. For instance, by using Gödel numbering one can in fact prove Gödel's first incompleteness theorem as a theorem of elementary number theory. But if those numbers of which the theorem is proved are merely self-referential number-theoretical statements in a nonstandard notation, how can their truth be truth about numbers? Shouldn't we think of them as truths about formulas rather than about numbers? Similar question arise if we operate with quotations instead of Gödel numbering. And these questions have been asked by intelligent people from Wittgenstein down. Of course, as Smullyan shows clearly in his books, these questions do not constitute any obstacle to carrying out quite strictly Gödel's argument. But there still lingers an aura of incomprehension among philosophers.

Indeed, even on a more technical level, complaints have been registered against Gödel's own exposition because he compares the crucial sentence he constructs to a "liar" sentence of the form "This sentence is false." This comparison is not part of Gödel's actual argument and it is not fully accurate, one reason being that in an arithmetical language there is no mechanism of literal self-reference of the kind that can be accomplished by demonstrative self-reference.

These questions may be illustrated by pointing out how they show up in Smullyan's work. There a perceptive reader finds a certain discrepancy between his marvelous ordinary-language analogues and the real metamathematical situation. In ordinary discourse, we have built-in devices for self-reference, in the first place the first-person pronoun. This makes it possible for Smullyan to reproduce Gödelian reasoning in ordinary language. But in an arithmetical language there are no comparable devices. In such languages self-referential sentences are not recognized by their logical form alone. They depend on the method of Gödel numbering that is being presupposed, and their existence must be proved by diagonal arguments. This added problematic is not fully caught by the methods Smullyan has so far used in his puzzles designed to illustrate Gödelian reasoning.

If I may be so bold as to make a suggestion here, it seems to me that there is a way of explaining informally the precise nature of the kind of self-reference involved in Gödel's sentence and more generally in the comparable sentences obtained by diagonalization. (Perhaps Ray can use his idea in his next marvelous book.) For the purpose, we recall the basic idea of Gödel numbering.[4] In a Smullyan mood, I can say that this idea is neither more nor less mysterious than what is involved in an amateur play. The members of the cast are considered in two different capacities. On the one hand, they can be spoken of (and they can themselves speak) as characters in a play, for instance as kings, princesses, dukes, and vassals. On the other hand, they can be considered as their everyday personae, as tinkers, tailors, soldiers, and sailors, so to speak. If one of them makes a statement, it has to be interpreted differently depending on whether it is taken to be part of the play or a part of ordinary life even though they speak the same language in the play and in life outside the play. No paradox nor even any difficulty in understanding what is going on is involved.

In the same way, in Gödel numbering the numbers in question are considered on the one hand in their everyday role as numbers plain and simple and on the other hand as codifications of number-theoretical formulas, as playing the role of formulas in a Gödelian arithmetical play. Now in a play a character can make a statement about people in their normal life. Such a statement may even concern the actors in the play themselves in their mundane everyday life. Sometimes the intended person may be the actor himself who is speaking. One can for instance imagine that Clint Eastwood is playing the role of a character in a movie, say Dirty Harry, and in so doing, uttering, as a part of the movie, "In this situation even Clint Eastwood could not keep a straight face." Such statements pertain to the denizens of the actual world, not to characters in the fictional world of a play or a movie. They must be tested, verified, falsified, proved, and disproved in the same way as any old statements about the actual world. The statement about Clint Eastwood concerns the behavior of a real-life person in certain real-life situations, not what a fictional character in a movie might do. Yet these statements themselves are part of the movie in question, and receive their interest and perhaps even poignancy from being utterances in that fictional world. One source of such interest is that Clint Eastwood the real flesh-and-blood person could disprove his own statement just by maintaining a stiff upper lip.

It is relevant to point out that if Clint had uttered in the same movie context, "In this situation even I could not keep a straight face," he would have made an entirely different statement. This statement would be about Dirty Harry, and its truth has to be assessed in the context of the movie by reference to what the imaginary character could or couldn't do.

In the same way, when a number plays a role as the codification of an arithmetical sentence, it can say something about this or that number considered in their weekday function as numbers. Sometimes, the codified number makes such a statement about is its own number. This is not any more paradoxical than that a character says as a part of the play something about himself in his normal identity outside the play, as I just imagined Clint Eastwood doing. Then the statement in question must be proved or disproved just in the same way as any other arithmetical statement. It is in this sense that the Gödelian sentence is proved as unproblematically as any other provable arithmetical statement. Any philosopher who hopes to find deep dark secrets by examining the details of the actual proofs of Gödel's sentence is barking up the wrong interpretation.

But the proof of the Gödelian sentence is a logical one, and hence independent of its interpretation for its truth. Since it is a logically valid numerical sentence, it is likewise logically true also as a sentence about the formulas of elementary number theory. As such, the Gödelian sentence says that there exists a true but unprovable sentence, assuming the consistency of the underlying system of elementary arithmetic. Hence it is simply false to say, as some philosophers have said, that all that there is to the Gödel sentence is merely a theorem of elementary number theory. It is just as much a theorem about the provability of arithmetical sentences, which is the source of its interest and importance. A philosopher who dismisses the Gödelian sentence as being merely an arithmetical truth is like a chap who dismisses Hamlet's soliloquy because he knows that the actor uttering the memorable lines is unlikely to commit suicide in real life.

Thus the play analogy helps us to find our bearings in interpreting Gödel's first incompleteness theorem. This problem turns out to be tantamount to understanding the specific kind of self-referentiality involved in it. It seems to me that we have here a telling example of how the clever lines of thought Smullyan uses in his popular puzzle books can instruct and not only amuse. Suitably extended, they can even be used to remove philosophers' misunderstandings of Gödel's theorem.

This strategy can be pursued further. One question that can be raised here is: If self-referentiality is so benign, how come it seems to give rise to paradoxes like the paradox of the liar? This paradox is not only a peculiarity of natural languages. It arises—or seems to arise—also in formal languages when one tries to introduce a truth predicate into them. Indeed, in Tarski's proof of his theorem about the impossibility of defining a truth predicate for a first-order language in the same language, he uses an argument which is in fact comparable to the liar argument, with the same qualifications as were explained above concerning Gödel's argument.

Once again, the problem turns out to lie elsewhere, not in self-reference.[5] The play analogy helps us here again. Not only can we speak of the same people on the one hand as characters in a play and on the other hand as ordinary people in ordinary life outside the play. We can quantify over the same people in their two different roles. This is possible without any difficulties, as long as we realize that two different interpretations are involved. (If someone speaks of "all my countrymen," it can make a difference whether he is speaking as an ordinary man in the street or as a character in a play.) More subtly, even when the difference between the respective interpretations of the two kinds of quantifiers is heeded, they must be informationally independent of each other: the choice of a verifying value of one kind of quantified variable must not depend on that of the other kind of quantifier, even though they range over the same values, in a sense. For what such quantifier dependencies express are actual dependencies, which there cannot be between the fictional play world and the real one.

Tarski maintained that we cannot consistently use the concept of truth in ordinary ("colloquial") language. His reasons have been shown to be mistaken by the development of independence-friendly logic. It turns out that the basic reason Tarski's impossibility theorem holds for first-order languages using ordinary Frege-Russell logic is that in such languages one cannot keep quantifiers ranging over numbers as numbers and quantifiers ranging over numbers as codifications of formulas independent of each other. And these quantifiers cannot be made independent of each other without violating compositionality. Tarski himself blamed the alleged impossibility of using the concept of truth consistently in ordinary discourse on the irregularities of natural languages.[6] I have argued that the only alleged irregularity that really mattered for Tarski is the failure of compositionality.[7] What independence-friendly logic shows among other things is that this failure is neither an irregularity nor even an unwanted feature of a language, natural or formal.

On a less abstract but nevertheless philosophically important level, much of Ray Smullyan's work can thus be considered as a kind pragmatic refutation of Tarski's pessimism. Dr. Johnson tried to refute Bishop Berkeley's idealism by kicking a stone. Much more convincingly, Ray Smullyan has refuted Tarski by kicking the concept of truth happily around in reasoning couched in ordinary language.

J. H.

NOTES

1. Raymond Smullyan, *First-Order Logic* (Heidelberg and New York: Springer-Verlag, 1968).

2. Raymond Smullyan, *Gödel's Incompleteness Theorems* (New York: Oxford University Press, 1992); *Diagonalization and Self-Reference* (New York: Clarendon Press, 1994).

3. See Raymond Smullyan, *The Riddle of Scheherazade and Other Amazing Puzzles, Ancient & Modern* (San Diego: Harcourt Brace & Co., 1998), pp. 79–81, 222–24.

4. Cf. here my *On Gödel* (Belmont, Calif.: Wadsworth, 2000).

5. Cf. here my 1998 paper, "Truth Definitions, Skolem Functions and Axiomatic Set Theory," *Bulletin of Symbolic Logic* 4 (1998).

6. Alfred Tarski, "The Concept of Truth in Formalized Languages," in *Logic, Semantics and Metamathematics* (Oxford: Clarendon Press, 1956).

7. See my 1998 paper with Gabriel Sandu, "Tarski's Guilty Secret: Compositionality" in *Alfred Tarski and the Vienna Circle, Vienna Circle Institute Yearbook* 6, ed. Jan Wolenski and Eckehart Köhler (Dordrecht: Kluwer Academic Publishers, 1999), pp. 217–30.

12

Solomon Feferman

WHAT KIND OF LOGIC IS "INDEPENDENCE-FRIENDLY" LOGIC?

I. TWO KINDS OF LOGIC

To a first approximation there are two main kinds of pursuit in logic. The first is the traditional one going back two millennia, concerned with characterizing the logically valid inferences. The second is the one that emerged most systematically only in the twentieth century, concerned with the semantics of logical operations. In the view of modern, model-theoretical eyes, the first requires the second, but not vice versa. According to Tarski's generally accepted account of logical consequence, inference from some statements as hypotheses to a statement as conclusion is logically valid if the truth of the hypotheses ensures the truth of the conclusion, in a way that depends only on the form of the statements involved, not on their content.[1] Interpreted model-theoretically this means that every model of the hypotheses is a model of the conclusion. However, there is an ambiguity in Tarski's explication, as he himself emphasized, since for the specification of form one needs to determine what are the logical notions. Once those are isolated and their semantical roles are settled, one can see how the truth of a statement (in a given model and relative to given assignments) is composed from the truth of its basic parts, in whatever way these are specified. The problem of what are the logical notions is an unsettled and controversial one.[2] In the classical truth-functional perspective, proposals range from those of first-order logic to generalized quantifiers to second and higher-order quantifiers to infinitary languages and beyond. Many of these stronger semantical notions have been treated in the volume *Model-Theoretic Logics*.[3]

In a series of singular, thought-provoking publications in recent years, Jaakko Hintikka has vigorously promoted consideration of an extension of first-order logic called IF logic, along with claims that its adoption promises to have revolutionary consequences. My main purpose here is to examine in what sense it deserves to be called a logic. On the face of it, IF logic fits squarely into the semantic approach, but I shall argue both that the fit is problematic, and that the neglect of the inferential aspect of logic in its use constitutes a serious defect. Along the way, I shall raise concerns of a philosophical nature concerning its underlying semantics.

II. IF LOGIC

The primary reference that I shall use in the following for Hintikka's work on IF logic is *The Principles of Mathematics Revisited* (referred to below as *PMR*).[4] The basic idea is very simple, and is sketched here in order to make this piece reasonably self-contained.

When sentences of the first-order predicate calculus are put in prenex normal form, the usual semantics makes each existential quantified variable y dependent on all the universally quantified variables in whose scope it lies, i.e., which precede it in the prefix. This dependence is made explicit in the language of Skolem functions, whose use in general in semantics requires the Axiom of Choice. To illustrate, if a sentence S takes the following prenex form,

(1) $\forall x \exists y \forall z \exists u \, R(x, y, z, u)$

where R is the quantifier-free matrix, its Skolem equivalent is of the form

(2) $\exists f \exists g \forall x \forall z \, R(x, f(x), z, g(x, z))$.

In the language of game theoretic semantics, S is true in a given structure $\underline{M} = \langle M, \ldots \rangle$ just in case V ("Verifier") has a winning strategy (f, g) in the associated evaluation game (cf. van Benthem, this volume). At each move by V in this game over M the choice of next move is based on complete information about the preceding moves by F ("Falsifier") who first chooses an $a \in M$ to which V responds with a choice of some $b \in M$; following that F chooses a $c \in M$, to which V responds finally with a choice of some $d \in M$. For this sequence of choices, V wins if $R(a, b, c, d)$ is true in $\underline{M}$, otherwise F wins.

Motivated in part by games with imperfect information, Hintikka and Sandu proposed consideration of semantic games where V's choices do not depend on all (or, indeed, any) of F's prior choices.[5] In the case of (1) above, this leads to the following possible independencies from earlier universally quantified variables: (i) y can be independent of x and (ii) u can be independent of the variables in a subset of {x, z}, for example, it can be independent of z. These particular independence relations are indicated by:

(3) $\forall x \, \exists y/\forall x \, \forall z \, \exists u/\forall z \, R(x, y, z, u)$

or equivalently,

(4) $\exists y \, \exists g \, \forall x \, \forall z \, R(x, y, z, g(x))$.

Since this depends on *declarations of independence*, Hintikka called the resulting semantics of sentences such as (3) "independence-friendly logic," or "IF logic" for short.[6] More recently, Hintikka has proposed to call this "hyperclassical logic" instead,[7] but I shall follow the earlier designation since it is more suggestive of the basic idea involved, and also because it was used in all the prior publications on the subject. One difference here: in *PMR* Hintikka refers to this consistently as "IF first-order logic," but since that is tendentious and the main bone of contention in this piece—see below—I will omit the "first-order" part except when quoting directly. Even the use of "logic" may be considered tendentious, in view of my arguments below, but I shall at least follow Hintikka in retaining that part of the name for the subject.

Another source of motivation for IF logic is the study of branching quantifiers, introduced by Henkin and pursued by Walkoe, Enderton, and Barwise, among others.[8] The paradigm example is given by

(5)
$$\left\{ \begin{array}{c} \forall x \, \exists y \\ \forall z \, \exists u \end{array} \right\} \quad R(x, y, z, u)$$

where y depends only on x and u only on z. Such quantifiers are subsumed by IF logic in terms of the independence notation, for example,

(6) $\forall x \, \forall z \, \exists y/\forall z \, \exists u/\forall x \, R(x, y, z, u)$.

Because ordinary first-order logic lacks the capacity to indicate such relations of independence between bound variables, Hintikka calls it "dependence handicapped" or "independence challenged."[9] By comparison, he asserts that

[u]nder any term [IF logic] is the general unrestricted first-order logic. Some philosophers have been so blindly committed to the "ranging over" idea as the whole truth about quantifiers that where this idea fails, as it fails in IF logic,

they have jumped to the conclusion that such a logic must somehow be higher-order. This is nonsense by their own criteria, for the only reasonable way of making the first-order vs. higher-order distinction is in terms of the entities one's quantified variables range over. And by this criterion IF first-order logic is indeed first-order.[10]

This remarkable claim cannot go unchallenged.[11]

Before getting into these issues, I need to introduce some more precise terminology concerning IF logic, in this respect following *PMR* only in part. As Hintikka explains, the logic in general applies to sentences in negation normal form (i.e., in which negation appears at most applied to atomic formulas) that are built up by means of the operations $\wedge$, $\vee/\forall \underline{x}$, $\forall u$, and $\exists y/\forall \underline{x}$, under the following restrictions: $\underline{x}$ is a sequence of variables, u and y are any variables, y is not in $\underline{x}$, and each $\vee/\forall \underline{x}$ and $\exists y/\forall \underline{x}$ is in the eventual scope of all the $\forall x_i$ for each x_i in $\underline{x}$. (Slashes are dropped if the sequence $\underline{x}$ is empty.) Formulas generated along the way are called "IF formulas," and those without free variables are called "IF sentences." The semantics of the "slashed" disjunctions is illustrated by the case of an IF sentence of the form

(7) $\forall x \forall z\, [A \vee/\forall z\, B]$,

where A and B are IF formulas. Given a distinguished constant 0, to show independence of the disjunction from the variable z, (7) is taken to hold just in case

(8) $\exists f \forall x \forall z[\, (f(x) = 0 \wedge A) \vee (f(x) \neq 0 \wedge B)\,]$.

This has the same truth conditions as the IF sentence,

(9) $\forall x \forall z \exists u/\forall z[\, (u = 0 \wedge A) \vee (u \neq 0 \wedge B)\,]$.

In view of these equivalents, for simplicity we ignore slashed disjunctions in the following, and take IF sentences to be built up from atomic formulas and their negations by $\wedge$, $\vee$, $\forall u$ and $\exists y/\forall \underline{x}$, under the restrictions on variables given above. Every IF sentence can be brought as usual to a prenex normal form in which there is an initial quantifier prefix consisting of quantifiers of the form $\forall u$ and $\exists y/\forall \underline{x}$, in which the latter occur within the scope of earlier $\forall x_i$ for each x_i in $\underline{x}$; the matrix of such a formula is quantifier-free. These are called here *prenex IF sentences*; the initial sequence of quantifiers is called the *IF-quantifier prefix* of such a sentence. The *Skolem form* of a prenex IF sentence S is of the form

(10) $\exists \underline{f} \forall \underline{u}\, R(\underline{f}, \underline{u})$,

where $\underline{f}$ is a sequence of function variables f_i of various numbers of arguments (possibly zero); each f_i is associated with a (possibly) slashed existential quantifier $\exists y_i / \forall \underline{x}^{(i)}$ in the original IF-quantifier prefix of S and each occurrence of that y_i in the matrix of S is replaced by $f_i(\underline{w}^{(i)})$, where $\underline{w}^{(i)}$ is the list of variables in $\underline{u}$ other than those in $\underline{x}^{(i)}$.

Sentences of the form (10) are said to be in Σ_1^1-form. Walkoe and Enderton showed how to associate with every Σ_1^1 sentence a prenex IF sentence to whose Skolem form it is equivalent, in the sense that they are true in the same models.[12] When the Skolem form of an IF sentence S is satisfied, the realization of the function quantifiers encodes the winning strategy for Verifier in the (possibly) imperfect information game for S. Such semantics is seemingly "top-down" or "from the outside in," in contrast to usual model-theoretic Tarskian style semantics which is "bottom up" or "from the inside out," that is, is *compositional*. On the face of it—as Hintikka repeatedly stresses (and argues as a virtue)—compositional semantics is *not* in general available for IF sentences built up from IF formulas. For, without the universal quantification of the variables in $\underline{x}$ preceding a slashed existential quantifier $\exists y / \forall \underline{x}$, no explanation of the semantics for the latter can be given by a recursive definition of satisfaction in the usual way. However, as has been shown by Hodges,[13] *there is a perfectly reasonable compositional semantics for IF formulas;* this is obtained by taking the satisfying objects to be *sets* of sequences of individuals, rather than sequences of individuals in the ordinary way following Tarski. Hodges's work has been extended by Väänänen to show that the semantics of IF formulas can be treated in terms of suitable *games of perfect information*.[14]

III. GENERALIZED FIRST-ORDER LOGICAL OPERATIONS

Let us follow up Hintikka's assertion that "the only reasonable way of making the first-order vs. higher-order distinction is in terms of the entities one's quantified variables range over" (see above). Syntactically, a generalized first-order logical operation O applies to predicates of individual variables $P_1, \ldots, P_k$ of $n_1, \ldots, n_k$ arguments respectively. As defined by Lindström,[15] the semantics for such an operation can be specified by a collection K of relational structures $\underline{M} = \langle M, R_1, \ldots, R_k \rangle$ closed under isomorphism, in which the domain M is nonempty and each R_i is an n_i-ary relation between elements of M. This determines, as follows, an operation $O_k \underline{x}^{(1)}, \ldots, \underline{x}^{(k)} (P_1(\underline{x}^{(1)}), \ldots, P_k(\underline{x}^{(k)}))$ where $\underline{x}^{(i)}$ is a sequence of n_i distinct variables and $\underline{x}^{(i)}$ is disjoint from $\underline{x}^{(j)}$ when i and j are different. For any structure $\underline{M} = \langle M, R_1, \ldots, R_k \rangle$ providing an interpretation of each P_i by an n_i-ary relation R_i between elements of M, $O_K \underline{x}^{(1)}, \ldots, \underline{x}^{(k)} (P_1(\underline{x}^{(1)}), \ldots, P_k(\underline{x}^{(k)}))$ is satisfied in $\underline{M}$ if and only if $\underline{M}$ is in K.

We call such O_K *generalized quantifiers*; the usual quantifiers $\forall$ and $\exists$ can be treated as special cases by taking K to be the class of all $\langle M, R \rangle$ with $R \subseteq M$ such that $R = M$, and $R \neq \varnothing$, respectively. By allowing the n_i to be 0, all the usual propositional operations also fall out as generalized quantifiers in this sense. Further familiar examples are determined by the following classes of structures:

(1) For any infinite cardinal number κ, let K be the class of all $\langle M, R \rangle$ with $R \subseteq M$ and $\text{card}(R) \geq \kappa$. Then $O_K x (P(x))$ expresses that there are at least κ x's such that $P(x)$. This operation O_K is usually denoted $\exists_{\geq \kappa}$.

(2) Let K be the class of all $\langle M, R_1, R_2 \rangle$ with $R_1 \subseteq M$ and $R_2 \subseteq M$ such that $\text{card}(R_1) \geq \text{card}(R_2)$. Then $O_K x,y (P(x), Q(y))$ expresses that there are at least as many x's such that $P(x)$ as there are y's such that $Q(y)$.

(3) Let K be the class of all $\langle M, R \rangle$ with $R \subseteq M^2$, such that $\exists f \forall n [(f(n+1), f(n)) \in R]$. Then $O_K x,y (P(x, y))$ expresses that the relation determined by P is not well founded.

It is evident from these examples that though the Lindström generalized quantifiers are *syntactically first-order* insofar as the quantified variables are first-order, they may be *semantically higher-order*. Indeed this is the case for the operations determined by (1)–(3), since the notions of cardinality and well-foundedness are essentially higher-order concepts, requiring either implicitly or explicitly quantification over arbitrary functions.

The IF-quantifier prefixes may be used to determine generalized quantifiers in Lindström's sense. For example, with (3) and (4) of the preceding section in mind, the prefix $\forall x \, \exists y/x \, \forall z \, \exists u/z$ may be considered to be the quantifier O_K, where K is the class of structures $\langle M, R \rangle$ with $R \subseteq M^4$ and

(4) $\exists y \, \exists g \, \forall x \, \forall z \, [\, (x, y, z, g(x)) \in R \,]$.

As such, the IF-quantifier prefixes are semantically no more first-order than the generalized quantifier (3) above, expressing non-well-foundedness. The issue as to whether IF logic deserves to be called a first-order logic is pursued further in the next section.

Though IF quantifiers can be subsumed under generalized quantifiers in the way just explained, there are some obvious differences between Hintikka's conception of the former and the usual treatment of the latter.

Namely, generalized quantifiers can be compounded unrestrictedly with themselves and with other quantifiers and the usual classical propositional operations. For example, taking κ to be the least uncountable cardinal $\aleph_1$, we can express that there are only countably many P's by forming $\neg \exists_{\geq \kappa} x \, (P(x))$, and we can express that there are uncountably many P's or uncountably many Q's by $\exists_{\geq \kappa} x \, (P(x)) \vee \exists_{\geq \kappa} y \, (Q(y))$; finally, for example, $\exists x \, \exists_{\geq \kappa} y \, P(x, y)$ expresses that for some x there are uncountably many y for which P(x, y). Once the semantics of the quantifier $\exists_{\geq \kappa}$ is specified as in (1) above, the truth conditions of such compounds are determined compositionally.

By contrast, IF operations as given by quantifier prefixes are not compounded with themselves or other operations except in a limited sense, and only to the extent that they can be treated via game-theoretic semantics (allowing imperfect information), for example, by taking the conjunction or disjunction of two IF sentences, brought to a common prenex form. The prime example of an operation which cannot be so treated is that of classical or "contradictory" negation ($\neg$), where $\neg S$ is true if and only if S is not true. The operation of contradictory negation does not in general take an IF sentence to another IF sentence (up to equivalence); that holds only for first-order sentences S in the ordinary sense (cf. *PMR*, p. 133). Rather a new "dual negation" operation $\sim S$ is introduced by Hintikka (*PMR*, ch. 7), whose semantics is given by the game dual to that for S, that is, $\sim S$ is true if Falsifier has a winning strategy in the game associated with S. We do not in general have $S \vee \sim S$ valid since neither Verifier nor Falsifier may have a winning strategy, as is commonly illustrated by the case of the IF sentence $\forall x \exists y / \forall x \, (x = y)$ when tested in a domain of more than one element. Similarly there are two operations of conditionals to be considered in application to IF formulas S and S', the one being the classical $S \rightarrow S'$ [denoted $S \supset_T S'$ by Hintikka] whose semantics is the same as that of $\neg S \vee S'$, while the other, denoted $S \supset S'$, is defined as $\sim S \vee S'$; the latter has game-theoretic semantics since the disjunction of two IF formulas can be treated as a single IF formula.

Sentences S* of the form $\neg S$ for S an IF-sentence can be brought to Π_1^1 form and conversely. When Hintikka considers the expressive power of IF sentences or their negations in this sense, he refers to it as "extended IF logic." Allowing full compounding of IF sentences with $\neg$, $\wedge$, and $\vee$ leads to what he calls "truth-functionally extended IF logic." As is easily seen, such sentences can be brought to Δ_2^1 form, in other words, are equivalent to sentences in both Σ_2^1 and Π_2^1 form. This is a nontrivial part of full second-order logic; the relation to that is examined more closely in the next section.

Another difference of IF logic from the semantics of generalized quantifiers is that it is not informative to speak of the logic of the latter as a whole. Rather, what is of interest is the logic of one or a few such specific quantifiers considered in combination with the connectives and quantifiers of ordinary first-order logic. This is illustrated by the work descending from Mostowski in which the center of attention is the logic of $\exists_{\geq\kappa}$ in that sense, for various cardinal numbers κ.[16] For example, as shown by Keisler, the logic of "there exist uncountably many" shares many good properties with usual first-order logic, including a completeness theorem for validity (which happens not to be the case for the logic of "there exist infinitely many").[17] By contrast, IF logic is simply the logic of *arbitrary* IF-quantifier prefixes and their relations to each other.

Thus, though IF logic shares with the logic of generalized quantifiers a model-theoretic perspective, the concerns in most respects are orthogonal to each other. In *PMR*, chapter 1, in opposition to the traditional *deductive, inferential* function of logic, Hintikka identifies model theory with its *descriptive* function, that is, with what structures can be described or characterized in terms of given sentences. To be sure, the fundamental relation of model theory is that of *satisfaction*, $\underline{M} \models S$, between structures $\underline{M}$ of a specified kind and sentences S from a specified language L. But that is only the beginning, as any text in model theory reveals.[18] In general, one wants to know—given a set Γ of sentences—what is the class K of models of all S in Γ, and inversely—given a class K of structures—what is the theory of K, namely, the set Γ of all sentences satisfied in all members of K. The first problem implicitly involves the relation of *logical consequence* in Tarski's model-theoretic sense, since every model of Γ is a model of all consequences of Γ. In other words, the inferential function of logic is implicit in this broad conception of model theory. Of course, without a completeness theorem for a given language L and satisfaction relation for L, there is no assurance that such inference can be conducted on a purely syntactic plane; but the point is that, whether or not one has a completeness theorem, this general model-theoretic problem takes us beyond purely descriptive concerns.

Other traditional concerns that are syntactic but not necessarily inferential occupy attention in model theory, e.g., one asks whether the theory of a class K of structures is decidable, or whether its theory can be axiomatized in a sublanguage of L. Beyond this, model theory has been concerned with which properties of structures are preserved under given relations between structures and operations on them. In the opposite (so to speak, internal) direction, as pointed out to me by Wilfrid Hodges, mainstream "geometric" model theory is concerned with describing relations within a particular structure, not with defining classes of structures.[19] None of this is suggested by talk of the descriptive function of logic. In other words, Hintikka's conception of model theory is narrow to the extreme, and is further narrowed by the insistence on dealing with sentences of a very particular form, namely the IF sentences.

The point of departure in this section was whether IF logic deserves to be called a first-order logic according to the criterion offered above by Hintikka, namely "in terms of the entities one's quantified variables range over." I have argued that this does not distinguish IF logic from the logics of generalized quantifiers in Lindström's sense, which by all ordinary measures go beyond first-order logic. The question is whether something more special about IF logic is supposed to make the difference. Of course, one can talk in picturesque terms about playing games with individuals, each play involving only a finite number of choices, as a way of arguing that verification of an IF sentence is a first-order matter. But it is not the particular plays that matter; rather it is whether there is or is not a winning strategy for Verifier in such games, both in any one structure and over all structures in general. And, as we shall see in the next section in pursuit of my argument, *that* lands us squarely in *full second-order logic*.

IV. THE EXPRESSIVE POWER OF IF AND EXTENDED IF LOGIC

In chapter 9 of *PMR*, Hintikka gives a number of examples of mathematical notions which can be expressed by IF sentences S or by their contradictory negations S*. In ordinary logical terms, this comes down to seeing which notions can be expressed in Σ_1^1 or Π_1^1 form.

The following are standard examples.

(1) The relation of equicardinality is Σ_1^1.
That is, we have a Σ_1^1 sentence S in two unary predicate symbols P and Q, which expresses that P and Q are in one-one correspondence.

(2) The property of being infinite is Σ_1^1.
That is, we have a Σ_1^1 sentence S in one unary predicate symbol P which expresses that P is infinite; using = alone, we can express by such a sentence that the domain of interpretation of the first-order variables is infinite.

(3) The notion of being a non-well-founded binary relation is Σ_1^1. Hence that of being a well-founded relation is Π_1^1; the same applies to the notion of being a well-ordering relation.

(4) There is a Π_1^1 sentence S* which characterizes up to isomorphism the structure of the natural numbers $\langle N, Sc, 0 \rangle$, where Sc is the successor

relation; the sentence uses one binary symbol P and one constant symbol c.

(5) There is a Π_1^1 sentence S* which characterizes up to isomorphism the two-sorted structure $\langle N, \wp(N), Sc, 0, \in \rangle$ for second-order number theory, where $\wp(N)$ is the set of all subsets of N. (If preferred, the structure in (5) can be treated as one-sorted by unification of domains.) The sentence S* for (5) may be taken to include the statement that every characteristic function $f: N \to \{0, 1\}$ determines a member a of $\wp(N)$ by $\forall x [x \in a \leftrightarrow f(x) = 0]$.

(6) Similarly, there is a Π_1^1 sentence S* characterizing the finite type hierarchy over the natural numbers, obtained by iterating the power set operation $\wp$ up to ω.

(7) Transfinite iterations of the power set operation can also be dealt with in this form, most smoothly within the one-sorted language for the system ZFC of set theory. As pointed out by Väänänen[20] among others, there is a Π_1^1 sentence S* characterizing (up to isomorphism) the structure for the cumulative hierarchy $\langle V_\kappa, \in \rangle$ up to the first inaccessible cardinal κ, where $V_0 = \varnothing$, each $V_{\alpha+1} = \wp(V_\alpha)$ and V_λ is the union of the V_α for $\alpha < \lambda$ when λ is a limit ordinal. The same can be done for still larger specific inaccessible cardinals κ.

Further examples mentioned in *PMR*, chapter 9, concern characterizations of the real numbers in extended IF logic and expressibility of various topological notions. All such examples lead Hintikka to conclude that "virtually all of classical mathematics can in principle be done in extended IF first-order logic,"[21] that is, can be expressed in Π_1^1 form, and that many mathematical concepts can already be expressed in Σ_1^1 form. However, there is a substantial difference between the two, since Π_1^1 sentences do not admit a direct game-theoretic interpretation. So, what is gained by these expressibility results? Hintikka points out (loc. cit.) a kind of *reduction to* IF logic, which may be formulated more generally as follows. Given a Π_1^1 sentence S* like that indicated above in (5)–(7) for second-order or finite-order number theory, or for the cumulative hierarchy of sets up to the first inaccessible cardinal, and given a mathematical conjecture C expressible in Σ_1^1 form in the language of S*, the implication S* $\to$ C is equivalent to $\neg$S* $\vee$ C, and thence to a Σ_1^1 sentence, or—if one prefers—an IF sentence. Hintikka concludes that, "a great many mathematical *problems* can be taken to relate to the logical status of a sentence of an *un*extended IF first-order language."[22]

However, in the use here of the words "logical status" there is a shift from *satisfaction* of Σ_1^1 sentences in some structure or another—Hintikka's main concern when speaking of the descriptive function of logic—to *validity* of such sentences, and this makes a world of difference when it comes to sentences of the form $\neg S^* \vee C$. For, the relevant logical status in these cases is that of validity, not satisfaction in one model or another. An IF-sentence or, equivalently, Σ_1^1 sentence S is valid if it is true in *every* possible interpretation of its nonlogical symbols. Here is what Hintikka has to say about the shift in concerns (taking S* from (6) as the example):

> The upshot of this line of thought is thus a kind of reduction of the entire finite theory of types, with standard interpretation, to IF first-order logic. Since most of mathematics can in principle be expressed in a standardly interpreted finite theory of types, this reduction throws some interesting light on mathematics in general. For what can we say of the output sentences [i.e., $\neg S^* \vee C$] of this reduction? They are IF *first-order* sentences. All their bound variables range over individuals. This should warm the heart of every philosophical nominalist. More importantly, their interpretation is completely free of the logical problems that beset the notion of *all subsets* of a given infinite set. An IF first-order sentence is valid if and only if a certain relational structure cannot help being instantiated in every model. The problem whether a given IF first-order sentence is valid or not is therefore a combinatorial problem in a sufficiently wide sense of the term.[23]

I take it that what Hintikka means by "a certain relational structure [that] cannot help being instantiated in every model" $\underline{M}$, for a given IF sentence S or its Σ_1^1 equivalent $\exists \underline{f} \forall \underline{x} \ R(\underline{f},\underline{x})$, is a realization of the existentially quantified function variables $\underline{f}$ in $\underline{M}$, if S is true in $\underline{M}$ at all. As to this, Väänänen has proven that the general question of validity of IF sentences is recursively isomorphic to that for validity in full second-order logic.[24] Moreover, he shows there (op. cit., p. 517) that the set of valid sentences of full second-order logic is a complete Π_2 set (in the sense of the Lèvy set-theoretical hierarchy), hence is not Σ_2 definable. The two results together imply that *validity of IF sentences is not Σ_2 definable*; that strengthens an old result of Montague, according to which the set of valid Σ_1^1 sentences is not definable in finite type theory over the natural numbers.[25] Thus, the validity problem for IF sentences is by no means a "combinatorial," nominalistically heart-warming matter. On the contrary, if the question of validity of such sentences is taken to have definite meaning, there is a concomitant commitment to full second-order logic. This seems to be contradicted by Hintikka's statement that "IF first-order logic is equivalent only to a small fragment of second-order logic, namely, the Σ_1^1 fragment."[26] By Väänänen's theorem, that is true only if one considers *satisfiability* of IF sentences, *not* of *validity*.[27]

What we have here is a clear case of trying to have your philosophical cake and eat it too. On the one hand, second-order logic in its supposed standard sense is suspect:

[m]any hard-nosed logicians will not be happy with the proposal of using a second-order language as a medium for their mathematical theorizing, and for a good reason. In order for such a language to serve its purpose, its second-order variables must be taken in their standard sense. They must be taken to range over *all* extensionally possible entities of the appropriate type (sets, functions, etc.). . . . But if so, we face all the problems connected with the ideas of arbitrary set and arbitrary function. . . . I can indicate this kind of commitment to arbitrary higher-order entities by saying that it involves the idea of "all sets." Another way of expressing myself might be to speak of the standard interpretation in Henkin's sense. But whatever the name that this idea passes under, its smell is equally foul to many logicians. And there is a great deal to be said for their perceptions. The idea of the totality of all (sub)sets is indeed a hard one to master.[28]

These suspect notions can be avoided simply by restricting them to first-order logic. But ordinary first-order logic is expressively totally inadequate to the task of grounding mathematics because the principal notions of concern, such as those listed (1)–(7) above, cannot be characterized in first-order terms. First-order axiomatic set theory provides no solution to this problem since we cannot prevent nonstandard interpretations; chapter 8 of *PMR* is a sustained polemic against axiomatic set theory, a.k.a. "Fraenkelstein's monster," primarily on these grounds.

Since nonstandard interpretations do not help us to deal with the problems of set existence, what can? Here IF logic seems to offer its services to us. As long as we can stay on the level of first-order logic, independence-friendly or not, then problems of set existence do not arise. We do not have to open the Gordian knot of set existence since it was not tied in the first place.[29]

In other words, by *declaring* IF logic to be a first-order logic one can have one's philosophical cake and eat it too. But endlessly declaring it to be so does not make it so. As I have argued, the assimilation of IF logic to first-order logic just doesn't hold water. On the contrary, once validity comes into the picture, and it does come in essentially if one is to account for mathematics in the way that Hintikka proposes above, then one is in the same boat as second-order logic. You cannot buy the one without buying the other.

V. WHAT DOES IT MEAN TO DO MATHEMATICS? THE NECESSITY OF INFERENCE

We have seen that Hintikka's claim, quoted above, that "virtually all of classical mathematics can be done in extended IF first-order logic" comes down to the validity of Σ_1^1 sentences of the form $S^* \to C$, where S^* is a Π_1^1 characterization of some substantial part of set theory, be it second-order or higher-order number theory or even the cumulative hierarchy up to the first inaccessible. But that is where the real work for doing mathematics comes into the picture; inference is its *sine qua non*. For, higher mathematics makes essential use of long and involved chains of reasoning from what is already accepted (eventually, special cases of S^*) to what is to be established (C). And such reasoning for human mathematicians does not and cannot work directly at the semantic level of the notions involved; it can only proceed syntactically, in a way that is justified by the semantics. In other words, what is needed for the *doing of mathematics* is logic in its traditional deductive sense. And for that it is not an issue whether the model-theoretic notion of validity has a complete axiomatization. This is not to say that deductive logic in the ordinary sense suffices; what separates mathematics from logic is the employment of general notions of set and function that are irreducible to logic, and the assumption of axioms concerning those notions that are accepted on the grounds of what they are supposed to be about. That such assumptions may be seriously problematic philosophically does not mean that they can be ignored; on the contrary.[30] But that is another matter; what is at issue here is whether there is any sense to talking about doing mathematics *without* considering deductive logic. This would hardly need emphasizing except that in *PMR* Hintikka is utterly dismissive of the deductive role of logic in mathematics for reasons that I fail to comprehend.

Given my view of the matter, I have to ask what might be of value in expanding everyday logical reasoning as represented in the ordinary first-order logic to a system of reasoning—necessarily incomplete—making use of the formalism of IF sentences. In *PMR*, chapter 4, Hintikka gives a few examples in everyday mathematical parlance where the ideas of independence are used loosely, and which can be represented by IF sentences. But all such examples are equally well taken care of in ordinary first-order terms with the observance of just a little care. And since no substantial fragment of IF logic as an inferential system is on offer, the matter is entirely speculative. If the promoters of IF logic were to grant that some inferential system of reasoning with IF formulas would be of value, they should encourage its pursuit. But I personally think such an effort would be regressive, since it was realized long ago in mathematical practice how to say in precise terms that one quantity is or is not dependent on another, without invoking a new syntax hinging on that idea. Sometimes, all that is required for that is to take care about the order of quantifiers with respect to first-order variables, while other times function quantification is needed; but it is rare in the latter cases that one has to appeal to substantial function existence axioms to reason with such dependence conditions.

Taking this idea one step further, it may be of interest (in the spirit of note 6) to set up deductive fragments of second-order logic to formalize dependence relations in practice. In particular, it is often the case that one argues for an implication $\exists \underline{f}\ \forall \underline{x}\ R(\underline{f}, \underline{x}) \rightarrow \exists \underline{g}\ \forall \underline{y}\ S(\underline{g}, \underline{y})$ between Σ_1^1 sentences on the basis of the fact that there is an elementary way H of choosing a witness for $\underline{g}$ from any $\underline{f}$ satisfying $\forall \underline{x}\ R(\underline{f}, \underline{x})$, i.e., the functional $H(\underline{f}) = \underline{g}$ is first-order definable and one has $\forall \underline{x}\ R(\underline{f}, \underline{x}) \rightarrow \forall \underline{y}\ S(H(\underline{f}), \underline{y})$. This way of reasoning immediately suggests a rule of inference:

(1) from $\forall \underline{x}\ R(\underline{f}, \underline{x}) \rightarrow \forall \underline{y}\ S(H(\underline{f}), \underline{y})$, with H first-order,
 infer $\exists \underline{f}\ \forall \underline{x}\ R(\underline{f}, \underline{x}) \rightarrow \exists \underline{g}\ \forall \underline{y}\ S(\underline{g}, \underline{y})$.

More generally, it is natural to consider the fragment dealing with implications between *essentially* Σ_1^1 formulas, that is, those whose prenex form has only existential second-order quantifiers. In particular, this permits formulation of the Axiom of Choice for Σ_1^1 formulas in the form

(2) $\forall z\ \exists \underline{f}\ \forall \underline{x}\ R(\underline{f}, \underline{x}, z) \rightarrow \exists \underline{f}'\ \forall z\ \forall \underline{x}\ R(\underline{f}'(z), \underline{x}, z)$.

A rule like (1) and axiom of the form (2) were featured in one formal system for predicativity, under special restrictions on the formulas involved,[31] but the preceding shows that such principles are clearly meaningful in a much more general context.

VI. WHAT'S LEFT?

Hintikka has offered more reasons than those considered above from logic and mathematics for promoting IF logic. One main claim surrounds the autonomy of the truth definition for IF sentences, in the sense that one has a Σ_1^1 formula T(x) such that for any Σ_1^1 sentence S

$$T(\#S) \Leftrightarrow S,$$

where #S is the Gödel number of S. The weak link here is the relation $\Leftrightarrow$ of equivalence, where $A \Leftrightarrow B$ is true if A and B are true in the same models; this cannot be treated as a connective of IF logic. For a full critique of the claims on behalf of the self-definability of truth within IF logic the reader is referred to Rouilhan and Bozon.[32]

Outside of logic and mathematics, Hintikka appeals among other things to language games, philosophically and in everyday life, and to the IF representation of certain phenomena in natural language.[33] For these, the points disputed in this paper are irrelevant, and a defense of the formalism of IF logic and its associated semantics on such other grounds may well be sustained. In particular, games of imperfect information have a clear interest in their own right, and their investigation (as well as the investigation of the related games of perfect information in Väänänen 2002) merits further study.[34]

SOLOMON FEFERMAN
DEPARTMENTS OF MATHEMATICS AND PHILOSOPHY
STANFORD UNIVERSITY
MAY 2003

NOTES

1. Alfred Tarski, "Über den Begriff der logischen Folgerung," *Actes du Congrès Internationale de Philosophie Scientifique*, vol. 7, *Actualités Scientifiques et Industrielles* 394 (Paris: Hermann & Cie, 1936): 1–11. (English translation, "On the Concept of Logical Consequence," in Tarski, *Logic, Semantics, Metamathematics*, 2nd ed., ed. J. Corcoran [Indianapolis, Ind.: Hackett Publishing Co., 1983], pp. 409–20.)

2. See Solomon Feferman, "Logic, Logics and Logicism," *Notre Dame Journal of Formal Logic* 40 (1999): 31–54; Mario Gómez-Torrente, "The Problem of Logical Constants," *Bulletin of Symbolic Logic* 8 (2002): 1–37.

3. Jon Barwise and Solomon Feferman, *Model-Theoretic Logics* (New York: Springer-Verlag, 1987).

4. Jaakko Hintikka, *The Principles of Mathematics Revisited* (Cambridge: Cambridge University Press, 1996), with an appendix by Gabriel Sandu. Hereafter cited as *PMR*.

5. Jaakko Hintikka and Gabriel Sandu, "Informational Independence as a Semantical Phenomenon," in *Logic, Methodology and Philosophy of Science* VIII, ed. J. E. Fenstad, et al. (Amsterdam: North-Holland, 1989).

6. Interestingly, at least to me, the shift from IF forms such as (3) to modified Skolem forms such as (4), corresponds to a shift from attention to questions of *independence* to those of *dependence*.

7. Jaakko Hintikka, "Hyperclassical Logic (A.K.A. IF logic) and its Implications for Logical Theory," *Bulletin of Symbolic Logic* 8 (2002): 404–23.

8. Wilbur Walkoe, Jr., "Finite Partially Ordered Quantification," *Journal of Symbolic Logic* 35 (1970): 535–55; Herbert B. Enderton, "Finite Partially Ordered Quantifiers, *Zeitschrift für Mathematische Logik und Grundlagen der Mathematik* 16 (1970): 393–97; Jon Barwise, "On Branching Quantifiers in English," *Journal of Philosophical Logic* 8 (1979): 47–80.

9. Hintikka, "Hyperclassic Logic and Its Implications for Logical Theory," p. 408.

10. Ibid., p. 409.

11. The claim that IF logic is a first-order logic has been challenged by a number of thinkers, including Roy Cook and Stewart Shapiro, "Hintikka's Revolution: The Principles of Mathematics Revisited" (review article), *British Journal of the Philosophy of Science* 49 (1998): 309–16; Harold Hodes, "Review of Hintikka's *The Principles of Mathematics Revisited*," *Journal of Symbolic Logic* 63 (1998): 1615–23; Jouko Väänänen, "Second-order Logic and Foundations of Mathematics," *Bulletin of Symbolic Logic* 7 (2001): 504–20; and Philippe de Rouilhan, *L'ordre de IF, Proceedings of the International Symposium, Philosophical Insights into Logic and Mathematics*, Nancy, Sept. 30–Oct. 4, 2002 (to appear). Väänänen's results in this respect have been of particular use to me, as will be seen in section 4 below.

12. Walkoe, "Finite Partially Ordered Quantification"; Enderton, "Finite Partially Ordered Quantifiers."

13. Wilfrid Hodges, "Compositional Semantics for a Language of Imperfect Information," *Logic Journal of the IGPL* 5 (1997): 539–63; Wilfrid Hodges, "Some Strange Quantifiers," in *Structures in Logic and Computer Science*, ed. J. Mycielski, et al., *Lecture Notes in Computer Science* 1261 (Berlin: Springer, 1997), pp. 51–65.

14. Jouko Väänänen, "On the Semantics of Informational Independence," *Logic Journal of the IGPL* 10 (2002): 339–52.

15. Per Lindström, "First-Order Predicate Logic with Generalized Quantifiers," *Theoria* 32 (1966): 165–71.

16. Andrzej Mostowski, "On a Generalization of Quantifiers," *Fundamenta Mathematicae* 44 (1957): 12–36.

17. H. Jerome Keisler, "Logic with the Quantifier 'There Exist Uncountably Many'," *Annals of Mathematical Logic* 1 (1970): 1–93.

18. Cf., e.g., the classic Chen-Chung Chang and H. Jerome Keisler, *Model Theory* (rev. 3rd ed.) (Amsterdam: North-Holland, 1990); and the more recent Wilfrid Hodges, *Model Theory* (Cambridge: Cambridge University Press, 1993).

19. Personal communication. Hodges added that the usual compositional semantics of first-order formulas is essential for the work on geometrical model theory.

20. See Väänänen, "Second-Order Logic and Foundations of Mathematics."

21. Hintikka, *PMR*, p. 196.

22. Ibid., p. 197, italics in the original.

23. Ibid., p. 198, italics in the original.

24. Väänänen, "Second-Order Logic and Foundations of Mathematics," p. 519. The argument indicated by Väänänen makes use of a Π_1^1 sentence S* in a binary predicate symbol E and two unary predicate symbols P and Q whose models are exactly those isomorphic to $\langle M, \in, P, Q \rangle$ with $Q = \wp(P)$. If A is an IF sentence true in the same models as ¬S*, then we can associate with any second-order sentence

B a first-order sentence B′ in E, P and Q such that B is valid in full second-order logic if and only if A ∨ B′ is a valid IF sentence.

25. Richard Montague, "Reductions of Higher-Order Logic," in *The Theory of Models*, ed. J. Addison, L. Henkin, and A. Tarski (Amsterdam: North-Holland, 1965), p. 263.

26. Hintikka, *PMR*, pp. 191–92.

27. In effect, Hintikka is hoisted here by his own petard via the "reduction of the entire finite theory of types, with standard interpretation" to IF logic (as quoted above from *PMR*, p. 198).

28. Ibid., p. 193, italics in the original.

29. Ibid., p. 194.

30. See Solomon Feferman, Harvey M. Friedman, Penelope Maddy, and John R. Steel, "Does Mathematics Need New Axioms?" (proceedings of a symposium), *Bulletin of Symbolic Logic* 6 (2000): 401–46.

31. Solomon Feferman, "A More Perspicuous Formal System for Predicativity," in *Konstrunktionen versus Positionen*, vol. I, ed. K. Lorenz (Berlin: de Gruyter, 1979), p. 78.

32. One consequence of the main result of Philippe de Rouilhan and Serge Bozon, "The Truth of IF: Has Hintikka Really Exorcised Tarski's Curse?" (this volume), Theorem 2, sec. 4, is that for a great variety of IF languages L with standard interpretation, the relation A ⇔ B for sentences A, B of L is not definable by any formula of finite order having the same signature as L, nor, a fortiori, by any formula of L. Their full result undermines Hintikka's claims in *PMR* for the autonomy of the model theory of IF languages.

33. Cf. also Jaakko Hintikka and Gabriel Sandu, "Game-theoretical Semantics," in *Handbook of Logic and Language*, ed. Johan van Benthem and Alice ter Meulen (Amsterdam: Elsevier, 1996).

34. I wish to thank Wilfrid Hodges, Philippe de Rouilhan, and Jouko Väänänen for their comments on a draft of this piece.

REPLY TO SOLOMON FEFERMAN

Once upon a time, Marx Wartofsky had the task of commenting on a paper by Mihailo Markovic. The paper dealt with the influence of natural sciences on social sciences. What Wartofsky did was to read the first couple of pages of Markovic's paper with the phrases "natural science" and "social science" reversed. Disconcertingly, Wartofsky's version made perfect sense.

It has occurred to me that the most instructive way for me to respond to Sol Feferman's paper is do something similar, in the sense of reversing the roles of traditional first-order logic and IF first-order logic. What Feferman is in effect doing is relying on the received framework used in what he calls the semantic approach and trying to locate IF logic in that framework. This framework also involves such familiar props as Tarski-type truth definitions, truth-preserving inference, a distinction between logical and nonlogical notions, compositionality ("how the truth of a statement is composed from the truth of its basic facts"), and axiomatic set theory, as well as such newer ideas as generalized quantifiers and infinitary logics. This framework involves a hierarchy in which the received first-order logic constitutes the bottom layer. Second-order formulas with increasingly complex quantifier prefixes continue the hierarchy. Technically, this part of the hierarchy is known as the $\Sigma_n^1 \Pi_n^1$ hierarchy. I am not in the least surprised that Feferman finds it difficult to fit game-theoretical semantics (GTS) and independence-friendly (IF) logic into this kind of traditional framework. In order to see the true reasons for this apparent misfit, it seems to me best to turn the tables and begin by examining whether (and if so how) some of the main elements of the traditional framework can be accommodated within the GTS—IF logic framework.

Feferman argues that IF logic is not the ground floor in the structure of different logics, but in effect a fragment of second-order logic. Such hierarchies are conceptually delicate, however. For instance, where would Feferman place intuitionistic logic in the received hierarchies? Presumably even lower down than ordinary first-order logic, since it supposedly is weaker than "classical" logic.

More generally speaking, one can compare the two logics for their deductive strength, but also for their expressive power. Moreover, the two kinds of superiority are not totally unrelated. The only novelty of IF logic seems to be greater freedom of expression. How can that affect its place in the relevant hierarchies? Feferman notwithstanding, there is a perspective from which IF logic appears in a perfectly good sense weaker than the received first-order logic.

Spelling out this point requires a few explanations. (See here my 2004 paper "What is the True Algebra of Logic?") In IF first-order logic there is only one negation. Even though it obeys in game-theoretical semantics precisely the same rules as the so-called classical negation, it behaves differently. For one important thing, it does not obey the law of excluded middle. However, this apparently makes no difference as long as no explicit independence indicators are used and no other changes are made in the usual notation of first-order logic, in particular, if no independence indicators are present. From this logic, we obtain what has been called extended IF logic by admitting also a sentence-initial contradictory negation.

Algebraically, extended IF logic is a Boolean algebra with an additional operator. It falls within the scope of treatment of Tarski and Jónsson.[1] According to their results, it admits of a set-theoretical realization. Moreover, the added operator is a closure operator. This structure is shared by the modal logic known as S4. Now it is known that if we restrict ourselves to propositional logic, intuitionistic logic can be interpreted in S4, and vice versa. Hence we have reached an important conclusion. IF propositional logic is in effect intuitionistic propositional logic in disguise. Thus one answer to Feferman's title question is a variant of intuitionistic logic. Of course this result is not entirely surprising in view of the failure of *tertium non datur* in IF logic.

This analogy cannot be extended to first-order logic. I am prepared to argue that this is because Heyting's intuitionistic logic does not have the right rules for quantifiers. The limited analogy is nevertheless highly interesting. It should help to demystify IF logic. The same result should also show that there is a perspective from which IF logic is weaker than the received first-order logic.

This result may at first sight look like a merely formal analogy. It can nevertheless be strengthened and put into perspective in different ways. For one thing, we can now see what kind of hierarchy can be built by starting from an IF logic and by extending it step by step. A starting point is offered by the observation that game-theoretical truth conditions do not work when a contradictory negation occurs within the scope of quantifiers. It turns out that such sentences can be assigned a truth condition and hence a meaning by means of a nonelementary rule which operates via all the substitution-instances of the relevant formula with respect to the members of the domain. The more nesting of contradictory negations we allow, the stronger the sentences we obtain. If we allow arbitrary occurrences of contradictory negation in sentences also containing independence indicators, we obtain a first-order logic which can be shown to be as strong as the entire second-order logic (with the standard interpretation, of course).

By a first-order logic I mean here a logic in which all quantifiers range over individuals in contradistinction to higher-order entities. This characterization of "first-order" is much simpler than the criteria—whatever they are or may be—that Feferman relies on. In any case, the result just mentioned shows how strange the traditional first-order vs. second-order distinction really is. In the simple sense in which I am using the term "first-order," the received second-order logic is tantamount to a kind of first-order logic. In the light of relationships like these, it is hard to know what *Realgehalt* there is to Feferman's claim that IF logic is part of second-order logic.

What is especially interesting here is the engine that produces this striking strengthening of IF first-order logic. It is not an ascent to higher-order logic, but the unrestricted use of *tertium non datur*. This is in line with the intuitions of the original intuitionists like Brouwer who located the infinitary element in classical mathematics in the unrestricted use of the law of excluded middle. It also shows how natural it is to consider IF logic as the true intuitionistic logic.

There is also another kind of evidence for the fundamental role of IF first-order logic. It looks as if IF first-order logic and the received first-order logic would yield the same results as long as there are no independence-indicators around. However, this is the case only as long the basic predicates of the language in question obey *tertium non datur*, that is, leave truth-value gaps, then the difference between the two can become significant. Typically, what this means is that a sentence that is valid (logically true) in the received first-order logic is no longer valid in IF logic. I have found a few examples, and in all of them our logical and linguistic common sense favors IF logic. Cases in point include the following sentence:

> There is somebody such that if he understands this problem, everyone does.

This is logically true in ordinary first-order logic but not in IF logic, if "understanding a problem" is assumed to be an unsharp predicate. Other examples include the equivalence of the following two sentences:

> Someone is such that if he fails in business, he commits suicide.
> Someone is such that if everyone fails in business, he commits suicide.

These two are logically equivalent (sic) in received first-order logic, but fail to be so in IF logic. The only assumption we have to make is that the notion of failing in business is unsharp. Furthermore, the reasoning that gives rise to the sorites (a.k.a. bald man) paradox does not go through in IF logic. This example is especially clear in the sense that intuitively the source of the paradox is in some sense the fuzziness of the predicate "bald."

But what about Feferman's arguments purporting to show that IF logic is not the ground floor in a hierarchy of stronger and stronger logics? One of the main reasons he gives is that a compositional semantics for IF logic can be formulated only in a second-order level, but not on the first-order level. But this argument is in effect circular. We have to resort to second-order logic in order to formulate a truth predicate for IF logic only if compositionality is required. But just to insist on the requirement of compositionality is to rule out IF logic without a shred of argument.

But why cannot we require compositionality? Here we come to a deep reason for IF logic, a reason which Feferman does not even mention. This reason emerges from an analysis of the meaning of quantifiers. The largely unspoken assumption among most logicians and philosophers is that this semantics is exhausted by the idea of quantifiers ranging over a class of values. This idea has, in fact, sometimes been expressed, for instance when Frege suggested treating quantifiers as higher-order predicates expressing the emptiness or exceptionlessness of a lower-order predicate, or when Kripke and others defended the substitutional interpretation of quantifiers. To claim that the "ranging over" idea exhausts the meaning of quantifiers is nevertheless a mistake. Quantifiers also serve another semantical task. It is to express the dependence and independence of variables of each other. This task is clearly an extremely important one. It is performed by expressing the actual dependence of a variable y on another one, say x, by the formal dependence of the quantifier (Q_2y) to which it is bound on the quantifiers (Q_1x) to which the other variable is bound. But how is this formal dependence among quantifiers expressed? In the received Frege-Russell logic it is expressed by means of the scopes of the quantifiers in question. The scope of quantifier $(Q_1x)(—)$ is indicated by a pair of parentheses. Another quantifier (Q_2y) depends on (Q_1x) if and only if it occurs within its scope. Scopes are assumed to be continuous segments of the formula in question, and they are assumed to be nested, in that the scopes of two quantifiers may not overlap only partially.

But these features of the received logic make it impossible to express by its means many perfectly possible patterns of dependence and independence among variables. For one thing, only transitive and antisymmetric dependence relations are expressible by means of the received first-order logic. For instance, branching quantifier structures and mutually dependent quantifiers cannot be expressed by its means. Hence a first-order logic can only fulfill its job description if it is made more flexible than the received one. The IF first-order logic serves this purpose, and hence is the natural basic logic of quantifiers.

From these observations it can be seen that the greater flexibility exhibited by IF logic can be achieved notationally in different ways. One is merely to relax the rules for scope-indicating parentheses. I explore this briefly in my 1997 paper "No Scope for Scope?" Thus in principle IF logic does not need to involve any other changes in the formalism of ordinary first-order logic than freer punctuation. This possibility illustrates the nature of the novelty of IF logic as involving only the mutual dependence relations among quantifiers. In practice, it is nevertheless more convenient to introduce a notation (Q_2y/Q_1x) that serves to exempt a quantifier (Q_2y) from its *prima facie* dependence on (Q_1x).

This puts Feferman's claim concerning the second-order character of IF logic once again in a strange light. How can a mere change in punctuation lift a logic from the first-order level to the second-order level? Is this ascent a peculiarity of parentheses, or can it be avoided by using dots instead of brackets, as in the *Principia Mathematica*?

The dependence of a variable y on another variable x can of course be expressed also by using a second-order quantifier $(\exists f)$ such that $y = f(x)$. These existential second-order quantifiers can be thought of as sentence-initial, for if x and y were bound to quantifiers, their dependence relations would be determined by the scopes of their quantifiers. But then their dependencies and independencies could be expressed by means of IF logic, for such Σ_1^1 formulas can be translated into the corresponding IF first-order language.

In the light of all this, there is no hope whatsoever to insist on compositionality as a general principle in semantics. For the very notion of a quantifier's dependence on another quantifier within whose scope it occurs violates compositionality. Feferman refers to the results of Hodges that show that a compositional semantics can be constructed for IF languages on the second-order level. He might have referred also to the result by Hodges and Cameron to the effect that such a semantics is not possible on the first-order level.[2] Hence the vagaries of compositional semantics cannot be used to support the claim that IF logic is second-order logic.

The two dimensions of the semantics of quantifiers show up already in the theory of the received first-order logic. The "ranging over" idea is reflected by different instantiation rules, whereas the dependence indications are reflected by quantifier-ordering rules, for instance, by the logical truth of

(1) $(\exists x)(\forall y)\, Rxy \supset (\forall y)(\exists x)\, Rxy$

This might be the formalization of the ordinary-language conditional

(1)*   If someone loves everybody, everybody is loved by someone

The logical truth of (1) or (1)* can be seen immediately from the vantage point of dependence relations. In order to find, for anybody mentioned in the consequent, who his or her lover is, it suffices to select the universal lover introduced in the antecedent. In contrast, logical truths dependent on such ordering relations are much more awkward to handle in a compositional semantics, for instance, from the point of view of the Fregean "higher-order predicate" idea.

This "transcendental deduction" of IF logic does not depend on any special logical principles. In general, it seems to me that we should trust model-theoretical analyses of particular, concrete situations more than abstract principles and general concepts, which often turn out to admit different interpretations and are more complicated than first meets the eye. For instance, the notion of scope as it is commonly used is a blend of two essentially different ideas, neither of which need to be applicable in all cases.[3] Hence scope cannot function as a primitive explanatory notion in the semantics of natural languages. Similar things can be said of such notions as negation and compositionality. Thus if you accept the viability of IF logic, several of the widely accepted principles of logical theory have to be qualified or rejected. For one thing, there is no realistic hope for maintaining compositionality. Actually, the question as to whether—and if so in what sense—compositionality can be maintained is a tricky one, for there are ways of maintaining it if one is willing to complicate one's semantics. But since compositionality restricts semantical dependence relations to inside-out ones, and hence to transitive and antisymmetric ones, it is in some sense obvious that it does not allow us to express all possible patterns of dependence and independence. And in any case, the occasional claim that only compositional languages can be learned is without a shred of evidence. As Tarski seems to have realized, natural languages are not compositional.[4]

Furthermore, when compositionality is given up as a main *desideratum* of semantical theory, we cannot any longer rely on Tarski-type characterizations of truth. Such compositional truth definitions do not do their job in noncompositional languages. Thus another feature of the framework on which Feferman is relying turns out to be subject to qualifications. Instead of Tarski-type truth definitions, we have to resort to a game-theoretical truth predicate. Such a game-theoretical truth definition captures in part our pretheoretical notion of the truth much more directly than a Tarski-type one. The GTS truth condition as applied to a sentence S amounts to saying that there exists a full set of Skolem functions for S. Now, what Skolem functions do is to produce as their values those "witness individuals" (usually dependent on other witness individuals) that vouchsafe the truth of S in an obvious sense. Not only is this in obvious agreement with our intuitive notion of truth, it is also a much more elementary characterization of truth than a Tarski-type one, in which each recursion step for quantifiers requires considering infinite closed totalities (if the domain is infinite), in the sense of quantifying over second-order entities (valuations). In contrast, the only second-order quantifiers involved in a GTS truth predicate are sentence-initial existential ones which can be eliminated in favor of IF first-order quantifiers.

Thus it is only natural that GTS and IF logic cannot be accommodated in received semantical approaches in a natural way. But this is not the fault of IF logic, even though Feferman seems to think so, but of the prevalent framework.

There is a strange disparity between the different things Feferman argues for. On the one hand, he suggests that IF logic is so strong that it cannot be a first-order logic. On the other hand, he criticizes my statements to the effect that much of normal mathematics can be done in IF logic. Here I realize that I have in the past made a serious expositional mistake in using the locution "doing mathematics." If one says that one can "do mathematics" in such-and-such logic, it is easily and perhaps justifiably taken to mean that that logic can in practice serve as the medium in which a working mathematician can write out his or her theorems and carry out proofs and other arguments. In this sense, IF logic cannot for obvious practical reasons serve very well as a framework for mathematical practice. But I never intended to claim that it can serve such a hands-on purpose. What was intended—as I assumed could be seen from the precise claims I made—is that all and sundry mathematical truths can be expressed by reference to IF logic. The main result—I do not want to call it much more than an observation—is that the validity of any mathematical theorem expressible in higher-order logic is tantamount to the validity of an IF sentence. Feferman misrepresents this result, claiming that it deals with satisfiability rather than validity. It does not. What it amounts to in the second-order case is this: You can construe a second-order language as a many-sorted first-order language, except that you have to have as standing second-order premises a number of Σ_1^1 sentences which say that for any arbitrary class of n-tuples of individuals there exists a member of the appropriate (higher) sort having them and only them as members. If X is the class of such premises, then a reconstructed second-order sentence S is valid if and only if $X \vdash S$. Here S is a many-sorted first-order sentence. In the case of any one S, only a finite number of such assumptions are needed and hence X can be thought of as a conjunction. Then S is valid if and only if $(\neg X \vee S)$ is valid. But $\neg X$ is an IF formula. Hence the validity of the unreconstructed origin of S in higher-order logic is tantamount to the validity of $(\neg X \lor S)$ in IF logic. Indeed, this result is practically equivalent with the result by Väänänen that Feferman refers to ostensibly for the purpose of criticizing me. This result says in effect that the problems of deciding validity in the entire second-order logic is recursively equivalent to the problem of deciding validity in IF first-order logic. The possibility of such a result should be fairly obvious to a reader of my 1955 paper "Reductions in the Theory of Types." Väänänen's result in fact nicely supports my point about the purview of IF first-order logic. I do not see why Feferman chooses to quote it to criticize my claim that IF logic is first-order logic but not to support my claim concerning the purview of IF logic.

Unfortunately, my poorly formulated comments on "doing mathematics" seem to have misled Feferman also in his comments on logic as a theory of inference. Nobody denies the importance in the actual bread-and-butter practice of logic of inferential relations. But where do these relations come from? The received first-order logic does not provide all the principles of inference that mathematicians—and not only mathematicians—need. Where can we go for stronger and better principles? It is very difficult to see what higher-order logics could offer in this respect. For their principles depend on what can be assumed about the existence and nonexistence of higher-order entities, which is a notoriously difficult and unintuitive problem. Most philosophers and mathematicians resort to axiomatic set theory. The search for stronger principles of inference thus takes the form of a search for stronger set-theoretical axioms. But first-order axiomatic set theory is open to very serious objections in its foundational role.[5] And in any case it is itself incomplete.

It seems to me that IF logic and game-theoretical semantics can do an indirect service to the theory of inference. They can provide a theoretical and heuristic framework for the search for stronger inferential principles. Since IF logic is deductively (semantically) incomplete, we have to discover there, too, ever new rules of valid inference. But the two kinds of searches for the new assumptions are not on a par. In IF logic, we have well-defined model-theoretical conditions of truth and validity (logical truth) to guide our search. It represents precisely the kind of internal "geometric" model theory which Feferman for some reason claims that I do not advocate. In order to find new logical principles, we can therefore use our model-theoretical intuitions and—even more importantly—actually experiment with different models, in the sense of envisaging models of different kinds, comparing them, and seeing how they could be modified. This is made possible by the first-order character of IF logic in any sense, to wit, in the sense that all the entities quantified over are particulars formally and interpretationally. If this is not the case, model-theoretical experimentation is not possible. For instance, even though axiomatic set theory is formally a first-order theory, interpretationally it is not. As a consequence, we do not have in set theory any equally obvious model theory to provide guidelines for similar experimentation.

Many logicians, following Gödel, seem to think of intuition as providing the new assumptions. However, this is a very questionable move. Gödel has compared the use of intuition, which he thinks can yield new set-theoretical principles, to the use of sense perception in empirical science. But real science does not rely only, or even primarily, on sense perception for the purpose of discovering new theories. What is involved is experimentation. Now model-theoretical argumentation can be thought of as counterpart in logic to scientific experimentation. Indeed, in practice, Gödel himself did not rely on intuition alone, but experimented with different models of set theory, including the constructible model.

Such an experimentation (for the lack of a better word) amounts to constructing different kinds of structures (of individuals), modifying them and seeing which formulas are true in such "possible worlds." This kind of quasi-experimentation in mathematical sciences is possible only with the help of model theory. It is much easier to carry out on the first-order level, for this first-order character means that the relevant models are studies of objects in the ordinary sense of structure, unlike models of higher-order theories. Since IF logic is a first-order logic in the basic sense that all its quantifiers range over individuals, its model theory admits of "experimentation" in this sense. Its greater expressive power means that first-order model theory can be extended to the study of logically and mathematically more interesting structures without raising any questions concerning the existence or nonexistence of higher-order entities. In particular, the search for new and stronger principles of inference can in principle take place by considering only different structures of individuals and typically within logic itself.

The reduction described earlier of the entire second-order logic to a first-order IF logic supplemented by unlimited contradictory negation shows that such model-theoretical experimentation is now possible (on the first-order level in the sense of involving only individuals as values of quantifiers, not any higher-order entities) also in the whole of what is usually taken to be second-order logic.

In contrast, in the case of axiomatic set theory, there is no clear idea what its intended models are or may be. Hence, model-theoretical experimentation is impossible, and we are at the mercy of some mysterious faculty of intuition.

But this is not the worst problem about axiomatic set theory. As was pointed out earlier in this response, first-order axiomatic set theory cannot have a model theory which is in agreement with our pre-theoretical notion of truth and that this failure cannot be blamed on the peculiarities of very large sets. Hence, I can turn the tables here and suggest that insofar as mathematical practice involves the search for new axioms and rules of inference, IF logic is a better guide than set theory.

There is another aspect of the theory of inference with respect to which IF logic is not only equal to the received ideas, but opens new lines of thought. Feferman operates with a notion of inference according to which the validity of an inference means that all steps of the same form are truth preserving. Now truth can be defined for IF languages quite as well as in the received logical languages. This implies that the notion of truth preservation makes sense and more generally that a theory of inference can be developed along the same lines as are used to study inference in traditional approaches.

However, IF logic enables us to raise further questions. For IF languages, the truth of a sentence means the existence of a winning strategy for the verifier in the correlated game. This suggests studying inferences not only from the point of view of truth preservation, but from the point of view of how knowing the truth-making strategies of verification for a premise enables us to find a truth-making strategy for the conclusion. In this perspective, a rule of inference should produce from any given winning strategy for the premise a winning strategy for the conclusion. The naturalness of such a suggestion is attested to by what can be said about the truth conditions of conditionals. An examination of the semantics of conditionals in natural language shows that in the subgame played on the consequent, typically the verifier, must be assumed to know the strategy that was used to verify the antecedent. The initial verifier thus has a winning strategy in the overall game if and only if he/she/it can transform a winning strategy in the subgame played with the antecedent into a winning strategy in the game with the consequent. Such truth conditions for conditionals seem to capture the conditions for one sense of inference. Furthermore, the rule for conditionals in Gödel's *Dialectica* interpretation can be viewed in the same light.

Thus it seems to me that raising questions about the nature of received logics and about their place in a hierarchy built on the top of IF logic is a much more interesting enterprise than to try to pidgeonhole IF logic in the old hierarchies. For this reason, I am still left with a question I cannot answer. Why is it more important for Feferman (as I cannot help thinking it obviously is) to locate my ideas on the map of old logics than to see what interesting uses they might have for the purpose of reaching new insights?

J. H.

NOTES

1. Alfred Tarski, *Collected Papers*, vol. 3 (Basel: Birkhäuser, 1986), pp. 369–419 and 421–58.

2. Kurt Gödel, *Collected Works*, vol. 2 (New York: Oxford University Press, 1990), pp. 217–51.

3. See here my 1997 paper "No Scope for Scope?"

4. See my 1999 paper with Sandu, "Tarski's Guilty Secret: Compositionality."

5. See here my paper "Independence-Friendly Logic and Axiomatic Set Theory," *Annals of Pure and Applied Logic* 126: 313–33.

13

Johan van Benthem

THE EPISTEMIC LOGIC OF IF GAMES

1. LOGIC MEETS GAMES

Game theory and logic met in the 1950s—and Jaakko Hintikka has been a pioneer ever since, introducing game-theoretic viewpoints into logic; from his early basic evaluation games for predicate logic to his more recent "independence-friendly" logic ("IF logic") based on extended games that go far beyond classical systems. The grand philosophical program behind these technical efforts is found in his books *Logic, Language Games and Information*,[1] *The Game of Language*,[2] the *Handbook of Logic and Language* chapter with Gabriel Sandu on "Game-Theoretical Semantics,"[3] and many recent papers and manifestoes.[4] Connections between logic and games are attracting attention these days, ranging from special-purpose "logic games" to "game logics" analyzing general game structure.[5] IF logic is intriguing in this respect, as it sits at the interface of ordinary logic games, whose players have perfect information about their position during play, and general game theory, where players may typically have various sorts of imperfect information. My aim in this paper is to explore the game content of Hintikka's systems using tools from epistemic logic, and more generally, clarify their thrust at the interface of logic and game theory.

Exegetically, however, this is a somewhat tricky business. There is much less game content to Hintikka's systems than one might expect. His true interest is closer to the classical logical agenda of meaning and expressive power, mainly for quantifier expressions, viz., the notion of *(in-) dependence*. Despite occasional declarations of love for games *as such* as the basis of rational enquiry, they remain mostly a didactic device for studying dependence in quantification—as well as a way of drawing battle-lines in that well-trodden war zone of semantic compositionality. By contrast, I myself am a post-Hintikkean radical, whatever the original motivations. Games are important *per se* as models for action and information flow, and the interface of logic and game theory has a logical agenda of its own, which may make the classical one less urgent. So, admittedly, by taking the games too seriously in this essay, there is a grave risk of missing the point of Hintikka's work by pursuing a shallow dispensable metaphor. But I will cheerfully accept that stigma, provided—fair is fair—I can take the credit for all the pleasant new views that arise by setting off resolutely on my shallow path.

But what vistas can be seen? One look at a game theory book shows that the field is driven by concerns far removed from Hintikka's evaluation games, or other logic games due to Lorenzen, Ehrenfeucht, and more recent authors such as Hodges, Blass, or Abramsky. Game theorists look at such issues as players' preferences, strategic equilibria, imperfect information, uncertainty and probability, bounded rationality, repeated behavior, or the powers of coalitions. The intersection between logic and game theory may be as thin as just the shared notion of a *strategy*. We shall see. In this paper, I will first analyze Hintikka's original first-order games (section 2), usually thought rather trivial, and uncover a good portion of general game-theoretic structure. Then I will analyze the more mysterious IF games (section 3) as imperfect information versions of the original games, using a mix of the game-theoretic notions just found and *epistemic logic*. Both analyses broaden the bridge between logic games and general game theory, and show the contours of a new game logic. In section 4, I will discuss IF logic once more, but now from a general game-theoretic perspective. Finally, I will state my conclusions and suggestions in section 5. The tools for this work are two: (a) some unbiased reflection on the role of games in logic, and (b) the use of an explicit epistemic language of actions and knowledge. Both are things we have learned from Jaakko Hintikka, and thus, the thrust of this essay has been explained.

2. FIRST-ORDER EVALUATION GAMES

We start with the simplest logic games, which Hintikka proposed back in the 1960s, taking off with some well-known facts, and becoming airborne in a few pages.

2.1 Evaluation Games, Truth, and Winning Strategies

Let two parties disagree about a statement in some model M under discussion: *Verifier V* claims it is true, *Falsifier F* that it is false. Evaluation games describe their moves of defense and attack—with a schedule of turns driven by the statement:

atoms	*test* to determine who wins
disjunction $A \lor B$	*V chooses* which disjunct to play
conjunction $A \land B$	*F chooses* which conjunct to play
negation $\neg A$	*role switch* between the two players, play continues with respect to A
existential quantifiers $\exists x\, A(x)$	*V picks an object d*, after which play continues with respect to $A(d)$
universal quantifiers $\forall x\, A(x)$	likewise, but now for F

E.g., consider the first-order formula

$$\forall x\, \exists y\, x \neq y$$

on a model with two objects s, t. The game may be pictured as a tree of possible moves of object picking and fact testing, with the schedule read from top to bottom:

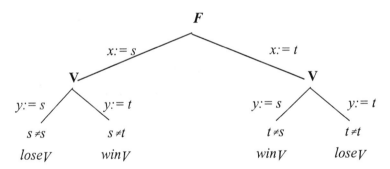

Falsifier starts, Verifier must respond. There are four possible runs of the game, with two wins for each player. Games like this are easy to play in class, and they sharpen the students' sense of first-order expressive power and model checking complexity. A bit more precisely (though one can go even further), think of the states as *pairs*

$$\langle s, \psi \rangle$$

where s is an assignment of objects in M to the variables in the original formula ϕ, and ψ is a subformula of ϕ. In particular, the game must start from some initial assignment, which can be modified by quantifier moves, and whose descendants eventually serve to identify the relevant atomic fact to be tested.

In the preceding game, players are not evenly matched. For, V has a *winning strategy*, a map from her successive turns to available moves that guarantees a winning outcome against every play by the opponent: she just needs to play the object different from the one picked by V. This makes sense, as she has Truth on her side. This illustrates a general connection between evaluation games and standard first-order semantics:

PROPOSITION   The following two assertions are equivalent:
  (a)   Formula ϕ is *true* in model M under assignment s
  (b)   Verifier has a *winning strategy* for ϕ's evaluation game played in M starting from the initial state $<s, \phi>$

This equivalence seems at best a Pyrrhic victory for game-theoretical semantics. It says that the game-theoretic analysis amounts to a notion that we knew already. So, it yields nothing new, except for a pleasant didactic tool for feeding our students the Tarskian fare we had decided they should eat anyway. But the result has many interesting features, and it is worthwhile to take our time and think about these.

2.2 *Exegetic Intermezzo: The Importance of Strategies*

Strategies. First, the Proposition highlights the role of winning strategies, or generally, strategies. In particular, it suggests a new semantic notion. Verifier may have more than one winning strategy in the game for a given formula. For example, for a disjunction with both disjuncts true, there are two winning strategies, 'choose left', 'choose right'. (The number of strategies can be computed for any formula and model.) Thus, winning strategies are *a more fine-grained semantic object* than the usual denotations (truth values, predicates): say, patterns of verification, or reasons for truth. Classical model theory does not deal with these winning strategies as such, unless in the auxiliary guise of Skolem functions, but they have many nice features.

In fact, as most logic games capture basic notions by winning strategies for some player (Proponent, Duplicator, and so forth), a general *calculus of strategies* is a mechanism underlying much of logic. For instance, take a classically valid inference like

$$A\&(B \vee C) \quad |= \quad (A\&B) \vee C$$

At the finer-grained level of semantic reasons, this says that any winning strategy σ for Verifier in an $A\&(B\vee C)$–game can be transformed explicitly into one in an $(A\&B)\vee C$–game. In the latter, V makes the same choice at the start that σ prescribes in the premise game if F were to play "right." After that she can sit back and wait.

Powers. Strategies do not just serve to win. Any strategy gives a player a *power*, a certain control over the outcomes of the game, no matter what the other player does. The Proposition says that a winning power for V amounts to truth. But F may still have powers, too. For example, in the above game, even though V can always win, it is up to F to decide where that winning takes place. This, too, may be a crucial feature of a game. Think of my having a strategy ensuring I will defeat you, but either in some boring meadow, or a picturesque location. If it is up to you to decide, you will go for the Last Stand at Thermopylae, as bards will sing about your defeat for centuries. To get its full impact, this story needs finer preferences for players than just zeroes and ones, but nothing prevents us from introducing these, and enlivening our logic games. But bare powers are of interest by themselves, and we will pursue them later on.

Games and Boards. Another striking feature of the Proposition is the juxtaposition of *two* relevant objects: an external *game board*—here, a model M plus all variable assignments over it—and a *game tree* with internal states for the game played over this board, generated by the formula ϕ. One board can accommodate many games. The Proposition says that some game-internal property, the existence of a winning strategy for player V, *reduces* to an external first-order property of the game board.

Activities versus Assertions. But the Proposition contains one more juxtaposition. It distinguishes *games* as dynamic activities from *assertions* about games. This is just as in dynamic logics of programs, which have two kinds of expression that are handled similarly: terms denoting actions and formulas denoting propositions. In the present setting, the distinction is easy to overlook, since the same letter 'ϕ' denotes a game in clause (b) and a standard proposition in (a). In fact, most of the literature on game-theoretic semantics wavers on this issue, using 'ϕ' both for the game and the assertion that V has a winning strategy in it, or the assertion expressed by ϕ without any games at all. This may reflect the earlier point that people are not really interested in the games, but in their good old logical propositions. I will try to be explicit about the difference where it matters. Indeed, when all is said and done, the Proposition makes a plea for having *three* kinds of entities to be handled in juxtaposition: games, assertions, and strategies.

Even this discussion has just skimmed the surface of the Proposition. For a more elaborate analysis of Adequacy Theorems for logic games, see "What Logic Games are Trying to Tell Us."[6]

2.3 *Logical Laws, Players' Powers, and Game Equivalence*

The Proposition is a bridge between logic and game theory. Let us take a walk across it. For a start, logical laws now acquire game-theoretic import.

Determinacy. Consider the classical law of *excluded middle $A \vee \neg A$*. That Verifier has a winning strategy for it in every model means she can choose to play either A as Verifier, or $\neg A$ as Verifier, i.e., A as Falsifier, and still have a winning strategy for the remainder. But this just expresses a well-known notion from game theory:

FACT   All evaluation games are *determined*: one of the players has a winning strategy.

This is true for a very general game-theoretic reason:

THEOREM[7]   All two-player games with perfect information that are *zero-sum* and have *finite branch depth* are determined.

Determinacy is important in descriptive set theory and foundations of mathematics: 'Zermelo's Theorem' above started a long line of results on classes of determined games. Nevertheless, this first link between logic and game theory may be misleading. Not all games are determined, and excluded middle is not the most significant logical law from a game-theoretic viewpoint. We will do better in a moment.

Powers Once More. Determinacy emphasizes powers of one player only. Indeed, Hintikka's work has a bias towards Verifier. But a more general description of games must state what *both* players can achieve—especially in nondetermined settings such as the IF games of section 3. Here is a somewhat more formal definition:

DEFINITION A player's *powers* in a game are all sets of outcomes X for which the player has a strategy in the game that ensures that all its outcomes, regardless of the opponent's moves, lie inside X.

Consider the following abstract version of our earlier game:

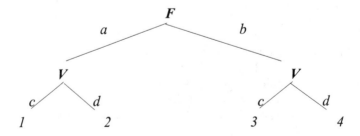

Here is the complete description of the power structure in this game.

  F has two strategies: 'left' with power *{1, 2}*, and 'right' with *{3, 4}*,
  V has four strategies: 'left, left' with power *{1, 3}*, 'left, right' with
  {1, 4}, 'right, left' with power *{2, 3}*, and 'right, right' with *{2, 4}*.

This tells us much more about the interaction encoded by the game. More generally, players' powers satisfy some general conditions which together are necessary and sufficient for representability in a determined game:[8]

Monotonicity If *j* has power *X* and $X \subseteq Y$, then *j* has power *Y*

Consistency   If *V* has power *X* and *F* has power *Y*, then *X*, *Y* overlap

Determinacy   If *V (F)* lacks power *X*, then *F (V)* has power *–X*

Now, here is the deeper connection with logical laws. Many of these have the form of equivalences. Consider a propositional law like *distribution*:

$$p \wedge (q \vee r) \leftrightarrow (p \wedge q) \vee (p \wedge r)$$

Here are the games corresponding to the formulas on the left and right:

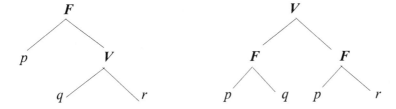

FACT   Both players have the same powers in both games.

On the left, *F* has strategies 'left' and 'right' yielding powers *{p}*, *{q, r}*, while **V** has 'left', 'right' yielding *{p, q}*, *{p, r}*. On the right, *V* has two strategies yielding again *{p, q}*, *{p, r}*, while *F* has *four*, yielding *{p}*, *{p, r}*, *{q, p}*, *{q, r}*. But as supersets represent weaker powers, two are redundant, and *F* has really powers *{p}*, *{q, r}*. Power equivalence is an excellent notion of game equivalence overall, and we have:

THEOREM   All valid equivalences of predicate logic, with their formulas interpreted as evaluation games, give players equal powers on both sides when played in any model.

  From Logic Games to Game Logics. There is much more to this style of analysis. One can design richer modal power languages[9] with operators *{G, j}φ* expressing that player *j* has the power to enforce proposition *φ* by the end of game G. Such a language for describing games expresses many further properties preserved under power equivalence.[10] Actually, this is a momentous move—even though we will downplay it in this essay to keep the focus on Hintikka games. Logic now plays two roles. We started with logic games: very specific games for analyzing logical formalisms. But now we also have game logics, formalisms that describe properties of games in general. And then the mill starts turning: there are also logic games for analyzing game logics, and so on: mind-boggling, but useful!

2.4 Compositionality and Operations on Games

Perhaps the most lively discussion concerning Hintikka games has been the issue of their *compositionality*. I, too, would love to write on this fascinating subject, but must honor the ten-year moratorium on the subject imposed at Amsterdam.

General Operations in Evaluation Games. Instead, let me point out a related and equally interesting aspect of the above evaluation games, viz., the completely general *game-forming operations* embodied in them:

  (a) offer a *choice* between two games G, H to one of the players:
        a disjunction $\lor$ gave this to V, and a conjunction $\&$ to F
  (b) negation *switches the roles* in G to get the dual game G^d
  (c) *compose* two games $G;H$, playing one after the other

The latter operation occurs in a quantified formula like $\exists x\, Px$, where V first picks some object for x, and then an atomic test is played. Properly understood, first-order evaluation games are operational compounds of two sorts of semantic base game:

  (i)   *object picking*   (single quantifiers)
  (ii) *fact testing*   (atomic formulas)

But there are other natural operations on games, which are less *sequential* and more *parallel*, such as playing two games interleaved ("having a family breakfast" while "reading one's paper"). The latter are more prominent in that other grand tradition of logic games, running from the pioneering work of Paul Lorenzen to modern game semantics for linear logic.[11]

Game Algebra. Where there are operations, there must be algebra. The above set of {choices, switch, composition} support a natural abstract game algebra. Its criterion for validity of an identity $G=H$ is—as above—that, when interpreted on any game board, the two expressions G, H define games in which both players have the same powers. The earlier distribution law is generally valid in this sense:

$$p \wedge (q \vee r) \leftrightarrow (p \wedge q) \vee (p \wedge r)$$

Game-theoretically, it says that one can reverse the scheduling order of players without affecting their powers. Many other equivalence laws of first-order logic are game-valid, too. But game algebra also includes some further principles, such as the following laws for composition that go beyond first-order syntax:

$(G \vee H) ; K$	$=$	$(G ; K) \vee (H ; K)$	left-distribution
$(G ; H)^d$	$=$	$G^d ; H^d$	dualization

Typically nonvalid, however, would be *right*-distribution

$$G ; (H \vee K) = (G ; H) \vee (G ; K)$$

To refute this, set $G = \forall x$, $H = Px$, $K = Qx$. Basic game algebra is decidable and axiomatizable.[12] Moreover, it tells us something new about first-order logic from a game-theoretic perspective. The corresponding set of valid equivalences $\phi \leftrightarrow \psi$ may be viewed as a new *decidable sublogic* of first-order logic. The above criterion of algebraic validity then amounts to the following logical version:

> The equivalence between two formulas should hold no matter what formulas we substitute for their atomic predicates, and also no matter what quantifiers (or general game expressions) we substitute for their quantifier occurrences.

The latter clause explains why right-distribution fails, even though predicate logic validates $\exists x(Px \vee Qx) \leftrightarrow \exists x Px \vee \exists x Qx$ for the special case of the existential quantifier. One more result of interest here is that each non-validity of general game algebra can be refuted by such predicate-logical equivalences. In that precise sense, logic games are complete for game logics.[13]

2.5 *Finer Levels of Game Structure: Extensive Games and Modal Logic*

Choosing an Invariance. What we have so far suffices for analyzing logic games as usually understood. But from a game-theoretic viewpoint, we have still missed an important issue. In any field, a crucial test on understanding its structures is asking when two presentations are the same. In the philosophers' terms, we need a *criterion of identity*. Now, the above power equivalence is one answer, but it seems rather coarse and global, disregarding details of players' turns and moves. Indeed, asking when two games are equivalent is an excellent test of one's understanding of any game-semantics. So, let us go back once more to our distribution example:

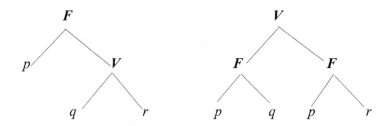

In terms of powers, these two games were the same. In game theory, this corresponds to looking at *strategic forms* of games, which only care about input-output relations.

But game theory also studies *extensive games*, the full trees of what can happen.[14] And then, the two games have important differences of detail. Their scheduling of turns clearly differs, and also the intermediate powers. For instance, *V* might get a choice between *q* and *r* on the left, but this will never happen in the game on the right.

Modal Logic. Extensive games are like process graphs in computer science or Kripke models which can be studied using modal and dynamic logics. Typically, modal logic allows us to express the key difference between the two games:

$<>(<>q \ \& \ <>r)$ is true in the root on the left, but not on the right

Also, *V*'s having a winning strategy in the game of section 2.1 is expressed by a modal-dynamic formula with assignment actions and choices U inside the boxes:

$$[x:=s \cup x:=t] \ <y:=s \cup y:=t> win_V$$

A more complex example is the earlier Zermelo Theorem on determinacy, whose proof involves this modal inductive clause for computing winning positions of player *E*, with *E* the union of all moves available to her, and *A* the same for player *A*:

$$WIN_E \leftrightarrow (end \ \& \ win_E) \lor (turn_E \ \& \ <E>WIN_E) \lor (turn_A \ \& \ [A]WIN_E)$$

Specialized to first-order evaluation games, this schema may be seen as an alternative formalization of the recursive mechanics of the truth definition.[15] For the moment, we just remark that game equivalence at this level is more like modal *bisimulation*, a much finer sieve than power equivalence. What level of detail one wants depends on the intended application.

2.6 *A First Summary*

Though we have not yet reached IF games, we have already found the beginnings of a research program about the connections between evaluation games and game theory. Moreover, this perspective passes one test: it tells us things about first-order logic that we did not know before. One striking example was the discovery of a decidable game algebra lying underneath its surface. But one can find such things basically anywhere. For instance, take our final excursion into modal logic, at the game level that "did not fit" first-order equivalence. Actually, the issue of finer levels than standard equivalence at which to identify *logical propositions* has a long history, going back at least to Russell. Bisimulation of evaluation games provides one such answer to this issue, and more generally, different levels of game representation might provide different accounts of logical *propositions*: some more "extensional," some more "intensional."[16] Thus there is much more game structure to evaluation games than one would think, once we stop waving the classical tourbook.

3. IF GAMES AND IMPERFECT INFORMATION

3.1 *IF Logic in a Nutshell*

It is high time to turn to Hintikka's more spectacular proposals, changing standard evaluation games into an engine for general *independence-friendly logic*. In what follows, we presuppose familiarity with this system on the part of the reader. Here is the program in a nutshell. Standard first-order logic imposes a linear operator order, which introduces hosts of dependencies, since "later means under." There are many reasons for breaking away from this—in logic, philosophy, linguistics, computer science, or even physics. We wish to allow for more complex nonlinear constellations of quantifiers with only partial dependencies. In terms of the above evaluation games, perfect information meant that players have access to all previous moves by their opponent and themselves. Breaking with this constraint requires new games where players may have to make their choices of objects independently from what the other player has done before. One typical way of achieving this involves *imperfect information*, where players need not know where they are in the game tree. This is the typical situation in card games, when we do not know each other's hands—and indeed, in game theory, imperfect information is a well-established subject.[17] In logic, however, it is a major innovation, whose repercussions are still widely debated.[18]

In this section, we make just one major logical point. Imperfect information means that players cannot distinguish between different states of a game. This is *precisely* the standard semantics of epistemic logic, and hence we can introduce explicit epistemic knowledge operators to formalize various aspects of IF games. The benefits of such a move are the same as those of epistemic logic generally: clarity of analysis, and suggestiveness for further topics. Using this tool, we will look at IF games more or less as in section 2, at various levels. Viewed as theaters for players operating under ignorance, we analyze them using a dynamic-epistemic language. Viewing them as just outcome-producing "machines," we extend the earlier "power equivalence" to deal with IF equivalence, and relate the result to known issues in game theory.

3.2 *Getting Acquainted*

Many discussions of IF games start with perplexities and attempts at formulating the design intuitions behind the system. Here we will just make a brief tour of the issues.

Slash Syntax and Nondetermined Games. IF logic has a lush syntax of slashes, indicating that quantifiers are independent, or that players may have imperfect information about previous moves. In what follows, we forego a priori limitations: players may be uncertain about their own, or the opponent's moves. There are some syntax restrictions in IF logic, such as F's never being uncertain about V—but these seem mainly remnants of a statement focus, making Verifier the *prima donna*. Having grasped the general scene, we will discuss systematic restrictions later. As an example, consider the earlier game with a two-object domain, but now for the game

$$\forall x \, \exists y/\pmb{x} \, x \neq y$$

where the slash indicates that Verifier no longer has access to the first object mentioned by Falsifier. She may have forgotten, the object may have been presented in a sealed envelope, or whatever else we may suppose. Intuitively, this game has the following tree:

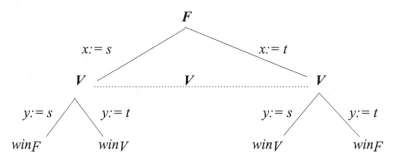

Here the dotted line is a standard game-theorist's device indicating

Verifier's natural equivalence relation of indistinguishability between the two game states in the middle. Equivalence classes of this relation are called players' "information sets" in game theory—a deviant terminology going back to an independent rediscovery of Hintikka's epistemic logic[19] by game theorists in the 1970s.

Crucially, the new game is *nondetermined*, in a sense appropriate to the extended setting. Verifier still has her old winning strategy, but it is not usable. What she needs is a *uniform winning strategy*, whose prescribed actions are the same across all game states that are indistinguishable to her. Game theorists would even call this the only strategy for V in this game, as strategies assign moves to information sets. But no such uniform strategy exists in this game. The only two candidates ('choose object s', 'choose object t') cannot guarantee a win. But neither does Falsifier have a winning strategy: anything he does might be countered by a move for Verifier.

Skolem Forms and Complexity. In logical terms, the statement that Verifier has a winning strategy corresponds closely to normal forms using *Skolem functions*. For example, a standard first-order formula $\forall x \, \exists y \, R(x, y)$ is equivalent to

$$\exists f \, \forall x \, R(x, fx)$$

Likewise, the statement that V has a uniform winning strategy in the above game for $\forall x \, \exists y/x \, \, x \neq y$ can be written as follows, dropping one variable dependency:

$$\exists f \, \forall x \, R(x, f)$$

This gets more exciting in more complex examples. Say, consider

$$\forall x \, \exists y \, \forall z \, \exists u/x \, R(x, y, z, u)$$

Here the statement that V has a winning strategy amounts to saying that

$$\exists f \, \exists g \, \forall x \, \forall z \, R(x, f(x), z, g(z))$$

There is a body of technical theory on this,[20] showing that the expressive power of IF logic goes up to fragments of second-order logic. That is, the statement that Verifier has a uniform winning strategy in an IF game can lead to branching non-first-order quantification patterns over Skolem functions.

Of course, in terms of section 2.2, this says something about the complexity of some statements about IF games. It does not tell us much about the games themselves. Imperfect information is all around us: in card games, or in parlor games, with sometimes quite sophisticated mechanisms of information hiding. The logic of those mechanisms is an exciting ongoing story,[21] but it has taught us at least this: The fact that some technical statements *about* imperfect information games need high complexity is orthogonal to the issue whether the games themselves, as activities, are easy or hard to play. Some such games might even be *easier* to play than their perfect information counterparts, as there may be fewer things to keep in mind in small memories.

Can IF Games Be Played at All? Even so, all this does not address the question *how, or even whether,* one can play *IF games.* IF syntax allows arbitrary slashing of quantifiers and connectives, suppressing dependencies on any earlier operators. Does this correspond to realistic settings where players find themselves in such circumstances? Hintikka and Sandu never provide a definition of IF games. We are not given the game trees, let alone specific mechanisms that would make arbitrary IF games playable. Parts of the syntax suggest imperfect information about moves (as in the above game), others memory loss, perhaps even just intermittent:

$$\forall x \; \exists y \; \forall z \; \exists u/x \; \forall v \; \exists s \; R(x, y, z, u, v, s)$$

One interpretation offered in the folklore is that all slashes make sense when we assume that V and F are really *teams* whose members work in parallel. This would be like the typical game-theoretic notion of a *coalition* (cf. section 4)—but no precise interpretation of this form has been specified so far by Hintikka or his critics.

My own view is the following: IF syntax is a specification for patterns of knowledge and ignorance. It does not address the issue of designing actual games that meet these specifications. Also, it ignores finer distinctions. Some ignorance is public, and part of the legitimate design of a game. Examples are putting moves in envelopes, shuffling cards, or dealing hands to players. Such games can be played by ideal players without limitations on their capacities for reasoning and observation. Another, quite different source of ignorance is players' limitations: they may not pay attention, or may have bounded memory, or may cheat, and so on. This might even happen with games of perfect information. These different sources of ignorance are run together in IF syntax, so that discussion is bound to remain confused.

A Way Out. At this stage, I should offer the reader an escape hatch. All these worries only hurt if one takes the games seriously. On the other exegetic hypothesis, IF logic is just about *(in-)dependence,* and the game metaphor can be thrown away as soon as it becomes a nuisance. I intend to pursue the games, but one does not have to follow. To focus what follows, here are a few more concrete test questions to play with.

Test Problems. Here is the first example. Many people claim that the above game

$$\forall x \, \exists y/x \; x \neq y$$

is not yet an issue, because it is "really" equivalent to the first-order formula

$$\exists y \, \forall y x \neq y$$

For, in order to win the first game, Verifier must put up an object that works against anything that Falsifier may have mentioned. But upon reflection, this story is strange! The first game is *nondetermined*, the second game has perfect information. So they differ in significant properties—and one would expect them to come out as being different. (They are.) Equivalence judgments are a nice test for understanding any proposed semantics. Typically, when quizzed on equivalence of slash formulas, people will either quote Hintikka, or try to look mysterious and appeal to private semantic intuitions. We will analyze what goes on in neutral game-theoretic terms, leading to a different outcome—which is actually better from the standpoint of pure logic.

A second example is the beautiful signalling phenomena found in Hodges.[22] Consider a slight modification of $\forall x \, \exists y/x \; Rxy$, with a vacuous quantifier inserted:

$$\forall x \, \exists z \, \exists y/x \; x \neq y$$

Some people's intuitions tell them a vacuous quantifier never makes a difference "since it is redundant in standard logic." This reasoning is hard to understand, since one of the purposes of IF logic was to extend standard logic, so that intuitions from that original area need to be sifted as to what should generalize and what should not. Indeed, vacuous quantifiers are additional moves, which do matter in game theory. This time, Verifier does have a uniform winning strategy:

"use your z-move to copy F's first move,
  then copy that for your own y-move."

This is admissible. If we want to prevent V from using her earlier z-response, we should rather consider a different IF game, with some obvious extended slash syntax:

$$\forall x \, \exists z \, \exists y/\{x, z\} \; x \neq y$$

There is nothing mysterious here, and we will provide precise game-theoretic details.

I will now show how to treat at least some IF games as imperfect information game trees, and we can then embark on the program outlined at the end of section 3.1.

3.3 *IF Games as Imperfect Information Games*

Intriguing Examples. In section 2, it was easy to define an extensive game tree *game (ϕ, M, s)* for any first-order formula ϕ, model **M**, and variable assignment *s*. We have not really specified the last details of this, but it can be done, given enough industry. Can we do the same when ϕ is a slash formula from IF syntax? We already did the example of $\forall x \, \exists y / x \, x \neq y$ on a two-object domain, whose form will also be clear for arbitrary models **M**. The underlying game tree was the ordinary one for $\forall x \, \exists y \, x \neq y$, while the slash told us where to put dotted lines in that tree for players' uncertainties. Next, consider the two (non-)signalling examples from section 3.2, again for convenience over a two-object domain. Lots of insights will emerge.

An Imperfect Information Game for $\forall x \, \exists z \, \exists y \, /x \, x \neq y$. It may not be immediately obvious from this first slash formula how to draw dotted lines for *V* in the underlying game tree. But a rather simple algorithm does exist—and it is implicit in the next picture:

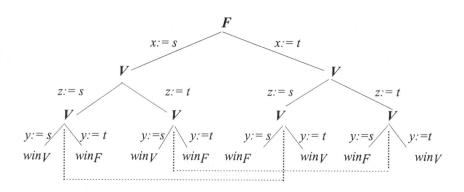

The dotted lines represent *V*'s uncertainty in the third round about *F*'s first move. But at the same time, in that round, the lines show that she knows her own move in the second round. We indicate a uniform winning strategy for her with boldface arrows:

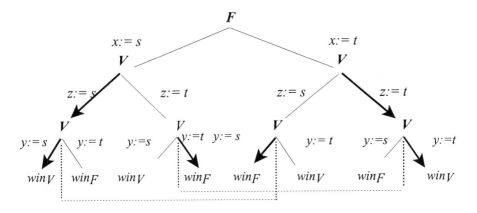

There are some subtleties here in interpretation. V's strategy is indeed uniform by definition, as it assigns the same move to states that she cannot distinguish. Moreover, it is a winning strategy, in that, if she follows it, she will in fact end in a winning state, whatever F does. But when the third round has come, V will not *know* that her strategy is winning, as she considers it possible that F played another move, so that her prescribed move will make her lose. In other words, one can have a uniform winning strategy without knowing at each stage of following it that playing the rest of the strategy is in fact winning. This is like following a guide through a bog, having forgotten the reasons that convinced us that the guide was going to get us across. Some people find such subtleties annoying; I myself find them delightful.

In game-theoretic terms, notice that the above is a game *without Perfect Recall*. In the third round, V has forgotten information which she did have in the second round. Such games are notoriously harder to interpret than games where players cope with uncertainty without memory failures, like expert card players.

Knowledge about Strategies. The interpretation of what happens under various scenarios in imperfect information games remains a contested issue, even in game theory. Incidentally, these difficulties reflect those of interpreting IF syntax, and so they strengthen, rather than weaken the connection that we are making. For instance, consider this: Since V is just as rational as you and me, she can see that the above strategy must make her win. Will not this knowledge assure her in the third round that she must win? Well, for that to happen, she must *remember* her strategy. But modeling the latter knowledge goes beyond knowing where one is in the game tree: it presupposes a richer representation, including information about possible strategies. Such "metamodels" of games have existed in game theory since the 1970s in discussions of rational behavior,[23] but they would take us too far afield here. In particular, if V remembers her strategy throughout the game, her information should only contain the game played according to that strategy. But then, the above picture changes, and we get a "cut-off version":

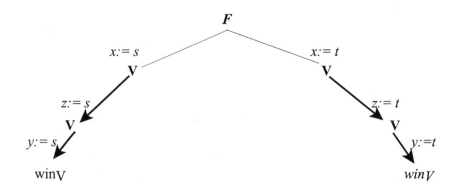

An imperfect information game for $\forall x\ \exists z\ \exists y\ /\{x,\ z\}\ x \neq y$ The preceding game contrasts with the next, where only the dot pattern for V changes:

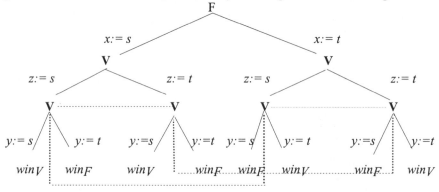

With the uncertainty lines in this second game, V has no strategy which she knows to work.

The phenomenon encountered with $\forall x\ \exists z\ \exists y/x\ x \neq y$ is called *self-signalling*. Players may be able to derive officially unavailable information by a roundabout route. To work well, signalling arguments depend on epistemic assumptions about knowledge, such as *players know their available moves, how many moves have been played,* and so on. In general games of imperfect information, players need not know how many moves were played. But IF syntax always seems to assume at least this much: *V* may know nothing about the object which *F* chose, but she does know that he made a choice.

I have not formulated a precise algorithm for drawing game trees for IF formulas, but the general method should be clear from these examples. One first draws the slash-free game tree, and then, at the level corresponding to an operator, one connects all histories for *E* which differ only in positions on which her choice should not depend.

3.4 *Powers, Game Equivalence, and Game Algebra*

Hintikka and Sandu sometimes call IF games *three-valued*: either *V* has a winning strategy (this is "truth"), or *F* has a winning strategy ("falsity"), or neither ("third truth value"). This is about the most niggardly way of giving imperfect information games some additional structure beyond that of perfect information games.

Uniform Powers. Instead, let us look at the power analysis of section 2.3. This extends immediately to imperfect information games, but this time considering only *uniform* strategies. Thus, in the game of section 3.2, *F* retains the powers he had in the perfect information version, but *V* loses two former powers, retaining only those for her remaining strategies "left, left" and "right, right":

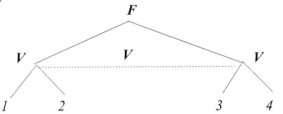

powers of *F*   *{1, 2}, {3, 4}*
powers of *V*   *{1, 3}, {2, 4}*

This list seems poorer than that of the perfect information version. But one can also see it as a more subtle form of power sharing where *V* and *F* have become more equal. In fact, imperfect information is often *needed* in designing organizations giving members just the right amount of influence. This time, the only general conditions that hold are Monotonicity and Consistency. I have shown elsewhere that these suffice to represent any power list for two players by an imperfect information game.[24]

Power Equivalence. Game equivalence may again be analyzed in terms of powers in this new sense. An interesting check is that there already exists a calculus to this effect in game theory, the "Thompson transformations."[25] These match the predictions of power equivalence precisely, at least for games with *Perfect Recall.* We are now in a position to answer an earlier question: *What is the correct game equivalent for* $\forall x\ \exists y/x\ x \neq y$? The answer is, not $\exists y\ \forall x\ x \neq y$, but the symmetric formula: $\exists y\ \forall x/y\ x \neq y$. This is the above game tree, but with turns and outcomes interchanged:

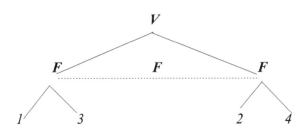

Clearly, players' uniform powers are exactly the same here as in the preceding game tree. This scheduling equivalence is about the most basic Thompson transformation.

A similar analysis of the Hodges example $\forall x\ \exists z\ \exists y/x\ x \neq y$ shows that it is equivalent to the formula $\forall x\ \exists y\ x \neq y$, which is slash-free and determined. On the other hand, this is not a Thompson transformation, as we are not assuming *Perfect Recall.*

IF Logic as Game Calculus. These observations raise some interesting logical issues. We can see the equivalential part of IF logic as a calculus for game equivalence, just as first-order logic encoded such a calculus for perfect information games in section 2.4. For instance, the equivalence between $\forall x\ \exists y/x\ \phi$ and $\exists y\ \forall x/y\ \phi$ is a valid distribution law of sorts. It also has propositional equivalents, such as

$$(A\ \mathbf{V}/\wedge\ B) \wedge (C\ \mathbf{V}/\wedge\ D) \quad \leftrightarrow \quad (A\wedge C/\vee) \vee (B\wedge/\vee D)$$

One interesting question is this: Does IF logic have a simple subsystem of operator equivalences which axiomatizes uniform power equivalence over general games?

Operations and Game Algebra. There are also pitfalls in extending the account of section 2. Hintikka's well-known quarrels with compositionality reflect the game-theoretic difficulty that imperfect information games "have no good notion of a subgame." Their dotted lines mess up the compositional structure of the underlying game tree. So, are there natural operations at all on imperfect information games?

Parallel Products. Perhaps a shift in perspective is needed. Abramsky embeds some IF games in linear game semantics, using parallel composition to achieve imperfect information.[26] This would embed part of IF logic into *linear logic*, although the sense in which it does this is a bit unclear, given the different complexities. Netchitajlov proposes further parallel products, allowing for interleaved play.[27]

Here is a simpler observation from an article of my own with a similar point.[28] A basic structure in game theory is to use strategy matrices. Two players move in parallel, with four possible outcomes. A parallel phenomenon in logic is "branching quantification":

$$\begin{array}{c} \forall x \, \exists y \\ \\ \forall z \, \exists u \end{array} \Bigg\rangle \; Rxyzu$$

This lets choices for prefixes take place independently—bringing them together at the end to evaluate the matrix assertion *Rxyzu*. Such games involve a mild form of imperfect information: ignorance of others' moves played at the same time. We can define the corresponding game operation more generally as

product G x H

whose runs are pairs of separate runs for *G, H* with the product of their end states as the total end state. In terms of players' powers, this works out as:

$$\rho^i{}_{GxH} \, (s, t), X \;\; \text{iff} \;\; \exists U \colon \rho^i{}_G \, s, \, U \, , \; \exists V \colon \rho^i{}_H \, t, \, V : UxV \subseteq X$$

Players' powers in such games are no longer determined, but they still satisfy Monotonicity and Consistency, and there is an analogue of the above representation result.

FACT   The following identities of game algebra hold for product games:

$A \times (B \cup C) \;\; = \;\; (AxB) \cup (AxC)$

$(A \cup B) \times C \;\; = \;\; (AxC) \cup (BxC)$

$(A \times B)^d \;\;\;\;\; = \;\; A^d \times B^d$

$G \times H \;\;\;\;\;\;\; = \;\; H \times G$

This follows by straightforward analysis of players' powers. The fourth line assumes that the component order in product states *(s, t)* is immaterial.

But now back to IF games. What would it mean to play an evaluation game $\phi x \psi$? Consider the above branching quantifier. Here is a corresponding slash formula:

$$\forall x \, \exists y \, \forall z/\{x, y\} \, \exists u/\{x, y\} \, Rxyzu$$

which suppresses all information flow between the two prefixes. In game-algebraic terms, this is written as follows, with a "test game" at the end:

$$((\forall x \, ; \, \exists y) \, x \, (\forall z \, ; \, \exists u)) \, ; \, Rxyzu?$$

Thus, again, at least this fragment of IF logic seems a mixture of general game algebra and special facts about first-order semantic procedures. Game-algebraic laws now have IF instances that allow one to manipulate quantifier prefixes, such as

$$(\forall x \, ; \, \exists y) \, x \, ((\forall z \, ; \, \forall u) \, \cup \, (\exists v \, ; \, \exists u)) \, =$$

$$((\forall x \, ; \, \exists y) \, x \, (\forall z \, ; \, \forall u)) \, \cup \, ((\forall x \, ; \, \exists y) \, x \, (\exists v \, ; \, \exists u))$$

Also, valid principles of IF logic show up as algebraic validities. For example, the above

$$\forall x \, \exists y/x \, Rxy \, \leftrightarrow \, \exists y \, \forall x/y \, Rxy$$

says in game-algebraic terms that

$$(G \, x \, H) \, ; \, K \, = \, (H \, x \, G) \, ; \, K$$

This principle follows easily from the above game algebra. But IF logic can also detect invalid algebraic principles. Here is an example of the latter:

$$(A \, x \, B) \, ; \, C \, = \, (A \, ; \, C) \, x \, (B \, ; \, C)$$

An IF-counterexample is the slash formula $\exists x \, \forall y/x \, Rxy$, whose evaluation game is not equivalent to that for the perfect information game for $\exists x \, Rxy$; $\forall y \, Rxy$. Given these observations, can we extend the representation theorem for perfect information games via evaluation games in my earlier example to IF logic after all?[29]

3.5 Dynamic-Epistemic Logic of Actions and Knowledge

Games as Dynamic-Epistemic Models. Within information games many interesting phenomena occur as players move through a game. To bring this out, we must move to the action level of section 2.5 with a formalism to describe what players *know*. Games of imperfect information have states, moves, and epistemic equivalence relations $\sim_i$ for players i between states. The resulting models look like this:

$M = (S, \{R_a| \, a \in A\}, \{\sim_i | \, i \in I\}, V)$

In principle, any uncertainty pattern might occur. Players need not know what the opponent has played, or they themselves; they need not know whether it is their turn, if the game has ended, and so on. Game theorists sometimes impose restrictions like common knowledge of the current turn or moves—which can be special axioms.

Dynamic-Epistemic Logic. These models support a standard combined dynamic-epistemic language, with action modalities *[a]*, *<a>* for moves as in section 2.6, and knowledge operators for each player:

$M, s \models K_i\phi$ iff $M, t \models \phi$ *for all t s.t. s $\sim_i$ t*

Now we can talk about knowledge and ignorance of players when the game has reached a certain state. This illuminates the intuitive situation depicted in section 3.1. At the intermediate states, Verifier's knowledge may be described as follows:

$K_V(<y:=s>win_V \vee <y:=t>win_V)$
$\neg K_V<y:=s> win_V \; \& \; \neg K_V<y:=t> win_V$

This is a familiar distinction from intensional logic. *V* knows *de dicto* that she has a winning move, but she lacks a *de re* version: there is no particular move that she knows to be winning. You may know the ideal partner is walking around in this dark rain-swept town without knowing of any passer-by whether she or he is that partner. Players can also have *iterated* knowledge about others' knowledge and ignorance via formulas like $K_iK_j\phi$, $K_i\neg K_j\phi$, which may be crucial to understanding the course of a game. Also players may achieve *common knowledge* about certain facts:

$C_{\{1, 2\}} \phi$ ϕ is true in all those states that can be reached from
the current one in a finite number of $\sim_1$ and $\sim_2$ steps

In the above game, *E*'s plight is common knowledge among the players.

As for systematic reasoning about players' actions, knowledge, and ignorance in such models, the complete set of axioms for validity in dynamic-epistemic logic is

(a) the *minimal dynamic logic* for the modal operators *[a]*
(b) *epistemic S5* for each knowledge operator K_i

With a common knowledge operator added, we also get the minimal logic of that.[30] There are no further axioms in general—but see below.

Defining Uniform Strategies. In these game models, we can also define players' strategies as in section 2.2. Recall that the relevant strategies now are the *uniform* ones, which have to prescribe the same moves at indistinguishable nodes for a player where it is her turn. Speaking generally, this restricts the possible behaviors. The above examples suggest that the uniform strategies are the ones of which a player *knows* that they lead to the desired result. This will show in available strategy definitions of this language, which may contain instructions like

"IF $K_{you}P$ THEN *do a* ELSE *do b*"

It was suggested in section 3.3 that uniform strategies are precisely those that force a set of outcomes such that their owners *know* at each stage of using them that they will produce that set. But this is still imprecise, and not always true—e.g., with "self-signalling" examples like the above $\forall x \exists z \exists y/x \; x \neq y$. A more precise description is found in an essay of mine[31] which shows that for players with *Perfect Recall*, uniform strategies and "fully predictive" strategies of this epistemic kind indeed coincide. This may be seen as a kind of epistemic analysis of Skolem functions.

Varieties of Imperfection. Within the total universe of behavior, specific imperfect information games may validate additional epistemic-dynamic axioms, such as the game-theoretic assumptions mentioned above, which also hold for IF games:

(a) The fact who is to move is common knowledge between players
(b) All indistinguishable nodes have the same possible actions

More generally, in this way, we can do an epistemic analysis of types of imperfect information game, distinguishing different strands inside full IF syntax. In particular, the cited reference shows how one can distinguish *ways of playing games*, and describe their effects. For instance, consider players who have the above-mentioned feature of *Perfect Recall*, operating with perfect memory amidst the structural uncertainties introduced by the game itself. In particular, the latter may arise through defective observation of other players' moves. This restricts the pattern of dotted uncertainty lines in ways expressed by two additional principles:

(a) $turn_i \; \& \; K_i[a]\phi \;\rightarrow\; [a]K_i\phi$
(b) $\neg turn_i \; \& \; K_i[A]\phi \;\rightarrow\; [A]K_i\phi$

  with A the union of all actions available to the other player

These axioms say that moves of player *i* in this game *commute* with her knowledge. This commutation fails in general dynamic-epistemic logic, since my normal actions can have epistemic side-effects. I may know that "having a beer" will lead to my "being a bore," without knowing I am being a bore once I have drunk the beer. The resulting restriction on games is a commutative diagram. For example, for (a) we get:

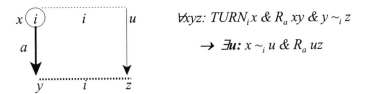

$$\forall xyz: TURN_i x \ \& \ R_a xy \ \& \ y \sim_i z$$
$$\rightarrow \exists u: x \sim_i u \ \& \ R_a uz$$

One can take this restriction to IF games, and ask just which syntactic slash patterns obey this commutative condition. In particular, the preceding diagram says that V's slashes at some level in a quantifier prefix must have ancestors at the preceding prefix position, if the latter is an existential quantifier. The result of the restricted syntax might be a simpler sublogic for game equivalence.

At an opposite extreme to *Perfect Recall*, players have *Bounded Memory*, allowing them to remember only the last k moves played for some k. This, too, can be expressed in dynamic-epistemic logic. For example, with $k=1$, we get a characteristic axiom

$$<a>\phi \ \rightarrow \ U[a]\neg K_i \neg \phi$$

with U a *universal* modality. This, too, is a pattern of IF syntax: slashes should start appearing beyond a certain distance in the quantifier prefix. Agents with different epistemic capacities, and their interactions, can be described naturally in dynamic-epistemic logic.[32] More generally then, it would be of interest to look at the fine-structure of IF games, and characterize those fragments of IF syntax which model natural ways of playing games, along with their corresponding axioms in our logic. The dynamic-epistemic language will allow us to reason about V and F's interaction in these games.

3.6 *A Second Summary*

We have shown how IF games may be seen as perfectly ordinary games of imperfect information. The fact that there are some difficulties of making intuitive sense of them merely reflects intriguing similar subtleties in game theory. At the level of players' powers, one can do an analysis of equivalence in terms of uniform strategies, and even an incipient game algebra. This led to open questions about IF logic serving as a complete algebra for varieties of imperfect information games. But perhaps the most interesting perspective is the more detailed action level. There we can use explicit epistemic logic to describe players' progress in a game, and define interesting types of special behavior. These correspond to IF sublanguages, with perhaps better-behaved logics. Thus, we get a handle on what might be called the fine-structure of IF logic.

4. DISCUSSION

Finally, we will point at some further issues concerning IF logic that we had previously to forego. After that, we will state our main claims, and draw our general conclusions.

Logical Aspects. There are many further logical aspects to IF logic.

First, it would be good to add an explicit component of *strategy calculus*, dealing, amongst others, with Skolem functions. But the latter would have to be generalized, as we are dealing not just with V but also with independent powers of F. Instead of embedding IF logic into second-order logic as it is now, this might enrich second-order logic to a system with a duality between Skolem functions for two players.

Another aspect is the question whether the first-order language, even when slashed, is really the right formalism for the enterprise. With many other deviant logics one is led to introduce *new logical operators* reflecting the new setting. Examples are the product operations of linear logic, which made their appearance in section 3.3. Other examples might be polyadic quantifiers, letting players pick bunches of objects at the same time. Redesign of the IF syntax is also taken up by Hintikka.[33]

Finally, a widely noted desideratum: one would like to have a more general account of "IF-ing" which can also be applied to study imperfect information versions of other logic games, such as proofs in which participants either do not know some earlier moves, or model comparisons requiring players to make do with a finite memory.

Game-theoretic Aspects. IF games introduce one type of more realistic structure over traditional logic games of semantic evaluation, viz., imperfect information. But there are other candidates. For instance, real game theory is about games in which players have finer *preferences* than the "win"/"lose" of logic games. This can also be done in logic games, giving V, F independent evaluations of atomic facts in a model. This fits with modern default logics using preferences for players in their models. An example was the non-zero-sum battle-field game of section 2.2:

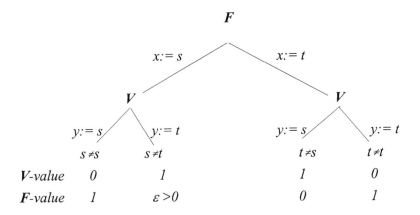

V-value	0	1	1	0
F-value	1	$\varepsilon > 0$	0	1

Now a deeper issue arises. In game theory, preferences lead to Nash's notion of *strategic equilibrium*, and finer predictions of behavior. For instance, the original game of section 2.2 has two Nash equilibria: *V* plays her winning strategy, *F* any strategy:

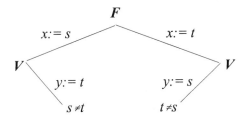

The game with the ε-preference has only one equilibrium, resulting in

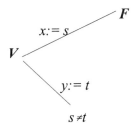

The set of Nash equilibria of its evaluation games might be a good candidate for a more radical game-theoretic denotation of a logical formula.

Another realistic game-theoretic feature is *coalitions*. Perhaps the most significant move in epistemic logic after Hintikka's pioneering work has been the introduction of operators that are typical to groups of agents, such as *common knowledge*.[34] It suggests a similar extension of IF logic with joint actions for groups of agents. In particular, the players *V, F* themselves might be teams. A first logical analysis of coalitions was proposed by Pauly,[35] but epistemic and dynamic logic have not yet taken in this notion in its full generality.

Probability? But things are even more intriguing. The basic insight in game theory has been that strategic equilibria may only exist in a game when we move from *pure* to *mixed strategies*, using probabilistic mixtures of pure strategies. This mixture will not arise in the standard logic games of section 2 with preferences added, as we can always find Nash equilibria there using the well-known algorithm of "backward induction," a numerical version of the proof of the Zermelo Theorem on determinacy. But, probabilistic solutions do arise in some IF games. The little game in section 3.2

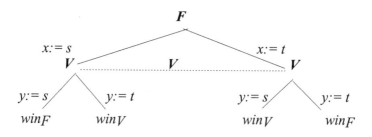

is just the game-theoretic classic of "Matching Pennies." This has an optimal value (1/2, 1/2), achieved by players using their uniform strategies with probability 1/2.

I find this observation extremely intriguing from a logical point of view. We know that probability sometimes emerges naturally in pure logic, telling us something about long-term behavior. An example is the *Zero-One laws* of first-order logic which state that with increasing finite domain size the probability that any given first-order formula is true goes to either 1 or 0. Could it be that IF games also involve an essential probabilistic feature, which we just have not been able to identify yet?

Architecture of Intended Applications. The original grand motivations of game-theoretical semantics had to do with describing large-scale cognitive systems such as natural language.[36] Evaluation games are just a small part of this story, but more can be said. Natural language or ordinary reasoning involves many different games. There are terminating finite-depth games for short-term tasks, such as evaluation or proof. Nice recent examples on very different principles from IF games are the interpretation games of van Rooy with speaker/hearer preferences from linguistic optimality theory,[37] and the argumentation games of Rubinstein analyzing Gricean pragmatics.[38] But there are also infinite games providing the hopefully never-ending "operating system" for these short-term tasks, such as the procedural rules of civilized conversation or debate. Another missing feature of IF logic, then, is an account of architecture: how do different games fit together into one coherent system? How can information be passed from one game to another?

5. CONCLUSION

What has been shown in this paper is that logical evaluation games, either Hintikka's original ones or their IF versions, can be linked systematically with game-theoretic themes, some of them present in existing game theory and some of them new. In particular, this has led to some insights and new questions about game-theoretical semantics, summarized in sections 2.6 and 3.5, which need not be repeated here. Whatever its merits as an exegesis of Hintikka's intentions, I hope this has been a convincing sample of the lively current interface between logic, computer science, and game theory, which naturally covers many more topics.[39]

As to IF games specifically, we propose viewing them in a systematic game-theoretic light, which suggests a host of new perspectives and questions. In doing so one encounters Hintikka's pioneering work once more, since the tool of choice in this area is his very own epistemic logic in its original form. This is somewhat surprising since many of the informal explanations behind the Hintikka and Sandu approach involve players' knowledge, but they are left implicit. Admittedly, there are published IF versions of epistemic languages, but my point is rather that one can illuminate the workings of any IF game by means of standard static epistemic operators. Of course, one can then play a carrousel research game of systems $EL(IF(EL(IF. \ldots$

Finally, let us briefly reconsider the central IF motivation of possible independence between and among quantifiers. As I said before, Hintikka's writings leave open an interpretation where *this* independence is the central topic, and the games become just a discardable wrapping. This is a crucial decision point. For, *if* we take the games seriously, then eventually dependence and independence will *not* be the central notions. They are rather derivatives from something still more central, namely, *interaction* between players. I will make no further defense of the latter here, but the issue cannot be evaded.

Nevertheless, I totally agree that independence is a crucial logical topic. But then we must be radical and account for the fact that the notice is quite diverse, with intuitively different sources. Hintikka describes one of these: *procedural dependencies* that arise in a process of evaluating assertions. These dependencies are absolutely important—but there are also *objective dependencies* in the nature of things, lying encoded in models whether or not we interpret anything at all. Objective dependencies have been studied by van Lambalgen on the logic of independent events in probabilistic reasoning.[40] Another example, with more published results, is "generalized assignment semantics" for first-order logic,[41] which drops the assumption of the standard Tarskian models that values for variables can be modified completely independently of what happens to other variables. This, too, generates a new base logic of dependent and independent quantifiers different from standard first-order logic, while supporting a richer logical vocabulary of polyadic quantifiers and substitutions. But the intriguing difference with IF logic is that in its case, the true first-order basic logic (without any built-in objective independence assumptions) has lower, rather than higher complexity: it becomes *decidable*! Were I to write a paper on independence—which I have not done—a comparison between these varieties of independence logics would be the first order of business.

Despite possible divergences in interests, one only writes a long paper like this if the subject seems worthwhile. IF logic offers an attractive laboratory for studying the logic of imperfect information and information flow generally. Hintikka's broad intellectual vision and challenging ideas over the years have been remarkable—and like many colleagues, I am still happy to experience his continued influence.

JOHAN VAN BENTHEM

AMSTERDAM AND STANFORD
DECEMBER 2002

NOTES

1. Jaakko Hintikka, *Logic, Language Games and Information* (Oxford: Clarendon Press, 1973).

2. Jaakko Hintikka and Jack Kulas, *The Game of Language* (Dordrecht: Kluwer, 1985).

3.   Jaakko Hintikka and Gabriel Sandu, "Game-Theoretical Semantics," in *Handbook of Logic and Language*, ed. J. van Benthem and A. ter Meulen (Amsterdam: Elsevier, 1997), pp. 361–410.

4.   See Jaakko Hintikka, "Hyperclassical Logic (a.k.a. IF Logic) and Its Implications for Logical Theory," *Bulletin of Symbolic Logic* 8, no. 3 (2002): 404–23.

5.   See the general program in Johan van Benthem, "Logic in Games," lecture notes, ILLC Amsterdam and Stanford University, 1999–2002.

6.   Johan van Benthem, "What Logic Games are Trying to Tell Us," invited lecture, 7th Asian Logic Conference, Taiwan, 1999. Research Report PP-2002-25, ILLC Amsterdam.

7.   Ernst Zermelo, "Ueber eine Anwendung der Mengenlehre auf die Theorie des Schachspiels," in *Proceedings of the Fifth International Congress of Mathematicians*, ed. E. Hobson and A. Love (Cambridge: Cambridge University Press, 1913), pp. 501–4.

8.   Johan van Benthem, "Games in Dynamic-Epistemic Logic," *Bulletin of Economic Research* 53, no. 4 (2001): 219–48.

9.   Rohit Parikh, "The Logic of Games and its Applications," *Annals of Discrete Mathematics* 24 (1985): 111–40; Marc Pauly, "Logic for Social Software," PhD diss., DS-2001-10, Institute for Logic, Language and Computation, University of Amsterdam, 2001.

10.   Cf. also work on links with modal languages in computational process theories. Johan van Benthem, "Extensive Games as Process Models," *Journal of Logic, Language and Information* 11 (2002): 289–313.

11.   Andreas Blass, "A Game Semantics for Linear Logic," *Annals of Pure and Applied Logic* 56 (1992): 183–220; Samson Abramsky, "Semantics of Interaction: An Introduction to Game Semantics," in *Proceedings 1996 CLiCS Summer School, Isaac Newton Institute*, ed. P. Dybjer and A. Pitts (Cambridge: Cambridge University Press, 1996), pp. 1–31.

12.   See Valentin Goranko, "The Basic Algebra of Game Equivalences," *Studia Logica* (Special Issue on Game Logic) 75 (2003): 221–38.

13.   Johan van Benthem, "Logic Games are Complete for Game Logics," *Studia Logica* 75, no. 2 (2003): 183–203.

14.   See Osborne and Rubinstein for this and other game-theoretic points. Martin Osborne and Ariel Rubinstein, *A Course in Game Theory* (Cambridge, Mass.: MIT Press, 1994).

15.   For more on this fine-grained analysis using modal logic as the game logic, cf. van Benthem, "Games in Dynamic-Epistemic Logic" and "Extensive Games as Process Models."

16.   See Yiannis Moschovakis, "Sense and Denotation as Algorithm and Value," *Lecture Notes in Logic* #2, ed. J. Oikkonen and J. Väänänen (Berlin: Springer Verlag, 1994), pp. 210–49.

17.   See Osborne and Rubinstein, *A Course in Game Theory*, ch. 11.

18.   Wilfrid Hodges, "Compositional Semantics for a Language of Imperfect

Information," *Journal of the IGPL* 5 (1997): 539–63; Theo Janssen, "Independent Choices and the Interpretation of IF Logic," *Journal of Logic, Language and Information* 11 (2002): 367–87.

19. Jaakko Hintikka, *Knowledge and Belief* (Ithaca: Cornell University Press, 1962).

20. See Gabriel Sandu and Jouko Väänänen, "Partially Ordered Connectives," *Zeitschrift für Mathematische Logik und Grundlagen der Mathematik* 38 (1992): 361–72.

21. See Alexandru Baltag, Lawrence Moss, and Slawomir Solecki, "The Logic of Public Announcements, Common Knowledge and Private Suspicions," *Proceedings TARK 1998* (Los Altos: Morgan Kaufmann Publishers, 1998), 43–56. Update in 2002: Department of Cognitive Science, Indiana University, Bloomington, and Department of Computing, Oxford University. Hans van Ditmarsch, "Knowledge Games," PhD diss., DS-2000-06, Institute for Logic, Language and Computation, University of Amsterdam, 2000. Johan van Benthem, "Logics for Information Update," *Proceedings TARK VIII* (Los Altos: Morgan Kaufmann Publishers, 2001), pp. 51–88.

22. Hodges, "Compositional Semantics for a Language of Imperfect Information."

23. See Osborne and Rubinstein, *A Course in Game Theory*, ch. 5; Robert Stalnaker, "Extensive and Strategic Form: Games and Models for Games," *Research in Economics* 53, no. 3 (1999): 293–319.

24. Van Benthem, "Games in Dynamic-Epistemic Logic," p. 241.

25. Osborne and Rubinstein, *A Course in Game Theory*, ch. 11.

26. Samson Abramsky, "Games in Computer Science and Logical Dynamics," invited lecture, 12th Amsterdam Colloquium, ILLC Amsterdam, 2000.

27. Youri Netchitajlov, "An Extension of Game Logic with Parallel Operators," Master of Logic thesis, Institute for Logic, Language and Computation, University of Amsterdam, 2000.

28. Johan van Benthem, "Logic Games are Complete for Game Logics."

29. Ibid.

30. See Ronald Fagin, Joseph Halpern, Yoram Moses, and Moshe Vardi, *Reasoning about Knowledge* (Cambridge, Mass.: MIT Press, 1995).

31. Van Benthem, "Games in Dynamic-Epistemic Logic, p. 246.

32. Johan van Benthem and Fenrong Liu, "Diversity of Logical Agents in Games," Research Report 2004-13, ILLC Amsterdam. To appear in *Philosophia Scientiae*.

33. See Hintikka, "Hyperclassical Logic (a.k.a. IF Logic) and Its Implications for Logical Theory."

34. Fagin et al., *Reasoning about Knowledge*; Osborne and Rubinstein, *A Course in Game Theory*.

35. Pauly, "Logic for Social Software."

36. Hintikka and Sandu, "Game-Theoretical Semantics."

37. Robert van Rooy, "Signalling Games Select Horn Strategies," *Linguistics and Philosophy* 27, no. 4 (2004): 493–527.

38. Ariel Rubinstein, *Economics and Language* (Cambridge: Cambridge University Press, 2000), ch. 3.

39. Cf. van Benthem, "Logic in Games," and dedicated conferences such as TARK, LOFT, and GAMES.

40. Michiel van Lambalgen, "Natural Deduction for Generalized Quantifiers," in *Quantifiers, Logic and Language*, ed. J. van der Does and J. van Eyck, CSLI Lecture Notes, vol. 54 (1995), Stanford University, 225–36.

41. István Németi, "The Equational Theory of Cylindric Relativized Set Algebras is Decidable," Preprint No. 63/85, Mathematical Institute, Hungarian Academy of Sciences, Budapest, 1985; J. van Benthem, *Exploring Logical Dynamics* (Stanford: CSLI Publications, 1996); J. van Benthem, "Modal Foundations for Predicate Logic," invited lecture, WoLLIC, Recife, 1995; appeared in *Bulletin of the IGPL* 5, no. 2 (1997), 259–86, London and Saarbruecken (R. de Queiroz, ed., *Proceedings WoLLIC, Recife 1995*).

REPLY TO JOHAN VAN BENTHEM

Johan van Benthem and I have in common an approach to logic using the concepts and tools of the mathematical theory of games. But in the same sense as the British and the Americans are proverbially separated by a common language, so van Benthem and I are separated by our supposedly shared approach. In his exemplary paper van Benthem examines what thus unites us and what separates us methodologically. To my mind he has diagnosed the relationship of our respective approaches to each other perceptively, accurately, and fairly. What remains for me to do in this response is to give an account of that relationship from my perspective.

Van Benthem studies logical games as special cases of a more general theory of games. This includes prominently my "semantical games," called by van Benthem "evaluation games." In such a theory, the knowledge states of the players are among the most crucial parameters. As his title indicates, van Benthem seeks to capture this aspect of logical games by means of epistemic logic. In contrast, my use of game-theoretical ideas culminates in a new basic logic, independence-friendly (IF) logic, which is a non-epistemic, nonmodal and extensional first-order language. In van Benthem's words, the central motivation of IF logic is the phenomenon of quantifier independence. He writes: "Hintikka's writings leave open an interpretation where *this* independence is the central topic, and the games become just a discardable wrapping. [In contrast] *if* we take the games seriously, then eventually dependence and independence will *not* be the central notions." This is a remarkably perceptive statement and it can serve as the starting point of a diagnosis of the differences between van Benthem's approach and mine. From my perspective this statement nevertheless requires several explanations and reformulations.

In one sense I take a strong exception to van Benthem's last sentence. No matter what line we take, dependence and independence will not fade from our logical theory. Like the poor according to the New Testament dependence and independence will always be with us. I have formulated the reason for this pervasive role of the notions of dependence and independence several other responses in this volume. Its importance nevertheless justifies a repetition. The reason is that expressing dependence and independence is an integral part of the semantics of quantifiers. One of the most important things that must be expressible in any fully satisfactory factual language is dependencies and independencies between variables in the world of which the language speaks. But how is the (actual material) dependence of a variable y on another variable, say x, expressed in a logical language? By the formal dependence of the quantifier $(Q_2 y)$ to which y is bound on the quantifier $(Q_1 x)$ to which x is bound. (A moment's silent mediation should enable a reader to see this.)

This point provides at once a clinching motivation for IF logic. For how are formal dependencies between quantifiers expressed in received logical language? By the nesting of their scopes, of course. But nesting can create only a heavily restricted class of patterns of dependence and independence between variables. For one thing, the nesting (inclusion) relation is transitive and antisymmetric. In order to express all possible structures of dependence and independence between variables we must therefore be able to formulate all possible patterns of formal dependence and independence between quantifiers. This is precisely what is accomplished in IF first-order logic. In the sense appearing from these remarks, one can never dispense with the notions of dependence and independence in logic, no matter whether one formulates it game-theoretically or not, as long as quantifiers are expressible in one's language.

Thus van Benthem's suspicion is correct up to a point. The fundamental idea in IF logic is dependence. What happens is that such (f)actual dependence can for the purpose of logical and semantical theorizing be handily modelled by informational independence in the sense of game theory. It is nevertheless highly misleading to say that because of this priority of the notion of dependence games are nothing but "discardable wrapping." I believe that Wittgenstein was right and that some of the basic language-world links are actually constituted by what I have called semantical games. And these links are precisely the games that serve as the semantics of IF logic. It also turns out that the game angle is most suggestive in analyzing further the ideas of dependence and independence, which on closer examination can be seen to be much more complicated than first meets the eye. This is especially true of the idea of mutual dependence. In order to express irreducible mutual dependence each of us has to go beyond IF logic as it is currently formulated. Interestingly, game-theoretical ideas still remain useful. In fact, one of the crucial generalizations is simply the admission of mixed strategies over and above pure ones.

There is nevertheless a much more general and much more important reason for the usefulness of the game angle. It is not much of an exaggeration to say that the term "game theory" is a misnomer. The central concept of all game theory is the notion of strategy. This notion applies well beyond the conceptions we normally call games. Often there are strategies of cooperation and not only strategies of competition. Now I believe that the strategic aspects of logic have been seriously neglected in logical theory. The best antidote is naturally the theory of strategies, even if it is misnamed "theory of games."

Here we also encounter a technical point which has little general theoretical interest, but which makes a difference to the actual applications of game ideas to logic. If the crucial questions in such applications concern the dependence and independence of variables, the only interesting form of ignorance in semantical games is a player's ignorance of earlier moves. Now in the game theory of von Neumann and Morgenstern a much wider class of forms of ignorance is allowed in that a player's information sets need not specify only the earlier moves by the actual players that a given player is aware of when making a specific move.[1] Apparently von Neumann and Morgenstern wanted to be able to apply their theory also to games (such as, e.g., bridge) where other kinds of ignorance are possible. But such applications, however interesting intrinsically, are not relevant to the applications to logic that are my central concern. In applications to logic we can build a much smoother theory simply by restricting all admissible information sets to sets specifying the earlier moves of which a player is aware. This restriction eliminates in one fell swoop a large number of questions, for instance all questions of uniformity, not because they are not of interest to a game theorist, but because they are not of immediate interest to a logician.

With the help of such a simplification, we can reach an overview of all possible patterns of dependence and independence of variables on each other, at least on the level of dependencies and independencies of moves on each other in a semantical game. Both van Benthem and Hodges in effect point out that there are forms of dependence that I apparently have not taken into account in IF logic, for instance, the dependence of an existential quantifier on another existential quantifier. On the face of it, my slash notation allows only one kind of independence not expressible already in the received first-order logic, viz., the independence of an existential quantifier ($\exists y/\forall x$) of a universal quantifier ($\forall x$) in whose syntactical scope it occurs. Such dependencies can even be manifested in actual games in the form of such familiar phenomena as signaling. (Just think here of the various bidding conventions in bridge.) In some cases, dependencies between existential quantifiers can obviously be expressed in my notation.

For instance, van Benthem's simple sample sentence (in his notation)

(1) $\forall x \exists z \exists y/x \; x=y$

has in my notation the Skolem form

(2) $(\exists f)(\exists g)(\forall x)(x=f(g(x)))$

This is according to what was said earlier equivalent with

(3) $(\exists f)(\exists g)(\forall x)(\forall w)((w=g(x)) \supset (x=f)w)))$

which in my notation translates back to the first-order level as

(4) $(\forall x)(\forall w)(\exists z/\!\!\forall w)(\exists y/\!\!\forall x) \; ((w=z) \supset (x=y))$

This will give as good an analysis of what goes on in the relevant game as van Benthem's without any appeal to intuitions. It illustrates the fact that the intriguing phenomenon of signaling can be dealt with without any difficulty and my approach, too.

It is not equally obvious, however, what can be said in general terms. This question is answered in my 2002 paper "Hyperclassical Logic (a.k.a. IF Logic) and its Implication for Logical Theory."[2] There I consider all possible patterns of dependence and independence between variables. This examination can even be applied when explicit dependence indicators as well as independence indicators are being used. I show in my paper that as far as only conditions of truth are concerned, all of them can be expressed by means of my original slash notation. This generalizes the treatment of signaling just presented. It provides an overview of all possible kinds of structures of dependent and independent variables, at least as far as dependencies between moves are concerned.

What is not covered by this treatment are dependencies of strategies in contradistinction to dependencies of moves, to use the game-theoretical jargon. Special cases of such strategic dependence, including dependencies instantiated in the semantics of natural-language conditionals, are studied in my book *The Game of Language* (1983). Such strategic dependence turns out to be crucial also in dealing with irreducibly mutual dependence and suggests interesting generalizations of key logical and mathematical concepts. As far as I know, dependencies between strategies have not been studied systematically in other applications of game theory to logic.

An example of strategic dependence is provided by what is known as complex donkey sentences, for instance

(5)   If you give a gift to each child for Christmas, some child will open it today.

In evaluating the antecedent, the verifier relies on a Skolem function that for each child as an argument yields as its value a gift given by you to that child. In evaluating the consequent the verifier must "remember" that Skolem function in order to pick out the gift given to that particular child that is the value of the quantifier phrase "some child."

One fundamental question of research strategy we encounter here is: How should the epistemic (informational) aspects of logical games be handled? As van Benthem's very title shows, he proposes to deal with them by means of epistemic logic. This brings out another major difference between van Benthem's approach and mine. In IF first-order languages, we need not resort to epistemic logic of any sort. The informational dependencies between variables are naturally expressed by the Skolem functions linking them to each other. Skolem functions do the job of spelling out the kinds of information transfer that are needed, in the first place at least. Of course, when my approach is extended to dependencies between strategies, the transfer of information has to be expressed by functionals instead of functions. The procedure has a precedent in Gödel's *Dialectica* interpretation.[3] It is of interest to note that Gödel was trying to capture by an interpretation of logic and arithmetic closely related to the intuitionistic one. The connection here lies in the fact that intuitionistic logic can be viewed as a kind of epistemic logic.

Indeed, it seems to me that by far the best research strategy is to invert van Benthem's priorities, not to try to study logical games by means of epistemic logic, but to use the notion of independence to formulate a satisfactory general epistemic logic. Once again, I have explained the main points elsewhere, among other places in my paper "A Second Generation Epistemic Logic."[4] Once again, the point is important enough to be repeated.

It can be seen by asking: What is the logical form of wh-questions? The answer given by the earlier epistemic logic looks obvious and impeccable. To *know who* (say x) satisfies the condition $F[x]$ is to *know of some one particular person x* that he or she did it, in symbols

(6) $(\exists x)K\, F[x]$

where K can be read "it is known that." But this analysis does not work for more complex wh-questions where the questioned element depends on an outside universal quantifier, as in the following:

(7)   It is known whom each person admires most.

(8)   It is known that the value of the observed variable y is related to the value of the controlled variable x by the law $F[x,y]$.

These may be what the corresponding wh-questions are calculated to bring about:

(9)   Whom does each person admire most?

(10)   How does the value of the variable y depend on the value of the variable x?

Here the only viable form is

(11) $K(\forall x)(\exists y/K)\, F[x,y]$

This form can easily be motivated by reference to the possible-worlds or possible-scenarios analysis of *knowing that*. It can also be explained by pointing out that $(\exists/-)$ is the questioned ingredient in (11). If we try to force (11) into a form similar to (6), $(\exists y)$ must therefore precede K. But it depends on $(\forall x)$ and hence follows it on a linear order. Yet $(\forall x)$ is not questioned and therefore must occur within the scope of K.

It can be shown how by means of the slash notation $(-/K)$ the logical forms of all possible wh-questions and propositional questions can be formulated and a general theory developed for them. This theory includes explicit formulations of such notions as the presupposition of a question, the conclusiveness conditions ("presuppositions") of its answers, and the desideratum of a question, that is, a specification of the epistemic state of affairs that an answer to the question is calculated to bring about. The question ingredient that is used in this theory is in the case of propositional questions $(\vee/K)$ and in the case of wh-questions $(\exists x/K)$. Thus it seems to me that a truly satisfactory theory of epistemic logic must be based on the notion of independence, not vice versa. I have not been building an epistemic logic of IF games, but (among other theories) rather an epistemic logic based on IF games.

I cannot exclude sight unseen other approaches. However, there is a close link between the possible-scenarios interpretation of knowledge and the IF approach to epistemic logic, which makes it very hard to explicate the semantics of knowledge any differently from my slash treatment. And the possible-scenarios analysis of knowledge is by far the most natural way of understanding the all-important role of knowledge in decision-making. These issues are briefly discussed in my forthcoming paper "Epistemology Without Knowledge and Without Belief."[5]

J. H.

NOTES

1. John von Neumann and Oskar Morgenstern, *Theory of Games and Economic Behavior* (Princeton: Princeton University Press, 1944).

2. Jaakko Hintikka, "Hyperclassical Logic (a.k.a. IF Logic) and its Implication for Logical Theory," *Bulletin of Symbolic Logic* 8 (2002): 404–23.

3. Kurt Gödel, *Collected Works* 1–4 (New York: Oxford University Press, 1986–2002), vol. 2, pp. 217–51.

4. Jaakko Hintikka, "A Second Generation Epistemic Logic and its General Significance," in *Knowledge Contributers*, Synthese Library, 322, ed. Vincent F. Hendricks, Klaus Frovin Jørgensen and Stig Andur Pedersen (Dordrecht: Kluwer Academic Publishers, 2003), pp. 33–56.

5. Jaako Hintikka, "Epistemology Without Knowledge and Without Belief," forthcoming.

14

Wilfrid Hodges

THE LOGIC OF QUANTIFIERS

I. THE LOGIC OF QUANTIFIERS

The logic of quantifiers has been a central theme of Jaakko Hintikka's work throughout his career, from his early technical contributions on model-building and distributive normal forms to his most recent commentaries on foundations of mathematics and semantics of natural languages. As a research student in mathematical logic in the late 1960s I knew and admired his technical innovations; it was only many years later that I learned how deeply he had connected them with philosophical issues such as the role of *Anschauung* in Kant's *Critique of Pure Reason*.[1]

At the heart of Hintikka's work on quantifiers there lie two related questions: "What do sentences containing quantifiers mean?" and "When is a sentence containing quantifiers true?" The sentence could come either from a formal language of logic or from a natural language. But Hintikka's approach to natural language semantics is markedly different from that of most late twentieth-century linguistics. He has very little interest in general theories of language, for example, questions of learnability or the relation between syntactic rules and everyday speech. For him the test of reality is what actually happens when people use language: "we have tried to rely more on quotations from contemporary fiction, newspapers and magazines than on linguists' and philosophers' ad hoc examples."[2] So he is not at all inhibited about using sentences that many linguists would regard as deviant or as creative uses of language, such as "Some relative of each villager and some relative of each townsman hate each other."[3] Hintikka is also happy to quote mathematicians' usage, so he will not mind me taking this example from Serge Lang:

Let $0 < a \leq 1$, and m an integer with $|m| \geq 2$. Let $s = \sigma + iT_m$ with $-a \leq \sigma \leq 1 + a$ and T_m as above. Then $|\xi'/\xi\,(s)| \leq B\,(\log|m|)^2$, where B is a number depending on a but not on m and σ.[4]

Here Lang's phrase "depending on a but not on m and σ" plays exactly the role of Hintikka's slash quantifiers (we shall come to them). This is mathematicians' talk, but in practice most English speakers would understand the sentence 'Every villager has a relative (depending only on the villager) and every townsman has a relative (depending only on the townsman) so that these two relatives hate each other.' If we can mean this or understand it, then for Hintikka our "logic of quantifiers" should say how.

Hintikka makes it a requirement on his logical language that it should be "adequate for the description of different natural phenomena."[5] But the natural phenomena that he cites include quite abstruse mathematical discussions. I guess that they would also include the language of Martians if we live to see any samples of it. This allows Hintikka to move fairly freely between natural languages and artificial formal ones, describing a semantical framework that he believes applies to all cases. (Of course, there are differences between quantification in English and in first-order logic, as Hintikka himself emphasizes.)

So Hintikka aims to give a correct description of how quantifiers work. He has other aims too. For example he often speaks of giving "insight" or "illumination," or of "throwing light." These words appear in his writings throughout his career. To give illumination is a noble aim, and many important advances have come through seeing a problem in the right light. But insight is a personal thing; one person's insight can be the next person's distracting irrelevance.

I believe much of Hintikka's work has a third aim. It is not a thing that he emphasizes, but to my mind it is one of his chief achievements. This third aim is to pick up what in one place he calls "curious phenomena that suggest that further explanations are needed."[6] Time and again he brings to our notice things that people hardly ever get quite right, and he forces us to look for "further explanations." For example, we often speak of pronouns or variables "referring back" to something mentioned earlier, even when nothing has been mentioned earlier (for example, when the variable is bound). So what we say is not literally correct, and it calls for further explanation. Hintikka's game semantics is meant to provide that explanation, among other things.

II. Existential Quantifiers

Here is a sample sentence containing an existential quantifier:

(1)   A man I met on a train sold me his hat.

In 1846 Augustus De Morgan made a revealing remark about sentences like (1).[7] He said: "If language were copious enough, particular [i.e., existential] propositions would seldom occur." To illustrate his point, suppose that the sentence above is true, and that two people I met on trains, viz., Mr. Bowler and Mr. Trilby, both sold me their hats. Introduce the term 'trainperson' for the class consisting of Mr. Bowler and Mr. Trilby. Then without any loss of information we can replace the sentence (1) by 'Every trainperson sold me his hat, and I met every trainperson on a train.' De Morgan is assuming, by the usual Aristotelian convention, that any mention of trainpersons implies that there is at least one trainperson. But note that he does not have to assume there is exactly one trainperson. We shall come back to this.

Hintikka's rule for interpreting existential phrases like that in (1) resembles De Morgan's in adding an expression to the language (if necessary) so as to remove the quantifier phrase. The sentence (1) counts as true if and only if there is an individual, whom we can name say as 'b', so that the sentence

(2) b sold me his hat, and I met b on a train.

is true. Hintikka casts this condition in the form of a game for Myself: Myself has one move, namely to choose an individual and name that individual. Myself wins if and only if the resulting sentence (2) is true. The sentence (1) is true if and only if Myself has a winning strategy for this game.[8]

I told a lie. Hintikka's game for the sentence (1) has one more step, namely to interpret 'his'. The details are a little complicated; they depend on whether we interpret 'his hat' as 'a hat of his' or as 'the hat of his'. But the effect is that after Myself has chosen b, the players must somehow choose an individual h for 'his hat'. Where should this individual come from?

Hintikka's suggestion is that we should think of this question in the same way as we ask: From what set is the individual b to be chosen? In both cases something about the context supplies a set that the relevant player can choose from. Of course, the rules that fix the set are different in the two cases. The individual b should presumably be chosen from human beings. But the word 'his' is a cue that h should be chosen from possessions of some person recently identified in the game. Since b was recently identified in this play of the game, h could be one of b's possessions.

But now Hintikka notes that the sentence (1) could occur in a dialogue that raises a completely different possibility: "I collect memorabilia of Elvis Presley. A man I met on a train sold me his hat." Hintikka's semantics allows two players to play a game for these two sentences, one after the other. Then exactly the same rule for 'his hat' allows the players to pick either a possession of b or a possession of the person chosen as Elvis Presley.

This suggestion (which Hintikka attributes in part to Lauri Carlson)[9] was a breakthrough when it came. It gave a semantics for sentences that could be transferred at once to situations where there is cross-referencing between sentences. Since then other formalisms have appeared that cover similar ground, notably the discourse representation theory of Hans Kamp and (independently) Irene Heim.

Hintikka often emphasizes how this behavior of words like 'his' makes them unlike bound variables in first-order logic. Bound variables cannot be bound to something outside the sentence containing them. Since Hintikka's own game semantics grew out of a version for first-order logic, maybe the difference is not so great; the choice set for bound variables is more strictly confined. But there is a major distinction of another kind, because of the syntax of first-order quantifiers. To interpret a sentence of the form $\exists x\, \varphi(x)$ in the game fashion, Myself has to delete the quantifier $\exists x$ and immediately replace all the free occurrences of 'x' by the chosen name 'b'. Myself can't drop 'b' into the sentence to be picked up later by the bound variables 'x', because there is nowhere to drop it.

One might think that linguists would welcome with open arms this game formalism, that allows them to say precise things about cross-referencing of pronouns without using unexplained or question-begging terms like "cross-referencing." They could disagree with some of the rules proposed by Hintikka, but surely they would welcome the games. By and large this has not happened. I think I see at least part of the reason why.

In his John Locke Lectures Hintikka suggests that understanding quantifiers amounts to understanding the language-games that go together with these quantifiers, and "the relation of the different quantifying expressions to these games."[10] This is where the problem lies. We know that a sentence S is true if and only if Myself has a winning strategy for the game $G(S)$ associated with S. But what does the game $G(S)$ itself do for us? How is it related to the quantifiers?

As Hintikka rightly says in many places, the game $G(S)$ does not have to be played at all. But there is a very strong temptation to think of the game $G(S)$ as describing a possible dialogue involving S, or a possible procedure for processing *S*. Here are some examples from Hintikka himself and his collaborators:

> It is thus possible to see in pragmatic terms how the Russellian use of *the*-phrases can be considered as a variant of the anaphoric use. Briefly, since there is no nonempty set *I* in the sense of (G.anaphoric the) available, the hearer interprets the *the*-phrase by making the next most obvious choice, that is, setting *I* equal to the whole domain of discourse.[11]

This conflates the hearer with a player in the game.

> [Discussing a dialogue in which a sentence (58) evokes a reply (59)] . . . it is reasonably clear that the utterer of the question (58) and the answerer who provides the reply are in some sense opponents. Hence, for the defender of the answer (59), the value of "a young mother" in the question (58) is selected by his or her opponent, whose strategy is remembered in the game connected with the answer (59).[12]

This conflates the speakers with the players in a game. "The rules of my semantical games are set up in such a way that the class of individuals quantified over is shown by the behavior of the players of these games."[13] But the games are not played, so there are no players and no behavior.

I am not saying that these and similar passages do not have perfectly acceptable explications. But I do say that the games are treacherous because they invite one to think of them as being played when the sentences are used, and this causes the opposite of illumination. If I were a linguist, I think I would be extremely cautious about using a game semantics that so easily leads us astray. This is a pity, because from a formal point of view these "Hintikka games" have great potential as a tool of linguistic theory, as Hintikka saw.

III. UNIVERSAL QUANTIFIERS

The traditional doctrine about universal quantifiers—it goes back essentially to the thirteenth century—is that (for example) the sentence 'All Nigerians respect their parents' is true if and only if every one of the sentences 'Jim respects his parents', 'Adegabe respects her parents', and so on, as we run through names of all Nigerians, is true. Tarski pointed out in the 1930s that to make this account correct, we have to allow ourselves to add new names for any unnamed Nigerians.

Hintikka rewrites the truth condition in terms of a game. A hostile Nature chooses an individual and a name *c* (possibly new) for this individual. Myself wins this play against Nature if and only if the sentence '*c* respects his/her parents, if *c* is a Nigerian' is true. The sentence is true if and only if Myself has a winning strategy for this game.

Hintikka's condition is certainly correct. The winning strategy for Myself—indeed the only possible strategy for Myself—is to sit tight in the game and do nothing at all. The sentence expresses that Myself always wins by doing nothing. So the next question is, what has Hintikka added by putting matters into a game setting?

Hintikka always insists that Nature is trying to win. "Nature can be thought of as trying to falsify *S*."[14] Nature is "perhaps best thought of as a Cartesian *malin genie* [who] is trying to show that it is false."[15] I cannot see what this adds. The intentions of Nature are completely irrelevant to the existence of a winning strategy. It is possible that Hintikka makes Nature hostile for fear that someone might think the strategy could be winning as a result of Nature's behavior. But anybody who thought this would have misunderstood the idea of a winning strategy.

In a recent paper Hintikka suggests that as a thought-experiment we can "play language-games against nature with different strategies against nature in order to obtain knowledge of reality."[16] It is clear that in this case at least, Myself's strategy has nothing of any kind to do with obtaining knowledge about whether the sentence is true. To find out whether it is true, doing nothing will not suffice; one must investigate Nigerians. In another place Hintikka and Kulas suggest that the game rules "have a great deal of psycholinguistic plausibility" in that "the situations the players may encounter in [playing the game] are precisely the situations one may have to face in investigating a world in which [the sentence] is true."[17] Unfortunately they make an explicit exception for the case we are considering: "of course with the proviso that the values of (unnegated) universal quantifiers are individuals one perhaps chances upon."[18] The problem is the same. There seems to be no plausible link between the game and any natural real-life activity involving the sentence. Evidently we are back to the problem raised earlier, of "the relation of the different quantifying expressions to these games."

IV. EXISTENTIAL AND UNIVERSAL COMBINED

To handle sentences that contain both universal and existential quantifiers, we have to look back not to De Morgan but to Thoralf Skolem[19] and his Skolem functions. Skolem worked only with formal languages. A typical application of Skolem functions runs as follows: The sentence '$\forall x \exists y \forall z \exists w \, R(x, y, z, w)$' (call it φ) is true in a structure A if and only if A can be expanded by adding to its language two functions written F, H so that the sentence '$\forall x \forall z\, R(x, F(x), z, H(x, z))$' is true in A.

Leon Henkin and Hintikka noticed that Skolem functions can be read as strategies for the player Myself in a game $G(\varphi)$ based on φ: following the order of the quantifiers in φ, Nature chooses an element a of A, then Myself chooses an element b, Nature chooses an element c and finally Myself chooses an element d. Myself wins the game if and only if the sentence '$R(a, b, c, d)$' is true in A.[20] We can read the functions named F, H as instructions to Myself to choose b to be $F(a)$ and d to be $H(a, c)$; so together they form a strategy for Myself. One can prove—in fact Skolem already proved essentially this—that the sentence φ is true in A in the usual Tarskian sense if and only if Myself has a winning strategy for $G(\varphi)$.

At first glance, Skolem functions and winning strategies for Myself might seem to be the same thing looked at from different angles. Closer inspection shows that there are three significant differences that are important for understanding Hintikka's contribution.

First, as Skolem himself pointed out, Skolem's theorem uses the axiom of choice. (In fact it is equivalent to the axiom of choice.) The reason is that Skolem functions form terms, and a term must have a single value for each choice of values of its arguments. People have sometimes deduced that we need the axiom of choice to tie Tarskian semantics to games. This is not so. Choice is needed if we assume that the strategy for Myself is *deterministic*, that is, that it tells Myself exactly which element to pick at each of Myself's turns. De Morgan would surely have pointed out that, just as with trainpersons, all that is needed for a game-theoretic definition of truth is that Myself should have a set of instructions which guarantee a win for Myself; they can still give Myself some freedom for maneuver. With nondeterministic strategies, the game criterion for truth agrees exactly with Tarski's without the intervention of the axiom of choice.

When we take this on board, it is no longer clear that Hintikka is right to choose deterministic strategies. He says, for example, "Coming to know that [a sentence] S is true means finding a winning strategy for this game."[21] Are we really sure that coming to know the truth of S means finding a *deterministic* winning strategy? At least we need an argument for this view.

Second, the purpose of Skolem functions is to eliminate existential quantifiers and their variables. So the variables of a Skolem function associated with an existential quantifier $\exists y$ are all the variables that come from *universal* quantifiers earlier in the sentence. This corresponds to the requirement that a winning strategy for Myself is a function of previous moves of Nature, ignoring previous moves of Myself. But in a game, a strategy can call on all previous moves of either player. Fortunately it is easy to prove that if Myself has a winning strategy that depends on all previous moves, then Myself also has a winning strategy of the more restricted kind. But we shall see in the next section that under conditions of imperfect information, the extra freedom given by allowing Myself to consult Myself's own earlier moves does make a difference. Skolem functions cannot handle this.

Third, a Skolem function is a function only of variables that are bound in the sentence in question. But a strategy in a game can use information from anywhere, for example, choices in games that are played earlier. We have already seen in section II that this feature of game strategies led Hintikka to a breakthrough in natural language semantics.

V. INDEPENDENCE-FRIENDLY LOGIC

Henkin noticed that we can also introduce a sentence φ which is true in A if and only if functions F, H can be added so that '$\forall x \forall z\, R(x, F(x), z, H(z))$' is true in A.[22] There is no first-order sentence that serves this purpose. Henkin suggested a nonlinear notation, and thus he invented branching quantifiers. Later Hintikka proposed a more printable notation along the lines of our example from Serge Lang: we write '$(\exists w/\forall x)$' to mean 'there is a w not depending on x'. In this notation we can write Henkin's sentence φ as

(3) $\forall x \exists y \forall z (\exists w/\forall x)\, R(x, y, z, w).$

Hintikka calls this the "slash notation." The space after the slash can contain any finite number of universal quantifiers.

Hintikka's game reading of disjunctions $\varphi \lor \psi$ is that Myself chooses either the lefthand formula or the righthand one, and the game proceeds with the chosen formula. (Likewise for conjunctions $\varphi \land \psi$, except that Nature makes the choice.) We write a slash disjunction $(\lor/\forall x)$ if we want to prevent Myself's strategy at this choice from using the element chosen earlier at $\forall x$; this is the natural analogue of the slash existential quantifiers.

Using the slash notation, Hintikka described an extension of first-order logic which he calls "Independence-Friendly Logic," IF for short.[23] It is what we get from first-order logic if we allow slash existential quantifiers and disjunctions as well as the usual ones, and also insist that negation signs never occur except in front of atomic formulas. For atomic and negated atomic formulas the semantics is the usual Tarskian one; for all other formulas the semantics is defined in game terms as above. (In first-order logic every formula is logically equivalent to one with all negation signs in front of atomic formulas; so IF logic is genuinely an extension of first-order logic. But this restriction on negation saves us having to consider a game rule for negation—though in fact Hintikka offers one that agrees with classical negation in first-order logic.)

The game semantics for IF logic works like a dream. It is exactly the same as the game semantics for first-order logic, except that the player choosing at w (taking the sentence [3] above as an illustration) is not allowed to call on a strategy that makes use of the element previously chosen by the other player at x. So we have a game of imperfect information, if we imagine that the player at w is simply not allowed to know or remember what element was chosen at x.

By results of Herb Enderton and Wilbur Walkoe on Henkin quantifiers,[24] we know exactly what things can be expressed by sentences of IF logic. Namely, for each sentence φ of IF logic there exists a second-order sentence '$\exists F_1 \ldots \exists F_n \psi$' that has the same models as φ, and vice versa (where $F_1, \ldots, F_n$ are function variables and ψ is a first-order sentence of the language of φ with the variables $F_1, \ldots, F_n$ added as function symbols). So, measured by what we can say with sentences, IF logic has exactly the strength of Σ_1^1 second-order logic. IF logic is distinctly more expressive than first-order logic; for example, there is a sentence of IF logic with no relation or function symbols, which is true in all and only infinite structures.

In a recent paper Hintikka describes IF logic as "the true basic logic."[25] Likewise he speaks of IF logic as "our true elementary logic," and he implies that it is "a logic which everybody has practiced and which almost everybody thinks of as the unproblematic core of logic, namely, the logic of quantifiers."[26] Descriptions like these suggest one of two things:

(i)   A logic that all logicians need to know; for example the logic that enlightened universities teach to their undergraduates, and the logic that further logical research refers back to as common knowledge.

(ii) A logic that embraces all the things that we—logicians, linguists, the rest of us—might find ourselves doing with quantifiers.

I do not believe that these two things are compatible; a huge amount is known about quantifiers, and much of it is best left to specialists. In fact it seems to me that Hintikka's IF logic is too complicated to serve for (i) and too limited for (ii).

Taking (i) first, we note that IF logic shares a number of appealing features with ordinary first-order logic. For example, the Enderton-Walkoe theorem implies that:

(a)   the set of refutable sentences of IF logic is recursively enumerable;

(b)   IF logic satisfies the compactness theorem, the downward Löwenheim-Skolem theorem and Craig's interpolation lemma;

In fact (a) reminds us of a deficiency of IF logic; unlike ordinary first-order logic, IF logic has no proof calculus. But it does have one interesting advantage over the ordinary logic:

(c) one can write a truth definition for IF logic within IF logic.

This is an intriguing fact. It seems at first that IF logic can circumvent Tarski's theorem on the undefinability of truth. But as Hintikka points out, the escape route is that IF logic is not closed under classical negation.[27]

So we have a vote: whether to teach our students a logic that is closed under negation and has a proof calculus, or to teach them one that can express its own truth definition. Fact (c) is first cousin to an old set-theoretic result of Azriel Levy,[28] that there is a Σ_1 truth definition for Σ_1 sentences. I believe nobody has proposed Levy's theorem as a reason for giving a privileged status to Σ_1 set theory. This illustrates how the vote went in the twentieth century (though to be fair, the vote could conceivably have gone differently if Levy's result had been better known among philosophers). Of course, it may be that the twenty-first century will vote a different way from the twentieth on this question, if, for example, the practical consequences of (c) become valuable. Then Hintikka will rightly be seen as a pioneer.

There is a further problem with taking IF logic as "the true basic logic" in sense (i). As Hintikka rightly emphasizes throughout his *Principles of Mathematics Revisited*, logic is needed just as much for defining and describing as for proving. There are two main ways in which first-order logic serves to define. First, sets of first-order axioms define classes of models; and second, first-order formulas with free variables define the class of assignments which satisfy the free variables in a structure. (Large parts of algebraic geometry fall within model theory through this second method of defining.)

So we look to single formulas of IF logic and see what they will define for us. Hintikka himself invites us to do this when he writes in italics "*one can develop a model theory for the powerful IF first-order languages on the first-order level.*"[29] For simplicity we can begin with a formula $\varphi(x)$ with one free variable. As Hintikka well explains, the game semantics of IF does not go by a route that involves satisfaction of formulas. So we have to put in some work to see what kind of interpretation $\varphi(x)$ inherits from the game semantics on sentences of IF logic.

Fortunately there is a canonical answer, though it is too complicated to describe here.[30] Like the Tarski semantics in the ordinary first-order case, it tells us exactly what information the formula $\varphi(x)$ contributes to the truth or falsehood of sentences containing it. But unlike the ordinary first-order case, the semantical interpretation of $\varphi(x)$ seems to give no clue what if anything the formula defines in a structure. We can see the problem as follows.

We get a rough measure of the descriptive power of IF by asking how many different interpretations there are for formulas of the form $\varphi(x)$ in a structure of n elements with each element named by a constant. In first-order logic the answer is 2^n, because any subset of the n elements could be the set of elements satisfying $\varphi(x)$. In second-order logic with x as a set variable, it is 2^{2^n} by a similar argument. For IF logic the number is intermediate: IF logic says more than first-order logic, but (by this measure) significantly less than second-order logic—in fact the number becomes a negligible fraction of 2^{2^n} as n tends to infinity. All this is as we would expect. Most of us would not expect the actual numbers that come out.[31] For $n = 8$, for example, the number of possible interpretations in first-order logic is $2^8 = 256$, and for second-order logic it is 2^{256}, which is roughly 10^{77}. In IF logic it is a little more than $10^{22} \times 5$. What are these more than 10^{22} different things that we can say about eight named elements with a formula of one free variable? This definitely has to be one of those "curious phenomena that suggest that further explanations are needed," and the explanations are needed before we even dream of teaching this logic to our students. (Incidentally these calculations depend only on the part of IF logic that does not use negation. Adding negation as in IF does not alter the count, but adding negation more freely roughly doubles the numbers. So negation is responsible for only a very small part of the complexity of IF logic.)

We turn now to our true basic logic in sense (ii). Some of Hintikka's remarks suggest that (ii) is the sense he intended. For example: "Everything you need to understand it, you already need to understand traditional Frege-Russell first-order logic."[32] I read this as implying that we should include all quantifiers that have semantics in the same general game-theoretic framework as the usual first-order quantifiers.

However, this criterion may force us to include some things not included in IF logic. Many of the generalized quantifiers studied in the last fifty years are expressible in IF, because they have Σ_1^1 second-order definitions. For example, the Chang quantifier, 'There are as many elements x satisfying Px as there are elements in the universe', says that a certain kind of bijection exists. But then the classical negations and De Morgan duals of these quantifiers have Π_1^1 definitions and are often not expressible in IF logic, because of the restrictions on negation in IF logic. A fortiori IF logic is unable to handle sequences of quantifiers that alternate between Σ_1^1-definable quantifiers and Π_1^1-definable ones. But let me finish by noting a subtler gap in IF logic.

At the end of the previous section we noted that a game strategy, unlike a Skolem function, can depend on earlier choices of 'the same player'. For games of imperfect information this makes a difference, because Myself can use his early choices to store up information about choices of Nature that later become hidden from him. An example within IF logic is the sentence '$\forall x\,(x=0 \lor (\exists y/\forall x)\,y \neq x)$'. In the game semantics, $\lor$ is a cue to Myself to pick one of the disjuncts. Myself should play as follows. See what element a Nature picks at x. If a is 0, choose the first disjunct and win at once. If a is not 0, choose the second. At the quantifier '$(\exists y/\forall x)$', Myself has the fixed strategy of choosing 0. Here Myself uses information about a at the step $\lor$ in order to 'signal' to himself information that was supposed to be hidden from the existential quantifier; he can choose 0 at $\exists y$ because he has indirect evidence that 0 was not chosen at $\forall x$.

By always requiring that strategies at quantifiers depend only on moves of the other player, Hintikka forbids exactly this kind of signalling when it occurs from one quantifier (rather than $\lor$) to another quantifier. In fact Hintikka notes this gap in IF logic himself when he points to "the impossibility of expressing [a certain sentence] in an IF notation without the convention" that "moves connected with existential quantifiers are always independent of earlier moves with existential quantifiers."[33] I read this as an admission that IF notation is inadequate, in this respect at least, for a satisfactory basic logic in sense (ii).[34]

VI. Conclusion

In 1900, near the beginning of his fertile Fourth Logical Investigation, Edmund Husserl distinguished between simple and complex meanings. His first example of a simple meaning is the meaning of the word *Etwas* ("something"); he says that the simplicity of this meaning is indubitable, and "no shadow of complexity lies across it."[35] With the hindsight of a hundred years, Husserl's example seems amazingly naive. If Husserl were to lean his head out of the clouds and ask us to explain to him what he had missed, I know exactly what I would do: I would tell him to read Hintikka's writings on quantifiers.

My warm thanks to Gabriel Sandu and Peter Cameron for some illuminating discussions, and to Jaakko Hintikka for his comments on a spoken early draft of this chapter.

WILFRID HODGES

SCHOOL OF MATHEMATICAL SCIENCES
QUEEN MARY, UNIVERSITY OF LONDON
DECEMBER 2000

NOTES

1. Jaakko Hintikka, *Logic, Language-games and Information: Kantian Themes in the Philosophy of Logic* (Oxford: Clarendon Press, 1973).
2. Jaakko Hintikka and Jack Kulas, *Anaphora and Definite Descriptions: Two Applications of Game-theoretical Semantics* (Dordrecht: Reidel, 1985), p. ix.
3. Esa Saarinen, ed., *Game-Theoretical Semantics* (Dordrecht: Reidel, 1979), p. 64.
4. Serge Lang, *Algebraic Number Theory* (Reading, Mass.: Addison-Wesley, 1970), p. 335.
5. Jaakko Hintikka, "What is IF Logic and Why Do We Need It?" (Preprint 2000), p. 1.
6. Jaakko Hintikka, *The Principles of Mathematics Revisited* (Cambridge: Cambridge University Press, 1996), p. 27.
7. Augustus De Morgan, "On the Syllogism: I. On the Structure of the Syllogism," *Transactions of the Cambridge Philosophical Society* 8 (1846): 379–408.
8. See Esa Saarinen, ed., *Game-Theoretical Semantics*, p. 37; Jaakko Hintikka and Jack Kulas, *The Game of Language* (Dordrecht: Reidel, 1983), p. 164f. Hintikka is wise to say 'Myself' rather than 'I'. Try discussing these games with students: 'I do this.' 'Do you do that?' 'No, I do that.' 'I see, I do that'. . . .
9. Saarinen, ed., *Game-Theoretical Semantics*, p. 155.
10. Hintikka, *Logic, Language-games and Information*, p. 58, n. 12.
11. Hintikka and Kulas, *Anaphora and Definite Descriptions*, p. 67.
12. Ibid., p. 108.
13. Saarinen, ed., *Game-Theoretical Semantics*, p. 136.
14. Hintikka and Kulas, *Anaphora and Definite Descriptions*, p. 4.
15. Saarinen, ed., *Game-Theoretical Semantics*, p. 34.
16. Jaakko Hintikka, "On the Epistemology of Game-theoretical Semantics" (Preprint 2000), p. 8.
17. Hintikka and Kulas, *Anaphora and Definite Descriptions*, p. 29.
18. Ibid.
19. Thoralf Skolem, Logisch-kombinatorische Untersuchungen über die Erfüllbarkeit oder Beweisbarkeit mathematischer Sätze nebst einem Theoreme über dichte Mengen, *Videnskapsselskapets Skrifter*, I. Matem.-naturv. klasse I no. 4 (1920): 1–36.
20. See Leon Henkin, "Some Remarks on Infinitely Long Formulas," in *Infinitistic Methods: Proceedings of A Symposium on the Foundations of Mathematics* (Pergamon Press and Państwowe Wydawnictwo Naukowe, 1961), pp. 167–83; and Saarinen, ed., *Game-Theoretical Semantics*, p. 53.
21. Hintikka, *The Principles of Mathematics Revisited*, p. 35.
22. See Henkin, "Some Remarks on Infinitely Long Formulas," pp. 179–83.
23. See, for example, Hintikka, *The Principles of Mathematics Revisited*, chapter 3.

WILFRID HODGES

24. See H. B. Enderton, "Finite partially ordered quantifiers," *Zeitschrift für mathematische Logik und Grundlagen der Mathematik* 16 (1970): 393–97; and W. J. Walkoe Jr., "Finite Partially-ordered Quantification," *Journal of Symbolic Logic* 35 (1970): 535–55.

25. Hintikka, "On the Epistemology of Game-theoretical Semantics," p. 1.

26. Hintikka, *The Principles of Mathematics Revisited*, p. 50.

27. Ibid., p. 131ff.

28. Azriel Levy, "A Hierarchy of Formulas in Set Theory," *Memoirs of the American Mathematical Society* 57 (1965).

29. Hintikka, *The Principles of Mathematics Revisited*, p. 129.

30. See Wilfrid Hodges, "Compositional Semantics for a Language of Imperfect Information," *Logic Journal of the IGPL* 5 (1997): 539–63; and "Some Strange Quantifiers," in *Structures in Logic and Computer Science*, ed. J. Mycielski et al., Lecture Notes in Computer Science 1261 (Berlin: Springer-Verlag, 1997), pp. 51–65.

31. Peter Cameron and Wilfrid Hodges, "Some Combinatorics of Imperfect Information," *Journal of Symbolic Logic* 66 (2001): 673–84.

32. Hintikka, *The Principles of Mathematics Revisited*, pp. 50–51.

33. Ibid., pp. 63–64.

34. In "Compositional Semantics for a Language of Imperfect Information," I suggested a simplification of Hintikka's notation that plugs this gap.

35. Edmund Husserl, *Logische Untersuchungen* II/1 (Tübingen: Max Niemeyer Verlag, 1995 [original 1900], p. 296.

REPLY TO WILFRID HODGES

In his perceptive contribution, Wilfrid Hodges raises in an admirably clear way some of the fundamental issues that confront every serious analyst of logic and on which I have tried to ponder. These issues also play an important role in the contributions by van Benthem and by Feferman. For this reason my response to Hodges inevitably overlaps with my responses to these two logicians. In some cases, my answers to Hodges have to be supplemented by what I say in response to van Benthem or to Feferman.

Hodges is right that my main concern has been the nature of quantifiers. He nevertheless does not mention the way in which I have tried to capture this "nature." (The fault is undoubtedly mine in that I have only recently made this point in print.) Contrary to what is usually thought, the meaning of quantifiers is not exhausted by their ranging over a class of values. Quantifiers serve another extremely important representative function. The only way we have of expressing on the first-order level the actual dependence or independence of variables—real-life or real-mathematics variables —on each other is by the mutual formal dependence or independence of the quantifiers to which they are bound. Of course one can express the dependence of a variable on another one on the second-order level by stating explicitly that there exist functions that mediate this dependence. But the resulting second-order sentence will be of the Σ_1^1 form and hence equivalent to an independence-friendly first-order sentence. The dependence relations asserted to obtain in a given sentence are codified in the Skolem functions of this sentence. These functions therefore play a crucial role in the semantics of quantifiers in formal as well as natural languages.

Game-theoretical semantics (GTS) of quantifiers can be considered a method of representing, on the first-order level, these dependence and independence relations between variables by means of informational dependence and independence in the sense of game theory. Full arrays of Skolem functions of a given sentence S then will codify the verifier's winning strategies in the game G(S) connected with S. The game-theoretical jargon is nevertheless mostly a dramatization of the role of quantifiers in expressing dependence relations between variables. In sober mathematical reality, we can rephrase all game-theoretical talk by speaking only about Skolem functions. However, since Skolem functions codify essentially parts of strategies in semantical games, it may be argued that the notion of strategy is indispensable here.

At one point Hodges envisages using the term "strategy" so widely as to include indeterministic strategies. This can be done, but at the first stage of our theory it seems wisest to avoid such extension of the term. The reason is that the extension would make it more difficult to keep an eye on the connection between strategies in a semantical game and dependencies between variables. This is connected with the fact that (in their usual form) Skolem functions codify deterministic rather than indeterministic strategies. However, it turns out that for the purpose of dealing with irreducibly interdependent variables, we have to resort to considering mixed strategies on the part of the players of semantical games.

The dispensability of game-theoretical jargon is among other things shown by the fact that there is another intuitive way of looking at Skolem functions, viz., to think of them as the functions that pick out suitable "witness individuals" that could show the truth of the sentence in question. Functions are needed here because these witness individuals often depend on other witness individuals.

Skolem functions do such a basic job that in a sense we can eliminate existential quantifiers in favor of Skolem functions. Hodges describes De Morgan's speculations about the elimination of existential quantifiers. Skolem functions offer a much more systematic and much more revealing way of doing so. In existential instantiation the job of an existential quantifier is taken over by a "dummy name" standing for "an arbitrary individual." But the usual rule of existential instantiation is applicable only to sentence-initial existential quantifiers. An existential quantifier $(\exists x)$ can nevertheless be omitted also inside a complex formula (in a negation normal form) if we replace the variable x bound to it by a dummy function term $f(y_1, y_2, \ldots)$ where $y_1, y_2, \ldots$ are all the variables bound to those quantifiers on which $(\exists x)$ depends in its context. Such a replacement can in fact result in an especially convenient framework for first-order reasoning.[1]

All this will serve to clarify what I have meant by saying that independence-friendly logic is the true basic logic of quantifiers. It is the logic that deals with the representation of all possible patterns of dependence and independence of variables. Such a representation is an integral part of the semantical job description of quantifiers. The fact that in a suitable independence-friendly first-order logic we can form a truth predicate for that very language is nice definitory frosting on a semantical cake, but it is not the only thing that is truly important here.

To return to the main feature of the semantics of quantifiers, once we realize the crucial role of the relations of dependence and independence, we can obtain an overview on all possible patterns of dependence and independence by means of IF logic. I have carried out such a survey in a recent (2002) paper in the *Bulletin of Symbolic Logic*. There we can also see *a fortiori* that there is no problem in representing in IF logic all the kinds of dependencies, including dependencies between two existential quantifiers or the universal quantifier, which Hodges has studied and which he claims are not representable in my older notation. In fact, if this notation is understood in a suitable way (which I admittedly did not explain in my earlier publications) it turns out to be capable of doing the whole job. At one point Hodges claims that I am forbidding what he calls signaling. I am not, but it was never made clear earlier how such dependence relations between quantifiers as are captured by signaling can be represented in my notation.

Hodges calls attention to the relevance of game-theoretical semantics to the study of the semantics of natural language. The applicability of game-theoretical ideas to natural language is more direct than he seems to think. For instance, whether a quantificational statement is given in formal or in natural language, the condition of its truth is the existence of its Skolem functions. Admittedly, in natural language we do not have variables for which names can be substituted. However, the players can substitute names of the individuals they choose for entire quantifier phrases. Then suitable conjuncts or disjuncts must be added, of course, to restrict the choices to relevant individuals. Indeed, an explicit semantics for English quantifier sentences has been outlined in my 1985 book with Jack Kulas, *Anaphora and Definite Descriptions*.[2] This approach has already thrown light on interesting natural-language phenomena, especially on the nature and behavior of anaphora in English. Unfortunately linguists have not pursued the possibilities opened up by this approach.

Needless to say, in natural-language semantics there nevertheless are phenomena that are not manifested in the formal languages that logicians (and linguists) usually consider. For instance, in order to formulate the semantics of anaphoric pronouns in natural languages like English, we have to consider quantification over (in gamespeak, choices of individuals from) classes of individuals which are not determined either absolutely or relative to a context of language use. Instead, they are relative to a situation in a play of a semantic game. For instance, if my first name is Ernest, I can begin a story by referring to "an old man." Later in the story, I can refer to the same *hombre* as "the old man" or "he," but only if the choice of the reference is unique among the other males that have been introduced. None of them need be known to the writer or to his readers even if we were dealing with a factual story. We are in effect quantifying over the set of the males referred to in the story so far. All this is spelled out in my 1985 book with Jack Kulas.

What is the status, not to say the reality, of such play-relative quantification? This question is a special case of the all-important question that Hodges raises. This question concerns the status of semantical games. Who plays them and when? As Hodges points out, I have not been unequivocal in my earlier explanation. In principle, semantical games can be played by two human players (on teams of human players). Indeed, Peirce presented his semantical games as games between two human players and apparently thought of the context of a play of such a game as being the interpretation of our utterance. But it seems to me clear that there is no hope of construing semantical games as being played in such a context, that is, in a context in which a sentence is uttered or written and interpreted by an audience. Game-theoretical semantics is not discourse semantics, and not even commensurable with it.

Indeed, discourse semantics just cannot be the whole truth about the semantics of natural language. The reason is that in ordinary reasoning we are all the time introducing "arbitrary individuals" not unlike what are supposed to be referred to by the "dummy names" of existential instantiation. In typical cases, the discourse context does not provide genuine individuals to serve as the actual references of such terms and by so doing make the semantics realistic.

The correct way of looking at semantical games is the rightly understood Wittgensteinian one. Semantical games are language-games in Wittgenstein's sense, that is, they are rule-governed practices or mini-institutions that mediate the semantical relations between language and reality. They must be known (typically implicitly) and mastered conceptually by the users of the language in question. They are relied on by whoever speaks or writes a sentence and by whoever understands such a language-act, but they are not played when language is used communicatively. To assert a quantificational sentence is to make a claim about what can and cannot happen if and when a certain language-game is played, but such an assertion is not itself a move in the game. More explicitly, when one asserts S, one asserts the existence of a winning strategy for the first player ("verifier") in the correlated game G(S). In order to understand such a claim, one must grasp what it means for such a strategy to exist. And since the notion of strategy (in the strict game-theoretical sense) refers in principle to all the possible eventualities that might come up in a play of the game, in order to understand S one therefore has to have some rudimentary idea of what the different situations are that might come up. This includes understanding quantification over individuals that are specified only relative to some one play of the game and more generally understanding what individuals might have a role in a play of the game. Such "arbitrary" individuals can even be referred to linguistically. In a sense, this is what anaphoric pronouns do when their head is a quantifier phrase.

This rudimentary idea of what might come up in the game does not presuppose that, when you assert a quantificational sentence S, you already know a winning strategy in G(S). You are only claiming that such a winning strategy exists. And the same applies *mutatis mutandis* to one who understand S.

Similar remarks can be leveled at another characteristic feature of natural language semantics not mentioned by Hodges. This feature is the possibility of transferring information from one subgame to another. Recognizing this possibility is crucial for understanding the semantics of conditionals in natural languages.[3] But the information so conveyed concerns what happens in the course of a play of a semantical game, not ordinary factual or linguistic information, not even information relative to the discourse context. This point shows that the job of game-theoretical semantics cannot possibly be done by any kind of discourse semantics, for the "missing" references that are supplied by a play of a game cannot always be supplied by the actual discourse context.

Hodges warns linguists to heed the differences between different kinds of games. This warning is undoubtedly in order. However, it seems to me that the work I did in the eighties on game-theoretical semantics of natural language should provide an example of how one can treat quantification and anaphora in natural languages without confusing the different kinds of games (or other activities) with each other.

Hodges raises the question as to the sense in which IF logic is our natural basic logic. I have already explained the grounds of its claims to such a fundamental status. They consist in its capacity of representing all different patterns of dependence and independence between variables. But another aspect of the role of IF logic in our basic logic concerns, as Hodges appropriately points out, the status of negation in it. Hodges speaks of "the restrictions on negation in IF logic." I do not quite understand what these restrictions are supposed to be. The negation built into (unextended) IF logic is the strong (dual) negation. It does not result from restrictions on the familiar contradictory negation, but on the contrary from unrestricted use of the usual "classical" game rules for negation. From the vantage point of GTS, this kind of negation has thus a better claim to being "classical" than the contradictory negation. Rather, it is the contradictory negation that needs qualifications and extensions when IF logic is extended by adding to it contradictory negation. If we stick to the rules of GTS, the best we can do is to allow the contradictory negation to occur only sentence-initially. If we are to allow it to occur without restrictions, we have to add to GTS certain infinitistic truth conditions. Then the result of such unlimited use of the negation that obeys *tertium non datur* (added to IF logic) turns out to be a logic which is as strong as the entire second-order logic. The details of this way of extending IF logic are given in my paper "Truth, Negation and Other Basic Concepts of Logic."[4]

It seems to me that from the vantage point of these results, too, it is natural to consider IF logic as the core area of logic.

J. H.

NOTES

1.   See here my paper on Kanger's work, "The Proper Treatment of Quantifiers in Ordinary Logic," in *Collected Papers of Stig Kanger: With Essays on His Life and Work*, vol. 2, ed. Ghita Holmström-Hintikka, Sten Lindström and Rysiek Sliwinski (Dordrecht: Kluwer Academic, 2001), pp. 87–95.

2.   Jaakko Hintikka and Jack Kulas, *Anaphora and Definite Descriptions: Two Applications of Game-Theoretical Semantics*, Synthese Language Library vol. 26 (Dordrecht: D. Reidel Publishing Co., 1985).

3.   Cf. here my 1985 book with Kulas.

4.   "Truth, Negation and Other Basic Concepts of Logic" in *The Age of Alternative Logics*, forthcoming.

15

Gabriel Sandu

HINTIKKA AND THE FALLACIES OF THE NEW THEORY OF REFERENCE

PROPER INDIVIDUALS

There is a continuous interplay between semantic (logical), ontological, and cognitive notions in Hintikka's writings from the early beginnings up to his latest writings. But where in some other cases the marriage between the two has occurred from a need to connect meaning and use (Frege's senses and one's apprehension of them, to give just an example), I understand that in Hintikka's case this dual aspect of his philosophical analysis has a rather unconventional source. The following contains, in a nutshell the quintessence of Hintikka's logical program:

> For instance, consider a man who has a number of beliefs as to what will happen tomorrow to himself and to his friends. Consider, on his behalf, a number of possible courses of events tomorrow. If I know what our man believes, I can sort these into those which are compatible with his beliefs as distinguished from those which are incompatible with them. But this is not all that is involved. Surely the same or largely the same individuals must figure in these different sequences of events. Under different courses of events a different individual may undergo different experiences, entertain different beliefs, and hopes and fears; he may behave rather differently and perhaps even look somewhat different. Nevertheless our man can be (although he need not be) and usually is completely confident that, whatever may happen, he is going to be able to recognize (re-identify) his friends under these various courses of events, at least in principle. . . . Given full descriptions of two different courses of events tomorrow, both compatible with what our man believes . . . he will be able to recognize which individuals figuring in one of these descriptions are identical with which individual in the other, even if their names are being

withheld. . . . We are given ways of *cross-identifying* individuals, that is to say, ways of understanding questions as to whether an individual figuring in one possible world is or is not identical with an individual figuring in another world.[1]

We have in this passage all the key notions which have ubiquitously figured in Hintikka's writings from the late fifties (1957) up to nowadays: propositional attitudes, possible worlds, and cross-identification of individuals.

One of Hintikka's basic insights in the early sixties was that he could extend the logical analysis of knowledge and belief that he undertook in his celebrated *Knowledge and Belief*,[2] and which is illustrated in the above quotation, to other attitude reports. More exactly, he drew an analogy between perceptual notions (*a sees b*, *a perceives b*), and modal notions (which for him include also propositional attitudes) like

> *a knows that p*
> *a believes that p*
> *a hopes that p*

I understand that the possibility of this analogy occurred to him while listening to Miss G. E. M. Anscombe's Howison Lectures on the intentionality of perception given in Berkeley in 1963. As Hintikka recalls,[3] Anscombe spoke in those lectures about the relation between perceptual objects and intentional objects, drawing, among other things, attention to the fact that the distinction between intentional and material objects holds with respect to perception too. She used an example where somebody mistakenly shot his father, after taking the dark patch of color in his visual field for somebody else.

Hintikka realized that the content of an agent's perceptual state and the distinction Miss Anscombe drew attention to can be *explained* by exploring the analogy with the aforementioned modal notions, especially if the semantic content of the latter is spelled out in terms of the notion of *possible world* or *scenario*, as in the quotation above. What was needed for the analogy to become operative, was a more flexible reconstrual of the latter. Possible worlds were not any longer supposed to be only possible courses of events, but also states of affairs with all their spatio-temporal infrastructure:

> A moment's thought also shows that *b*'s having such a location in my visual space is just what my seeing *b* means. (Direct object construction!) We are tempted to say that *a* has a place in my visual space if and only if *a* is one of my *visual objects*, and that being one of my visual objects is precisely what 'my seeing *a*' means. . . . Likewise, I remember *b* (direct object construction

again!) if and only if I can place him in the context of my personally remembered past.[4]

Of course, over the years, he has warned us repeatedly against the danger of reifying possible worlds. He takes them only to be part of the logician's jargon and they are not to be thought of as belonging to the cognitive apparatus of the agent, or entities to be quantified over. The fact is that very often a logician will not be able to make sense of what one believes, sees, or is acquainted with, unless he or she considers different 'possible worlds'.[5]

A straightforward consequence of analyzing propositional attitudes in this way is that the notion of individual becomes much more subtle. I would say that another major insight Hintikka had in the early sixties was that the notion of an (individuated or well-defined) *individual* is relative to such an intentional background; that is, it is constituted within the network of cognitive attitudes arising in the interaction between an agent and his world. And since the intentionality of the attitudes in question is disintentionalized *via* the framework of possible worlds, so is the notion of a well-defined, proper individual. In the new setting, an individual has a life in different possible worlds, or alternatively, the specific individual one encounters in a specific possible world is just a 'manifestation' or a 'stage' of such a genuine individual. Of course, considering only contexts outside propositional attitudes amounts to a collapse between the two.

Formulating the problem in this way obviously gives rise to the question of whether a stage of an individual in a scenario is the same as (the stages of) another individual in another scenario. A genuine individual is one whose 'manifestations' are identical from world to world. As the quotation at the beginning of this section shows, putting the problem in these terms draws purposive attention to the fact that the question of cross-identification of an individual in different possible worlds is the logical counterpart of the problem of re-identification of an individual that one is usually facing in one's own cognitive experiences. Technically speaking, the logical counterpart of the notion of proper individual is the mathematical notion of a function (individuating function) whose arguments are relevant possible worlds and whose values are the appearances of the individual in question in one world or another.

For Hintikka, matters of reference are always intermingled, in a Russellian manner, with cognitive matters, and the question whether a proper name refers rigidly or not always occurs, not at the beginning, but at the end of the inquiry. One cannot start with a stock of individuals and then populate stipulatively possible worlds with them. In Hintikka's logical analysis "one's notion of an individual is, in a certain sense, relative to the context of discussion."[6] And at the end of the day it turns out that well-defined reference is tantamount to known reference. But the difference with Russell should also be obvious. Russellian individuals are *sense data*. Hintikka is reluctant to accept sense data just because that would imply that they are "epistemologically privileged":

> It is . . . impossible to make perceptual mistakes about the identity of sense data. If there were such entities, they would be epistemologically privileged, at least in this sense. It might thus be said that sense-data are at least as respectable, and as difficult to avoid, as intensional entities are in modal logic. . . . We have already seen, however, that these are a pretty disrespectable bunch of entities.[7]

We see here another justification for introducing proper individuals in Hintikka's framework. The mechanism of cross-identification codified in the individuating functions is supposed to ensure that the notion of an individual is an objectively defined entity (more on this below). If we accept it, then many other things fall into place. If a name in our language refers to such a well-defined individual, that is, if a singular term specifies the same individual in all the different 'possible worlds' we have to consider, or equivalently, if a name refers to an individual who does not 'split' from one world to another, then there are no problems any longer with substitutivity of identity or with quantification into modal contexts. This is not a refutation but rather a revindication of Quine, in the sense that, as Hintikka writes: "Quine is absolutely right in insisting that the only way of carrying out the normal, intended interpretation of quantification is to require that bound variables range over genuine individuals."[8] And when quantifiers range over proper individuals, and singular (and complex) terms refer to such individuals (which does not necessarily happen), then everything goes as smoothly as it should, in the sense that there is no violation of the classical laws of logic. And the important thing to notice is that, for example, substitutivity of identity "is restored, in brief, not by requiring that our singular terms refer to the entities postulated by the so-called theory of meaning, but by requiring (in the form of an explicit premise) that they really succeed in specifying uniquely the kind of ordinary individual with which the theory of reference typically deals."[9] In other words, there is no need in this case for Fregean *Sinne*. One may nevertheless ask: Are not the individuating functions exactly like Church's individual concepts, that is, functions from possible worlds to individuals which were devised for doing the job of Fregean *Sinne*? But Hintikka would say that, unlike individual concepts, his individuating functions are not arbitrary but are associated only with certain well-behaved singular terms. In addition, individuating functions are not modes of presentation but belong to the ontological (referential) level of the language.[10]

One of the objections pressed against this logical apparatus is that it is hard to make sense of the question of when one specific individual in one possible world is identical with another individual in another possible world. This question seems to be extremely difficult in Hintikka's setting where, most typically, possible worlds are *epistemic, perceptual*, and so on, *alternatives* to an actual situation, and not situations that could show up in the actual course of events. "They are possible alternatives to our given scenario or situation, not other actual situations."[11] So how is one supposed to make sense of the comparison in this case? This difficulty in both its metaphysical and epistemic variants has been discussed by Chisholm in his review of Hintikka's *Knowledge and Belief*:

> But what does it mean to say of something in one possible world that it is identical with something in another possible world? Or, if we know what it means, how are we to *decide* whether an individual in one possible world is identical with an individual in another?[12]

I do not know whether Hintikka has an answer to all such questions. Since the time of Chisholm's remarks he has written extensively on modes of identification. He certainly thinks that re-identification succeeds in usual cases ("one is able to recognize one's friends") and that it succeeds for physical objects too (public re-identification). He even discusses cases in which one is following a physical object in space and time back and forth towards a common ground. Here re-identification would take place by means of spatio-temporal continuities.[13] There were moments at the stage of "On the Logic of Perception"[14] when he wanted to remain agnostic on these questions, writing that

> to describe the criteria of personal identity is part of the business of a philosopher of psychology, and the task of describing the other kinds of the individuation methods belongs to the province of other branches of philosophy, maybe to the philosophy of biology and of physics. I do not see much reason to worry whether suitable methods of individuation exist.[15]

But his tone became more optimistic in the nineties when he thought that some of his ideas on this topic even received empirical support.[16]

Be this as it may, I interpret Hintikka as turning the tables on everybody who is asking such questions. That is, I take him to say that, since we do succeed in re-identifying and cross-identifying persons from situation to situation, it means that methods of cross-identification exist as part of our cognitive apparatus. The machinery of possible worlds is just one of the logician's ways to specify that cognitive content, and the trans-world individuating functions are the mathematical counterpart of those cognitive identification mechanisms, whatever they may be. In this respect, Hintikka's attitude is not so different from that of some of the defenders of the New Theory of Reference. For instance, Kripke writes, "Don't ask: how can I identify this table in another possible world . . .? I have the table in my hands, I can point to it, and when I ask whether *it* might have been in another room, I am talking, by definition, about *it*."[17] He goes on to say that "we begin with objects, which we *have,* and can identify."[18] The difference, however, is that where the proponents of the New Theory take the mechanism of identification for granted, Hintikka is mostly interested in the way the most basic statements of identification are expressed in one's logical language. His main claim is that, once the matter of cross-identification is settled, and once we have available the notion of well-defined individuals, then we no longer need rigid designators in our logical language. I will turn to this matter now.

RIGID DESIGNATION

Let me start with the following extended quotation:

> Each free singular term picks out a member (an individual or perhaps rather a particular 'stage' or 'manifestation' of an individual) from each possible world we are considering. (I am disregarding the possible emptiness of singular terms here, if only in order to simplify my discussion.) However, the individuals so picked out need not be identical (i.e., they need not be 'manifestations' of the same individual in all these worlds). Only some free singular terms always pick out the same individual. They are the ones that satisfy the appropriate uniqueness conditions (22) (or (24)). In order for this to be an objectively defined notion and in order to speak of the totality of individuals which can in this way manifest themselves in different possible worlds, we must assume that we are given a particular objectively determined set of functions each of which picks from all the appropriate possible worlds the manifestations of *one and the same* individual.[19] [The uniqueness condition (22) will be explicated below.]

Obviously in this passage Hintikka is considering the idea of rigid designation, although he does not use that jargon (The quotation is from "The Modes of Modality," which appeared in 1963!) as it appears in the New Theory of Reference where a proper name necessarily refers to whatever it refers. In other words, in this theory a proper name refers to one and the same individual in all possible circumstances.

For Hintikka the idea of rigid designation reduces simply to the idea of a name referring to a proper individual. Although he considers rigid designation, he does not embrace it, for that would make his logical system too restrictive. As mentioned above, the outcome of his logical analysis is that well-defined reference (i.e., rigid designation) is tantamount to known reference (when the relevant propositional attitude is knowing) and the latter is a property even proper names may *fail* to have.[20] In other words, even for '*c*' a proper name, the statement $\exists x Know_a$ ($x = c$) may fail to be true, according to Hintikka. (Here '$Know_a$' is an abbreviation of 'a knows that'.)

Hintikka's main objection to the New Theory has been expressed in the more recent paper "The Fallacies of the New Theory of Reference" that he co-authored with me.[21] We claimed there that once we have the idea of cross-identification in the form of a bunch of individuating functions, we then can let quantifiers range over such well-defined individuals, and that, in turn, would allow us to express rigid designation: it does not need to be introduced or presupposed as a separate ingredient in one's logical system.

> There is no need to assume any particular class of "rigid designators." If a singular term "*b*" is a "rigid designator" as far as the given class of possible worlds is concerned, this can be expressed in the language by means of quantifiers as $\exists x\, N(b=x)$. . . . [Such formulas] show how this can be done independently of there being any syntactic class of "logically proper names" or "rigid designators." They show that rigid designators can be expressed, and *a fortiori* accounted for, in terms of quantifiers. And quantifiers make sense as soon as the criteria of cross-identification have been understood completely independently of questions of any possible rigid designation by free singular terms including names.[22]

Although I suscribed to this claim when we wrote the article, I now think it is true only up to a point.

One of the problems with this claim is that the rigid reference we were talking about in "The Fallacies of the New Theory of Reference," exploring some of Hintikka's earlier ideas, is not the rigid reference Kripke and other proponents of it have been talking about. For I take the latter to hold the view that there is a stock of proper names which refer rigidly *in all contexts*, as a matter of how our ordinary language functions. But if this is so, the idea expressed in the quotation above, which is to define rigid designation in terms of '$\exists x\, N(b = x)$' cannot always work, for it makes the name '*b*' to refer rigidly only in alethic contexts. This is a consequence of the more general fact that the notion of a well-defined individual makes sense, for Hintikka, only relative to a context, and therefore the definability of rigid designation in terms of quantifiers which, in turn, relies on the notion of well-defined individual, can work only in those contexts too. The context in this case is the set of relevant alethic alternatives. But for the New

Theorists a proper name works as a rigid designator in many other contexts. To put the same point in a different way, 'b' is supposed to designate rigidly also in the context 'a believes that b proved the Incompleteness Theorem'. In this case our initial condition '$\exists x \, N(b = x)$' does not help us any longer, and we would need instead '$\exists x B_a (b = x)$', where 'B_a' is an abbreviation of 'a believes that'; that is, we need to consider the set of possible worlds which are a's relevant epistemic alternatives.

True, we find a partial solution to this problem in Hintikka's early writings, more specifically in his notion of the *modal profile* of an individual constant 'b'. We first define the modal profile of an occurrence of 'b' within a sentence p to be the natural number n_i which codifies the sequence of modal operators M (and N) within whose scope that occurrence of 'b' occurs. Then we take the modal profile of the individual constant 'b' with respect to the sentence p to be the finite sequence $n_1, n_2, \ldots$ where each n_i represents the modal profile of an occurrence of 'b' within p. The idea here should be clear enough: the modal profile of 'b' with respect to the sentence p codifies all the sequences of embeddings of modal operators within which occurrences of 'b' in p may occur. For each such modal profile $n_1, n_2, \ldots$, we then have a sentence denoted by '$Q^{n_1, n_2, \cdots}(b)$' which is intended to say that the referent of 'b' is unique with respect to the modal profile of 'b' in the sentence p. The sentence '$Q^{n_1, n_2, \cdots}(b)$' is

(22) $(\exists x)[N^{n_1}(x = b) \wedge N^{n_2}(x = b) \ldots]$.

where each N^{n_i} corresponds to the modal profile of one occurrence of 'b' in p.

In the particular case in which i = 1 and n_1 = N ('it is necessary that'), then '$Q^{n_1, n_2, \cdots}(b)$' becomes our initial

$\exists x N(b = x)$.

One consequence of defining rigid designation in this way is that, what counts as a rigid designator in one context may turn out not to be one in another. Of course, we can think of the modal profile to be constituted by the class of propositional attitudes of the agents in a communicative context during a period of time, and we may hope that by generalizing enough (i.e., enlarging the modal profile to the modal attitudes of other agents) to end up eventually with a constant class of rigid designators common to the whole community over a given period of time. This, of course, presupposes that the mechanism of cross-identification will run not only through the possible worlds of one agent but over those of all the others. I think that this is one of the senses, if I understood Hintikka correctly, in which *perspectival identification* (cross-identification relative to an agent) becomes *public identification*.

Despite what was said above, the basic difference with Kripke, Putnam, and other proponents of the New Theory still remains: the notion of rigid reference captured by the modal profile is a contextual one, which is tantamount to reference to an individual known (seen, perceived, remembered, etc.) by the members of the community.

These remarks are not intended to show that there is something essential missing in Hintikka's treatment of rigid designation, but rather to make clear what his theory commits him to, and what are the limits of our joint claim that rigid designators are not needed in language once we have available well-defined individuals and quantifiers. Given that the notion of a well-defined individual goes hand in hand with a set of "direct" propositional attitudes pertaining to those individuals' identifiers, one cannot obtain a notion of rigid designation which works in all contexts. For the latter notion works consistently, according to the New Theory, even when one does not have any identifying attitudes:

> Someone, let's say, a baby, is born; his parents call him by a certain name. They talk about him to their friends. Other people meet him. Through various sorts of talk the name is spread from link to link as if by a chain. A speaker who is at the far end of this chain, who has heard about, say Richard Feynman, in the market place or elsewhere, may be referred to Richard Feynman even though he can't remember from whom he first heard of Feynman or from whom he ever heard of Feynman. He knows that Feynman was a famous physicist. A certain passage of communication reaching ultimately to the man himself does reach the speaker. He then is referring to Feynman even though he can't identify him uniquely. He doesn't know what a Feynman diagram is, he doesn't know what the Feynman theory of pair production and annihilation is. Not only that: he'd have trouble distinguishing between Gell-Mann and Feynman.[23]

That Hintikka's notion of rigid designation works only in those cases in which the propositional attitudes of the identifiers can be invoked, may be seen also from what he says about the kind of expressions the individual constant 'b' is a place holder for in the schema (22). That is, his answer to the question "What are the expressions in one's language which function as rigid designators?" reminds one of Russell: indexicals and demonstratives, that is, expressions like 'I', 'you', 'this', and so forth.

Consider, for illustration, a case of visual cognition. Here the possible worlds are the perceiver's visual space with their relevant "coordinate system": persons and objects occupying the same slot in two different scenarios are deemed identical. When somebody, say John, utters, "I see that man," pointing to a person in his visual field, then, if he is truthful, there will be an individual occurring in John's visual scenarios in the same visual slot. Of course, all this presupposes that alternative scenarios (possible worlds) are now narrowed down to 'small worlds', i.e., momentarily bounded states of affairs restricted to one agent's perspective, that is, to John's perceptual perspective. There is even a conceptual connection between John's utterance (accompanied by the act of pointing) and John's seeing the person in question in the sense that whenever the utterance is true, it is conceptually true.[24]

Let me finally turn to a question I postponed until now, that is the question: Does the condition (22) really ensure that the same (stage of an) individual is picked up (from each of a contextually given set of possible worlds) as the referent of the constant 'b'? This question is different from the one I addressed earlier, which was: Is the class of rigid designators as understood by Kripke, Putnam, and others dispensable? And the answer was, as we saw, that they are dispensable but only in some very limited contexts. The present question is an important one, for there is a close relation between the condition (22) and the individuating functions which deliver the set of well-defined individuals needed to make rigid designation redundant or to solve problems of substitutivity of identity. As pointed out in the quotation at the beginning of this section, we see Hintikka claiming that condition (22) is supposed to ensure that certain individual constants pick up the same (stages of) individuals from all the relevant possible worlds, while the individuating functions, on the other side, are supposed to ensure that the (stages of) individuals so picked up are genuine individuals, that is, the stage of an individual which is the value of such a function for a possible world must be the same individual which is the value of the function for all the other possible worlds. Once an individual has been individuated via the corresponding individuating function, it is then possible to associate it with a linguistic label (singular term) which satisfies condition (22). However, for all these explications to work out, and for the claim that Kripkean rigid designation can be expressed in this logical formalism to be correct, condition (22) has to ensure that the singular term in question picks out the same (stages of an) individual from all relevant possible worlds. Does it?

The answer to this question is somehow obscured by the fact that in his logical system Hintikka is operating with a rather syntactical notion of possible world which is reminiscent of Carnapian state descriptions. In other words, he does not operate with 'real' possible worlds but with the syntactical notion of state-description specified as a set of formulas satisfying certain closure conditions. (The only exception relevant for the present topic is "Semantics for Propositional Attitudes," in Hintikka 1969.) Here is an example of a maximal state-description or model set μ:

(C.1) If p is an atomic formula or an identity, then not both p and $\neg p$ belong to μ.

(C.2) If p is an atomic formula or an identity and if all the free variables of p occur in the other formulas of μ then either p belongs to μ or $\neg p$ belongs to μ.

(C.3) If p is an atomic formula or an identity, and if q is like p except that a and b have been interchanged in one or more places, and if p belongs to μ and $a = b$ belongs to μ, then also q belongs to μ.

(C.9) If $(\exists x)p$ belongs to μ, then $p(a/x)$ for at least one free individual variable a.

(C.10) If $p(a/x)$ belongs to μ for at least one free individual variable a, then $(\exists x)p$ belongs to μ.[25]

In order to deal with modalities we have to consider several such model sets, that is, a model system Ω and have clauses like:

(C.M*) If Mp belongs to μ which in turn belongs to Ω then there is in Ω at least one alternative v to μ such that p belongs to v.

(C.N+) If Np belongs to μ which in turn belongs to Ω then and if v is an alternative of μ in Ω, then p belongs to v.

(Here 'N' stands for "it is necessarily that, and 'M' stands for 'it is possible that'.)

(C.$\exists$q) If $(\exists x)p$ belongs to μ, and if the modal profile of p with respect to 'x' is $n_1, n_2, \ldots$, then $p(a/x)$ belongs to μ and '$Q^{n_1, n_2, \cdots}(a)$' belongs to μ for some 'a'.[26]

('a' is a place holder for any singular term, including proper names like 'Phosphorus' or definite descriptions like 'The President of the United States'.)

A set of formulas λ is satisfiable if and only if there is a state-description in which all the members of λ hold.

I do not see how such a syntactically driven logical apparatus fits together with the semantical considerations needed to ensure that a singular term picks out the *same* (stage of an) individual in all the possible worlds, or that the individuating functions do the same thing. For all we are given are state-*descriptions*, that is, sentences intended to describe 'real' possible worlds. Hintikka mentions in one of his articles that Dagfinn Føllesdal had criticized him for speaking of model sets and not of 'real' models. His answer is that Føllesdal has underestimated the power of model sets, and that his method can be related to usual semantic methods.[27] I guess that his observations about the relation between the two methods are condensed in the quotation at the beginning of this section, that is, in the claim that for the notion of a singular term that picks out the same individual to become "an objectively defined notion" one needs "a particular objectively determined set of functions each of which picks from all the appropriate possible worlds the manifestations of one and the same individual." In order to illustrate what I have in mind, consider the following argument:

> We may, or we may not, assume that individuals existing in one state of affairs always exist in the alternative state of affairs. Conversely, we may, or we may not, assume that individuals existing in one of the alternatives to a given state of affairs always exist in this given state itself. In a system *without* existential presuppositions these assumptions may be formalized very simply by assuming the transferability of formulas of the form $(Ex)(x=a)$ or $(Ex)(a=x)$ from a model set to its alternatives or *vice versa*.[28]

We have to keep in mind that the sentence '$(\exists x)(x = a)$' is for Hintikka the formal counterpart of 'a exists'. The minor point I want to make is that I do not think that by requiring that '$(\exists x)(x = a)$' belongs to μ for every relevant μ we enforce that the referent of 'a' is the same (stage of an) individual in every μ. For, assume 'a' is the President of United States (or any other proper name, for that matter); assume that $(\exists x)(x =$ the President of the United States) belongs to μ_1 and '$(\exists x)(x =$ the President of the United States) belongs to μ_2. Then from (C.9) and these two assumptions we get '$b_1 =$ the President of the United States' belongs to μ_1 and '$b_2 =$ the President of the United States' belongs to μ_2, for some individual terms 'b_1' and 'b_2'. But we do not need to have '$b_1 = b_2$' belongs to μ_1 neither '$b_1 = b_2$' belongs to μ_2.

Even the stronger axiom '$(\exists x)N(x = a)$' does not ensure that the referent of the singular term 'a' is the same in all the relevant alternatives. For suppose '$(\exists x)N(x = a)$' belongs to μ_1. Then from (C.9) we get

$$'b_1 = a' \text{ belongs to } \mu_1$$

and

$$'b_1 = a' \text{ belongs to } \mu_2.$$

(We assume that μ_1 and μ_2 are the only alternatives to μ).

But it still may be the case that the referent of 'b_1' in μ_1 is different from its referent in μ_2, and because of that there is no guarantee that the singular term 'a' picks out one and the same individual from every possible world. I guess Hintikka is somehow aware of these difficulties when he writes "the main question which my treatment of modal logics leaves without a sufficiently explicit discussion is the question as to what the truth of these sentences [(22)] 'really' amounts to."[29] Immediately after this passage he tries to give a partial answer, i.e., the one I discussed above: it is the individuating functions which are supposed to do the job of ensuring that one and the same objectively defined individual is picked out from every possible world. The problem, however, as I see it, is that there is no way to make that transparent in his logic, that is, to have formulas "saying" that the individual picked up by such a function is one and the same in every possible world. I am wondering whether the fact that there is no way to say in the logic that a constant picks up one and the same (stage of an) individual from all relevant worlds is not a symptom of the fact that, perhaps, a class of "rigid" designators is still needed in the first place.

GABRIEL SANDU

UNIVERSITY OF HELSINKI
APRIL 2002

NOTES

1. Jaakko Hintikka, *Models for Modalities* (Dordrecht: D. Reidel, 1969), p. 99.
2. Jaakko Hintikka, *Knowledge and Belief: An Introduction into the Logic of the Two Notions* (Ithaca, N.Y.: Cornell University Press, 1962).
3. Hintikka recalls this episode in "On the Logic of Perception," in *Models for Modalities*.
4. Jaakko Hintikka, *Knowledge and the Known* (Dordrecht: D. Reidel, 1974), p. 219.
5. See Hintikka, *Models for Modalities*, p. 154.
6. Ibid., p. 139.
7. Ibid., p. 168.
8. Ibid., p. 132.
9. Ibid., p. 108; see also pp. 68–70.
10. See *Models for Modalities*, pp. 105–6.
11. Jaakko Hintikka, *Selected Papers 4: Paradigms for Language Theory and Other Essays* (Dordrecht: Kluwer Academic Publishers, 1998), p. 235.
12. Roderick Chisholm, "The Logic of Knowing," *The Journal of Philosophy* 60 (1963): 793–94.
13. See Jaakko Hintikka and Merrill Hintikka, "Towards a General Theory of Individuation and Identification," in *Logic and Ontology: Proceedings of the Sixth International Wittgenstein Symposium*, ed. W. Leinfellner, E. Kraemer, J. Schank (Vienna: Hölder-Pichler-Temsky, 1982), pp. 141–42.
14. Cf. Hintikka, *Models for Modalities*.
15. Hintikka, *Models for Modalities*, p. 170.
16. See Hintikka, *Selected Papers 4*, p. 223.
17. Saul Kripke, *Naming and Necessity*, 2nd ed. (Cambridge: Harvard University Press, 1980), pp. 52–53.

18. Ibid., p. 53.

19. Hintikka, *Models for Modalities*, pp. 135–36.

20. See ibid., p. 78.

21. Jaakko Hintikka and Gabriel Sandu, "The Fallacies of the New Theory of Reference," *Synthese* 104 (1995): 245–83; reprinted in Hintikka, *Selected Papers 4*, pp. 175–218.

22. Ibid.; the references are from Hintikka 1998, p. 181.

23. Kripke, *Naming and Necessity*, p. 91.

24. See Hintikka, *Selected Papers 4*, p. 222.

25. See Hintikka, *Models for Modalities*, p. 60.

26. See ibid., pp. 122–23.

27. See ibid., p. 114.

28. Ibid., pp. 78–79.

29. Hintikka, "Existential and Uniqueness Presuppositions," in *Models for Modalities*, p. 135.

REPLY TO GABRIEL SANDU

In his characteristically careful and perceptive essay Gabriel Sandu outlines my views on identification and its role in the semantics of modality and then raises certain specific questions about what he (following Kripke) calls "rigid designation." His exposition of my views is fair and on the whole accurate. However, on a number of issues my emphasis is different from his, and I would therefore prefer to express myself in a different way.

Maybe it is true to say that I have warned philosophers over the years about "the danger of reifying possible worlds." One thing that this can mean is that I have emphasized that, even though modal and intensional operators can for many logical purposes be handled as if they were quantifiers ranging over possible worlds, the notion of quantification involved here is unusual and has to be dealt with carefully. The reason is that we cannot always individuate possible worlds so that we could use concepts that are relative to one particular "possible world." Half seriously, I have expressed this point by saying that "possible world" is a mass term.

But even though I have tried not to reify possible worlds, I have always taken them in a robust sense. (I prefer not to use the term "realistically" here, for it is laden with too many misleading preconceptions.) Possible worlds (possible scenarios) play an important role in our lives. They can be objects of hopes and fears and I may have to prepare for them in the most concrete sense. To parody Dr. Johnson, if a man knows that there is a possible world (possible course of events) in which he is going to be hanged if he does not do anything, it braces his wits marvelously.

It has not been my purpose to "deintentionalize" propositional attitudes *per se*. I would rather see the possible-worlds approach as a way of spelling out what is involved in the so-called intentionality of propositional attitudes. I have even suggested using this framework for the purpose of comparing the relative degree of intentionality of different attitudes.[1]

Sandu says that "for Hintikka, matters of reference are always intermingled . . . with cognitive matters." I do not object, but at the same time I want to emphasize that I consider the rules governing reference objective, independent of language users' knowledge and beliefs (unless we happen to be speaking of what they know or believe).

Instead of speaking of the involvement of the reference system with "cognitive matters," I prefer calling attention to the transcendental element in the reference system and even more so in the identification system. When Kripke tells us not to ask how one can identify this table in another possible world, he is speaking (and thinking) as if Immanuel Kant never existed. Or to change the metaphor, he is speaking like the proverbial umpire who claims to call pitches as they are. In the case of language, references are what the rules of our reference system call them. If we extend this parable to Sandu, he is open to the danger that he is taken to be like the umpire who thinks that he calls pitches as he sees them.

Sandu wonders whether I have an answer to all his questions concerning identification that Chisholm poses in Sandu's quote from him. What I do believe is that language users have in paradigmatic cases such answers. What I have tried to do is to find the tacit transcendental preconditions of such successful identification.

Sandu's questions concerning what he calls "rigid designation" provides me with an opportunity to return to the vexing problems of identification, individuation and quantification in intensional contexts. These problems are still worth discussing at some length. Accordingly, I will examine briefly the background of the problems Sandu raises.

One main reason why these problems have provoked so much discussion and have led to so many different views is that in this area several different issues are intertwined. This multiplicity of issues has remained unappreciated in the philosophical literature, even though it is very real. To give one important example, the Kripke-type "New Theory of Reference" involves a confluence of at least two different mistakes. On the one hand, it involves an illicit shift from public identification to perspectival identification, for instance, visual identification. A question like "Who is Saul Kripke?" is normally understood as referring to his public identity, be this identity thought of as being specified by his DNA profile, his Social Security Number, his entry in *Who's Who?* or in some similar way, or for that matter by some combination of such criteria. But this question is ambiguous between the two modes of identification. If it is asked by a foreign visitor at an APA reception, the intended mode of identification might be the perspectival one. Then the hoped for answer might consist in pointing to a certain person and uttering "That man over there is Saul Kripke." One mistake of Kripke's is that in effect he interprets all questions of identification to be at bottom perspectival ones. He dramatizes this misinterpretation in the form of his idea of naming by dubbing. This is a straightforward fallacy of ambiguity, however, for in most philosophically relevant contexts, questions of identity must be taken to rely on the public framework. Kripke has correctly seen that if ostension is successful, it picks out a unique object, just as his dubbing is supposed to do. But such uniqueness is perspectival, not public.

In Kripke, this identification fallacy is combined with an insistence on the feasibility of a substitutional interpretation of quantifiers. The problem with substitutional interpretation of quantifiers is extremely subtle. Kripke has realized that the usual ways of characterizing the semantics of ordinary first-order logic are in effect equivalent with a suitable substitutional one. However, a game-theoretical treatment is more economical ontologically and model-theoretically, in the sense of not being as assumption-laden as the substitutional one. Moreover, a closer look at the game-theoretical truth definition shows that the substitutional interpretation of quantifiers is not our basic pretheoretical interpretation of quantified statements, as I have shown in my forthcoming paper "Truth, Negation and Other Basic Notions of Logic." Because of his insistence on the substitutional interpretation, Kripke needs rigid designators as substitution-values of bound variables. Ostensively defined proper names seem to him to serve the purpose.

Here I will briefly discuss yet another complication which has not been fully dealt with in the earlier literature but which is relevant to Sandu's paper. It is introduced by the question: What are the possible worlds like that are assumed in the semantics of intensional concepts?

The crucial fact is that in speaking of possible worlds philosophers have implicitly been concerned with two entirely different kinds of dimensions. In order to see what one of them is we may borrow a page from Quine and emphasize the analogies between a language and a scientific theory. At first sight, both of them might seem to be about "the world." But on a closer examination this impression turns out to be seriously misleading. A scientific theory, such as Maxwell's theory of electromagnetism or quantum theory, is seldom applied to the world at large. And when they are so applied, they become a part of a specialized discipline called cosmology instead of being general physical theories. Usually, what a physical theory is applied to is what a physicist is likely to call a system. Such systems are what a scientist has in mind when he or she considers what is possible or impossible according to a physical theory. In this sense, they are the "possible worlds" that are involved in the semantics of physical theories.

Such systems are not alternative states of the entire universe. They can be relatively small parts of our four-dimensional world. What is required of such systems is that they can be considered independently of the rest of the universe. This independence can be obtained in different ways. The outside influence is perhaps known to be negligible, or it may be known how it can be subtracted from the influences due to the internal workings of the system itself. In other cases the system can be conceptually isolated by specifying its boundary conditions. The same can be said of the application of a language to reality. The relevant models (aka "possible worlds") are like physicists' systems. They are not worlds in the sense of universes. Rather, they are scenarios as to what might happen in some system or "small world," as L. J. Savage used to call them. If an instructive example is needed, applications of our probabilistic concepts can serve as one. Using Kolmogorov's measure-theoretical interpretation, in such applications possible worlds are sample space points. But they are in practically no applications entire universes; typically they are scenarios in the sense of possible scenarios as to what might happen in some nook and cranny of the world, for instance, if dice are tossed.

Thus we can think of possible worlds not only as universes but also as scenarios. Clearly, the views of someone like David Lewis are predicated on the former whereas the latter sense is not very far from the notion of situation in the sense of "John and Jon" (Perry and Barwise). However, their situation semantics misses another dimension implicit in the idea of possible world, viz., the idea of how things could be or what might happen instead of what transpires in the actual course of events. We might call this the modal dimension. On this view, unactualized possible worlds in either sense are those alternatives to what actually happen which we have to take into account in our thinking, including our planning and preparation. This dimension is crucial in the semantics of modal notions, unless we could make some metaphysical assumption like the venerable Principle of Plenitude which requires each permanent possibility to be realized sooner or later. But such assumptions lose all their plausibility when possible worlds are conceived of as scenarios and not as world histories.

It is not hard to argue that failures to make these distinctions have played an important but unacknowledged role in the recent discussions about modality and modal logic. For instance, when Kripke talks about us "constructing" possible worlds, what he says may have some plausibility if we take possible worlds in the sense of scenarios but forget the modal dimension. Kripke's idea becomes ridiculous when applied to realistic cases of possible scenarios, for instance, when my "possible worlds" are the different states of weather tomorrow. Whether or not the possible hurricane, for which I am making physical and mental preparations, actually material-izes, it makes no sense to say that I construct it.

These distinctions have also influenced philosophers' views on identification. As long as our possible worlds are realistic scenarios, as they are in many applications, cross-identification presents no problems in practice. But when the question is asked in general terms it is seen clearly that we need criteria of cross-identification over and above criteria of reference. And as soon as we see this, we can also see the entire question as to whether or not there are "rigid designators" is in a deeper sense irrelevant. It was seen earlier that Kripke needs rigid designators because he fallaciously assumes a substitutional interpretation of quantifiers. But this is beside the point here. We do not need (and should not use) the substitutional interpretation, and hence we do not have any special need of rigid designators. What matters is what it means for a term to operate as if it were a rigid designator in a given context. And that meaning is determined by the very idea of possible worlds as alternatives to the actual one. It means that the term in question (say b) picks out the same reference in all the relevant alternatives. And this is expressed by sentences of a form like

(1) $(\exists x)N(b = x)$ or

(2) $(\exists x)K(b = x)$

(3) $(\exists x)B(b = x)$

(Here N expresses necessity, K *knowing that* and B *believing that*.)

There is apparently nothing here that Kripke (or anyone else who takes the possible-worlds idea seriously) could object to. Such identificatory sentences play a predictably crucial role in intensional logic, as illustrated by epistemic logic and its applications to the logic of questions and answers. This role is much more important than the question of the possible existence of rigid designators. It is somewhat surprising that this role has not been emphasized or even studied by the new theorists of reference.

All this is calculated to put into perspective the crucial questions Sandu is asking in his paper. As a true logician, he realizes the importance of identification statements like (1) and (2). And he is asking further questions about them. How precisely are we to express that "b" behaves like a rigid designator? Does the answer to this question depend on the conceptual context? Is (1) enough for this purpose if N expresses a suitable kind of necessity? But, as Sandu points out (1) does not entail (3). (It does not entail (2), either.) How is this to be understood? Isn't identity of reference through all logically possible worlds enough to guarantee rigid reference? These are not only questions concerning the metaphysics of modality. Their answers have repercussions for the deductive relations studied in intensional logics.

Sandu suggests that rigidity is best captured by means of identification statements involving what might be called the entire modal profile of a statement. Here some explanations are in order which I undoubtedly should have given long ago. I certainly owe some such explanations to Sandu.

Why doesn't (1) imply (2) or (3)? Model-theoretically the answer is clear. The only explanation possible is that there are epistemically or doxastically possible worlds which are not conceptually possible. This may sound paradoxical, but the explanation is perfectly simple. In speaking of logically or metaphysically possible worlds, we are speaking of worlds in which the terms of our language have their regular references. But a knower (or believer) might not know (or believe) what those regular references are.

Hence in epistemic (or doxastic) contexts we have to consider scenarios that differ from the actual situation in one respect even more radically than we do in the case of logically (conceptually) possible worlds.

In some epistemic (or doxastic) contexts, certain terms will refer to objects different from the ones prescribed by their literal meaning, viz., those terms whose meanings are not known by the person in question (and analogously for belief). This provides an explanation for the logical relationships between sentences like (1) through (3). This explanation also shows that it is not necessary to try to express what it would be like for a term to behave rigidly in all contexts. These different "contexts" are in practice so many different applications of our language to reality. And, as was in effect pointed out earlier in this response, each such application has to be considered independently of the others. Hence it is unnecessary to ask for a condition that would generalize (1) through (3) to all possible contexts of application. Such a request is as unrealistic as it would be to think that our language has only one application viz., to "*the* world."

All these observations reinforce the main point I find missing in Sandu's paper. It is that the problem of "rigid designation" in his sense has nothing to do with designation or reference. A term (say b) behaves as a rigid designator when it refers to the same object in all the relevant possible worlds. This sameness is not determined by the way in which b designates whatever it designates. Its reference in some one possible world is what it is, and not another thing, determined by the reference system independently of to what sets that possible world might belong. Whether or not b behaves like a rigid designator in speaking of what d knows depends on the class of possible worlds compatible with everything d knows. This happens when d has been able to restrict this class so narrowly that b picks out the same individual in all of them. Hence Kripke's fixation on rigid *designators* means that he is asking the wrong question. What he should ask is not how different terms designate (refer to) whatever they designate, but what the possible worlds are in which they are supposed to pick out the same object. The so-called problem of "rigid designators" is not about designation.

For this reason, I would not say that my "individuating functions are associated only with certain well-behaved singular terms," even though I agree with what Sandu seems to mean by such statements. A term can behave like a rigid designator even when it agrees with an individuating function only in a subclass of all possible worlds, namely when we can for contingent (e.g., epistemic) reasons restrict our attention to that subclass.

J. H.

NOTE

1. See my 1978 paper "Degrees and Dimensions of Intentionality."

16

James Higginbotham

THE SCOPE HYPOTHESIS

We should be surprised that language is as complicated as it is. That is to say, there is no reasonable doubt that a language with a context-free grammar, together with a transparent inductive characterization of the semantics, would have all of the expressive power of historically given natural languages, but none of the quirks or other puzzling features that we actually find when we study them. This circumstance suggests that the relations between apparent syntactic structure on the one hand and interpretation on the other—the "interface conditions," in popular terminology—should be seen through the perspective of an underlying regularity of structure and interpretation that can be revealed only through extended inquiry, taking into consideration especially comparative data. Indeed, advances made especially during the past twenty-five years or so indicate that, at least over a broad domain, structures either generated from what is (more or less) apparent, or else underlying those apparent structures, display the kind of regularity in their interface conditions that is familiar to us from the formalized languages. The elements that I concentrate upon here are two: the triggering of relative scope (from the interpretive point of view); and the distinction between those elements that contribute to meaning through their contribution to reference and truth conditions, on the one hand, and those that contribute to meaning through the information that they provide about the intentional states of the speaker or those the speaker is talking about, on the other. As will be seen, I will in part support Jaakko Hintikka's view that the latter distinction involves scope too, but in a more derivative fashion than he has explicitly envisaged.

Now, Hintikka and his students and colleagues have over a number of years contributed a variety of important discussions on the topic of scope. Without entering except by the way into great details on the English (or other) data, I should like first to place Hintikka's skepticism about scope within a general setting, one where, whether right or wrong, it constitutes an empirical issue for the study of the syntax-semantics interface.

To fix ideas, consider context-free grammars with a suitably parallel semantics. The grammar is a (positive) inductive definition of membership in various *categories*, given in advance. The generated structures are *trees* in the linguistic sense; i.e., trees are finite graphs (with labels for the points) with a partial ordering ≤, read *dominates*, such that the elements dominating any point x are linearly ordered by ≤. If the grammar **G** admits some tree **T**, then there will be a syntactic computation building **T** up in stages corresponding to the rules of **G** invoked. Each combinatorial rule of **G** will put together trees $\mathbf{T}_1, \ldots, \mathbf{T}_n$, forming a new tree $\mathbf{T}_0$, whose root bears some label, and dominates every point in the $\mathbf{T}_i$, $1 \le i \le n$. We are assuming that the semantics is parallel to the syntax, and therefore that the interpretation of $\mathbf{T}_0$ is determined by the interpretations of the $\mathbf{T}_i$ in a locally compositional way.[1] Hence, the semantic effect that the interpretation of any $\mathbf{T}_i$ may have upon $\mathbf{T}_0$ or any subsequent structure is encountered at the stage of the construction of $\mathbf{T}_0$, and there exhausted; for, if and when $\mathbf{T}_0$ combines with other elements to form a superordinate tree, the semantics may not look any longer at the $\mathbf{T}_i$.

If we think, now of the *scope* of an element $\mathbf{T}_i$ in a syntactic structure as comprising those points in the structure upon which the semantics associated with $\mathbf{T}_i$ can have a semantic effect, then, on the hypothesis that the semantics is indeed parallel to the syntax in the way sketched above, we may say: the scope of $\mathbf{T}_i$ is just the tree $\mathbf{T}_0$; and that the elements *within the scope of* $\mathbf{T}_i$ (or its root) are just those points outside $\mathbf{T}_i$ itself that are properly dominated by the root of $\mathbf{T}_0$.

Our semantic characterization of scope is very general, relying as it does upon a notion of local compositionality, and especially upon the assumption that the semantics, and what I called above the "semantic effects" of an element, are sufficiently well understood in actual cases. Indeed, it is easy enough to see that one could, in cooked-up settings, construct grammars and accompanying semantics that passed the test for local compositionality, but only by "cheating" in various ways, as by encoding features of the semantics of a subordinate tree $\mathbf{T}_i$ into those of the root of $\mathbf{T}_0$, to be cashed out by semantic rules at a much later stage. Much therefore depends upon what we think "interpretations" are, and upon what kinds of principles of semantic combination are permitted. However, as the reader familiar with contemporary syntactic theory will have noticed, our characterization of *scope* coincides with that of the *c-command domain* of a constituent in (almost) the sense of Reinhart, subsequently exploited, and in some ways refined, by many others.[2] I believe that this coincidence of the semantic notion with that determined by the topology of linguistic structures, constitutes a substantial discovery whose limits have not yet been reached.[3] Blown up into a general empirical thesis, the coincidence invites the conjecture: the scope of any element in any linguistic structure in any natural language is determined by its c-command domain at the level at which interpretation is computed. This is the *scope hypothesis*, as I will understand it here. I turn now to examples by way of illustration, and afterwards to the question raised first by Hintikka as to what limits there may be to the hypothesis.

In first-order languages (and others) the scope of a quantifier Q in a term or formula ...Q... is defined as: the least subformula of ...Q... containing Q. Putting the matter in terms of what Montague called analysis trees (rather than strings with parentheses), the scope of Q is just the point X that immediately dominates Q and its sister F, as in (1):

(1) X
      / \
     /   \
    Q F

The (absolute truth-theoretic, or model-theoretic) semantics is a paradigm of compositionality; and the c-command domain of Q is the formula F. Thus the syntactic notion of scope for these languages coincides with the semantic notion as described above. The scope hypothesis may now be elucidated as follows: it is the hypothesis that the coincidence between c-command domain and semantic scope obtains in all human first languages in just the way it obtains in first-order languages and others.

Since the c-command domain of an element is determined by hierarchical structure alone, i.e., by the relation ≤, the scope hypothesis says nothing about the linear order of constituents. However, since linear order has a visible effect on scope, as illustrated extensively in the literature and considered further below, the scope hypothesis invites inquiry into how linear order and scope interact cross-linguistically. Hintikka and his colleagues have often illustrated their semantic views by applying game-theoretic techniques that were sensitive to linear order within clauses. Of course, in a syntax that is largely right-branching (like that of English), linear order is generally a faithful guide to c-command. However, not only must far more theoretical steps be taken for other languages, but also even within English there are examples that go the other way; that is, where it is the rightmost element that takes wider scope. An example is afforded by iterated quantificational adverbs, as in (2):

(2) (When he lived in Oxford,) John walked to work frequently occasionally.

(2) can mean only that (when he lived in Oxford,) there were occasional periods when John's journeys to work were frequently walks, and not that there were frequent periods when he occasionally walked to work. If the scope hypothesis is correct, then either: (a) the structure is left-branching, as in (3), or else (b) it arises as a result of syntactic movement from an underlying right-branching structure as in (4).[4]

(3) [[[John walked to work][frequently]][occasionally]]

(4) [[occasionally][[frequently][John walked to work]]]

In either case, linear order is ultimately not relevant.

The scope hypothesis is an empirical hypothesis; for it is trivial to design languages for which it fails in all sorts of ways. But now we should note that insofar as we have leaned upon the formalism of context-free grammars we have incorporated into the scope hypothesis a second feature that may after all be detached from it, namely the feature that syntactic structures are always trees rather than simple partial orders. For tree structures **T**, the following is an elementary observation:

(5) If Z is in the c-command domain of both X and Y, and $X \neq Y$, then X is in the c-command domain of Y, or Y is in the c-command domain of X.

Assuming the scope hypothesis, (5) forces distinct elements having scope over something Z to have scope relative to one another. Precisely this condition is abandoned in branching quantification, where on the contrary quantifiers act independently upon subformulas. How could branching quantification, if it exists, be incorporated into the formalism?

The natural suggestion, I think, would be to weaken the assumption that the inductive clauses of grammars always act so as to build trees $\mathbf{T}_0$ from input trees $\mathbf{T}_1, \ldots, \mathbf{T}_n$. For simplicity, suppose $n = 3$. Then we may allow construction of a pair of trees $\mathbf{T}_0$, $\mathbf{T'}_0$, joined at the root **r** of $\mathbf{T}_2$ and having separate roots $\mathbf{r}_0$ and $\mathbf{r'}_0$ as illustrated in (6):

(6)
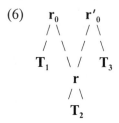

Under this modification of the usual principles, the scope hypothesis may survive intact: the scopes of the roots of each of $\mathbf{T}_1$ and $\mathbf{T}_3$ are $\mathbf{T}_2$. However, none of these roots is within the scope of the other.

A survey article by Beghelli, Ben-Shalom, and Szabolcsi reviews some of the standard data and proposals in favor of branching quantification in English.[5] Branching is not required, they suggest, to obtain the desired readings of the data sentences. In some crucial cases the interpretations are not branching but *cumulative*, as they are often called. A simple example would be (7):

(7) (At the party), many men danced with many women.

Evidently (7) can be interpreted as meaning that there are many men x, each of whom danced with many women; and, with some marginality, as meaning that there are many women y, each of whom many men danced with. It is intuitively clear, however, that there is a third interpretation, in which neither of the above is true, but there were many men-women pairs (for instance). For other scenarios, judgments are touchy, and differ amongst speakers; but even the simple case is enough to show that the quantifiers can be scopally independent. Now, one *could* treat the matter with branching quantifiers, as suggested by Barwise for instance;[6] but the system suggested by Schein would achieve the desired results as well.[7] We may take the verb in (7) to range over situations e of dancing, and we may separate the semantic roles of the subject and object, call them θ_1 and θ_2, from the predicate itself. Thus (8) would come out as (9):

(8) Mary danced with John.

(9) $(\exists e)\{$dance(e) & $\theta_1($John$,e)$ & $\theta_2($Mary$,e)$ & $(\forall x)[(\theta_1(x,e)\leftrightarrow x=$Mary$)$ & $(\theta_2(x,e)\leftrightarrow x=$John$)]\}$

that is: there is a situation e of dancing (with), whose actors comprised exactly John and whose partners comprised exactly Mary. The extension to (7) gives (10):

(10) $(\exists e)\{$dance(e) & $(\exists S)$many-men(S) & $(\exists T)$many-women(T) & $(\forall x)[(\theta_1(x,e)\leftrightarrow x\in S)$ & $(\theta_2(x,e)\leftrightarrow x\in T)]\}$.

That is: there is a situation e of dancing (with), whose actors (standing in the relation θ_1 to e) were just the elements of a class S of men counting as many of them, and whose partners (standing in the relation θ_2 to e) were just the elements of a class T of women counting as many of them. On the assumption that a given situation of dancing (or dancing-with) can involve an actor x only if x has some partner, and likewise that a partner must be a partner of some actor in that situation, it follows that, in e, each member of S is involved with some member of T, and vice versa. There seems little doubt that if the condition in (10) is fulfilled, then (7), on the reading where the quantifiers are independent, is vindicated; and of course (10) takes in as a special case that in which there were just many man-woman pairs.[8]

In a further working out of the above proposal, one takes into account a far wider range of data, involving quantifiers of different types for example. Independently of this matter, the task remains of associating a presumed syntactic structure with the interpretations given, a detailed "interface" question. A natural suggestion is that the quantificationally independent interpretations arise just when the arguments are not assigned scope; i.e., they are interpreted *in situ*, as existentials, with the erstwhile quantifier playing an adjectival role, measuring the size of classes.

In the restricted setting of quantification theory (i.e., with just the universal and existential quantifiers), we know that branching quantification can be replaced with quantification over functions. From a metaphysical point of view, given that reference to functions is part of our general scientific scheme of things, the replacement comes at no ontological cost. From the point of view of the design of human language, however, the matter is different. Rather similar remarks can be made about the replacement of branching quantification with quantification over classes, as suggested above. The resolution of the matter is not, so far as I am aware, determined at the moment. I have been concerned to argue that the scope hypothesis is consistent with branching or independent quantification, the crucial point of divergence lying not there, but with the question whether the linguistic structures relevant to interpretation are trees or graphs of a somewhat more abstract nature.

If the above discussion is correct in outline, then nominal expressions such as *many men* and others may play either of two roles in language; that is, they may function as quantifiers, taking scope in the usual fashion, or else as measures of cardinality, with quantificational force being supplied by interpretive principles applying to linguistic structures. They live, in this sense, a dual life, at least insofar as superficial syntax is concerned. There is another quantificational duality, or apparent duality, that has over the years attracted considerable attention. This is a duality in the class of *indefinites*, expressions *an F*, *some F*, and *a certain F*, the so-called "specific indefinites." I will consider what is to be said about these in the light of the scope hypothesis.

First of all, even if the assumptions in the literature have not always taken care about the matter, there can be no doubt about the *phenomenon* of specific indefiniteness. There is a difference in meaning between (11) and (12), for example, that must somehow be characterized and explained:

(11) I met a man.

(12) I met a certain man.

It has been suggested that (11) is ambiguous, having the interpretation of (12) (whatever that turns out to be), as well as the simple indefinite interpretation. However that may be, it is the peculiarity of (12) that stands out clearly, and for this reason I shall mostly advert to indefinites that wear their "specificity" on their sleeves.

Hintikka took on the obvious conjecture, examined in Hornstein, that the peculiarity of *a certain F* is that it takes wide scope with respect to other (local) quantifiers, or containing clauses.[9] The conjecture is natural enough in view of examples like (13) and (14):

(13) I want to meet a man.

(14) I want to meet a certain man.

Because, as one might say, an assertion of (14) is appropriately met by the query, "Which man?" and is to that extent indistinguishable from (15):

(15) There is a man I want to meet.

Similarly, there is a felt difference, naturally reflected in quantifier order, between (16) and (17):

(16) Every student solved a problem.

(17) Every student solved a certain problem.

(For example, in the case of (17), problem 26, as it might be). But the conjecture is wrong, Hintikka argues, because examples like (17) can be expanded as in (18):

(18) Every student solved a certain problem—namely, the one that she thought was the easiest.

On the other hand, the conjecture is partly correct, as shown by the difference between (13) and (14), although the operative principle is that *a certain* must take wide scope ("priority," in Hintikka's terms, since he is assuming a game-theoretic semantics) over epistemic operators. If the relevant class of operators is extended to include for instance the *want*, or *I want* of (14), then Hintikka's takes in this and similar examples, as well as those with operators that are explicitly epistemic. At the same time, the interpretation of (17) suggested by the continuation in (18) rules out the thesis that the contribution of *a certain* is just that of a wide-scope existential.

Writing with somewhat different purposes in mind, but self-consciously adopting a version of Hintikka's approach, Kratzer interprets *a certain*, and some uses at least of more neutral quantifiers such as *some*, as denoting choice functions of a sort.[10] In explaining her proposal, I shall be somewhat more explicit than she is in her text. Consider again an example like (17) above, understood as expanded in (18); or Kratzer's illustration (19), following Hintikka:

(19) Each husband had forgotten a certain date—his wife's birthday.

The idea is that the expression *his wife's birthday* redeems for each husband x a choice function f_x, that selects some date out of the year (or perhaps intensions with dates of the year as their values; I will not dwell upon this distinction here) that the speaker of the bare statement preceding the dash in (19) employed, without specifying it further in linguistic terms. Thus Kratzer's formula giving the truth conditions of (19) is (20):[11]

(20) ($\forall x$: husband(x)) had forgotten(x, f_x(date))

In a footnote, Kratzer suggests that for Hintikka the first part of (19) would be as in (21):

(21) ($\exists f$)($\forall x$: husband(x)) had forgotten (x, $f(x)$)

Where f is an ordinary function from individuals to individuals. However, this is a misinterpretation (or a typographical error). For: (21) is logically equivalent to (22):

(22) ($\forall x$: husband(x))($\exists y$: date(y)) had forgotten(x, y)

and that is precisely what is expressed by the general indefinite reading of *each husband had forgotten a date*. As I understand it, Hintikka's account would invoke for the first part of (19) a wide-scope quantification over functions (or quantificational independence as in his (21)),[12] but outside a hidden epistemic operator. In that case, there will be no equivalence like that of (21) and (22). To illustrate the point schematically, note that whereas according to (23) John knows merely that everything bears R to something, (24) has it that there is a *particular* function f such that John knows that everything x bears R to $f(x)$, so that, for familiar reasons, (23) might be true while (24) is false:

(23) John knows ($\forall x$)($\exists y$) $R(x,y)$

(24) ($\exists f$) John knows ($\forall x$) $R(x, f(x))$

To return to the main question: I have sketched two proposals for handling the so-called specific indefinite, exemplified by phrases *a certain F*. Hintikka's suggestion is that they are to be understood as contrasting in scope with ordinary indefinites, the domain over which this occurs being certain operators, but not necessarily including other quantifiers. Kratzer, however, understands them as truly referential, operating through certain choice functions that may in turn be the values of functions of other arguments, as in (20) above. But how does either proposal distinguish (11) from (12), repeated here?

(11) I met a man.

(12) I met a certain man.

As Hintikka recognizes, there are in any case no overt epistemic operators around; and whereas the hypothesis of choice functions would give the truth conditions of (12) as indicated in (25), we must ask where the functional element f is coming from:

(25) I met f(man).

and more particularly, what relation it may have to the speaker's communicative intentions.

There is indeed a dimension of the commonsensical explanation of *a certain* that I have thus far left out of explicit account, namely the idea that by using this expression the speaker warrants that something more can be added, but is not saying what it is; or, in Hintikka's words, that "the identity of . . . [the man in question in (12)] . . . is known but not divulged."[13] I take it that this pretheoretic observation is what, for him, is ultimately to be understood in terms of scope contrasts with epistemic operators. We need to ask whether it could emerge in some way from the choice-functional treatment suggested by Kratzer.

In building up to the approach I will eventually advocate here (one that, I believe, takes in what is right about Hintikka's and Kratzer's approaches as a special case), I begin further back, with an example from "Indefiniteness and Predication."[14] Suppose my colleague George says to me (26):

(26) A certain student of mine cheated on the logic exam.

We may take it that the identity of some student who (George believes) cheated is "known but not divulged" by George. But now I can report George in indirect discourse as in (27):

(27) George told me that a certain student of his cheated on the logic exam.

But *I* have no identities in mind! Still, when I say (27) I do not say just what would be said using the simple indefinite (28):

(28) George told me that a student of his cheated on the logic exam.

How are we to understand my, so to speak, passing the identificatory buck to George?

On Kratzer's choice-functional suggestion, George's statement has the truth conditions shown in (29):

(29) f(student of mine (i.e., George)) cheated.

for some choice function f, selecting a student from a class of students. But I, the reporter, would appear to be in no position to use George's f, and if so then my (28) cannot be as in (30):

(30) George told me that (f(student of George) cheated).

Compare this situation: I hear someone say, "This is red," but I have no idea what was being referred to. I cannot report what I heard in indirect discourse by saying, "She said that was red," or anything of the kind. The best I can do, it would appear, is to report, "She said that something or another was red," or perhaps, "She said of something or another that it was red." Free pronouns, as in "He is tall," behave in the same way. If passing the buck is impermissible in these cases, I cannot see that it could be permitted with specific indefinites.

Even waiving the last point, however, note that, if f(student of George) is a rigid designator, as it appears it appears it ought to be, inasmuch as George is communicating that he has perfectly definite beliefs concerning someone whose identity is known to him though not divulged, (30) would imply (31):

(31) ($\exists x$: student of George(x)) George told me (x cheated).

But (31) we take to be false: there is no particular student whom George told me cheated. Moreover, (27) in isolation must be said to have two distinct "specific" interpretations, one as described above, and the other, for which something like (20) might be offered as indicating the truth conditions, for the case in which George said to me, "Smith cheated on the logic exam," and in which I, the speaker, know but do not divulge that identity in saying (27). But how is the distinction between these cases to be indicated? Finally, I note with Kratzer that one cannot understand (27) by quantifying out the choice function, as in (32):

(32) ($\exists f$) George told me (f(student of George) cheated).

For that is simply equivalent to (31). For all these reasons, a choice-functional solution to the problem of *a certain* seems very doubtful.[15]

How could Hintikka's proposal handle the case of (27), on the scenario described? Well, when George spoke to me, I took him to be asserting something, hence to be putting himself forward as believing it. If we advert to a representation that puts this part of the story out in the open, then there may be room for *a certain* to take intermediate scope, for instance in (33):

(33) George told me that (he believes that (a certain student of his cheated)).

that is, George told me that there is a student whom he believes cheated (but not who it was). We have already seen that Hintikka would appeal to hidden operators in cases like (19) above. Our example would show, then, only that the appeal must extend beyond main clauses, so that the operators appear between clauses and their complements.

However, there is a problem with Hintikka's appeal even at the first step, as in (12), "I met a certain man." The problem is that there are no hidden operators in what I say. If I assert p, I do not assert that I assert p (which would in any case threaten an infinite regress). I do not *say* that I am asserting p; I simply do it. The same goes, *mutatis mutandis*, for other speech acts: asking, ordering, and so on.

We can put the matter another way.[16] Someone who asserts to me, "I met a certain man" gives me, through that act, no more information about the world than if he had asserted simply, "I met a man." Nevertheless, if he is speaking sincerely, he gives me more information about his state of belief. For simplicity, suppose there are just two men in question, Smith and Jones. In saying, "I met a man," the speaker informs me that his state of belief—or the worlds doxastically accessible to him, to advert to the modal account of the attitudes—do not include any in which he met neither Smith nor Jones. All others, so far as that utterance is concerned, are accessible. But in saying, "I met a certain man," he gives me to understand that *either* the doxastically accessible worlds include only those in which he met Smith, *or* they include only those in which he met Jones—but he does not tell me which. Because he does not tell me which, I cannot rule out either the worlds in which he met Smith, or those in which he met Jones. To accept what he said as true, therefore, gives me no more information about the world than the simple indefinite would have given; but it does give more information about the speaker's doxastic state. And, since that is done by means of an expression used in the speech itself, the semantics of that expression must take into account not only "what is said," but also the fact that it was said with a certain force.

If this is correct, then the moral of the story of *a certain*, and the other specific indefinites, is that they take wide scope not with respect to the utterance in which they occur, but rather with respect to what the speaker of that utterance is doing, or taken to be doing. This, I think, is the proper perspective to take on Hintikka's appeal to hidden epistemic (or other) operators. Kratzer's idea finds a place of a sort here too, because the appeal to choice functions is a way of indicating that the speaker is referring to a thing, at the same time withholding its identity. Ultimately, as we have seen, the choice-function view appears to fail (except perhaps as an intermediate stage of the semantics) in light of cases such as my report in all ignorance of what George said in deliberate concealment. The role of the specific indefinite is in the end explained in terms of scope, but only when more than what is uttered is taken into account. And, as the functional examples like (19) show, the wide-scope functional element may be understood through quantifiers within the structure itself.

What goes for root utterances, such as "I met a certain man," applies also to reports such as (27). In the critical interpretation, I do not represent myself as believing of any student that George told me he cheated, but I do represent George as having represented himself as believing of a student that he cheated. The "semantics for English" cannot just take what is said and assign it a propositional content: the background circumstances must be brought on board too.

In this article I have examined two areas where there is controversy over quantification. If I am right, then it turns out that, with the scope hypothesis on board as a matter of human language design, our familiar friend the scope distinction, appears onstage once again. The further resolution of the issues of branching on the one hand and specific indefinites on the other will, I hope, be carried forward with respect to a wide variety of human languages. In the meantime, we are indebted to Hintikka for his pioneering inquiries.

JAMES HIGGINBOTHAM

SCHOOL OF PHILOSOPHY
UNIVERSITY OF SOUTHERN CALIFORNIA
AUGUST 2003

NOTES

1. I offer a formal definition of local compositionality in James Higginbotham, "Some Consequences of Compositionality," ms., University of Southern California, 2003. For present purposes, however, it will be sufficient to indicate it roughly, as the property that a semantics has if the interpretation of the root of a local configuration is determined by the interpretations of its immediate successors, independently of how the latter interpretations were derived or what superordinate structure that configuration may be embedded in.

2. See Tanya Reinhart, *Anaphora and Semantic Interpretation* (London: Croom Helm, 1983).

3. The discovery, or perhaps one should say the molding of language into the format in question, owes much also to Richard Montague's work, whose focus was, however, more strongly on the metaphysical side. See Montague, "The Proper Treatment of Quantification in Ordinary English" (1970); reprinted in Montague,

Formal Philosophy, ed. Richmond Thomason (New Haven: Yale University Press, 1974), pp. 247–70.

4. For similar examples and discussion, see especially Guglielmo Cinque, *Adverbs and Functional Heads* (New York: Oxford University Press, 1999), section 1.4, pp. 16–28. Current research appears to favor (b) over (a), but discussion of this matter would take us too far afield.

5. Filippo Beghelli, Dorit Ben-Shalom, and Anna Szabolcsi, "Variation, Distributivity, and the Illusion of Branching," in *Ways of Scope Taking*, ed. A. Szabolcsi (Dordrecht: Kluwer, 1997), pp. 29–69.

6. Jon Barwise, "On Branching Quantifiers in English," *Journal of Philosophical Logic* 8, no. 1 (1979): 47–80.

7. Barry Schein, *Plurals and Events* (Cambridge, Mass.: The MIT Press, 1992).

8. For a wealth of further details, see Schein, *Plurals and Events*. See also Higginbotham, "On Higher Order Logic and Natural Language," *Proceedings of the British Academy* 95: *Philosophical Logic*, ed. T. J. Smiley (published for the British Academy by Oxford University Press, 1998), pp. 1–27, where I apply the discussion to issues of higher-order quantification in English. However, I have here used reference to classes, for ease of exposition.

9. Jaakko Hintikka, "The Semantics of *A Certain*," *Linguistic Inquiry* 17, no. 2 (1986): 331–36; Norbert Hornstein, "Interpreting Quantification in Natural Language," *Synthese* 59 (1984): 117–50.

10. Angelika Kratzer, "Scope or Pseudosope? Are there Wide Scope Indefinites?" in *Events and Grammar*, ed. Susan Rothstein (Dordrecht: Kluwer, 1998), pp. 163–96.

11. Ibid., p. 168.

12. Hintikka, "The Semantics of *A Certain*," p. 333.

13. Ibid., p. 335.

14. James Higginbotham, "Indefiniteness and Predication," in *The Representation of (In)definiteness: Papers from the Fifth Groningen Round Table*, ed. Eric Reuland and Alice ter Meulen (Cambridge, Mass.: The MIT Press, 1987), pp. 43–70.

15. Thanks to Angelika Kratzer for clarifying for me her discussion in the article cited.

16. I discuss the following point of view briefly also in James Higginbotham, "Priorities in the Philosophy of Thought," *Proceedings of the Aristotelian Society Supplementary Volume* (1994): 85–106.

REPLY TO JAMES HIGGINBOTHAM

I find James Higginbotham's essay extremely interesting in several different respects. He discusses my views on the general subject of scope in the context of other views on this important subject, using as his focal point what he calls the "scope hypothesis." This thesis is calculated to express how the scope of a quantifier or a similar linguistic ingredient is determined syntactically in natural languages. Higginbotham illustrates the issues that this thesis prompts by reference to the problem of the scope of the English quantifier expression *a certain*, a problem which I had discussed in my 1986 note in *Linguistic Inquiry*. Small though this problem might seem at first, it turns out to be connected with certain profound issues in semantics.

Furthermore, Higginbotham's essay illustrates vividly the relationships (or the lack thereof) that connect linguistic approaches to language theory with the logical and philosophical theories that have recently been developed. Thirty years ago the two approaches were closely related, especially perhaps in the form of Montague grammar. I still find the question Higginbotham is raising not only relevant to the general logical and methodological issues, but potentially highly illuminating.

However, on the level of working methodology, a gaping gulf has opened between the modes of conceptualization, explanation, and theorizing practiced by a linguist like Higginbotham and those relied on by a logico-semantical theorist like myself. A typical linguist is primarily concerned with generalizations from particular examples. In contrast, I have been concerned more and more with the most general logical and semantical features of logical as well as natural languages. This does not disassociate my problems from those of linguistics, for the insights I claim to have reached must prove their mettle by elucidating the surface phenomena of language and of languages, including natural ones. However, in natural language there are so many ambiguities that unexceptional generalizations from the data are rarely possible. Still more blatantly impossible is it to discover the underlying factors and their regularities by reference to empirical generalization only.

In this situation, constructive cooperation between linguists and logically oriented philosophers promises to be most fruitful. However, in order to realize this promise we have to bridge the conceptual and methodological gap that now separates the two. I hope that my exchange of views with Higginbotham will contribute to this integration.

These abstract remarks can be illustrated by reference to Higginbotham's paper. The scope hypothesis, in its simple form, assumes that the syntactical structure of the relevant sentences can be represented in the form of a labeled tree. This tree structure enables one to define such syntactical notions as the c-command domain of any element of a linguistic structure. The hypothesis then says that this domain determines the scope of the element in question (at the relevant level of interpretation). In order to accommodate the phenomenon known as branching quantification, Higginbotham relaxes this hypothesis by admitting arbitrary partial orderings and not only tree structures as syntactic forms of sentences.

This hypothesis is eminently consequential. Before asking whether it is true or not, I must note its most striking feature. In it, the notion of scope is taken for granted. The only problem raised is how this concept is indicated in the structure of natural-language sentences. But surely this does not take us to the bottom of things. The very concept of scope itself is in dire need of critical examination. (Here I am following the same line of thought as in the 1997 paper "No Scope for Scope?")[1] This concept is an extension of the notion of formal scope which is used in the received first-order logic and which is there indicated by a pair of parentheses (,). But what does such a formal scope express? A moment's critical thought shows that it in fact serves two different purposes. Consider for instance a quantifier (Qx) (—). On the one hand, its scope marks the segment of the relevant formula in which the variable x is bound to this particular quantifier. Such a notion of scope might be called *binding scope*.

But the nesting of scopes also expresses something else. It expresses the relative logical priority of the quantifiers (or other elements) in question. This notion of scope could be called *priority scope*.

Since in the ordinary first-order logical notation these two notions are expressed in the same way, it is in effect assumed there that they always go together. Whoever uses an unanalyzed notion of scope makes tacitly and perhaps unwittingly the same assumption. Yet, if you pause and think for a moment, you will realize that there is no a priori reason why the two notions of scope should always coincide. Even in formal languages the two notions of scope should be distinguished from each other. We might for instance express priority scope by square brackets [,] and binding scope by ordinary brackets (,). Then we can write out expressions like the following:

(1) $(\exists x)[(Ax] \supset Bx)$

But what does (1) mean? Since the square brackets determine the logical relations (priorities) obtaining in a formula, the existential quantifier is in (1) restricted to the antecedent of a conditional. If we extend its priority scope to include also the consequent, we must, according to the usual first-order logic, change it to a universal quantifier. Hence (1) is logically equivalent with

(2) $(\forall x)\,[(Ax \supset Bx)]$,

which expresses just the usual general conditional of ordinary first-order logic

(3) $(\forall x)\,(Ax \supset Bx)$.

In other cases, a two-bracketed formula need not be equivalent with any ordinary first-order formula. Cases in point are easier to formulate if we also realize that there is no reason why either kind of scope should be a continuous segment of the formula in question. In order to avoid ambiguity, brackets then have to be indexed to the bound variable in question. Then examples of the irreducible formulas in the new notation are offered by the following:

(4) $(\forall x)\,(\forall y)\,[(\exists z)]_x\,[(\exists u)\,[F[xyzu]]_x]_y$
(5) $(\forall x)\,(\forall y)\,[(\exists z)]_y\,[(\exists u)\,[(x = z)\ \&\ (y = u)\ \&\ F[x,y]]_x]_y$

As you can see, these irreducible formulas can be expressed more perspicuously in the IF notation as follows:

(6) $(\forall x)\,(\forall y)\,(\exists z\,/\forall y)\,(\exists u\,/\forall x)\,F[x,y,z,u]$
(7) $(\forall x)\,(\forall y)\,(\exists z\,/\forall x)\,(\exists u\,/\forall y)\,((x = z)\ \&\ (y = u)\ \&\ F[x,y])$

In (4) and (6) we are thus dealing with branching quantifier structures and in (5) and (7) with mutually dependent ones.

Once you realize all this, you can easily see that there are natural-language sentences where the two scopes do not go together. For instance, consider the notorious "donkey sentence"

(8) If Peter owns a donkey, he beats it.

The antecedent is naturally taken to present to the hearer or the reader a certain kind of situation, viz., Peter as a donkey owner. Hence the conditional has the priority over the elements of the antecedent in the logical form of (8). The consequent then tells as an afterthought what will happen in any such situation. This description will refer to the situation envisaged in the antecedent, including the individuals introduced by quantifiers in the antecedent. Hence the binding scope of the quantifier *a donkey* must also comprehend the consequent. This is also seen from the fact that the anaphoric pronoun *it* picks up the reference of *a donkey*. Hence, the logical form of (8) is in the two-parentheses notation

(9) If [(Peter owns a donkey], then he beats it).

In other words, the logical form of (8) is (1). This solves most of the problems about donkey sentences, including the telltale question as to why the apparent logical force of (8) seems to be that of (3). In this way, the entire "donkey sentences" problematic can be dissolved, including the problems connected with more complicated sentences like the following:

(10)   If you give a gift to each child for Christmas, some child will open it today.

Moreover, there is no *a priori* reason why priority scope should be expressed by means of the syntactic structure in the first place and not for instance by means of the lexical items used. Once again there are plenty of examples to be found in natural languages. Nevertheless, particular examples might not seem to have a knockdown force, the reason being that such examples have to be relative to assignment of a syntactic structure to the sample sentence in question. An obstinate critic can therefore try to ward off putative counter-examples by adding new epicycles to one's syntactic theory. However, I believe that the futility of such maneuvers will ultimately become evident.

For instance, consider the following pair of sentences:

(11)   Mary will be surprised if anyone comes.
(12)   Mary will be surprised if everyone comes.

The difference in meaning between the two is explained most naturally by acknowledging that in (11) *anyone* has a priority over ("wider scope" than) the conditional (*if-then*), whereas in (12) *everyone* does not. This difference in priority scope can scarcely be explained by reference to the respective syntactic structures of (11) and (12), because these structures are the same. (Of course this identity can be challenged, but there does not seem to be either independent evidence or theoretical pay off in such a complication.) A fair comparison can only be made by reference to the overall theoretical treatments that would back up the ascription of different syntactic structures to sentences like (11) and (12). I have outlined a systematic treatment (in game-theoretical terms) of quantifiers, anaphora, and a number of related phenomena in English in the books *The Game of Language*[2] and *Anaphora and Definite Descriptions*.[3]

In this treatment, an important role is played by priority rules in the guise of what I have called "special ordering principles" that operate by reference to lexical items rather than syntactical form. They constitute massive counter-evidence to Higginbotham's scope hypothesis.

The representation of priority scope can be considered in an even more general perspective. The inverse of the formal priority relation which scope is supposed to express is the relation of formal dependence. For instance, a quantifier, say (Q_2x) occurring in the scope of another one, say (Q_1x), is said to be formally dependent on (Q_1x). This relation of formal dependence is extremely important in the semantics of quantifiers for it serves to express the actual real-life dependence of the variable y on the variable x. This function of expressing dependence relations is a vital part of the meaning of quantifiers.

It is an important part of the rationale of a satisfactory working language that by its means all possible patterns of dependence and independence can be expressed. But if the scope hypothesis is true, this cannot be possible. For according to the scope hypothesis only partially ordered dependence structures can be expressed. Hence, if the scope hypothesis is true, natural language is importantly restricted in what it can express, somewhat like the received Frege-Russell first-order languages. Similar remarks can be addressed to the dependence relations among other elements of a sentence.

This does not prove that the scope hypothesis is wrong. Indeed, I suspect that there is some truth in it in the sense that patterns of dependence and independence between variables, such that their quantifiers do not satisfy the scope hypothesis, are awkward to express in ordinary discourse or to grasp in our spontaneous thinking. This difficulty might in turn explain why the conceptual problems of quantum theory are as puzzling as they have in fact proved to be. There would be an explanation if it could be assumed that, as I believe, those puzzles involve nontransitive patterns of dependence between variables. However, there is no reason why dependence relations that depend on the presence of particular lexical items must be partly ordered.

In sum, it seems clear that the scope hypothesis fails for priority scope, albeit in a rather small scale. But what about binding scope? The answer is that the notion of binding scope does not apply to natural languages in the first place. It is widely believed that the logical forms of natural-language sentences are rather like ordinary first-order logical formulas. For instance, the mode of operation of anaphoric pronouns is assimilated to that of variables of quantification. In an important sense this is a mistake. There are no variables in natural language, not even disguised as pronouns. In the right semantics, anaphoric pronouns operate as choice terms somewhat like definite descriptions or Hilbert's epsilon-terms. Anaphoric pronouns are evaluated one by one in their own right, not as an aspect of the interpretation of quantifiers. There are no unanalyzable relations of anaphoric pronouns to their so-called heads. Insofar as we can speak of pronoun-head relations or relations of coreference, they are consequences of the ordering principles governing applications of rules for pronouns in relation to other semantical rules. This serves in fact to explain a large number of features of the behavior of quantifiers and coreference in natural language, as is indicated in my book with Jack Kulas, *Anaphora and Definite Descriptions*.

Thus the deep question relevant here is not so much whether the scope hypothesis is true or not. The striking question is whether the concept of scope is self-explanatory enough to serve as a part of the explanatory framework in linguistics. And the answer that results inexorably from the observations made above is that it is not. The scope relations of natural language are derivative relations created by more basic semantical regularities, such as the ordering principles governing the relative logical priority of different elements of natural-language sentences.

The significance of the questions Higginbotham raises extends beyond the scope hypothesis. If the scope hypothesis fails and if no improved version of it does any better, it means that the semantics of natural-language sentences cannot be specified by reference to the kind of syntactical manifestations that are commonly used in linguistics, in particular by reference to labeled tree structures. This point becomes especially clear when we have to deal with mutually dependent quantifiers or other mutually dependent elements. In general, when priority scope relations are not partially ordered, they cannot be expressed by the usual labeled tree (or labeled partially ordered) structures. Insofar as such structures can adequately capture the syntactical forms of well-formed sentences the entire relationship between syntax and semantics becomes more complex than is usually assumed.

Higginbotham is aware that in the semantics of both logical and natural languages we have to go beyond the received Frege-Russell first-order languages. But in a certain sense he seems to belittle the significance of the step beyond conventional first-order logic. For instance, he points out that the semantics of branching quantifiers can be formulated by quantifying over functions. This is unobjectionable. But I cannot agree with Higginbotham when he says that this "replacement comes at no ontological cost." I am not sure what Higginbotham means by ontological cost. But it does make a huge difference both philosophically and methodologically whether we are quantifying over individuals (particulars) only or whether we are also quantifying over such higher-order entities as functions or sets. Philosophically the possibility of the former restriction is important because it opens the possibility of a nominalist view of logic. Methodologically, this possibility means dispensing with all the vexing problems concerning the existence of higher-order entities. One of the services that IF logic performs

for the foundations of logic and mathematics is that it enables us to define
several crucial mathematical concepts on the first-order level that earlier
had to be defined in higher-order terms. More generally speaking, only by
dispensing with higher-order quantification can we literally think of logic
and mathematics as a study of different kinds of structures.

The limitations of the concept of scope and in general the tremendous
subtleties of natural-language semantics can be illustrated by reference to
the problem of the behavior of *a certain* in English. I find Higginbotham's
choice of this test an inspired one. I doubt very much that simple rules for
the semantical behavior of *a certain*, including its "scope," can be formulated. Certainly what I said in 1986 is not the whole story by a half. Yet it
is possible to relate the behavior of *a certain* to deep problems in the
foundations of semantics.

One such relationship is suggested by Angelika Kratzer as reported by
Higginbotham. According to this proposal, *a certain* is interpreted as
denoting a choice function of a certain sort. This idea is also applied to
"some uses at least of more neutral quantifiers such as *some*." At first sight,
this might seem to be little more than a do-it-yourself version of a fragment
of game-theoretical semantics. Indeed, on the game-theoretical interpretation any sentence like

(13)   Each husband had forgotten a certain date—his wife's birthday

will have a second-order equivalent, for example,

(14) $(\exists f)\ (\forall x)\ (x$ is a husband $\supset (x$ hand forgotten the date $f(x)$ & $f(x)$ is
        his wife's birthday))

where existential quantifiers are replaced by choice terms. The introduction
of choice terms is therefore unobjectionable, and might go some mileage in
explaining some features of the behavior of *a certain*. But it does not seem
to tell us much, for according to game-theoretical semantics any existential
quantifier in English is likewise interpreted by means of an associated
choice function. So what else is new?

What is new is that realization that I have slowly reached recently to the
effect that in our pretheoretical interpretation of quantifiers in natural
languages, we have to distinguish two different possible interpretations.[4]
One of them is captured by game-theoretical semantics, while the other one
is essentially captured by treating quantifiers as higher-order predicates
expressing the nonemptiness or the exceptionlessness of lower-order
predicates. I have called them the game-theoretical interpretation and the
substitutional interpretation, respectively. There are certain highly important
theoretical differences between the two. These two coincide in ordinary
first-order logic, and hence the differences have not been noted. What I

have come to realize is that the difference between the two shows up already in ordinary first-order propositions (no matter whether they belong to logical or natural language) without independence indicators and without a relaxed notion of formal scope, viz., when the basic predicates and functions do not obey the law of excluded middle. By considering suitable test cases, including the sorites paradox, I have argued that our spontaneous interpretation of quantifiers in such cases is the game-theoretical one. By and large, the game-theoretical interpretation is needed when a quantifier serves as the head of anaphoric pronouns.

But the game-theoretical interpretation is not always possible. In particular, it is not applicable to a quantifier occurring in the scope of contradictory negation. In such cases, we seem to resort, as the next best thing, to the substitutional interpretation.

Now it seems to me that the quantifier phrase *a certain* exhibits an interesting semantic peculiarity. By using it one can indicate that one is relying on the game-theoretical interpretation rather than the substitutional one. This may be illustrated by contrasting it to such existential quantifier expressions as *at least one* and *some or other*. Unlike *a certain*, those quantifiers favor the substitutional interpretation. The contrast can be seen from such pairs of sentences as (13) contrasted to

(15)   Each husband had forgotten some date or other—his wife's birthday.

Sentence (15) is less natural than (13). Again, we may contrast with each other (10) and the following variant of it:

(16)   If you give a certain gift to each child for Christmas, some child will open it today.
(17)   If you give at least one gift to each child for Christmas, some child will open it today.

Since *a*, *a certain*, and *at least one* are all existential quantifiers, (10), (16), and (17) might be expected to be on a par. Yet the anaphora is impossible or at least most awkward in (17) but eminently acceptable in (16). Again, (10) might at first seem ambiguous between (16) and (17), but on second thought the unacceptability of (17) leaves only the sense of (16).

This distinction between the two interpretations does not presuppose hidden epistemic operators. It is operative in perfectly extensional contexts. In order to see this, compare with each other the following three sentences:

(18)   I met a man.
(19)   I met a certain man.
(20)   I met at least one man.

Further evidence is obtained by considering the negations of (18) through (20)

(21)   I did not meet a man.
(22)   I did not meet a certain man.
(23)   It's not the case that I met at least one man.

According to the general principles mentioned, *a certain man* cannot occur in (22) within the semantical scope of the negation. (This negation is obviously a contradictory one, and a game-theoretically interpreted quantifier cannot occur within its scope.) Accordingly, it is spontaneously read as if *a certain man* had the widest "scope." Thus (22) does not mean the same as (23). And it seems to me that (21) is ambiguous between (22) and (23).

These examples are interesting in that they show that at least in some cases it need not be assumed that *a certain* has the wide scope. That it has such a scope follows from its presupposing the game-theoretical interpretation together with the behavior of this interpretation in relation to the usual contradictory negation. I have come to believe that this observation can be generalized and that all the characteristic features of the semantic behavior of *a certain* can be explained on the basis of the assumption that it has to be interpreted game-theoretically. This would be interesting for more than one reason. One of them is that this kind of explanation of the surface phenomena of natural language semantics is unlike everything that can be found in the literature, although it seems to me that such an account is what Kratzer is at bottom trying to give. However, this is not a suitable occasion for a full-fledged presentation of the new interpretation of *a certain*. In any case, we have seen that a study of the behavior of the *prima facie* rather simple expression *a certain* quickly leads us to some of the most general issues in the interpretation of quantificational discourse.

In sum, the relatively technical-looking problems that Higginbotham discusses turn out to illustrate and even to exemplify some of the most central problems of semantics. The examination of these problems carried out above also demonstrates to my mind that there is a wealth of insights in the logico-semantical theories, such as game-theoretical semantics and independence-friendly logic, that are highly relevant to the concerns of theoretical linguists.

                                                              J. H.

NOTES

1. "No Scope for Scope?" *Linguistics and Philosophy* 20 (1997): 515–44. Also appears in Jaakko Hintikka, *Paradigms for Language Theory and Other Essays, Selected Papers* IV (Dordrecht: Kluwer Academic Publishers, 1998), pp. 22–51.

2. Jaakko Hintikka and Jack Kulas, *The Game of Language: Studies in Game-Theoretical Semantics and Its Applications,* Synthese Language Library 22 (Dordrecht: D. Reidel Publishing Co., 1983).

3. Jaakko Hintikka and Jack Kulas, *Anaphora and Definite Descriptions: Two Applications of Game-Theoretical Semantics,* Synthese Language Library 26 (Dordrecht: D. Reidel Publishing Co., 1985).

4. See here my paper "Truth, Negation and Other Basic Notions of Logic," in *The Age of Alternative Logics,* ed. J. van Benthem et al. (Dordrecht: Springer, forthcoming).

17

Hans Sluga

JAAKKO HINTIKKA (AND OTHERS) ON TRUTH

I

In the Spring of 1967, Jaakko Hintikka published two contributions to the journal *Synthese,* of which he was then the editor, that have proved to be of singular importance to the further development of analytic philosophy. The first was Donald Davidson's well known essay on "Truth and Meaning," the second Jean van Heijenoort's no less influential note on "Logic as Calculus and Logic as Language." In publishing these two programmatic statements side by side Hintikka as editor of *Synthese* helped to propel analytic philosophy into an entirely new phase of its evolution. He did not, of course, foresee this at the time nor did he anticipate that the two pieces would eventually also become crucial to his own philosophical thinking. But so great is their bearing on Hintikka's concerns with questions of language, meaning, and truth that no serious examination of his work can bypass an assessment of Davidson's and van Heijenoort's essays. These influences are particularly evident in the eight papers collected now in Hintikka's *Lingua Universalis vs. Calculus Ratiocinator* on which I will focus my attention in this essay.[1] In its theoretical parts, Hintikka's volume examines once more the Davidsonian question whether and how we can construct a theory of meaning for ordinary language and, like Davidson, it takes such a theory of meaning to require a definition and theory of truth.

In the other sections, the volume follows van Heijenoort in trying to situate such theoretical concerns in a larger historical context. To appreciate Hintikka's contribution to the ongoing philosophical debate means then to triangulate his writings with Davidson's and van Heijenoort's essays, and since the latter can help us to locate the two others in a broader context it is plausible to consider it first.

II

Jean van Heijenoort's essay—in fact a five-page note—presents itself modestly as providing "a useful insight into the history of logic."[2] Its stated purpose is to alert us to the absence of systematic work in formal semantics in the early phases of the development of modern logic (the period, roughly, from 1879 to 1913). The essay depicts logicians like Peano, Frege, and Russell as altogether unconcerned with metatheoretical investigations and argues that this branch of logic was first explored by Leopold Löwenheim in his essay on "Möglichkeiten im Relativkalkül" and subsequently expanded by Skolem, Herbrand, and Gödel. Van Heijenoort concludes with the simple but provocative observation that Frege's "*Begriffsschrift* (1879), Löwenheim's paper (1915), and chapter 5 of Herbrand's thesis (1929) are the three cornerstones of modern logic."[3] This leaves Tarski and his work on the concept of truth out of consideration, which is unfortunate given that *philosophical* interest in formal semantics is certainly more deeply indebted to Tarski than to either Löwenheim or Herbrand.[4] Carnap, in particular, to whom we can trace back much of the contemporary philosophical concern with questions of semantics, came to these matters precisely through Tarski's intervention.[5]

"Logic as Calculus and Logic as Language" begins with a review of the logical achievements of Frege's *Begriffsschrift*. Frege is given credit for formulating "with all the necessary accuracy, a cardinal notion of modern thought, that of a formal system" and for developing classical propositional and predicate logic. At the same time van Heijenoort charges Frege with advancing a conception of logic that, in effect, helped to stop the development of metamathematical reasoning. He traces this obstacle to metatheory back to Frege's belief in "the universality of logic." This belief, he writes, is "perhaps not discussed explicitly but nevertheless constantly guides Frege."[6] But to what extent was Frege actually guided by a belief in the universality of logic? What we find in his texts is, in fact, something significantly weaker though in some ways related to that doctrine. It is a characterization of the logical laws as "laws of thought that transcend all particulars."[7] Frege writes similarly also in his *Foundations of Arithmetic* that logic concerns "general *(allgemeine)* logical laws" and that its truths are "of a general logical nature."[8] He observes, moreover, that "the truths of arithmetic govern all that is numerable. This is the widest domain of all; for to it belongs not only the actual, but everything thinkable." And he asks, in consequence: "Should not the laws of number, then, be connected very intimately with the laws of thought."[9] This generality of logic expresses itself in Frege's notation most immediately in the fact that the quantifiers binding individual variables range over all objects. Van Heijenoort comments: "For Frege it cannot be a question of changing universes. One could not even say that he restricts himself to *one* universe. His universe is *the* universe."[10]

While all this is correct, van Heijenoort's conclusion that in Frege's logic "nothing can be, or has to be, said outside the system" and that for this reason Frege "never raises any metasystematic question" is problematic.[11] For Frege emphasizes in the preface to the *Begriffsschrift* that his logical symbolism is by no means meant to be a universal language in such a strong, Leibnizian sense. He considers it rather to be a tool for specialized investigations that is not intended to replace ordinary language at all. Comparing his logic to a microscope and ordinary language to the human eye, Frege writes: "[A]s soon as scientific purposes place great demands on sharpness of resolution, the eye turns out to be inadequate. The microscope, on the other hand, is perfectly suited for just such purposes, but precisely because of this is useless for all others."[12] Frege's notation is thus to be taken as "an aid for particular scientific purposes," and nothing else.[13] If we follow this metaphor through, we ought to say that the logical notation is for Frege a technical aid to ordinary language; it can, therefore, not replace ordinary language which retains its own original and distinctive function. There is also no reason to think that the structure (or deep structure) of ordinary language is identical with that of the logical notation. On the contrary, while the sentences of ordinary language have a subject-predicate structure, those expressed in the logical notation do not.[14] The formal notation is a constructed device and this means, presumably, that we first have to design a set of symbols and then attach appropriate meanings to them, meanings that are always specified with the help of the resources of ordinary language. By contrast, ordinary language itself has arisen in an organic fashion from sense perceptions and ideas and from groups of memory-images that have gathered around our perceptions. The symbolic devices of ordinary language allow us to pursue these images further and to prevent them from sinking into darkness as new perceptions arise. "But if we produce the symbol of an idea which a perception has called to mind, we create in this way a firm, new focus about which ideas gather."[15] That is why language is not governed by logical laws in the way our artificial notation can be.

It is true that, in order to describe his logical notation, Frege adopts the Leibnizian term "lingua characterica," but that does not mean he also adopts Leibniz's ambitions for such a language. The preface to the *Begriffsschrift*, in fact, dismisses Leibniz's view that it would be easy or useful to construct a universal language. "The enthusiasm that seized its originator in considering what an immense increase in the mental power of mankind would arise from a symbolism suited to things themselves let him underestimate the difficulties that such an enterprise faces."[16] Frege admittedly conceives of extensions of his symbolism that would make it applicable to physics, chemistry, and possibly other sciences, but even then he does not commit himself to the Leibnizian conception of a universal language. His notation is universal only in the restricted sense that the individual variables range over all objects. In contrast to Leibniz, he is not committed to the idea that all possible predicates should be expressible in that notation. Thus, semantic predicates (like "means," "refers," "is true"), in particular, find no representation in Frege's logical language. He is, in fact, quite clear about what the notation must express and what it cannot. Logic concerns for him "the laws of correct inference," as he puts it occasionally.[17] The *Begriffsschrift*, he writes in the preface to his book, "is thus intended to serve primarily to test in the most reliable way the validity of a chain of inference."[18] And it follows that "[e]verything that is necessary for a valid inference is fully expressed; but what is not necessary is mostly not even indicated."[19]

The decisive point in van Heijenoort's argument is, in fact, not that Frege conceives of his notation as a *universal* language, but that he thinks of it as a *language*. This is to say, that Frege takes his notation to be, like ordinary language, a system of signs with fixed meanings. By contrast, Löwenheim treats the logical notation as a *calculus,* that is, as a system of signs that can (a) be studied as a pure formalism and (b) be given various interpretations. He, thus, "takes the liberty to change the universe of discourse at will and to base considerations on such changes."[20] This makes it possible for him to establish that a well-formed formula is valid in every domain, if it is valid in a denumerable domain (Löwenheim-Skolem theorem). Van Heijenoort argues, moreover, that the calculus conception of the logical symbolism derives ultimately from Boole. Frege himself, he points out, had characterized Boole's symbolism as a mere calculus for the purpose of making deductions (a *calculus ratiocinator*), whereas he had called his own symbolism a characteristic language. With Löwenheim's paper we have, thus, "a return to, or at least a connection with pre-Fregean or non-Fregean logic."[21] Here again it is possible to grant van Heijenoort's historical observations but to question their philosophical interpretation. He is certainly right in saying that not only Frege but also Russell treated the logical symbolism as a language with a fixed interpretation. But from this it does not follow that "[s]emantic notions are unknown" to them.[22] This is a travesty of the truth, at least if we take van Heijenoort's words literally. For semantic considerations were, in fact, of prime importance to both Frege and Russell, as any serious reader of their writings will know. But van Heijenoort means, presumably, that neither Frege nor Russell worked in model-theoretical semantics and this is also correct and in this respect Löwenheim's 1915 paper does, indeed, mark "a sharp break with the Frege-Russell approach to the foundations of logic."[23] However, to this we must add that there is nothing in Frege's and Russell's conception of the symbolism as a language that bars them from considering questions of meaning and from examining notions like reference and truth. And that should come as no surprise, for if the symbolism is a language, as they believe, then a semantics of the symbolism is no more problematic than the semantics of ordinary language.

We may grant van Heijenoort that there are semantic problems that can be attacked only with model-theoretical methods, but from this it follows in no way that Frege's understanding of his logic prohibited him in principle from raising metasystematic questions and that it was a matter of principle that "[q]uestions about the system are as absent from *Principia Mathematica* as they are from Frege's work."[24] In contrast to what van Heijenoort suggests, Frege does, in fact, occasionally engage in meta-systematic arguments. One such argument can be found in his *Basic Laws of Arithmetic,* another in his debate with Hilbert over the foundations of geometry.[25] In his introduction to the *Tractatus,* Russell, in turn, takes up Wittgenstein's challenge that it is impossible to describe the syntactic and semantic characteristics of a language within that language and suggests that we might solve the problem by constructing a hierarchy of languages. Thus, it may turn out that "every language has, as Mr. Wittgenstein says, a structure concerning which, *in the language,* nothing can be said, but that there may be another language dealing with the structure of the first language, and having itself a new structure, and that to this hierarchy of languages there may be no limit."[26] Russell's remark draws our attention to what may well be the real source of van Heijenoort's claims, i.e., Wittgenstein's *Tractatus.* In that work, the anti-metatheoretical view is spelled out boldly in the programmatic statement that "[l]ogic must look after itself."[27] It follows for Wittgenstein that "[l]ogic is not a body of doctrine, but a mirror-image of the world. Logic is transcendental."[28] It follows, in particular, that "[p]ropositions can represent the whole of reality, but they cannot represent what they must have in common with reality in order to be able to represent it."²⁹ However, no corresponding statements can be found in the writings of either Frege or Russell. Van Heijenoort's claim that both Frege and Russell are committed to the belief in "the universality of logic" and can thus not encounter the possibility of metatheoretical reasoning derives from an illegitimate (or, at least, questionable) imposition of Tractarian ideas on their work.

What is more, in 1939 Löwenheim wrote to Paul Bernays that the "precise formulation of a strict formalism" which he had developed was ultimately due to Frege and that he had corresponded extensively with Frege on this matter. That correspondence, consisting of ten letters each by Frege and Löwenheim written between 1908 and 1910, was unfortunately lost in the Second World War. But Heinrich Scholz, who had collected it, reports that its authors considered it so important that they had planned to publish it.³⁰ Its significance, as Scholz tells us in another place, lay in the fact that "starting from *Basic Laws,* vol. II, § 90, Löwenheim had succeeded in convincing Frege of the possibility of constructing formal arithmetic in an unobjectionable manner."³¹ Though Frege seems to have been initially skeptical about the possibility of the model-theoretical reasoning that Löwenheim had developed, it appears that he eventually became convinced of its possibility. Scholz's short statement does not allow us to state with full confidence what Frege thought that admission came to. There is, however, no reason to think that it changed his general views on the concepts of meaning and truth as one can see from his post-1910 writings.

One must then admit that Frege never pursued metamathematics systematically and that Russell never pursued the proposal he had sketched in his introduction to the *Tractatus.* However, it is not implausible to conjecture that this was due to a natural division of labor in the development of modern logic. Frege and Russell had first to create their systems of symbolic logic before the project of a scientific examination of such systems could be formulated (plausible-development theory). Van Heijenoort quotes Kurt Gödel as saying that metamathematical questions arise "at once" when we adopt the methods of symbolic logic and he wonders why Frege and Russell did not see this point. He explains: "If the question of the semantic completeness of quantification theory did not 'at once' arise, it is because of the universality . . . of Frege's and Russell's logic."³² Is it not apparent that the plausible-development theory is sufficient to explain this fact? It is surely obvious that formal systems had first to be constructed before meta-theoretical questions could meaningfully be asked about them. Van Heijenoort thinks, however, that much more is at stake. According to him, Frege and Russell failed to develop metamathematics (including formal semantics) because they conceived of their logical notation as a universal language. By contrast, the metamathematicians treated the logical notation as an interpretable calculus. In other words, van Heijenoort adheres to what might be called an ultimate-presuppositions theory of the history of modern logic. This latter view has implications for the whole of twentieth-century analytic philosophy. While van Heijenoort's essay is meant to give us insight, in the first instance, into the history of modern logic, it proves just as relevant to an understanding of twentieth-century analytic philosophy because of the great bearing that the new logic has had on this branch of philosophy. Van Heijenoort speaks, in fact, of Frege not only as the founder of a new logic but also as the beginning of the analytic tradition in modern philosophy. "Frege's philosophy is analytic," he writes, "in the sense that logic has a constant control over his philosophical investigations; this marked a sharp break with the past, especially in Germany, and Frege influenced philosophers as different as Russell, Wittgenstein, and Austin."[33] This point was first fully appreciated by Burton Dreben who in turn communicated it to his students at Harvard; but because Dreben was such a reluctant writer, it took some while before his appropriation of van Heijenoort's scheme became visible.[34] It revealed itself first in Warren Goldfarb's article on "Logic in the Twenties: The Nature of the Quantifier" twelve years after the original essay which, however, like its source, still concentrated on the development of modern logic. It was only in the eighties and nineties that some of Dreben's students and a few other scholars began to weigh the broader implications of van Heijenoort's claims for the development of analytic philosophy and among these scholars was Jaakko Hintikka.

III

Throughout the essays that make up *Lingua Universalis vs. Calculus Ratiocinator* Hintikka emphasizes that van Heijenoort's essay has unearthed "an ultimate presupposition" of twentieth-century philosophy, not only of twentieth-century logic. This presupposition presents itself not as a shared belief but rather as a choice which all contemporary philosophy is said to face—"a choice between two competing overall views concerning our relationship to our language. I shall call them (i) the view of *language as a universal medium of communication* (in brief, language as the universal medium), or otherwise expressed, the view of *the universality of language,* and (ii) the view of *language as calculus.*"[35] Hintikka is aware, at the same time, that "the universalist position," understood in this way, "should perhaps be described as a syndrome of different ideas."[36] What really matters to him is one single element in this syndrome: the belief in what he calls "the ineffability" or "inexpressibility" of semantics. In this respect, his concern appears narrower than van Heijenoort's, who is, after all, trying to explain more generally why Frege, Russell, and their followers raised no "metasystematic" questions. Among those questions would, of course, be semantic ones; but they would also include questions of consistency and independence that can be cast in purely syntactic terms. According to van Heijenoort, none of these questions was asked by Frege and Russell and this, he thinks, needs explanation. The great division in the history of logic is for him between the systematic and the metasystematic thinkers, and he finds that division marked by two different conceptions of the logical symbolism. For Hintikka, on the other hand, the critical issue is that of the inexpressibility of semantics. Thus, Frege is for him a paradigmatic universalist because he thinks of language that "[i]ts semantics cannot be defined in that language itself without circularity, for this semantics is assumed in all its uses, and it cannot be defined in a metalanguage, because there is no such language beyond our actual working language. In brief, the semantics of our one and only actual language is inexpressible in it."[37]

Opposed to this view is for Hintikka the conception of language as a calculus or, rather "*the model-theoretical tradition* in logic and philosophy of language" of which he writes: "According to this tradition, we are not prisoners of our own language in the same way as [we are] according to the universalist tradition. We can speak in a suitable language of its own semantics; we can vary its interpretation; we can construct a model theory for it; we can theorize about its semantics. . . ."[38] But even this is not yet the crux of the matter for Hintikka. The ultimate and decisive question is rather whether a philosopher considers the notion of truth to be definable. He assumes "that the notion of truth is the single most important semantic relation" which is for him the "relation between language and the world."[39] Thus, the question whether language is universal turns out to be "to a considerable extent equivalent with the question" whether truth is "ineffable" or "indefinable."[40]

In speaking of the problem of "the universality of language" or, more specifically, the problem of "the inexpressibility of semantics" or, even more specifically the problem of "the definability of truth" as an ultimate presupposition of twentieth-century philosophy, Hintikka is borrowing consciously from R. G. Collingwood. On this account, the distinction between the language universalists and the model-theorists is so basic to analytic philosophy that it determines much of what goes on in the field. Those who proceed from one or the other of these two opposing conceptions may often not be aware of this or only partially so. In any case, they generally fail to reason about their respective presuppositions and instead take their own positions for granted. On one side of this dispute stand, as far as Hintikka is concerned, the early authoritative figures in analytic philosophy: Frege, Russell, and Wittgenstein, but also the members of the Vienna Circle as well as more recent authors like Quine and Church; on the other side stand the later Carnap but also, ultimately, Hintikka himself. Tarski and Gödel are said to have played an "ambivalent role . . . in the unfolding of the model-theoretical vision."[41] For Hintikka the division is also responsible outside the analytic tradition for "one of the most consequential and most intriguing love-hate relationships in twentieth-century philosophy, the relationship between Edmund Husserl and Martin Heidegger."[42] Because of Heidegger's and Wittgenstein's wide influence, the universalist conception of language is, according to Hintikka, reflected furthermore in philosophers as diverse as Richard Rorty and Jacques Derrida. That the front between the universalist and the model-theoretical view should be so long and cut across the boundary of contemporary philosophical schools will not surprise us, if we remember that, as Hintikka puts it, "an important part of the background of the ineffability view is Kant's transcendental philosophy."[43] Hintikka can, of course, not argue that the universalist conception is entirely under the influence of Kant since such stoutly anti-Kantian philosophers as Russell and Quine are, according to him, also committed to it. But he draws support for his reading from Wittgenstein's characterization of "[t]he impossibility of expressing in language the conditions of agreement between a meaningful proposition—a thought—and reality" as "the Kantian solution to the problem of philosophy."[44] The ultimate presupposition of twentieth-century philosophy is then, in a sense, the Kantian heritage in philosophy and the question to what extent it is necessary to take over and maintain that heritage.

Hintikka's goal is, however, not simply to diagnose the ultimate presuppositions of twentieth-century philosophy and of analytic philosophy more specifically. He wants rather to resolve the dispute between the two fundamentally different viewpoints. He asks accordingly in *Lingua Character vs. Calculus Ratiocinator* whether "the believers in language as the universal medium or the philosophers who see the wave of the future in the model-theoretic approach" are right and answers forthrightly: "The results reported here constitute a powerful argument for the conception of language as calculus and against the thesis of the ineffability of semantics."[45] I quote these words to show that he is not speaking of a decisive argument against the universalist view but only of a "powerful" one. For if it is the case that the opposing positions represent ultimate presuppositions in analytic philosophy and more generally in contemporary philosophy as a whole, we should not expect to come up with decisive arguments for or against them. It is in the nature of ultimate presuppositions that they are ultimate and, hence, cannot be dislodged by refutations. Arguments can be relevant to an ultimate presupposition only by showing that further adherence to it requires accommodations in one's theory which one may or may not find attractive.

IV

Before turning to Hintikka's theoretical claims about language, meaning, and truth, we must look more closely at his historical observations. The first thing to emphasize here is that the classing together of a large number of twentieth-century philosophers into two great, opposing camps is, at best, a hazardous undertaking. Philosophers are notorious individualists and philosophical schools or movements are, for that reason, characterized as often by their internal tensions and divisions as by their agreements. I have doubts, in any case, that the defining issues of twentieth-century philosophy can be described in the way Hintikka assumes. He is certainly right in thinking that language, meaning, and truth are of pervasive concern in twentieth-century thought—and that across the boundaries of individual schools—and that differences in how these concepts are understood may well be definitive of the different philosophical schools. We can also note that much of twentieth-century philosophy shows a particular interest in the concept of truth, that this is due to large-scale dissatisfaction with the classical conception of truth as correspondence, and that different philosophers seek to grasp the concept of truth in radically different ways. A short list of what philosophers and groups of philosophers have said about truth will make this evident:

- Pragmatists: truth is usefulness.
- Nietzsche: truth is interpretation.
- Frege: truth is simple and indefinable and unlike any other predicate.[46]
- Early Moore and Russell: truth is simple, indefinable, and exactly like any other predicate.
- Logical positivists: replace the concept of truth by that of verification/ falsification.
- Heidegger: truth is unhiddenness (*a-letheia*).
- Early Wittgenstein: truth is mirroring but to say that is really meaningless.
- Later Wittgenstein: attempts to characterize truth are empty.
- Foucault: truth is a system of procedures linked in a circular relation to power.

These variations show not only how intensively the concept of truth is discussed; they also make clear that we cannot easily reduce this multiplicity to an opposition between those who consider truth definable and those who do not. The definability or indefinability of truth is only one of the issues that divides philosophers. Equally fundamental divisions arise from the question whether truth should be considered a semantic, a pragmatic, or an ontological concept. Another fundamental division seems to exist between those who want to adhere to some notion of truth and those, like the logical positivists, who seek to set it aside as a residue of traditional metaphysics.

The variety and complexity of philosophical thinking about the concept of truth becomes more evident when we look closely at those philosophers who want to retain the notion of truth but also consider it indefinable. We then discover that this thesis allows for a number of very different readings and that those who agree on the formula "truth is indefinable" may be motivated by different and irreconcilable concerns. We will also be able to see that of all the thinkers who adhere to the indefinability thesis, Frege has the most worked out and most complex view, an account which seeks to incorporate a number of justifications for that thesis and which is, for that reason, multiply overdetermined. According to the first and weakest reading the thesis amounts to the following:

(1) The concept of the truth of a sentence is a semantic notion, but it cannot be explained in terms of the semantic properties of sub-sentential components such as the reference of proper names and the meanings of predicates (however the latter are to be specified).

In this form the indefinability thesis opposes itself to the traditional correspondence theory of truth according to which a sentence is true if and only if it corresponds to the facts (if and only if it says how things are) and in which this is, in turn, meant to say that an elementary sentence is true if the thing named by the subject term has the property indicated by the predicate. Such a characterization would, of course, need to be expanded, if elementary sentences can be of other than subject-predicate structure but even with this modification, proposition (1) may seem to be compelling.

On this reading of the indefinability thesis, it opposes, in effect, only certain kinds of definitions and does not, in principle, rule out the possibility of defining truth in some other semantic terms. Thus, an adherent of (1) could, perhaps trivially, write:

(1a) p is true $=_{Df}$ p is not false.

Or he could proceed disjunctively:

(1b) p is true $=_{Df}$ p is either analytic or synthetic a priori or empirically true.

The two definitions are certainly formally unobjectionable, even if they seem to be of little explanatory value. It might, however, be argued that (1a) and (1b) are, philosophically speaking, not proper definitions because they employ the notions of falsehood, analyticity, the synthetic a priori, and empirical truth. And these, in turn, it might then be said, *implicitly* presuppose the notion of truth, as is certainly suggested by the term "empirical truth." But how is one to determine whether one concept implicitly presupposes another one? The question has, unfortunately, no technical answer. We have to rely here, instead, on our intuitions and on philosophical argumentation and these also allow someone like Frege to maintain that the notion of the meanings of sub-sentential components implicitly presupposes that of the truth and falsity of sentences. This is, indeed, what Frege implies when he writes in his 1918 summary of his philosophical achievements that his logic begins with the notions of a thought and proceeds from there directly to that of the truth of the thought, and that he comes to the parts of a thought through a process of decomposition.[47] When we translate this into semantic terms, Frege seems to be saying that the notions of the sense and the reference of proper names and predicates have to be explained in terms of the more primitive notion of truth. Here truth is considered a semantic notion, but it is one which cannot be explicated in terms of the semantic properties of sub-sentential components. Already in his *Begriffsschrift* Frege shows us how we are to conceive of this possibility. He treats the judgment sign there as his first and most fundamental logical symbol and with it comes immediately the notion of a "judgeable content." He then argues that we can recognize relations of inference between such contents and that we must assign just enough structure to judgeable contents to account for these relations. It is for this reason that he rejects a subject-predicate analysis since it ascribes, on his view, more structure to judgeable contents than is needed to explain their inference relations. This account prefigures Frege's famous context principle which he made explicit in *The Foundations of Arithmetic*. It is often objected to such an account that it conflicts with the "principle of compositionality" according to which the meaning of a sentence is a function of the meanings of its parts. This principle must be true, it is said, if we are to explain how we are able to form and understand an indefinite number of new sentences. It is also said that Frege himself actually gave expression to the principle of compositionality in his essay "On Sense and Reference." But such objections overlook that the question is not whether the principle of compositionality is true or not but whether it is basic or derivative. On the interpretation of Frege put forward, the principle can be said to follow from more basic assumptions, for once we have decomposed a sentence in the manner suggested, we can, of course, also describe its meaning as a function of the elements into which we have decomposed it.

But because the principle is derivative, the attempt to define the truth of a sentence in terms of the meanings of its components would be philosophically speaking circular, though, perhaps, technically feasible. In other words, such an attempted definition would have the same shortcomings as the suggested definitions (1a) and (1b).

Proposition (1) was meant to spell out one interpretation of the thesis that truth is indefinable. There is, however, another and more radical reading of that thesis which is also advanced by Frege. That this is so has, however, been mostly overlooked by the interpreters. We can summarize this second reading of the indefinability thesis in the following proposition.

> (2) The concept of truth cannot be defined because it is presupposed in the **use** of any attempted definition.

We can describe the difference between (1) and (2) as follows: according to (1) the concept of truth is semantically prior to other semantic concepts and according to (2) the concept is pragmatically prior to other semantic concepts. These two claims are, of course, not incompatible and so Frege is able to subscribe to both of them. Frege accepts (2) because of his belief that judgment (or, linguistically speaking, assertion) is the most basic logical notion. The concept of truth is, in turn, contained in our practice of judgment or assertion. To judge (or assert) that p is to judge (or assert) that p is true. So, consider any attempted definition of truth, that is consider any formula of the form

> (2a) P is true $=_{Df}$ X.

Now, before we can judge in a particular case that P is true, we must ask ourselves whether X can be asserted. If we can assert X, then we are also entitled to assert that P is true. But in asserting X, we are already presupposing that we have a concept of truth and so the concept of truth is presupposed in our attempt to explain what it means to say that P is true. But does Frege's argument not founder on the distinction between object- and meta-language? All he seems to be proving is that in order to define a notion of truth in our object language we must already be able to employ it in our meta-language. And that is surely not incompatible with advancing a meta-linguistic truth definition for sentences in the object language. That is precisely what Tarski has shown. Frege knows, of course, no such distinction as that between object- and meta-language and for him this objection is, in consequence, hardly decisive. But Frege's argument must, in any case, be of concern to anyone who holds that it is unnecessary to maintain a separation of object- and meta-language and that the concept of truth must be definable within the language in which it is being used (and Hintikka, we will see, is one of these).

Frege's considerations in support of (2) come close here to a third interpretation of the thesis that truth is indefinable. For we may also mean by that claim:

(3) The concept of truth is not a semantic notion at all and can therefore not be defined in semantic terms.

Frege's views come close to this, if we take proposition (2) to imply that truth is really a pragmatic notion, or rather that truth is a notion that needs to be explained in terms of and, perhaps, reduced to pragmatic notions. There are passages in which Frege suggests that conclusion, such as the intriguing note "My Logical Insights" in which he argues that we have a concept of truth only because our language is imperfect and that we would need no such concept in a logically adequate language. His reason is that the concept of truth is merely a device for trying to make the assertive function of language explicit. In a perfect language we would be able to do this by just making judgments.[48] It is sometimes supposed that Frege was here advancing a redundancy theory of truth according to which the concept of truth is defined as:

(3a) P is true $=_{Df}$ P.

But the redundancy theory is best considered in conjunction with another, a fourth interpretation of the thesis that truth is indefinable. Frege's assertion in "My Logical Insights" that the concept of truth is without (semantic) content is rather to be understood as akin to the pragmatist assertion that truth is usefulness and akin to the logical positivists' desire to replace the notion altogether by that of verification/falsification.

There is, in addition, a second, and quite different take on proposition (3) according to which truth is neither a semantic nor a pragmatic but an ontological notion and that the concept is for this reason not definable in semantic terms. This is a view first put forward in the writings of the early Moore and the early Russell at the turn of last century when they were breaking with their own idealist past. It is a view, moreover, which was later taken up for different reasons by Martin Heidegger. Moore and Russell argued in their revolt against idealism that the semantic conception of truth—and more specifically the correspondence conception of truth—leads eventually and inevitably to the monistic idealism proposed by Bradley. We need not concern ourselves here with the question of how compelling these objections are, but their consequence is that Moore$_1$ and Russell$_1$ take judgments (or propositions) to be constituents of reality, not things that are about or correspond to reality and thus stand apart from it. Their judgments (or propositions) are, in other and more familiar words, states of affairs. Truth and falsity are accordingly, for them, simple and semantically indefinable properties of such states of affairs. To say that a state of affairs is true means as much as that it is there in the world and that it can be apprehended and known. Russell makes the point most brutally by saying that some propositions are true and others false just as some roses are red and others white. Logically, he argues, there is nothing more to be said.

This conception of truth is as close as it can get to Heidegger's concept of truth as unhiddenness, a notion much derided by analytic philosophers. For Heidegger, as for the early Moore and Russell, propositional truth is an uninteresting and derivative concept. It presupposes that there is something (which Heidegger calls "Being itself") that is presented to us or reveals itself to us. And this unhiddenness, this truth of Being, is the fundamental meaning of truth. What distinguishes Heidegger from Moore₁ and Russell₁ is simply that for the former the truth of Being is historical, in that different things reveal or fail to reveal themselves over time. For Moore₁ and Russell₁, on the other hand, truth and falsity are timeless characteristics of equally timeless judgments or propositions. On both understandings, however, truth turns out to be an ontological characteristic rather than a semantic one and the concept of truth, for that reason, cannot be explicated in semantic terms. It should be added that Frege, too, comes close to such unorthodox ways of speaking about truth. This manifests itself in the doctrine of truth values according to which the truth and falsity of a sentences consists in its referring to "the True" or "the False." These truth values are clearly not semantic in character and the semantic notion of truth is thus also for Frege derivative; primary for him, rather, is an ontology of value objects that has affinities to Neo-Kantian value theory.

There is still a fourth, "Kantian" reading of the claim that truth is indefinable and it may well be that this is the reading Frege was also groping for:

(4) The concept of truth may or may not be formally definable but such a definition can tell us in principle nothing about the relation of our language to the world.

This view was first expressed by Kant who writes in *The Critique of Pure Reason* that we may take "the *nominal* definition of truth, that it is the agreement of knowledge with its object" for granted.[49] But this admission is for Kant of limited philosophical significance since truth substantively concerns the content of the knowledge and "it is impossible, and indeed absurd, to ask for a general test of the truth of such content."[50] It follows that "a sufficient and at the same time general criterion of truth cannot possibly be given."[51] The purely logical criterion of truth is only formal or negative in character. "[F]urther than this logic cannot go."[52] Hence, "no one can venture with the help of logic alone to judge regarding objects, or to make any assertion."[53] The gist of this is for Kant that we may be justified in saying that the sentence "S is P" is true if and only if S has the property P, but this can tell us nothing about whether there (metaphysically) exists an object S and a property P. We can speak, in other words, of the correspondence of a sentence to appearance; but this reveals nothing about the constitution of the thing in itself. This may, indeed, be close to Wittgenstein's views, as Hintikka seems to recognize. For in the same period in which Wittgenstein expresses the "Kantian" view that it is impossible to describe a fact corresponding to a sentence without repeating that sentence, he also asserts in the *Tractatus* that "[a] proposition can be true or false only in virtue of being a picture of reality."[54]

I suspect, moreover, that Frege's assertion that the concept of truth is unique and indefinable really points to the same conclusion. To state that conclusion more generally: while it may or may not be possible to give a satisfactory formal definition of the concept of truth, such a definition can in no way add to our philosophical understanding of reality. Or even more generally: a characterization of the semantics of a sentence P will not tell us anything more about the world than the original sentence P. There is, to put it a third way, no semantic super-knowledge which can take us beyond the knowledge we communicate in our nonsemantic language. No metaphysical or ontological benefits are to be derived from a definition of truth. This point has been understood even by some of those philosophers who have sought to construct a theory of truth for ordinary language. Thus, Davidson writes about his proposed theory of meaning and truth: "The theory reveals nothing new about the conditions under which an individual sentence is true; it does not make those conditions any clearer than the sentence itself does."[55]

All in all, we are thus left with a series of doubts about Hintikka's thesis that allows us to divide contemporary philosophers into two camps according to whether they believe truth to be definable or not. Such a classification may be too broad to capture the multiple and varying views that twentieth-century philosophers have expressed concerning the concept of truth. Our examination also raises doubts about how useful it is to divide philosophers into those who engage in semantic theorizing and those who do not, and also raises doubts about distinguishing between thinkers who engage in metatheoretical reasoning and those who do not. It is, in any case, clear that the indefinability thesis does not imply that there can be no (other) semantic theorizing; even less does it imply that there can be no metatheoretical reasoning. It is the latter view we should identify with the doctrine of the universality of language and we can see now that this doctrine follows in no way from doubts about truth definitions or about semantics. Van Heijenoort's reconstruction of the ultimate presuppositions of twentieth-century logic is thus doubtful and so is Hintikka's story about the ultimate presuppositions of twentieth-century philosophy.

V

Hintikka's concern with the question of the definability of truth is (as I have said) both historically and theoretically motivated. On the theoretical side he proceeds from the assumption that it is possible to construct a theory of meaning as a theory of truth and that the latter will have to include a definition of the concept of truth. That conviction is indubitably shaped by Donald Davidson's programmatic statement of these claims in his essay, "Truth and Meaning."[56] In retrospect we can see that this essay has had a formative influence on the course of analytic philosophy after 1967. For one thing it initiated a research program on which its author would work for decades to come. In elaborating that program in ever new ways Davidson also motivated a whole generation of other philosophers to expand, revise, or contest it. Hintikka is, no doubt, one of those who has taken up the challenge posed by that essay.

When we set aside the philosophical concerns that have subsequently accreted around "Truth and Meaning," we will find that two fundamental ideas characterize Davidson's essay. The first is that the meaning of a sentence is to be understood in terms of the conditions of its truth, the second that the notion of truth is to be explicated by means of an application and extension of Tarski's theory of truth for formalized languages. These were not obvious claims to make in 1967, nor was it obvious how they could be made together. For the first claim is, in effect, the outcome of a set of deliberations that began with a critique of the correspondence theory of truth, whereas Tarski's work was generally regarded as a modern reformulation of that theory. It was (as I have shown) precisely the critics of the correspondence theory of truth who insisted that the concept of the truth of a sentence is the fundamental semantic notion and that this notion cannot therefore be explicated in terms of the reference of the components of the sentence. Tarski's model-theoretical definition appears therefore, at least at first sight, incompatible with this belief in the priority of the concept of truth. The complexity of Davidson's undertaking is due to the fact that he sets out to maintain the priority claim while at the same time subscribing to a Tarski-style theory of truth. On the one hand he is committed to treating a theory of meaning as a theory of truth, on the other he also wants to agree with those philosophers who hold that "a satisfactory theory of meaning must give an account of how the meanings of sentences depend upon the meanings of words."[57] Much of Davidson's later work on the concept of truth results from the need to resolve the resulting tensions.

It is easy to forget today how provocative Davidson's two theses must have originally sounded, for by now they have become almost a commonplace among analytic philosophers. They are, nevertheless, by no means obvious. In "Truth and Meaning" Davidson himself admits that there exists "a staggering list of difficulties and conundrums" for his theory.[58] For one thing, such a theory presupposes an understanding of the formal structure of the sentences to which it is applied. But Davidson has to admit that "we do not know the logical form of counterfactual or subjunctive sentences; nor of sentences about probabilities and about causal relations; we have no good idea what the logical role of adverbs is, nor the role of attributive adjectives; we have no theory for mass terms like 'fire', 'water', and 'snow', nor for sentences about belief, perception, and intention, nor for verbs of action that imply purpose. And finally, there are all the sentences that seem not to have truth values at all."[59] Davidson himself and others have, since then, sought to fill these gaps. For all that, it remains true that it is still an open issue whether a theory of meaning for ordinary language can be successfully executed as a theory of truth. For one thing, such a theory is not likely to tell us what the connections are between the assumed semantic properties of our sentences and their use. It may be easy, moreover, to explain the truth conditions and the meaning of simple sentences like "snow is white," but how about all those sentences we find in scientific, technical, and other kinds of theoretical writing? How about the propositions and formulas that make up sophisticated physical theories? How about meaning in the sense in which it is the concern of interpreters and translators of literary or philosophical texts? Could a theory of meaning conceived as a theory of truth make us understand Kant's transcendental deduction any better? Do the dark lines of an Ezra Pound become more transparent by means of a theory of truth? Davidson's hope in "Truth and Meaning" was, of course, that all these questions could be answered satisfactorily, but such answers are still not forthcoming.

There is another challenge that Davidson takes up in "Truth and Meaning." Tarski himself had always denied the possibility of extending his results to ordinary language. Davidson argues by contrast that this caution is unwarranted and that one can conceive of the possibility of a truth-theoretical account of the meaning for the sentences of ordinary language. He concludes his essay accordingly with the admission, "I have taken an optimistic and programmatic view of the possibilities for a formal characterization of a truth predicate for natural language."[60] Such an optimistic view would not have seemed plausible without Noam Chomsky's work in transformational grammar. Commenting on his own paper "Semantics for Natural Languages," Davidson wrote, in fact, in 1984, that it urged, "that truth theories could provide a formal semantics for natural languages to match the sort of formal syntax linguists from Chomsky on have favoured."[61] It was the publication of Chomsky's *Syntactic Structures* in 1957 that evidently prepared the way for Davidson's undertaking.[62]

One forgets today the challenge that Chomsky's work in linguistics together with Davidson's programmatic statement in "Truth and Meaning" presented to the analytic philosophers of the nineteen sixties. The shock was not, however, due to a sudden disillusionment with the doctrine that language is a universal medium, as Hintikka's account might suggest. It was due, rather, to the fact that most analytic philosophers had been convinced that ordinary language was too fluid a medium to allow for a formal characterization of its syntactic and semantic properties. The target of Davidson's pointed remarks was, indeed, the ordinary language philosophers at Oxford and all those philosophers whose picture of language was shaped by the thought of Moore and, perhaps, even more importantly, by the work of the later Wittgenstein. It is not too much to say that Chomsky and Davidson together brought the dominance of ordinary language philosophy to an end and helped to make Wittgenstein a more contested figure in the field. This development had certainly been prepared by a number of factors. One of them was the shift of the center of analytic philosophy from Great Britain to the United States with its accompanying shift towards a more scientistic conception of philosophy. Another significant factor was changes in the philosophical curriculum both in England and in the United States. The younger generation of philosophers emerging in the nineteen sixties were more highly trained in symbolic logic than their teachers had been. They were familiar not only with the rudiments of the propositional and predicate calculus, but also learned set theory and metamathematics. They read Hilbert, Gödel, and Tarski. They were, in other words, catching up with the developments in symbolic logic in the first third of the century that van Heijenoort discusses in "Logic as Calculus and Logic as Language." The ground was thus well prepared for the acceptance of Chomsky's and Davidson's program.

These observations help us to reflect more broadly on the development of philosophy in the twentieth century. They help us understand that the most significant division in philosophy in this period is not, as Hintikka will have it, between those who consider language a universal medium and those who conceive it as a calculus; the most radical division is rather between those who think of philosophy on the model of the formal and natural sciences and those who do not; those who consider the objective of philosophy to be the generation of theories and those who do not; those who think that human reason can be fully formalized and those who do not; those who conceive of language as a formal system and those who do not.

In sum, the fundamental division in twentieth-century philosophy is between, as we might say, the formalizers and the anti-formalizers. While the formalizers think of philosophy as a science, as aiming at the construction of theories, as a spelling out of the formal rules of human reason, as committed to the picture of language as a formal structure which can be analyzed by means of metatheoretical tools, the anti-formalizers speak of philosophy as a questioning, as describing, as phenomenology, as a concern with difference, or as deconstruction, and proceeding in this way they see philosophy as distinct from the sciences. These anti-formal philosophers aim not at the generality of theories, but at the grasp of particularity, of the historically unique, of the distinctive. They understand that some parts of human reason may follow formal rules, but they are wary of generalizing that claim, they are wary of the very distinction between the formal and the substantive, and they are wary most of all of supposing that rules govern everything. These anti-formalist philosophers are, finally, attuned to the loose play of language, observant of the ever-changing surfaces of language and skeptical about postulating a fixed, underlying, logical deep structures. They are, in a word, wary of depth. Such philosophers are, for that reason, interested not only in the regulated uses of language in science or for making statements, but just as much in informal, metaphorical, literary, poetical, and political uses of language.

The division of twentieth-century philosophy along these two broad fronts is due to the peculiar historical condition of contemporary philosophizing. For all modern philosophy takes place in the shadow of the sciences. These sciences have absorbed some of the old philosophical concerns (about the constitution of matter, the origin of the world, about space and time, etc.) and their methods have generally proved effective and progressive. Hence, the inevitable question: what if anything is left for philosophical labor? If we are to look for "ultimate presuppositions" in our philosophizing, it is presumably to be found in this peculiar and historically unique condition of twentieth-century thought. In the face of these worries there arises the possibility of two very different understandings of the philosophical enterprise: one is the conviction that philosophy, too, can be given a scientific character and the other that philosophy lies in principle outside the scope of the scientific enterprise. Both conceptions of philosophy permit a number of variations. Philosophy can be seen as a science in its own right (logical analysis), but also as something continuous with scientific investigation (positivism, naturalism) or, again, as laying the conceptual groundwork of the sciences (Neo-Kantianism, foundationalism). Philosophy, understood in the second way, thinks of itself as a radical questioning (skepticism, Heideggerian "piety of thought"), as a therapeutic undertaking (later Wittgenstein), as a practical pursuit, or as the recovery of a way of life. This conception can be accompanied by a radical critique of reason, science, and technology or it can involve the decision to bypass the results of science and to consider them as having no bearing on philosophy (Heidegger, Wittgenstein). It is in these multiple forms that the distinction between philosophical formalizers and the philosophical anti-formalists expresses itself. As such it cuts across the classification that Hintikka considers decisive and is quite different in character from the popular distinction between analytic and continental philosophy (which divides philosophical thought into two classes by pitting a methodological term against a geographic one). On the distinction here suggested, Frege and Russell belong in the same camp as Husserl, the French structuralists, Carnap, Chomsky, Davidson, and Hintikka. On the other side of the division we have thinkers as diverse as Moore and (the later) Wittgenstein, the Oxford ordinary language philosophers of the nineteen fifties, Heidegger, Foucault, Feyerabend, Rorty, and Derrida.

Admittedly, if this distinction marks a fundamental division in twentieth-century philosophy, it still remains to write its history and until this is done, the classification has at best a suggestive and polemical function. A history of twentieth-century philosophy written in terms of division between formalizers and anti-formalizing thinkers will, of course, have plenty of reasons for dissolving the apparent dualism into a scheme involving multiple and intersecting divisions. Everything I have said in criticism of Hintikka's dualistic scheme will no doubt apply. But in whatever way such a history of philosophy will be written, it will not be based on the divisions suggested by Hintikka and van Heijenoort.

VI

It should be evident by now that Davidson's essay on "Truth and Meaning" and van Heijenoort's note on "Logic as Calculus and Logic as Language" were symptoms, expressions, and motivating forces of a reorientation in philosophy which began around the time of the publication of these two pieces, and Hintikka, as editor of *Synthese,* played a seminal role in helping to bring about that reorientation. His own theoretical concern with questions of language, meaning, and truth has to be considered, thus, part of that sea change.

It would certainly be difficult to imagine Hintikka's writings on these topics without that assumption. His guiding conviction that a theory of meaning must be conceived as a theory of truth and his resulting pre-occupation with the definition of truth reflect directly the programmatic statements of Davidson's essay. But this does not mean that Hintikka ever intended to adopt Davidson's program in its entirety. Where Davidson sees himself as applying Tarski-style truth theory to ordinary language, Hintikka remains largely critical of such an approach. At first sight, Hintikka writes, "Tarski might seem to have aided and abetted theorists of language as calculus." But since Tarski thought that a truth definition for one language can be given only in a stronger metalanguage and since he considered the actual working language as our highest metalanguage, it followed for him that "in the case that really matters philosophically, truth-definitions are impossible. In this sense, truth is literally ineffable, and the universalists have won."[63]

Davidson, it turns out, had also been somewhat ambiguous on this matter. In characterizing his project of a truth-theoretical account of meaning, he had written that "it is assumed that the language for which truth is being characterized is part of the language used and understood by the characterizer."[64] This suggests that, like Hintikka, he wanted to lift Tarski's restriction that the concept of truth is definable for a language only within another language. But Davidson had continued immediately: "Under these circumstances, the framer of a theory will as a matter of course avail himself when he can of the built-in convenience of a metalanguage with a sentence guaranteed equivalent to each sentence in the object language."[65] This move leaves open the question whether the metalanguage has to be, in Tarski's sense, "essentially richer" than the object language. Davidson notes that there were two reasons for Tarski's pessimism about the possibility of giving a truth definition for our actual working language. The first was that "the universal character of natural languages leads to contradiction" and the second that these languages are "too confused and amorphous to permit the direct application of formal methods."[66] Though Davidson grants that he has no "serious answer" to the first point, he is confident that the claim that natural languages are truly universal is suspect, now that we know such universality leads to paradox.[67] His argument is unfortunately vitiated here by a confusion, for Tarski's claim was, of course, not that natural languages lead to paradoxes, but that the attempt to define truth for such language in that very language leads to paradoxes, and nothing that Davidson says contradicts that possibility. Davidson counters Tarski's second objection, that natural language is too amorphous for the application of formal methods to it, by arguing that we can always construct a formal language that approximates our ordinary idiom. "Philosophers have long been at the hard work of applying theory to ordinary language by the device of matching sentences in the vernacular with sentences for which they have a theory."[68] In making that point Davidson refers once again to "recent work by Chomsky and others."[69]

In contrast to Davidson, Hintikka holds out no hope for a Tarski-style truth definition for ordinary language. He is convinced, rather, that "[r]esults like Gödel's and Tarski's in fact constitute the hard core of any rational basis of the overall ineffability thesis."[70] He proposes, therefore, to rethink the problem of a definition and theory of truth by departing from Tarski's model. His first step in this direction is to reconstruct the theory of quantification we have inherited from Frege. For Hintikka the classical Fregean account is problematic because in any formula containing more than one quantifier, a quantifier R within the scope of another quantifier Q will always be considered dependent on Q. As Hintikka says of the classical theory: "In that notation, each quantifier is associated with a segment of the formula as its *scope*. It is then required that these scopes are ordered, that is, that the scopes of two different quantifiers must either be exclusive or else that the scope of one is included in the scope of the other."[71] This makes it sounds as if the classical theory was based on a tautology according to which two quantifiers are always either exclusive or inclusive of each other's scope. Hintikka adds therefore in explanation that he means to say that the scopes of two quantifiers may overlap only partially. Even that explanation is, however, open to misinterpretation. What Hintikka really intends is, however, made clear by the notational variation he introduces into quantification theory. Thus, in the standard formula:

(5) (Vx)(Vz)(Ey)(Eu) S[x,y,z,u]

the two existential quantifiers are both dependent on the two universal quantifiers preceding them. Hintikka adds to the standard quantifier notation a slash operator notation that exempts the quantifier immediately preceding the slash from dependence on the quantifier that immediately follows the slash. Thus, in:

(6) (Vx) (Vz) (Ey/Vz) (Eu/Vx) S[x,y,z,u]

the first existential quantifier depends on (Vx) but not on (Vz) while the second depends on (Vz) but not on (Vx). Hintikka calls a logic including such a slash operator "an independence friendly logic" and argues that the exclusion of such a device from classical quantification theory is arbitrary and that the use of generality in ordinary language corresponds, in fact, more closely to IF logic than to classical quantification theory.

He also writes: "Interpretationally, IF logic does not mark a single step beyond ordinary first-order logic, and notationally it can be considered merely as a liberated variant of the same logic."[72] That is, however, a modest understatement of the differences. For one of the characteristics of IF first-order logic is that its valid formulas are not recursively enumerable—a fact that may well explain logicians' preference for classical quantification theory. Another is that IF logic violates the principle of compositionality, that is, we can no longer assume that the semantic interpretation of a complex expression can be determined from the semantic interpretation of its component expressions and the order of their composition. It follows from this that we will also find it impossible to construct a Tarski-style truth definition for such a logic. None of this worries Hintikka, for he is convinced that IF logic possesses certain decisive advantages over classical quantificational logic. The most important of these advantages is that there exists a "kinship of IF languages and natural languages."[73] There is, as Hintikka also writes, an "important similarity between extended IF first-order logic and our *Sprachlogik.*"[74] I will have to come back to this claim, but it is in any case obvious what role it plays in Hintikka's reasoning. For if we are to show that a theory of meaning for ordinary language can be conceived as a theory of truth, we can make that claim plausible only by constructing a theory of truth for a logical notation that possesses "important similarity" to ordinary language.

That a Tarski-style truth theory cannot be constructed for IF logic may, at first, seem an obstacle to this line of reasoning. For the question must then be asked what other procedures there might be for defining the concept of truth. Hintikka argues that while Tarski-style truth theory is unavailable, we can apply a game-theoretical semantics of the sort that he first developed in *The Game of Language* and that we can do so without any changes in IF logic.[75] What is more, in IF logic the game-theoretical truth conditions of any first-order sentence S can be expressed by a second-order sentence S* in that logic. In order to turn this observation into an actual truth definition, we must first apply the technique of Gödel numbering to the sentences of our logic (which requires that IF contains, at least, elementary arithmetic); we can then formulate a truth predicate Tr in IF such that

(7) $\text{Tr}(\ulcorner S \urcorner) \leftrightarrow S$

where $\ulcorner S \urcorner$ is the Gödel number of S. Hintikka's goal is then to find a finite conjunction of sentences containing $\text{Tr}(x)$ that together can be taken to provide an implicit characterization of the concept of truth for IF first-order sentences. He proceeds to show how this is to be done and concludes that he has, thus, established that the concept of truth can be defined in IF itself (and not just in a metalanguage of IF). With this, he thinks, he is in a position to show that at least one of the requirements for an ideal semantic theory for a language L can be satisfied, namely that "[t]he truth-definition should be formulated in L itself, not in some metalanguage with a stronger and hence presumably more problematic semantics."[76] Since Hintikka's ultimate goal is to convince us that he can provide a truth definition for ordinary language and since ordinary language will, in a way, be the highest metalanguage, we can see how important it is for Hintikka to show that one can define truth for a language L in L itself. But this argumentation exposes him, as he is aware, to the danger that a form of the liar paradox can be reconstructed as well. Thus, we can show that there is a numeral $\ulcorner g \urcorner$ which is the Gödel number of the sentence

(8) $\sim T(\ulcorner g \urcorner)$.

This sentence says therefore roughly of itself that it is false. But here a decisive aspect of IF logic comes in. It is that the law of excluded middle holds only in the fragment of such a logic that consists of the corresponding ordinary first-order language. A contradiction follows from (8) only by assuming that it must be either true or false. But in IF logic it need not be either and thus no contradiction can be derived. While there are other logics in which truth-value gaps or third truth values lead to violations of the law of excluded middle, Hintikka considers IF logic distinctive in that the failure of the law of excluded middle in it "is a consequence of the eminently natural basic assumptions of the entire theory."[77]

The failure of the principle of excluded middle in IF logic is, in particular, reflected in the way that negation works in such a logic. Here, Hintikka sees once again affinities between IF logic and natural usages. Extended first-order IF languages, he argues, offer "an interesting novel framework for analyzing the behavior of negation in natural languages."[78] He thinks, in particular, that they can explain the difference between verbal and sentential negation in English. But he is forced to admit, in the end, that the analogy is only loose (and therefore, presumably, also inconclusive). For he is forced to admit that "the overt facts of the grammar of negation in English are too complex to be subject to any correlation with what happens in logical languages."[79] Still, he is confident he has shown that "the main theoretical underpinning of the idea of the ineffability of semantics is eliminated if truth is defined in a suitable language, approximating the logical power of natural languages."[80]

Hintikka is thus confident that he has shown us how truth can be technically defined in a formal symbolism which approximates ordinary language and he concludes that his work bears thus directly on the philosophical problem of truth. "What we have here is an interesting example of how apparently technical results can have truly striking consequences of the fundamental assumptions of entire philosophical traditions."[81] The remark leaves us, however, with two questions: How strong are the technical results? And how significant are the philosophical implications? As far as the first question is concerned, we must note that Hintikka's Gödelized truth theory cannot entirely avoid making a distinc-tion between object- and meta-language for the assignment of Gödel numbers to expressions in the symbolism must itself be carried through outside the symbolism. And in this outside language we must have such metalinguistic expressions as "sentence," "quantifier," and "variable" at our command. We must, moreover, be able to say in this metalanguage that the Gödel number of sentence S is n and such sentences will have, in turn, truth conditions which, however, are not captured by the proposed definition. The Gödelization of our symbolic notation is, moreover, a mere thought experiment that proves too complicated to be carried out in actual practice. On practical grounds then we find ourselves forced to employ the meta-linguistic idiom that Hintikka's theory is meant to circumvent. It is in this metalanguage that we will actually express the truth theory of our symbolism and this is evident from Hintikka's own words. For when he sets out to explain to us his theory of truth for IF logic he has to fall back on ordinary English to do so. But once we have granted that much, we are back to Tarski's observation that our truth theory will then be a theory only for the notation which is the object of our study and not a theory of truth for the language in which we are speaking.

Hintikka will, presumably respond to this by arguing that ordinary language, the language in which we are speaking can itself be conceived as an IF logic. But this he has, of course, not yet shown. On the contrary, he has been forced to admit that the similarity between ordinary language and IF logic is only an approximate one. And even that result holds only for a carefully chosen fragment of ordinary language. Hintikka has, in fact, made no step beyond Davidson's expression of hope that it will eventually become possible to describe the logical structure of all the formations of ordinary language. What is more, he has also given us no further reasons, beyond those advanced by Davidson, to think that a comprehensive theory of meaning for ordinary language can be developed as a theory of truth. Hintikka has certainly not shown us how ordinary language could be Gödelized and how a truth predicate could be defined for that language.

All these concerns do not yet touch the fundamental philosophical issue at stake in this discussion. Even if Hintikka succeeded in ironing out the technical difficulties of a comprehensive theory of truth for ordinary language, he would in no way be settling the broader questions concerning the notion of truth that have motivated philosophers since Kant. For the ultimate philosophical concern is, as we have seen, with the relation of language to the world. This relation, the philosophers have concluded, reveals itself in the way we speak. In other words, in speaking we speak about the world. No theory of truth can tell us more about the world than our ordinary speaking does. The sentence "snow is white" tells us no less about the world than the sentence that "the sentence 'snow is white' is true." No additional understanding of the world is achieved when we consider the "semantics" of that sentence. In other words, if we want to understand the physical universe, we should consult the words of the physicists not the analyses of the semanticists. There is nothing the semanticists can add to physicists' story. A theory of truth will certainly not help us in any way with understanding the universe any better. This may appear to be a trivial point, but philosophers from Russell onwards have thought that we can determine what there is by considering the logical structure of our sentences. In opposition to such armchair science we should be firm in concluding that what we mean is contained in our words and that we do not, in general, require to say also what we mean with our words. That would, in any case, be futile for in trying to say what we mean we would, once again, have to rely on the meaning of what we are saying to be contained in our words. It is this discovery that Kant sought to embody in the conclusion that truth may be nominally definable but, for all that, we still lack a general and sure criterion of truth. It is this which lies at the heart of the thesis that "truth is indefinable," which again and again has motivated philosophers since Kant, though not always in a manner that is recognizably Kantian. Such a philosophical concern with truth does, however, not stand on its own; it is not itself the ultimate presupposition of twentieth-century philosophy. The concern arises rather from the broader question whether we can step away from or outside the forms through which we understand and describe the world and describe and analyze these structures. The dream of the formalizers in philosophy has always been that of a science behind all science; but that may be, just as the anti-formalizers have always said, merely a dream.

HANS SLUGA

UNIVERSITY OF CALIFORNIA, BERKELEY
APRIL 2003

NOTES

1. Jaakko Hintikka, *Lingua Universalis vs. Calculus Ratiocinator: An Ultimate Presupposition of Twentieth-century Philosophy*, Jaako Hintikka Selected Papers, vol. 2 (Dordrecht: Kluwer, 1997).

2. Jean van Heijenoort, "Logic as Calculus and Logic as Language," *Synthese* 17 (1967): 324–30. Here, p. 324.

3. Ibid., p. 329.

4. The omission is hardly accidental as one can see from van Heijenoort's *From Frege to Gödel* (Cambridge MA: Harvard University Press, 1967) where Tarski is also given short shrift. It is unclear from this text whether van Heijenoort intended to downplay Tarski's significance or whether he considered him to belong to a later phase of the history of logic.

5. Hans Sluga, "Truth before Tarski," in *Alfred Tarski and the Vienna Circle: Austro-Polish Connections in Logical Empiricism*, ed. Jan Woleński and Eckehart Köhler (Dordrecht: Kluwer, 1999).

6. van Heijenoort, "Logic as Calculus and Logic as Language," p. 324.

7. Gottlob Frege, *Begriffsschrift*, trans. Michael Beaney, in *The Frege Reader*, ed. Michael Beaney (Oxford: Blackwell, 1997), p. iv; 48. In quoting this text I will each time give the page number of the German original followed by the page number of the Beaney collection.

8. Gottlob Frege, *The Foundations of Arithmetic,* trans. J. L. Austin, in *The Frege Reader*, p. 4.

9. Ibid., p. 21.

10. van Heijenoort, "Logic as Calculus and Logic as Language," p. 325.

11. Ibid., p. 326.

12. Frege, *Begriffsschrift*, p. v; 49.

13. Ibid. In the somewhat later essay "On the Scientific Justification of a Conceptual Notation," Frege compares ordinary language to the human hand which despite its "adaptability to the most diverse tasks" proves inadequate for some purposes. We then "build for ourselves artificial hands, tools for particular purposes." These prove useful through their "stiffness and inflexibility of parts" but lack the dexterity of the human hand" (Gottlob Frege, *Conceptual Notation and Related Articles*, trans. and ed. Terrell Ward Bynum [Oxford: The Clarendon Press, 1972], p. 86). He also speaks of the invention of his notation as "an advance in technology" that makes possible "the construction of new instruments" (p. 89).

14. "In my first draft of a formula language I was misled by the example of ordinary language into constructing judgments out of subject and predicate. But I soon convinced myself that this was an obstacle to my particular goal and only led to useless prolixity." (Frege, *Begriffsschrift*, p. 4; 54)

15. Frege, "On the Scientific Justification of a Conceptual Notation," p. 83f.

16. Frege, *Begriffsschrift*, p. v; 50.

17. Gottlob Frege, "Logik," *Nachgelassene Schriften,* ed. Hans Hermes, et al. (Hamburg: Felix Meiner, 1969), p. 3.

18. Frege, *Begriffsschrift*, p. iv; 48.

19. Ibid., p. 3; 54.

20. van Heijenoort, "Logic as Calculus and Logic as Language," p. 328.

21 Ibid. Readers have generally overlooked the Hegelian, dialectic tone of van Heijenoort's account in which the Frege-Russell conception of logic as language represents the thesis and the calculus view the appropriate antithesis which together generate the inevitable synthesis: "During the 'twenties'," so van Heijenoort concludes his story of the two conceptions of logic, "the work of Skolem, Herbrand, and Gödel produced an amalgamation and also a *dé passement* of these two trends" (Ibid.).

22. Ibid., p. 326.

23. Ibid., p. 328.

24. Ibid., p. 326.

25. Jamie Tappenden, "Metatheory and Mathematical Practice in Frege,"

Philosophical Topics 29 (1997): 213–64; also Tappenden, "Frege on Axioms, Indirect Proof, and Independence Arguments in Geometry: Did Frege Reject Independence Arguments?" *Notre Dame Journal of Formal Logic* 41 (2000).

26. From the introduction by Bertrand Russell to Ludwig Wittgenstein, *Tractatus Logico-Philosophicus*, trans. D. F. Pears and B. F. McGuinness (London: Routledge, 1961), p. xxii.

27. Ibid., 5.473. References to Wittgenstein's own words will be indicated by the numbered propositions.

28. Ibid., 6.13.

29. Ibid., 4.12.

30. Gottlob Frege, *Wissenschaftlicher Briefwechsel*, ed. Gottfried Gabriel et al. (Hamburg: Felix Meiner, 1976), p. 161.

31. Heinrich Scholz and Friedrich Bachmann, "Der wissenschaftliche Nachlaß von Gottlob Frege," *Actes du Congrès International de Philosophie Scientific* (Paris 1936), p. 29.

32. van Heijenoort, "Logic as Calculus and Logic as Language, p. 327.

33. Ibid., p. 324.

34. See van Heijenoort's and Dreben's joint "Introductory note to 1929a, 1930, and 1930a," in *Kurt Gödel, Collected Works,* vol. 1, ed. Solomon Feferman et al. (Oxford: Oxford University Press, 1986), p. 44.

35. Hintikka, *Lingua Universalis vs. Calculus Ratiocinator*, p. 21.

36. Ibid., p. 193.

37. Ibid., p. x.

38. Ibid., p. xi.

39. Ibid., p. 7.

40. Ibid., p. 23.

41. Ibid., p. xii.

42. Ibid., p. xiii.

43. Ibid., p. xviii.

44. Ibid.

45. Ibid., p. xvii.

46 I discuss the Fregean version of the doctrine that truth is indefinable and its place in Frege's overall reflections on the concept of truth in "Frege and the Indefinability of Truth," in *From Frege to Wittgenstein,* ed. Erich Reck (Oxford: Oxford University Press, 2000). A revised version of my argument can be found in "Frege's These von der Undefinierbarkeit von Wahrheit," in *Das Wahre und das Falsche: Studien zu Freges Auffassung von Wahrheit,* ed. Dirk Greimann (Hildesheim: Georg Olms, 2003).

47. Gottlob Frege, "Notes for Ludwig Darmstaedter," in Michael Beaney, *The Frege Reader*, p. 362.

48. The word 'true' "allows what corresponds to the assertoric force to assume the form of a contribution to the thought." But this attempt fails. That we cannot do without the notion of truth "is due to the imperfections of language." (Gottlob Frege, "My Basic Logical Insights," in Beaney, *The Frege Reader*, p. 323.

49. Immanuel Kant, *Critique of Pure Reason*, trans. Norman Kemp Smith (New

York: St. Martin's Press, 1965 [1929]), p. A58 (my emphasis).

    50. Ibid., p. A59.

    51. Ibid.

    52. Ibid., p. A60.

    53. Ibid.

    54. Wittgenstein, *Tractatus Logico-Philosophicus*, 4.06.

    55. Donald Davidson, "Truth and Meaning," in *Inquiries into Truth and Interpretation* (Oxford: Clarendon Press, 1984), p. 25.

    56. Davidson, "Truth and Meaning," *Synthese* 17 (1967): 304–23. Reprinted in *Inquiries into Truth and Interpretation* (Oxford: Clarendon Press, 1984), and in *Meaning and Truth: Essential Readings in Modern Semantics*, ed. J. Garfield and M. Kitely (New York: Paragon House, 1990), and in numerous other publications.

    57. Davidson, "Truth and Meaning," in *Inquiries into Truth and Interpretation*, p. 17.

    58. Ibid., p. 35.

    59. Ibid., pp. 35–36.

    60. Ibid., p. 35.

    61. Davidson, in his introduction to *Inquiries into Truth and Interpretation*, p. xv, referring to "Semantics for Natural Languages" (essay 4 in *Inquiries*). He presented this essay in Milan in October 1968, proceedings of which were published in *Linguaggi nella Società e nella Tecnica*, Edizioni di Comunità, Milan, 1970.

    62. Noam Chomsky, *Syntactic Structures* (The Hague: Mouton, 1957).

    63. Hintikka, *Lingua Universalis vs. Calculus Ratiocinator*, p. 13.

    64. Davidson, "Truth and Meaning," in *Inquiries*, p. 25.

    65. Ibid.

    66. Ibid., p. 28.

    67. Ibid., p. 29.

    68. Ibid.

    69. Ibid., p. 30.

    70. Hintikka, *Lingua Universalis vs. Calculus Ratiocinator*, p. 17.

    71. Ibid., p. 49.

    72. Ibid., p. 54.

    73. Ibid., p. 86.

    74. Ibid., p. 87.

    75. Jaakko Hintikka and Jack Kulas, *The Game of Language: Studies in Game-Theoretical Semantics and Its Applications* (Dordrecht: Reidel, 1983).

    76. Hintikka, *Lingua Universalis vs. Calculus Ratiocinator*, p. 46.

    77. Ibid., p. 61.

    78. Ibid., p. 88.

    79. Ibid., p. 91.

    80. Ibid., p. 93.

    81. Ibid., p. 7.

REPLY TO HANS SLUGA

Hans Sluga's paper deals ostensibly with my views on truth. But when you read it, you will soon discover that in reality it has a much more ambitious and much more interesting aim. Sluga is trying to place my entire approach to logic and language on the map of different trends and traditions in contemporary philosophy. Or, rather, one should not speak of *the* map here, for the current and recent scene in philosophy can be viewed from several different vantage points. Sluga considers and weighs two such frameworks. One of them is a contrast between conceptions of language as the universal medium (a.k.a. the universalist view) and of language as calculus (a.k.a. the model-theoretical view). This contrast was pointed out clearly by van Heijenoort in his 1967 paper whose importance is highlighted by Sluga. I have used this contrast as a frame of reference for the purpose of discussing from a historical vantage point different issues in logical theory and philosophy of language. One of the most clear-cut differences between the two contrasting conceptions is that all model theory (logical semantics) when pursued as a genuine theory expressible in a suitable language presupposes the calculus view. Admittedly, a universalist can have model-theoretical ideas, but for such a thinker they will belong, to use Wittgenstein's jargon, to what cannot be said in language, only shown. Alternatively, a universalist can view model theory as a bunch of technical tricks, best suitable for illuminating such local issues as the independence of axioms of one another.

Sluga discusses this contrast, but does not make it a lynchpin of his interpretation. However, I am not sure that Sluga understands the contrast between universality views and calculus views quite in the same way van Heijenoort and I have understood it. For one thing, he speaks in connection to Peano, Frege, and Russell as if one of the crucial issues were the possibility (or desirability) of metatheoretical theorizing. But this is not the most relevant way of understanding the contrast even historically. The real issue is whether the metatheory of a language can be expressed in the same language. This is the reason why the possibility of a self-applicable universal language of science was an important issue in the discussions among Carnap, Tarski, and Gödel.

By and large, my own systematic work has aided and abetted the model-theoretical viewpoint. For one prominent example, by means of the new, richer basic logic which I have developed, known as IF logic, the concept of truth can be defined in a suitable first-order language for the self-same language. Indeed, Sluga sees in the definability of truth the main tenet or at least one of the main aims of the calculus approach.

A methodological caveat is perhaps in order here. Sluga calls the contrast I have drawn a "classification" and "dualistic." Maybe these terms are accurate enough. However, I have come to realize that the most illuminating applications of such contrasts in intellectual history are to the ambivalent cases. It does not tell very much of a thinker to label him a "hedgehog" or a "fox" in the sense of the old proverbial saying. Isaiah Berlin was nevertheless able to put Archilochos's dictum to brilliant use by diagnosing Tolstoy as a fox who believed that he was a hedgehog. Likewise the contrast between conceptions of universal medium or calculus is at its most intriguing in the mixed cases, for instance, in the cases of Tarski and Gödel, who helped to create the explicit conceptual tools for the calculus view, but who in their overall approach remained to a considerable degree committed to a universalist viewpoint. Their motives and their influence are especially instructive historically, throwing light on such questions as why Carnap's self-conscious "logical semantics" remained relatively uninfluential or why model theory in the narrower technical sense was originally developed as a model theory of algebraic theories rather than as a tool of philosophical analysis.

For another example, even when Carnap tried to restrict his theorizing to the formal mode of speech, he at the same time entertained a hope—or should one speak of a wish here?—for a universal language that could serve as its own metatheory.

Sluga nevertheless disparages the significance of the contrast between the universalist idea and the (possibly misnamed) calculus conception. He argues that truth definitions do not constitute a major advance in understanding language, reality, or their interrelations. In the place of this contrast he proposes to place another one. To use his own words, Sluga wants to write a history of twentieth-century philosophy "in terms of division between formalizers and anti-formalizing thinkers." He sees the deeper motivation of this contrast in a difference between different philosophers' attitudes to science and scientific methods.

I do not think that it is constructive or clarifying to ask here which distinction is the right one or the more enlightening one. For me, one of the main uses of the universality versus calculus contrast has in any case been trying to understand specific aspects of philosophers' and logicians' views, such as Frege's astonishing failure to begin to understand Hilbert's axiomatic project, Wittgenstein's distinction between what can be said and what can only be shown, its aftermath in the form of the Vienna Circle's preference of *die formale Redeweise*, and Quine's refusal to avail himself of the resources of logical model theory, rather than as a pigeonholing principle for all and sundry philosophers. It seems to me that if Sluga's distinction between formalizers and anti-formalistic thinkers is to provide the deepest insights possible, it must be complemented by a further distinction. There is an important difference between, on the one hand, those formalizers who conceive of their task as explicating, regimenting, systematizing, or otherwise accounting for the overt phenomena of use and usage, in natural as well as in technical and even formal languages, in other words, as finding the regularities that govern the surface data of language, perhaps by means of including the use of language for drawing logical inferences and, on the other hand, those who are trying to use formalism as a means of uncovering those deeper, usually hidden, factors whose distant consequences manifest themselves in the form of surface structures.

The contrast I am describing can be operative also on the anti-formalists' side, and can help us to understand their ideas. For instance, it is often claimed that Wittgenstein's later anti-formalist stance is due to his realization of the multiplicity and elusiveness of the different uses of language. This is a typical surface argument. In reality, Wittgenstein's new stance is due to a deep theoretical change in his views, viz., giving up the belief that language can express directly the given phenomenological data of experience.

Once again, this contrast admits of all sorts of gradations and mixed cases. In some cases the contrast is nevertheless obvious. For instance, most logicians seem to think that the essence of negation can be captured by the one single notion of contradictory negation. Alas, this does not help very much a linguist who is trying to master the overt phenomena of negation in a natural language, the "natural history of negation," as Horn has put it.[1] By means of IF logic, I have tried to make the logic of negation more helpful for the purpose of understanding the actual behavior of negation both in formal and in natural languages. I have shown that in any sufficiently rich language there are inevitably two different notions of negation present whose nature and interplay with each other explains certain surface data that are otherwise hard to account for without blatant adhockery.

Again, some of the mixed cases are among the most interesting ones. Chomsky has obviously sought to find "deep" explanations, not only in terms of the ill-fated deep structure expounded in *Aspects of the Theory of Syntax* (1964).[2] He has, for instance, extolled the methodological significance of explanatory depth. The very idea of universal grammar is a bold stab at a depth explanation. However, in the hands of his followers and in some cases in Chomsky's own hands, the generative enterprise has deteriorated into a bunch of empirical generalizations, which cannot sustain claims of significant explanatory depth.

Much of the recent and current work in the so-called philosophical logic is no more than study of surface phenomena. In contrast, I have in my own work consistently sought to capture the underlying structures, often semantical ones, that manifest themselves only indirectly and often modified by pragmatic pressures on the surface level. I tried to give an account of this methodology a long time ago.[3] I have been repeatedly surprised by the unwillingness of many philosophical logicians to look under the surface phenomena. For an important example, I have shown what conditions have to be imposed on existential generalization and universal instantiation in intensional contexts; these have not received their due and have even been repeatedly misunderstood.

The most outrageous example in my first-hand experience would be a good parody of such surface theorizing, if it were intended as a parody. George Lakoff once criticized my theory of the semantics of questions because it did not explain why one can say "Why the hell...?" but not "Who the hell...?" or "What the hell...?" Not only did Lakoff get his facts wrong (he obviously does not read Raymond Chandler in whose story "Red Wind" both these allegedly nonexistent locutions occur), but even if his facts had been right, explaining the use of expletives is scarcely the business of semantic depth rules.

But the surface-depth dimension is relevant in other ways than for the purpose of classifying different thinkers' approaches. Some results deal with a subject matter which is intrinsically close to the surface phenomena of language, whereas others are only indirectly connected with the immediately accessible data. For instance, the presence of two different negations in natural language does not manifest itself in any simply interpretable evidence.

Here we come to the crucial fact about which Sluga is in an important sense both right and wrong in one of the main thrusts of his paper. He belittles the theoretical significance of truth definitions, including those provided by IF logic. However, there are different ways of understanding what kind of significance we are dealing with here. Sluga is to my mind dangerously wrong when it comes to the significance of explicit truth definitions for philosophical discussions of truth. I will indicate my reasons later.

In contrast, Sluga is in a sense and in a certain respect right when it comes to the systematic significance of truth definitions for the purposes of actual language theory. He is right in the sense that such truth definitions as are provided by IF logic are at bottom only codifications of fairly obvious and "intuitive" features of the semantics of the language they pertain to. As I have pointed out in an earlier paper, it is for instance instructive to try to convert Tarski's T-schema (strictly speaking, a suitable class of instances of the T-schema) directly into a truth definition for an arithmetical language. It turns out that such an attempt fails if the traditional Frege-Russell first-order logic is being used, but only because of the limitations of this logic, in which the independence of two nested quantifiers cannot be expressed. And as soon as this flaw is corrected in IF logic, a perfectly straightforward truth definition becomes available. Furthermore, such a truth definition for a given language does not require any semantical assumptions beyond what is needed already for the purpose of formulating the semantics of the language in question (without the concept of truth). As a Wittgensteinean might put it, the language-games that give the notion of truth its meaning as applied to a given language are the same ones that are already needed for the semantics of the language in question. Or, to look at the same matter from a different point of view, it is seen that in a philosophical perspective there is a great deal of truth in the ideas of the minimalists. Of course, if they had taken their own ideas seriously and tried to systematize them, they would have run into the same problems which can be solved only by means of IF logic.

Thus Sluga, in an important sense, is right about the relative superficiality of truth definitions for constructive purposes. However, I cannot agree with him in other respects. First, the very superficiality of truth definitions makes them a poor candidate for being the poster issue in the context of model-theoretic approaches to language. This role belongs to other ideas. As far as logical languages are concerned, the deep insight is into the role of different logical notions in expressing relations of dependence and independence between variables. When this role is acknowledged, we are immediately forced to enrich the traditional Frege-Russell logic of quantifiers so as to become an IF logic. I have myself been amazed how deep the problems quickly become in this direction, for instance, when one tries to express relations of irreducibly mutual dependence.

Thus Sluga's use of truth and truth definitions as his focal issue does not help to bring out the deeper theoretical significance of the new developments in logical theory like the IF logic. Even though the issue is probably too massive to be dealt with adequately here, it also seems to me that Sluga is underestimating the philosophical significance of the new truth definitions, especially of their liberating effects. Previously, it was generally thought that the impossibility of truth definitions (expressible in a given language for the same language) was due to the excessive strength of the language in question. Hence it was deemed hopeless to use the concept of truth systematically in the strongest language of all, that is, in our actual working language. However, it now turns out that the Tarskian indefinability of truth is instead due to the expressive poverty of the underlying logic. This removes all reasons to think that the notion of truth could not be employed without any risk of paradoxes in ordinary language. As I once put it, in philosophy, "true" is no longer a four-letter word.

Moreover, being able to give an explicit definition of truth enables us to get rid of all the mystifications that have clouded philosophical discussions of truth. I expect that we can still make good sense of most of the philosophical issues still concerning truth. We can presumably ask whether truth is a semantical or ontological concept, whether the essence of truth is unhiddenness, or what the relation of truth is to the ends of inquiry. But these questions will no longer pertain to some ineffable idea that cannot be expressed in literal terms in our sober ordinary discourse. Attempts to answer such questions can, and must, start from a precise definition of truth. In particular, we do not have to resort to any oblique hermeneutical modes of thinking. And the more general motivation for so proceeding need not be any admiration of scientific techniques, but simply a respect for the ways in which our language actually works, a respect that would have been appreciated by ordinary language thinkers like John Austin who liked to surprise his audience by meaning what he said.[4]

But there is more to be said here even on the level of systematic logical theory. Truth definitions are in certain respects less superficial than Sluga makes them out to be. They do not tell us anything about the world, but they can tell a great deal about how our language is related to the world. In fact, different truth definitions go together with different assumptions of what those links are. Now if you take an unprejudiced look at a quantificational statement, no matter whether it is a formalized or unformalized one, traditional first-order statement or an IF one, a moment's reflection should show you what its truth condition is according to our pre-theoretical assumptions, viz., the existence of a full array of its Skolem functions. For these functions yield as their values the "witness individuals" that vouchsafe the truth of the sentence in question. And this conception of truth is precisely the game-theoretical one, which accordingly is little more than a codification of our spontaneous notion of truth as applied to quantificational sentences.

Now in traditional first-order languages, such truth conditions are equivalent to what is yielded by Tarski-type truth definitions and also to what might be called substitutional truth conditions, which operate by reference to the set of all substitution-instances of quantificational formulas. But when these traditional types of truth conditions are used in connection with IF languages, they are no longer equivalent with the game-theoretical ones. And this nonequivalence makes a huge difference. Semantical games do not involve any completed infinite totalities even when they are played in an infinite domain. They are hence in an important sense finitistic or perhaps rather elementary. In contrast, both Tarski-type truth conditions and substitutional ones require appeals to closed infinite totalities. They are therefore infinitistic or perhaps rather nonelementary in a clear-cut sense. This throws interesting light on the entire complex of problems in the foundations of mathematics. Among other things, in a forthcoming paper I will show that a suitable use of game-theoretical truth conditions enables us to carry out Hilbert's foundational project in a way that would have satisfied Hilbert himself.[5] More generally, we can understand better the difference between elementary ("finitistic") and nonelementary conceptualizations.

Moreover, it can be argued that our innate notion of truth embodied in the semantics of natural language is captured more accurately by the game-theoretical truth definition than by the others. From this it follows that Tarski-type truth definitions do not fully capture the philosophically relevant notion of truth. Instead of continuing the deluge of papers and books on Tarski-type truth definitions, philosophers might thus be well advised to concentrate instead on game-theoretical ones.

Furthermore, the very equivalence of a theory of truth for a given language on the one hand and a semantics for it on the other hand makes the concept of truth a useful tool in meaning theory. This way of approaching meaning theory as a theory of truth was the leading idea of Davidson's early approach, as Sluga aptly emphasizes. However, Davidson's 1967 article[6] did not make much of an impact on me personally, both because I had always thought of meaning as being specified by truth conditions and because I found the specifics of Davidson's approach unimpressive. Subsequently it has in fact become clear that it was Davidson's commitment to compositionality that above everything else prevented him putting forward actual truth predicates. However, any Davidsonian who is willing to sacrifice compositionality (which I have argued is a lost cause anyway) should in my judgment welcome the IF truth definition as a definitive realization of Davidson's project.

Davidson himself apparently remained unaware of the fact that it was his commitment to compositionality that prevented him and others from carrying out his own original leading idea much more fully. In this respect, I suspect that Tarski was to some extent better aware of the situation. I have argued (with Gabriel Sandu) that Tarski's belief in the inapplicability of the concept to natural languages was based on his insight that natural languages are not compositional.[7] No wonder Tarski objected strongly to Davidson's use of his ideas for the purpose of constructing a truth theory for natural languages. However, even though Tarski's insight is undoubtedly valid, it constitutes no objection to IF truth definitions, for IF logic is not compositional.

Even though the possibility of an IF truth definition is relatively speaking a surface phenomenon, its presuppositions are far from obvious, and alter in fact the methodological presuppositions of entire logical semantics, especially the principle of compositionality. Thus we have found yet more to be said for Sluga's choice of truth definitions as his paradigm case than I have so far given him credit for.

In conclusion, it may be helpful for the reader if I explain briefly in what sense an IF truth definition—strictly speaking, a definition of a truth predicate in an IF language which is rich enough to express its own syntax—belies the four different forms of undefinability of truth that Sluga formulates.

The first form says that the truth of a sentence cannot be explained in terms of the semantical properties of its subsentential components—plus, although Sluga does not spell it out, its syntactical form. This amounts to stating that compositional definitions of truth are impossible. Such impossibility may very well hold, but it does not rule out noncompositional definitions of truth like IF truth definitions.

The second form claims that the concept of truth cannot be defined because it is presupposed in the use of any attempted definition. Here we must ask: presupposed in what sense? What I have pointed out is that understanding the concept of truth for a language cannot be separated from understanding its semantics in the first place. This lends a reasonable meaning to, and justifications for, saying that the concept of truth is presupposed in any use of a proposed definition, just as it is in meaningful use of the language in question. But this does not make a valid truth definition impossible, for the only thing that is presupposed there strictly speaking is the *definiens*.

The third form claims that the concept of truth is not a semantic notion at all and therefore is not definable in semantic terms. This claim is confused in several ways. Of course the notion of truth is semantic in that it pertains to language-world relations. But from its being semantic it does not follow that the notion of truth is a matter of fixed relations of meaning or reference. Game-theoretical truth definitions are given in terms of certain rule-governed activities that might be characterized as verification games. This does not make them impossible or separate them from the most purely logical concepts imaginable. To ask whether such truth definitions are semantic or not is a matter of terminology not of substance.

The fourth form claims that even though truth may be formally definable (whatever that means), such a definition cannot tell us anything about the relation of our language to the world. To this I can reply that game-theoretical truth definitions can tell us about the relation of language and world because they do in fact do so. These definitions are formulated in terms of the very language-games (to use Wittgensteinean jargon) that relate our language to the world. Whether other truth definitions can do so need not be discussed here. Tarski-type truth definitions have been criticized precisely for the reason Sluga mentions. Game-theoretical ones are not subject to such objections.

Sluga examines the role of these different forms of the undefinability thesis in Frege. In the unfair light of hindsight, his lucid and illuminating discussion is an excellent illustration of my historical thesis that the great interest that still prevails in the ideas of early analytic thinkers like Frege lies by this time almost exclusively in diagnosing their shortcomings. These shortcomings influenced the subsequent history of philosophy profoundly, and we are still engaged in an effort to overcome them.

These all too brief remarks will hopefully help not only to clarify my views on truth, but also, and more importantly, to locate my work more accurately on the map of current (and future) trends in logical theory and in the methodology of linguistics. I am deeply grateful to Hans Sluga for providing me with an incentive to try to do so.

J. H.

NOTES

1. Laurence Horn, *A Natural History of Negation* (Chicago: University of Chicago Press, 1989).

2. See Noam Chomsky, *Aspects of the Theory of Syntax* (Cambridge: MIT Press, 1964).

3. See my 1968 paper, "Epistemic Logic and the Methods of Philosophical Analysis," *Australian Journal of Philosophy* 46 (1968): 37–51. Also appears in Jaakko Hintikka, *Models for Modalities*, 3–22 (Dordrecht: D. Reidel Publishing Co., 1969).

4. John Austin, "Performative Utterances," in *Philosophical Papers* (Oxford: Clarendon Press, 1961), pp. 220–39.

5. With Besim Karakadilar, "How to Prove the Consistency of Arithmetic," *Acta Philosophica Fennica,* Societas Philosophica Fennica, Helsinki, forthcoming.

6. Donald Davidson, "Meaning and Truth," *Synthese* 17 (1997): 303–23.

7. See Hintikka and Sandu, "Tarski's Guilty Secret: Compositionality" in *Alfred Tarski and the Vienna Circle* (Vienna Circle Institute Yearbook vol. 6, for 1998), ed. Jan Wolenski and Eckehart Köhler (Dordrecht: Kluwer Academic Publishers, 1999), pp. 217–30.

18

Pascal Engel

IS TRUTH EFFABLE?

I

Professor Hintikka's work has so much breadth and scope that it is tempting to think of him as a contemporary Leibniz, if he had not warned us against the nostalgia for systematic philosophy:

> Once upon a time a serious philosopher was expected to produce a system of his own. Twentieth-century philosophers are likely to find this expectation not only old-fashioned but more than a little ridiculous. Professional standards of clarity and argumentation are in our time and age such that it is hard enough to produce first-class work in one limited area of philosophy. Hence the idea of marshalling deep philosophical thoughts on command about each and every philosophical topic seems to be about as relevant to us as the principles of Napoleonic warfare are to twentieth-century global strategy.[1]

Nevertheless, Hintikka's work is very systematic, both in his constant defense and illustration of the model-theoretic tradition in logic, in its application to so many fields as modal logic, epistemic logic, logical semantics, and in his analysis of the "ultimate presuppositions" (a term he borrows from Collingwood) that lie behind the traditions of thought that he examines. One such great presupposition, which he has brought into light better than anyone else, is the universalist assumption in logic and the thesis of the ineffability of semantics. Hintikka argues that his own game-theoretical approach in logic and in semantics allow us to claim that semantics is not ineffable, and to reject the universality assumption. In an illuminating series of essays,[2] he has analyzed how the thesis of the ineffability of semantics affects our understanding of the concept of truth, which becomes itself ineffable. Now the question we may ask is this: what conception of truth emerges from Hintikka's rejection of the ineffability thesis? I want to try to characterize the *philosophical* concept of truth that underlies Hintikka's analyses, and in particular to confront it with the "deflationary" and "minimalist" conceptions of truth that have recently occupied the front scene. I shall try to show that, in spite of his criticism of Wittgenstein's conceptions of truth and semantics, Hintikka is still very close to Wittgenstein's conception of meaning as use, and that Hintikka's view can still be characterized as a form of minimalism about truth and meaning.

II

Let us try first to characterize the ineffability thesis about truth and semantics, starting, as Hintikka most often does, from Wittgenstein's views. In a famous passage of the *Philosophical Remarks*, Wittgenstein says:

> [I]n a certain sense, the use of language is something that cannot be taught, i.e., I cannot use language to teach it in the way in which language could be used to teach someone to play the piano.—And that of course is just another way of saying: I cannot use language to get outside language.[3]

There are at least two lines of thought, closely associated with each other, in such passages. The first is the thesis of the *ineffability of semantics* proper, that semantic relations cannot be established from without, but only from within a language, and actually from within our language, the language that we speak. The ineffability of semantics goes hand in hand with the thesis of the universality of language, that language is the universal medium of communication and thought. Actually, as Hintikka notes, the former assumption is stronger, and entails the second:

> [I]f semantics is ineffable, it makes no sense to try to speak in our language of a situation in which the expressions of one's language would have meanings different from what they in fact have. In other words, if semantics is ineffable, it makes no sense to try to say or to assume, by using my actual home language, that there are languages other than it or that I am changing the semantics of my language. "A language that I do not understand is no language," as Wittgenstein once put it. Thus it may be argued that the ineffability of semantics entails the universality of language.[4]

The second line of thought present in Wittgenstein's passage is that "the use of language cannot be taught," and that for this reason one cannot use language to teach the meanings of the expressions of language. Wittgenstein is not here saying that language cannot be taught, for this would be obviously false, but only that "in a certain sense" it cannot be taught. Why? What he seems to say is that any rule for the use of a word must be expressed in language, and that we cannot use language itself to explain the rules: in some sense the way the signs are used is primary. This means that signs can only convey meaning if at some point there is a natural uptake on how they are used, which cannot be taught. Although it is in a sense just another way of formulating the ineffability thesis, what Wittgenstein says can be formulated thus: there is no way to explain what it is to know the meaning of a word, and to understand a language, which would be independent from our knowing already how words are used. Hence there is no language-independent account of what it is to know meaning. In particular (and this is a familiar theme emerging from Wittgenstein's "rule-following" considerations), there is no account of meaning which could invoke our grasping concepts or propositions, conceived either as psychological entities ("ideas," "representations") or as abstract Platonic entities independent from language. In other words, there is no priority of a structure of thought—or of a structure of ontological entities independent from language—over language. Hintitkka has commented widely upon this idea in Wittgenstein's writings.[5] Following John Skorupski who himself adapts a phrase from Dummett, let us call this the *thesis of the priority of language* (or *the priority thesis*, for short): it says that any account of thought and concepts is intrinsically dependent upon an account of language rules and language-understanding.[6] Although, as I have just said, the priority thesis seems to entail the ineffability thesis (there is no way of formulating the semantics of our language outside our language), they are not equivalent and the latter does not necessarily entail the former. It is open to a theorist to defend the view that semantics is ineffable although thoughts and concepts are independent from language. For Frege, for instance, thoughts are language-independent entities, although he subscribes to the ineffability thesis and to the universality assumption.[7]

III

Now, what are the consequences for the nature of the concept of truth of the thesis of the ineffability of semantics and of the thesis of the priority of language? As Hintikka shows, the first thesis implies the ineffability of truth, as the main semantic relation. This line of thought is clearly present in Wittgenstein, when he argues, against a correspondence theory of truth, that such a theory is impossible, because it is "impossible to describe the fact which corresponds to . . . a sentence, without repeating the sentence."[8] Because the relationship between sentences and facts, propositions and reality, cannot be spelled out, truth admits of no other "definition" than this one: "For what does a proposition's 'being true' mean? 'p' is true = p. (That is the answer.)"[9] As Hintikka points out commenting on this passage, the basis of this Wittgensteinian view is "this impossibility of expressing in languages the conditions of agreement between a meaningful proposition— a thought—and reality."[10] And in this sense it does not amount to a *definition*, or to a *theory* of truth. It is simply the denial that any sort of such definition or theory could be given.

Insofar as one could ascribe a "theory" (and not simply an elucidation) of truth to Wittgenstein in such passages, it would fall within the category of so-called "minimalist" or "deflationist" theories of truth. Actually, Wittgenstein is often considered as a representative of the "redundancy" theory of truth, alongside Ramsey and Ayer.

The redundancy conception of truth should not be confused with the *disquotational* conception. According to the former, truth is a (nongenuine) property of *propositions*, the meaning of which we already know, whereas according to the latter, truth is a (nongenuine) property of *sentences*. The role of "true" is to express T-sentences of the form " 'p' is true iff p"or infinite disjunctions and conjunctions of sentences of the form: x is true iff $(x = $'$s_1$' $\& s_1)$ or $(x = $'$s_2$' $\& s_2)$ or. . . .[11] What these views have in common, as Paul Horwich has pointed out,[12] is the claim that truth is not a genuine property, but only a quasi-property: truth has no essence, substance, or explanatory role, and so cannot be explained in terms of such properties or relations as correspondence, coherence, utility, and the like.

Against such minimalist views of truth, Hintikka argues that they belie the ineffability assumption about semantics. Tarski's hierarchy of metalanguages is itself but a version of the view that truth cannot be defined and that the ultimate semantical relations cannot be spelled out. This is because both disquotational and other "minimalist" conceptions of truth suffer from the same difficulty as Tarski's definitions: they cannot be formulated in the language to which they are supposed to apply.[13] They operate at a purely syntactical level. Indeed, for the minimalist the truth predicate only obeys the discipline of syntax: it allows us to quote and to disquote sentences, and to embed them within propositional attitude and other contexts.[14] Against this, Hintikka argues that truth can be defined, both for a formal and for a natural language, by dropping Tarski's hierarchy, through an Independence-Friendly (IF) logic and a game-theoretical semantics, by developing a theory of truth "in some suitable metalanguage which does not have to be thought of as being sharply separated from the object language itself."[15] By contrast,

Disquotational treatments of truth are . . . subject to the standard criticism which has been levelled at Tarski's treatment of truth. They do not tell anything about the way our sentences are in fact shown to be true or false. Indeed, when nothing is said of the "language games" through which truth and falsity are constituted, it is natural to resort to disquotational ideas.[16]

Not only do disquotional accounts of truth do little to illuminate truth, but also they do little to illuminate meaning. Where famously a number of philosophers, following Davidson, have hoped to build an empirical theory of meaning on the basis of theories of truth satisfying (to a certain extent) Tarski's Convention T, Hintikka has objected that such accounts fail for a number of simple quantificational sentences (such as "Any corporal can become a general") and that the principle of semantic compositionality upon which they rest fails as well.[17]

IV

My concern here is not to examine the specific nature of Hintikka's proposals in logic and in model-theoretic semantics. The question that I intend to raise is this: what kind of analysis of the *ordinary* concept of truth emerges out of Hintikka's position, and what kind of philosophical conception of truth does it support? Given his criticism of minimalist theories of truth, one should expect that Hintikka should propose some kind of substantive theory of truth, where by "substantive" I mean any conception of truth which would reject the minimalist view and the ineffability thesis, and which would claim that truth is a genuine property of some sort which could be defined and spelled out fully. But which one? One suggestion which comes naturally to mind could be that Hintikka defends a variety of verificationist theories of truth. As he says in the passage above when he contrasts the game-theoretical approach with the disquotational approach to truth, the former does, in a way in which the latter does not, tell us how sentences are *shown* to be true or false. In a nutshell, the game theoretical analysis of the truth conditions of a sentence says that a sentence S is true in a given model M if and only if there exists a winning strategy for the initial verifier in the game G(S) when played on M. Now this definition, because of the role played in it by the notion of verification, has often been compared with an anti-realist conception of meaning in terms of assertability conditions, such as Dummett's. But although he admits that his views are very much "in the spirit of the constructivist way of thinking," Hintikka has stressed that his own conception of truth is not constructivistic or anti-realist.[18] Dummett's famous analogy between the notion of truth and the notion of winning a game is not the good one if truth is supposed to be *identified* in some way with the strategy of verification. This is not so: "The interesting analogy is between the notion of truth and the *existence* [my italics] of a winning strategy."[19] In other terms, the winning strategy is already there, it is not constructed or created in any sense by the steps in which it consists. So it is not part of the game-theoretical conception that truth conditions should be understood in some sense as investigation-dependent or as *known*. In spite of the analogy between the notion of game and the notion of verification, truth, Hintikka insists, is not *known* truth; so his concept of truth is not to be identified with the constructivist's or the intuitionist's version. Actually Hintikka's substantive conception of truth seems to be closer to the *realist* conception of truth, which presupposes that there are verification-transcendent truth conditions for sentences. This point emerges in particular in Hintikka's analysis of such first-order sentences with dependent quantifiers as

(1) $(\forall x)(\exists y)F[x, y]$

These are true not only when it is possible to find a "witness" individual y depending on x such that $F[x, y]$. But one can *find* such an individual only if *there is* a certain function f such that

(2) $(\forall x)F[x, f(x)]$

where f is a Skolem function, namely a choice function of individuals.[20] So the truth condition of (1) is the existence of such a Skolem function. In other terms, appropriate witness individuals exist for a quantificational sentence S only if there is an "array" of Skolem functions. The quantifier "there exists" should be understood here objectually. As Hintikka suggests in a recent essay, one could even use the notion of a truth-maker, which has been invoked in the context of recent realistic conceptions of truth.[21] When it comes to the establishment of the truth conditions of our sentences, Hintikka's account is genuinely semantical, in the sense in which David Lewis said famously that "semantics without truth conditions is no semantics." But when it comes to seeking truth, Hintikka's account is constructivistic: it involves the activities of finding truths. But the first cannot be reduced to the second, and it is only when one confuses semantical games with interrogative games that one is led to the idea that truth is in some way dependent upon our human activities.[22]

Now, is Hintikka a straightforward realist about truth in the sense of a correspondence theory? There are several reasons to doubt this. In the first place, Hintikka has little sympathy, to say the least, for an ontology of facts and states of affairs, and even less for an ontology of real possible worlds à la Lewis, which are the entities usually invoked by genuine correspondence theories of truth. In the second place, he has often reiterated Wittgenstein's criticism against such theories. Commenting upon the difference between his game-theoretical approach and pragmatist conceptions of truth he says:

> The possibility of a game-theoretical concept of truth which accords with our natural concept of truth, together with the distinction between semantical (truth-conditioning) and interrogative (truth-seeking) games also has profound philosophical repercussions. For one thing, it shows what is true and what is false in pragmatist conceptions of truth. What is true is that to speak of truth is not to speak of any independently existing correspondence relations between language and the world. There are no such relations. Or, as Wittgenstein once put it, the correspondence between language and the world is established only by the use of our language—that is, by semantical games. Truth is literally constituted by certain human rule-governed activities.
>
> What is false in pragmatist ideas about truth is the claim that the relevant activities are the activities by means of which we typically find out what is true—that is to say, verify, falsify, confirm, disconfirm and so forth, our propositions. This claim is based on overlooking the all-important distinction between truth-establishing games (that is, semantical games) and truth-seeking games (that is, interrogative or perhaps other epistemic games). . . . Our actual truth-seeking practices, whether or not they are relative to a historical era, epistemic or scientific community, social class or gender, are not constitutive of our normal concept of truth—that is, of *the* concept of truth.[23]

Here Hintikka's reasons for rejecting the correspondence theory seem very close to the reasons that led Wittgenstein to say that it is "impossible to describe the fact which corresponds to . . . a sentence, without simply repeating the sentence."[24]

But not only does Hintikka reject the correspondence conception in such a passage, he also seems to commit himself to what I have called the priority thesis. The priority thesis, remember, is not a thesis about truth, but a thesis about meaning. It says that there is no account of meaning independent from an antecedent grasp of the meanings that we give to the sentences and expressions of *our* language. This is partly what is involved in Wittgenstein's emphasis that meaning is, in a certain sense, nothing but *use*. The only way in which we can spell out the meaning of our sentences is by displaying how they are used in certain rule-governed practices. Now, given that among meaning relations the relation between a sentence and its truth conditions is central, what would be the consequence of this for the truth relation (or the truth property)? To say that a certain sentence is true is just to be able to use it within a certain language game, the language game of assertion. But to know what truth "is" *is* just to understand how the rule or rules for assertion function. And this kind of knowledge seems only to be available *from within* our assertoric practices. In this respect, Hintikka's game-semantical ideas seem to be very close to Wittgenstein's version of the ineffability and priority theses. When he comments upon his game-theoretical account of truth conditions for first-order sentences—in terms of Skolem functions as above with (1) and (2)—Hintikka seems as ready to draw the same conclusions about the use-character of the concept of truth as those he draws about the use-character of the concept of meaning:

> It may nevertheless be questioned whether the concept of truth in general is really illuminated by the game-theoretical conditions. The job that they do is to specify what quantificational sentences *mean* by specifying their *truth-conditions*. The notion of truth is here a merely auxiliary one, it seems. In other words, the first-order semantical games seem to be language games for quantifiers, and not for the concept of truth. This is apparently in keeping with the nature of these games as games of seeking and finding. The conceptual connection between quantifiers and the activities of seeking and finding is easy to appreciate, but there does not seem to be any equally natural link between semantical games and the notion of truth in general. This can be thought of as being illustrated also by the impossibility of defining truth for quantificational sentences in those first-order languages which receive their meaning from my semantical games. One can suspect here, as Wittgenstein would have done, that the concept of truth can only receive a use—and *ergo* a meaning—in the context of certain other language games.[25]

The very fact, however, that we cannot spell out the meaning of the concept of truth from without its use and from without our language games does not imply that the concept of truth is ineffable or inexpressible. Actually when he comments upon his truth definitions for IF languages, which can be given *from within* these languages and not from without in a distinct metalanguage, Hintikka emphasizes that this feature dispels the "myth that the notion of truth for a sufficiently strong language is inexpressible in that language itself" and hence the ineffability thesis about truth. But what is interesting is that Hintikka recruits this point in favor of the priority thesis. He raises precisely the Wittgensteinian point about semantical games:

> [H]ow can these very same games also serve to give an altogether different kind of concept its meaning, namely, the concept of truth—at least the notion of truth as applied to first-order languages. How can one and the same language game serve to lend a meaning to two different kinds of concepts, one

of which (the concept of truth) seems to be a metalogical one? This two hats problem can also be called Wittgenstein's problem (cf. here Hintikka and Hintikka 1986, ch. 1). For Wittgenstein insisted that you cannot speak meaningfully and nontrivially of the truth of the sentences of a language in that language itself. Or, since for Wittgenstein there is ultimately only one language ("the only language that I understand"), we cannot speak of truth nontrivially, period. What looks like a metalogical discourse pertaining to the truth and falsity of a fragment of language is for Wittgenstein merely a different "calculus," a different language based on a different language game. How, then, can the meaning of first-order logical constant *and* the notion of truth as applied to first-order languages be constituted by the same language games? Doesn't speaking of truth take us ipso facto to a metatheoretical level?[26]

And his answer to these questions is that giving the meaning for various expressions (here quantifiers) is not the same as giving *definitory* rules; it is giving *strategic* rules for the sentences which contain these expressions, and what it is to understand the meanings of these expressions is just what it is to understand the concept of truth for the languages which contain them. Thus the step from an understanding of the expressions to an understanding of the truth of the sentences that contain them is not a step "to a metalogical level": "understanding . . . the strategies available to the players of a semantical game . . . [is] just what is needed to understand the concept of truth. . . ."[27] In other terms, the definability of truth—which refutes the ineffability thesis—does not imply that our understanding of the *concept of truth* is not implicit to our mastery of our language, hence it is compatible with the the priority thesis.

If this is correct, Hintikka's rejection of the ineffability thesis about truth and meaning is still compatible with a form of minimalism. Contrary to the universalist tradition in logic and semantics, Hintikka takes truth to be definable. Contrary to the deflations and disquotational conceptions of truth, he does not take the meaning of the truth predicate to be exhausted by Tarski's T-schema. But he holds in order to understand the concept of truth, we do not have to use resources that would exceed our own grasp of the rules of our language. As I have suggested, although Hintikka rejects the ineffability thesis, he still subscribes to a form of the priority thesis. Now the priority thesis does not, by itself, entail any minimalism about truth, but it does entail a minimalism about meaning, in the following sense: in grasping a language rule, I grasp its applications, but I do not grasp any further rules determining what its applications to particular cases consist in. Similarly when I understand a strategic rule for a semantical game, I do not need *further* rules to grasp their applications. Minimalism about meaning does not, by itself, justify minimalism about truth. But there is a straight-forward incompatibility between a (nonminimalist) conception of meaning in terms of truth conditions and the minimalist theory of truth, which has been spelled out by Dummett a long time ago:

> [I]n order that someone should gain from the explanation that P is true in such-and-such circumstances an understanding of the sense of P, he must already know what it means to say of P that it is true. If when he enquires into this he is told that the only explanation is that to say that P is true is the same as to assert P, it will follow that in order to understand what is meant by saying that P is true, he must already know the sense of asserting that P, which was precisely what was supposed to be being explained to him.[28]

Dummett actually uses the same point against a truth-conditional conception of meaning when he claims that such a conception can only lead to a minimalist (or "modest") conception of meaning. On a truth-conditional conception of meaning—in particular when it takes the form of the Tarski-like requirement that truth conditions be given by such T-sentences as:

(3) "Theaetetus flies" is true (in English) if and only if Theaetetus flies

what it is to know what "Theaetetus flies" means consists in knowing that (1) (on the basis of its structure) expresses a truth. But of course one can know that this metalinguistic sentence expresses a truth without knowing what the object-language sentence "Theaetetus flies" means, or the proposition that it expresses. In order to know the meaning of "Theaetetus flies" through (1), I must already know the meaning of this sentence (on the right-hand side). This is why Dummett says that the attempt to specify what a speaker understands through T-sentences like (1) can only yield a *modest* theory of meaning, one which "is not intended to convey the concepts expressible in the object-language, but to convey an understanding of that language to one who already possesses those concepts." On the contrary, a "rich" or "full-blooded" theory should "in the course of specifying what is required for a speaker to grasp the meaning of a given word . . . explain what it is to possess the concept it expresses."[29]

Of course Hintikka is not a "modest" theorist of meaning in the sense in which Dummett considers that Davidson is one; neither is Hintikka a minimalist theorist of truth. But he is no more a full-blooded theorist in Dummett's sense (nor, as we have seen, would he subscribe to a constructivist conception of truth). Nevertheless, if I am right, Hintikka shares Wittgenstein's view that grasping the meaning of an expression is not grasping a language-independent concept that this expression expresses. There is no more to grasp of meaning than to grasp the strategic rules that are immanent to our implicit understanding of our own language. In this respect, in accepting a version of the priority thesis, Hintikka has not completely withdrawn the thesis of the universality of language.

V

I am not sure that Hintikka has completely withdrawn a (certain form of) minimalist conception of truth either. In order to see this, let us first contrast a genuine minimalist conception of truth, such as Horwich's deflationism, with a more substantive conception. According to Horwich,[30] the meaning of the truth predicate and the nature of truth itself are completely exhausted by (a form of the) the disquotational schema:

The proposition that p is true iff p

The problem with this view is that there is more to truth than that. Truth does not simply register the fact that we make certain assertions, the contents of which are either quotable with the predicate "is true" or disquotable when one drops this predicate. Truth registers a distinctive norm, which has a definite content.[31] The norm in question is that our assertions, when true, are not simply subject to disquotation and to the discipline of syntax, but also to certain standards of objective correctness. The fact that a speaker who makes an assertion is supposed to be justified in making it, and liable to answer queries about it, is an important fact which shows that truth has a more substantive content than the deflationist conception allows. The recognition of this fact does not imply that truth is a substantive concept in the sense of the realist or anti-realist conceptions of truth, such as correspondence, verificationist, or coherence conceptions. But it implies that our use of the truth predicate carries an implication that our statements can be objective, answerable, and that speakers can potentially converge on them. In other terms, the concept of truth is substantial in the sense that in the use of it, we commit ourselves to a minimal form of realism. But this realism need not be of a metaphysical kind, as in a correspondence theory of truth couched in terms of facts or states of affairs. We only need to recognize that when someone asserts a certain sentence to be true, he carries the implication that its content is *knowable*. The norm of assertion is not so much truth as *knowledge*: in making an assertion I make a claim to knowledge, and I do not simply express my belief that the assertion is true. Given that knowledge implies truth, it is open to us to say that truth is the norm of assertion, through its aiming at knowledge.[32] I cannot develop these ideas here.[33] But if they are correct, there is room for a form of minimalism about truth—which would grant that there is not much more to truth than the disquotational feature —which would nevertheless be substantive in the sense that it registers the norm of knowledge.

At first sight, and on the one hand, it seems to me that Professor Hintikka should agree with the view that I have just sketched. The idea that truth is not just disquotation and that it registers a distinctive norm is but a version of Dummett's famous remark that truth is what our assertions aim at, just like winning is what our playing a game aims at. Hintikka agrees with this analogy in so far as it is understood as the analogy between truth and the existence of a winning strategy.[34] And we have seen that this reading is compatible with a form of realism, although not of the metaphysical kind. On the other hand, I suspect that he would disagree, and would say that my reading into the concept of truth a commitment to a knowledge claim belies a confusion—already alluded to above—between *semantical* games, which give the truth conditions of the relevant sentences of the language, and *interrogative* games, which give the conditions of our reaching knowledge through inquiry.[35] The former are prior to the latter, and more fundamental. They characterize truth in general, and not the way we come to know truth. Hintikka denounces the confusion between semantic and interrogative games in the context of a criticism of the verificationist conception of truth, which in some sense equates truth with knowledge of truth. This is not, however, the point that I put forward when I say that truth registers a norm of knowledge. I do not mean to say that truth is in some sense epistemic, since the conception of truth presupposed here is realistic. But the distinction that Hintikka makes between semantic games as dealing with truth and interrogative games as dealing with knowledge, shows that he is closer to a minimalist conception of truth than the conception that I have advanced. Another sign of this would be his recent claim that in epistemology we need neither the notion of knowledge nor the notion of belief, but only the notion of information.[36] Insofar as Hintikka wants to dissociate the notion of truth from the notion of knowledge, and epistemology from this very notion, it seems to me that he is prepared to adopt a relatively thin concept of truth.

Let us, finally, turn to the credentials of what I have called the priority thesis. The priority thesis seems compelling only if the alternatives to an account of language understanding from within our language games are a Platonist conception of concepts or a psychologistic account of them. These were actually the two kinds of views that Wittgenstein meant to attack in the rule following considerations. But these are not the only options. If we could give a better account of what it is to possess a concept than a Platonist or a psychologistic one, the priority thesis would seem less attractive. Such an account would have to be substantive, in the sense that it would not explain our grasp of a meaning or of a concept in terms of capacities that would presuppose an a priori grasp of these meanings. On a minimalist theory of meaning, we do not in any sense explain the meaning of "Theaetetus flies" through a sentence like (1) because we must already know what the right-hand side means. The case is similar when a minimalist conception of meaning is formulated in terms of language rules. In order for a conception of meaning to be substantive, one has to frame it in terms of necessary and sufficient conditions that do not presuppose the meaning of the target sentences, along the lines of something like (for instance, for the rule for assertion):

> (A) S is correctly used to make an assertion in language L if and only if . . .

Now a game-theoretical semantics is just what can provide us with what we need on the right-hand side. But if what precedes is correct, even though game-theoretical semantics uses such notions as that of a verifier or of a winning strategy, these are notions that a speaker is supposed to understand already, and hence are redescriptions of what a language user already knows. A better account seems to be directly available in terms of what a speaker knows:

> (A) One correctly uses an S to make an assertion if and only if one is justified in believing of the proposition expressed by that use that it is true.

And here again the account yields an analysis only if the relevant notion of "justified belief," or indeed of *knowledge*, is spelled out. On such an account, meaning is understood in terms of *epistemic capacities* or in terms of *epistemic* norms. To grasp the meaning of an expression is to grasp a certain concept individuated in terms of its *cognitive* role.[37] Here too I cannot develop this proposal, but I suspect again that Professor Hintikka would say that it is to confuse semantical games and interrogative games, truth conditions and knowledge conditions. But this too would show the extent of his commitment to the priority thesis.

Hintikka's discussions of truth are shaped by his concern to give an overall account of the languages of logic and mathematics on the one hand, and of the semantic structure of natural languages on the other. I have not discussed his particular proposal for a truth definition, but only his remarks on our "normal" concept of truth. Let us grant that truth is indeed definable, along the lines that he has proposed. The ineffability thesis would then be disproved. But I have suggested that Hintikka is still committed to the view that "one cannot use language to get outside language," with respect both to truth and meaning.

PASCAL ENGEL

UNIVERSITY OF PARIS-SORBONNE
SEPTEMBER 2002

NOTES

1. Jaakko Hintikka, "Self Profile," in vol. 8 of *Profiles: Jaakko Hintikka*, ed. Radu Bogdan (Dordrecht: Reidel, 1987), p. 9.

2. Especially those in Jaakko Hintikka, *Lingua Universalis vs Calculus Ratiocinator: An Ultimate Presupposition of Twentieth Century Philosophy*, vol. 2 of *Jaakko Hintikka's Selected Papers* (Dordrecht: Kluwer, 1997), such as "Contemporary Philosophy and the Problem of Truth," pp. 1–19, but in many other places as well. Hintikka has shown that the idea of language as a universal medium plays a structuring role in much of contemporary philosophy, and in this sense it is comparable to the role played, in the context of philosophical thought about modality, to the principle of plenitude. I tried once to examine the status of this principle in Engel, "Plenitude and Contingency: Modal Concepts in Nineteenth Century French Philosophy," in *Modern Modalities*, ed. Simo Knuuttila (Dordrecht: Kluwer, 1988), pp. 179–237.

3. Ludwig Wittgenstein, *Philosophical Remarks* (Oxford: Blackwell, 1975), p. 54.

4. Jaakko Hintikka, "Is Truth Ineffable?" in *Les formes actuelles du vrai, entretiens de Palermo*, ed. N. Scardona (Palermo: Enchiridion, 1989), repr. in vol. 2 of Hintikka, *Selected Papers*, pp. 20–45 (quoted after this edition), p. 23.

5. See in particular Jaakko Hintikka and Merrill Hintikka, *Investigating Wittgenstein* (Oxford: Blackwell, 1986), ch. 1.

6. John Skorupski, "Meaning, Use, Verification," in *A Companion to the Philosophy of Language*, ed. C. Wright and B. Hale (Oxford: Blackwell, 1997), pp. 29–59.

7. On this point, see e.g., Jaakko Hintikka, "Semantics: A Revolt against Frege," in *Contemporary Philosophy*, vol. 1, ed. G. Floistad (The Hague: Nijhoff, 1981), pp. 57–82.

8. Ludwig Wittgenstein, *Vermischte Bemerkungen*; including English translation: *Culture and Value* (Oxford: Blackwell, 1980), p. 10, quoted and translated by Hintikka in "Is Truth Ineffable?" p. 24.

9. Ludwig Wittgenstein, *Remarks on the Foundations of Mathematics* (Oxford: Blackwell, 1978), 3rd ed. Appendix I, sec 5, quoted by Hintikka, "Is Truth Ineffable?" p. 23.

10. Hintikka, "Is Truth Ineffable?" p. 23.

11. For various versions of the disquotational conception, see Marian David, *Correspondence and Disquotation* (Oxford: Oxford University Press, 1994.)

12. Paul Horwich, *Truth* (Oxford: Blackwell, 1990; Oxford: Clarendon Press and New York: Oxford University Press, 1998).

13. Jaakko Hintikka, "Defining Truth, the Whole Truth and Nothing but the Truth," *Reports from the Department of Philosophy*, Helsinki, 1 (1991); repr. in *Selected Papers*, vol. 2 (1997), pp. 46–97 (quoted after this edition), p. 76.

14. This very feature has been called "syntacticalism" by some minimalist

theorists. See in particular Crispin Wright, *Truth and Objectivity* (Oxford: Oxford University Press, 1992).

15. Hintikka, "Defining Truth, the Whole Truth and Nothing but the Truth," p. 87.

16. Ibid., p. 76.

17. See in particular Jaakko Hintikka, "The Prospects of Convention T," *Dialectica* 30 (1976): 61–66.

18. See Jaakko Hintikka, *The Principles of Mathematics Revisited* (Cambridge: Cambridge University Press, 1996), p. 210; "Defining Truth, the Whole Truth, and Nothing but the Truth," p. 65.

19. Hintikka, *The Principles of Mathematics Revisited*, p. 27.

20. See Hintikka, "Post-Tarskian Truth," *Synthese* 126 (2001): 17–36.

21. Jaakko Hintikka, "Truth, Negation and Other Basic Notions of Logic" (manuscript, 2002). I thank professor Hintikka for having allowed me to read this manuscript. As Hintikka notes, however, this cannot really be considered as equivalent to, say, David Armstrong's notion of truth-making, for according to Armstrong sentences are made true by a host of different kinds of "truthmakers": objects, properties, relations, states of affairs, and facts. See e.g., David Armstrong, *A World of States of Affairs* (Cambridge: Cambridge University Press, 1997).

22. See e.g., Hintikka, *The Principles of Mathematics Revisited*, pp. 42–44.

23. Ibid., pp. 44–45.

24. Wittgenstein, *Culture and Value*, p. 10. Quoted by Hintikka in "Is Truth Ineffable?" p. 24.

25. Hintikka, *The Principles of Mathematics Revisited*, pp. 31–32.

26. Ibid., pp. 127–28.

27. Ibid., p. 128. [The full passage reads, "Understanding a quantificational language means mastering the language games that give quantifiers their meaning. Now, such mastery was just seen to involve a grasp of the strategies available to the players of a semantical game. But those strategies are just what is needed to understand the concept of truth as applied to quantificational languages."]

28. Michael Dummett, "Truth," in M. Dummett, *Truth and Other Enigmas* (1959; London: Duckworth, 1978), p. 7.

29. Michael Dummett, *The Seas of Language* (Oxford: Oxford University Press, 1993), p. viii. See also M. Dummett, "What Is a Theory of Meaning (I)," in *Mind and Language*, ed. S. Guttenplan (Oxford: Oxford University Press, 1974); reprinted as ch. 1 in *The Seas of Language*, esp. pp. 22 ff.)

30. Horwich, *Truth*.

31. Crispin Wright, *Truth and Objectivity*; Pascal Engel, "Is Truth a Norm?" in *Interpreting Davidson*, ed. P. Pagin, G. Segal, and P. Kotatko (Stanford: CSLI., 2001), pp. 37–51; Pascal Engel, *Truth* (Bocks: Acumen, 2002).

32. These issues have been discussed in Hintikka's classic *Knowledge and Belief* (Ithaca: Cornell University Press, 1962). But as far as I know, he does not

defend the view that assertion implies a claim to knowledge.

33. See Timothy Williamson, *Knowledge and its Limits* (Oxford: Oxford University Press, 2000); Engel, *Truth*.

34. Hintikka, *The Principles of Mathematics Revisited*, p. 27.

35. For this distinction and the confusion in question, see for instance, ibid., pp. 36–37.

36. Jaakko Hintikka, "Epistemology Without Knowledge and Without Belief" (manuscript, 2002).

37. For such views, see in particular C. Peacocke, *A Study of Concepts* (Cambridge, Mass.: MIT Press, 1992); Skorupski, "Meaning, Use, Verification."

REPLY TO PASCAL ENGEL

Pascal Engel is, in his knowledgeable and perceptive paper, seeking to place my ideas of truth, meaning, and the inexpressibility of semantics on the map of the different prevalent views on these and related topics. This is a legitimate enterprise, which is part and parcel of the task of a historian of recent philosophy. Engel's main conclusions are that "Hintikka is still very close to Wittgenstein's conception of meaning as use" and that "Hintikka's view can still be characterized as a form of minimalism about truth and meaning." Furthermore, Engel finds that in a certain respect "Hintikka has not completely withdrawn the thesis of the universality of language."

I find these attributions not only fair, but remarkably insightful. If Engel's interpretations are understood correctly, they may even constitute a useful supplement (in one case correction) to what I have asserted publicly in so many words.

Even though I thus find myself agreeing to considerable extent with Engel, I experience a strong reaction of wanting to put what he says in a different perspective. As witnessed by his quoted conclusions, Engel is in effect endeavoring to understand my ideas by considering them from the standpoint of different current philosophical views. I find it much more instructive to do nearly the opposite, that is, to analyze and to put into perspective other philosophers' views from the vantage point of the results I have reached. One of the main reasons for thus turning the tables on Engel is that the prevalent views that he is using as his Archimedean fixed points of comparison are full of uncertainties and often open to widely different interpretations. For instance, let us consider the views of the minimalists. They claim to use as the basis of their treatment of truth in natural language the intuitively obvious instances of the T-schema. But this claim is nonsense, for—as Engel reminds us—there are intuitively false instances of the T-schema, as witnessed by examples like the following:

"Any corporal can become a general" is true if any corporal can become general.

On its most natural reading, this instance of the T-schema is simply false. It has never been explained how minimalists can hope to extract a true theory out of such sometimes false assumptions. I shudder to think what scorn Karl Popper would have poured on minimalists' failure—or is it a refusal?—to face a clear-cut prima facie counter-example to their views.

Again minimalists refuse to systematize their views, for instance, refusing to try to formulate an explicit truth predicate. Whether this is done in natural language or in its regimented versions in logic does not matter here. When one speaks of truth predicates, admittedly most people will think of formal logical languages. But, as I will point out below, it turns out that the reasons why Tarski-type truth definitions fail in first-order formal languages when applied to the same language has nothing to do with their formal character, but depends entirely on questions that apply as well to natural languages as to formal ones. Hence, if minimalists had tried to develop a genuine theory of truth from natural language, including a formulation of a truth predicate, they would have run into the very same problematic as Tarski, and they would have had to resort to the same concepts and arguments as are used in game-theoretical semantics. Hence they can pretend that their approach is self-sufficient only because they refuse to develop their own theory beyond a certain point.

Likewise, it is far from clear what Wittgenstein meant, or what anyone can mean, by the slogan "meaning as use" which Engel claims I countenance in some sense or other. Wittgenstein himself changed his views in this respect during his late (post-1929) period. When he said in 1930 that "language cannot be taught," he was simply emphasizing that one "cannot use language to get outside language." But by the time of the *Philosophical Investigations* he was maintaining something much more striking.[1] He was claiming that the primary connections between language and reality are not conveyed by teaching in any cognitive sense but by training—training to make the right moves in certain language games. This is what he means by saying that the rules of language are followed "blindly." If so, there is no "natural uptake of how they [signs] are used," as little as a dog needs a natural uptake to learn how to jump on command.

Furthermore, when one tries to apply the "meaning as use" to the meaning of specific expressions it is not sufficient simply to say that the language-world ties are constituted by use. In order to understand the meaning of an expression, one has to know what its intended use is, in Wittgenstein's own jargon, what the relevant language-game is. In the case of the crucial logical and semantical words, such as "true" or logical words like quantifiers, neither Wittgenstein nor any Wittgensteinean has told us precisely what language games are their "logical home." In the *Tractatus*, he assumed that quantified sentences receive their meaning by being considered long disjunctions and conjunctions, but he gave up that view later. It was never replaced by a clear answer to the sixty-four thousand dollar question: What language-games lend quantifiers their meaning? Hence to say that I am "still very close to Wittgenstein's conception" may very well be true insofar as abstract philosophical classifications are concerned, but it overlooks the fact that I have been trying to implement "Wittgenstein's conception" as applied to our basic logical languages *in concreto* and in a large scale.

Similarly, simply stating whether a philosopher believes in the ineffability of semantics or is not very informative. This idea, and more generally the universalist syndrome, offers a highly instructive frame of reference for locating different philosophers' views. It is the more instructive, however, the subtler a philosopher's attitude to this "ultimate presupposition" is. For instance, in the case of Tarski the most intriguing question is not whether he believed in the inexpressibility of truth in the same language in general, but why he did so.

Furthermore, what is it that is significant about the kinds of truth predicates that I (as well as Gabriel Sandu) have defined for suitable first-order IF languages in the same language? Not just the fact that such a truth predicate can be defined for them in contradistinction to received first-order languages. What is remarkable is an explanation why these truth predicates are possible. This explanation is at the same time a diagnosis why Tarski's T-schema cannot yield such a predicate. The explanation and the diagnosis are based on the very meaning of quantifiers, which is only partially captured by the received first-order logic. This partial failure can be seen to be due to assumption of compositionality that even historically turns out to be Tarski's motivation.

Again, the game-theoretical interpretation of quantifiers is not just one possible way of looking at the semantics of "classical" logic, as distinguished from, for instance, constructivistic logic. Constructivistic logic can in fact be considered in a most natural way as a variant of "classical" logic when it is interpreted game-theoretically. All that is needed is a restriction of the verifiers' strategies to constructive ones. Thus a game-theoretical approach helps us to appreciate other approaches. The relation of my views to those of the constructivists is much more complicated than a simple opposition.

In what sense then are Engel's attributions of different views to me correct? In the case of truth and in the case of the meaning of quantifiers, I am going way beyond Wittgenstein in that I specify in so many words what the language games are like that are the logical home of these different concepts. Most significantly, language games with quantifiers can be described as games of seeking and finding. (Such games were thought of by

Wittgenstein as the logical home of the notion of object, but he did not realize that to be an object is the same as to be a value of a quantified variable.) Now the language games that are needed to give the notion of truth a foothold in quantificational languages are those very same games. What is needed in order to understand the notion of truth as applied to quantificational languages is therefore nothing over and above understanding those languages in the first place. If this is what Engel means by characterizing my views as minimalistic, he is not only right but importantly right.

But do I hold as allegedly Wittgenstein did that "meaning is use"? What I do hold, like Wittgenstein (on what I have argued is the correct interpretation of his views), is that the basic language-world links are constituted by certain rule-governed human activities of the kind Wittgenstein called language-games. In this simple sense I do indeed hold that "meaning is use," to use that nearly meaningless phrase. Part of its meaning is presumably that the mode of existence of meaning is in the form of language-games mastered by some actual or potential players. I am not objecting to saying so, but from such a view it is apparently very tempting to slide into thinking that the rules of language-games somehow have to exist in our minds or to be "immanent to our implicit understanding of our own language," as Engel puts it. This view, whether or not Engel subscribes to it, is rejected by Wittgenstein who in his inimitable way says that "if God had looked into our minds, he would not have been able to see there whom we are speaking of."[2] I find this view likewise unacceptable when applied to actual uses of language, but for reasons different from Wittgenstein's. When someone asserts a quantificational sentence he or she (or it if the language user is an automaton) in effect asserts the existence of a winning strategy in a certain game. Neither the asserter nor the addressee of the assertion need have any idea what that winning strategy is or might be like in order to understand fully the assertion. Indeed, even if there exists such a strategy, it might be that no one will even know what it is. In this sense, the strategies that play a crucial role in the semantics of quantificational discourse do not exist in the human mind. They are functions in the mathematical sense of the word, and as such understanding and mastering them is not bound to any particular language. In this respect, I am withdrawing completely from the universalist idea that one's language is limited by the extent of our implicit understanding of our own particular language. One's understanding of any language depends on mastering implicitly the space of all its strategy functions, but understanding that space goes well beyond understanding any particular language. The use that can be said to constitute meaning on my view is not grounded on our implicit understanding of language but on certain mathematical entities, viz., the rules of certain language-games abstracted completely from the appliers of such rules, be they human language users, automata, or omniscient angels. I do not know what Engel would say here, but to my mind this looks like a fairly complete rejection of the universality thesis.

Furthermore, the particular truth predicate I have used—existence of Skolem functions for the sentence in question—not only shows that truth is somehow expressible in IF languages in the same language but also brings out through its form (the existence of certain functions) the objectivity and language independence of the concept of truth so defined. At the same time, this conception of truth in quantificational languages, that is, truth as the existence of Skolem functions, can on reflection be seen to be nothing more than an expression of our pretheoretical notion of truth for these languages. Hence the expressibility of truth can be expected to apply much more widely than just IF languages, and it can be seen to be deeply rooted in the nature of our logical concepts.

J. H.

NOTES

1. Ludwig Wittgenstein, *Philosophical Investigations* (Oxford: Blackwell, 1953).
2. Ibid., p. 217.

19

Jan Woleński

TARSKIAN AND POST-TARSKIAN TRUTH

Truth is neither Pre-Tarskian nor Tarskian. It is also not Post-Tarskian. Although it looks like a tautology, truth is simply truth and nothing else. On the other hand, we have explications of the concept of truth, which are Pre-Tarskian, Tarskian, or Post-Tarskian. Although I am Tarskian in my views about truth, I still take modestly the division of truth theories into Pre-Tarskian, Tarskian, and Post-Tarskian. Many philosophers deny that the semantic or Tarskian conception of truth (**TCT**, for brevity) has any philosophical importance. Others reject it in favor of other proposals, for example, the coherence theory of truth. Hence, it would be an exaggeration to maintain that **TCT** is the turning point in the history of philosophical attempts to define truth. Yet we are in position to think that Tarski's ideas have significance within the camp of philosophers who advocate the classical or correspondence theory of truth. Strictly speaking, I am inclined to distinguish between the classical and the correspondence theories of truth.[1] The former follows Aristotle's famous *dictum* from *Metaphysics* 1011b: "Falsehood is saying of that which is that it is not, or of that which is not, that it is; truth is saying of that which is that it is, or of that which is not that it is not."[2] The latter explains the concept of truth with more or less sophisticated ideas of correspondence, mapping, and so forth, between truth-bearers and reality. Although Tarski sometimes employed the concept of correspondence or agreement,[3] it seems that he was somehow reluctant to use it. In any case he explicitly said:

> [A]ll these formulations can lead to various misunderstandings, for none of them is sufficiently precise and clear (though it applies much less to the original Aristotelian formulation than to either of the others); at any rate, none of them can be considered a satisfactory definition of truth.[4]

In fact, we can explain **TCT** without any appeal to correspondence (adequacy, and the like) as a relation between truth-bearers and reality. Of course, one can say that truth as the satisfaction of a sentence by all sequences of objects defines what is meant by correspondence, but this is only a convention which, at least on the level of pure semantics, does not add anything particularly interesting to the original explication.[5]

Jaakko Hintikka does not deny that **TCT** has some importance. He regards it as an essential achievement in the development of the model-theoretic view in logic.[6] However, Hintikka argues that **TCT** does not satisfy all desirable constraints to be obeyed by any successful philosophical truth theory. Hintikka's desiderata are these:

(H1) The truth definition should apply to a language **L** which closely approximates the real language in which we think, reason, and argue. It is admissible that this approximation be a regimented form of our actual language. In particular, **L** should be sufficiently rich to cover the whole of mathematics.

(H2) The truth definition should be complete, that is applicable to every well-formed sentence *S* belonging to **L**, providing an affirmative answer to the question whether *S* is true always when *S* is true. Thus, our definition should define "the whole truth."

(H3) The truth definition is to be formulated in **L** itself. In particular, we should avoid defining truth in a stronger metalanguage **ML** since this is semantically more problematic than our initial language **L**.

(H4) The definition should be straightforward in the sense that it will tell us directly what it means for a sentence *S* to be true. In particular, the definition should avoid the concept of correspondence between truth-bearers and facts and appeal entirely to procedures which verify or falsify sentences. Thus, the definition should grasp "nothing but truth." This also means that the truth conditions for sentences associated with the definition should be nontrivial or informative.

(H5) The definition should be independent of the specific model (possible world) **M** of **L**. This means that we need a method which will enable us, independently of any model **M**, to pair each sentence *S* of **L** with another sentence which expresses a truth condition of the former.[7]

Hintikka argues that **TCT** does not satisfy the requirements (H1) – (H5). In fact, Hintikka does not explicitly link his evaluation of **TCT** with (H1) – (H5),[8] but it is rather obvious that these constraints stand behind his thinking about the semantic definition of truth. Hintikka makes several critical remarks concerning **TCT**. The most important seem as follows:

(H1') **TCT** is applicable to languages which are not "good approximations" of our natural language. In particular, **TCT** assumes compositionality,

"Tarski's guilty secret,"[9] which is clearly violated by our real language. Moreover, Tarski himself denied that truth could be correctly defined with respect to natural language.

(H2') **TCT** defines truth indirectly via the concept of satisfaction.

(H3') **TCT** defines truth for a given **L** in its **ML**. This means that truth (and, more generally, semantics) is ineffable.[10] Elsewhere Hintikka attributes to Tarski the universal medium conception of language (*eo ipso*, the view that semantics is ineffable) with respect to natural language, but the calculus conception with respect to formal languages.[11]

(H4') **TCT** defines truth via the relation of correspondence between sentences and external facts.

(H5') **TCT** defines truth relative to a model **M**.

Hintikka does not end with the criticism of **TCT** given above. His main task is to develop an alternative to the semantic definition of truth (I will use the letters **HCT** as an abbreviation for Hintikka's account of truth). One should point out that the character of this alternative must be well understood here. Although Hintikka is very critical of Tarski, in many respects he remains within the same paradigm. Perhaps this is why he calls his theory of truth "Post-Tarskian."[12] This might suggest (and I think it does) that there is no other way to explain what truth is than to locate this concept within semantics and to make heavy use of the tools of mathematical logic. My further plan is as follows: First, I will briefly present Hintikka's ideas about truth, semantics and logic in their historical context. Second, I will defend **TCT** against Hintikka's criticism. I will not consider (H2'), but (H1'), (H4'), and (H5') will be commented upon rather briefly. I have chosen (H3') as basic and requiring more attention than the other points. I think that this concurs with Hintikka's intentions, since in his criticism of **TCT** he clearly considers (H3') to be the most important and devotes more space to it than to any of the others.

The general attitude of Finnish analytic philosophy was always favorable toward semantics.[13] This was a result of the realistic standpoint introduced in Finland by Eino Kaila, although he himself did not work on formal semantics. Georg Henrik von Wright and Erik Stenius became semanticists to a greater extent than Kaila, but their involvement in this field was rather occasional. It was Hintikka who turned Finnish philosophy onto an explicit semantic path. Let me only recall (without details; other papers in this volume deal with the subject more closely) Hintikka's model sets or his possible worlds semantic constructions for various kinds of modal logic (in a broad sense). Although these ideas provide new tools for metalogical studies on logic, they are fairly coherent with the received paradigm of standard (Tarskian) semantics. However, in the sixties and seventies Hintikka began to doubt whether this paradigm did justice to natural language and its alleged logic. As regards the problem of the truth definition, Hintikka's first explicit criticism of Tarski concerned the convention T as adequate for some sentences of natural language.[14] As an example consider the sentence

(1) "anyone can become a millionaire" is true if and only if anyone can become a millionare.

Hintikka argues that (1) is false, because the implication

(2) if anyone can become a millionaire, then "anyone can become a millionaire" is true,

fails. As Hintikka maintains, (2) "is not true: one person making a cool million does not imply that everyone can do it."[15] This assessment is closely related to the fact that the logical role of the quantifier "any" depends on its place in the whole sentence. In general, the game rule for "any" is prior to the game rule for the conditional in question. An important corollary here is that the logic of "any" violates the principle of compositionality.

Hintikka's analysis of (1) and (2) invokes game-theoretical semantics (**GTS**).[16] I will not enter into the history of this construction in Hintikka's writings. The final product is the following: Let **L** be a first-order language and **M** its model. **L** is conceived as a language with extralogical constants interpreted in **M**. Game-theoretical semantics for **L** is understood as a two-person game played by Myself (**ms**; the initial verifier) and Nature (**nt**; the initial falsifier). Both players handle sentences (possibly containing new individual constants) according to the following rules (S, S_0, S_1, S_2 are arbitrary sentences belonging to **L**; the expression G(T; **M**) schematizes a game for a given sentence T interpreted in the selected model **M**; S_0 is an atomic sentence):

(R.∨)   G($S_1 \vee S_2$; **M**) begins with **ms's** choice of $i = 1$ or $i = 2$. The game continues as G(S_i, **M**);

(R. ∧)   G($S_1 \wedge S_2$; **M**) begins with **nt's** choice of $i = 1$ or $i = 2$. The game continues as G(S_i, **M**);

(R. ∃)   G(($\exists$x)S_0 (x); **M**) begins with **ms's** choice of an individual c from the universe of **M**. The game continues as G($S_0(c)$, **M**);

(R. ∀)   G(($\forall$x)$S_0(x)$; **M**) is like G(($\exists$x)$S_0(x)$; **M**), except that **nt** makes the choice;

(R. ¬)   G($\neg S_0$; **M**) is like G(S_0; **M**), except that the roles of the players are reversed;

(R. At)   If S is an atomic formula or an identity **ms** wins and **nt** loses when S is true in **M**. On the other hand, **nt** wins and **ms** loses when S is false in **M**.

The following quotations exhibit the intuitions behind the above rules:

> At each stage of the game, intuitively speaking, the player who all that time is the verifier is trying to show that the sentence considered then is true and the falsifier is trying to show that it is false. . . . The distinctive feature of **GTS** is the definition of the central semantical notion of truth. The truth or falsity of S in **M** usually cannot be seen from any play of **G**(S; **M**). Rather truth in **M** is defined by reference to what the initial verifier *can* do in **G**(S; **M**). It refers to the strategies, in the sense of game theory, that Myself and Nature have available in **G**(S; **M**). A strategy in this sense is a rule that tells a player what to do in every conceivable situation which might arise in a play of the given game. More exactly, a strategy for a player m (m is either Myself or Nature) in the game **G**(S; **M**) is a set F_m of functions f_Q corresponding to to different logical constants Q which can prompt a move by player m in **G**(S; **M**). A winning strategy in a two-person zero-sum game is one which results in a win for that player no matter which strategy one's opponent uses.[17]

We have three basic facts about truth ($\vdash$), falsehood ($\dashv$) in **GTS** and its relation to Tarskian semantics:

(3) **M** $\vdash_{GTS} S$ if and only if there is a winning strategy for **ms** in G(S; **M**);

(4) **M** $_{GTS}\dashv$ if and only if there is a winning strategy for **nt** in G(S; **M**);

(5) Assuming the axiom of choice (**AC**), **M** $\vdash_{TARSKI} S$ if and only if **M** $\vdash_{GTS} S$.

On Hintikka's account, **GTS** is closely related (see below for details) to independence-friendly logic (**IFL**). It is conceived as an important reform (in fact, an improvement) of the received paradigm of logic.[18] What is wrong in standard first-order logic (**SFOL**)? According to Hintikka, it should be blamed for its fundamentally improper treatment of quantifiers.[19] This point seems of crucial significance for Hintikka, as can be seen from the strong formulations (not to say evidently negative propaganda), which accompany his criticism of the received logical theory. For instance, we read:

> Frege's formulation of first-order logic contains a fundamental error. It is manifested already in his formation rules. And this same virus has infected all the subsequent formulations and versions of first-order logic.[20]

A similar tenor emanates from the following passage:

> [T]he received first-order logic, as formulated by the likes of Frege, Russell and Whitehead, or Hilbert Ackermann, involves an important restrictive assumption which is largely unmotivated—or perhaps rather motivated by wrong reasons. . . . For simplicity, I will refer to it as Frege's fallacy or mistake.[21]

The fallacy or mistake (elsewhere "an outright mistake of Frege and Russell") consists in ignoring certain relations between quantifiers.[22] In order to see it, consider the sentence

(6) $\forall x \exists y S(x, y)$.

This formula is constructed and interpreted so that its existential quantifier is dependent on its universal quantifiers. This means that the values of y are related to the set being the range of the variable x; in particular, this variable indicates the objectual scope on which the quantifier $\forall$ operates. In other words, the interpretation selects an object ascribed to y dependently on the domain determined by the universal quantifier. However, it can happen that both quantifiers are independent (the choice of the value of y has nothing to do with the scope of $\forall$). This situation requires a new notation, which yields the formula

(7) $\forall x(\exists y/\forall x)S(x, y)$,

where the symbol $\exists y/\forall x$ means: "the existential quantifier $\exists y$ is independent of the universal quantifier $\forall x$." When independence is allowed, (7) is equivalent to (6). However, there are more complicated cases, which are not equivalent to formulas without slashes. One such case, for example, is the sentence

(8) $\forall x \forall z(\exists y/\forall z)(\exists y/\forall z)(\exists u/\forall x)S(x, y, z, u)$.

Although (8) is equivalent to

(9) $\forall x \exists y \forall x \forall z(\exists u/\forall x)S(x, y, z, u)$,

there is no slash-free linear formula which could serve as an equivalent to (8). We can eventually use branching (Henkin) quantifiers, but logic with these devices also exceeds **SFOL**. Thus, if someone wants to have quantificational independence in logic, he or she must enrich linear notational patterns by slashes, special brackets, etc., or abandon linearity by admitting branching quantifiers. However, according to Hintikka, we should introduce these new relations between quantifiers because the logic of quantifiers is precisely about quantifiers; it must cover all relations between $\forall$ and $\exists$, dependences as well as independences (for simplicity, I entirely neglect independences between quantifiers and connectives). Hence the name "independent-friendly logic." Admitting quantificational independence entails various consequences. First of all, one must say "goodbye" to Frege's account of quantifiers as second-order predicates. Moreover, the idea that the role of quantifiers is exhausted by the concept of "ranging over" should also be given up.

Technically speaking, **IFL** is exactly equivalent to Σ^1_1 logic, that is, to a system classified as between first-order and second-order logic and such that the prefixes of prenex normal form of its formulas consist only of existential quantifiers. However, as Hintikka claims, **IFL** is still first-order and a conservative extension of **SFOL**, because its quantifiers bind individual variables only. The metalogical properties of this logic are as follows: **IFL** has no complete axiomatization and it thereby lacks an effective proof-procedure and the deduction theorem is not valid for it. Its validities are not recursively enumerable. Hence it is incomplete, syntactically (deductively) and semantically. On the other hand, it has an effective disproof procedure. **IFL** is compact (the consistency of finite subsets of a given set guarantees the consistency of the whole set) and has the interpolation property (roughly speaking, two mutually not satisfiable **IFL**-formulas are separable by ordinary first-order formulas). Both Löwenheim-Skolem theorems hold for **IFL** (downward: if a system has an infinite model, it also possesses a denumerable one, and upward: if a system has an infinite model, it also possesses a model of arbitrary infinite cardinality). Negation in this logic is not contradictory. Thus, the law of excluded middle (**LEM**) fails in this logic. This fact decides that **IFL** does not contradict the Lindström characterization theorem (more strictly: one of the theorems of this kind) which says that standard **SFOL** logic is the strongest logical system having the compactness and has the downward Löwenheim-Skolem property. This is so because negation in **IFL** is not Boolean; the regularity of logic consists in the Boolean character of its connectives and this is one of the assumptions of the Lindström theorem. Since **IFL** is not compositional, this feature prevents the application of Tarskian semantics to it. In particular, we cannot formulate the definition of satisfaction as recursive.[23] On the other hand, **GTS** is a suitable semantic basis for **IFL**, if we change the assumption that logical games assume perfect information on the part of the players. It means that moves generated by the winning strategies are independent of former steps of ms and nt. Thus, the rules (R. ∨, etc.) operate under imperfect (incomplete) information. This is the reason why Hintikka uses the label "the logic of imperfect information" for his independence-friendly logic. This new **GTS** preserves (3) and (4), but (5) does not hold any longer for it. Also, the presence of imperfect information is responsible for the failure of **LEM** in **IFL**. In fact, the lack of *tertium not datur* in **IFL** means that semantic games under imperfect information are not determinate. This is natural and expected.[24]

Hintikka recommends **IFL** as highly desirable and even revolutionary. Commenting the defects of the former paradigm, he writes:

> Here [that is, on the occasion of introducing the slash notation – J. W.] we are beginning to see the whole horror of Frege's mistake. The notation he

introduced (like the latter notation of Russell and Whitehead) arbitrarily rules out certain perfectly possible patterns of dependence and independence between quantifiers or between connectives and quantifiers. These patterns are the ones represented by irreducible slashed quantifier combination (and similar combinations involving quantifiers and connectives). Anyone who understands received first-order logic understands sentences which involve such patterns, for instance understands sentences of the form (8) and (9), in the concrete sense of understanding the precise conditions that their truth imposes on reality. Hence they ought to be expressible in the language of our basic logic. And the only way of doing so is to build our true logic of quantification so as to dispense with the artificial restrictions Frege imposed on the received first-order logic. The real logic of quantification, in other words the real ground floor of the edifice of logic, is not the ordinary first-order logic. It is **IF** first-order logic. Terminologically speaking, we are doing ourselves an injustice by calling the received first-order logic "ordinary." The limitations we have been discussing make Fregean logic systematically speaking quite extraordinary, as is also reflected by the fact that the properties of the received first-order logic do not reflect at all faithfully what one can expect to happen in logic in general.[25]

Hintikka stresses that the importance of **IFL** is not exhausted by its revolutionary character as pure logic. The new logic also has significant applications in the foundations of mathematics, philosophy (for example, in epistemic logic or philosophy of science), semantics of natural language, physics (the logic of quantum mechanics) and many other fields.[26] And, last but not least, according to Hintikka, **IFL** allows us to construct a fresh theory of truth, which is able to replace **TCT**. Let me recall that I regard (H3) and (H3') as fundamental in Hintikka's criticism of **TCT** and the development of his own ideas concerning the concept of truth. Indeed, Hintikka wants to find a definition of truth for a language **L** in **L** itself and thereby to overcome the Tarski undefinability theorem, which asserts that the set of arithmetical truths is not definable in arithmetic (this rough formulation will be replaced below by a much more precise one). Hintikka is very dissatisfied with limitations introduced by the Tarski theorem. He says:

> Generally speaking, Tarski's result seems to confirm one's worst fears about the dependence of model theory on higher-order logic and thereby on questions of sets and set existence. It has even been alleged that this makes model theory little more than a part of set theory. Indeed, the apparent dependence of Tarski-type truth definitions on set theory is in my view one of the most disconcerting features of the current scene in logic and the foundations of mathematics. I am sorely tempted to call it "Tarski's curse." It inflicts model theory with all the problems and uncertainties of set theory. More generally, Tarski's curse might be understood as the undefinability of truth for a given language in that language (given Tarski's assumptions).[27]

HCT is based on statement (3) as the starting point. Of course, (4) also holds, but (5) is not longer valid. Since **HCT** is intended as a radically different alternative to **TCT**, this last fact is not surprising. Thus, according to (3), a sentence S is true if and only if the initial verifier (**ms**) has a winning strategy for S according to the rules of **GTS**. Since winning strategies do not define truth conditions directly, Hintikka offers a more formal treatment of the circumstances in which sentences are true. In particular he tries to find a **GTS**-substitute for the T-scheme, which is an essential ingredient of **TCT** (in the next formula, the symbol S^* is a name of the sentence S):

(10) S^* is true if and only if S.

There are at least three reasons for rejecting (1) in the framework of **IFL** and **GTS**. First, the T-scheme has nothing to do with games and, therefore it does not fit the ideas underlying game-theoretical semantics (although I did not find this argument in Hintikka's writings, it seems fairly natural from his standpoint). Second, on the basis of simple formal manipulations governed by classical propositional logic, (10) is decomposable into (I replace "S^* is true" by "$\mathrm{Tr}(S^*)$"):

(11) $\mathrm{Tr}(S^*) \wedge S \vee \neg\mathrm{Tr}(S^*) \wedge \neg S$,

which assumes **LEM**.[28] Third, the T-scheme as based on the principle of compositionality prevents a satisfactory analysis of sentences represented by "anyone can become a millionaire" (see (1) and (2) above). In order to formulate truth conditions in a new and different way, Hintikka employs the fact that **IFL** formulas have second-order translations.[29] For instance, the formula (with independent quantifiers),

(12) $\forall x \forall z(\exists y/\forall z)\exists u \forall x S(x, y, u, z)$

is translated into second-order language as

(13) $\exists f \exists g \forall x \forall z S(x, f(x), z, g(z))$,

where the letters f and g refer to functions. Now, we can say that truth conditions of independence-friendly first-order sentences are expressed by their second-order translations. A more refined treatment consists in introducing Skolem functions. It is a well-known fact that every first-order sentence may be "skolemized" (I neglect cases other than those similar to (12)), that is, replaced by a formula in which existential quantifiers are eliminated in favor of functions like f and g in (13). More exactly, the formula $\forall x \forall z S(x, f(x), z, g(z))$ is the Skolem counterpart of (12); (13) is obtainable from (12) by second-order existential generalization. In general, S and its Skolem counterpart are equisatisfiable.

Hintikka's proposal is to identify descriptions of truth conditions of arbitrary formulas with suitable skolemizations, which are, of course of Σ_1^1 complexity. Thus, we have (I disregard here, as nonessential, some of the extensions of skolemization introduced by Hintikka)[30]:

(14) S^* is true if and only if Sk(S)

as a **GTS** (or **HCT**) counterpart of the T-scheme. In particular Hintikka considers Skolem functions as determining winning strategies; this proviso connects skolemization with **GTS**. Of course, the question arises whether (14) is decomposable like (10). Although Hintikka does not give any direct answer, a hint may be derived from his treatment of logical equivalence.[31] Under the standard account, S and T are logically equivalent if and only if they are true in the same models and false in the same models. Hintikka adopts a weaker clause, which requires that truth in the same models be sufficient for logical equivalence. This account is parallel to the lack of **LEM** in **IFL**.

Formula (14) is not the definition of truth which Hintikka is looking for. It is rather something that imitates the T-scheme (Hintikka requires that particular instances of (14) be provable from the definition). The proposed truth predicate falls under the following scheme[32]:

(15) $\exists X \mathrm{Tr}(X) \wedge X(y)$,

where "$\mathrm{Tr}(X)$" means that X is a truth predicate and y ranges over natural numbers. If y is the Gödel number of a given sentence S, we write $g(S)$. Hintikka's strategy consists in defining $X(y)$ as true of g if and only if g is a number of a true sentence. The procedure employs the rules of **GTS**. For example, taking (R. $\wedge$), we have (other cases are handled similarly):

(16) $X(g(S_1 \wedge S_2))$ if and only if $X(g(S_1) \wedge g(S_2))$.

Arithmetization transforms clauses like (17) into formulas of arithmetic. Now, the crucial connection between skolemization and (16) is given by

(17) For any sentence S of **IFL**, the truth predicate applies to $g(S)$ if and only if all Skolem functions of S exist.[33]

Another result is covered by

(18) If S is a closed and quantifier-free sentence, then $\mathrm{Tr}(g(S))$ if and only if S.[34]

Hintikka calls (18) the T-theorem "because of its similarity with Tarski's T-scheme."

According to Hintikka, (17) and (18) demonstrate that his truth predicate is of Σ_1^1 complexity. Thus, since Σ_1^1 formulas are convertible to **IFL** formulas, Hintikka concludes that he has succeeded in giving a truth definition for the arithmetical extension of **IFL** in itself. In particular, the Tarski undefinability result is tamed. The usual proof of Tarski's result consists in showing that the truth-definability would lead to the Liar Paradox. However, since **IFL** has no contradictory negation, the Liar Paradox does not arise in it. More specifically, although the diagonal lemma

(19) S if and only if $X(S^*)$

applied to $\neg Tr$ produces

(20) S if and only if $\neg Tr(S^*)$,

$\neg Tr(S^*)$ is neither true nor false and thereby does not lead to any trouble. Since (see above) the failure of **LEM** in **IFL** is a natural phenomenon, this way of avoiding the Liar Paradox is regarded by Hintikka as an equally natural outcome.

Hintikka's ideas sketched above call for several comments. I shall begin with some critical remarks about **IFL**.[35] Although it is to a considerable degree a matter of convention how we decide to use the word "logic," we should remember Lesniewski's noteworthy and remarkable warning that the properties of things do not depend on their labels. Logic is not about quantifiers or dependences and independences between them (these are matters of metalogic), or about perfect or imperfect information. The primary goal of logic is to study truth-preserving patterns (rules, principles, forms, etc.) of inference. These patterns are coded by the theorems of logic as universally valid sentences. Clearly, **IFL** does not help in this respect and even considerably confuses the issue. Consider (6) and (7) once more. Let the former be instantiated by

(21) for every natural number x, there is a natural number y, such that $x < y$.

If we change the order of quantifiers, we obtain a false sentence

(22) there is a natural number y such that for every natural number x, $x < y$.

Of course, there are cases in which formulas falling under the scheme

(23) $\exists x \forall y S(x, y)$

are true as well as equivalent to instances of (6). For example, we can take the set $\{a\}$ and the predicate $=$ as the model in which (23) is true and equivalent to (6). Nonstandard models of arithmetic in which "natural number" is understood as "standard or nonstandard natural number" are the next and more interesting illustration. However, this has nothing to do with the dependence or independence of quantifiers, but is related to properties and relations holding in given models (various models given by Hintikka in order to illustrate his ideas invite similar comments). Note that **IFL** has no resource to express in a single formula the banal fact that (6) and (23) are sometimes equivalent, but sometimes not. Nothing is achieved by saying that (6) and (7) are equivalent, provided that independence is taken into account, because saying so disregards dependence. In a sense independence-friendly logic is dependence-nasty. If this point is clarified, Hintikka's complaints concerning Frege's interpretation of quantifiers as second-order predicates are baseless, at least as concerns dependence and independence. Moreover, Hintikka ignores the treatment of quantifiers as functions, which is more standard nowadays than the Fregean account. Let me also note that there are cases which seem completely neutral to the matters of dependence or independence. I mean here formulas preceded by blocks of the same quantifiers, for instance $\forall x \forall y S(x, y)$ or $\exists x \exists y S(x,y)$. It is clear that in such a case quantifiers behave in a perfectly regular way (in the sense that their order can be freely changed, modulo the syntactic correctness of formulas), regardless of whether they are dependent or independent. Once more: logical validity, not dependence or independence, is what is crucial.

Contrary to Hintikka, I think that incompleteness and the lack of a codified proof-procedure on the part of **IFL** do not fit the requirements of any reasonable logic, if we expect logical theorems to be universally valid (by the way, I have never seen any proof that an effective rejection procedure is available for **IFL**; I wonder whether it is possible, if the set of **IFL**-truths is not recursive). Furthermore, the lack of a deduction theorem in **IFL** makes it impossible to define this logic as the set of consequences of the empty set exhibiting an important sense of the need for universality in any logic.[36] Even if a given logic is semantically incomplete, its deductive apparatus should be elaborated as far as possible (see the case of second-order logic). Due to experiments with equivalence, negation and **LEM** (note that it does not close possible questions: what about implication or mutual definability of connectives and quantifiers?), this is particularly important in the case of **IFL**. As regards negation, I think it is improper to say that **IFL** has a special negation, different from the classical (contradictory) one. It is clear when we look at **IFL** from the perspective of Σ_1^1-logic. We easily see that Σ_1^1 formulas are not closed by external negation, that is, preceding the whole formula. It suffices to reject **LEM** as universally valid, because it does not hold for the formula $\exists x S \lor \neg \exists x S$ (the second disjunct is not well-formed). However, this does not close the matter, because the lack of external negation raises the question how proofs by *reductio ad absurdum* are available. There are also other reservations concerning the formal machinery of **IFL**. As this logic is considered by Hintikka to be an extension of **SFOL**, differences should be somehow manifested on the formal level. Let us assume that the syntax does not matter very much. To be fair, let me add that Hintikka does consider modifications of the rules of instantiation. On the level of **GTS**, everything reduces itself to the scant comment (see above) that imperfect information is involved in the winning strategies. However, if the difference between the two kinds of information is of a logical nature, this fact should affect the form of semantic rules. Thus, there are still many gaps in **IFL**, too many to agree that "**IF** first-order logic is a true Mafia logic: It is a logic you cannot refuse to understand."[37] Even if someone (for example, myself) understands it, he will have many reasons for rejecting **IFL** as "a Mafia logic," or at least for suspending judgment about its unquestionable virtues.

Hintikka defends his general position[38] by pointing out that so called descriptive completeness, that is, the suitability of a system for capturing an interesting content, for instance, mathematical content, is much more important than semantic or deductive completeness. I do not agree, at least in the case of logic understood as the codification of valid patterns of inference. On the other hand, the descriptive power of **IFL** logic is not particularly great. Since it is compact, we cannot define the property of being finite in it. Also, the failure of **LEM** is not without effects. For example, we cannot[39] prove that **AC** (the axiom of choice) in its usual form is equivalent to the version with the choice function or to the well-ordering principle. In my opinion **IFL** should be considered as an extralogical theory arising by adding the slash symbol to pure first-order logic with identity. It is justified by the fact that perfect and imperfect information (if we decide to use these categories in speaking about logic) are not parallel phenomena, but rather the former is a special case of the latter; similarly, **SFOL** being associated with perfect information is a special case of **IFL**.[40] Thus, **IFL**, at least from the point of view of **SFOL**, is an extralogical theory (this was already implicitly suggested by considerations about the logical status of the slash). Incidentally, since independence is rather a special case of dependence, but not inversely, **IFL**, according to this relation, should be a special case of **SFOL**, which is at odds with Hintikka's intentions. In my opinion, it shows that dependences and independences between quantifiers, perhaps contrary to perfect and imperfect information, are accidental from the point of view of logic, that is, they are actually extralogical. It does not mean that such phenomena do not deserve formal treatment. It is one of merits of **IFL** that it provides tools for defining dependencies and independences between quantifiers (or their domains) in first-order language and thereby express branching quantifiers in a linear notation. However, I think that logical studies of semantic games with imperfect information[41] open prospects for

IFL. Finally, needless to say, all of the criticism which I direct against **IFL** is not intended to suggest that this logic is a "horror," "mistake," or "curse." In fact, it is a valuable invention, which can help us with many problems in formal analysis. However, I do not see any convincing reason which could justify abandoning **SFOL** in favor of **IFL**, at least, to repeat, if we assume that logic should be universal as to validity of its theorems.

Now let me pass to **HCT** and related topics. I will start by clarifying some matters related to **TCT**. This is the proper place to touch upon objections (H1') and (H5'). At first, I must say something about the T-scheme. (10) is not its proper wording and should be replaced by the following formula:

(24) S^* is true if and only if S^{ML},

where the expression S^{ML} refers to the translation of the sentence named by the symbol S^* into a given metalanguage **ML**. This will help us to interpret sentences (1) and (2). Since everything depends how we translate "any" into metalanguage, it is possible to preserve Hintikka's claim concerning this word. Eventually one can conventionally decide that "any" means "every." My impression is that the trouble with (1) and (2) is largely due to the ambiguity of "any," although I do not suggest that there is no problem at all. In fact, it is nothing new, because the question of how to translate ordinary quantifiers into a regimented formal language has bothered logicians and linguists for centuries.

A more important problem concerns the strength of **ML**. As we recall, Tarski claimed that the metalanguage proper for **TCT** should be essentially richer than the object-language. I quoted above Hintikka's worries concerning the Tarski curse, basically pointing out the disadvantages which appear when a truth theory is involved in difficult problems of set theory. Hintikka is certainly right in the sense that when we try to formulate a truth-definition for set theory, the complex issues in the foundations of this theory cannot all be ignored. However, the situation is not so dramatic in the case of the general framework of first-order languages. Although **TCT** employs set theory as its metalanguage, the tools used are rather elementary and mostly consist of means allowing constructions of sequence, mappings, and the like. It is a well-known fact that **TCT** for an elementary language can be constructed in weak second-order arithmetic.[42] As I will argue **HTC** is not in a better situation. In spite of Hintikka's efforts,[43] his reform of set theory via **IFL** is very far from being complete and convincing. Hence, we can conclude that an independence-friendly set theory is still a very cloudy project with largely unknown consequences. As far as model theory is concerned, its rudiments, already developed by Hintikka for **IFL**, are based, as in the case **SFOL**, on strong results including **AC**.

The last (direct) question about the T-scheme concerns its relation to
LEM.[44] First of all, Hintikka does not distinguish of the logical and
metalogical versions of this principle. Since the T-scheme is a metalogical
statement, only the latter can be taken into consideration. In fact, **TCT** is
formulated in classical metalanguage and automatically assumes (metalogical) **LEM**, like any other assertion dressed in this linguistic frame.
Quite another problem is whether the T-scheme itself needs or entails **LEM**.
I think that the answer is negative. The decomposition of (10) (or (24)) into
(11) is related to definitions of implication by negation and disjunction (or
negation and conjuction). More specifically, we first define $S \Leftrightarrow T$ as $(S \Rightarrow$
$T) \wedge (T \Rightarrow S)$, and then, $S \Rightarrow T$ as $\neg S \vee T$ (or $\neg(S \wedge \neg T)$). Only the latter
definitions assume **LEM**. However, the T-scheme can function without the
decomposition indicated by (11). Although **TCT** entails (metalogical)
LEM, it is due to the definition (I repeat: S is true if and only if it is
satisfied by all sequences of objects), not to the T-scheme. A fascinating
problem is whether **TCT** entails **LEM** constructively. I am inclined to
answer this question affirmatively, but the discussion of this issue is beyond
the scope of the present paper.[45] Hintikka says that **LEM** is responsible for
the fact that logical games are determinate. I think that this is a mistake. Let
us look at (5). It says that Tarskian semantics and **GTS** are equivalent,
provided that **AC** holds. In fact, **AC** entails that first-order games with
perfect information are determinate, because this axiom decides that there
is a winning strategy for any logically true sentence, independent of the
moves of the second player. **LEM** contributes to the principle of bivalence
(every sentence is true or false) in this way. However, I can imagine a
situation in which the principle of bivalence (it implies **LEM**) holds,
semantic, but games are not determinate. Incidentally, it is interesting that
no result, like (5), is established for **GTS** with imperfect information, even
partially. Certainly the Martin determinacy axiom does not help, because it
also involves perfect information.

The issue of compositionality is serious but I will not devote much
space to it. Hintikka distinguishes the usual and extended principles of
compositionality (**PC**).[46] The former considers the meanings of complex
expressions as functions of the meanings of their constituents. Hintikka
proposes to extend this for any relevant semantic attribute. Tarski never
accepted either "the usual" or "the extended" version of **PC**. Extensionality
was one of the guiding ideas of the Polish school of logic (it is only a
historical explanation and an argument for compositionality). As can be
easily demonstrated, **PC** restricted to denotations is a corollary of the
principle of extensionality. Obviously, the limited **PC** considerably
constrains formal semantic analysis. However, something can be said in
defense of it and the related restrictions. The strict parallelism between

syntactic and semantic constructions modulo recursivity is an important ingredient of **TCT** and the whole Tarskian paradigm in semantics. I fully understand the objections that this approach limits the scope of semantics, but, at least on my part, I prefer elegance and simplicity over a somewhat heavier approach when **PC** is abandoned. This can be illustrated, for example, by the complicated tools used by Cantini[47] in order to handle intensionality in a formal way, or even some features of **IFL** (e.g., there is no algorithm converting Skolem forms into **IFL** formulas). Even if **PC** is a matter of taste, it is unfair to blame it as a sin, even if a hidden one. Does one complain that theoretical physics is not effective as a description of the motions which constitute ordinary walking? Should mathematical semantics cover every detail of ordinary language? Since the concept of a "good approximation" of a semantic construction to our ordinary language is vague, any further discussion of (H1') is pointless without additional clarifications. It is of course true that Tarski was skeptical about the possibility of a semantics of natural language, and in particular about a correct truth definition for it. However, his later position[48] was more friendly toward ordinary language than his earlier one,[49] because he (later) admitted formal semantic constructions for more or less extensive fragments of natural language, suitably improved, although not for the monster consisting of all ethnic idiolects and all semantic levels. Even if one regards Tarski's relation to natural language as somehow ambiguous or too skeptical, the unconditional qualification "**TCT** is not applicable to ordinary language" is historically dubious and systemically misleading, because one should distinguish Tarski's views from the actual scope of his theory. Several works (including plenty of the writings of Hintikka) were devoted to formal analysis of natural language and perhaps local exceptions to **PC** are not at odds with a general requirement of compositionality in abstract semantics.

I must confess that (H2') and (H5') sound rather strange in the context of Hintikka's own practice. Tarski fully explained why he first defined satisfaction and then truth. Roughly speaking, he maintained that some types of sentences did not admit a recursive definition of truth, contrary to the recursive treatment of satisfaction. Moreover, since satisfaction is a fully general concept, applicable to any formulas of the syntactic category covering both sentences (closed formulas) and open formulas, and since closed formulas are a special case of open ones, truth as a property of sentences should be considered to be a particular instance of satisfaction. This is what forces the definition of satisfaction in **TCT** to be given before the definition of truth. That is all. Hintikka does not explain why the indirect definition of truth (in particular, via satisfaction) is wrong or worse than the direct one. One could equally say: well, Hintikka's own truth definition is wrong, because it relies on the concept of winning strategy derived from mathematical game theory and, moreover, it is implicit, not explicit. Objection (H5') is even more strange, because the whole of Hintikka's construction (in particular skolemization as its essential ingredient) relies heavily on models. In fact, the rules of **GTS** explicitly contain **M** as a parameter, which refers truth conditions to arbitrary but established interpretations. Other examples of the presence (tacit or even explicit) of model theory in Hintikka's thoughts about truth will be given below. Thus, if Hintikka directs (H5') against Tarski's theory, he should also direct it against his own theory.

There remains (H3') and the whole issue of the undefinability theorem. This task requires a closer analysis of Hintikka's truth definition. The first thing to be said is that Hintikka's general truth definition (see (3) above) is not purely game-theoretical, because the rule (R. At) is formulated without any real reference to games. Although game-theoretical terms, "wins" and "loses," occur in this rule, they are completely redundant. In fact, as clearly follows from the formulation of (R. At) (if S is an atomic formula or an identity, **ms** wins and **nt** loses, when S is true in **M**, etc.), truth and falsity are prior to winning strategies in the case of atoms. Hintikka anticipates this objection and says:

> The rule (R. At) requires a special comment. It introduces an apparent circularity into my treatment in that it contains a reference to the truth or falsity of atomic sentences. However, as was pointed out above, the concept of truth can be applied to the relevant atomic sentences as soon as all the nonlogical constants of the given sentence have been interpreted on the given model **M** [see the next reference not only to **M**, but also to an interpretation forced by it – J. W.] with respect to which the truth or falsity of S is being evaluated and on which $G(S)$ is being played. This interpretation is part and parcel of the definition of **M**. It is determined by the meanings of the nonlogical constants of S.
>
> What (R. At) hence codifies is a kind of division of labor. The game-theoretical analysis of truth takes the meanings of primitive nonlogical constants of an interpreted first-order language for granted. This fixes the truth-values of the relevant atomic sentences, that is, of all sentences that can serve as endpoints of a semantical game. What my characterization does is to extend the notion of truth to all other sentences of the language in question.[50]

However, the excuse which appeals to the division of labor, instead of explaining something, begs the question. Note first that atomic sentences play a crucial role in **GTS**, because, except for (R. At), the rules (R. ∃), (R. ∀) and (R. ¬) directly refer to S_0. Their treatment must therefore be explicit, not indirect. Contrary to Hintikka's statement, the meaning of atomic sentences, taken for granted (in fact, this is very Tarskian) or not, does not fix truth-values. Thus, (R. At) only says that the truth-values of atomic sentences are fixed and nothing more. A Tarskian philosopher of truth, like me, could say

(25) if $S_0 = R(a_1, ..., a_n)$, then $\mathrm{Tr}(S_0)$ if and only if $R(a_1, ..., a_n)^{\mathrm{ML}}$,

and explain the rest by **GTS** rules. (5) guarantees that first-order logic will be reproduced in this way. Since I am not in a position to propose a solution how to improve **GTS** in this respect, I only indicate a gap in Hintikka's treatment.

Hintikka's claim (18) seems to me to be wrong. The observation that the truth of a sentence is closely related to the Skolem function associated with them it is certainly very interesting (see below). However, if no reference to models is introduced, it is hard to see an exact sense of the statement that a truth predicate applies to $g(S)$ if and only if all Skolem functions of S exist. On the syntactic level, we can describe the Skolem counterpart of any false sentence. Thus, suitable functional expressions are available completely independently of whether S is true or false (or neither true nor false in the light of **IFL**). Since S and $\mathrm{Sk}(S)$ are always equisatisfiable (let us ignore here sentences which are neither true nor false), perhaps we could say

(26) $\mathrm{Tr}(S^*)$ if and only if $\mathrm{Sk}(S)$.

What (26) says is precisely how the truth (or the satisfaction) of a sentence is connected with its skolemization and thereby related Skolem functions. Yet if we are interested in the logical value of a given sentence, it is not sufficient to consider possible Skolem functions, but we must know how things and relations between them are in **M**, taken as a semantic interpretation. This clearly suggests that the language of Skolem functions is suitable to serve as a metalanguage of truth theory, in particular of **TCT**. In fact, as Hintikka rightly points out (see above), Skolem counterparts describe truth conditions. This is an essential role of the right part of T-sentences.

The suggestions made in the last paragraph are at odds with Hintikka's course of thinking because he is looking for a truth definition inside the object language. This job is to be done by $\mathrm{Tr}(X)$ (see (15), (16) and similar clauses, (17) and (18); by the way (18) is perfectly Tarskian, provided that equivalence is standard). An inspection of Hintikka's construction shows that it is reducible to the following statement:

(27) the set *Tr* of Gödel numbers to which $\mathrm{Tr}(X)$ applies is the subset of Gödel numbers for formulas. *Tr* is generated by the rules of **GTS**.

(27) seems plausible at first sight. There is no problem with defining the set

of Gödel numbers for sentences understood as syntactic items of a given language **L**. Then, we can calculate the numbers of true sentences, according to the explicit rules of **GTS**. Since the resulting truth predicate is of Σ_1^1 complexity, we can translate (16) into an **IFL** formula. Thus, the aim is achieved and we have the truth definition for **L** in **L** itself. In particular, Tarski's fatal mistake is corrected: we do not need a stronger metalanguage in order to define truth. The Liar Paradox is also avoided, because **LEM** and contradictory negation are expelled from our Mafia logic and its conceptual apparatus. *Quod erat demonstrandum*, which means a philosophical happy end:

> Philosophically the most important upshot of the results of this chapter is undoubtedly that they disprove, once and for all, the myth that the notion of truth in a sufficiently strong language is inexpressible in that language itself. Applied to our actual working language, this myth entails the companion myth of the ineffability of truth in the ordinary sense of the word. These myths are ready to be discarded. Not only has it been shown in this work that such a self-applicable notion of truth is possible in some recondite formal languages—the construction presented above can serve as a paradigm case for the definition of a truth predicate for any language whose logic contains **IF** first-order logic. And this logic is, as I have argued, nothing but our most basic ground-floor elementary logic. Hence the strong suggestion of what has been seen here is virtually the contrary of the ineffability myth. As soon as you understand your own language and its logic, you have all that it takes to understand and even to define the concept of truth, or so the suggestion goes.[51]

However, all of this is much too quick, because "as soon as one understands a sufficiently strong language and its logic," several doubts (modestly speaking) arise. Although there are various moves to define self-referential truth for **L** in **L** itself,[52] let **IFL** serve as our basic logic and be applied to sufficiently rich languages, that is, languages strong enough for elementary arithmetic. In order to handle the problem of truth for arithmetic based on **IFL** as its logical foundation, one must extend logic at least by primitive recursive arithmetic. This allows us to define arithmetization, representability and strong representability of functions and relations, and so forth.[53] First of all, one can wonder whether **IFL** is sufficiently powerful (let us remember the oddities of equivalence and the lack of contradictory negation) to do the job. In any case, Hintikka is obliged to show all of this. Unfortunately, he only claims that everything is in order. As regards a definition of the set of true Gödel numbers (that is, numbers of true arithmetical sentences in the standard model), one must observe that **GTS** does not generate all arithmetical truths, particularly those provable by induction. Hintikka notes himself that mathematical induction is definable in extended (not pure) logic.[54] No **GTS** rule is equivalent to mathematical induction. Moreover, Hintikka should be alarmed by the problem of universal standard arithmetical truths which fall under the scheme $\forall x S$.[55] How to show that $\mathbf{N} \models \forall x S$ on the basis of **IFL** and **GTS**? The rule (R. $\forall$) says only that the initial falsifier makes the choice. However, if $\mathbf{N} \models \forall x S$, then even an infinite number of choices makes its task undecided. This seems to suggest that **GTS** should be supplemented by the ω-rule, which generates all arithmetical truths, but it makes **IFL** redundant, because a suitably extended **SFOL** is enough and provides an arithmetical truth definition in arithmetic itself.

Let us disregard for a moment the above inaccuracies and assume that **IFL** as the ground for arithmetic has been sufficiently elaborated. What about the Tarski theorem that arithmetical truth is not definable in arithmetic? We should formulate it in a precise manner. Here is the official version, so to speak:

> (28) Let *Tr* be the set of Gödel numbers of formulas that are true for the standard model of arithmetic. Then *Tr* is not arithmetical.[56]

The actual content and proof of the undefinability theorem is closely related to the theorem:

> (29) Let **S** be a consistent theory with equality in the arithmetical language in which the diagonal function is representable. Then the property of being the set of Gödel numbers of theorems of **S** is not expressible in **S**.[57]

The proof of (28) goes as follows: Assume that **S** is sufficiently rich and its axioms are true for the standard interpretation of arithmetic.[58] Since our logic is sound, T-theorems are also standardly true and *Tr* = **S** (we identify theories with a set of their theorems). Furthermore, we observe that **S** is consistent and represents the diagonal function (all recursive functions are representable in **S**). Thus, (29) holds for **S**. As the set of Gödel numbers is not expressible in **S**, the same concerns the set of Gödel numbers of true sentences (the set *Tr*).

Comparing Hintikka's claims with the reality outlined by (28) and (29), either we must assume that the diagonal function is not representable in **IFL**-arithmetic or we must accept (28). If we choose the first route, then the resulting arithmetic is descriptively incomplete (to use Hintikka's own vocabulary), but if we decide to take the second horn of the dilemma, the whole project of defining arithmetical truth in arithmetic fails. Since it also fails in the first case, it fails in the second. Perhaps descriptive incompleteness is the case, because the formula $\neg \mathrm{Tr}_n(n)$ ($\neg \mathrm{Tr}(S^*)$ after arithmetization; (see [20], where *n* belongs to *Tr* and *n* is a numeral related to n) is neither true nor false in **IFL**; this formula says "the formula having a 'true' Gödel number is not true." Incidentally, Hintikka should be alarmed by Ehrenfeucht's result that branching quantifiers introduce infinitistic elements.[59] This fact has been interpreted as demonstrating that the universal validity of Σ_1^1 sentences is not arithmetical.[60] Thus, it would be hard to expect its arithmetical definability. Yet I am very far from suggesting that **IFL** does not contribute to the problem of truth and its definability. Sandu, following some of Hintikka's suggestions, established various results concerning definability in partially interpreted languages.[61] However, his line of thought does not contradict (28). Thus, Hintikka's hopes were too optimistic. In fact, Tr(X) from (15) is only a partial truth-predicate, but it does not diminish related studies, because it is very important to see how far partial truth-definitions go. It is also interesting to note that the issue of compositionality is neutral with respect to (28), because noncompositional IFL does not overcome (28).

It is important to note that the proof of (28) has nothing to do with the Liar Paradox. The instances of the T-scheme produced by the diagonal lemma and contradicting (see [19] and [20] above) the assumptions that the set *Tr* is definable in arithmetic are perfectly well-formed (via arithmetization) formulas of arithmetic. They are at most similar to the Liar sentence. Originally, Tarski considered the Liar Paradox, that is, the sentence, "I am now saying a false sentence," as an ill-formed expression. Thus, it is highly misleading to say that arithmetical truth is not definable because of the Liar Paradox. The Liar sentence (or other similar sentences) illustrates the problem, when we (as Tarski did in 1933) show the undefinability of truth for languages of infinite order. The proof proceeds by demonstrating that the definition produced an inconsistency stemming from the Liar sentence. Rejecting this sentence as ill-formed is equivalent to abandoning the possibility of the universal metalanguage **UML** in which all semantical relations (also those encoded in **UML** itself) are definable. A weakening of logic by cancelling **LEM** is the only good recipe in this case, if one wants to keep the universal metalanguage. When Gödel invented the method of arithmetization, any appeal to the Liar Paradox became redundant.

The last topic leads us to the issue of the ineffability of semantics and the general philosophical significance of the Tarski theorem. Hintikka writes:

> As a corollary to these results [about the definability of truth predicates inside **IFL** – J.W.], it is seen that Tarski's impossibility theorem loses its philosophical significance. It is of course a technically valid result, but it rests on so restrictive premises that its applicability to interesting cases remains dubious.[62]

JAN WOLEŃSKI

Leaving aside "so restrictive premises" (see the remarks about compositionality in the context of [28] above), let me go directly to the indicated problem. Since "(in)effability" is a vague word, I would prefer another term when speaking about the philosophical importance of the Tarski impossibility theorem. It (like the Gödel incompleteness theorems) shows how semantics of a sufficiently rich **L** is related to its syntax. In general, the limitative theorems of Gödel and Tarski arguably demonstrate that the semantics of **L** is not fully reproducible in its syntax, at least modulo classical logic. The word "fully" cannot be eliminated here, because arithmetization as a syntactic device partially captures semantic relations. Thus, Hintikka should restrict his talk about the ineffability of semantics as created by the limitative theorems to a more modest verdict, asserting only partial ineffability. Finally, I would like to suggest that the philosophy behind the limitative theorems is related to the old idea that truth is among the so-called transcendentals, that is, concepts or categories that exceed the usual ones. *Verum transcendit omnia genera*—as the Schoolmen used to say. Something similar is suggested by (28). I regard this as very interesting from the philosophical viewpoint.

JAN WOLEŃSKI

INSTITUTE OF PHILOSOPHY
JAGIELLONIAN UNIVERSITY CRACOW
FEBRUARY 2002

The critical tone of this paper cannot hide my great respect for Jaakko Hintikka as a very human being, great scholar, and reliable friend. Many philosophers coming from the former communist block (I belong to them) owe much to Jaakko. He always helped us in many respects and continuously built bridges that overcame political divisions. Many, many thanks, Jaakko, for everything you did.

NOTES

1. See Jan Woleński and P. M. Simons, "De Veritate: Austro-Polish Contributions to The Theory of Truth from Brentano to Tarski," in *The Vienna Circle and the Lvov-Warsaw School*, ed. K. Szaniawski (Dordrecht: Kluwer Academic Publishers, 1989), pp. 391–442; and J. Woleński, "Semantic Conception of Truth as a Philosophical Theory," in *The Nature of Truth (If Any)*, ed. J. Peregrin (Dordrecht: Kluwer Academic Publishers, 1999), pp. 51–66.

2. Aristotle, *Metaphysics*, vol. 1, A Revised Text with Introduction by W. D. Ross (Oxford: Clarendon Press, 1924), p. 283.

3. See Alfred Tarski, 1933, *Pojęcie prawdy w językach nauk dedukcyjnych* (Warsaw: Towarzystwo Naukowe Warszawskie), p. 153; Eng. tr. by J. H. Woodger, *The Concept of Truth in Formalized Languages*, in A. Tarski, *Logic, Semantics, Metamathematcs. Papers from 1923 to 1939*, 2nd ed., ed. J. Corcoran (Indianapolis: Hackett Publishing Company, 1984), pp. 152–278; and Alfred Tarski, "The Semantic Conception of Truth and the Foundations of Semantics," *Philosophy and Phenomenological Research* 4 (1944): 341–76 (*CP* 2: 665–99, see esp. p. 667. [*Editor's note:* For ease of reference, citations of Tarski will be followed by an indication of where the information can be located in his *Collected Papers* (*CP*), 4 vols., ed. S. R. Givant and R. McKenzie (Basel: Birkhäuser, 1986). For example, the information cited here may be located in *CP*, vol. 2, pp. 665–99, esp. p. 667. This will be cited as *CP* 2: 665–99, esp. 667, and likewise hereafter.]

4. Tarski, "The Semantic Conception of Truth and the Foundations of Semantics," p. 343.

5. See Woleński, "Semantic Conception of Truth as a Philosophical Theory," p. 85.

6. See Jaakko Hintikka, "Truth-Definitions, Skolem Functions and Axiomatic Set-Theory," *Bulletin of Symbolic Logic* 4 (1988): 303–37.

7. See Jaakko Hintikka, *Defining Truth, the Whole Truth and Nothing But the Truth*, Reports from the Department of Philosophy, University of Helsinki, no. 1, 1991; repr. in Jaakko Hintikka, *Lingua Universalis vs. Calculus Ratiocinator: An Ultimate Presupposition of Twentieth-Century Philosophy, Selected Papers* 2 (Dordrecht: Kluwer Academic Publishers, 1997), pp. 46–103, esp. 46.

8. See Jaakko Hintikka, *The Principles of Mathematics Revisited* (Cambridge: Cambridge University Press, 1996), pp. 13–19, 105–6.

9. See Jaakko Hintikka and Gabriel Sandu, "Tarski's Guilty Secret: Compositionality," in *Alfred Tarski and the Vienna Circle: Austro-Polish Connections in Logical Empricism*, ed. J. Woleński and E. Köhler (Dordrecht: Kluwer Academic Publishers, 1999), pp. 217–30.

10. Hintikka, *The Principles of Mathematics Revisited*, pp. 17–18.

11. Jaakko Hintikka, "On the Development of the Model-Theoretic Viewpoint in Logical Theory," *Synthese* 77 (1988): 1–36; repr. in Hintikka, *Selected Papers* 2, pp. 104–39; see esp. p. 108.

12. See Jaakko Hintikka, "Post-Tarskian Truth," *Synthese* 126 (2001):17–36.

13. See Jan Woleński, "Formal Metaphilosophy in Finland," in *Analytic Philosophy in Finland*, ed. L. Haaparanta and I. Niiniluoto (Amsterdam: Rodopi, 2002).

14. See Jaakko Hintikka, "The Prospects of Convention T," *Dialectica* 30 (1976): 61–63. See also Hintikka, *The Principles of Mathematics Revisited*, p. 139.

15. Hintikka, *The Principles of Mathematics Revisited*, p. 139.

16. See Jaakko Hintikka and Gabriel Sandu, "Game-Theoretical Semantics," in *Handbook of Logic and Language*, ed. J. Van Benthem and A. Ter Meulen (Amsterdam: Elsevier Science, 1997), pp. 361–410.

17. Ibid., pp. 363, 364. (I have made slight though nonessential changes in the notation which do not alter the meaning of the quoted fragments; the same in some further quotations.)

18. See Jaakko Hintikka, "What is Elementary Logic? Independence-Friendly Logic As the True Core Area of Logic," in *Physics, Philosophy and the Scientific Community*, ed. K. Gavroglu et al. (Dordrecht: Kluwer Academic Publishers, 1995), pp. 301–26; Hintikka, *The Principles of Mathematics Revisited*, chs. 3–4; Jaakko Hintikka and Gabriel Sandu, "A Revolution in Logic?" *Nordic Journal of Philosophical Logic* 1 (1996): 169–83; and Hintikka, "What is IF Logic and Why Do We Need It?" in Chinese translation by Chen Bo, *Journal of Dialectics of Nature* 22, no. 3 (2000): 20–28.

19. See also Jaakko Hintikka and Gabriel Sandu, "What is a Quantifier," *Synthese* 98 (1994): 113–29.

20. Ibid., p. 169.

21. Hintikka, *The Principles of Mathematics Revisited*, p. 46.

22. Hintikka and Sandu, "Game-Theoretical Semantics," p. 366.

23. See, however, Wilfrid Hodges, "First-Order Logic," in *Handbook of Philosophical Logic*, vol. 1, 2nd ed., ed. D. M. Gabbay and F. Guenther (Dordrecht: Kluwer Academic Publishers, 2001), p. 91, and reference there to the possibility of compositional semantics for **IFL**. See also critical comments about Hodges's proposals in Gabriel Sandu and Jaakko Hintikka, "Aspects of Compositionality," *Journal of Logic, Language and Information* 10 (2001): 56–59, and Hintikka, "Post-Tarskian Truth," pp. 11–12.

24. See Hintikka, "Truth-Definitions, Skolem Functions and Axiomatic Set-Theory," p. 311.

25. Hintikka and Sandu, "A Revolution in Logic?" pp. 171–72; although this paper is co-authored, it is rather certain that the general evaluative and critical remarks are Hintikka's.

26. See Hintikka, *The Principles of Mathematics Revisited*; and Jaakko Hintikka, "Independence Friendly Logic and Axiomatic Set Theory," in *Annals of Pure and Applied Logic* 126 (2004): 313–33.

27. Hintikka, *The Principles of Mathematics Revisited*, p. 16.

28. Hintikka, *Defining Truth, the Whole Truth and Nothing But the Truth*, p. 61.

29. Ibid., p. 64.

30. See Hintikka, "Truth-Definitions, Skolem Functions and Axiomatic Set-Theory," p. 309.

31. See Hintikka, *The Principles of Mathematics Revisited*, p. 65.

32. See Hintikka, *Defining Truth, the Whole Truth and Nothing But the Truth*, pp. 68, 114; and "Truth-Definitions, Skolem Functions and Axiomatic Set-Theory," p. 308.

33. See Hintikka, "Truth-Definitions, Skolem Functions and Axiomatic Set-Theory," p. 308.

34. Ibid., p. 310.

35. See also Neil Tennant, "Games Some People Would Have All of Us Play" [Review of J. Hintikka, *The Principles of Mathematics Revisited*], *Philosophia Mathematica* 6 (1998): 90–115, although I regard his criticism as unfair at some points; see A.-V. Pietarinen, *Semantic Games in Logic and Language* (Helsinki: University of Helsinki, Department of Philosophy, 2001) for a defense of Hintikka.

36. See Woleński, "Semantic Conception of Truth as a Philosophical Theory."

37. Hintikka, *The Principles of Mathematics Revisited*, p. 51.

38. Ibid., pp. 88–105.

39. See William Tait, "The Law of Excluded Middle and the Axiom of Choice," in *Mathematics and Mind*, ed. A. George (New York: Oxford University Press, 1994), pp. 45–70.

40. This is also pointed out by Hintikka; see Hintikka, *The Principles of Mathematics Revisited*, p. 65.

41. See Gabriel Sandu, "IF-Logic and Truth-Definition," *Journal of Philosophical Logic* 27 (1998): 142–64; Tapani Hyttinen and Gabriel Sandu, "Henkin Quantifiers and the Definability of Truth," *Journal of Philosophical Logic* 29 (2000): 507–27.

42. See V. Halbach, *Axiomatische Wahrheitstheorien* (Berlin: Akademie Verlag, 1996), ch. 3.

43. See Hintikka, *The Principles of Mathematics Revisited*, ch. 8; "Truth-Definitions, Skolem Functions and Axiomatic Set-Theory"; "Independence Friendly Logic and Axiomatic Set Theory."

44. In some points, I follow Tennant, "Games Some People Would Have All of Us Play," pp. 107–110.

45. See Jan Woleński, "Remarks on the Concept of Satisfaction," in *The Logica Yearbook 1999*, ed. T. Childers (Prague: Filosofia, 2000), pp. 80–86.

46. See Hintikka, *The Principles of Mathematics Revisited*, p. 106; see also Sandu and Hintikka, "Aspects of Compositionality."

47. A. Cantini, *Logical Framework for Truth and Abstraction: An Axiomatic Study* (Amsterdam: Elsevier, 1996).

48. See Tarski, "The Semantic Conception of Truth and the Foundations of Semantics"; Tarski, "Truth and Proof," *Scientific American* 6 (1969): 63–77 (revised in *CP* 4: 401–23).

49. See Tarski, *The Concept of Truth in Formalized Languages.*

50. See Hintikka *The Principles of Mathematics Revisited*, pp. 25–26.

51. Ibid., pp. 126–27.

52. See F. Fitch, "Universal Metalanguage for Philosophy," *Review of Metaphysics* 17 (1964): 397–402 or J. Myhill, "A System Which Can Define Its Own Truth," *Fundamenta Mathematicae* 37 (1952): 190–92, for instance.

53. See R. Murawski, *Recursive Functions and Metamathematics: Problems of Completeness and Decidability, Gödel's Theorems* (Dodrecht: Kluwer Academic Publishers, 1999) for all details.

54. See Hintikka, *The Principles of Mathematics Revisited*, p. 188.

55. See also Tennant, "Games Some People Would Have All of Us Play," p. 106.

56. E. Mendelson, *Introduction to Mathematical Logic*, 4th ed. (London: Chapman & Hall, 1997), p. 217.

57. Ibid., p. 216.

58. Ibid., p. 217.

59. Reported in L. Henkin, "Some Remarks on Infinitely Long Formulas," in *Infinitistic Methods*: *Proceedings of the Symposium on Foundations of Mathematics, Warsaw, 2-9 September 1959* (Oxford-Warsaw: Pergamon Press-Pañstwowe Wydawnictwo Naukowe, 1961), p. 182.

60. H. Enderton, "Finitely Partially Ordered Quantifiers," *Zeitschrift für mathematische Logik und Grundlagen der Mathematik* 16 (1970): 393; and J. Van Benthem and K. Doets, "Higher-Order Logic," in *Handbook of Philosophical Logic*, ed. Gabbay and Guenther, p. 210.

61. Sandu, "IF-Logic and Truth-Definition"; see also Hyttinen and Sandu, "Henkin Quantifiers and the Definability of Truth"; Pietarinen, *Semantic Games in Logic and Language*.

62. Hintikka, "Post-Tarskian Truth," p. 22.

REPLY TO JAN WOLEŃSKI

I am grateful to Jan Woleński for providing a natural occasion for me to clarify the relationship of my treatment of truth with Alfred Tarski's influential treatment and also to correct a number of misunderstandings concerning the logical and semantical basis of the truth definition I have proposed (in collaboration with Gabriel Sandu and others).

In dealing with Woleński's contribution, the strategy I found myself following in the case of Feferman's essay is again appropriate. In effect Woleński discusses my ideas about truth on the basis of received logical and semantical ideas, especially those of Tarski. It is a much better way of getting to the bottom of the relevant problems to turn the tables and show what Tarski's ideas look like in light of the insights reached in game-theoretical semantics (GTS) and independence-friendly (IF) logic. This strategy is encouraged by Woleński's title, which promises to the reader also a perspective on "Tarskian truth." Such an account of Tarski's work in the light of hindsight promises to be instructive also because most philosophers do not seem to have reached a full understanding of what Tarski did. They tend to think of his truth definition as an eternal truth (no pun intended) carved in stone. In reality, Tarski's work is heavily conditioned by his own particular intellectual preferences.

So what was Tarski like as a logician?[1] By and large, one can distinguish three kinds of methodological orientation among thinkers in this field, widely understood. A logician or philosopher of logic can rely on set-theoretical concepts and conceptualizations; he or she can use the logic of quantifiers as the core area methodologically; or he or she can prefer algebraic techniques and algebraic ways of thinking. Tarski made important contributions to all these three types of approaches, but his preferred orientation is nevertheless conspicuous. His favorite way of thinking was unmistakably algebraic. He even tried in a sense to reduce the other approaches to the algebraic one. It is highly significant that he was the driving force in the development of algebraic logic in the form of cylindrical algebras, and in his posthumous book (with Steven Givant) he even tried to deal with set theory algebraically, without quantifiers.[2] Some of his most significant results dealt with quantifier elimination. Furthermore, from this perspective we can understand why, in the beginning, when Tarski and his associates and students developed model theory as a technical discipline in logic, this model theory took largely the form of a metatheory of algebra.

Now how does such an algebraically oriented logician approach semantics? The answer is predictable: by means of the principle of compositionality. In a purely algebraic symbolism, the reference of different terms is literally a function of the reference of their component terms. This is precisely what is prescribed by the principle of compositionality. The purest form of such semantics is a categorial grammar. Now such grammars were first developed largely by Leśniewski whose ideas Tarski is echoing in his discussion of the T-schema and of the undefinability of truth in natural languages in section 1 of his famous monograph on truth.[3] Tarski clearly believed, true to his algebraic ideas, that the only viable types of semantics are compositional. He was also shrewd enough to realize that natural languages are not compositional. Officially Tarski blames this undefinability not on his undefinability theorem, but on the irregularity of natural languages. I have argued that in fact Tarski has only one kind of irregularity in mind: the failure of compositionality. No wonder he was incensed when Davidson tried to develop compositional truth definitions for natural languages.

In his monograph, Tarski treats in the first place class-logical languages. Only in a postscript added to the German version of his book did he envisage extending his treatment to the more common types of logical languages, clearly meaning first-order languages.[4]

The requirement of compositionality also determines the general character of Tarski's truth definition. It is an inside-out recursive definition. The precise form of Tarski's truth definition is well known, and will not be explained here. Some comments are nevertheless in order.

Tarski's methodological orientation is in evidence in his truth definition in several ways. For instance, he could not implement compositionality in its simplest form, for he could not literally state how the truth or falsity of a sentence is determined by the truth or falsity of its component expressions. The reason is that those component expressions typically contain variables (i.e., they are not closed formulas), to which the notion of truth does not apply. But he could define satisfaction recursively for open formulas, too, in accordance with the (unspoken) principle of compositionality, which is what he in fact does.

Tarski's truth definition is as such unobjectionable in the area in which it was calculated to apply. Woleński says that I criticize Tarski's conception of truth by arguing that it "does not satisfy all desirable constraints to be obeyed by any successful philosophical truth-theory." This is not a fair description of what I have been doing. I do not pretend that I know, sight unseen, what any successful philosophical truth theory must be like. As far as Tarski's treatment of truth is concerned, I am in the first place trying to understand it in its historical and conceptual setting. Among other things, I am concerned with exposing its tacit presuppositions and the limitations due to these presuppositions.

One way of approaching Tarski's truth definition is a comparative one. We can ask: How does Tarski's truth definition differ from the game-theoretical one that I have proposed? Let us consider traditional first-order languages. In this case, the two truth definitions are equivalent. Hence there might not seem to be much to help us choose between them in this area. However, already in this case, a major difference is in evidence. Each of the recursive steps for quantifiers in Tarski's definition involves quantification over a domain that can be infinite. Technically, Tarski uses quantification over valuations, which seems to bring in second-order quantification. However, since the only thing that matters is the value of a valuation function for one particular argument, essentially we do not have to go beyond first-order quantification. But this does not close the issue. Woleński says, "Although TCT [Tarski's conception of truth] employs set theory as its metalanguage, the tools used are rather elementary." This is essentially correct. However, in applying a Tarski-type truth definition one must consider at each recursive step for a quantifier a closed infinite totality of individuals (i.e., members of the domain). If we imagine a human agent applying a Tarski-type truth definition to a particular interpreted sentence *S*, that agent literally has to operate with closed infinite totalities. These totalities are the classes of individuals *x* satisfying certain formulas *F[x]* which are subformulas of *S*.

In contrast, when a game-theoretical truth definition is applied to *S*, no infinitary operations are presupposed, the truth conditions for *S* merely assert the existence of a winning strategy for one of the players in a certain game G(*S*) correlated with S. This game, unlike an application of Tarski-type truth definition, does not rely on any infinite closed totalities or any infinitary operations. It even could be played, as Peirce envisaged, by two finite human beings. It comes to an end after a finite number of moves. It can be played in this way even if the domain is infinite.

In this sense, a Tarski-type truth definition is nonelementary while the game-theoretical one is in an important sense elementary. (I use the term "elementary" rather than "finitary" because the finiteness or infinity of the domain is not the crucial matter here). This highly relevant difference is easily obscured in a formal treatment. Formally, both a Tarski-type truth definition and a game-theoretical one seem to involve second-order quantification, the former over valuations or equivalent, the latter over strategy functions. But by means of IF logic existential quantification over strategy functions can be eliminated in favor of first-order quantification. This cannot be done in either case by means of the logic Tarski is using.

Most importantly, the strategies that figure in the game-theoretical truth definition are not assumed to be known to the players of actual semantical games. They are not chosen by the players ahead of time. In practice, they are typically created by the players "across the board" in the course of a semantical game.

This difference is subtle, but it is very real. The relevance of Tarski-type truth definitions on closed infinite totalities is a sufficient reason for an intuitionist to reject them. In contrast, it can be shown that the extended IF propositional logic is essentially the same as intuitionistic logic. This kinship between IF logic and intuitionistic logic merits further scrutiny.

The nonelementary character of Tarski-type truth definitions has not been appreciated sufficiently in the philosophical discussion. Furthermore, the relation of the two types of truth definitions deserves more discussion. There is a major confusion in Woleński's paper. He obviously thinks that he has to criticize IF logic and perhaps even GTS in order to defend Tarski's approach to truth and truth definitions. This is a mistake. It is perfectly possible to accept IF languages with their game-theoretical truth definition and yet to use Tarski-type truth conditions to interpret some particular types of sentences. What Tarski-type truth definitions cannot do is to define truth for all sentences of a noncompositional language. This failure is not due to any special feature of IF languages, except for one. Tarski-type truth definitions fail in IF languages because these languages are not compositional. And the restriction of the applicability of these definitions to compositional languages is a self-imposed limitation, part and parcel of Tarski's intellectual orientation. In a sufficiently long historical perspective, Tarski's commitment to compositionality is a historical accident—in both senses of "accident."

Woleński or someone else might reply here that there is nevertheless a kind of parity between the two approaches. Admittedly, Tarski-type truth definitions fail for compositional languages, but on the other hand in certain cases game-theoretical truth conditions become inapplicable. This happens when IF logic is extended by admitting a contradictory negation $\neg$ into our logic. Then GTS allows us to interpret such a negation only when it occurs sentence-initially, but not when it occurs within the scope of a quantifier, for instance, $(\forall x) \neg F[x]$. Here the ideas codified in Tarski-type truth conditions can nevertheless be used. We can say that $(\forall x) \neg F[x]$ is truth if and only if $\neg F[b]$ is true for the name "b" of each member of the domain. (This is possible because in $\neg F[b]$ contradictory negation is no longer prefixed to an open formula.) There is no objection to the use of such truth conditions. In fact, they are what enables us to extend the use of the contradictory negation so that it can also occur within the scope of a quantifier. There is no reason why suitable Tarski-type truth conditions could not apply to sentences containing such occurrences of the contradictory negation.

Hence both types of truth conditions have a job to do. What makes a difference is the massively nonelementary character of the non-game-theoretical ("Tarski-type") truth conditions. In fact, if they are applicable to contradictorily negated expressions in any position, we obtain a logic that is as strong as the entire second-order logic (with the standard interpretation, of course). Thus such truth conditions are not only nonelementary, they transcend the purview of elementary methods by a mile. Hence if there is a rock-bottom theoretical objection to Tarski-type conceptions of truth, it lies in this nonelementary character, not in any failure to satisfy some imaginary a priori philosophical *desiderata*.

But which kind of truth definition is being presupposed in ordinary discourse? There are not syntactical independence indicators in natural language. Hence it seems that this question typically concerns languages like traditional first-order languages. But in them the two truth definitions coincide. Hence there is no way of deciding between them, it might seem.

However, the situation is more complicated than that. The two conceptions of truth yield somewhat different results even in traditional first-order language, if the basic predicates of the language leave truth value gaps, that is, do not obey the law of excluded middle. Now in the cases where the two differ, it turns out that it is the game-theoretical conception of truth that normally yields the right reading. For instance, in IF logic the following is not a truth of logic:

(1) For each problem, there is someone such that if he or she can solve it, anyone can.

In symbols

(2) $(\forall p)(\exists x)(S[x,p] \supset (\forall y\, S[y, p]))$

This is the case even though (2) is a logical truth when the traditional first-order logic is used. Nor are the following two sentences logically equivalent in IF logic:

(3) There is someone such that if he fails in business, he will commit suicide.
(4) There is someone such that if everyone fails in business, he will commit suicide.

Yet, as Peirce already pointed out, in the usual first-order logic the two are logically equivalent. Thus it seems that IF logic rather than the received first-order logic with a Tarski-type truth definition that is the best approximation to the logic of natural language. Similarly, apparent paradoxes like the sorites paradox are solved simply by dealing with them by means of IF logic.

Admittedly, there are some uses of negation or of conditionals in natural language that can only be interpreted by appealing to the "Tarski-type" truth conditions. However, they seem to be exceptions rather than the rule.

In sum, Woleński tries to defend Tarski's approach to truth and truth definitions against the imagined threat posed by game-theoretical truth definitions. It turns out that such a threat does not exist. It is possible to use at the same time both kinds of truth conditions. If Tarski-type truth definitions are threatened by anything, they are threatened by their own nonelementary character. However, game-theoretical truth definitions cannot be replaced by compositional ones. As far as the logic of natural language is concerned, it seems to be predominantly game-theoretical, even though in some cases Tarski-type truth conditions are needed to do justice to the meaning of certain natural language sentences. Thus Woleński's interesting paper is not the last word concerning either post-Tarskian or Tarskian truth.

Instead of comparing with each other the two approaches to truth, Woleński for some reason thinks that he has to criticize IF logic in order to defend Tarski-type truth definitions. This assumption is mistaken, and his criticisms of IF logic mostly misleading and ill-informed. Maybe I should accept some blame here myself, for apparently I have not been as successful as an expositor as I have hoped.

One source of Woleński's troubles is probably his conception of logic. He says that "the primary goal of logic is to study truth-preserving patterns (rules, principles, forms, etc.) of inference." This is true in the sense that the primary applications and the primary human uses of logic are calculated to carry out and to understand inferences and other kinds of reasoning. However, it does not follow that a systematic theory of logic should take the form of a theory of inference. Inferences are valid or invalid in virtue of the ways in which logical concepts contribute to the way in which language can represent the world. The basic part of logic will therefore involve a study of such representative relations, that is, a study of model theory. Applications should not drive a theory. Perhaps a partial analogy may illustrate this. Somebody might claim that the main application of physiology is to internal medicine. But if this were the case, it would not follow that the science of physiology is a branch of internal medicine.

Woleński overlooks the deeper issues, including how an interpreted IF language can represent reality. In particular, there is in his paper no single word about the leading insight of IF logic. This insight is that the only way of representing in a first-order logical language the actual "real-life" dependence relations between different variables is by means of formal dependence between the quantifiers to which they are bound. A paper on IF logic that does not come to grips with this idea is like the proverbial performance of *Hamlet* without the prince of Denmark.

An aspect of this general oversight is Woleński's failure to see the role of Skolem functions in a suitable IF truth-definition. He says that "if no reference to models is introduced, it is hard to see an exact sense of the statement that a truth predicate applies to *g(S)* [i.e., to the Gödel number of *S*] if and only if all Skolem functions of *S* exist." Taken literally, this is nonsense since the truth predicate says that all Skolem functions of *S* exist, wherefore the "exact sense" in question is one of identity. Apparently Woleński fails to appreciate the notion of Skolem function of a given sentence *S*, thinking that they somehow must be defined syntactically independently of the different models of *S*. This does not make any sense, for obviously the notion of a Skolem function of *S* is relative to a model *M* of *S*. Hence their existence is a condition on *M*, as is the truth of *S* in *M*. The truth definition says that these two conditions coincide. Woleński's talk about functional expressions being available for *S* independently of whether *S* is true or false is neither here nor there. It is like saying that purely syntactically speaking we can express false as well as true sentences.

This failure is a pity, for the existence of Skolem functions can, on reflection, be seen to be the formal codification of our "intuitive" pretheoretical idea of truth for quantificational sentences. Woleński's failure at this point has obviously made it impossible to understand what is involved in an IF truth definition. Small wonder, therefore, that he fails to appreciate my feeble joke about IF logic as a mafia logic, which I can now see was somewhat overly optimistic in the first place. What he has produced is merely evidence of my poor performance as an expositor.

For reasons of space, I can here make only a few corrections to specific misunderstandings. It is simply a misunderstanding to maintain, as Woleński claims, that "it is improper to say that [IF logic] has a special negation, different from the classical (contradictory) one." This claim is so bizarre that I had to read it repeatedly before I could believe that it is what Woleński really says. In order to recognize the mistake it should be enough to note that the truth conditions of the two kinds of negated sentences, that is, sentences with a strong IF negation and sentences with a contradictory negation, are simply different. It can also be pointed out that in the extended IF logic there are two different negations, the one defined by the "classical"

semantical rules and the other the contradictory one. It is not only not
improper to distinguish them, one absolutely must distinguish the two.
Again, in the geometrical (set-theoretical) representation shown possible by
Tarski's results on Boolean algebras with operators the two negations
behave differently.[5] The contradictory negation becomes complementation
whereas the strong negation can be considered as a generalization of the
notion of orthogonality.

At one point, Woleński writes: "I have never seen any proof that an
effective rejection procedure is available for IF logic." This statement is
ambiguous. Nobody has ever claimed that there is a recursive disproof
procedure (decision method for inconsistency) that can be formulated for
IF logic any more than it can be formulated for the first-order logic. What
is true is that there exists a complete disproof procedure for IF first-order
logic in the same sense as there exists a complete proof procedure for
ordinary first-order logic. And Woleński has certainly seen plenty of proofs
of the existence of such a complete disproof procedure for IF logic, for such
a completeness proof is *ipso facto* a typical proof of the completeness of
ordinary first-order logic. In a typical proof of this kind, it is shown that if
(F & $\neg G$) is inconsistent (logically false), then this falsity is seen by trying
to construct a model for it by means of a certain fully explicit procedure,
such as *tableau* construction or tree method. As a special case (no $\neg G$
present), we can see that if F is inconsistent, then this inconsistency can be
brought out by means of the same technique. This argument goes through
without changes in IF first-order logic.

Woleński tries to insinuate that I smuggle stronger assumptions into the
IF truth theory than is warranted. For instance, at one point he writes that
the rudiments of model theory, "already developed by Hintikka for [IF
logic], are based . . . on strong results including [the] axiom of choice." All
that this shows is that Woleński does not appreciate what is involved in IF
logic. The axiom of choice is not a "result" smuggled into IF logic, nor is
it especially "strong" from the vantage point of IF logic. It is simply a truth
of IF logic in the sense that all of its instances are. The fact that people talk
about it as a special assumption (though never as a "result") is that they
think uncritically of first-order axiomatic set theory as the canonical
notation for mathematics. Due to its first-order character (in the sense of
received first-order logic), the axiom of choice cannot be completely
expressed in it as a logical truth and has to be introduced as a separate
"axiom."

Woleński raises various questions about the truth conditions of
sentences without quantifiers, such as the result which in his numbering is
(18) and the truth conditions of atomic sentences. I will not discuss his
remarks on these questions, not because they are correct, but because they

are not relevant to the main issue of his essay. This main issue concerns the possibility of a truth predicate for quantified sentences. Whatever questions one can raise about truth in propositional logic or about the truth conditions of atomic sentences simply are not relevant to this issue.

It is regrettable that Woleński has felt called upon to criticize IF logic before fully understanding it, even if the fault perhaps lies in my inadequacy as an expositor. I agree wholeheartedly when he writes that I remain within the same paradigm as Tarski. Tarski is without any doubt one of the giants on whose shoulders I am standing. Woleński is doing a disservice not so much to myself as to Tarski by trying to criticize those who are pointing out humanly unavoidable limitations of Tarski's work. He should instead try to understand better, not just the nature of IF logic, but also the motivation and the intellectual context of Tarski's work.

J. H.

NOTES

1. See here also the suggestive article by Steven Givant, "Unifying Threads in Alfred Tarski's Work," *Mathematical Intelligencer* 21 (1999): 47–58.

2. Alfred Tarski and Steven Givant, *A Formalization of Set Theory Without Variables* (Providence, R.I.: American Mathematical Society, 1987).

3. Alfred Tarski, "The Concept of Truth in Formalized Languages," in *Logic, Semantics, Metamathematics* (Oxford: Clarendon Press, 1956), section 1. (See especially the first footnote to this section.)

4. Ibid., sec. 7, Postscript, pp. 268–77, especially pp. 268–69.

5. Alfred Tarski, *CP* 3: 369–419, 421–58.

20

Philippe de Rouilhan and Serge Bozon

THE TRUTH OF IF: HAS HINTIKKA REALLY EXORCISED TARSKI'S CURSE?

We all remember Kripke's observation made towards the end of his 1975 article on truth: "The ghost of the Tarski hierarchy is still with us."[1] Kripke had shown that a nonclassical language containing a minimum of arithmetic could contain its own truth predicate, but not that it could contain an *adequate* definition of this predicate. What Kripke had not done, others have done subsequently, in particular Hintikka, in a privately circulated 72- page paper of 1991, the content of which is taken up again in his 1996 book, *The Principles of Mathematics Revisited*. Has "Tarski's curse" been thus "exorcised," as Hintikka claims?[2] In this essay we maintain that the model-theoretical criterion of adequacy involved should be internally expressible, and this leads us to argue, contrary to Hintika's claim, that the ghost of the Tarski hierarchy is still with us.

1. HINTIKKA'S PLACE IN THE HISTORY OF THEORIES OF TRUTH SUBSEQUENT TO TARSKI

1.1. Tarski's work is essentially known for having yielded a positive result and a negative result, both of them involving the theory of truth. *Let $\mathcal{L}$ be any object-language[3] of a certain kind, let us say classical, and $\mathcal{M}$ an appropriate metalanguage*, meaning a metalanguage (1) containing the elementary syntax of $\mathcal{L}$,[4] (2) into which the expressions of $\mathcal{L}$ can be translated, and (3) essentially richer, from the logical point of view, than $\mathcal{L}$.[5] The positive result is that:

(a) *it is possible adequately to define a truth predicate for $\mathcal{L}$ in $\mathcal{M}$.* The criterion of adequacy adopted, called "Convention T," for the predicate

'... is true' in question is that the formal implication

$(\forall x)(x$ is true $\Rightarrow x$ is a sentence of $\mathcal{L})$

and all the T-equivalences (i.e., the equivalences of the form

... is true $\Leftrightarrow$ ---

with the name for a sentence of $\mathcal{L}$ in place of the dots and its translation in $\mathcal{M}$ in place of the dashes), are logically deducible from this definition and the principles of elementary syntax of $\mathcal{L}$.[6]

The negative result can be presented in two parts: *if $\mathcal{L}$ contains its own elementary syntax, then*

(b) *it is impossible adequately to define a truth predicate for $\mathcal{L}$ in a metalanguage that is not essentially logically richer than $\mathcal{L}$;*[7]
(c) *it is not even possible to admit such a predicate in $\mathcal{L}$ as primitive and govern its use by an adequate, consistent axiom system.* The criterion of adequacy adopted here is that a system of axioms governs adequately the use of a truth predicate if it enables one to deduce the corresponding formal implication and T-equivalences, as in (a).[8]

1.2. Instead of applying the idea of adequacy to a putative definition of truth as Tarski did, we can apply it to the definiens of this definition. We shall retain what is essential in the negative results via the following corollaries:

(b') *it is impossible for $\mathcal{L}$ to contain an adequate truth predicate for $\mathcal{L}$ itself,* i.e., a predicate such that the corresponding formal implication and T-equivalences are logically deducible from the principles of elementary syntax of $\mathcal{L}$;[9]
(c') *it is not even possible for $\mathcal{L}$ to contain a truth predicate for $\mathcal{L}$ itself,* i.e., a predicate whose extension would coincide with the set of sentences of $\mathcal{L}$ that are true in a sense adequately defined in $\mathcal{M}$.[10]

(b') is a direct consequence of (b). As for (c'), let us assume (c). If $\mathcal{L}$ contained a predicate, say Tr, whose extension was the set of true sentences of $\mathcal{L}$, then the formal implication '$(\forall x)(\text{Tr}[x] \Rightarrow x$ is a sentence of $\mathcal{L})$' and all the T-equivalences of the form 'Tr[...] $\Leftrightarrow$ ---', with the name for a sentence of L in place of the dots and this sentence itself in place of the dashes, would be true, and one could adopt these without inconsistency as axioms for Tr, contrary to (c).

1.3. What Hintikka has called "Tarski's curse" lies in this (double) negative result. Rather curiously, in his own presentation of this curse, Hintikka fails to distinguish carefully between the two negative results, the two curses, so to speak, coming out of Tarski's work. Yet it is this very distinction that would have enabled him to accord his own work its genuine place in the history of truth theories subsequent to Tarski.

Result (b') amounts to saying that it is impossible for $\mathcal{L}$ to contain a predicate such that the corresponding formal implication and T-equivalences are true for, let us say, "quasi-logical" reasons (ones involving logic or elementary syntax), while (c') goes so far as to state that it is not even possible for $\mathcal{L}$ to contain a predicate such that the corresponding formal implication and T-equivalences are true *simpliciter*. The second result is stronger than the first, and the associated curse a priori easier to "exorcise" (to imitate Hintikka's language once again). It must be easier to find non-classical languages containing their own elementary syntax and a truth predicate for themselves than to find ones for which the truth predicate in question is adequate.

One can actually distinguish two major stages in the history of post-Tarskian truth theories. The first stage concerns the easier of the two tasks. The decisive breakthrough there was due to Kripke, in 1975.[11] The second stage concerns the harder of the two. The key year there is 1991. That is when Hintikka privately circulated a 72-page paper entitled "Defining Truth, the Whole Truth and Nothing but the Truth,"[12] the content of which would appear in his 1996 book.[13]

Toward the end of his seminal 1975 article, Kripke had to confess: "The ghost of the Tarski hierarchy is still with us." Hintikka can legitimately, it seems, proclaim: "Tarski's curse [can] be exorcised" (*PMR*, p. 129), and he indeed thinks that he has exorcised it: Hintikka's "IF languages" ('IF' for '*independence friendly*') which contain their own elementary syntax contain not only a truth predicate, but even an adequate truth predicate. It is astonishing, let us repeat, that Hintikka does not feel the need, either in the 1991 paper or in the 1996 book, to be more specific about what favorably distinguishes him from Kripke.[14]

The difference in question here is as significant as the one Tarski saw between extensionally correct definitions of truth for $\mathcal{L}$ which he held to be adequate and those which he held not to be so. The former capture the intension[15] (or more precisely what we would like to call the *quasi-intension*, because of the intervention of principles of elementary syntax of $\mathcal{L}$ in the Convention T) of the truth predicate for $\mathcal{L}$, while the latter capture only its extension. Some philosophers have believed they were entitled to blame Tarski for accounting only for the extension of the concept of truth for $\mathcal{L}$, not for its intension, but this reproach is essentially unjustified.

Kripke and Hintikka each show that a certain language $\mathcal{L}$ containing its elementary syntax contains a truth predicate Tr for itself. In the appendix to Hintikka's book, specifically devoted to a comparison between Kripke and Hintikka, Gabriel Sandu does note that for Kripke the truth predicate in question figures as primitive in $\mathcal{L}$, while in Hintikka, it is defined, but the difference does not lie there.[16] It lies in the fact that, on the one hand, $\mathcal{L}$ contains a predicate whose extension coincides, for one reason or another, with the set of sentences true in $\mathcal{L}$, while, on the other hand, $\mathcal{L}$ contains a predicate whose extension is identical for logical—or rather quasi-logical—reasons to this set. At this level of description, the simplicity or complexity, the primitive or derived nature, of the predicate in question need not come into play (even though it is true that a primitive truth predicate can not be adequate, or that an adequate predicate must be derived).

The difference between Kripke and Hintikka deserves to be dwelt upon. Let us say that a truth predicate Tr for $\mathcal{L}$ is *e-adequate* (*i-adequate*, respectively) if, and only if, in the interpretation of $\mathcal{L}$ under consideration (in every interpretation of $\mathcal{L}$ verifying the principles of elementary syntax of $\mathcal{L}$, respectively), Tr is true only of sentences of $\mathcal{L}$ and, for every sentence s of $\mathcal{L}$, Tr[s] is true if, and only if, s is true. The methodological status of the notions of e- vs. i-adequacy formally defined in this way must not be confused with that of adequacy as used so far. The latter notion pertains to a Carnapian methodology of explication and does not admit of formal definition. Behind Convention T, as expressed by Tarski in proof-theoretical terms, and granting a sufficient condition of adequacy, one guesses that Tarski had in mind a corresponding convention fixing a model-theoretical, necessary and sufficient condition of adequacy, namely: a truth predicate for $\mathcal{L}$ is adequate if, and only if, it is i-adequate. Be that as it may, the difference between Kripke and Hintikka can now be restated as follows: the predicate Tr of Kripke and that of Hintikka are both e-adequate, but in addition Hintikka's predicate Tr is i-adequate, while Kripke's is not.

We do not mean to say that in every respect Hintikka's achievements constitute definite progress over and above what Kripke has accomplished. For example, both Kripke's and Hintikka's truth predicates are partial in the sense that, in the interpretation under consideration, some sentences of $\mathcal{L}$ are undefined (neither true, nor false). For every sentence s of $\mathcal{L}$, in Kripke Tr[s] and s are both true or both false or both undefined, while in Hintikka they are both true or both untrue, but one can be false and the other undefined. In this regard, Kripke is in the more advantageous position.

Regardless of the ultimate outcome of any thorough comparison, Hintikka undoubtedly deserves credit for the breakthrough represented by his definition of truth with respect to adequacy, which is likely to pass unnoticed, since he himself allows it to go unmentioned. However, our main concern in this article is inversely what Hintikka did *not* succeed in doing in order to sustain his claims about exorcising Tarski's curse.

2. How Hintikka Proves That a Truth Predicate for an IF Language is Adequately Definable Within That Language Itself

For the sake of brevity, we shall implicitly limit ourselves in what follows, as indicated in the title of this section, to languages containing their own elementary syntax. It will not be our goal to cast doubt upon the fine, specific, positive result Hintikka arrives at regarding the definability of an adequate truth predicate in an IF language. Our goal will be to examine whether Tarski's curse is really exorcised owing to it, or whether the ghost of the Tarski hierarchy is still with us in spite of it. We shall begin by quickly setting out the way in which Hintikka arrives at his result, or rather we shall propose a rational reconstruction of it modeled upon the way Tarski himself posed the problem of an adequate definition of the concept of truth in terms of object-language, metalanguage, translation of the former into the latter, criterion of adequacy, and so on.

(1) The object-language, $\mathcal{L}$, will be an IF language. Morphologically, such a language is a first-order language enriched by a new logical sign, the slash '/', enabling one to express the independence of an existential quantification or a disjunction with regard to one or several instances of universal quantification within whose scope it appears.[17] One finds there, for example (this is the example that serves as paradigm), sentences of the form:

(1) $(\forall x)(\forall z)(\exists y/\forall z)(\exists u/\forall x)F[x, y, z, u]$.

The metalanguage, $\mathcal{M}$, will be a classical language of at least second order, in which the ordinary (i.e., nonslashed) first-order part of $\mathcal{L}$ is included and in which the totality of $\mathcal{L}$ can be comprehended, understood, translated.

The basic ideas for this translation are those of *game-theoretical semantics* (GTS) for ordinary first-order languages, well known since the end of the 1960s and now applied to IF languages. To any sentence s of $\mathcal{L}$, whose variables range over a certain domain $\mathcal{D}$ and whose extralogical primitive terms are interpreted in $\mathcal{D}$, is associated a certain *semantical game*, G(s), opposing *Me* (the *initial verifier*) and *Nature* (the *initial falsifier*). The rules of the game are the usual rules of GTS except that, to state it with Hintikka in an improperly epistemological way, a player can now have to make a move while having at his or her disposal only imperfect information about the course of the playing up to that point. As usual, if I (Me) have a winning strategy, s is true by definition; if it is Nature that has a winning strategy, s is false by definition. What is new, now, is that a sentence, even a very simple one, can be neither true nor false, for example:

(2) $(\forall x)(\exists y/\forall x)\, x = y$

in any domain having at least two elements.[18]

Naturally, the foregoing does not, *properly speaking*, in any way constitute a definition of truth (falsity, respectively) for $\mathcal{L}$ in $\mathcal{M}$. At best, it would be a matter of a *schematic* definition, the instances of which would be, to imitate Tarski's language, *partial* definitions, in other words T-equivalences (F-equivalences, respectively), the second members of which express the truth (falsity, respectively) conditions of the sentences mentioned in the first ones according to GTS. This will be precisely the case if the strategies in question are encoded by Skolem functions (in a certain generalized sense enabling one to align the treatment of disjunction with that of existential quantification). Thus, for example, supposing the predicate F to be atomic, the truth (falsity, respectively) conditions of sentence (1) are expressed in $\mathcal{M}$ by sentence (1)* ((1)#, respectively) below:

(1)* $(\exists f)(\exists g)(\forall x)(\forall z)F[x, f(x), z, g(z)]$,
(1)# $(\exists x)(\exists z)(\forall y)(\forall u)\sim F[x, y, z, u]$.

The translation, in the strong sense of the word, of the sentences of $\mathcal{L}$ into $\mathcal{M}$, corresponding to their full comprehension, would consist of associating every sentence s of $\mathcal{L}$ with, not *one* sentence of $\mathcal{M}$, but *two*, $s*$ and $s\#$, the first expressing the truth conditions of s and the second its falsity conditions. The translation in the weak sense, the only one acknowledged by Hintikka as a "translation," amounts to associating a sentence s of $\mathcal{L}$ with a single sentence, $s*$, of $\mathcal{M}$ that is supposed to express its truth conditions.

The translation function $s|{\rightarrow}s*$ can be defined in a purely syntactical manner, independently of the semantical ideas underlying it. There is no need to go into details about this here. One need only underscore two features of this translation brought out by the syntactical definition. On the one hand, although the ordinary part of $\mathcal{L}$ is contained in $\mathcal{M}$, the translation restricted to this part is not homographic (as we say, see note 9): even if s is an ordinary sentence, in general, $s \neq s*$. On the other hand, the translations of sentences of $\mathcal{L}$ are always sentences of $\mathcal{M}$ of definite complexity, namely Σ_1^1. There is nothing unexpected about these two features given the game-theoretical ideas that determine the truth conditions of a sentence s of $\mathcal{L}$: s is true if, and only if, there exists a winning strategy for the initial verifier in the semantical game associated with this sentence. The sentence $s*$ affirms the existence of Skolem functions (in the generalized sense already mentioned) encoding such a strategy. This sentence is not, in general, identical to s, even if s is ordinary; and it is a Σ_1^1 sentence.

(2) One then defines in $\mathcal{M}$ a truth predicate, '... is true', for $\mathcal{L}$, requiring this definition to satisfy a certain criterion of adequacy of Tarskian inspiration, namely that the following sentences are quasi-logical consequences (in the model-theoretical sense, compare the first part of note 6) of this definition:

(1°) the formal implication:

$(\forall x)(x$ is true $\Rightarrow x$ is a sentence of $\mathcal{L})$

(2°) for any sentence s of $\mathcal{L}$, the corresponding T-equivalence (obtained from the schema:

... is true $\Leftrightarrow$ ---

by replacing the dots with the name for s in $\mathcal{M}$ and the dashes with the translation s^* of s in $\mathcal{M}$). For this definition, one proceeds in four steps: (a) one uses a result of Krynicki,[19] enabling one to reduce the infinitely many nonordinary primitive quantifiers of $\mathcal{L}$ to the single quantifier, called *Henkin's quantifier*, in question in sentence (1); at that point (b) one can give a definition by induction of the notion of satisfaction, as in Tarski; then (c) this inductive definition is transformed into a definition in the strict sense following a classical procedure; from which (d) one easily draws the sought after definition of truth for $\mathcal{L}$ in $\mathcal{M}$.

(3) One then finds that, so defined, the formula 'x is true' (where 'x' is a variable) is of a certain complexity, namely Σ_1^1. However, a theorem due (independently) to Enderton and to Walkoe implies that any formula of this complexity is the translation of a formula of $\mathcal{L}$ and can therefore be trans-lated back into this formula, say '$\mathrm{Tr}[x]$'.[20] Whence the putative definition of truth for $\mathcal{L}$ in $\mathcal{L}$ that was being sought.

Constructed in this way, is this definition really an adequate definition of truth for $\mathcal{L}$ in $\mathcal{L}$? We would like to reply yes, certainly, since Tr is just the translation back into $\mathcal{L}$ of a truth predicate for $\mathcal{L}$ adequately defined in $\mathcal{M}$. Of course, it does not follow from this that the corresponding formal impli-cation and T-equivalences as expressed in $\mathcal{L}$ are quasi-logical consequences of the definition, for the only connectives available in $\mathcal{L}$ for negation and therefore also for implication and equivalence, express connections stronger than the classical connectives, and this would be asking too much. But it definitely follows, that, in every structure in which the principles of elementary syntax are true, first, the extension of the predicate '... is true' is included in the extension of the predicate '... is a sentence of $\mathcal{L}$', and second, the two members of each T-equivalence are both true or both untrue. Hintikka says that these two members are "logically equivalent."[21] We shall be more specific and say that they are quasi-logically equivalent. After all, why ask for more? One is tempted to cry victory.

3. IS THE GHOST OF TARSKI'S HIERARCHY STILL WITH US?

3.1. That is just what Hintikka does, cry victory, right in the middle of the battle. He even believes that the war has been won. While he has just barely defined the truth predicate for $\mathcal{L}$ in $\mathcal{L}$, he is enthusiastically proclaiming a "declaration of independence" to supposedly free model theory from the yoke of set theory or higher-order logic: "[O]ne can see the significance of my truth predicate. . . . It shows that *one can develop a model theory for the powerful IF first-order languages on the first-order level*. . . . Tarski's curse [can therefore] be exorcised."[22] What exactly does he mean?[23] That one can develop the model theory of $\mathcal{L}$ in $\mathcal{L}$? And in particular that one can express the relation of logical (or quasi-logical) equivalence between two sentences of $\mathcal{L}$ in $\mathcal{L}$? In the next section, we shall show that, for the languages we call "fundamental," it is not the case.

But we are not going to be content to show that, presuming Hintikka has won the battle of truth, the war over model theory is to be lost. Let us go further and say that the battle of truth is itself also lost in that very way. Even restricting oneself to the problem of truth, Tarski's curse has not yet been exorcised.

The curse would be exorcised only if it were possible for the speakers of $\mathcal{L}$, presumed to be perfectly monolingual, not only adequately to define a truth predicate (for $\mathcal{L}$ in $\mathcal{L}$), but first of all to come up with a plan to do so and, therefore, to have the idea of adequacy, at least such as it took shape through the criterion adopted at the end of the preceding section. However, in order to formulate such a criterion, they would at least have to be capable of expressing the relation of quasi-logical equivalence between two sentences. If the notions of model theory were at their disposal, as Hintikka joyously presumes in his book, those speakers of $\mathcal{L}$ could in particular express the said relation, but if, precisely, $\mathcal{L}$ is a "fundamental" language, this is not the case. It is in vain that those speakers have at their disposal an *adequate* definition of truth according to the criterion adopted: *we*, speakers of $\mathcal{M}$, know that, but, *they*, do not know it. They cannot even ask themselves the question. This is what we shall show in section 4.

3.2. It will perhaps be objected that we are asking too much. After all, when Tarski formulated the plan for an adequate definition of truth for an object-language in a metalanguage, he was not concerned with providing a *model-theoretical, necessary and sufficient* condition of adequacy beforehand. He was content to provide a *proof-theoretical, sufficient* condition (Convention T). Why should Hintikka do any better? One can only ask him to provide a proof-theoretical, sufficient condition.

In response, let us make four points:

(1) First of all, we are not requiring anything more than Hintikka himself does for T-equivalences, for instance, namely the quasi-logical equivalence of the two members of each T-equivalence.[24] As for Tarski's Convention T, Hintikka expressly rejects it,[25] charging him with presupposing classical principles (compositionality and the law of the excluded

middle) from which the taking into consideration of IF languages precisely shows, according to him, one must free oneself.

(2) Were a *proof-theoretical* criterion to provide a sufficient condition of adequacy to be drawn up, it could not be dependent, like Tarski's Convention T, on the logical deducibility of the formal implication and T-equivalences, as expressed in $\mathcal{L}$, from the principles of elementary syntax. It is not the established incompleteness of IF logic that is in question. It is merely that these sentences are not in general quasi-logical truths (see the end of section 2). Moreover, in Hintikka's book, the proof-theoretical considerations for the IF languages are conspicuous by their absence, and no indication is given as to how they might be introduced. And this is not an accident. For, on the one hand, this corresponds to a general predilection on Hintikka's part for the *model-theoretical* approach to problems; and, on the other hand, being a matter of IF languages, the *proof-theoretical* approach seems to be doomed to run into serious difficulties.

(3) Without having to supply a reasonable system of inference rules for $\mathcal{L}$, we have presumed that a notion of deducibility for $\mathcal{M}$ had been set. Taking one's inspiration from Hintikka's own way of defining truth for $\mathcal{L}$ in $\mathcal{L}$, it is then possible (if only up to a coding), since $\mathcal{L}$ contains its elementary syntax, to express in $\mathcal{L}$ a *proof-theoretical criterion of adequacy*, as opposed to the model-theoretical criterion of adequacy adopted by Hintikka: a predicate is an adequate truth predicate for $\mathcal{L}$ in $\mathcal{L}$ if it is the translation back into $\mathcal{L}$ of a monadic predicate φ of $\mathcal{M}$ such that the following sentences are logically deducible from the principles of elementary syntax of $\mathcal{L}$:

(1°) the formal implication:

$$(\forall x)(\varphi[x] \Rightarrow x \text{ is a sentence of } \mathcal{L}),$$

(2°) for any sentence s of $\mathcal{L}$, the corresponding T-equivalence (obtained from the schema:

$$\varphi[...] \Leftrightarrow -$$

by replacing the dots with the name for s in $\mathcal{M}$ and the dashes with the translation s^* of s in $\mathcal{M}$). Does such a predicate φ exist? $\mathcal{L}$ being an IF language and $\mathcal{M}$ a language of at least second order, the answer is not self-evident, for here the proof-theoretical criterion is more demanding than the model-theoretical criterion. Hyttinen and Sandu prove that the answer is affirmative.[26]

But there is a problem. It is not that the sufficient condition would not be necessary, for, in consideration of the result of Hyttinen and Sandu, it is indeed a necessary and sufficient condition. It is that such a proof-theoretical criterion is extrinsic and seems arbitrary until one has correlated it with a model-theoretical criterion. The situation is comparable to that of a proof-theoretical criterion of logical truth for first-order languages before the corresponding model-theoretical definition was given and a soundness (and indeed completeness thrown into the bargain) theorem demonstrated. For a full comparison taking into account the ineffability referred to in 3.1 above, imagine people having at their disposal the proof-theoretical criterion, but no possible access, even in principle, to the model-theoretical definition.

(4) Far from being exaggerated, the first requirement for a model-theoretical criterion was a perfectly legitimate one. In Tarski's case, the criterion of adequacy formulated in the beginning essentially appealed to a *proof-theoretical* notion (viz. deducibility for the metalanguage). Obviously a *model-theoretical* notion (viz. consequence for the metalanguage) loomed behind the proof-theoretical one—and a criterion appealing to the former notion behind the criterion appealing to the latter. The model-theoretical notion was to be formulated later on in a meta-metalanguage essentially logically richer than the metalanguage. And, providing that such a meta-metalanguage was available, nothing stood in the way, in Tarski's work, of the carrying out of this program.[27] In Hintikka's case, an analogous requirement holds, with the additional constraint, now, that everything be done in a single language, $\mathcal{L}$, its very own, one and only metalanguage, and its own, one and only meta-metalanguage. The first requirement was therefore legitimate. And we are going to see that, in the "fundamental" cases, it cannot be satisfied.

4. An Ineffable Criterion of Adequacy

4.1.1. Let S be a signature (elementary or not, with one or many sorts).[28] We say that an S-structure $\mathcal{a}$ is *fundamental* if, and only if, $\mathcal{a}$ is characterizable up to isomorphism by an S-sentence of finite order, and that a language of signature S is *fundamental* if, and only if, (a) it is interpreted in a fundamental S-structure, (b) it contains its elementary syntax. The informal clause (b) could be specified as follows (along classical lines): an S-language $\mathcal{L}$ interpreted in an S-structure $\mathcal{a}$ contains its elementary syntax if, and only if, $\mathcal{a}$ is acceptable in Moschavakis's sense (see Yiannis Moschovakis, *Elementary Induction on Abstract Structures* [Amsterdam: North-Holland, 1974]).[29] Among the fundamental structures are found the structures which, in Bourbaki's words, are "at the basis of classical Mathematics"[30]: simply infinite systems in Dedekind's sense, or progressions (isomorphic to $\mathbf{N}$)[31]; infinite, cyclic groups (isomorphic to $\mathbf{Z}$); prime fields of characteristic zero (isomorphic to $\mathbf{Q}$); complete ordered fields[32] (isomorphic to $\mathbf{R}$); algebraically closed, connected, locally compact topological fields (isomorphic to

C); noncommutative, connected, locally compact topological division rings (isomorphic to the division ring of quaternions **H**); three-dimensional Euclidean spaces (isomorphic to the space of classical Euclidean geometry). But there are others, which never held the attention of the author of the *Elements*, like, for example, $\langle V_\mu, \in \rangle$, where μ is the nth ($n \geq 1$) (strongly) inaccessible, or (strongly) Mahlo's, or weakly compact cardinal, and V_μ the μ-th level of the cumulative hierarchy of types (models of ZFC axiomatic set theory).[33]

4.1.2. Let $\mathcal{L}$ be a fundamental IF language. We wish to demonstrate that the (coded) notions of logical truth, of logical implication and of logical equivalence for $\mathcal{L}$ are not definable in $\mathcal{L}$ (for the interpretation under consideration) and, *a fortiori*, that the notions in question are not adequately definable in $\mathcal{L}$, no matter what criterion of adequacy is decided upon.

Let us use "logic" in a Church-like sense[34]: IF logic has infinitely many individual constants and, for any $n > 0$, infinitely many n-ary predicate and function symbols. Every IF sentence has its logical form represented by a sentence of IF logic. A direct corollary of the theorem we want to prove is that the (coded) notions of logical truth, of logical implication, and of logical equivalence for IF logic are not definable in $\mathcal{L}$ (for the interpretation under consideration). Now a monolingual speaker of $\mathcal{L}$ should only be able to ask himself the question of the logical status of sentences he can understand, namely sentences of $\mathcal{L}$, so Hintikka does not need the strong definability result (concerning IF logic), but only the weak one (concerning $\mathcal{L}$), which is correspondingly more difficult to disprove. That is why we shall begin by the direct corollary.

Recall (as a corollary of results obtained by Enderton and by Walkoe, referred to on many an occasion by Hintikka)[35] that any Σ^1_1 formula s can be "translated back" (relatively to $s| \rightarrow s^*$) into an IF formula, s', having the same signature, the translation back $s| \rightarrow s'$ being, moreover, effective. It therefore amounts to the same thing to show that the notions in question are not definable by a Σ^1_1-formula having the same signature as $\mathcal{L}$. We shall show more generally that these formulas are not even definable by any formula of finite order having the same signature as $\mathcal{L}$.[36]

THEOREM 1. *Let $\mathcal{L}$ be a fundamental IF language. The (coded) notions of logical truth, of logical implication, and of logical equivalence for IF logic are not definable by any formula of finite order having the same signature as $\mathcal{L}$, nor, a fortiori, by any formula of $\mathcal{L}$.*

DEMONSTRATION. It will suffice to show that this is so for the (coded) notion of logical truth. For, if the (coded) notion of logical implication, in other words the set of $<\ulcorner\varphi\urcorner, \ulcorner\psi\urcorner>$ such that φ and ψ are IF sentences and that ψ is true in every structure where φ is true, were definable by an ordinary formula, $\Phi[x,y]$, of finite order having the same signature as $\mathcal{L}$, it would be the same for the set of $\ulcorner\psi\urcorner$ such that ψ is an IF sentence true in every structure (the latter set would be definable by $\Phi[\ulcorner(\forall x)(x=x)\urcorner, y]^{37}$). The indefinability in question of the logical truth will likewise entail that of logical equivalence, i.e., of the set of $<\ulcorner\phi\urcorner, \ulcorner\psi\urcorner>$ such that ϕ and ψ are IF sentences true in the same structures.[38]

Recall that (as a corollary of the results of Hintikka, 1955), for any finite-order sentence s of signature S, there exists a Σ_1^1 sentence, $s^\square$, of signature $S^\square \supseteq S$ such that s is a logical truth if, and only if, $s^\square$ is a logical truth, the reduction $s|{\to}s^\square$ being, moreover, effective.

Let S be the signature of $\mathcal{L}$, $\mathcal{A}$ the interpretation structure of $\mathcal{L}$, $\mathcal{D}$ the domain of $\mathcal{A}$, $\mathcal{A} \vDash_T \ldots$ truth in Tarski's sense in $\mathcal{A}$, $\vDash_T \ldots$ logical truth in Tarski's sense, $\vDash_{GTS} \ldots$ logical truth in the sense of GTS. Let us assume that there exists a finite-order formula $\Psi[x]$ of signature S such that, for any $a \in \mathcal{D}$, $a \in \{\ulcorner\phi\urcorner / \phi$ is an IF sentence and $\vDash_{GTS} \phi\}$ if, and only if, $\mathcal{A} \vDash_T \Psi[a]$. Let θ be the finite-order sentence of signature S characterizing $\mathcal{A}$ up to isomorphism and ϕ a finite-order sentence of signature S. Under these conditions,

$$\mathcal{A} \vDash_T \phi \text{ iff } \vDash_T (\theta \Rightarrow \phi) \qquad \text{(by definition of } \theta\text{)}$$
$$\text{iff } \vDash_T (\theta \Rightarrow \phi)^\square \qquad \text{(by Hintikka 1955)}$$
$$\text{iff } \vDash_{GTS} ((\theta \Rightarrow \phi)^\square)' \qquad \text{(by Enderton 1970 and Walkoe 1970)}$$
$$\text{iff } \mathcal{A} \vDash_T \Psi[\underline{\ulcorner((\theta \Rightarrow \phi)^\square)'\urcorner}] \qquad \text{(by hypothesis)}$$

Now, the function $f\colon \mathbb{N} \to \mathbb{N}$ defined by:[39]

$$f(n) = \ulcorner((\theta \Rightarrow \phi)^\square)'\urcorner \text{ if } n = \ulcorner\phi\urcorner, \text{ where } \phi \text{ is a finite-order sentence}$$
of signature S,
$$f(n) = 0 \text{ otherwise}$$

is recursive, therefore a result of Moschovakis 1974 (p. 67) implies that its graph is definable in $\mathcal{A}$ by an ordinary first-order formula $\vartheta[x, y]$ of signature S, since $\mathcal{A}$ is acceptable (by definition of $\mathcal{L}$).[40] Let us define $T[x]$ as $(\exists y)(\vartheta[x, y] \wedge \Psi[y])$. So, for any finite-order sentence ϕ of signature S, $\mathcal{A} \vDash_T \phi$ if, and only if, $\mathcal{A} \vDash_T T[\ulcorner\phi\urcorner]$, therefore $\mathcal{A} \vDash_T (\phi \Leftrightarrow T[\ulcorner\phi\urcorner])$. The ω-order language of signature S (interpreted in $\mathcal{A}$) would contain a truth predicate for itself, namely $T[x]$, which Tarski's negative theorem (§1.2, (c')) forbids. (QED)

4.1.3. Let us come now to the main result that we wanted to prove, namely that the (coded) notions of logical truth, of logical implication, and of logical equivalence for $\mathcal{L}$ are not definable in $\mathcal{L}$ (for the interpretation under consideration). Indeed, we would like to prove, more generally, that they are not even so by any formula of finite order having the same signature as $\mathcal{L}$. This is what we intend to do but for a slight restriction that we shall go back on in §4.1.4.

THEOREM 2. *Let $\mathcal{L}$ be a fundamental IF language with at least two predicate symbols. The (coded) notions of logical truth, of logical implication, and of logical equivalence for $\mathcal{L}$ are not definable by any formula of finite order having the same signature as $\mathcal{L}$, nor, a fortiori, by any formula of $\mathcal{L}$.*

DEMONSTRATION. Again, it will suffice to show that this is so for the (coded) notion of logical truth. Using the same notations as before, let $cl(\varphi)$, where φ is a finite-order S-sentence, be the purely logical finite-order monadic closure of φ obtained, first, by quantifying universally (as if they were variables) all the nonlogical symbols of φ (respecting arities, of course), and then by ascending in type to find, using classical effective methods,[41] a monadic higher-order sentence that is a logical truth if, and only if, φ is a logical truth.[42] Theorems 5 and 6 of Montague (1965) imply that, for any finite-order monadic S-sentence φ, we can by an effective procedure find a Σ_1^1-sentence $\varphi^{\blacktriangle}$ of signature $S \cup \{\in, P\}$, where $\{\in, P\} \not\subseteq S$, P is a 1-place predicate symbol, $\in$ a 2-place predicate symbol, such that φ is a logical truth if, and only if, $\varphi^{\blacktriangle}$ is a logical truth.

Let us assume that there exists a finite-order formula $\Psi[x]$ of signature S such that, for any $a \in \mathcal{D}$, $a \in \{\ulcorner \varphi \urcorner / \varphi \in \mathcal{L} \wedge \vDash_{GTS} \varphi\}$ if, and only if, $\mathcal{A} \vDash_T \Psi[a]$. Let θ be the finite-order sentence of signature S characterizing $\mathcal{A}$ up to isomorphism and φ a finite-order sentence of signature S. Under these conditions,

$$\mathcal{A} \vDash_T \varphi \text{ iff } \vDash_T (\theta \Rightarrow \varphi) \text{ (by definition of } \theta)$$
$$\text{iff } \vDash_T cl(\theta \Rightarrow \varphi) \text{ (by definition of } cl)$$
$$\text{iff } \vDash_T (cl(\theta \Rightarrow \varphi))^{\blacktriangle} \text{ (by Montague 1965)}$$

But $(cl(\theta \Rightarrow \varphi))^{\blacktriangle}$ is a Σ_1^1-sentence of signature $\{\in, P\}$, since the signature of $cl(\theta \Rightarrow \varphi)$ is empty. $\mathcal{A}$ being acceptable, by definition of $\mathcal{L}$, one could prove that there can not be only unary predicate symbols in S.[43] Thus S contains at least a n-ary predicate symbol G, where $n > 1$. By hypothesis, S contains at least another n-ary predicate symbol F, where $n \geq 1$. But it is easy to see that the Σ_1^1-sentence $((cl(\theta \Rightarrow \varphi))^{\blacktriangle})^{\clubsuit}$ of signature $\{G, F\} \subseteq S$ obtained by replacing each occurrence of (an atomic formula of the form) '$\in(v, w)$' ('$P(z)$', respectively) in $(cl(\theta \Rightarrow \varphi))^{\blacktriangle}$ by an occurrence of '$G(v, w, v, \ldots, v)$' ('$F(z, z, \ldots, z)$', respectively), where v, w, z are first-order variables, is such that:

$$\vDash_T (cl(\theta \Rightarrow \varphi))^{\blacktriangle} \text{ iff } \vDash_T ((cl(\theta \Rightarrow \varphi))^{\blacktriangle})^{\clubsuit} \text{ (by definition of } \clubsuit)$$
$$\text{iff } \vDash_{GTS} (((cl(\theta \Rightarrow \varphi))^{\blacktriangle})^{\clubsuit})' \text{ (by Enderton and Walkoe)}$$
$$\text{iff } \mathcal{A} \vDash_T \Psi[\ulcorner (((cl(\theta \Rightarrow \varphi))^{\blacktriangle})^{\clubsuit})' \urcorner] \text{ (by hypothesis, since}$$
$$(((cl(\theta \Rightarrow \varphi))^{\blacktriangle})^{\clubsuit})' \text{ is a sentence of } \mathcal{L}).$$

The end of the proof is perfectly analogous to that of theorem 1. (QED)

4.1.4. Let us go back on the restriction concerning predicate symbols in Theorem 2. As we have seen, one can already prove that there is at least an n-ary predicate symbol, where $n > 1$, in any fundamental language. Thus we could obtain the intended theorem in its full generality if we could dispense with the unary predicate symbol P involved in Montague's result. But $\varphi^\blacktriangle$ is logically equivalent to a sentence of the form 'T $\Rightarrow$ ...', where T is a set theory with *Urelemente* and P the predicate (representing) 'is a set' in T. Standard set-theoretical methods relating set theories with *Urelemente* to set theories without *Urelemente* teach us that, loosely speaking, what can be done (at least up to the equivalidity involved here) with *Urelemente* can be done without *Urelemente*. We are thus led to conjecture that the (small) restriction in Theorem 2 is in fact unnecessary.

4.2. Let us accept that conjecture, or, if one prefers, just for the sake of brevity, let us omit that restriction in what follows. No fundamental IF language contains its own model theory and, in particular, no fundamental IF language can express the model-theoretical criterion of adequacy of its internal definition of truth. But the ineffability of such a criterion was only demonstrated for those languages whose interpretation structure is fundamental. What would happen if the interpretation structure of an IF language containing its elementary syntax were not fundamental?

And first of all, are there any such structures? Yes, it is easy to see that some very large structures are not fundamental.[44] Thus, languages containing their elementary syntax interpreted within such structures also exist, for languages containing their elementary syntax interpreted in structures of arbitrarily large cardinality exist.[45] But one would like to know whether there are smaller nonfundamental structures, for example, denumerable ones. The answer is yes, and is indeed provable as a corollary of Theorem 1.[46]

Be that as it may, let $\mathcal{L}$ be an IF language containing its elementary syntax. Let us formulate the question again to ask: If the interpretation structure of $\mathcal{L}$ is not fundamental, does $\mathcal{L}$ contain its own model theory, and in particular, can it express the model-theoretical criterion of adequacy of its internal definition of truth? This is not known. But if $\mathcal{L}$ is fundamental, one does know it, and the answer is no, and that is enough for us (for this essay).

4.3. On the whole, the transition from ordinary fundamental languages to fundamental IF languages of the same signature is far from being enough to overcome the ineffability of (coded versions of) semantical notions for these languages in themselves. If the initial ordinary languages are first-order ones, the transition in question even adds a new bit of ineffability, since the notions of logical truth, of logical implication, and of logical equivalence for these languages *are* definable (up to a coding) within these languages themselves.

One might hope to find a way out in changing the notions of logical truth, implication, and equivalence for IF languages. The following table takes an inventory of the naturally conceivable notions for such languages. It must be read by starting from the notions of the central column, in terms of which those of the lateral columns are defined.

Logical Truth	Logical Implication	Logical Equivalence
$\models_1 \psi$ (i.e. for every φ, $\varphi \models_1 \psi$) truth in every structure **Undefinable**	$\varphi \models_1 \psi$ preservation of truth and nonfalsity **Undefinable**	$\varphi \models_1 \psi$ (i.e. $\varphi \models_1 \psi$ and $\psi \models_1 \varphi$) same value in every structure **Undefinable**
$\models_2 \psi$ (i.e. for every φ, $\varphi \models_2 \psi$) truth in every structure **Undefinable**	$\varphi \models_2 \psi$ preservation of truth **Undefinable**	$\varphi \models_2 \psi$ (i.e. $\varphi \models_2 \psi$ and $\psi \models_2 \varphi$) truth in the same structures **Undefinable**
$\models_3 \psi$ (i.e. for every φ, $\varphi \models_3 \psi$) nonfalsity in every structure **Definable**	$\varphi \models_3 \psi$ preservation of nonfalsity **Undefinable**	$\varphi \models_3 \psi$ (i.e. $\varphi \models_3 \psi$ and $\psi \models_3 \varphi$) nonfalsity in the same structures **Undefinable**
$\models_4 \psi$ (i.e. for every φ, $\varphi \models_4 \psi$) nonfalsity in every structure **Definable**	$\varphi \models_4 \psi$ passage from truth to false in no structure **Definable**	$\varphi \models_4 \psi$ (i.e. $\varphi \models_4 \psi$ and $\psi \models_4 \varphi$) no structure where one sentence is true and the other false **Definable**

The transition from a row to a lower row does not always imply a weakening: in the left column, the notions of the first (third, respectively) and second (fourth, respectively) row are equivalent; and, in the central (right, respectively) column, the notions of the second and third row are incomparable; in all other cases, there is indeed a weakening.

The notions of the second row correspond to the choice of Hintikka, and fall prey to undefinability Theorem 2. The same is true of the notions of the first row ($\models_2 \psi$ iff $\models_1 \psi$; and argument analogous to that of the first paragraph of the proof of Theorem 1). The same is also true, on the third row, of the central notion ($\varphi \models_2 \psi$ iff $\sim\!\psi \models_3 \sim\!\varphi$) and of the right one ($\varphi \dashv_2 \psi$ iff $\sim \varphi \dashv_3 \sim\!\psi$). All the other (coded) notions of the table are definable in any IF language containing its elementary syntax, since the left one on the third row is definable (as a corollary of a remark of Hintikka),[47] and thus the notions of the fourth row are also definable ($\models_4 \psi$ iff $\models_3 \psi$; $\varphi \models_4 \psi$ iff $\models_3 \varphi \to \psi$; $\varphi \dashv_4 \psi$ iff $\models_3 (\varphi \to \psi) \wedge (\psi \to \varphi)$).

So, among all these notions, the only ones that a monolingual speaker of an IF language $\mathcal{L}$ containing its elementary syntax could use to express a model-theoretical criterion of adequacy for his own definition of truth for $\mathcal{L}$ in $\mathcal{L}$ would be those of the fourth row. But these notions are so weak (for example, $\models_4$ (2) [see section 2.1]), whereas (2) is true only in structures having just one element) that such a criterion would hardly correspond to an adequacy worthy of the name.

One could also think, as Hintikka himself does, to solve problems other than the one interesting us here, which he completely neglects, of going from IF languages to *extended* or even *verifunctionally extended* IF languages, obtained by adding a classical negation operator in a more or less restrictive way. But, however interesting such extensions might otherwise be, they would be of no help here. On the contrary, not only would the preceding negative result still hold, obviously, but the fundamental result of Hintikka's book, namely the definability of an adequate truth predicate for an IF language within this very language, would *no longer* hold, no more than would the theorem of compactness, the downward theorem of Löwenheim-Skolem, and Craig's interpolation lemma.

IF logic is certainly one of Hintikka's most fascinating contributions to philosophy, but it does not enable one to exorcise Tarski's curse. Even after *The Principles of Mathematics Revisited*, the ghost of Tarski's hierarchy is again and still with us.

PHILIPPE DE ROUILHAN AND SERGE BOZON
CENTRE NATIONAL DE LA RECHERCHE SCIENTIFIQUE UNIVERSITY OF PARIS I
UNIVERSITY OF PARIS I (PANTHÉON-SORBONNE) (PANTHÉON-SORBONNE)
AUGUST 2003 AUGUST 2003

NOTES

The main ideas of this essay date back to the early 2000s. They were the subject of talks by either of us on May 22, 2000 (in Prof. Hintikka's presence) and January 15, 2001 at the Institut d'Histoire et de Philosophie des Sciences et des Techniques, then on June 3, 2001 in Munich (international conference *One*

Hundred Years of Russell's Paradox), and October 1, 2002 in Nancy (international conference *Philosophical Insights into Logic and Mathematics*). We thank Gabriel Sandu and Denis Bonnay for fruitful exchanges regarding the issues under discussion here, and Yiannis Moschovakis for responding to some technical questions about acceptable structures. We are specially indebted to Solomon Feferman, who thoroughly read a previous version of our paper and led us to improve it on many points. Claire Ortiz Hill helped us to express our thoughts in English.

1.   Saul Kripke, "Outline of a Theory of Truth," *Journal of Philosophy* 72 (1975): 690–716.

2.   Jaakko Hintikka, *The Principles of Mathematics Revisited* (Cambridge University Press, 1996), p. 129. [Hereafter cited as *PMR*.]

3.   Unless otherwise mentioned, the "languages" in question in this article are *interpreted* languages, as in Tarski, but in contrast to what was done at the time, the ideas of an axiom system and of rules of inference are not included in the notion of language.

4.   Or, more generally, containing a coded version of it. To lighten our prose, the point regarding possible coding of elementary syntactic notions is systematically implied in what follows except in section 4.

5.   The notions involved (elementary syntax, translation, essential logical richness) obviously merit precise characterization. Suffice it to say here that such a characterization is harder to arrive at than is generally thought. We shall return to the question of elementary syntax in section 4.1.1.

6.   (a) Tarski spoke in terms of "logical consequence" rather than "logical deducibility," but that was in a proof-theoretical sense. Whence our change of terminology. As in Tarski, far from being restricted to the first-order predicate calculus, in what follows, the logical deducibility concerned will refer to a background higher-order logic that is presumed to be available. (b) A result of this kind appears for the first time in the Polish version of Tarski's paper on truth, (Alfred Tarski, *Projecie prawdy w jezykach nauk dedukcyjnych* [*The Concept of Truth in the Languages of the Deductive Sciences*], Warsaw, 1933). In the postscript to the German version, "Der Warheitsbegriff in der formalisierten Sprachen," *Studia Philosophica* 1 (1935): 261–405, it underwent a twofold transformation: not only would certain languages excluded earlier be taken into account from then on, but the logical form of the result also changed surreptitiously (regarding this twofold transformation, see Philippe de Rouilhan's article, "Tarski et l'universalité de la logique: Remarques sur le post-scriptum au '*Warheitsbegriff*,'" *Le formalisme en question. Le tournant des années* 30, ed. F. Nef and D. Vernant [Paris: Vrin, 1998], pp. 85–102.)

7.   The result appears for the first time in the German version of the paper.

8.   In this presentation, we are departing significantly from what Tarski literally did. He only appealed to the axiomatic method in view of a positive result, namely, that it is possible to introduce a truth predicate for $\mathcal{L}$ as primitive in a metalanguage of the *same* essential logical richness as $\mathcal{L}$ and to govern its use by an adequate, consistent system of axioms.

9. When it is a matter, as it is here, of a (classical) language's ability to contain its own adequate truth predicate, we obviously presume the translation involved to be homophonic, or, as we prefer to say, homographic. In the counter-examples involved in Solomon Feferman, "Arithmetization of Metamathematics in a General Setting," *Fundamenta Mathematicae* 49 (1960): 35–92, the translations are *not* homographic. (Cf. Peter Hájek and Pavel Pudlák, *Metamathematics of First-Order Arithmetic* [Berlin: Springer-Verlag, 1993], §III.2.)

10. In the counter-example proposed by Gupta in 1982, the language in question does *not* contain (all) its elementary syntax. See Anil Gupta, "Truth and Paradox," *Journal of Philosophical Logic* 11 (1982): 1–60, p. 15; Anil Gupta and Nuel Belnap, *The Revision Theory of Truth* (Cambridge, Mass.: MIT Press, 1993), p. 76.

11. See also, the same year (and independently), Robert L. Martin and Peter W. Woodruff, "On Representing 'True-in-*L*' in *L*," *Philosophia* 5 (1975): 213–17, but Kripke's more impressive article is rightly the one that has best stood the test of time. See also, later, Hans G. Herzberger, "Notes on Naive Semantics," *Journal of Philosophical Logic* 11 (1982): 61–102; Gupta, "Truth and Paradox"; Nuel Belnap, "Gupta's Rule of Revision Theory of Truth," *Journal of Philosophical Logic* 11 (1982): 103–16; Solomon Feferman, "Toward Useful Type-free Theories I," *Journal of Symbolic Logic* 49 (1984): 75–111; Keith Simmons, "On a Medieval Solution to the Liar Paradox," *History and Philosophy of Logic* 8 (1987): 121–40; Vann McGee, *Truth, Vagueness and Paradox* (Indianapolis: Hackett, 1991); Gupta and Belnap, *The Revision Theory of Truth*; Simmons, *Universality and the Liar: An Essay on Truth and the Diagonal Argument* (Cambridge: Cambridge University Press, 1993); and so on.

12. Hintikka, "Defining Truth, the Whole Truth, and Nothing But the Truth," *Reports from the Department of Philosophy of the University of Helsinki* 2, reprinted in revised form in Hintikka, *Selected Papers*, vol. 2, *Lingua Universalis* vs. *Calculus Ratiocinator: An Ultimate Presupposition of Twentieth-Century Philosophy* (Dordrecht: Kluwer Academic Publishers, 1997), pp. 48–103.

13. The careless way in which this book was written up has already been sufficiently disparaged elsewhere. There is no need to bring this up again. In this essay, the argument turns only on essential issues.

14. A historical remark is necessary. One could object that people like Myhill, Lévy, and Smorynsky had already proved the existence of nonclassical languages containing an adequate truth predicate for themselves. (See John Myhill, "A System Which Can Define its Own Truth," *Fundamenta Mathematicae* 37 [1950]: 190–92; Azriel Lévy, *A Hierarchy of Formulas in Set Theory*, Memoirs of the American Mathematical Society, vol. 57 [1965], Providence, R.I.; Craig Smorynski, "The Incompleteness Theorems," in *Handbook of Mathematical Logic*, ed. J. Barwise [Amsterdam: North-Holland, 1977], pp. 821–65.) But, since the mere morphology of those languages lacks the classical closure properties, none of them being closed by universal quantification and by negation, all those languages are deviant in a sense that, to our mind, invalidates them. In short, their formation rules are *ad hoc*: these languages are mere "bits" of languages, not "real" languages. A detail can cloud the judgment. It happens that, in his book, to simplify matters, Hintikka limits

THE TRUTH OF IF

himself to languages (the IF languages) that are of course closed by quantification, but not by (GTS-)negation. However, the transition to languages closed by (GTS-) negation does not harbor any basic difficulty, and there is no break between the body of the book and the appendix in which Sandu shows that a certain language closed by all its (GTS-)logical operations contains an adequate definition of a truth predicate for itself. (See Gabriel Sandu, "IF First-Order Logic, Kripke, and 3-Valued Logic," appendix to *PMR*, pp. 254–70.) Hintikka's and Sandu's results therefore definitely constitute a breakthrough, contrary to what may have been said here or there, and no matter the limitation of the expressive power of IF languages to a certain fragment of corresponding second-order languages.

15. The notion goes back to Carnap, 1947 (Rudolf Carnap, *Meaning and Necessity: A Study in Semantics and Modal Logic* [Chicago: The University of Chicago Press, 1947; 2nd ed. 1956]). Unlike Carnap, there is no question for us here of meaning postulates. So, two monadic predicates have the same intension if, and only if, the corresponding formal equivalence is *logically* true, while they have the same extension if, and only if, the formal equivalence is true *simpliciter*.

16. Even if one takes into account the fact that when Sandu speaks of "definition," he, like Hintikka, is thinking of an "adequate definition." See Gabriel Sandu, op. cit. note 14, p. 267.

17. Hintikka, in his book (but not Sandu, in the appendix), requires that the formulas of $\mathcal{L}$ be in "the normal form for negation," i.e., that the negation only concerns atomic constituents. See note 14 above.

18. The example is from Hintikka and Sandu, "Game-theoretical Semantics," in *Handbook of Logic and Language*, ed. J. Van Benthem and A. Ter Meulen (Amsterdam: Elsevier, 1997), p. 369.

19. Michal Krinicky, "Hierarchies of Partially Ordered Connectives and Quantifiers," *Mathematical Logic Quarterly* 39 (1993): 287–94. This reduction of Krynicki presupposes that $\mathcal{L}$ contains the definition of an *ordered pair* functor, which is a consequence of the hypothesis according to which $\mathcal{L}$ contains its elementary syntax.

20. Herbert B. Enderton, "Finite Partially-ordered Quantifiers," *Zeitschrift für mathematische Logik und Grundlagen der Mathematik* 16 (1970): 393–97; William Walkoe, "Finite Partially Ordered Quantification," *Journal of Symbolic Logic* 35 (1970): 535–55. One sees that, strictly speaking, Hintikka should have extended the translation function to open formulas of $\mathcal{L}$. That presents no fundamental difficulty.

21. This is to be understood in a weak sense, as opposed to a logical equivalence in a stronger sense, which would in addition involve falsity in the same structures. Likewise, the notion of logical implication below will be taken in the weak sense of truth preservation from the antecedent to the consequent, as opposed to a stronger sense which would in addition involve the falsity preservation from the consequent to the antecedent. See below, section 4.3.

22. Hintikka, *PMR*, p. 129.

23. Hintikka repeats this first statement on several occasions in the remainder of *PMR* (pp. 163, 171, 204, 205). He is never more specific about its content, nor does he present the least argument in support of it.

24. Hintikka, *PMR*, pp. 41, 119.

25. Ibid., pp. 138–40.

26. Tapani Hyttinen and Gabriel Sandu, "Deflationism and Arithmetical Truth," *Dialectica* 58 (2004): 413–26.

27. About this reservation, once again see the article "Tarski et l'universalité de la logique" (cited in note 6).

28. A signature is elementary if, and only if, it is the signature of a first-order language. One will note that many-sorted languages are not ruled out here. To simplify the exposition, we will, without loss of generality, assume in what follows that all the signatures are relational, where a signature S is relational if, and only if, S does not contain function symbols.

29. To speak loosely, an acceptable structure is a structure with a coding scheme built into it. Let us add incidentally that (among much stronger results, see S. J. Garland, "Second-order Cardinal Characterizability," in *Axiomatic Set Theory, Proceedings of Symposia in Pure Mathematics*, vol. 13, II [Providence, R.I.: American Mathematical Society, 1974], pp. 127–46) the structures $\aleph_n$ or $\beth_n$ ($n \geq 0$), of empty signature, are characterizable up to isomorphism by purely logical finite-order sentences and that, by a result of Johan van Benthem and Kees Doets ("Higher-Order Logic," in *Handbook of Philosophical Logic 1*, ed. D. Gabbay and F. Guenthner [Dordrecht: D. Reidel, 1983], p. 300), the set of (codes of the) purely logical IF logical truths is definable in any IF language containing its elementary syntax.

30. Nicolas Bourbaki, *Eléments de mathématique*, Livre I, *Théorie des ensembles*, Actualités scientifiques et industrielles, no. 1258 (Paris: Hermann, 1957), ch. 4, ("Structures"), §1, n°5. (English version in: Bourbaki, *Elements of Mathematics: Theory of Sets*, Adiwes International Series in Mathematics, ed. A. J. Lohwater [the translator is unnamed] [Paris: Hermann, and Reading, Mass.: Addison-Wesley Publishing, 1968].)

31. $\mathbf{N} = \langle \mathbb{N}, 0, S \rangle$, where S is the successor relation. For the following examples, we likewise assume that $\mathbf{Z}$, $\mathbf{Q}$, $\mathbf{R}$, $\mathbf{C}$, $\mathbf{H}$ and the space of classical Euclidean geometry have been appropriately defined.

32. Bourbaki speaks of "the structure of a complete *Archimedean* ordered field" (loc. cit., our emphasis), but the statement is redundant.

33. See, for example, Stewart Shapiro, *Foundations without Foundationalism* (Oxford: Clarendon Press, 1991), chs. 4, 6; and Jouko Väänänen, "Second-order Logic and Foundations of Mathematics," *Bulletin of Symbolic Logic* 7 (2001): 504–20, 516.

34. Alonzo Church, *Introduction to Mathematical Logic*, revised and enlarged ed. (Princeton: Princeton University Press, 1956), §30.

35. Enderton, "Finite Partially-ordered Quantifiers"; Walkoe, "Finite Partially Ordered Quantification"; Hintikka, *PMR*.

36. Väänänen, "Second-order Logic and Foundations of Mathematics," indirectly proves an abstract and strong result (§8, Corollary 4) that implies, among other things, the ineffability of the (coded) notion of logical truth for any IF language with at least a binary predicate symbol in the ordinary arithmetical language of order ω (and therefore in the IF arithmetical language itself). Our theorem I is a routine generalization of this last limitation that we shall prove directly by

appealing to classical methods in the literature devoted to higher-order logic—cf., e.g. Georg Kreisel and Jean-Louis Krivine, *Elements of Mathematical Logic: Model Theory* (Amsterdam: North-Holland, 1967), ch. 7. The irony is that the person to which the principal one of these methods is due is none other than Hintikka himself in a 1955 paper ("Reductions in the Theory of Types," *Acta Philosophica Fennica* 8: 61–115) that is as remarkable as it is underestimated. Let us add some historical remarks: Montague proved (among stronger results) that the set (of codes) of Σ_1^1- logical truths does not appear anywhere in the whole Kleene arithmetical hierarchy (i.e., is not Σ_n^m for any $n, m \in \omega$); in the first paper devoted to branching quantifiers to come after Henkin's initial one, Enderton inferred from Montague's result that the set (of codes) of logical truths of a language with such quantifiers and at least one binary predicate symbol is not Σ_n^m for any $n, m \in \omega$. But one should not forget that IF logic is not at all a notational variant of the logic with branching quantifiers L^*, the metalogical properties of the latter being very different from those of the former: IF logic, contrary to L^*, is compact, has the interpolation property, the downward Löwenheim-Skolem property. See Richard Montague, "Reductions of Higher-order Logic," in *The Theory of Models (Proceedings of the 1963 International Symposium at Berkeley)* (Amsterdam: North-Holland, 1965), pp. 251–64; Leon Henkin, "Some Remarks on Infinitely Long Formulas," *Infinitistic Methods, Proceedings of the Symposium on Foundations of Mathematics, Warsaw, 2–9 September 1959* (Oxford: Pergamon Press, 1961), pp. 167–83; Enderton, "Finite Partially-ordered Quantifiers."

37. Naturally, ' $\ulcorner(\forall x)(x=x)\urcorner$ ' stands for the numeral of the code $\ulcorner(\forall x)(x=x)\urcorner$ of the sentence '$(\forall x)(x = x)$'. Analogous notations follow.

38. The notions concerned (logical truth, etc.) are definitely those of Hintikka (*PMR*, pp. 65, 67). The indefinability of logical implication obviously entails that of logical consequence.

39. $\mathcal{L}$ containing its elementary syntax, we can use its coding scheme to code at once $\mathcal{L}$ and the ω-order S-language.

40. Identified here are N and its copy in $\mathcal{D}$, copy whose existence is guaranteed by the fundamental character of $\mathcal{L}$ (cf. clause (b) in section 4.1.1, and Moschovakis, *Elementary Induction on Abstract Structures*, ch. 5).

41. See Shapiro, *Foundations without Foundationalism*, ch. 6, note 2.

42. A monadic sentence is a sentence whose higher-order variables are all unary predicate variables. We will use some results of Montague ("Reductions of Higher-order Logic"), who does not countenance predicate variables of arity > 1 into his ω-order logic, hence our choice of *cl*.

43. There is no acceptable structure $\langle \mathcal{D}, R_1, R_2, \ldots, R_n \rangle$, $n \geq 1$, where each R_i, $1 \leq i \leq n$, is a subset of $\mathcal{D}$. The proof of this, which uses only standard model-theoretical techniques, will be omitted (we are grateful to Yiannis Moschovakis here). This implies of course that S can not be empty.

44. The reason for this is very simple. Let S be a signature. Then the class of finite-order S-sentences being a set, the class R of these sentences that are satisfiable is also a set. With each element x of R, let us associate the smallest cardinal that is the cardinal of a model of x. By the replacement axiom schema, the

class C of such cardinals is also a set. Let κ be the least upper bound (i.e., the union) of C, and $\mathcal{a}$ an S-structure of cardinality $> \kappa$. If $\mathcal{a}$ were characterizable up to isomorphism by a finite-order S-sentence, then an element z of R would exist, all the models of which would have the same cardinal as $\mathcal{a}$. However, by definition of κ, z has a model of cardinal $\leq \kappa$. (QED) This proof appeals to a routine technique (passed down from Hanf and Hasenjaeger) in abstract model theory. (See William Hanf, "Models of Languages with Infinitely Long Expressions," *International Congress for Logic, Methodology and Philosophy of Science* [Stanford, Calif.: Stanford University Press, 1962], 24; and Gisbert Hasenjaeger, "On Löwenheim-Skolem-type Insufficiencies of Second-order Logic," in *Sets, Models and Recursion Theory*, ed. J. Crossley [Amsterdam: North-Holland, 1967], pp. 173–82.) Let us add that κ is a cardinal whose size is amply underdetermined by ZFC, for classical results imply that, for any $n > 0$, κ is greater than the nth (strongly) inaccessible and than the nth measurable cardinal, if such cardinals exist. Although it is possible to prove in ZFC that the existence of (strongly) inaccessible or measurable cardinals is not provable in ZFC (if ZFC is consistent), let us recall that it is not possible to prove in ZFC (if ZFC is consistent) that their inexistence is not provable in ZFC. We are thus doubly "blind" with regard to the size of κ.

45. Acceptable structures of arbitrarily large cardinality in fact exist.

46. Let $\mathcal{L}$ be the IF language of signature $\langle 0, S, +, \times, P \rangle$, where P is an unary predicate symbol, interpreted in $\mathbf{N}^* = \langle \mathbb{N}, 0, S, +, \times, \mathrm{Val}_{\mathrm{IF}} \rangle$, where $\mathrm{Val}_{\mathrm{IF}}$ is the set of (codes of) IF logical truths. The (coded) notion of logical truth for IF logic is definable in $\mathcal{L}$, therefore, by Theorem 1, $\mathcal{L}$ is not fundamental. But $\mathcal{L}$ contains its elementary syntax, since $\langle \mathbb{N}, 0, S, +, \times \rangle$, and *a fortiori* $\langle \mathbb{N}, 0, S, +, \times, \mathrm{Val}_{\mathrm{IF}} \rangle$, is acceptable. So $\mathbf{N}^*$ is not fundamental. But $\mathbf{N}^*$ is denumerable. (QED)

It is natural to ask the more general question: Are there denumerable structures that are not categorically characterizable by any set of finite-order sentences? Surprisingly, this question turns out to have no answer in ZFC. Let us demonstrate this.

Let S be a finite signature. Two S-structures are ω-equivalent if, and only if, any finite-order S-sentence true in one is true in the other. Now, Miklos Ajtai, in "Isomorphism and Higher-order Equivalence," *Annals of Mathematical Logic* 16 (1979): 181–203, proves the undecidability in ZFC of:

(a) If two denumerable S-structures are ω-equivalent, then they are isomorphic. Let us show that (a) is equivalent to:

(b) Any denumerable S-structure is characterizable up to isomorphism by a set of finite-order S-sentences.

Let $\mathcal{a}$ be a denumerable S-structure, $\mathrm{Th}(\mathcal{a})_\omega$ the set of finite-order S-sentences satisfied in $\mathcal{a}$ and $\mathcal{a}'$ a S-model of $\mathrm{Th}(\mathcal{a})_\omega$. One easily verifies that $\mathrm{Th}(\mathcal{a})_\omega = \mathrm{Th}(\mathcal{a}')_\omega$. Therefore, by (a), $\mathcal{a}'$ is isomorphic to $\mathcal{a}$, whence (b). Consequently, (a) implies (b). Reciprocally, let $\mathcal{a}$ and $\mathcal{a}'$ be two ω-equivalent denumerable S-structures. By (b), $\mathcal{a}$ is characterizable up to isomorphism by a set of finite-order S-sentences T. Thus $\mathcal{a}'$ is a model of T, therefore $\mathcal{a}'$ is isomorphic to $\mathcal{a}$, whence (a). Consequently, (b) implies (a). (QED)

47. See *PMR*, p. 68. A sentence φ is true-or-neutral in every structure iff its GTS negation $\sim\varphi$ is not true in any structure. Now Hintikka (*loc. cit.*) points out

that a complete and effective *"disproof"* procedure exists for the set of unsatisfiable IF sentences. It follows that the set of the (codes of) IF sentences true-or-neutral in every structure is recursively enumerable, and so definable in ordinary arithmetical first-order languages, and *a fortiori* in any IF language containing its elementary syntax. Of course, this implies that the set of (codes of) logical truths in the sense of the third row of any IF language $\mathcal{L}$ containing its elementary syntax is also definable in that very language. (QED)

REPLY TO PHILIPPE DE ROUILHAN
AND SERGE BOZON

There are two ways of responding to a critical paper like the one by Philippe de Rouilhan and Serge Bozon. (In what follows, I will refer to them as "the authors.") There are destructive responses, calculated to uncover the mistakes in the purported criticisms. There are also constructive ones, trying to place the disputed issues in a wider context. In my response, I will use both approaches. I will first show what is wrong in the authors' main argument. After that, I will try to place the entire bunch of issues they are discussing in the appropriate historical and conceptual context, including the authors' actual constructive results.[*]

The overall heading under which the authors' paper falls is the question whether we need a hierarchy of languages in order to deal with the notion of truth in explicit logical languages. Tarski showed in his famous impossibility theorem that truth is not definable for a formalized first-order language in the same language. Tarski assumed as a matter of course that the logic he was using is the received ("Frege-Russell") first-order logic. The usual way of trying to cope with the problem created by Tarski's result has been to postulate a hierarchy of increasingly rich languages. The concept of truth for one of them can only be defined in higher ones.

The need of such a hierarchy was disproved by the discovery of IF logic. Of course Tarski's theorem is correct as it stands, but it rests on the assumption that the logic used is the received first-order logic. Hence it does not apply to IF languages. Indeed, it turns out that if the syntax of an IF first-order language L can be expressed in L, for instance by means of Gödel numbering, then a truth predicate for L can be formulated in L itself. Hence no hierarchy of languages is needed in truth theory.

---

[*] Some of the formulations in the following paragraphs refer to an earlier version of the authors' paper, rather than the final one which was not available to me at the time. This does not make substantial differences to the argument, however.

As the title of the authors' paper shows, they are challenging this conclusion. As a part of doing so, they have to show that the definability result just mentioned does not amount to what it seems to do.

The purported conclusion of the authors' "general argument" is that the IF truth predicate "is nothing other than the translation back into [an IF language] L of a truth predicate for L adequately defined in [a metalanguage]" which is presumably an ordinary second-order language. Unfortunately, here the words "nothing other than" have no cognitive meaning. The problem here is a well-defined one. An IF first-order language L is a well-defined language with fully defined truth conditions. Let us assume that the syntax of L can be expressed in L itself, for instance, by means of Gödel numbering. Then the question whether the concept of truth for L can be defined in L has an absolutely clear meaning. It means asking whether there exists in L a formula T[x] such that, for any sentence S of L, it is the case that T[g(S)] if and only if it is the case that S. (Here g(S) is of course the Gödel number of S.) This is a question concerning the internal properties of the language L completely independent of the language in which it is discussed and proved. Hence the fact—assuming that it is a fact—that T[x] is a translational equivalent of a second-order formula is simply irrelevant to the question whether truth in L can be defined in L. It offers absolutely no basis for saying that F[x] is "nothing other than" a second-order formula in disguise (or in translation). Hence the only relevant response to the authors' "general argument" is: So what?

The authors' "general argument" is thus merely rhetorical. The announced issue of the authors' essay is whether a hierarchy of languages is needed for the purpose of defining truth in different languages. This issue is closed by a proof that a truth predicate is definable in an IF language strong enough to express its own syntax. The way in which this definability is proved is strictly irrelevant.

From this definability it follows that some aspects of the model theory of an IF language can be handled in the very same language. This should apply also to the argument that shows that the truth predicate actually does its job. What the authors flaunt is the fact that in my own expositions I reach the truth predicate by a line of thought which is not in terms of IF logic. But of course this happened merely in the interest of intelligibility, for the same reason (so to speak) that the great majority of proofs in expositions of recursive number theory are not strictly speaking proofs at all, but "proofs by Church's thesis." What the authors do is to insinuate that this somehow invalidates my result. Not only is this claim mistaken, the authors could easily have constructed a truth predicate by using only the resources of expression of IF first-order logic. Consider, in order to see this, the kind of truth predicate in which there is only one initial second-order existential quantifier.[1] One can formulate the same predicate in terms of IF logic by replacing this initial second-order existential quantifier by a suitable Henkin quantifier. One can then carry out the entire discussion in terms of the resulting IF predicate. This discussion can include the proof that the predicate so defined really defines truth. Admittedly, if we do this, our line of thought becomes less intuitive, but the kind of intuitiveness involved here is a matter of expository ease, not of a matter of the cogency of the argument.

All that this shows is nevertheless only that the particular arguments offered by the authors do not establish the negative conclusion the authors would like to draw. But what can be said of the overall problem that the authors pose? Is a hierarchy of languages necessitated by Tarski's impossibility theorem or by similar results? This theorem is formulated by the authors as Tarski's "negative result." It says, roughly, that in a language using the received first-order logic it is impossible to define a truth predicate. In order to do so, we have to resort to an "essentially richer" metalanguage. If this metalanguage is of the same kind as the original object language, defining a truth predicate for it requires a new ascent to a richer metalanguage, and so on. The authors argue that some hierarchy of this kind is unavoidable.

The first puzzling thing here in a wider perspective is the very notion of metalanguage. It is a concept forced on philosophers and logicians. In the late nineteenth century it was by and large assumed that philosophers can conduct their business in our common home language. And the same was required of the different logical languages that were proposed. If something is inexpressible in some presumed *lingua universalis*, then either that something was not real or else the language in question was not adequate. For instance, Russell was prepared to use the inexpressibility of some features of Frege's semantical theory in the same theory as a reason for rejecting the theory. Likewise he worried about his own theory of types because it did not seem expressible in the same type theory.

It was only when some absolutely crucial matters could not be expressed in a given language that the idea of a separate metalanguage became tempting. Russell proposed it as a desperate last resort for the purpose of avoiding the inexpressibility of what can only be shown but not said according to Wittgenstein's *Tractatus*. But even later, ambitious philosophers like Carnap could dream of a universal language that could incorporate its own metatheory. His dream was shattered by the results of Gödel and Tarski. In particular, Tarski's result of the undefinability of a truth predicate for a first-order language in the same language was generally taken to force on us a hierarchy of stronger and stronger metalanguages. The essay of Rouilhan and Bozon is calculated to argue for the inevitability of this hierarchy.

Now the absolutely crucial question in this entire area concerns the reasons a truth predicate cannot be defined in a first-order language (which is assumed to be rich enough for a formulation of its own syntax) for the same language. It might at first sight look like a most damaging criticism of the authors' essay that they do not offer or even attempt diagnosis of the reasons for the problem they are discussing. This apparent oversight may perhaps be excusable in light of the fact that no such diagnosis is to be found elsewhere in the literature, either, with the partial exception of my 1998 paper "Truth-definitions, Skolem Functions, and Axiomatic Set Theory."[2] Disappointingly, we do not find an adequate analysis of the reasons for the inexpressibility of truth even in Tarski's own exposition. Such a diagnostic analysis can be carried out by means of the play analogy I explain in my comment on Raymond Smullyan in this volume. Indeed, a diagnosis of the kind of impossibility Tarski's theorem expresses is briefly carried out there. The main idea can be recounted here, using an arithmetical language as a test case.

There is no inconsistency and indeed no problem in letting numbers serve two different functions, on the one hand as ordinary workday numbers and on the other hand as playing the role of arithmetical formulas. Not very much more is involved here that is not completely routine than a two-sorted language, the two "sorts" or domains being numbers in their two different uses, corresponding to the fictional universe of a play and to the real world of actors in their everyday life. It was explained in my reply to Smullyan what kind of self-reference is possible here. Moreover, it might seem that an arithmetical language has enough expressive power to formulate a truth predicate, that is, a predicate $T[x]$ of the Gödel number of a sentence S that $g(S)$ applies to $g(S)$ if and only if it is the case that S. But in formulating the predicate $T[x]$, calculated to codify truth, we have to quantify over numbers in their two roles (or, strictly speaking, in their role in the Gödelian drama and in their everyday life as numbers pure and simple). I have to use quantifiers whose variables operate in their playacting role to express the Gödel number $g(S)$ of S as a function of the numbers which codify the structure of S. But the variable x in the predicate $T[x]$ ranges over numbers as numbers *simpliciter*. For reasons explained in my response to Smullyan, here the "structural" quantifiers must be independent of x. This independence does not follow from the fact that the different variables are thought of as ranging over different domains, for the dependence relations between quantifiers do not depend on the classes of values they range over.

But there is in the received first-order logic no way of expressing that the structural quantifiers inside $T[x]$ must be independent of the variable x. This is the basic reason why a truth predicate cannot be defined for an ordinary first-order language in the same language. In spite of its simplicity and intuitiveness, this diagnosis reveals several things about the alleged role of Tarski's impossibility theorem as forcing us to resort to a hierarchy of languages.

First, it may perhaps be said that a language in which a desired truth predicate can be defined must be richer than the given "object language," if this object language is the one Tarski is using. But the diagnosis just outlined shows that only one very special kind of richness matters. What must be expressible (but is not expressible in the received first-order language) is the independence of quantifiers of each other and of free variables. To call this "essential richness" seems to me somewhat misleading. Any respectable logic of quantifiers should have this kind of richness.

Moreover, requiring this kind of richness does not create a hierarchy of languages. Once our first-order language is extended so as to allow expressing the independence of quantifiers, there is no need of extending the language further. Or, strictly speaking, no such reason is provided by Tarski's impossibility theorem. In this sense, the diagnosis we reached shows that there is no need of a Tarski hierarchy even if we start from received first-order languages.

All this pertains much more to the title of the authors' paper than to its content. What can be said of the constructive results of the two authors? It is not difficult to see the drift of their paper. They are changing the subject. They are raising questions about such metatheoretical concepts as logical truths instead of ordinary folks' notion of truth *simpliciter*. This means a step from the theory of truth to an essentially different kind of logical theorizing. We speak of logical truth only by courtesy of a pun, for logical truth is not a species of truth. Logical truth is, or at least can be looked upon, as an archetypal modal notion. Logical truth is not truth in any one world; it is truth in all possible worlds.

The authors prove two theorems that in different ways show that logical truth in an IF language is not expressible in the same language. These interesting and important theorems do not belong to the theory of truth, however, and certainly not to a discussion of whether or not Tarski-type results necessitate a hierarchy of languages. The notion of logical truth is a modal notion, and the authors' results belong to the theory of modal logic. They are in effect results showing that the modal notion of logical necessity cannot be captured syntactically. As such, they are parallel to Montague's important 1963 results.[3] The authors' results show that this Montagovian impossibility of capturing logical modalities syntactically cannot be avoided by switching from the received first-order logic to IF logic. This is not entirely surprising, for—as Montague brings out very well—his results are little more than generalizations of Gödel's incompleteness theorems. Now Gödel's incompleteness theorems, unlike Tarski's impossibility result, are essentially combinatorial, and hence cannot be overcome by enriching one's language semantically.

The authors are technically right when they say that their results show that not all metatheory of an IF language can be done in that same language. Both the observations just made show that the particular kind of impossibility they have in mind is of a kind essentially different from the kind of incompleteness that is at issue in the impossibility of truth definitions.

Moreover, impossibility of defining logical truth does not necessarily lead to a hierarchy of languages. Logical truth for an IF language can be discussed by first enriching it by adding to it contradictory negation ¬. Without entering any details, for each fragment of the resulting language, logical truth can be discussed in another fragment in which ¬ is allowed to occur in more complicated contexts. For this purpose, no step to a separate metalanguage is needed.

Thus in its strict sense Tarski's curse has been overcome. But the authors' essay may serve as a reminder that there may be other so far unexorcised spells cast over attempts to do modal theory for a language in the same object language.

J. H.

NOTES

1. Such a predicate is described in chapter 6 of my book, *The Principles of Mathematics Revisited* (Cambridge: Cambridge University Press, 1996).

2. "Truth-definitions, Skolem Functions, and Axiomatic Set Theory," *Bulletin of Symbolic Logic* 4 (1998): 303–37.

3. Richard Montagne, "Syntactical Treatments of Modality," *Acta Philosophica Fennica* 16 (1963): 153–67.

21

Martin Kusch

HINTIKKA ON HEIDEGGER AND THE UNIVERSALITY OF LANGUAGE

I

There are many things I admire about Jaakko Hintikka's philosophical oeuvre. But two features stand out. One is Hintikka's distinctive way of combining systematic philosophy with studies in the history of philosophy. The other is his unique ability to bridge the gap between "analytic" and "continental" traditions in contemporary Western philosophy. Both of these virtues are impressively displayed in Hintikka's recent work on the contrast between two conceptions of the semantic relations between language and the world. He calls these two conceptions "language as universal medium" and "language as calculus."

Over the last twenty-odd years, Hintikka has produced detailed studies of the history of these two conceptions in twentieth-century philosophy. He has demonstrated how crucial the universal-medium assumption was for Wittgenstein and Quine, and how the calculus conception has slowly emerged in model theory and logical semantics.[1] Hintikka has also suggested ways in which the distinction between the two positions might illuminate central junctures in continental philosophy. As Hintikka's student I was the beneficiary of these suggestions.[2]

During the 1990s Hintikka increasingly turned to evaluating the merits of the two views. In so doing, he has drawn on many aspects of his own earlier historical and systematic work, such as Game-Theoretical Semantics (GTS), Independence-Friendly (IF) Logic, and the interpretation of Kant's transcendental philosophy. In a nutshell, Hintikka's evaluation comes to this: the view of language as the universal medium has become obsolete and indefensible. Hintikka thinks that this result is particularly damaging for Heidegger and his followers; in Hintikka's view, the "hermeneutic" way of doing philosophy has been comprehensively refuted.[3]

In this essay, I want to investigate Hintikka's refutation of language as the universal medium. I am intrigued by Hintikka's arguments, but not (yet) fully convinced that my former teacher has clinched his case. My aim is to stimulate further discussion by suggesting ways in which Heidegger might defend his position against Hintikka. In so doing, I will have to cross the same divides—between systematic and historical philosophy, and between the continental and the analytic traditions—that Hintikka has bridged so successfully. Undoubtedly, my feeble attempt at negotiating these gulfs will not be equally impressive.

II

In his 1967 paper "Logic as Calculus and Logic as Language," Jean van Heijenoort contrasted two traditions in the recent history of logic.[4] The first takes logic to be a universal language, the second conceives of logic as a calculus, in the sense of being reinterpretable on a large scale like a calculus. Hintikka has generalized van Heijenoort's distinction in order to conceptualize a fundamental opposition between two different ways of looking at one's language, regardless of whether this home language is formal or natural. Thus he speaks of a conception of "language as the universal medium" and of a conception of "language as calculus." As Jaakko and the late Merrill B. Hintikka put it in their book on Wittgenstein, according to the view of language as the universal medium,

> one cannot as it were look at one's language from outside and describe it. . . . The reason for this alleged impossibility is that one can use language to talk about something only if one can rely on a given definite interpretation, a given network of meaning relations obtaining between language and the world. Hence one cannot meaningfully and significantly say in language what these meaning relations are, for in any attempt to do so one must already presuppose them.[5]

It is easy to see how such a view can lead one to believe in the "ineffability of semantics." This is the idea that the relations between language and the world cannot be expressed. Needless to say, this notion does not imply that the advocate of this view cannot have all sorts of *unspoken* ideas concerning semantics and semantic relations.

According to proponents of language as calculus, we are not trapped in our language in this way. An advocate of this viewpoint conceives of language as a tool, that is, as something that can be manipulated and re-interpreted, improved, changed, and replaced, as a whole or at least on a large scale. We can disentangle ourselves from our home language and discuss in language its semantic relations to the world. Semantics is not ineffable.

Which of the two positions a given philosopher adopts will pre-structure—though not determine—her choices concerning a number of further important philosophical issues. I shall here focus only on language as the universal medium; the implications of the calculus view can be easily derived *via negationis*.

One of the central corollaries of the presumed ineffability of semantic relations between our home language and the world is that we cannot conceive of different systems of semantic relations, or at least not express them in language and therefore not use them as an ingredient of a serious theoretical enterprise. This idea, in turn, can easily lead one to reject model theory and talk of possible worlds. After all, model theory is based precisely on the idea of a systematical variation of semantic relations. And since our language is thus interpreted, and interpretable, only with respect to *one* world, our language cannot be used to speak meaningfully about other, merely possible worlds.

The belief in the ineffability of semantics inclines many advocates of language as universal medium to adopt versions of linguistic relativism and semantic Kantianism. Linguistic relativism can appear inevitable to universalists because they have no way of comparing the semantic relations of different languages to the world. Semantic Kantianism might seem inescapable because of the close conceptual link between not knowing the mechanisms and activities used by our faculty of knowledge and not knowing the things-in-themselves. That is to say, we must, according to the view in question, also accept the ineffability of things considered independ-ently of the (possible) distorting influence of our language because we cannot reach a full knowledge of the relation between language and reality.

Finally, a believer in language as the universal medium will also be strongly tempted to reject metalanguage and to distrust the idea of truth as correspondence. To the defender of this view, the development of a meta-language presupposes that one can station oneself outside of one's home language. Yet since there is no way of stepping beyond this language, there cannot be a metalanguage either. Moreover, since language is tied to the world, speaking about language by means of language is a misuse of language. Precisely because we cannot step outside of our language, truth as correspondence must also be regarded as a highly questionable notion, for, according to this classical account, "true" is a metalinguistic term that expresses a certain correspondence between a sentence (or proposition, or belief) and the world.

III

As already mentioned, Hintikka directs much of his criticism of the universality view against Heidegger in particular. And in so doing, Hintikka has done me the honor of drawing on my interpretation of Heidegger. I therefore need to introduce a few central themes of this interpretation.[6]

The *Leitmotiv* of Heidegger's thinking during the 1920s was his opposition to what he regarded as an unsophisticated and excessive use of the traditional "subject-object" distinction in Husserl's analysis of intentionality. As Heidegger saw it, the subject-object distinction has its natural home in a particular kind of perception, that is, in controlled and scientific observation. In such perception we seek to be "objective" by distinguishing sharply between the observer and the observed, by separating clearly between the observed and its background, and by explicitly focusing our attention on the observed only. (The subject-object distinction was the central figure of thought in German Idealism; for instance, most German Idealists defined knowledge as a coincidence of subject, the knower, and object, the known.)

Although Husserl claimed to give "pure" descriptions of phenomena in the intentional consciousness—that is, descriptions that do not involve traditional preconceptions—he relied centrally on the opposition between "a subject with its immanent sphere and an object with its transcendent sphere."[7] In Heidegger's view, Husserl treated all of the following items as "objects": the world, worldly things, history, time, language, tools, other subjects, and the subject itself (insofar as it becomes an object of knowledge for itself).

According to Heidegger, Husserl was wrong to construe these items as objects. Heidegger claimed that an unbiased description of the ingredients of this list would reveal that they are anything but objects. The world, history, time, and language are not objects; they are the background against which objects stand out, or the medium in and through which objects are individuated and defined. Other subjects and tools are not objects outside the immanent sphere of my consciousness either; they are "always already" present in the ways in which I relate to myself and my environment. They are part of what makes me the person I am, and what defines my doing and thinking. I am not even an object for myself. The vague self-awareness that I have during my actions is not an awareness of an independent and external object.

Throughout his life, Heidegger tried to reconceptualize world, history, time, and language in ways that are not tied to the subject-object scheme. In other words, he attempted to think about these categories in ways that do not tie them to contexts of control or contexts of science. Heidegger's main alternative was to describe world, history, time, and language as *historically variable, universal media of meaning* (my expression, not his) that we can neither control technologically nor grasp scientifically. At best, we can get glimpses of these universal media in the writings of poets like Friedrich Hölderlin or Stefan George. We cannot understand these universal media scientifically-objectively since scientific research is attuned only to the study of objects (in the technical sense of object captured in the subject-object scheme). To mark this insight (or insistence), Heidegger often resorted to tautologies. He wrote that *"die Welt weltet," "die Sprache spricht,"* or *"die Zeit zeitigt."* These expressions are meant to signal that world, language, and time should not be thought of on the model of objects.

It (still) seems to me correct to say that the above considerations lead Heidegger to think of language as a universal medium. For Heidegger we can never pass behind, or beyond, language; we cannot understand how language structures our world; we have to accept linguistic and historical relativism; and we cannot make sense of truth as correspondence with an independent and unconceptualized reality. Let me here elaborate only on the last point. According to Heidegger, it is a fundamental mistake to think of truth as a relation of correspondence between a linguistic (or mental) item and a chunk of uninterpreted reality. There is no standpoint from which we could meaningfully talk about the latter. This is not to say that there is no truth, however. We can even hold on to truth as correspondence. But we must acknowledge that both relata of the correspondence relation (sentence or belief, and fact) are internal to our historically variable and imperceptibly changing media of meaning:

> [T]he fact must show itself to be fact if knowledge and the proposition that forms and expresses knowledge are to be able to conform to the fact; otherwise the fact cannot become binding on the proposition. How can fact show itself if it cannot itself stand forth out of the concealedness, if it does not itself stand in the unconcealed?[8]

Heidegger thinks that this insight allows us to grasp a more fundamental sense of truth—more fundamental, that is, than correspondence. This is the notion of truth as "disclosure" or "unconcealedness." Truth marks the phenomenon that we always already find ourselves within a world that makes sense to us; a world within which most things have a taken-for-granted familiarity and reliability; and a world which acts as the background for our identifications of salient objects and facts.

IV

Hintikka's critical assessment of language as the universal medium in general, and Heidegger's version of this view in particular, is contained in a number of papers, written over the past twelve years, and now conveniently collected into volume two of Hintikka's *Selected Papers*.[9] Three lines of argument and criticism can be distinguished.

The first line of argument insists that the universalist position is out of touch with contemporary philosophical reality. Philosophers are developing model theory and logical semantics; they are defining truth for formal languages; they are using metalanguage without remorse; they are treating truth conditions as "the cornerstone of all meaning theory"; and they are not finding "cross-linguistic breakdowns of understanding."[10]

The second line of argument alleges that the initial plausibility of the universalist position is based upon conflating two different views of semantics: the view that semantics is inexhaustible, and the view that semantics is ineffable. The inexhaustibility claim is correct but innocuous. We cannot access the semantics of our (natural) language in one fell swoop, and coming to understand the relations between our words and the world might well be an infinite process. In order to think about, and formulate, semantic relations we must use language, and thus rely on these very semantic relations. This circularity would be a problem only if we tried to study all semantic relations at once. However, there is no circularity involved in capturing the meaning of an expression E1 by relying on the meanings of expressions other than E1.[11]

Hintikka's second line of reasoning is closely related to his earlier criticism of Kant's claim according to which things-in-themselves are ineffable—and not just inexhaustible.[12] Hintikka argues that things-in-themselves are ineffable only if our faculties for acquiring knowledge are also ineffable. For if we could come to understand the working of these faculties ever better, then we could also increasingly learn to take account of the ways in which they might distort things-in-themselves. This would then allow us to deduct these distortions from the things-for-us and get ever closer to the things-in-themselves. Hintikka's model here is a measuring apparatus:

If we know nothing about this apparatus, we do not know what its registrations tell us about the reality at its other end, for instance, [we] do not know which part of the data it apparently yields are really due to the mode of functioning of the apparatus rather than to the objects as they would be independently of the apparatus which is monitoring them. The more we come to know about the apparatus, the more of the merely apparent registrations we can dismiss and the more narrowly we can pinpoint the input from "things in themselves."[13]

Unsurprisingly, Hintikka takes it as obvious that we do indeed come to know the workings of our faculties ever better, and that we thus get closer and closer to the things-in-themselves. All of this is important for assessing the view of language as the universal medium. Since this universalist conception insists that the working of our semantic relations is ineffable, it is also committed to the ineffability of reality. And this is "semantic Kantianism." Hintikka thinks that semantic Kantianism fares no better than Kant's transcendental philosophy. The upshot is Hintikka believes that through a piecemeal study of semantic relations we increasingly acquire an understanding of how our language distorts reality.

V

Hintikka's third line of argument against the universality assumption is the most important and the most recent of his criticisms. It is also of special interest to us here because Hintikka uses this line of argument against Heidegger in particular. Hintikka claims to have identified a crucial experiment for deciding the validity of the universality view. This crucial experiment is the definability of truth.[14]

The starting point of Hintikka's argument is to suggest that the universalist can do no better than rest her general case for the ineffability of semantics on the special case of the ineffability of truth. For only in the latter case can the universalist rely on hard logical results. The most important hard result in the present case is Tarski's proof, according to which the truth predicate for any given (object) language can only be defined in a stronger metalanguage. Add to this the obvious premise that we do not know how to construct a metalanguage with respect to our natural language, and the universalist position follows immediately: "in the case that really matters philosophically, truth-definitions are impossible. In this sense, truth is literally ineffable. . . ."[15]

Hintikka is convinced that this is the only serious argument for the universal-medium conception, and he dismisses what he regards as "relatively superficial" ways of defending the universalist stance. In

Heidegger's case he mentions two such ways. One is "the notorious hermeneutical circle"; this is the idea that all understanding of meaning already presupposes meaning. Hintikka thinks his second line (above) has already disposed of this defense. The other "superficial" defense invokes "the involvement of human action in meaning." Hintikka reconstructs this argument as follows: "human action is constitutive of the meanings of the world of our concepts. . . . For this reason . . . we cannot detach ourselves from our concepts, for we cannot possibly stop our conceptual practices without losing our concepts."[16] Hintikka takes this to be a bad argument. Even if there were this tight link between meaning and practice, it is not obvious why there could not be meta-practices and meta-concepts that allow us to talk about our first-order practices: "There is sight unseen no reason why the concepts we need to master in order to talk about our language could not also be grounded on human activities."[17]

Good or bad arguments for the universality assumption aside, Hintikka goes to some length to establish an essential link (of mutual implication) between Heidegger's commitment to the universal-medium view and Heidegger's "hermeneutic method," that is, his evocative, poetic, and non-scientific way of writing:

> [Heidegger] looked upon the world as a text to be interpreted. . . . But a hermeneutical task is a task of understanding meanings. Hence, according to the universalist thesis, it falls within the scope of the ineffability of meanings. Hermeneutical understanding is hence a task which cannot be carried out by means of the normal rational uses of language, and its results cannot be codified in normal language. It requires a technique of its own.[18]

Hintikka insists that, since the hermeneutic method and the universality assumption are so closely intertwined, they stand and fall together. If semantics turns out not to be infallible, then the hermeneutic method—a method that Hintikka sees continuing in Derrida's deconstruction[19]—is without justification. Heidegger's work will then have to be translated back into either Husserl's phenomenology or "some other kind of phenomeno-logical or analytical enterprise."[20] If semantics is accessible after all, then: "We have every right to say to hermeneutically oriented philosophers: *Hic Rhodos, hic salta*, the *hic* being the familiar ground of our normal logical, mathematical, scientific, linguistic, historical and legal methods of argumentation."[21]

I have now explained the context of Hintikka's third (or main) argument against the universality assumption, but it remains for me to explain the argument itself. As already mentioned, Hintikka holds that defenders of the universality view can do no better than make use of

Tarski's proof according to which truth definitions presuppose metalanguages. This is not without irony for Hintikka's third argument is in fact meant as a refutation of Tarski's proof. Hintikka claims that Tarski's proof does not apply to all kinds of formal languages. More precisely, Tarski's proof does not hold for some so-called "Independence-Friendly Logics," logical languages that Hintikka and a number of his Helsinki-based collaborators have studied over the past few years, using Hintikka's Game-theoretical Semantics as a framework. In the case of these languages one can define a truth predicate *for* these languages *in* these languages.

The full technical details of this work obviously lie beyond the scope of this essay. (Undoubtedly they will loom large elsewhere in this volume.) Suffice it to point out only a few central features of Hintikka's argument. First of all, Hintikka's truth definitions are not of the general, abstract variety. They do not "define some abstract correspondence relation between the sentence and a fact 'out there.'"[22] Rather, in keeping with the game-theoretical approach, truth is defined as the existence of a winning strategy for "the initial verifier" (the player who first puts forward the sentence to be verified).[23] Lest this switch from correspondence to winning strategy sounds like a switch from realism to idealism, it must be remembered that Hintikka's logical games are "'outdoor' games of exploring the world in order to verify or falsify certain (interpreted) statements by producing suitable individuals."[24]

Second, Hintikka's actual practice of defining truth for a given object IF-language does use metalanguage. He defines truth in the metalanguage only to go on then to show that the metalinguistic truth definition can be expressed in the object-language.[25]

Third, Hintikka also gives an informal justification for dissolving the boundary between object- and metalanguage. This informal justification is based on the distinction between rules that define the game (i.e., object-level rules), and rules that codify winning strategies (i.e., meta-level rules):

> [I]n every game of strategy the real understanding of the game involves more than knowing which moves are admissible and which ones are not. If you only know which movements of the different chessmen are admissible, you are not even a mediocre chess player; you cannot even honestly say that you know how to play chess. In order to be able to defend such claims, you need to have some grasp of the *strategies* that can be pursued in the game.[26]

Fourth, Hintikka insists that his observations concerning IF-logics are relevant concerning his disagreement with Heidegger. As Hintikka sees it, IF-logics are not some special case; IF-logics are closer to ordinary language than any other logical systems. And thus any insight concerning the peculiarities and potentialities of IF-logics is also a good indicator for what is possible in the case of natural languages.[27]

Put all this together, and we have, in Hintikka's view, "a most severe blow to the entire hermeneutical methodology":

> Whether it is a knockdown blow remains to be seen, even though by my count we are reaching the conclusive ten very soon. . . . [T]he definability of truth in IF first-order languages is in effect a proof that the ineffability thesis is wrong. . . . And this in turn amounts to a total dispensability of any specifically hermeneutical methodology, together with all the doctrines that depend on that methodology, for instance the view of truth as disclosedness.[28]

VI

I now turn to a discussion of Hintikka's three lines of argument against language as the universal medium. I will try to convince my former teacher (and other readers) that Heidegger could duck many of his punches, and that a knockdown argument against the universality view is unlikely to come from formal work on IF-logics.

Consider Hintikka's first argument, according to which philosophers in fact do many of the very things that universalists must deem impossible. This observation would not impress Heidegger. Like Tarski and Quine on the side of analytic philosophy, Heidegger could simply reply that although, say, model-theoretical conceptualizations are feasible on a small scale, they fail to illuminate natural language at large.[29] Heidegger might also reject the claim that model theory teaches us anything about the relations between language and the world. Models are defined by using some (formal or natural) language, making any study of language-model relations an intra-linguistic investigation of sorts. Varying semantic relations in model theory is not varying relations between language and an unconceptualized world; it is varying relations between language and a linguistically constituted artificial mini-world.

Moreover, although Hintikka is absolutely right to insist that philosophers often use metalinguistic expressions, such use does not imply that there is any viewpoint from which we could describe how our natural home language relates to an unconceptualized world. Nor would Heidegger have to be impressed by analytic philosophers who treat truth conditions as the cornerstone of all meaning theory. Not only are such theories controversial even amongst analytic philosophers, but at least one famous proponent of such theory, Donald Davidson, rejects both the correspondence theory and the definability of truth.[30] Finally, Heidegger would not be impressed either with Hintikka's insistence that we have yet to experience cross-linguistic breakdowns of understanding. For Heidegger claims to have experienced such breakdown in his attempts to understand Eastern philosophies.[31]

VII

Hintikka's second line of criticism is based on the distinction between the inexhaustibility and the ineffability of semantics. This distinction is in turn based on Hintikka's earlier dichotomy of ineffable and inexhaustible things-in-themselves. One thought that connects both distinctions is that language and faculties for acquiring knowledge can be thought of as measuring instruments. These are fascinating and powerful ideas, but again I fear, Heidegger would have no difficulties in evading their force.

To begin with, take the very model of the measuring instrument. Undoubtedly, Heidegger would reject this model as totally inadequate for capturing the nature of mental faculties and languages. As seen in section III above, Heidegger tried to free the philosophical study of our natural (everyday) attitude (towards others, our environment, and ourselves) from the traditional subject-object scheme. And he thought that this scheme often enters our philosophizing in the form of a mistaken assimilation of everyday perception to scientific observation. Thus Heidegger would have to regard the parallel between natural language and a measuring instrument as inadequate. Natural language does not measure anything, and natural language cannot be studied in the way we study instruments. How could Hintikka persuade Heidegger to think otherwise?

Moreover, and aside from this first misgiving, far from clinching the debate in favor of the inexhaustibility view, the analogy is in fact neutral between the two positions. It all depends on how we think of measuring instruments. Assume, for instance, that the measuring instrument were a "universal instrument." That is to say, imagine our cognition—individually or collectively—were (all of) the measuring instrument; imagine that the measuring instrument were our only faculty of understanding and knowing, and thus the only means for gaining access to the world and ourselves. Under this hypothesis, it would no longer be persuasive to claim that better knowledge of the instrument would enable us to gain better knowledge of whatever the instrument measures. If the instrument distorts in unknown ways and dimensions, then it may do so also when turned on itself. Even an infinite self-investigation might not yield the correct answer. Heidegger could claim that if we think of language as a universal measuring instrument then his view of language has been vindicated. Of course, in order to avoid refuting himself, Heidegger had better not say this in so many words.

VIII

Hintikka might not be too worried about the fact that Heidegger can escape his first two lines of attack, for he places his strongest hopes on his third criticism, the truth argument. Again, I admire the ingenuity of the argument, but doubt that it is conclusive as it stands.

Let me first make some comments on Hintikka's reconstruction of Heidegger's position. Hintikka is absolutely right about the importance of circularity and practices in Heidegger. But I am unable to find in Heidegger the specific "pragmatist" argument for the universality of language that Hintikka attributes to him. If I had to couch Heidegger's thinking in terms of "practices," I would put things as follows: Heidegger tries to understand how our pretheoretical practices provide the tacit background of intelligibility for all of our doing, including thinking, observing, and theorizing. As Heidegger saw it, every attempt to understand this background must already presuppose it. Moreover, although we constantly engage in piecemeal understanding of the background, it is a mistake to assume that such piecemeal understanding can progress (however slowly) towards a full understanding. Practical, pretheoretical, tacit understanding must always outrun theoretical, propositional, and explicit understanding. This Heideggerian argument has, of course, found favor with critics of strong artificial intelligence like Hubert Dreyfus and John Haugeland.[32] It has also been influential in anthropological and sociological studies of scientific practice.[33] I cannot help thinking that these studies have confirmed Heidegger's views both on the importance and on the ineffability of pre-theoretical practices.

Hintikka has shown convincingly how a commitment to language as the universal medium can lead one to speak in tautologies. And it is correct to suggest that Heidegger's use of semi-poetic modes of writing is in part motivated by his commitment to the universality of language. It is crucial to keep in mind, however, that Heidegger's peculiar style of investigating and writing had more than one motivation. Here I have to emphasize once more how vital it was for Heidegger to free philosophy from the temptation to model itself on science and technology. Only if we resist this temptation can we get to an adequate understanding of our everyday attitude and life, and only if we resist this temptation can we rediscover and protect other important modes of defining ourselves and the world around us. It is for this reason that Heidegger wrote so much about the poetry of Hölderlin and George. Whether or not one agrees with Heidegger on this score, it seems to me obvious that the just-mentioned motivation for a poetic style of writing can well stand on its own feet; it does not need the universality of language to back it up. It also puzzles me why Hintikka thinks that all philosophers should speak the languages of the sciences, logic, and the law. Talk to the practitioners in any of these fields, and you will learn that there is as much jargon in any of these areas as there is in deconstruction or hermeneutics. If scientists, logicians, and lawyers are allowed to introduce new expressions and new languages, why not Derrida and Heidegger?

If the ideas put forward in the last two paragraphs are anywhere near the mark, then the following claim seems plausible: even if Hintikka's argument from the definability of truth in IF-logic were successful, it would not necessarily prevent Heidegger from continuing with his hermeneutic approach. But what are we to say about Hintikka's truth argument itself? Here my comments will have to be tentative and provisional. I am not a logician and I can follow the technical details of the work of Hintikka and his collaborators only up to a point.

First, Hintikka's proof according to which truth definitions for (some) IF first-order languages can be expressed in those very languages themselves has the following form. Hintikka gives formulas of those languages; identifies winning strategies (in semantic games) for those formulas in a second-order meta-logic; and then shows that the strategy-identifying second-order formulas can be translated back into formulas of the IF first-order language. This raises the question, why do we need to take a detour through the metalanguage? And how essential is this detour to the whole project? If it is essential to the project, then we have not gotten rid of metalanguage. And then Heidegger can continue to maintain that truth is ineffable. After all, Hintikka grants that there is no metalanguage with respect to ordinary language.

Second, two of Hintikka's collaborators, Gabriel Sandu and Tapani Hyttinen, have reminded us of an important feature of the proof according to which the strategy-identifying, second-order formulas can be translated back into formulas of the IF first-order language. This important feature is that the proof is carried out in set theory. This crucial proof thus does presuppose metalanguage.[34] What damage does this do to the idea that we can get to truth definitions without relying on metalanguage?

Third, in his fascinating book *The Principles of Mathematics Revisited*, Hintikka writes as follows:

> The game-theoretical analysis of truth takes the meanings of primitive nonlogical constants of an interpreted first-order language for granted. This fixes the truth-values of the relevant atomic sentences, that is, of all sentences that can serve as endpoints of a semantical game. What my characterization does is to extend the notion of truth to all other sentences of the language in question.[35]

Taking these meanings (of primitive nonlogical constants) for granted might be fine as far as the purposes of mathematics are concerned, but it seems to me to beg an important question when GTS (and IF logic) are used to refute the view that semantics is ineffable. Surely, when it comes to refuting the ineffability view we cannot presuppose symbolic meaning in order to get to propositional meaning and truth.

Fourth, in order to refute the Heideggerian position on truth, Hintikka must defend not just any theory of truth, but the correspondence theory of truth. Hintikka is of course aware of this himself. He begins his argument against the universalist by noting that the latter "cannot speak of . . . truth as correspondence between sentences and facts."[36] When it comes to defining desiderata for truth definitions, however, Hintikka himself does not seem to favor correspondence either. Hintikka writes that we should want a definition that "should in a straightforward sense tell us what it means for a sentence to be true, rather than merely to define some abstract correspondence relation between the sentence and a fact 'out there.'"[37] Hintikka goes on to define truth in terms of winning strategies. This must provoke the question how the GTS formula (a) relates to the classical correspondence formula (b):

(a) A sentence S is true if, and only if, the initial verifier has a winning strategy for S in a semantic game defined by GTS.
(b) A sentence S is true if, and only if, S corresponds to a fact.

Speaking, as Hintikka does, of semantic games as "outdoor games" is helpful to forestall idealistic misunderstandings, but it is not informative enough to explain fully the relation between (a) and (b). We still need to be told how a sentence relates to the world when (a) is fulfilled.

Fifth, it seems to me that the degree of similarity between IF logics and natural languages is still very much open to debate. Hintikka has convinced me that IF logics are successful in modeling the behavior of quantifiers and negation in natural languages. Alas, there is much more to the semantics of natural language than meets the logician's eye. For instance, the terms of natural language do not have the fixed extensions that logicians take for granted when they set up their models and define their nonlogical constants. What our natural-language terms mean is the product of negotiation and fluctuation in the linguistic community; typically, no one speaker can control the outcome of such negotiation and fluctuation.[38] This indeterminacy of meaning in natural languages marks an important difference between formal and natural languages. It prevents quick generalizations from the semantics of formal languages to the semantics of all languages.

Finally, let us assume that Hintikka's truth argument were successful, and that truth definitions for natural languages could be given in (the same) natural languages. I doubt that even this result would constitute a knock-down blow against the Heideggerian universalist position. On the one hand, Heidegger might respond by claiming that Hintikka has in fact vindicated the universalist position: Hintikka's result shows that natural language is truly universal—universal, that is, in the sense that we can even speak of truth within it.[39] On the other hand, Heidegger might point out that by accepting Hintikka's analysis of truth, we have made truth definitions internal to specific languages. And does not this move invite precisely the linguistic and ontological relativism that Hintikka wants to avoid?

IX

In this essay, I have continued the critical dialogue that Hintikka has recently opened up with the hermeneutic tradition. I have sought to suggest ways in which Heidegger might escape Hintikka's attempts at refuting the view of language as the universal medium. I have done so not because I value continental thought more than the analytic tradition, or because I have learnt more from Heidegger than from Hintikka. (The opposite is much more likely to be true.) My purpose has rather been to invite more discussion of the arguments of the man to whom I owe so much of my philosophical education. This is the man to whom this volume is dedicated.

MARTIN KUSCH

DEPARTMENT OF HISTORY AND PHILOSOPHY OF SCIENCE
UNIVERSITY OF CAMBRIDGE
AUGUST 2000

NOTES

1. See the papers collected in Jaakko Hintikka, *Lingua Universalis vs. Calculus Ratiocinator: An Ultimate Presupposition in Twentieth-Century Philosophy (Jaakko Hintikka Selected Papers,* vol. 2*)* (Dordrecht: Kluwer, 1997). See also Merrill B. Hintikka and J. Hintikka, *Investigating Wittgenstein* (Oxford: Blackwell, 1986); and J. Hintikka, "Wittgenstein's Semantical Kantianism," in Edgar Morscher and Rudolf Stranzinger, eds., *Ethics: Foundations, Problems, and Applications (Proceedings of the Fifth International Wittgenstein Symposium)* (Vienna: Hölder-Pichler-Tempsky, 1981), pp. 375–91.

2. Building upon Hintikka's hypotheses, I showed in detail that Husserl and Heidegger were radical proponents of language as calculus and language as the universal medium, respectively. See Martin Kusch, *Language as Calculus vs.*

Language as Universal Medium: A Study in Husserl, Heidegger and Gadamer (Dordrecht: Kluwer, 1989).

3. See especially Jaakko Hintikka, "Contemporary Philosophy and the Problem of Truth," in Jaakko Hintikka, *Lingua Universalis vs. Calculus Ratiocinator*, pp. 1–19.

4. Jean van Heijenoort, "Logic as Calculus and Logic as Language," *Synthese* 17 (1967): 324–30; reprinted in J. Hintikka, *Lingua Universalis vs. Calculus Ratiocinator*, pp. 233–39.

5. M. Hintikka and J. Hintikka, *Investigating Wittgenstein*, p. 1. My explanation of the implications of this view (in the rest of this section) is based on chapter 1 of the Hintikkas' book. Cf. Part I of Kusch, *Language as Calculus vs. Language as Universal Medium*.

6. The following interpretation of Heidegger is a very brief summary of Part II of Kusch, *Language as Calculus vs. Language as Universal Medium*. For further details and references, the reader should consult this text.

7. Martin Heidegger, *Basic Problems of Phenomenology*, translated by Albert Hofstadter (Bloomington: Indiana University Press, 1982), p. 64.

8. Martin Heidegger, "Origin of the Work of Art," in M. Heidegger, *Poetry, Language, Thought*, ed. A. Hofstadter (New York: Harper & Row, 1971), pp. 17–87, here p. 51.

9. J. Hintikka, *Lingua Universalis vs. Calculus Ratiocinator*.

10. Ibid., pp. 33–34.

11. Ibid., pp. 34–36; see also 38–41.

12. J. Hintikka, "Das Paradox transzendentaler Erkenntnis," in Eva Schaper and Wilhelm Vossenkuhl, eds., *Bedingungen der Möglichkeit* (Stuttgart: Klett-Cotta, 1984), pp. 123–49.

13. J. Hintikka, "Wittgenstein's Semantical Kantianism," p. 377.

14. J. Hintikka, *Lingua Universalis vs. Calculus Ratiocinator*, pp. xv, 4, 12.

15. Ibid., p. 13.

16. Ibid., p. 5.

17. Ibid., p. 6.

18. Ibid., pp. 10–11.

19. Ibid., pp. 2, 16.

20. Ibid., p. 11.

21. Ibid., p. xvii.

22. Ibid., p. 46.

23. Ibid., p. 96.

24. J. Hintikka, *Logic, Language-Games and Information: Kantian Themes in the Philosophy of Logic* (Oxford: Clarendon Press, 1973), p. 81.—I am grateful to Gabriel Sandu for stressing this point in correspondence.

25. See J. Hintikka, *Lingua Universalis vs. Calculus Ratiocinator*, pp. 54–59, 64–73; and J. Hintikka, *The Principles of Mathematics Revisited* (Cambridge, England: Cambridge University Press, 1996), pp. 104–30.

26. J. Hintikka, *Lingua Universalis vs. Calculus Ratiocinator*, pp. 65–66.

27. Ibid., p. 15.

28. Ibid., p. 16.

29. Cf. ibid., p. 217.

30. See e.g. Donald Davidson, "The Structure and Content of Truth," *Journal of Philosophy* 87 (1990): 279–328; and "The Folly of Trying to Define Truth," in Simon Blackburn and Keith Simmons, eds., *Truth* (Oxford: Oxford University Press, 1999), pp. 308–22.

31. See Kusch, *Language as Calculus vs. Language as Universal Medium*, pp. 204–5.

32. Hubert Dreyfus, *Being-in-the-World: A Commentary on Heidegger's Being and Time Division I* (Cambridge, Mass.: MIT Press, 1991); John Haugeland, *Having Thought: Essays in the Metaphysics of Mind* (Cambridge, Mass. and London, England: Harvard University Press, 1998).

33. See especially the studies by Harry Collins: *Changing Order: Replication and Induction in Scientific Practice* (Beverley Hills: Sage, 1985); *Artificial Experts: Social Knowledge and Intelligent Machines* (Cambridge, Mass.: MIT Press, 1990); H. Collins and M. Kusch, *The Shape of Actions: What Humans and Machines Can Do* (Cambridge, Mass.: MIT Press, 1998).

34. Gabriel Sandu and Tapani Hyttinen, "IF Logic and Foundations of Mathematics," *Synthese* 126 (2001): 37–47. I am grateful to Sandu for correspondence on this point.

35. Hintikka, *The Principles of Mathematics Revisited*, p. 26.

36. Hintikka, *Lingua Universalis vs. Calculus Ratiocinator*, p. 4.

37. Ibid., p. 46.

38. This idea has been developed in the writings of Barry Barnes and David Bloor. See, e.g., Barry Barnes, David Bloor, John Henry, *Scientific Knowledge: A Sociological Analysis* (London: Athlone Press, 1996), ch. 3; D. Bloor, *Wittgenstein, Rules and Institutions* (London: Routledge, 1997). See also, M. Kusch, *Psychological Knowledge: A Social History and Philosophy* (London: Routledge, 1999), Interlude; and M. Kusch, *Knowledge by Agreement: The Programme of Communitarian Epistemology* (Oxford: Clarendon Press, 2002).

39. This is Hans-Georg Gadamer's version of language as the universal medium. See Kusch, *Language as Calculus vs. Language as Universal Medium*, Part IV.

REPLY TO MARTIN KUSCH

I am most grateful to Martin Kusch for providing an occasion for me to take up once again the intriguing contrast between the ideas of language as calculus and language as a universal medium which he has himself successfully explored.[1] He is right in saying that there is a genuine need of further clarification of the issues related to this contrast. I am particularly glad to have this opportunity to set the record straight because some of the views Martin Kusch airs seem to be widely accepted.

Indeed, I find that the issues are even deeper than Kusch brings out. I do not think that he does full justice either to me or to the thinker whose views he contrasts to mine, his namesake Martin Heidegger. To begin with one of the clearest issues, in connection with the question of the definability of truth Kusch admits that truth is indeed definable in so-called independence-friendly (IF) first-order languages. He presents IF logic as a special member of a variety of logics, leaving their "technical details" for others to discuss. But IF logic is not just one "system" among others. And what is important about IF logic are nevertheless not any "technical details," but the simple and striking interpretational import of IF languages. They are the only first-order logical languages in which we can express all possible patterns of dependence and independence between variables. This is plainly what a fully adequate language for science and everyday life should be able to do, but which received first-order logics do not enable a language to do. Hence IF logic is the only viable candidate for an unrestricted first-order logic of factual discourse.

Kusch raises the question whether model-theoretical results like the definition of truth really "illuminate natural language at large." But this is not the issue here. The line of thought that leads to IF logic strikingly illuminates what *any* language, natural, formal, or imaginary, has to be able to do in order to meet its job description. Whether or not this or that natural or unnatural language fails to do this job is not the crucial question. (So much the worse for it if some particular language fails this task!) IF logic illuminates natural languages not by approximating them, but by setting up a standard to which they are compared.

In this matter, appeals to received authorities are worthless, especially if the authority figures are unaware of, or have not responded to, this challenge by IF logics. For instance, an appeal to Davidson against the possibility of defining truth is vacuous as long as Davidson has not presented as much as a scintilla of argument against the specific, explicit truth predicates which I have put forward (together with Gabriel Sandu). My comments on truth definitions are not observations concerning some obscure system of logic, as Kusch seems to insinuate. They are observations concerning what any language must be able to do in order to be capable of expressing all the different things we might have to say about reality. Independence-friendly languages are not any closer to ordinary language than other logical systems, except perhaps in that certain things are expressible in them that are apparently expressible in natural languages but not in other first-order logical languages.

All this puts my past comments on Heidegger up to a light different from Kusch's reading of them. I have not criticized Heidegger's arguments directly. What I have tried to do is to show independently of his arguments that their purported conclusion is wrong in the sense that truth is definable after all. What I have also done, admittedly rather feebly, is to try to understand Heidegger's line of thought and find out what is interesting in it. Kusch quotes what I say of the role of human action in the constitution of our conceptual world and of this role as a reason for a universalist view, and says that I take it to be a bad argument. No, I take the role of human action as a determinant of meaning to be a fascinating idea that cries out for further development and discussion. If I may be so bold, I suggest that this idea, rather than the presuppositional considerations Kusch seems to prefer, would have provided better ways for his virtual Heidegger to challenge my views. For me, the basis of first-order logic is the language-games of seeking and finding. They involve human activities and "institutions" in a wide sense of the word. It is inconceivable, or so it seems, to change something that is as central as these conceptual practices. Thus the examination of the language-world links mediated by human activities might be put to use as criticizing the calculus view.

I do not consider this line of thought conclusive, however, though it is very interesting. It might even be correct when construed in a suitable way. One possibility for my virtual Heidegger would be to claim that understanding the language-games of seeking and finding is the proto-logic that is the indispensable basis of all discursive thinking. I could agree with some such view, but only with the all-important proviso that such an alleged proto-logic will simply coincide with our correctly understood basic logic.

This connection between our basic logic and the "institutions" of seeking and finding is not merely a philosophical *aperçu* but an idea that can be put to use. Kant claimed that the validity of the mathematical method of reasoning, which he more or less correctly saw in the use of instantiation rules, is founded on the form of the human sensory intuition. I have shown that a similar idea becomes viable if we replace sensory intuition by the language-games of seeking and finding.[2]

These games thus are the true basis of our very own logic. And since they seem to be an integral part of our life in the world, they might very well seem to be inescapable, a veritable conceptual mediator between our thinking and the world. Even though it may be a coincidence, I find it instructive that such Heideggerians as Paul Lorenzen have sought the foundation of logic in certain games, though games different from the one envisaged in game-theoretical semantics.

A presuppositional motivation for the universality of our logic thus is an interesting possibility, not "a bad argument." The same goes of course for semantics more generally. But this is not the end of the story. Another important question is whether we can formulate alternatives to the usual language-games in question. A universalist like Heidegger would presumably have to deny such a possibility. In the case of first-order logical languages and their language-games I have in fact explained how such alternative first-order languages might be obtained, for instance, by restricting the verifiers's strategies in a semantical game.[3] A careful study of such alternative semantical games, especially of how they can be defined, might throw more light on the entire issue of the presuppositional motivation of the universalist position. For instance, one can ask whether such nonclassical games can be defined by reference to the "classical" ones. Are our usual logic and, for instance, intuitionistic logic genuinely incommensurable? And what would happen if such an alternative logic turned out to be but a part of a richer classical logic, for instance, if intuitionistic logic should be interpreted as a part of our usual epistemic logic? Whatever answers to such questions will ultimately be, they do not concern only the "technical details" of different logics, but also the fundamental philosophical issues that Heidegger was struggling with.

This role of human activities—whether we call them language-games or not—in determining the meaning of our language is indeed the deep idea here. If I share it with Heidegger, so much the better for both of us. It is also the idea I have tried to highlight by using the locution "semantical Kantianism"—not the idea of the unknowability of meanings in analogy with the unknowability of things-in-themselves, but the idea that meanings are constituted by rule-governed human activities.

In the same way it can be seen what the obvious answer is to Kusch's question: How is the GTS idea of truth as the existence of a winning verificatory strategy in a semantical game related to the idea of truth as a correspondence between a sentence and a fact? The answer is simple: They amount ultimately to the same. It is an essential part of the job description of semantical games to constitute a correspondence between a sentence S and a world W in which S is true. The semantical game G(S) correlated with S succeeds in establishing such a correspondence if and only if there exists a winning strategy for the verifier in it. In fact, a winning strategy shows how to find the "witness individuals" that according to our normal intuitive understanding vouchsafe the truth of a proposition. For instance, for $(\forall x)(\exists y)$ S[x,y] a winning strategy (codified by a function f) tells you which individual y=f(x) satisfies S[x,y] for any given x.

Admittedly, this is correspondence in a rather abstract sense. This sense is so abstract that you might legitimately balk at using the term "correspondence" here at all. Jan Woleński (see his contribution to this volume) may very well be right in de-emphasizing the notion of correspondence in connection with truth definitions. The "correspondence" in question is not mediated by any naturalistic relations, but by the rules of a language-game. For instance, the correspondence is not based on any correlation between the elements of a sentence and the ingredients of the world of which the language speaks. As Wittgenstein once said,[4] the correspondence (Wittgenstein's term is "agreement") between language and reality is constituted by the use of language. He also added: "As everything metaphysical." This is the reason why I have not emphasized the idea of correspondence more than I have done. But this abstractness does not make the "correspondence" in question any less objective or in any way different from our pre-theoretical bread-and-butter sense of truth.

Focusing on the language-world relations instead of the world (Heidegger presumably would speak of beings), seems in fact to offer the best ways for Heidegger to explain and to defend his philosophy. From the perspective of language-world and language-thought links mediated by human activities, the being of beings can take different forms. There is *Zuhandensein*, there is *Vorhandensein*, and there is *Dasein*. Behind all this there is the unspoken idea that Dasein constitutes the world through its activities and hence can find itself mirrored in the beings and even in Being. In non-Heideggerian terms, the different forms of being thus represent different relations of oneself to the world. I cannot see why Heidegger could not have admitted that our discourse about *Zuhandensein* is in principle open to explicit meta-discussion and tool-like manipulation—in other words open to the calculus view. (It may even be that he does.) Arguably, the same could hold of *Vorhandensein*. It is only *Dasein* that is inexpressible in the usual sense, and the same goes to the meanings of the language we use of it.

Whether or not this is a fair representation (or extension) of Heidegger's thought, it is a highly interesting view, or perhaps rather vision. I do not believe that there is any knockdown argument against it. However, its representatives are excluding themselves from rational argumentation in a subtle way.

My analogy between language (and the associated conceptual system) and a measuring apparatus is calculated to illustrate this subtlety. Properly speaking, I should not call it "my" analogy, for I am not the first philosopher to use it. No lesser a figure than Hegel used it against the Kantians.[5] Not only is it not an argument; it is merely an analogy, not a simile. I am somewhat surprised that Kusch should go out of his way to admonish me that language is not literally a measuring instrument. Would he scold Hegel, too, for thinking that our conceptual system is literally like a measuring instrument? Kusch seems to overlook or at least underplay the subtlest aspect of the analogy. He describes correctly and eloquently how according to Heidegger "our pretheoretical practices provide the tacit background of intelligibility for all of our doing, including thinking, observing, and theorizing." Now any concrete knowledge that we can reach about those pre-theoretical practices is analogous to knowledge we can reach about the measuring apparatus. And, as in the case of physical tools of inquiry, so in the case of our *Vorwissen* what we can find about it will enable us to eliminate the distorting effects of the mediator, be it an apparatus or the structure of our *Vorwissen*. Thus Heidegger or whoever else holds such views has banished himself from the enterprise of normal rational inquiry. The more concrete evidence he offers for his views, the less important these views become. Thus a Heideggerian ineffability has to be accepted on blind faith or else on evidence incommensurable with all our normal knowledge. While I cannot disprove such a view, I find blind reliance on the word of a character like Heidegger unworthy of serious philosophers.

The alternative to such an obscurantism is to do what Kusch apparently wants to do and to study seriously the actual preconditions of our thinking. These preconceptions and presuppositions are tradition-bound. They are conditioned by our historical and linguistic context. Eliciting them is an enterprise I thoroughly approve of. However, the poster boy of such a tradition-oriented approach to hermeneutics is not Heidegger but Hans-Georg Gadamer concerning whose views I can only agree with his master (as quoted by Kusch): "Das ist nicht mehr Heidegger." I have analyzed the conceptual problem of the presuppositions of rational inquiry in my forthcoming paper "Presuppositions of Questions and Other Limitations of Inquiry." One main result is that the preconditions of inquiry are multiple but not traceable back in any interesting sense to any "absolute presuppositions" à la Collingwood.[6]

There seems to be some misunderstanding on Kusch's part as to what

I am holding concerning the object language—metalanguage distinction. I do not claim that there is anything wrong with the distinction between object language and metalanguage. Of course we have to use the distinction all the time. The only question is what the different things are that one can or cannot express about a language in the same language, without climbing up to a metalanguage or, to put the same question in a different way, whether in some cases a language can serve as it own metalanguage. It is the alleged impossibility of using a language seriously and across the board as its own metalanguage that separates universalists from their opponents, in that for them there is no metalanguage available, at least not in the case of our actual working language.

In any case, Kusch is misleading when he claims that in my "actual practice of defining truth for a given IF language" I use a metalanguage. Of course I explain informally the way of defining a truth predicate in plain English. But such motivating explanations are not part of the definition. If you had learned an IF first-order language as your mother tongue, I could use that language to do the same, including formulating a truth predicate for your own language. It looks as if Kusch had confused second-order languages and metalanguages, for I do formulate—albeit only for explanatory purposes—my truth predicate first in a second-order language and then show that such a truth predicate can be translated into the corresponding IF first-order language. But second-order languages are object languages as much as any. For additional comments on the possibility of formulating a truth predicate for a language in the same language, the reader is referred to my response to Rouilhan and Bozon in this volume.

In sum, for all my disagreement with Heidegger, my concerns and his are much closer to each other than Kusch seems to think.

J. H.

NOTES

1. See Martin Kusch, *Language as Calculus vs. Language as Universal Medium: Study of Husserl, Heidegger and Gadamer* (Dordrecht: Kluwer Academic Publishers, 1989).

2. See e.g., my paper "Quantifiers, Language-games and Transcendental Arguments" in my *Logic, Language-Games and Information*, 1973.

3. See here my 1996 book *Principles of Mathematics Revisited*, chapter 10.

4. Wittgenstein said this on p. 122 of the manuscript referred to as MS 116 in von Wright's catalogue; see his article "The Wittgenstein Papers" in G. H. von

736JAAKKO HINTIKKA

Wright, *Wittgenstein* (Oxford: Blackwell, 1982).

5. G.W.F. Hegel, *Phänomenologie des Geistes, Einleitung*, ed. von Hoffmeister (Hamburg, 1952), pp. 63–64. (In the 1807 edition, pp. 3–4.)

6. See R. G. Collingwood, *An Essay on Metaphysics* (Oxford: Clarendon Press, 1939).

22

Patrick Suppes

HINTIKKA'S GENERALIZATIONS OF LOGIC AND THEIR RELATION TO SCIENCE

I have known Jaakko Hintikka for at least forty years and during that time he has written far too many papers and books for me to have any sense of having read most of them in any detailed way. However, I have found a relatively smaller subset that addresses his lively and interesting recent work on generalizations of standard first-order logic to a wider setting, especially in the applications of these generalizations to the sciences. Requiring that the papers be relevant directly to the sciences in itself restricts quite considerably the papers to be considered. There is still more than enough for me to cover.

It is also important to state at the beginning that I do not have some general theses to set forth and defend, nor do I abstract from Hintikka's writings general theses on his part. What I find attractive is that he has a great deal to say, in detail, about many issues of interest to me as a philosopher of science. I consider a number of individual questions, not necessarily closely related, but all, in my judgment, of some importance in any general philosophy of science.

I. IF LOGIC AND SET THEORY

I have long been associated with the use of set theory to analyze scientific theories. My ideas about this, with many detailed examples as well, are set forth in my recent book, *Representation and Invariance of Scientific*

Structures,[1] but I have been publishing various parts of it and preliminary editions of this book have been widely used. It is also clear that the implicit general framework for my analysis of scientific structures has been standard axiomatic set theory. I say all of this, not to talk about myself, but to set the scene for introducing Hintikka's alternative. This framework that I have been mentioning is certainly, with exceptions that can be easily noted (which will be mentioned explicitly later), the set-theoretical setting that dominates the writing of modern mathematics. Most branches of pure mathematics are provided a setting that is naturally either set-theoretical or category-theoretical in character. But these two approaches are too closely linked to distinguish in the present discussion. It will, I think, be satisfactory just to refer to the standard set-theoretical view of modern pure mathematics.

As a breath of fresh air in philosophical discussions of modern logic, Hintikka has recently written a whirlwind of papers on independence-friendly (IF) logic, which is a generalization of first-order logic that does not require a linear ordering of quantifiers in the sentences codified in the usual first-order logic notation. This kind of logic in earlier forms has been known as logic with branching quantifiers and sometimes also as Henkin quantifiers, after the logician Leon Henkin. Hintikka and his collaborators are the ones, however, who have made extensive use of this framework in recent writings about the philosophical foundations of logic. This applies to IF logic as an alternative to standard axiomatic set theory in some form, to logic as inquiry, to logic as reasoning, and all the way to the logic of quantum mechanics. I will comment on each of these endeavors. One thing that has not been discussed very much in Hintikka's many publications is how his notion of independence, as in IF logic, relates to the various notions of independence in probability theory. I will comment on the varying concepts of independence later.

It is too much for me to undertake a systematic discussion of IF logic here, but the intuitive content of it can be easily and naturally expressed. It also leads to a way of expressing many things to which I am very sympathetic. Instead of writing down the formal syntax of IF logic, which Hintikka mentions as being rather tricky, we can think of always writing down the formal sentences by replacing the quantifiers with Skolem functions, so that the dependency questions that arise in the linear ordering of quantifiers can be avoided and the natural expression as intended is just expressed by the Skolem functions, which show the dependence.

Here is a simple example to show that what I have just said is not as complicated as it may sound. Suppose that we want to say that for every x there exists a y and for every z there exists a u for some $F(x, y, z, u)$. Then we can immediately write this as a quantifier-free expression with Skolem functions *f* and *g* as $F(x, f(x), z, g(z))$. Now such Skolem functions can be very natural and useful in eliminating quantifiers. In fact, it is an important mathematical technique in logic to have such an elimination of quantifiers within a classical framework. One is, of course, still left with the problem, at a more conceptual level, of saying what functions are the Skolem functions. For the present, I leave that aside. What Hintikka is emphasizing in this advertisement for IF logic is its greater flexibility and strength, and this seems appropriate. I should also note that he discusses the semantics of IF logic in the context of his earlier work on game-theoretic semantics and this, too, has some applications to the obsession in current economics with game theory, but I shall not pursue this topic here.

There is an important issue, from a scientific standpoint, about the kind of flexibility on independence and dependence permitted in IF logic. The example I have given is too simple. We may want to have dependency between the arguments of various functions; every possible variety of such dependence can be exhibited in quite natural physical relations. So, for example, we can have constraints on the motions of particles or non-idealized bodies, such that two constraints can be independent or such that they are highly dependent, and there can be nesting, hierarchical relations, and the like, among these dependencies. IF logic gives much greater flexibility in expressing this than does ordinary classical logic. On the other hand, I do not want to overemphasize this flexibility, for I might be mistaken as saying that all the kinds of independence and dependence that arise in scientific contexts can be expressed at the level of logic. This is certainly not the case. The substantive expression of dependencies depends upon something more than logical structure. Probability provides excellent examples to be discussed later—and physics just as many.

Hintikka points out the most obvious logical failings of the standard axiomatizations of set theory within first-order logic.[2] Almost everything he has to say about these failures, including the absence of a definition of truth—problems of many natural statements being independent of the axioms, and so forth—I accept, but, more importantly, these views are accepted quite widely. On the other hand, in my own perspective, these purely logical matters have turned out to be not very important for the use of the language of set theory as the standard formulation for characterizing mathematical and scientific structures.

The applications of logic, especially in science, have usually a rather special and particular character. So, for example, general discussions of truth will not be of much interest in analyzing specific problems in the framework of specific physical theories, economic theories, and so on. So, what I think is as yet missing from Hintikka's method of IF logic is how the apparatus can be used to settle some significant questions in particular parts of science. This is the kind of thing he does not discuss in his general paper just cited on axiomatic set theory. On the other hand, some applications are evident in two areas. One is that of game-theoretic semantics and the other in the applications to quantum mechanics. The latter I examine later.

I leave this question about the general framework now, saying that I do not think there will be much changing the general use of set-theoretical language in mathematics and science, except where special needs for that change are found, as they can be found in the foundations of mathematics and also in the logic of quantum mechanics.

II. Logic as Interrogative Inquiry

One of the important generalizations of classical logic, in terms of formulation, is Hintikka's work on the development of the logic of questions and answers, as a new game-theoretic way of thinking about semantics. In the present context, without going into the details of this approach to semantics, I want rather to examine Hintikka's interesting paper "Presuppositions of Questions—Presuppositions of Inquiry."[3] Here Hintikka discusses, especially, presuppositions of questions that may be asked. He emphasizes the point in several places that the question-answering methods developed and the discussion of presuppositions, as well, have application to empirical work in the sciences. This kind of idea goes back, in a general way, to Francis Bacon, as Hintikka remarks. But the popular notion of the scientist putting questions to nature, for which answers are then sought, but not necessarily given by nature, is a familiar way of formulating some aspects of scientific method. Hintikka has something more ambitious in mind. He wants the formal structure of questions and answers, as he has developed them in numerous publications, especially in his discussion of the presupposition of questions, to provide an apparatus that may be used by the scientist.

There are a number of useful and interesting lines of inquiry he begins in this investigation, emphasizing as he does the important contrast between definitory rules and strategic rules. He also emphasizes that, for any complex situation, there will not be feasible, optimal strategic rules (feasible in the sense of feasible computation).

In this context, Hintikka has an interesting discussion of reducing all experimental scientific questions to yes-no questions. Although he does not explicitly mention quantum mechanics here, this is a standard mathematical move in analyzing the foundations of quantum mechanics. The basis is that any observable can be replaced by an equivalent set of yes-no questions.

Intuitively, it is easy to see how this could be done. Suppose we want to predict the trajectory of a particle in classical mechanics or the time-dependent sequence of probability distributions of a particle in position space in quantum mechanics. Classically, let us think of having a very fine finite grid of cubes in the (x, y, z) coordinates.[4] Then we can ask for each one of these small cubes, whether a given particle can be found there. Of course, we ask this in terms of space-time trajectories, really. So, we are actually using four-dimensional space, but this still does not change anything. We can get, in principle, a yes-no answer for each small four-dimensional cube. It is easy to see, however, that, although this procedure is theoretically equivalent to a very fine approximation of writing down a standard expression for the trajectory, it is something very different in terms of intuitive representation or computation. It is not a way you will find anyone using to do actual computations in quantum or classical mechanics. So, to move from the general framework of yes-no questions, as discussed by Hintikka, to their detailed application in physics, for example, would be a big step. And, in fact, I would expect him to shift away from yes-no questions in turning to scientific details. He does this for the kind of applications in logic and ordinary discourse he discusses. So, my point is that there is both a theoretical resonance with the question-answer procedure and something as far removed from ordinary Socratic questions as quantum mechanics, but it does not mean this provides a good route to answering complicated quantum mechanical questions.

Consider now this matter of questions from a related angle. Here is an interesting quote at the end of section 4 of "Presuppositions of Questions" I want to comment on.

> This strategic power of experimental questions can be considered as the epistemological explanation of the success of early modern science. The methodological "secret" of scientists like Galileo and Newton is not their empiricism, but their use of experiments, especially controlled experiments. Such experiments can be thought of, it was seen earlier, as wh-questions with a functional (general) answer.[5]

There is something in this, but think of Newton's work on the inversesquare law of gravity and the marvelous results he was able to obtain about the dynamics of solar bodies. In this context the role of experimental questions was very limited. First of all, Newton himself essentially made no astronomical observations of any importance. And, he certainly did not, in the context of astronomy, conduct any controlled experiments. What he did was have marvelous ideas about mathematical models to fit the data that had been collected—some of it over hundreds of years—by astronomers of many different times and places. Moreover, I emphasize again, in the ordinary sense of things, there are no really good controlled experiments in Newton's work on astronomy. Of course, there is another sense in which we can discuss Newton's asking of questions, but I want to express some skepticism about the ordinary logical formalism of questions that Hintikka introduces in this article. Interesting though it may be for the purposes he mainly uses it for, it does not seem to have much direct use in any actual astronomical inquiries or investigations of the kind Newton conducted.

It is worth noting in this connection the beginning of Book III of Newton's *Principia* (1686/1946), which is about his detailed astronomical calculations for the "system of the world." Newton states four rules of reasoning in philosophy. The first two concern causes. The third, universal qualities of bodies, such as extension and impenetrability, and the fourth, induction in experimental philosophy. Now, my only point is that these set the tone of Newton's qualitative way of looking at what he is doing. A better example of Newton's use of specific experiments that he himself made is, of course, to be found in his *Optics,* and in many ways, this work better supports Hintikka's remark.

But the point I am getting at is this: In spite of my appreciation for what Hintikka has done about the logic of questions, which gives a good account of many kinds of reasoning and of dialectic, he has not as yet carried out detailed developments to analyze or reconceptualize his work in any detail so as to have it fit with actual experimental methods in any branch of science. There is also another point. If we talk in general about experimental methods, something much broader has to be considered. It is important to emphasize the pragmatic *doing* of experiments. Being a good experimenter often means developing better instrumentation, which Newton remarks on, by the way. This is a matter not of questions, but of actual construction of something new. Running experiments is like building a house or making a pair of shoes. There are a great number of practical skills that are fundamental to the real endeavor and that go far beyond any logic of questions. As far as I know, Hintikka has not yet developed his ideas about such pragmatic considerations.

There is, however, one rather direct extension of his view about questions and answers and the logic of inquiry to consider. This is Bayesian inductive methods, which do have a deductive framework. As the saying goes, all a subjectivist about probability needs is a prior distribution and the outcomes of observations from properly designed experiments to compute mathematically the appropriate posterior distribution. This is all, in principle, that induction consists of. There are many things about this Bayesian picture that are close to Hintikka's model. I think that with a little pushing and shoving here and there, the two could be made very congenial to each other. This would immediately bring Hintikka's views closer to a well-known methodology in experimental work. Both sides could in all likelihood profit from further common developments.

III. LOGIC AND GOOD REASONING

In an important and sensible paper on this topic, Hintikka has lots of useful things to say about why the model of purely formal logic made prominent in the nineteenth century by Boole and Frege has not provided a place for many of the things that were traditionally thought to be important aspects of logic.[6] Hintikka draws the desirable distinction between the definitory and strategic rules of logic. The simple example to clarify this is that it is easy enough to understand the definitory rules of chess. It is quite another thing to understand the strategic principles of the game. What one long tradition expected from logic was the latter rather than the former, that is, the development of good methods of reasoning, not in the sense of simply being formally correct principles, but in the sense of being practically useful for inquiry.

This move of Hintikka, with which I am entirely in sympathy, is a move in the direction of something congenial to the actual practices of scientists and of mathematicians, it might be said. So, it is worth examining more carefully his ideas in this direction. To begin his analysis in a systematic way, Hintikka makes the good point that Aristotle, the first formal logician, whose main results are to be found in the *Prior Analytics,* was actually concerned with strategic aspects of reasoning, which he thought of dialectically as an interrogative process. But, just as good lawyers never like to ask a witness a question whose answer they do not know, so Aristotle was interested in the kinds of questions that can be asked in a dialectic procedure such that the answer to a question is fully determined logically by earlier answers. Of course, as Aristotle makes clear in *The Posterior Analytics,* and as Hintikka fully recognizes, no one can expect to receive only logically necessary answers, in the sense of being logically implied by earlier questions and their answers.

I want to emphasize that in this analysis of logic as good reasoning, Hintikka is making the excellent point that, in the teaching of logic, the emphasis on strategic rules has been neglected in favor of the purely formal rules of inference that guarantee logical validity. He goes on to make a number of suggestions of a positive nature about how to think about strategic rules. The main focus of his suggestions centers around his use of interrogative logic, with a claim that certainly has some justification. It is that such logic represents a natural generalization to the kind of inquiry to be found in the sciences and in many other walks of life. He also makes, in this connection, the point that, as his own work has shown, such an interrogative approach can be used as a formal basis of logic, but it also is easily extended in a seamless way to nonlogical inferences that satisfy weaker canons of rationality. He appends to the article a useful study; an earlier article by Hintikka, Halonen, and Mutaten[7] is full of detailed developments.

However, in spite of my positive attitude, I want to add that analysis at this level of generality constitutes a prolegomenon to future detailed studies. Holding on to the interrogative framework, I think it would be possible to enter into the details of various parts of science at an elementary level, to exhibit how such a framework can provide unification, and to show how it can also be used as a framework within which particular details about reasoning in a given domain can be amplified and learned. This extends beyond the sciences and certainly applies to many other domains of reasoning, from the law and government policy to architectural design. I would like to be able to be optimistic about the number of workers in the vineyard ready to follow out this general expansion of strategy analysis within the framework of interrogative inquiry. I think it will be, unfortunately, some time before it really happens.

There is one aspect of this expansion that I think is important that Hintikka does not dwell on. This is the fact that learning to reason well about a particular domain depends upon a great deal of nonverbal learning, that is, experience that comes from many detailed encounters with the subject matter and, possibly, the environment of the domain such that much of what is learned is learned unconsciously and without any specific verbal formalization whatsoever. Think of the person becoming familiar with hunting, pruning, or guiding, tourists in a dense forest. What that person knows about the forest is mainly nonverbal and, above all, he is not even able to verbalize the fine points of his knowledge. Such nonverbal learning is needed to deepen, not only students' experiences, but our own understanding of how such matters work at the frontiers of scientific research or in novel applications in any domain of knowledge. So, I am not arguing against anything that Hintikka has to say about logic as good reasoning, but I am emphasizing something that is, in many ways, against too much focus on formality, which, fortunately, Hintikka is also saying. Hintikka mentions one fine example of such learning, already, in his discussion of chess. I would add only to his analysis of the chess playing my insistence that the deeper levels of analysis are never completely verbalized by a master chess player. The formal rules of chess are easy for anyone to learn, but because of the complexity of the game, there are no closed sets of strategies. You can choose the one you care for. It remains open-ended, full of associations that are unconscious, but built upon past experience and usable in the next game in ways you can only partly explain.

IV. INDEPENDENCE IN IF LOGICS COMPARED TO PROBABILISTIC STRUCTURES

My comments are related to the important emphasis on independence in IF logics. Independence is necessary to get the generalization that is natural for classical logic. What I want to raise are some questions about the more detailed structure of this independence, especially how it relates to classical notions of independence in probability theory.

Let us suppose, first, that we have a structure that is a classical probability space $(\Omega, \mathcal{F}, P)$ where Ω is the set of possible outcomes, $\mathcal{F}$ is the Boolean family of events, and P is the probability measure on the family of events. The axioms are familiar and I will not state them here. For such spaces, slightly less familiar, is the definition of the concept of an experiment. We call an *experiment*, with respect to the given probability structure, any partition of Ω, i.e., any collection of nonempty subsets of Ω such that

(i)   the collection is a subset of the algebra $\mathfrak{F}$ of sets,

(ii) the intersection of any two distinct sets in the collection is empty, and

(iii) the union of the collection is Ω itself.

What we now define is the important concept of mutual independence in the following way.

DEFINITION 1 *The n experiments $M^{(1)}, \ldots, M^{(n)}$ are (mutually) independent if and only if for every $A_i \in M^{(i)}$ where $1 \leq i \leq n$,*

$$P\left(\bigcap_{i=1}^{n} A_i\right) = \Pi_{i=1}^{n} \, P(A_i).$$

Also, we can easily extend this definition to events. The n events $A_1, A_2, \ldots, A_n$ are *(mutually) independent* if and only if the n experiments $M^{(1)}, M^{(2)}, \ldots, M^{(n)}$ are mutually independent, where

$$M^{(i)} = \{A_i, -A_i\}.$$

This definition looks rather different from the one given in several places by Hintikka for IF logic. So, I have again a natural question for him. How does he relate the concept of independence for IF logics to the classical definition of independence of probabilistic experiments or events?

The apparatus just defined is very quantitative in character. It is natural to move to considerations that seem more readily compared to the type of independence to be found in IF logic. The kind of qualitative properties to which I now turn relates to distributive properties and the like, such as those discussed by Hintikka in his article on quantum logic.[8] I list here some standard properties of the qualitative probabilistic independence of two events, taken from Suppes and Alechina:[9] (I use the customary symbol $\perp$ for such independence.)

1. If $A \perp B$ then $B \perp A$;

2. $A \perp \Omega$;

3. If $A \perp B$ then $A \perp \neg B$;

4. If $B \cap C = \emptyset$, $A \perp B$, $A \perp C$ then $A \perp (B \cup C)$;

5. If $A \perp B \cap C$, $B \perp C$, $A' \cap B' \perp C'$, $A' \perp B'$, $A \approx A'$, $B \approx B'$, $C \approx C'$ then $A \cap B \cap C \approx A' \cap B' \cap C'$;

6. If $A \perp B$, $B \perp C$, $A \perp B \cap C$ then $C \perp A \cap B$.

Do these elementary qualitative properties have actual analogues in IF logic? If not, what are the salient qualitative independence properties of IF logic?

V. APPLICATION OF IF LOGIC TO QUANTUM LOGIC

In Hintikka's "Quantum Logic as a Fragment of Independence-friendly Logic" we have one of his most substantial applications of the ideas of IF logic to a scientific domain.[10] It is a domain standing ready-made for his kind of application, because of the contradictions between first-order classical logic, as usually formulated, and quantum logic in any one of several different forms. I will not attempt here to review and give a technical discussion of quantum logic, but I will instead focus on a few points. First of all, I agree with Hintikka that he has successfully shown how his ideas of IF logic can be used to give a natural framework within which to interpret quantum logic. The philosophical significance of this is clear. Ordinarily, quantum logic is advertised as a logic that is separate from classical logic. In Hintikka's extension of classical logic to IF logic, quantum logic is now no longer a separate domain, but a subdomain of IF logic, and, therefore, of classical logic in this extended sense.

There is one main point I want to consider about IF logic and quantum mechanics. In the final paragraphs of his paper, Hintikka briefly mentions that, just as the received first-order logic can be embedded in a suitable probability logic, so can the extended IF logic be so embedded. However, there are some natural questions that arise and that have implications for the development of probability theory in a way that is suitable for IF logic. This can be stated in a concrete and simple way by considering what is needed for limited cases of quantum logic.

I shall try to make this discussion explicit by a few simple elementary definitions. The basic idea is that we generalize for restricted cases the concept of a set-theoretical structure that is a Boolean algebra to a quantum mechanical algebra. A Boolean algebra of sets is closed under complementation and union of any two sets of the algebra. In the quantum mechanical case, the closure under union is restricted to disjoint sets. This means that troublesome cases such as the joint observation of two noncommuting observables do not need to be considered, since the disjointness eliminates any problem of considering their joint distribution. So, for example, the set-theoretical framework can handle all the elementary cases of the noncommuting observables of position and momentum in quantum mechanics, but not the general case of any collection of observables. It is not critical to discuss the general case for the point that I want to make.

So, to formalize these ideas, I first define explicitly quantum-mechanical algebras of sets and, secondly, quantum-mechanical probability spaces.

DEFINITION 1 *Let Ω be a nonempty set. $\mathcal{F}$ is a quantum-mechanical algebra of sets on Ω if and only if $\mathcal{F}$ is a nonempty family of subsets of Ω and for every A and B in $\mathcal{F}$:*

    1. $\neg A \in \mathcal{F}$;

    2. If $A \cap B = \emptyset$ then $A \cup B \in \mathcal{F}$.

Moreover, if $\mathcal{F}$ is closed under countable unions of pairwise disjoint sets, that is, if $A_1, A_2, \ldots$ is a sequence of elements of $\mathcal{F}$ such that for $i \neq j$, $A_i \cap A_j = \emptyset$

$$\bigcup_{i=1}^{\infty} A_i \in \mathcal{F},$$

then $\mathcal{F}$ is a quantum-mechanical σ-algebra of sets.

(Note that '$\neg$' is the symbol for set complementation (relative to Ω), and '$\emptyset$' is the symbol for the empty set.)

An obvious elementary theorem is that any classical algebra (or σ-algebra) of sets on Ω is also a quantum-mechanical algebra (or σ-algebra) of sets on Ω, but easy counterexamples can be constructed to show that the converse is not true.

DEFINITION 2 *A structure* $\Omega = (\Omega, \mathcal{F}, \mathcal{P})$ *is a finitely additive quantum-mechanical probability space if and only if for every A and B in* $\mathcal{F}$:

P1. $\mathcal{F}$ *is a quantum-mechanical algebra of sets on* Ω;

P2. $P(A) \geq 0$;

P3. $P(\Omega) = 1$;

P4. If $A \cap B = \emptyset$, *then* $P(A \cup B) = P(A) + P(B)$.

Moreover, Ω *is a* quantum-mechanical probability space *(without restriction to finite additivity) if the following two axioms are also satisfied:*

P5. $\mathcal{F}$ *is a quantum-mechanical σ-algebra of sets on* Ω;

P6. If $A_1, A_2, \ldots,$ *is a sequence of pairwise incompatible events in* $\mathcal{F}$, *i.e.,* $A_i \cap A_j = \emptyset$ *for* $i \neq j$, *then*

$$P\left(\bigcup_{i=1}^{\infty}\right) = \sum_{i=1}^{\infty} P(A_i).$$

Again, we have the obvious and trivial theorem that every classical probability space, which I have not defined precisely, but follows the obvious and standard line, is also a quantum-mechanical probability space, but not conversely. The critical differences between classical and quantum-mechanical probability spaces, brought out in these two definitions, carry over naturally to the more general setting of ortho-complemented partial orderings of the sort discussed in Hintikka's article. But I do not need these generalizations to ask the relevant question, exactly how does Hintikka propose to handle probability in IF logics, in relation to what I am saying here? In the previous section, I brought up another, but related, question about probability and independence.

The point of the quantum-mechanical probability spaces is that they do not assign probabilities where you do not want them, as in the case of joint distribution and position of momentum. The classical space that satisfies the quantum-mechanical axioms would do so, and this would be undesirable. In the same way, IF logic is a generalization of classical logic and the probability structure that goes with such logics might have the same weakness of assigning probabilities when it is not desirable to do so. In other words, there seems to be a tension between the generalization of classical logic, given by Hintikka, in terms of probability on the one hand, and the reduction in the scope of probability on the other hand in the quantum-mechanical characterization just given. Of course, Hintikka can answer by so restricting, in the same kind of way, the probability that goes with an IF logic when it is applied to quantum mechanics. My question to him is, "Is this the kind of restriction you think is natural and appropriate?"

Of additional interest is how more detailed quantum-mechanical questions of dependence and independence relate to the structure of IF logic. I restrict the discussion to one simple but important case. This is the dependence between the probability distribution of position and that of momentum for an individual particle. As is well known, there is, for all but special degenerate cases, no joint distribution of position and momentum for a quantum-mechanical particle such as an electron or proton. So discussion of any dependency of one on the other lies outside a classical probabilistic analysis, which would, if it were possible, be framed around the properties of the joint distribution of position and momentum, as is standard for the phase spaces of classical statistical mechanics. (A conceptually important special case is the existence of the joint distribution of position and momentum in the ground state of a one-dimensional quantum harmonic oscillator. Here position and momentum are probabilistically independent.)

Of course, an important probabilistic constraint does exist in the general case, namely, the Heisenberg uncertainty principle, which asserts that the product of the standard deviations σ_q and σ_p for position and momentum must be greater than a certain constant, namely,

$$\sigma_q \sigma_p \geq \frac{\hbar}{2},$$

where $\hbar$ is Planck's constant h divided by 2π.

But a much more detailed result is also available. By well-known methods due to Wigner,[11] it may be shown that the marginal probability density $f(p)$ of momentum may be expressed as an integral of the position variable q by using the quantum state ψ that is a function of q.

$$f(p) = \frac{1}{2\pi} \int \int \psi^* \left(q - \frac{1}{2}\hbar u\right) e^{-iup} \psi\left(q + \frac{1}{2}\hbar u\right) du\, dq$$

(Details of this derivation are given in "Probability Concepts in Quantum Mechanics."[12]) Intuitively, this says that the distribution of momentum is a function of the entire distribution of position, a strong kind of dependence lying outside the framework of joint probability distributions. A dual integral formulation of $f(q)$ in terms of p may also be given. There may also be some interesting remarks to make about this example from the standpoint of IF logic, but Hintikka is more equipped than I am to ascertain whether or not this is true.

PATRICK SUPPES

STANFORD UNIVERSITY
JUNE 2003

NOTES

1.   Patrick Suppes, *Representation and Invariance of Scientific Structures* (Stanford, Calif.: CSLI Publications, 2002).
2.   See Jaakko Hintikka, "Truth Definitions, Skolem Functions and Axiomatic Set Theory," *Bulletin of Symbolic Logic* 4 (1998): 303–37.
3.   Jaakko Hintikka, "Presuppositions of Questions—Presuppositions of Inquiry," *Proceedings of the 2001 IIP Annual Meeting*, forthcoming.
4.   G. W. Mackey, *Mathematical Foundations of Quantum Mechanics* (New York: W. A. Benjamin, Inc., 1963).
5.   Hintikka, "Presuppositions of Questions—Presuppositions of Inquiry," p. 19.
6.   Hintikka, "Is Logic the Key to All Good Reasoning?" *Argumentation* 15 (2001): 35–57.
7.   J. Hintikka, I. Halonen, and A. Mutanen, "Interrogative Logic as a General Theory of Reasoning," ch. 3 in *Inquiry as Inquiry* (Dordrecht: Kluwer, 1999); reprinted in *Handbook of the Logic of Argument and Inference*, ed. D. M. Gabbay, R. H. Johnson, H. J. Ohlbach, and J. Woods, Studies in Logic and Practical Reasoning, vol. 1 (Amsterdam: North-Holland, 2002).
8.   Jaakko Hintikka, "Quantum Logic as a Fragment of Independence-friendly Logic," *Journal of Philosophical Logic* 31 (2000): 197–209.
9.   P. Suppes and N. Alechina, "The Definability of the Qualitative Independence of Events in Terms of Extended Indicator Functions," *Journal of Mathematical Psychology* 38 (1994): 366–76.
10. Hintikka, "Quantum Logic as a Fragment of Independence-friendly Logic."
11. E. Wigner, "On the Quantum Correction for Thermodynamic Equilibrium," *Physical Review* 40 (1932): 749–59.
12. Patrick Suppes, "Probability Concepts in Quantum Mechanics," *Philosophy of Science* 28 (1961): 378–89.

REPLY TO PATRICK SUPPES

Patrick Suppes's paper differs from the others in a way that I find eminently constructive. He is not asking in the first place what precisely my ideas are and how my ideas are related to those of other philosophers. He is not asking whether those ideas are right or wrong. What he is asking is what they are good for, in the sense of asking what further results or other developments they could lead us to. This makes his contribution singularly inspiring, but at the same time a challenging one. Significant new results do not come without effort and without new ideas. Since it has to anticipate future developments, my response will thus be somewhat speculative and involve more promissory notes than my responses to other contributors.

The applications Suppes has in mind are primarily scientific ones. Once again, I share his attitude. Philosophers are in these days concerned far too much (even in the philosophy of mathematics and in parts of the philosophy of science) with self-inflicted problems which have no relevance to the actual work in mathematics or in science and certainly do not threaten the foundations of these disciplines. It is a breath of fresh air to have Suppes challenge me to point out some uses of my ideas for the purposes of actual working science.

The ideas whose further promise are relevant here emerge by and large from my work in logic. It may nevertheless be clarifying to distinguish three different kinds of ideas, for their applications are likely to be somewhat different. There are, first, some "classical" ideas, that is, concepts and results that can be formulated in terms of received logical theories. Second, there is the approach which I have called game-theoretical and that has given rise to a new basic logic, which I have called (misleadingly, it has turned out) independence-friendly (IF) logic. Third, I have developed a new and better logic of questions and answers and used it as a framework for an approach to empirical inquiry, which I have called the interrogative model of inquiry. The uses of these different kinds of results are best discussed apart from each other, it seems to me.

Theoretically the deepest new ideas of these three are the ones leading to, or prompted by, IF logic. Suppes says, eminently fairly, that "what . . . is as yet missing from Hintikka's method of IF logic is how the apparatus can be used to settle some significant questions in particular parts of science." I have in effect anticipated this challenge, among other things by devoting a great deal of thought to how the ideas of IF logic can throw light on the conceptual problems of quantum theory. I have reached the working hypothesis that the key to dealing with these problems is the fact that noncommuting variables of quantum theory are irreducibly mutually dependent. If this working hypothesis pans out, as I believe that it will, we will have a most interesting example of cooperation between scientific and logical ideas. The working assumption, however abstract, is a physical assumption concerning the interaction of physical quantities. The reason why logical theory comes in in a big way here is that irreducibly mutual dependence turns out to be extremely difficult to express by means of the received mathematical and logical means. This difficulty is in my view the underlying reason for the conceptual problems of quantum theory.

Unfortunately, I have not yet developed my ideas far enough to have published them, with the sole exception of the paper on quantum logic that Suppes mentions. For one thing, in order to express the notion of irreducibly mutual dependence we have to relax even the conceptual framework of IF logic in the form in which this logic has so far been presented. It is in any case already clear that some of the characteristic phenomena uncovered by quantum theory, such as the uncertainty relations, and the need of relying on eigenvectors of operators are consequences of my working hypothesis. I am confident that the eventual outcome of this work will serve to meet Suppes's challenge, even though at this time I can only issue a promissory note.

On a general philosophical level we can also see here why the classical notion of cause is so inadequate for the purpose of quantum theory. IF logic can be thought of as the logical study of all different types of dependence and independence between variables. Now cause represents only one particular kind of dependence relation, being as it is antisymmetric. In particular, genuine mutual dependence can scarcely be hoped to be amenable to a treatment in terms of such a relation.

Suppes mentions some specific conceptual issues in quantum theory. The reason I am not yet ready to comment on them directly is that they are mostly in terms of probabilistic notions. Now so far we have not yet developed an explicit probability logic or "probability calculus" to go with IF logic. Nevertheless it is possible to see that such an extension of IF methods is highly interesting. The appropriate logic to use as a basis here is IF logic extended by a sentence-initial contradictory negation. Algebraically, this logic is a Boolean algebra with an additional operator. By

Tarski's old results, such an algebra admits of a set-theoretical ("geometrical") interpretation.[1] In this interpretation all the logical constants have the familiar set-theoretical meaning, except for the strong (dual) negation ~. Now it turns out that this operator can be thought of as a generalization of the familiar geometrical notion of orthogonality. This is not a mere matter of terminology, for the strong negation behaves in certain characteristic respects like an orthogonality. For instance, we can use it to define the notion of dimension as the maximal number of pairwise orthogonal sentences, and following the same line of thought to define coordinate representation on a purely logical level. This should be enough to indicate that IF logic is giving rise to generalizations of the concepts we use to solve significant questions in different parts of science. In particular, when the concept of probability is introduced into IF logic, we obtain a richer structure than the classical probability calculus, for the probability measures must now be defined also on the strong negations of propositions (events). This can be hoped to remove some of the difficulties in the foundations of probability that were emphasized by von Neumann.[2] Thus it is not so much a new conception of probability that is needed in quantum theory. It is a new conception of what it is to which probabilities are assigned.

I can try to relate this point even more closely to Suppes's paper. Suppes raises sharp questions about the use of probability concepts in quantum theory. He points out that, while IF logic gives us a greater flexibility than before in describing phenomena, the applications of probability concepts apparently have to be restricted. For instance, we cannot assign a joint probability distribution to position and momentum. Is there not a tension here? I cannot give a technical treatment here, but I can indicate what I believe the answer to be. What happens is not that we have to restrict the probability distributions we use, but that we have to restructure the events to which we assign probabilities. For instance, in this proposed treatment there will not exist any state in which both the position variable and the momentum variable assume a definite value at the same time.

At the same time we encounter here a reminder of the subtleties of the notions of dependence and independence. For one thing, in vector spaces orthogonality can be thought of as a kind of independence. (Needless to say, this is a different kind of independence from the one captured in IF logic.) For this kind of independence, we can write down various structural laws. They are not unlike the properties of probabilistic independence listed by Suppes in his section 4, even though they are not precisely the same. They are simply among the logical truths of IF propositional logic (extended by a sentence-initial contradictory negation).

A direct comparison between the notion of independence used in IF logic and probabilistic independence is not possible in that the two are defined for different kinds of entities. IF independence is a relation defined for pairs of variables, whereas probabilistic independence is defined for pairs of events (philosophers' "propositions"). More thought is needed, however, to uncover their precise relationship.

Somewhat similar things can be said of the applications of the interrogative model. As Suppes points out, one of the advantages of this approach is that it makes it possible to use strategic concepts in the study of the scientific process and in principle in scientific research itself. Once again, he would like to see specific applications. I am not in a position to provide quite as detailed realistic applications as Suppes undoubtedly has in mind. However, I can point to a result that should in principle guide such applications but which is not emphasized by Suppes. It is the extremely close connection between the optimal strategies of deduction and of interrogation. I agree with Suppes that it will probably take some time before the promise of such insights is put to use on the concrete working level. But, as I have suggested before, this connection has tacitly been recognized in the popular consciousness in the form of the "Sherlock Holmes" idea of logic as the secret of all good reasoning.

In this direction, too, I have been slowly planning a specific scientific application, even though it probably is different from what Suppes has in mind. He mentions in passing Bayesian methods as an approach that perhaps could be integrated with the interrogative model. Now Bayesian methods have admittedly many handy applications in actual scientific methodology. However, on the general theoretical level, working with the interrogative method has made me sensitive to the limitations of a Bayesian approach as a general analysis of rationality. Bayesian inference relies on prior probabilities. What I have slowly come to realize is that the choice of such priors amounts to a factual assumption concerning the world. (See here my response to Isaac Levi in this volume.) Hence, in order to avoid a priori commitments, Bayesian inference must in principle be complemented by a method of changing priors in the light of experiences. We cannot always go by asymptotic results either. Such results may be applicable in a context of choosing a scientific generalization on the basis of relatively stable data, but in other contexts we cannot rely on what happens in the long run. For instance, in the deliberations of a jury the priors include the reliability of the testimony of different witnesses, and the conclusion to be drawn may depend on how that reliability is judged in the short run of a court case.

I believe that much more thought has to be devoted to the kind of supplementary reasoning than has been the case so far. As a potential scientific application, I have come to the conclusion that the would-be cognitive fallacies studied by Tversky and Kahneman are predicated on an insufficient analysis of the epistemological situation.[3] (I am thinking here primarily of what are known as the "conjunctive fallacy" and the "base rate fallacy.") I hope to put the interrogative model to use to show this. Perhaps it will qualify as the kind of actual scientific application Suppes has in mind.

Perhaps it should be added that, largely independently of the development of IF logic and of the interrogative model, there are plenty of important insights in logical theory that have general theoretical significance. For instance, a strengthened version of Craig-type interpolation results (for ordinary first-order logic) has opened interesting perspectives into the nature of explanation.[4] Furthermore, it seems to me that a critical examination of the widely used notion of supervenience is badly needed. I suspect that it cannot sustain the theoretical uses that it has been put to recently.

These developments are not directly related to the points Suppes raises. More closely relevant to his and other philosophers' practice is the question of axiomatic set theory as the framework of choice in mathematics and in philosophy of science. Suppes notes the difference between himself and me in this respect. An earlier version of his magnum opus was in fact called *Set-Theoretical Structures in Science*,[5] whereas I have relied much more on straightforward logical languages and their model theory. This choice is, I believe, more than a matter of intellectual taste. At least for the purposes of the foundations of mathematics, axiomatic set theory is subject to serious objections. They are expounded in my forthcoming paper in the proceedings of the Tarski centenary meeting under the title "Independence-Friendly Logic and Axiomatic Set Theory."[6] Whether these shortcomings seriously impair axiomatic set theory also as a tool in the philosophy of science remains to be seen.

One way in which epistemological ideas can prove their mettle is by enabling us to understand better the actual history of science. One such application is worth discussing here. In that direction, I have called attention to the remarkable affinity between the interrogative model and the description by Newton of his experimental method at the end of the *Opticks*, and indeed the affinity between the interrogative model and the experimental method Newton practiced in his optical work. Suppes belittles somewhat the extent of this similarity, characterizing Newton's work in the *Principia* as mathematical model-building and not so much as deductions from the results of experiments. Here I am prepared to stick to my guns and point to two things. First, Newton speaks of drawing conclusions from phenomena, which include not only experiments but systematic observation. Now for the methodology I am ascribing to Newton the crucial thing about experiments is that they result in data about dependencies between different variables. Similar dependence data can of course be obtained by systematic observations, which in Newton's case included (among other things) Kepler's laws.

Hence the term "experimental method" is too narrow. What is crucial in the method I have ascribed to Newton is the use of dependence laws as part of the most important "phenomena" that are the input in the scientific process.

Second, Newton himself insists that he is in the *Principia* using the same method as in the *Opticks*.[7] In his preface to the first edition, he describes his procedure as follows: "For the basic problem of philosophy seems to be to discover the forces of nature from the phenomena of motions and then to demonstrate the other phenomena from these forces."[8] And in a letter to Cotes, Newton says that "Experimental philosophy proceeds only upon Phenomena & deduces general propositions from them only by Induction. And such is the proof of mutual attraction."[9] It is also unmistakable that among "phenomena" Newton includes experimentally or observationally established dependence relations. Newton's own conception of his activity was definitely not a freestanding model-building, but a procedure starting from phenomena.

J. H.

NOTES

1.   See here Tarski's papers with Bjarni Jonsson on Boolean algebras with operators, reprinted in his *Collected Papers*, vol. 3, pp. 369–458.

2.   See von Neumann's Amsterdam talk on unsolved problems in mathematics, published in *John von Neumann and the Foundations of Quantum Physics*, ed. Miklos Redei and Michael Stöltzner (Dordrecht: Kluwer Academic, 2001), pp. 231–46, as well as Redei's paper in the same volume.

3.   For a popular survey, with references to the literature, see Massimo Piatelli-Palmarini, *Inevitable Illusions* (New York: John Wiley, 1994).

4.   See here my 1999 paper with Ilpo Halonen, "The Structure of Interpolation and Explanation."

5.   Patrick Suppes, *Representation and Invariance of Scientific Structures* (Stanford, Calif.: CSLI Publications, 2002).

6.   "Independence-friendly Logic and Axiomatic Set Theory," *Annals of Pure and Applied Logic* 126: 313–33.

7.   Isaac Newton, *Opticks* (New York: Dover Publications, 1952), pp. 404–5.

8.   Isaac Newton, *The Principia: Mathematical Principles of Natural Philosophy*, a new translation by I. Bernard Cohen and Anne Whitman (Berkeley: University of California Press, 1999), p. 382.

9.   See *The Correspondence of Isaac Newton*, ed. A. Rupert Hall and Laura Tilling (Cambridge: Cambridge University Press, 1975), vol. 5, p. 400.

23

Isaac Levi

INDUCTION, ABDUCTION, AND ORACLES

In 1966 Jaakko Hintikka proposed a way of modifying Carnap's program for inductive logic so as to allow for the possibility that universal generalizations can receive positive probabilities on the basis of data.[1] Hintikka and Hilpinen explained how accepting hypotheses when the probability is high enough could be secured while retaining the consistency and deductive closure conditions on accepted sentences.[2] In addition, Hintikka and Pietarinen initiated a line of research that came up with a method of justifying inductive inferences where the conclusion is the coming to full belief that the conclusion is true by showing that adopting that conclusion maximizes expected epistemic utility where the epistemic utility function represents a certain kind of cognitive goal.[3]

Since the mid-1980s, Hintikka has shifted gears. He seems to have come to the conclusion that neither the methods for assessing on the basis of data within the framework of an improved Carnapian inductive logic he had proposed, nor the decision theoretic approach to inductive expansion that he, Juhani Pietarinen, and Risto Hilpinen had developed some twenty years earlier, is satisfactory. In recent years, Hintikka has been advocating an "interrogative model" of inquiry.[4] To those of us familiar with the emphasis by Peirce and Dewey on inquiry as problem solving where one of the central tasks is the identification of the potential answers to the questions being raised, Hintikka's emphasis on questions and answers sounds a sympathetic chord. I hope Hintikka will forgive the egocentricity involved in my developing an account of the similarities and differences between my approach to answering questions and his as I understand it.

In my earliest publications on inference, I focused on testing statistical hypotheses after the fashion of Neyman and Pearson where the difference between the null hypothesis and the alternative called for recognition of the importance of the question being asked in evaluating inductive behavior.[5] Emphasis on the importance of questions and their potential answers was commonplace among advocates of the approach to statistical reasoning developed by Neyman and Pearson. The same emphasis was also central to the approach to scientific inquiry developed by Charles Peirce who anticipated the Neyman-Pearson-Wald approach a half century earlier. I began with the same attitude even though the approach to decision-making I adopted there was predicated on the injunction to maximize expected utility.[6] I insisted that legitimate inductive inference depended for its legitimacy on the kind of question raised and the roster of potential answers posed to the question.

Following Peirce, I have maintained that inquiry begins with a settled stock of assumptions perfectly free of doubt. I suggest that the inquirer is committed by that stock of assumptions to being absolutely certain of the truth of those assumptions and their logical consequences. Such commitments may be represented linguistically by a set of sentences K closed under logical consequence in a suitably regimented language L. Although the inquirer will find it important to clarify and identify his or her doxastic commitments, that explicative task is not to be conflated with the task of determining whether to and how to change those doxastic commitments. Inquiry outside of logic and mathematics is concerned with changing doxastic commitments.

In the first instance, inquiry seeks to remove doubts. By this I mean that bona fide inquiry is concerned to eliminate doubts in doxastic *commitments*. To doubt whether h is true or false is to be committed to acknowledging the serious possibility that h is true and that h is false while ruling out as a serious possibility that both are false. Such commitments to doubt are to be distinguished from the anxieties that are associated with subjective feelings of doubt. They are also to be distinguished from the "paper doubts" of philosophers who think well of Descartes's methodological skepticism. And while insisting that no inquiry is serious unless it addresses a genuine question, inquirers recognize some problems and questions as more urgent than others. In the arena of publicly funded research, the politics of how to prioritize projects for research is practiced with great vigor. But even the solitary inquirer will need to confront hard choices concerning which question to investigate. And the choices will often be grounded in moral considerations, economic interest, aesthetic demands, ego gratification, or other values. To be sure, the effort to remove doubt is highly selective. It remains, nonetheless, an effort to remove doubt.

In any given inquiry some problem or group of problems is raised. Efforts are made to identify potential answers or solutions. That is the task in inquiry that Peirce called "abduction" in the last decade of his life.

Peirce also assigned a task to what he misleadingly called "deduction." The epithet is misleading because deduction included so called "probable syllogism" and "statistical syllogism." The respect in which such reasoning qualifies as syllogism or deduction or even deduction from statistical premises via the calculus of probabilities is far from clear. (Peirce fussed over this issue for a couple of decades before settling on a more or less stable view.) Whatever the deductive task might be, in the statistical case, it does involve deriving judgments as to the subjective or credal probability that specified outcomes of a given experiment will occur on the basis of information to the effect that the experiment has taken place and assumptions about the statistical probabilities of outcomes of the kind specified occurring on trials of the kind specified. (Peirce would not have stated the matter in this fashion, but his view is more or less equivalent to this.) Like ordinary deduction, such "direct inference" or "statistical syllogism" as Peirce called it is useful in deriving "consequences" of conjectures obtained by abduction and, hence, may be classified with deduction when "inferences" are classified in terms of the tasks they perform in inquiry.

Induction has as its task the determination of which of the conjectures proposed by abduction for investigation should be rejected on the basis of the experimental data. The conclusion drawn from the data is that one of the conjectures surviving rejection is true. When the induction is a good one, the inquirer is warranted in changing his "corpus" or set of full beliefs by adding this conclusion to his body of certainties. The inquirer is then committed to a new state of full belief represented by the deductive consequences of his initial corpus and the newly added sentence.

According to Peirce, the new beliefs, like the old beliefs, are liable to be revised or corrected in subsequent inquiries. That is the doctrine he called "fallibilism." Unfortunately, fallibilism is all too often taken to mean that every (extralogical or extraconceptual) judgment might be false. Possibility of being revised is not the same as possibility of being false. Although he certainly should have, whether Peirce fully appreciated this point is not clear. He ought to have done. According to Peirce, if one takes for granted some proposition, one needs a good reason to give it up. Otherwise the doubt is a paper doubt. Moreover, it is not enough to point out that the belief itself was acquired improperly. One needs a good reason for converting a paper doubt into a serious one.

Consider, however, an inquirer X in a given state of doxastic commitment K at time or in context t. X is at t committed to ruling out as impossible the falsity of each and every consequence of K. Of course, X at t can and should acknowledge the logical possibility that each and every extralogical consequence h of K is false. But X rules out the logical possibility that h is false as a serious possibility.

X is, in this sense, absolutely certain that X is not born of a virgin
mother. But X should be *able* to revise X's beliefs even on this issue and
recognize that he is able to do so. That is to say, X should acknowledge that
it is or should be possible *for* X to change X's mind even though it is not
possible *that* X is born of a virgin mother.

Moreover, X at t can and should acknowledge the serious possibility
that in the future X will acquire good reason to change X's mind and
become committed to recognizing the logical possibility that *h* is false to be
a serious possibility. In this sense, X's mind should be open. *But an open
mind should not be an empty mind.* Openness would collapse into emptiness
if every logical possibility were considered a serious possibility.

Corrigibilism, as I understand it, is the view that we should keep an
open mind. Fallibilism, as I understand it, is the view that we should
maintain an empty mind. (I do not pretend that my usage conforms with
presystematic precedent.) I favor corrigibilism. I reject fallibilism.[7] Whether
rejecting fallibilism while endorsing corrigibilism is a coherent philosophical perspective is an important philosophical issue. When this perspective
is not deemed philosophically acceptable, it is easy to conflate the two
views. Peirce is a self-proclaimed fallibilist who does not distinguish clearly
between fallibilism and corrigibilism, as I understand them. I contend that
drawing the distinction enables us to be more faithful to Peirce's original
insight than Peirce himself seems to have been.

In contrast to fallibilists, corrigibilists can coherently acknowledge a
distinction between conjectures or potential answers that might be true or
false and settled assumptions perfectly free from doubt. From the point of
view of inquirer X at t, there is no serious possibility that any settled
assumption is false. Conjectures might be true and might be false. One may
coherently distinguish between conjectures with respect to probability. Full
beliefs or settled assumptions are indistinguishable with respect to
probability. They are all maximally certain. However, occasions may arise
where the inquirer has good reason to give up erstwhile settled assumptions.
When such a situation does occur, a distinction must be made between
certainties with respect to degrees of vulnerability to being given up or
degrees of corrigibility.

Fallibilists, by way of contrast, must think of the distinction between
conjectures and settled assumptions as matters of degree. Strictly speaking,
settled assumptions are propositions judged so highly probable that the
difference between such high probability and absolute certainty is barely
discernible.

But even fallibilists appear to be committed to acknowledging some
sort of space of possibilities. Judgments of probability are, after all, fine-
grained distinctions between serious possibilities. So given any partition of

the space of possibilities, the inquirer should be absolutely certain that at least one cell in the partition contains the truth. I take it that fallibilists should concede that rational agents should be absolutely certain of the truth of some propositions. They insist, however, that such propositions are logical or conceptual truths. For fallibilists, no extralogical proposition can become a settled assumption strictly speaking. Fallibilists are closet skeptics.

Fallibilists must deny the usefulness of a distinction between explicative and ampliative reasoning. Explicative reasoning involves coming to recognize the deductive implications of one's state of full belief. Such reasoning does not involve any *change* in that state of doxastic commitment even though it does entail a change in the extent to which such one is fulfilling such commitments. Inductive or ampliative reasoning does involve a change in doxastic commitment. Adding new information to one's current state of doxastic commitment terminates doubt on some issue. Since the fallibilist (in my sense—not Peirce's) insists that inquirer X is fully committed to believe all and only logical and other conceptually necessary truths, there is little scope for change in doxastic commitment either through adding or removing information from X's doxastic commitments. In particular, there can be no inductive or ampliative inference.

Peirce emphasized the distinction between the explicative and the ampliative and between conjecture obtained via abduction and the belief formed when doubt is terminated via induction. As late as the 1880s, Peirce insisted that induction and hypothetic reasoning are both ampliative.[8] But, as he later admitted, the inferences he had called hypothetic in 1883 were after all inductive.[9] By the turn of the century, Peirce had introduced the term "abduction" to characterize the kind of reasoning involved in the task of forming conjectures as candidate answers to questions under investigation. Having recognized that he had misclassified certain inductions ("qualitative inductions") as nondeductive hypothetic inferences, Peirce distinguished more carefully between these qualitative inductions (which he explicitly classified with the quantitative inductions he had discussed in 1883) and another task that he mixed up with that one. The other task is the task of abduction or forming potential answers that Peirce discusses explicitly beginning at the turn of the century.

Peirce continued to think of both qualitative inductions and abductions as inferences. No doubt they both are species of reasoning. But I prefer to restrict "inference" to reasonings where one justifies coming to full belief in the conclusion on the basis of the information contained in the premises (relative to the initial state of full belief). The "conclusion" of abduction is a conjecture. Conjecturing is not fully believing or even coming to full belief. So I prefer to deny that abduction is a form of inference (although it is a species of reasoning). In my terminology, the early Peirce thought of hypothetic inference as reasoning where the conclusion was forming a belief (or at least, he sometimes thought of hypothetic inference in this way). When he replaced that category of reasoning with abduction, the conclusion of abduction is no longer the forming of a belief.

Hintikka thinks of abduction as conjecturing just as the later Peirce and I do. But he insists not only that it is a form of inference but that it is the only genuine form of ampliative inference. I agree with Hintikka that it is ampliative in the sense that the conclusion does not follow deductively from the premises. But it is not inference in the sense that new information is added to the inquirer's state of full belief. The conclusion of an ampliative inference in this sense must be a new belief.

Peirce failed to distinguish fallibilism from corrigibilism in any clear and explicit way and explicitly identified himself as a fallibilist. I think it charitable to interpret his fallibilism as my corrigibilism. On this assumption, I have reformed his terminology. In Hintikka's case, the classificatory issues are somewhat more complicated and it is not so easy to identify the substantive presuppositions and goals underlying the differences between his classificatory system and mine.

According to Peirce and Dewey, inquiry is concerned with changing states of full belief in order to solve urgent problems or answer important questions. Strictly speaking, the preoccupation here is not merely with changes of states of full belief but with changes in other attitudinal states such as states of credal probability judgment and value judgment as well. The important point of concern here is that the study of justifiable changes calls for a study of the features, if any, that all attitudinal states of a certain kind (such as states of full belief) should possess. In the case of full belief, these features are specified by identifying the minimal conditions that rationally coherent states of full belief should satisfy. As I understand "logic" it focuses on identifying such conditions not only for states of full belief (where a logic of full belief is required) but for states of probability judgment (where a probability logic is needed), for value commitments, assessments of feasibility of options, and judgments as to which among such options ought to be considered admissible.

Is there a logic of abduction as Peirce and Hintikka both think there is? If the task of abduction is to identify conjectures that are potential answers to the question under study, then the first principle of abductive logic is, as Peirce said it was, the pragmatic principle. Given the initial state of full belief (which, from the inquirer's point of view, ought to be identical with the inquirer's initial state of knowledge), a potential answer should be testable. Otherwise, the conjecture will not serve the purpose for which it was intended.

The tasks of deduction and abduction have two sides. On the one hand there are universal norms of minimal rationality. Thus, all rational agents are committed to believing the deductive consequences of what they believe. Of course, none of us can perfectly fulfill our commitments. We need advice, therapy, prosthetic devices, and training in order to improve our capacities to implement these prescriptions. Precisely the same is true in the case of abduction. The pragmatic principle spells out our minimal commitments in endorsing a proposed conjecture as a potential answer to a given question. But we may well need help in fulfilling these commitments.

The canons regulating the task of deduction serve as standards for determining the legitimacy of reasonings from conjectural suppositions to testable consequences. These include not only principles of deductive logic but principles of direct inference regulating the legitimacy of statistical syllogisms. The pragmatic principle is intended to serve as a standard for distinguishing between legitimate and illegitimate formation of conjectures or potential answers to questions. In both deduction and abduction, skill is required to fulfill the commitments that the appropriate standards set for the inquirer. Therapy, training, and technology can help enhance the skills. Logic (in the normative and broad sense) by way of contrast sets the standards for having the requisite skills.

In this sense, both deductive and abductive logic are "definitory." Hintikka disagrees. Hintikka insists as I do that there is an abductive logic. Nonetheless, he maintains that, in contrast to deduction, the rules are "strategic." For Peirce, however, the pragmatic principle sets the standards for legitimate abductions.

Another important contrast comes into play when we focus on changing doxastic commitments, the roster of potential answers under consideration, and so forth. In my judgment, there is no logic of change in the sense of minimal requirements imposed on rational agents concerning how to change *commitments* to belief or value. Changing such commitments calls for justification. My contention is that such justification is a *decision theoretic* justification that shows which of the available options are admissible in the light of the deliberating agent's goals and values. I do not think it helpful to think of the deliberating agent as participant in some game, unless one is prepared to adopt the view advocated by Kadane and Larkey according to which a participant in a game should always treat the moves of the other players as so many unknown states of nature or parts of states of nature and reduce his problem to a problem of decision making under risk or uncertainty.[10] I do not think as game theorists tend to do that we should ideally recommend Nash equilibria or some other kind of equilibrium as "solutions" to games. In spite of his insistence that he is discussing game theoretic models for inquiry, I am not certain how seriously Hintikka takes his metaphor. Perhaps, his strategic principles are my decision-theoretic ones. But in my view, decision making, whether it is in the service of changing beliefs or forming policy, needs to satisfy minimal standards of rational decision making. In this sense, there is a logic of decision making but it is definitory, not strategic.

This logic, however, concerns minimal conditions for rationally coherent evaluation of options. Justification identifies the subset of the options the agent X is committed to recognizing as available to X that are admissible for choice given X's values and beliefs in the context of deliberation. The conclusion of deliberation is, therefore, the *identification* of a subset of the available options as admissible options. If X judges members of a set of options to be admissible prior to choice, X is committed at that time to altering X's commitments by choosing and implementing one of those options subsequently. The logic of rational choice commits X to restricting choice to the admissible options (whatever the logic of rational choice says these are) relative to X's beliefs and values. From that prior point of view, X has not as yet chosen. Yet from that point of view, X will subsequently violate X's initial commitments if X does not choose and implement an option identified as admissible from that initial point of view.

X *alters* X's commitments upon making a choice. Whereas beforehand, X was committed to recognizing a certain roster of acts as optional for X, once X has made a decision, none of these acts are any longer optional from X's new point of view. This is at least one respect in which X's commitments have changed. By making the decision, X has also committed to believing fully that the choice undertaken will be fulfilled. This is so whether or not the decision taken is admissible relative to X's prior beliefs, goals, and values.

If X should fail to make a choice of an option judged admissible from the prior point of view, X can recognize that X has violated X's prior commitments and has chosen in a manner that is not rationally justified by these prior commitments. X's "weakness of will" displays irrationality relative to the beliefs, goals, and values X endorsed prior to choice. And retrospectively as well as prospectively X may recognize that X has not changed X's point of view justifiably. But X's new commitments need not be internally incoherent.

Thus, even the principles of rational choice are principles of logic in a definitory sense. It is unclear to me that any principles of logic need to be considered anything other than minimal constraints on synchronic rationality. In addition to such logical principles, we often need help, advice, technological and therapeutic fixes, and the like to enable us to satisfy the principles. And such contributions are important. But I do not think it advisable to call such advice "logic." In any case, such advice is needed when the task is the deductive one as well as the abductive one. Hintikka's contrast once more seems to me misleading.

I also think that inductive inference ought to be rationalized on decision-theoretic principles (as Hintikka, Pietarinen, Hilpinen, and Niiniluoto also thought many years ago). I could endorse Hintikka's brief criticism of Gärdenfors's views as calling for critical scrutiny from a strategic viewpoint (p. 4) if "strategic" means "decision-theoretic."[11] I myself am on record as complaining that AGM accounts of belief change do not provide a decision-theoretic rationale for either expansion by observation or by induction or a corresponding rationale for contraction.

There is another aspect of the relation of Peirce's views and mine with Hintikka's that should be mentioned. According to Peirce, the conjectures obtained via abduction will typically involve statistical claims specifying the chances of outcomes of experiments. Hintikka's focus on specifying potential answers and their complexity in terms of the character of the quantificational structure of their prefixes cannot, I believe, do justice to statistical claims.

Moreover, data do not refute the hypotheses in virtue of deductive considerations as usually conceived. In this respect, statistical conjectures exhibit a superficial similarity to existential generalization. But the resemblance is spurious. Nor does an appeal to probability logic (also called "inductive logic") provide us with a sure footing when it comes to relating statistical hypotheses to the outcomes of experiments.

I agree with Ramsey and the recent views of Hintikka in registering skepticism concerning the importance of inductive logic if this skepticism is directed at the efforts of Laplace, Keynes, Johnson, Jeffreys, Carnap, and the early Hintikka to construct an inductive or probability logic so strong as to recommend unique probability distributions over hypotheses on the basis of the available data. Ramsey departed from this project. He recognized the usefulness of probability logic as a logic of consistency specifying minimal requirements of rational probability judgment such as conformity to the requirements of the calculus of probability. I am inclined to add a family of new principles to Ramsey's logic of consistency. These principles impose constraints on subjective probability judgments that concern the outcomes of stochastic experiments. The type of constraint would depend on the available information about the system subject to the experiment and the kind of experiment being conducted. But probability logic so conceived is a far cry from the dreams of Carnap when he first explored the prospects for inductive logic. In particular, one cannot support, on the basis of probability logic alone, posterior judgments of credal probability for the potential answers to questions on the basis of experimental data if these judgments are expected to be numerically determinate.

This does not mean *pace* Ramsey that we cannot make sense of the idea of logical probability. A brief digression may help to explain why.[12] According to those who have defended the notion, we can consider a logical probability to be a function from potential states of full belief to states of credal or subjective probability judgment. I call such a function a *confirmational commitment* $C: K \rightarrow B$ where K is the set of conceptually available potential states of full belief and B is the set of potential credal states. Those who have advocated the use of logical probability have assumed at a very minimum that such functions satisfy the following three requirements:

> *Probabilistic Coherence*: For each K in K, C(K) should be a set of finitely additive probability functions $Q(x/y)$ defined for every x in the algebra and each y consistent with K.

> *Probabilistic Consistency*: C(K) should be nonempty if and only if K is consistent.

> *Probabilistic Convexity*: For every y consistent with K, the set of probability measures of the form $Q_y(x) = Q(x/y)$ is convex.

In addition, to these three minimal and relatively non controversial requirements, adherents to what may be called a *weak Bayesian* view, endorse the following requirement:

> *Confirmational Conditionalization*: Let K be consistent and in K and let h be any proposition consistent with K. Let K^+_h be the result of expanding K by adding h together with all consequences of K and h. For every Q in C(K), there is a Q_h in $C(K^+_h)$ such that $Q(x/yh) = Q_h(x/y)$ and conversely for every Q_h there is a Q satisfying the same equation.

There are important writers (most notably R. A. Fisher and H. E. Kyburg) who would reject confirmational conditionalization. Others such as I would endorse it but would not impose the temporal version according to which whenever an inquirer at t_0 is in state K with confirmational commitment C and expands K at t_1 by adding h, X's new credal state should be the conditionalization of the one at t_0. On my view, temporal credal conditionalization may fail when inquirer X changes X's confirmational commitment.

Those in the past who have taken the notion of logical probability seriously made two assumptions that seriously compromise the prospects for taking the idea seriously:

First, they embraced *strict Bayesianism* by insisting the following:

> *Probabilistic Uniqueness*: For every consistent K in K, C(K) is a singleton.

Second, they insisted that there be a standard confirmational commitment certified by probability logic. Carnap's confirmation functions are familiar representations of confirmational commitments embedded in toy languages.

Ramsey was rightly skeptical of the existence of logical confirmational commitments satisfying probabilistic uniqueness. But he wrongly thought that principles of rationality (or of the probabilistic logic of consistency) require that no matter what confirmational commitment one endorses, probabilistic uniqueness should be satisfied. Ramsey's view (and the somewhat similar views of De Finetti and Savage) lead to the conclusion that rational agents are obliged as rational agents to be opinionated in their probability judgments. That is to say, they should always be committed to a numerically determinate state of credal probability judgment as credal uniqueness requires. Nonetheless, the confirmational commitment that delivers that opinionated probability judgment is not rationally mandated by the norms of rational probability judgment. There is no single numerically determinate confirmational commitment that serves as the standard for opinionated probability judgment for all inquirers. But every rational inquirer is obliged as a rational agent to have determinate confirmational commitment. It is ironic that subjectivists or personalists who take this position are often probabilists as well. They urge us to shun being absolutely certain (i.e., fully believing) any extralogical proposition. Yet they are happy to insist that probability judgment be opinionated.

I have suggested that we allow for confirmational commitments where $C(K)$ violates credal uniqueness. With confirmational conditionalization in place, we can follow Carnap in characterizing a confirmational commitment in terms of the value of $C(LK)$ where LK is a minimal state of full belief relative to the family of inquiries under consideration. Attention may be restricted to the set K of potential states of full belief that are expansions of LK by rejecting elements of a *basic partition* U_{LK} and adding the join of the unrejected elements of LK. The value of a confirmational commitment C for K in K is obtained by confirmational conditionalization from $C(LK)$. Any confirmational commitment, such that $C(LK)$ is a singleton, is a maximally determinate consistent confirmational commitment. When $C(LK)$ is the set of all such singletons obeying the requirements of probability logic, $C(LK)$ is the logical confirmational commitment.

On this view, there is always a logical confirmational commitment. The concept of logical probability does make perfectly good sense. Nonetheless, if Ramsey is right in denying that probability logic singles out a unique determinate confirmational commitment for use, then the logical confirmational commitment must be numerically indeterminate. And this indeterminacy means that inquirers are not obliged as rational agents to endorse the logical confirmational commitment as their standard any more than they are obliged to restrict their full beliefs to logical truths. They may coherently adopt stronger extralogical confirmational commitments as long as they are prepared to recognize their revisability.

Nonetheless, differences can arise concerning the conception of logical probability to adopt. That is due to disagreements concerning the conditions for probability logic to be complete. De Finetti and Savage would have urged something like the requirements just mentioned. Those who have thought that a stronger set of principles should be incorporated have proceeded along two different lines.

First, following J. Bernoulli and P. S. de Laplace, H. Jeffreys, R. Carnap, E. T. Jaynes, and Jaakko Hintikka, among others, have sought in different ways to appeal to symmetry conditions to impose constraints on confirmational commitments. In recent years, Hintikka seems to have renounced his own previous efforts to improve upon the principle of insufficient reason so we shall not address this matter here.

The main alternative approach to strengthening probability logic involves adding a principle of direct inference mandating how credal probabilities should be assigned outcomes of stochastic experiments, given information about the statistical probability distributions over the outcomes of such experiments. Approaches of this kind presuppose the usefulness of some conception of statistical probability or chance. Variations in the principles deployed often reflect disagreements concerning how statistical probability is to be understood. And these differences can be relevant to the way the principle of direct inference is formulated.

De Finetti and Savage were skeptical of the usefulness of conceptions of statistical probability. They were also skeptical of the status of principles of insufficient reason, maximum entropy, or other appeals to symmetry as principles of probability logic. Consequently, they held that the minimal constraints I listed above constitute a complete probability logic. As I have mentioned, they also insisted on credal uniqueness with unfortunate results.

To my way of thinking, the completeness of probability logic pivots on the status of objective chance or statistical probability and the principle of direct inference associated with it. We should turn our back on insufficient reason and all its misbegotten progeny. Peirce may be counted among those who have adopted a similar view. Peirce was a firm opponent of the use of inverse inference deriving determinate posteriors from determinate Laplacian priors. He did not object to using Bayes's theorem to derive posteriors from priors provided the prior probabilities could be derived from information about precise simple statistical hypotheses via direct inference. Indeed, Peirce insisted that the *only* setting in which judgments of numerically determinate credal probability is warranted is when credal probability is grounded in information about statistical probabilities and is derived via direct inference (which he called statistical syllogism).

Thus, Peirce seems to have insisted on endorsing the logical confirmational commitment—i.e., the maximally indeterminate one according to the probability logic he embraced. He would also have opposed the use of indeterminate priors to derive indeterminate posteriors as I have urged. On this point, I think Peirce was not true to his own position. If inquirer X is entitled to embrace extralogical full beliefs subject to modification in the course of subsequent inquiry, why cannot the same be true of confirmational commitments?

Peirce himself made no explicit use of confirmational commitments. He would have simply rejected the appeal to prior probabilities for use in deriving posteriors unless they are grounded in statistical knowledge. Even so, his own insistence that in the absence of statistical knowledge no probability judgment can be made may plausibly be taken to be equivalent to the view that, in the absence of statistical knowledge, probability judgment should be maximally indeterminate. And this view is tantamount to adding a principle of direct inference to minimal probability logic and recommending the logical confirmational commitment.

The problem facing Peirce, as it has faced others who have taken his position, is how to acquire new information from data in the absence of useful priors. Peirce suggested a method for rejecting elements of the set of strongest consistent potential answers to a question identified by abduction.[13] It is not, however, a method in the sense of a criterion for distinguishing legitimate from illegitimate rejections on the basis of evidence. The investigator does not gather information from the observations or experiment that he or she then uses as premises to draw a conclusion as to the true value of the parameter. The data are used as *input* (rather than as *evidence*) into a program whose output is an estimate of the parameter according to the program.

Thus, an inquirer X who is interested in estimating the percentage of cloven-hoofed animals who are herbivorous might sample from the cloven-hoofed at random. Consider a rule for estimating the proportion of herbivorous animals in the population from the proportion in the sample that instructs X to come to believe that the population proportion is approximately r/n in response to data that the sample proportion is r/n. The weak law of large numbers warrants X in judging that following such a rule has a high statistical probability of avoiding error. By statistical syllogism or direct inference, X judges *before sampling* that following the rule is unlikely to lead to error. So X *precommits* to following the rule. That is to say, X undertakes to obey the requirements of the rule regardless of what happens in the course of implementation.

To implement the rule, X will have to determine the proportion of herbivorous animals in the sample. But X does not use this information as evidence. Taken as evidence, the data are nuisance information. The statistical probability of avoiding error in following the rule given the precise proportion of herbivorous animals in the random sample of cloven-hoofed animals depends on the true proportion of herbivorous animals in the population. When the interval estimate prescribed by the rule covers the true value, the statistical probability of avoiding error will be 1 and otherwise 0. Using the data as evidence renders the data useless. On the other hand, if the inquirer X follows the rule and refuses to use the data as evidence, using it only as input into a rule for making estimates adopted before sampling, the chance of avoiding error is the chance of avoiding error on following the rule (not on following the rule given that the proportion of herbivorous animals is r/n) can be very close to 1 depending on the size of the sample.

The inquirer knows that in facing problems of statistical estimation of the kind he or she is currently addressing, the chance of rejecting the true value of the parameter to be estimated is very low—say, no more than 5 percent on an application of the program for rejecting values of the parameter under consideration. The inquirer intends to apply the program to the specific program under consideration. Prior to implementing the program, he or she can argue on the basis of statistical syllogism that the chance of the output being a false estimate is no more than 5 percent. On that basis, the investigator runs the program and makes an estimate.

Peirce's method amounted to a procedure or a program for responding to external inputs, such as stimulation of sensory apparatus or reports by other individuals, in a manner that rejects some potential answers but not others. The inquirer is precommitted to the program in precisely the same way Neyman and Pearson recommended that inquirers concerned to estimate the value of some parameter should be. Prior to implementing the program, the inquirer can be confident that he or she will obtain an interval estimate of the parameter with a chance of, say, 95 percent.

To my way of thinking, the use of such precommitment strategies to fix beliefs is interrogating nature and adopting nature's answers in a sense that ought to be congenial to Hintikka. Peirce, like Hintikka, began the line of reflection that led to this view (that Peirce articulated in 1878 and more fully in 1883) by adapting Aristotle's characterization of the formal structure of induction in terms of the transposition of the major premise and conclusion of a syllogism in Barbara. Peirce dismissed Aristotle's use of conversion of the minor premise to make the minor premise into a report of an exhaustive sample (the minor term) from the middle term. He proposed a reform of Aristotle's idea. He took the minor term to represent a *random* sample from the "population" represented by the middle term and using the weak law of large numbers concluded that the frequencies reported for the presence of the major term in the random sample are "representative" of the population frequencies of the major. Because the sample statistics for the major term are, in probability, representative of the proportion of the population satisfying the major term according to the weak law of large numbers, the risk of error involved in adopting the sample statistics as a good approximation for the population statistics is negligible. Peirce replaced the conversion of the minor premise that made Aristotle's account of induction so dubious by a statistical argument.

All of this is predicated on the assumption that information available to the investigator is the information available prior to collecting the sample statistics. To implement the program for taking the sample statistics to be approximately the same as the population statistics, one has to precommit to making the substitution prior to finding out the result of sampling. If one had the opportunity to use the data from sampling as additional evidence, the conclusion would be unwarranted. The data are used as input into the program but not as evidence.

Peirce presented this version of confidence interval estimation in 1878 and 1883. His proposal seems to have derived from a succession of modifications of Aristotle's conception of induction in the *Prior Analytics*. Whatever its differences are with Hintikka's account of Aristotelian induction, Peirce agrees with Hintikka's approach in being non-Humean. Indeed, it allows for the interval estimation of statistical parameters in direct (albeit controlled) response to the data without using the data as premises of an inference. In this sense, it is, like Hintikka's approach, allowing nature to answer a question put to it by the inquirer. The answer does not conveniently fit into Hintikka's quantifier classification scheme since the hypotheses are statistical claims and as such involve statistical operators that are not easily construed within first-order predicate logic. Even so, as in Hintikka's approach, there is no particular restriction imposed on the content of nature's response. There is no conceptually mandated distinction here between observational and nonobservational terms. As Hintikka says, the process involves consulting oracles. It is not to be confused with the hypothetico-deductive method. It is not induction by simple enumeration. And it is not induction by complete enumeration as some commentators on Aristotle took him to be defending.

Peirce himself did not recognize the close analogy between his account of what, at the turn of the century, he called "quantitative induction" and observation. But the analogy is present. In both cases, a program is implemented that has external stimuli as input and beliefs as outputs. And both cases resemble, in this regard, the consultation of expert witnesses. In consulting experts, the testimony of the senses or in confidence estimation, a program the inquirer takes to be reliable for what I have called "routine expansion" is deployed.

Hintikka does see inductive conclusions after the fashion of Aristotle as analogous to the observation of the truth of general conclusions. Peirce's conception of quantitative induction can also, I am suggesting, be compared to eliciting information from nature. For Peirce the conclusions specify estimates of statistical parameters.

Of course, to understand acquisition of information via observation in the manner suggested is a species of the view that pragmatists always favored. Observation is *direct* in the sense that new information is acquired without inference from premises but is *mediated* in the sense that the procedures used to acquire such information presuppose background knowledge that implies the reliability of the program used for "routine expansion." This view lurks at the core of Peirce's anti-Cartesian epistemology. Peirce, who did think of observation in this fashion, failed, as far as I can tell, to appreciate the close affinity between his account of quantitative induction and observation. But the analogy is striking. And the affinity with Hintikka's vision of putting questions to nature is suggestive.

Hintikka's position seems to be that the addition of new information to the stock K of information available at the onset of inquiry is through interrogation of nature and deduction. There are activities that look like ampliative inference, but appearances are deceiving. Thus, the generalizations obtained by Aristotelian induction typically have limited scope. But several distinct limited scope generalizations may be consolidated into a more comprehensive system of principles supported by the fact that the theory is inferred from the several generalizations thus consolidated. This process of consolidation is a species of anticipating an answer that nature might give if consulted. In Peirce's terms, it is abduction rather than observation or induction. Consolidation does not terminate in settled conclusions. The conjectures formed appear to be conjectures that should once more be put to nature for an answer.

If this is a fair rendition of Hintikka's view, it seems to me that Hintikka's view resembles the ideas of the pre-twentieth century Peirce. Hypothetic reasoning (the alleged precursor to abduction) is ampliative and includes modes of argument that appear to be consolidations in Hintikka's sense. In the 1878–83 theory of Peirce, induction is characterized in a manner that makes it appear to be a species of consultation with nature's oracles. Peirce called this consultation inductive inference; but there is no inductive inference from premises to a conclusion.

Peirce abandoned the view of hypothetic inference he initially had and saw it as inductive inference of a qualitative sort that contrasted with the conjecturing of abduction. Moreover, it seems to contrast with quantitative induction in virtue of the fact that data are not used as input but as evidence. The textual evidence is far from conclusive; but Peirce did seem to make room for genuine ampliative inductive inference in a sense that Hintikka and the younger Peirce were prepared to de-emphasize.

In my judgment, the view Peirce adopted in the twentieth century seems preferable to that of the young Peirce and of Hintikka. One reason for this is that it is often difficult to devise the experiments whose implementation would decide the fate of the conclusions of hypothetic inference according to a program for routine expansion. Yet, theoretical conjectures formed via abductive reasoning are, nonetheless, incorporated into the settled background information used as premises in subsequent inquiries. The inquirer thus expands his or her state of full belief without implementing a program for routine expansion. Presystematically, when the data are used as evidence in a qualitative induction, there seems often enough to be good reason to expand inductively.

Moreover, the fragility of quantitative induction as Peirce conceived it suggests that it cannot carry the burden that Peirce seemed to place on it or that Hintikka places on Aristotelian induction. In order to apply inductive rules as Peirce conceived of them, the commitment to adopting the rules and following through with them must be taken prior to finding out the results of experiment. It is then and only then that statistical syllogisms as Peirce rightly understood them license the judgment that following the rule has a very high probability of avoiding error on the basis of the information available to the inquirer. As soon as the inquirer finds out the data, then, in the absence of determinate prior probabilities, there can be no determinate probability judgment and the data are useless.

Peirce understood this point. His response was that if one seeks a retrospective assessment of the conclusion based on the data, one could say either the estimate is right or, if the program is run again, the chance of the error being uncovered is very high. This response is acceptable in those contexts in which the program for routine expansion was designed and implemented prospectively before the data were collected. But this reduces the opportunities for using data effectively to reach conclusions quite considerably. If one wishes to use data retrospectively, it becomes necessary to use it as evidence rather than as input. As a consequence, putting questions to nature is not going to be a very effective means of acquiring new information. Perhaps Hintikka thinks that Aristotle had a vision of how to squeeze information out of data that obviates this difficulty. But I don't see it.

Keep in mind, moreover, that relying on the testimony of the senses and of competent witnesses or experts is itself utilizing a program for routine expansion. And such routine expansion is often conflict injecting. X regularly checks his blood pressure. His checking indicates that X is not certain whether his blood pressure is within tolerable range or not. But X is confident that the apparatus he uses for checking his pressure is highly reliable and safe to use. Moreover, X is absolutely certain that his diastolic is below 250 and above 80 whereas his systolic is below 150 and above 30. X takes a reading and obtains a diastolic reading of 270. Having placed his trust in the program by precommitment, X expands into inconsistency.

To be sure, inconsistency is, as Peter Gärdenfors insists, "epistemic hell."[14] And, as Erik Olsson has insisted, one cannot retreat from epistemic hell in deliberate fashion where one should choose from among alternative contractions from the inconsistent state.[15] Olsson has rounded out a subtle discussion with the conclusion that instead of recognizing expansion into inconsistency as a possibility, one should provide an account of routine expansion that allows for routine expansion into anomaly. In my judgment, Olsson does not succeed in finessing the problem of retreat from epistemic hell by denying that one needs ever to do so. Instead, I now favor a precommitment strategy for retreat that obviates the main problems raised by Olsson.[16]

In the blood pressure example, X might take another reading with a different machine to check both on the reliability of the original apparatus and on whether his blood pressure is as high as recorded. In doing this, X has revealed that X was precommitted to questioning both the apparatus and the abnormality of his blood pressure. In this example, X may no longer trust the old apparatus and program for routine expansion; but he has another to which he can appeal. But sometimes, especially when several apparatuses or programs for routine expansion that previously were assumed to be reliable yield conflicting verdicts, there may be no more routine expansion to which X can resort. X may have to rely on the use of data as evidence in deliberate or inductive expansion to resolve the issue.

I do not mean to dismiss the use of oracles in acquiring information altogether. But the need often to use retrospective evaluations of data and the circumstance that routine expansion is conflict injecting argue for the view that routine expansion should be supplemented by deliberate or inductive expansion.

As I understand it, deliberate, inferential or inductive expansion that justifies expansion of a body of belief by appealing to trade-offs between risk of error and informational value—along lines that Hintikka, Pietarinen, Hilpinen, and Niiniluoto, on the one hand, and I, on the other, began investigating in the early 1960s—is a way of supplementing the resources of routine expansion and deductive calculation in information acquisition. In his enthusiasm for his interrogative model of inquiry, it seems to me that

Hintikka has underrated the need for genuine ampliative inference in the context of theory choice as well as in problems of statistical estimation.

Recognizing inductive expansion as a means for answering a question is in a generous sense quite in keeping with an interrogative model of inquiry. I say in a generous sense because, as I understand Hintikka's view of an interrogative model, the inquirer only asks a question. Nature or some oracle then responds to the question or request for an answer. That is why Hintikka's interrogative model shares so much in common with routine expansion. In deliberate or inductive expansion, however, adopting a potential answer is no mere response to the deliverances of nature. In deliberate expansion, the relevant information already available to the inquirer is used together with the inquirer's "confirmational commitment" to warrant an assessment of credal probabilities for the several hypotheses. This assessment determines the risk of error incurred by adopting one answer as compared to another. The inquirer also takes into account the explanatory value of the several candidate answers if the inquirer is seeking explanations. More generally, the inquirer is seeking valuable information. The kind of informational value being sought depends upon what I have called the "demands for information" imposed by the inquirer. Even if explanatory value is the primary focus of these demands, it is far from clear that such a focus will yield a univocal standard for informational value to use in evaluating rival potential answers. This is not surprising if one is focusing on problem-solving or question-answering inquiry.

The fact that my approach was, in this respect, highly sensitive to the question being asked, the answers identified and the demands for information imposed was the basis for complaints leveled against my proposals by Hilpinen and Niiniluoto in the 1970s. If Hintikka's interrogative model is serious about making the answering of questions central to inquiry, he, at any rate, ought not to object to my approach on these grounds. Any differences between us ought to be found in the details.

ISAAC LEVI

COLUMBIA UNIVERSITY
SEPTEMBER 2002

NOTES

1.   Jaakko Hintikka, "A Two Dimensional Continuum of Inductive Methods," in Jaakko Hintikka and Patrick Suppes, *Aspects of Inductive Logic* (Amsterdam: North Holland, 1966), pp. 113–32.

2. Jaakko Hintikka and Risto Hilpinen, "Knowledge, Acceptance and Inductive Logic," in Hintikka and Suppes, *Aspects of Inductive Logic*, pp. 1–20.

3. Jaakko Hintikka and Juhani Pietarinen, "Semantic Information and Inductive Logic," in Hintikka and Suppes, *Aspects of Inductive Logic*, pp. 96–112. See also Risto Hilpinen, *Rules of Acceptance and Inductive Logic* (Amsterdam: North Holland, 1968) and Ilkka Niiniluoto, "Truthlikeness and Bayesian Estimation," *Synthese* 67 (1986): 321–46.

4. Jaakko Hintikka, *Inquiry as Inquiry: A Logic of Scientific Discovery* (Dordrecht: Kluwer, 1999).

5. See the initial chapters of Isaac Levi, *Decisions and Revisions* (Cambridge: Cambridge University Press, 1984).

6. Isaac Levi (1967), *Gambling with Truth*, reprinted in 1973 (Cambridge, Mass.: MIT Press).

7. See Isaac Levi, *Enterprise of Knowledge* (Cambridge, Mass.: MIT Press, 1980); *The Fixation of Belief and Its Undoing* (Cambridge: Cambridge University Press, 1991); *The Covenant of Reason* (Cambridge: Cambridge University Press, 1997).

8. C. S. Peirce, *Writings of Charles S. Peirce* (Bloomington and Indianapolis: University of Indiana Press, 1982–2000) vols. 1–6 ed. Fish, Kloessel, *et al.* See vol. 4, ch. 64.

9. C. S. Peirce, *Collected Papers of Charles Sanders Peirce* (Cambridge, Mass.: Harvard University Press), vol. 2, p. 102. Vols.1–6 (1931–35) ed. Hartshorne and Weiss, vols. 7–8 (1958) ed. Burkes.

10. Joseph B. Kadane and Patrick D. Larkey, "Subjective Probability and the Theory of Games," *Management Science* 25, no. 2 (Feb. 1982): 113–20.

11. Hintikka, *Inquiry as Inquiry*, p. 4.

12. See also Levi, *Enterprise of Knowledge*.

13. For a more elaborate discussion, see Isaac Levi, "Induction as Self Correcting According to Peirce,"in *Science, Belief and Behaviour*," ed. D. H. Mellor (Cambridge: Cambridge University Press, 1980).

14. Peter Gärdenfors, *Knowledge in Flux* (Cambridge, Mass.: MIT Press, 1988), p. 5.

15. Erik Olsson, "Avoiding Epistemic Hell," *Synthese* 135 (2003): 119–40.

16. Isaac Levi, "Contracting from Epistemic Hell is Routine," *Synthese* 135 (2003): 141–64.

REPLY TO ISAAC LEVI

I find much in Isaac Levi's rich paper that is congenial to me. We share a critical attitude toward several of the traditional approaches to induction and hypothesis choice. We also share an interest in, and sympathy with, pragmatist ideas about these subjects, especially in the ideas of Charles S. Peirce.

However, our reasons for adopting these shared likes and dislikes are not the same. It may therefore be helpful if I spell out some of mine. I will follow Levi's example and couch some of my discussion in autobiographical terms. Levi notes that earlier I worked in inductive logic but that I have since the mid-1980s approached epistemological problems by means of what has been called the interrogative model of inquiry.

Why did I lose interest in inductive logic? Levi surmises that it was because "neither the methods for assessing on the basis of data within the framework of an improved Carnapian inductive logic . . . nor the decision theoretic approach to inductive expansion . . . is satisfactory." This is not incorrect, but there is much more to be said. There is also more to be said about Carnap's work. It is routinely dismissed by philosophers because the languages he studied are too weak for real science and because in his choice of priors he relied on unrealistically strong symmetry assumptions. However, in spite of these simplifications Carnap's "noble experiment," which culminated in his lambda-continuum of inductive methods, brought out a philosophically highly significant result. It was not the result Carnap hoped for, however. It was a negative one. Even with his strong symmetry assumptions, Carnap could fix his inductive method only up to a non-negative real-valued parameter. And an examination of this parameter quickly shows that there is no hope of assigning a unique value to it on logical or other a priori grounds. The optimal choice of this parameter depends on how orderly the world is. In the simple cases considered by Carnap, this orderliness can be measured by the entropy of the universe of discourse. Because of this connection between the best choice of the inductive method and the nature of the world, there cannot be an a priori determination of the right method of inductive inference.

Could this result be a peculiarity of the special cases studied by Carnap? When I extended Carnap's methods to inductive generalization, it turned out that the lambda parameter did not disappear, but that further parameters were needed also. The optimal choice of each of them depends on some specifiable kind of order in the world. There is no way of fixing the value of any of them on a purely logical basis. This outcome does not mean that probabilistic induction of the Carnapian kind is invalid. However, Carnapian induction needs a number of contingent premises to back it up, each specifying some general feature of the world. But if these premises are spelled out explicitly, we no longer need any independent rules of inductive inference. Ordinary deductive logic together with probability theory does the whole job.

I leave it to Levi to decide whether this state of affairs might posthumously vindicate Peirce, who is criticized by Levi for including "probable syllogisms" and "statistical syllogisms" under the heading of "deduction."

Thus, improved Carnapian methods have not so much proved unsatisfactory as philosophically uninteresting in their role as a hoped-for Archimedean point for induction. And the same can be said of decision-theoretical approaches. Typically, they involve the maximization of epistemic utilities, the first and foremost of which is information. But semantic information is the inverse of a priori probability. From what has just been said it follows that the choice of an appropriate measure of information cannot be made a priori.

When I reached this point, I realized that similar criticisms can in principle be leveled at the use of inverse probabilities in philosophical contexts. Fortunately, the dependence on priors is a blessing in disguise. For, as J. Savage emphasized, the choice of priors can serve as a handy way of bringing our background information to bear on the particular problem at hand. But in philosophy, one of the crucial problems is to choose the priors independently of contingent background information. Hence, I came to lose my interest in Bayesian inference as a potential panacea in the theory of induction.

How serious are these philosophical criticisms? I suspect that I might very well be criticized for rejecting Bayesian ways of thinking too abruptly. In general, it seems to me, Levi is modifying the received approaches less drastically than I have done. For instance, Levi retains a rule of confirmational conditionalization, only relaxing it so as to apply to sets of conceptually available potential states of full belief (and to the corresponding probability functions) instead of particular states.

This comparison deserves some further thought. In a situation that is traditionally thought of as characteristic of scientific inference, it might seem that my radical surgery is not needed. In such a situation, we have available to us an ever increasing number of indubitable particular data, the task being to find a generalization to fit them into. The choice of priors does not loom large because we can prove various convergence results that are largely independent of the priors at least as long as they do not assign zero prior probabilities to viable potential hypotheses. But when we no longer have such a classical Humean situation to deal with, for instance, when we have to assign priors to the statements of a witness in a cross-examination or to the reliability of the experimental apparatus, the situation will be much more delicate. Yet Bayesian methods must apply to such situations, if they are to be a measure of all inference. And in this direction the issues are much more problematic than philosophers seem to think. At the very least the usual Bayesian methods have to be supplemented by a procedure of modifying the priors in the light of evidence. I have no proof that such procedures cannot be found, but I think they have yet to be developed. I am prepared to go so far as to claim that when appropriate methods are developed for the purpose, they will show that there is nothing necessarily fallacious in some of the typical (in)famous "cognitive fallacies" of Amos Tversky and Daniel Kahneman.

This radical departure from tradition makes it singularly difficult to respond to the specifics of Levi's paper. The conceptual framework I am using is partly different from his. I welcome Levi's decision to discuss my ideas about inductive and other ampliative inference by comparing them with his own ideas. But his fully thought-out ideas are so elaborate that I have some difficulty in commanding a general view of them. Conversely, my ideas have been impossible for Levi to take into account because they have not yet been generally accessible while others are in a state of flux. Yet I am excited by his paper, for it is eminently suitable for the purpose of raising several deep issues in the foundations of the entire epistemological enterprise.

One of these issues is the basic one: what kind of activity are we studying in epistemology, anyway? Levi reminds us of the pragmatist idea that inquiry serves to remove doubts. But if so, what do we need philosophers' strong notion of knowledge for? Reaching justified belief apparently serves this purpose quite as well.

But the role of the notion of belief, either in a commonsensical sense or in the form of Levi's "doxastic commitments," also prompts a number of questions. Subjectivists consider probabilities as degrees of belief. Decision theorists study how presumably rational action is determined by our degrees of belief and our utilities. But why beliefs? Would it not be much more rational to base our decisions on what we know rather than on what we believe? Surely the rationality of a decision based on one's beliefs depends on how those beliefs are formed. It seems to me that we should study belief, and not only knowledge, as a product of inquiry.

We should obviously also study strategies of inquiry, and not only epistemological inferences, as most contemporary epistemologists tend to do. Yet almost all attention has recently been paid to step-by-step rules of scientific procedure even when the rules can be interpreted as strategic rules rather than rules for making one move at a time.

As far as the concept of induction is concerned, a closer examination of its logic is carried out from an interrogative point of view in my unpublished paper "The Place of the A Priori in Epistemology." It shows that, for instance, an experimental induction striving to establish how an observed variable y depends on a controlled variable x involves two different tasks: First, it involves establishing y as a function of x, $y = f(x)$, in the sense of function-in-extension, comparable to a curve on graph paper. Second, it involves finding out what the function f is mathematically speaking, e.g., what its power series expansion is like. These two tasks are not separate, but they can proceed at different paces. If the mathematical formula has been found, the rest of the induction typically reduces to the estimation of its parameter.

This case shows, among other things, that even the kind of straightforward inductive generalization to which Bayesian ideas seem to apply fairly unproblematically is in reality more complicated than first meets the eye. For one thing, probabilities can be assigned only to known mathematical entities. Hence no probability can presumably be assigned to the result of experimental inquiry before its outcome until the function that expresses the dependence sought for has been mathematically identified.

Perhaps the most striking departure from tradition results from an inventory of the concepts actually used in interrogative inquiry. All the concepts of epistemic logic are in fact used there, but not applied to philosophers' notion of knowledge, nor to their notion of belief. In short, the usual concepts of knowledge and belief are not needed in a theory of knowledge acquisition. This insight is spelled out and put into perspective in my 2004 paper "Epistemology without Knowledge and without Belief." Knowledge enters the picture as a criterion of whether the inquiry, which includes both discovery and justification, has proceeded far enough for its output to be used in decision making. Furthermore, normally this criterion depends on the subject matter. There is no general definition of knowledge.

Likewise, belief amounts to another, more subjective way of judging the outcome of inquiry. In the course of the inquiry, the notions of acceptance and rejection ("bracketing") are needed, but acceptance does not mean belief in any normal sense nor rejection disbelief. Belief, too, has to be formed by means of inquiry.

Since practically all of Levi's conceptual framework depends on some notion of belief (doxastic commitment), the reader can perhaps appreciate my difficulty in trying to relate what he says to my ideas. It is thanks to the lucidity and force of Levi's exposition that I have managed to write as close a comparison as I have managed.

Indeed, in spite of all these *prima facie* indications of incommensurability, Levi manages to suggest an interesting comparison between my ideas and those of his own and even those of Charles S. Peirce. What is there to be said of his comparison? First, one apparently minor correction to Levi's comments might be in order. I never intended to present the old Aristotelian and Newtonian sense of induction[1] as an alternative to induction in the Humean sense. I merely pointed out that this systematically and historically important mode of reasoning has a natural place within the interrogative approach. However, it is in a different ballpark altogether from induction in John Stuart Mill's or Carnap's sense.

This correction may have a bearing on Levi's main suggestions concerning my views. Are they more like Peirce's earlier views, as Levi maintains, or his later (twentieth-century) views? Peirce's later ideas depend on the idea of abduction. It was supposed by Peirce (according to Levi) to accomplish the same as "routine expansion," only better. "Yet, theoretical conjectures formed via abductive reasoning are, nonetheless, incorporated into the settled background information used as premises in subsequent inquiries." But how does Levi conceive of such abduction? His answer is: "In any given inquiry some problem or group of problems is raised. Efforts are made to identify potential answers or solutions. That is the task in inquiry that Peirce called 'abduction'. . . ." I am not sure of the precise interpretation of Peirce's notion. But that is not the important question here. The real question is what abduction must be like in order to serve the purpose that Peirce and Levi assign to it. Mercifully, neither succumbs to the tempting but superficial view of abduction as "inference to the best explanation," even though some of Peirce's pronouncements might seem to presuppose such a view. I have discussed this matter in my paper on Peirce. The main problem is to reconcile with each other the different things Peirce says about abduction. Abduction is for him a mode of inference, but it amounts to making good guesses. Most intriguingly, Peirce unmistakably acknowledges that abductive inference is interrogative in nature. The best way of integrating these different elements is to take an abduction to be a question to be answered by one's conjecturing capacity. The character of abduction as inferences is then due to the formal and especially strategic analogies between questions and deductive inferences. Of course, Peirce did not know the basis of all these analogies, but I do not put it past him that he might very well have been intuitively aware of them.

If abduction is looked upon in this light, my interrogative approach is beginning to look much more like Peirce's late views and not his earlier ones. What may have influenced Levi is the fact that there are also similarities between the interrogative model and Peirce's earlier views. For instance, we may take Levi's comments on using data as input for what he calls routine expansion as distinguished from using them as evidence. The data in question can be thought of as an oracle's—usually nature's—answers to certain questions. If we trust our oracle, we will use its answers as stepping stones in subsequent inquiries. But if difficulties should arise, we can and must resort to tentatively rejecting ("bracketing") some of the earlier answers. And in deciding which answers to bracket, the very same answers that were earlier compared with routine expansions can now perhaps play the role of evidence.

This point can be elaborated. The bracketing of answers need not be guesswork. There is a way of using the very same logical and interrogative techniques as can establish normal interrogative conclusions for the purpose of establishing "how possible" (in this case, "how possibly false") conclusions. (This simple variant of interrogative techniques has not been acknowledged by philosophers, and I have unfortunately not had a chance of publishing it). One way of motivating the bracketing of an answer A is to show by means of such technique how it is possible that not-A, using only such earlier answers as are considered reliable.

J. H.

NOTE

1.   See my 1992 paper "The Concept of Induction in the Light of the Interrogative Approach to Inquiry," in *Inference, Explanation and Other Frustrations: Essays in the Philosophy of Science*, ed. John Earman (Berkeley: University of California Press, 1992), pp. 23–43. Also appears in Jaakko Hintikka, *Inquiry As Inquiry: Toward a Logic of Scientific Discovery, Selected Papers*, vol. 5 (Dordrecht: Kluwer Academic Publishers, 1999), pp. 161–82.

24

Risto Hilpinen

JAAKKO HINTIKKA ON EPISTEMIC LOGIC AND EPISTEMOLOGY

> *I do not ask any questions, because when a guy goes around asking questions in this town people may get the idea that he is such a guy as wishes to find things out.*

> Damon Runyon, "The Lily of St. Pierre,"
> in *More Than Somewhat* (1937)

I

It is not an exaggeration to say that the publication of Jaakko Hintikka's *Knowledge and Belief: An Introduction to the Logic of the Two Notions* in 1962 launched a new branch of philosophical logic, *epistemic logic*. Hintikka's book was not the first study of the logic of epistemic concepts. For example, many fourteenth-century treatises on philosophical logic contained a chapter on the problems of epistemic logic, sometimes entitled *De scire et dubitare*, which discussed and analyzed sophisms about the concepts of knowledge and doubt.[1] In the late nineteenth century, Charles S. Peirce put forward an epistemic interpretation of modal concepts, according to which a proposition is regarded as possible if and only if the proposition is not known to be false "in a given state of information," and Georg Henrik von Wright's *An Essay in Modal Logic* contains a short discussion of the epistemic interpretation of modalities.[2] In these early contributions epistemic concepts were construed as modal concepts, and their logic was regarded as a branch of modal logic, but epistemic logic was not applied in a significant way to the analysis of methodological and epistemological issues. (It may be observed, however, that in the fourteenth century logic epistemic principles were often studied in a methodological context, as part of the theory of disputation.)[3] Hintikka has used epistemic logic as an analytic tool in several areas of epistemology: he has characterized the concepts of knowledge and belief and different uses of the verb "know," studied the logic of perception and perceptual knowledge, investigated the epistemology of reference, and developed a theory of questions and inquiry based on epistemic logic. As the basis of the logic of inquiry, epistemic logic forms the core of Hintikka's epistemology.

In this paper I shall understand epistemic logic in a wide sense, as including the logic of knowledge, belief, perception, and related propositional attitudes. I shall focus on two central topics in Hintikka's work: epistemology as the theory of inquiry and his analysis of different ways of identifying the objects of knowledge and belief.

II

The concept of knowledge represented in Hintikka's epistemic logic is an articulation of the simple idea that knowing that something is the case, knowing that p, means that one is in a position to rule out the possibilities (courses of events, scenarios, situations, or possible worlds) in which it is not the case that p. The possibilities allowed by a knowledge claim are called the epistemic alternatives to the situation in which the claim is being evaluated. The truth of the proposition that an inquirer i knows that p (abbreviated '$K_i p$') in a situation u, is taken to mean that p is true in all epistemic alternatives to u, and the epistemic possibility of p ('$P_i p$') means that p holds in some epistemic alternative to u. Thus epistemic operators are in effect quantifiers over possible scenarios or situations. The alternatives relativized to an inquirer i are called the i-alternatives to u. (The expression 'p is true' is used here as an abbreviation of the expression 'it is true that p'.) The concept of belief can be characterized in a similar way: believing that p means that the believer rejects the possibilities inconsistent with what he believes; the possibilities that remain unrejected in a given situation may be called the doxastic alternatives to the situation. According to the standard view about the concepts of knowledge and belief (acceptance as true), knowledge claims and expressions of belief rule out possibilities in different ways: an inquirer's beliefs rule out more possibilities than his knowledge, or what he can legitimately claim to know; knowledge entails belief or acceptance. For example, an inquirer's beliefs may rule out the actual situation, but what is known cannot: according to the ordinary sense of "know," the epistemic alternatives to a given situation are bound to include that situation itself, in other words, epistemic alternativeness (or accessibility), unlike doxastic alternativeness, is an essentially reflexive relation.

In general, philosophers have regarded knowledge as a cognitively superior form of belief, as "good belief," and the relevant superiority or goodness has been characterized in different ways. For example, it has been suggested that if an inquirer knows that p, then the possibilities inconsistent with p are ruled out *conclusively* in the sense that they should not have to be considered at a later time, whereas beliefs, even true and well-justified beliefs, can be undermined new information. This difference is illustrated by Major Willie Brownley's remark to Sergeant Hoke Moseley in Charles Willeford's *Sideswipe*:

> You and Bill Henderson aren't half as smart as you think you are. I signed your emergency leave because I believed him when he told me your father was dying. But just because I believed him at that time didn't mean I wouldn't check it later. And I did.[4]

A person who claims that he knows something does not think that he should "check it later"; it would not make much sense to say "I know that p and will act accordingly, but when I have more time, I better check whether p is indeed the case." The assertion that one knows that p expresses the conviction that new information or evidence would not lead one to change one's view.[5] Major Brownley's act of signing Hoke Moseley's emergency leave was based on his belief that Bill Henderson was telling the truth: in many situations action cannot wait for knowledge, but must be based on belief or conjecture. Charles S. Peirce expressed this aspect or dimension of the concept of knowledge as follows:

> The only difference, that there seems to be room for between these two [what one *knows* and what one *has sufficient reason to be entirely confident of*] is that what one *knows*, one always will have *reason to be confident of*, while what one now has ample reason to be entirely confident of, one may conceivably in the future, in consequence of a new light, find reason to doubt and ultimately to deny.[6]

Thus a knowledge claim, unlike the claim that a certain belief is justified within an inquirer's belief system, involves a prediction about the inquirer's future beliefs. In the recent discussion on the concept of knowledge Peirce's observation has sometimes been expressed by saying that true knowledge claims should be "indefeasible,"[7] and that genuine knowledge is "extendable" and consists of "stable" beliefs which cannot be lost simply as a result of learning something new.[8] The thirteenth-century philosopher Siger of Brabant characterized knowledge in a closely related way, as an inquirer's ability to find the truth and defend his view against objections:

> Finding truth presupposes the ability to solve any objection or dubitation
> against the proposition accepted as true. For if you do not know how to solve
> objections that may arise, you are not in possession of the truth, since in that
> case you have not assimilated *the procedure of finding* truth and thus will not
> know whether or when you have arrived at truth.[9]

The requirement that an inquirer does not know that p unless he can defend his acceptance of p against objections may be called "Siger's condition."

The justification condition of the standard (justified true belief) analysis of knowledge can be regarded as serving a similar purpose. The justification condition has often been interpreted as the requirement that an inquirer should have adequate (sufficient) evidence for his belief that p, and "having evidence" has been taken to mean that the inquirer's belief system (acceptance system) contains evidential propositions that justify p. According to this interpretation, evidence consists of beliefs, that is, accepted evidential propositions.[10] If an inquirer does not have evidence (in the form of accepted evidential propositions) for his opinion, it is not clear how he can defend it against conflicting opinions and doubts. However, when an inquirer wants to defend his opinion against a skeptical opponent, the defense need not be based on his current beliefs. He may be able to defend his claim successfully even if the evidence that originally justified his belief has been lost, if, to use Siger's locution, "he has assimilated the procedure of finding truth," in other words, if he knows how to find sufficient new evidence for p (assuming that p is true). In a disputation, the ability to find the truth consists in analyzing and solving arguments, but in real life, truth is found by means of inquiry, for example, by means of experiments and observations, or by consulting external sources of information. According to this interpretation of Siger's condition, an inquirer knows that p only if his belief that p results from or can be sustained by his exercise of the ability to find the truth—more specifically, the ability to determine whether p is true. This condition resembles Frank P. Ramsey's suggestion that a belief is knowledge only if it is obtained by a reliable process.[11] The main difference between Ramsey's condition and Siger's condition is that the former is expressed in terms of a belief producing *process*, whereas the latter refers to a *procedure*, an action (or a sequence of actions) by means of which an inquirer can find the truth, that is, a true answer to some question. Such actions are called inquiries.

A belief can be epistemically superior to another in different respects: there are many dimensions of epistemic goodness. In a disputation about what an inquirer knows, the claim that his belief that p counts as knowledge is supported by showing that the belief that p has a certain desirable feature (is true, is well-justified, has been obtained by a reliable process, and so on), and contested by arguing that the belief is in some respect cognitively unsatisfactory (for example, is disconfirmed by some evidence available to the inquirer's opponent). In a dispute with a skeptical opponent, the inquirer is an advocate of the proposition that he knows something, but the situation can also be reversed, as in the case of Inspector Cramer and Nero Wolfe: Inspector Cramer often claims that Nero Wolfe knows something relevant to the police investigation in hand, and has the duty to give the information to him, but Nero Wolfe argues that he has no such obligation, because what he has is merely a conjecture which has not been verified in a completely satisfactory manner.

Hintikka's K-operator can be regarded as expressing a cognitively satisfactory belief. What makes a belief satisfactory depends on various situational factors and on the context of application of epistemic concepts, for example, on the circumstances under which the results of inquiry can be regarded as a satisfactory basis for action. For this reason the concept of knowledge cannot be defined by means of a fixed set of necessary and sufficient conditions—according to Hintikka, such considerations belong to applied rather than general epistemology.[12] The task of general epistemology is to analyze the basic features of the process of inquiry.

III

Much of recent epistemology has focused on the concept of epistemic justification, especially on the ways in which beliefs or accepted propositions have to be supported by other beliefs in order to count as knowledge. Epistemic logic has not played a significant role in this discussion. The situation changes if the concept of inquiry is regarded as a central concept of the theory of knowledge. In a recent paper, Hintikka has observed:

> Surely the first order of business of any genuine theory of knowledge—the most important task both theoretically and practically—is how new knowledge can be achieved, not merely how previously obtained information can be evaluated. A theory of information (knowledge) acquisition is both philosophically and humanly much more important than a theory of whether already achieved information amounts to knowledge or not. Discovery is more important than the defense of what you already know.[13]

However, even if the inquirer's aim is the defense of an accepted opinion (i.e., justification) and not the discovery of an answer to an open question, the best procedure is often the acquisition of new evidence by inquiry. As was observed above, an inquirer's defense of a proposition against objections need not be based on his or her "old" evidence. Hintikka says:

> Suppose that a scientist has a reason to think that one of his or her conclusions is not beyond doubt. What is he or she to do? Will the scientist try to analyze his or her data so as to extract from them grounds for a decision? Sometimes, perhaps, but in an overwhelming majority of actual scientific situations, the scientist will ask what further information one should in such circumstances try to obtain in order to confirm or disconfirm the suspect proposition, for instance what experiments it would be advisable to perform or what kinds of observation one should try to make in order to throw light on the subject matter.[14]

In the same way, in most cases the best way to convince an inquirer's critic about the truth of a proposition p is to obtain suitable new evidence for p and not merely to invite the critic to (re)consider the old data. Should the new evidence turn out to disconfirm p, the inquirer has to admit that he does not (and did not) know that p.

Hintikka's theory of knowledge is essentially a theory of inquiry, understood in a wide sense so that it includes scientific inquiries as well as other varieties of knowledge acquisition. The purpose of an inquiry is to find a satisfactory answer to some question in which the inquirer is interested. Moreover, according to Hintikka's interrogative model of inquiry, an inquiry consists of questions presented to external sources of information. Thus an inquiry involves two kinds of questions: the question which generates the inquiry, and the questions which constitute it. The former may be termed the *principal* or *main* question of the inquiry, and latter questions the *operative* or *secondary* questions. If an inquirer asks a question in order to find an answer to another question, the latter question may be said to be *prior* to the former question. An inquirer needs secondary questions in order to find a satisfactory answer to the main question because the respondent either does not know the answer to the main question or, even if he knows the answer, is not in a position to give the inquirer a satisfactory answer to the main question. For example, suppose that Sir Roderick wants to know whether Bertie is mentally unbalanced. Bertie knows perfectly well that he is not, but Sir Roderick cannot find this out simply by asking Bertie or his acquaintances whether he is a lunatic, because they might give the same answer regardless of Bertie's mental condition. Thus, Sir Roderick has to use suitable secondary questions to find out what he wants to know, for example, "Does Bertie keep fish under his bed?"

Inquiries can be divided into theoretical (or factual) and practical inquiries. In practical inquiries, the main question concerns the course of action to be adopted in a given situation, whereas theoretical inquiries concern the state of the world (matters of fact). It is often helpful for an inquirer to find an answer to a (theoretical) question about the state of the world in order to find a solution to a practical decision problem. The question whether it is going to rain is a secondary question in relation to the practical question whether one ought to take an umbrella when one goes out, and an inquirer can try to find an answer to the former question by means of (secondary) questions addressed to the weather bureau.

Questioning is understood in a wide sense so that it includes observations and experiments. Here Hintikka follows Kant's characterization of experimental knowledge: according to Kant, reason "must approach nature in order to be taught by it. It must not, however, do so in the character of a pupil who listens to everything that the teacher chooses to say, but as an appointed judge who compels the witnesses to answer questions which he himself has formulated."[15] The situations in which an inquirer behaves like a pupil "who listens to everything the teacher chooses to say" can be regarded as degenerate instances of this model, because any accepted proposition can be regarded as an answer to some question.[16]

Kant's characterization expresses one essential aspect of the semantics and pragmatics of questions, namely, that questions are a form of imperatives or requests. The purpose of a question is to make something known to the inquirer; thus the questions which constitute an inquiry are *epistemic requests*. This was a common view about questions among the philosophers who studied the logic and psychology of questions in the late nineteenth and early twentieth century.[17] For example, Friedrich Löw observes that when I ask someone: "Is radium an element?" the addressee "can gather that I demand to know something and what I demand to know, and that I expect him to convey this knowledge."[18] This view forms the basis of Hintikka's theory of questions and inquiry. An essentially similar approach to the semantics of questions has been developed by Lennart Åqvist.[19] It is clear that not all utterances of interrogative sentences express genuine epistemic requests,[20] and some philosophers have made a distinction between spurious and genuine questions ("unechte und echte Fragen").[21] The Hintikka-Åqvist theory is an account of genuine questions, questions as means of knowledge acquisition, and this is our present concern.

An inquiry can be represented as an exchange between two participants, an inquirer or questioner and a respondent. In his writings Hintikka often calls the respondent "the oracle" or, in the case of observational and experimental inquiries, "the nature." Understood in this way, an inquiry can be regarded as a game (a questioning game) between the inquirer and the respondent.

By presenting questions to the respondent, the inquirer wishes to reach a certain (kind of) epistemic state, called the *desideratum* of the question.

Questions can be divided into *propositional* questions and *wh*-questions. For example, an inquirer's propositional question

(3.1)   Is the light red or yellow?

expresses the request (addressed to the respondent)

(3.2)   Bring it about that I know that the light is red or I know that the light is yellow.

The form of (3.2) can be represented by the schema

(3.3) $\mathbf{ID_n(K_ip \lor K_iq)}$,

where 'n' represents the respondent, 'i' refers to the inquirer, '$\mathbf{I}$' is a sign of a directive (or an imperative), and '$\mathbf{D_n}$' may be read 'n brings it about that' or 'n sees to it that'. (The latter reading does not presuppose initial ignorance on the part of the questioner, and is therefore appropriate to the situations in which the questioner already knows the answer.) Thus a simple question consists of an imperative-optative element, expressed above by '$\mathbf{ID_n}$', and an epistemic part as the desideratum of the question. Epistemic logic enters the theory of inquiry through the latter constituent of questions. The desideratum of (3.2) is

(3.4)   I know that the light is red or I know that the light is yellow.

More generally, the desideratum of a propositional question has the form

(3.5) $\mathbf{K_ip_1 \lor \ldots \lor K_ip_n}$.

The directive constituent is the same in all simple questions, whereas the desideratum varies; thus the desideratum determines the distinguishing features of different kinds of questions. The deletion of all occurrences of the K-operator from the desideratum gives us the *presupposition* of the question, that is, a proposition whose truth is a necessary condition of the existence of a truthful answer to the question. Thus the presupposition of (3.2) is:

(3.6)   The light is red or the light is yellow.

It is clear that the desideratum (3.2) cannot be satisfied unless (3.6) is true. A yes-no question "Is it the case that p?" has an empty or tautologous presupposition, $p \lor \neg p$. An inquirer such as Socrates, who pretends to be totally ignorant about a subject matter, can ask only yes-no questions.[22] Note that question (3.1) is ambiguous: above it was understood as a disjunctive question, but it can also be understood as a yes-no question, in which case its desideratum is "I know that the light is red or yellow or I know that the light is not red or yellow." In general, a question can be identified by its desideratum.

This analysis requires certain qualifications. For example, it is clear that a question directs the respondent to change the epistemic state of the inquirer (questioner) in such a way that it fits the world in a certain respect (or see to it that the inquirer's beliefs fit the world), not the other way around. Thus the force of the imperative operator is relative to the presupposition of the question. It is roughly the following: 'Assuming that the presupposition of the question is satisfied, bring it about that d', where d is the desideratum.[23]

Questions of the second main type, *wh*-questions, are those containing a *wh*-word, that is, an interrogative pronoun or a pronominal adverb, for example, 'who', 'which', 'why', 'when', and so forth. According to Hintikka's analysis, the *wh*-question

(3.7)   Who is the president?

expresses the request

(3.8)   Bring it about that I know who is the president;

thus the desideratum of (3.8) is

(3.9)   I know who is the president,

and it has as its presupposition

(3.10) Someone is the president,

that is, taking persons as the universe of discourse,

(3.11) $(\exists x)(x = \text{the president})$.

According to the present analysis of questions, (3.11) is the result of deleting (the occurrences of) the K-operator from the desideratum of (3.7). Thus it should be possible to obtain the desideratum of (3.7) from (3.11) by inserting instances of the K-operator back to the position from which they have been deleted. The simplest plausible result of such a replacement is

(3.12) $(\exists x)K_i(x = \text{the president})$.

This suggests that (3.12) may be regarded as a formal representation of (3.9). It is obvious that

(3.13) $K_i(\exists x)(x = \text{the president})$

will not do as a formalization of (3.9); (3.13) states only that I know (or the inquirer i knows) that someone is the president, whereas (3.9) asserts that

I know which individual is the president. According to Hintikka, the desideratum of a simple *wh*-question is represented by the formula

(3.14) $(\exists x)\mathbf{K}_i(x = c),$

where c is a singular term (a name or a definite description). (3.14) can be regarded as a generalization of (3.5).[24] For example, assume that Bingo Little wishes to make a bet on the outcome of the Goodwood Cup, and is interested in the *wh*-question

Which horse will be the winner of Goodwood Cup?

that is, a question whose desideratum has the form

(3.15) $(\exists x)\mathbf{K}_b(x = w),$

where 'w' is short for 'the winner'. If Bingo knows that (say) six horses will be running, namely, Ocean Breeze, Red Dawn, Gargoyle, Cara Mia, Spotted Dog, and Trafalgar, (3.15) holds if and only if

(3.16) $\mathbf{K}_b$(Ocean Breeze = w) $\vee$ $\mathbf{K}_b$(Red Dawn = w). $\vee$ $\mathbf{K}_b$(Gargoyle = w) $\vee$ $\mathbf{K}_b$(Cara Mia = w) $\vee$ $\mathbf{K}_b$(Spotted Dog = w) $\vee$ $\mathbf{K}_b$(Trafalgar = w),

where at least the horse that Bingo regards as the winner satisfies condition (3.14). To be in a position to know that (for example) Ocean Breeze will be the winner, Bingo must obviously have a conception of Ocean Breeze as one of the horses running in the Goodwood Cup as well as some relevant information about it.

(3.14) means that the same individual is c in all epistemic possibilities open to the inquirer. The existential quantifier in (3.14) identifies an individual across the inquirer's epistemic possibilities. Quantification into an epistemic context connects the appearances of the same individual in different possibilities (possible worlds) by means of a "world line."[25] According to this interpretation, (3.14) holds for c if and only if it is a genuine or "full-fledged" individual for the inquirer,[26] or rather has (for the inquirer) a *full-fledged sense*. What does this mean?

The concept of a "full-fledged individual" (or full-fledged sense of a term) has been characterized in popular fiction and in philosophy by similar metaphors or models. According to C. S. Peirce, a name functions as a "true" proper name (as opposed to an indefinite singular term) for an inquirer if and only if the inquirer is able to place the object of the name in its "proper place in [the inquirer's] mental chart" of objects and events.[27] Hintikka has characterized the identification of an object in a similar way in terms of its place in the inquirer's "framework or 'map'."[28] The chart (or map) model is particularly apposite in the case of where-questions: travelers and navigators usually find out where they are by identifying their position on a map or chart. David Kaplan has suggested that knowing who someone is (or rather having an opinion as to who someone is) can be taken to mean that one can place the individual in question "among the leading characters of [one's] inner story." Kaplan calls the names of such individuals "vivid names."[29] Without such anchoring a proper name does not function as a genuine name of an individual for an inquirer. For Rex Stout's fictional detective Archie Goodwin, knowing who someone is means that one has an entry for the person in the "card index" one carries in one's skull.[30] In the recent philosophical and psychological literature, many authors have adopted the Stout-Goodwin model and characterized the representations of individuals in terms of information files or dossiers.[31] In Kaplan's terminology, we can say that Hintikka's condition (3.14) means that c is vivid for the inquirer.

Not all individual terms satisfy condition (3.14), and consequently some familiar inference rules for quantifiers must be restricted in epistemic logic in such a way that they apply only to what can be regarded "genuine individuals" from the point of view of the epistemic subject (the inquirer). For example, it is not possible to apply the rule of existential generalization to derive

(3.17) $(\exists x)\mathbf{K}_i Fx$

from

(3.18) $\mathbf{K}_i Fc$

without (3.14) as an additional premise.[32]

IV

As was observed above, an inquiry is an attempt to find a satisfactory answer to some question (or questions), the principal question(s) of the inquiry, and it can be represented as a game between two participants, an inquirer and a respondent (the "oracle" or "nature"). According to Hintikka, the inquirer can perform two kinds of actions or make two kinds of "moves" in such a game: (a) deductive inferences from his background information (or background theory), and (b) interrogative moves, which consist in questions ("small questions" or secondary questions), addressed to the respondent (oracle).

The deductive steps of an inquiry can be conveniently represented by the tableau method developed by Hintikka, Evert Beth, and others.[33] It is plausible to use the tableau method as a model of inquiry and discovery, because it can be regarded as a discovery procedure for natural deduction and Gentzen-style proofs.[34] In a two-sided deductive tableau, a potential answer to an inquirer's main question (the conclusion to be established) is written on the right-hand side of the tableau, and the premises which may be used in the reasoning are codified on the left-hand side. The tableau construction can be regarded as an attempt to build a counter-model to the inference in which the sentences on the left-hand side are true and those on the right-hand side are false. A tableau which shows that all possible attempts to construct such a counter-example lead to an impasse, that is, contain the same sentence on both sides, is said to be closed and constitutes a proof of the conclusion.[35] It should be observed that the initial sentences written on the left-hand side of a tableau represent the inquirer's knowledge at the beginning of the inquiry, and should therefore be thought of as epistemic sentences, preceded by the K-operator.[36] Below, the K-operator has usually been omitted unless it is essential for the exposition.

Hintikka's model of interrogative inquiry is obtained by adding to the deductive tableau rules interrogative rules which determine under what conditions the inquirer is in a position to address a question to the oracle. An interrogative move in the tableau construction consists in asking a question and recording the oracle's answer on the left-hand side of the tableau (or of the relevant subtableau). If the left-hand side of the tableau represents the inquirer's knowledge in the strong sense discussed above in section II, writing the oracle's answer in the tableau expresses the assumption that the oracle's answers are true and known to the inquirer to be true. It is clear that an inquirer is in a position to ask a question only if he knows that the presupposition of the question holds, or in other words, if the presupposition of the question occurs on the left side of the (sub)tableau under consideration. Thus the basic rule of questioning can be expressed as follows:

(4.1)   If the presupposition of a question occurs on the left side of a tableau (or a subtableau), the inquirer may address the question to the oracle. If the oracle gives an answer, the answer is added to the left side of the (sub)tableau.[37]

There is a close correspondence between the interrogative moves in the questioning process and certain deductive moves. For example, if the inquirer finds a disjunctive proposition $p \vee q$ on the left-hand side of a tableau, he may apply the deductive rule for a disjunction, that is, introduce two alternative extensions (branches) of the tableau, and add p to one branch and q to the other. However, since a disjunction is a presupposition of a propositional question, the inquirer may also use it as a basis of a question addressed to the oracle, and add the answer to the tableau. If he learns from the oracle that (for example) p is true, he may add it to the left-hand side of his tableau as new information (or knowledge), and attempt to close the tableau without having to apply the deductive rule for a disjunction. In this way the information given by the oracle can help the inquirer to close the tableau and arrive at an answer which could not be established without the help of the oracle. In a deductive tableau, the inquirer can introduce at any stage of the construction a tautology $p \lor \neg p$ on the left side; this deductive move corresponds to the interrogative move of asking a yes-no question. Since such questions have tautological presuppositions, they are always permissible. In the same way, if a subtableau contains an existential sentence

(4.2) $(\exists x)Fx,$

the inquirer may apply the rule of existential instantiation and add to the subtableau the formula

(4.3) $F\alpha,$

where α is a new individual parameter (a "dummy name") representing an "arbitrary (or suitably chosen) individual." On the other hand, having (4.2) in a tableau enables the inquirer to ask the question "Who is F?" since (4.2) is the presupposition of such a question. A satisfactory answer to such a question adds to the subtableau a proposition of the form

(4.4) $Fc,$

where c is one of the individuals known to the inquirer, that is, an individual such that

(4.5) $(\exists x)\mathbf{K}_i(c = x)$

holds for it. Unlike (4.3), (4.4) is a genuine proposition, and having (4.4) in the tableau enables the inquirer to use his background information about c in his attempt to close the tableau and find a satisfactory answer to his main question. Since the dummy name 'α' in (4.3) is not a genuine name (singular term), but represents an "arbitrary individual," (4.3) can be considered as an implicitly interrogative formula in the sense that it gives rise to a question about the identity of an F. In the same way, when the inquirer applies the tableau rule for a disjunction and considers two alternative extensions of the tableau, the formulas p and q in the two branches do not represent the inquirer's current state of knowledge, but are put forward as it were interrogatively: what would follow if I (the inquirer) knew that p? If the oracle is not able to give any answer to the question whether p or q, the inquirer must consider both subtableaux in the process of inquiry.

At the beginning of the tableau construction, the sentence written on the right-hand side of the tableau, i.e., the proposed answer to the inquirer's main question, can also be said to be considered interrogatively, as a hypothesis. The inquirer's epistemic state at the beginning of the inquiry can be represented by a system of alternative tableaux, each of which contains a different potential answer on the right-hand side, and the same initial sentences on the left. For example, if the inquirer's main question is "who is the G?" there will be a tableau for each of the "suspects" considered by the inquirer.

According to Hintikka's model, interrogative inquiry can be regarded as an extension of deductive reasoning, and the logic of inquiry is an extension of deductive logic. The function of the questions addressed to nature is to eliminate epistemic possibilities which the inquirer would otherwise have to consider in his attempt to reach a satisfactory answer to his main question. In the present context, "finding a satisfactory answer" means determining that an answer is satisfactory; thus, when the inquirer has reached such an answer and found out that the answer is satisfactory, he has also found a justification for the answer. Thus there is no difference between the logic of discovery and the logic of justification. We might say that Hintikka's logic of discovery is a logic of the discovery of a justification. (However, this does not seem to be Hintikka's view.)[38]

                                        V

As we have seen, Hintikka construes the logic of inquiry and discovery as an extension of deductive logic. According to many accounts of scientific reasoning, inquiry involves three different varieties of reasoning: deduction, induction, and abduction. What is the role of abduction and induction in Hintikka's model?

The concept of abduction was introduced into epistemology and philosophy of science by Charles S. Peirce, who regarded it as a tentative acceptance of a hypothesis as an explanation of some surprising phenomenon. More generally, we can say that abduction consists in a tentative acceptance of an answer to a question. In his early writings Peirce called abductive inference "hypothesis" or "hypothetic inference." An answer reached by abduction is not epistemically satisfactory from the inquirer's point of view before it has been verified (or confirmed) by inductive reasoning. According to Peirce, the conclusions of abductive inferences should be entertained only "interrogatively"; he observed that "in pure abduction, it is never justifiable to accept the hypothesis otherwise than as an interrogation," and "a hypothesis ought, at first, to be entertained interrogatively, before being tested by experiment."[39] Isaac Levi has taken abduction to consist in the identification of the potential answers to a given question and their evaluation as potential answers; thus Levi has in effect taken an abductive step in an inquiry to consist in the identification of the desideratum of a question.[40] The abductive and inductive steps in Peirce's model of inquiry play the same role as the interrogative moves in Hintikka's model: a hypothesis (an abductive conclusion) is "tested by experiment" by presenting questions to nature and by recording the answers.

In Hintikka's model, writing a tentative answer to the investigator's main question on the right-hand side of a tableau can be regarded as an abductive step. Similar abductive steps can be included in the tableau construction. As was observed above, a disjunctive proposition on the left side of a tableau can be used as a basis of a propositional question addressed to the oracle. If the oracle is unable to give a satisfactory answer, the inquirer can proceed by assuming one of the disjuncts is a satisfactory answer (that is, holds in an arbitrary epistemically acceptable situation), and may then construct a subtableau based on that hypothesis. In both cases there is a close connection between an interrogative step and an abductive step in the process of inquiry: when the inquirer makes an abductive step in his reasoning, the hypothesis under consideration is not yet established as something the inquirer knows, but merely as a conjecture or as an "interrogation."

How does the other main form of nondeductive reasoning, induction, enter Hintikka's model of inquiry?

The customary conception of induction construes it as a form of non deductive reasoning which is capable of justifying propositions about unobserved objects, including general propositions, on the basis of observational or experimental evidence. This evidence is obtained by means of questions addressed to nature. To understand the role of inductive reasoning in inquiry, it is necessary to consider what kinds of questions nature is capable of answering in a satisfactory way, in other words, what is the scope of "direct" observational or experimental knowledge. According to a widespread epistemological view, observational knowledge is restricted to singular propositions as expressed by the atomic sentences of one's language. Hintikka calls this assumption the "Atomistic Postulate."[41] Furthermore, it is assumed that the predicates of the observation propositions should represent observable characteristics of objects or features whose presence can be detected by the senses. Sometimes it has also been argued that the objects of immediate perceptual knowledge form a special category (e.g., "sense data" or other "immediate" objects), and cannot be identified by ordinary physical objects. This assumption will be discussed below in section VIII.

Hintikka regards the Atomistic Postulate as indisputable in purely observational (that is, nonexperimental) research, but he argues that it need not hold for knowledge acquisition by means of controlled experiments. Thus he makes a distinction between observational moves (questions) and experimental moves in a game of inquiry.[42]

Some philosophers have made a distinction between *data* and *phenomena*.[43] The former are essentially singular propositions about a particular experiment, whereas the latter are "relatively stable and general features of the world that are potential objects of explanation and prediction by general theory."[44] The "raw data" produced in an experiment are usually regarded as evidence for (or against) the existence of a phenomenon. For example, Max Wertheimer's (1912) discovery of the *phi*-phenomenon, the perception of apparent movement in stationary, successively exposed visual stimuli, was the discovery of a general law or regularity. The purpose of his experiments was to verify the existence of this phenomenon and determine under what conditions it occurs.[45] (As Hintikka observes, the general phenomena whose existence can be demonstrated by experiments are often limited generalizations.)[46] If the "raw" data produced by an experiment are regarded as evidence that justifies an inference to propositions about the phenomenon under investigation, it is plausible to regard the former as the nature's answer to the inquirer's question. On the other hand, experiments are designed to give information about general phenomena; that is the very purpose of an experimental design.

A well-defined experiment is defined by a general description or "precept" that specifies how the experiment is to be performed; thus experiments are usually instantiations of general types. The familiar methodological norm that the result of an experiment is "valid" only if it is repeatable, that is, can be reproduced by new instantiations of the same experiment, presupposes that both the experiment and its results are general phenomena (or types).[47] Often the analysis of the data, including the statistical methodology to be employed, is an essential part of the design of an experiment, and the statistical analysis can be performed automatically. For example, assume that an investigator is interested in the dependence of some characteristic on another, and performs an experiment using the latter as an independent variable and the former as a dependent variable. The raw data of such an experiment can be represented as a scatter diagram, and the data in the diagram can be used to generate the regression equation for the relationship between the two variables automatically by means of a computer program. In such cases the determination of the functional relationship between the two features on the basis of the data is what Isaac Levi has called a "routine expansion" of a belief system, not a deliberate or genuinely inferential expansion.[48] This suggests that we can regard the regression equation, not just the scatter diagram, as nature's answer. The acceptance of the regression equation as nature's answer depends on the inquirer's background assumption that the dependence between the two features is linear, but all experimental results, however they might be conceptualized, depend on empirical assumptions (or background knowledge) about the functioning of the experimental apparatus. These considerations support Hintikka's view that nature's answers to experimental questions need not be restricted to singular propositions, but can at least in some cases be general propositions about phenomena. According to this view, an experiment is a cognitive artifact which extends what the inquirer can find out from the nature beyond what can be learned by "naked observation." A microscope enables an inquirer to see things that are invisible to the naked eye, and according to Hintikka, well-designed experiments make it possible for an inquirer to "perceive" general phenomena in an analogous manner.

However, the acceptance of a generalization on the basis of experimental data is not always a routine expansion in Levi's sense. Sometimes scientists reject or correct their data. Robert A. Millikan's famous oil-drop experiments that established the quantization of electric charge serve as an example. Millikan excluded part of his data from the published report for various reasons, for example, suspected equipment malfunction, the presence of dust in the experimental apparatus, voltage irregularities, and other factors. Millikan considered the individual oil-drops as nature's answers to his questions, and he accepted some of these answers as input for further analysis, but rejected others.[49]

Hintikka has acknowledged this possibility by making a distinction between the "macrolevel" and the "microlevel" of inquiry.[50] If experiments are considered on the "macrolevel," that is, as part of a research program or the process of inquiry in general, it is clear that their function is to give information about the existence and nature of general phenomena. On the other hand, on the "microlevel," an experiment can be considered as a complex process involving a series of questions, answers, and inferences from the answers, including questions and inferences about particular data, as in the case of Millikan's oil-drop experiments. Inductive (or probabilistic) inference in the customary sense is confined to the microlevel of

inquiry. On the macrolevel, the reconciliation of partial or limited generalizations by means of a general theory can be regarded as a form of inductive
reasoning. Such macro-induction (or "inductive reconciliation") does not
fit the modern (Humean) account of inductive reasoning, but it resembles
"Aristotelian induction" or *epagoge*, the process of finding a common
character of interrelated phenomena.[51] In contemporary epistemology this
process is usually regarded as a form of abduction rather than induction.[52]

Regardless of whether nature's answers to experimental questions are
taken to be general propositions about phenomena or singular propositions
about particular data, such answers, even when they appear satisfactory, are
fallible and subject to possible revision in light of new information and new
experiments. This revisability necessitates the introduction of a new kind
of move in the tableau procedure: if an answer is found to be false or
otherwise unsatisfactory, it should be possible to delete it, together with all
other sentences on the left-hand side of the same subtableau that depend on
it. For this purpose, Hintikka introduces "rules of bracketing" which allow
the inquirer to "bracket" (that is, delete) any of the initial premises or the
answers given by the respondent.[53] In this way the tableau procedure can be
adapted to the representation of uncertain information. In the deductive
tableaux extended by interrogative moves alone, there is no mechanism for
deleting or revising the propositions written in the tableau; thus all
propositions, including the answers given by nature, are in effect regarded
as incorrigible and certain. This is not a serious shortcoming if the left-hand
side of the tableau represents what the inquirer knows, or is assumed to
know, in the strong sense discussed above in section II. However, including
rules of bracketing (and "unbracketing") in the tableau method makes it
more realistic as a theory or inquiry because the answers obtained from
nature and other sources of information are usually fallible and uncertain.
The rules of bracketing make Hintikka's theory of inquiry an interesting
potential model of belief revision. Unlike Hintikka's theory, many recent
theories of belief revision, for example, the Alchourrón-Gärdenfors-
Makinson theory, do not give any account of the way in which belief
conflicts are solved by *inquiry*, that is, by means of questions addressed to
suitable respondents.[54] In many standard belief-revision models, an inquirer
does not actively search for information by means of questions and
experiments, but only tries to adapt his belief system to the new information
he happens to receive. For example, according to Gärdenfors, the
"epistemic inputs" which lead to belief revision depend on some "external
forces,"[55] but his model fails to account for an important feature of inquiry,
namely, that such external forces are dependent on and controlled by the
inquirer's interrogative activities.

VI

Since the Middle Ages philosophers have distinguished between two kinds of rules in the practice of an activity or art. For example, Walter Burley observed that the art of disputation, which is a form of inquiry, involves two kinds of rules: "[T]here are some rules that constitute the practice of this art and others that pertain to its being practiced well."[56] Hintikka has formulated this distinction as a distinction between the *definitory* and the *strategic* rules of the game of inquiry.[57] The deductive and interrogative rules mentioned above are definitory or constitutive rules. They are merely permissive rules in the sense that they tell what an inquirer can legally do at each stage in a game of inquiry.[58] For example, the usual tableau rules for logical constants are definitory rules. They do not tell in any interesting sense what an inquirer *ought* to do to find a satisfactory answer to his main question. Norms about satisfactory answers are the function of strategic rules, which advise the inquirer about the best (most effective or economical) ways of finding such an answer to his main question. By way of an example, Hintikka notes that according to Gentzen's first *Hauptsatz*, the cut-rule is eliminable as a definitory rule: all logical proofs in first-order logic can be carried out by cut-free methods. For example, Beth's and Hintikka's tableau rules do not include a cut-type rule. However, various forms of the cut rule are strategically useful because their application can simplify logical proofs.[59] Strategic considerations are vitally important in interrogative games. Any question whose presuppositions are satisfied (i.e., known by the inquirer to be true) is "logically permitted" in inquiry, but to be able to reach his goal the inquirer should choose his secondary questions in such a way that the respondent is able to give satisfactory answers to them. The answers given by the respondent enable the inquirer to find a satisfactory answer to his main question. In experimental inquiry, the purpose of experimental design is to ensure that these requirements are fulfilled: the design of an experiment can be regarded as the design of secondary questions which lead, insofar as possible, to a satisfactory answer to the inquirer's main question. The rules which define the main types of experimental design (e.g., Randomized Blocks, Latin Squares, etc.) are definitory rules, but the choice of a design and its associated statistical and inferential methodology, for the purpose of answering the inquirer's main question, depends on strategic considerations.

A rational inquirer wants to find a satisfactory answer to his main question by means of the simplest and most efficient methods and procedures available to him. These factors can be regarded as aspects of the cost of inquiry, if the expression 'cost' is understood in a suitably wide sense.[60] Thus the *principle of economy* can be regarded as one of the fundamental strategic principles of inquiry. This seems to have been the view of C. S. Peirce, who formulated the basic (strategic) principle of abduction as follows:

> In view of the fact that the hypothesis is one of innumerable possibly false ones, in view, too, of the enormous expensiveness of experimentation in money, time, energy, and thought, is the consideration of economy. Now economy, in general, depends upon three kinds of factors: cost, the value of the thing proposed, in itself, and its effect upon other projects. Under the head of cost, if a hypothesis can be put to the test of experiment with very little expense of any kind, that should be regarded as giving it precedence in the inductive procedure.[61]

One should add to this that the way in which a hypothesis (a potential answer to a question) ought to be investigated is also a question of economy. In the interrogative model, this means that the inquirer's choice of secondary questions should depend on considerations of economy.

The value of secondary questions is relative to an inquirer's primary question, and the significance or importance of a primary question can be evaluated in a similar way: it depends on whether an answer to the question helps to find satisfactory answers to other primary questions in which the investigator (or someone else) is interested.

VII

Many interesting and distinctive features of Hintikka's epistemic logic depend on the use and interpretation of quantifiers in epistemic logic and on the study of the interplay between quantifiers and epistemic operators; the analysis of *wh*-questions outlined above is an example of this approach. Hintikka has used quantified modal logic for the purpose of conceptual clarification in several other areas of philosophical logic; for example, in deontic logic he has used quantifiers together with deontic operators for analyzing different concepts of obligation and permission.[62] Another distinctive feature of Hintikka's work in epistemic logic is the use of game-theoretical semantics, that is, the game-theoretical interpretation of logical constants.[63] As mentioned above, questioning can be understood as a game between an inquirer and a respondent (the "oracle" or "nature"), and quantifiers and other logical constants can also be interpreted in terms of games between two participants or players. Interrogative games represent the way an inquirer can acquire knowledge about the world (i.e., about a model), whereas semantic games assign meanings to the sentences of a language by explaining how the actions of the players (i.e., language users) connect them to their objects.[64]

In game-theoretical semantics, the meanings of logical constants are explicated by means of the interpretive actions of two players, called the advocate or the verifier and the opponent or the falsifier of a sentence. To use Charles Peirce's expression, logical constants are regarded as *precepts* that tell the advocate and the opponent how they ought to act to become acquainted with an object of a given sentence in such a way that its truth-value can be determined.

A semantic game is played about a complex proposition, and the two players, the verifier and the falsifier (or the advocate and the opponent), analyze the sentence until they reach the level of atomic propositions. Each logical symbol is regarded as a precept or a directive that tells how a complex sentence formed by means of that symbol should be analyzed. The verifier of a sentence tries to find an interpretation which makes it true, that is, leads to a true literal (an atomic proposition or the negation of an atomic proposition), and the falsifier has the opposite aim. Thus the game is a zero-sum game. The sentence is true if and only if the verifier has a winning strategy in the game associated with the sentence. Charles S. Peirce, who seems to have been the first philosopher to analyze the semantics of logical constants in terms of the actions of two players, explained this opposition between the interests of the two players by the use of a sentence in an assertive speech act.[65] In an assertive speech act, the utterer of a proposition "assumes responsibility" for its truth and is assumed to suffer some untoward consequences if the sentence turns out to be false, and the hearer or the "interpreter" will suffer the negative effects of the acceptance of false proposition unless he detects its falsity. Thus, the utterer is interested in finding an interpretation which makes the sentence true, and the falsifier must look for the interpretations that might falsify it. This means that in assertive speech acts, the utterer of a sentence can be thought of as its verifier, and the hearer as the falsifier.

For example, quantifiers direct the advocate and the opponent to select objects (values of the variables of quantification) from the domain of quantification in such a way that an existential quantifier assigns the choice of an object to the advocate (the verifier), and a universal quantifier means that the opponent is free to choose an object. The games of ordinary first-order logic are games with prefect information, that is, at each stage of the game the players are fully informed about the moves made by the other players. In the case of quantifiers, this means that the quantifiers are linearly ordered and do not branch. Game-theoretical semantics led Hintikka to consider sentences for which the interpretive actions of the two players are independent of each other, and this generalization of semantical games led

him to what is called independence-friendly quantification theory and epistemic logic, and thus to the "second-generation epistemic logic."[66]
Consider the sentence

(7.1) $(\forall x)(\exists y)Fxy$.

Here the verifier (the utterer) of the proposition lets the falsifier choose an individual, and after the falsifier has chosen an individual, the verifier has an opportunity to find an individual related to the falsifier's individual by F. If the advocate has to make the choice without knowing what the opponent has done, he will have the winning strategy in the game only if he is able to find an individual y such that 'Fxy' holds regardless of how the opponent has chosen x. Hintikka expresses a precept of this kind by the expression

(7.2) $(\forall x)(\exists y/\forall x)$,

where the slash indicates that the verifier's choice is made independently or in ignorance of the falsifier's choice. The sentence

(7.3) $(\forall x)(\exists y/\forall x)Fxy$

is obviously equivalent to

(7.4) $(\exists y)(\forall x)Fxy$.

(7.3) can be translated into the language of standard first-order quantification theory, but not all sentences involving independent quantifiers have such translations.[67]
Propositional connectives and modal operators, including epistemic operators, can be defined by game rules analogous to the quantifier rules. The main difference between ordinary quantifiers on one hand and propositional connectives and modal operators on the other is that the latter are precepts for making choices among propositions (in the case of propositional connectives) or among possible situations (possible worlds). A disjunction signifies a verifier's choice of a disjunct, a conjunction transfers the choice to the falsifier, and a negation exchanges the roles of the verifier and the falsifier so that the original verifier (the utterer of an assertive speech act) assumes the role of the falsifier and vice versa. The epistemic possibility operator signifies the verifier's choice of a possible situation (epistemic possibility), and its dual, representing the concept of knowledge, the opponent's choice. The verifier is here the player who is thought of as making an epistemic assertion, not necessarily the epistemic subject (the inquirer).
Consider the epistemic sentence

(7.5) $K_i(\exists x)Fx$.

This sentence lets the falsifier choose an epistemically acceptable situation (a situation which is epistemically acceptable for i), and the proposition is true if the verifier can then choose from the domain of individuals of that situation one which is F. Suppose now that the advocate (the verifier) has to make his choice without knowing which situation has been chosen by the falsifier, as expressed by the sentence

(7.6) $K_i(\exists x/K_i)Fx$

To ensure that he can win this game, the verifier has to select an individual which turns out to be F regardless of how the falsifier makes (or has made) his choice. Thus (7.6) is equivalent to

(7.7) $(\exists x)K_iFx$.

According to (7.7), the verifier chooses an individual and to falsify the sentence, the opponent has to find an epistemically i-acceptable alternative situation in which the individual chosen by the verifier is not F. In other words, when the verifier chooses an individual or an object, he in effect chooses a "world line" that identifies the individual in all of the epistemic possibilities open to the inquirer. (7.7) can be read as

The inquirer knows who is F

The individuals connected by the world lines are individuals known to the inquirer. In the same way, the sentence 'i knows who c is' can now be written as

(7.8) $K_i(\exists x/K_i)(x = c)$,

which is equivalent to (3.14).

As was observed above, not all sentences in an independence-friendly language (abbreviated 'IF-language') can be translated into the standard first-order logic. For example,

(7.9) $K_i(\forall x)(\exists y/K_i)Gxy$

is such a sentence. In (7.9), the existential quantifier (the verifier's choice) depends on the universal quantifier (the falsifiers's choice), but not on the K-operator (the falsifier's choice of an epistemically i-acceptable world). The game for (7.9) can be described as follows: The falsifier chooses an epistemically i-acceptable world and an arbitrary individual from that world, and to have a winning strategy the verifier must be able to choose an individual y to which the individual chosen by the falsifier is related by G, regardless of the world chosen by the falsifier. For example, if we take the domain of individuals to be members of a certain social group and 'Gxy' is the predicate 'y is x's confidant', (7.9) is the proposition

i knows who is everyone's confidant

in a situation where different persons may have different confidants. (7.9) differs in meaning from both

(7.10) $(\exists y)\mathbf{K}_i(\forall x)Gxy$

and

(7.11) $\mathbf{K}_i(\forall x)(\exists y)Gxy;$

the former states that someone is known by i to be everyone's confidant, and the latter states only that i knows that everyone has a confidant.

VIII

As we have seen, quantification into an epistemic context is interpreted as a player's choice of a "world line" which identifies an individual across epistemically possible situations. According to Hintikka, the world is not given to us divided into "prefabricated" individuals; the individuals are not, as it were, "metaphysically given," but are constituted by a method of cross-identification over situations.[68]

In his paper "On the Logic of Perception," Hintikka introduced a distinction between two methods of individuation which he called perceptual individuation and public or "descriptive" individuation. (We might also use the terms subject-centered and object-centered individuation.)[69] This distinction was the result of Hintikka's study of epistemic logic as the logic of perception. The constructions 'i sees that p' or 'i perceives that p' behave in many ways in the same way as 'i knows that p', and can be analyzed in a similar way by means of an alternativeness relation between possible situations. In this case the alternatives under consideration may be termed *perceptual* alternatives, or situations compatible with what an inquirer (or a perceiver) perceives or sees in a given situation. Thus the concept of perception, like the concepts of knowledge and belief, can be represented by a division of possible situations (or, in the case of perception, possible perceptual *scenes*) into those that are compatible with what an inquirer perceives and those that are ruled out by the inquirer's perceptions. The former situations may be termed the inquirer's (or the perceiver's) "perceptually acceptable situations." Human beings acquire most of their perceptual information visually, and I shall consider below mainly visual perception.

The objects of perceptual knowledge are usually identified by means of demonstrative expressions (complex demonstratives) of the form 'this F' or 'that F', where 'F' is a suitable sortal predicate, for example, 'animal' or 'spot'. An inquirer's perceptual (visual) knowledge that such an object has a certain property, for example, is a tiger, is expressed by a sentence of the form

(8.1) See_i(the indicated object is G),

where 'the indicated object' represents the inquirer's way of identifying the object, for example:

(8.2) See_i(this F is G).

When demonstrative phrases are used in this way, they identify objects perceptually across the perceptual alternatives to a given situation. The identity of a perceptual object depends on its location in the perceiver's perceptual space and on the way it appears to the perceiver. Quantifiers can be used for individuating objects across the inquirer's perceptually acceptable situations (perceptual alternatives), but this method of individuation differs from the public (or "descriptive") individuation mentioned earlier; thus Hintikka distinguishes the "perceptual" quantifiers notationally from those corresponding to the public or descriptive methods of individuation.[70] Using '(Ex)' and '(Ux)' as the perspectival quantifiers and 'S_i' for the perceptual (visual) modality, the perceptual counterpart of the proposition that i knows who c is can be written as

(8.3) $(Ex)S_i(x = c)$

or, using the slash notation explained above,

(8.4) $S_i(Ex/S_i)(x = c)$,

which means that i recognizes one of his visual objects as c.

According to Hintikka, (8.4) may be read as

(8.5)   i sees c,

where 'seeing c' is taken to entail the recognition of the object as c, that is, it is being assumed that the object has a definite place in the inquirer's "visual chart of characters." A sense of 'seeing c' that does not entail such recognition can be expressed by means of Hintikka's perspectival (or visual) quantifiers as

(8.6) $(Ex)(x = c \& (Ey)S_i(y = x))$

The free variable 'x' in

(8.7) $(Ey)S_i(y = x)$

indicates a place or position in i's visual space that can be occupied by a visual object.[71]

It should be observed that the distinction between perceptual and public modes of individuation does not mark an ontological distinction between two kinds of objects, but rather a distinction between different ways of individuating objects, or our ways of "dealing" with them.[72] Thus 'visual object' means a visually identified object.

The distinction between perceptual and descriptive individuation has a counterpart in the constructions involving the verb 'know'. Just as I can say that I see someone, I can say that I know someone, using a direct object construction. This suggests that the distinction between perspectival (perceptual) and descriptive identification can be generalized. Using again '(Ex)' and '(Ux)' as the perspectival quantifiers, 'i knows c' can be expressed by

(8.8) $(Ex)\mathbf{K}_i(x = c)$

or by

(8.9) $(Ex)(x = c \ \& \ (Ey)\mathbf{K}_i(y = x))$,

depending on how the phrase is understood.

This analysis shows that the distinction between knowledge of facts (propositional knowledge) and knowledge of objects ('knowing c') is not a difference between two kinds of knowledge or between two senses of 'know': both can be expressed by means of the same epistemic K-operator.[73]

The distinction between perspectival and public methods of cross-identification sheds new light on the doctrine that proper names are semantically constant singular terms ("rigid designators"), that is, refer to the same object in all possible situations. This view of names, incidentally, is a very old theory of reference, not a new theory; for example, William of Ockham held the view that in the case of demonstrative pronouns and proper names, there is no semantic difference between the *de re* and *de dicto* constructions.[74] In epistemic contexts, the constancy assumption can be expressed by

(8.10) $(\exists x)\mathbf{K}_i(x = c)$,

or, in the case of perspectival individuation, by

(8.11) $(Ex)\mathbf{K}_i(x = c)$.

The constancy assumption is relative to the underlying method of cross-identification. In general, (8.11) holds for demonstrative expressions (complex demonstratives) used by the inquirer for identifying his perceptual (or perspectival) objects.[75] We do not usually introduce proper names for the purpose of perspectival identification, but sometimes this is done. Consider the example about Bingo Little introduced above in section III. Let us assume that the horses running in Goodwood Cup get numbers from 1 to 6, and that Bingo's favorite horse, Ocean Breeze, is No. 4. The numbers can be regarded as temporary (or perspectival) names assigned to the horses; according to some philosophers, names are essentially *tags*,[76] and the numbers are literally tags attached to the horses. We might say that in the race, the numbers get a *perspectival sense* by being assigned to the horses. (The numbers are so to speak the "official" perspectival names assigned to the horses; they are not subjective or "private" names, but Bingo could also use some private system of temporary names.)[77] When Bingo is watching the race, he sees the six horses and can identify them perspectivally by their numbers, for example, he knows which horse is No. 4 in the following sense:

(8.12) $(Ex)\mathbf{K}_b(x = \text{No. 4})$.

Horse No. 4 is (for Bingo) in the situation in question a perspectivally well-defined object. However, in another sense Bingo may not know which horse No. 4 is, in other words, if Bingo does not recognize No. 4 as Ocean Breeze,

(8.13) $\neg(\exists x)\mathbf{K}_b(x = \text{No. 4})$.

In some of Bingo's perspectival alternatives No. 4 is Ocean Breeze, in others it could be (say) Trafalgar. Bingo does not know what Ocean Breeze looks like. Thus

(8.14) $\neg(Ex)\mathbf{K}_b(x = \text{Ocean Breeze})$.

From the standpoint of perspectival identification, 'No. 4' is a constant individual term, whereas 'Ocean Breeze' is not, but from the standpoint of public identification, the situation is the opposite. When Honoria Glossop says that Bingo does not know which horse is Ocean Breeze, she probably means that Bingo is not able to recognize Ocean Breeze; this lack of recognition is expressed by (8.14). This is of course compatible with the truth of

(8.15) $(\exists x)\mathbf{K}_b(x = \text{Ocean Breeze})$,

which in the present example means that Bingo knows that Ocean Breeze is one of the horses running in the Goodwood Cup, and can identify Ocean Breeze for the bookmaker. (Here it may be assumed that Bingo knows which horse is the winner if he is able to identify the winner by its public name 'Ocean Breeze', the name used by the bookmaker.) This example shows that the import of the statement that someone knows who (or which F) c is depends on the context, and it would be futile to try to analyze it in terms of necessary and sufficient "naturalistic" conditions: what holds for the concept of knowledge in general holds for knowing who (or which).[78]

It is important to note here that the perspectival constancy of a singular term (e.g., 'No. 4') does not depend on whether it is construed as a (perspectival) proper name or as a definite description 'the horse marked with number 4'. Thus semantic constancy over possible situations is not a general feature of proper names: some names are constant terms, others are not, depending on the way in which their objects are individuated.

IX

Hintikka's distinction between perspectival and public methods of cross-identification helps to clarify certain old issues in epistemology, for example, questions about the foundation of knowledge and the nature of perceptual beliefs.

Many philosophers, for example, Edmund Husserl and Moritz Schlick,[79] have argued that epistemologically the most basic propositions, the propositions directly based on a subject's experience, are indexical propositions that identify their objects by demonstrative expressions (e.g., 'this horse') accompanied by gestures. If epistemologically basic beliefs and knowledge are expressed by such propositions, they must rely on the perceptual or perspectival modes of cross-identification. Schlick observed that such propositions cannot be "written down," because the context and the gestures that are needed to identify the object of 'this F' are part of the proposition.[80] Consequently such propositions cannot be part of a system of beliefs in which information about the world is stored over time. Schlick expressed this by saying that observation propositions ("Konstatierungen," as he called them) "have no duration."[81] The information provided by such observation propositions can be stored and preserved only if their objects are identified as public, intersubjective objects. This usually means that an object that has been referred to by a demonstrative phrase is recognized as an object with a public identity and identified by an expression with an associated public (cross-situational) sense. This step or inference is an interrogative-abductive step, prompted by the question "Who is this F?" or "Which G is this F?"

Hintikka has assimilated the distinction between the two methods of cross-identification to a distinction between two systems of visual processing which Lucia Vaina has called the "where" system and the "what" system.[82] The former supports the localization of objects in the visual space ("where"), the latter is needed for the categorization and identification of an object on the basis of its nonspatial and nonvisual predicates, for example, those based on its function and use ('glove', 'hammer', etc.). Vaina reports that patients whose "what" system was impaired as a result of a lesion of certain areas of the visually responsive brain were apt to confuse objects with similar visual textures, e.g., a cauliflower and a sheep.[83]

The distinction between the "where" system and the "what" system, or spatial vision and object vision, as Vaina also expresses the distinction,[84] is based on the characterization of objects by means of different predicates, strictly visual predicates (form, texture, etc.) and nonvisual predicates. (The former are usually unverbalized; according to Vaina, verbal processing takes place on the level of "object vision.")[85] The perspectival and the public modes of identification are based on partly different predicates, but Hintikka's distinction seems much more general than Vaina's, and it operates on many levels of cognitive organization. The perspectival identification of an object by means of indexical expressions is a case of "object vision." In the example about the Goodwood Cup in the previous section, I regarded Hintikka's distinction as a distinction between two kinds of object representations, a temporary indexical representation, used in a limited perceptual context (that of watching a single race), and a long-term representation that makes it possible for an inquirer to store information across situations over extended periods of time. Proper names usually serve the latter purpose. In the discussions about the foundation of knowledge among the members of the Vienna Circle, the propositions formulated in terms of the long-term representations were called "system propositions."[86] This interpretation of Hintikka's distinction has a counterpart in the recent work in cognitive psychology. In the research on perception and attention, a distinction has been made between temporary perceptual representations ("episodic representations" or "object files") and long-term representations of objects.[87] A temporary object-file is not instantaneous, but is maintained as long as the perceiver's attention is directed at the same perceptual object. Moreover, a perceptual object file can undergo changes as a result of new incoming sensory information.[88] Anne Treisman gives the following example of a change in a temporary object file: "A distant aeroplane retains its continuity as a single perceptual object, even when we see it flap its wings and alight on a nearby tree, thus forcing us to change the label [i.e., the sortal predicate] we initially assigned."[89] In a situation of this kind, the observer usually identifies the object by means of a demonstrative pronoun and a suitable sortal predicate. In Treisman's example, the sortal predicate is 'airplane', which turns out to be a miscategorization; a cautious observer might have used the predicate 'spot' or 'mark'.[90] However, the observer could also introduce a temporary perspectival name for the object.[91]

The indexical propositions based on a perspectival method of cross-identification form, in a sense, the "foundation" of a person's belief system or corpus of knowledge, but it is not the sort of foundation suggested by the foundation metaphor and some foundational theories of knowledge. It is not

a lasting structure of indubitable propositions but consists of constantly
changing indexical beliefs. We might say that a person's belief system is
connected to the world through a process in which perspectival beliefs are
constantly being replaced by new ones. Temporary perceptual information
that does not get translated into system propositions is left behind. The
foundation metaphor is a highly misleading account of epistemologically
basic propositions and of the nature of immediate knowledge.

RISTO HILPINEN

UNIVERSITY OF MIAMI (CORAL GABLES)
AUGUST 2003

NOTES

I wish to thank Ms. Anneli Hilpinen for discussions on statistical methodology
and other procedures of knowledge acquisition.

1. See William Heytesbury, "The Verbs 'Know' and 'Doubt'," in *The
Cambridge Translations of Medieval Philosophical Texts*, vol. 1: *Logic and The
Philosophy of Language*, ed. N. Kretzmann and E. Stumpf (Cambridge: Cambridge
University Press, 1988), pp. 435–79; Ivan Boh, *Epistemic Logic in the Later Middle
Ages* (London: Routledge, 1993), pp. 63–77.
2. Charles S. Peirce, *Collected Papers of Charles Sanders Peirce*, vols. 1–6, ed.
Charles Hartshorne and Paul Weiss (Cambridge, Mass.: Harvard University Press,
1931–1935), vol. 4, ¶ 65; Georg Henrik von Wright, *An Essay in Modal Logic*
(Amsterdam: North-Holland, 1951).
3. See Boh, *Epistemic Logic in the Later Middle Ages*, p. 65.
4. Charles Willeford, *Sideswipe* (New York: Bantam Books, 1987), pp. 221–22.
5. Jaakko Hintikka, *Knowledge and Belief* (Ithaca: Cornell University Press,
1962), pp. 20–21.
6. Peirce, *Collected Papers*, vol. 4, ¶ 523.
7. See Risto Hilpinen, "Knowledge and Conditionals," in *Philosophical
Perspectives*, vol. 2: *Epistemology*, ed. James Tomberlin (Atascadero, Calif.:
Ridgeview Publishing Co., 1988), pp. 157–82, esp. 166–67; Michael Williams,
Problems of Knowledge: A Critical Introduction to Epistemology (Oxord and New
York: Oxford University Press, 2001), pp. 48–49.
8. See Risto Hilpinen, "Knowledge and Justification," *Ajatus* 33 (1971):
25–26; Timothy Williamson, *Knowledge and Its Limits* (Oxford and New York:
Oxford University Press, 2000), pp. 78–80.
9. Quoted from Anthony Kenny and Jan Pinborg, "Medieval Philosophical
Literature," in *The Cambridge History of Later Medieval Philosophy*, ed. N.

Kretzmann et al. (Cambridge: Cambridge University Press, 1982), p. 27. The reference is to Siger of Brabant, *Quaestiones super librum de causis.*

10. See Keith Lehrer, *Theory of Knowledge* (Boulder and San Francisco: Westview Press, 1990), pp. 12–13.

11. See Frank P. Ramsey's 1929 essay, "Knowledge," in F. P. Ramsey, *Philosophical Papers*, ed. D. H. Mellor (Cambridge: Cambridge University Press, 1990), p. 110.

12. See Jaakko Hintikka, "Epistemology without Knowledge and without Belief" (forthcoming).

13. Ibid.

14. Ibid.; see also Jaakko Hintikka, "Is Logic the Key to All Good Reasoning?" in Jaakko Hintikka, *Inquiry as Inquiry: A Logic of Scientific Discovery, Selected Papers*, vol. 5 (Dordrecht: Kluwer Academic Publishers, 1999), p. 9.

15. Immanuel Kant, *Critique of Pure Reason*, 2nd ed., trans. Norman Kemp Smith (New York: St. Martin's Press, 1965), B xiii.

16. See Robin George Collingwood, *An Essay in Metaphysics* (Oxford: Clarendon Press, 1940), p. 23.

17. See Peirce, *Collected Papers*, vol. 5, ¶ 584; Alexius Meinong, *On Assumptions*, 2nd. ed. (Berkeley and London: University of California Press, 1983), p. 98, translation of *Über Annahmen*, 2nd. ed. (Leipzig: Barth, 1910); Friedrich Löw, "Zur Logik der Frage," *Archiv für die Gesamte Psychologie* 66 (1928): 357–58; see also Martin Kusch, "Theories of Questions in German-Speaking Philosophy around the Turn of the Century," in *Knowledge and Inquiry: Essays on Jaakko Hintikka's Epistemology and Philosophy of Science*, ed. M. Sintonen (Amsterdam: Rodopi, 1997), pp. 41–60.

18. Löw, "Zur Logik der Frage," pp. 357–58.

19. Lennart Åqvist, *A New Approach to the Logical Theory of Interrrogatives: Part I: Analysis* (Uppsala: The Philosophical Society Series, 1965); Lennart Åqvist, "On the Analysis and Logic of Questions," in *Contemporary Philosophy in Scandinavia*, ed. R. Olson and A. Paul (Baltimore and London: Johns Hopkins Press, 1972), pp. 27–39.

20. Cf. David Lewis and Stephanie R. Lewis, Review of R. Olson and A. Paul, *Contemporary Philosophy of Scandinavia, Theoria* 41 (1975): 48–51; Lennart Åqvist, "On the 'Tell Me Truly' Approach to the Analysis of Interrogatives," in *Questions and Answers*, ed. Ferenc Kiefer (Dordrecht: Kluwer Academic Publishers, 1983), pp. 9–14.

21. See Manfred Moritz, "Zur Logik der Frage," *Theoria* 6 (1940): 125.

22. See Jaakko Hintikka, "Presuppositions of Questions—Presuppositions of Inquiry," *Proceedings of the 2001 IIP Annual Meeting* (Dordrecht: Kluwer Academic Publishers, forthcoming).

23. Jaakko Hintikka, *The Semantics of Questions and the Questions of Semantics. Acta Philosophica Fennica* 28, no. 4 (Amsterdam: North-Holland, 1976), p. 29; Jaakko Hintikka, "New Foundations for a Theory of Questions and Answers," in *Questions and Answers*, ed. Ferenc Kiefer (Dordrecht: D. Reidel,

1983), p. 175.

24. See Jaakko Hintikka, "Different Constructions in Terms of the Basic Epistemological Terms: A Survey of Some Problems and Proposals," in *Contemporary Philosophy in Scandinavia*, ed. R. Olson and A. Paul (Baltimore and London: Johns Hopkins Press, 1972), pp. 107–8; Jaakko Hintikka and Ilpo Halonen, "Semantics and Pragmatics of Why-Questions," in Hintikka, *Inquiry as Inquiry, Selected Papers*, vol. 5, p. 187, originally published in *Journal of Philosophy* 92 (1995): 636–57.

25. Jaakko Hintikka, "On Denoting What?" *Synthese* 46 (1981): 179; Hintikka, "New Foundations," in *Questions and Answers*, pp. 164–65; Jaakko Hintikka, "World Lines and Their Role in Epistemic Logic," in *Philosophical Logic and Logical Philosophy: Essays in Honour of Vladimir Smirnov*, ed. P. I. Bystrov and V. N. Sadovsky (Dordrecht: Kluwer Academic Publishers, 1996), pp. 121–38.

26. Jaakko Hintikka, "Individuals, Possible Worlds, and Epistemic Logic," *Noûs* 1 (1967): 38.

27. Charles S. Peirce, "The Basis of Pragmaticism" (MS 280, 1905), *The Charles S. Peirce Papers*, Microfilm Edition (Cambridge: Harvard University Library, 1966), pp. 42–43; cf. Risto Hilpinen, "Peirce on Language and Reference," in *Peirce and Contemporary Thought: Philosophical Inquiries*, ed. Kenneth L. Ketner (New York: Fordham University Press, 1995), p. 285.

28. Jaakko Hintikka and John Symons, "Systems of Visual Identification and Neuroscience: Lessons from Epistemic Logic," *Philosophy of Science* 70 (2003): 96.

29. David Kaplan, "Quantifying In," in *Words and Objections: Essays on the Work of W. V. Quine*, ed. D. Davidson and J. Hintikka (Dordrecht: D. Reidel Publishing Co., 1969), pp. 227–30.

30. Rex Stout, *Where There's a Will* (New York: Lawrence E. Spivak, 1940; New York: Bantam Books, 1992), p. 70.

31. Paul Grice, "Vacuous Names," in *Words and Objections: Essays on the Work of W. V. Quine*, ed. by D. Davidson and J. Hintikka (Dordrecht: D. Reidel, 1969), pp. 141–42; Gareth Evans, "The Causal Theory of Names," in Gareth Evans, *Collected Papers* (Oxford: Clarendon Press, 1985), p. 16, originally published in *The Aristotelian Society*, Supplementary vol. 47 (1973): 187–208; Daniel Kahneman and Anne Treisman, "Changing Views of Attention and Automaticity," in *Varieties of Attention*, ed. R. Parasurman and D. R. Davies (London: Academic Press, 1984), pp. 54–55; Anne Treisman, "Features and Objects: The Fourteenth Bartlett Memorial Lecture," *Quarterly Journal of Experimental Psychology* 40 A (1988): 218–20.

32. See Hintikka, "Individuals, Possible Worlds, and Epistemic Logic," pp. 35–37. See n. 26.

33. Jaakko Hintikka, "A New Approach to Sentential Logic," *Societas Scientiarum Fennica, Commentationes Phys.-Math.* 17 (1953): 2; Jaakko Hintikka, "Form and Content in Quantification Theory," in *Two Papers on Symbolic Logic*, *Acta Philosophica Fennica* 8 (1955): 8–55; Evert Beth, "Semantic Entailment and Formal Derivability," *Mededelingen der Koninklijke Nederlandse Akademie van*

Wetenschappen, Afdeling Letterkunde, New Series 18 (1955): 13, reprinted in *The Philosophy of Mathematics*, ed. J. Hintikka (London and New York: Oxford University Press, 1969), pp. 9–41; Evert Beth, *The Foundations of Mathematics: A Study in the Philosophy of Science* (Amsterdam: North-Holland, 1959). See also Melvin Fitting, "Introduction," in *Handbook of Tableau Methods*, ed. M. D'Agostino, D. Gabbay, R. Hähnle, and J. Posegga (Dordrecht: Kluwer Academic Publishers, 1999), pp. 1–43.

34. Cf. Beth, *The Foundations of Mathematics*, pp. 190–91; Fitting, "Introduction," p. 9.

35. For details of the tableau method, see Fitting's "Introduction" and the other articles in D'Agostino et al., *Handbook of Tableau Methods*.

36. Cf. Jaakko Hintikka, Ilpo Halonen, and Arto Mutanen, "Interrogative Logic as a General Theory of Reasoning," in Hintikka, *Inquiry as Inquiry*, pp. 74–76.

37. Ibid., p. 51.

38. See Hintikka, *Inquiry as Inquiry*, p. xi.

39. Peirce, *Collected Papers*, vol. 6, ¶¶ 528 and 524; see also ¶ 6.469 and vol. 2, ¶ 634.

40. Isaac Levi, *The Enterprise of Knowledge: An Essay on Knowledge, Credal Probability, and Chance* (Cambridge, Mass.: MIT Press, 1980), p. 49; Isaac Levi, *Decisions and Revisions: Philosophical Essays on Knowledge and Value* (Cambridge: Cambridge University Press, 1984), p. 92.

41. Jaakko Hintikka, "What is the Logic of Experimental Inquiry?" in Hintikka, *Inquiry as Inquiry*, p. 145. Originally published in *Synthese* 74 (1988): 173–90.

42. Ibid., pp. 145, 151.

43. James Bogen and James Woodward, "Saving the Phenomena," *Philosophical Review* 97 (1988): 305–6; James Robert Brown, "Phenomena," in *Realism and Anti-Realism in the Philosophy of Science*, ed. R. S. Cohen et al. (Dordrecht: Kluwer Academic Publishers, 1996), pp. 119–20.

44. Jim Woodward, "Data and Phenomena," *Synthese* 79 (1989): 393.

45. Max Wertheimer, "Experimentelle Studien über das Sehen von Bewegung," *Zeitschrift für Psychologie* 91 (1912): 161–265.

46. See Jaakko Hintikka, "The Concept of Induction in the Light of the Interrogative Approach to Inquiry," in Hintikka, *Inquiry as Inquiry*, p. 168. Originally published in *Inference, Explanation, and Other Frustrations: Essays in the Philosophy of Science*, ed. John Earman (Berkeley: University of California Press, 1992), pp. 23–42.

47. Allan Franklin, *Experiment, Right or Wrong* (Cambridge: Cambridge University Press, 1990), pp. 103–5.

48. Levi, *The Enterprise of Knowledge*, pp. 37–41.

49. See Allan Franklin, *The Neglect of Experiment* (Cambridge: Cambridge University Press, 1986), pp. 148–57.

50. See Hintikka, "What is the Logic of Experimental Inquiry?" in *Inquiry as Inquiry*, pp. 152–54.

51. See Hintikka, "The Concept of Induction in the Light of the Interrogative

Approach to Inquiry," in *Inquiry as Inquiry*, pp. 173–75; Hintikka, "Aristotelian Induction," *Revue Internationale de Philosophie* 34 (1980): 422–39.

52. See Jaakko Hintikka, "What is Abduction? The Fundamental Problem of Contemporary Epistemology," in *Inquiry as Inquiry*, p. 95; originally published in *Transactions of the Charles S. Peirce Society* 34 (1998), pp. 503–33.

53. Hintikka et al., "Interrogative Logic as a General Theory of Reasoning," in *Inquiry as Inquiry*, pp. 63–64.

54. See Peter Gärdenfors, *Knowledge in Flux: Modeling the Dynamics of Epistemic States* (Cambridge, Mass.: MIT Press, 1988); Peter Gärdenfors, "Belief Revision: An Introduction," in *Belief Revision*, ed. P. Gärdenfors (Cambridge: Cambridge University Press, 1992), pp. 1–28.

55. Gärdenfors, *Knowledge in Flux*, p. 13.

56. Walter Burley, "Obligations," in *The Cambridge Translations of Medieval Philosophical Texts*, vol. 1: *Logic and the Philosophy of Language*, ed. N. Kretzmann and E. Stumpf (Cambridge: Cambridge University Press, 1988), p. 379.

57. Hintikka, "Is Logic the Key to All Good Reasoning?" in *Inquiry as Inquiry*, p. 2; "The Role of Logic in Argumentation," ibid., pp. 27–29, originally published in *Monist* 72 (1989): 3–24.

58. Hintikka, "What is Abduction?" in *Inquiry as Inquiry*, p. 98; "Is Logic the Key to All Good Reasoning?" ibid., p. 5; cf. Peirce, *Collected Papers*, vol. 4, ¶¶ 414–17.

59. Hintikka, "Is Logic the Key to All Good Reasoning?" pp. 12–13.

60. See Jaakko Hintikka and Merrill B. Hintikka, "Sherlock Holmes Confronts Modern Logic: Toward a Theory of Information-Seeking through Questioning," in *The Sign of Three: Dupin, Holmes, Peirce*, ed. Umberto Eco and Thomas Sebeok (Bloomington and Indianapolis: Indiana University Press, 1984), pp. 167–68; Hintikka, "Is Logic the Key to All Good Reasoning?" pp. 12–13.

61. Charles S. Peirce, *Collected Papers of Charles Sanders Peirce*, vols. 7–8, ed. Arthur Burks (Cambridge, Mass.: Harvard University Press, 1958), vol. 7, ¶ 220 n. 18. See also Peirce, *Collected Papers*, vol. 6, ¶ 528.

62. Jaakko Hintikka, "Quantifiers in Deontic Logic," *Societas Scientiarum Fennica, Commentationes Humanarum Litterarum* (Helsinki) 23 (1957): 4; Jaakko Hintikka, "Some Main Problems in Deontic Logic," in *Deontic Logic: Introductory and Systematic Readings*, ed. R. Hilpinen (Dordrecht: D. Reidel, 1971), pp. 59–104.

63. For game-theoretical semantics, see Jaakko Hintikka and Gabriel Sandu, "Game-Theoretical Semantics," in *Handbook of Logic and Language*, ed. J. van Benthem and A. ter Meulen, (Amsterdam and New York: Elsevier, 1997), pp. 361–410.

64. Cf. Jaakko Hintikka, "The Games of Logic and the Games of Inquiry," *Dialectica* 49 (1995): 229–49.

65. See Risto Hilpinen, "Peirce's Theory of the Proposition: Peirce as a Precursor of Game-Theoretical Semantics," in *The Relevance of Charles Peirce*, ed. Eugene Freeman (La Salle, Ill.: The Hegeler Institute, 1983), pp. 266–68. Originally published in *Monist* 62 (1982): 182–89.

66. Jaakko Hintikka, *The Principles of Mathematics Revisited* (Cambridge: Cambridge University Press, 1996), pp. 46–87; Hintikka, "A Second Generation Epistemic Logic and Its General Significance," in *Knowledge Contributors*, ed. V. F. Hendricks et al. (Dordrecht: Kluwer Academic Publishers, 2003), pp. 33–55.

67. For examples see Hintikka, *The Principles of Mathematics Revisited*, ch. 3; Hintikka and Sandu, "Game-Theoretical Semantics," in *Handbook of Logic and Language*.

68. Jaakko Hintikka, *The Intentions of Intentionality and Other New Models for Modalities* (Dordrecht: D. Reidel, 1975), p. 209.

69. Jaakko Hintikka, "On the Logic of Perception," in Jaakko Hintikka, *Models for Modalities* (Dordrecht: D. Reidel, 1969), pp. 151–83, originally published in *Perception and Personal Identity: Proceedings of the 1967 Oberlin Colloquium in Philosophy*, ed. Norman S. Care and Robert H. Grimm (Cleveland: Press of the Case Western Reserve University), pp. 140–73. Cf. Jaako Hintikka, "Knowledge Acknowledged: Knowledge of Propositions and Knowledge of Objects," *Philosophy and Phenomenological Research* 56 (1996): 261.

70. See Hintikka, "On the Logic of Perception."

71. Hintikka and John Symons, "Systems of Visual Identification and Neuroscience," *Philosophy of Science* 70 (2003): 99.

72. Hintikka, "On the Logic of Perception," pp. 172, 177–79.

73. Hintikka, "Knowledge Acknowledged," p. 268.

74. William Ockham, "Modal Consequences" (ch. 10 of *Summa Logicae*), in *The Cambridge Translations of Medieval Philosophical Texts*, vol. 1: *Logic and The Philosophy of Language*, ed. N. Kretzmann and E. Stumpf (Cambridge: Cambridge University Press, 1988), p. 316.

75. See Jaakko Hintikka, "Perspectival Identification, Demonstratives and 'Small Worlds'," in Jaakko Hintikka, *Paradigms for Language Theory and Other Essays*, *Selected Papers*, vol. 4 (Dordrecht: Kluwer Academic Publishers, 1998), pp. 219–21; and Jaakko Hintikka and Gabriel Sandu, "The Fallacies of the New Theory of Reference," in Hintikka, *Paradigms for Language Theory and Other Essays*, pp. 204–7 (reprinted from *Synthese* 104 [1995]: 245–83).

76. See Ruth Barcan-Marcus, "Modalities and Intensional Languages," in Ruth Barcan-Marcus, *Modalities: Philosophical Essays* (New York: Oxford University Press, 1993), p. 11. Originally published in *Synthese* 8 (1961): 303–22.

77. See François Recanati, *Direct Reference: From Language to Thought* (Oxford, U.K. and Cambridge, Mass.: Blackwell Publishers, 1993), p. 172.

78. See Hintikka, "Knowledge Acknowledged," pp. 263–64.

79. Edmund Husserl, *Logische Untersuchungen*, 2nd ed. (Tübingen: Max Niemeyer Verlag, 1968 [1913]), vol. 2, part II, ch. VI:1, §§4–6); Moritz Schlick, "On the Foundation of Knowledge," in Moritz Schlick, *Philosophical Papers*, vol. 2, ed. H. Mulder and B. F. B. van de Velde-Schlick (Dordrecht: D. Reidel, 1979), pp. 385–86, translation of "Über das Fundament der Erkenntnis," *Erkenntnis* 4 (1934): 79–99.

80. Schlick, "On the Foundation of Knowledge," p. 386.

81. Ibid., p. 382.

82. Hintikka, "The Cartesian *Cogito*: Epistemic Logic and Neuroscience," *Synthese* 83 (1990): 144–45; Lucia Vaina, "'What' and 'Where' in the Human Visual System: Two Hierarchies of Visual Modules," *Synthese* 83 (1990): 49–91.

83. Vaina, "'What' and 'Where' in the Human Visual System," p. 65.

84. Ibid., p. 49.

85. Ibid., p. 75.

86. Risto Hilpinen, "Über die Indexikalität der Wahrnehmungsurteile bei Schlick und Neurath," *Zeitschrift für Semiotik* 21, no. 1 (1999): 22–23.

87. See Treisman, "Features and Objects," 218–22; Kahneman and Treisman, "Changing Views of Attention and Automaticity," pp. 54–55.

88. Daniel Kahneman and Avishai Henik, "Perceptual Organization and Attention," in *Perceptual Organization*, ed. Michael Kubovy and James R. Pomerantz (Hillsdale, N.J.: Lawrence Earlbaum Associates, 1981), pp. 210–11; Treisman, "Features and Objects," pp. 218–19.

89. Treisman, "Features and Objects," p. 219.

90. See, for example, Virginia Woolf's 1919 story, "The Mark on the Wall," in *The Virginia Woolf Reader*, ed. Mitchell A. Leaska (San Diego: Harcourt Brace Jovanovich, 1985), pp. 152–59.

91. See Recanati, "Direct Reference," p. 172.

REPLY TO RISTO HILPINEN

R isto Hilpinen's task in his paper is exceptionally difficult because of the extent and complexity of the area he is trying to cover. He is the only contributor who deals with my work in epistemic logic and one of the few who deals with my epistemological ideas. He presents lucid surveys of several central topics in this problem area. I expect them to be useful for many readers, among other things because of the instructive examples Hilpinen uses. His expositions are by and large eminently accurate. I will make a few minor corrections as I proceed. It seems to me that the best service I can do to my readers is to try to indicate how the different topics Hilpinen discusses are related, how they fit into a wider framework and what other topics can be approached by means of the same framework. I will try to follow a roughly systematic order.

Hilpinen begins most appropriately from the analysis of knowledge in terms of excluded and admitted alternatives (scenarios, "possible worlds"). What he could have added to his informative exposition is that the possible-scenarios analysis is firmly based on the role of knowledge as a guide of life, for instance, as a guide of decision-making. The scenarios that are not among a person's, say b's, epistemic alternatives, are the ones he is entitled to disregard. Thus b may restrict his or her (or its, if the decision-maker is a computer) attention to the epistemic alternatives belonging to the world in which the decision-maker is located.

One remarkable thing here is that most of the logical aspects of knowledge depend only on this dichotomous character of the semantics of knowledge. As a consequence, much of the logic of belief (doxastic logic) is structurally similar to the logic of knowledge, and so are the logics of such other epistemic notions as remembering, perceiving, and seeing. For instance, the behavior of quantifiers and identity is analogous in all such epistemic contexts. What distinguishes knowledge from other propositional attitudes is the nature of the entitlement needed to disregard the scenarios that are not one's epistemic alternatives. To characterize the criteria that govern such a legitimate dismissal of possibilities is to define knowledge.

Hilpinen discusses this problem in an interesting way. However, from what has been said it follows that the precise definition of knowledge makes little difference to most of the strictly logical aspects of knowledge. Furthermore, the question of the definition of knowledge has some interesting light thrown on it by the interrogative model of knowledge-seeking (see below).

Several of the specific things Hilpinen says about the definition of knowledge are nevertheless connected with general epistemological insights. For one thing, Hilpinen's point that a knowledge claim must be able to withstand future scrutiny in order to be true (it "involves a prediction about the inquirer's future beliefs") is connected with the fact that measures of information cannot be defined a priori but involve assumptions concerning the unknown part of the world. Hilpinen's reminder of Frank Ramsey's characterization of knowledge points to the need of considering knowledge in the context of processes of inquiry, especially in the context of the interrogative model.

Again, Hilpinen's perceptive discussion of the meaning of "knowing who" and "knowing what" (as being similar to locating the person or object or some map or "chart" in a sufficiently general sense) suggests a more general point about cross-identification. Identification does not rely primarily on the properties (like the supposedly "essential properties") of individuals, but mainly on some geometry in which they can be located.[1]

In contrast, the behavior of quantifiers is determined almost immediately by the possible-scenarios ("possible-worlds") analysis. Unless we take the hopelessly uncritical view that possible worlds are somehow assembled from the same individuals, we have to assume that our semantics of quantifiers is based on some principle of cross-world identification. Whatever this method is, it leads immediately to representations like Hilpinen's (3.12) and (3.14) in the case of simple *wh*-knowledge.

Hilpinen presents carefully and fairly the idea of questions as requests for information and explains how this idea leads to the logical form of questions that I have proposed. Since not all actually asked questions are literally requests for information, some analysts have (as Hilpinen points out) distinguished spurious and genuine questions from each other. This terminology seems to me misleading. Questions and answers form as it were a kind of semantical mechanism, a conceptual tool. This tool can have different uses. The primary use of this semantical mechanism is information acquisition. However, the same tool can be put to other legitimate uses. There need not be anything "spurious" about examination questions, or rhetorical questions, as little as there is anything unnatural, nonsemantical, or spurious for a pedestrian to cross a river using a railway bridge instead of a walkway.

At one point, Hilpinen says that answers to an inquirer's questions are "external." Unfortunately or fortunately, I do not see any hope of developing a realistic theory of knowledge-seeking by questioning without treating a human inquirer's tacit knowledge or a computer's database as a source of answers. Such answers activate potential information for the purposes of inquiry, even though their source can only be called "internal."

Hilpinen does not explicitly mention the notion of conclusiveness conditions or answers ("presuppositions of answers"). This makes it difficult for him to place some of the most interesting features of the logic of questions and answers in the most general perspective. Hilpinen examines in a clear and instructive way experimental questions and points out that nature's replies to them can either be considered *prima facie* as "scatter diagrams" or else mathematical specifications of the dependence. He opts for the latter, for instance, suggesting in the case of a regression analysis "that we regard the regression equation, not just the scatter diagram, as nature's answer." This is eminently agreeable to me, but it misses the deeper logical point here. Considering (in a typical case) the mathematical expression of dependence as nature's conclusive answer is not merely a natural way of talking about answers to experimental questions. It is strictly mandated by the logic of questions and answers. This point is worth emphasizing in that such unexpected (although in themselves intuitive) consequences of one's logical model strikingly illustrate the power of logical analysis in epistemology. Nature's raw response is at best a fragment of a curve that represents a function-in-extension. According to a straightforward logic of questions, such response amounts to a conclusive answer only if the experimenter knows what mathematical function the experimentally obtained curve represents. This insight does not only make the logic of controlled experiments an integral part of the logic of questions and answers in general. It throws interesting light on the nature of experimental induction in general. This subject is discussed in my forthcoming paper, "The Place of the A Priori in Epistemology."

Hilpinen has available in his paper all the ingredients that are needed in order to explain the logic of experimental inquiry in his presentation of the role of independence indicators in the logic of questions. However, he explains this role only after he has discussed experimental questions.

One of the developments Hilpinen briefly explains is the interrogative model of inquiry. It has far more sweeping consequences for epistemology than have been spelled out in the literature. Interrogative inquiry is a process of knowledge acquisition. Hence knowledge figures in it as a goal. Thus in the process itself an inquirer cannot rely on the notion of knowledge. Therefore what ought to be the central part of epistemology, the theory of inquiry, should be studied without using philosophers' strong concept of knowledge. I have argued that the same applies to philosophers' notion of belief. The result is very nearly "Epistemology without Knowledge and without Belief," to quote the title of an unpublished paper of mine.

Knowledge and belief enter into the interrogative model as ways of evaluating the outcome of an interrogative inquiry. If we recall the connection between knowledge and decision-making indicated above, there seems to be little reason to believe that such an evaluation can be independent of the subject matter of inquiry. If it is not, there cannot exist a purely epistemological general definition of knowledge. This point might help to put in a longer perspective the issues that Hilpinen surveys.

Hilpinen briefly explains the use of Beth-type semantical tableaux as a book-keeping device for interrogative inquiry. He could have explained more fully the reasons for prefixing statements by the K-operator on both sides. For one thing, without doing so, we cannot use a tableau in modeling an attempt to answer a principal question by means of a number of operative questions. (Hilpinen explains very well this difference between the two kinds of questions.) With the help of the K-operator, this task can be done simply by using the desideratum of the principal question as the aimed-at ultimate conclusion of inquiry.

Hilpinen's paper should be especially useful to our readers in that it contains expositions of two developments that have not yet received the attention they deserve in the literature. One of them is the use of independence indicators in representing the logical form of questions via representing their desiderata. Hilpinen's able exposition of this subject does not fully bring out the motivation of the use of independence indicators. The fact is that only with their help can we analyze the logical forms of all the different kinds of *wh*-questions.

Furthermore, and most importantly, only by using independence indicators to help us analyze these logical forms can we reach a general theory of questions, in the sense of being able to define in a uniform way such notions as the all-important desideratum of a question, its presupposition, and the conclusiveness condition ("presupposition") of its answers. I do not think it is much of an exaggeration to say that only the "second generation" epistemic logic using the notion of independence can yield a truly general logic of questions and answers. Among other things, it is only in the framework involving the notion of independence that we can deal with several of the problems Hilpinen takes up, including the nature of the answers to experimental questions and the need for knowledge operators in tableau-type book-keeping in interrogative inquiry.

The other major relative novelty Hilpinen discusses at some length is the presence in our actual conceptual scheme of two different principles of cross-identification. I hope that Hilpinen's exposition raises the awareness of philosophers of this crucial distinction. Hilpinen explains carefully the distinction which is especially clear in the case of visual cognition but not restricted to it. He also points out that this distinction between two modes of cross-identification necessarily involves a distinction between two kinds of quantification. This distinction in turn implies a distinction between two kinds of questions.

The implications of these parallel distinctions are so sweeping that no one can exhaust them in one article. Hilpinen points out a few of them. One of them is the need of making the distinction between two kinds of cross-identification also when speaking of the objects of perception, memory, and knowledge. Another is the manifestation of the distinction in cognitive neuroscience in the form of two visual systems that are often called in the neuroscientific literature the "where" system and the "what" system. This analogy cuts even deeper than Hilpinen brings out. For one thing, from the perspective of the different modes of identification, the very terms "where-system" and "what-system" are somewhat misleading, in that the words "where" and "what" can themselves rely on either method of cross-identification. More importantly, from the logical distinction it is immediately seen that the difference between the two systems does not lie in their involving different kinds of information, since only one epistemic operator is used. Rather, what is involved is a difference between two kinds of frameworks of identification. In contrast, neuroscientists initially took the contrast to be between two different kinds of information and were only gradually dissuaded by empirical evidence.[1]

Hilpinen points out the interesting fact that accounts of an epistemic constitution of the world typically start from perspectival knowledge. Now perspectival identification has to take place in a local environment, by reference to someone's visual space in the cases of seeing or by reference to a person's world line in the case of memory. The logical constitution of the world will therefore involve the task of integrating these local environments into one big public world. This way of looking at the constitution problem deserves much more attention than it has received.

As is noted by Hilpinen in effect, a study of the logic of perspectival identification amounts to a theory of indexical reference. I have sketched the basic ideas of such a theory. Much more work remains to be done here, however.

One of the main uses of the distinction lies in the sharply critical light it throws on sundry ideas of philosophers. Hilpinen points out, correctly, that the question of which singular terms refer "rigidly" depends on the mode of identification. Here one can push this line of thought further and for instance point out the fallacy of Kripke's account of fixing the reference of a term by ostensive dubbing. Of course such a ceremony can only uniquely determine the perspectival reference of a term. The only "rigid designators" whose references he can thus fix are in reality Russell's "logically proper names," *this*, *that*, and (perhaps) *I*. Kripke nevertheless thinks in effect that he is explaining public reference. Kripke's appeal to causal chains in extending the use of a name beyond the dubbing situation is an empty gesture as long as a much more detailed account is not given of the re-identification of the named object.

These remarks will, I hope, give the reader a sense of the depth and width of the issues to which a rightly developed epistemic logic and epistemological analysis lead us.

J. H.

NOTES

1. I have examined this matter in my 1982 paper (with Merrill B. Hintikka) "Towards a General Theory of Individuation and Identification," reprinted in the 1989 collection *The Logic of Epistemology and the Epistemology of Logic.*

2. See here, e.g., S. Zeki, *A Vision of the Brain* (Oxford: Blackwell, 1993).

25

Matti Sintonen

FROM THE LOGIC OF QUESTIONS TO THE LOGIC OF INQUIRY

I. INTRODUCTION

Jaakko Hintikka's interrogative model (I-model) of inquiry builds on the basic idea that all knowledge seeking is a process of searching for answers to questions.[1] This was the default view of inquiry in Greek philosophy from Plato's *elenchus* to Aristotle's dialectics. It was a leading principle and metaphor in early modern experimental philosophy when the idea became popular that one should read the book of Nature and not (just) the Bible or the books of Aristotle. This resulted in the official ethos of the rising science: the optimism about man's intellectual powers to reveal the secrets of nature, the idea that the key to success is the right method, and the notion that this method could be captured in an organized procedure of putting questions to Nature.

So what is the news? The news is in Hintikka's way of using logic and formal tools to give the idea a precise content. It has been fashionable to doubt the power of logic to capture everyday life and scientific concepts. Consequently, the current has been away from logic to informal expositions and explorations. Hintikka swims against this current, arguing that when in trouble, one needs more logic, not less. Moreover, Hintikka's way of conceiving logic is special and carries much of the spirit of the nineteenth century and earlier. Perhaps somewhat paradoxically, he puts more emphasis than is customary in much of twentieth-century philosophy on the intimate connection between logic and thinking: though not a science of thought, logic nevertheless is the backbone of rational thought and reasonable action.

There are two more specific ideas that provide interpretive keys for the
I-model. The first one is Hintikka's Kantian view of knowing as making, as
the activity of seeking and finding, or indeed constructing. The second key
is von Neumann's theory of games, which gives a formally well-behaved
handle for this activist epistemology. In game theory inquiry, like any goal-
directed activity, is viewed in terms of a strategically conceived procedure:
one starts from some initial position and proceeds by alternating steps
against another player, here called "Nature." There is also a structural
bridge from Hintikka's game-theoretical semantics (not dealt with here at
all) to inquiry as a game against Nature: language games and knowledge
games are both viewed as goal-directed rather than rule-bound; neither
meaning nor knowledge is a single-shot affair but a matter of assessing
strategies.

Viewing Hintikka's I-model from this perspective occasions a
preliminary note on the general character of his enterprise. The motivation
behind Hintikka's explorations is increased philosophical consilience, a
systematic view in which the various aspects of knowledge seeking have a
place. Hintikka is also singularly persistent in the pursuit of the consequences of his ideas and in the cultivation of his analytical tools. There is
hardly an idea or tool (and often the idea is the tool) which does not bear on
the articulation of others. One can almost see a Hegelian teleological
process of the Spirit becoming conscious of itself: ideas that have emerged
early on to deal with some region on the map of philosophy are seen, in the
light of newly honed ideas and generalizations, as inevitable stages on the
way to the fully articulated end stage. In Hintikka's system the final stage
is given in terms of independence-friendly logic (IF logic), for the crucial
notions of a question, its presupposition and desideratum receive a fully
general treatment within that logic.

When this perspective is applied to the history of philosophy the
outcome looks ahistorical or Whiggish, at times. It may be objected that
Aristotle, Newton, and Peirce hardly dealt with the same problem of, say,
induction. I shall not try to address this historiographical problem at all. As
I understand him Hintikka is not grading past masters with the current
yardstick but, rather, using the tools of logic to make distinctions and to
explicate conceptions which, in some form, had a genealogy in earlier
thought. The best way to describe this process is William Whewell's:
scientific progress consists of some fundamental ideas being explicated (by
the tools of logics in Hintikka's case) as well as of colligation of facts. In
science the result is consilience of inductions. Here it is philosophical
consilience.

I shall start with the grand philosophical metaphor of "putting questions
to Nature" and the insight that structures his philosophy: Kant's activist

epistemology (section II). This is followed by a précis of Hintikka's logic of questions and the I-model (section III) and its applications: the logic of experimental inquiry (section IV), induction (section V), abduction and scientific discovery (section VI), the role of the mathematical or a priori in science (section VII), and scientific explanation (section VIII). The question is: does the I-model provide a philosophically illuminating explication of these fundamental concepts? Here we find Kant's and Whewell's views of progress of knowledge again. William Whewell's notions of induction and discovery in particular bear striking similarity to Hintikka's account. This viewpoint also gives rise to a possible limitation of the interrogative approach. It is a captive view, but one may wonder if it is based on an illicit and potentially misleading metaphor. It is also an extremely rationalistic account of science and inquiry. Unlike current historically and sociologically inclined views which make much of science a process conditioned by historical contingencies and social negotiations, Hintikka's vision is characterized by logic and order (section VIII).

II. PUTTING QUESTIONS TO NATURE

The notion that inquiry is a process in which an inquirer attempts to find (conclusive) answers to her questions is an idea that has its roots in thinkers otherwise as different as Aristotle and Bacon. R. G. Collingwood added to this list Descartes when he wrote that Bacon's *Novum Organum* (and Descartes's *Discourse on Method*) built their views on method on the "principle that a body of knowledge consists not of 'propositions,' 'statements,' 'judgments,' or whatever name logicians use in order to designate assertive acts of thought." Rather, knowledge consists of propositions "together with the questions they are meant to answer; and that a logic in which the answers are attended to and the questions neglected is a false logic."[2] Another golden period for the interrogative view was nineteenth-century German philosophy. Husserl, Meinong, and Rickert displayed a live interest in the way philosophy and science arise from wonder and questioning, and Bolzano suggested that questions not just express a questioner's desire to know, but that they also fall in the province of logic because they have a truth value; the important distinction between propositional and "wh-questions" (what-, where-, who-questions) emerged in the writings of Groos, Sigwart, and Meinong. Questions and questioning were particularly close to the heart of the neo-Kantians Hermann Cohen and Paul Natorp who held that questions, just as Kant had said, do not just mark the beginning of an inquiry but also pave the way towards knowledge. Questions therefore both initiate inquiry and provide heuristic guidance.[3]

The questions-answers view of Bacon and the neo-Kantians has a number of attractions, not just as a general model of knowledge seeking but also as a metatheory for scientific inquiry. Airing questions and answers are primordial modes of actions—and the language games of questioning are deeply entrenched in our cognitive capacity.[4] The view also accords with working scientists' self-understanding, for any well-structured research project can be cast in the form of an interrogative portrayal, which starts from some big initial questions and then proceeds to answer them by help of small operational questions. It also opens a promising angle into heuristics and discovery. The standard objection to discovery programs has been that the generation of new ideas and specific hypotheses is ultimately a matter of guessing and luck. But this need not be true, and certainly the neo-Kantians and Hintikka think otherwise. Nor did this Kantian influence pass by the scientists. The Danish physicist Christian Oersted wrote, "To observe is to detect the actions of nature; but we shall not advance far in this path, unless we have a notion of its character. To make experiments is to lay questions before nature; but he alone can do that beneficially who knows what he should ask."[5]

I have gone to some length along Kantian lines because his Copernican Revolution is a unifying theme in Hintikka. Hintikka rethinks the relationship between knowing and making, and extends the new constructivism beyond understanding to perception and to inquiry.[6] Hintikka has argued that there is a close relationship between Kant's transcendentalism and his own theories of space, time, and mathematics. As he puts it, Kant's transcendental method in epistemology requires not just that one examines the objects of our putative knowledge but also that one focuses on what one must do to obtain knowledge. The gist of the transcendental method and the entire Copernican Revolution is, on this interpretation, in the active contribution of the mind. Transcendental arguments are designed to demonstrate that a priori knowledge draws on the contribution to the overall structure of human knowledge. As Kant expresses his point, "reason has insight only into that which it produces after a plan of its own."[7]

Now what is the structure? What is it that reason produces in accordance with its plan and which therefore can be known with certainty, and a priori? Hintikka thinks that these are not recipes for preparing concrete or even cultural objects, a theme important to the tradition from Vico to Ricoeur. Rather, he reads Kant as referring to the "conceptual tools" that the human mind employs in knowledge-acquisition. It is the mind's own input or contribution that makes the synthetic a priori element in knowledge possible, whether that knowledge concerns the spatiotemporal *rerum natura*, mathematical truths, or indeed, human beings. An important aspect of Kant's mathematical method is the use "particular representatives" of central concepts. In modern logical terms this amounts to the employment of instantiation rules. The reason why logic (more precisely, first-order logic) and hence Kant's mathematics applies to all experience is that it reflects the inquirer's "method" of obtaining knowledge. This I think is an interesting turn: it is not always clear if Kant, when insisting on the synthesizing role of mind, refers to the process of cognition of its outcome (not anything would go, for Kant). Both are possible, but in Hintikka's case the process and the method governing it have special weight.

The Copernican turn is therefore the key to Hintikka's insistence on the idea that the strategic principles which govern good—that is, efficient and intelligent—deductive reasoning are the same principles which govern good empirical inquiry. Kant followed Bacon but emphasized, even more clearly if possible, the ineliminable role of the inquirer in the interpretation of nature. Kant insisted that when Reason approaches nature it must do so not "in the character of a pupil who listens to everything that the teacher chooses to say, but of an appointed judge who compels the witnesses to answer questions which he has himself formulated."[8] Note the plural for questions, for it carries the implication that in issues of any consequence, those which involve secrets, Nature cannot be cornered in a single move.

The thoroughly Kantian mood is not made quite explicit in Hintikka's more recent writings of the interrogative model. Since it bears directly on the claim of the model to be a logic of knowledge seeking, of discovery and not just of justification, it is well worth a deeper look. The twentieth-century dogma was that there is no logical way of having ideas—how they come is no concern to logic. But passive waiting is not Hintikka's way. Interestingly, he also thinks that Kant indeed was on the right track in his interventionist epistemology but did not carry it all the way. Again there is the parallel between mathematical and empirical knowledge. Since the mathematical method deals with particulars, potential objects of knowledge in this area are, logically speaking, individuals. But how does the mind access individuals? Kant refers here to human sensibility as the sole source of "empirical intuition" (A19 = B33)—with the upshot that mathematical knowledge mirrors the structure of this faculty of sense-perception. But if the structure of our outer sense (empirical intuition) is identified with space, and that of inner sense with time, the result is neatly symmetrical—but mistaken. Hintikka's line of thinking in the 1960s and 1970s was that knowledge of particulars cannot be based on mere reception or passive perception. In fact, the tradition to which Kant clearly belongs requires that mental activity is not mere receptivity but also intervention—whether in accordance with an antecedently drawn plan, or improvisation. To find out how things are out "in the world"—and the world of mathematical truths is no different in this respect—one must engage in active search to find them.

Therefore "the activities of seeking and finding" are the general methods through which particulars are accessed. As will become clear, this view is all the more natural in the method of science.

III. THE LOGIC OF QUESTIONS AND THE INTERROGATIVE MODEL OF INQUIRY

With these virtues and such a prestigious pedigree, one would have expected that the I-model had become the dominant view of inquiry. This is not the case—and it behooves us to ask why. One reason seems to be that it has been thought to be an illicit and misleading metaphor. It could be considered illicit because inert Nature cannot be an equal partner in dialogue, and misleading because Nature does not understand some crucial types of questions, viz., questions that aim at revealing general truths concerning Nature's workings. Another reason holding the I-model down, especially in the logic and pragmatics of explanation, has been that the notion of a satisfactory answer appears to be overly pragmatic and subjective: what counts as a good (in Hintikka's terms a conclusive) answer has been thought to depend on the (possibly) idiosyncratic knowledge and interests of the questioner. A third reason may well be the fact that neo-Kantianism in philosophy of science gave way to the new exact philosophy, scientific or logical empiricism. Logic of questions was in the air, but not in a form that would have met the new exacting standards.

It is here that Hintikka has made a decisive contribution, in two steps which at least promise to alleviate these skeptical worries concerning the scope of logic. The first step was a logic of questions and answers in which answerhood is precisely defined but pragmatically flexible. The second step elaborates Kant's and Oersted's idea that there are two kinds of questions in the interrogative procedure, the big initial questions and the small operational questions that are used to find information needed in the process of finding potential answers to the initial question. I shall start by outlining Hintikka's version of this logic and deal with the first two worries in later sections. The focus here is not on the logical and linguistic detail of the model but rather on its philosophical applications within epistemology and philosophy of science. Consequently I shall not even attempt to motivate this version against other candidates.[9]

Following the imperative suggestion of Lennart Åqvist (a suggestion that relied heavily on Hintikka's earlier work on knowledge and belief),[10] Hintikka designed a logic that was based on the idea that information-seeking questions are requests (or commands) to an addressee to provide information that has causal or rational efficacy. The information provided should be sufficient to produce in the questioner a desired epistemic state.

To explore the proposal we need some notation. To begin with, Hintikka distinguishes between propositional questions (such as whether-questions and yes-no–questions) that take complete propositions as answers and wh-questions that receive singular terms as answers.

To proceed via examples, let us represent (the logical forms of) the desiderata of the whether-question "Is gold white or yellow" and the wh-questions "Who is the Waynflete Professor of Metaphysical Philosophy?" by (1) and (3), and their presuppositions (propositions "without which the questions have no direct answers") by (2) and (3):

(1) $K(S_1(v/K)S_2)$
(2) $K(S_1 \vee S_2)$
(3) $K(\exists x/K) S[x]$
(4) $K(\exists x) S[x]$

An answer, say "Gold is white," is one of the offered alternatives of the whether-question (and in the special case of a yes-no–question the queried proposition or its negation), or a name ("Gilbert Ryle") or definite description in the wh-question. Wh-questions have the feature that they allow us to use epistemic logic to study conditions under which an answer is conclusive for an inquirer H. An answer is conclusive for H if H is, after hearing it, in a position to say, truly, "I know what, who (where, when, etc.) X is." A correct direct answer does not automatically fulfill this condition. For instance a name ("Gilbert Ryle") or a (unique) definite description, say "The writer of *The Concept of Mind*," to (3) is not conclusive for H, if H wants more than a name or a definite description (some queries could also be raised about the uniqueness condition). The model provides a logically simple but pragmatically flexible tool for the study of answerhood. A direct answer satisfies the questioner when and only when the answer, together with the inquirer's background knowledge, suffices to entail the state of affairs she or he desires. Clearly, an answer is conclusive only if it does not give rise to such further questions as "But who, then, wrote *The Concept of Mind?*" In short, the questioner must be able to identify the individual (person, place, instant of time, etc.) to which the answer refers. The special slash-notation in (1)–(4) serves the purpose of expressing informational independence, needed to distinguish between H's knowing that someone is the Waynflete Professor and H's knowing who that someone is. The distinction is based on the idea that H's knowledge of identity presupposes ability of identifying the individual independently of any particular epistemic scenario compatible with what H knows. I shall not, however, need the fine details of this distinction in what follows.

Hintikka's I-model of knowledge-seeking builds on erotetic logic. Knowledge-seeking is a game in which an Inquirer attempts to find a conclusive answer to an initial research question, such as finding out whether B or not-B, or which individuals have a property P, or why a state of affairs C obtains. The details of knowledge-seeking games depend on the interlocutor (Nature, the Inquirer's *alter ego*), a fellow investigator, on the formal restrictions on admissible answers, etc.[11] But whatever the more specific model, the rules of the art divide admissible knowledge-seeking steps into two categories, deductive and interrogative moves (in some more complicated games there are also definitory moves). Experiments, unsolicited observations, memory consultations and help from friends and colleagues feed in new information and can be therefore be construed as answers to questions put to a source of information. These are codified by rules for asking questions. Apart from them there are deductive moves in which the Inquirer infers new conclusions from those already possessed.

The art of querying and answering can be codified in terms of semantical tableaux employed by Evert Beth and Hintikka, where explicit tableau-construction rules govern deductive rules and further rules governing admissible interrogative moves. Again, there is variation in the detail, but some ground rules are universal or nearly so. The Inquirer cannot demand an answer to the big initial question. There is also no moving of items from the right-hand column to the left-hand one in a tableau. It is also assumed that before an inquirer can raise a small operational question she must establish its presupposition, and write it down in the left column. It is also usually agreed that the game is, at any given time, tied to a particular model M and its language, usually first-order language, that Nature cooperates when she can, and that Her answers are true in M. The Inquirer, then, attempts to find or construe an answer to the initial big question by forcing Nature to yield unambiguous answers to her small questions, answers which the Inquirer then can avail in the interrogative derivation of the chosen conclusion. A crucial feature of these games of interrogation is also that apart from the rules which specify admissible moves there are strategic principles which advise players on the best moves to make. The Inquirer can choose, at any stage, a deductive move and derive a proposition from what she already has, or make an interrogative move in order to obtain new information.

Relativization to background knowledge explains why different answers are conclusive for different inquirers. It is at the root of the second worry concerning the I-model. Braithwaite formulated the worry as follows:

> Any proper answer to a 'Why?' question may be said to be an explanation of a sort. So the different kinds of explanation can best be appreciated by considering the different sorts of answers that are appropriate to the same or to different 'Why?' questions. What is demanded in a 'Why?' question is

intellectual satisfaction of one kind or another, and this can be provided, partially or completely, in different ways. . . . And what gives partial or complete intellectual satisfaction to one person may give none whatever to a person at a different stage of intellectual development.[12]

But the lesson to draw is not erotetic relativism. Although answers come in all sizes and shapes, there is the nontrivial relationship between the question, the desideratum and the conclusive answer.

IV. THE ATOMISTIC POSTULATE AND THE LOGIC OF EXPERIMENTAL INQUIRY

What kinds of questions are within reach when Nature is the interlocutor? For us at least "reading the Book of Nature" and "putting Questions to Nature" are metaphorical. One reason is that Nature is not an intentional agent who could engage in dialogue, or play a game with us in a literal sense. Nature, with the exception of humans and possibly some other primates, does not have communicative intentions (at least not of degree three in Grice's sense). Scientific progress in fact has been the elimination of the anthropomorphic picture of which these metaphors were part.

But granting that interrogating Nature is a metaphor, is it a good one? Does Nature understand the sort of questions we are interested in in episte-mology and philosophy of science? One view, the default one since the sensationalists and David Hume, is that Nature's understanding, even in this metaphorical sense, is confined to particular matters of fact. Nature can only testify to what She has seen herself. The issue arises within the interrogative model as follows. Observations and experiments can be viewed as questions put to Nature because here the answerer's (Nature's) task is confined to recording one of the two outcomes of a yes-no question, or one of the possible meter readings of an apparatus (25°C, say). The way we understand observations and experiments relies on the idea that we are in causal interaction with inert Nature, with or without intervening with its course. On this view Nature cannot offer answers of a general form because the presuppositions of general questions are beyond Nature's capacities. In interrogative terms the presuppositions and desiderata of the questions are of form (1) – (4), and answers to them, coming as causal responses in observational and experimentational arrangements, are restricted to spatiotemporal particulars. On this view the onus of inferring and generaliz-ing is always on the Inquirer, requiring as it does, extrapolation, bold judgment, and conjecture.

Hintikka wants to have none of this. The I-model is not committed to sensationalism. Within the interrogative model this amounts to giving up the Atomistic Postulate according to which Nature's answers are confined to sentences with no quantifiers, the $A^0 = E^0$ case.[13] In general the logical complexity of answers can be cashed out in terms of the number of changes of quantifier kind (changes from an existential to a universal quantifier or vice versa) in the quantifier prefix of the answer. Atomistic answers are quantifier-free whereas the next more complicated answers have universal quantifiers in the prefix. Moving up in the hierarchy towards increasingly complex quantifier prefixes we first come to the AE case in which universal quantifiers are followed by existential ones.

Restricting Nature's answers to the $A^0 = E^0$ case appears obvious at first, but turns out to be problematic, Hintikka thinks, because controlled experiments presuppose AE complexity. An experimental question (in the macro-inquiry sense to be specified shortly) put to Nature is of the form, "How does the variable y observed depend on the controlled variable x?" where x is the object of our intervention and manipulation. What the inquirer is trying to find out is an answer to this question such that, upon receiving the answer, she or he would know the functional relationship. Functional relationships express generalities, not particular matters of fact. In the IF interrogative model this means the fulfillment of the desideratum which has one of the following forms:

(5) $(\exists f)K(\forall x) S[x, f(x)]$
(6) $K(\exists f/K)(\forall x) S[x, f(x)]$
(7) $K(\forall x) (\exists y/K) S[x, y]$

where "/" expresses informational independence and "K" is the knowledge operator. Experiments therefore are answers that bring about these desiderata. Controlled experiments aim at establishing a functional relationship between the controlled and the observed variable and therefore require at least AE complexity. Consequently, Hintikka argues, the logic of experimental science is an AE logic.

But how radical is this departure from the standard view criticized by Hintikka? What is the motivation for maintaining that Nature only understands queries concerning particulars? Note first that Hintikka softens the claim about the logic of experimental inquiry by distinguishing between the primary data, particular recordings obtained from observations and measurements, and the "role which the results of controlled experiments play in the entire scientific process."[14] And he considers the objection that these particular recordings are one thing and the further inferential step of plotting the curve is another thing. This reading is strengthened by the distinction between observational moves whose results are atomistic answers and experimental moves whose results have A^2 complexity.[15] Further support comes through the distinction between the microlevel and the macrolevel of inquiry such that the former deals with the level of inquiry "on which an experiment operates as a single direct question to nature."[16] As Hintikka puts it, this is not at odds with the view that there is a macrolevel: "The measurement results may be nature's answer in the micro-level game that an experiment can be thought of as being, not in the macro-level game in which an entire controlled experiment is but a single move."[17] But if this view is adopted the idea of putting questions to Nature appears less radical: it would be natural to think that Nature's direct responses are of the former type while it is the inquirer's task to come up with a conclusion with respect to how these direct answers are to be interpreted.

However, there is much more to Hintikka's idea than terminology. Giving up the Atomistic Postulate is important not just for understanding his views on the logic of experimentation but also on induction, abduction, and inquiry more generally (see the next section). What follows is conjecture and not certainty. But it seems to me that Hintikka reasons as follows: Inquiry is a rational goal-directed activity, hence amenable to reconstruction by means of logic. But if Nature cannot be called to testify on generalizations, ending up with them must be alogical and arational.

I shall pursue this line in the following sections. But why did the Atomistic Postulate harden into a methodological dogma? Here is another conjecture that focuses on the way the logic of inquiry has shaped during the past centuries. To begin with, there is a partial rationale within the I-model. There are some obvious questions that cannot be put to Nature, namely the initial big question. The reason is that that would amount to committing the fallacy of Begging the Question (although, as Hintikka puts it, this is no logical fallacy but a breach of the rules of questioning). This is one reason why we cannot ask Nature the yes-no question "Is Einstein's special theory of relativity true?" But there is another reason which, in a deep sense, gives a justification for this questioning rule. The main reason is that deducing a generalization from particular observations would amount to too much, to a logic of discovery in the strong generativist sense where one and the same procedure could both generate and justify a hypothesis.[18] Such a logic was the dream in Descartes's *Rules for the Direction of Mind* and Bacon's *Novum Organum* but, so we are told, this turned out to be precisely that—a dream. Descartes had to acknowledge that a set of facts might be accounted for by competing and incompatible generalizations. And if empirical generalizations and "phenomenological" laws are underdetermined by necessarily finite observations, then explanatory or "fundamental" theories which postulate unobservable entitities, forces and causal mechanisms to account for these generalizations are doubly underdetermined. Since generalizations and especially theories are risky extrapolations or bold conjectures, there can be no logical way of having ideas, or no demonstrative way of deriving true theories. These problems quickly led into the great epistemological and methodological debates about the proper understanding of empirical inquiry and to the new realization that uncertainty is here to stay—and that probability is the mode of inquiry.

There is a sense of drama here, since sensationalism carries with it a number of epistemological and metaphysical consequences for the applications of the I-model. In Larry Laudan's useful summary, the new fallibilism, together with consequentialism according to which there is no direct way of comparing theories with nature, resulted in the hypothetico-deductive view of inquiry.[19] All we can do is try and deduce (or induce) empirical consequences and thereby assess, albeit indirectly, their tenability. Empirical claims, whether conceived by intuition, analysis, synthesis, induction, or whatever, could not be proved the way mathematical truths can be proved. What I am suggesting is that Hintikka again navigates against the modern fallibilist current of empirical knowledge, towards Bacon's and Descartes's dream, using Kant's methodological insights as the steering-gear. Newton is on record for maintaining that he deduced generalizations from phenomena, and Hintikka thinks he got it right. Hypothetico-deductivism might not be completely false, but it is not much use either. It better be replaced by interrogationism.

V. INDUCTION AND INTERROGATION

Perhaps the most surprising view of Hintikka's is that the traditional notion of induction is at odds with the I-model. This is a surprising statement from a founding member of the Finnish school of inductive logic (whatever that is). And after all, induction is the mode of modern science. In Hintikka's view the notion of induction that is needed went into hibernation with Hume. In fact, for the pre-Humeans there was no such thing as the problem of induction in the twentieth-century sense.

What does it mean to say that induction plays no role in the interrogative view? It does not mean that premises and a conclusion could not be in an inductive relationship, nor that induction in the current sense has no role in inquiry. But it does mean that it plays second fiddle. So what is induction on the received view? David Hume and the sensationalists have taught us that induction deals with generalizations inferred from particular observations. The Atomistic Postulate is part of this received view of inductive philosophy. But this is contrary to the old view on which, first, generality is in the picture from the very beginning and, second, induction properly speaking refers to the process of reconciling restricted generalizations into more encompassing ones. Aristotelian *epagogue* meant this, and that is also what Newton meant by induction in his methodological comments on optics and mechanics.[20] Here the idea is precisely to start from restricted generalizations and to proceed, inductively, to more general laws by subsuming the generalizations under these laws. There is of course a sense in which inductive reasoning still is with us, namely, the sense in which reconciliation is ampliative in nature. In Hintikka's view this means simply that induction is uncertain. As Newton put it, we argue from experiment and observations by induction, and although this is not infallible it is the best way of arguing which the nature of things admits of.

There are some intriguing systematic and historical issues of interpretation. Here we need to go back to Hintikka's Kantian way of viewing Nature's interrogation, and to the view that there can be no nonconceptual but still cognitive commerce with Her. Kant was of the view that intuitions without concepts are blind. Here it would mean that already *seeing that* a particular is a particular of a certain sort involves a conceptual ingredient and hence a degree of generality. Making even a particular claim, e.g., that the position of a planet at a certain time is such-and-such involves the concept of a planet—and the conceptions of space and time. Pure nonconceptual observation therefore is impossible. But although there is some generality already at this level, there is the further type of generalization which sums up such observations under a more general conception, such that the position of a planet at two times falls on an elliptical curve. Now this sort of generalization cannot be simply *seen* so that there is no generality-free way of perceiving *that* this is the case. This means that the mind must first have the concept of an ellipse and entertain the idea that the positions *might* fall on the elliptical curve. Only then is it possible to raise the question if that *actually* is the case. Testing through consequences can therefore not be the entire story of rational inquiry, for the concepts needed to frame the hypotheses—indeed the questions—have logical priority. And once the mind has established that two observed points are on an elliptical curve, it can check if this is true of the planet's position at other times. Finally, once this possibility has been established the mind can ask if this is true of other planets in our planetary system, or if it is true more generally amongst the entire set of applications of sun-planet systems.

It is also possible that there are parallel trains of thought amongst other applications, for comets, falling bodies, springs, penduli, or magnets, and so forth. And with the craving for an Architechtonic the faculty of Reason is bound to look for still more general (and exciting) generalizations: it may turn out that there are more general conceptions such that planets and comets are essentially similar, that planets and falling bodies are essentially similar, and that planets and penduli are similar. Reason therefore ventures

increasingly bold conjectures, in the hope that Nature fulfills its Architechtonic wishes. The point remains nevertheless that Reason is here
following its own master plan, and little by little filling in the particular
details (such as: what particular function the ellipse is, and the like).

This description of the progress of knowledge is essentially that of
William Whewell. Whewell's philosophy was an original blend of British
empiricism and Kantian conceptualism, and it exerted a great influence on
science and philosophy of science in the nineteenth century. According to
Whewell consilience is the hallmark of progress in science. There are two
basic processes by which science is constructed, viz., "the Explication of
Conceptions and the Colligation of Facts." Each science has its own
fundamental ideas (conceptions) which determine what kinds of facts are
gathered. Colligation of facts means the gathering of facts under such
conceptions. The two processes unite in induction. It sometimes happens
that inductions obtained from different classes of facts coincide, that "rules
springing from remote and unconnected quarters" leap together. "I will take
the liberty of describing it by a particular phrase; and will term it the
'Consilience of Inductions'."[21] Whewell quite evidently shared the view that
there are two types of induction, or perhaps two kinds of steps in the
inductive procedure, one for colligating facts under appropriate conceptions
(provided by the mind) and the other one for generalizing beyond what has
been established in the process of colligation.

Whewell's *Philosophy of the Inductive Sciences* is the best example of
induction at work, in Hintikka's (Newtonian) sense. Whewell was aware
that his induction was not exactly Aristotelean *epagoge*. He appreciated
Bacon's description of the way inquiry proceeds by putting questions to
Nature, and he canonized the Newtonian view of the inductive procedure.
However, inspired by Kant's Copernican turn he took exception to Bacon's
(alleged) and Hume's (evident) sensationalism. Neither perception nor
reasoning or inference can proceed without guidance from the concepts
provided by the mind. Whewell stresses, just as Kant did in the first
Critique, that unification is no mere "juxta-position of materials" but
contains "a new conception, a principle of connection and unity, supplied
by the mind."[22] Moreover, the required principles have a very strong
binding force: it is not sufficient that we can show an analogy between the
phenomena in the two realms. Rather, the unity supplied by the mind is
actual sameness. What appeared as two unrelated and distinct types of
phenomena are in fact one type.

The entire interrogative procedure outlined by Whewell fits Hintikka's
description. Hintikka observes that experience in early modern philosophy
referred to common knowledge of *phainomena* which included general and
not just particular propositions. The starting point of inquiry was not a set
of singular observations for the early moderns—and it was not for the

ancients (indeed *endoxa*). But there is a deeper methodological lesson. Bacon was keen to point out that responsible inquiry is not anticipation but interpretation of Nature. Anticipation amounts to rushing into generalization in the direction the mind finds agreeable, without due respect to empirical checks, whereas interpretation consists of ascending, little by little and with caution, to increasingly encompassing generalizations. This seems to fit Hintikka's views very well, and not just because for Whewell an important part of induction was reconciliation of inductive generalizations. First, Hintikka has been keen to emphasize the concept-ladenness of observations as well as the theory-ladenness of concepts.[23] But second, the reason why induction in the modern sense has a secondary role in the interrogative model is that the sensationalist reading of experience, and with it the atomist construal of interrogationism, only starts with Hume.[24] Third, the idea of "Putting Questions to Nature" mixes easily with another metaphor, that of interpreting or "Reading the Book of Nature." Bacon gave his *New Organon* the subtitle "true directions concerning the interpretation of Nature," and one of his great admirers, William Whewell, tied the phrase up with the possibility of mastering Nature's language (and gave the third book of *Philosophy* the title *Novum Organum Renovatum*). In interpreting the book of nature, Whewell wrote, an inquirer tries to find laws which are identical with the real laws of nature. "To trace order and law in that which has been observed, may be considered as interpreting what nature has written down for us, and will commonly prove that we understand her alphabet."[25]

VI. AND THE LANGUAGE OF NATURE IS—MATHEMATICS!

If Hintikka shares William Whewell's views on the inductive method and scientific progress, we can understand some of his further claims about the I-model. I already pointed to Hintikka's intellectual debt to the Copernican Revolution and to the notion that there already is a degree of generality in any perception, whether inner or outer. This degree of generality is something that the mind imposes on the findings. Further influence from Kant and Whewell comes from the role of mathematics, the a priori element in science. The received view of the so-called Scientific Revolution is that it resulted from the marriage between the platonizing and mathematizing tradition and the new experimental philosophy which emphasized the notion that all inquiry should be checked through experience. This view of the Scientific Revolution has largely been discredited but there still is the view that we have the experimentalists and we have the theoreticians—and that seldom do these two meet.

Now Hintikka suggests that this view misses the mark completely. It may be true that experimental science leads a life of relative autonomy, but experimental inquiry itself cannot be conducted without mathematical knowledge. In fact, it would seem to follow, from Hintikka's view, that progress in mathematics can be the driving force of inquiry by making possible new questions to put to Nature. Experimental questions, we saw, require functions as answers, and desiderata in the form of (5) – (7). Now it is conceivable that Nature could provide an infinite list of argument and function values such that the inquirer could know, for each value of x, the value of y. However, such an answer (of form)

(8) K $(\forall x)$ S$[x, g(x)]$

would not entail the required desiderata. What more could a rational experimental ignoramus want? On Hintikka's view she or he would need to know what that function is. It is here that Hintikka's notion of a conclusive condition comes into play again. An answer of form (8) may be one step towards a fully satisfying answer but, intuitively speaking, may fall short of one because the questioner still might be unable to master the functions, to know not just that there are such functions but also which functions they are. These conclusiveness conditions could have any of the following four forms:

(9) $(\exists f)K(\forall x) (g(x) = f(x))$
(10) $K(\exists f/K) (\forall x) (g(x) = f(x))$
(11) $K(\exists f/K) (g = f)$
(12) $K(\forall x) (\exists y/K) g(x) = y$

Equipped with knowledge of (9) – (12), (8) does entail (5) – (7) and therefore becomes a conclusive answer. Hintikka calls these conclusiveness conditions (a kind of) presupposition of answers to an experimental question. Just as presuppositions of questions rule out a range of answers, so "presuppositions" (conclusiveness conditions) of questions rule out some answers as unsatisfactory. To the extent mathematical knowledge constrains the satisfactoriness of empirical queries we can see why mathematics is so important to, say, experimental physics or econometrics. For the answer to be conclusive she or he would need a piece of mathematics—and this is the a priori as against the a posteriori part of the answer.

Again we find this very idea in William Whewell. He wrote that Kepler was able to recognize the ellipse in the observed data not just because the elliptic form is really there—and this means that Whewell was a realist with respect to aims of inquiry—"but also . . . because he had, in his mind, those relations of thought." And Whewell resorted to the familiar analogy from Galileo and Kepler: "We too find the law in Kepler's book [the *Astronomia Nova*]; but if we did not understand Latin, we should not find it there. . . . In like manner, a discoverer must know the language of science, as well as look at the book of nature, in order to find the scientific truth."[26] And how do we know that we have come to master the language of Nature? The assurance we have is based on a sort of inference to best explanation, here put to metaphysical service. If it so happens that the various so far unrelated inductions conspire and fall under more general laws, that is, if there is Consilience of Inductions, we witness a process in which Nature indeed conforms to the Reason's architechtonic wishes. This, Whewell writes, is a sure sign that we are on the right track (and understand Her alphabet).

If this view is correct, these conclusiveness conditions are not just constraints on answers but also heuristic devices. This would be in line with Whewell, for he made it clear that only a mathematically prepared mind can search for the right types of generalizations and identify them as such when encountering them. He writes that "to supply this conception, required a special preparation, and a special activity in the mind of the discoverer. . . . To discover such a connection, the mind must be conversant with certain relations of space, and with certain kinds of figures."[27] Laura Snyder has made the relationship between the a priori element (provided by the mind) and the a posteriori element (submitted by observation) clearer than anyone else: "The fact that Kepler had more fully explicated his conception of an ellipse explains why he was able to recognize in the observed facts the elliptical property of the orbit, whereas Tycho Brahe and his assistant Longomontanus were not."[28]

VII. ABDUCTION AND SCIENTIFIC DISCOVERY: FROM WHERE DO QUESTIONS COME?

On the hypothetico-deductive view of theory formation there is no logic of discovery, and none is needed—precisely because knowledge is fallible and justification goes via consequences. This view was popularized by Popper in *The Logic of Scientific Discovery*[29] and it has become one of the most deeply entrenched assumptions in the philosophy of science. Hintikka joins the "friends of discovery" in thinking that discovery is too important to leave out from the rational reconstruction of inquiry, or to leave it to historians and psychologists.[30] But again he goes a few steps further in subscribing to a logic and not just to the heuristics of discovery. He also suggests that Peirce and Hanson were right in insisting that there is a pattern of abduction conceptually distinct from deduction and induction.[31] If so, discovery is rational and amenable to logical treatment. However, Peirce misplaced the peculiarity of abduction in the constitutive rules of logic (which serve to define permissible moves). In Hintikka's construal the *differentia* of abduction, and hence the title to an independent status, resides in the strategic rules which advise on the steps which are likely to bring results. For that reason it is also able to serve as a logic of discovery.

It turns out also that Peirce discerned two early steps in the abductive process, the starting (i.e., generation) of a hypothesis and "the entertaining of it," whether probatively or *as a simple interrogation*," or "with any degree of confidence."[32] With hindsight this could be extended to an even more fine-grained analysis to include also the cultivation and elaboration hypotheses into forms that are testable, to actual testing, and to final acceptance or rejection. All these steps could well be considered forms of interrogation (as Peirce did for "inductive" testing; more on cultivation below).

But there is also an interpretive issue. Hintikka suggests that, *pace* Isaac Levi,[33] abduction contains more than the construction of the potential set of answers to a question—so that the early generative stages may have special epistemic weight. Hintikka has a point here—as can be appreciated by adopting the nineteenth-century perspective again. We can understand Peirce, and Hintikka, better if we view them, again, in the light of Whewell's *Philosophy of the Inductive Sciences*. To start with, to Peirce, Whewell's (and Mill's) views on the "method of thought in science" ranked among the highest there was. There are good grounds also for thinking that Peirce followed, up to terminology, Whewell's criticism of the simple method of hypothesis. If inquiry is to be rational there *must* be more to abduction than mere enumeration of possibilities—and luck. Indeed, it appears that Peirce's notion that abduction is a *sui generis* pattern of inference seems to have started with Whewell's notion of *Discoverer's Induction*—which in turn derives from Newton. The evidence, some circumstantial, is that Whewell was thoroughly opposed to the view that discovery is a matter of luck and unreasoned serendipity. He followed Newton and made it clear that novel general hypotheses can be "collected from facts."[34] Indeed, Whewell subscribes to something which in the hypothetico-inductive view is a complete nonstarter, viz., that an inquirer can "infer true theories from observed facts."[35] It is not true in his view, either, that such collection is akin to perceptual taking, seeing. Rather, it is inference in which the mind provides the conception. The outcome therefore is that "the discovery of laws and causes of phenomena is not loose haphazard sort of guessing" but a process of reasoning. In this sense science proceeds "from experience and observation by Induction."[36]

Hintikka has criticized available metatheories for backwards looking timidity and one-sided focus on the definitory rules of logic. What discovery needs is looking forward. The I-model captures this desideratum by refining the idea that asking the right questions at the right time serves the purposes of inquiry better than aimless deductions. One salient scientific skill is that of organizing one's questions in a cost-efficient way: Supposing that Nature's answer to a small question—the outcome of an experiment or an observation—is this or that, how does this answer help to construe a conclusive answer to the initial big question?[37]

But there are some aspects to the process of inquiry not yet fully addressed. First, the I-model engages *two* types of questions, initial big ones and small operational ones, but strategic considerations only apply to the choice of the small ones. Can anything illuminating be said of the choice of the big questions to ask? Second, once the initial question is chosen, how far do the resources of the I-model go towards advising on choices? This is of utmost importance and at the heart of Oersted's rendering of Kant's procedure: "To make experiments is to lay questions before nature; but he alone can do that beneficially *who knows what he should ask*" (emphasis added).[38]

The first question is, admittedly, in part a pragmatic one: what questions are cognitively or practically worth pursuing? There might be important logical considerations involving, say, the importance of questions vis-à-vis a field of inquiry. The question also involves epistemic utilities (truth, information content, simplicity, and other aesthetic virtues) as well as practical utilities (cash values) which could enter as pay-offs in the games of knowledge seeking. Hintikka has dealt with the varieties of information elsewhere,[39] but one would like to see how these values could be incorporated into the I-model, as pay-offs of these games. Such an account would no doubt also open doors towards psychological, sociological, and historical applications of the model.

The second question is intriguing. Natural scientists have the strong intuition that theories are evolving and ramifying research projects in which inarticulate (groups of) questions are processed into more specific ones. New constraints—indeed presuppositions about answers—are also added during the process of inquiry. Furthermore, the I-model is committed to the view that questions and answers in any particular knowledge seeking game are tied to a model M and its underlying language. However, as the historicist philosophers of science have been keen to point out, a question can linger in the air for a long time before an answer can be provided. Intuitively speaking a satisfactory answer may surpass the conceptual and linguistic resources in which the initial question was phrased. Again this is not a difficulty for the small operational question but it does pose an issue of descriptive adequacy for the relationship between the initial big question and the answer. It would appear that these are enormously important questions, ones which also involve straightforwardly strategic principles. But is there a mechanism for question-generation in this sense in the I-model? What would such cultivation or nurturing of a question involve?

One proposal comes from Andrzej Wisniewski's erotetic logic (based on multiple-conclusion logic) in which questions can serve as premises and conclusions: one can, for example, derive a more specific question from a general one on the basis of declarative premises. His erotetic search scenarios also contain strategic principles for moving from question to question without actually pausing to answer every one of them when and where they arise.[40] Sometimes, Wisniewski thinks, it serves the purposes of inquiry better to derive a more specific question which in turn gives rise to a further question—as when an answer to the latter counts as an answer to the former. Wisniewski's simple example goes as follows. If you want to find person X and you know that he has gone to Paris, London, Kiev, or Moscow, you might raise a four-fold whether-question. But if Nature does not volunteer an answer, you may want auxiliary information, based on further knowledge such as: if X traveled to London or Moscow he could not have taken a train. By deriving further questions, e.g., about his time of departure ("When was he last seen?"), possibilities of travel ("Did he take a train in the morning?"), the Inquirer may manage to rule out some alternatives. These search scenarios (not to speak of their explicit logic) would take too much space to produce here, but the upshot is that they yield an answer to the initial question through a series of inferences, some of which are inferences from questions to more specific questions. Unfortunately Wisniewski's logic is not the same as in the I-model. Its attractions nevertheless are considerable: erotetic search scenarios give tangible though conditional advice as to which questions to ask and when. These features give an alternative Sherlock Holmes logic for questioning, and one would like to see how they could be emulated within the I-model.

VIII. The Logic (and Pragmatics) of Explanation

The final application I wish to turn to is the notion of scientific explanation, if only because it has been the favorite one since Aristotle's four types of causes (four types of explanatory answers, as Moravcsik has suggested).[41] Indeed, the tradition to Hempel and Oppenheim[42] and beyond has been that explanations are answers to why-questions. But although Hempel and Oppenheim start with the claim that explaining phenomena amounts to answering (explanation-seeking) why-questions, the interrogative perspective did not find its way to either the *analysandum* or the *analysans*. We saw some possible reasons already: there was no logic of questions of the required precision to cash the intuition, and answerhood appeared to be woolly and even idiosyncratic. As a result, explanations were conceived as deductive (or inductive) inferences or arguments with the explanandum as the conclusion. What followed was an industry around the difficulties which plagued the initial model: partial and complete self-explanations, failures of relevance, difficulties in conceiving lawlikeness. It dawned that it is extremely difficult to design a notion which does not presuppose either causation or something like that to exclude nonexplanatory inferences.

But what if we take the interrogative view literally and build on erotetic logic? Elsewhere I have suggested that erotetic logic is not of much use because there is no logic of why-questions to match the precision of the logic of wh-questions.[43] Here the I-model threatens to sink into a misleading metaphor. Some explanation-seeking why-questions are requests to Nature to pick out an item from a set of alternatives (if one knows, say, all the possible causes but not which one of them is the actual one). However, the tough nuts, those that require a search for new explanatory concepts and theories, are puzzles or predicaments in which the answerhood is ill-specified.[44] Here the Inquirer may not even know what would count as an answer, and hence what kinds of facts to look for.

Hintikka and Halonen[45] start by acknowledging that why-questions are degenerate propositional questions with scant logical structure: the presupposition of the why-question "Why do stars twinkle?" is "Stars twinkle," and its desideratum is the same: the answer should bring about, in the questioner H, the knowledge state that stars twinkle. But that much H already knows, so offering the answer would be conversationally perverse. What more could H want? H would want illumination and understanding, knowledge *why* on top of knowledge *that*, as Aristotle said. How could that be achieved? It should be required that this desideratum be brought about in a way that is independent of the knowledge that stars twinkle, via background knowledge, theoretical premises, and initial conditions. For this reason also, the I-model advises, a conclusive answer to an explanation-seeking question cannot be a reply in the usual sense, i.e., one which, together with the conclusiveness conditions, entails the desideratum. Rather, the answer consists of the covering law and the initial conditions which, through an interrogative derivation starting from an initial premise (background knowledge) T, entail the explanandum P(b). After all, when the explanatory task is set, the explanandum is known—and what need to be derived are the covering law and the initial conditions.

Halonen and Hintikka have recently elaborated on the needed covering law model, and derived a number of theorems which in effect, they say, salvage Hempel's covering law model.[46] Using Craig's interpolation theorem they prove that when a theory T and Nature's answer A entail an explanadum P(b) there always is a covering law, which in a sense summarizes the entire derivation. The result is an ingenious way around the metaphysical difficulty that Nature does not understand why-questions. This approach also shows that the request for more logic rather than less works, for the Craig's theorem was not available when the covering law model was conceived.

Yet one may wonder if the model proves too much. For reasons already specified in section 4, explanatory theories are underdetermined by data. And even if we distinguish between the tasks of theory formation (that of arriving at T) and explanation (finding the covering law and the initial conditions), there can be no unique covering law. For any singular explanation there could be any number of covering laws which could be used to derive P(b). The problems which plagued Hempel's model remain. After all, interrogative derivation produces a deductive argument and only some deductions are explanatory.

The difficulty can also be put in terms of the I-model as follows. In explanation the initial why-question is approached via a strategically arranged series of small questions. But what about the conclusiveness conditions? For the operational questions the answer is obvious: the answer is conclusive and should satisfy a rational ignoramus when and only when she or he is in the position to say, "Now I know this piece of information." But what about the conclusiveness conditions for the big questions? What guarantees that they satisfy the inquirer? Is there any way, using the logical tools of the I-model, to tell what sets potentially explanatory interrogative derivations apart from nonexplanatory ones?

The trouble, as I see it, is that there is no way to guarantee, for singular explananda, that even the basic requirements of explanation, that P(b) is true *because* T and the covering law and the initial conditions are all true. The I-model is superb in illustrating a process of explanation—but only if we already know that the interrogative derivation counts as explanation. This outcome is disconcerting—but I cannot see a way around it. It is also ironic in that it brings us back to square one: the entire interrogative tradition from Aristotle to the German neo-Kantians took it for granted that the question-answer relationship is not a deductive relationship but something more (or something else). This something more (or else) must respect the requirement that the answer is an answer to the question—and a correct one. Hintikka very nicely shows that for Aristotle, logical inference was a species of interrogation, the species in which the answer of a rational respondent can be anticipated with certainty.[47] I would very much like to see this line of thought carried through also in the theory of explanation.

MATTI SINTONEN

UNIVERSITY OF HELSINKI
MAY 2003

NOTES

1. Many of Hintikka's key papers on the I-model have been reprinted in *Inquiry as Inquiry: A Logic of Scientific Discovery*, Jaakko Hintikka, *Selected Papers 5* (Dordrecht: Kluwer Academic Publishers, 1999).

2. R. G. Collingwood, *An Autobiography* (London: Oxford University Press, 1939), pp. 30–31.

3. I am indebted for this account of questions and questioning in nineteenth-century German philosophy to Martin Kusch's highly perceptive 1997 article, "Theories of Questions in German-Speaking Philosophy Around the Turn of the Century," in *Knowledge and Inquiry: Essays on Jaakko Hintikka's Epistemology and Philosophy of Science*, ed. Matti Sintonen, Poznan Studies in the Philosophy of the Sciences and the Humanities, vol. 51, pp. 41–60. As to speculation concerning why questions and questioning became suspect, see Matti Sintonen, "Explanation: In Search of the Rationale," in *Scientific Explanation*, ed. P. Kitcher and W. C. Salmon, vol. 13, Minnesota Studies in the Philosophy of Science (Minneapolis: University of Minnesota Press), pp. 253–82.

4. In "Why Questions, and Why Just Why-Questions?" *Synthese* 120, no. 1 (1999), I have suggested that Quine's methodological procedure in his jungle linguistics, as well as the philosophical thought experiment on radical interpretation, one of the most extensively discussed philosophical programs in the analytic philosophy of this century, only makes sense if both the jungle linguist and the informant have two crucial abilities. They must be able to identify some of each other's utterances as questions and some as answers, that is, as specific types of speech acts. They must also be able to identify the contents of the speech acts, that is what the content of a specific speech act is.

5. Christian Oersted, "On the Spirit and Study of Universal Natural Philosophy," in C. Oersted, *The Soul in Nature, with Supplementary Contributions*, trans. Leonora and Joanna B. Horner (London: H. G. Bohn, 1852), p. 457. (Reprinted by Dawsons of Pall Mall, London, 1966.)

6. See Jaakko Hintikka, *Logic, Language-Games and Information: Kantian Themes in the Philosophy of Logic* (Oxford: Clarendon Press, 1973) and *Knowledge and the Known: Historical Perspectives in Epistemology* (Dordrecht: D. Reidel, 1974).

7. Immanuel Kant, *Critique of Pure Reason* (published in 1787), trans. Norman Kemp Smith (New York: St. Martin's Press, 1968), B xiii.

8. Ibid., B xiii–xiv.

9. Most notably, Nuel D. Belnap and Thomas B. Steel, Jr., *The Logic of Questions and Answers* (New Haven and London: Yale University Press, 1976); but see also David Harrah, "Hintikka's Theory of Questions," in *Jaakko Hintikka*, ed. Radu J. Bogdan (Dordrecht: D. Reidel, 1987), pp. 199–213; Andrzej Wisniewski, *The Posing of Questions: Logical Foundations of Erotetic Inferences* (Dordrecht/ Boston/ London: Kluwer Academic Publishers, 1995); A. Wisniewski,

"Some Foundational Concepts of Erotetic Semantics," in *Knowledge and Inquiry: Essays on Jaakko Hintikka's Epistemology and Philosophy of Science*, ed. M. Sintonen, vol. 51, Poznan Studies in the Philosophy of the Sciences and the Humanities (Amsterdam and Atlanta, Ga.: Rodopi, 1997), pp. 181–211.

10. Lennart Åqvist, *A New Approach to the Logical Theory of Interrogatives*, Filosofista Studie 3 (Uppsala, 1965); Jaakko Hintikka, *Knowledge and Belief: An Introduction to the Logic of the Two Notions* (Ithaca, N.J.: Cornell University Press, 1963).

11. See Hintikka, *Selected Papers 5*, ch. 3.

12. R. B. Braithwaite, *Scientific Explanation: A Study of the Function of Theory, Probability and Law in Science* (Cambridge: Cambridge University Press, 1953), p. 319.

13. See Hintikka, *Selected Papers 5*, pp. 149–53.

14. Ibid., p. 149.

15. Ibid., p. 151.

16. Ibid., p. 153.

17. Ibid.

18. See Thomas Nickles, "Introductory Essay: Scientific Discovery and the Future of Philosophy of Science," in *Scientific Discovery, Logic, and Rationality*, vol. 56, ed. Thomas Nickles, Boston Studies in the Philosophy of Science (Holland/Boston/London: D. Dordrecht, 1980).

19. Larry Laudan, "Why Was the Logic of Scientific Discovery Abandoned?" in *Scientific Discovery, Logic, and Rationality*, ed. Thomas Nickles, pp. 173–83.

20. See Hintikka, *Selected Papers 5*, ch. 8, pp. 161–82.

21. William Whewell, *The Philosophy of the Inductive Sciences, Founded Upon Their History*, 2 vols. (1847; reprint, London: Frank Cass and Co., 1967), vol. 2, p. 65.

22. Ibid., p. 779.

23. Hintikka, *Selected Papers 5*, ch. 12, pp. 241–50.

24. There are some obvious points of dissimilarity between Whewell and Hintikka. As can be seen from the methodological debate between John Stuart Mill and Whewell, the credentials of the method of hypothesis as a general method were coupled with the particular worry over the possibility of inferring to unobserved causes. Whewell thought that there is a way of reasoning to causes on the basis of analogies and similarities in effects, whereas Mill insisted that such inference is illegitimate. Hintikka does not deal with the question of causes at all. As will be seen in section 7, Hintikka nevertheless sides with Whewell in thinking that the method of hypothesis as such is too weak a notion to make reasoning into generalizations and theories a rational procedure.

25. Whewell, *The Philosophy of the Inductive Sciences*, vol. 2, pp. 64–65; see Sintonen, "Taming a Regulative Principle: From Kant to Schlick," in *Aesthetic Factors in Natural Science*, ed. N. Rescher (Maryland: Lanham, 1990), pp. 47–56.

26. William Whewell, *Of Induction, with Especial Reference to Mr. J. Stuart*

Mill's System of Logic (London: John W. Parker, 1849), p. 34.

27. Ibid., pp. 28–29.

28. I am indebted for Laura Snyder's perceptive "The Mill-Whewell Debate: Much Ado about Induction," *Perspectives on Science* 5, no. 2 (1997): 159–98, for some of these quotations from Whewell. My debt to her goes also deeper: reading her paper gave me the idea of reading Hintikka through nineteenth-century lenses. For an early interrogative account of Whewell, see Sintonen, "A New Look at Consilience," *Abstracts of the VIIth International Congress of Logic, Methodology and Philosophy of Science*, vol. 3 (Salzburg, Austria, 1983), pp. 235–38.

29. Karl Popper, *The Logic of Scientific Discovery* (London: Hutchinson, 1959).

30. See the overview in Nickles, *Scientific Discovery, Logic, and Rationality*.

31. Hintikka, *Selected Papers 5*, ch. 4; Norwood Russell Hanson, *Patterns of Discovery* (Cambridge: Cambridge University Press, 1958).

32. Peirce, *Collected Papers*, vol. 6, paragraph 525, in Hintikka, *Selected Papers 5*, p. 103. [Pierce quoted by Hintikka, Hintikka's emphasis.]

33. Isaac Levi, *The Fixation of Belief and its Undoing* (Cambridge: Cambridge University Press, 1991), p. 71.

34. Whewell, *Of Induction*, p. 17.

35. William Whewell, *History of the Inductive Sciences, from the Earliest to the Present Time* (1857; reprint London: John W. Parker, 1873), 1:51.

36. William Whewell, *On the Philosophy of Discovery: Chapters Historical and Critical* (1860; reprint, New York: Burt Franklin, 1971), p. 274.

37. It is of some interest to note that these strategic skills were important in Piaget's characterization of human cognitive development. On his view children move from a concrete-operational phase to abstract thinking (through several stages) in which the crucial skill is that of understanding and planning controlled experiments. In controlled experiments children face precisely the task of asking themselves: what do I have to find out (and know), to be able to answer the question of what factors influence a phenomenon. For an interrogative elaboration of knowledge seeking in educational contexts, see Kirsti Lonka, Kai Hakkarainen, and Matti Sintonen, "The Progressive Inquiry Learning for Children—Experiences, Possibilities, Limitations," *European Early Childhood Education Research Journal* 8, no. 1 (2000): 7–23; and Kai Hakkarainen and Matti Sintonen, "The Interrogative Model of Inquiry and Computer-Supported Collaborative Learning," *Science and Education* 11 (2002): 25–43.

38. Oersted, "On the Spirit and Study of Universal Natural Philosophy," p. 457.

39. Hintikka, "The Varieties of Information and Scientific Explanation," reprinted as chapter 10 of Hintikka, *Selected Papers 5*.

40. Andrzej Wisniewski, "Erotetic Search Scenarios," *Synthese* 134, no. 3 (2002): 389–427.

41. Julius M.E. Moravcsik, "Aristotle on Adequate Explanation," *Synthese* 28 (1974): 3–17.

42. Carl Hempel and Paul Oppenheim, "Studies in the Logic of Explanation,"

in C. Hempel, *Aspects of Scientific Explanation and Other Essays in the Philosophy of Science* (1948; reprint New York: The Free Press, 1965), pp. 245–95.

43. Matti Sintonen, "On the Logic of Why-Questions," *PSA* 1, ed. P. D. Asquith and P. Kitcher (East Lansing, Mich., 1984), pp. 168–76.

44. Sylvain Bromberger, *On What We Know We Don't Know: Explanation, Theory, Linguistics, and How Questions Shape Them* (Chicago: University of Chicago Press, 1992). See also Belnap and Steel, *The Logic of Questions and Answers*.

45. Hintikka, *Selected Papers 5*, ch. 9.

46. Ilpo Halonen and Jaakko Hintikka, "Toward a Theory of the Process of Explanation," forthcoming in *Synthese*.

47. Hintikka, *Selected Papers 5*, ch. 1.

REPLY TO MATTI SINTONEN

Matti Sintonen presents a survey of the interrogative model of inquiry, which I have developed in collaboration with others, including Sintonen himself, and raises a number of questions about it. The survey is lucid, fair, and mostly unexceptionable. It is given a special flavor by the historical perspectives from which Sintonen views the interrogative model. I find his historical comparisons highly interesting, and I will be pleased if I can consider such thinkers as William Whewell as my predecessors. Further research is needed to see how close the anticipations that Sintonen considers come to the actual interrogative model. It is in any case clear that further precedents can be found. For instance, Jevons's comments on the experimental method clearly anticipate some of the features of the logic experiments that are uncovered by the interrogative model.[1] I am especially intrigued by the connection Sintonen sees between the need of a priori mathematical knowledge in experimental inquiry and the old idea that the language of nature is mathematics.

However, even truly accurate historical comparisons can result in emphases that do not do full justice to the topical issues. For instance, I certainly do not want to object when Sintonen speaks about "Hintikka's insistence on the idea that the strategic principles which govern good . . . deductive reasoning are the same principles which govern good empirical inquiry." However, it may be in order to stress that the basis of this insistence is not any kind of deliberative equilibrium between different philosophical arguments, but a bright and shiny logical insight into the structural similarities between deduction and interrogation.

Likewise, Sintonen calls attention both to Whewell's idea that "inquiry proceeds by putting questions to Nature" and to Whewell's view that we need conceptual, for instance, mathematical, assumptions in inquiry. Both ideas are congenial to me, and have counterparts in the interrogative model. However, as Sintonen partly indicates, the need of those conceptual assumptions ensues from the very logic of questioning. I do not find any counterpart to this crucial insight in Whewell.

Again, Sintonen speaks in connection with Whewell of reason's "bold conjectures." I can agree in the sense that the optimal questioning strategies are often quite bold. But strictly speaking there is no place for conjectures in the interrogative model. I have gone as far as to suggest that even Peirce's abductions, which he sometimes speaks of as "queries," should perhaps be construed as question-answer steps.

Some of the issues raised by Sintonen deserve further comments. For instance, the idea of separating levels of inquiry from each other can be viewed in a light different from Sintonen's. The difference between the microlevel and the macrolevel does not have to be viewed as only a difference between nature's direct answers and an inquirer's interpretation. There are structural differences. Typically, on the macrolevel we do not have strong initial premises, but this is compensated by the fact that answers can already be, logically speaking, general truths. In contrast, on the micro-level nature's answers are particular truths, such as meter readings, but this is compensated by there being available initial premises in the form of experimental technology and unproblematic other theories.

The differentiation of levels of inquiry need not be a dichotomy between a microlevel and a macrolevel. We can view even the macrolevel as being subordinate to some kind of superlevel. Then we can happily apply to the choice of principal questions in the overall scientific enterprise the same methodology as to the choice of operative questions.

The notion of induction might also be worth clarifying further. Take first induction in the usual Humean sense. There is good evidence, most directly perhaps from inductive logic, that to choose a particular inductive method rather than another is to make a conjecture concerning the regularity of the actual world as a whole. Given the truth of this conjecture, induction becomes a variant of deductive reasoning. In this sense, a rich flora and fauna of different kinds of inductive inferences becomes possible. However, no separate supply of irreducible inductive inferences is needed in the interrogative model. On the level of the basic rules of the interrogative model, induction does not even play a second fiddle. It plays no irreducible role whatsoever.

Sintonen brings out very well the older sense of induction instantiated by the usage of Aristotle and Newton. A still further aspect of the notion of induction is in evidence in experimental inquiry, where finding the function -in-extension that governs a certain dependence relation is not enough, but must be accompanied by an identification of the mathematical function governing the dependence. This identification can and must be taken to be a part of the inductive task.

Sintonen raises a number of questions concerning the theory of scientific explanations. Recent developments enable me to answer (at least partly) some of them. He speaks as if the intention of my joint work with Ilpo Halonen were to "salvage Hempel's covering law model." Salvaging

Hempel's theory was certainly not one of my motives. In the broadest possible terms, our approach is the opposite of Hempel's in a sense. One can, roughly speaking, distinguish two types of thinking about explanations, viz., explanation as subsumption under a law, and explanation as turning on actual dependence relations. My very distinct preference is for the latter approach. However, this difference is obscured by two things. First, the dependence approach is typically assumed to amount to the exploration of causal connections. This is to my mind far too narrow, for causal relations represent only one type of dependence relation. Second, it so happens that one kind of dependence explanation yields as a by-product certain covering laws connecting the observational basis of explanation with the explanandum. These covering laws are not the gist of any type of explanation, however. Therefore, I cannot hope or want to "salvage" Hempel's view as a general theory of explanation

Admittedly, at first sight an explanation of the kind that one can formulate (according to us) within the interrogative framework does not seem to bring out dependence relations particularly well. In my earlier work with Halonen, we referred to Craig's well-known interpolation theorem as serving this purpose.[2] This is blatantly insufficient. However, we have since proved a much sharpened interpretation theorem.[3] Suppose that $F \vdash G$. Then the interpolation formula I_L brings out what it is about the models of F that made them models of G, in the sense of spelling out what individuals there are in a model of F whose existence forces it, together with certain general laws that hold in the models of F, to be a model of G. (Each quantifier in I_L either expresses the existence of such an individual or expresses the general law in question.) There is likewise also a mirror-image interpolation formula I_R that, in a similar way, spells out what it is about models of G that makes them include the models of F. In this way, the dependence between the models of F and G is spelled out. The interpolation formula in a perfectly reasonable sense shows why G logically follows from F.

Applied to a scientific explanation the interpolation formula between the *ad explanandum* data A (e.g., initial conditions) and the conditional $(T \supset E)$, where T is the background theory and E is the *explanandum*, shows what it is about the *ad explanandum* data A that necessitates the truth of the *explanandum* E, given the background theory T.

This shows that the logic of why-questions is not really lagging as hopelessly behind the logic of wh-questions and propositional-questions as Sintonen seems to think. This logic can be enriched further by evoking the important distinction between depth information and surface information and by studying the increase in surface information that the interpolation formula yields.

J. H.

NOTES

1. See W. Stanley Jevons, *The Principles of Science* (Dover Publications, 1958), especially chs. 19 and 22.

2. William Craig, "Three Uses of the Herbrand-gentzen Theorem in Relating Model Theory and Proof Theory," *Journal of Symbolic Logic* 22 (1957): 269–85.

3. For it, see our 1999 paper "The Structure of Interpolation and Explanation."

26

Theo A. F. Kuipers

INDUCTIVE ASPECTS OF CONFIRMATION, INFORMATION, AND CONTENT

INTRODUCTION

This contribution consists of three parts. In section 1, which is a kind of summary of part I of *From Instrumentalism to Constructive Realism*,[1] I will characterize Hintikka's quantitative theory of confirmation as one of the four main theories. Moreover, I will disentangle the *structural* and genuine *inductive* aspects in these theories of confirmation. In section 2 I will develop Hintikka's ideas about two major types of information called *information* and *content*.[2] In 1997 Hintikka wrote, "In hindsight, I regret that I did not develop further the ideas presented in Hintikka (1968)."[3] I will point out the close relation between *transmitted* information and content on the one hand and *confirmation* on the other. Additionally, I will characterize Hintikka's aims and claims regarding the choice between hypotheses when dealing with *explanation* and *generalization* in relation to (transmitted) information and content. In section 3 I will first disentangle the structural and genuine inductive aspects of prior and posterior probabilities and of transmitted information and content, then I will discuss Hintikka's answers to the question of what to maximize in the service of explanation and generalization, viz., maximizing information by maximizing likelihood and maximizing (transmitted) content, respectively. I will suggest alternative answers, viz., in terms of structural and inductive aspects, respectively. I will conclude with some remarks about the choice of a probability function, a problem that tends to remain hidden when dealing with the choice between hypotheses on the basis of a fixed probability function underlying a theory of confirmation.

1. ORDERING THE LANDSCAPE OF CONFIRMATION

The aim of this section is to give a coherent survey of qualitative and quantitative notions of confirmation, partly by synthesizing the work of others, in a standard or nonstandard way, and partly by showing the distance between this synthesis and the work of others. I will start with qualitative, more specifically, deductive confirmation, of which the standard form is supplemented with two comparative principles. Keeping deductive confirmation as extreme partial explication in mind, I then turn to quantitative, more specifically, probabilistic confirmation, and introduce the crucial distinction between inductive and noninductive, or structural confirmation. This will lead to a survey of the four main theories of confirmation for universal hypotheses, viz., those of Popper, Carnap, Bayes, and Hintikka. Finally, the section deals with the question of a general (quantitative) degree of confirmation and its decomposition into degrees of structural and inductive confirmation, leading to four kinds of inductive confirmation.

1.1. *Types of Confirmation*

1.1.1. *Deductive Confirmation*

Contrary to many critics, and partly in line with Gemes,[4] I believe that the notion of *deductive (d-)confirmation* makes perfectly good sense as partial explication, provided the classificatory definition is supplemented with some comparative principles. More specifically, "(contingent) evidence E d-confirms (consistent) hypothesis H" is defined by the clause: H (logically) entails E, and further obeys the following principles:

> *Comparative principles*:
>
> P1: if H entails E and E entails E* (and not vice versa) then E d-confirms H more than E*.
>
> P2: if H and H* both entail E then E d-confirms H and H* equally.

To be sure, this definition-with-comparative-supplement only makes sense as a *partial* explication of the intuitive notion of confirmation; it leaves room for nondeductive, in particular, probabilistic extensions, as we will see below. However, let us first look more closely at the comparative principles. They are very reasonable in light of the fact that the deductive definition can be conceived as a (deductive) *success* definition of confirmation: if H entails E, E clearly is a success of H, if not a predictive success, then at least a kind of explanatory success. From this perspective, P1 says that a stronger (deductive) success confirms a hypothesis more than a weaker one, and P2 says that two hypotheses should be equally praised for the same success. In particular P2 runs against standard conceptions. However, in chapter 2 of *From Instrumentalism to Constructive Realism*, I deal extensively with the possible objections and show, moreover, that the present analysis can handle the confirmation paradoxes discovered by Hempel and Goodman.

Deductive confirmation can also be supplemented with "conditional deductive confirmation": E d-confirms H, assuming a condition C, that is, H & C entails E. This type of conditionalization, also applicable for non-deductive confirmation, will not be treated further in this survey.

1.1.2. *Probabilistic Confirmation*

Probabilistic confirmation presupposes, by definition, a probability function, indicated by p, that is, a real-valued function obeying the standard axioms of probability, which may nevertheless be of one kind or another (see below). But first I will briefly deal with the general question of a probabilistic criterion of confirmation. The *standard* (or *forward*) *criterion* for probabilistic confirmation is that the *posterior* probability $p(H \mid E)$ exceeds the *prior* probability $p(H)$ (relative to the background knowledge), that is, $p(H \mid E) > p(H)$. However, this criterion is rather inadequate for 'p-zero' hypotheses. For example, if $p(H) = 0$ and E d-confirms H, this confirmation cannot be seen as an extreme case of probabilistic confirmation, since $p(H \mid E) = p(H) = 0$. However, for p-nonzero hypotheses and assuming $0 < p(E) < 1$, the standard criterion is equivalent to the *backward* or *success* criterion, according to which the so-called *likelihood* $p(E \mid H)$ exceeds the initial probability $p(E)$ of E: $p(E \mid H) > p(E)$. Now it is easy to verify that any probability function respects d-confirmation according to this criterion, since $p(E \mid H) = 1$ when H entails E, and hence exceeds $p(E)$, even if $p(H) = 0$. More generally, the success criterion can apply in all p-zero cases in which $p(E \mid H)$ can nevertheless be meaningfully interpreted.

To be sure, as Maher stresses, the success criterion does not work properly for 'p-zero evidence',[5] e.g., in the case of verification of a real-valued interval hypothesis by a specific value within that interval. However, although this is less problematic,[6] it seems reasonable to accept the standard criterion for p-zero evidence. Note that this leads to the confirmation verdict in the indicated case of verification. From now on "confirmation" will mean forward or backward confirmation when $p(H) \neq 0 \neq p(E)$, backward confirmation when $p(H) = 0$ and $p(E) \neq 0$ and forward confirmation when $p(E) = 0$ and $p(H) \neq 0$; and it is left undefined when $p(H) = 0 = p(E)$.

1.1.2.1. *Structural Confirmation*

I now turn to a discussion of the kinds of probability functions and corresponding kinds of probabilistic confirmation. I start with non-inductive or *structural confirmation*, which has an "objective" and a "logical" version.

Consider first an objective example dealing with a fair die. Let E indicate the even (elementary) outcomes 2, 4, 6, and H the "high" outcomes 4, 5, 6. Then (the evidence of) an even outcome confirms the hypothesis of a high outcome according to both criteria, since $p(E \mid H) = p(H \mid E) = 2/3 > 1/2 = p(H) = p(E)$.

I define structural confirmation as confirmation based on a probability function assigning equal and constant probabilities to the elementary outcomes. Such a probability function may either represent an *objective* probability process, such as a fair die, or it may concern the so-called *logical* probability or logical measure function, indicated by m (corresponding to Carnap's c^+-function).[7] Kemeny's m-function assigns probabilities on the basis of ([the limit, if it exists, of] the ratio of) the number of structures making a statement true, that is, the number of models of the statement.[8] These logical probabilities may or may not correspond to the objective probabilities of an underlying process, as is the case of a fair die. Hence, for structural confirmation, we may restrict the attention to generalizations of Kemeny's m-function.

Structural confirmation is a straightforward generalization of d-confirmation. For suppose that H entails E. Then

$$m(E \mid H) = (\text{lim}) \; |\text{Mod}(E \;\&\; H)| \, / \, |\text{Mod}(H)| =$$
$$1 > (\text{lim}) \; |\text{Mod}(E)| \, / \, |\text{Mod}(\text{Tautology})| = m(E),$$

where e.g., '$|\text{Mod}(H)|$' indicates the number of models of H. Hence, structural confirmation might also be called "extended" or "generalized d-confirmation." Moreover, structural confirmation is a probabilistic explication of Salmon's idea of confirmation by "partial entailment," according to which an even outcome of a throw with a fair die typically is partially implied by a high outcome.[9] For this reason we might call nondeductive cases of structural confirmation also cases of "partial d-confirmation."

It is important to note that the m-function leads in many cases to 'm-zero' hypotheses.[10] For instance, every universal generalization "for all x Fx" gets zero m-value for an infinite universe. As we may conclude from the general exposition, such hypotheses may well be structurally confirmed by some evidence, by definition, according to the success criterion, but not according to the standard criterion. For example, a black raven structurally confirms "all ravens are black" according to the success criterion, even if the universe is supposed to be infinite. Typical for the m-function is that it lacks the property, which I will present as characteristic for inductive probability functions.

1.1.2.2. *Inductive Confirmation*

Inductive confirmation is (*pace* Popper and Miller's 1983 paper[11]) explicated in terms of confirmation based on an inductive probability function, i.e., a probability function p having the general feature of "positive relevance," "inductive confirmation" or, as I like to call it, *instantial confirmation*: $p(Fb \mid E \& Fa) > p(Fb \mid E)$, where 'a' and 'b' represent distinct individuals, 'F' an arbitrary monadic property and 'E' any kind of contingent or tautological evidence. Note that this definition is easy to generalize to *n*-tuples and *n*-ary properties, but I will restrict the attention to monadic ones. Since the m-function satisfies the condition $m(Fb \mid E \& Fa) = m(Fb \mid E)$, we get for any inductive probability function p:

$$p(Fa \& Fb \mid E) = p(Fa \mid E) \cdot p(Fb \mid E \& Fa) > m(Fa \& Fb \mid E)$$

as long as we may also assume that

$$p(Fa \mid E) = p(Fb \mid E) = m(Fa \mid E) = m(Fb \mid E).$$

Inductive (probability) functions can be obtained in two ways, which may also be combined. They can be based on:

- "inductive priors." i.e., positive prior values $p(H)$ for m-zero hypotheses

and/or on

- "inductive likelihoods," i.e., likelihood functions $p(E \mid H)$ having the property of instantial confirmation

Note first that forward confirmation of m-zero hypotheses requires inductive priors, whereas backward confirmation of such hypotheses is always possible, assuming that $p(E \mid H)$ can be interpreted. Second, although we now have a definition of inductive probability functions, we do not yet have a general definition of inductive confirmation. In the next subsection I will give such a general definition in terms of degrees of confirmation, but the basic idea is, of course, that the confirmation is (at least partially) due to instantial confirmation.

With reference to the two origins of (the defining property of) inductive probability functions I now can characterize the four main theories of confirmation in philosophy of science:

	inductive priors	inductive likelihoods
Popper	no	no
Carnap	no	yes
Bayes	yes	no
Hintikka	yes	yes

TABLE 1: The Four Main Theories of Confirmation in Philosophy of Science.

Popper rejected both kinds of inductive confirmation, roughly, for three reasons: two problematic ones and a defensible one. The first problematic reason to note (although not convincingly presented) is that p(H) could not be positive.[12] The best positive argument against zero prior probabilities is perhaps that zero priors amount to dogmatic scepticism with respect to the relevant hypotheses.[13] The second problematic argument against inductive confirmation is that any probability function has the property 'p(E → H | E) < p(E → H)'.[14] Although the claimed property is undisputed, the argument that a proper inductive probability function should have the reverse property, since 'E → H' is the "inductive conjunct" in the equivalence 'H ↔ (E ∨ H) & (E → H)', is not convincing. The indicated reverse property may well be conceived as an unlucky first attempt to explicate the core of (probabilistic) inductive intuitions, which should be replaced by the property of instantial confirmation. The defensible reason is that the latter property merely reflects a subjective attitude and, usually, not an objective feature of the underlying probability process, if there is such a process at all.

Carnap, following Laplace, favored inductive likelihoods, although he did not reject inductive priors. The so-called Bayesian approach in philosophy of science reflects inductive priors.[15] Finally, Hintikka introduced "double inductive" probability functions, by combining the Carnapian and the Bayesian approach. This leads to "double inductive confirmation," which might well be called "Hintikka-confirmation."[16]

Hintikka (in his "Comment on Theo Kuipers") likes to stress that his approach is not only deviating technically from Carnap and Bayes, but also philosophically, and I agree with the main points. First, in contrast to Carnap, Hintikka does not believe that a convincing logical argument can be given for the choice of the relevant parameters, i.e., nonlogical criteria dealing with subjective attitudes, such as caution, or expectations (e.g., about the order in the universe) are unavoidable. Second, in contrast to Carnap and Bayes, Hintikka believes that there can be good reasons to change the parameters, i.e., to make non-Bayesian moves, as it is sometimes called in the literature. Finally, Hintikka's further ambitions are to take different kinds of information into account when dealing with confirmation (see section 2) and to express "assumptions concerning the orderliness of order in one's universe of discourse . . . by explicit premises rather than [by] choices of the value of a parameter."[17]

1.2. Degrees of Confirmation

I now turn to the problem of defining degrees of confirmation, in particular a *degree of inductive confirmation*, even such that it entails a general definition of *inductive confirmation*. The present approach does not follow the letter but is in the spirit of Mura.[18] The idea is to specify a measure for the degree of inductive influence by comparing the relevant *p*-expressions with the corresponding (structural) *m*-expressions in an appropriate way. I will proceed in three stages.

1.2.1. *Stage 1: Degrees of General and Structural Confirmation*

In the first stage I propose, instead of the standard difference measure $p(H \mid E) - p(H)$, the (nonstandard version of the) ratio measure $p(E \mid H) / p(E)$ as the degree (or rate) of (backward) confirmation in general (that is, according to some p), indicated by $Cp(H, E)$. It amounts to the degree of structural confirmation for $p = m$. This ratio has the following properties: for p-non-zero hypotheses, it is equal to the standard ratio measure $p(H \mid E) / p(H)$, and hence is symmetric ($Cp(H, E) = Cp(E, H)$), but it leaves room for confirmation (amounting to: $Cp(H, E) > 1$) of p-zero hypotheses. (For p-zero evidence we might turn to the standard ratio measure.) Moreover, it satisfies the comparative principles of deductive (d-)confirmation P1 and P2. Note first that $Cp(H, E)$ is equal to $1 / p(E)$ when H entails E, for $p(E \mid H) = 1$ in that case. This immediately implies P2: if H and H* both entail E then $Cp(H, E) = Cp(H^*, E)$. Moreover, if H entails E and E*, and E entails E* (and not vice versa) then $Cp(H, E) > Cp(H, E^*)$, as soon as we may even assume that $p(E) < p(E^*)$. This condition amounts to a slightly weakened version of P1. In agreement with P2 we obtain, for example, that an even outcome with a fair die equally d-confirms the hypotheses {6}, {4,6}, and {2,4,6}, with degree of (structural and deductive) confirmation 2. This result expresses the fact that the outcome probabilities are multiplied by 2, raising them from 1/6 to 1/3, from 1/3 to 2/3, and from 1/2 to 1, respectively. Note also that in the paradigm example of structural nondeductive confirmation, that is, an even outcome confirms a high outcome, the corresponding degree is $(2/3) / (1/2) = 4/3$. But, in agreement with P1, the stronger outcome {4,6} confirms it more, viz., by degree $(2/3) / (1/3) = 2$. It even verifies the hypothesis.

As suggested, there are a number of other degrees of confirmation. Fitelson evaluates four of them, among which the logarithmic forward version of our backward ratio measure, in the light of seven arguments or conditions of adequacy as they occur in the literature.[19] The ratio measure fails in five cases. Three of them are directly related to the "pure" character of Cp, that is, its satisfaction of P2.[20] In chapter 2 of *From Instrumentalism to Constructive Realism*, I defend P2 extensively. However, I also argue in chapter 3 of that book, that as soon as one uses the probability calculus, it does not matter very much which "confirmation language" one chooses, for that calculus provides the crucial means for updating the plausibility of a hypothesis in the light of evidence. Hence, the only important point which then remains is always to make clear which confirmation language one has chosen.

1.2.2. *Stage 2: The Degree of Inductive Confirmation*

In the second stage I will define, as announced, the degree of inductive influence in this degree of confirmation, or simply the degree of inductive (backward) confirmation (according to p), as the ratio:

$$R_p(H, E) = \frac{C_p(H, E)}{C_m(H, E)} = \frac{p(E \mid H) / p(E)}{m(E \mid H) / m(E)}$$

A nice direct consequence of this definition is that the total degree of confirmation equals the product of the degree of structural confirmation and the degree of inductive confirmation.

In the following table I summarize the kinds of degrees of confirmation that I have distinguished. For later purposes I also add the log ratio version of the ratio measure and the difference measure and, for enabling easy comparison I mainly list the forward versions of the (log) ratio measures.

	A	B	C	D
1	Notion: n(.)	ratio doc	log ratio doc	difference doc
2	degree of confirmation C-p(H; E)	$C_p(H; E) =$ df $p(E \mid H) / p(E) =$ $p(H \mid E) / p(H) =$ $p(H \& E) / [p(H)p(E)]$	$C_{lp}(H; E) =$ df $\log p(E \mid H) / p(E) =$ $\log p(H \mid E) / p(H) =$ $\log p(H \mid E) - \log p(H)$	$C_{dp}(H; E) =$ df $p(H \mid E) - p(H)$
3	Relation between prior and posterior probability and degree of confirmation	$p(H \mid E) =$ $p(H) \times C_p(H; E)$	$\log p(H \mid E) =$ $\log p(H) + C_{lp}(H; E)$	$p(H \mid E) =$ $p(H) + C_{dp}(H; E)$
4	degree of *structural* confirmation C-m(H; E)	$C_m(H; E) =$ df $m(H \mid E) / m(H)$	$C_{lm}(H; E) =$ df $\log m(H \mid E) / m(H)$	$C_{dm}(H; E) =$ df $m(H \mid E) - m(H)$
5	degree of *inductive* confirmation R-p(H,E)	$R_p(H, E) =$ df $[p(H \mid E) / p(H)] /$ $[m(H \mid E) / m(H)]$	$R_{lp}(H, E) =$ df $\log [p(H \mid E) / p(H)] -$ $\log [m(H \mid E) / m(H)]$	$R_{dp}(H, E) =$ df $[p(H \mid E) - p(H)] -$ $[m(H \mid E) - m(H)]$

TABLE 2: Survey of Degrees of Confirmation (doc; 'p' fixed).

1.2.3. *Stage 3: Four Kinds of Inductive Confirmation*

In the third and final stage I generally define *inductive confirmation*, that is, E inductively confirms H, of course, by the condition: $Rp(H, E) > 1$. This definition leads to four interesting possibilities for confirmation according to p.

Assume that $Cp(H, E) > 1$, that is, assume E confirms H according to p. The *first* possibility is *purely structural* confirmation, that is, $Rp(H, E) = 1$, in which case the confirmation has *no inductive features*. This trivially holds in general for structural confirmation, but it may occasionally apply to cases of confirmation according to some p different from m. The *second* possibility is that of *purely inductive* confirmation, that is, $Cm(H, E) = 1$, and hence $Rp(H, E) = Cp(H, E)$. This condition typically applies in the case of (purely) instantial confirmation, since, for example, $m(Fa \mid Fb \ \& \ E) \ / \ m(Fa \mid E) = 1$.

The *third* possibility is that of a combination of structural and inductive confirmation: $Cm(H, E)$ and $Cp(H, E)$ both exceed 1, but the second more than the first. This type of *combined* confirmation typically occurs when a Carnapian inductive probability function is assigned, for example, in the case of a die-like object of which it may not be assumed that it is fair. Starting from equal prior probabilities for the six sides, such a function gradually approaches the observed relative frequencies. If among the even outcomes a high outcome has been observed more often than expected on the basis of equal probability then (only) knowing in addition that the next throw has resulted in an even outcome confirms the hypothesis that it is a high outcome in two ways: structurally (as I showed already in 1.2.1) and inductively. Consider the following example:

Let n be the total number of throws so far, let n_i indicate the number of throws that have resulted in outcome i (1, ..., 6). Then the Carnapian probability that the next throw results in i is $(n_i + \lambda/6) / (n + \lambda)$, for some fixed finite positive value of the parameter λ. Hence, the probability that the next throw results in an even outcome is $(n_2 + n_4 + n_6 + \lambda/2) / (n + \lambda)$, and the probability that it is 'even-and-high' is $(n_4 + n_6 + \lambda/3) / (n + \lambda)$. The ratio of the latter to the former is the posterior probability of a high next outcome given that it is even and given the previous outcomes. It is now easy to check that in order to get a degree of confirmation larger than the structural degree, which is 4/3 as I have noted before, this posterior probability should be larger than the corresponding logical probability, which is 2/3. This is the case as soon as $2n_2 < n_4 + n_6$, that is, when the average occurrence of '4' and '6' exceeds that of '2'.

It is easy to check that the same example when treated by a Hintikka-system (for references, see section 1.1.2.2.) shows essentially the same combined type of structural and inductive confirmation.

Let me finally turn to the *fourth* and perhaps most surprising possibility: confirmation combined with the "opposite" of inductive confirmation, that is, $R_p(H, E) < 1$, to be called *counterinductive* confirmation. Typical examples arise in the case of deductive confirmation. In this case $R_p(H, E)$ reduces to $m(E) / p(E)$, which may well be smaller than 1. A specific example is the following: let E be Fa & Fb and let p be inductive then E d-confirms "for all x Fx" in a counterinductive way. On second thought, the possibility of, in particular, deductive counterinductive confirmation should not be surprising. Inductive probability functions borrow, as it were, the possibility of inductive confirmation by reducing the available "amount" of possible deductive confirmation. To be precise, deductive confirmation by some E is counterinductive as soon as E gets "inductive load" (see section 3.1) from p, that is, $m(E) < p(E)$.

Table 3 summarizes the distinguished kinds of confirmation: general and deductive.

	A: kind	B: condition	C: degree of confirmation =
	General confirmation	$C_p(H, E) > 1$	
1	*Purely inductive* confirmation: e.g., instantial confirmation	$C_p(H, E) > C_m(H, E) = 1$	degree of inductive confirmation
2	*Combined* (inductive and structural) confirmation:	$C_p(H, E) > C_m(H, E) > 1$	degree of structural confirmation × degree of inductive confirmation
3	*Purely structural* confirmation:	$C_p(H, E) = C_m(H, E) > 1$	degree of structural confirmation
4	*Counterinductive* confirmation:	$C_m(H, E) > C_p(H, E) > 1$	degree of structural confirmation × degree of "inductive" confirmation
	Deductive confirmation	H $\models$ E, and hence $p(E\|H) = m(E\|H) = 1$	$C_p(H, E) = 1 / p(E) = [1/m(E)] (m(E)/p(E)) = C_m(H, E) R_p(H, E)$
5	*Purely inductive* confirmation	impossible, if $m(E) < 1$	
6	*Combined* (inductive and structural) confirmation	$m(E) > p(E)$	
7	*Purely structural* confirmation	$m(E) = p(E)$	
8	*Counterinductive* confirmation	$m(E) < p(E)$	

TABLE 3: Survey of Kinds of Inductive Confirmation in Terms of Ratio Degrees of Confirmation ('p' Fixed, 'm': Logical Measure Function).

2. KINDS OF INFORMATION AND THEIR RELEVANCE FOR EXPLANATION AND GENERALIZATION

Drawing upon the work of Carnap, Bar-Hillel, Popper, Törnebohm, and Adams, Hintikka has introduced in a systematic way two kinds of information, indicated as surprise value and substantive information, and briefly called information and content.[21] When representing them I will point out the close relation between *transmitted* information and *transmitted* content on the one hand and certain *degrees of confirmation* on the other. Moreover, I will characterize Hintikka's aims and claims regarding the choice between hypotheses when dealing with *explanation* and *generalization* in relation to (transmitted) information and content.

2.1. *Kinds of Information*

2.1.1. *Surprise Value Information*

The first kind of information is related to the surprise value or unexpectedness of a statement. As now is usual in computer science, Hintikka focuses on the logarithmic versions of the relevant notions for their nice additive properties. However, as in the case of confirmation, I prefer and start each time with the nonlogarithmic versions for their conceptual simplicity. I begin with the prior (or absolute), the posterior (or conditional) and the transmitted notions of information. The prior information contained in a statement, e.g., a hypothesis H, is supposed to be inversely related to its probability in the following way:

$$i(H) = \text{df } 1/ p(H)$$

$$\inf (H) = \text{df} \log i(H) = \log 1/ p(H) = - \log p(H)$$

The posterior version aims to capture how much information this hypothesis, "adds to" or "exceeds" another, e.g., an evidential statement E, assuming E:

$$i(H \mid E) = \text{df } 1/ p(H \mid E) = p(E) / p(H \& E) = i(H \& E) / i(E)$$

$$\inf (H \mid E)^{22} = \text{df} - \log p(H \mid E) = \log i(H \mid E) = \inf(H \& E) - \inf(E)$$

Hintikka calls the inf(H | E) the incremental or conditional information. Now I turn to the idea of information transmission: how much information does E "convey concerning the subject matter" of H, or transmit to H, assuming E?

$$\text{trans-}i(E; H) = \text{df } i(H \mid E) / i(H) = p(H \mid E) / p(H)$$

$$\text{trans-}\inf(E; H)^{23} = \text{df} \inf(H) - \inf(H \mid E) = \log \text{trans-}i(H; E) =$$
$$\log p(H \mid E) - \log p(H)$$

According to Hintikka, we may say that trans-inf(E; H) (and hence trans-i(E; H)) "measures the reduction of our uncertainty concerning H which takes place when we come to know, not H, but E."[24]

It is directly clear that trans-i(E; H) coincides with the forward ratio measure of confirmation C_p (H; E), and hence that it is symmetric, that is, it equals trans-i(H; E) when p(E) and p(H) are nonzero. However, if p(H) is 0 and p(E) nonzero, trans-i(E; H) is undefined (hence, it may be equated with 1), but trans-i(H; E) may well be defined, viz., when p(E | H) is defined. For instance, in case H entails E trans-i(H; E) = 1/p(E), that is, H reduces the uncertainty regarding E from 1/p(E) to 1 (certainty). Trans-*inf*(E; H) coincides of course with the logarithmic version of the ratio measure, viz., C_{lp} (H; E), and similar remarks apply.

2.1.2. *Substantive Information*

The second kind of information is related to the content or substantive information contained in a statement. Now there are no relevant logarithmic versions. Again I define the prior, the posterior (or conditional) and the transmitted notions of substantive information.

The prior content of a statement, for example, a hypothesis H, is made inversely related to its probability by equating it with the probability of its negation:

$$\text{cont(H)} = _{df} 1 - p(H) = p(\neg H)$$

It is called the substantive information or the content of H.

For the posterior version, called the "conditional content" by Hintikka, aiming to capture how much information this hypothesis, "adds to" or "exceeds" evidential statement E, assuming E, we get:

$$\text{cont(H | E)}^{25} = 1 - p(H | E) = 1 - p(H \ \& \ E) / p(E)$$

Now I turn again to the idea of information transmission: how much information does E convey concerning H, or transmit to H, assuming E:

$$\text{trans-cont(E; H)}^{26} = _{df} \text{cont(H)} - \text{cont(H | E)} = p(H | E) - p(H)$$

According to Hintikka, we may say that trans-cont(E;H) indicates the *"change in the information-carrying status of H which takes place when one comes to know E."*[27]

It is trivial to see that trans-cont(E; H) coincides with the (forward) difference measure of confirmation. In contrast to the ratio measure (as far as straightforwardly defined), the difference measure is not symmetric, i.e., p(H | E) − p(H) is in general not equal to p(E | H) − p(E). Moreover, if p(H) is 0 and p(E) nonzero, trans-cont(E; H) is 0, that is, the "information-carrying status" of H does not change by coming to know E. This sounds plausible, and so for the reverse: trans-cont(E; H) may well be substantial, viz., when p(E | H) is defined. For instance, in case H entails E trans-cont(H; E) = 1 − p(E) = cont(E), that is, the "information-carrying status" of E changes by coming to know H, by cont(E).

Table 4 summarizes the notions introduced so far. I have included Hintikka's main characterizing terms and also the information and content of a conjunction of two independent hypotheses.

	A	B	C	D
1	Notion: n(.)	Information: i(.)	log-information: inf(.)	content: cont(.)
2	Prior value: n(H)	i(H) = df 1/p(H)	inf(H) = df − log p(H)	cont(H) = df 1 − p(H)
	Hintikka		the *surprise value* or *unexpectedness* of (the truth of) H	the *substantive information* or *content* of H
3	n(H & H') for independent H and H', hence, p(H & H') = p(H) × p(H')	i(H) × i(H')	inf(H) + inf(H')	cont(H & H') = cont(H) + cont(H') − cont(H) × cont(H')
4	Posterior value of H given E: n(H | E)	i(H | E) = df 1/p(H | E) = i(H & E) / i(E)	inf(H | E) = df − log p(H | E) = inf(H & E) − inf(E)	cont (H | E) = df 1 − p(H/E) = 1− p(H & E) / p(E)
	Hintikka		*incremental* information (*conditional* information)	*conditional* content
5	Transmitted value (from E to H): trans-n(E; H) corresponds to doc	trans-i(E; H) = df i(H) / i(H | E) = p(H | E) / p(H) = Cp(H; E)	trans-inf(E; H) = df inf(H) − inf(H | E) = log p(H | E) − log p(H) = Clp(H; E)	trans-cont(E; H) = df cont(H) − cont(H | E) = p(H | E) − p(H) = Cdp(H; E)
	Hintikka		the information E conveys concerning the subject matter of H	the change in the content of H due to E
	Transmitted value = df prior value / (resp. −) posterior value = (log) posterior probability / (resp. −) (log) prior probability = df degree of confirmation			

TABLE 4: Survey of Definitions of "Information" and "Content" ('p' Fixed).

In the last row I have also included a compact indication of the plausible relations between the various notions. For the nonlogarithmic version of information we get more specifically:

transmitted value = df prior value / posterior value =
posterior probability / prior probability = df
(forward) ratio degree of confirmation

For the logarithmic version of information we get:

> transmitted value = df prior value – posterior value =
> log posterior probability – log prior probability = df
> log ratio degree of confirmation

Finally for the notion of content we get:

> transmitted value = df prior value – posterior value =
> posterior probability – prior probability = df
> difference degree of confirmation

Let me illustrate the different notions by the fair die (recall, E/H: even/high outcome), where p = m. For the i-notions we get:

> $i(E) = i(H) = 2$, $i(H \mid E) = i(E \mid H) = 3/2$, $\text{Cm}(H; E) =$
> trans-$i(E; H) = (2/3) / (1/2 = 4/3$.

For the inf-notions we simply get the logarithms of these values. For the cont-notions we get: $\text{cont}(E) = \text{cont}(H) = 1/2$, $\text{cont}(H \mid E) = \text{cont}(E \mid H) = 1/3$, $\text{Cdp}(H; E) = \text{trans-cont}(E;H) = 2/3 - 1/2 = 1/6$.

2.1.3. *Implication Related Notions*

Strangely enough, Hintikka introduces as a variant of "conditional content" $\text{cont}(H \mid E)$ an alternative definition, called "incremental content," where E is not assumed as "posterior" condition, but only figuring as condition in the implication E → H, viz.,

> $\text{cont}_{\dashv}(H \mid E)^{28} = \text{cont}(E \to H) = 1 - p(E \to H)$

Hintikka introduces a separate notation for "cont(E → H)," I am puzzled about why he does not even mention its formal analogue "inf(E → H)," let alone "i(E → H)":

> $i_{\dashv}(H \mid E) = df\ i(E \to H) = 1 / p(E \to H)$

and its (logarithmic) inf-version

> $\inf_{\dashv}(H \mid E) = df\ \inf(E \to H) = -\log p(E \to H)$

It is unclear why Hintikka compared, in fact, the pair "inf(H | E)" and "cont(E → H)," even two times (viz., (4) and (5), (6) and (7), respectively). The plausible comparisons seem to be both the pair "inf(E → H)" and "cont(E → H)" and the pair "inf(H | E)" and "cont(H | E)." He only compares the last pair (by (9) and (10)). The only reason for the first mentioned comparison seems to be the "additive" character of both its members (as expressed by (4) and (5)).

For later purposes I introduce Hintikka's definition of the corresponding transmission concept of incremental content.

$$\text{trans-cont}_\to(E; H)^{29} = \text{df } \text{cont}(H) - \text{cont}_\to H \mid E) =$$
$$\text{cont}_\to(H) - \text{cont}(E \to H) = 1 - p(H \vee E)$$

Similarly we can define:

$$\text{trans-inf}_\to(E; H) = \text{df } \text{inf}(H) - \text{inf}(E \to H) = \log p(E \to H) / p(H)$$

and hence

$$\text{trans-i}_\to(E; H) = \text{df } i(H) / i(E \to H) = p(E \to H) / p(H)$$

Table 5 presents a survey of the implication-related notions.

	A	B	C	D
1	Notion: n(.)	information: i(.)	log-information: inf(.)	content: cont(.)
2	Prior value: n(H)	$i(H) = \text{df } 1/p(H)$	$\text{inf}(H) = \text{df} - \log p(H)$	$\text{cont}(H) = \text{df } 1 - p(H)$
	Hintikka		the *surprise value* or *unexpectedness* of (the truth of) H	the *substantive information* or *content* of H
3	Value of implication: $(E \to H)$	$i_\to(H; E) = \text{df}$ $i(E \to H) =$ $1/p(E \to H)$	$\text{inf}_\to(H; E) = \text{df}$ $\text{inf}(E \to H) =$ $- \log p(E \to H)$	$\text{cont}_\to(H; E) = \text{df}$ $\text{cont}(E \to H) =$ $1 - p(E \to H) =$ $\text{cont}(H \& E) - \text{cont}(E)$
	Hintikka			*incremental* content
4	"Transmitted value by $\to$" (from E to H *by* $E \to H$): trans-$n_\to$(E; H)	$\text{trans-i}_\to(E; H) = \text{df}$ $i(H) / i(E \to H)$	$\text{trans-inf}_\to(E; H) = \text{df}$ $\text{inf}(H) - \text{inf}(E \to H) =$ $\log p(E \to H) / p(H)$	$\text{trans-cont}_\to(E; H) = \text{df}$ $\text{cont}(H) - \text{cont}_\to(H \mid E) =$ $\text{cont}(H) - \text{cont}(E \to H) =$ $1 - p(H \vee E)$
	Hintikka			the information E conveys concerning the subject matter of H

TABLE 5: Definitions of "Information" and "Content" Related to the Implication ('p' Fixed).

2.2. *Explanation and Generalization*

From section 7 on, it becomes clear where Hintikka is basically aiming with his distinction between information and content. According to him there is a strong relation with different targets of scientific research. Let me quote him on this matter:

One of the most important uses that our distinctions have is to show that there are several different ways of looking at the relation of observational data to those hypotheses which are based on them and which perhaps are designed to explain them. In different situations the concept of information can be brought to bear on this relation in entirely different ways. . . . In general, the scientific search for truth is much less of a single-goal enterprise than philosophers usually realize, and suitable distinctions between different senses of information perhaps serve to bring out some of the relevant differences between different goals.

Let us consider some differences between different cases. One of the most important distinctions here is between, on one hand, a case in which we are predominantly interested in a particular body of observations E which we want to explain by means of a suitable hypothesis H, and on the other hand a case in which we have no particular interest in our evidence E but rather want to use it as a stepping-stone to some general theory H which is designed to apply to other matters, too, besides E. We might label these two situations as cases of local and global theorizing, respectively. Often the difference in question can also be characterized as a difference between explanation and generalization, respectively. Perhaps we can even partly characterize the difference between the activities of (local) explanation and (global) theorizing by spelling out (as we shall proceed to do) the differences between the two types of cases.

It is important to realize, however, that in this respect [explanation versus generalizing, TK] the interests of a historian are apt to differ from those of a scientist.[30]

Hintikka argues at length in section 8 that in the cases where we want to explain some evidence E by a hypothesis, we have good reasons, in his own words (replacing symbols): "to choose the explanatory hypothesis H such that it is maximally informative concerning the subject matter with which E deals. Since we know the truth of E already, we are not interested in the substantive information that H carries concerning the truth of E. What we want to do is to find H such that the truth of E is not unexpected, given H."[31] This brings him immediately to a plea for maximizing the transmitted information trans-inf(E; H), which was seen to be equal to log p(E | H) / p(E). For fixed E, this amounts, of course, to support of the so-called *maximum likelihood principle* in this type of case: choose H such that p(E | H) is maximal.

For global theorizing or generalization Hintikka argues extensively in section 9 that we should concentrate on maximizing relevant content notions. As a matter of fact, he has four arguments in favor of the claim that we should choose that hypothesis that maximizes the transmitted content, given E, that is, p(H | E) − p(H). Strangely enough, he only hints upon the only direct argument for this by speaking of "the fourth time" that this expression is to be maximized, whereas he only specifies three, indirect, arguments. However, it is clear that maximizing the transmitted content is an argument in itself, not in the least, because it amounts to maximizing the difference degree of confirmation. But his three indirect arguments are more surprising, or at least two of them are.

These three arguments are all dealing with notions of "expected value gains."[32] First he notes that the "(posterior) expected content gain," plausibly defined by

$$p(H \mid E) \times \text{cont}(H) - p(\neg H \mid E) \times \text{cont}(\neg H)$$

is maximal when $p(H \mid E) - p(E)$ is maximal. Then he argues that the "expected transmitted content gain," similarly defined by

$$p(H \mid E) \times \text{trans-cont}(E; H) - p(\neg H \mid E) \times \text{trans-cont}(E; \neg H)$$

is also maximized by the same condition. The latter does not need to surprise us very much because the "expected posterior value gain," viz., $p(H \mid E) \times \text{cont}(H \mid E) - p(\neg H \mid E) \times \text{cont}(\neg H \mid E)$, is easily seen to be 0, whereas $\text{cont}(H) = \text{trans-cont}(E; H) + \text{cont}(H \mid E)$.

The third indirect argument is again surprising. It turns out that maximizing $p(H \mid E) - p(E)$ also leads to maximizing the "expected transmitted incremental content gain," that is:

$$p(H \mid E) \times \text{trans-cont}_\rightarrow(E; H) - p(\neg H \mid E) \times \text{trans-cont}_\rightarrow(E; \neg H)$$

In sum, in the context of generalization, Hintikka has impressive "expectation" arguments in favor of maximizing the transmitted content.

However, I have strong doubts about his considerations. Hintikka's plea for maximization of the transmitted content and hence of the difference degree of confirmation has strange consequences. Consider the case that hypotheses H and H* have equal likelihood in view of E. Suppose, more specifically, that H and H* entail E, and hence that $p(E \mid H) = p(E \mid H^*) = 1$. Then it is easy to check that maximization of $p(H \mid E) - p(H) = p(H)(p(E \mid H) / p(E) - 1)$ leads to favoring the more probable hypothesis among H and H*. This is a direct illustration of the fact that the difference measure does not satisfy P2 (see section 1.1.1.). Its "impure" character[33] in the form of the Matthew-effect, the more probable hypothesis is rewarded more for the same success, is, surprisingly enough, shared by Popper's favorite measures of corroboration.[34] If any preference is to be expected I would be more inclined to think of the reverse preference in the "context of generalization": if two hypotheses are equally successful with regard to the evidence, then the stronger hypothesis seems more challenging to proceed with. Apart

from the fact that Popper would not appreciate the notion of "generalization," this would be very much in Popperian spirit. On the other hand, in the
"context of explanation" one might expect a preference for the weaker
hypothesis: if one wants to explain something on the basis of the available
knowledge one will prefer, among equally successful hypotheses regarding
the evidence, the hypothesis that has the highest initial probability, that is,
to be precise, the highest updated probability just before the evidence to be
explained came available. However, this is not intended to reverse
Hintikka's plea into a plea for maximizing likelihood in the case of
generalization, for this would, of course, not work in the case of equal
likelihoods. But a partial criterion would be possible: when the likelihoods
are the same, such as is the case for deductive confirmation, we should
favor the weaker hypothesis for explanation purposes and the stronger for
generalization purposes.[35] However, even this partial criterion can be
questioned because the choice still depends very much on the used
probability function. Moreover, it is not easy to see how to proceed in the
case of different likelihoods. Simply maximizing likelihood then would
discard probability considerations that seem to be relevant at least when the
likelihoods do not discriminate.

In the next section I will start to elaborate an alternative view on
explanation and generalization, by taking structural and inductive aspects
into account. I conclude this section with a totally different critical
consideration regarding the notion of "transmitted content." One attractive
aspect of the notion of content, whether prior or posterior, is that it has a
straightforward qualitative interpretation. If Struct(L) indicates the set of
structures of language L and Mod(H) the set of models on which H is true,
then the latter's complement Struct(L) − Mod(H) not only represents
Mod(¬H) but is also, as Hintikka is well aware, precisely the model
theoretic interpretation of Popper's notion of empirical content of H. Hence,
cont (H) = $p(\neg H)$ may be reconstrued as the $p(Mod(\neg H)) / p(Struct(L))$,
where the $p(Struct(L)) = 1$. Similarly, cont(H | E) may be seen as the
probabilistic version of the posterior empirical content of H, viz., Mod(E) −
Mod(H). However, I did not succeed in finding a plausible qualitative
interpretation of Hintikka's notion of transmitted content. If such an
interpretation cannot be given, it raises the question whether "transmitted
content" is more than a somewhat arbitrary notion. Note that a similar
objection would apply to the notion of "transmitted information" if it should
turn out not to be possible to give an interpretation of it in terms of
(qualitative) bits of information, of which it is well known that such an
interpretation can be given for the underlying notions of prior and posterior
information, assuming that 2 is used as the base of the logarithm.

3. Structural and Inductive Aspects of Explanation and Generalization

Whereas Hintikka tries to drive a wedge between explanation and generalization by the distinction between (logarithmic) information and content, in particular the transmitted values, I would like to suggest that the distinction between structural and inductive aspects of these and other notions is at least as important. Hence, first I will disentangle these aspects for some crucial notions in a similar way as I did for confirmation. Next, I will discuss what to maximize in the service of explanation and generalization. Since there do not seem to be in the present context (extra) advantages of the logarithmic version of "surprise value" information, I will only deal with the nonlogarithmic version, from which the logarithmic version can easily be obtained if one so wishes.

3.1. *Structural and Inductive Aspects of Probability and Types of Information*

As we have seen in section 1.2 confirmation has structural and inductive aspects, resulting from a comparison of the values belonging to one's favorite p-function, with the corresponding structural values, that is, the values belonging to the logical measure (m-)function. I will extend this analysis to prior and posterior probabilities and to transmitted information and content. From now on I will call the p-function the "subjective" probability function. However, I hasten to say that "subjective" is not supposed to mean "merely subjective," because such a function may well have been designed in a rather rational way, as Carnap and Hintikka have demonstrated very convincingly.

Let me start by defining the "inductive load" of prior and posterior subjective probability and of the "extra inductive load" of the latter relative to the former. There are of course two versions: a ratio and a difference version. In table 6 I have depicted all of them.

	A	B: ratio loads	C: difference loads
1	Prior inductive load: $ni(H)$	$p(H) / m(H)$	$p(H) - m(H)$
2	Posterior inductive load: $ni(H \mid E)$	$p(H \mid E) / m(H \mid E)$	$p(H / E) - m(H \mid E)$
3	Extra inductive load of posterior probability = Degree of *inductive* confirmation $Rp(H; E) / Rdp$ $(H; E) = $ Inductive load in transmitted i / cont	$[p(H \mid E) / m(H \mid E] /$ $[p(H) / m(H)] =$ $[p(H \mid E) / p(H)] /$ $[m(H \mid E) / m(H)]$	$[p(H \mid E) - m(H \mid E)] -$ $[p(H) - m(H)] =$ $[p(H \mid E) - p(H)] -$ $[m(H \mid E) - m(H)]$

TABLE 6: (Extra) Inductive Loads in Probabilities ('p' Fixed, 'm': Logical Measure Function).

THEO A. F. KUIPERS

It is easy to check whether the extra inductive load of the posterior probability relative to the prior probability, as indicated in row 3, is equal to the relevant degree of inductive confirmation as defined in section 1.2. However, the latter degrees also equal the ratio or the difference of the transmitted type of information to the corresponding transmitted type of structural information. Hence, it is plausible to define them also as the "inductive load" of the transmitted type of information. Accordingly, for the ratio versions of loads and degrees we get the conceptual relations:

extra inductive (ratio) load (of posterior probability to the prior)
= df posterior inductive load / prior inductive load
= degree of subjective confirmation / degree of structural
  confirmation
= df degree of inductive confirmation
= transmitted subjective information / transmitted structural
  information
= df inductive load of transmitted information

And for the difference versions:

extra inductive (difference) load (of posterior probability to the
  prior)
= df posterior inductive load − prior inductive load
= degree of confirmation − degree of structural confirmation
= df degree of inductive confirmation
= transmitted subjective content − transmitted structural content
= df inductive load of transmitted content

Turning to the question of how to define the (extra) inductive loads of prior and posterior information and content, it is not immediately clear how to proceed. For example, in the difference version it was rather plausible to define the inductive load of the prior subjective probability by $p(H) − m(H)$. In view of the definition of content, $1 − p(H)$, it now seems plausible to define the inductive load in the prior content by $[1 − p(H)] − [1 − m(H)] = m(H) − p(H)$, and hence equal to "minus the inductive load" in the prior subjective probability. However, one might also argue for equating the inductive (difference) loads of probability and content, or one might define the inductive load as the absolute value $| p(H) − m(H) |$. Similar considerations and possibilities apply to the ratio versions. However, it is not clear whether we really need all these definitions. Let us see how far we can come by restricting inductive aspects to the probabilities constituting information and content and to the "corresponding" degrees of confirmation, and hence to the transmitted types of information.

3.2. *Explanation and Generalization Reconsidered*

In section 2.2, I discussed Hintikka's arguments in favor of maximizing transmitted information, and hence the (log) ratio degree of confirmation and even the likelihood, for explanation purposes and maximizing the transmitted content, and hence the difference degree of confirmation, for generalization purposes. It turned out that these preferences have strange consequences, in particular in the case of equal likelihoods, notably deductive confirmation. Moreover, Hintikka's perspective seemed rather restricted by taking only one probability function into account. In my opinion at least the subjective and the structural probability function should be taken into account. My claim in this subsection will be that the structural and inductive aspects may be particularly relevant when we want to compare appropriate explanation and generalization strategies. Roughly speaking, I will suggest that inductive features should be minimized in the case of explanation in favor of structural features, and the reverse in the case of generalization.

Our leading question is: What do we want to maximize or minimize in choosing a hypothesis, given the structural m-function and a fixed subjective p-function, when explaining E, and when generalizing from E, respectively? I will certainly not arrive at final answers, but only make a start with answering these questions.[36] The basic candidate values for comparison seem to be the prior and posterior probabilities and the degree of confirmation or, equivalently, the transmitted type of information. In all cases we can compare subjective, structural and inductive values, and in the case of inductive loads and degrees of confirmation we can choose at least between ratio and difference measures. We should keep in mind that maximizing probabilities amounts to minimizing both information and content. In table 7 I have depicted the basic candidate values for maximization or minimization, and indicated Hintikka's preferences for explanation and generalization (indicated in cells 9F and 12F, respectively) and my tentative partial answers (1F and 2F, respectively), which are strongly qualified in the text.

TABLE 7: (next page) Possibilities for Maximizing or Minimizing when Choosing H, for Given p and m (p/m: Subjective/Structural Probability).

	A	B	C	D	E	F
1	prior probability	structural			$m(H)$	TK: maximize for deductive explanation
2		subjective			$p(H)$	TK: maximize for inductive generalization
3		inductive load	ratio		$p(H) / m(H)$	
4			difference		$P(H) - m(H)$	
5	posterior probability	structural			$m(H \mid E)$	
6		subjective			$p(H \mid E)$	
7		inductive load	ratio		$p(H \mid E) / m(H \mid E)$	
8			difference		$p(H \mid E) - m(H \mid E)$	
9	degree of confirmation	structural	ratio	= transmitted structural information	$m(H \mid E) / m(H)$	
10			difference	= transmitted structural content	$m(H \mid E) - m(H)$	
11		subjective	ratio	= transmitted subjective information	$p(H \mid E) / p(H)$	JH: maximize when explaining
12			difference	= transmitted subjective content	$p(H \mid E) - p(H)$	JH: maximize when generalizing
13		inductive	ratio	= extra inductive (ratio) load of posterior probability = inductive load of transmitted information	$[p(H \mid E) / m(H \mid E)] / [p(H) / m(H)] = [p(H \mid E) / p(H)] / [m(H \mid E) / m(H)]$	
14			difference	= extra inductive (diff.) load of posterior probability = inductive load of transmitted content	$[p(H \mid E) - m(H \mid E)] - [p(H) - m(H)] = [p(H \mid E) - p(H)] - [m(H \mid E) - m(H)]$	

TABLE 7: Possibilities for Maximizing or Minimizing when Choosing H, for Given p and m (p/m: Subjective/Structural Probability).

Our start will be restricted to the case of equal likelihoods, more specifically, deductive confirmation, and is particularly intended to invite Hintikka to develop his intuitions regarding inductive aspects further. When H and H* both entail E, all relevant likelihoods are simply 1. This result maximizes whatever likelihood will then not work. Moreover, as I have pointed out in section 1.2 (see table 3) deductive confirmation based on p will be counterinductive as soon as p(E) has inductive load in the sense of exceeding m(E). We have also seen in section 2.2 that maximizing the transmitted subjective content, as Hintikka proposed for generalizing, would favor, quite counterintuitively, the weaker hypothesis.[37] But for explanation purposes this might not be so counterintuitive.

So let us first concentrate on explanation. When we merely want to explain (deductively) a certain phenomenon on the basis of the available knowledge, including hypotheses with various probabilities, we would like to be safe. However, instead of saying that this explanation is based on the difference measure of confirmation, I rather prefer to see the preference as essentially based on the following sextuple: $\langle p(H), p(E), p(E \mid H), m(H),$ $m(E), m(E \mid H)\rangle$, in terms of which the other notions can be defined. Hence, my tentative answer is that in the context of deductive explanation in the face of deductive confirmation, or more generally in the case of equal likelihoods, the more probable hypothesis should be preferred. This is a robust strategy as far as the comparisons of p- and m-values coincide, or are at least not opposite, which will automatically be the case when one of the hypotheses entails the other. However, the following are among the interesting questions that remain.

(1) What to do when the comparison of m-values diverges from that of p-values?

I will deal separately with an extreme and a special case, respectively:

(2) What to do when $p(H) = p(H^*) = 1$ and hence, when both are considered to be established background knowledge, and hence when we will also have $m(H) = m(H^*) = 1$?

(3) What to do when the m-values of both hypotheses are 0 and the p-values nonzero?

Regarding the first case, I would like to suggest that the hypothesis with the highest prior m-value is the most plausible one to choose. The reason is that the higher subjective prior probability is apparently not due to logico-structural considerations, but due instead to inductive considerations of one kind or another, e.g., order (simplicity, homogeneity) or analogy influences. In the second case, the proper conclusion is that there is apparently more than one valid explanation available. In the third case, and more generally when the prior m-values do not differ, our preferences may well depend on the reason why one subjective prior probability exceeds another. The reason may be due to the fact that one hypothesis is weaker than the other in some logico-structural sense, which cannot be accounted for by the m-function; this may well be the case for m-zero hypotheses. For example, "All A and B are F" and "All C are F" may both get m-value 0, but the first claims in a sense more than the second. In such a case, preferring the one with the higher p-value, due to this aspect, seems plausible for explanation purposes. However, the higher p-value may also be (mainly) due to typical inductive considerations, whereas the relevant hypotheses are logico-structurally comparable. As an example, the one may have more analogical features than the other, accounted for by a higher prior subjective probability. In such a case it will be difficult to choose. However, if the other hypothesis is logico-structurally weaker, but not accounted for by 0 m-values, that one seems preferable again.

Similarly interesting questions remain when I turn to the suggested answer in the case of generalizing: in the context of (inductive) generalization[38] from E by hypotheses that are deductively confirmed by E, the less probable hypothesis should *prima facie* be preferred. However, before I discuss these questions, I have to address the so-called "converse consequence property" of deductive confirmation of H by E, that is, the fact that any stronger hypothesis than H is also deductively confirmed by E, including any one resulting from conjugating H with a totally unrelated additional hypothesis. Of course, we should not prefer such a type of stronger hypothesis. As I have argued in *From Instrumentalism to Constructive Realism* 2.1.2, in such a case the confirmation remains perfectly localizable. Hence, in this case we should only compare hypotheses that are relevant in a sense to be specified, where our limited knowledge of deductive relations should ideally also be taken into account. Assuming that such a definition can be given, the suggestion is that the less probable of the relevant hypotheses should be preferred. Preference here of course means preference for further testing and evaluation, not yet for acceptance, even if that is only for the time being.

Let me now turn to the three remaining questions or cases applied to relevant hypotheses in the context of generalization. Regarding (1), what to do when the p-comparison differs from the m-comparison, I would now like to suggest that the hypothesis with the lowest prior p-value is the most plausible one to choose. The reason is the mirror image of the one in the case of explanation. The lower subjective prior probability is apparently not due to logico-structural considerations but to inductive considerations in favor of other hypotheses; after all, assigning higher probabilities to some hypotheses on the basis of order or analogy considerations has to be paid by other hypotheses. In case (2), the "hypotheses" in question will not be considered as interesting new generalizations because they belong already to the background knowledge. In case (3), when both prior m-values are 0, and more generally when the prior m-values do not differ, our preferences will again depend on the reason why one subjective prior probability exceeds another. It may be due to the fact that the one hypothesis is weaker in some logico-structural sense, which cannot be accounted for by the m-function. In such a case, focussing on the one with the lower p-value, due to this way of being stronger, seems plausible for generalization purposes. However, the lower p-value may also be (mainly) due to typical inductive considerations, working positive for other hypotheses. If another hypothesis is logico-structurally stronger, but is not accounted for by 0 m-values, that one seems now preferable to proceed with.

In sum, as far as choosing between different deductive explanations of new evidence is concerned, my preference goes in the direction of higher structural prior probabilities, with a number of qualifications. On the other hand, as far as choosing between different inductive generalizations is concerned, my preference goes in the direction of lower subjective prior probabilities, with even more qualifications. In both cases the relevant degrees of confirmation and hence the transmitted information do not differ, for the corresponding likelihoods do not differ. I leave the question of how to deal with cases of different likelihoods open.

CONCLUDING REMARKS

From sections 2 and 3 it is rather clear that we are far from a final answer to the question how to use probabilities, and measures of confirmation, information and content in the contexts of explanation and generalization. However, I hope to have convinced the reader, and in particular Jaakko Hintikka, whatever the role of different kinds of information, structural and inductive aspects should also play a role. I conclude this paper by enlarging the problem of choices to be made.

It is surprising that Hintikka did not explicitly consider the information-theoretic notion of *entropy*, although he took the corresponding logarithmic notion of information extensively into account. Entropy not only naturally leads to new preference criteria between different hypotheses, but it also suggests preference criteria between different probability functions for the same set of (mutually exclusive and together exhaustive) hypotheses.

$$- p(H)\log p(H) - p(\neg H)\log p(\neg H)$$

Similarly, the *posterior entropy* is defined as the posterior expected posterior information:

$$- p(H \mid E)\log p(H \mid E) - p(\neg H \mid E)\log p(\neg H \mid E)$$

It is plausible to call the difference of the prior entropy minus the posterior entropy, the (amount of) *entropy reduction* due to E. Since entropy measures something like the amount of disorder a hypothesis represents, one plausible option could be to favor the hypothesis that obtains the highest entropy reduction from E. However, I do not have strong feelings in this respect.

So let me turn to the alternative use. Assuming a finite number of mutually exclusive and together exhaustive hypotheses H1, . . . , Hn ({H, ¬H} forms such a set above), the corresponding prior entropy is of course

$$\Sigma_i - p(Hi) \log p(Hi)$$

with similar definitions for the posterior entropy and the entropy reduction. From this perspective the natural question is of course which probability function leads to the highest or lowest prior or posterior entropy and which one to the highest entropy reduction. In fact, the so-called maximum entropy principle, advocated in particular by E. T. Jaynes,[39] is frequently used for selecting the prior distribution with the highest entropy. However, if one is willing to consider non-Bayesian moves, one may of course also consider, in addition, to posteriorily prefer the probability distribution that received the highest entropy reduction.

However this may be, in my opinion, entropy considerations of one kind or another might well turn out to be crucial for finding a satisfactory account of preferences regarding confirmation, information, and content in both the context of explanation and of generalization. That these contexts have to be distinguished carefully I consider to be one of the main challenging and even revolutionary points in Hintikka's contribution to the year 1968.

THEO A. F. KUIPERS

UNIVERSITY OF GRONINGEN
MAY 2001

NOTES

1.   Theo A. F. Kuipers, *From Instrumentalism to Constructive Realism*, Synthese Library 287 (Dordrecht: Kluwer, 2000). A provisional version of this section, also entitled "Ordering the Landscape of Confirmation," has appeared as Subsection 7.1.2 (pp. 206–13) of Kuipers, *Structures in Science*, Synthese Library 301 (Dordrecht: Kluwer, 2001). The present version, which appears here with the permission of Kluwer Academic Publishers, underwent some minor revisions and tables 2 and 3 have been added. The section prepares the conceptual ground for sections 2 and 3 which were written for this occasion.

2.   See Jaakko Hintikka, "The Varieties of Information and Scientific Explanation," in *Logic, Methodology and Philosophy of Science III*, ed. B. van Rootselaar and J. F. Staal (Amsterdam: North-Holland, 1968), pp. 311–31.

3.   Jaakko Hintikka, "Comment on Theo Kuipers," in *Knowledge and Inquiry: Essays on Jaakko Hintikka's Epistemology and Philosophy of Science*, ed. M. Sintonen, Poznan Studies, vol. 51 (Amsterdam: Rodopi, 1997), pp. 317–18.

4.   Ken Gemes, "Horwich and Hempel on Hypothetico-Deductivism," *Philosophy of Science* 56 (1990): 609–702.

5.   Patrick Maher, "Kuipers on Qualitative Confirmation and the Ravens Paradox," in *Confirmation, Empirical Progress, and Truth Approximation: Essays in Debate with Theo Kuipers*, ed. R. Festa, A. Aliseda, J. Peijnenburg. Poznan Studies (Amsterdam: Rodopi, forthcoming).

6.   Theo A. F. Kuipers, "Reply to Patrick Maher," in *Confirmation, Empirical Progress, and Truth Approximation*.

7.   John Kemeny, "A Logical Measure Function," *Journal of Symbolic Logic* 18, no. 4 (1953): 289–308.

8.   Cf. the random-world or labeled method in Adam Grove, Joseph Halpern, and Daphne Koller, "Asymptotic Conditional Probabilities: The Unary Case," *Journal of Symbolic Logic* 61, no. 1 (1996): 250–75.

9.   Wesley Salmon, "Partial Entailment as a Basis for Inductive Logic," in *Essays in Honor of Carl G. Hempel*, ed. N. Rescher (Dordrecht: Reidel, 1969), pp. 47–82.

10. Cf. Kevin Compton, "0-1 Laws in Logic and Combinatorics," in *Proceedings 1987 NATO Adv. Study Inst. on Algorithms and Order*, ed. I. Rival (Dordrecht: Reidel, 1988), pp. 353–83.

11. Karl R. Popper and David Miller, "A Proof of the Impossibility of Inductive Probability," *Nature* 302 (1983): 687–88.

12. See Karl R. Popper, *Logik der Forschung* (Vienna, 1934); translated as *The Logic of Scientific Discovery* (London: Hutchinson, 1959). See also John Earman, *Bayes or Bust: A Critical Examination of Bayesian Confirmation Theory* (Cambridge, Mass.: MIT Press, 1992); C. Howson and P. Urbach, *Scientific Reasoning: The Bayesian Approach* (La Salle, Ill.: Open Court, 1989); Theo Kuipers, *Studies in Inductive Probability and Rational Expectation*, Synthese Library 123 (Dordrecht: Reidel, 1978).

13. Cf. Ilkka Niiniluoto, *Critical Scientific Realism* (Oxford: Oxford University Press, 1999), pp. 187–88.

14. Popper and Miller, "A Proof of the Impossibility of Inductive Probability."

15. But Bayesian statistics uses inductive likelihoods as well; see Roberto Festa, *Optimum Inductive Methods: A Study in Inductive Probability Theory, Bayesian Statistics and Verisimilitude* (Dordrecht: Kluwer, 1993).

16. For a survey of "Hintikka-systems" and related systems, such as the systems resulting from the joint work of Hintikka and Ilkka Niiniluoto, see Kuipers, "The Carnap-Hintikka Programme in Inductive Logic," in *Knowledge and Inquiry: Essays on Jaakko Hintikka's Epistemology and Philosophy of Science*, ed. M. Sintonen, Poznan Studies, vol. 51 (Amsterdam: Rodopi, 1997), pp. 87–99, or Kuipers, *From Instrumentalism to Constructive Realism*, section 4.5. For elaborated versions and a study of their properties and relations, see Kuipers, *Studies in Inductive Probability and Rational Expectation*.

17. Hintikka, "Comment on Theo Kuipers," p. 318.

18. Alberto Mura, "When Probabilistic Support Is Inductive," *Philosophy of Science* 57 (1990): 278–89. See also e.g., G. Schlesinger, "Measuring Degrees of Confirmation," *Analysis* 55, no. 3 (1995): 208–12; P. Milne, "*Log[P(h|eb)/P(h|b)]* is the One True Measure of Confirmation," *Philosophy of Science* 63 (1996): 21–26; and Roberto Festa, "Bayesian Confirmation," in *Experience, Reality, and Scientific Explanation*, ed. M. C. Galavotti and A. Pagnini (Dordrecht: Kluwer, 1999), pp. 55–87.

19. Brandon Fitelson, "The Plurality of Bayesian Measures of Confirmation and the Problem of Measure Sensitivity," *Philosophy of Science*, supplement to volume 66, no. 3 (1999): S362–S378.

20. The P2-related arguments concern the first and the second argument in Fitelson's table 1, and the second in table 2. Of the other two, the example of "unintuitive" confirmation is rebutted in chapter 3 of *From Instrumentalism to Constructive Realism* with a similar case against the difference measure. The other one is related to the "grue-paradox," for which chapters 2 and 3 claim to present an illuminating analysis in agreement with P2.

21. Hintikka, "The Varieties of Information and Scientific Explanation," in *Logic, Methodology and Philosophy of Science III*. See also Hintikka, "On Proper (Popper?) and Improper Uses of Information in Epistemology," *Theoria* 59 (1993): 158–65. (All further references are to "Varieties," except when otherwise stated.)

22. Here I start to deviate somewhat from Hintikka's notation. Hintikka's "$inf_{add}(H \mid E)$," (4), p. 313, and "$inf_{cond}(H \mid E)$," (9), p. 315, both correspond with "$inf(H \mid E)$," as he notes on p. 315 on the basis of (6) on p. 314.

23. "trans-inf(E; H)" corresponds with Hintikka's notion (11) on p. 316, indicated by him as "$transinf(E \mid H)$" on p. 317.

24. P. 316, where I have replaced the relevant symbols.

25. Hintikka's "$cont_{cond}(H \mid E)$," (10), p. 315, corresponds with my "$cont(H \mid E)$."

26. My "trans-cont(E; H)" corresponds with Hintikka's notion (13) on p. 316, indicated by him as "$transcont_{cond}(E \mid H)$" on p. 317; note that I cancelled his sub-

script "cond" because no confusion will arise.

27. P. 316, where I have replaced the relevant symbols.

28. Hintikka's "cont$_{add}$(H | E)," (5), p. 313, corresponds with "cont(E → H)," and hence with my cont$_-$(H | E), as he notes by (7) on p. 314.

29. "trans-cont$_-$(E; H)" corresponds with Hintikka's notion (12) on p. 316, indicated by him as "transcont$_{add}$(E | H) on p. 317.

30. Pp. 321, 324 (symbols adapted, TK).

31. P. 321.

32. In section 6 Hintikka writes down the (posterior) expected transmitted values for trans-inf(E; H), trans-cont(E; H) and trans-cont$_-$(E; H) and it would be easy to add those for trans-i(E; H), trans-i$_-$(E; H) trans-inf$_-$(E; H). However, as we will see in the text some of the so-called "expected value gains" are much more interesting.

33. Comparing the "impure" degree p(H | E) – p(H) = p(H)(p(E | H) / p(E) – 1) with the "pure" degree p(E | H) / p(E) makes clear that p(H) can even be considered as a measure of the impurity in the former, at least when the likelihoods are the same.

34. See Kuipers, *From Instrumentalism to Constructive Realism*, appendix 1 of ch. 3.

35. Another option would be to maximize the "expected i-gain," the analogue of expected content gain, which equals p(H | E) / p(H) – p(¬H | E) / p(¬H) = p(E | H) / p(E) – p(E | ¬H) / p(E), which leads to favoring the one with the lowest likelihood of the negation, also called the degree of *dis*confirmation. This sounds plausible: when the degree of confirmation does not discriminate, we should prefer the hypothesis with the lowest degree of disconfirmation. However, it remains unclear whether this option is more appropriate for explanation rather than for generalization.

36. Moreover, I will neglect the possibility of combining the perspectives of explanation and generalization. This might be done in similar ways as truth value and informativeness have been combined by Isaac Levi for epistemic utility and Ilkka Niiniluoto for truthlikeness (see Niiniluoto, *Critical Scientific Realism*, pp. 168–70). I thank Allard Tamminga for drawing my attention to this type of possibility.

37. Note that when one hypothesis is stronger than the other due to logically entailing the other, comparing m-values will lead to this same conclusion as comparing p-values.

38. Note that using here the phrase "deductive generalization" would be highly misleading, but "inductive generalization" is appropriate, in particular as far as generalizations are concerned that are formulated in the same language as the evidence.

39. See *E. T. Jaynes: Papers on Probability, Statistics and Statistical Physics*, ed. R. D. Rosenkrantz (Dordrecht: Kluwer, 1989).

REPLY TO THEO A. F. KUIPERS

$\mathbf{I}$am afraid that my response to Theo A.F. Kuipers will disappoint him and disappoint many readers, and I apologize to them. Kuipers presents an impressive, knowledgeable survey of the state of the art of confirmation and information maximization with a view on the contributions I made to this field in the sixties. As Isaac Levi points out in his contribution to this volume, my main interests in the field of epistemology and philosophy of science have since shifted away from inductive probability and confirmation to an interrogative approach to inquiry. I have not done any detailed work on the subject of Kuipers's excellent paper for a quarter of a century. Hence I cannot comment on the technicalities of his contribution. However, it is possible to put Kuipers's enterprise in an interesting perspective from the vantage point of the interrogative approach to inquiry.

The first aspect of that perspective is explained in my response to Levi. From the vantage point of the interrogative approach, there are no irreducible rules of inductive inference. Inductive inference, including rules for probabilistic induction, depends on tacit assumptions concerning the nature of the world. Once these assumptions are spelled out, inductive inference becomes in principle a species of deductive inference.

From this it follows that one of the focal points of the kind of studies Kuipers is engaged in is to identify the tacit assumptions on which inductive inference rests. Traditional philosophers used to speak in this context of an assumption of the uniformity of nature. In the research tradition represented by Kuipers, assumptions of this kind are in the simplest cases represented by choices of Carnap's parameter λ. It was in fact a tremendous achievement on Carnap's part to identify this crucial parameter, even if only in the artificially simple case he studied. It has turned out that the optimal choice of λ is a monotonic function of the entropy of the universe. This choice cannot be made a priori. However, this analysis shows precisely what features of the world are relevant to the kind of inductive inference in question.

Thus we can see one important possible aim of the kind of analyses Kuipers and others in the same tradition are engaged in. It is to find, in other cases, too, this kind of connection between inductive methods and assumptions concerning the world. In my work on inductive generalization (with Ilkka Niiniluoto and others) I uncovered similar connections between the different parameters on which our inductive inferences depend and certain kinds of order in the world. Entropy then becomes the measure of only one particular kind of order. Indeed, Kuipers recognizes clearly the importance of the concept of entropy in confirmation theory. What I miss is a similar recognition of the role of the kinds of order and disorder that are not measured by entropy.[1]

Even though it has not been pointed out by anyone—including Kuipers and myself—we have here a result directly relevant to traditional discussions of induction. Contrary to what many philosophers seem to have thought, we cannot vindicate inductive inference simply by assuming that the world is regular. For it now turns out that there are many different kinds of regularity which are largely independent of one another.

Another, related perspective on Kuipers's discussion is the following. Kuipers uses the idea of thinking of a scientist's choices in a decision-theoretical spirit as aiming at the maximization of information. I have advocated this idea, and I still think it is a promising approach to scientific inference. Hence it is of great interest to examine different ways of defining information and to examine the consequences of choosing one way rather than another one. This is what Kuipers does at some length in an interesting manner. But this does not get to the bottom of the matter. The reason is that measures of information and measures of a priori inductive probability are interdependent. Since the latter codify in effect assumptions concerning the world, so do the former. In other words, there are no presuppositionless measures of factual information. (There may be exceptions to this in special cases, such as zero information.) Hence even before we can ask how information might serve as an epistemic utility, we face the more fundamental problem of how to measure information and prior probability.

Another general perspective brought out by the interrogative approach is that typical rules of scientific inference can, and perhaps should, be thought of as strategic rules and not step-by-step "definitory" rules. It would be an interesting task to try to see what can be said of Kuipers's discussion in the light of this distinction.

These comments do not reflect on the value of the work that Kuipers and others in the same tradition are doing. What it does is to place this work on a wider map of problems and results. Perhaps it can also help to give a direction for future research in this area. For instance, it would be highly interesting to see what kind of assumptions can be codified in the choice of prior probabilities (and of measures of information).

J. H.

NOTE

1. See here my 1976 paper with Ilkka Niiniluoto, "An Axiomatic Foundation for the Logic of Inductive Generalization," in *Formal Methods in the Methodology of Empirical Sciences*, ed. M. Przełecki et al. (Dordrecht: D. Reidel Publishing Co., 1976), pp. 57–81. Appears also in *Studies in Inductive Logic and Probability* 2, ed. Richard C. Jeffrey (Berkeley: University of California Press, 1980), pp. 157–81.

27

Michel Meyer

QUESTIONING ART

The interrogative model conceptualized by Jaakko Hintikka has been the source of an epistemological renewal. Its logic has proved a real asset in the understanding of propositions as answers. But questioning is at work in many a field of inquiry, ranging from metaphysics to aesthetics.

My purpose here is not to envisage all those domains of applications, however interesting they appear. I would like to consider how questioning is at work in art, in its conception as well as in its reception. The history of art will be our material and philosophy our tool. The questioning model will receive its due extension in order to have its place in aesthetics recognized as foundational there too.

I. WHERE AND WHY IS QUESTIONING FOUNDATIONAL?

Adorno used to say that the basic property of works of art is the fact that each is an enigma.

> What has irritated the theory of art on end is the fact that all art works are riddles; indeed, art as a whole is a riddle. Another way of putting this is to say that art expresses something while at the same time hiding it. The enigmatic quality grimaces like a clown. It becomes the more invisible, the more one tries to be on the inside of art works, seeking to re-enact them. But even if one steps outside and purposely breaks the contract with the immanent totality of the work, then the enigma returns like an imp.[1]

Art raises the question of its own answerhood, of to what it is an answer. Hence, "the enigmatic quality of art renders the very notion of *Verstehen* (understanding) problematic."[2] And "even felicitously interpreted works continue to require understanding; they are waiting for the word that breaks the spell of the riddle."[3] To understand art means to grasp the problem it tackles and this is already an answer, although it is not *the* solution, because there is none. "To solve a riddle in art is to identify the reason why it is insoluble."[4] One can say that "in the final analysis works of art are enigmatic not in terms of their composition, but in terms of the truth they contain."[5] Hence, the question of meaning, which is an invitation to the mind to recognize *what* is in question in the very problematic. This reminds us of Wittgenstein's famous saying: meaning is what answers the question of meaning. This holds even when there is no other answer to that question than questioning itself, as in Kafka's famous *Parables* or as in Borgès' enigmatic conclusion of *The Book of Sands*. Truth, says Adorno, is the answer in its very content, while meaning is the question, and this is also an answer, although a problematic one. The latter opens up toward a multiplicity of choices that are called the interpretation of the work of art.

The idea concerning the problematic character of art can also be found in Collingwood's philosophy of art, as expressed in his *Autobiography*. A work of art is an answer to an implicit question. To "read" art—and this means seeing, hearing, or touching—means to raise the question of the implied question embodied within the work of art which *is* the work of art itself. Art as a question addressed to the audience supposes that art is rhetorical and needs to be addressed to someone it moves, pleases, or influences.

II. RHETORIC AS THE SUBJECTIVIZATION OF QUESTIONING

Rhetoric has been defined since Aristotle as a debate on a given thesis, but also as eloquence, and later on, as the expression of the beautiful through figures of speech or through any other type of figurativity as found in art. All those definitions are, of course, not false and all cover a real aspect of rhetoric at a given moment of its history.[6] But all these definitions suffer from the same flaw. They put emphasis on one particular feature of rhetoric, reducing all the other features to the chosen parameter and subordinating them to it. To define rhetoric as manipulative, as Plato did in the *Gorgias*, reveals an emphasis put on the treatment of the audience. To define rhetoric by eloquence, as Quintilian did it in the *Oratory Institutes*, rather emphasizes the role and the action of the orator. Theoreticians have also stressed the importance of reasoning or style when asked what rhetoric was about. Who is right? Everybody and nobody, because all those aspects of the rhetorical relationship obviously matter and are complementary to one other. We need an encompassing view of rhetoric in which the speaker (or *ethos*, to use Aristotle's term), the audience (or *pathos*) and the message that mediates (or *logos*) their relationship, are on equal footing. Hence my definition of rhetoric: "*rhetoric is the negotiation of the distance between individuals on a given question.*" The speaker, the author, the artist is defined by an *ethos* that characterizes him or her *as such*, in his or her very *capacity*, not merely by his or her expertise. *Ethos* is that in virtue of which that role of speaker or author or artist is taken up. *What* is in *question* in the debate or the relationship is expressed by the *logos*. *Logos* must therefore be capable of differentiating what is problematic from what is not: let us call this feature the *apocritical* (from *apokrisis*, solution in Greek) one. And finally, someone must be challenged, moved, or interested by that problem the speaker or the author put forth to his or her attention. The problem submitted is received by the audience, whose passive role, at least in the beginning, is designated by Aristotle through the term *pathos*: passivity and emotion seem to meet and fuse in rhetoric.

Now, when a question is submitted to some audience, it can be done in two ways. Either the question can be put on the table and openly discussed, as in court, where the two terms of the alternative are represented by the opposing parties and their advocates. Or, the question can be repressed and treated as if it were solved by the answer, when in fact answers only appear in the relationship. This repression of the question makes the answer taken alone fictional and sometimes even fictive. Everybody knows the example of funeral oration. What is the problem of its rhetoric? The problem is precisely to see that no problem be raised concerning the deceased, who will be gratified with all the possible virtues as if he never had made any fault during his lifetime. Consensual and unproblematic discourse will be the basic rhetoric of the funeral oration. In order to achieve such a resolution, a beautiful rather than a convincing speech is expected. It will be, as it is often called, "pure rhetoric." Rhetoric of this sort tackles a question by repressing it into answers presented as solving it, whereas an argument (or argumentation) explicitly raises the question beforehand. It is probably to such a distinction that Aristotle himself referred when he wrote, in the first line of his *Rhetoric*, that dialectic is the counterpart of rhetoric. For lack of recourse to an interrogative model of thought and speech, Aristotle was not in a position to conceptualize rhetoric and argumentation (or dialectic) as being related conceptually. He could only characterize this relationship between rhetoric and dialectic in a metaphorical way, as being analogical and complementary.

Thus, rhetoric alone cannot put forward answers as if they were solving some underlying question, without resorting to style and form. Eloquence is grounded within the requirement of proceeding as if questions are solved by only offering answers. The fiction of style is therefore necessary to make the account believable.

Rhetoric, in the broad sense of the term, usually includes argument theory: the rhetoric of figures and the rhetoric of conflicts, in which questions are discussed and debated openly, both belong to rhetoric as defined above. People negotiate on a given question that divides them, or at least, that creates a gap between them. When we speak or write, or even create, we have a question or a problem in mind we wish to address. Language and other expressive forms are meant to express and communicate either the problem or the solution we have in mind. As the audience takes up the question raised thereby, it can approve or disapprove the answer or even the relevance of the question (one can discard a question, as uninteresting for instance), agree or disagree, like it or dislike it, and so forth.

Thus, we may conclude that there is no rhetoric without questioning, because questions are both the measure of the difference between individuals and the topic of *what* divides them, or, in the case of answers, what unites and pleases them.

III. THE QUESTIONING MODEL IN LITERARY RHETORIC

Literature is born from the progressive death of mythology (or *mythos*). Mythology ceases to be taken literally, and the stories we find therein become stories to be taken as such, i.e., as fictions. Homer, then, became possible, so to speak, as myth declined. *Mythos* became the basis of the plot, as Aristotle says it in his *Poetics*. Now, what is striking here is the fact that corresponding to the *ethos*, the *pathos*, and the *logos*, we find three modes of fictionalization. For the *ethos*, emphasis being put on the speaker, on the "I," we have *lyric* poetry. For the *logos*, emphasis being laid on the description of the world and mundane actions or events, we have the "he" or "she" of the *epic*. And finally, we have the *pathos* (or "thou") where the role of the other is determining. In this case, fiction embodies the Other in theater, and we have the *tragedy*.

Now, we must also distinguish poetry from the prose. How does such a distinction arise? In order to answer this question, it is necessary to acknowledge the basic dynamic feature of History that lies behind or under that distinction. I should rather speak of the *grammar* of History. History imprints differences upon what is. Whatever is ceases to be or is different in some respect. Hence, may we say that what was, is still there but metaphorically so? It *is* what it was but fictionally, because it *is* different nonetheless. So identity cannot be taken literally.

We have two responses to historical change. The first consists of looking for a new answer, since the old ones have disappeared or have ceased to be answers. The second response consists of considering the old answers still as answers but as problematic ones, as figurative answers but not as real ones. As a result of these different responses, we also have a figurative treatment and a realistic treatment of *what* has been answered so far. Let us take as an example the evolution of painting at the Renaissance. In Italy we observe an increasing figurativity in painting that gave rise eventually to mannerism. Botticelli's *Venus* is inconceivable in the North, although the dynamic of capitalism was fastened there by the commercial role of the free towns too. Realism was strong in Flanders and became even stronger in the Netherlands, for example, with Vermeer and his famous *View of Delft*. We find the same double movement in literature. An increased figurativity verges on an increased realism, i.e., respectively, resort to verse and figures of speech, such as allegory, and to prose, that developed too. This gives rise to the following classifications based on whether the first or second response is taken:

	ethos	*logos*	*pathos*
Figurative speech (problematicity)	lyric	epic	tragedy
Realist speech (apocriticity)	novel	history	comedy

How can we verify our hypothesis, as embodied in the table above? Let us consider how Greek, French, and Italian literature developed. Classical Greece had lyrical poets (Sappho, for instance), epic poets (Homer, for instance), and authors of theater (Aeschylus, for instance). Realism emerged in all the three genres : comedy with Aristophanes, history with Herodotus, while the novel seems to have emerged very late. Realism was, after all, the realm of comedy for the Greeks. As to literal narrativity, it came to be associated with philosophy.

Greece	*ethos*	*logos*	*pathos*
Figurativism	Archilochus Sappho Simonides Pindar	Homer	Aeschylus Sophocles Euripides
Literalism	Socrates Plato	Herodotus	Aristophanes

Roman Republic [7]	*ethos*	*logos*	*pathos*
Figurativism	*Lyric*	*Epic*	*Tragedy*
	Catullus Virgil Lucilius	Lucretius	Ennius Naevius Livius
Realism or Literalism	*Rhetoric*	*History*	*Comedy*
	Cicero	Cato (Later in Imperial Rome: Livy, Sallust)	Plautus Terence

The birth of literature in France, Italy, and England are more familiar but clearly we can apply the same principle with Imperial Rome. Let us consider the case of France, since it is less familiar to the English reader:

France	*ethos*	*logos*	*pathos*
Figurativism	*Lyric poetry*	*Epic*	*Tragedy*
	Chansons des troubadours The Roman of the Rose	Chansons de gestes (Roland)	Tristan and Ysolde
Realism	*Novels*	*History*	*Comedy*
	Roman de Renart Chrétien of Troyes's novels	Villehardouin Commynes	soties farces fabliaux

As Michel Zink has put it, "the *roman* (novel) appears somewhat later than the *chanson de geste* and later than lyric poetry."[8] In fact, everything began with the epic of the *Chanson de Roland*, the French *Beowulf*. Later, there were songs sung in the castles by minstrels and jesters. On the public places, there were *soties* and *farces* that were played. One laughed at the powerful people and especially at the clergy. Later in Italy, we also find allegorical poetry with Dante and realism with Boccacio.

What is striking in the birth of European literature is that we always find the tripartition *ethos, logos, pathos*, giving rise to a certain type of literary style. The questions dealt with are distinct. The *ethos*-questions are I-questions: issues of self-expression were put in terms of poetry, before the novel, in the modern sense of the term, could take over. The *logos*-questions deal with the state of the world, they are "it-questions" (he or she questions too): epic poetry turned into historical narrative. As to the *pathos*-questions, they imply the other in a theatrical form, figuratively in tragedy, realistically in comedies.

The questions to which the *ethos*, *logos*, and the *pathos* refer are the self, the world, and the other. They are the most basic questions raised by the human mind. In his *Treatise of Human Nature*, David Hume said the same when he considered the most fundamental divisions of such a treatise to be the understanding (for the knowledge of the world), the passions (for what we "know" about ourselves), and morals (for the relationship with others). Those questions cover alternatives, like all problems. For the self and its perpetuation, the individual is questioned by the feminine and the masculine. It is the problem of love in all its implications. The quest of the self is to perpetuate itself as a living organism in a society. This implies maintaining an identity through the sexual difference. The problem of the "other" emerges as the relationship we have towards the family, our parents, and our children. It is the familiar form taken by History. As to the question of the world, and things in general, the problem is that of economic survival in an universe dominated by scarcity. Life and death express the alternatives we face when we live in an objective world, and we have, as we say, to "earn our living." All this has determined the contents of lyric, epic, and comedy (or tragedy). The lyrical ethos, being self-expression, is animated by the quest of love. In the Middle Ages, courtly love permeated all the lyrical and poetical works. The epic, on the other hand, is defined by the capacity to face death and to live an honorable life. To be above life is to live according to the code of honor. As to comedy or tragedy, it is always a family business of some sort. "Oedipus-Rex" is a good example, but also the comedies have the same topic, even if it is to mock the cheated husband as in Chaucer or Boccacio, or in the French *Fabliaux*.

Literature is what I would call a complete structure because it contains all three dimensions, self, world, and other. Other arts do not. Architecture is cosmological and expresses the *logos*, it reflects some order of the world. Sculpture embodies the *ethos* and represents the self, the body, the character. As to painting, it raises emotions by representation. It plays with the other's response. These are incomplete structures.

Let us consider all this in more detail and we shall then be able to integrate literature into the general picture of the history of art.

IV. QUESTIONING AND FINE ARTS

If literature contains the three dimensions of *ethos*, *logos*, and *pathos*, the other fine arts need one another to express those three aspects. Architecture, sculpture, and painting differ from literature in this respect. Architecture is certainly not representational, while sculpture is. The *logos* is present in architecture through geometric relations and proportions, while sculpture is more realistic, at least when used within buildings or on their outside. Architecture is dominated by the geometrical *logos*. Sculpture is the language of *ethos*, for it expresses the way the human self represents itself. Painting on the other hand depicts the emotions. It embodies the look of the other and what is asked from such a look.

All this explains why buildings will contain sculptures or frescoes. There is no figurality without a corresponding form designed to represent reality. A given art is exhausted when it is no longer able to produce that representation and when it becomes merely formal. For the Greeks, sculpture provided the required realistic outlook, because painting was merely ornamental and architecture, formal and figurative. Hence we grasp the Greek ideal of beauty, whose purpose was to reestablish some difference between the gods and the mortals, who seem so alike in so many respects.

Christianity had another view of the divinity, less ritualistic, more allegorical, consecrating the Jewish prohibition to represent God. Notwithstanding this prohibition, ritualism emerged within Christianism through the adoration of the Saints. Hence, we grasp the emergence of painting in Western history. What about the representation of Jesus himself? The iconoclast quarrel (is Jesus a God or a messiah of God?) in the Byzantine empire is rooted in the indetermination of the answer, in the problematic aspect of ritualism in the Christian creed. Too much ritualism led to the Protestant reaction in which religion is a matter of conscience and interiority. But the Christian religion began by being symbolic and figurative, at least in the Western world. Roman churches were massive, so much so that the figurative aspect of art was left to the sculptures, on the columns for instance, representing aspects of Christian life in allegorical forms. The churches themselves were buildings that were more immediately seen—and not interpreted—as the place to pray and meet for religious practice. The gothic churches, on the other hand, were more symbolic of the aspiration toward God, but just as the churches became more symbolic, the sculptures, in counterpart, became more realistic. Painting came out of the books copied and illustrated in Christianism, and turned out to be more symbolic in Italy and more realistic in the North, in Flanders, and in the Netherlands. At the Renaissance, painting came to play a major role in the realistic trend, although more so in the North than in the South; hence, the need to have a more realistic counterpart, played by sculpture in the South, whereas we hardly find such sculpture in the North.

But History does not stop. Its pace even increased with the development of capitalism. What *is* becomes more and more different from what it is, or was, becoming at most a metaphorical identity with itself. Such an identity is then a fiction. A rhetorical identity such as this leads to more figurativism. The Italian Renaissance came from a mild allegorical vision of reality before revealing eventually the increased figurativity of mannerism and baroque. Painting was less and less realistic in Italy and became more and more formal, a form of exhaustion and saturatedness. Music then took over, because it is based on differences in a more abstract figurative way. Painting was too figurative and was not enough so at the same time. But music could not survive as more fit to the historical pace without a corresponding realism. Opera provided it. Born in the middle of the seventeenth century with Monteverdi, opera represented the mimetic (or representational) aspect of music, until photography and cinema led to the death of opera, something that the realistic expression of painting could not accomplish. The novel turned out to be the literary form par excellence when it finally turned realistic: in the eighteenth century in England and in the nineteenth in France with Stendhal, Balzac, Flaubert, and Zola. Simultaneously, figurality increased in literature with the new formalistic poetry, leading to Baudelaire and Mallarmé, Yeats, and Eliot. Painting too became more abstract and figurative, like music.

Art cannot evolve without stressing realism and figurativism at the same time. A form of art becomes dominant when it achieves both tasks. Baroque painting in Bavaria and Austria, for instance, had to have its neo-classical counterpart (in France or in England), while literature became romantic in poetry and realistic in novels. Sculpture evolved too, passing from the baroque and the allegorical to the realism of portraits, before knowing abstractness too (Brancusi, Giacometti).

All this shows that there is a double face to art expressed in the problematological difference of questions and answers. Enigmatic figurality coexists with realistic and representational answers as the two faces of the same coin.

The questioning model is not only an interpretative one but also the basis of artistic production through the ages. History imposes increased differentiation, hence increased realism. This explains the success of some forms of art at a given epoch: the opera in the eighteenth and the nineteenth centuries, while Beethoven's symphonies flourished alongside romantic music, the realistic novel in France, the impressionist and abstract forms of paintings at the end of the nineteenth century. And cinema came, as the most realistic form of art, leading creative literature (Joyce, Kafka, Borgès, Proust) to more allegorical forms of expression, as in painting or sculpture.

This paper was meant as an essay. As such, it should lead to controversy and discussion, i.e., questioning. It has no specific bibliography. It would be without purpose or help in this matter. The only aim of such an article is to honor Jaakko Hintikka's achievement in original thinking by offering something provocative as his own thought has always been. Other considerations would be superfluously academic in my mind. I only hope not to shock too many of the readers here by taking such a liberty with their habits, but that is how I now conceive of making philosophy.

MICHEL MEYER

UNIVERSITY OF BRUSSELS
JANUARY 2001

NOTES

1. Adorno. *Aesthetic Theory*, trans. C. Lenhardt (London and New York: Routledge, 1984), p. 176.

2. Ibid., p. 177.

3. Ibid., p. 178.

4. Ibid., pp.178–79.

5. Ibid. p. 185.

6. See my contribution in *Histoire de la rhétorique des Grecs à nos jours*, ed. Michel Meyer (Paris: Hachette, Le Livre de Poche, Biblio-Essais, 1999), p. 289.

7. G. Conte, *Latin Literature* (Baltimore: Johns Hopkins University Press, 1994).

8. M. Zink, *Introduction à la littérature française du Moyen Age* (Paris: Hachette, Le Livre de Poche), p. 61.

REPLY TO MICHEL MEYER

Michel Meyer and I have been for a long time thinking along the same general lines. We have both seen in questions and questioning not only a philosophical method (perhaps the philosophical method), but the archetypal form of philosophical activity. Michel Meyer has put forward this vision in his problematology,[1] while I have sought to develop an explicit theory of questioning activity in the form of what I have called the interrogative model of inquiry. We have both traced our ideas back to Socrates. An apparent difference is that I have been dealing in the first place with knowledge-seeking inquiry while Meyer has emphasized the general applicability of the questioning idea in many different walks of life and letters. His eloquent and provocative essay might at first sight have little to do with my philosophical work. In a deeper sense, it can nevertheless be considered an important challenge to me.

I would like to view Meyer's essay as posing the unspoken question as to whether my ideas of questioning as the essence of knowledge-seeking can be extended beyond epistemology, for instance, to the arts. This is a genuine problem. I find attempts at such generalization congenial, but that does not automatically mean that they are in fact feasible.

Are they feasible? Is some approach like the interrogative model applicable in the realm of the aesthetic? A detailed and reasoned answer would require writing a learned treatise, which for a variety of reasons I cannot do here and now. What I can do is to indicate what form or forms such an application of the logic and semantics of questions and questioning to the arts might take.

In his essay Meyer discusses from the vantage point of a questioning model relatively large-scale issues such as the nature of literary genres and their relation to each other. I have in my earlier work explored comprehensive analogies between entire artistic and philosophical movements, such as a partial analogy between cubism and phenomenology proposed in my paper "Concept as Vision."[2] However, I am convinced that the most direct applications of the interrogative model are likely to be on a much more detailed level, namely, on the level of the interpretation of actual works of art, be they literary works or works of fine art. Simply by asking the questions that the logic of questions and answers leads us to we are *ipso facto* engaged in interpreting a work of art, and much of actual interpretation activity can be understood as tacitly asking precisely such questions. All one has to do, so to speak, is to take Collingwood literally and consider every proposition and every visual representation as an answer to a question. Let us for instance consider a novelist describing a fictional character. If a statement describing such a character is an answer to a question, we often can—and sometimes must— ask what the presupposition of his question is. Insofar as it can be gathered from the text, that presupposition is in a very real sense part of what the writer is conveying to his or her readers. An interpreter can for instance ask: What is the tacit question that a given statement is an answer to? Is the presupposition of this question stated in so many words in the text? Is the author simply assuming that his reader will know what this presupposition is and accept it? Why is he asking this particular question and none of the others whose presuppositions he had available to him? Answers to such questions will be components of any interpretation of the texts, and conversely many existing hermeneutical texts can be thought of as series of such questions.

Moreover the entire description of a fictional character, even when it is scattered over different pages of the story in question, can be thought of as an answer to the principal question "Who is that character?" Insofar as we can take the writer as giving us a full (conclusive) answer, it must satisfy the writer's criteria of conclusiveness. And these criteria are criteria of identity, that is, of what it takes to know who the character in question is. Hence they can tell a lot of what the writer takes to constitute the identity of persons in general. For one small example, when Montaigne says in his self-description that he is describing the whole person, that very description shows what he took that "whole person" to include.

Thus asking and answering even the very simplest questions prompted by the interrogative logic is an integral—and important—part of the process of understanding a literary work of art. And this is not restricted to questions concerning persons. We can for instance understand a study like Erich Auerbach's *Mimesis*[3] concerning different people's and different periods' conception of reality by looking at the tacit questions that in a literary text are being asked and answered, including their presuppositions and the conclusiveness criteria of their answers.

Similar remarks can be made about pictorial representation. It is little more than common sense to say that what a painter chose to include in his or her portrait shows what the painter thought of as expressing the sitter's character. However, what is not trivial is that this point is at bottom nothing more and nothing less than a consequence of the basic logic of questions and answers.

A modest personal experience may illustrate what I mean. Once I was in the Rembrandt room of the Hermitage Museum in St. Petersburg. Suddenly it struck me how very expressively the hands of one of the models were depicted. I looked at another portrait, and found the representation of the sitter's hands was equally revealing. As I could say in my erotetic logician's jargon, in answering the principal questions of the character of the subject, Rembrandt obviously used as one of the operative questions: What are his or her hands like? I ended up spending forty minutes in that single room going back and forth among different portraits and examining how Rembrandt depicted the hands of different sitters as a part of his attempt to convey a general impression of them visually.

I agree with Michel Meyer that there are many ways in which questions and questioning—and problematology, I feel free to say—can be brought to bear on the appreciation and the study of art. If I were to try to do so, I would begin at the grassroots level, at the level of an application of the basic notions of the logic of questions and answers to the interpretation of works of art.

J. H.

NOTES

1. See Michel Meyer, *De la problématologie* (Sprimont: Pierre Mardaga, 1986); also Michel Meyer, *Questionnement et historicité* (Paris: Presses Universitaires de France, 2000).

2. Reprinted in *The Intentions of Intentionality* (1975).

3. Erich Auerbach, *Mimesis. Die dargestellte Wirklichkeit in der abendländischen Literatur* (Bern: A. Francke, 1946).

PART THREE

BIBLIOGRAPHY OF THE WRITINGS OF JAAKKO HINTIKKA

Compiled and edited by

Lynne Sullivan

on the basis of earlier bibliographies by Olav Flo and Radu Bogdan

BIBLIOGRAPHY OF THE WRITINGS OF JAAKKO HINTIKKA

A. BOOKS

1953

(a) *Distributive Normal Forms in the Calculus of Predicates.* Acta Philosophica Fennica 6. Helsinki: Philosophical Society of Finland.

1955

(a) *Two Papers on Symbolic Logic.* Acta Philosophica Fennica 8. Helsinki: Philosophical Society of Finland. (Includes "Form and Content in Quantification Theory," 11–55, and "Reductions in the Theory of Types," 57–115.)

1962

(a) *Knowledge and Belief: An Introduction to the Logic of the Two Notions.* Ithaca: Cornell University Press. (Appears in Japanese translation, translated by Shigeo Nagai and Taneomi Uchida, Tokyo: Kinokuni ya Bookstore, 1975. Appears in Spanish translation as *Saber y Creer: Una introdución a la lógica de las dos nociones*, translated by Joan J. Acero, Madrid: Editorial Tecnos, 1979. Also appears as a new reprint edition, edited by Vincent F. Hendricks and John Symons, London: King's College Publications, 2005.)

1966

(a) Edited with Patrick Suppes. *Aspects of Inductive Logic.* Amsterdam: North-Holland Publishing Co.

1969

(a) *Models for Modalities.* Dordrecht: D. Reidel Publishing Co.
(b) *Tieto on valtaa: ja muita aatehistoriallisia esseitä* (*"Knowledge is Power" and Other Essays in the History of Ideas*). Helsinki: Werner Söderström Osakeyhtiö.
(c) Edited. *Philosophy of Mathematics.* Oxford: Clarendon Press.
(d) Edited with Donald Davidson. *Words and Objections: Essays on the Work of W. V. Quine.* Dordrecht: D. Reidel Publishing Co.

1970

(a) Edited with Lauri Routila. *Filosofian tila ja tulevaisuus* (*The State and Future of Philosophy*). Tapiola/Helsinki: Weilin+Göös Ab:n kirjapaino.
(b) Edited with Patrick Suppes. *Information and Inference.* Dordrecht: D. Reidel Publishing Co.

1973

(a) *Logic, Language-games, and Information.* Oxford: Clarendon Press. (Appears in Italian translation as, *Logica giochi linguistici e informazione: Temi kantiani nella filosofia della logica*, translated by Marco Mondadori and Paolo Parlavecchia, in the series Biblioteca di filosofia e metodo scientifico 40. Milan: il Saggiatore, 1975.)

(b) *Time and Necessity: Studies in Aristotle's Theory of Modality*. Oxford: Clarendon Press.

(c) Edited with Julius M. E. Moravcsik and Patrick Suppes. *Approaches to Natural Languages: Proceedings of the 1970 Stanford Workshop on Grammar and Semantics*. Dordrecht: D. Reidel Publishing Co.

1974

(a) *Induzione, accettazione, informazione*. Edited and translated by Marco Mondadori and Paolo Parlavecchia, Societa editrice. Bologna: il Mulino.

(b) *Knowledge and the Known: Historical Perspectives in Epistemology*. Dordrecht: D. Reidel Publishing Co.

(c) With Unto Remes. *The Method of Analysis: Its Geometrical Origin and Its General Significance*. Dordrecht: D. Reidel Publishing Co.

1975

(a) *The Intentions of Intentionality and Other New Models for Modalities*. Dordrecht: D. Reidel Publishing Co.

(b) Edited. *Rudolf Carnap, Logical Empiricist: Materials and Perspectives*. Dordrecht: D. Reidel Publishing Co.

1976

(a) *The Semantics of Questions and the Questions of Semantics: Case Studies in the Interrelations of Logic, Semantics and Syntax*. Acta Philosophica Fennica 28, no. 4. Helsinki: Philosophical Society of Finland.

(b) Edited with others. *Essays on Wittgenstein in Honour of G. H. von Wright*. Acta Philosophical Fennica 28, nos.1–3. Helsinki: Philosophical Society of Finland.

1977

(a) With Unto Remes and Simo Knuuttila. *Aristotle on Modality and Determinism*. Acta Philosophica Fennica 29, no. 1. Helsinki: Philosophical Society of Finland.

(b) Edited with Robert Butts. *Proceedings of the Fifth International Congress of Logic, Methodology and Philosophy of Science, London, Ontario, Canada, 1975*. 4 vols. Dordrecht: D. Reidel Publishing Co. (Includes vol. 1, *Logic, Foundations of Mathematics and Computability Theory*; vol. 2, *Foundational Problems in the Special Sciences*; vol. 3, *Basic Problems in Methodology and Linguistics*; vol. 4, *Historical and Philosophical Dimensions of Logic, Methodology and Philosophy of Science*.)

1979

(a) Edited with Ilkka Niiniluoto and Esa Saarinen. *Essays in Mathematical and Philosophical Logic. Proceedings of the 4th Scandinavian Logic Symposium and of the 1st Soviet-Finnish Logic Conference, Jyäskylä, Finland, June 29–July 6, 1976*. Dordrecht: D. Reidel Publishing Co.

1980

(a) *Logical-Epistemological Studies*. Edited by V. N. Sadovski and V. A. Smirnova.

Translated into Russian by V. I. Bryushinkina, et al., in the series Logic and Methodology of Science, edited by V. M. Leontyev. Moscow: Publishing House 'Progress'.

1981

(a) Edited with David Gruender and Evandro Agazzi. *Theory Change, Ancient Axiomatics, and Galileo's Methodology: Probabilistic Thinking, Thermodynamics, and the Interaction of the History and Philosophy of Science. Proceedings of the 1978 Pisa Conference on the History and Philosophy of Science.* Synthese Library. 2 vols. Dordrecht: D. Reidel Publishing Co. (Includes Synthese Library 145 and Synthese Library 146.)

1982

(a) *Kieli ja mieli: Katsauksia kielifilosofiaan ja merkityksen teoriaan (Language and Meaning: Surveys of the Philosophy of Language and the Theory of Meaning).* Helsinki: Otava.

1983

(a) With Jack Kulas. *The Game of Language: Studies in Game-Theoretical Semantics and Its Applications.* Synthese Language Library 22. Dordrecht: D. Reidel Publishing Co. (Second, corrected ed. 1985.)

1984

(a) Edited with Lucia Vaina. *Cognitive Constraints on Communication.* Dordrecht: D. Reidel Publishing Co.

1985

(a) With Jack Kulas. *Anaphora and Definite Descriptions: Two Applications of Game-Theoretical Semantics.* Synthese Language Library 26. Dordrecht: D. Reidel Publishing Co.

(b) Edited with Fernand Vandamme. *Logic of Discovery and Logic of Discourse.* New York: Plenum Press.

1986

(a) With Merrill B. Hintikka. *Investigating Wittgenstein.* Oxford: Basil Blackwell. (Appears in French translation as *Investigations sur Wittgenstein,* translated by Martine Jawerbaum and Yaron Pesztat, edited by Pierre Mardaga, Liège: Mardaga, 1986. In Italian translation as *Indagine su Wittgenstein,* translated by Mario Alai, Bologna: Società editrice il Mulino, 1990. In German translation as *Untersuchungen zu Wittgenstein,* translated by Joachim Schulte, Frankfurt (Main): Suhrkamp Verlag, 1990. In Portuguese translation as *Uma investigação sobre Wittgenstein,* translated by Enid Abreu Dobránszky, São Paulo: Papirus Editora, 1994. Also chapter 1 "Wittgenstein and Language as the Universal Medium" appears in Jaakko Hintikka, *Lingua Universalis vs. Calculus Ratiocinator: An Ultimate Presupposition of Twentieth-Century Philosophy, Selected Papers* II, 162–90. Dordrecht: Kluwer Academic Publishers, 1997.

(b) Edited with Leila Haaparanta. *Frege Synthesized: Essays on the Philosophical and Foundational Work of Gottlob Frege.* Dordrecht: D. Reidel Publishing Co.

(c) Edited with Simo Knuuttila. *The Logic of Being: Historical Studies.* Synthese Historical Library 28. Dordrecht: D. Reidel Publishing Co.

1989

(a) *L'intentionnalité et les mondes possibles*. Translated and introduced by Nadine Lavand, in the series Opuscule 6, edited by André Laks and Jean Quillien. Paris: Presses Universitaires de Lille.
(b) With Merrill Hintikka. *The Logic of Epistemology and the Epistemology of Logic: Selected Essays*. Synthese Library 200. Dordrecht: Kluwer Academic Publishers.

1991

(a) With James Bachman. *What If...? Toward Excellence in Reasoning*. Mayfield: Mountain View.
(b) With Gabriel Sandu. *On the Methodology of Linguistics*. Oxford: Basil Blackwell.
(c) Edited. *Wittgenstein in Florida. Proceedings of the Colloquium on the Philosophy of Ludwig Wittgenstein, Florida State University, 7–8 August 1989*. Dordrecht: Kluwer Academic Publishers. (Reprinted from *Synthese* 87, nos. 1–2, 1991.)

1994

(a) *Fondements d'une théorie du langage*. Translated from English by Nadine Lavand. Paris: Presses Universitaire de France.
(b) *La vérité est-elle ineffable? et autres essais*. Translated from English by Antonia Soulez and Francois Schmitz, Collection 'tiré à part', edited by Jean-Pierre Cometti. Combas: Éditions de l'Éclat.

1995

(a) Edited with Klaus Puhl. *The British Tradition in 20th Century Philosophy. Proceedings of the 17th International Wittgenstein Symposium*. Vienna: Hölder-Pichler-Tempsky.
(b) Edited. *From Dedekind to Gödel: Essays on the Development of the Foundations of Mathematics*. Dordrecht: Kluwer Academic Publishers.

1996

(a) *The Principles of Mathematics Revisited*. Cambridge: Cambridge University Press. (Appears in French translation as *Les Principes des mathématiques revisités*, introduced and translated by M. Rebuschi, with notes by M. Rebuschi, Paris: Librairie Philosophique J. Vrin, 2006.)
(b) *La philosophie des mathématiques chez Kant. La structure de l'argumentation transcendantale*. Translated from English by Corinne Hoogaert, in the series L'interrogation philosophique, edited by Michel Meyer. Paris: Presses Universitaires de France.
(c) *Ludwig Wittgenstein: Half-Truths and One-and-a-Half Truths, Selected Papers* I. Dordrecht: Kluwer Academic Publishers.

1997

(a) *Lingua Universalis vs. Calculus Ratiocinator: An Ultimate Presupposition of Twentieth-Century Philosophy, Selected Papers* II. Dordrecht: Kluwer Academic Publishers.

1998

(a) *Language, Truth and Logic in Mathematics, Selected Papers* III. Dordrecht: Kluwer Academic Publishers.

(b) *Paradigms for Language Theory and Other Essays, Selected Papers* IV. Dordrecht: Kluwer Academic Publishers.
(c) *Questions de logique et de phénoménologie.* Edited by Élisabeth Rigal. Translated by Élisabeth Rigal, et al., in the series Problèmes et Controverses, edited by Jean-François Courtine. Librairie Philosophique. Paris: J. Vrin.
(d) *El viaje filosófico más largo: De Aristóteles a Virginia Woolf.* Translated by Marcelo M.M. Hurtado. Barcelona: Gedisa Editorial.

1999

(a) *Inquiry As Inquiry: Toward a Logic of Scientific Discovery, Selected Papers* V. Dordrecht: Kluwer Academic Publishers.

2000

(a) *On Gödel.* Wadsworth Philosophers Series. Belmont, Calif.: Wadsworth/Thomson Learning.
(b) *On Wittgenstein.* Wadsworth Philosophers Series. Belmont, Calif.: Wadsworth/Thomson Learning.

2001

(a) *Filosofian köyhyys ja rikkaus: Nykyfilosofian kartoitusta* (*The Poverty and Richness of Philosophy: Perspectives on Contemporary Philosophy*). Edited by Janne Hiipakka and Risto Vilkko. Helsinki: Art House Oy.

2003

(a) Edited with T. Czarnecki, K. Kijania-Placek, T. Placek, and A. Rogszczak. *Philosophy and Logic: In Search of the Polish Tradition: Essays in Honour of Jan Woleński on the Occasion of his 60th Birthday.* Synthese Library 323. Dordrecht: Kluwer Academic Publishers.

2004

(a) *Analyses of Aristotle, Selected Papers* VI. Dordrecht: Kluwer Academic Publishers.

2006

(a) *Les Principes des mathématiques revisités.* Introduced and translated by M. Rebuschi, with notes by M. Rebuschi. Paris: Librairie Philosophique J. Vrin.

B. PAPERS

1953

(a) "A New Approach to Sentential Logic." *Societas Scientiarum Fennica, Commentationes Physico-Mathematicae* 17, no. 3.

1954

(a) "An Application of Logic to Algebra." *Mathematica Scandinavia* 2:243–46.

1955

(a)   "Notes on Quantification Theory." *Societas Scientiarum Fennicae, Commentationes Physico-Mathematicae* 17, no. 12.

1956

(a)   "Identity, Variables, and Impredicative Definitions." *Journal of Symbolic Logic* 21: 225–45.

(b)   "Loogisen kielentutkimuksen näköaloja" (Perspectives on the Logical Study of Language). *Ajatus* 19:81–96.

1957

(a)   "Arvokäsitteistä sosiaalitieteiden metodiopissa" (On Value-Concepts in the Methodology of the Social Sciences). *Ajatus* 20:27–47.

(b)   "Modality as Referential Multiplicity." *Ajatus* 20:49–64.

(c)   "Necessity, Universality, and Time in Aristotle." *Ajatus* 20:65–90. (Appears in Finnish translation as "Välttämättömyys, yleisyys ja aika Aristoteleella" in Jaakko Hintikka, *Tieto on valtaa: ja muita aatehistoriallisia esseitä*, 113–32, Helsinki: Werner Söderström Osakeyhtiö, 1969. A much revised version appears in Jaakko Hintikka, *Time and Necessity: Studies in Aristotle's Theory of Modality*, 93–113, Oxford: Clarendon Press, 1973. The revision incorporates most of "A. O. Lovejoy on Plenitude in Aristotle," *Ajatus* 22 [1967]: 5–11. The original version appears in *Articles on Aristotle: Metaphysics*, edited by Jonathan Barnes, Malcolm Schofield, and Richard Sorabji, 108–24, London: Gerald Duckworth and Company, 1979.)

(d)   "Quantifiers in Deontic Logic." *Societas Scientaiarum Fennicae, Commentationes Humanarum Litterarum* 23, no. 4. (Appears also in a greatly expanded form as "Deontic Logic and its Philosophical Morals in *Models for Modalities*, Dordrecht: D. Reidel Publishing Co., 1969.)

(e)   "Vicious Circle Principle and the Paradoxes." *Journal of Symbolic Logic* 22: 245–49.

1958

(a)   "On Wittgenstein's 'Solipsism.'" *Mind* 67:88–91. (Appears also in *Essays on Wittgenstein's Tractatus*, edited by I. M. Copi and R. W. Beard, 157–61, London: Routledge & Kegan Paul, 1966.)

(b)   "Remarks on a Paradox." *Archiv für Rechts- und Sozialphilosophie* 44:514–16.

(c)   "Towards a Theory of Definite Descriptions." *Analysis* 19:79–85.

1959

(a)   "Aristotle and the Ambiguity of Ambiguity." *Inquiry* 2:137–51. (Appears also, in a revised and expanded form, in Jaakko Hintikka, *Time and Necessity: Studies in Aristotle's Theory of Modality*, 1–26, Oxford: Clarendon Press, 1973. This version also incorporates most of "Different Kinds of Equivocation in Aristotle," *Journal of the History of Philosophy* 9 [1971]: 368–72.)

(b)   "An Aristotelian Dilemma." *Ajatus* 22:87–92. (An expanded version under the title "On Aristotle's Modal Syllogistic" appears in Jaakko Hintikka, *Time and Necessity: Studies in Aristotle's Theory of Modality*, 135–46, Oxford: Clarendon Press, 1973.)

(c)   "Existential Presuppositions and Existential Commitments." *Journal of Philosophy* 56:125–37.

(d)   "Filosofian ajankohtaisista ja ajattomista tehtävistä" (On the Timely and Timeless Tasks of Philosophy). *Suomalainen Suomi* 27:538–42.

(e) "Kantin oppi matematiikasta: tutkimuksia sen peruskäsitteistä, rakenteesta ja esikuvista" (Kant's Theory of Mathematics: Studies in its Basic Concepts, Structure, and Precedents). *Ajatus* 22:5–85.

1960

(a) "Aristotle's Different Possibilities." *Inquiry* 3:17–28. (Appears also in *Aristotle: Modern Studies in Philosophy*, edited by Julius M.E. Moravcsik, 34–50, Garden City, N.Y.: Doubleday Anchor Books, 1967. Also in Jaakko Hintikka, *Time and Necessity: Studies in Aristotle's Theory of Modality*, 27–40, Oxford: Clarendon Press, 1973.)

1961

(a) "Cogito, ergo sum, 1–11." *Nya Argus* 54:143–46 and 159–62. (An early Swedish version of "Cogito ergo sum: Inference or Performance?" *Philosophical Review* 71 [1962]: 3–32.)
(b) "Filosofia ja maailmankatsomukset" (Philosophy and *Weltanschauungen*). *Uusi Suomi*, 22 October 1961.
(c) "Käsitteilläkin on kohtalonsa" (Concepts Have Their Fates, Too). *Suomalainen Suomi* 29:459–64. (Appears also in Jaakko Hintikka, *Tieto on valtaa: ja muita aatehistoriallisia esseitä*, 35–46, Helsinki: Werner Söderström Osakeyhtiö, 1969.)
(d) "Modality and Quantification." *Theoria* 27:119–28. (An expanded version appears in Jaakko Hintikka, *Models for Modalities*, 57–70, Dordrecht: D. Reidel Publishing Co., 1969.)

1962

(a) "Cogito, ergo sum: Inference or Performance?" *Philosophical Review* 71:3–32. (Appears also in *Meta-Meditations: Studies in Descartes*, edited by Alexander Sesonke and Noel Fleming, 50–76, Belmont, Calif.: Wadsworth Publishing, 1965. Also in *Descartes: A Collection of Critical Essays*, edited by Willis Doney, 108–39, Notre Dame, Ind.: University of Notre Dame Press, 1968. Also in *Philosophical Applications of Free Logic*, edited by Karel Lambert, 145–70, New York: Oxford University Press, 1991. Appears in Finnish translation as "Ajattelen, olen siis olemassa" in Jaakko Hintikka, *Tieto on valtaa: ja muita aatehistoriallisia esseitä*, 206–34, Helsinki: Werner Söderström Osakeyhtiö, 1969. In Hebrew translation in *From Parmenides to Contemporary Thinkers: An Ontology Reader*, edited by Abraham Zvie Bar-On, 308–32, Jerusalem: Magnes Press, 1977. A modified English version appears in Jaakko Hintikka, *Knowledge and the Known: Historical Perspectives in Epistemology*, 98–125, Dordrecht: D. Reidel Publishing Co., 1974. In French translation, translated by P. Le Quelle-Wolf, in *Philosophie* 6 [1985]: 21–51.)
(b) "Huomioita kreikkalaisten ajankäsityksestä" (Observations on the Concept of Time in Ancient Greek Philosophy). *Ajatus* 24:39–65. (Appears also as "Kreikkalaisten ajankäsityksestä" in Jaakko Hintikka, *Tieto on valtaa: ja muita aatehistoriallisia esseitä*, 88–112, Helsinki: Werner Söderström Osakeyhtiö, 1969.)
(c) "Johdonmukaisen järkevyyden ihanteet: 90-vuotias Bertrand Russell" (The Ideals of Consistent Reasonableness: Bertrand Russell at Ninety). *Uusi Suomi* (18 May 1962).
(d) "Kaksi Spengleriä?" (Spengler Against Himself?) *Suomalainen Suomi* 30: 86–92. (A revised version appears as "Spenglerin itsepeto" in *Filosofian tila ja tulevaisuus*, edited by Jaakko Hintikka and Lauri Routila, 186–94, Tapiola/Helsinki: Oy Weilin+Göös Ab:n kirjapaino, 1970.)
(e) "Kepler ja Galilei" (Kepler and Galileo). *Suomalainen Suomi* 30:278–81.
(f) "Kieliopin uudet tiet" (New Paths in the Study of Grammar). *Suomalainen Suomi* 30: 106–107.

(g) "Miksi hyve oli kreikkalaisten mielestä tietoa?" (Why Was Virtue Knowledge for the Ancient Greeks?) *Suomalainen Suomi* 30:341–49. (Appears also in Jaakko Hintikka, *Tieto on valta: ja muita aatehistoriallisia esseitä*, 59–74, Helsinki: Werner Söderström Osakeyhtiö, 1969.)

(h) "On the Interpretation of 'De Interpretatione xii–xiii.'" *Acta Philosophica Fennica* 14: 5–22. (An expanded version appears in Jaakko Hintikka, *Time and Necessity: Studies in Aristotle's Theory of Modality*, 41–61, Oxford: Clarendon Press, 1973.)

1963

(a) "'Cogito ergo sum' as an Inference and a Performance: Reply to Comments by J. R. Weinberg and J. D. Carney." *Philosophical Review* 72:487–96. (Appears in French translation, translated by P. Le Quellec-Wolff, in *Revue de Métaphysique et de Morale* [2000]: 3–12.)

(b) "Filosofian tehtävästä" (On the Task of Philosophy). *Suomalainen Suomi* 30:379–82.

(c) "The Modes of Modality." In *Proceedings of a Colloquium on Modal and Many-Valued Logics, Helsinki, 23–26 August, 1962. Acta Philosophica Fennica* 16:65–82. (Appears also in Jaakko Hintikka, *Models for Modalities*, 71–86, Dordrecht: D. Reidel Publishing Co., 1969.)

1964

(a) "Aristotle and the 'Master Argument' of Diodorous." *American Philosophical Quarterly* 1:101–14. (Appears with new material in Jaakko Hintikka, *Time and Necessity: Studies in Aristotle's Theory of Modality*, 179–213, Oxford: Clarendon Press, 1973.)

(b) "Definite Descriptions and Self-Identity." *Philosophical Studies* 15:5–7.

(c) "Distributive Normal Forms and Deductive Interpolation." *Zeitschrift fur mathematische Logik und Grundlagen der Mathematik* 10:185–91.

(d) "Galilein kohtalo 400 Vuotta sitten" (The Fate of Galileo 400 Years Ago). *Uusi Suomi* (15 February 1964). (Appears also as "Galilein kohtalo historian ironian ilmauksena" in Jaakko Hintikka, *Tieto on valtaa: ja muita aatehistoriallisia esseitä*, 198–205, Helsinki: Werner Söderström Osakeyhtiö, 1969.)

(e) "The Once and Future Sea Fight: Aristotle's Discussion of Future Contingents in 'De Interpretatione.'" *Philosophical Review* 73:461–92. (Appears in Finnish translation as "Mennyt ja tuleva meritaistelu: Aristoteleen keskustelu tulevaisuutta koskevista satunnaislauseista," translated by Erkka Maula, in Jaakko Hintikka, *Tieto on valtaa: ja muita aatehistoriallisia esseitä*, 166–97, Helsinki: Werner Söderström Osakeyhtiö, 1969. Appears also in Jaakko Hintikka, *Time and Necessity: Studies in Aristotle's Theory of Modality*, 147–78, Oxford: Clarendon Press, 1973. In German translation in *Logik und Erkenntnislehre des Aristoteles*, edited by Fritz-Peter Hager, 259–95, Darmstadt: Wissenschaftliche Buchgesellschaft, 1972. In Spanish translation as "La batalla naval pasada y futura: La discusión de Aristóteles sobre las contingencias futuras en *De Interpretatione IX*," in Jaakko Hintikka, *El viaje filosófico más largo: De Aristóteles a Virginia Woolf*, translated by Marcelo M.M. Hurtado, 57–90, Barcelona: Gedisa Editorial, 1998.)

(f) "Päämäärä, sattuma ja välttämättömyys: eräiden kreikkalaisten ajatustapojen tarkastelua" (Purpose, Chance and Necessity: Observations on Certain Greek Ways of Thinking). *Ajatus* 26:61–81.

(g) "Tieto on valtaa: Eräitä aatehistoriallisia näköaloja" (Knowledge is Power: Reflections on the History of an Idea). *Valvoja* 185–96. (Appears also in Jaakko Hintikka, *Tieto on valtaa: ja muita aatehistoriallisia esseitä*, 19–34, Helsinki: Werner Söderström Osakeyhtiö, 1969.)

1965

(a) "Analyyttisyyden käsitteen eri merkityksistä" (On the Different Senses of the Concept of Analyticity). *Suomalainen Tiedeakatemia,* Esitelmät ja päytäkirjat 1964, Helsinki, 122–37.

(b) "Are Logical Truths Analytic?" *Philosophical Review* 74:178–203. (Appears also in Jaakko Hintikka, *Knowledge and the Known: Historical Perspectives in Epistemology,* 135–59, Dordrecht: D. Reidel Publishing Co., 1974.)

(c) "A Closure and Complement Result for Nested Topologies." *Fundamenta Mathematicae* 57:97–106.

(d) "Distributive Normal Forms in First-Order Logic." In *Formal Systems and Recursive Functions: Proceedings of the Eighth Logic Colloquium, Oxford, July 1963,* edited by J. N. Crossley and M.A.E. Dummett, 47–90. Amsterdam: North-Holland Publishing Co. (Appears also in Jaakko Hintikka, *Logic, Language Games and Information,* 242–86, Oxford: Clarendon Press, 1973. Appears in Italian translation as "Forme normali distributive nella logica del primordine," in Jaakko Hintikka, *Linguistici e informazione: Temi kantiani nella filosofia della logica,* translated by Marco Mondadori and Paolo Parlavecchia, in the series Biblioteca di filosofia e metodo scientifico 40, 266–313, Milan: il Saggiatore, 1975. In Russian translation in Jaakko Hintikka, *Logical-Epistemological Studies* edited by V. N. Sadovski and V. A. Smirnova, translated by V. I. Bryushinkina, et al., in the series Logic and Methodology of Science, edited by V. M. Leontyev, 105–57, Moscow: Publishing House 'Progress', 1980.)

(e) "Kant's 'New Method of Thought' and his Theories of Mathematics." *Ajatus* 27: 37–47. (Appears also in Jaakko Hintikka, *Knowledge and the Known: Historical Perspectives in Epistemology,* 126–34, Dordrecht: D. Reidel Publishing Co., 1974. Appears in French translation as "La 'nouvelle façon de penser' de Kant et sa théorie des mathématiques" in *La philosophie des mathematiques chez Kant. La structure de l'argumentation transcendantale,* translated from English by Corinne Hoogaert, in the series L'interrogation philosophique, edited by Michel Meyer, 23–34, Paris: Presses Universitaires de France, 1996.)

(f) "On a Combined System of Inductive Logic." In *Studia Logico-mathematica et Philosophica in Honorem Rolf Nevanlinna,* 21–30. Helsinki.

(g) "Tieto, taito ja päämäärä: Kaksi tutkielmaa vanhojen kreikkalaisten tiedonkäsitteestä" (Knowledge, Skill, and Purpose: Two Studies on the Ancient Greek Concept of Knowledge). *Ajatus* 27:49–67. (Also reprinted in part as "Knowing How, Knowing That, and Knowing What: Observations on their Relation in Plato and other Greek Philosophers" in *Modality, Morality and Other Problems of Sense and Nonsense: Studies Dedicated to Sören Hallden,* edited by Bengt Hansson, 1–12, Lund: C.W.K. Gleerup, 1973. Also part of expanded version of above appears as "Plato on Knowing How, Knowing That, and Knowing What" in *Knowledge and the Known: Historical Perspectives in Epistemology,* 31–49, Dordrecht: D. Reidel Publishing Co., 1974.)

(h) "Towards a Theory of Inductive Generalization." In *Proceedings of the 1964 International Congress for Logic, Methodology and Philosophy of Science,* edited by Yehoshua Bar-Hillel, 274–88. Amsterdam: North-Holland Publishing Co.

1966

(a) "An Analysis of Analyticity." In *Deskription, Analytizität und Existenz: 3–4 Forschungsgepräch des Internationalen Forschungszentrums für Grundfragen der Wissenschaften Salzburg,* edited by Paul Weingartner, 193–214. Salzburg and Munich: Pustet. (Appears also in *Sitzungsberichte der Finnischen Akademie der Wissenschaften* 1964, 101–122. Also in Jaakko Hintikka, *Logic, Language Games and Information,*

123–49, Oxford: Clarendon Press, 1973. Appears in Italian translation as "Una analisi dell'analiticità," in Jaakko Hintikka, *Logica giochi linguistici e informazione: Temi kantiani nella filosofia della logica*, translated by Marco Mondadori and Paolo Parlavecchia, 140–66, in the series Biblioteca di filosofia e metodo scientifico 40, Milan: il Saggiatore, 1975.)

(b) "Are Logical Truths Tautologies?" In *Deskription, Analytizität und Existenz: 3–4 Forschungsgepräch des Internationalen Forschungszentrums für Grundfragen der Wissenschaften Salzburg*, edited by Paul Weingartner, 215–33. Salzburg and Munich: Pustet. (Appears also in Jaakko Hintikka, *Logic, Language Games and Information*, 150–73, Oxford: Clarendon Press, 1973. Appears in Italian translation as "Le verità logiche sono tautologie?" in Jaakko Hintikka, *Logica giochi linguistici e informazione: Temi kantiani nella filosofia della logica*, translated by Marco Mondadori and Paolo Parlavecchia, 167–92, in the series Biblioteca di filosofia e metodo scientifico 40, Milan: il Saggiatore, 1975. In French translation as "Les vérités logiques sont-elles des tautologies?" *La philosophie des mathematiques chez Kant. La structure de l'argumentation transcendantale*, translated from English by Corinne Hoogaert, in the series L'interrogation philosophique, edited by Michel Meyer, 171–200, Paris: Presses Universitaires de France, 1996.)

(c) "Aristotelian Infinity." *Philosophical Review* 75:197–219. (Appears also in Jaakko Hintikka, *Time and Necessity: Studies in Aristotle's Theory of Modality*, 114–34, Oxford: Clarendon Press, 1973. Also in *Articles on Aristotle: Metaphysics*, edited by Jonathan Barnes, Malcolm Schofield and Richard Sorabji, 125–39, London: Gerald Duckworth and Company, 1979.)

(d) "Individen och statens ändamål." *Ajatus* 28:23–37. (In Swedish: "The Individual and the Aims of the State.") (Appears in English translation as "Some Conceptual Presuppositions of Greek Political Theory," translated by Jaakko Hintikka, *Scandinavian Political Studies* 2 [1967]: 11–25. Appears again in Finnish as "Yksilö ja valtion päämäärät: Eräitä kerikkalaisten ajattelutapojen piirteitä," translated by Jaakko Hintikka, in Jaakko Hintikka, *Tieto on valtaa: ja muita aatehistoriallisia esseitä*, 75–87, Helsinki: Werner Söderström Osakeyhtiö, 1969.)

(e) "Kant Vindicated." In *Deskription, Analytizität und Existenz: 3–4 Forschungsgepräch des Internationalen Forschungszentrums für Grundfragen der Wissenschaften Salzburg*, edited by Paul Weingartner, 234–53. Salzburg and Munich: Pustet. (Appears also in Jaakko Hintikka, *Logic, Language Games and Information*, 174–98, Oxford: Clarendon Press, 1973. Appears in Italian translation as "Kant rivisitato," in Jaakko Hintikka, *Logica giochi linguistici e informazione: Temi kantiani nella filosofia della logica*, translated by Marco Mondadori and Paolo Parlavecchia, 193–219, in the series Biblioteca di filosofia e metodo scientifico 40, Milan: il Saggiatore, 1975. In French translation as "Justification des thèses kantiennes" in *La philosophie des mathematiques chez Kant. La structure de l'argumentation transcendantale*, translated from English by Corinne Hoogaert, 201–32, in the series L'interrogation philosophique, edited by Michel Meyer, Paris: Presses Universitaires de France, 1996.)

(f) "Kant and the Tradition of Analysis." In *Deskription, Analytizität und Existenz: 3–4 Forschungsgepräch des Internationalen Forschungszentrums für Grundfragen der Wissenschaften Salzburg*, edited by Paul Weingartner, 254–72. Salzburg and Munich: Pustet. (Appears also in Jaakko Hintikka, *Logic, Language Games and Information*, 199–221, Oxford: Clarendon Press, 1973. Appears in Italian translation as "Kant e la tradizione dell'analisi," in Jaakko Hintikka, *Logica giochi linguistici e informazione: Temi kantiani nella filosofia della logica*, translated by Marco Mondadori and Paolo Parlavecchia, 220–43, in the series Biblioteca di filosofia e metodo scientifico 40, Milan: il Saggiatore, 1975. In French translation as "Kant et la tradition de l'analyse" in *La philosophie des mathematiques chez Kant. La structure de l'argumentation transcendantale*, translated from English by Corinne Hoogaert, 233–60, in the series

L'interrogation philosophique, edited by Michel Meyer, Paris: Presses Universitaires de France, 1996.)

(g) "Knowing Oneself and Other Problems in Epistemic Logic." *Theoria* 32:1–13.

(h) "Kommunikaatiovälineet ja yleinen kulttuurikehitys" (Methods of Communication and General Cultural Development). *Parnasso* 16:21–27. (Appears also in Jaakko Hintikka, *Tieto on valtaa: ja muita aatehistoriallisia esseitä*, 9–18, Helsinki: Werner Söderström Osakeyhtiö, 1969.)

(i) "Parmenideen peruslause ja kreikkalaisten tiedonkäsitys" (The Axiom of Paramenides and the Ancient Greek Concept of Knowledge). *Valvoja* 86:138–46.

(j) "Semanttisen informaation teoriasta" (On the Theory of Semantic Information). *Arkhimedes* 18:12–22. (Appears also in Jaakko Hintikka, *Kieli ja mieli: Katsauksia kielifilosofiaan ja merkityksen teoriaan*, 234–55, Helsinki: Otava, 1982.)

(k) "Studies in the Logic of Existence and Necessity: Existence." *Monist* 50:55–76. (A revised version appears as "Existential Presuppositions and their Elimination" in Jaakko Hintikka, *Models for Modalities*, 23–44, Dordrecht: D. Reidel Publishing Co., 1969.)

(l) "A Two-Dimensional Continuum of Inductive Methods." In *Aspects of Inductive Logic*, edited by Jaakko Hintikka and Patrick Suppes, 113–32. Amsterdam: North-Holland Publishing Co.

(m) "Yhteiskunta-ja käyttäytymistieteet" (Social and Behavioral Sciences). *Luotain* 5: 16–23. (Appears also as "Yhteiskunta- ja käyttäytymistieteiden metodinen tila," in *Filosofian tila ja tulevaisuus*, edited by Jaakko Hintikka and Lauri Routila, 175–85, Tapiola/ Helsinki: Weilin+Göös Ab:n kirjapaino, 1970.)

(n) With Risto Hilpinen. "Knowledge, Acceptance, and Inductive Logic." In *Aspects of Inductive Logic*, edited by Jaakko Hintikka and Patrick Suppes, 1–20. Amsterdam: North-Holland Publishing Co.

(o) With Juhani Pietarinen. "Semantic Information and Inductive Logic." In *Aspects of Inductive Logic*, edited by Jaakko Hintikka and Patrick Suppes, 96–112. Amsterdam: North-Holland Publishing Co.

1967

(a) "A. O. Lovejoy on Plenitude in Aristotle." *Ajatus* 29:5–11. (Also incorporated into "Aristotle on the Realization of Possibilities in Time" in Jaakko Hintikka, *Time and Necessity: Studies in Aristotle's Theory of Modality*, 93–113, Oxford: Clarendon Press, 1973. Appears also in *Philosophy*, no. 106, Bobbs-Merrill Reprints.)

(b) "Existence and Identity in Epistemic Contexts: A Comment on Føllesdal's Paper." *Theoria* 33:138–47.

(c) "Individuals, Possible Worlds, and Epistemic Logic." *Nous* 1:33–62.

(d) "Kant on the Mathematical Method." *Monist* 51:352–75. (Appears in Finnish translation as "Kant ja matemaattinen metodi," translated by Irma Korte, in Jaakko Hintikka, *Tieto on valtaa: ja muita aatehistoriallisia esseitä*, 235–59, Helsinki: Werner Söderström Osakeyhtiö, 1969. Appears also in *Kant's Philosophy of Mathematics*, edited by Carl J. Posy, 21–42, Dordrecht: Kluwer Academic Publishers, 1992. Also in Jaakko Hintikka *Knowledge and the Known: Historical Perspectives in Epistemology*, 160–83, Dordrecht: D. Reidel Publishing Co., 1974. In French translation as "Kant et la méthode mathématique" in *La philosophie des mathematiques chez Kant. La structure de l'argumentation transcendantale*, translated from English by Corinne Hoogaert, in the series L'interrogation philosophique, edited by Michel Meyer, 105–34, Paris: Presses Universitaires de France, 1996. In Spanish translation as, "Las reflexiones de Kant sobre el método de la matemática" in Jaakko Hintikka, *El viaje filosófico más largo: De Aristóteles a Virginia Woolf*, translated by Marcelo M.M. Hurtado, 157–85, Barcelona: Gedisa Editorial, 1998.)

(e) "Luovat mahdollisuudet ja päätöksenteko" (Creative Possibilities and Decision Making). In *Aikamme kaksi kulttuuria*, edited by Eero Saarenheimo, 96–103. Helsinki: Werner Söderström Oy.

(f) "New Essays on Old Philosophers." *Inquiry* 10:101–13.

(g) "A Program and a Set of Concepts for Philosophical Logic." *Monist* 51:69–92. (Appears with some small changes, as "Logic in Philosophy—Philosophy of Logic," in Jaakko Hintikka, *Logic, Language Games and Information*, 1–25, Oxford: Clarendon Press, 1973. Appears in Italian translation as "Logica nella filosofia e filosofia della logica," in Jaakko Hintikka, *Logica giochi linguistici e informazione: Temi kantiani nella filosofia della logica*, translated by Marco Mondadori and Paolo Parlavecchia, 11–35, in the series Biblioteca di filosofia e metodo scientifico 40, Milan: il Saggiatore, 1975. In Russian translation in Jaakko Hintikka, *Logical-Epistemological Studies*, edited by V. N. Sadovski and V. A. Smirnova, translated by V. I. Bryushinkina, et al., 35–67, in the series Logic and Methodology of Science, edited by V. M. Leontyev, Moscow: Publishing House 'Progress,' 1980.)

(h) "Some Conceptual Presuppositions of Greek Political Theory." *Scandinavian Political Studies* 2:11–25. (Appears in Finnish as "Yksilö ja valtion päämäärät," *Ajatus* 28: 23–37. Also in Finnish in Jaakko Hintikka, *Tieto on valtaa: ja muita aatehistoriallisia esseitä*, 75–87, Helsinki: Werner Söderström Osakeyhtiö, 1969.)

(i) "Suomen filosofisen tutkimuksen tila ja tavoitteet" (The State and the Aims of Philosophical Research in Finland). *Ajatus* 29:11–25.

(j) "Time, Truth, and Knowledge in Ancient Greek Thought." *American Philosophical Quarterly* 4:1–14. (Appears under the title "Time, Truth, and Knowledge in Aristotle and Other Greek Philosophers" in Jaakko Hintikka, *Time and Necessity: Studies in Aristotle's Theory of Modality*, 62–92, Oxford: Clarendon Press, 1973. In addition to small changes, a new section and a half have been added to it here. Also appears under the title "Time, Truth, and Knowledge in Aristotle and Other Greek Philosophers," in Jaakko Hintikka, *Knowledge and the Known: Historical Perspectives in Epistemology*, 50–79, Dordrecht: D. Reidel Publishing Co., 1974. The version in *Knowledge and the Known* appears in Russian translation in Jaakko Hintikka, *Logical-Epistemological Studies*, edited by V. N. Sadovski and V. A. Smirnova, translated by V. I. Bryushinkina, et al., 392–429, in the series Logic and Methodology of Science, edited by V. M. Leontyev, Moscow: Publishing House 'Progress,' 1980.)

1968

(a) "Are Mathematical Truths Synthetic a Priori?" *Journal of Philosophy* 65:640–51. (Appears also as "A Priori Truths and Things-in-Themselves" in Jaakko Hintikka, *Knowledge and the Known: Historical Perspectives in Epistemology*, 184–96, Dordrecht: D. Reidel Publishing Co., 1974. Appears in French translation as "Les vérités *a priori* et les choses en soi" in *La philosophie des mathematiques chez Kant. La structure de l'argumentation transcendantale*, translated from English by Corinne Hoogaert, in the series L'interrogation philosophique, edited by Michel Meyer, 135–50, Paris: Presses Universitaires de France, 1996.)

(b) "Behavioral Criteria of Radical Translation." *Synthese* 19:69–81. (Appears also in *Words and Objections: Essays on the Work of W. V. Quine*, edited by Donald Davidson and Jaakko Hintikka, 69–81, Dordrecht: D. Reidel Publishing Co., 1969. A longer version appears in Jaakko Hintikka, *Logic, Language Games and Information*, 83–97, Oxford: Clarendon Press, 1973. Appears in Italian translation as "Criteri comportamentali per la traduzione radicale: un commento a *Parola e Oggetto* di W. V. Quine," in Jaakko Hintikka, *Logica giochi linguistici e informazione: Temi kantiani nella filosofia della logica*, translated by Marco Mondadori and Paolo Parlavecchia, 98–114, in the series Biblioteca di filosofia e metodo scientifico 40, Milan: il Saggiatore, 1975.)

(c) "Conditionalization and Information." *Synthese* 19:303–6.

(d) "Epistemic Logic and the Methods of Philosophical Analysis." *Australian Journal of Philosophy* 46:37–51. (Also appears in Jaakko Hintikka, *Models for Modalities*, 3–22, Dordrecht: D. Reidel Publishing Co., 1969.)

(e) "Filosofinen ja mietekirjallisuus." In *Suomen Kirjallisuus VII: Kirjallisuuden kenttä*, edited by Matti Kuusi, 399–433. Helsinki: Suomalaisen Kirjallisuuden Seura ja Otava, 1968. ("Philosophical and meditative literature," in *Literature in Finland*.)

(f) "Induction by Enumeration and Induction by Elimination." In *The Problem of Inductive Logic. Proceedings of the International Colloquium in the Philosophy of Science, London, 1965*, edited by Imre Lakatos, 191–216. Amsterdam: North-Holland Publishing Co.

(g) "Language-Games for Quantifiers." In *Studies in Logical Theory*, edited by Nicholas Rescher, 46–72. American Philosophical Quarterly Monograph Series 2. Oxford: Basil Blackwell. (A longer version appears in Jaakko Hintikka, *Logic, Language Games and Information*, 53–82, Oxford: Clarendon Press, 1973. Appears in Italian translation as "Giochi linguistici per i quantificatori," in Jaakko Hintikka, *Logica giochi linguistici e informazione: Temi kantiani nella filosofia della logica*, translated by Marco Mondadori and Paolo Parlavecchia, 11–35, in the series Biblioteca di filosofia e metodo scientifico 40, Milan: il Saggiatore, 1975. In Russian translation in Jaakko Hintikka, *Logical-Epistemological Studies*, edited by V. N. Sadovski and V. A. Smirnova, translated by V. I. Bryushinkina, et al., in the series Logic and Methodology of Science, edited by V. M. Leontyev [Moscow: Publishing House 'Progress,' 1980], 245–58.)

(h) "Logic and Philosophy." In *Contemporary Philosophy – La philosophie contemporaine* 1, edited by R. Klibansky, 3–30. Florence: La Nuova Italia Editrice.

(i) "Meaning as Multiple Reference." In *Proceedings of the Fourteenth International Congress of Philosophy* 1, 340–45. Vienna: Hölder-Verlag. (Appears also as "Semantics for Propositional Attitudes" in *Philosophical Logic*, edited by W. Davis et al., 21–45, Dordrecht: D. Reidel Publishing Co., 1968.)

(j) "On Semantic Information." In *Physics, Logic and History: Proceedings of the International Colloquium on Logic, Physical Reality, and History, University of Denver*, edited by W. Yourgrau, 147–68. New York: Plenum Press.

(k) "The Possibility of Acceptance Rules." In *The Problem of Inductive Logic: Proceedings of the International Colloquium in the Philosophy of Science, London 1965*, vol. 2, edited by Imre Lakatos, 98–119. Amsterdam: North-Holland Publishing Co.

(l) "Reply." In *The Problem of Inductive Logic. Proceedings of the International Colloquium in the Philosophy of Science, London, 1965*, vol. 2, edited by Imre Lakatos, 223–31. Amsterdam: North-Holland Publishing Co.

(m) "Review: *The Encyclopedia of Philosophy*. Paul Edwards, Editor-in-Chief. London/ New York: Collier-Macmillan/ The Macmillan Co., 1967, vols. 1-8." *Synthese* 19 (1968–69): 466–69.

(n) "The Varieties of Information and Scientific Explanation." In *Logic, Methodology, and Philosophy of Science III: Proceedings of the 1967 International Congress*, edited by B. van Rootselaar and J. F. Staal, 151–71. Amsterdam: North-Holland Publishing Co. (Appears also in Jaakko Hintikka, *Inquiry As Inquiry: Toward a Logic of Scientific Discovery, Selected Papers* V, 205–26, Dordrecht: Kluwer Academic Publishers, 1999.)

1969

(a) "Deontic Logic and its Philosophical Morals." In *Models for Modalities*, 184–214. Dordrecht: D. Reidel Publishing Co.

(b)   "Inductive Independence and the Paradoxes of Confirmation." In *Essays in Honor of Carl G. Hempel*, edited by Nicholas Rescher et al., 24–46. Dordrecht: D. Reidel Publishing Co.

(c)   "Leibniz, Plentitude, Relations and the 'Reign of Law.'" *Ajatus* 31:117–44. (Also appears in *Leibniz: A Collection of Critical Essays*, edited by H. Frankfurt, 155–90, Garden City, N.J.: Anchor Books, 1972.)

(d)   "On Kant's Notion of Intuition (Anschauung)." In *The First Critique: Reflections on Kant's Critique of Pure Reason*, edited by Terrence Penelhum and J. J. Macintosh, 38–53. Belmont, Calif.: Wadsworth. (Appears in French translation as "La notion d'intuition chez Kant *(Anschauung)*" in *La philosophie des mathematiques chez Kant. La structure de l'argumentation transcendantale*, translated from English by Corinne Hoogaert, 55-80, in the series L'interrogation philosophique, edited by Michel Meyer, Paris: Presses Universitaires de France, 1996.)

(e)   "On the Logic of Perception." In *Perception and Personal Identity*, edited by Norman S. Care and Robert H. Grimm, 140–75. Cleveland, Ohio: Case Western Reserve University Press. (Appears also in Jaakko Hintikka, *Models for Modalities*, 151–83, Dordrecht: D. Reidel Publishing Co, 1969.)

(f)   "On the Logic of the Ontological Argument: Some Elementary Remarks." In *The Logical Way of Doing Things*, edited by Karel Lambert, 185–97. New Haven: Yale University Press. (Appears also in Jaakko Hintikka, *Models for Modalities*, 45–56, Dordrecht: D Reidel Publishing Co, 1969.)

(g)   "Partially Transparent Senses of Knowing." *Philosophical Studies* 20:4–8.

(h)   "Quantification Theory and the Picture Theory of Language." *Monist* 55:204–30. (Appears also in Jaakko Hintikka, *Logic, Language Games and Information*, 26–52, Oxford: Clarendon Press, 1973. Appears in Italian translation as "La quantificazione e la teoria raffigurativa del linguaggio," in Jaakko Hintikka, *Logica giochi linguistici e informazione: Temi kantiani nella filosofia della logica*, translated by Marco Mondadori and Paolo Parlavecchia, 36–65, in the series Biblioteca di filosofia e metodo scientifico 40, Milan: il Saggiatore, 1975.)

(i)   "Semantics for Propositional Attitudes." In *Philosophical Logic*, edited by W. Davis et al., 21–45. Dordrecht: D. Reidel Publishing Co. (Appears also in Jaakko Hintikka, *Models for Modalities*, 87–111, Dordrecht: D. Reidel Publishing Co., 1969. Appears in French translation as "Sémantique des attitudes propositionnelles," translated by J. Savatovsky, in *Sujet, Forme, Sens* 13 [1985]: 87–124. Again in French translation as "Une sémantique adaptée aux attitudes propositionnelles" in Jaakko Hintikka, *L'intentionnalité et les mondes possibles*, translated and introduced by Nadine Lavand, 37–64, in the series Opuscule 6, edited by André Laks and Jean Quillien, Paris: Presses Universitaires de Lille, 1989. In Russian translation in Jaakko Hintikka, *Logical-Epistemological Studies*, edited by V. N. Sadovski and V. A. Smirnova, translated by V. I. Bryushinkina, et al., in the series Logic and Methodology of Science, edited by V. M. Leontyev [Moscow: Publishing House 'Progress,' 1980], 68–104. An abbreviated and modified version appears as "Meaning as Multiple Reference" in *Proceedings of the Fourteenth International Congress of Philosophy* I, 340–45, Vienna: Verlag-Herder, 1968.)

(j)   "Statistics, Induction and Lawlikeness: Comments on Dr. Vetter's Paper." *Synthese* 20: 72–85.

(k)   "Tieteen metodi analyyttisena toimituksena" (Scientific Method as an Analytical Procedure). In *Societas Scientiarum Fennica, Yearbook*, 95B, no. 2. Helsinki, 1969. (Appears also in Jaakko Hintikka, *Tieto on valtaa: ja muita aatehistoriallisia esseitä*, 272–91, Helsinki: Werner Söderström Osakeyhtiö, 1969.)

(l)   "Wittgenstein on Private Language: Some Sources of Misunderstanding." *Mind* 78: 423–25. (Appears also in *The Philosophy of Wittgenstein, Vol. 5: The Private*

Language Argument, edited by John V. Canfield, 149–51, New York: Garland Publishing, 1986.)

1970

(a) "Creative Process, Crystallization and Cumulation?" In *Scientists at Work: Festschrift in Honour of Herman Wold*, edited by Tore Dalenius et al., 62–65. Stockholm: Almqvist och Wiksell.

(b) "Existential Presuppositions and Uniqueness Presuppositions." In *Philosophical Problems in Logic: Some Recent Developments. Proceedings of the Irvine Colloquium, May 1968*, edited by K. Lambert, 20–55. Dordrecht: D. Reidel Publishing Co. (Appears also in Jaakko Hintikka, *Models for Modalities*, 112–51, Dordrecht: D. Reidel Publishing Co., 1969.)

(c) "Filosofian looginen välineistö" (Logical Tools of Philosophy). In *Filosofian tila ja tulevaisuus*, edited by Jaakko Hintikka and Lauri Routila, 195–220. Tapiola/ Helsinki: Weilin+Göös Ab:n kirjapaino.

(d) "Inductive Generalization and Its Problems: A Comment on Kronthaler's Comment." *Theory and Decision* 1:393–98.

(e) "Information, Deduction, and the A Priori." *Nous* 4:131–52. (Appears also in Jaakko Hintikka, *Logic, Language Games and Information*, 222–41, Oxford: Clarendon Press, 1973. Appears in Italian translation as "Inforimazione, deduzione e a priori," in Jaakko Hintikka, *Logica giochi linguistici e informazione: Temi kantiani nella filosofia della logica*, translated by Marco Mondadori and Paolo Parlavecchia, 244–65, in the series Biblioteca di filosofia e metodo scientifico 40, Milan: il Saggiatore, 1975. In Russian translation in Jaakko Hintikka, *Logical-Epistemological Studies*, edited by V. N. Sadovski and V. A. Smirnova, translated by V. I. Bryushinkina, et al., 158–79, in the series Logic and Methodology of Science, edited by V. M. Leontyev, Moscow: Publishing House 'Progress,' 1980. In French translation as "L'information, la déduction et l' *a priori*" in *La philosophie des mathematiques chez Kant. La structure de l'argumentation transcendantale*, translated from English by Corinne Hoogaert, 261–84, in the series L'interrogation philosophique, edited by Michel Meyer, Paris: Presses Universitaires de France, 1996.)

(f) "'Knowing That One Knows' Reviewed." *Synthese* 21:141–62.

(g) "Knowledge, Belief, and Logical Consequence." *Ajatus* 32:32–47. (Appears also in Jaakko Hintikka, *The Intentions of Intentionality and Other New Models for Modalities*, 179–91, Dordrecht: D. Reidel Publishing Co., 1975.)

(h) "Kolme itävaltalaista rautatieasemaa ja kiinalainen onnenpeli: Huomioita Grazin filosofikokouksesta 1-4.10.1970" (Three Austrian Railway-stations and a Chinese Game of Chance: Observations From the Meinong-Colloquium in Graz, 1-4 October 1970). *Parnasso* 20:512–15.

(i) "Kontinuumiongelma ja joukko-opin aksiomatiikan probleemat" (The Continuum Problem and the Problems of Axiomatic Set Theory). *Arkhimedes* 22:1–7.

(j) "Kybernetiikka ja yhteishuntatieteiden metodologia" (Cybernetics and the Methodology of Social Sciences). *Sosiologia* 7:217–25.

(k) "Nykyinen logiikka filosofian apuvälineenä" (Modern Logic as a Tool in Philosophy). In *Logiikka ja matematiikka-Studia Logica et Mathematica*, 41–60. Porvoo-Helsinki: Werner Söderström Oy.

(l) "Objects of Knowledge and Belief: Acquaintances and Public Figures." *Journal of Philosophy* 67:869–83. (Appears also in Jaakko Hintikka, *The Intentions of Intentionality and Other New Models for Modalities*, 43–58, Dordrecht: D. Reidel Publishing Co., 1975. Appears in French translation as "Les objects de la connaissance et de la croyance, accointances et personnes de notoriété publique" in Jaakko Hintikka,

L'intentionnalité et les mondes possibles, translated and introduced by Nadine Lavand, 65–84, in the series Opuscule 6, edited by André Laks and Jean Quillien, Paris: Presses Universitaires de Lille, 1989.)

(m) "On Attributions of 'Self-Knowledge.'" *Journal of Philosophy* 67:73–87.

(n) "On Kant's Background." *Ajatus* 31:164–70.

(o) "On Semantic Information." In *Information and Inference*, edited by Jaakko Hintikka and Patrick Suppes, 3–27. Dordrecht: D. Reidel Publishing Co.

(p) "Philosophy of Science (Wissenschaftstheorie) in Finland." *Zeitschrift für allgemeine Wissenschaftstheorie* 1:119–32.

(q) "'Prima Facie' Obligations and Iterated Modalities." *Theoria* 36:232–40.

(r) "The Semantics of Modal Notions and the Indeterminacy of Ontology." *Synthese* 21: 408–24. (Appears also in Jaakko Hintikka, *The Intentions of Intentionality and Other New Models for Modalities*, 26–42, Dordrecht: D. Reidel Publishing Co., 1975. Also in *The Semantics of Natural Language*, Synthese Library, edited by Donald Davidson and Gilbert Harman, 398–414, Dordrecht: D. Reidel Publishing Co., 1972.)

(s) "Statistics, Induction and Lawlikeness: Comments on Dr. Vetter's Paper." In *Induction, Physics, and Ethics. Proceedings and Discussions of the 1968 Salzburg Colloquium in the Philosophy of Science*, edited by P. Weingartner and G. Zech, 91–102. Dordrecht: D. Reidel Publishing Co.

(t) "Surface Information and Depth Information." In *Information and Inference*, edited by Jaakko Hintikka and Patrick Suppes, 263–97. Dordrecht: D. Reidel Publishing Co. (Appears also in Russian translation in Jaakko Hintikka, *Logical-Epistemological Studies*, edited by V. N. Sadovski and V. A. Smirnova, translated by V. I. Bryushinkina, et al., 182–227, in the series Logic and Methodology of Science, edited by V. M. Leontyev, Moscow: Publishing House 'Progress,' 1980.)

(u) "Two Studies in Probability." In *Reports from the Institute of Philosophy, University of Helsinki*, (1970). (Includes [1] "Unknown Probabilities, Bayesianism and de Finetti's Representation Theorem," 2–25. [This study also appears in *In Memory of Rudolf Carnap*, edited by Roger C. Buck and Robert S. Cohen, 325–41, Boston Studies in the Philosophy of Science 8, Dordrecht: D. Reidel Publishing Co.] [2] "Probability as a Decision – Theoretical Concept," 26–45. [3] "A Short Working Bibliography on Probability and Induction," 46–58.)

(v) With Raimo Tuomela. "Towards a General Theory of Auxiliary Concepts and Definability in First-order Theories." In *Information and Inference*, edited by Jaakko Hintikka and Patrick Suppes, 298–330. Dordrecht: D. Reidel Publishing Co.

1971

(a) "Different Kinds of Equivocation in Aristotle." *Journal of the History of Philosophy* 9:368–72.

(b) "Inductive Generalization and Its Problem: A Comment on Kronthaler's Comment." *Theory and Decision* 1:393–98.

(c) "Knowledge and its Objects in Plato." *Ajatus* 33:168–200. (Appears also in *Patterns of Plato's Thought*, edited by Moravcsik, 1–30, Dordrecht: D. Reidel Publishing Co., 1973. Also in Jaakko Hintikka, *Knowledge and the Known: Historical Perspectives in Epistemology*, 1–31, Dordrecht: D. Reidel Publishing Co., 1974. Appears in Russian translation in Jaakko Hintikka, *Logical-Epistemological Studies*, edited by V. N. Sadovski and V. A. Smirnova, translated by V. I. Bryushinkina, et al., 355–91, in the series Logic and Methodology of Science, edited by V. M. Leontyev, Moscow: Publishing House 'Progress,' 1980.)

(d) "The 'Lottery Paradox' and the Concept of Shared Information." *Ajatus* 33:266–70.

(e) "On Defining Information." *Ajatus* 33:271–73.

(f) "On the Ingredients of an Aristotelian Science." *Reports from the Institute of Philosophy: University of Helsinki*, no. 3 (1971). (An early version of "On the Ingredients of an Aristotelian Science," *Nous* 6 [1972]: 55–69.)

(g) "Semantics for the Propositional Attitudes." In *Reference and Modality*, edited by Leonard Linsky, 145–67. London/New York: Routledge & Kegan Paul.

(h) "Some Main Problems of Deontic Logic." In *Deontic Logic: Introductory and Systematic Readings*, edited by Risto Hilpinen, 59–104. Dordrecht: D. Reidel Publishing Co.

(i) "Sosa on Propositional Attitudes de dicto and de re." *Journal of Philosophy* 68: 489–97.

(j) With Risto Hilpinen. "Rules of Acceptance, Indices of Lawlikeness, and Singular Inductive Inference: Reply to a Critical Discussion." *Philosophy of Science* 38: 303–7.

1972

(a) "Concept as vision. Todellisuuden esittämisen ongelmasta modernissa kuvataiteessa ja modernissa filosofiassa" (On the Problem of Representation in Modern Art and Modern Philosophy). *Aika* 66:133–46. (Appears also in Jaakko Hintikka, *Kieli ja mieli: Katsauksia kielifilosofiaan ja merkityksen teoriaan*, 7–10, Helsinki: Otava, 1982. Appears in English translation in Jaakko Hintikka, *The Intentions of Intentionality and Other New Models for Modalities*, 223–51, Dordrecht: D. Reidel Publishing Co., 1975.)

(b) "Constituents and Finite Identifiability." *Journal of Philosophical Logic* 1:45–52.

(c) "Different Constructions in Terms of the Basic Epistemological Concepts: A Survey of Some Problems and Proposals." In *Contemporary Philosophy in Scandinavia*, edited by Raymond Olsen and Anthony M. Paul, 105–22. Baltimore and London: The Johns Hopkins Press. (Appears also in Jaakko Hintikka, *The Intentions of Intentionality and Other New Models for Modalities*, 1–25, Dordrecht: D. Reidel Publishing Co., 1975. Appears in French translation as "Les diverses constructions admises par les principaux terms du champ épistémologique" in Jaakko Hintikka, *L'intentionnalité et les mondes possibles*, translated and introduced by Nadine Lavand, 85–112, in the series Opuscule 6, edited by André Laks and Jean Quillien, Paris: Presses Universitaires de Lille, 1989.)

(d) "Die Intentionen der Intentionalität." *Neue Hefte für Philosophie*. Netherlands: Martinus Nijhoff Publishers. (Appears in English translation as "The Intentions of Intentionality," in *Essays on Explanation and Understanding*, edited by Juha Manninen and Raimo Tuomela, Dordrecht: D. Reidel Publishing Co., 1975. Also in English translation in Jaakko Hintikka, *The Intentions of Intentionality and Other New Models for Modalities*, 192–223, Dordrecht: D. Reidel Publishing Co., 1975. In Finnish translation as "Intentionaalisuuden intentiot" in Jaakko Hintikka, *Kieli ja mieli: Katsauksia kielifilosofiaan ja merkityksen teoriaan*, 68–106, Helsinki: Otava, 1982. In Japanese translation, in *Die Perspective der Phänomenologie*, edited by H. Rombach and L. Landgrobe et al., 255–307, Tokyo: Orion Press, 1986. In French translation as "Les intentions de l'intentionnalité" in Jaakko Hintikka, *L'intentionnalité et les mondes possibles*, translated and introduced by Nadine Lavand, 141–80 in the series Opuscule 6, edited by André Laks and Jean Quillien, Paris: Presses Universitaires de Lille, 1989.)

(e) "Kantian Intuitions." *Inquiry* 15:341–45.

(f) "Knowledge by Acquaintance—Individuation by Acquaintance." In *Bertrand Russell: A Collection of Critical Essays*, edited by David Pears, 52–79. Garden City, N.J.: Anchor Books/ Doubleday and Co. (Appears also in Jaakko Hintikka, *Knowledge and the Known: Historical Perspectives in Epistemology*, 212–35, Dordrecht: D. Reidel Publishing Co., 1974. Appears in German translation in *Jenseits von Sein und Nichtsein: Beiträge zur Meinong Forschung*, edited by R. Haller, 205–21, Akademische Druck und Verlagsanstalt. In French translation as "Connaissance par accointance, individualization par accointance" in Jaakko Hintikka, *L'Intentionnalité et les mondes possibles*, translated and introduced by Nadine Lavand, 113–40, in the series *Opuscule* 6, edited by André Laks and Jean Quillien, Paris: Presses Universitaires de Lille, 1989.)

(g) "Leibniz on Plenitude, Relations, and the Reign of Law." In *Leibniz: A Collection of Critical Essays*, edited by Harry Frankfurt, 155–90. Garden City, N.J.: Anchor Books, Doubleday and Co. (Appears also in *Ajatus* 31:117–44.)

(h) "Mitä on kybernetiikka?" (What is Cybernetics?) In *Mitä-Missä-Milloin: Kansalaisen vuosikirja* 23, edited by Paul Kojo et al., 294–95. Helsinki: Otava.

(i) "On the Ingredients of an Aristotelian Science." *Nous* 6:55–69.

(j) "Transcendental Arguments: Genuine and Spurious." *Nous* 6:274–81.

(k) "Valtasuhteet, määräenemmistösuhteet ja parlamentarismin luonne" (Power Relations, Qualified Majority Rules, and the Nature of Parliamentary Democracy). *Aika* 66: 406–11.

(l) "Some Main Problems in Epistemic Logic: Two Comments." *Ajatus* 34:144–48.

1973

(a) "Aristotle on the Realization of Possibilities in Time." In Jaakko Hintikka, *Time and Necessity: Studies in Aristotle's Theory of Modality*, 93–113. Oxford: Clarendon Press. (A fuller version of "Necessity, Universality and Time in Aristotle," *Ajatus* 20 [1957]: 65–90.)

(b) "Carnap's Semantics in Retrospect." *Synthese* 25:372–97. (Appears also as "Carnap's Heritage in Logical Semantics," in Jaakko Hintikka, *The Intentions of Intentionality and Other New Models for Modalities*, 76–101, Dordrecht: D. Reidel Publishing Co., 1975. Appears again as "Carnap's Heritage in Logical Semantics," in *Rudolf Carnap, Logical Empiricist: Materials and Perspectives*, edited by Jaakko Hintikka, 217–42, Dordrecht: D. Reidel Publishing Co., 1975. Appears in Finnish translation as "Carnapin perinne loogisessa semantiikassa" in Jaakko Hintikka, *Kieli ja mieli: Katsauksia kielifilosofiaan ja merkityksen teoriaan*, 32–67, Helsinki: Otava, 1982.)

(c) "Grammar and Logic: Some Borderline Problems." In *Approaches to Natural Languages*, edited by Jaakko Hintikka, Julius M. E. Moravcik and Patrick Suppes, 197–214. Dordrecht: D. Reidel Publishing Co. (Revised version appears in Jaakko Hintikka, *The Intentions of Intentionality and Other New Models for Modalities*, 159–78, Dordrecht: D. Reidel Publishing Co., 1975.)

(d) "Knowing How, Knowing That, and Knowing What: Observations on Their Relation in Plato and Other Greek Philosophers." In *Modality, Morality, and Other Problems of Sense and Nonsense: Essays Dedicated to Sören Halldén*, edited by C.W.K. Gleerup, 1–12. Lund. (An amended, enlarged version appears in Jaakko Hintikka, *Knowledge and the Known: Historical Perspectives in Epistemology*, 31–50, Dordrecht: D. Reidel Publishing Co., 1974.)

(e) "On the Different Ingredients of an Empirical Theory." In *Logic, Methodology, and the Philosophy of Science* III, edited by Patrick Suppes et al., 313–22. Amsterdam: North-Holland Publishing Co.

(f) "Quantifiers, Language-games, and Transcendental Arguments." In *Logic and Ontology*, edited by Milton K. Munitz, 37–57. New York: New York University Press. (Appears also in Jaakko Hintikka, *Logic, Language Games and Information*, 98–122, Oxford: Clarendon Press, 1973. Appears in Italian translation as "Quantificatori, giochi linguistici e argomenti trascendentali" in Jaakko Hintikka, *Logica giochi linguistici e informazione: Temi kantiani nella filosofia della logica*, translated by Marco Mondadori and Paolo Parlavecchia, 114–39, in the series Biblioteca di filosofia e metodo scientifico 40, Milan: il Saggiatore, 1975. In Russian in Jaakko Hintikka, *Logical-Epistemological Studies*, edited by V. N. Sadovski and V. A. Smirnova, translated by V. I. Bryushinkina, et al., 281–309, in the series Logic and Methodology of Science, edited by V. M. Leontyev, Moscow: Publishing House 'Progress,' 1980.)

(g) "Quantifiers vs. Quantification Theory." *Dialectica* 27:329–58. (Appears also in *Linguistic Inquiry* 5 (1974): 153–77. Also in *Game Theoretical Semantics: Essays on Semantics by Hintikka, Carlson, Peacocke, Rantala, and Saarinen*, edited by Esa Saarinen, 49–80, Dordrecht: D. Reidel Publishing Co., 1979.)

(h) "Remarks on *Poiesis, Praxis* and *Ergon* in Plato and Aristotle." In *Studia Philosophica in Honorem Sven Krohn*, edited by Timo Airaksinen and Risto Hilpinen, 53–62. Turku: Turun Yliopisto.

(i) "Surface Semantics: Definition and its Motivation." In *Truth, Syntax, and Modality: Proceedings of the Temple University Conference on Alternative Semantics*, edited by Hughes Leblanc, 128–47. Amsterdam: North-Holland Publishing Co.

(j) "Theoretical Terms from Ramsey's Reductions: Outline of Scientific Logic" (in Russian). Translated by V. A. Markov. In *Scientific Lectures for Higher Education: Philosophy of Science*: 49–61.

(k) With Ilkka Niiniluoto. "On the Surface Semantics of Proof Procedures." *Ajatus* 35: 197–215.

1974

(a) "Concept as Vision." *Iyyun* 25:139–57. (Translation into Hebrew of an early version of "Concept as Vision: On the Problem of Representation in Modern Art and in Modern Philosophy," in *The Intentions of Intentionality and Other New Models for Modalities*, 223–51, Dordrecht: D. Reidel Publishing Company, 1975.)

(b) "'Dinge an Sich' Revisited." In *Akten des 4. Internationalen Kant-Kongresses*, Mainz, 6–10 April 1974, Teil 1, hg. Gerhard Funke and Joachim Kopper, 86–96. Berlin: Walter de Gruyter. (Appears also in Jaakko Hintikka *Knowledge and the Known: Historical Perspectives in Epistemology*, 197–211, Dordrecht: D. Reidel Publishing Co. Appears in French translation as "La notion de *Dinge an sich* reconsidérée" in *La philosophie des mathematiques chez Kant. La structure de l'argumentation transcendantale*, translated from English by Corinne Hoogaert, 285–304, in the series L'interrogation philosophique, edited by Michel Meyer, Paris: Presses Universitaires de France, 1996.)

(c) "Logic, Philosophy of." In *Encyclopedia Britannica* 11. Edited by Helen Hemingway Benton, 72–77. Chicago, 1974.

(d) "Logiikka ja kielitieteen vallankumous" (Logic and the Revolution in Linguistics). In *Suomalainen Tiedeakatemia, esitelmät ja pöytäkirjat 1973*. The Finnish Academy of Science and Letters, 1974.

(e) "On the Proper Treatment of Quantifiers in Montague Semantics." In *Logical Theory and Semantic Analysis: Essays dedicated to Stig Kanger on his Fiftieth Birthday*, edited by Sören Stenlund, 45–60. Dordrecht: D. Reidel Publishing Co. (Appears also in Jaakko Hintikka, with Merrill Hintikka, *The Logic of Epistemology and the Epistemology of Logic: Selected Essays*, 97–112, Synthese Library 200, Dordrecht: Kluwer Academic Publishers, 1989.)

(f) "Practical vs. Theoretical Reason: An Ambiguous Legacy." In *Proceedings of the 1972 Bristol Colloquium on Practical Reason*, edited by Stephan Körner, 83–102. Oxford: Basil Blackwell. (Appears also in Jaakko Hintikka, *Knowledge and the Known*, 80–97, Dordrecht: D. Reidel Publishing Co., 1974. Appears in Spanish translation as "Razón práctica versus razón teórica: Un legado ambiguo," *Teorema* 6 [1976]: 213–47.)

(g) "Questions on Questions." In *Semantics and Philosophy*, edited by Milton K. Munitz

and Peter Unger, 103–58. New York: New York University Press.
(h) "Reply to Dorothea Frege." *Synthese* 28:91–96.
(i) "Transparent Knowledge Once Again." *Philosophical Studies* 24:125–27.
(j) With Lauri Carlson. "Conditionals, Generic Quantifiers and Other Applications of Subgames." In *Meaning and Use*, edited by A. Margalit, 179–214. Dordrecht: D. Reidel Publishing.

1975

(a) "Answers to Questions." In *The Intentions of Intentionality and Other New Models for Modalities*, 137–58. Dordrecht: D. Reidel Publishing Co. (Appears also in *The Semantics of Questions and the Questions of Semantics: Case Studies in the Inter-relations of Logic, Semantics and Syntax. Acta Philosophica Fennica* 28, no. 4 [1976]: 41–60. Also in *Questions*, edited by Henry Hiż, 279–300, Dordrecht: D. Reidel Publishing Co., 1978.)
(b) "Carnap and Essler versus Inductive Generalization." *Erkenntnis* 9 (1995): 235–44.
(c) "Comment on Professor Bergström." *Theoria* 41:35–38.
(d) "Concept as Vision: On the Problem of Representation in Modern Art and in Modern Philosophy." In *The Intentions of Intentionality and Other New Models for Modalities*, 223–51. Dordrecht: D. Reidel Publishing Co. (Partly based on an earlier essay in Finnish which appeared in *Aika* [1972]: 133–46. Appears in French translation as "Le concept comme vision, à propos des problems de la représentation dans l'art moderne et la philosophie contemporaine" in *La vérité est-elle ineffable? et autres essais*, translated from English by Antonia Soulez and Francois Schmitz, Collection 'tiré à part', edited by Jean-Pierre Cometti, Éditions de l'Éclat, Combas, 1994, 95–121.)
(e) "A Counterexample to Tarski-type Truth-definitions as Applied to Natural Languages." *Philosophia* 5:207–12.
(f) "G. H. von Wright on Logical Truth." In *The Philosophy of G. H. von Wright*. Edited by Paul Schilpp, 25–39. La Salle, Ill.: Open Court.
(g) "Impossible Possible Worlds Vindicated." *Journal of Philosophical Logic* 4:475–84. (An extended version appears in *Game Theoretical Semantics*, edited by Esa Saarinen, 367–79, Dordrecht: D. Reidel Publishing Co., 1979. Appears also in Russian translation in Jaakko Hintikka, *Logical-Epistemological Studies*, edited by V. N. Sadovski and V. A. Smirnova, translated by V. I. Bryushinkina, et al., in the series Logic and Methodology of Science, edited by V. M. Leontyev, 228–42, Moscow: Publishing House 'Progress,' 1980. Also in Jaakko Hintikka, with Merrill Hintikka, *The Logic of Epistemology and the Epistemology of Logic: Selected Essays*, Synthese Library 200, Dordrecht: Kluwer Academic Publishers, 1989, 63–72.)
(h) "Quine on Quantifying: A Dialogue." In *The Intentions of Intentionality and Other New Models for Modalities*, 102–36. Dordrecht: D. Reidel Publishing Co. (Appears in Finnish translation as "Quine ja kvanttorit" in Jaakko Hintikka, *Kieli ja mieli: Katsauksia kielifilosofiaan ja merkityksen teoriaan*, 107–60, Helsinki: Otava, 1982.
(i) With Veikko Rantala. "Systematizing Definability Theory." In *Proceedings of the Third Scandinavian Logic Symposium, Uppsala, April 1973*, edited by Stig Kanger, 40–62. Amsterdam: North-Holland Publishing Co.
(j) With Unto Remes. "Ancient Geometrical Analysis and Modern Logic." In *Essays in Memory of Imre Lakatos*, edited by R. S. Cohen et al., 253–76. Dordrecht: D. Reidel Publishing Co.
(k) With Esa Saarinen. "Semantical Games and the Bach-Peters Paradox." *Theoretical Linguistics* 2:1–20. (Also appears in *Game Theoretical Semantics*, edited by Esa Saarinen, 153–78, Dordrecht: D. Reidel Publishing Co., 1979.)

1976

(a)   "Back to Frege? A reply to Dr. Potts." In *Proceedings of the Bristol Colloquium on Philosophical Logic*, edited by Stephan Körner. Oxford: Basil Blackwell.

(b)   "Gaps in the Great Chain of Being: An Exercise in the Methodology of the History of Ideas." *Proceedings and Addresses of the American Philosophical Association* 49: 22–38. (Also appears in *Reforging the Great Chain of Being*, edited by S. Knuuttila, 1–17, Dordrecht: D. Reidel Publishing Co., 1981. Appears in Finnish as "Olevaisen suuren ketjun aukot: Havaintoesimerkki aatehistorian periaateongelmista," translated by Markku Enval, *Ajatus* 40 (1983): 1–19. Reprinted in Finnish in *Filosofian köyhyys ja rikkaus: Nykyfilosofian kartoitusta*, edited by Janne Hiipakka and Risto Vilkko, 366–88, Helsinki: Art House Oy, 2001.)

(c)   "Information, Causality, and the Logic of Perception." *Ajatus* 36:76–94. (Appears also in Jaakko Hintikka, *The Intentions of Intentionality and Other New Models for Modalities*, 59–75, Dordrecht: D. Reidel Publishing Co., 1975.)

(d)   "Language-games." In *Essays on Wittgenstein in Honour of G. H. von Wright*, edited by Jaakko Hintikka, et al. *Acta Philosophica Fennica* 28, nos. 1–3:105–25. (Appears also in *Dialectica* 31 (1977): 225–45. Also in *The Philosophy of Wittgenstein*, edited by John V. Canfield, *Vol. 6: Meaning*, 231–51, New York: Garland Publishing, 1986. Also in *Game Theoretical Semantics*, edited by Esa Saarinen, 1–27, Dordrecht: D. Reidel Publishing Co., 1979. Also in Jaakko Hintikka, *Ludwig Wittgenstein: Half-Truths and One-and-a-Half-Truths, Selected Papers* I, 275–95, Dordrecht: Kluwer Academic Publishers, 1996. Appears in Finnish translation as "Wittgensteinin kielipelit" in Jaakko Hintikka, *Kieli ja mieli: Katsauksia kielifilosofiaan ja merkityksen teoriaan*, 161–83, Helsinki: Otava, 1982.)

(e)   "Partially Ordered Quantifiers vs. Partially Ordered Ideas." *Dialectica* 30:89–99.

(f)   "Possible Worlds Semantics as a Framework for Critical and Comparative Philosophy." In *Contemporary Aspects of Philosophy*, edited by Gilbert Ryle, 57–69. London: Routledge & Kegan Paul.

(g)   "The Prospects of Convention T." *Dialectica* 30:61–66. (Appears in French translation as "L'avenir de la convention T," in *Fondements d'une théorie du langage*, translated from English by Nadine Lavand, 128–35, Paris: Presses Universitaire de France, 1994.)

(h)   "Quantifiers in Logic and Quantifiers in Natural Language." In *Philosophy of Logic: Proceedings of the 1974 Bristol Colloquium*, edited by Stephan Körner, 208–32. Oxford: Basil Blackwell. (Appears also in *Game Theoretical Semantics*, edited by Esa Saarinen, 27–49, Dordrecht: D. Reidel Publishing Co., 1979.)

(i)   "The Question of Question Mark: A Comment on Urs Egli." *Dialectica* 30:101–3.

(j)   "Quine vs. Peirce?" *Dialectica* 30:7–8.

(k)   "Who is Afraid of Ludwig Wittgenstein? Reply to Professor Fogelin." In *Proceedings of the Bristol Colloquium on Philosophical Logic*, edited by Stephan Körner. Oxford: Basil Blackwell.

(l)   With Heikki Kannisto. "Kant on 'The Great Chain of Being' or the Eventual Realization of all Possibilities: A Comparative Study." *Philosophic Exchange* 2:69–85.

(m)   With Ilkka Niiniluoto. "An Axiomatic Foundation for the Logic of Inductive Generalization." In *Formal Methods in the Methodology of Empirical Sciences*, edited by M. Przțęcki, et al., 57–81. Dordrecht: D. Reidel Publishing Co. (Appears also in *Studies in Inductive Logic and Probability* 2, edited by Richard C. Jeffrey, 157–81, Berkeley: University of California Press, 1980.)

(n)   With Veikko Rantala. "A New Approach to Infinitary Languages." *Annals of Mathematical Logic* 10:95–115.

(o)   With Unto Remes. "Ancient Geometrical Analysis and Modern Logic." In *Essays in*

Memory of Imre Lakatos, edited by R. Cohen and M. Wartofsky, 253–76. Dordrecht: D. Reidel Publishing Co.

1977

(a) "Quantifiers in Natural Languages: Some Logical Problems II." *Linguistics and Philosophy* 1:153–72. (Appears also in *Game Theoretical Semantics*, edited by Esa Saarinen, 81–118, Dordrecht: D. Reidel Publishing Co., 1979.)
(b) "The Ross Paradox as Evidence for Reality of Semantical Games." *Monist* 60: 370–79. (Appears also in *Game Theoretical Semantics*, edited by Esa Saarinen, 329–46, Dordrecht: D. Reidel Publishing Co., 1979.)
(c) With Lauri Carlson. "Pronouns of Laziness in Game-theoretical Semantics." *Theoretical Linguistics* 4:1–29.

1978

(a) "Aristotle's Incontinent Logician." *Ajatus* 37:48–65.
(b) "Degrees and Dimensions of Intentionality." *Versus: Quaderni di studi semiotici* 19: 73–76. (Appears also in Jaakko Hintikka, with Merrill Hintikka, *The Logic of Epistemology and the Epistemology of Logic: Selected Essays*, Synthese Library 200, 183–204, Dordrecht: Kluwer Academic Publishers, 1989. In French translation as "Degrés et dimensions de l'intentionnalité" in Jaakko Hintikka, *L'intentionnalité et les mondes possibles*, translated and introduced by Nadine Lavand, in the series Opuscule 6, edited by André Laks and Jean Quillien, 181–208, Paris: Presses Universitaires de Lille, 1989.)
(c) "A Discourse on Descartes' Method." In *Descartes: Critical and Interpretative Essays*, edited by Michael Hooker, 74–88. Baltimore: Johns Hopkins University Press. (In Spanish translation as, "Un discurso sobre el método de Descartes" in Jaakko Hintikka, *El viaje filosófico más largo: De Aristóteles a Virginia Woolf*, translated by Marcelo M.M. Hurtado, 93–111, Barcelona: Gedisa Editorial, 1998.)
(d) With Merrill Provence (Hintikka). "Wittgenstein on Privacy and Publicity." In *Wittgenstein and His Impact on Contemporary Thought*, edited by Elisabeth Leinfellner et al., 353–62. Vienna: Hölder-Pichler-Tempsky. (The same material is used, much revised, in Jaakko Hintikka, with Merrill B. Hintikka, *Investigating Wittgenstein*, Oxford: Basil Blackwell, 1986.)

1979

(a) "Frege's Hidden Semantics." *Revue Internationale de Philosophie* 33:716–22.
(b) "'Is', Semantical Games, and Semantical Relativity." *Journal of Philosophical Logic* 8:433–68. (Appears also in *Game Theoretical Semantics*, edited by Esa Saarinen, 161–200, Dordrecht: D. Reidel Publishing Co. Appears in Russian translation in Jaakko Hintikka, *Logical-Epistemological Studies*, edited by V. N. Sadovski and V. A. Smirnova, translated by V. I. Bryushinkina, et al., 310–51, in the series Logic and Methodology of Science, edited by V. M. Leontyev, Moscow: Publishing House 'Progress,' 1980. Also in Jaakko Hintikka, *Paradigms for Language Theory and Other Essays, Selected Papers* IV, 71–106, Dordrecht: Kluwer Academic Publishers, 1998.)
(c) "Quantifiers in Natural Languages: Some Logical Problems." In *Game-Theoretical Semantics*, edited by Esa Saarinen, 81–117. Dordrecht: D. Reidel Publishing Co.
(d) "Quantifiers in Natural Language: Some Logical Problems I." In *Essays in Mathematical and Philosophical Logic,* edited by Jaakko Hintikka, Ilkka Niiniluoto and Esa Saarinen, 295–314. Dordrecht: D. Reidel Publishing Co. (Appears also as the first part

of "Quantifiers in Natural Languages: Some Logical Problems," in *Game-Theoretical Semantics*, edited by Esa Saarinen, Dordrecht: D. Reidel Publishing Co., 1979.)

(e) "Rejoinder to Peacocke." In *Game-theoretical Semantics*, edited by Esa Saarinen, 135–51. Dordrecht: D. Reidel Publishing Co.

(f) "Virginia Woolf and our Knowledge of the External World." *Journal of Aesthetics and Art Criticism* 38:5–14. (Appears in French translation as "Virginia Woolf et notre connaissance du monde estérieur" in Jaakko Hintikka *La vérité est-elle ineffable? et autres essais*, translated from English by Antonia Soulez and Francois Schmitz, Collection 'tiré à part', edited by Jean-Pierre Cometti, 73–94, Combas: Éditions de l'Éclat, 1994. In Spanish as "Virginia Woolf y nuestro conocimiento del mundo externo," in Jaakko Hintikka, *El viaje filosófico más largo: De Aristóteles a Virginia Woolf*, translated by Marcelo M.M. Hurtado, 266–84, Barcelona: Gedisa Editorial, 1998.)

(g) With Lauri Carlson. "Conditionals, Generic Quantifiers, and other Applications of Subgames." In *Meaning and Use*, edited by Avishai Margalit, 179–214, Dordrecht: D. Reidel Publishing Co. (Appears also in *Game Theoretical Sematics*, edited by Esa Saarinen, 179–214, Dordrecht: D. Reidel Publishing Co., 1979.)

(h) With Esa Saarinen. "Information-seeking Dialogues: Some of their Logical Properties." *Studia Logica* 38:355–63.

1980

(a) "Aristotelian Induction." *Revue Internationale de Philosophie* 34:422–39.

(b) "C. S. Peirce's 'First Real Discovery' and its Contemporary Relevance." *Monist* 63: 304–15.

(c) "Degrees and Dimensions of Intentionality." In *Language, Logic, and Philosophy. Proceedings of the Fourth International Wittgenstein Symposium, 28th August to 2nd September, 1979*, edited by Rudolf Haller and Wolfgang Grassl, 283–96. Vienna: Holder-Pichler-Tempsky. (Also appears in Jaakko Hintikka, with Merrill Hintikka, *The Logic of Epistemology and the Epistemology of Logic: Selected Essays*, 183–205, Synthese Library 200, Dordrecht: Kluwer Academic Publishers. Appears in French translation as "Degrés et dimensions de l'intentionnalité" in Jaakko Hintikka, *L'intentionnalité et les mondes possibles*, translated and introduced by Nadine Lavand, in the series Opuscule 6, edited by André Laks and Jean Quillien, 181–208, Paris: Presses Universitaires de Lille, 1989.)

(d) "In What Sense can Values be Absolute?" In *Proceedings of the Eighth International Conference on the Unity of Sciences*, 35–39. New York, 1980.

(e) "On the *Any*-thesis and the Methodology of Linguistics." *Linguistics and Philosophy* 4:101–22. (Appears also in Jaakko Hintikka, with Jack Kulas, *The Game of Language: Studies in Game-Theoretical Semantics and Its Applications*, 231–58, Synthese Language Library 22, Dordrecht: D. Reidel Publishing Co., 1983. [Second, corrected ed. 1985.] Appears in French translation as "A propos de la thèse on sur *any* et de la méthodologie de la linguistique," in *Fondements d'une théorie du langage*, translated from English by Nadine Lavand, 98–127, Paris: Presses Universitaire de France, 1994. Also in Jaakko Hintikka, *Paradigms for Language Theory and Other Essays, Selected Papers* IV, 124–45, Dordrecht: Kluwer Academic Publishers, 1998.)

(f) "On Sense, Reference, and the Objects of Knowledge." *Epistemologia* 3:143–64. (Appears also in Jaakko Hintikka, with Merrill Hintikka, *The Logic of Epistemology and the Epistemology of Logic, Selected Essays*, 45–61, Synthese Library 200, Dordrecht: Kluwer Academic Publishers, 1989.)

(g) "Parmenides' Cogito Argument." *Ancient Philosophy* 1:5–16.

(h) "Philosophy in Finland since 1945." In *Handbook of World Philosophy*, edited by John R. Burr, 15–32. Westport, Conn.: Greenwood Press.

(i) "Standard vs. Nonstandard Logic: Higher-order, Modal, and First Order Logics." In *Modern Logic*, edited by Evandro Agazzi, 283–96. Dordrecht: D. Reidel Publishing Co. (Also appears in Jaakko Hintikka, *Language, Truth and Logic in Mathematics, Selected Papers* III, 130–43, Dordrecht: Kluwer Academic Publishers, 1998. Appears in French translation as "Où la distinction standard/non-standard se trouve transportée des logiques d'order supérieur á un á la logique modale, et á la logique du primier ordre" in *Fondements d'une théorie du langage*, translated from English by Nadine Lavand, 252–70, Paris: Presses Universitaire de France, 1994.)

(j) "Theories of Truth and Learnable Languages." In *Philosophy and Grammar: Papers on the Occasion of the Quincentennial of Uppsala University*, edited by Stig Kanger and Sven Ohman, 37–57. Dordrecht: D. Reidel Publishing Co. (An expanded version appears in Jaakko Hintikka, with Jack Kulas, *The Game of Language: Studies in Game-Theoretical Semantics and Its Applications*, 259–92, Synthese Language Library 22, Dordrecht: D. Reidel Publishing Co., 1983. [Second, corrected ed. 1985.])

(k) With Merrill B. Hintikka. "Different Language-games in Wittgenstein." In *Language, Logic, and Philosophy: Proceedings of the Fourth International Wittgenstein Symposium*, edited by Rudolf Haller and Wolfgang Grassl, 417–22. Vienna: Hölder-Pichler-Tempsky. (Appears also in Jaakko Hintikka, *Ludwig Wittgenstein: Half-Truths and One-and-a-Half-Truths, Selected Papers* I, 335–43, Dordrecht: Kluwer Academic Publishers, 1996. The same material is used, much revised, in Jaakko Hintikka, with Merrill B. Hintikka, *Investigating Wittgenstein*, Oxford: Basil Blackwell, 1986.)

1981

(a) "Aristotelian Axiomatics and Geometrical Axiomatics." In *Theory Change, Ancient Axiomatics, and Galileo's Methodology: Probabilistic Thinking, Thermodynamics, and the Interaction of the History and Philosophy of Science: Proceedings of the 1978 Pisa Conference on the History and Philosophy of Science* I, Synthese Library 145, edited by Jaakko Hintikka, David Gruender, and Evandro Agazzi, 133–44. Dordrecht: D. Reidel Publishing Co.

(b) "Intuitions and Philosophical Method." *Revue Internationale de Philosophie* 35:74–90.

(c) "Kant on Existence, Predication, and the Ontological Argument." *Dialectica* 35:127–46. (Appears also in *The Logic of Being*, edited by Simo Knuuttila and Jaakko Hintikka, 249–68, Dordrecht: D. Reidel Publishing Co., 1986.)

(d) "The Logic of Information-seeking Dialogues: A Model." In *Konzepte der Dialektik*, edited by Wilhelm Essler and Werner Becker, 212–31. Frankfurt A.M.: Vittorio Klostermann.

(e) "On Common Factors of Dialectics." In *Konzepte der Dialektik*, edited by Wilhelm Esler and Werner Becker, 109–10. Frankfurt A.M.: Vittorio Klostermann.

(f) "On Denoting What?" *Synthese* 46:167–83. (Appears also in Jaakko Hintikka, with Merrill Hintikka, *The Logic of Epistemology and the Epistemology of Logic: Selected Essays*, Synthese Library 200, 165–81, Dordrecht: Kluwer Academic Publishers, 1989.)

(g) "On the Logic of an Interrogative Model of Scientific Inquiry." *Synthese* 47:60–84.

(h) "Phenomenology vs. Possible-worlds Semantics: Apparent and Real Differences." *Revue Internationale de Philosophie* 35:113–19.

(i) "Russell, Kant, and Coffa." *Synthese* 46:265–70.

(j) "Semantical Games and Transcendental Arguments." In *Theory of Argumentation*, edited by E.M. Barth and J. Martens. Amsterdam: John Benjamins.

(k) "Semantics: A Revolt Against Frege." In *Contemporary Philosophy: A New Survey*, 1, in the series Philosophy of Language/Philosophical Logic, edited by G. Floistad and

G. H. von Wright, 57–82. The Hague: Martinus Nijhoff.

(l)   "Theories of Truth and Learnable Languages." In *Philosophy and Grammar: Papers on the Occasion of the Quincentennial of Uppsala University*, edited by Stig Kanger and Sven Ohman, 37–57. Dordrecht: D. Reidel Publishing Co. (Appears also in Jaakko Hintikka, with Jack Kulas, *The Game of Language: Studies in Game-Theoretical Semantics and Its Applications*, Synthese Language Library 22, 259–92, Dordrecht: D. Reidel Publishing Co., 1983. [Second, corrected ed. 1985.])

(m) "Tieteen prosessiluonne ja sen seuraukset tiedesuunnittelulle" (The Process Character of Science and its Consequences for Science Policy). *Tieteen tila, KTTS:n monistesarja* 9:58–80, Helsinki: Foundation for Research in Higher Education and Science Policy.

(n)   "What is an Answer? and Other Questions in the Theory of Questions and Answers." In *Philosophy as Science and Philosophy of Science*, edited by Edgar Morscher, et al., 261–77. Bad Reichenhall: Comes Verlag. (Appears in French translation as "Questions de reponses et bien d'autres questions encore," translated by Michel Meyer, in *Language francaise, numero sur l'interrogation*, Paris: Larousse, 1981.)

(o)   "Wittgenstein's Semantical Kantianism." In *Ethics: Foundations, Problems and Applications. Proceedings of the Fifth International Wittgenstein Symposium*, edited by Edgar Morscher and R. Stranzinger, 375–90. Vienna: Hölder-Pichler-Tempsky. (Material used but much revised, in Jaakko Hintikka, with Merrill B. Hintikka, *Investigating Wittgenstein*, Oxford: Basil Blackwell, 1986.)

(p)   With Merrill B. Hintikka. "Wittgenstein: Some Perspectives on the Development of his Thought." In *Essays in Philosophical Analysis: Dedicated to Erik Stenius on the Occasion of his 70th birthday*, edited by Ingmar Pörn, 79–95. *Acta Philosophica Fennica* 32. (Appears also in Jaakko Hintikka, *Ludwig Wittgenstein: Half-Truths and One-and-a-Half-Truths, Selected Papers* I, 297–313, Dordrecht: Kluwer Academic Publishers, 1996. Also in *The Philosophy of Wittgenstein*, edited by John V. Canfield, 253–69, *Vol.6: Meaning*, New York: Garland Publishing, 1986. Material used, much revised, in Jaakko Hintikka, with Merrill B. Hintikka, *Investigating Wittgenstein*, Oxford: Basil Blackwell, 1986.)

(q)   With Merrill B. Hintikka. "Wittgenstein and the 'Universal Language' of Painting." In *Ethics, Foundations, Problems and Applications. Proceedings of the Fifth International Wittgenstein Symposium*, edited by E. Morscher and R. Stranzinger, 492–97. Vienna: Hölder-Pichler-Tempsky. (Appears also in Jaakko Hintikka, *Ludwig Wittgenstein: Half-Truths and One-and-a-Half-Truths, Selected Papers* I, 345–53, Dordrecht: Kluwer Academic Publishers, 1996.)

1982

(a)   "A Dialogical Model of Teaching." *Synthese* 51, no.1:39–59.

(b)   "Game-Theoretical Semantics: Insights and Prospects." *Notre Dame Journal of Formal Logic* 23:219–41. (Appears also in Jaakko Hintikka, with Jack Kulas, *The Game of Language: Studies in Game-Theoretical Semantics and Its Applications*, Synthese Language Library 22, 1–32, Dordrecht: D. Reidel Publishing Co., 1983. [Second, corrected ed. 1985.])

(c)   "Is Alethic Modal Logic Possible?" In *Intensional Logic: Theory and Applications*, edited by Ilkka Niiniluoto and Esa Saarinen. *Acta Philosophica Fennica* 35:89–105. (Appears also in Jaakko Hintikka, with Merrill Hintikka, *The Logic of Epistemology and the Epistemology of Logic: Selected Essays*, 1–15, Synthese Library 200, Dordrecht: Kluwer Academic Publishers, 1989.)

(d)   "Kant's Theory of Mathematics Revisited." In *Essays on Kant's Critique of Pure Reason*, edited by J. N. Mohanty and Robert W. Shehan, 201–15. Norman: University of Oklahoma Press. (Appears also in *Philosophical Topics* 12 [1982]. Appears in

French translation as "La théorie kantienne des mathématiques reconsidérée" in *La philosophie des mathematiques chez Kant. La structure de l'argumentation transcendantale*, translated from English by Corinne Hoogaert, in the series L'interrogation philosophique, edited by Michel Meyer, Paris: Presses Universitaires de France, 1996, 151–70.)

(e)   "Questions with Outside Quantifiers." In *Papers from the Parasession on Nondeclaratives*, edited by Robinson Schneider, Kevin Tute, and Robert Chametzky, 83–92. Chicago:

(f)   "Semantical Games and Transcendental Arguments." In *Argumentation: Approaches to Theory Formation*, edited by E. M. Barth and J. L. Martens, 77–91. Amsterdam: John Benjamins. (Also appears in Jaakko Hintikka, with Jack Kulas, *The Game of Language: Studies in Game-Theoretical Semantics and Its Applications*, Synthese Language Library 22, 33–47, Dordrecht: D. Reidel Publishing Co., 1983. [Second, corrected ed. 1985.])

(g)   "Tag-questions and Grammatical Acceptability." *Nordic Journal of Linguistics* 5:129–32.

(h)   "Temporal Discourse and Semantical Games." *Linguistics and Philosophy* 5:3–22. (Appears also in Jaakko Hintikka, with Jack Kulas, *The Game of Language: Studies in Game-Theoretical Semantics and Its Applications*, 113–36, Synthese Language Library 22, Dordrecht: D. Reidel Publishing Co., 1983, [Second, corrected ed. 1985.])

(i)   "Transcendental Arguments Revived." In *Philosophers on Their Own Work: Philosophers critiques d'eux-mêmes* 9, edited by Andre Mercier and Maja Svilar, 116–33. Bern: Peter Lang, 1983. (In French translation as "Renaissance de l'argumentation transcendentale," in *Philosophers on Their Own Work: Philosophers critiques d'eux-mêmes* 9, edited by Andre Mercier and Maja Svilar, 135–50, Bern: Peter Lang, 1983. Also in French translation in *La philosophie des mathematiques chez Kant. La structure de l'argumentation transcendantale*, translated from English by Corinne Hoogaert, in the series L'interrogation philosophique, edited by Michel Meyer, 7–22, Paris: Presses Universitaires de France, 1996.)

(j)   With Merrill B. Hintikka. "Sherlock Holmes Confronts Modern Logic: Toward a Theory of Information-seeking Through Questioning." In *Argumentation: Approaches to Theory Formation*, edited by E. M. Barth and J. L. Martens, 55–76. Amsterdam: John Benjamins.

(k)   With Merrill B. Hintikka. "Towards a General Theory of Individuation and Identification." In *Language and Ontology: Proceedings of the Sixth International Wittgenstein Symposium*, edited by Werner Leinfellner, Eric Kraemer and Jeffrey Schank, 137–50. Vienna: Hölder-Pichler-Tempsky. (Appears also in Jaakko Hintikka, with Merrill Hintikka, *The Logic of Epistemology and the Epistemology of Logic: Selected Essays*, 73–95, Synthese Library 200, Dordrecht: Kluwer Academic Publishers, 1989.)

(l)   With Jack Kulas. "Russell Vindicated: Towards a General Theory of Definite Descriptions." *Journal of Semantics* 1:387–97. (A revised version appears as "Definite Descriptions in Game Theoretical Semantics" in *The Game of Language: Studies in Game-Theoretical Semantics and Its Applications*, 137–61, Synthese Language Library 22, Dordrecht: D. Reidel Publishing Co., 1983. [Second, corrected ed. 1985.] Material used from original and revised articles in Part II of Jaakko Hintikka, with Jack Kulas, *Anaphora and Definite Descriptions: Two Applications of Game-Theoretical Semantics*, 33–78, Synthese Language Library 26, Dordrecht: D. Reidel Publishing Co., 1985.)

1983

(a)   "*Any* Problems—No Problems." In Jaakko Hintika, with Jack Kulas, *The Game of Language: Studies in Game-Theoretical Semantics and Its Applications*, 77–112. Synthese

Language Library 22. Dordrecht: D. Reidel Publishing Co. (Second, corrected ed. 1985.)
(b) "New Foundations for a Theory of Questions and Answers." In *Questions and Answers*, edited by F. Kiefer and Hans Karlgren, 159–90. Stockholm: KVAL.
(c) "Paras teoria" (The Best Theory). In *Huippuluokan tutkielmia*, edited by Lilli Alanen et al., 8–14. Reports from the Department of Philosophy, University of Helsinki, no. 2.
(d) "Semantical Games, the Alleged Ambiguity of 'is', and Aristotelian Categories." *Synthese* 54:443–67. (Appears also as "Semantical Games and Aristotelian Categories" in Jaakko Hintikka, with Jack Kulas, *The Game of Language: Studies in Game-Theoretical Semantics and Its Applications*, 1–32, Synthese Language Library 22, Dordrecht: D. Reidel Publishing Co., 1983, [Second, corrected ed. 1985.] Partial Greek translation in *The Actuality of Ancient Greek Philosophy*, edited by Myrto Dragona-Monachou and George Roussopoulos, 261–78, Athens: Ellinika Grammata, 1997.)
(e) "Semantical Games, Subgames, and Functional Interpretations." In Jaakko Hintikka, with Jack Kulas, *The Game of Language: Studies in Game-Theoretical Semantics and Its Applications*, 47–76. Synthese Language Library 22. Dordrecht: D. Reidel Publishing Co.
(f) "Sherlock Holmes Formalized." In *The Sign of Three: Dupin, Holmes, Peirce*, edited by Umberto Eco and Thomas Sebeok, 170–78. Bloomington: Indiana University Press.
(g) "Situations, Possible Worlds, and Attitudes." *Synthese* 54:154–62. (Appears also in Jaakko Hintikka, with Merrill Hintikka, *The Logic of Epistemology and the Epistemology of Logic: Selected Essays*, 205–14, Synthese Library 200, Kluwer Academic Publishers, 1989.)
(h) "Super Models." In *Vexing Questions: An Urnful of Essays in Honour of Veikko Rantala*, edited by Ilkka Patoluoto et al., 12–18. Reports from the Department of Philosophy, University of Helsinki, no. 3.
(i) "Transsendentaalitiedon paradoksi" (The Paradox of Transcendental Knowledge). *Ajatus* 40:20–48.
(j) With Merrill B. Hintikka. "The Development of Ludwig Wittgenstein's Philosophy: The Hidden Unity." In *Epistemology and Philosophy of Science. Proceedings of the Seventh International Wittgenstein Symposium*, edited by Paul Weingartner and Hans Czermak, 425–37. Vienna: Hölder-Pichler-Tempsky. (Material used, much revised, in Jaakko Hintikka, with Merrill B. Hintikka, *Investigating Wittgenstein*, Oxford: Basil Blackwell, 1986.)
(k) With Merrill B. Hintikka. "How Can Language be Sexist?" In *Discovering Reality: Feminist Perspectives on Epistemology, Metaphysics, Methodology, and Philosophy of Science*, edited by Sandra Harding and Merrill B. Hintikka, 139–48. Dordrecht: D. Reidel Publishing Co. (Appears also in Jaakko Hintikka, with Merrill Hintikka, *The Logic of Epistemology and the Epistemology of Logic: Selected Essays*, 155–64, Synthese Library 200, Kluwer Academic Publishers, 1989.)
(l) With Merrill B. Hintikka. "Some Remarks on (Wittgensteinian) Logical Form." *Synthese* 56:155–70. (Appears also in *The Philosophy of Wittgenstein*, edited by John V. Canfield, 405–20, *Vol. 1: The Early Philosophy — Language as Picture*, New York: Garland Publishing, 1986. Material used, much revised, in Jaakko Hintikka, with Merrill B. Hintikka, *Investigating Wittgenstein*, Oxford: Basil Blackwell, 1986.)
(m) With Merrill B. Hintikka. "Wittgensteinin Tractatus-teoksen salaisuus" (The Enigma of Wittgenstein's *Tractatus*). In *Suomalainen, Tiedeakatemia – Academia Scientiarum Fennica — Vuosikirja – Yearbook 1982*, edited by Lauri A. Vuorela, 121–33. Helsinki, 1983. (Appears also in Finnish in *Filosofian köyhyys ja rikkaus: Nykyfilosofian kartoitusta*, edited by Janne Hiipakka and Risto Vilkko, 297–317, Helsinki: Art House Oy, 2001. Material used, much revised, in Jaakko Hintikka, with Merrill B. Hintikka, *Investigating Wittgenstein*, Oxford: Basil Blackwell, 1986.)

1984

(a) "Are There Nonexistent Objects? Why Not? But Where are They?" *Synthese* 60 (1984): 451–58. (Appears also in Jaakko Hintikka, with Merrill Hintikka, *The Logic of Epistemology and the Epistemology of Logic: Selected Essays*, 37–44, Synthese Library 200, Kluwer Academic Publishers, 1989.)

(b) "Das Paradox transzendentaler Erkenntnis." In *Bedingungen der Möglichkeit: 'Transcendental Arguments' und Transzendentales Denken*, edited by Eva Schaper and W. Vossenkuhl, 123–49. Stuttgart: Klett-Cotta. (In Japanese translation as *Transzendental-philosophie and Analytic Philosophy: An Exchange between German and Anglo-Saxon Philosophers*, 259–300. First part appears in English translation as "Kant's Transcendental Method and His Theory of Mathematics," *Topoi* 3 [1984]: 99–108. First part also appears in French translation as "Le paradoxe de la connaissance transcendantale" in *La philosophie des mathematiques chez Kant. La structure de l'argumentation transcendantale,* translated from English by Corinne Hoogaert, 35–54, in the series L'interrogation philosophique, edited by Michel Meyer, Paris: Presses Universitaires de France, 1996.)

(c) "Hundred Years Later: The Rise and Fall of Frege's Influence in Language Theory." *Synthese* 59:27–49.

(d) "The Logic of Science as a Model-Oriented Logic." In *Philosophy of Science Association 1984* 1. Edited by Peter Asquith and Philip Kitcher, 177–85. East Lansing, Mich.: Philosophy of Science Association.

(e) "Luovuus ja ihmiskäsitykset" (Creativity and Conceptions of Man). *Ajatus* 41:83–88. (Appears also in Finnish in *Filosofian köyhyys ja rikkaus: Nykyfilosofian kartoitusta*, edited by Janne Hiipakka and Risto Vilkko, 391–96, Helsinki: Art House Oy, 2001.)

(f) "Kant's Transcendental Method and His Theory of Mathematics." *Topoi* 3:99–108. (Appears also in *Kant's Philosophy of Mathematics*, edited by Carl J. Posy, 341–59, Dordrecht: Kluwer Academic Publishers, 1992. Appears in French translation as "La méthode transcendantale de Kant dans sa théorie des mathématiques" in *La philosophie des mathematiques chez Kant. La structure de l'argumentation transcendantale*, translated from English by Corinne Hoogaert, in the series L'interrogation philosophique, edited by Michel Meyer, 81–104, Paris: Presses Universitaires de France, 1996. In Spanish translation as "El método trascendental de Kant y su teoría de la matemática" in Jaakko Hintikka, *El viaje filosófico más largo: De Aristóteles a Virginia Woolf*, translated by Marcelo M.M. Hurtado, 186–211, Barcelona: Gedisa Editorial, 1998.)

(g) "Questioning as a Philosophical Method." In *Principles of Philosophical Reasoning*, edited by James H. Fetzer, 25–43. Totowa, N.J.: Rowman and Allanheld. (Appears also in Jaakko Hintikka with Merrill Hintikka, *The Logic of Epistemology and the Epistemology of Logic: Selected Essays*, 215–33, Synthese Library 200, Kluwer Academic Publishers, 1989. Also in *The Examined Life: Readings from Western Philosophy from Plato to Kant,* edited by Stanley Rosen, 453–72, New York: Random House, 2000.)

(h) "Rules, Utilities, and Strategies in Dialogical Games." In *Cognitive Constraints on Communication*, edited by Lucia Vaina and Jaakko Hintikka, 277–94. Dordrecht: D. Reidel Publishing Co.

(i) With Charles Harvey. "Review Article on David W. Smith and Ronald McIntyre, *Husserl and Intentionality.*" *Husserl Studies* 2:201–12.

(j) With Lucia Vaina. "Introduction." In *Cognitive Constraints on Communication*, edited by Lucia Vaina and Jaakko Hintikka, vii–xvii. Dordrecht: D. Reidel Publishing Co.

1985

(a) "Legal Reasoning and Legal Systems." In *Man, Law and Modern Forms of Life*, edited by E. Bulygin et al., 209–20. Dordrecht: D. Reidel Publishing Co.
(b) "Philosophical Logic" (in Hebrew). *Modern Trends in Philosophy* 2, edited by A. Kasher and Shalom Lappin, 71–93. Tel Aviv: Yachdav United Publishers.
(c) "A Spectrum of Logics of Questioning." *Philosophica* 35:135–50. (Appears also in Jaakko Hintikka, *Inquiry As Inquiry: Toward a Logic of Scientific Discovery, Selected Papers* V, 127–42, Dordrecht: Kluwer Academic Publishers, 1999.)
(d) "True and False Logics of Scientific Discovery." *Communication and Cognition* 18:3–14. (Appears also in Jaakko Hintikka and Fernand Vandamme, *Logic of Discovery and Logic of Discourse*, 3–15, Dordrecht: D. Reidel Publishing Co., 1985. Also in Jaakko Hintikka, *Inquiry As Inquiry: Toward a Logic of Scientific Discovery, Selected Papers* V, 115–26, Dordrecht: Kluwer Academic Publishers, 1999.)
(e) With Merrill B. Hintikka. "Ludwig Looks at the Necker Cube: The Problem of 'Seeing as' as a Clue to Wittgenstein's Philosophy." *Acta Philosophica Fennica* 38:36–48. (Appears also in Jaakko Hintikka, *Ludwig Wittgenstein: Half-Truths and One-and-a-Half-Truths, Selected Papers* I, 179–89, Dordrecht: Kluwer Academic Publishers, 1996.)
(f) With Merrill B. Hintikka. "Wittgenstein über private Erfahrung." In *Sprachspiel und Methode: Zum Stand der Wittgenstein-Diskussion*, edited by Dieter Birnbacher and Armin Burkhardt, 1–26. Berlin: Walter de Gruyter.
(g) With Merrill B. Hintikka. "Wittgenstein's 'annus mirabilis': 1929." In *The Tasks of Contemporary Philosophy. Proceedings of the Tenth International Wittgenstein Symposium*, 437–47. Vienna: Hölder-Pichler-Tempsky. (Appears also in Jaakko Hintikka, *Ludwig Wittgenstein: Half-Truths and One-and-a-Half-Truths, Selected Papers* I, 107–24, Dordrecht: Kluwer Academic Publishers, 1996.)
(h) With Simo Knuuttila. "Introduction." In *The Logic of Being: Historical Studies*, ix–xvi. Synthese Historical Library 28, edited by Simo Knuuttila and Jaakko Hintikka. Dordrecht: D. Reidel Publishing Co.
(i) With Jack Kulas. "Different Uses of the Definite Article." *Communication and Cognition* 18:69–80. (Appears simultaneously in *Logic of Discovery and Logic of Discourse*, edited by Jaakko Hintikka and Fernand Vandamme, 71–82, New York: Plenum Press, 1985. Material used in Part II of Jaakko Hintikka, with Jack Kulas, *Anaphora and Definite Descriptions: Two Applications of Game-Theoretical Semantics*, 33–78, Synthese Language Library 26, Dordrecht: D. Reidel Publishing Co., 1985.)

1986

(a) Comments and Replies." *Philosophia* 2, Part 1, nos. 1–2: 105–19; and Part 2, nos. 3–4: 277–87.
(b) "Filosofian tulevaisuus." In *Tulevaisuus* (a *Festschrift* for G. H. von Wright), edited by Ilkka Niiniluoto and Heikki Nyman, 265–75. Helsinki: Otava.
(c) "The Languages of Human Thought and the Languages of AI" (résumé). In *AI and Philosophy. STEP-86 Invited Papers*, 1, edited by M. Karjalainen, J. Seppänen and M. Tamminen, 1–3. Espoo: Finnish Society of Information Processing Science. (A complete version appears in French translation as "Langages de la pensèe humaine, langages de l'intelligence artificielle" in *Fondements d' une théorie du langage*, translated by Nadine Lavand, 318–45, Paris: Presses Universitaires de France, 1994.)
(d) "Logic of Conversation as a Logic of Dialogue." In *Philosophical Grounds of*

Rationality, Intentions, Categories, and Ends, 259–76. Oxford: Clarendon Press.
(e) "Quine on Who's Who." In *The Philosophy of W. V. Quine*, edited by L. E. Hahn and P. A. Schilpp. Library of Living Philosophers. La Salle, Ill.: Open Court. (Appears also in Jaakko Hintikka, with Merrill Hintikka, *The Logic of Epistemology and the Epistemology of Logic: Selected Essays*, 137–54, Synthese Library 200, Kluwer Academic Publishers, 1989.)
(f) "Reasoning about Knowledge in Philosophy: The Paradigm of Epistemic Logic." In *Reasoning About Knowledge*, edited by Joseph Halpern, 63–80. Los Altos, Calif.: Morgan Kaufmann Publishers. (Appears also in Jaakko Hintikka, with Merrill Hintikka, *The Logic of Epistemology and the Epistemology of Logic: Selected Essays*, 17–35, Synthese Library 200, Kluwer Academic Publishers, 1989.)
(g) "The Semantics of 'a certain.'" *Linguistic Inquiry* 17, no. 2 (1986): 331–36.
(h) "The Varieties of Being in Aristotle." In *The Logic of Being: Historical Studies*, 81–114. Synthese Historical Library 28, edited by Simo Knuuttila and Jaakko Hintikka. Dordrecht: D. Reidel Publishing Co. (Appears in Spanish translation as "Las variedades del ser en Aristóteles" in Jaakko Hintikka, *El viaje filosófico más largo: De Aristóteles a Virginia Woolf*, translated by Marcelo M.M. Hurtado, 13–56, Barcelona: Gedisa Editorial, 1998.)
(i) With Leila Haaparanta. "General Introduction." In *Frege Synthesized: Essays on the Philosophical and Foundational Work of Gottlob Frege*, edited by Jaakko Hintikka and Leila Haaparanta, 3–8. Dordrecht: D. Reidel Publishing Co.
(j) With Merrill B. Hintikka. "Wittgenstein and Language as the Universal Medium." In *Investigating Wittgenstein*, 1–29. Oxford: Basil Blackwell. (Appears also in Jaakko Hintikka, *Lingua Universalis vs. Calculus Ratiocinator: An Ultimate Presupposition of Twentieth-Century Philosophy, Selected Papers* II, 162–90, Dordrecht: Kluwer Academic Publishers, 1996.)
(k) With Simo Knuuttila. "Introduction." In *The Logic of Being: Historical Studies*, ix–xvi. Synthese Historical Library 28, edited by Jaakko Hintikka and Simo Knuuttila, Dordrecht: D. Reidel Publishing Co.

1987

(a) "Comment je vois la philosophie." In *Encyclopédie Philosophique*, edited by A. Jacob. Paris: Presses Universitaires de France.
(b) "Comment on Jeffrey's 'Alias Smith and Jones: The Testimony of the Senses.'" *Erkenntnis* 26:407.
(c) "Comments on Kamlah's 'What can Methodologists Learn From the History of Probability.'" *Erkenntnis* 26:327.
(d) "Extremality Conditions in the Foundations of Mathematics." In *Philosophy of Science Association 1986* 2, edited by A. Fine and M. Forbes. East Lansing, Mich.: Philosophy of Science Association.
(e) "The Fallacy of Fallacies." *Argumentation* 1:221–38.
(f) "Game-theoretical Semantics as a Synthesis of Truth-conditional and Verificationist Meaning Theories." In *New Directions in Semantics*, edited by E. LePore, 235–58. London and Orlando, Florida: Academic Press. (Also appears in Jaakko Hintikka, *Paradigms for Language Theory and Other Essays, Selected Papers* IV, 250–73, Kluwer Academic Publishers, 1998. Appears in French translation as "La sémantique des jeux, synthèse des théories vériconditionnelle et vérficationnelle de la signification" in *Fondements d'une théorie du langage*, translated from English by Nadine Lavand, 136–67, Paris: Presses Universitaire de France, 1994.)
(g) "The Interrogative Approach to Inquiry and Probabilistic Inference." *Erkenntnis* 26: 429–42.

(h) "Is Scope a Viable Concept in Semantics?" In *ESCOL '86. Proceedings of the Third Eastern States Conference on Linguistics*, edited by Ann Miller and Zheng-Shen Zhang, 259–70. Columbus: Ohio State University, 1987. (Appears in French translation as "Le concept de domaine est-il apte à survivre en milieu sémantique?" in *Fondements d'une théorie du langage*, translated from English by Nadine Lavand, 60–75, Paris: Presses Universitaire de France, 1994.)

(i) "Language Understanding and Strategic Meaning." *Synthese* 73:497–529. (Appears in French translation as "Compréhension linguistique et signification stratégique" in *Fondements d'une théorie du langage*, translated from English by Nadine Lavand, 168–208, Paris: Presses Universitaire de France, 1994.)

(j) "Logic Translation: An Impossible Dream?" *LMPS 87, 5, Abstracts*, 1987, 30–32.

(k) "Mental Models, Semantical Games and Varieties of Intelligence." In *Matters of Intelligence: Conceptual Structures in Cognitive Neuroscience*, edited by Lucia Vaina, 197–215. Dordrecht: D. Reidel Publishing Co. (Appears also in French translation as "Modèles mentauz, jeux sémantiques, forms d'intelligence artificielle," in *Fondements d'une théorie du langage*, translated from English by Nadine Lavand, 318–45, Paris: Presses Universitaire de France, 1994.)

(l) "Model Minimization: An Alternative to Circumscription." *Journal of Automated Reasoning* 3:1–13. (Also appears in Jaakko Hintikka, *Language, Truth and Logic in Mathematics, Selected Papers* III, 212–24, Dordrecht: Kluwer Academic Publishers, 1998.)

(m) "A Note on Anaphoric Pronouns and Information Processing by Humans." *Linguistic Inquiry* 18:111–19.

(n) "Replies and Comments." In *Jaakko Hintikka: A Profile*, edited by Radu Bogdan, 227–344. Dordrecht: D. Reidel Publishers.

(o) "Self-profile." In *Jaakko Hintikka: A Profile*, edited by Radu Bogdan, 3–40, Dordrecht: D. Reidel Publishing Co.

1988

(a) "Advice to Prospective Philosophers." In *Proceedings and Addresses of The American Philosophical Association*, Supplement to vol. 62, no.1 (September, 1988): 272–73.

(b) "'Die Wende der Philosophie': Wittgenstein's New Logic of 1928." In *Philosophy of Law, Politics and Society. Proceedings of the 12th International Wittgenstein Symposium*, 380–96. Vienna: Hölder-Pichler-Tempsky. (Appears also in *Wittgenstein and Contemporary Philosophy*, edited by Souren Teghrarian, 1–40, Bristol: Thoemes, 1994. Also in Jaakko Hintikka, *Ludwig Wittgenstein: Half-Truths and One-and-a-Half-Truths, Selected Papers* I, 79–105, Kluwer Academic Publishers, 1996.)

(c) "Oikeustieteellinen päättely ja oikeusjärjestelmät." *Lakimies* 3:219–31.

(d) "On the Development of the Model-theoretic Viewpoint in Logical Theory." *Synthese* 77:1–36. (Appears also in Jaakko Hintikka, *Lingua Universalis vs. Calculus Ratiocinator: An Ultimate Presupposition of Twentieth-Century Philosophy, Selected Papers* II, 140–61, Dordrecht: Kluwer Academic Publishers, 1996. Appears in French translation as "La théorie des modèles en logique, tradition et perspectives" in *Fondements d'une théorie du langage*, translated from English by Nadine Lavand, 209–51, Paris: Presses Universitaire de France, 1994.)

(e) "On the Incommensurability of Theories." *Philosophy of Science* 55:25–38. (Appears also in Jaakko Hintikka, *Inquiry As Inquiry: Toward a Logic of Scientific Discovery, Selected Papers* V, 227–40, Dordrecht: Kluwer Academic Publishers, 1999.)

(f) "Todistiko Gödel matematiikan epätäydelliseksi?" In *Suomalainen Tiedeakatemia vuoikirjassa 1988-89, Esitelmät ja pöytäkirjat*, 117–26. (Reprinted in *Filosofian köyhyys ja rikkaus: Nykyfilosofian kartoitusta* [The Poverty and Richness of Philosophy: Perspectives on Contemporary Philosophy], edited by Janne Hiipakka and

Risto Vilkko, 318–31, Helsinki: Art House Oy, 2001.)
(g) "Was Leibniz's Deity an *Akrates*?" In *Modern Modalities: Studies of the History of Modal Theories from Medieval Nominalism to Logical Positivism*, edited by Simo Knuuttila, Synthese Historical Library 33, 85–108. Dordrecht: Kluwer Academic Publishers. (In Spanish as "¿Fue la deidad de Leibniz un *akrates*? in Jaakko Hintikka, *El viaje filosófico más largo: De Aristóteles a Virginia Woolf*, translated by Marcelo M.M. Hurtado, 131–56, Barcelona: Gedisa Editorial, 1998.)
(h) "What is the Logic of Experimental Inquiry?" *Synthese* 74:173–90. (Appears also in Jaakko Hintikka, *Inquiry As Inquiry: Toward a Logic of Scientific Discovery, Selected Papers* V, 143–60, Dordrecht: Kluwer Academic Publishers, 1999.)
(i) With Stephen Harris. "On the Logic of Interrogative Inquiry." In *Philosophy of Science Association 1988* 2, edited by A. Fine and J. Lepkin, 233–40. East Lansing, Mich.: Philosophy of Science Association.

1989

(a) "The Cartesian *cogito*, Epistemic Logic, and Neuroscience: Some Surprising Interrelations." In Jaakko Hintikka, with Merrill Hintikka, *The Logic of Epistemology and the Epistemology of Logic: Selected Essays*, Synthese Library 200, 113–36. Dordrecht: Kluwer Academic Publishers. (Appears also in *Synthese* 83, no. 1 [1990]: 133–57.)
(b) "Concepts of Scientific Method from Aristotle to Newton." In *Knowledge and the Sciences in Medieval Philosophy. Proceedings of the Eighth Congress of Medieval Philosophy*, Helsinki, 24–29 August 1987, edited by Monica Asztalos, John Murdoch, and Ilkka Niiniluoto. *Acta Philosophica Fennica* 48:72–84.
(c) "Exploring Possible Worlds." In *Possible Worlds in Humanities, Arts and Sciences. Proceedings of Nobel Symposium 65*, edited by Sture Allén, 52–73. Berlin: Walter de Gruyter.
(d) "G. H. von Wright on Logical Truth and Distributive Normal Forms." In *The Philosophy of G. H. von Wright*, edited by P. A. Schilpp and L. Hahn, 517–37. The Library of Living Philosophers 19. La Salle, Ill.: Open Court.
(e) "Is There Completeness in Mathematics after Gödel?" *Philosophical Topics* 17, no. 2: 69–90. (Also appears in Jaakko Hintikka, *Language, Truth and Logic in Mathematics, Selected Papers* III, 62–83, Dordrecht: Kluwer Academic Publishers, 1998.)
(f) "Is Truth Ineffable?" In *Les formes actuelles du vrai. Entretiens de Palermo 1985*, (no editor indicated), 89–120. Palermo: Endichiridion. (Appears also in *The Opened Curtain: A U.S.-Soviet Philosophy Summit*, edited by Keith Lehrer and Ernest Sosa, Boulder, Colorado/San Francisco/Oxford: Westview Press, 1991. Appears in French translation as "La vérité est-elle ineffable?" in *La vérité est-elle ineffable? et autres essais*, translated from English by Antonia Soulez and Francois Schmitz, Collection 'tiré à part', edited by Jean-Pierre Cometti, 9–42, Combas: Éditions de l'Éclat, 1994. In Polish as "Czy prawda jest niewystasialna?" in *Znaczenie i prawda: Rozprawy semiotyczne*, edited by Jerzego Pelca, translated by Marek Witkowski, in the series Biblioteka Myśli Semiotycznej 26, 331–54, Warsaw: Znak–Jezyk–Rzeczywistość, 1994. Also in Jaakko Hintikka, *Lingua Universalis vs. Calculus Ratiocinator: An Ultimate Presupposition of Twentieth-Century Philosophy, Selected Papers* II, 20–45, Dordrecht: Kluwer Academic Publishers, 1996.)
(g) "Knowledge Representation and the Interrogative Model of Inquiry." In *Knowledge and Skepticism*, edited by Marjorie Clay and Keith Lehrer, 155–83. Boulder, Colo.: Westview Press.
(h) "Logical Form and Linguistic Theory." In *Reflections on Chomsky*, edited by Alex George, 41–57. Oxford: Basil Blackwell. (Appears also in Jaakko Hintikka, *Paradigms*

for Language Theory and Other Essays, Selected Papers IV, 107–23, Dordrecht: Kluwer Academic Publishers, 1998. Appears in French translation as "Forme logique, théorie linguistique" in *Fondements d'une théorie du langage*, translated from English by Nadine Lavand, 35–59, Paris: Presses Universitaire de France, 1994.)

(i) "Ludwig's Apple Tree: Evidence Concerning the Philosophical Relations between Wittgenstein and the Vienna Circle." In *Traditionen und Perspektiven der Analytischen Philosophie: Festschrift für Rudolf Haller*, edited by Wolfgang L. Gombocz, Heiner Rutte and Werner Sauer, 187–202. Vienna: Hölder-Pichler-Tempsky. (Appears also in *Scientific Philosophy: Origins and Developments*, edited by Friedrich Stadler, 27–46, Dordrecht: Kluwer Academic Publishers, 1993. A much expanded version appears in Jaakko Hintikka, *Ludwig Wittgenstein: Half-Truths and One-and-a-Half-Truths, Selected Papers* I, 125–44, Dordrecht: Kluwer Academic Publishers, 1996.)

(j) "On the Limitations of Generative Grammar." In *Proceedings of the Scandinavian Seminar on Philosophy of Language*, Filosofiska Förening and Filosofiska Institutionen vid Uppsala Universitet, Uppsala 26, no. 1: 1–92.

(k) "On the Role of Modality in Aristotle's Metaphysics." In *Of Scholars, Savants and Their Texts*, edited by Ruth Link-Salinger, 123–34. New York: Peter Lang.

(l) "The Paradox of Transcendental Knowledge." In *An Intimate Relation*, edited by J. R. Brown and J. Mittelstrass, 243–57. Dordrecht: Kluwer Academic Publishers. (Appears also in *Boston Studies in the Philosophy of Science* 116 [1989]: 243–57. Appears in Spanish translation as "La paradoja del conocimiento trascendental," translated by Alicia Herrera Ibáñez, translator, 283–300, in *Argumentos trascendentales,* compiled by Isable Cabrera, in the series Filosofia Contemporànea, 1999.)

(m) "The Role of Logic in Argumentation." *The Monist* 72:3–24. (Appears in Finnish translation as "Logiikan rooli päättelyssä," translated by Janne Hiipakka, in *Malli, Metodi, Merkitys — Esseitä Veikko Rantalan 60-vuotispäivän kunniaksi*, edited by Leila Haaparanta, Ismo Koskinen, Erna Oesch and Tere Vadén, 3–26, *Filosofisia tutkimuksia Tampereen yliopistosta* 49, Tampereen yliopisto, 1993. Appears also in Jaakko Hintikka, *Inquiry As Inquiry: Toward a Logic of Scientific Discovery, Selected Papers* V, 25–46, Dordrecht: Kluwer Academic Publishers, 1999. Reprinted in Finnish in *Filosofian köyhyys ja rikkaus: Nykyfilosofian kartoitusta*, edited by Janne Hiipakka and Risto Vilkko, 148–78, Helsinki: Art House Oy, 2001. Appears in Swedish translation as "Spelar logiken någon roll I argumentation?" in *Huvudinnehåll, Tolv filosofiska uppsatser*, edited by Åke E. Anderson and Nils-Eric Sahlin, 93–119, Nora: Nya Doxa, 1993.)

(n) "Rules, Games and Experiences: Wittgenstein's Discussion of Rule-following in the Light of His Development." *Revue Internationale de Philosophie* 43:279–97. (Appears also in Jaakko Hintikka, *Ludwig Wittgenstein: Half-Truths and One-and-a-Half-Truths, Selected Papers* I, 315–33, Dordrecht: Kluwer Academic Publishers, 1996.)

(o) "Todistiko Gödel matematiikan epätäydelliseksi?" (Did Gödel Show that Mathematics is Incomplete?) In *Finnish Academy of Science and Letters, Year Book 1988–89*, 117–26. Helsinki.

(p) With Gabriel Sandu. "Informational Independence as a Semantical Phenomenon." In *Logic, Methodology and Philosophy of Science VIII*, edited by J. E. Fenstad et al., 571–89. Amsterdam: Elsevier. (Appears also in Jaakko Hintikka, *Paradigms for Language Theory and Other Essays, Selected Papers* IV, 52–70, Dordrecht: Kluwer Academic Publishers, 1998. Appears in French translation as "L'indépendence informationnelle, phénomène sémantique" in *Fondements d'une théorie du langage*, translated from English by Nadine Lavand, 76–97, Paris: Presses Universitaire de France, 1994.)

1990

(a)   "The Languages of Human Thought and the Languages of Artificial Intelligence." *Acta Philosophica Fennica* 49:307–30. (Appears in French translation as "Langages de la pensée humaine, langages de l'intelligence artificielle" in *Fondements d'une théorie du langage*, translated from English by Nadine Lavand, 318–45, Paris: Presses Universitaire de France, 1994.)

(b)   "Nonstandard Models and the Completeness of Mathematical Theories." In Russian translation, from *The Joint Soviet Finnish Colloquium on Logic and New Tendencies in Logical Semantics, July, 1989* in *Humanism, Science, Technology* I, 96–110, V. S. Stepin, editor-in-chief. Moscow: Academy of Science.

(c)   "Obstacles to Understanding" (on the fate of Wittgenstein's *Nachlass*). *Times Literary Supplement*, September 28–October 4, 1990, 1030. (An earlier, shorter form of "An Impatient Man and His Papers." *Synthese* 87 [1991]: 183–201.)

(d)   "Paradigms for Language Theory." In *Language, Knowledge and Intentionality: Perspectives on the Philosophy of Jaakko Hintikka*, edited by Leila Haaparanta, Martin Kusch and Ilkka Niiniluoto. *Acta Philosophica Fennica* 49 (listed as 1990, appeared in 1991): 181–209. (Also appears in French translation as "Deux paradigms pour une théorie du langage" in *Fondements d'une théorie du langage*, translated from English by Nadine Lavand, 3–34, Paris: Presses Universitaire de France, 1994. Also appears in Jaakko Hintikka, *Paradigms for Language Theory and Other Essays, Selected Papers* IV, 146–74, Dordrecht: Kluwer Academic Publishers, 1998.)

(e)   "Quine as a Member of the Tradition of the Universality of Language." In *Perspectives on Quine*, edited by Robert Barrett and Roger Gibson, 159–75. Oxford: Basil Blackwell. (Appears also in Jaakko Hintikka, *Lingua Universalis vs. Calculus Ratiocinator: An Ultimate Presupposition of Twentieth-Century Philosophy, Selected Papers* II, 214–30, Dordrecht: Kluwer Academic Publishers, 1996.)

(f)   "Wittgenstein as a Philosopher of Immediate Experience." In *Wittgenstein: Towards a Re-evaluation. Proceedings of the 14th International Wittgenstein Symposium* 1, edited by 1, Rudolf Haller et al., 155–67. Vienna: Hölder-Pichler-Tempsky. (Appears in French translation as "Wittgenstein, philosophe de l'expérience" in *La vérité est-elle ineffable? et autres essais*, translated from English by Antonia Soulez and Francois Schmitz, Collection 'tiré à part', edited by Jean-Pierre Cometti, 48–72, Combas: Éditions de l'Éclat, 1994. Also appears in Jaakko Hintikka, *Ludwig Wittgenstein: Half-Truths and One-and-a-Half-Truths, Selected Papers* I, 191–208, Dordrecht: Kluwer Academic Publishers, 1996.)

(g)   "Wittgenstein and the Problem of Phenomenology." In *Language, Knowledge and Intentionality: Perspectives on the Philosophy of Jaakko Hintikka*, edited by Leilla Haaparanta, Martin Kusch and Ilkka Niiniluoto. *Acta Philosophica Fennica* 49:15–46. (Appears also in Jaakko Hintikkka, *Ludwig Wittgenstein: Half-Truths and One-and-a-Half-Truths, Selected Papers* I, 209–40, Dordrecht: Kluwer Academic Publishers, 1996.)

(h)   With Gabriel Sandu. "Metaphor and the Varieties of Lexical Meaning." *Dialectica*: 55–77. (Appears also in *Aspects of Metaphor*, Synthese Library 238, edited by Jaakko Hintikka, 151–87, Dordrecht: Kluwer Academic Publishers, 1994. Also in *Paradigms for Language Theory and Other Essays, Selected Papers* IV, 274–310, Kluwer Academic Publishers, 1998.)

1991

(a)   "Carnap, the Universality of Language and Extremality Axioms." *Erkenntnis* 35:325–36.
(b)   "Defining Truth, the Whole Truth, and Nothing But the Truth." In *Reports from the*

Department of Philosophy, University of Helsinki, no. 2. (Appears also in Jaakko Hintikka, *Lingua Universalis vs. Calculus Ratiocinator: An Ultimate Presupposition of Twentieth-Century Philosophy, Selected Papers* II, 46–103. Dordrecht: Kluwer Academic Publishers, 1996. Appears in Italian translation in *Iride*, 1992.)

(c) "Geach and the Methodology of the Logical Study of Natural Language." In *Peter Geach: Philosophical Encounters*, edited by Harry Lewis, 137–49. Dordrecht: Kluwer Academic Publishers.

(d) "Husserl: The Phenomenological Dimension." In *Phenomenology/Fenomenologia. Proceedings of the Symposium on Phenomenology, Jyväskylä, 5 May 1988*, edited by Matti Kosonen, 15–28. Department of Philosophy, University of Jyväskylä, 1990 (appeared in fact in 1991).

(e) "An Impatient Man and His Papers." *Synthese* 87:183–201. (Appears also in *Wittgenstein in Florida. Proceedings of the Colloquium on the Philosophy of Ludwig Wittgenstein, Florida State University, 7–8 August 1989*, edited by Jaakko Hintikka, 183–202, Dordrecht: Kluwer Academic Publishers, 1991. Also in Jaakko Hintikka, *Ludwig Wittgenstein: Half-Truths and One-and-a-Half-Truths, Selected Papers* I, 1–19, Dordrecht: Kluwer Academic Publishers, 1996. [A postscript has been added.] An earlier short version, "Obstacles to Understanding" [on the fate of Wittgenstein's *Nachlass*], *Times Literary Supplement*, September 28–October 4, 1990, 1030.)

(f) "The Languages of Human Thought and the Languages of Artificial Intelligence." In *Language, Knowledge and Intentionality: Perspectives on the Philosophy of Jaakko Hintikka*, edited by Leila Haaparanta, Martin Kusch and Ilkka Niiniluoto. *Acta Philosophica Fennica* 49 (Noted as 1990, appeared in 1991): 307–30. (In French translation as "Langages de la pensée humaine, langages de l'intelligence artificielle" in *Fondements d'une théorie du langage*, translated from English by Nadine Lavand, 318–45, Paris: Presses Universitaires de Frances, 1994.)

(g) "Overcoming 'Overcoming Metaphysics Through Logical Analysis of Language' Through Logical Analysis of Language." *Dialectica* 45:203–18.

(h) "Towards a General Theory of Identifiability." In *Definitions and Definability: Philosophical Perspectives*, edited by James H. Fetzer, et al., 161–83, Dordrecht: Kluwer Academic Publishers. (Appears also in Jaakko Hintikka, *Inquiry As Inquiry: Toward a Logic of Scientific Discovery, Selected Papers* V, 267–89, Dordrecht: Kluwer Academic Publishers, 1999.)

(i) "Wittgenstein and the Problem of Phenomenology." *Acta Philosophica Fennica* 49 (listed as 1990, appeared in 1991): 15–46.

(j) With Charles W. Harvey. "Modalization and Modalities." In *Phenomenology and the Formal Sciences*, edited by Thomas M. Seebohm, 59–77. Dordrecht: Kluwer Academic Publishers.

1992

(a) "Carnap's Work in the Foundations of Logic and Mathematics in a Historical Perspective." *Synthese* 93:167–89. (Appears also in Jaakko Hintikka, *Lingua Universalis vs. Calculus Ratiocinator: An Ultimate Presupposition of Twentieth-Century Philosophy, Selected Papers* II, 167–213, Dordrecht: Kluwer Academic Publishers, 1996.)

(b) "The Concept of Induction in the Light of the Interrogative Approach to Inquiry." In *Inference, Explanation and Other Frustrations: Essays in the Philosophy of Science*, edited by John Earman, 23–43. Berkeley: University of California Press. (Also appears in Jaakko Hintikka, *Inquiry As Inquiry: Toward a Logic of Scientific Discovery, Selected Papers* V, 161–82, Dordrecht: Kluwer Academic Publishers, 1999.)

(c) "Different Constructions in Terms of 'Knows.'" In *A Companion to Epistemology*, edited by Jonathan Dancy and Ernest Sosa, 99B–104B. Oxford: Basil Blackwell.

(d) "Eino Kaila's 'Blue Fire.'" In *Eino Kaila and Logical Empiricism*, edited by Ilkka Niiniluoto et al. *Acta Philosophica Fennica* 52:152–59. (Appears also in Finnish as "Eino Kailan 'Sininen tuli,'" translated by Risto Vilkko, in *Filosofian köyhyys ja rikkaus: Nykyfilosofian kartoitusta*, edited by Janne Hiipakka and Risto Vilkko, 332–42, Helsinki: Art House Oy, 2001.)

(e) "Independence-Friendly Logic as a Medium of Knowledge Representation and Reasoning about Knowledge." In *Information, Modelling and Databases*, edited by S. Ohsuga et al., 258–65. Amsterdam, Washington, Tokyo: IOS Press.

(f) "The Interrogative Model of Knowledge Acquisition as a Framework for Concept Identification." In *Information, Modelling and Databases*, edited by S. Ohsuga et al. Amsterdam, Washington, Tokyo: IOS Press, 174–81.

(g) "The Interrogative Model of Inquiry as a General Theory of Argumentation." *Communication and Cognition* 25:221–42. (In Portuguese translation as "Estratégia e teoria da argumentação," translated by Fernando Martinho, 71–94, *Retórica e comunicação*, 1994.)

(h) "Knowledge-Seeking by Questioning." In *A Companion to Epistemology*, edited by Jonathan Dancy and Ernest Sosa, 241A–244A. Oxford: Basil Blackwell.

(i) "Theory-Ladenness of Observations as a Test Case of Kuhn's Approach to Scientific Inquiry." In *PSA 1992. Proceedings of the 1992 Biennial Meeting of the Philosophy of Science Association* 1, edited by David Hull et al., 277–86. East Lansing, Mich.: Philosophy of Science Association. (Appears also in Jaakko Hintikka, *Inquiry As Inquiry: Toward a Logic of Scientific Discovery, Selected Papers* V, 241–50, Dordrecht: Kluwer Academic Publishers, 1999.)

(j) With Gabriel Sandu. "The Skeleton in Frege's Cupboard: The Standard vs. Nonstandard Distinction." *Journal of Philosophy* 89:290–315. (Appears also in Jaakko Hintikka, *Language, Truth and Logic in Mathematics, Selected Papers* III, 144–73, Dordrecht: Kluwer Academic Publishers, 1998. A modified version in French translation appears as "La vérité est au fond du puit, Frege et les interpretations standard et non-standard," translated by Lionel Perrin, in *Frege. Logique et philosophie*, edited by Mathieu Marion and Alain Voizard, 171–210, in the series Collection tradition sémantique, Montreal: Harmattan Inc., 1998.)

1993

(a) "Gödel's Functional Interpretation in a Wider Perspective." In *Yearbook 1991 of the Kurt Gödel Society*, edited by H. D. Schwabl, 1–39. Vienna: Kurt Gödel Society.

(b) "A Historical Note on Scott's 'Game-theoretical Interpretation of Logical Formulae.'" In *Yearbook 1991 of the Kurt Gödel Society*, edited by H. D. Schwabl, 45. Vienna: Kurt Gödel Society.

(c) "New Foundations for Mathematical Theories." In *Logic Colloquium 90: Lecture Notes in Logic*, no. 2, edited by J. Väänänen and J. Oikkonen, 122–44. Berlin: Springer. (Appears also in Jaakko Hintikka, *Language, Truth and Logic in Mathematics, Selected Papers* III, 225–47, Dordrecht: Kluwer Academic Publishers, 1998.)

(d) "The Original *Sinn* of Wittgenstein's Philosophy of Mathematics." In *Wittgenstein's Philosophy of Mathematics* 2, edited by Klaus Puhl, 24–52. Vienna: Hölder-Pichler-Tempsky. (Appears also in Jaakko Hintikka, *Ludwig Wittgenstein: Half-Truths and One-and-a-Half-Truths, Selected Papers* I, 145–77, Dordrecht: Kluwer Academic Publishers, 1996.)

(e) "Socratic Questioning, Logic, and Rhetoric." *Revue Internationale de Philosophie* 47: 5–30.

1994

(a) "An Anatomy of Wittgenstein's Picture Theory." In *Artifacts, Representations and Social Practice*, edited by C. C. Gould and Robert S. Cohen, 223–56. Dordrecht: Kluwer Academic Publishers. (Also appears in Jaakko Hintikka, *Ludwig Wittgenstein: Half Truths and One-and-a-Half-Truths, Selected Papers* I, 21–54, Dordrecht: Kluwer Academic Publishers, 1996.)

(b) With Ilpo Halonen. "Quantum Logic as a Logic of Identification." In *Patrick Suppes: Scientific Philosopher* 3, edited by Paul Humphreys, 125–45. Dordrecht: Kluwer Academic Publishers.

(c) With Gabriel Sandu. "Uses and Misuses of Frege's Ideas." *Monist* 77:278–93.

(d) With Gabriel Sandu. "What is a Quantifier?" *Synthese* 98:113–29.

(e) With Gabriel Sandu. "Why Parallel Processing?" In *Philosophy and Cognitive Sciences. Proceedings of the Sixteenth International Wittgenstein Symposium*, edited by Robert Casati, Barry Smith, and Graham White, 265–72. Vienna: Hölder-Pichler-Tempsky. (Appears also in French translation as "Le traitement parallèle, pourquoi?" in *Fondements d'une théorie du langage*, translated from English by Nadine Lavand, 367–94, Paris: Presses Universitaire de France, 1994.)

1995

(a) "Commentary on Allen." *Proceedings of the Boston Colloquium on Ancient Philosophy* 11, edited by John J. Cleary and William Wians, 206–13. Lanham, Md.: University Press of America.

(b) "Commentary on Smith's 'What Use is Aristotle's *Organon*?'" In *Proceedings of the Boston Area Colloquium in Ancient Philosophy* 9, edited by John J. Cleary and William Wians, 286–95. Lanham, Md.: University Press of America.

(c) "Constructivism *aufgehoben*." In *Logica '94*, edited by T. Childers and O. Majer, 1–15. Praha: Filosofia.

(d) "Finnish Philosophy." In *The Oxford Companion to Philosophy*, edited by Ted Honderich, 281–82. Oxford University Press.

(e) "The Games of Logic and the Games of Inquiry." *Dialectica* 49:229–49. (Also appears in Jaakko Hintikka, *Paradigms for Language Theory and Other Essays, Selected Papers* IV, 1–21, Dordrecht: Kluwer Academic Publishers, 1998.)

(f) "The Longest Philosophical Journey: Quest of Reality as a Common Theme in Bloomsbury." In *The British Tradition in Twentieth Century Philosophy. Proceedings of the Seventeenth International Wittgenstein Symposium*, edited by Klaus Puhl and Jaakko Hintikka, 1–26. Vienna: Hölder-Pichler-Tempsky. (In Spanish as "El viaje filosófico más largo. La búsqueda de la realidad como tema común en Bloomsbury" in Jaakko Hintikka, *El viaje filosófico más largo: De Aristóteles a Virginia Woolf*, translated by Marcelo M.M. Hurtado, 243–65, Barcelona: Gedisa Editorial, 1998. In Finnish as "The Longest Philosophical Journey: todellisuuden tavoittelu Bloomburyn piirin yhteisenä teemana," translated by Janne Hiipakka, in *Filosofian köyhyys ja rikkaus: Nykyfilosofian kartoitusta*, edited by Janne Hiipakka and Risto Vilkko, 343–65, Helsinki: Art House Oy, 2001.)

(g) "Meinong in a Long Perspective." *Grazer Philosophische Studien* 50, edited by Rudolf Haller (listed 1995, appeared in 1996): 29–45.

(h) "On Proper (Popper?) and Improper Uses of Information in Epistemology." *Theoria* 59 (for 1993, appeared 1995): 158–65.

(i) "The Phenomenological Dimension." In *The Cambridge Companion to Husserl*, edited by Barry Smith and David W. Smith, 78–105. Cambridge University Press.

(j) "Standard vs. Nonstandard Distinction: A Watershed in the Foundations of Mathematics." In *From Dedekind to Gödel: Essays on the Development of the Foundations of*

Mathematics, edited by Jaakko Hintikka, 21–44. Dordrecht: Kluwer Academic Publishers. (Appears also in Jaakko Hintikka, *Language, Truth and Logic in Mathematics, Selected Papers* III, 106–29, Dordrecht: Kluwer Academic Publishers, 1998.)

(k)   "What Is Elementary Logic? Independence-friendly Logic as the True Core Area of Logic." In *Physics, Philosophy, and the Scientific Community*, edited by Kostas Gavroglu, John Stachel, and Marx W. Wartofsky, 301–26. Dordrecht: Kluwer Academic Publishers. (Also appears in Jaakko Hintikka, *Language, Truth and Logic in Mathematics, Selected Papers* III, 1–26, Kluwer Academic Publishers, 1998. Appears in French translation as "Qu'est-ce que la logique élémentaire? La logique faite pour l' indépendence est le coeur même de la logique" in *Fondements d'une théorie du langage*, translated from English by Nadine Lavand, 271–317, Paris: Presses Universitaire de France, 1994.)

(l)   With Ilpo Halonen. "Semantics and Pragmatics for Why-Questions." *Journal of Philosophy* 92:636–57. (Appears also in Jaakko Hintikka, *Inquiry As Inquiry: Toward a Logic of Scientific Discovery, Selected Papers* V, 183–204, Dordrecht: Kluwer Academic Publishers, 1999. Also in Ilpo Halonen, *Interrogative Model of Explanation and Covering Laws* [dissertation], 97–124, Department of Philosophy, University of Helsinki, 2001.)

(m)   With Byong-Chul Park. "The Background of Wittgenstein's Phenomenology." *Phenomenological Inquiry* 19:134–48.

(n)   With Gabriel Sandu. "The Fallacies of the New Theory of Reference." *Synthese* 104: 245–83. (Also appears in Jaakko Hintikka, *Paradigms for Language Theory and Other Essays, Selected Papers* IV, 175–218, Dordrecht: Kluwer Academic Publishers, 1998.)

(o)   With Gabriel Sandu. "What Is the Logic of Parallel Processing?" *International Journal of Foundations of Computer Science* 6:27–49. (Appears also in Jaakko Hintikka, *Language, Truth and Logic in Mathematics, Selected Papers* III, 189–211, Dordrecht: Kluwer Academic Publishers, 1998.)

1996

(a)   "Ajatuksia Aristoteleen ajattelua koskevista ajatuksista" (Thoughts on Aristotle's Thoughts about Thinking). In *Sielun liikkeitä*, edited by Taina and Toivo Holopainen, 28–42. Helsinki: Gaudeamus. (Appears in French translation.)

(b)   "Cogito, ergo quis est?" *Revue Internationale de Philosophie* 50:5–21. (Appears also in Spanish translation as ¿*Cogito ergo quis est*? in Jaakko Hintikka, *El viaje filosófico más largo: De Aristóteles a Virginia Woolf*, translated by Marcelo M.M. Hurtado, 112–30, Barcelona: Gedisa Editorial, 1998. In French translation, P. Le Quellec-Wolff, translator, *Revue de Métaphysique et de Morale*, no. 1 [2000]: 13–28.)

(c)   "Contemporary Philosophy and the Problem of Truth." In *Methods of Philosophy and the History of Philosophy*, edited by Simo Knuuttila and Ilkka Niiniluoto. *Acta Philosophica Fennica* 61:23–39. (Appears also in Jaakko Hintikka, *Lingua Universalis vs. Calculus Ratiocinator: An Ultimate Presupposition of Twentieth-Century Philosophy, Selected Papers* II, 1–19, Dordrecht: Kluwer Academic Publishers, 1997. Appears in Russian translation in *Voprosi filosofii*, no. 9 [1996]: 46–58. In French translation as "La philosophie contemporaine et le problème de la vérité," translated by Jean-Pierre Cometti, in Jaakko Hintikka, *Questions de logique et de phénoménologie*, edited by Élisabeth Rigal, 47–67, in the series Problèmes et Controverses, edited by Jean-François Courtine, Librairie Philosophique, Paris: J. Vrin, 1998. In Slovakian translation as "Súčasná filosofie a problém pravdy" in *Organon F: Filozofický Časopis* 4, no.2 [1997]: 137–56. In Finnish translation as "Totuuden ongelma nykyfilosofiassa," translated by Janne Hiipakka, in *Filosofian köyhyys ja rikkaus: Nykyfilosofian kartoitusta*, edited by Janne Hiipakka and Risto Vilkko, 241–66, Helsinki: Art House Oy, 2001. Reprinted in English in *Annalytic Philosophy in Finland*, Poznań Studies in the Philosophy of the Sciences and the Humanities 80, edited by Leila Haaparanta and Ilkka Niiniluoto, 89–106, Amsterdam: Rodopi, 2003.)

(d) "Knowledge Acknowledged: Knowledge of Propositions vs. Knowledge of Objects." *Philosophy and Phenomenological Research* 56:251–75. (Appears in Finnish translation as "Tiedostavasta tiedosta: propositiotieto vs. objektitieto" in *Tiedon loogisesta esittämisestä: Filosofisia tutkimuksia tampereen Yliopistosta* 62, edited by Jari Palomäki and Ismo Koskinen, 43–66, Tampereen yliopisto, 1997. In French translation as "La connaissance reconnue, la connaissance de propositions par opposition à la connaissance d'objets," translated by Fabienne Poin Boeuf and Christine Chauviré, in Jaakko Hintikka, *Questions de logique et de phénoménologie*, edited by Élisabeth Rigal, 99–126, in the series Problèmes et Controverses, edited by Jean-François Courtine, Librairie Philosophique, Paris: J. Vrin, 1998. Reprinted in Finnish in *Filosofian köyhyys ja rikkaus: Nykyfilosofian kartoitusta*, edited by Janne Hiipakka and Risto Vilkko, Helsinki: Art House Oy, 2001.)

(e) "On the Development of Aristotle's Ideas of Scientific Method and the Structure of Science." In *Aristotle's Philosophical Development: Problems and Prospects*, edited by William Wians, 83–104. Savage, Md.: Rowman and Littlefield.

(f) "Ovatko uutiset analyyttisen filosofian kuolemasta liioiteltuja?" (Is the news about the death of analytic philosophy exaggerated?). In *Tieto, totuus ja todellisuus*, edited by I. A. Kieseppä et al., 267–80. Helsinki: Gaudeamus. (Reprinted in *Filosofian köyhyys ja rikkaus: Nykyfilosofian kartoitusta*, edited by Janne Hiipakka and Risto Vilkko, 21–39, Helsinki: Art House Oy, 2001.)

(g) "The Place of C. S. Peirce in the History of Logical Theory." In *The Rule of Reason: The Philosophy of Charles Sanders Peirce*, edited by Jacqueline Brunning and Paul Forster, 13–33. Toronto: University of Toronto Press. (Appears also in *Lingua Universalis vs. Calculus Ratiocinator, Selected Papers II*, 140–61, Dordrecht: Kluwer Academic Publishers, 1997. In Spanish translation as "El lugar de C. S. Peirce en la historia de la lógica," in Jaakko Hintikka, *El viaje filosófico más largo: De Aristóteles a Virginia Woolf*, translated by Marcelo M.M. Hurtado, 215–43, Barcelona: Gedisa Editorial, 1998.)

(h) "Possible Worlds – Possible Individuals." In *Philosophy of Language: An International Handbook of Contemporary Research* 2, edited by Marcelo Dascal et al., 1271–78. Berlin: Walter de Gruyter.

(i) "Strategic Thinking in Argumentation and Argumentation Theory." *Revue Internationale de Philosophie* 50:307–24.

(j) "Wittgenstein on Being and Time." In Jaakko Hintikka, *Ludwig Wittgenstein: Half-truths and One-and-a-half-truths*, 3–18. Dordrecht: Kluwer Academic Publishers. (Also appears in *Theoria* 62, nos. 1–2 [1996]: 241–74.)

(k) "World Lines and Their Role in Epistemic Logic." In *Philosophical Logic and Logical Philosophy: Essays in Honour of Vladimir A. Smirnov*, edited by Peter Bystrov and Vadim Sadovsky, 121–37. Dordrecht: Kluwer Academic Publishers.

(l) With Marcelo Dascal and Kuno Lorenz. "Games in Language." In *Philosophy of Language: An International Handbook of Contemporary Research* 2, edited by Marcelo Dascal et al., 1371–91. Berlin: Walter de Gruyter.

(m) With Gabriel Sandu. "Game-Theoretical Semantics." In *Handbook of Logic and Language,* edited by Johan van Benthem and Alice ter Meulen, 361–410. Amsterdam: Elsevier.

(n) With Gabriel Sandu. "A Revolution in Logic?" *Nordic Journal of Philosophical Logic* 1:169–83. (Also appears in Jaakko Hintikka, *Language, Truth and Logic in Mathematics, Selected Papers* III, 27–44, Dordrecht: Kluwer Academic Publishers, 1998.

Appears in Chinese translation, translated by Chen Po, in *Translated and Collected Essays in Philosophy* 4, 1999, 43–50. Appears in Finnish as "Vallankumous logiikassa," translated by Risto Vilkko, in *Filosofian köyhyys ja rikkaus: Nykyfilosofian kartoitusta* [The Poverty and Richness of Philosophy: Perspectives on Contemporary Philosophy], edited by Janne Hiipakka and Risto Vilkko, 87–111, Helsinki: Art House Oy, 2001.)

1997

(a)   "Commentary on Allen." In *Proceedings of the Boston Area Colloquium in Ancient Philosophy* 11, edited by John J. Cleary and William Wians, 206–13. Lanham, Md.: University Press of America, 1997 (for 1995).

(b)   "A Game Theory of Logic – A Logic of Game Theory." *Vienna Circle Institute Yearbook* 5:315–23.

(c)   "Hilbert Vindicated?" *Synthese* 110, no. 1:15–36. (Appears also in Jaakko Hintikka, *Language, Truth and Logic in Mathematics, Selected Papers* III, 84–105, Dordrecht: Kluwer Academic Publishers, 1998.)

(d)   "The Idea of Phenomenology in Wittgenstein and Husserl." In *Phänomenologie und Logischer Empirismus: Zentrarium Felix Kaufman*, edited by Friedrich Stadler, 127–51. Vienna: Springer-Verlag. (Also appears in Jaakko Hintikka, *Ludwig Wittgenstein: Half-Truths and One-and-a-half-truths, Selected Papers* I, 55–77, Dordrecht: Kluwer Academic Publishers, 1996. Appears in French translation as "L'idée de phénoménologie chez Wittgenstein et Husserl," translated by Élisabeth Rigal, in Jaakko Hintikka, *Questions de logique et de phénoménologie*, edited by Élisabeth Rigal, 199–222, in the series Problèmes et Controverses, edited by Jean-François Courtine, Librairie Philosophique, Paris: J. Vrin, 1998.)

(e)   "No Scope for Scope?" *Linguistics and Philosophy* 20:515–44. (Also appears in Jaakko Hintikka, *Paradigms for Language Theory and Other Essays, Selected Papers* IV, 22–51, Dordrecht: Kluwer Academic Publishers, 1998.)

(f)   "On Creativity in Reasoning." In *The Complexity of Creativity*, edited by Å. E. Andersson and N.-E. Sahlin, 67–78. Dordrecht: Kluwer Academic Publishers.

(g)   "Replies." In *Knowledge and Inquiry: Essays on Jaakko Hintikka's Epistemology and Philosophy of Science*, edited by Matti Sintonen, 311–40. Poznan Studies in the Philosophy of Science. Amsterdam: Rodopi.

(h)   "A Revolution in the Foundations of Mathematics?" *Synthese* 111, no. 2:155–70. (Also appears in Jaakko Hintikka, *Language, Truth and Logic in Mathematics, Selected Papers* III, 45–61, Dordrecht: Kluwer Academic Publishers, 1998.)

(i)   "Three Dogmas of Quine's Empiricism." *Revue Internationale de Philosophie* 51: 457–77. (Appears in Finnish as "Quinen empirismin kolme dogmia," translated by Janne Hiipakka, in *Filosofian köyhyys ja rikkaus: Nykyfilosofian kartoitusta*, edited by Janne Hiipakka and Risto Vilkko, 53–86, Helsinki: Art House Oy, 2001.)

(j)   "What was Aristotle Doing in his Early Logic, Anyway? A Reply to Woods and Hansen." *Synthese* 113, no. 2:241–49.

(k)   "Who Is About to Kill Analytic Philosophy?" In *The Story of Analytic Philosophy*, edited by Anat Biletzki and Anat Matar, 253–69. London: Routledge. (Appears in Chinese translation in *Analytic Philosophy: Review and Reflection*, edited by Chen Bo, 263–82, CIP, 2001. In Finnish translation as "Ovatko uutiset analyyttisen fiosofian kuolemasta liioiteltuja?" in *Tieto, totuus ja todellisuus*, edited by I. A. Kieseppä, Sami Pihlström, and Panu Raatikainen, 267–80, Helsinki: Gaudeamus, 1996. Reprinted in *Filosofian köyhyys ja rikkaus: Nykyfilosofian kartoitusta*, edited by Janne Hiipakka and Risto Vilkko, 21–39, Helsinki: Art House Oy, 2001.)

1998

(a) "*Argumentum ad hominem:* Will the Real Fallacy Please Stand Up?" *Armenian Mind* II, no. 1:45–60.
(b) "Der Formelkram ist nur eine Sprache." In *Einladung zum Denken: Ein kleiner Streifzug durch die Analytische Philosophie,* edited by Dagmar Borchers, Olaf Brill, and Uwe Czaniera, 133–42. Vienna: Verlag Hölder-Pichler-Tempsky.
(c) "On Gödel's Philosophical Assumptions." *Synthese* 114:13–23.
(d) "Perspectival Identification, Demonstratives and 'Small Worlds.'" In Jaakko Hintikka, *Paradigms for Language Theory and Other Essays, Selected Papers* IV, 219–49. Dordrecht: Kluwer Academic Publishers. (Appears also in *Synthese* 114, no.2 (1998): 203–32.)
(e) "The Pragmatic Fallacies of the New Theory of Reference." *Pragmatics and Cognition* 6, nos. 1–2 :9–20.
(f) "Ramsey Sentences and the Meaning of Quantifiers." *Philosophy of Science* 65: 289–305. (Appears also in Jaakko Hintikka, *Inquiry As Inquiry: Toward a Logic of Scientific Discovery, Selected Papers* V, 251–66, Dordrecht: Kluwer Academic Publishers, 1999.)
(g) "Réponses et commentaires," translated by Élisabeth Rigal. In Jaakko Hintikka, *Questions de logique et de phénoménologie,* edited by Élisabeth Rigal, 309–29. In the series Problèmes et Controverses, edited by Jean-François Courtine, Librairie Philosophique. Paris: J. Vrin.
(h) "Truth Definitions, Skolem Functions and Axiomatic Set Theory." *Bulletin of Symbolic Logic* 4:303–37.
(i) "What is Abduction? The Fundamental Problem of Contemporary Epistemology." *Transactions of the Charles Peirce Society* 34:503–33. (Appears also in Jaakko Hintikka, *Inquiry as Inquiry: Toward a Logic of Scientific Discovery, Selected Papers* V, 91–113, Dordrecht: Kluwer Academic Publishers, 1999.)
(j) With Ilpo Halonen. "Epistemic Logic." In *Routledge Encyclopedia of Philosophy* 3, edited by Peter Klein and R. Foley, 354–59. London: Routledge.
(k) With Arto Mutanen. "An Alternative Concept of Computability." In Jaakko Hintikka, *Language, Truth and Logic in Mathematics, Selected Papers* III, 174–88. Dordrecht: Kluwer Academic Publishers. (Appears also in *Bulletin of the Interest Group in Pure and Applied Logics.*)
(l) With Gabriel Sandu. "Quantifiers." In *Routledge Encyclopedia of Philosophy* 7, edited by Peter Klein and R. Foley, 870–73. London: Routledge.

1999

(a) "The Emperor's New Intuitions." *Journal of Philosophy* 96:127–47.
(b) "Is the Axiom of Choice a Logical or Set-Theoretical Principle?" *Dialectica* 53:283–29.
(c) "Is Logic the Key to all Good Reasoning?" In Jaakko Hintikka, *Inquiry as Inquiry: A Logic of Scientific Discovery: Selected Papers* V, 1–24. Dordrecht: Kluwer Academic Publishers. (In Russian translation in *Voprosi filosofii* 11 (2000): 105–25. Appears also in Finnish as "Onko logiikka kaiken luovan päättelyn avain?" translated by Risto Vilkko, in *Filosofian köyhyys ja rikkaus: Nykyfilosofian kartoitusta,* edited by Janne Hiipakka and Risto Vilkko, 112–47, Helsinki: Art House Oy, 2001.)
(d) "On Aristotle's Notion of Existence." *Review of Metaphysics* 52:779–805.
(e) "Quine's Ultimate Presuppositions." *Theoria* 65:3–24.
(f) With Ilpo Halonen. "Interpolation as Explanation." *Philosophy of Science* 66:414–23.
(g) With Ilpo Halonen. "Unification: It's Magnificent But Is It Explanation?" In *Proceedings of the Lund Conference on Explanation,* edited by J. Persson, *Synthese* 120,

no. 1:27–47. (Appears also in Ilpo Halonen [dissertation], *Interrogative Model of Explanation and Covering Laws*, 213–39, Department of Philosophy, University of Helsinki, Vantaa, 2001. In Finnish as "Unifikaatio: selittääkö se selittämisen?" translated by Ilpo Halonen, in *Filosofian köyhyys ja rikkaus: Nykyfilosofian kartoitusta*, edited by Janne Hiipakka and Risto Vilkko, 212–40, Helsinki: Art House Oy, 2001.)

(h) With Ilpo Halonen and Arto Mutanen. "Interrogative Logic as a General Theory of Reasoning." In Jaakko Hintikka, *Inquiry as Inquiry: A Logic of Scientific Discovery, Selected Papers* V, 47–90. Dordrecht: Kluwer Academic Publishers. (Also in Ilpo Halonen [dissertation], *Interrogative Model of Explanation and Covering Laws*, 39–95, Department of Philosophy, University of Helsinki, Vantaa, 2001.)

(i) With Gabriel Sandu. "Tarski's Guilty Secret: Compositionality." In *Alfred Tarski and the Vienna Circle* (Vienna Circle Institute Yearbook vol. 6, for 1988), edited by Jan Wolenski and Eckehart Köhler, 217–30. Dordrecht: Kluwer Academic Publishers.

2000

(a) "Epistemology: Introduction." In *The Examined Life: Readings from Western Philosophy from Plato to Kant*, edited by Stanley Rosen, 401–14. New York: Random House.

(b) "Gadamer: Squaring the Hermeneutical Circle." *Revue de Internationale de Philosophie* 54:487–97.

(c) "Game-Theoretical Semantics as a Challenge to Proof Theory." *Nordic Journal of Philosophical Logic* 4:127–41.

(d) "History of Logic Before and After Bochenski." In *Joseph (I.M.) Bochenski: Life and Work*, edited by J. Kozak and G. Küng. Verlag A. Stanic Scientific Publishers.

(e) "Intuitions as Model-theoretical Insights." In *Intuitive Formation of Meaning: Symposium Held in Stockholm, April 20-21, 1998*, edited by Sven Sandström. *Konferenser* 48:75–90.

(f) "Knowledge Functions in the Growth of Mathematical Knowledge." In *The Growth of Mathematical Knowledge*, edited by E. Grosholz and H. Berger, 1–15. Dordrecht: Kluwer Academic Publishers.

(g) "Language as a "Mirror of Nature." *Sign Systems Studies* 28:62–72.

(h) "On the Educational Missions of Philosophy." *Diogenes* 48/4, no. 192:63–70. (Appears also in the French edition as "La mission éducative de la philosophie" translated by Denis Trierweiler, *Diogenes* 48/4, no. 192:83–99.)

(i) "Questioning as a Philosophical Method." In *The Examined Life: Readings from Western Philosophy from Plato to Kant*, edited by Stanley Rosen, 453–70. New York: Random House.

(j) "The Theory-Ladenness of Intuitions." In *Logique en perspective: Mélanges offerts à Paul Gochet*, edited by François Beets and Éric Gillet, 259–87. Brussels: Ouisia.

(k) "What is IF Logic and Why Do We Need It?" In Chinese translation by Chen Bo. *Journal of Dialectics of Nature* 22, no. 3:20–28.

(l) "What is True and False about So-Called Theories of Truth?" In *Analytic Philosophy and Logic*, edited by Akihiro Kanamori, 155–60. *Proceedings of the Twentieth World Congress of Philosophy* 6.

(m) "Review: *Routledge Encyclopedia of Philosophy*, Edward Craig, General Editor. London/New York: Routledge, vols. 1–10." In *Synthese* 124, no. 3:433–45.

(n) With Ilpo Halonen. "Aristotelian Explanations." *Studies in History and Philosophy of Science* 31:125–36. (Also in Ilpo Halonen, *Interrogative Model of Explanation and Covering Laws* [dissertation], 241–57, Department of Philosophy, Vantaa: University of Helsinki, 2001.)

2001

(a)   "Ernst Mach at the Crossroads of Twentieth-Century Philosophy." In *Future Pasts: Perspectives on the Analytic Tradition*, edited by Juliet Floyd and Sanford Shieh, 81–100. Oxford: Oxford University Press.

(b)   "Introduction and Postscript: Defining Truth and its Difficulties." *Synthese* 126, nos. 1–2:1–16.

(c)   "Intuitionistic Logic as Epistemic Logic." *Synthese* 127, no. 1:7–19.

(d)   "Is Logic the Key to All Good Reasoning?" *Argumentation* 15:35–57. (Appears in Russian translation in *Voprosi Filosofii* 11 [2000]: 105–25.)

(e)   "Post-Tarskian Truth." *Synthese* 126, no.1:17–36. (Appears as "Totuus Tarskin jälkeen," translated by Janne Hiipakka, in *Filosofian köyhyys ja rikkaus: Nykyfilosofian kartoitusta*, edited by Janne Hiipakka and Risto Vilkko, 267–96, Helsinki: Art House Oy, 2001.)

(f)   "What Is Truth? Stay for an Answer." In *What Is Truth*, edited by Richard Schantz, 238–45. Berlin: Walter de Gruyter.

(g)   With Ilpo Halonen. "Toward a Theory of the Process of Explanation." In Ilpo Halonen, *Interrogative Model of Explanation and Covering Laws* (dissertation), 141–212. Department of Philosophy, University of Helsinki, Vantaa, 2001. (Forthcoming in *Synthese*.)

(h)   "The Proper Treatment of Quantifiers in Ordinary Logic." In *Collected Papers of Stig Kanger: With Essays on His Life and Work* 2, edited by Ghita Holmström-Hintikka, Sten Lindström, and Rysiek Sliwinski, 87–95. Dordrecht: Kluwer Academic.

2002

(a)   "Causes, Causes, Causes: Three Aspects of the Idea of Cause." In *Infinity, Causality and Determinism: Cosmological Enterprises and their Preconditions*, edited by Eeva Martikainen, 111–18. Frankfurt: Peter Lang.

(b)   "Comment on Eklund and Kolak." *Synthese* 131, no. 3:389–93.

(c)   "Die Dialektik in Gödels *Dialectica* Interpretation." In *Kurt Gödel: Wahrheit und Beweisbarkeit* 2, edited by Bernd Buldt et al., 67–90. Vienna: öbv & hpt. (A corrected and expanded version in German translation of "Gödel's Functional Interpretation in a Wider Perspective," in *Yearbook 1991 of the Kurt Gödel Society*, edited by H. D. Schwabl, 1–39, Vienna: Kurt Gödel Society, 1993.)

(d)   "Hyperclassical Logic (a.k.a. IF logic) and Its Implications for Logical Theory." *Bulletin of Symbolic Logic* 8:404–23.

(e)   "Looginen empirismi kuusi vuosikymmentä myöhemmin." In *Wienin piiri*, edited by Ilkka Niiniluoto and Heikki J. Koskinen, 250–60. Helsinki: Gaudeamus.

(f)   "Negation in Logic and in Natural Language." *Linguistics and Philosophy* 25: 585–600.

(g)   "Quantum Logic as a Fragment of Independence-Friendly Logic." *Journal of Philosophical Logic* 31:197–209.

(h)   With Anna-Maija Hintikka. "Wittgenstein the Bewitched Writer." In *Wittgenstein and the Future of Philosophy: A Reassessment after 50 Years*, edited by Rudolf Haller and Klaus Puhl, 131–50. Proceedings of the 24th International Wittgenstein Symposium. Vienna: öbv & hpt.

2003

(a)   "A Distinction Too Few or Too Many? A Vindication of the Analytic vs. Synthetic Distinction." In *Constructivism and Practice: Toward a Historical Epistemology*,

edited by Carol C. Gould, 47–74. Lanham, Md.: Roman & Littlefield.
(b) "The Notion of Intuition in Husserl." *Review Internationale de Philosophie* 224: 169–91.
(c) "On the Epistemology of Game-Theoretical Semantics." In *Philosophy and Logic: In Search of the Polish Tradition: Essays in Honour of Jan Woleński on the Occasion of his 60th Birthday*, Synthese Library 323, edited by J. Hintikka, T. Czarnecki, K. Kijania-Placek, T. Placek, and A. Rogszczak. Dordrecht: Kluwer Academic Publishers.
(d) "A Second Generation Epistemic Logic and its General Significance." In *Knowledge Contributers*, Synthese Library, 322, edited by Vincent F. Hendricks, Klaus Frovin Jørgensen, and Stig Andur Pedersen, 33–56. Dordrecht: Kluwer Academic Publishers.
(e) "Squaring the Vienna Circle with Up-to-date Logic and Epistemology." In *Language, Truth and Knowledge: Contributions to the Philosophy of Rudolf Carnap*, edited by Thomas Bonk, 149–66. Dordrecht: Kluwer Academic Publishers.
(f) "What Does the Wittgensteinian Inexpressible Express?" *Harvard Review of Philosophy* 11:9–17.
(g) With John Symons. "Systems of Visual Identification and Neuroscience: Lessons from Epistemic Logic." *Philosophy of Science* 70:89–104.

2004

(a) "Aristotle's Theory of Thinking and Its Consequences for his Methodology." In Jaakko Hintikka, *Analyses of Aristotle: Selected Papers* VI, 45–85. Dordrecht: Kluwer Academic Publishers.
(b) "Did Wittgenstein Follow the Rules? (Or Was He Guided by Them?)" In *Experience and Analysis: Contributions of the Austrian Ludwig Wittgenstein Society*, 27th International Wittgenstein Symposium, edited by Elisabeth Leinfellner, Rudolf Haller, Werner Leinfellner, Klaus Puhl, and Paul Weingartner, 140–41. Kirchberg am Wechsel: Austrian Ludwig Wittgenstein Society.
(c) "Une épistémologie sans connaissance et sans croyance." In *Journée de la philosophie à l'UNESCO, 2002*, edited by Moufida Goucha, 9–62. Paris: UNESCO.
(d) "A Fallacious Fallacy?" *Synthese* 140:25–35.
(e) "Independence-Friendly Logic and Axiomatic Set Theory." *Annals of Pure and Applied Logic* 126:313–33.
(f) "Kielto kiellon päälle" (Denial on Denial). In *Kielto*, edited by Heta Gylling, S. Albert Kivinen, and Risto Vilkko, 79–86. Helsinki: University of Helsinki Press.
(g) "Logical vs. Nonlogical Concepts: An Untenable Dualism?" In *Logic, Epistemology, and the Unity of Science*, edited by Shahid Rahman et al., 51–56. Dordrecht: Kluwer Academic Publishers.
(h) "Ludwig Wittgenstein – lainsuojaton filosofi." *Ajatus* 61:7–24.
(i) "On the Different Identities of Identity: A Historical and Critical Essay." In *Language, Meaning, Interpretation*, edited by Guttorm Fløistad, 117–39. Dordrecht: Kluwer Academic Publishers. (Appears also in French translation in the Proceedings of Societé Française de Philosophie.)
(j) "On Tarski's Assumptions." *Synthese* 142:353–69.
(k) "What Is the True Algebra of Logic?" In *First-Order Logic Revisited*, edited by Vincent Hendricks et al., 117–28. Berlin: Logos Verlag.
(l) "Wittgenstein's Demon and His Theory of Mathematics." In *Essays on Wittgenstein and Austrian Philosophy: In Honour of J. C. Nyiri*, edited by Tamás Demeter, 89–107. Amsterdam and New York: Rodopi.

2005

(a) "Hintikka, Merrill Bristow." In *Dictionary of Modern American Philosophers*, edited by John Shook. Bristol: Thoemmes Press.

(b) "Jaakko Hintikka." In *Formal Philosophy*, edited by Vincent F. Hendricks and John Symons, 111–15. U.S. and U.K.: Automatic Press.
(c) "Kurt Gödel: An Introduction." *Revue Internationale de Philosophie* 59:451–57.
(d) "Omitting Data: Ethical or Strategic Problem?" *Synthese* 145:169–76.
(e) "La philosophie finnoise chez elle et à l'étranger." *Diogéne* 211:48–55.
(f) "What Platonism? Reflections on the Thought of Kurt Gödel." *Revue Internationale de Philosophie* 59: 535–52.
(g) With Ilpo Halonen. "Explanation: Retrospective Reflections." *Synthese* 143:207–22.
(h) With Ilpo Halonen. "Toward a Theory of the Process of Explanation." *Synthese* 143:5–61

Forthcoming

(a) "The Crash of the Philosophy of the *Tractatus*: Wittgenstein's Change of Mind in 1929."
(b) "G. H. von Wright on Logic, Philosophy and Mathematics." In *Acta Philosophica Fennica* 77, edited by Ilkka Niiniluoto and Risto Vilkko. Helsinki: Philosophical Society of Finland, 2006.
(c) "Hilbert was an Axiomatist, not a Formalist." *Festschrift for Ilkka Niiniluoto*, edited by Sami Pihlström, et al.
(d) "IF Logic in a Wider Setting: Probability Functions and Dependence."
(e) "An Intellectual Autobiography." In *The Philosophy of Jaakko Hintikka*, edited by Randall E. Auxier and Lewis Edwin Hahn. Library of Living Philosophers. Chicago: Open Court, 2006.
(f) "Logicism." In *Handbook of the Philosophy of Mathematics*, edited by Andrew Irvine. Handbook of the Philosophy of Science Series, edited by Dov Gabbay, Paul Thagard, and John Woods. Elsevier.
(g) "On Argumentation in a Multicultural Setting." In *Proceedings of the New Delhi Meeting of the IIP*, edited by D. P. Chattopadhyaya, Jaakko Hintikka, and Hans Lenk. Litt Verlag, 2006.
(h) "The Place of the A Priori in Epistemology."
(i) "Presuppositions of Questions and Other Limitations of Inquiry." In *Proceedings of the 2001 IIP Annual Meeting*, edited by Matti Sintonen and Jaakko Hintikka.
(j) "Ta Meta Ta Metaphysika: The Argumentative Structure of Aristotle's Metaphysics." In *Mind and Modality: Studies in the History of Philosophy in Honour of Simo Knuuttila*, edited by Vesa Hirvonen, Toivo J. Holopainen, and Miira Tuominen. Leiden: Brill, 2006.
(k) "Truth, Negation and Other Basic Notions of Logic." In *The Age of Alternative Logics: Assessing Philosophy of Logic and Mathematics Today*, edited by J. van Benthem et al. Dordrecht: Springer.
(l) "Truth, Axiom of Choice and Set Theory."
(m) "Who Has Kidnapped the Notion of Information?"
(n) With Besim Karakadilar. "How to Prove the Consistency of Arithmetic." In *Truth and Games: Essays in Honour of Gabriel Sandu*, edited by Tuomo Aho and Ahti-Veikka Pietarinen. *Acta Philosophica Fennica*.
(o) With Gabriel Sandu. "What Is Logic?" In *Handbook of the Philosophy of Logic*, edited by Dale Jacquette. Handbook of the Philosophy of Science Series, edited by Dov Gabbay, Paul Thagard, and John Woods. Elsevier.
(p) With Risto Vilkko. "Existence and Predication from Aristotle to Frege." *Philosophy and Phenomenological Research*.
(q) With Risto Vilkko. "Kant's Influence in the Development of Modern Logic." In *Kant To-Day*, edited by Hans Lenk.

INDEX

(by Kathleen League)